D1345609

A1011001

Foreign &
Commonwealth
Office

NAZI GOLD

THE LONDON CONFERENCE

2–4 December 1997

London: The Stationery Office

The Stationery Office

Published by The Stationery Office and available from:

The Publications Centre
(mail, telephone and fax orders only)
PO Box 276, London SW8 5DT
General enquiries 0171 873 0011
Telephone orders 0171 873 9090
Fax orders 0171 873 8200

The Stationery Office Bookshops
123 Kingsway, London WC2B 6PQ
0171 242 6393 Fax 0171 242 6394
68–69 Bull Street, Birmingham B4 6AD
0121 236 9696 Fax 0121 236 9699
33 Wine Street, Bristol BS1 2BQ
0117 9264306 Fax 0117 9294515
9–21 Princess Street, Manchester M60 8AS
0161 834 7201 Fax 0161 833 0634
16 Arthur Street, Belfast BT1 4GD
01232 238451 Fax 01232 235401
The Stationery Office Oriel Bookshop
The Friary, Cardiff CF1 4AA
01222 395548 Fax 01222 384347
71 Lothian Road, Edinburgh EH3 9AZ
0131 228 4181 Fax 0131 622 7017

The Stationery Office's Accredited Agents
(see Yellow Pages)

and through good booksellers

Printed in the United Kingdom for The Stationery Office
J54822   C35   8/98

CONTENTS

OPENING REMARKS

Opening speech by the Foreign Secretary, the Rt. Hon Robin Cook, MP   5
Opening plenary statement by Stuart Eizenstat   9
Address to conference by Lord Janner of Braunstone, QC   11

ALBANIA

On the plundered Albanian gold by the Nazis; Jews in Albania   17

ARGENTINA

Nazi war criminals and assets: 1   21
Nazi war criminals and assets: 2   23

AUSTRIA

Statement by Mr Hans Winkler   27

BANK OF ENGLAND

The Bank of England's role as custodian of the Tripartite Gold Commission's
holdings of gold   31

THE BANK FOR INTERNATIONAL SETTLEMENTS
DURING THE SECOND WORLD WAR

Conference paper by Dr Piet Clement   43

BELARUS

Speech by Valentin Gerasimov   61
Speech by O.A. Nekhay   63

BELGIUM

The gold of the Belgian monetary institutes   67

BRAZIL

How is Brazil dealing with the Nazi gold issue?   71

BULGARIA

Anti-Semitic legislation in Bulgaria, 1940–44: a case study of some aspects   73

CANADA

Due diligence: a report on the Bank of Canada's handling of foreign gold
    during World War II   79
Finding aid: gold arrangements and transactions files   183

REPUBLIC OF CROATIA

Statement by the Croatian delegation   235
Supplement to the report of the Croatian delegation   238

CZECH REPUBLIC

Czechoslovak gold reserves and their surrender to Nazi Germany   245
Steps taken hitherto to compensate occupied countries and individual
    victims   249

DENMARK

Statement by the Danish delegation   251

FEDERAL RESERVE BANK OF NEW YORK

Paper   253

FRANCE

Plunder of Jewish property and its restitution   273

GERMANY

Introductory statement by Dr Hans-Werner Lautenschlager   279
Statement by Prof. Dr Horst Moller   280
German restitution for National Socialist crimes   286

GREECE

Speech by Ambassador Alexandros Philon   293
Contribution of the Historical Archive Directorate of the Hellenic Ministry
    of Foreign Affairs   295
Results of the steps taken to compensate the country and individual victims   300

HUNGARY

Contribution from the Hungarian delegation   303

INTERNATIONAL ROMANI UNION

Statement by the Hon. Ian F. Hancock 307

INTERNATIONAL UNION OF FORMER JUVENILE PRISONERS OF FASCIST CONCENTRATION CAMPS

Statement 309

ISRAEL

Bobby Brown's speech 315
Speech of MK Avraham Hirschenson 317
Speech by Nili Arad 320

ITALY

The story of the gold deposited at the Bank of Italy (1943–58) 323

LUXEMBOURG

Luxembourg gold despoiled by Germany during the Second World War 345
The restitution of the monetary gold stolen from Luxembourg by the Nazis 351

THE NETHERLANDS

Introduction by Count Jan d'Ansembourg 355
Dutch gold 357
Looting and restitution 360
Compensation schemes for victims of persecution in the Netherlands and
   the former colony of the Netherlands East Indies 367
Concern for Dutch groups of war victims from the Second World War 369
Bank balances in the Netherlands East Indies 371
Information on the activities of the Contact Group World War II deposits 373

NORWAY

Summary of the Majority Report 375
Summary of the Minority of the Committee of Inquiry 379

PINK TRIANGLE COALITION

Paper 383

POLAND

Statement of the Polish delegation 389

RUSSIA

Victims of Nazism and the issue of compensation   391

SLOVAK REPUBLIC

Statement from the Ministry of Foreign Affairs   403
German occupational regime and the history of monetary and
   non-monetary gold in Slovakia 1944–45   404

SLOVENIA

Some crimes committed by the German occupying force in Slovenia   409
Yugoslav monetary gold 1939–51   411

SPAIN

Approach and views of the Spanish Commission in the light of the
   London Conference   417

SWEDEN

Statement by the Swedish delegation   421
Sweden and the Nazi gold   426
The gold transactions of Sveriges Riksbank with Nazi Germany   449

SWITZERLAND

Switzerland – World War II (Ascona Declaration)   487
Address by Ambassador Thomas G. Borer   489
Measurements taken by Switzerland relating to the problem of Nazi gold
   and unclaimed assets   493
Statement by Ambassador Thomas G. Borer   497
Declaration of the Federal Council on the Eizenstat Report   501
Reaction of Federal Councillor F. Cotti to Eizenstat Report   505
Gold transactions in the Second World War: statistical review with
   commentary   507
The Swiss National Bank's gold operations during the Second World War   535
Statement by Professor Jean-Francois Bergier   543

TRIPARTITE GOLD COMMISSION

The Tripartite Commission for the Restitution of Monetary Gold   547

TURKEY

Conference Paper 1: The Jews of Turkey (historical background)   553
Conference Paper 2   579

Conference Paper 3: Historical facts   587
Conference Paper 4: Complementary statement by Turkey   655
Conference Paper 5: Gold purchased from Switzerland   665

UKRAINE

Report of the Ukraine delegation   673
Nazi victims in Ukraine   684

UNITED KINGDOM

Allied discussions and decisions on gold, 1945–46   687
Changes in the conceptual landscape   691
Documentation of the records of the Tripartite Gold Commission   697

UNITED STATES OF AMERICA

What U.S. officials knew about the movement of German monetary gold,
    looted or otherwise, during World War II and the restitution of looted gold
    after the war   699
Research into US and Allied efforts to recover and restore gold and other
    assets stolen or hidden by Germany during World War II   709
Insurance as a forcibly surrendered or plundered asset in the Holocaust 715

WORLD JEWISH CONGRESS

Indemnification and reparations: Jewish losses   719
Movements of Nazi gold   766

CLOSING STATEMENTS

Closing statement by the Foreign Secretary, the Rt. Hon. Robin Cook MP 789
Closing plenary statement by Stuart Eizenstat   790
Summing up by the Conference Chairman, Lord Mackay of Clashfern   795
Conclusions by the Conference Chairman, Lord Mackay of Clashfern   800

OBSERVERS' PAPERS

Nazi gold – a call for justice   809
Present position of surviving former political prisoners of German
    concentration camps   823
Campaign for Jewish slave labour compensation   825

APPENDIX

List of delegates   827

Opening Speech by the Foreign Secretary, the Rt. Hon Robin Cook, MP

FOREIGN AND COMMONWEALTH OFFICE

I am honoured to be opening this conference. We are here to help clarify one of the darkest episodes in human history. We are here to look for compensation for a suffering that can never be expiated. We are here to ensure we do not forget the most awful memory known to man. I hope that memory will instil in us the humility and urgency to do our work in a spirit of honesty and trust.

We are here, the experts, the governments, the victims. We represent everyone with an interest in resolving the question of Nazi gold. The Foreign Office has worked closely with many British and international organisations in setting up the conference. From over forty countries, six NGOs representing the survivors, four institutions that actually handled the Nazi gold – more expertise than has ever been gathered on this subject before.

I would like to pay particular tribute to those countries for whom Nazi gold is a difficult subject. They have shown courage and concern in agreeing to take part.

AN INCOMPLETE JIGSAW

Together, we can pool our knowledge on the gold stolen by the Nazis. Many countries here have been digging through their records, piecing together bits of the jigsaw. Whom the gold came from. What happened to it under the Nazis. What happened to it following the Allied victory. The British Foreign and Commonwealth Office has now published two papers. The US State Department has published the Eizenstat report. Our co-operation with the State Department has been close, constant and immensely productive. The Matteoli Commission is at work in France. The Swiss government have launched the Bergier Commission. Others are now starting to look at these questions. The jigsaw may never be complete. But we are building a clearer picture, and answers to some of the most difficult questions are fitting into place.

I hope this Conference will help this process develop. I hope it will help answer some of the most contentious questions, such as whether any gold stolen from individual victims of the Nazis was included in the monetary gold that was distributed to countries that had been occupied following the war. There is a limit to what a single conference can achieve. But we can use this meeting to take the process forward. To share what research we have already. To ensure that future research is co-ordinated and fruitful.

We must be open. The subject is not an easy one. It requires that we shine a light in corners which have stayed dark too long. But honesty and openness is the bare minimum we all owe. They must be the foundations of our discussions. Because truth is the only basis for justice. And in Hebrew, Truth is one of the names of God.

One difficult question is the distribution of gold immediately following the Allied victory. The records tell a story of genuine efforts by the Allies to do the right thing in the midst of post-war chaos. The needs of the survivors were urgent, and decisions were taken that allowed those needs to be met. Those decisions were not perfect, or exact. With the 20/20 vision of hindsight there are things we might have done differently. But they met the desperate needs of the time, and did so in good faith.

The same good faith has been shown since then. By the three countries of the Tripartite Gold Commission, who have made great efforts to distribute fairly what was left of the Nazis' gold. By Switzerland, which has set up a special fund for individual victims of the Nazis. And by Germany, which has gone to great lengths to compensate the victims of Nazi atrocities, paying out over 100 billion Deutschmarks. I hope this conference will recognise the good that has been done as well as the bad, and give credit where individuals and countries have made reparation.

But the Conference will have to ask whether more needs to be done by all of us together. It will have to measure up the case for further compensation. We must avoid the second tragedy of those who survived the Nazis being left to live out their days in poverty.

THE FUND

One aspect of this is the disposal of the remainder of the Tripartite Commission's monetary gold pool. There are five and a half tons left, worth about $30 million. It is held in the Bank of England and the US Federal Reserve. Some have said that it should be distributed to needy survivors, because of the "victim gold" which may have been included in the monetary gold. The British, French and US governments considered the evidence, which showed that small amounts of monetary gold may have come from the victims. This was not the result of callous neglect by the Allies after the War. Gold by its very nature can be made anonymous without losing its value. The three countries believe that this does not affect their legal obligation under the Paris Agreement of 1946 to distribute the remainder of the gold pool to the countries that had been looted by the Nazis.

But we felt we should still look at how we can help surviving victims who are in financial need. We have proposed to the recipient countries that when they received their final share of the gold, they should give some or all of it to survivors – either in their own countries, or through an international fund we are establishing. The recipient countries responded positively. I can announce today that the fund has been established. An account has been opened in the Federal Reserve Bank of New York with the British Government as the account holder. It will be voluntary, but a number of countries have already said that they will make contributions.

Britain is not a recipient of any of the Tripartite Commission gold. We used up our entire gold deposits and incurred large debts defeating the Nazis. But I still believe it is right that Britain should contribute to the fund. As the country that has taken the lead in setting up the fund, it is right that Britain should start the fund going. So I am pleased to announce that Britain will be contributing one million pounds.

THE LEGACY OF THE NAZIS

Fifty years on, the legacy of the Nazis still leaves a heavy hand on the world. The divisions that disfigured Europe after the War have only recently been erased, as the Cold War has come to an end.

But the legacy is not all bad. Britain and Germany are now leading partners in a European Union which has made another war in Europe unthinkable. The people of Israel have created their own state, built out of the hopes of a people that survived. And we have the inspiration of those who will not allow the Holocaust to be forgotten.

REMEMBERING

Last week, I visited the Warsaw Ghetto. Fifty-five years ago, a young man wrote a poem about the last butterfly he saw there. He ended by writing:

> For seven weeks I've lived in here,
> Penned up inside this ghetto.
> But I have found what I love here.
> The dandelions call to me
> And the white chestnut branches in the court.
> Only I never saw another butterfly.

> That butterfly was the last one.
> Butterflies don't live here,
>   in the ghetto.

Pavel Friedmann died in Auschwitz just under four months later. He was 21. He is the reason we are here. Because the real victims of the Nazis were not the Central Banks. They were individuals. Countless individuals, who died because of their religion, their race, their beliefs. And we must always remember that they were individuals, because the Nazis tried so hard to reduce them to numbers, to remove their humanity.

We have two duties to the victims of the Nazis. To those who are still alive, we must ensure that the unbearable tragedy of living through the Holocaust is not compounded by an old age marked by the fear and sadness of poverty. We must let them know that the international community is not indifferent to their plight.

To those who died, we have a different duty – to document the facts, to gather the evidence, to locate the truth. The duty we owe them is to remember.

This must be done with urgency. Fifty years on from Auschwitz, fewer and fewer of the survivors are left. This is the last chance we have to recreate the jigsaw from first hand. As their numbers diminish, we who were not survivors have even more responsibility to keep their memory alive.

The evil the Nazis did must not be consigned to text-books and dry academic debate, it must not become just another subject for the historians. It must be remembered in a living way. That is our duty. To remember that we can never let our guard down against bigotry and hatred. To keep a lamp burning, and show it to our children.

Opening Plenary Statement by Stuart Eizenstat

U.S. UNDER SECRETARY OF STATE

We have just heard Foreign Secretary Cook announce an historic breakthrough on which we have worked together over the last several months to achieve. On behalf of the United States and Secretary Albright, I want to congratulate the Foreign Secretary and the British Government, especially Francis Richards and Anthony Layden, for their part in our common effort to establish this Fund and to conclude the work of the Tripartite Gold Commission after five decades.

Today we are taking an important step toward completing a significant portion of the unfinished business of the Second World War. We are doing so in a way which extends both a moral gesture and a material contribution to justice, however little and late, for Holocaust survivors.

I want to commend the nations which have indicated their intention, on a voluntary basis, to contribute to the account now open for deposit to the Fund. I hope that other nations will choose to join them in the coming weeks so that the work of the TGC can be completed in a way which brings dignity to all nations involved, and demonstrates that we have learned the lessons of this darkest chapter in history.

I also want to announce the decision by the United States Government to deposit $4 million in the Fund, as a down-payment on what we hope, with the support from our Congress, will be up to a $25 million contribution over three years. We have decided to take this action, even though we have no claim on the gold in the TGC pool, because of the light that recent research has shed on the gold pool's origins; because of our own actions and inactions after the War; and because of the urgent needs of those Holocaust survivors who have received little or no compensation in the intervening years.

The launch of the Fund is not the only reason this is an historic occasion. Rarely has an historical conference itself been so poised to make history. Today the eyes of millions of people around the world, people with an interest in history and a commitment to justice, are upon us.

It is in large part due to the personal leadership of the Foreign Secretary, Lord Greville Janner and the efforts of the British Government that representatives from over forty countries – historians and experts, diplomats and NGOs – have come together to address these still painfully unresolved issues from half a century ago. And it is in large part due to the heroic and tireless efforts of so many organisations, especially the NGOs represented here, that these issues have come to command the attention of the world and touch the conscience of humanity.

Over the next three days, we can make history by illuminating long-obscured facts; coordinating our research efforts; addressing difficult methodological issues; and encouraging all countries involved to open their archives and make their records fully available. Nothing is more important than full disclosure and declassification of documents. In these ways, we can move ever closer to the fullest possible accounting of the assets under question from this period.

History is already being made by the extraordinary work of the historical commissions which have been established in some dozen nations – work which will be spotlighted throughout our agenda this week.

We can also make history in the months ahead, beyond this Conference, by serving the cause of justice. Justice can be served by wider scholarship and public education on all aspects of this period, especially the Holocaust. Justice can also be served by open and frank democratic debate within our pluralistic societies and by diplomatic dialogue among our sovereign nations.

Justice *is* being served as more and more countries are recognizing their responsibility and examining their own actions. Our own U.S. historical report spared no self-criticism of America's attempts to restitute looted Nazi gold after the War. This is a painful process for *any* nation, including the United States. At the same time, this can be and should be a healing process that will strengthen *all* our nations.

Justice *is* also being served as we create funds like the one announced this morning and like Switzerland's Special Holocaust Fund, which made its first payment to Holocaust survivors just two weeks ago. Justice *will* be advanced if the facts established and the views exchanged here and elsewhere further crystallize and galvanize the international consensus for justice and action.

I hope that we can all agree that the most important test for any country today is *not* what it did or failed to do in the past, but what it is doing *now* and will do in the future to face the past honestly.

Ladies and gentlemen, as we approach not only the end of a century but the beginning of a new millennium, we must meet our collective responsibility to history, to justice, and to the victims and survivors whom we must never forget.

Thank you very much, and let me once again express my appreciation to Foreign Secretary Cook and the United Kingdom for their leadership.

Address to Conference
Lord Janner of Braunstone, QC

CHAIRMAN, HOLOCAUST EDUCATIONAL TRUST

Lord Mackay, Foreign Secretary, Your Excellencies, delegates from so many respected nations, colleagues and friends.

I thank you, Foreign Secretary, for your very kind references to my part in this most significant Conference. The credit for convening and inspiring our gathering is yours. To you and to your colleagues, our profound thanks for your leadership and your determination, and your understanding of the crucial importance of the work which lies ahead of us all.

I thank you for setting us on the trail of a constructive international venture and adventure in the search for truth as a massive step towards restitution and justice.

Ambassador Eizenstat – we thank you and your government for all the prodigious work that you and your colleagues have undertaken. We especially recognise and salute your personal, sustained concern. The breadth and courage of your enquiries and of your reports have set a standard for us all.

This Conference is unique. It is a great international recognition of moral debt. It provides new hope for a concerted, energetic and international quest for the truth – the truth about Nazi gold and other looted assets. Truth which must lead to at least some measure of restitution, to some degree of justice, for survivors of Nazi persecution, Jewish and non-Jewish – justice so long delayed and denied. Without the truth, there can be no justice. But the truth alone is only the first step on the road to justice and to restitution.

Is it not devastating, ladies and gentlemen, that fifty years after the end of the war, we still do not know the full and real truth about what happened to Nazi gold – especially non-monetary gold, torn from individuals, most of them murdered. We still do not know the full truth about other assets – bank accounts and deposits, art treasures, insurance policies, the savings and the property of human beings, whose lives the Nazis destroyed. When we achieve that truth, there is then hope for an end to the trail of suspicion, of hatred and of ill-will.

No one can ever return to the victims and their families, their wrecked lives, their murdered relatives, their homes and their hopes. But we shall be judged together – our nations and ourselves – on our effort to uncover the truth. This Conference should enable us achieve much more effectively together than we can do separately. I hope that we shall spur each other on, in the quest for transparency. That we shall accept the challenge of our moral obligations – together.

So I thank the nations here represented. Every country invited by Foreign Secretary Robin Cook to attend this Conference is here today.

We all know of the hesitations and anxieties, the concerns and the problems

with which some nations wrestled before they decided to attend. We will understand how difficult it is for some nations to accept the reality today that their
countrymen behaved so dishonourably, even so long ago. We know that some
nations still fear what research may reveal. But we are here from every nation,
to examine our consciences and our archives, in the international search for an
honourable future, through opening up what was often a deeply dishonourable
past.

For today's governments to make honourable amends as too many of their
predecessors failed to do, presents a great moral challenge – a challenge that has
brought us together today and which will bind us together in the future.

So I thank all nations represented. Together we must make a constructive
contribution towards the work of the Conference and I trust that none will seek
to divert or to diminish that work.

This Conference is one of the greatest, most worthy and challenging international quests for truth in the history of mankind. It is a privilege for all of us to
be part of that quest. But what is its purpose?

For historians, it is the unearthing of a vile chapter of the past, for the sake of
the future. For academics, it is an academy of learning. But for practical human-
itarians seeking to ensure that some measure of justice will emerge from the
ashes of the past, it is a step on the path to restitution.

Restitution for whom? For the survivors of Nazi persecution and for their families – for human beings in need – for people whose lives have been wrecked but
who are now entitled to some quality of life, for that portion of life that remains
for them.

Time, then, is of the essence of our search. There is a burning urgency in all
that we do. The survivors, after all, will not survive for much longer.

We must all face up now, and with no more delay, to failings of the past –
whether they resulted from deliberate malice, or from the ambivalence of immediate convenience.

I salute the Tripartite Gold Commission authorities – the United States,
France and Great Britain – and those claimant countries who have agreed to
their portion of the residue in the TGC funds being used for the benefit of survivors in need.

This decision is the direct outcome of the work of distinguished historians and
diligent researchers, who examined both the provenance of the gold recovered
after the war and the methods of its return. I salute the groundbreaking work in
the reports of the Holocaust Educational Trust, the British Foreign Office
Historians and Librarians, and of course, the Eizenstat report.

It is a tribute to the integrity of the three Government authorities of the
Tripartite Gold Commission that they responded positively and swiftly to my
request to delay the final distribution of the remaining gold until these questions
were properly examined.

I hope that this process will continue to be an example to many countries,
over the many issues that we need most urgently to investigate.

Chairman, my own passionate involvement in this work began when I was a
young 18 year old soldier, serving in Germany – in the British Army of the

Rhine, mainly as a War Crimes Investigator. I was taken by the Jewish Relief Unit to the site of the Belsen concentration camp on the first anniversary of its liberation. I have ever since been haunted by the grief of the survivors. By the pain of their past and the poverty of their present and the grim outlook for their future. There was no Israel, no Jewish State, no country that wanted them. For many months, I spent my weekends and my leave working in Belsen among the human devastation of that Jewish Displaced Persons Camp.

It was then that I determined that one day, some day, somehow, I would do something, to seek to bring some sustenance, some help, some hope to the survivors and to their families.

If this Conference moves swiftly towards that end – if the nations here represented recognise the great moral dimension and challenge of this extraordinary Conference – then we shall all return home, proud to have been part of this worthy assembly.

These three days, then, mark the start and not the finish of our effort. But a most worthy start it certainly is. And I thank all of you who will be working together, on the tortuous trail of the truth, as an urgent start towards the honourable and worthy search for transparency, for restitution – and for justice.

CONTRIBUTIONS

From countries and organisations

ALBANIA

On the plundered Albanian gold by the Nazis; Jews in Albania

PROF. ARBEN PUTO AND QIRJAKO QIRKO

After the capitulation of fascist Italy on September 8, 1943, Albania was invaded by the Nazis. Unlike the previous invaders, the Nazis did not proclaim the union of Albania with the Reich. They declared Albania independent and neutral. In this context they overturned a number of financial agreements reached between Albania and Italy on the eve of Albania's fascist occupation and declared invalid all the legal acts enacted during that period.

Through these measures they wanted to create the impression that the finances of the country were being put under the Albanian national sovereignty and regulated by the country's own laws.

On the other hand, maintaining and keeping the Nazi machine in working mode required funds. To this end, on September 12, 1943, the then man in charge of South-eastern Europe at the German Ministry for Foreign Affairs, Noibaher, in a cable sent to his government said that for army supplies and the carrying out of important strategic works we will be in an ever greater need of financial means. He considered the transfer of Albanian bank-notes available in the Bank of Rome to Albania as an urgent need. He also proposed the transfer of the Albanian gold reserves from the Bank of Rome, where they were deposited during the Italian occupation to Reichsbank because – he explained – they were needed for political and military purposes. The Nazi government considered Noibaher's proposals as appropriate and the same day, its Foreign Ministry asked the German embassy in Rome to get hold of the Albanian gold and bank-notes that were in the Bank of Rome.

The operation for the withdrawal of the Albanian gold and bank-notes from the Bank of Rome was carried out on September 16, 1943, on orders from the German Consul General in Rome, Wishter. It was carried out by special SS troops led by Major Herbert Kapler and in presence of the German Foreign Ministry official in charge, Josef Oertman. The operation led to the plundering of 120,514,902 francs-worth of Albanian banknotes, 8,062,826 gold francs-worth of Albanian gold reserves weighing 2.5 tons. Of those, there were 24 bags full of gold coins worth 435,070 gold francs and 78 bags of gold bars worth 7,637,756 gold francs. The gold reserves of the Albanian National Bank were transported by special plane to Berlin and were deposited in Reichsbank whereas the banknotes were sent to the German Consulate in Tirana, which handed them over to the Albanian National Bank.

Other large financial means were plundered by the Nazi army later on through the credit and loan system. Thus the Nazi military authorities withdrew large amounts of money from the Albanian Bank before it left Albania. On October 21, 1944, Captain Lederch withdrew from the Albanian National Bank the sum of 280,000 gold francs.

Summing up, the Albanian gold plundered by the Nazi constitutes of the following:

- 8,062,826 gold francs plundered from the Albanian National Bank reserves in Rome;
- 280,000 gold francs plundered from the Albanian National Bank itself and
- 5,075,169 gold francs-worth of gold coins and jewellery plundered from the people.

At the end of the war all these quantities of gold were found and identified as belonging to Albania. This was officiated by the Protocol, signed by the Albanian and German governments on April 16, 1944, according to which Albanian gold reserves be put 55 cases sealed with steel strips, which would be initiated and numbered as AN1, AN2, ...AN55. The cases would be stored in the secret tunnels of Reichsbank and could be used by the Albanian government only with the approval of the German Ministry for Foreign Affairs.

Although a long time has passed, Albania has not yet got hold of its gold as determined by the Tri-lateral Commission. Such a delay has come about because the Albanian communist government, in power for 45 years, politicised the problem.

The Albanian gold issue embarked on the way towards a solution after the collapse of the communist regime. In the early 1990's members of the Trilateral Commission were contacted, in 1992 a protocol was concluded with the British government, in 1995 an agreement with the American government was reached and the approval of the French government was given for the withdrawal of the gold. At present, only a final document remains to be signed between the Tri-lateral Commission and the Albanian government.

Albania is considered as one of the most damaged countries during the World War II (judging by the population it had). For this reason it will always support all initiatives in favour of the rehabilitation of all victims of the war and especially of the Jewish people, as one of the most victimised people by the Nazi madness.

Allow me to make a brief historical description of the contacts between the Albanian and Jewish peoples.

The first contacts of the Albanian government with the Jews date back to the mid 1930's. Hitler's coming to power marked for the Jews in general, and those of Germany in particular, the beginning of a cruel persecution and genocide. From the historical documents in the Albanian State Archives we learned that the International Jewish circles (including the Committee for Jewish Refugees in London) began to show an interest in Albania in 1934. Some Zionist organisations planned to bring and settle in Albania thousands of Jews displaced from Nazi Germany. Efforts to carry out these plans were mediated by the High Commission of Refugees at the League of Nations. Albania was chosen as a possible shelter for two reasons: first, because it was regarded as a safe haven, far enough away from the racist influences that were then spreading along the coastal border on the Adriatic Sea. Thus Albania was going to be used as a temporary stop for the German Jews, who would later be moved towards Palestine by sea. Those efforts continued for two years (until 1935), but without any concrete result. This was because the League of Nations did not agree to bring to Albania a large Jewish community, to settle there for good, whereas the Albanian government insisted on the opposite hoping that the Jewish immigrants would bring with them financial means that would help the poor Balkan country's economic development.

However, the early thirties saw an influx of Jewish refugees to Albania. They came from Germany, Poland and Czechoslovakia. Being under the pressure of fascist Italy, the Albanian government set some restrictive regulations with regards to the entry of the Jews in Albania. But the then Albanian government was inconsistent in applying these regulations.

The Jews continued to come to Albania even after the fascist invasion of Albania, on April 9, 1939. Most of them came from Serbia and Montenegro where their life was being put in danger as a result of a wave of deportations to Germany. In the circumstances, the Italians invaded Albania, which still continued to attract Jews, and was known for its moderate stand. However, in the documents of the then administration one can note a tendency to control the Israel immigration. Not all the Jews were treated even-handedly. A difference could be seen in the handling of the Jews who had been in the country for a long time and those who had arrived just before or after the outbreak of the war. The former were not subject to the so-called restrictive measures that were introduced. They were considered as Albanians. Whereas the latter (those who had arrived just before or after the outbreak of the war), were put in refugee camps. It must be stressed that the camps set up by the Italian fascist administration cannot be compared to those set up by the Nazis. Such camps were built in central Albania (Berat and Kavaje) and in northern Albania (Burrel).

After the capitulation of fascist Italy and the country's invasion by Nazi Germany, the anti-Semitic propaganda was intensified. It was aimed at creating a gap between the local population and the Jews so that they could be easily identified and sent to the mass-extermination camps. It was these circumstances that highlighted the human solidarity of Albanians in all its values. Almost all the Jews that were in Albania were sheltered by the Albanian families, both in towns and countryside. It is worth mentioning here the humane attitude of some Italian military authorities who released the Jewish immigrants from the camps before they fell into the hands of the Nazi troops.

At the end of the war, most of the Jews were evacuated by UNRA.

Judging by the archival sources that we have as well as by the memories of the former Jewish refugees we come to the conclusion that Albania became a safe haven for the Jews during World War II. This ranks the Albanian people among those peoples who were distinguished for the precious help they provided for thousands upon thousands of Jewish families, sharing with them the poverty and danger, by not allowing any of them to fall prey to the Nazi extermination fury.

ARGENTINA

Nazi War Criminals and Assets: 1

ROGELIO PFIRTER

Argentine Ambassador to the United Kingdom

I should like first to congratulate the British Government on its initiative in organising this Conference which will undoubtedly be an important step on the way to throwing light on one of the darkest and most inhuman chapters of recent history.

The guiding spirit behind the calling of this conference coincides with my Government's firm determination to establish the facts connected with the activities of Nazism in Argentina.

In fact, it is the Government's and, indeed, the whole Argentine people's conviction that to investigate and clarify these facts, which represent an extremely negative moment in our history, constitutes a duty not only towards the victims of Nazism but also towards the vast majority of Argentines who aspire to live in a fully democratic society founded on unconditional respect for human rights.

I wish to draw attention to some of the specific measures which the Argentine Government has adopted during the present decade, which demonstrate its clear intention to get to the full facts concerning the activities of Nazism in Argentina.

To that end, in 1992, it approved Decree 232/92, a measure which allowed publicity to be given to documentation connected with Nazi activities, which the official institutions were keeping confidential.

The following year, it issued Decree 1290/93, a legal instrument which made it possible to make public documentation relating to cases linked to racially or politically motivated persecution or crimes.

Immediately thereafter, that same year, the joint resolution of 6 December 1993 of the Ministries of the Interior, Foreign Affairs, International Trade and Worship, Economic Affairs and Public Works and Services, Defence and Justice, made possible the adoption of various measures which would help to throw light on the activities of the Nazi regime.

On 6 May 1997, President Menem decided to set up the Commission of Enquiry into the Activities of Nazism in the Argentine Republic (CEANA), a decision based on his firm conviction that the long period of time which had elapsed since the events occurred meant that there could be no delay in making every effort to get to the full facts concerning those illegal activities, in as effective and impartial a manner as possible.

The Commission is non-governmental and autonomous in character and receives financial and logistical support from the Argentine State.

Under the decree establishing it, in the event that the CEANA "finds, as a result of the research carried out, any evidence concerning the commission of offences, that circumstance shall be reported to the judicial authorities." The Commission is constituted at three levels:

- An International Panel made up of international personalities of recognised prestige, experience and ethical and moral qualities, to whom the reports, conclusions and findings of the Academic Committee will be made available so that it can give its approval if it considers it appropriate.
- An Advisory Committee, composed of institutions connected with this subject area, to provide advice and co-operate in the research.
- An Academic Committee responsible for carrying out the studies and research.

The Minister of Foreign Affairs, Mr Guido Di Tella, invited prestigious personalities to participate in the CEANA and, on 15 July of last year, announced its definitive membership to the press.

Subsequently, Mr Di Tella met on various occasions with the members of the CEANA in order to exchange ideas and proposals.

To that end, he held meetings

- with the members of the "Argentine Chapter" in Buenos Aires on 19 August 1997;
- with the members of the "North American Chapter" in New York on 22 September 1997;
- with the members of the "European Chapter" in London on 31 October 1997.

On 24 November of last year, the Minister of Foreign Affairs held the second meeting of the "Argentine Chapter" on the occasion of his meeting in this country with the Vice-Chairmen of the CEANA Academic Committee, Professors Ronald Newton and Robert Potash.

Otherwise, it should be stressed that the process of engaging the main researchers who will carry out the field tasks has been concluded.

Likewise, the national Government has already introduced the relevant measures to enable these professionals to have unrestricted access to all the national, provincial and municipal archives, as well as to those of private bodies and institutions, and to receive whatever co-operation and assistance are necessary for their research.

Finally, I should like formally to announce that the Argentine Government has decided to make a contribution to the compensation fund for survivors of the holocaust, the amount of which will be determined by legislation.

This measure will be incorporated into the initiatives which the Executive Power will present to the Congress of the Nation for discussion during its 1998 ordinary session.

This latter measure is a further demonstration of the seriousness and firmness of the commitment of my country, joining forces with the international community, to throw light on, and in some measure relieve, the pain and suffering of the innocent victims of one of darkest moments in contemporary history.

Nazi War Criminals and Assets: 2

IGNACIO KLICH

Academic Co-ordinator of the Commission of Enquiry
into the Activities of Nazism in Argentina

To understand the coming into being of the Commission of Enquiry into the Activities of Nazism in Argentina (CEANA), a government created and supported through non-governmental commission, and the difference in mandate between CEANA and other commissions, namely Argentina's interest in reaching an informed estimate of Nazi war criminal arrivals, in addition to determining whether Nazi loot entered the country during and post-World War II, it is necessary to look into Argentina's mixed wartime and postwar record.

During the war the country did not sever diplomatic relations with the Axis until January 1944, a date generally missed in many recent accounts of Argentina's performance; this afforded Axis agents a unique base of operations in Latin America, especially after Pearl Harbour. At the same time, though, all Argentine exports went to the Allies and were supplied on credit, while the foremost achievement of Buenos Aires-based Nazi agents was to smuggle to the Third Reich small quantities of strategic materials. Moreover, Argentina witnessed the entry of not less than 40,000 Jewish refugees during 1933–45. In hindsight they were too few to have a decisive impact on Nazi extermination plans, but the Jews who entered Argentina, some of them surreptitiously, represented a record figure in Latin America, and this at a time when the country's authorities generally opposed the admission of refugees, whether Republican Spaniards, Jews, etc. In addition, Argentina's postwar efforts to lure former Third Reich scientists and technicians came hand-in-hand with the arrival of alleged, indicted and convicted Nazi war criminals. Finally, successive Argentine governments, whether elected or de facto, were generally reluctant to extradite war criminals, notwithstanding the stigma carried by such a behaviour.

Of course, Argentina's reticence to admit Jewish refugees was far from unique: its interest in Nazi brainpower mirrored other countries' more successful efforts, while the unwillingness to part company with wanted Nazis duplicated that of others, whether in Latin America or elsewhere. Nevertheless, a greater readiness to grant extraditions began to become evident after the return to elected governments in December 1983. Visible under President Raul Alfonsin, during whose term in office Josef Schwammberger's extradition to Germany was decided, such readiness was furthered by President Carlos Menem's deportation of Schwammberger and extradition to Italy of Erich Priebke. Today, Argentina's extraditions, not more than three, have turned the country into the Latin American state that has sent most war criminals to stand trial, and this as part of a concerted effort to come to terms with a past which, rightly or wrongly, proven or unproven, is connected in many minds with far more recent instances of terrible violence in the country.

Not surprisingly, a bipartisan approach has meant that the notion of establishing a commission to investigate whether Nazi gold had been stashed away or laundered via Argentina was first heard of last year, initially presented by opposition legislators, with the Menem government responding to the challenge with a commission with an enlarged remit, and resorting to local and foreign specialists, whether to carry out research or judge results. Concerning the latter, CEANA's International Panel is made up of seventeen personalities, including among others Marcos Aguinis, a former Alfonsín administration Secretary of Culture; Adolfo Gass, a former Radical party lawmaker and current vicepresident of Argentina's Permanent Assembly for Human Rights; Sir Sigmund Sternberg, chairman of the International Council of Christians and Jews; Lord Dahrendorf, a former warden of St. Antony's College, Oxford; and the World Jewish Congress' Edgar Bronfman. Against the background of an isolationist and inward-looking past, the above mentioned is rather unprecedented in Argentine history, and is pregnant with implications for those who would like to see Argentina's decades old culture of secrecy replaced by transparency, not only in respect of the country's record during and post-World War II.

While it would be idle to pretend that the body of Argentine documents on the Nazi subject is beyond enlargement, diplomatic and presidential papers at official repositories have become increasingly easier to access; those pertaining to extradition requests became readily available in 1993, irrespective of the year when such requests were lodged, while Banco Central books covering wartime and postwar transactions in gold were released into the public domain last year.

An enlarged body of Argentine documents, as covered by government decrees issued since 1992 is certainly crucial to the fulfilment of CEANA's mandate; but it is also the case that 'the jigsaw may never be complete,' to quote Foreign Secretary Robin Cook's words this morning, without linking the findings in Argentina with those afforded by papers of foreign governments, as well as Jewish and other institutions. If this were not the case, we could simply declare ourselves satisfied with the state of the art on the major topics under scrutiny, i.e. proclaim that the best scholarly work on the migration to Argentina of German and Austrian war criminals disallows speculation of an Argentine intake of 1,000 to 60,000 Nazi war criminals; likewise, we could simply declare ourselves amply satisfied with the results of the scouring of US archival materials by Ambassador Stuart Eizenstat's team, namely that Argentina has not been a haven for Nazi gold or other looted assets, including gems and art treasures, which contradict some of the undocumented and extravagant claims made in respect of Argentina.

None of the aforementioned is meant to minimise the setting of Nazi war criminals in the country, or its possible though yet to be proven role in the subject of Nazi assets. However, if truth is a prerequisite for justice, we need a better estimate of the number of Nazi war criminals who came to Argentina, as well as to explain transactions in gold with, among other countries, Chile, Portugal and Switzerland. In the interest of avoiding duplication, CEANA has started where others have left; at this point in time, eight research units, headed by local or foreign scholars, have their sights set on the following subjects.

1. Quantification of Nazi war criminals according to Argentine government documents.
2. Quantification of Nazi war criminals according to foreign, namely German and Austrian sources.
3. Spain as a possible stepping stone for Nazi war criminals and loot aimed at Argentina.
4. Italy as a country of transit for Nazi and other war criminals arrived in Argentina.
5. German U-boats and the arrival in Argentina of Nazi war criminals, hierarchies and assets.
6. Bank Central transactions in gold and hard currency with Axis and neutral countries and Argentina's international economic exchanges.
7. Nazi investments in Argentina through third parties.
8. The impact of war criminal and other Nazi arrivals on Argentine politics and society.

Whether too ambitious or too modest, a successful conclusion of such research has already demanded prior knowledge that hitherto unused Argentine sources are available, as well as the search of important collaborative ventures with others. In connection with the latter, the meeting organised by Switzerland's Independent Commission of Historians in October 1997 afforded Argentina, the sole Spanish-speaking and/or Latin American country represented at that gathering, a valuable opportunity for initiating contact with the CEANA's counterparts elsewhere with a view to exchanging materials, a process we look forward to further during this conference.

AUSTRIA

Statement by Mr. Hans Winkler

ON BEHALF OF THE AUSTRIAN DELEGATION

First of all, I would like to thank the member governments of the Tripartite Gold Commission for having initiated this conference and the government of the United Kingdom for hosting this important gathering. We welcome this opportunity to make our own position on the subject matter of this conference known and to exchange views with other government representatives and with important NGOs in the course of the coming days.

Austria has followed with great interest the studies undertaken by various international bodies – governmental and non-governmental – on the issues connected to the gold transactions by the Nazi regime before and during Second World War. Taking the findings of the Commission established by the President of the United States and headed by Secretary Eizenstat as a starting point, Austria has investigated with care the historical sequence of events surrounding the illegal seizure of the official Austrian gold reserves by the Nazi regime right after the occupation of Austria by Germany in March of 1938 up to the restitution of part of the stolen gold by the Allies after the end of the war. What we found with the help of the appropriate authorities, in particular the Austrian National bank which actually owned the gold in 1938, corresponds entirely with the records kept by the Tripartite Gold Commission and with the historical facts as they appear in the already mentioned Eizenstat report.

This is not the time to enter into all the details of the history of the monetary gold reserves of the first Republic of Austria. Suffice it to say that the Gold Commission recognised that Austria has claims to the restitution of some 65% of the gold stolen from her by the Nazis in 1938. This means that of the 78.2 tons of gold reserves transferred to Berlin, Austria has a valid claim recognised by the Gold Commission to approx. 51 tons of gold, of which 50.1 tons have already been restituted in several instalments in the years 1948 to 1958. The final amount still pending according to the notification received by the TGC therefore amounts to exactly 26,829 ounces of gold which represents a value of roughly 9 million US-Dollars.

Even before our authorities were able to establish all the facts about the Austrian gold reserves that were transferred to the German Reichsbank and before the exact amount of the remaining Austrian claim was known, my government publicly expressed a positive attitude to the proposal of the United States, later supported by the other members of the TGC, to put a substantial portion of the $70 million that remain at the disposal of the Gold Commission into a fund for victims of the holocaust. We have from the beginning shared the view that taken as a global amount, the sum to be distributed seems a pittance, but it could nevertheless significantly help in particular those ageing survivors of the Nazi atrocities who have not received anything so far close to the justice they deserve.

The unrefutable proof that at least a portion of the gold restituted to the claimant countries since the end of the war as well as of the gold still in the vaults of the Federal Reserve and other banks was non-monetary, belonging to individual victims of the Nazi persecution, confirmed our conviction that a moral oblation exists to making available the amount still held by the TGC to the benefit of needy survivors of the holocaust. We regard this as a humanitarian gesture as expression of shared international solidarity with the victims of the holocaust.

As a consequence of this positive attitude, Austria has actively and in a constructive way participated in the work of the task force established three months ago in order to elaborate guidelines for the setting up and the functioning of an account which would collect contributions by individual Governments. The contributions should then be used in a manner consistent with the overall objective that I have mentioned. Although not all the details have been clarified up to now, we are satisfied with the work the task force was able to carry out so far. In particular, we share the approach that the whole undertaking should be a joint one by the international community – and we hope that a large number of countries will be able to subscribe to it – but at the same time preserve the freedom of action of participating countries to take into account their priorities within the framework of the general principle that the beneficiaries should be victims of Nazi persecution. Austria has also insisted that the bureaucratic mechanism for the distribution of funds should not involve heavy overhead costs. It is our desire that the money is used for the benefit of the victims and that the necessary arrangements are taken as soon as possible. Finally, it was our wish that money should not go only to individuals but also projects that are connected with the fight against racism, anti-Semitism, intolerance and xenophobia should be qualified to receive contributions from the international account.

*   *   *   *   *

Austria has from the beginning actively supported a speedy elaboration of the terms of reference and the structure of the international account in order to provide the necessary legal basis for a final decision by the Austrian Government on its financial contribution for the benefit of holocaust survivors. Not all points have been resolved at this stage. In particular, it remains to be decided within our own administration which administrative and legislative steps must be taken in order to come to a final decision. There is, in any event, broad political consensus in Austria that the share in the gold still held by the gold Commission to which Austria has a legitimate claim, should be used for such purposes. As I said, we also see great benefit in a broad international effort and we therefore welcome the setting up of the international account by the British Government. Details remain to be worked out but we firmly believe that we should not stand aside in this unique demonstration of international solidarity. We fully subscribe to the words of Secretary Eizenstat in this respect, when he said "it is important that a healing process begin, and that genuine reconciliation be achieved. Here there is genuine reason for optimism, especially with so many countries now willing to honestly confront their past and to draw lessons from it."

BANK OF ENGLAND

The Bank of England's role as custodian of the Tripartite Gold Commission's holdings of gold

As the government's bankers, the Bank of England acted as advisors to HM Government when the original efforts were made to determine the origin of the gold recovered from Germany at the end of the Second World War. Since 1947, the Bank's role has been limited to that of safe custodian for the Tripartite Commission for the Restitution of Monetary Gold, (TGC). In that year, two accounts were opened in the Bank's books, both in the name of "HM Treasury o/a the Governments of US, UK and France (Tripartite Commission)." One account was used to hold gold in bar form, and the other held coins. Decisions covering the operation of these accounts, (and in particular the paying away of any gold amounts), have been made by the 3 governments and the TGC.

The amount of looted gold recovered by the three Allied Governments during and after the War eventually totalled about 337 tonnes, of which nearly 158 tonnes was deposited at one time or another at the Bank of England. Most of this gold came from the Foreign Exchange Depository in Frankfurt where the gold recovered by the US military authorities had been collected.

Acting on instructions from the TGC, the Bank made initial distributions from the TGC's accounts to 9 countries, (Austria, Belgium, Czechoslovakia, Greece, Italy, Luxembourg, Holland, Poland and Yugoslavia), between June 1948 and March 1952. Second, quasi-final distributions were similarly made to these countries between 1958 and 1982. An outstanding claim from Albania was satisfactorily resolved in 1995–6, with the quasi-final Albanian distribution being made in October 1996.

When the preliminary and quasi-final shares were distributed, allocations were rounded down to the nearest 50 kgs. of gold. This, plus a previously planned small balance to cover operating costs and other contingencies, leaves approximately 5.5 tonnes for final distribution to claimant countries – 3.5 tonnes at the Bank of England and 2 tonnes at the Federal Reserve.

Pre-war, individually numbered gold bars were held in the Bank on individual accounts, a system known as allocated gold. However, in early 1940, it was clear that in order to safeguard the gold being held at the Bank it would be best if it was dispersed overseas for safety. In order to expedite this mammoth operation, the Bank's policy on the custody of gold changed in May 1940. Gold now became fungible. In other words, gold was held on fine ounce basis, with a particular weight recorded as belonging to each customer, rather than specific bars.

At the end of the War, repatriation of these gold stocks from overseas began. In addition, the Bank began to receive large accumulated stocks of gold from various producer countries. It was at this time that the TGC gold was also received at the Bank.

One of the main concerns of the TGC when the recovered gold was first shipped to the Bank was to confirm the validity of the gold content. For gold to be regarded as "good delivery" it needs, inter alia, to be of a minimum fineness of 995 parts per thousand pure gold. A world-wide system of acceptable melter and assayer marks is in use, and these marks on bars are taken as confirming the fineness figure either stamped on them or shown on an accompanying Certificate of Assay. This system prevents the cost of a re-assay being needed each time a bar changes ownership. Pre-War, the two German refiners, the Prussian State Mint and Degussa, had been acceptable refiners, and their marks regarded accordingly. At the end of the War, this acceptability was revoked.

Although no complete definitive records exist, it is likely that the majority of bars delivered to the Bank for the TGC would have borne either one of these two refinery marks or no mark at all. As the decision had already been made by the TGC that this gold was to be redistributed as monetary gold, it was necessary for all the bars to be melted and re-refined into "good delivery" bars. The identity of the original bars was, therefore, lost. All of the coin, (which consisted mostly of US dollars and UK sovereigns) has left the Bank as a result of distribution to claimants by the TGC.

In 1950, the Bank reverted to its earlier practice of holding gold on a specific bar basis. The individual bars allocated to the TGC's account at the time of this change of policy would not necessarily have been those produced as a result of the re-refining programme of the late 1940s because, as mentioned above, most of the TGC bars bore stamps of disqualified or unknown refiners and needed to be re-refined to acceptable size and status. These bars would then have been pooled with all other bars held, on an unallocated basis, with their original identity lost.

Two bars, with Nazi markings and date stamped 1938, are held by the Bank on behalf of the TGC. These bars would appear to have been part of the reserves of the Belgian Central Bank stolen by the Nazis and then remelted and restamped with a false date. They had been part of the gold recovered by US forces in Germany in 1945. The bulk of the recovered gold was sent to Frankfurt, but these two bars were seemingly delivered to the then Reichsbank offices in Munich where they were held on special closed deposit. The Bank of England first became aware of the existence of these bars in 1988. The bars were transferred to the US authorities in September 1996, who in turn transferred them to the TGC in accordance with the 1946 Paris Agreement on Reparation from Germany. The TGC then deposited the bars with the Bank of England.

There is little evidence in the Bank's records of the Bank taking receipt of items that might be regarded as personal gold. A small quantity of "certain gold coins, medals and tokens" was received in 1948 which could not easily be assessed for gold content. The total weight of these items was approximately 134 kgs. The TGC referred these items to a Curator at the British Museum who decided that none of the items had a numismatic or historical value within the meaning of the Paris Agreement. The TGC instructed that these items be melted into good delivery bars.

The practice of lending gold for an interest payment has grown in recent years. Recently, the TGC decided to place most of its gold at the Bank out in the London market, on deposit. Although our current policy is to allocate gold bars to specific accounts, this is not the case for bullion lent in the market on fixed term deposit. When the deposit matures, the borrower is obliged to repay only the same weight of gold, not the same bars. So the TGC bars put on deposit are unlikely to be the ones eventually returned to their account here at the Bank.

The following table shows details of all transactions across the TGC's gold account at the Bank of England.

Bank of England Transactions – according to TGC Gold Book

1948

20 May	Transfer from Swiss National Bank of 578, 700.153 oz in bars on behalf of Rumanian Government.
30 June	Transfer to Banque de France of 463,664.343 oz in bars
1(?) July	Charges for handling, re-melting and storage 488.856 oz
12 July	Shipment from Frankfurt – 416,333.537 oz in coins
15 July	Shipment from Frankfurt – 149,259.939 oz in coins
23 July	Shipment from Frankfurt – 508,362.615 oz in coins
23 July	Storage charges – 28.637 oz
28 July	Transfer to National Bank of Austria 330,862.199 oz in coins and 358,434.052 in bars (but see below 17 Aug)
28 July	Transfer to Bank of Italy of 269,710.784 oz in coins (but see 31 August)
28 July	Amount of gold resulting from re-smelting of Prussian bars delivered by BIS – 89,541.258 oz (but see 20 December for amendment)
28 July	Bars from BIS – 30,683.887 oz
28 July	Charges for re-smelting and storage – 91.480 oz
28 July	Shipment from Frankfurt – 289,843.727 oz in bars
3 Aug	Shipment from Frankfurt – 575,740.933 oz in coins
11 Aug	Shipment from Frankfurt – 44,928.851 oz in coins
11 Aug	Handling and storage charges – 847.312 oz
17 Aug	Quantities transferred to National Bank of Austria amended – 330,862.153 oz coins and 358,434.098 bars (see 28 July)
24 Aug	Shipment from Frankfurt – 68,535.798 oz bars and 33,919.156 oz coins
24 Aug	Handling and storage charges – 348.817 oz
30 Aug	Shipment from Frankfurt – 227,374.261 oz bars and 58,735.636 oz coins
30 Aug	Handling and storage charges – 215.372 oz
31 Aug	Shipment from Frankfurt – 44,385.563 oz coins
31 Aug	Handling and storage charges 22.192 oz
31 Aug	Amendment of amount transferred to Bank of Italy (see 28 July) 269,710.696 oz coins

1948 continued

23 Sept	Transfer to National Bank of Federative and Popular Republic of Yugoslavia – 269,841.059 oz coins and 6,919.692 oz bars
1 Oct	Storage charges 206.053 oz
8 Oct	Transfer to Bank of Italy – 14,917.944 oz in bars
15 Oct	Shipment from Frankfurt – 696,154.048 oz bars
15 Oct	Handling and storage charges – 577.480 oz
14 (?) Oct	Transfer to National Bank of Austria – 190,784.716 oz coins
18 Oct	Shipment from Frankfurt – 13,009.870 oz coins and 3,937.431 oz and 409.381 oz bars
18 Oct	Handling and storage charges – 17.430 oz
19 Oct	Amount of gold shipped from Frankfurt and melted down – 33,723.042oz (Prussian bars/coins?)
19 Oct	Handling and storage charges – 104.947 oz
21 Oct	Storage charges – 71.527 oz
20 (?) Oct	Storage charges – 127.664 oz
22 Oct	Shipment from Frankfurt – 664,583.899 oz bars
22 Oct	Handling and storage charges – 545.572 oz
25 Oct	Shipment from Frankfurt – 25,679.605 oz bars
25 Oct	Handling and storage charges – 12.840 oz
28 Oct	Storage charges – 7.671 oz
3 Nov	Storage charges – 355.035 oz
4 Nov	Storage charges – 11.199 oz
15 Nov	Cost of new sacks for coins – 53.254 oz
20 Dec	Amendment of amount of gold in Prussian coins transferred by BIS, melted down – 89,559.890 oz
20 Dec	Loss in smelting of Prussian coins transferred by BIS – 18.632 oz

1949

1 Jan	Storage charges – 162.297 oz
20 Jan	Storage charges – 127.664 oz
21 Jan	Storage charges – 71.527 oz
28 Jan	Storage charges – 7.671 oz
3 Feb	Storage charges – 355.035 oz
4 Feb	Storage charges – 11.199 oz
28 Feb	Transfer from Spain (Instituto de Moneda Extranjero Madrid) – 3,267.271 oz bars
28 Feb	Handling and transport charges – 1.044 oz
18 Mar	Reimbursement by Bank of England to TGC of handling and storage charges – 3,196,437 oz
18 Mar	Settling of account of losses incurred by France in re-smelting Prussian mint bars – 154.748 oz
1 June	Storage charges – 57.571 oz
1 Sept	Storage charges – 57.571 oz
1 Dec	Storage charges – 40.000 oz

1950

6 Jan	Transfer to Netherlands Bank – 450,110.403 oz bars and 310,132.656 coins
7 Mar	Storage charges – 40.000 oz
20 Mar	Shipment from US Zone of Austria – 2,903.063 oz bars and 61.842 oz coins
20 Mar	Handling and transport charges – 2.524 oz
1 June	Storage charges – 40.000 oz
1 Sept	Storage charges – 40.000 oz
4 Dec	Storage charges – 40.000 oz

1951

4 Jan	Transfer to National Bank of the Federative and Popular Republic of Yugoslavia – 1,629.648 oz bars
4 April	Storage charges – 40.000 oz
4 June	Storage charges – 40.000 oz
18 Sept	Storage charges – 40.000 oz
6 Dec	Storage charges – 40.000 oz

1952

4 March	Storage charges – 40.000 oz
12 March	Shipment from Austria of 585,487 oz coins (sovereigns and US gold dollars)
12 March	Handling charge – 0.146 oz
17 March	Transfer to Banque de France for Belgian account – 520,975.361 oz bars and 282,793.189 oz coins
30 March	Transfer to Netherlands Bank of replacements for false coins – 9.675 oz (?25 August)
4 June	Storage charges – 20.000 oz
18 Sept	Storage charges – 20.000 oz
3 Dec	Storage charges – 20.000 oz

1953

8 March	Storage charges – 20.000 oz
7 June	Storage charges – 20.000 oz
4 Sept	Storage charges – 20.000 oz
10 Dec	Storage charges – 20.000 oz

1954

4 March	Storage charges – 20.000 oz
4 June	Storage charges – 20.091 oz
19 Sept	Storage charges – 20.009 oz
15 Nov.	Sale of 2 gold bars – 806.182 oz
29 Dec	Sale of 2 gold bars – 807.251 oz

1955

17 May	Sale of 2 gold bars – 806.953 oz

1956

17 Aug   Sale of 2 gold bars – 807.953 oz
17 Dec   Sale of 2 gold bars – 808.974 oz

1957

21 Oct   Sale of 2 gold bars – 810.591 oz

1958

12 May   Sale of 2 gold bars – 802.283 oz
6 June   Exchange of 106 bars in the Commission's account for 107 Bank of
                England bars – 82.506 oz
2 July   Transfer to Belgium and Luxembourg. (France), of 211,659.148 oz bars
                and 13,458.848 oz coins
7 July   Transfer to Italy of 409,920.847 oz bars
7 Aug   Transfer to Austria 197,725.755 oz bars
5 Nov.   Transfer to Yugoslavia 31,613.597 oz bars and 24,650.190 oz coins

1959

15 Jan   Sale of 1 gold bar – 400.731 oz
29 June   Transfer to Greece of 815.508 oz bars and 792.022 oz coins
17 Aug   Sale of 2 gold bars – 804.425 oz
24 Dec   Transfer to Bank of England from Portugal of 128,500.638 oz bars
31 Dec   Transfer to Bank of England from Portugal of 61.583 oz bars and sale of
                this amount on the same day

1960

9 March   Transfer to Bank of England from British Zone of Germany of 7 coins
                weighing 0.918 oz
25 April   Sale of 2 gold bars – 805.059 oz

1961

6 Jan   Sale of 2 gold bars – 808.272 oz
25 Sept   Sale of 2 gold bars – 804.207 oz

1962

30 April   Sale of 2 gold bars – 808.564 oz

1963

16 Jan   Sale of 2 gold bars – 808.049 oz
18 Sept   Sale of 2 gold bars – 809.336 oz

1964

11 May   Sale of 2 gold bars – 806.399 oz

1965

22 Jan   Sale of 2 gold bars – 807.419 oz
19 Oct   Sale of 2 gold bars – 806.970 oz

1966

1 July   Sale of 3 gold bars – 1,214.280 oz

1967

19 May   Sale of 3 gold bars – 1,210.808 oz

1968

13 June   Sale of 2 gold bars – 808.414 oz

1969

17 March   Sale of 2 gold bars – 810.081 oz
9 Dec   Sale of 3 gold bars – 1,209.087 oz

1971

9 March   Sale of 3 gold bars – 1,210.751 oz

1972

6 Jun   Sale of 3 gold bars – 1,207.421 oz
18 July   Sale of 2 gold bars – 805.445 oz

1973

30 May   Transfer to the Netherlands of 4,410.351 oz bars and 73,692.148 oz coins

1976

25 Aug   Transfer to Poland of 29,327.197 oz coins
21 Dec   Sale of 1 gold bar – 406.259 oz

1982

20 Feb   Transfer to Czechoslovakia of 327,633.729 oz coins

1987

18 Dec   Sale of 1 gold bar – 403.968 oz

1996

3 Oct   Receipt of 2 Prussian State Mint bars – 797.539 oz
29 Oct   Transfer to Albania – 31,168.508 oz bars and 18,636.069 oz coins

1997

5 Feb   Placed on interest bearing Fixed Term Deposits – 113,839.674 oz

Bank of England Archive: Records on Wartime Gold Transactions

This is a guide to records in the Bank of England Archive bearing on wartime gold dealings and movements. The transactional records listed will, it is believed, enable researchers to identify all the Bank's dealings from 1927 to 1966. The selection of policy and subject files has of necessity been subjective: files included are those where the compiler believes they will be of relevance or at least interest, or where an interest has already been expressed.

Other records exist and are available for public access. Full finding aids are available. Please contact the Bank's Archivists, Henry Gillett and Sarah Millard on 0171 601 4889/5096 for details or appointments to see records.

Notes on this list:
The date spans given are those of the file(s) but the papers relevant to this subject do not necessarily cover the same range. Bank records are, in general, open for public access after 30 years.

Henry Gillett
Bank of England Archive
Threadneedle St
London EC2 8AH
e-mail archive@bankofengland.co.uk

17 November 1997

Records dealing principally with the Tripartite Gold Commission (TGC)

C52/9 is the Bullion Office file dealing with the visit of Bank staff to Frankfurt to help with inventorying the gold held at the Frankfurt Exchange Depository in 1945. There are preliminary lists, working papers, a general report on conditions and working procedures and detailed coin and bar lists.

OV34/251 is the Overseas Department file on the TGC, 1941–48. Contains details of claims presented by the governments of Albania, Czechoslovakia and Poland.

OV34/218–219 are Overseas Department files entitled "Germany; looted property and its restitution." 1942–47. Joint Allied Declaration on looted gold. German methods of securing control of property rights and interests situated in or belonging to residents of occupied allied territory. Gold finds; inventories. Bank staff visit; correspondence. Rumours of further hoards. Frankfurt inventories. Estimates of gold looted by Germany. Estimates of looted Dutch, Austrian and Italian gold.

OV34/247–250 are files of the Overseas Department entitled "Germany; restitution of monetary gold." 1945–77. Proposals to pool gold as found. Paris Conference on Reparations. List of gold held in British zone. Definition of "monetary" and other terms relevant to pooling and reparation. Tripartite Commission established. Analysis of claims received. Gold available for restitution. Distributions. Dutch claim in 1963.

Other records, relating to the TGC's relationship with the Bank as a customer, remain subject to customer confidentiality.

Records on specific countries

ALBANIA

OV116/1–2 Overseas Department file on Albania, 1923–64.
Albanian gold with Banca d'Italia. Albanian claim, Italian counter claim etc.

BELGIUM

OV88/48 Overseas Department file on Belgium, 1927–51.
Holdings in Belgium and in the Belgian Congo. Gold with the Bank of France looted by Germany, equivalent restored post war.

C43/425 Gold and foreign exchange file on Belgium, 1940–43. Anglo-Belgian gold agreement 1941: Gold belonging to National Bank of Belgium to be delivered to Bank of Ottawa for prosecution of war and to be repaid in instalments after conclusion of hostilities.

C43/376–382 Gold and foreign exchange file on Belgium, 1933–54. Gold purchase and sale. Shipments to London during the war.

CANADA

C43/167 Gold and foreign exchange file on Canada, 1939–40. Gold shipments to Canada: line and port to be used.

C43/240–242 Gold and foreign exchange file on Canada, 1939–42. Shipments by naval vessels.

C43/247 Gold and foreign exchange file on Canada, 1937–71. Opening of new account with Bank of Canada, Montreal, prior to shipments of gold from France, 1938; press speculation; choice of shipping line.

C43/629 Gold and foreign exchange file on Canada, 1940–46. Evacuation of foreign central bank gold set aside at Bank, following that of Treasury gold to Ottawa, with particular reference to occupied France, and arrangements after war for repatriation of gold and re-set aside.

CZECHOSLOVAKIA

OV112/5–8 Overseas Department file on Czechoslovakia, 1939–47. Some papers on the Czech gold transfer, but mostly dealing with arrangements for blocking Czech assets. Czech gold holdings in Switzerland.

C43/374–375 Gold and foreign exchange file on Czechoslovakia, 1933–70. Narodni Banka Ceskoslovenska; gold and foreign exchange accounts with the Bank. Holdings on the account vested with Custodian. Resumption of relations after the war.

OV4/101 Overseas Department file on BIS/Czechoslovakia, 1939–47. Detailed account of the sequence of events leading to and following the transfer of Czech gold held in London on BIS account to Reichsbank BIS account.

OV4/102 Press cuttings on the Czech gold affair, 1939.

G14/166 Committee of Treasury file on Czech gold affair, 1939. Extracts from the Bank's Committee of Treasury on Czech gold, and some correspondence between the Governor and the Chancellor.

G15/327 Secretary's Department file of miscellanea, 1943. Includes an internal memorandum on the Czech gold affair, prepared for internal circulation.

FRANCE

C43/451–452 Gold and foreign exchange file on France, 1935–45. Gold moved to Canada from France and from London. Gold holdings and movements.

OV45/95–96 Overseas Department file on France, 1932–52. Location of French gold. Movements, transactions etc.

C40/1008 Cashier's Department file on France, 1940–41. Bank of France Gold: Bank/HMG correspondence on transfer of title to Custodian of Enemy Property.

C43/629 Gold and foreign exchange file on French Equatorial Africa, 1941–44. Purchase of gold from French Equatorial Africa.

HOLLAND

C43/371 Gold and foreign exchange file on Holland, 1933–59.

POLAND

C43/682 Gold and foreign exchange file on Poland, 1940–45. Gold reserves moved from Paris to Dakar, then under Vichy government control. Poles offered (blocked) French gold in return.

PORTUGAL

C43/308 Gold and foreign exchange file on Portugal, 1935–48. Gold movements etc.

SWEDEN

C43/359–360 Gold and foreign exchange files on Sweden, 1933–55.

SWITZERLAND

C43/365–367 Gold and foreign exchange files on Switzerland, 1933–54.

OV58/4 Overseas Department file on Switzerland, 1939–45. Papers on a wartime Swiss gold swap were weeded in the 1980s, but index references still exist.

OV4/99–100 Overseas Department files on BIS gold, 1935–52. These contain copies of BIS papers sent to Sir Otto Niemeyer, who was a Director of the BIS from 1932–65 and Chairman from 1937–40, and correspondence with him. They also include internal Bank memoranda commenting on transactions and policy.

C43/332 Gold and foreign exchange file on the BIS, 1934–46. Management of the BIS gold at the Bank – amounts, movements, instructions etc.

Records on broader subjects

OV48/12–13 Overseas Department files entitled "Gold", 1938–61. Wartime estimates of holdings by occupied and other countries, and amounts looted. International gold movements. Frozen accounts. Post war papers are largely concerned with gold production and prices and re-establishing the Bullion Market.

Particular schemes, etc.

C43/10–11 Gold and foreign exchange files, 1940–55. These files deal with a scheme whereby gold held in London by non UK residents could be relocated to Canada against subsequent repayment after the war. *Details of the individuals involved remain sensitive on customer grounds.*

C40/370–377 Cashier's department files, 1947–58. The files cover the Dollfus Mieg case, which is concerned with that company's claim for the restitution of specific bars looted by the Germans.

Transactional records

C139/1–8 Exchange Equalisation Account Gold ledgers, 1937–65. These ledgers record gold holdings and movements on the Exchange Equalisation Account.

C142/1–5 Bullion Office: set aside ledgers, 1927–71. Records of gold held at the Bank and set aside for specific customers. These include the BIS numbered accounts and the accounts of other central banks.

These records contain dealings with a number of the Bank's customers and may still be subject to restrictions on access.

THE BANK FOR
INTERNATIONAL
SETTLEMENTS
DURING THE SECOND WORLD WAR

Conference Paper

DR. PIET CLEMENT

Historian, Head of Records and Archives, BIS

The aim of this paper is to provide a brief overview of the wartime activities of the Bank for International Settlements (BIS), focusing in particular on the gold transactions undertaken with the German Reichsbank. The paper describes why and under what circumstances the BIS received gold from the Reichsbank during the war, what is known about the origin and final destination of this gold and, finally, what steps were taken by the BIS after the war when part of this gold was identified as having been looted by the Germans.[1]

I. INTRODUCTION[2]

The Bank for International Settlements is the world's oldest international financial institution, owned and controlled by central banks. The BIS was created in 1930 in implementation of the Young Plan, which was adopted at the second Hague Conference in January of that year and which provided for a settlement of the problem of German reparations ensuing from the First World War. The Bank took up its activities in Basle, Switzerland, in May 1930. By early 1932, 24 European central banks and two banking syndicates representing Japan and the United States had subscribed to the Bank's capital. The primary tasks of the BIS, as summed up in its original Statutes, were to promote the cooperation of central banks and to provide additional facilities for international financial operations. Very soon, the Bank's functions as trustee in respect of the German reparation payments virtually ceased when those payments were first temporarily (Hoover, Moratorium, June 1931) and then indefinitely (Lausanne Agreement, July 1932) suspended. However, it is important to underline the fact that Germany's obligations towards the BIS and the creditor nations were formally only suspended and not cancelled. As a result, the BIS continued to comply with its own obligations under the Young Plan, in order to safeguard the creditor nations' financial interests with a view to the expected resumption of reparation payments at some point in the future. In practical terms this meant that the BIS had to maintain the high level of investments it had made in Germany in 1930–31 in connection with the Young Plan. As will be seen, this point is crucial in order to understand the BIS's wartime transactions with the German Reichsbank.

The suspension of reparation payments in 1932 meant that the emphasis in the Bank's activities shifted to the deepening of central bank cooperation, mainly through the monthly Board meetings organised in Basle in which most Western European central bank governors participated, and to the further developments of banking services offered to its central bank customers. The creation of a gold clearing system for international postal payments was an example of this, as was the expansion of the BIS's role in central bank gold transactions. By the late 1930s, the banking transactions in which the BIS most commonly engaged included:

- carrying out transfer orders from or between central bank deposit accounts held with the BIS;
- foreign exchange transactions with or for the account of central banks;
- gold transactions with or for the account of central banks (gold sales and purchases, gold exchanges, gold shipments);
- carrying out transfer orders from or between central bank gold accounts held with the BIS.

Throughout the 1930s, the BIS's business activities remained on a fairly modest scale when compared with the large or even medium-sized commercial banks of that time.

2. THE BANK FOR INTERNATIONAL SETTLEMENTS DURING THE WAR[3]

When war broke out in September 1939, the BIS Board of Directors, including central bank representatives from Belgium, France, Germany, Italy, Japan, the Netherlands, Sweden, Switzerland and the United Kingdom, decided unanimously that all further Board Meeting be suspended for the duration of hostilities. At the same time, the BIS would continue its activities, albeit on a reduced scale, in order to safeguard the pre-war financial interests of its members and to guarantee its own survival. Indeed, it was in particular the creditor nations – France, the United Kingdom, Belgium – which stood to lose from a precipitate dissolution of the BIS, while the survival of the BIS was also judged vital for a prompt resumption of European central bank cooperation once the war was over. In the meantime, it would be left to the BIS President – from January 1940 the American Thomas McKittrick – together with the Bank's Management, all resident in Basle, to steer the BIS through this difficult period, while the Board members would be called on to endorse the major management decisions by correspondence. In December 1939, these same Board members approved a declaration of neutral conduct sent out to all BIS correspondents, in which the

Bank proclaimed its intention to refrain from any business transactions involving the currencies or markets of two countries at war with each other, and further from any transaction which might be judged reproachable from either a belligerent's or a neutral state's point of view.[4]

The BIS maintained its business relationships, albeit on a much reduced scale, with most of its traditional central bank customers, regardless of their country's position in the Allied, Axis or, neutral camp. Whenever the legitimacy of a given central bank was cast into doubt, however, all further transactions were suspended (as was the case with the central banks of the Baltic states).

It comes as no surprise that the outbreak of war in September 1939 had a dramatic effect on the BIS's level of activity. The average monthly volume of business declined sharply in September 1939, and again in June 1940, after the Germans had overrun the Low Countries and France. By the summer of 1941 the business volume had fallen to less than one-tenth of the monthly average recorded during the last three pre-war years, and by 1943 it stood at less than 5%. The evolution of gold shipments organised by the BIS is very illustrative in this respect. In the last years before the war, the BIS had specialised in this type of operation. Thus, from June 1938 until August 1939, the Bank was instrumental in shipping for the account of its member central banks and for its own account well over 100 tonnes of gold from the European continent to the United States for safekeeping. From September 1939 to June 1940, the BIS shipped an additional 29 tonnes of gold to New York under increasingly difficult circumstances. The occupation by the Germans of most of Western Europe in the spring of 1940 and the escalation of war at sea brought the transatlantic shipments to an end. From the summer of 1940 until the end of the war in May 1945, gold shipments organised by the BIS were very few and far between: 18 shipments in five years, mostly overland, for an overall amount of 21 tonnes of gold, of which 16 tonnes was transported for the BIS's own account and 3 and 2 tonnes respectively for the account of the central banks of Portugal and Bulgaria.

The graphs below illustrate that the BIS's balance-sheet totals (assets and liabilities) remained largely unchanged throughout the war (Graph 1), while the level of the Bank's activity declined sharply (Graph 2). Under these circumstances, profits also fell steeply, to the extent that the interest the BIS earned on the pre-war investments made in the German market became the single most important source of income left to the Bank (Table 1).[5] From the financial year 1940/41, the annual 6% dividend could only be paid by gradually drawing down and finally exhausting the Dividend Reserve Fund. From 1943 the dividend had to be reduced and in 1945 it had to be suspended altogether.

3. WARTIME GOLD TRANSACTIONS WITH THE GERMAN REICHSBANK[6]

Table 2 and Graph 3 summarise all gold transactions undertaken between the Bank for International Settlements and the German Reichsbank during the Second World War.[7] As can be seen, an overall amount of 21.5 tonnes of gold flowed through the Reichsbank gold account with the BIS. However, of this total

Graph 1
Bank for International Settlements' balance-sheet totals

On 31st March, in millions of Swiss francs at par (= "Statutory francs", now designated gold francs)

A. Assets

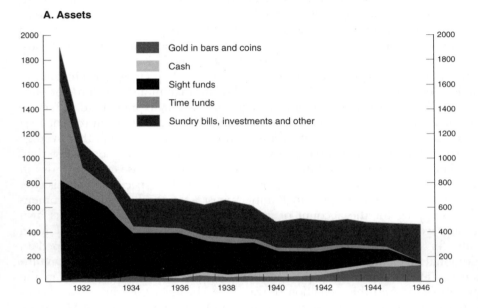

B. Liabilities

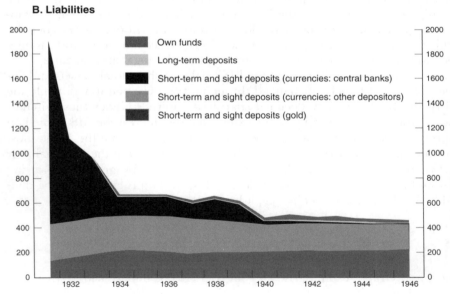

Graph 2 Bank for International Settlements' indices of activity

In millions of Swiss francs at par (= "Statutory francs", now designated gold francs)

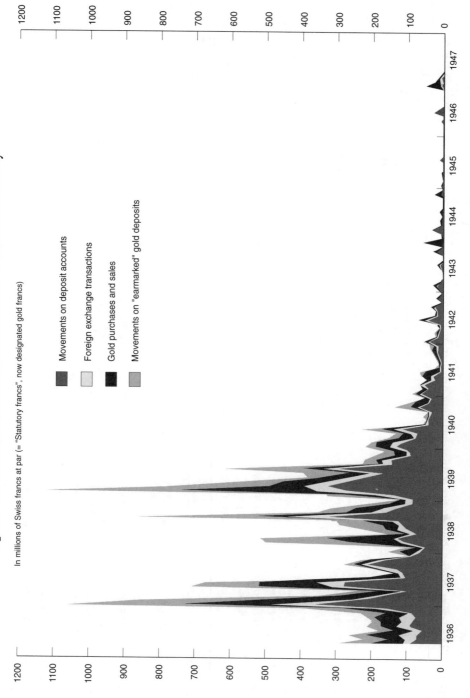

Movements on deposit accounts

Foreign exchange transactions

Gold purchases and sales

Movements on "earmarked" gold deposits

Table 1: BIS – Gross Profits, Net Profits & Appropriation Account, 1937-46

In Swiss Francs at par = "Statutory Francs"

Financial year	1 Interest earned on investments in Reichsmark	2 Other earnings (interest, misc., commissions)	3 Total earnings	4 Less: interest allowed and discount paid	5 Less: provision for contingencies	6 Less administration costs	7 Net profit
1937/38	8,979,900	7,340,700	16,320,600	1,563,200	3,550,000	2,195,400	9,012,000
1938/39	8,781,000	6,351,000	15,132,700	1,131,000	3,350,000	2,067,800	8,583,900
1939/40	8,565,400	4,725,600	13,291,000	441,100	2,900,000	1,987,800	7,962,100
1940/41	7,894,000	3,308,900	11,202,900	782,700	3,100,000	2,026,300	5,293,900
1941/42	7,456,000	3,213,400	10,669,400	682,200	2,900,000	1,901,500	5,185,700
1942/43	7,234,000	1,852,100	9,086,100	39,300	2,600,000	1,946,900	4,508,900
1943/44	7,201,000	1,999,700	9,200,700	24,900	1,985,000	1,936,900	5,523,900
1944/45	6,878,000	1,474,300	8,352,300	17,500	6,464,600	1,870,200	0
1945/46	0	1,259,500	1,259,500	16,800	0	1,859,300	-616,600

Financial year	7 Net profit	8 Dividend payments	9 Allocation to reserve funds	10 Other
1937/38	9,012,000	7,500,000	1,087,400	424,600
1938/39	8,583,900	7,500,000	822,000	261,900
1939/40	7,962,100	7,500,000	436,500	25,600
1940/41	5,293,900	5,029,200	264,700	0
1941/42	5,185,700	4,926,400	259,300	0
1942/43	4,508,900	4,283,500	225,400	0
1943/44	5,523,900	4,991,200	262,700	0
1944/45	0	0	0	0
1945/46	-616,600	0	0	0

amount only 13.5 tonnes constituted new gold delivered to the BIS by the Reichsbank during the war. The remainder was either already on the Reichsbank gold account with the BIS from before the war (1.9 tonnes), obtained by the Reichsbank from the BIS (6 tonnes) or credited to the Reichsbank gold account with the BIS by other central banks (0.1 tonnes).

The 21.5 tonnes of gold which the Reichsbank thus held or deposited with the BIS during the war served mainly two purposes: German interest payments to the BIS in respect of the BIS's pre-war investments in Germany (7.8 tonnes) and payments to other central banks in respect of the international postal and railway settlements system operated through the BIS (6 tonnes). The remainder was either withdrawn by the Reichsbank from its BIS account early in the war (5.8 tonnes) or directly ceded to the BIS as a result of sale and exchange transactions (1.9 tonnes).

3.1 Gold credited to the Reichsbank gold deposits with the BIS

Let us turn first to the gold credited to the Reichsbank gold deposits held with the BIS during the war. Throughout the 1930s the Reichsbank had held several gold deposit accounts with the BIS at various depositories (Amsterdam, Berne, Brussels, London and Paris), but most of these had been emptied before the end of August 1939. The balances on these accounts were either sold, exchanged or – most frequently – sent to the Reichsbankhauptkasse in Berlin. Consequently, at the time of the outbreak of the Second World War, the only gold deposits the Reichsbank still held with the BIS were a number of earmarked gold deposits held in Berne (Nos. 5, 7, 10 and 11) and a gold sight account used for the transfer of international postal payments held in London, which, however, was also transferred to Berne in October 1939.[8] On 1st September 1939 the amount of gold held by the Reichsbank on these accounts totalled 1,861.70292 kg. fine gold.

During the war, the Reichsbank deposited new gold with the BIS at regular intervals. All Reichsbank gold newly deposited with the BIS was first sent by the Reichsbank to its own gold deposit account held with the Swiss National Bank in Berne and from there, on the orders of the Reichsbank, transferred to the aforementioned Reichsbank gold deposits held with the BIS (also held at the Swiss National Bank in Berne – the BIS had no vaults at its own premises in Basle). From 1st September 1939 until 8th May 1945, new Reichsbank gold deposits with the BIS loco Berne amounted to 12,016.59862 kg. fine gold.

Apart from the deposits in Berne, the BIS received, during the war, one further deposit of new gold from the Reichsbank: on 12th April 1945 the Reichsbank placed 1,525.62030 kg. fine gold at the disposal of the BIS at the Reichsbanknebenstelle in Konstanz (Germany), close to the Swiss-German border. This gold, consisting of 34 gold bars (417.98290 kg. fine) and 31 cases of gold coins (1,107.63740 kg. fine), was intended as an advance settlement of interest payments due by Germany to the BIS in the course of 1945. At this late stage of the war, the physical transport of this gold to Berne was refused by the Swiss authorities on the grounds of the agreement on the restriction of further German gold deliveries to Switzerland which they had concluded with the Allies in March 1945. Consequently, this gold was held under earmark in the name of the BIS at the Reichsbanknebenstelle in Konstanz and remained blocked there until after the war.

The amount of gold newly deposited by the Reichsbank with the BIS during the war thus totalled: *13,542.21892 kg. fine gold*.

During the war, the Reichsbank gold deposits held with the BIS were further increased by *5,479.72850 kg. fine gold* which the Reichsbank bought directly from the BIS between October 1939 and January 1941, and by another *499.88150 kg. fine gold* which the Reichsbank exchanged with the BIS in February 1940. Finally, from October 1939 to June 1940, *88.51264 kg. fine gold* was credited to the Reichsbank gold account by the central banks of Denmark, Finland, Norway, Hungary, Estonia and Argentina in respect of the international postal settlements system operated through the BIS.

Thus, during the wartime period, the sum total of the amount of gold available to the Reichsbank on its gold deposits held with the BIS was *21,472.04448 kg. fine gold*.

3.2 Gold debited from the Reichsbank gold deposits with the BIS

As indicated above, these 21,472.04448 kg. fine gold were mainly used by the Reichsbank for interest payments to the BIS and for payments to other central banks in respect of the international postal and railway settlements system.

German interest payments in gold

The German interest payments to the BIS had their origin in the Young Plan. From the early 1930s, the BIS had made substantial investments in the German market. These investments were directly linked to the Young Plan for the final settlement of German reparation payments, adopted at the second Hague Conference of January 1930. Together with the so-called Young Loan, they were intended as a concrete expression of the international community's commitment to assisting Germany's economic recovery, which, in turn, was considered vital to ensure that Germany would continue to be able to meet its financial obligations towards the creditor nations. These hopes were not fulfilled, and very soon German reparation payments were suspended (1931–32). Nonetheless, the BIS had to maintain its investments in Germany in order to preserve its own and the creditor nations' rights under the Young Plan with a view to a possible future settlement.

The BIS's investments in Germany consisted of interest-bearing funds held at the Reichsbank and the Golddiskontbank and in bills and bonds of the German Treasury and the German Railway and Postal Administrations. The overall sum involved had remained substantially unchanged ever since July 1931. It amounted to 294 million Swiss gold francs on 31st August 1939, on the eve of the Second World War (US$ 96 million). Until March 1940 the interest due on these investments was settled by the Reichsbank through monthly payments in Swiss francs to the BIS (up to SF 1,000,000–700,000 Swiss gold francs or US$ 230,000 – each month). During the war, however, the Reichsbank settled part of the interest payments due to the BIS in gold. This was the case from March to June 1940, in October 1941, and for all payments due between January 1943 and March 1945. Between 1st September 1939 and 8th May 1945, interest payments to the BIS settled by the Reichsbank in gold thus amounted to 6,266.82753 kg. fine gold.

As mentioned earlier, a further 1,525.62030 kg. fine gold was transferred to the BIS by the Reichsbank on 12th April 1945 as an advance settlement of the interest payments due in 1945. This gold was deposited under the BIS's name in the Reichsbank depot at Konstanz, and remained blocked there until after the war. This brings the total for German interest payments in gold during the war to *7,792.44783 kg. fine gold*.

International postal and railway payments

From before the war, the Reichsbank participated in the gold clearing system for international postal payments which the BIS had set up in the late 1930s at the request of the World Postal Union. In this system, sums due on account of international postal traffic were settled bilaterally between countries through the gold sight accounts which their respective central banks held with the BIS. From September 1939 to January 1945, the Reichsbank instructed the BIS to debit its gold account with an overall amount of 1,362.062226 kg. fine gold in postal payments to Argentina, Belgium, Denmark, Estonia, Hungary, Finland, Norway, Slovakia and Sweden. Over 70% of this total amount was transferred to the Hungarian National Bank in favour of the Hungarian Postal Service. Apart from the international postal payments, but following the same procedure, a total of 4,655.83657 kg. fine gold was transferred from the Reichsbank's gold account with the BIS to the account of the National Bank of Yugoslavia in favour of the Yugoslav Railway Administration. These transactions were carried out between June 1940 and March 1941, that is, until German troops occupied Yugoslavia (April 1941). During the whole of the war, payments in gold in respect of the international postal and railway settlements system made by the Reichsbank through its gold account with the BIS amounted to *6,017.89883 kg. fine gold*.

Gold withdrawn and gold sold by the Reichsbank

What happened to the remainder of the gold available to the Reichsbank on its gold account with the BIS? *5,809.04639 kg. fine gold* was withdrawn by the Reichsbank between November 1939 and May 1940. *1,852.65145 kg. fine gold* was ceded by the Reichsbank to the BIS: 502.65145 kg. fine gold held by the Reichsbank in Berne in exchange for 499.88150 kg. fine gold held by the BIS in Stockholm, in February 1940; and 1,350 kg. fine gold held by the Reichsbank in Berne against Swiss francs in November 1941 and January 1942.

Thus, between 1st September 1939 and 8th May 1945, the total amount of *21,472.04448 kg. fine gold* was debited from the Reichsbank gold account held with the BIS (bringing the closing balance at the end of the war to 0.00000 kg. fine gold).

Table 2: Summary of Reichsbank Gold Transactions carried out with or through the Bank for International Settlements – 1 September 1939 – 8 May 1945

A – Gold In for the Reichsbank (in kilogramme fine gold)

Date	1 Opening Balance 1st Sept. 1939	2 Gold newly deposited by the Reichsbank	3 Gold received by the Reichsbank from the BIS in exchange transaction	4 Gold sold to the Reichsbank by the BIS	5 Gold credited Reichsbank to a/c in respect of postal payments	6 Total
1939*	1,861.70292	0.00000	0.00000	2,006.95686	27.59375	3,896.25353
1940	0.00000	4,134.38706	499.88150	2,772.77164	60.91889	7,467.95909
1941	0.00000	1,307.51290	0.00000	700.00000	0.00000	2,007.51290
1942	0.00000	1,099.69198	0.00000	0.00000	0.00000	1,099.69198
1943	0.00000	2,707.09391	0.00000	0.00000	0.00000	2,707.09391
1944	0.00000	2,767.91277	0.00000	0.00000	0.00000	2,767.91277
1945**	0.00000	1,525.62030	0.00000	0.00000	0.00000	1,525.62030
TOTAL:	1,861.70292	13,542.21892	499.88150	5,479.72850	88.51264	21,472.04448

1939* = from 1.09.1939   1945** = until 8.05.1945

Table 2: Summary of Reichsbank Gold Transactions carried out with or through the Bank for International Settlements – 1 September 1939 – 8 May 1945

B – Gold Out for the Reichsbank (in kilogramme fine gold)

Date	1 Gold withdrawn by the Reichsbank from its BIS a/c	2 Gold received by the BIS from the Reichsbank in exchange transaction	3 Gold sold by the Reichsbank to the BIS	4 Gold debited from Reichsbank a/c in respect of postal & railway payments	5 Reichsbank interest payments in gold to the BIS	6 Total
1939*	2,006.95686	0.00000	0.00000	66.42475	0.00000	2,073.38161
1940	3,802.08953	502.65145	0.00000	3,405.35992	808.37176	8,518.47266
1941	0.00000	0.00000	300.00000	1,371.78375	600.00000	2,271.78375
1942	0.00000	0.00000	1,050.00000	528.96683	0.00000	1,578.96683
1943	0.00000	0.00000	0.00000	285.40202	2,247.19307	2,532.59509
1944	0.00000	0.00000	0.00000	311.70569	2,206.33498	2,518.04067
1945**	0.00000	0.00000	0.00000	48.26187	1,930.54802	1,978.80989
Total:	5,809.04639	502.65145	1,350.00000	6,017.89883	7,792.44783	21,472.04450
rounding:						−0.00002
						21,472.04448

1939* = from 1.09.1939   1945** = until 8.05.1945

Graph 3
Summary of Reichsbank gold transactions carried out with or through the Bank for International Settlements

In 1,000 kilogrammes fine gold

A. Gold in for the Reichsbank

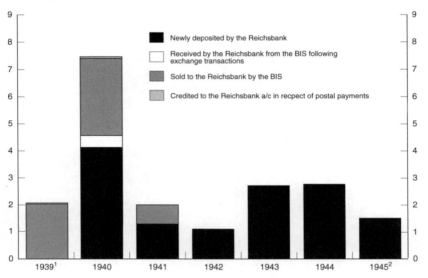

Legend:
- Newly deposited by the Reichsbank
- Received by the Reichsbank from the BIS following exchange transactions
- Sold to the Reichsbank by the BIS
- Credited to the Reichsbank a/c in recpect of postal payments

B. Gold out for the Reichsbank

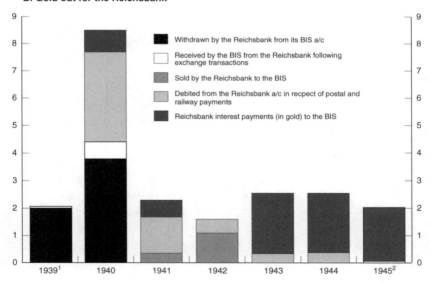

Legend:
- Withdrawn by the Reichsbank from its BIS a/c
- Received by the BIS from the Reichsbank following exchange transactions
- Sold by the Reichsbank to the BIS
- Debited from the Reichsbank a/c in recpect of postal and railway payments
- Reichsbank interest payments (in gold) to the BIS

[1] From 1st September   [2] Until 8th May

4. POSTWAR INVESTIGATIONS INTO THE ORIGIN OF THE GOLD RECEIVED FROM THE REICHSBANK[9]

While the war was still being fought, the Allied governments made it clear that they did not recognise the transfer of assets looted by the Axis powers and that after the end of hostilities they would require the restitution of such assets, including looted gold, to their rightful owners (see the joint United Nations declaration of 5th January 1943 and the declaration issued by the UK, US and USSR Treasuries on 22nd February 1944). These warnings were addressed explicitly to the Axis countries and neutrals alike. Once the war was over, the necessary measures were taken to put this intention into effect. In December 1945, the Paris Conference on Reparations created a Tripartite Commission for the Restitution of Monetary Gold, consisting of representatives from France, the United Kingdom and the United States and charged with collecting all looted monetary gold into a gold pool for restitution to the original owners. This concerned not only the looted monetary gold recovered in Germany by the Allied occupation forces, but also the gold that during the war had found its way to neutral countries such as Switzerland, Portugal, Spain or Sweden (Paris Reparations Agreement, 14th January 1946).

Even before the Paris Conference on Reparations was convened, it had become common knowledge that the Nazis had looted monetary gold from the central banks in the occupied territories on a large scale, and had used this gold in their wartime transactions with neutral countries. One of the most notorious cases was that of the gold of the National Bank of Belgium. The odyssey of the Belgian gold – entrusted to the Bank of France for safekeeping before the war, then captured by the Germans, sent to Berlin and resmelted by the Prussian Mint – has been recounted innumerable times.[10] After the liberation of France and Belgium in late 1944, the Bank of France indemnified the National Bank of Belgium in full for the amount of the gold with which it had been entrusted (approximately 200 tonnes fine gold). Once the records of the Reichsbank and the Prussian Mint captured by the Allied forces became available, in mid-1945, the Bank of France began a detailed investigation in order to trace and recover the Belgian gold for its own account. From January 1946, this investigation was embedded in and supported by the work undertaken by the Tripartite Commission on the Restitution of Monetary Gold, based in Brussels.

As early as 25th September 1945, BIS President Thomas McKittrick had written to the central banks of Belgium and France, offering the BIS's full cooperation in any official investigation regarding the gold looted by the Germans from the National Bank of Belgium. In preparation for such an investigation, the BIS compiled a list containing all details of the individual gold bars the Bank had received during the war from the Reichsbank through its gold deposit at the Swiss National Bank in Berne.[11] On 14th June 1946, two experts from the Bank of France visited Basle in order to examine the BIS's books and to compare the details of the German gold bars received by the BIS with the information from the National Bank of Belgium's files and the relevant extracts from the Reichsbank and Prussian Mint records. As a result of this investigation it was established that between 2nd August 1943 and 22nd March 1944 the BIS had received from the Reichsbank 129 gold bars – 1,607.38516 kg. fine gold in all – minted with the official Reichsbank seal and bearing the years 1934 to 1939, which in fact had originally been Belgian gold bars which were resmelted at the Prussian Mint between January and June 1943. The BIS immediately offered to restitute an equivalent weight of gold to the Bank of France.

In the meantime, however, another case of monetary gold looted and subsequently falsified by the Nazis had come to light. In July 1946, the President of the Netherlands Bank wrote to the BIS to announce that the Netherlands Bank had started an enquiry into the final destination of the Dutch gold requisitioned by the Germans during the war. The BIS replied by inviting Dutch experts to Basle and by declaring itself ready to restitute all gold that could be shown to have originated from Dutch looted gold. Dutch experts exchanged information with BIS representatives in Basle on 7th March 1947, but it proved very difficult to establish conclusively whether Dutch looted gold had been part of the gold delivered to the BIS by the Reichsbank. The reason for this was that some of the gold in question had been resmelted by the Prussian Mint between December 1942 and February 1944 fused with looted gold from different origins. Finally, in the spring of 1948, after the Dutch had submitted additional evidence from their own files and from the Reichsbank and Prussian Mint records, it was established that the gold delivered by the Reichsbank to the BIS during the war contained 2,093.86258 kg. fine gold of the gold looted from the Netherlands Bank. Between November 1941 and January 1943 the Reichsbank had delivered to the BIS 80 gold bars originating from the pre-war gold reserves of the Netherlands Bank, and between 9th March 1943 and 12th October 1944 an additional 119 gold bars originating from resmelting operations, undertaken by the Prussian Mint between December 1942 and February 1944, in which looted Dutch gold coins had been fused with looted gold from other sources.

Once the 13.5 tonnes of gold which the BIS had received from the Reichsbank during the war had been fully investigated in respect of the Belgian and Dutch claims, a final agreement was concluded in Washington on 13th May 1948 between the BIS and the Tripartite Commission for the Restitution of Monetary Gold. The BIS agreed to restitute the rounded figure of 3,740 kg. fine gold to the Tripartite Commission Gold Pool.[12] Whereupon the representatives of the Governments of France, the United Kingdom and the United States agreed

". . . in their own behalf and in behalf of all of the other Governments signatory to the Paris Reparations Agreement of 14th January 1946, and of the banks of issue of the signatory Governments, that, in accepting delivery of such amount of gold, they waive all claims against the Bank for International Settlements with regard to looted gold transferred to it by Germany". [13]

5. CONCLUDING REMARKS

At the time the Washington Agreement was concluded in May 1948, most of the gold the Reichsbank had newly delivered to the BIS during the war was no longer in the possession of the BIS. As is current practice in a system of gold sight accounts, there was no necessary link between the individual gold bars delivered by the Reichsbank and those used by the BIS in carrying out banking instructions from the Reichsbank. As a result, the gold delivered by the Reichsbank was subsequently used by the BIS in banking transactions with other central banks. These transactions can be summarised as follows:

- 3,893.46171 kg. fine gold was transferred to the National Bank of Romania between 24th November 1941 and 17th January 1947;
- 3,138.28017 kg. fine gold was transferred to the National Bank of Yugoslavia between 7th June 1940 and 29th April 1941;
- 1,118.55459 kg. fine gold was sold to the National Bank of Bulgaria between 13th January 1942 and 4th March 1943;
- 799.27177 kg. fine gold was sold to the Banco de Portugal on 10th February 1941;
- 699.38898 kg. fine gold was exchanged with the Swiss National Bank against gold held in New York on 9th April 1941.

This means that of the 13,542.21892 kg. fine gold the BIS received from the Reichsbank during the war, *3,893.26170 kg. fine gold* was still in the possession of the BIS on 1st February 1947:

- 2,367.64140 kg. fine gold (198 gold bars) at the Swiss National Bank in Berne;
- 417.98290 kg. fine gold (34 gold bars) at the Reichsbanknebenstelle in Konstanz, Germany;
- 1,107.63740 kg. fine gold (gold coins) at the Reichsbanknebenstelle in Konstanz, Germany.

On 24th June 1948, the BIS transferred 3,740 kg. fine gold to the Tripartite Commission for the Restitution of Monetary Gold at the Bank of England, London, as agreed in the Washington Agreement of 13th May 1948. For this purpose, the BIS used the 232 gold bars (2,785,62430 kg. fine gold) delivered by the Reichsbank and still in its possession, while the balance of 954,37570 kg. fine gold was made up by taking gold from the BIS's own gold deposit with the Bank of England. Finally, the remaining 1,107.63740 kg. fine gold in coins held in Konstanz was first transferred to the gold depot of the Bank of France in Strasbourg, then exchanged with the Bank of France for gold bars "good delivery", which, on 13th and 30th September 1948, were sold on the private market. Thus, by 1st October 1948 none of the 13.5 tonnes of gold delivered by the Reichsbank to the BIS during the Second World War remained physically in the possession of the BIS.

The gold transactions described in this paper and all the figures quoted here can easily be verified on the basis of the BIS's wartime archives, which have been open to outside researchers since July of this year. These same facts and figures can also be found in a paper released by the BIS on 12th May 1997, that was examined and certified by Coopers & Lybrand, London.[14]

To conclude, there remains one issue that has not been touched upon here: looted non-monetary gold or, in other words, gold looted by the Nazis from individual citizens including Holocaust victims. As is known, the Tripartite Commission for the Restitution of Monetary Gold devoted itself primarily to the recovery and restitution of monetary gold as defined by the Paris Reparations Agreement of 14th January 1946. In practice, this meant that first and foremost gold looted from central banks or official reserves was traced and restituted to the monetary authorities concerned. If the international community were to decide today to reopen the official investigation into the origins and destination of non-monetary looted gold, the Bank for International Settlements would of course be ready to cooperate fully. However, it should be stressed that the BIS archives do not hold the necessary information to determine whether any of the 13.5 tonnes of gold which the Bank received from the Reichsbank during the war may or may not have contained a fraction of non-monetary looted gold.

Having said this, some specifications can be made on the basis of the BIS archives. The BIS archives do indeed allow a crude analysis of the gold received from the Reichsbank on the basis of the detailed list of the individual gold bars involved which was drawn up immediately after the war. If we consider the 13,542.21892 kg. of fine gold which the Reichsbank delivered to the BIS during the war, the following conclusions can be put forward:

- *3,701.24774* kg. fine gold was identified by the Tripartite Gold Commission as monetary gold looted by the Germans from the central banks of Belgium and the Netherlands and restituted in full by the BIS. Consequently, any conflicting claim as to the origin of this gold can be safely dismissed.

- *5,012.88208* kg. fine gold consisted of gold bars delivered to the BIS between February 1940 and December 1943. None of these bars had been minted in Germany: all were pre-war gold bars minted in France, the Netherlands, Russia, South Africa, Switzerland, the United Kingdom or the United States. This gold was explicitly cleared by the Tripartite Gold Commission of all claims regarding looted monetary gold. For these reasons, it would seem very unlikely that the 5 tonnes in question contained any looted gold, be it monetary or non-monetary.

- *1,391.56773* kg. fine gold consisted of gold bars minted in Germany, with no year marked on the bars, and delivered to the BIS between 31st May 1940 and 19th January 1942. The Tripartite Gold Commission cleared this gold of any claims regarding looted monetary gold. The fact that this gold reached the BIS well before the summer of 1942 would seem to rule out the possibility that it contained some of the gold looted from Holocaust victims, given the fact that the first recorded delivery of such gold to the Reichsbank was made by the SS on 26th August 1942.[15]

- *3,436.52137* kg. fine gold consisted of 172 gold bars minted in Germany (2,328.88397 kg. fine) and 62 sacks of German gold coins (1,107.63740 kg. fine). Most of the bars were marked with the year 1937 (131 bars) and some with the year 1942 (41 bars). In the case of the gold coins, on the other hand, no further details are available. We only know that they were German gold coins, but it is unclear whether they were minted before or during the war and what their origin was. The total amount of 3,436.5 kg. of gold was cleared by the Tripartite Gold Commission of any claims regarding looted monetary gold, but given the fact that this gold was delivered to the BIS between March 1943 and April 1945, it cannot be ruled out that the 3.4 tonnes in question might have contained some looted non-monetary gold. However, as already mentioned, no information whatsoever is available in the BIS Archives that would make it possible to determine this.

Overall total = 13,452.21892 kg. fine gold.

NOTES

[1] I am grateful to Stephan Arthur for assistance with the graphs.

[2] Roger Auboin, *The Bank for International Settlements, 1930–55, – Essays in International Finance, Princeton University, 22 (1955),* and *The Bank for International Settlements and the Basle Meetings, published on the occasion of the fiftieth anniversary, 1930–1980,* Basle 1980.

[3] See BIS ARCHIVES, 1/3(4) *Report on BIS Operations from 1.11.1939 to 30.11.1946; BIS ARCHIVES, 1/3(5) Banking Policy of the BIS during the Second World War;* Bank for International Settlements, *Note on gold shipments and gold exchanges organised by the Bank for International Settlements, 1st June 1938–31st May 1945,* Basle, 9th September 1997.

[4] These "rules of conduct" were sent out in a circular to all central banks having business relations with the BIS on 18th December 1939. See BIS ARCHIVES, 1/19c *Banking policy of the BIS during the Second World War.*

[5] The figures in the table and graphs are given in "Statutory francs" = "Swiss francs at par" or "Swiss gold francs". This was the unit of account used by the BIS from its foundation in 1930: 1 Statutory franc = 1 Swiss franc at its fixed gold value of 0.29032258 . . . grammes fine gold (= fixed value of the Swiss franc until 27th September 1936). The exchange rate of the Statutory franc during the Second World War was roughly as follows: 1 Statutory franc = US$ 0.32755 = Swiss franc 1.41.

[6] See Bank for International Settlements. *Note on gold operations involving the Bank for International Settlements and the German Reichsbank, 1st September 1939–8th May 1945,* Basle, 12th May 1997.

[7] During the Second World War, the Swiss National Bank applied the following official gold prices: SF 4,920.63 per kilogram fine gold sales and SF 4,869.80 per kilogram fine gold for purchases. Thus, the average price applied by the Swiss National Bank was approximately US$ 1,130 per kilogram fine gold (US$ 35 per ounce). These prices were followed closely by the BIS in its gold transactions.

[8] Gold on "earmarked" accounts is allocated gold. The Bank's obligation with respect to gold held in such accounts is to place on demand at the disposal of its depositors, at the central bank where the deposit was constituted, the identical bars which had originally been deposited with it. Gold on sight accounts is unallocated gold. The Bank's obligation with respect to gold held in such accounts is to place on demand at the disposal of its depositors, at the central bank where the deposit was constituted, gold bars of the same type as it has received, up to the total fine weight standing to the credit of the account.

[9] See BIS ARCHIVES, 7/15.2(7) *Specific Questions: Looted Gold.*

[10] For instance in Werner Rings, *Raubgold aus Deutschland, Die "Golddrehscheibe" Schweiz in Zweiten Weltkrieg,* Zurich, 1985.

[11] This list, giving the characteristics of the gold bars received during the war from the Reichsbank totalling 13,542.21892 kg. fine gold, is preserved in BIS ARCHIVES, Legal Service. After the war, the BIS insisted that in receiving gold from the Reichsbank the Bank had always acted in good faith, asking the Reichsbank for assurances that the gold delivered to the BIS originated from the Reichsbank's pre-war gold reserves. Such assurances, however, were only given orally, never in writing.

[12] The (rounded) final amount of 3,740 kg. fine gold agreed upon in the Washington Agreement of 13th May 1948 included, apart from the Belgian and Dutch claims (1,607.38516 and 2,093.86258 kg. fine gold respectively), a small additional claim in respect of Italian gold confiscated by the Germans towards the end of the war (37,23783 kg. fine gold).

[13] See BIS ARCHIVES, 7/15.2(1) *Specific Questions: BIS Assets in the USA*, box RB1.

[14] Bank for International Settlements, *Note on gold operations involving the Bank for International Settlements and the German Reichsbank, 1st September 1939–8th May 1945*, Basle, 12th May 1997.

[15] Stuart E. Eizenstat (coor.), *U.S. and Allied Efforts to Recover and Restore Gold and Other Assets Stolen or Hidden by Germany During World War II, Preliminary Study*, May 1997.

BELARUS

Speech

VALENTIN GERASIMOV

Chairman of the Fund for Mutual Understanding
and Reconciliation of the Belarusian Republic

Just over fifty years stands between us and that glorious day which marked the
end of World War II, the bloodiest war of the twentieth century.

This Conference has representatives from more than 40 States, the majority
of which suffered as a result of fascism during that war.

My republic, Belarus – which, though small, is situated at the very heart of
Europe – felt the horrors of war: three years of occupation and bloody battles
when Hitler's hordes invaded and when they retreated.

What criteria can be used to measure the damage inflicted by the war on my
country, my State? There is no way of measuring it! Just one or two statistics and
the memories of eye witnesses.

The Belarusian Republic suffered damage which totalled more than 150 thousand million roubles in 1945, with damage to civilian property amounting to
almost 90 million roubles. 209 towns and 9,200 villages in the republic were
almost completely destroyed and 682,000 buildings were burnt down, including
hospitals, theatres, schools, institutions of higher education, Orthodox churches,
Roman Catholic churches, mosques, synagogues, museums and libraries, not to
mention the countless historic and cultural treasures belonging to our nation
which were destroyed or taken out of the country.

What I would like to stress in particular is the damage inflicted on the
Belarusian people, both material and non-material.

Throughout the war years Belarus was a camp surrounded by barbed wire
which contained 350 concentration camps, prisons, ghettos, civilian camps and
prisoner-of-war camps, all created for the extermination of human beings.
According to calculations, the total number of inhabitants of Belarus who died
during World War II was almost 2.5 million; in other words, one in four inhabitants. 800,000 of them were Jews. Generally, each had on their person items
made of gold and precious stones which were, at times, the only things that
could save them from starvation and death. It is those valuables, confiscated
from Jews and members of all the other ethnic groups represented in the population of Belarus, which constitute a considerable proportion of the so-called
Nazi gold which found its way by various means into banks in Switzerland and

other countries. People in the western part of Belarus, which had become part of Poland before the start of World War II, had deposits in the banks of various countries; those deposits were confiscated by the Nazis and, in several States, including Switzerland, remained unclaimed by their owners, either because those owners had died or for other reasons. Therefore, the inhabitants of Belarus, having suffered as a result of Nazi persecution, are fully entitled to demand that their country be one of the States which receives its share of compensation.

Doubt may be cast on the validity of references to post-war agreements since, in our understanding, they concerned war reparations relating to Germany itself, i.e. valuables which were found in its territory. This Conference is concerned with gold and deposits of money which were in banks outside Germany and the location and volume of which was unknown by the time the post-war agreements relating to war reparations were concluded and which, consequently, could not be taken into account by the contracting parties.

In this connection, the delegation of the Republic of Belarus would like to propose the following:

1. A review of the list of countries whose population will receive compensation for Nazi gold and the inclusion in that list of Belarus and other countries whose inhabitants suffered in particular as a result of Nazi crimes.
2. The establishment of a Commission made up of representatives of interested countries, which will study the questions examined at this Conference on a permanent basis.
3. Similar conferences held on a regular basis (annually) to examine the Commissions's reports and to draw up recommendations for an intergovernmental meeting to adopt the corresponding intergovernmental agreements.
4. The provision of funding for the activities of the above-mentioned Commission and for conference expenses of the delegations from money connected to Nazi gold.

Truth and justice must prevail. Human relations between peoples of various countries are like a fast-flowing river running its eternal course. Try to stop this natural course and a quagmire forms, a still backwater. Without the truth as a means of mutual self-cleansing, there can be no new way of thinking or no new human relations.

All efforts by interested world organisations to distribute the "Swiss gold" must be directed at a just resolution of this question and the strengthening of trust and mutual understanding.

Speech

O. A. NEKHAY

President of "Lyos",* the Belarusian Association
of Former Prisoners of Fascism

World War II brought grief to the peoples of those countries which were drawn into its bloody slaughter. The Belarusian Republic suffered damage which totalled approximately 150 thousand million roubles in 1945, and damage to civilian property amounted to about 90 million roubles. Nevertheless, there is no cost higher than human life. Many concentration camps were set up in Belarus during the war. Around 1.5 million innocent civilians were killed or tortured in those camps and, in addition, in every district mass graves have been discovered containing murdered women and children of various ages. Around 700,000 people were sent off into German slavery.

It is not known to which category the prisoners of Auschwitz, Buchenwald, Ravensbrück, Dora and other concentration camps belonged – either the tortured or the dead. Their lives were doomed, just like the Jews in the ghettos.

The Fascists threw people of various nationalities into the concentration camps. No nationality received preferential treatment when faced with death. According to calculations, the total number of inhabitants of Belarus who died during World War II was 2.5 million – one in four. 800,000 of them were Jews. Generally, each had on their person items made of gold and precious stones which were, at times, the only things that could save them from starvation and death. It is those valuables, confiscated from Jews and members of all the other ethnic groups represented in the population of Belarus, which constitute a considerable proportion of the so-called Nazi gold which found its way by various means into banks in Switzerland and other countries.

People in the western part of Belarus, which had become part of Poland before the start of World War II, had deposits in the banks of various countries; those deposits were confiscated by the Nazis and, in several States, including Switzerland, remained unclaimed by their owners, either because those owners had died or for other reasons. Therefore, the inhabitants of Belarus, having suffered as a result of Nazi persecution, are fully entitled to demand that their country be one of the States which receives its share of compensation.

The prisoners in the concentration camps included people from the arts and sciences, businessmen, bankers, white-collar workers and blue-collar workers. Before their arrest, they all worked for the good of their homeland. Not only Germany but also the industrial and economic structures of other countries in the world profited from their property and labour. No distinction was made: money was taken from the French, from Jews, from people of German nationality, etc.

---

* *Translator's Note*: "Fate" or "Destiny" in English.

Former prisoners of fascism from Western countries received and continue to receive ten times more compensation than the one-off financial assistance given to the victims of fascism from Central and Eastern Europe. Those Deutschmarks come as payment for childhood and youth blighted by war and even for life destroyed by it. Those Deutschmarks are a drop in the ocean in a period of deep economic crisis such as the one in which our Republic now finds itself. Nevertheless, that drop has helped many people to survive and has even afforded some a decent burial.

Germany is now allocating a further DM 80 million but with the proviso that such aid does not go to the victims of fascism in Eastern Europe. It is also odd that democratic Germany, which in its foreign policy condemns totalitarianism and its manifestations, is invoking agreements with the former government of the USSR.

Doubt may be cast on the validity of references to post-war agreements since, in our understanding, they concerned war reparations relating to Germany itself, i.e. valuables which were found in its territory. This Conference is concerned with gold and deposits of money which were in banks outside Germany and the location and volume of which was unknown by the time the post-war agreements relating to war reparations were concluded and which, consequently, could not be taken into account by the contracting parties.

It would be very unpleasant if the policies of the former totalitarian Germany were repeated in the distribution of Nazi gold. The authorities under Hitler differentiated between foreign workers according to nationality: they divided them into workers from the countries of Central and South-Eastern Europe and "Eastern workers" who were living in the USSR before the start of the war. All Eastern workers, except the inhabitants of Lithuania, Latvia and Estonia, had the distinctive badge "Ost" on their clothing. Those badges enabled the Nazis to single out a race they considered "inferior" and which was given the right to life only while it was useful to Germany and its militarist economy.

To grant aid selectively to one nationality now may be likened to genocide if the victims of fascism who lived in Belarus are denied the opportunity to receive compensation for their suffering.

We would like to say to the Fund for Assistance to Victims of the Holocaust that your services in the search for Nazi gold have been invaluable. We would like to say to all those present at this Conference that the countries in which fascist Germany hid the stolen hoards of gold are known. One of those countries should recompense those who suffered Nazi repressions on Belarusian soil, for both material and non-material damage.

One generation replaces another. But death is powerless whilst memories live on in the next generation. The young and the older generation can and must help one another understand:

- why it is vital, for the sake of the future, not to forget the past;
- why, for the sake of peaceful coexistence, the younger generation should not be allowed to continue harbouring the grievances of the older generation;
- why it is important to make every effort to heed any signs in history which mark the appearance of totalitarianism and the onset of racial hatred.

All efforts by governments and interested representatives to distribute Nazi gold must be directed at strengthening the friendship between all peoples and preserving peace throughout the world.

In this connection, the delegation of the Republic of Belarus would like to propose the following:

1. A review of the list of countries whose population will receive compensation for Nazi gold and the inclusion in that list of Belarus and other countries whose inhabitants suffered in particular as a result of Nazi crimes.

2. The establishment of a Commission made up of representatives of interested countries, which will study the questions examined at this Conference on a permanent basis.

3. Similar conferences held on a regular basis (annually) to examine the Commissions's reports and to draw up recommendations for an intergovernmental meeting to adopt the corresponding intergovernmental agreements.

4. The provision of funding for the activities of the above-mentioned Commission and for conference expenses of the delegations from money connected to Nazi gold.

BELGIUM

The gold of the Belgian monetary institutes

Following the invasion of Belgium on 10 May 1940, the despoliation of the Belgian population and economy by the occupying power took on various forms.

This note sets out to describe concisely two of those forms, that is the removal of Belgian gold deposited at the *Banque de France* and the transfer to Berlin of the gold and foreign currency which Belgian residents were forced to sell to the *Banque d'Emission* in Brussels.

There were many other forms of despoliation.

1. Belgian gold deposited at the Banque de France and stolen by Germany

In late 1939, the majority of the official Belgian gold reserves were abroad, in particular at the Bank of England, the *Banque de France* and the Federal Reserve Bank of New York.

On the eve of the invasion of Belgium by German troops, the monetary gold balance remaining in Belgium was transferred to France, as were the gold assets of the Belgian Treasury and the *Caisse d'Epargne Luxembourgeoise* [Luxembourg Savings Bank] which had been deposited with the *Banque Nationale de Belgique* [Belgian National Bank].

The *Banque de France* thus agreed to the deposit of 5,079 sealed deposit boxes containing 209.5 tonnes of fine gold and undertook to return them on closure of the deposit. If the 36 tonnes which had already been deposited under the name of the *Banque Nationale de Belgique* with the *Banque de France* are taken into account, the latter held on 10 May 1940 a total of 245.5 tonnes on behalf of Belgium.

In order to meet its needs and, in particular, for the purpose of the exchange of banknotes from the very large numbers of Belgian refugees in France, the *Banque Nationale de Belgique* was forced to transfer 42.7 tonnes to the *Banque de France* between 10 May and 5 June 1940, using for that purpose the gold held under its name and deducting the balance from the contents of the sealed deposit boxes which belonged to it.

The *Banque Nationale de Belgique* at that time asked the *Banque de France* – as well as the other depositaries of its gold reserves – to take the same security measures as it was taking in respect of its own assets. The *Banque de France* therefore entrusted the remaining sealed deposit boxes, i.e. 202.7 tonnes of gold, to the French admiralty, which alone was capable of transporting the gold out of the reach of the invader. The *Banque Nationale de Belgique*, like the *Banque de France*, did not know the real destination of the cargo it wished to ship to the United States.

The deposit boxes were loaded at Lorient on 18 June 1940 onto a French auxiliary cruiser which, some ten days later, finally cast anchor at Dakar, where the gold was entrusted to the local French authorities.

The Germans then endeavoured to have the *Banque Nationale de Belgique* repatriate the gold reserves. However, Governor Janssen who, with the consent of the Belgian government which was at that time in refuge in France, had returned to Brussels, rejected that request and demanded that the *Banque Nationale de Belgique* retain full and unfettered control over any gold brought back to Belgium.

Governor Janssen later also objected to the Wiesbaden Agreement concluded on 29 October 1940 between the French and German Armistice Delegations because it provided for the return of the gold coveted by Germany.

The Germans then issued an order authorising the German Commissioner to the *Banque Nationale* – at that time a Mr von Becker – *"to represent the Banque Nationale de Belgique in legal proceedings and in extra-judicial affairs, in particular to undertake legal transactions, including disposition of the Bank's property"*. Furthermore, they forced the French Delegation to sign on 11 December 1940 an Additional Protocol to the Wiesbaden Agreement under which the *Reichsbank* replaced the *Banque de France* as depositary for the Belgian gold transferred to Dakar.

Since the *Banque de France* was of the opinion that the measures taken previously, in accordance with the decisions of the Belgian Government, to guarantee the security of the gold in wartime were still in force, it maintained its opposition, arguing *inter alia* that it could not be bound by an agreement to which it was not a party. The *Banque Nationale de Belgique* accordingly considered that the *Banque de France* was still the depositary for the gold and was responsible for it. It refused to afford material assistance to the transfer of the gold from Dakar to Berlin. Officials from the *Banque Nationale de Belgique* took part in the auditing of the gold transferred to Germany only by order of the German Commissioner and only as ordinary witnesses.

In September 1942, Germany requisitioned the Belgian gold stored at the *Reichsbank*. However, the *Banque Nationale de Belgique*, like the *Banque de France* moreover, rejected all compensation in *reichsmarks*. A sum of RM 500 million which had been credited automatically to the *Banque Nationale's* account at the *Reichsbank* was returned.

Meanwhile, the Belgian government which had finally taken refuge in London did not remain inactive. As regards the official reserves of the *Banque Nationale de Belgique*, its task was undoubtedly made easier by the fact that before the country was invaded, Governor Janssen, with the government's consent, had duly charged three foreign agents, Theunis, Baudewyns and Ansiaux, with the task of taking all protective measures necessary to protect the foreign assets of the *Banque Nationale de Belgique* during the occupation. Following the death of Governor Janssen in 1941 in Brussels, Mr Theunis was appointed governor of the *Banque Nationale de Belgique* in London. On 5 February 1941 the *Banque Nationale de Belgique* brought an action against the *Banque de France* before the Supreme Court in New York for recovery of the gold.

After Belgium's liberation in September 1944, the *Banque de France* and the *Banque Nationale de Belgique* began negotiations as part of a highly positive approach to resolving the problem of the gold taken by the Germans. Those negotiations resulted in an agreement of 8 and 9 October 1944. It its capacity as depositary, the *Banque de France* undertook to replenish the assets with which it had been entrusted by the *Banque Nationale de Belgique*.

The *Banque Nationale de Belgique* withdrew the proceedings brought in New York and all similar actions against the *Banque de France*, and lifted the preventive attachments it had issued in the United States. The *Banque de France* consequently handed over 198.4 tonnes of gold to the *Banque Nationale de Belgique* on 22 December 1944.

On 2 March 1946, a similar agreement settled the case of the Luxembourg gold which the *Banque de France* also returned in full.

The governments concerned agreed on the implementation of the aforementioned agreements.

By the agreement of October 1944, the *Banque Nationale de Belgique* also undertook to lend its full assistance to the *Banque de France* in any steps or action which the latter might consider it, necessary to take against the German government or the *Reichsbank*.

In accordance with the Agreement on Reparations signed in Paris on 14 January 1946, all monetary gold recovered by the allied forces was pooled, ready for distribution to the States entitled in proportion to their claims.

As part of the commitments undertaken in respect of the *Banque de France* and in close co-operation with it, Belgium in 1947 submitted to the Tripartite Commission for the Restitution of Monetary Gold a claim for the recovery of 198.4 tonnes of gold (in this instance 183.2 tonnes in the name of the *Banque Nationale de Belgique* and 15.2 tonnes mainly in the name of the Belgian Treasury). That claim was granted.

To date approximately 127 tonnes have been awarded on that basis to Belgium and delivered directly to the *Banque de France*. As a result of the co-operation of the *Banque de France*, which sought neither to rely on *force majeure* nor to resort to the dilatory stance which it could legitimately have adopted in the legal proceedings under way, Belgium recovered the monetary gold which Germany had stolen from it.

2. Germany's appropriation of gold and foreign currency belonging to the Belgian population.

From the very beginning of Belgium's invasion in May 1940, the occupying power ordered that safety-deposit boxes hired at banks would be temporarily frozen in so far as their owners could open them only in the presence of an agent of the *Devisenschutzkommando* [Currency Protection Command], which was responsible for recording the existence of German gold, foreign currency and securities. Safety-deposit boxes whose owners failed to comply with those orders were forced open by order of the *Devisenschutzkommando* a few months later so that an inventory of their contents could be drawn up.

Under a German order of 17 June 1940, Belgian residents (physical persons and companies) were forced to declare their foreign monetary assets (foreign currency, foreign securities and shares, claims and negotiable instruments entitling payment in foreign currency or abroad) and their assets in gold and in other precious metals such as silver and platinum. That order was of general application and was in no way restricted to assets held in the aforementioned safety-deposit boxes.

The enforcement measures taken by the Germans provided that declarants were also required to sell the gold (coins, ingots) and the foreign currency to the Banque d'Emission in Brussels. That bank had been established on the initiative of the occupying power and, during the war, it served alongside the Banque Nationale de Belgique as a central bank, being responsible more specifically for clearing business with foreign countries and foreign currency transactions.

Assets declared which were situated abroad, in other occupied countries such as France and the Netherlands to be more precise, were in several cases repatriated later by the Devisenschutzkommando, which had obtained authority to do so from their owners.

From early August 1940, the German Commissioner, Mr von Becker, instructed the *Banque d'Emission* to transfer the gold and foreign currency sold by the declarants to the *Reichsbank* in Berlin.

The shipments reached their peak in September/October 1940 and at that time took place every week. Later, they gradually became more irregular, until eventually they occurred only occasionally.

The demand made by Governor Janssen in 1940 that the Belgian economy receive foodstuffs and raw materials in return was effectively not acted upon in the years that followed.

The implementation of the abovementioned German orders was also the subject of much wrangling between the *Banque d'Emission* and the German authorities, particularly in 1943 over cases of assets repatriated by the *Devisenschutzkommando* being sold to the *Banque d'Emission* without the consent of their owners, sterling banknotes being seized from individuals again by the *Devisenschutzkommando*, and even platinum assets being purchased outside the proper powers of a monetary institution.

Since the Germans considered that the *Banque d'Emission* was not taking the desired action, the *Reichskreditkasse* was designated by order of 30 June 1943 to acquire the securities declared, instead of the *Banque d 'Emission.*

Nevertheless, it was still the latter bank which was instructed soon after by a further German order to collect the declarations and offers relating to foreign currency and gold assets situated in Belgium but owned by persons living in the Belgian Congo. Those last two orders admittedly had only very limited effects.

In total, during the occupation, the equivalent of some 305 million francs is alleged to have been transferred to Berlin in accordance with those orders, partly in the form of currency and partly in the form of gold.

In 1947, Belgium submitted to the Tripartite Gold Commission on behalf of the provisional director of the *Banque d'Emission* (which had been put into liquidation) a claim in damages for the 6.4 tonnes of gold which it had been forced to transfer to Berlin without any real consideration after buying it from Belgian residents. The Tripartite Gold Commission rejected the claim lodged by the *Banque d'Emission* as it considered that that claim did not concern monetary gold.

BRAZIL

How is Brazil dealing with the Nazi Gold Issue?

THE BRAZILIAN GOVERNMENT'S APPROACH TO THE ISSUE

The Brazilian Government attaches considerable importance to the efforts that have been made by the international community to increase its understanding and knowledge of the historical facts relating to gold looted by the Nazis.

It also acknowledges the relevance of the work carried out by the Tripartite Commission for the Restitution of Monetary Gold (TGC), its member countries and other interested parties, with respect to the distribution of monetary gold recovered after the Second World War.

It shares the main concerns of all countries that have so far undertaken relevant work with the view both to investigate the issue and, in some cases, reimburse countries and compensate individual victims.

In order to deal with this issue at home, the Brazilian Government has set up a Special Commission charged with identifying and investigating Nazi assets believed to have been brought into the country.

This approach is in line with Brazil's international and national commitment to promote and protect human rights.

THE COMMISSION FOR THE INVESTIGATION OF NAZI ASSETS

The Commission was created by Presidential Decree on the 7th of April 1997.

It operates from the Ministry of Justice, which provides it with the needed administrative and financial support for its work.

The Commission is composed of seven members appointed by the President of the Republic, among which are government officials, historians and representatives from civil society, including the Jewish community of Brazil. The Minister of Justice is responsible for monitoring the activities carried out by the Commission.

The Commission was in principle established for a one-year period, that is, until June 1998, but may be prolonged by ministerial request.

WORK AND AIMS OF THE COMMISSION

The principal aims of the work being carried out by the Commission are:
- a. to investigate the entry and the existence in Brazil of assets illicitly confiscated from Nazi régime victims; and
- b. to ascertain their value, origin and destination.

In order to achieve these aims, the Commission has wide-ranging competence. It may request documents and information from any public and private institution in Brazil, and it is also authorized to search for information abroad through the pertinent diplomatic channels. Furthermore it is authorized to:

a. promote investigations and eventual audits;
b. examine witnesses; and
c. request technical advice.

At the end of its deliberations, the Commission will draw conclusions and put forward recommendations that will be submitted to the President.

RECENT ACTIVITIES

In accordance with its mandate, the Commission has already undertaken research and investigations. It has assessed, on a preliminary basis, the historical archives and sources of information available in Brazil, particularly in the Ministries of Justice and of External Relations, the Bank of Brazil and the Public Archives of the States of Rio de Janeiro and São Paulo. Exchanges of information with other pertinent institutions abroad have also begun.

Preliminary findings have indicated that there may have been immigration of members, or associated militants, of the Nazi Party into Brazil after the Second World War, mainly from 1946 to 1950. The level of association of these Germans with the Nazi régime and their involvement in the looting of gold are still to be determined. The archives also contain data on some monetary assets and financial transactions related to Germans and Jews who came to Brazil, or maintained relations with their own Nationals and others in the country, in the period from 1930 to 1950. Further investigation of these facts and connections is required.

At the request of the Commission, Brazilian judicial authorities have recently granted permission for the examination of some bank accounts and safety deposit boxes in Brazil. Many valuables came to light, such as those in a safety deposit box found in a branch of the Bank of Brazil in Sao Paulo last week. These valuables, which it is suspected might have been illicitly remitted to Brazil, are now being subjected to technical examination.

CONCLUSIONS

As stated, the work of the Commission is ongoing and still in its early stages.

Much work is still to be done, not only in pursuing investigations on the value, origin and destination of suspect assets, but also in improving research and evaluation of factual elements and connections discovered in historical archives and in the information made available by Brazilian and foreign institutions.

It is too early to say whether some of the assets found in Brazil – in the form of Bank accounts, safety deposit boxes, cash and even works of art – contain or are connected with the gold and other valuables stolen by the Nazis.

The Commission will be investigating all cases which might have some bearing on the gold and other valuables taken from victims of the Nazi régime and smuggled into Brazil. By setting up the Commission the Brazilian Government is responding to the legitimate demands of public opinion for an investigation into possible Nazi assets in Brazil.

BULGARIA

Anti-Semitic Legislation in Bulgaria, 1940–44: A Case Study of Some Aspects

DR VITA TOSHKOVA

Department of International Relations
Institute of History, Bulgarian Academy of Science

The looting of Jewish gold has been greatly facilitated by the Anti-Semitic legislation enacted in Bulgaria since 1940. The Bulgarian rulers didn't save the Bulgarian Jews the humiliation and deprivation of the anti-Jewish restrictions modelled on the Nuremberg laws. As a matter of fact, there was no official anti-Semitism in Bulgaria until the fall of 1939. Nevertheless, the declared neutrality on September 15, 1939, couldn't hide the more friendly attitude of Sofia toward the Third Reich. The Bulgarian authorities tried to expel 4,000 foreign Jews from the country. They had left Central Europe before the Nazis advance and had come to Bulgaria to find passage to Palestine. Some of them, however, remained in Bulgaria.

The Germans were anxious to see their potential allies accepting an anti-Jewish legislation tailored on the German pattern. In fact, King Boris initiated the project. There were speculations about the King's motives. He had told one of his closest advisors that "since the anti-Jewish law had to come, the Bulgarians should initiate it themselves, rather than let the Germans dictate a harsher one".[1]

The real author of the project was Alexander Belev, the associate and "protégé" of the Minister of Internal Affairs since February 1940 Peter Gabrovski. Belev visited Germany to study the Nuremberg laws in the summer of 1940; after his return Gabrovski declared the idea to propose a "Law for Defence of the Nation" (LDN). In general, the project was directed against the Jews.

The main justification for the law was that "the Jews, as a part of the international community, are alien to the Bulgarian spirit and their cosmopolitan connections constitute a danger to the State".[2] Part II of the draft entitled "About Persons of Jewish Origin" first defined who is of Jewish origin. Chapter II included general restrictions for the Jewish limiting their right "to participate in Bulgaria's economic and political LIFE", i.e. to vote or be elected to occupy posts in state administration, to marry a Bulgarian, to serve in the army, to have restricted access to educational institutions, to participate in funds for trade, industry and crafts, *to export funds abroad*, etc. Exceptions under Article 33 were provided for Jews who had converted to Christianity, married Bulgarians or served in the military.

The Jewish access to crafts and professions was limited to the same percentage of workers throughout the country as the percentage of the Jewish population in the Kingdom. According to the last pre-war census for 1934 there were *49,398* Jews (0.80% of the entire population); 97% of them lived in the cities and only 3% in the countryside. The social structure of the Jews in 1936–1946 was as follows:

34.95% – workers: of them 12.27% worked in industry
13.57% – in crafts
4.02% – in trade
0.65% – in social and Government institutions
3.84% – in other jobs.

The class between the workers and the lower middle class comprised 15.18%. The middle class made up 32.66% (lowest – 11.84%, lower – 15.07%, middle – 5.26%, upper – 0.49%). 17.21% were intellectuals, mainly clerks, 2.25% – in open professions, 0.97% – in industry and 0.86% – in other branches. Thus, the LDN sentenced most of the Jewish families to losses of livelihood.

The Cabinet approved the project, and it was published in October 1940. The draft started a great controversy in Bulgaria and engaged the entire capital in a debate concerning the Jews and the bill. The opposition couldn't stop the passage of the bill in the Parliament. Gabrovski sent the Law to the Palace on January 15, 1941. King Boris ratified it, and both the King and the Minister of Internal Affairs signed the bill. On January 23, 1941 it was published in the "Durzhaven vestnik" – "the official gazette for promulgation of laws and decrees" as "ukaz" No. 3.[3]

The application of the LDN was connected with time limits: one month for Jews to leave their posts, six months to liquidate forbidden property.

The Bulgarians followed with persistence one aspect of their anti-Jewish policy – the confiscation. In July 1941 the Bulgarian Government proposed a special tax on the Jewish community. The National Assembly enacted a Law which required the Jews to submit to the Ministry of Finance a statement of their total wealth within seven days after the Law's publication.[4] All Jews with property valued over 200,000 leva ($2,430) were subject to the tax:

20% – on property valued above 200,000 leva but under 3,000,000 ($36,500),
25% – on property valued above 3,000,000 leva.

The Law was valid for all Jewish property in Bulgaria regardless of the citizenship of the owners; Bulgarian Jews abroad were also liable to the tax. Half of the tax was due within thirty days, the rest in six months. Penalties for non-payment or false information were severe: triple taxation on the undeclared property, a fine of 3,000,000 leva, 5 year prison term, and confiscation of the property. The Jews couldn't emigrate until the tax was paid. This Law – for the unique tax on Jews – was the most cruel measure against the Jews after the promulgation of the LDN.

The application of the LDN met some difficulties due to intercession by foreign Governments – Spain, Rumania and Hungary – on behalf of their citizens. The foreign minister Popov, on a visit to Berlin in November 1941, suggested that the Germans convene a European conference to consider the Jewish problem as a whole. The proposition was rejected because of the preparations for the Wannsee conference connected with the "Final Solution of the Jewish Question". The German officials preferred bilateral treaties concerning Jews. According to the decision for equal treatment of foreign Jewish citizens, on June 19, 1942, Martin Luther of the German Foreign Office notified A. H. Beckerle, the German minister to Sofia, that several hundred Bulgarian Jews lived in the Reich and Protectorate (Bohemia and Moravia). Luther proposed an exchange of notes according to which the German and Bulgarian Governments would not claim any rights for Jews who were citizens of either country. Sofia agreed and promised to prepare *a detailed list* of Bulgarian Jews residing in the German controlled territories.[5] Thus, one of the consequences of the Wannsee conference (met on January 20, 1942 in Berlin) affected the Bulgarian-German cooperation on the "Final Solution".

Al. Belev was in Berlin during the conference to learn the latest decisions on the Jewish question. He reported (June 1942) that the Bulgarian Government must prepare the Jews for deportation and to take measures for the complete confiscation of Jewish property. Belev also suggested new restrictions which included limiting the privileged Jews as well the privileges, transferring Jews from the capital, putting Jewish organisations under government control and unifying supervision of the Jewish measures under a single agency.

The implementation of the above mentioned propositions was facilitated by the Bulgarian Government. The Cabinet introduced into the National Assembly (June 1942) a bill for a *"Law to Charge the Council of Ministers to Take all Measures for Solving the Jewish Question and Matters Connected with it"*. The bill passed on June 28 1942 and gave the Cabinet "plenipotentiary authority" to pass decrees on Jewish matters, including the existing Jewish legislation.[6]

Beckerle sent a German translation of the law to Berlin. He noted that the Bulgarian Government was considering "some more radical measures and actions" against the Jews, and, more precisely "confiscating and taking possession of those people's properties in the near future".

The main result of this Law was the government decree of August 26, 1942.[7] The decree was designed to amplify the LDN and to create a *Commissariat for Jewish Questions*. The main task of this body was to achieve "a complete isolation" of the Jews from the economy, "elimination of all their rights and privileges, and their extradition". Meanwhile, Al. Belev was appointed a commissioner of the Commissariat and took up his duties on the 3rd of September 1942.

The decree of August 26, 1942 also changed the definition of "Jew" considering ancestry rather than religion as the most important criterion. It included measures for total confiscation of Jewish wealth – an integral part of the Nazi's plans for Europe: the Jews had to wear a six-pointed yellow star and carry a pink identity card; their homes, offices and products were marked by a sign "Jewish Home" . . . etc.

Rumania, Hungary, France, Spain and Italy protested the application of the decree to their Jewish citizens in Bulgaria. The Italian Foreign Ministry, for example, was allowing Jews to enter Italy very easily, permitting many Jews to become Italian citizens.

One of the important sections of Commissariat was the "Treasury", so called *"Jewish community fund"*. Income for the fund came chiefly from *frozen Jewish bank accounts*, from taxes and assessments on Jews, from sale of revenue stamps on Commissariat's documents and forms.

Besides the marking of Jews, the CJQ registered all Jews subject under Bulgarian administration.

Approximately, the total indicated 63,400 Jews:

    51,500 – pre-1940 boundaries
    500 – Southern Dobrudzha
    4,000 – Western Thrace
    7,200 – Macedonia
    200 – Pirot (Serbia)

Next to designation and location, the CJQ confiscated and administered Jewish property, because it planned to deport the Bulgarian Jews. The total value of Jewish property (assuming that it was proportional to the total number of declarations filed) would be 7.5 billion leva or about $91 million. The CJQ required the Jews deposit all cash and valuables in frozen accounts which were controlled by the CJQ. By March, 1943, the frozen Jewish bank accounts were over 307 million leva ($3,730,000), and the value of property and valuables under CJQ control was over 801 million leva ($9,730,000). According to some studies, the total value of expropriated Jewish property which can be calculated was 4.5 billion leva ($54,700,000).[8]

Under CJQ control were all Jewish economic organisations: popular banks, credit institutions, and insurance companies.

*   *   *   *   *

The first action in applying the Final Solution to the Bulgarian population included those Jews resident in Germany and Reich-occupied lands, which the Bulgarian Cabinet allowed the Germans to deport in July 1942. The second step was taken on February 22, 1943, when Belev and Dannecker (sent to Sofia by the German Foreign Office) signed an official agreement for the deportation of the first 20,000 Jews into German hands.[9] On March 2, 1943, the Council of Ministers issued seven decrees concerning deportation of the Jews. By them was approved the expatriation of 20,000 Jews living in the "new lands" (Thrace and Macedonia); the Cabinet also arranged to take away the citizenship of all Jews deported across the border, according to article 15 of the Law for Bulgarian Citizenship, which provided that Bulgarian citizens who were not of Bulgarian nationality lost their citizenship if they emigrated; a special decree declared that all real estate of the deported Jews would be confiscated.

The deportation of the Jews from the "new territories" began on March 4, 1943. The Bulgarians deported approximately 4,075 Jews from Thrace; 158 Jews

from Pirot; and 7,160 Jews from Macedonia – total 11,393. The profit for liquidation were deposited in the frozen accounts of the Jewish owners when known;
the Bulgarian National Bank sent deposit statement addressed to the Jewish
owners, in care of the CJQ.[10]

The deportation of Jews from "old" Bulgaria was a failure. The reasons are
well studied.[11] The course of the war urged the Bulgarians away from Germany.
In the summer of 1944 the Prime Minister Ivan Bagrianov showed more con-
ciliatory attitude toward the Allies. On August 31, 1944, the Bulgarian Government abrogated restrictive legislation affecting the Jews. The legal situation
prior to January 23, 1941, was restored. The Cabinet also promised to return
confiscated Jewish property. The Muraviev Government, the Cabinet over-
thrown by Fatherland Front forces on September 8–9, 1944, issued only few
orders to promote a complete return to the conditions before 1941. The government granted amnesty to Jews indicated under anti-Semitic legislation on
September 7, 1944.

The real implementation of the return to pre-1941 conditions was one aspect
of the Fatherland Front Government's program. On September 23, 1944 was
announced that the Government would return the Jews' property. In March
1945, a Law authorising the return of Jewish property was published in
Durzaven Vestnik. The value of property was set at 1943 levels. The
Government promised to return rents collected on Jewish property and pay
compensation in the amount of 30,000,000 leva ($364,000) for unreturned prop-
erty. In general, the Government was unable to return all of the property and
money confiscated. Later, the nationalisation of industry and business eliminat-
ed the possibility of return for much of the expropriated Jewish property.

NOTES

[1] See Frederick B. Chary, *The Bulgarian Jews and the Final Solution, 1940–1944* (University of
Pittsburgh Press, 1972), p. 37.

[2] Stenografski Dnevnitsi [Stenographic Records], XXV Obiknoveno Narodno Subranie
[Ordinary National Assembly], 2nd reg. session (October 28, 1940, to May 28, 1941) p. 204.

[3] Chary, p. 41; see also: *The Survival*. A Compilation of Documents, 1940–1944. "Shalom"
Publishing Centre, Sofia, 1995. (Compiler: David Cohen); Durzaven Vestnik [State Gazette]
(hereafter cited as DV), No. 16, January 23, 1941.

[4] DV, No. 151, July 14, 1941.

[5] *The Survival*, p.66.

[6] DV, No. 148 July 9, 1942.

[7] DV, No. 192, August 29, 1942.

[8] David B. Koen, *Ekspropriatsiata na evreiskite imushtestva prez perioda na hitleristkata okupatsiia
[Expropriation of Jewish Property during the Period of Hitlerist Occupation]*, in: Godishnik (of Bulgarian
Jewish Organization), 2 (1967), pp. 109–110.

[9] *The Survival*, pp. 204–205.

[10] Chary, pp. 126–128.

[11] See Chary, pp. 129–199; Bela Vago, The Reaction to the Nazi Anti-Jewish Policy in East-
Central Europe and in the Balkans, in: Unanswered Questions: Nazi Germany and the
Genocide of the Jews. Ed. Francois Furet. Schooken Books, New York, 1989, pp. 206–207,
223–227.

CANADA

Due Diligence

*A Report on the Bank of Canada's Handling of
Foreign Gold During World War II*

PREPARED FOR THE BANK OF CANADA BY DUNCAN MCDOWALL
CARLETON UNIVERSITY, OTTAWA

CONTENTS

Summary   80

Preamble   87

Earmarked Gold in Canada, 1935–56   97

The European Perspective, 1942–45   132

Commentary: Due Diligence?   147

The Documents   156

Acknowledgements   163

Notes   164

Appendix: Reconstruction of Gold Safekeeping Records 1935–56   170

Summary

CONTEXT

The issue of "Nazi gold" has galvanized the Western world since 1995. Through a conjuncture of activism on the part of the World Jewish Congress and American Senator Alfonse D'Amato, chair of the Senate Banking Committee, the long-unresolved issue of where an alleged US$580 million in gold looted by the Axis during World War II went has come to life with a vengeance. Much of this gold had been plundered during the early stages of the war from the vaults of European central banks that had fallen under the heel of the German army. A portion of this monetary gold – state-owned gold used to support a country's monetary operations – had been recaptured by the Allies in the dying months of the war and repatriated to its rightful owners. A greater portion, however, proved untraceable, largely because it had been laundered by means of surreptitious refining and transfer to banks in the neutral countries of Europe – Switzerland, Portugal and Sweden. Much of the trade in looted gold supported Germany's acquisition of foreign raw materials and equipment to run its war machine. By the end of the war, therefore, much of this looted gold was in fact in the hands of neutral countries.

The question of looted gold had other dimensions. There was a significant amount of non-monetary gold – gold plundered from individuals caught in the trap of war – mingled with the looted monetary gold. Most worrisome was evidence that some of this non-monetary gold was stripped from the Jewish victims of Nazi death camps. This sinister gold had also passed through the mill of Nazi refining and had been filtered through bank accounts and commercial transactions with European neutral banks. These same banks also became the focus of another financial legacy of the war: the issue of dormant bank accounts and so-called "heirless assets". As appeasement failed in the late 1930s, many Europeans, principally German Jews, sought some financial insurance in the face of the impending conflict by placing some or all of their assets in bank accounts in safe-haven countries like Switzerland. The appalling extermination inflicted upon these same people by the Holocaust made the postwar restitution and disposition of these assets a problematic process, especially given the secretiveness of the initial deposits and the cocoon of secrecy that the Swiss banking system erected around foreign accounts.

In the late stages of the war, the Allies made a concerted attempt to locate and repatriate gold looted by the Axis. Declarations were issued warning of the consequences of trading or taking possession of looted gold and, as peace neared, more active efforts were launched to actually reclaim "Nazi gold." The American Safehaven program spearheaded this campaign. Much of the attention fell on Switzerland. The Swiss central bank, the Banque National Suisse, had bought more gold from the Germans than any other country. The Swiss had also acted as Germany's principal trade conduit to non-Axis economies. And Switzerland's commercial banks had also commanded a near-monopoly on safe-haven bank accounts held by victims of the war and with the return of peace these banks found themselves under pressure to restore deposits to their legal owners. Emerging beside this negotiation was the thorny issue of "heirless assets", the disposition of assets for which there now appeared to be no living claimant. Through the late 1940s, Allied governments, principally those of the United States, Britain and France, therefore engaged in prolonged negotiations with the European neutral powers that had maintained financial ties with the Axis. Some restitution of gold was made to the central banks of once-occupied countries. Some distribution of "heirless assets" was made to stateless refugees. But much of the looted gold remained elusive, and the rights of account holders and heirs of personal accounts in neutral banks were by and large overlooked by Allied negotiators. By the early 1950s, emerging new issues of European and Cold War diplomacy tended to shunt the issue of looted gold to the sidelines of big-power statecraft.

The end of the Cold War in the early 1990s, the crumbling of the East Bloc and the determination of the World Jewish Congress to bring justice to some of the long-suffering Jewish community all combined in 1995 to reignite interest in the question of looted gold and dormant bank accounts.

Once again, Switzerland was the fulcrum of the debate. The tone of the controversy was set by a powerful mixture of politics, morality and history. After a brief and disastrous reprise of denial and obfuscation by Switzerland's bankers, the universal response to the issue has become one of inquiry and restitution. The means to this end has largely been historical investigation. Formal historical commissions have been active in Switzerland, Portugal, Sweden, Britain and the United States. These commissions have focused not only on the wartime activities of central and commercial bankers, but also on the broader picture of Allied and Axis diplomacy and war bureaucracy. Archives have been scoured, evidence taken and reports produced – most noticeable to date has been the mammoth Eizenstat report produced by the American government at President Clinton's behest. The process of restitution has also begun. The Swiss Banker's Association has finally begun a thorough identification of dormant bank accounts on the books of its members, thereby allowing long-frozen assets to be reunited with their rightful owners.

Through all the initial postwar investigations and the more recent rebirth of the "Nazi gold" issue, the word "Canada" has practically never surfaced. Canada played no active role in the late 1940s negotiations with European neutrals, nor did its name ever surface in connection with the trade in looted gold. The massive Eizenstat report issued by the American government earlier this year does not contain a single mention of Canada in connection with the issue of looted gold, despite the survey of over 15 million documents in reaching its conclusions. In July 1997 the silence over Canada's role broke abruptly. A document retrieved by World Jewish Congress researchers in Washington gave rise to the allegation, based on an anonymous late-war intelligence report "from a very confidential source," that the Bank of Canada had been party, by means of paper transfer, to a complex gold transfer involving six tons of gold shuffled between Switzerland and Portugal in 1942. Later in the war, the document alleged, this same gold became part of a second questionable swap between Portugal and Sweden with Canada's central bank again playing the role of intermediary. In a letter forwarding this document and its incriminating allegation to Bank of Canada Governor Gordon Thiessen on July 11, 1997, the Canadian Jewish Congress echoed the opinion of the World Jewish Congress that the gold transfers involving the Bank looked like a "classic money-laundering operation." The Canadian Jewish Congress therefore asked that the Bank of Canada "undertake an investigation to ascertain the involvement of the Bank in these transactions."

The Bank of Canada immediately acquiesced, announcing not only that a thorough internal investigation would be undertaken but also that an outside historian would be asked to complete an independent analysis of the Bank's role in the wartime movement of gold. On August 12, I began this investigation. My mandate was both wide-ranging and unfettered. I was to review all the Bank of Canada's documents related to gold transactions during the period from the founding of the Bank in 1935 through 1950 and to have unconditional access to the Bank's archives and personnel. Since the Department of Finance was also party to the wartime gold transfers in question, Minister of Finance Paul Martin issued similar assurances that the investigation would meet with the unreserved cooperation of his department. The investigation was to culminate in a public report that was "to respond to public concern about possible Bank of Canada involvement in transactions related to looted 'Nazi gold' during and after the Second World War" and at the same time advise the Bank on "the appropriate way to make the records [of the Bank] accessible to other researchers." Under these terms, I commenced the research underlying this report.

METHODOLOGY

This report is rooted in an intensive archival survey of all documents relating to gold transfers facilitated by the Bank of Canada in World War II. The archival search extended well beyond the Bank of Canada into the records of federal government departments and offices that had a role, however remote, in the gold transfers in question. Papers of prominent politicians and senior bureaucrats were also consulted. Oral interviews were conducted with retired Bank of Canada officials who might possibly have had recollections of the Bank's wartime operations. While the project's principal objective was to supply the Canadian perspective on these transfers, a concerted effort was made to contact the European central banks that were party to these transactions and to collect opinions and documents on their roles in these events. To this end, detailed inquiries were submitted to the Bank of England, the Banque National Suisse, the Banco de Portugal and the Sveriges Riksbank in Stockholm. Full and willing cooperation was received from all these bodies and the historical commissions now working on their national investigations into the issue of Nazi gold. The following conclusions can be drawn about the documentary record supporting this report.

The Reliability of the Source Material Used in this Report

• A very complete record of the Bank of Canada's role as a wartime safe-keeper of foreign gold exists. The documents reflect the expected thoroughness of a central banker. There are virtually no gaps in the record.

• This record is fully complemented by documents in the archives of other federal agencies, notably the Department of Finance, which played a subsidiary role in policy vis-à-vis the safekeeping of foreign gold in Ottawa.

• There is no evidence whatsoever of document tampering. There is one possible departure in record-keeping practice that led to a gap in the file covering the Bank of England's large wartime account in Ottawa. The gap, can, however, be closed by drawing evidence from other document series.

• The documentary record of the contentious gold swaps of 1942–45 involving Switzerland, Portugal and Sweden through the Bank of Canada reveals absolutely no departure in procedure (e.g., legal transfer documents, gold export permits) from other non-contentious gold accounts.

• There is ample evidence that the Bank of Canada has in the years since World War II devoted considerable energy to the systematic retention of its records.

• Original documentation obtained from the Bank of England, the Banque Nationale Suisse, Banco de Portugal and Sveriges Riksbank all tends to confirm the Bank of Canada's documentary record of the events surrounding the swaps of 1942–45.

• There is a striking absence of marginalia, unusual commentary or other written signs of anxiety in the records concerning these transfers, indicting that they were not viewed in an unusual light by the Canadian participants.

• Records of senior officials at the Bank of Canada as well as those of prominent Canadian politicians and bureaucrats reveal no undue concern over the swaps in question (e.g., the W.L.M. King diaries or the papers of Finance Minister J.L. Ilsley).

• The Bank of Canada has accompanied this research with a massive effort to reconstruct its gold ledgers (i.e., the ledgers used to record all gold entering and leaving the Bank's vault) for the years 1935–56. This work is largely complete and will eventually give the Bank the ability to track the majority of gold bars that physically arrived and left the Bank during these years. A statistical synopsis of this reconstruction is appended to this report.

• A finding aid listing all the documents consulted in the course of this research is available upon request from the Bank of Canada. Some of these documents are already in the public domain (e.g., at the National Archives of Canada), others are still within controlled archives.

• This report endorses the Bank of Canada's determination to make all the documents consulted during the course of this research available for public consultation. This process is well under way, but cannot proceed any quicker than the provisions of Canada's Access to Information and Privacy Acts dictate. The principle of client confidentiality has necessitated the seeking of permission for the release of documents from the European central banks discussed in this report.

FINDINGS

• During World War II, Canada played a major role in the earmarking of foreign gold for safekeeping at the Bank of Canada. Between the first rumblings of war in 1938 and peace in 1945, foreign central banks deposited 2,586 tons of gold in Ottawa for safekeeping. For many nations that had fallen under German occupation, this cache of safe gold was the ultimate guarantee of national survival. In particular, the central banks of Belgium, the Netherlands, France, Norway and Poland availed themselves of this unique type of Canadian wartime hospitality. The Bank of England was also a frequent earmarker of gold in Ottawa and in the dark days of 1940 even made plans to create a "shadow" Bank of England in Ottawa that could draw upon Britain's gold cache in Canada. Such deposits involved no profit for Canada beyond small handling charges.
• The flow of earmarked gold to the Bank of Canada was almost exclusively one-way. Large amounts of gold crossed the Atlantic in the early war period, especially from the Bank of England and the Banque de France. After 1941, virtually no more gold arrived from Europe, with the exception of a shipment of 525 bars from the Bank Polski in London in 1944. During the course of the war, virtually none of the gold stored in Ottawa was shipped back across the Atlantic, with the exception of two small shipments of gold coin returned to England in 1942. All the transactions in question in this report were paper transfers of gold ownership between one central bank account at the Bank of Canada and other central bank accounts. There is therefore no possibility that tainted gold – gold looted by Germany – ever found its way into the Canadian gold stream.
• The 1942–43 transfer of Bank of England gold earmarked in Ottawa to the Ottawa earmark account of the Banque Nationale Suisse involved 56 tons of gold, a small fraction of the overall wartime deposit of foreign gold in Ottawa. This gold was swapped for Swiss francs delivered to the British in Switzerland. This swap was necessitated by Britain's desperate need for Swiss francs to maintain its trade and diplomatic relationship with Switzerland and was entered into reluctantly by the Swiss. Switzerland already had large quantities of gold stockpiled beyond its borders in London and New York, but this was blocked and of no wartime use to Switzerland. The Swiss accepted the deal only as a *pro tem.* measure in the hope of keeping stalled trade negotiations with the British alive.
• To safeguard the gold that had passed from Allied hands to neutral hands under earmark in Ottawa, the Bank of Canada altered the minimal prewar arrangements for foreign gold deposited in Canada to reflect the exigencies of war. The primary concern was that the 56 tons of gold held by Switzerland in Ottawa might find its way back to Europe and ultimately be applied to the ends of the Axis. These conditions stipulated that the gold received by the Banque Nationale Suisse from the Bank of England might be physically exported only to other central banks in the Western Hemisphere or transferred on paper to central banks in the Western Hemisphere and to the central banks of European neutral countries – namely Portugal, Sweden and Spain. These conditions were to apply until the end of hostilities. The Swiss agreed to these conditions.

• The Bank of Canada's willingness to facilitate such swaps was strongly condi-
tioned by its relationship with the Bank of England. Canada was one of the last
Western powers to create a central bank and, since its inauguration in 1935, the
Bank of Canada had relied heavily on the guidance of the Bank of England.
This relationship was epitomized by the close personal friendship of Bank of
Canada Governor Graham Towers and Bank of England Governor Montagu
Norman. The Bank of England was, for instance, the first foreign central bank
to open – in 1936 – an earmarked gold account in Ottawa. Similarly, the Bank
of Canada's first deputy governor was seconded from the Bank of England in
1935. While Towers was never oblivious to protecting Canada's interests, there
was an almost filial inclination to respond to England's bidding. This would pre-
condition the Bank of Canada's positive response to Britain's request to facilitate the gold-for-francs swap with Switzerland and other European gold
exchanges involving Canada.
• The 1942 gold-for-francs swap had been preceded by another request from the
Bank of England in September 1940. Confronted with an influx of small holdings of gold deposited in English commercial banks by Europeans anxious for
the safety of their wealth and well-being, the British asked the Bank of Canada
to earmark these deposits of personal gold under the umbrella of its own Ottawa
accounts. This was a departure from usual earmark procedure in that it allowed
foreign individuals the prerogative of the security of an earmark account well
beyond the fray in Europe. Control of the deposits remained in the hands of the
Bank of England. A handling charge of 5% of each individual's gold was
imposed by the Bank of England the depositor had to sign an agreement
acknowledging that the gold would not be released until after the war, except in
extraordinary circumstances approved by the Bank of England. During the
course of September 1940 to June 1941, 155 of these so-called "sundry persons"
deposits of personal gold at the Bank of England were included in shipments to
the Bank of Canada from London. The total deposit was the equivalent of 1,315
bars of gold. Many of the depositors appear – by name and testimonial – to have
been European Jewish refugees who had fled their homelands in the early stages
of the war. They were generally well-to-do and had left their homelands early
enough to avoid the Holocaust. Other deposits appear to have been made by
Swiss and other nationals. A small number of the depositors – 34 sundry persons – were able to convince the Bank of England to release their gold in Ottawa
before the end of the war. The remaining deposits were all closed after the war
without incident or complication. The last deposit was closed in 1955.
• Almost as soon as the process of swapping English gold for Swiss francs had
begun in the spring of 1942, the Banque Nationale Suisse [BNS] began seeking
ways to apply the gold it was accumulating in Ottawa to its domestic needs at
home, principally the building up of internal gold reserves as a check on Swiss
inflation. This desire was limited by the conditions set on the earmark account
by the Bank of Canada. An initial attempt to establish Swiss commercial bank
accounts in Ottawa and thereby open the way for transfers between off-shore
central bank and commercial bank accounts was locked by vigilant officials at
the Bank of Canada. In the wake of this decision, Governor Towers informed

the general managers of Canada's chartered banks that it was the government's wish that they stop opening new gold safekeeping accounts for non-residents and to report any future requests for such services to Ottawa. Rebuffed in this direction, the BNS began negotiations with the Banco de Portugal, which had gold accounts with it in Switzerland. In two equal transactions in April and May 1942, the BNS subsequently traded four tons of its earmarked gold in Canada for a similar amount of gold held by the Portuguese earmarked in its vault in Switzerland. Thus, the Swiss succeeded in obtaining the free use of four tons of gold in Switzerland in return for surrendering four tons of assuredly clean gold in Canada. To achieve this swap, the BNS was obliged to pay a steep commission to the Banco de Portugal of $1^1/2\%$ on the first swap and $2^1/2\%$ on the second swap. These commissions reflected the fact that the gold Portugal was obtaining in Ottawa was blocked for the duration of the war. In the wake of these swaps, the BNS board of directors decided to abandon the tactic of offering gold in Ottawa for gold in Europe because the transaction costs were exorbitant. The crucial question of whether the Portuguese gold released to the Swiss was tainted gold of German origin is elucidated by reference to classified British wartime documents drawn from British intercept of cables between the Swiss and Portuguese central banks and from banking records recently released by the Banco de Portugal. These reveal that, while the Banco de Portugal did receive large amounts of Reichsbank gold into its BNS accounts, the gold transferred to the Swiss in 1942 was generally believed to be drawn from an account "thought to be without German taint". There is no absolute assurance that this swapped gold was beyond all possible taint, but this evidence and the complete absence of any indication of concern on the part of Allied bankers involved in the swap indicate that this was likely the case. Once again, national liquidity needs, not schemes to launder dirty German gold, seemed to drive the transaction.

• In 1944, Portugal itself encountered liquidity problems in its trade with Switzerland. Increasingly unable to trade in gold because of the tightening Allied injunctions on looted gold, Portugal was driven to finance its trade with hard currencies like the Swiss franc and the Swedish krona. By August, the value of the Portuguese escudo was plummeting against the franc and the krona. Both the Swiss and Swedish proved reluctant to accept Portuguese offers of gold-for-currency swaps. In desperation, the Banco de Portugal therefore offered the Sveriges Riksbank, Sweden's central bank, clean gold in Ottawa in exchange for kronor. This offer of a ton and a half of gold in September and October of 1944 was accepted by the Swedes on the condition that the Portuguese applied the resultant kronor to the process of Swedish-Portuguese trade alone. Subsequently, the Sveriges Riksbank and the Banco de Portugal agreed to ease Portugal's ongoing exchange needs by using the swapping of gold earmarked in Ottawa back and forth to provide kronor for Lisbon. By the end of this process in September 1945, the Sveriges Riksbank had accumulated two and a half tons of gold previously owned by the Banco de Portugal in Ottawa.

• One last gold swap rounded out the Bank of Canada's role in gold transfers between neutral European central banks. In the midst of its swaps with the

Sveriges Riksbank in September 1944, the Banco de Portugal swapped another two tons of its gold in gold holdings in Switzerland for Swiss gold held in Ottawa. As in 1942, the gold in Switzerland was taken from Portugal's untainted account. This time, Portugal received a smaller commission of only $3/8\%$, probably because it saw the advantage of topping up its Ottawa reserve of gold at a time when its newly made agreement with Sweden might have required more gold if the escudo's exchange value had continued to deteriorate.

• With the lifting of all conditions restraining foreign gold on earmark in Ottawa after the war, there was no rush by neutral central banks to clear out their accounts in Ottawa. In fact, all parties to the wartime swaps maintained their Ottawa earmarks well into the peace, often increasing their balances.

• Throughout all these transactions, officials at the Bank of Canada, usually in consultation with officials at the Department of Finance and the Bank of England, exhibited due diligence in handling these transfer requests from Europe. The context of the times must be borne in mind. These transactions took place at the height of the war, when the pressures of wartime decision-making bore heavily on Ottawa's mandarins. These gold swaps between friendly and neutral central banks constituted fleeting decisions in a myriad of wartime challenges and must be seen in this light. By and large, the decisions taken around Canada's custodianship of foreign gold earmarked in the Bank of Canada conform to the stereotype of the cautious, deliberate and well-balanced demeanour of the senior bureaucrats who have come to be known by history as the "Ottawa men." They never possessed the absolute knowledge or the power to eliminate any possibility that Ottawa might facilitate the movement of looted gold, but their instincts led them to policies that made that possibility remote. In this sense, Canadians can take justifiable pride in the efficient manner in which the rather prosaic service of earmarking of gold was turned to commendable Allied and, at times, humanitarian ends during the war.

Preamble

UNFINISHED BUSINESS

In 1995, the fiftieth anniversary of the end of World War II produced a joyous and predictable celebration of the liberation from the heel of Axis repression of Europe and parts of the Far East. The parades, wreath-layings and reunions all seemed designed to bring closure to the agonies of the century's second global conflict. Yet, the year also produced some painful and unpredicted outcomes that stimulated rather than stilled half-century-old injustices and anxieties. While the military, diplomatic, social and economic history of the war has long been accorded extensive treatment, events in 1995 reawakened nagging concerns that the financial and fiscal history of World War II still contained unresolved mysteries and unadjudicated injustices. Much of this moral, political and legal disquiet centred on the financial strategies and procedures of the Axis war machine and some of the neutral powers – principally Switzerland – situated around its periphery.

At the centre of the controversy was what Stuart Eizenstat, the U.S. under secretary of commerce for international trade who has headed that government's massive investigation into the issue, has called "One of the greatest thefts by a government in history" – the looting of an estimated US$580 million of central bank gold from territories conquered by Germany during World War II.[1] Postwar reports indicated that the largest involuntary contributor to this trove was the Belgian central bank with US$223 million, followed by the Netherlands with US$168 million, then US$64 million of Italian gold, US$53 of French gold and a succession of smaller contributions from Austria, Hungary, Yugoslavia, Czechoslovakia, Poland, Luxembourg and Danzig.[2]

Added to this hoard of "monetary gold" – gold held by governments to support the monetary operations of the state – was a smaller, indeterminate amount of "non-monetary" gold, gold looted from individuals trapped in Germany and Axis-occupied lands. This pillaging of personal gold ranged from the casual acquisition of family treasures by the advancing German army to the systematic collection of gold – jewellery and dental gold – from the victims of the Nazi death camps in which so many European Jews perished in the Holocaust. It is important to emphasize, as Stuart Eizenstat has forcefully pointed out, that Germany's acquisition of looted gold was no accidental by-product of war: "the massive and systematic plundering of gold and other assets from conquered nations and Nazi victims was no rogue operation. It was essential to the financing of the German war machine."[3]

Two factors clouded understanding of the ultimate disposition of this so-called "Nazi gold." During the course of the war, Germany used much of this precious loot to finance its war economy. Having quickly drawn down its own store of central bank gold (generally estimated to have been around US$100 million in 1939) in the early stages of the war and unable to finance its international purchases with its shunned currency, the Reich began recycling captured gold into its trade financing. This usually involved the resmelting of looted gold by the Reichsbank to disguise the metal's national origin – gold, for instance, bearing the marks of the Belgian and Dutch central banks – and then passing it off to Axis trade partners as legitimate prewar gold. A second complicating factor was introduced by the deliberate blending of non-monetary gold into this flow of seemingly pure monetary gold thereby creating "tainted" gold. Given the purity and uniformity of refined gold and the ease of imprinting re-refined bars with counterfeit marks, the degree of this tainting in the overall hoard of looted gold by Germany is virtually impossible to determine.

Much of the outflow of Germany's looted gold was directed to and willingly received by neutral Switzerland. The almost exclusive conduit for these transfers was the Swiss central bank, the Banque Nationale Suisse (BNS), which received an estimated US$400 million in German looted gold between 1939 and 1945. Of this transferred gold, US$276 million or about three-quarters was bought directly by the BNS and the rest was simply channelled through the bank to the accounts of other trading partners of the Axis.[4] Portugal was the largest of these recipients, followed by Spain. During the course of the war, the BNS also resold gold it had probably acquired from the Axis to other neutral countries, again principally Portugal. The Banque Nationale Suisse's own records reveal that Germany was the largest supplier of gold to Switzerland with sales of SFr1,210.3 million between 1939 and 1945; Portugal was the largest acquirer of Swiss gold with purchases of SFr451.5 million.[5] During the war, the gold reserves of the Swiss national bank consequently grew dramatically, although much of the growth took place beyond Switzerland's borders in blocked accounts in London, New York, and Ottawa and often as the result of direct Swiss purchases of gold from the Allies, notably SFr1,178.2 million worth from the United States. Gold stocks held physically in Switzerland actually declined slightly. These strong gold reserves secured the Swiss franc's value and ensured that when the war ended Switzerland would emerge with an economy well positioned for the opportunities of peace.

The Allies were never oblivious to Germany's disposition of looted gold. As early as 1942, the British government began agitating for a joint Allied injunction that would have proscribed any recognition of transfers of property in Axis-occupied territories. On January 5, 1943, seventeen nations did in fact sign the "Inter-Allied Declaration Against Acts of Dispossession" which contained the threat that legal recognition of transfers of looted goods would be withheld by the victorious Allies when peace returned. The declaration was intended to cool the willingness of neutral powers, like Switzerland, to act as outlets for assets plundered by the Axis. As such, it joined an existing array of "freezing" measures that had been imposed on Axis and neutral countries earlier in the war in an effort to crimp Germany's ability to finance its war economy.

The 1943 declaration did not specifically target looted gold. Conscious that large amounts of German gold were still crossing the Swiss border, U.S. Secretary of the Treasury Henry Morgenthau began to assert American leadership in the campaign to contain the spread of Germany's plundered wealth. In a declaration of February 22, 1944, the American government vowed not to recognize the title or to purchase any gold passed by Germany onto world markets. Rigorous conditions were set out for gold held by countries that had not officially broken relations with the Axis. Britain and the Soviet Union issued similar declarations. American leadership on the question of looted gold became further evident in the spring of 1944 when U.S. Treasury officials hatched a more active program of containing the spread of Germany's ill-gotten wealth. Fears that Germany might be stockpiling looted gold beyond its borders to provide a foundation for the erection of a postwar Fourth Reich explained some of the pressure for this new style of active containment. Postwar restitution of such wealth also now joined containment as an objective of Allied policy. At the heart of Operation Safehaven, as the American initiative became known, was fact-finding by officials despatched to Europe. Facts were not, however, easy to come by as neutral trading partners of the Axis proved uncooperative and jealousies between Allied agencies undermined the effort.

The Safehaven initiative was however reinforced in July 1944 by Resolution

VI of the Bretton Woods conference at which the Allies mapped out the contours of the postwar monetary system. The resolution called upon neutral powers to "take immediate measures to prevent any disposition or transfer . . . of looted gold, currency, art objects, securities and financial or business enterprises [and] to take immediate measures to prevent the concealment by fraudulent means or otherwise" of stolen assets. Safehaven now became an active Anglo-American intelligence program aimed at dissecting the patterns of Axis-neutral trade and financial interaction. Switzerland increasingly became the fulcrum of these investigations. In the wake of the D-Day landings and the imminence of the Axis defeat, increasing diplomatic pressure was placed on Switzerland to reveal the workings of its financial relationship with Germany. At the same time, intense effort was poured into the clandestine collection of evidence of Switzerland's complicity in the movement of Nazi gold from the Reichsbank to the vaults of neutral European banks. Central to this collection was the Office of Strategic Services (OSS), an American intelligence agency formed in 1942 to monitor among other tasks the Axis economy. The OSS station in Berne was run by Allen Dulles, a hard-driving, Wall Street banking lawyer, who soon turned the post into a clearing house for the flood of hard evidence, rumours and speculation that began to emerge from the crumbling Axis and from Swiss sources, now aware that the tide of conflict had clearly turned in the Allies' favour. Other OSS operations were conducted elsewhere in Europe, especially in neutral centres such as Madrid and Lisbon. It was from this net of intelligence that the first real appreciation of the magnitude of the flow of looted gold out of Germany began to emerge.

The Safehaven investigations set the stage for a period of intensive postwar negotiations between the victorious Allies and neutral countries believed to be in possession of German assets. These long and arduous negotiations stretched into the early 1950s and generally involved two objectives: the restoration of looted monetary gold to its rightful owners – the central banks of now-liberated European countries – and the extraction of non-monetary gold out of the pool of monetary gold and its application to the plight of refugees displaced by the war. The Swiss were to prove wily negotiators, constantly pleading that the preservation of Swiss neutrality governed their ability to satisfy Allied demands. Consequently, the untainting of monetary gold was to prove an aggravating challenge. The intricate details of these postwar negotiations lie beyond the scope of this preamble,[6] except to note that certain acknowledgements and restitutions were achieved. In 1946, a "Gold Pool" was established by the Allies for the restitution of looted monetary gold on a prorated basis to its legitimate national owners. A Tripartite Commission on the Restitution of Monetary Gold (TGC) was established by the United States, Britain and France to administer the pool. In 1947, under the terms of the 1946 Allied-Swiss Accord signed in Washington, Switzerland paid US$58 million – a figure far below the US$185-289 million in looted gold that Safehaven intelligence reports indicated were in BNS coffers at the war's end – into the TGC. This contribution was reciprocated by the Allies' gradual unblocking of Swiss assets held outside the country. At the same time, Switzerland agreed that it would, in cooperation with an Allied joint commission, liquidate German assets still held within its borders. These assets were estimated by the Allies to be worth US$250–$500 million; the Swiss claimed their worth to be US$250 million.

In 1948, Switzerland agreed to pay another US$4.7 million to the International Refuge Organization for the support of refugees displaced by the war. But after this, Swiss intransigence gained an upper hand in the negotiations. Swiss negotiators argued that Switzerland's own debt claims on defeated Germany must first be satisfactorily settled, that the exchange rates embedded in the 1946 accord with the Allies were unfair and that the Allies must recognize certain German assets seized by the Allies in the war as actually Swiss-owned. Through all this, the Swiss acknowledged no moral culpability in the handling of wartime looted assets.

The diminishing returns of Allied-Swiss gold restitution negotiations were generally paralleled by similar negotiations with the other neutral countries – Spain, Portugal, Sweden, Turkey and Argentina – implicated in the wartime dealing in looted gold. As the peace faded into the Cold War, new, unrelated geopolitical considerations (e.g., NATO's desire to build a strategic air base in Portugal's Azores islands) began to colour and debase negotiations over looted gold. Finally in 1952, the frustrated Allies agreed to a compromise with the Swiss by which the Swiss would pay another US$23.6 million towards the relief of war refugees in lieu of any liquidation of German assets held in Switzerland. A parallel agreement between Switzerland and the new West German government allowed the Swiss to recover about half of the outstanding war debt owed it by Germany.

The 1952 agreements effectively brought to an end active Allied efforts to identify and restore the monetary gold that had been devoured by the Axis and pumped abroad to finance its ambitions. The Tripartite Gold Commission would continue its work, fitfully restoring monetary gold to the once-occupied countries of Europe. As late as 1995 monetary gold was returned to Albania by the Bank of England. Despite this, there had been a dreadful slippage from the early postwar determination to track down and restore the estimated US$580 million in looted monetary gold. Despite a mountain of intelligence material gathered both by operations such as Safehaven and during the protracted, postwar negotiations with the Swiss and other neutral powers that had worked with the Axis, there was still no clear understanding of exactly how looted gold found its way into the mainstream of legitimate European finance. Switzerland had effectively warded off such discovery by means of artful negotiation and dogged insistence on the sanctity of its neutral status.

The troubled search for monetary gold was paralleled by another attempt at postwar restitution of assets dislocated by the war – the so-called question of "heirless assets." Just as the war had divorced national governments from their legitimate gold stocks, so too did it conspire to separate individuals from their personal wealth and make them economic victims of the conflict. After the war, attention focused on two particular types of such victims. First, there was strong evidence that gold and other precious assets of the victims of German death camps had been seized and put to the economic service of the Axis. The gold was then mingled – by resmelting and counterfeit marking – with seized stocks of monetary gold. After the war, the differentiation of legitimate, prewar monetary gold from "tainted" victims' gold proved devilishly difficult. To some degree, this dilemma was addressed by the commitment contained in the Paris Reparations Agreement of January 1946 to establish a US$25 million fund to assist stateless peoples. Into this fund, later administered by the International Refugee Organization, Switzerland, for instance, made its contribution of US$4.7 million in 1948.

A second category of victims' assets proved equally awkward to resolve. As the war tensions mounted in the late 1930s, many Europeans sought a measure of security by dispersing their assets to foreign domiciles, where they imagined their wealth would be safe from enemy incursion. This flight of capital largely originated in Germany, where Jews sensed the menace of the anti-Semitism that national socialism nurtured. With its reputation for neutrality and banking integrity, Switzerland became a favourite destination for such assets, but the dispersal reached as far afield as the United States. These arrangements were largely made with commercial banks, where foreign nationals simply opened accounts or rented safety deposit facilities. With the advent of war, Allied governments froze the assets of foreign nationals within their borders and administered them as "alien" or "enemy" property.

With the return of peace, Allied governments loosened these controls and returned the assets to the control of their owners or their heirs. The disposition of assets of those who had died heirless proved more difficult, particularly in light of the decimation of European Jewry by the Germans. Much the same situation pertained in Switzerland. Under the terms of the 1946 Allied-Swiss Washington Accord, Switzerland agreed to examine "sympathetically" the idea of transferring heirless assets found in Swiss banks to postwar Allied efforts at refugee relief. While it seemed likely that these assets were predominantly those of Jewish victims of the Holocaust, there was no accurate way, given Switzerland's insistence on the sanctity of its commercial banking system, of ascertaining the number of these accounts or their magnitude.

In the immediate postwar decade the issue of heirless assets was shunted aside by the Allied-Swiss fixation on the restitution of monetary gold. Even in the United States, action was slow in coming. In 1954, a law was passed designating the Jewish Restitution Successor Organization (JRSO) in New York as the "successors in interest" of heirless Jewish assets held in the United States. By 1957, the JRSO had vetted approximately 11,000 claims on these assets and had approved approximately 2,000 of them as worthy of compensation. In 1962, another American law made US$500,000 available for the settlement of these claims.

In Switzerland, settlement of the heirless assets proceeded more slowly. The 1946 Paris Reparations Agreement had placed responsibility for reparations for individual victims of the war with individual national governments and international agencies (such as the International Refugee Organization). Thus, any effort to discover and lay claim to heirless assets depended upon the willingness of individual states, particularly those touched by the postwar diaspora of Jews, to choose to prosecute the issue. In the free world, pressure was applied by the World Jewish Congress, but behind the Iron Curtain there was virtually no willingness to champion an attempt to locate and secure title to heirless assets in the interest of Jewish citizens. In 1949, for instance, the Polish government struck a deal with Switzerland whereby the heirless assets of Polish origin were transferred to the Polish government which then applied them to settling Swiss claims against Poland. Individuals who took it upon themselves to attempt this task of identifying and freeing heirless assets in Switzerland, where most of the accounts were believed to be, were soon confronted by the impenetrable regulations of Swiss commercial banking.

The 1952 German-Swiss agreement on the settlement of German assets held in Switzerland allowed Germans to liquidate their assets in Switzerland. Holocaust victims with Swiss holdings of less than SFr10,000 were exempted from the provisions of the agreement that obliged those claiming their assets to make a compulsory Swiss franc contribution to the German government equal to one-third of the value of their assets. Through all these procedures, the Swiss government insisted that the integrity of its commercial banking system could not be breached by probes designed to connect heirless assets with potential claimants. The onus was placed on the banks themselves to identify and come forward with information on the existence of such accounts, a request that was enshrined in a 1963 law that required Swiss banks to report such accounts and to pay them, if unclaimed, into a federal fund. Under these conditions, and despite Swiss assurances to the contrary, many of the heirless assets lodged in Swiss banks remained dormant, the existence and extent only dimly comprehended by those beyond the halls of Swiss commercial banking.

Thus, despite sporadic diplomatic sallies – principally by the American government – and periodic representations by the World Jewish Congress, the issue of the postwar fate of looted gold and heirless assets slipped into a kind of limbo in the mid-1950s. Allied preoccupation with other issues – notably fighting the Cold War – and Swiss obfuscation combined to stymie any concerted effort to locate and free heirless assets.

The hibernation lasted until 1995, when a fortuitous combination of global events brought the issue of looted gold and dormant heirless assets once again to the fore and supplied it with a dynamic sufficient to ensure some sort of resolution to the unfinished business of the immediate postwar decade. The first factor was the end of the Cold War. The all-consuming East-West tension of the Cold War had powerfully served to suppress Allied willingness to pursue the twin issues of looting and restitution to their full conclusion in the 1950s. The West's eagerness to support the fledgling West German republic in the 1950s tended, for instance, to work against any over-vigorous enforcement of the reparation process. Undue economic strain could not be placed on the "German economic miracle" and West Germany had to be transformed into a pillar of the NATO alliance. Similarly, the Cold War trapped many Jewish victims of the war behind the Iron Curtain, where communist regimes had little interest in supporting their restitution claims. The collapse of the Soviet empire in the early 1990s thus freed the West to turn its attention to some of the unaddressed legacies of World War II. At the same time, the disintegration of authoritarianism in Eastern Europe freed Jews in these countries to engage in the search for restitution of assets stripped from them or their families in the Holocaust or believed to have lain dormant in foreign banks since the conflict.

Two factors in North America added to the forcefulness of events in Europe. While the World Jewish Restitution Organization had long exerted pressure for action on behalf of Holocaust victims and their financial claims, it took the emancipation of Eastern European Jewry and the publicity and research efforts of its sister organization, the World Jewish Congress (WJC), to finally give the campaign sufficient mass to command the attention of the world press and national governments. Led by Canadian-born businessman Edgar Bronfman, the WJC launched a concerted campaign against Eastern European governments for the return of property confiscated by Communist regimes. The WJC soon directed its energies towards Switzerland and the mysteries of dormant bank accounts. Determined to prepare itself as thoroughly as possible for these negotiations, the WJC set to work in the National Archives in Washington to document the wartime looting of gold and the postwar denial of access to unclaimed Jewish assets as fully as possible. In Washington, WJC researchers laboriously worked their way through the trove of Safehaven, OSS and diplomatic files that chronicled the tangled financial history of Nazi Germany and its neutral accomplices. In September 1995, Bronfman met the Swiss Bankers Association in Berne to demand disclosure and restitution of Jewish monies in long-dormant Swiss bank accounts. The bankers first suggested that their research had revealed the presence of US$32 million in these accounts and offered to settle on that basis. Bronfman rebuffed this offer, arguing that it was neither accurate nor did it acknowledge the moral dimensions of the situation. The bankers then agreed to another comprehensive audit of the dormant accounts preparatory to a final, mutually endorsed settlement.

As had been the case in the initial late-war crusade to uncover the secrets of Nazi wartime finance, the last and crucial ingredient in the reawakening of world interest in the fate of looted gold and dormant Jewish bank accounts was supplied by the moral and political fervour of the United States. New York Republican Senator Alfonse D'Amato, chairman of the influential Senate Banking Committee and a politician with a large Jewish American constituency, aligned himself with Bronfman and the WJC. The Banking Committee's power to revoke foreign bankers' licences to operate in the United States meant that D'Amato's interest in revisiting Switzerland's role as a neutral power and banker could not be lightly dismissed. In the spring of 1996, the coalition of D'Amato, Bronfman and the WJC prompted U.S. President Bill Clinton to empower Stuart E. Eizenstat, Under Secretary of Commerce for International Trade, to create a presidential task force to conduct a massive archival investigation of the whole wartime and immediate postwar history of Nazi gold. Over the next seven months, a staff of historians drawing on resources from eleven U.S. government agencies pored over 15 million pages of documents in Washington's National Archives. Their report, issued in May 1997, reconstructed in exact detail (as their report's title indicated) *U.S. and Allied Efforts to Recover*

and Restore Gold and Other Assets Stolen or Hidden by Germany During World War II.
Under Secretary Eizenstat's conclusion at the end of this huge investigation
bears repetition:

> The cumulative facts and conclusions contained in this report should evoke a
> sense of injustice and a determination to act. Now, half a century later, this gov-
> ernment's challenge is to complete the unfinished business of the Second World
> War to do justice while its surviving victims are still alive. To do justice is in part
> a financial task. But it is also a moral and political task that should compel each
> nation involved in these tragic events to come to terms with its own history and
> responsibility.[7]

Even before the Eizenstat team reported, other nations had responded.
British historians and archivists at the Foreign and Commonwealth Office
mined the records of the Public Record Office to produce two "History Notes"
entitled "Nazi Gold: Information from the British Archives" in September 1996
and May 1997. Similar research was undertaken by the Bank of England. In
Switzerland, such investigations quickly assumed the dimensions of an investigation into the soul of the nation itself. While Swiss bankers revisited the files of
their dormant accounts in conjunction with the WJC under the chairmanship
of former U.S. Federal Reserve Chairman Paul Volcker, the Swiss Parliament
established a historians' commission – the Bergier Commission – to unravel the
whole Swiss-German interaction in the war. Other commissions were directed
to examine other aspects of Switzerland's war – for instance, Switzerland's postwar agreements with Eastern European countries. Elsewhere in Europe, other
historians set to work. The German metal refiner Degussa, the alleged convert-
er of looted gold into seemingly legitimate new gold, hired an independent historian to examine its records. Thus, by the spring of 1997, the issue of Nazi gold,
Swiss neutrality and the postwar Allied efforts at restitution had become the
focus of a nearly global historical effort – an effort with huge moral, financial
and political implications.

Amid all this agitation and research, the word "Canada" never emerged.
Although a signatory to the various Allied declarations on looted gold signed
between 1943 and 1945, Canadian officials had not actively participated in
either the investigations or the negotiations that revolved around the looted gold
issue down to 1952. Canada is, in fact, not even mentioned in the thick and
authoritative Eizenstat report or in its index. The encyclopaedic bibliography
accompanying the report contains only several innocuous files concerning military operations involving Canada but unrelated to gold. The British "History
Notes" reports similarly do not mention Canada. Neither of the two best-selling
books on the Nazi gold controversy – Tom Bower's *Nazi Gold : The Full Story of
the Fifty-Year Swiss-Nazi Conspiracy to Steal Billions from Europe's Jews and Holocaust
Survivors* (1997) and Adam LeBor's *Hitler's Secret Bankers : The Myth of Swiss
Neutrality During the Holocaust* (1997) – contain a single mention of Canada in relation to looted gold or in any other context. Perhaps the closest Canadians get to
the pain of the issue is the chilling reminder in LeBor's narrative that the group
charged with sorting the loot stripped from Holocaust victims at Auschwitz was
called the "Canada Kommando"[8] – perhaps an allusion to the belief that

Canada was a remote land of plenty. Only by the summer of 1997 did Canada begin to appear in any of the Nazi gold literature and then only innocuously, in tables issued by the Swiss Department of Foreign Affairs showing wartime gold purchases by the country's central bank, the Banque Nationale Suisse.

Canada's quiescent role in the Nazi gold controversy ended abruptly on July 11, 1997, when Gordon Thiessen, the Governor of the Bank of Canada, received a letter co-signed by the president of the Canadian Jewish Congress (CJC), Goldie Hershon, Irving Abella, the CJC's past president and the co-chairs of Canada's National Holocaust Remembrance Committee, Myra Giberovitch and Nathan Leipeiger. The letter reported "with dismay" that the CJC had received from the WJC in New York news that documents recently uncovered in the scouring of the National Archives in Washington "indicate that Portugal and Switzerland swapped a significant amount of looted gold for gold held in the Bank of Canada and the Federal Reserve Bank of New York." Attached to the letter was a grainy facsimile of a document – probably generated during the era of Safehaven intelligence gathering – which gave details of the swaps. About six tons of gold appeared to be involved in a series of swaps between Switzerland, Portugal and Sweden in 1942 and 1944. The undated document was said to be "from a very confidential source" and suggested that "measures" had been taken to disguise the origin of the gold bars in Switzerland that were at the heart of the swap. The bars in Switzerland were described as "probably tainted."

In response to the July 11th letter's request that "the Bank of Canada undertake an investigation to ascertain the involvement of the Bank in these transactions," the Bank immediately launched an examination of its archives. On July 28, a press release from the Bank confirmed that the Bank did have a role in the 1942 Swiss-Portuguese transfer of gold held in its vaults for safekeeping, but cautioned that much work remained to be done in the Bank's archives before the full story of the transfers could be known. Virtually nothing was known of the Canadian context in which these gold swaps took place, about the procedures followed by Canadian officials or about whether they were even aware of the implications of trading gold into neutral Europe in time of war. To do this, about "50 cubic feet" of documents would have to be examined at the Bank of Canada. Other departments of the Canadian government would have to be consulted and their documents surveyed.

The Bank then outlined the "next steps" in its investigation. It openly acknowledged the need for transparency in its investigations and in making public disclosure of the conclusions of these searches. It committed itself to making all documentation surrounding the transactions "publicly available as soon as possible to facilitate further research in this area." And it would secure the services of an outside historian to prepare an "independent assessment" of the Bank's role in the gold transactions of 1942–44 identified by the WJC document. The historian would be guaranteed "full access" to the Bank's archives and an "external review group" would be appointed to comment on the final draft of the historian's report.

•   •   •   •   •

On July 22, I was contacted by the Bank of Canada and asked to undertake the above investigation. After a brief negotiation in which the Bank's determination to sponsor an absolutely open and independent investigation of its wartime gold operations became abundantly apparent, I agreed to proceed with the investigation. In the subsequent memorandum of agreement, the Bank of Canada stated its "objectives" in undertaking the investigation. These were:

- to respond to public concern about possible Bank of Canada involvement in transactions related to looted Nazi gold during and after the Second World War
- to meet the Bank's requirement for openness and accountability by providing a report of its activities and by making its records readily available to other researchers
- to respect all applicable laws
- to protect the Bank's relationship with its existing central bank clients and
- to act expeditiously on the issue and obtain closure as quickly as possible.

As historical consultant, I agreed to "review all the Bank of Canada's documents related to gold transactions during the relevant period from the founding of the Bank in 1935 to 1950." Review of peripheral federal government documents, particularly in the Department of Finance, was also to be undertaken. A team of Bank employees was to be made available to help me gain access to relevant documentation. My report was to focus on the Canadian aspects of the gold transfers in question; the purpose of the exercise was "not to document the history of international gold movements during the war", although there might be cause to consult the "secondary results" of foreign research on the topic. I was also to advise the Bank "on the appropriate way to make the records accessible to other researchers." Last, I was asked to produce "a formal, annotated paper summarizing the results" of my investigation. I was to have "complete freedom" in drawing my conclusions. The report was to be published.

On August 12, I arrived at the Bank of Canada to begin the research that underlies this report.

Earmarked Gold in Canada 1935–56

THE BANK OF CANADA'S EARLY YEARS, 1935–39:
ENGLISH FRIENDS AND ENGLISH GOLD

Canada was a latecomer to the world of central banking. By the time the Bank of Canada opened its doors on March 11, 1935, virtually every other industrialized, Western country had a central bank regulating its monetary affairs. In Canada, it had taken the collapse of national credit in the Depression and recognition that the gold standard no longer automatically regulated trade to dislodge the long-standing opposition on the part of Canada's commercial banks to the notion of state-sponsored intervention in the credit and currency of the nation. A royal commission report in 1933 had urged Canadian politicians to establish a central bank. A central bank would "regulate credit and currency in the best interests of the economic life of the nation, to control and protect the external value of the national monetary unit and to mitigate by its influence fluctuations in the general level of production, trade, prices and employment . . . and generally promote the economic and financial welfare of the Dominion."[9] Even with the pressure of the Dirty Thirties at their backs, Canadian legislators exhibited their habitual caution by making the new Bank of Canada a privately owned institution, thereby distancing it from possible political interference. Only the election of a new Liberal government in Ottawa in late 1935 paved the way for public ownership of the fledgling bank in 1936.

The young bank was headed by a young governor. Thirty-eight year old Graham Towers, a political economics graduate of McGill University, was deflected from a promising career at the Royal Bank of Canada and given the governorship in the hope that his presence at the helm of the new central bank would both serve Ottawa's monetary ambitions and allay the fears of the commercial banks. For Towers, there was a good deal of learning on the job. The Bank's organization had first to be designed and implemented, relations established with the chartered banks and contacts made with foreign central banks. Instinctively, Towers turned to the Bank of England for guidance. The venerable Bank of England on Threadneedle Street in the heart of the City – London's financial district – was the linchpin of world-wide central banking. Its redoubtable governor, Montagu Norman (1871–1950), had presided over its affairs since 1920, having come to the Bank after years in the City. Norman had long taken a keen interest in the promotion of central banking in the Commonwealth, lending his ideas and practical advice in the 1920s to the creation of central banks in Australia, India and South Africa. Only New Zealand and Canada remained holdouts by the 1930s. Norman saw the addition of new members to the central bank club as a contribution to international monetary stability in the turbulent post-World War I period. As the Bank of England's historian, R. S. Sayers, has remarked, Norman "gave to Commonwealth affairs a measure of priority in the time he devoted to international affairs. He concerned himself not merely with the foundation of the new central banks but also, at greater expense to his time, to maintaining close contacts with them." In particular, the Bank of England was always ready "to help on specific problems as they arose" in the new Commonwealth central banks.[10]

Towers was quick to avail himself of the senior bank's good offices. In November 1934 Norman agreed to lend J. A. C. Osborne, the Bank of England's secretary, to the Ottawa bank as its first deputy governor. Osborne had wide previous experience with the Federal Reserve Bank of New York and with European central banks. It was intended that he would apply this expertise to Canada's new central bank as Towers' first lieutenant. Osborne would stay until 1938, when he returned to become Norman's special adviser. Osborne later returned to Canada during the war as part of the British Supply Board and always maintained friendly, informal ties with the Canadian central bankers. "I have been happy to hear accounts of you from time to time," Norman's adviser, Harry Siepmann, wrote to Osborne in the spring of 1936, "which show that you like the Canadians almost as well as they like you . . ."[11] Canada had other London financial friends who were close to the Bank of England governor. The Canadian-born expatriate financier Sir Edward Peacock, for instance, sat on the Bank of England board from 1929 to 1946 and frequently figured in Anglo-Canadian monetary relations, as well as acting as financial adviser to the Royal Family.

Tower soon became a frequent visitor to Threadneedle Street. Shortly after his designation as governor in 1934, he went to London to consult with Norman. The Bank of England's official history notes that "Towers was disappointed at the limits to Norman's capacity to advise" on technical matters, but despite this the correspondence between the two on matters of general banking interest "went far beyond common courtesies." Towers quickly became "the most highly regarded" Dominion central banker in London.[12] (In 1943, it was even rumoured that John Maynard Keynes favoured Towers as a successor to Norman.[13] In the summer of 1935, Norman visited North America and made a call on Towers in Ottawa – "to call & make a bow to you."[14] While in Ottawa, Norman presented the Bank of Canada with a ceremonial inkstand, a gift that Towers told his directors the Canadians would reciprocate.[15] On Norman's return to England, he confirmed his esteem for his new acolyte in the Dominion: "I like to think that someday we shall get a harvest of cooperation from these early seeds of contact between our Banks!"[16] Throughout the late 1930s, whenever Towers returned from a visit to London, he presented his "impressions," often formed in Norman's office, of European monetary conditions to the Bank of Canada board.[17]

The intimacy of two central bank governors soon had practical outcomes for the young Canadian organization. In July 1935, Towers proudly told the executive committee of the board of directors that the Bank of England topped the list of 16 central banks that had opened drawing (i.e., cash deposit) accounts at the new central bank in Ottawa.[18] Soon after, discussion between the two banks turned to the idea of Britain acquiring Canadian gold and accumulating it in the vault of the Bank of Canada. The practice was not entirely new; in World War I Britain had established its first overseas gold reserve in Ottawa to serve as security for its purchases of war material in the United States. As deputy governor of the Bank of England from 1918 to 1920, Montagu Norman was privy to the late stages of these arrangements.[19]

Early in 1936, Britain again became interested in the idea of holding gold in Canada. In February, Towers informed Norman the Bank of Canada was receiving "$8–9 million in producer gold a month" and inquired whether the Bank of England might be interested in purchasing some of it to hold on reserve in Ottawa. Norman was immediately interested and by April was assuring Towers that the Bank of England welcomed the prospect of "bidding regularly for your weekly offerings of gold."[20] In a personal letter to Deputy Governor Osborne, Harry Siepmann wrote that the Bank of England found the gold purchase plan "welcome". It was "of obvious advantage to you" – finding buyers for Canadian gold – and appealed to London because it might provide gold at slightly below the New York price.[21] Within days, Osborne noted in an internal memorandum that the Bank of Canada had "earmarked for the Bank of England gold valued at some $9 million, and this may be increased from time to time before the account is closed. While it seems unlikely that the Bank of England would normally keep some gold here, such development is not impossible, especially in case of war."[22] Thus began the practice of the Bank of England's "earmarking" gold in the vaults of the Bank of Canada.

In some respects, the importance of gold in Canada's monetary arrangements had steadily faded in the early decades of the twentieth century. In 1914, the federal government had suspended its long-standing commitment to redeem its notes – the national currency – in gold. Since the 1850s, the Canadian banking system had been anchored by the gold standard – the assurance that gold was always available in exchange for circulating currency, thereby stabilizing the external value of Canada's currency. After the war, there was pressure for a return to the gold standard. Indeed it was restored briefly in the late 1920s, but the linkage of gold to the external value of national currency proved too difficult in the volatile postwar economy. One of the pressures behind the creation of a Canadian central bank was the need to restore some degree of national leverage over the external value of the dollar. The Bank of Canada was therefore empowered to deal in gold and foreign exchange on international markets in order to "offset" other pressures on the external value of the currency.

What is Fine Gold?

The public envisages central bank gold as piles of gold bars secreted in subterranean vaults. The gold bar, and occasional other forms of refined gold such as coins, minted bars and buttons, has evolved principally as a means of transporting and storing gold in relatively constant proportion. A gold bar usually weighs about 400 ounces or 11.4 kilograms, but most bullion markets – London, New York, Tokyo and Zurich – will accept bars ranging in weight from 350–430 ounces. Virtually all bars are, however, close to 400 ounces, so that an imperial ton (2,000 pounds or 32,000 ounces) contains about 80 bars of gold. For purposes of calculating the actual *worth* of gold, banks deal gold in terms of "fine ounces."

A gold bar, however meticulously refined, will always contain some small impurities, so that the purchaser in fact receives very slightly less than 400 ounces of real gold. To alleviate this problem, gold bars are assayed and the actual purity is then stamped on the bar together with a registration number. For a bar today to be considered "good delivery" by the London Bullion Market Association, it must be "not less than 995 parts gold in 1000 parts." All bars bear this "purity mark" plus the name of the melter/assayer. Thus, the actual worth in "fine gold" (i.e., free from dross or impurity) of any gold bar is obtained by multiplying the nominal weight of the bar by its purity. Gold trades are subsequently recorded in fine ounces, not bars. Bar counts are noted simply for purposes of storing and shipment. During the years covered by this study, the price of gold was fixed at US$35 per ounce. A gold bar was therefore worth approximately US$14,000 and a ton of gold approximately US$1.1 million.

Gold featured in other aspects of the Bank of Canada's charter.[23] The Bank was empowered to buy and sell gold. Any citizen tendering "the purchasing price in legal tender" could buy a bar of gold from the Bank, although this clause was almost immediately suspended. As the sole issuing-authority for the national currency, the Bank was to maintain a reserve of gold coin or bullion that was equivalent to not less than 25% of the value of its notes and deposit liabilities. To this end, plans for the Bank's head office on Ottawa's Wellington Street included provision for a subterranean vault built right into the Laurentian Shield. The act also stipulated that the same vault would be used to hold all gold coin and bullion transferred by Canada's chartered banks to the new central bank. Last, the Bank of Canada was given the power to open accounts in other central banks and in the Bank for International Settlements [BIS] or to act "as agent, depository or correspondent of such other central banks" or the BIS. Thus, the earmarked gold account was considered a normal and anticipated part of the Bank of Canada's mandate from the date of its inception.

Gold had other implications for the young Bank of Canada. In a decade in which the Depression drained the vitality out of the primary sectors of Canada's economy, gold production provided some positive news. Despite the disappearance of gold coinage, a kind of "gold mentality," as one author described it, gripped the developed economies. This mentality was rooted in the belief that gold alone could provide individuals and nations alike with a movable, valuable commodity that in times of economic hardship would retain its international value.[24] Canada's ability to feed the world hunger for gold was also facilitated by a steady drop in the cost of gold production during the deflationary Depression and by the fact that in 1935 the United States hiked the price of gold from US$20 an ounce to US$35 an ounce. Throughout the 1930s, gold production therefore increased dramatically in Canada. Its dollar value, calculated on the fixed rate of US$35 an ounce, rose from US$39 million in 1928 to US$178 million in 1939; world production in the same years grew from US$406 million to US$1.36 billion.[25] By the decade's end, Canada was rivalling the United States as the third largest producer of gold in the world, trailing only South Africa and the Soviet Union. Most of Canada's production was exported as non-monetary gold, while a small proportion of it was purchased to add to the stock of monetary gold held by the Bank of Canada.

As world demand for gold grew in the Depression, Ottawa asserted its control over the trade. The Royal Canadian Mint became the principal refiner of Canadian gold into "good delivery" bars and the Department of Finance became the sole regulator of gold exports out of Canada. In 1932, "an act respecting the export of gold" was passed to stipulate that no gold could be exported out of Canada without a licence from the minister of finance. Only chartered banks might apply for such licences; in 1935 the act was amended to entitle the new Bank of Canada to apply for such licences; in 1935 the act was amended to entitle the new Bank of Canada to apply for such licences.[26] The act was designed to assure the Canadian government that it would have a secure supply of foreign exchange from gold sales with which to service Canada's large foreign debt. In 1937, another federal act prohibited the use of "gold clauses" in

What is Earmarked Gold?

Earmarking is a courtesy function performed by one central bank for another central bank. It entails the delivery of gold owned by one central bank into the safe-keeping of another central bank. The Bank of England's historian, R. S. Sayers, has suggested that the modern practice of earmarking began in the 1920s, when England was temporarily off the gold standard and the Bank of England decided to allow its central bank clients to store gold in its vaults to allow them to use such gold as security on advances made to them by the Bank.[1] Earmarking soon acquired other purposes: providing off-shore cover for commercial transactions, providing a holding facility for purchases of newly minted gold and in times of international tension allowing the dispersing of national gold to foreign safe havens. Once a sufficient number of central banks had established earmark accounts abroad, the possibility existed that they could simply swap amounts of earmarked gold by legal transfer on paper rather than by actual physical exchange.

Host banks did not pay interest on earmark deposits, usually only levying a small handling charge to cover the cost of physically handling the gold on its arrival and departure from the host bank. The host bank assumed no legal control over the earmarked gold in its keeping. The arrangement was much like that enjoyed by a commercial bank client renting a safety deposit box. On instruction by the client the bank was obliged to open the box and deliver the contents into the client's hands without question.

When the Bank of Canada opened an earmarked gold account of its own at the Federal Reserve Bank of New York in 1935, the deputy governor of the Fed described the earmark function with succinctness: "We will earmark gold which is your property and will hold it subject solely to your instructions, giving to any such gold which is left in our custody the same care which we give to our own similar property but beyond that assuming no responsibility".[2] A year later, Harry Siepmann of the Bank of England put it more simply in a letter to the deputy governor of the Bank of Canada: "Earmarking is a routine activity of any full grown Central Bank and one of the normal forms of co-operation for mutual advantage."[3]

[1] R. S. Sayers, *The Bank of England 1891–1944*, vol. I, London, 1976.
[2] J. E. Crane to Towers, January 26, 1935, BOC file A19–12A.
[3] H. A. Siepmann to J. A. C. Osborne, July 31, 1936, BOC file A18–17.

---

financial arrangements, thereby ending the right of a creditor to claim settlement of a claim in gold. Such obligations were now to be settled only in the legal tender of the country. Thus, gold production was brought under tight federal control and as such was used as a powerful point of leverage on national economic performance in a decade of generally dismal economic times.

Thus, the prospect in 1936 of the Bank of England opening an earmark account at the Bank of Canada was doubly tantalizing. Not only would it bring the kudos of the world's senior central bank bestowing an account on the world's newest central bank, but it also offered the prospect of inducing the Bank of England to use the account as an export conduit for Canadian gold minted at the Royal Canadian Mint, to be bought by the British and stored in the vault of the Bank of Canada. The trick would be to partially wean Britain from its dependence on South African gold. As an inducement to this end, Ottawa offered to cover the shipping expenses to New York and London on gold bought at the Royal Canadian Mint, thus making it marginally cheaper than American and South African gold. Furthermore, in order to allay any earmark client's fear that their Canadian-held gold might not be immediately exportable, the Bank of Canada obtained a "general undertaking" from the minister of finance that an export licence would always be granted when the earmark client wanted to remove its gold from Canada.[27]

These arrangements proved sufficiently attractive that the Bank of England began buying Canadian gold and placing it on earmark in Ottawa in the spring of 1936. At first, the British thought of the account as a short-term commitment, one that gave them a small bargain in the price of new gold and also helped them to capitalize on shifts in value between the pound and North American currencies. The intention was to ship English gold held in Ottawa to the Federal Reserve Bank of New York, where it would be applied to supporting a large credit that the Bank of England had given the Bank of France. Early on in this pattern of purchases, Montagu Norman told Towers that the arrangement "was working quite satisfactorily and I have no wish to set any particular limits on the amount for the present."[28] Within the Bank of Canada, a regularized earmarking procedure was developed whereby the Bank of England's gold purchases were delivered from the mint to the Currency Division, where they were duly registered in the Bank's gold ledgers. "I have this day received from the Royal Canadian Mint 109 gold bars Nos. 2735 to 2843, of the gross weight of 44,236.375 ounces, containing 44,093.461 fine ounces," the Bank's secretary, Donald Gordon, was typically informed by the Currency Division in May 1936. "This gold is being held in safekeeping for the Bank of England."[29]

The Bank of Canada clearly saw the opening of the British earmark account as serving both its own ends and those of Canada's gold producers. Towers, for instance, assured Norman that the Canadian government was "committed to settle with mines on the basis of [the] best market price obtainable converted at current rate of exchange . . ." for the Bank of England.[30] In 1937, the mint in Ottawa even agreed to change the shape of the gold bars it produced to conform to "those favoured on the London market."[31] At the same time, Deputy Governor Osborne promised that the English earmark account would be cloaked in secrecy and that the Bank of Canada would not publish the names of its earmark clients and "should treat with silent contempt the suggestion that the Bank of England might be one of them." Only the Canadian government would be told *confidentially* if the Bank of England had a substantial amount of gold on earmark in Canada.[32]

Given these auspices, it was not surprising that the Bank of England continued to expand its Canadian earmark account. Canada was a safe and convenient place to earmark gold. Safe because Ottawa and London had established a close and friendly central banking relationship. Convenient because the Royal Canadian Mint supplied gold at an attractive price and also because the Bank of Canada was, relatively speaking, on the doorstep of the Federal Reserve Bank of New York, where the Bank of England had frequent business to transact. Late in 1936, the Bank of England therefore asked Ottawa to "continue to give us the opportunity to bid for newly produced Canadian gold as it comes forward" and announced that London would now pay its own shipping charges on the purchases.[33] By the end of 1936, the Bank of England had 3,304 bars, or, 1,335,588 fine ounces, of gold on earmark in Ottawa. A year later, the total reached, 4,748 bars or 1,915,435 ounces.[34] The Bank of England's early satisfaction with its Canadian earmark account would in the near future act to Canada's advantage in other ways, as the London bank began to refer would-be European earmarkers to the Canadian bank for their needs. As the clouds of war began to gather over Europe later in the decade, the Bank of England was predisposed to point anxious European bankers in Ottawa's direction. The phrase "whenever we were asked to introduce one of our Continental friends to the Bank of Canada" regularly appeared in London's correspondence with Ottawa.[35]

In the short term, however, only one other prewar earmark account materialized. The Bank for International Settlements (BIS) was a Swiss-based legacy of World War I. It had been established in 1931 in Basle to oversee the reparation payments agreed to by Germany after the war. All of the European central banks contributed to its establishment and were represented on its board. In effect, the BIS became the central bankers' central bank. Although Germany never fulfilled all its reparations commitments, the BIS remained active in interbank and various commercial transactions. Since it had no central bank in 1930, Canada was not a signatory to the Hague Agreement that established the BIS, but the BIS nonetheless kept a money account at the Bank of Montreal to facilitate its Canadian operations. When the Bank of Canada opened in 1935, the BIS requested the transfer of its Bank of Montreal account to the new Canadian central bank.[36] The BIS's money was converted into 12,819 fine ounces of earmarked gold by the Bank of Canada and in November was shipped to New York. A year later, the BIS arranged for the mint in Ottawa to melt down U.S. gold coins obtained in San Salvador into gold bars, which were then earmarked – 16,908 fine ounces – at the Bank of Canada. After this deposit, the BIS earmark account in Ottawa remained inactive until after the war.

Thus, by 1939 the Bank of Canada had established earmark accounts with two prestigious European counterparts in the world of banking. The small BIS account with only 42 bars of gold was dwarfed in importance and size by the thousands of bars of British gold that sat in the Bank of Canada vaults. These early earmark accounts in Ottawa reflected straightforward, accepted banking practice. They were intruded upon only by the federal government's monopoly right over gold exports from Canada: here the minister of finance had given assurance that an export licence would not be denied an earmark account-holder. To this uncomplicated arrangement, each party brought its own self-interest. Earmarking flattered the Bank of Canada's desire to join the club of international central banking and Ottawa's strategy of selling Canadian-mined gold onto world markets. From the European perspective, an earmark account in Ottawa offered access to attractively priced Canadian gold and the opportunity of storing it in close proximity to the Federal Reserve Bank of New York. As the first tremors of war were felt in 1938, other factors began to intrude into the business of earmarking gold in Canada. What had initially been simple banking was about to acquire a geopolitical cast.

EARMARKING AND WAR: 1938–40

The Bank of England's earmark account in Ottawa saw little activity through 1937; the correspondence file for that year is thin and routine. The spring of 1938 brought it alive. Austria fell under Germany's shadow. The Sudetenland followed. The aggressive German impulse that built to the Munich crisis that September may have been temporarily appeased on the diplomatic front by the blandishments of Britain's prime minister, but it set Britain's bankers wondering about the potential monetary safety of the realm. On March 31, 1938, Graham Towers received a "very secret and personal" cable from Harry Siepmann, special adviser to Montagu Norman. "The Governor asks me to put to you the following," Siepmann began, "please consider and reply by cable on Monday if possible what would be the attitude of the Bank of Canada if the Bank of England were to propose to accumulate gold in Ottawa by purchase, transfer and shipment from other centres, up to an amount of $250,000,000 or more." Siepmann also offered to let the Canadian mint melt down gold coins held by Britain in Ottawa and add them to this deposit.[37] Norman was clearly shifting Britain's attitude to the earmarking of gold in Ottawa. The account was no longer to be just a means of acquiring Canadian gold, but was now to become a line of national monetary defence – an offshore store of national gold beyond the reach of potential European belligerents. Gold was now to be shipped to Ottawa, not just bought there.

It is indicative of the empathy between the two central banks that Towers replied on schedule to Siepmann on April 2. Before doing so, he telephoned Canada's minister of finance, Charles Dunning, to gain assurance that any addition to the Bank of England's earmark account in Ottawa would automatically be given an export licence. Dunning agreed. Towers therefore cabled Siepmann that his bank was "willing to receive gold in amount of two hundred and fifty million dollars or more." He did however warn London that "substantial imports of gold over short period of time would no doubt attract attention." This was not an "objection," he added, simply something to consider. Towers also pointed out that until the Bank of Canada's new Ottawa headquarters building was opened, there would be insufficient space to store such gold. The new vault would be adequate. Towers then assured London that the matter had been discussed "very confidentially" with Finance Minister Dunning.[38] "As a parting note," he again cabled London two days later, "let me say we are most willing to be of assistance in any way we can."[39]

In early May 1938, the Bank of England began moving gold to Ottawa.

Governor Norman had forewarned his fellow governor Towers that his plan was to shift gold earmarked for the Bank of England at the Banque de France in Paris to Ottawa by shipping it to the Channel port of Cherbourg, loading it on board Canadian National steamships and delivering it to Quebec or Montreal. He agreed that such large movements of gold would attract "some publicity", but that his bank would do its "best not to attract undue attention and comment." Since direct shipment of gold out of London might excite alarm in England, Norman would try to avoid this option. Some gold, he cautioned Ottawa, "will reach you by devious and unexpected ways." In all this, he was "most grateful to you" and the minister of finance.[40] On May 9, the first shipment of British gold arrived in Canada. The Bank of Canada's new vault was ready just in time to receive it. Specially chartered trains brought the gold to Ottawa and the Bank hired some Mounties to oversee its unloading. Unfortunately, Towers reported to London, a "stray journalist" had seen the train arrive in Ottawa. Telephone calls from the press followed. The "press loves mystery," Osborne complained to Siepmann when garbled accounts of the gold's purpose began appearing in the press.[41]

Throughout the summer of 1938 the gold kept coming, until in October Deputy Governor Donald Gordon reported to London that the last two shipments had arrived and been stored "without a single word of press comment."[42] Throughout this accumulation, the Bank of England continued to buy gold at the mint and also began to use its Ottawa earmark as a means of satisfying its gold needs in New York. At the year's end, the Bank of England had 10,219 bars of gold – 4,087,731 fine ounces – worth $143,069,592[43] safely ensconced under Wellington Street. The amount rivalled the gold held by the Bank of Canada on its own account in the vault. Towers proudly reported the growth of the Bank's foreign gold on earmark to the board of directors, almost as if the Bank were coming of age.[44] The spring of 1939 brought no easing of tensions in Europe and served to broaden the anxiety of its central bankers. The idea of dispersing national gold out of harm's way began to find appeal in other European financial centres. On March 22, Towers talked by telephone with Bank of England senior official G. F. Bolton, who told him that the Banque Nationale de Belgique had inquired about the safekeeping of gold in Canada. The Belgians were thinking of placing $25–$50 million in gold in Ottawa. Towers noted in a memo that he immediately said "yes" and promised to let London know what fees would be involved in such safekeeping.[45] Within two weeks, Bolton was back in touch with Towers with news that additional inquiries about Ottawa safekeeping had been received from the Swiss central bank – the Banque Nationale Suisse – and the Banque de France. The Banque de France had "definitely made up its mind" to send £30 million in gold to Canada and preparations were under way to make the first shipment in mid-April.[46] Although all three of these banks – the French, Belgian and Swiss – had maintained regular financial relations (e.g., drawing accounts) with the Bank of Canada since soon after it had opened in 1935, it is interesting to note that all these approaches concerning safekeeping facilities in Ottawa were made *through* the Bank of England.[47] For his part, Governor Towers devoted his thoughts to ensuring that the Bank of Canada would have sufficient storage space for more foreign gold and how much to charge for such services. On a visit to New York and Washington that same month, Towers made enquiries of the Americans about proper fees and concluded he had no desire to "make money out of the situation" and would simply try to recover the actual cost of handling foreign gold.[48]

Amid these inquiries, the British reinitiated their own transhipment of gold to Ottawa. In late April the British battleship *Repulse* slipped quietly into the port of Quebec and unloaded gold bullion onto a train for Ottawa. Back in Ottawa, plans were drawn up for special shelving to be added to the new vault. When one young Bank employee first glimpsed the Bank's new vault in 1938, he had thought it was "as cavernous as Fort Knox." By mid-1939, he remembered that gold was by necessity being stacked on the floor to save space. Crawl spaces were left between the stacks to enable the Bank's auditors to verify that the stacks were all gold.[49] Throughout the rest of 1939, the British earmark account in Ottawa became the centre of intense activity. Gold bars and coin continued to arrive from abroad as well as gold from England itself, delivered by warship to Halifax, Vancouver and Quebec. From this growing hoard, some gold was despatched to New York where England was already using it to support its wartime spending in the United States. British gold reserves in Ottawa peaked at $346 million in early September and then slipped back to end the year at $251 million.[50]

Nothing came of the Swiss and Belgian inquiries about safekeeping in 1939, but the French acted on their declared intention, thereby becoming the Bank of Canada's third foreign earmark client. Without even waiting for complete Canadian approval, France began shipping its first consignment of gold – 403,516 fine ounces – across the Atlantic in April. Towers hurriedly confirmed with the deputy minister of finance, W. C. Clark, that the finance minister would extend the right of an export licence to the French when they desired to remove their gold from Canada.[51] On May 1, 1939, Towers therefore wrote to the governor of the Banque de France to confirm the opening of the account, citing the stock description of the earmark arrangement– "We will earmark and hold gold for your account, providing the same facilities for the custody of such gold as we provide for the custody of our own similar property, but beyond that assuming no responsibility."[52] Given this assurance, the Banque de France built up its earmark account in Canada with astonishing rapidity. By the end of 1939, it rivalled the Bank of England's account in Ottawa with 17,531 bars of gold – 7,088.094 fine ounces – worth approximately $250 million. Such heavy volume movements of gold attracted press attention, but the Bank of Canada did its best to appear shy in the face of such interest. Towers would only tell the Montreal *Gazette* that "quite a bit" of gold had come to Ottawa. The *Wall Street Journal* was not as easily put off and wrote that Canada had more than doubled its holding of earmarked gold in 1939 in "the largest earmarking operations conducted in Canada."[53]

Other French gold was shipped directly from dockside in Canada to the Federal Reserve Bank of New York to service France's early war contracts in the United States, thereby joining British shipments of gold from its Ottawa earmark to settle accounts in New York. Just after war broke out in September, Congress in Washington had convened in special session to modify America's usually stringent neutrality law to allow Allied powers the right of purchasing war matériel in the United States on a "cash and carry" basis – pay on the spot and take your purchases away in your own vessel. Such transactions required abundant amounts of U.S. dollars or gold convertible into such hard cash. Ottawa's nearby store of British and French gold, which could be safely shipped to the Federal Reserve free of attack from Axis submarines, now assumed an added advantage.

The coming of war thus dramatically expanded the volume of the Bank of Canada's earmarked gold business. It added a new client – France – and, thanks to the Bank of England, put the idea of earmarking in Canada in the minds of other European central banks. But this increase in business did not oblige the Bank to forsake the original definition of its responsibility as host bank to an ear-mark account. It assumed "no responsibility" beyond a simple custodian one. Through the "phoney war" of late 1939 and early 1940 this definition held. But there were already signs that difficult decisions lay ahead. In December 1939, for instance, Towers received a letter from the head of Sweden's central bank, the Sveriges Riksbank, asking about the prospects of opening a U.S. dollar account in Canada. In a "personal and strictly confidential" reply, Deputy Governor Donald Gordon assured the Swedish bank governor that if Sweden were invad-ed and taken over by another power that the Bank of Canada "would do our utmost to protect your interests and that any order to transfer, which we had reason to believe had been given under duress, would be ignored as a matter of ordinary banking procedure." It was hard, Gordon added, to answer such hypo-thetical questions "categorically."[54]

The German *blitzkrieg* of the spring of 1940 would bring new earmark clients and the first pressure on Ottawa to adapt the definition of earmarking to the cir-cumstances of war. What had been hypothetical soon became matters of hard choice.

EARMARKING UNDER PRESSURE: 1940–1941

At the beginning of 1940, the Bank of Canada had three foreign earmark accounts on its books. By the end of the same year, there were eleven accounts, ranging from the burgeoning Bank of England account with an all-time peak of 60,575 bars at the end of the year, to several accounts – for the Bank of Bolivia, the Banque Melli Iran and the Bank of London and South America (explained in greater detail later) – that were open but as yet contained no gold. In 1940, an incredible inflow of 134,798 bars of foreign gold arrived at the Bank of Canada for safekeeping. This proliferation of accounts was driven by the German army's incursion into the countries of the north European plain and Scandinavia. Countries once free became occupied and their governments des-perately sought ways to protect their central bank gold from predatory hands. They were only partially successful; large amounts of French, Belgian and Dutch gold fell into Axis hands and were quickly consumed by the German war machine. Here was the origin of the looted gold that Germany masterfully laundered through neutral countries and which would prove so difficult to trace after the war. Gold that escaped such looting did so in many ways. In many cases, panicky European central bankers were pointed in Ottawa's direction by the Bank of England. The common urge behind this flight of capital was to find a safe haven where the gold was beyond German reach and where it would be at the service of a government in exile. From the outset, this rush of gold across the Atlantic would place the Bank of Canada, and other wartime decision-makers in Ottawa, in the awkward position of redefining the Bank's responsibilities to holders of earmark accounts.

The first and thorniest problem was France. As the French government disintegrated in the face of the German assault of the late spring of 1940, the Banque de France desperately sought to remove its gold from its homeland. Some was captured, some was already abroad in Ottawa and other portions were put aboard warships and ended up in Dakar, West Africa. France had become an "occupied" country in Allied eyes. Back in France, the puppet Vichy government tried to assert a claim as the legitimate owner of France's central bank gold held abroad. In mid-July, Canada's senior foreign policy official, O. D. Skelton, the undersecretary of state for external affairs, was informed by the secretary of state for Dominion affairs in London that Britain was "blocking the assets of the Bank of France and should be glad if the Canadian Government would do likewise."[55] On July 31, Canada obliged Britain by passing Privy Council Order #3515 which "in consequence of the invasion of France by enemy forces" stipulated that all French assets domiciled in or controlled from Canada should be placed under the control of the custodian of enemy property, an office established in 1939 to "freeze" assets in Canada that might be employed to the enemy's advantage. By definition, this included France's earmarked gold and U.S. dollar account in Ottawa. But it quickly became apparent that there was no unanimity of opinion on the issue. A day later Finance Minister J. L. Ilsley issued an order that exempted the French gold from control of the custodian and instructed the governor of the Bank of Canada to act as his "agent for the control of these assets." Towers was not, however, to allow any disposition of the French gold and foreign currency without the finance minister's permission.[56] For the first time, the earmarking of gold had been coloured by political considerations.

From August to October of 1940, Ottawa's wartime policy-makers wrestled with the question of France's earmarked gold. On the one hand, there was persistent pressure from London to free the French gold so that it could be put to the use of the general Allied cause, thereby ultimately expediting France's return to freedom. In particular, France's cash and gold in Ottawa might be applied to "cash and carry" purchases of war matériel in the United States, where the French government had made contracts before its fall. Such contracts could still be honoured with French assets in Ottawa. To make this case, the British sent Sir Frederick Phillips, a senior Treasury official, to Ottawa to argue the case for freeing the French gold from wartime freezing. Late in August, British Prime Minister Churchill even cabled Ottawa, urging it to apply French resources in

Canada to Britain's immediate wartime fiscal needs. Contrary to this view was the belief that Canada had a fiduciary responsibility to the people of France and that wartime expediency should not override the inevitable postwar obligation to restore France's gold to its rightful owners.

At the Bank of Canada, Towers saw the debate over the French gold as a debate "purely" between two governments and that his role was to act "as a messenger." He was conscious that Prime Minister King and his principal foreign policy aide, O. D. Skelton, had long held an autonomous line in their relations with Britain. Canada must distance itself from Britain's international agenda; it must cease acting out of colonial obedience. King told Sir Frederick Phillips that the French gold question "should not be opened up at this time" and then in typical King fashion he bought time by telling Churchill in early September that his War Cabinet had given the issue a "most careful examination" and that subcommittee would study the issue.[57] It can also plausibly be suggested that King's hard-line position was moulded by his sensitivity to Quebec's possible reaction to any perceived move to liquidate French assets in Canada. King's Liberal Party was crucially dependent on Quebec support and any precipitous move on French currency or gold in Canada might easily be presented by King's political foes in Quebec as caving in to rabid, pro-British forces in English Canada. Skelton reinforced the prime minister's political instincts with arguments based on what he considered the moral obligations of a banker. "I consider that a trustee who substitutes an IOU for gold is not living up to the terms of his trusteeship, explicit or implicit," he told Towers in mid-September.[58] Only in absolute dire circumstances could French gold be employed by the Allies.

For his part, Towers (carefully noting that he was speaking as "an individual citizen") begged to differ with his prime minister. "I feel strongly," he wrote in early September, "that there is nothing in the slightest degree immoral in making use of such assets . . . If at the time of the debacle in France there had been four thousand fighting planes owned by the French in Canada, would anyone suggest that these planes should have been packed away for the duration of the war?"[59] Planes, Skelton responded, were not the same thing as gold. Gold carried a "sacred" value that made a depositor of gold "consider he has been gypped if he isn't given back gold or some instrument as certain to be exchangeable for equal value" when hostilities ended.[60]

And so the debate went through the fall of 1940, until on November 16 the prime minister had his way. All French gold and cash balances were to be put under the authority of the custodian of enemy property and the Bank of Canada was instructed by Finance Minister Ilsley to transfer control of French assets to the custodian.[61] Mackenzie King had prepared the way for the decision by telling Churchill that it was best to maintain the status quo and implied that if the Allies were ever in dire need of the French assets the custodian could be directed to deliver them into Allied hands.[62] This threshold was never crossed in Ottawa's mind and for most of the war France's earmarked gold – 10,581 bars of it – remained frozen in the vaults of the Bank of Canada until the fall of 1944, when control of the gold was duly returned to the Banque de France once it had reestablished itself in Paris. Canada had thus altered the conditions under which it was prepared to provide safe haven for foreign gold; it had weighed its own, admittedly political, needs against the needs of its British allies and had decided to be guided by domestic interests. The decision was taken after vigorous discussion between the prime minister's office, the departments of Finance, External Affairs and Justice and the Bank of Canada. Britain had been listened to and, judging by correspondence around the November 1940 decision, the British were prepared to agree that action on the French account could "wisely be deferred."

Other fugitive gold from Europe found a quicker and more open reception in Ottawa in the summer of 1940. While the drama of the Banque de France situation unfolded, the Bank of England headed three other European central banks in Ottawa's direction as they sought to protect their nations' monetary wealth from the German onslaught. First came the Norwegians, whose country had fallen under occupation in April. On June 10, the Norwegian minister in London cabled the Bank of Canada telling it that he had instructed the Bank of England to forward bullion worth £2.5 million to Ottawa for safekeeping and setting out the names of those who would have signing authority over the account.[63] Almost immediately, the gold was shipped. The Bank of Canada was initially confused. "We are uncertain as to whether any of the instructions we have received can be considered as instructions emanating from authorized officials of the Royal Norwegian Government," the Bank's secretary queried the Department of External Affairs, "...we should like your advice."[64] By mid-August, the Bank had 951 boxes of Norwegian gold in its vault and still no clear idea of who controlled it. Governor Towers wrote to Finance Minister Ilsley to inquire whether the gold should be delivered to the control of the custodian of enemy property or whether, if Canada recognized the legitimacy of the Norwegian government in exile in London, it was still under Norwegian control. On August 19, Ilsley confirmed that the Bank should oblige the Norwegian government in London and that the gold was therefore "freely disposable" and beyond the reach of the custodian.[65] "This appears to settle the question satisfactorily," a Bank official wrote to Norman Robertson at External Affairs.[66] Later in the fall, the governor of the Bank of Norway came to Ottawa to inspect the 589,834 fine ounces of gold earmarked for it in the Bank of Canada.[67] By the end of 1940, the Norwegian government had 1,335 bars of gold – 1,098,263 fine ounces – on earmark in Ottawa.

July 1940 brought two more European central bank clients displaced by war. On July 8, the deputy governor of the Bank of England cabled to request that 59,524 fine ounces be transferred out of its account and credited to Bank Polski, the Polish central bank. More gold arrived by ship from England in early August, giving Bank Polski 325,006 fine ounces in safekeeping in Ottawa.[68] Bank Polski's Ottawa earmark had convoluted origins. In June, it had arranged with the Banque de France to tranship much of its central gold reserve to Canada. Unfortunately, the French diverted the Polish gold to Dakar, West Africa, where it became mired in a wartime diplomatic tug-of-war. England then applied pressure for French gold now blocked in Ottawa to be released into Polish ownership. In the face of these demands, Canada took a passive attitude. "The attitude taken by the United Kingdom Government is understandable," Towers told O. D. Skelton, "and we have no comments to make."

The Bank of England then appears to have begun transferring gold from its account to the Polish account in Ottawa. On August 15, Governor Towers wrote to Finance Minister Ilsley telling him that Bank Polski had been a client since before the war and that on July 5 "we were advised by the Bank Polski that the President and managers of the Bank had come to London and were occupying space in the Bank of England." The Bank of Canada was therefore "taking the view that they are for the time being domiciled in London, England, and that the assets which they have with us are freely disposable and do not come within the control of the Enemy Property Custodian." Ilsley agreed.[69]

Unlike the inactive Norwegian account, the Polski Bank account took on a more active wartime role. Late in September 1940, Deputy Governor Donald Gordon met with the Polish consul general in Canada and the Polish minister plenipotentiary in England. The Poles asked to open a second account at the Bank of Canada to serve the needs of the Polish government in exile. The Poles indicated that the account would "probably remain inactive during the course of the war and that the fund was being held as far as possible for the rehabilitation of Poland after the war." And then to clinch their Allied *bona fides*, the Poles told Gordon that "in the event of need they would throw in the gold to the British cause." The Bank agreed, and 71,855 fine ounces of gold were transferred from Bank Polski to an account of the Polish government. Contrary to earlier professions, the Poles used their Ottawa gold frequently during the war, principally to help finance the activities of the Polish military mission in Canada by selling gold back to the Bank of England.[70]

Another government in exile made its wish to earmark gold in Canada evident in July 1940. Again, the Bank of England made the introductions. When the German attack came in the spring, the Netherlands government had scrambled to find a safe haven for its central bank gold. It was only partially successful. Some gold was captured outright and then shipped to Germany. Other gold fell into Axis hands when the ship carrying it was stranded on a sand bar in the Channel. The rest soon found itself in the vaults of the Bank of England. The Dutch government, however, remained anxious and in July prevailed on the British Treasury to inquire in Ottawa whether an earmark account might be opened on the other side of the Atlantic.[71] Towers instinctively cabled for Montagu Norman's reaction to the proposal. Norman replied that "after weighing all the factors that Netherlands gold in London should be at free disposal of the Netherlands Government."[72] Towers responded that "we see no difficulties" and proceeded to obtain the now-usual commitment from Finance Minister Ilsley that the Netherlands gold would be considered "freely disposable" and beyond the reach of the custodian of enemy property if a request was made to remove it from Canada. By the end of August, the Netherlands government had rapidly built up its new earmark account in Ottawa to 5,732 bars – 2,812,124 fine ounces. This would prove to be the high-water mark for Dutch gold in Canada, as throughout the war the Netherlands government drew the account down for various purposes, including the despatch of some Dutch gold to Australia for safekeeping in 1943. Nonetheless, the Netherlands in turn brought earmark accounts to Ottawa from various colonial banks affiliated with it. In September 1942, the Bank of Dutch Guiana (De Surinaamsche) opened a gold account at the Bank of Canada. A year later the Royal De Javaasche Bank of the Netherlands Indies followed suit. Finally, in 1945 De Curacaosche Bank in the Dutch West Indies came to Ottawa. All three of these accounts were relatively small compared with the main Netherlands account and were largely intended to facilitate wartime commercial interaction between the Netherlands and its dependencies.[73]

The constellation of small colonial accounts around the main Netherlands account was paralleled by two accounts set up at the request of the Bank of England. In October 1940, the Bank of Canada opened gold accounts for the central bank of Bolivia and the Banque Melli Iran in Tehran. Here, too, the purpose was largely commercial – to provide payment for British purchases of Bolivian tin and Iranian oil.[74] Neither account was active during the war, with the Bolivian account finally coming alive only in 1945. A 1940 account opened for the Bank of London and South America had a similarly British-oriented commercial motivation. In 1945, the Bank of Mexico opened a gold safekeeping account in Ottawa.[75] A last commercially driven account appeared in the summer of 1943 when the Banque Nationale de Belgique, on behalf of the Belgian government in exile, opened an earmark account in Ottawa to provide commercial cover on purchases of Canadian wheat they had made and for which they had no assurance from Washington that U.S. dollars would be released to make payment.[76]

The Bank of Canada thus found itself at the centre of a wartime proliferation of earmarked gold accounts. The surge of British and French gold pushed the Bank's total earmarked gold holdings to its high-water mark at the end of 1940, when 43,363,105 fine ounces of gold or the equivalent of just over 108,000 bars of gold rested in its vaults.[77] Despite the inflows and outflows, the total earmark remained remarkably steady, in the range of 37–42 million fine ounces from 1941 to 1945. However, the number of foreign accounts, as the foregoing narrative has indicated, grew steadily to 19 by the end of 1945 from the three active in late 1939.

Three common denominators run through this impressive expansion in the once rather pedestrian service of earmarking gold for foreign clients. Most obviously, the increase was the result of a flight of capital set in motion by the descent of Europe into war in 1939. Ottawa was a faraway, safe place to store gold and it was solidly in the Allied camp. Ottawa was also well situated for some of the commercial purposes of the Allied war effort, particularly Allied purchases in the still–neutral United States. Furthermore, the Bank of Canada, and other branches of the Canadian government like the Department of Finance, had developed predictable and relatively transparent procedures governing these accounts. Under the pressure of war, the Bank had developed new criteria for evaluating requests for earmarking and had applied them as a condition of opening the account. These usually focused on the *bona fides* of the depositing bank's government. Only in the case of the French gold despatched to Ottawa in 1939–40 were other factors, driven by domestic political concerns, introduced into the evaluation, in this case leading to the placing of foreign gold under the custodian of enemy property. But this decision in late 1940 was the exception that proved the rule. The rule was that the earmarking of gold in Ottawa was seen as a useful financial tool of war, one that geography and institutional affinity had bestowed on the young Bank of Canada. And the chief instrument of that affinity had been the Bank of England, which had invariably either introduced the Bank of Canada to its new earmark clients directly or had taken a facilitating role in bringing the accounts to life. Indeed, it has been speculated that in the dark days of late 1940 Britain even considered establishing a "shadow" Bank of England in Ottawa, where it would be safe from German air attack and free to draw upon its store of earmarked gold and thereby sustain Britain's financial war if the motherland should slip under Axis control. The presence of senior British financial officials, like Sir Otto Niemeyer, in Ottawa through that autumn tends to lend some credence to the notion.[78] It is worth mentioning that England had also transferred all its negotiable securities (e.g., Treasury bills) to safekeeping in Montreal during these same years.

In the fall of 1940, these three circumstances – the flight of European capital, the sanctity of Ottawa as a financial safe haven and the Bank of England's established influence in the Canadian capital – would combine to produce what was perhaps the most unusual of the Bank of Canada's wartime earmark accounts.

REFUGEE GOLD: THE SUNDRY PERSONS ACCOUNT

Since its inception in 1935, the only clients the Bank of Canada had served were other central banks, the Bank for International Settlements, Canadian chartered banks and the Canadian minister of finance. It was not in the business of retail banking and the closest it got to that function – Section 25 of its incorporation act empowering it to buy or sell gold to anyone tendering its price at is head office – had been suspended by annual orders-in-council since 1935. Nevertheless, the coming of war would bring the Bank of Canada as close to having individual clients as it would ever come. Once again, the initiating and controlling factor was the Bank's relationship with the Bank of England.

The rise of Nazi Germany in the 1930s and the ideological, diplomatic and racial tensions it overtly promoted in the late years of the decade compelled many Europeans to flee their homelands in search of safe haven. Many took their worldly wealth with them. Others, as the recent controversy over dormant accounts in Swiss commercial banks has revealed, transferred some or all of their wealth abroad as an insurance against possible displacement from their homeland if war should come. As tensions grew in Europe, the Bank of Canada quietly discussed the possibility of allowing foreigners to store and perhaps buy gold in Canada's commercial banks. The idea received guarded approval in Ottawa; there was some fear that news of such activity might trigger gold hoarding by the Canadian public. Nonetheless, the fact that an export licence would be required to move such gold back out of the country was help up as assurance that the ultimate disposition of such gold was within Canada's control. Ottawa therefore seemed to adopt a policy of low-keyed, tacit approval of such foreign deposits. In July 1938, Governor Towers asked the general managers of Canada's chartered banks to provide him with a monthly report of foreign-owned gold in their safekeeping. When war eventually came, he told them that it was their "very definite duty" to report any "suspicious or improper" holdings of foreign gold in the vaults.[79]

England, not Canada, however, became a favourite destination for these pre-war refugees and their valuables; it was close to Europe and seemingly safe. Once there, European exiles tended to deposit their valuables – often precious metals like silver and gold – in the safekeeping of English commercial banks. With the advent of war in 1939, these European refugees became subject to var-ious constraints placed on their activities as alien holders of gold in Britain. One of these was the necessity of obtaining an export licence from the British gov-ernment if they wished to take their gold out of Britain. Given the parlous state of Britain in the summer of 1940, this demand grew steadily as European refugees sought to further distance themselves from the menace of the Axis. At this point, the British government began to worry about the ultimate destina-tion or application of such gold once it left Britain. The principal concern was that these small amounts of refugee gold might find their way into the service of the Axis. "We have been concerned for some time," Bank of England senior offi-cial G. L. F. Bolton wrote to Donald Gordon at the Bank of Canada in September 1940, "with the degree of veracity to be placed on non-enemy Declarations executed by foreign owners of gold here when applying for per-mission to export." It was not that their loyalty to the Allied cause was in ques-tion, but that they might involuntarily be placed in positions that jeopardized the Allied cause. "In many cases," Bolton continued, "the relative documents have to go through enemy countries and it is probable that pressure is brought to bear on some owners to place their gold where it can be used directly or indi-rectly for enemy purposes." Consequently, by the late summer of 1940 the Bank of England was refusing all refugee requests to remove gold from the country.[80]

As Bolton acknowledged, the Bank realized that there was "a strong element of unfairness in maintaining a flat refusal" to all requests to move personal gold out of the country. The predicament of a few penalized the majority, who were presumably immune to pressure from the Axis. The Bank of England was there-fore prepared to offer "an alternative" to those refugees eager to move their gold to what they perceived as more secure safe havens. On September 12, 1940, the Bank issued Foreign Exchange Control Notice 234/44. Foreign holders of gold in British commercial banks could surrender their gold to the Bank of England, which would then earmark 95% of the value of that gold in its account at the Bank of Canada in Ottawa. Five per cent of the value would be kept by the Bank of England to cover the cost of handling the transaction. A receipt in the form of a "lodgement form" would be issued to the gold owner, but it would explicitly state that its ownership was "not transferable and not negotiable." "It must be understood, however," the notice warned, "that such gold will not be placed at the free disposal of the beneficiary until one month after the date upon which the Emergency Powers (Defence) Act of 1939 expires although the Bank of England would be prepared, in exceptional circumstances, to consider an application for earlier release."[81]

Foreign gold holders were thus given a safer refuge for their gold and Britain obtained some assurance, since legal control of the account remained with the Bank of England, that the gold could not be redirected to nefarious purpose. As Bolton candidly admitted later in the fall, the "gold offer is intended rather to immobilize than to mobilize foreign holdings and we do not intend to allow release before the end of the war unless for very good and exceptional reasons . . . the whole administration is centralized with us." [82]

From a Canadian point of view, what is remarkable about this policy is that it was made public six days *before* Bolton at the Bank of England wrote to the Bank of Canada informing Deputy Governor Donald Gordon of its intent and conditions. "The offer pre-supposes," Bolton told Gordon on September 18, "as you will see, that owners will be able to obtain free export facilities from Canada and I assume that as all releases will be authorized by us, under advice to you, there will be no difficulty about the issue of export permits from Canada if necessary." Such was the nature of the close relation of the two central banks that Gordon was predisposed to acquiesce to the British proposal, although he had in fact been presented with a fait accompli. "I can see no particular difficulty about the arrangement proposed," he wrote on October 10, "and we shall, of course, be happy to receive and hold in custody for you the duplicates of all Lodgement Forms received . . . I assume that we will not be asked to open special gold accounts for each of the individuals concerned, but that you would simply advise us to release from your stock a certain amount of gold to a specific individual." There was also "no difficulty" about obtaining gold export licences.[83] In fact, in January 1940 the Bank had made a similar plan available to the Banque de France, but there had been only a single depositor who chose in May of that year to deposit eight bars of gold in Ottawa in return for francs paid out in France.[84]

Almost immediately, refugee gold began arriving in Ottawa. "The offer is now seven weeks old and we have accepted 33 deposits, mostly from Swiss residents, to a total amount of something over £½ million," Bolton wrote in early November.[85] Thus, the value of a refugee's gold surrendered to the Bank of England in London was now under safekeeping in Ottawa. The Bank of Canada was made aware of the identity of individual gold holders by means of duplicate copies of the lodgement forms the depositors had received in London when they or their agents had surrendered their gold. The first deposit was registered on October 18, 1940, and the last appears to have been registered on June 17, 1941. In total, there would be 155 deposits. The records indicate the name of the depositor, their address (not always given in its entirety, e.g., simply a city) and the amount of gold earmarked. The amounts of gold varied dramatically. The smallest deposit was just over 11 ounces of fine gold; the next smallest was 22.5 fine ounces. The largest holding was 267,619 fine ounces – approximately 670 bars of gold. Most holdings were in the range of three to four bars of gold. Some of the deposits were in the form of gold coins. The total sundry persons deposit amounted to just over 526,400 fine ounces of gold or the equivalent of 1,316 bars of gold, of which 499,925 ounces – approximately 1,250 bars – were still the property of the "sundry persons" depositors after the Bank of England retained its 5% handling charge.

Some of the deposits were in a corporate name– usually a bank or a manufacturing concern – but most deposits bore the name of an individual. There was nothing more than a name and an address to suggest the identity of the depositor. It is a dangerous game to extrapolate about race, religion or nationality on the basis of a name and address alone. Nonetheless, a preponderance of the names would *appear* to be Jewish. Many of these appear to have been living in temporary accommodation (e.g., a New York hotel). There were, however, also names which are seemingly Anglo-Saxon, Slavic and Germanic, although, given marriage patterns, this is of course no absolute determinant of faith or nationality. Many of the deposits held in the name of a financial institution were held in the name of a foreign – usually in New York or London – branch of that banking corporation. The addresses were scattered across the face of the earth. They ranged across thirteen countries. There was a concentration in London and New York, but others gave addresses in prominent South American cities like Rio de Janeiro and Buenos Aires. Others lived as far afield as Iran and Hungary. There are no Canadian addresses. Of the minority of corporate clients (i.e., manufacturing companies) within the account, many had addresses in Switzerland.

Despite its seemingly simple terms, the arrangement was from the outset surrounded by confusion. Refugees, who were naturally caught up in the confusion and insecurity of war, were often unsure which central bank actually had control over their gold, despite the fact that this had been carefully spelled out on the lodgement form that was issued to each depositor. The Bank of Canada's first sundry person inquiry was dated October 9, 1940, and came from a Dutch national resident in Portugal en route to America. It contained a request that it was registered directly in the name of the letter writer. "It is not, of course, our intention that you should act on instructions received in this manner," Bolton instructed Ottawa, "and we have clearly stated that before delivery of the gold can be effected the receipt must be presented to us. Neither do we wish to place you in the position of having to verify that you are holding gold for any particular individual."[86]

Both legal and practical control over the account thus rested entirely with the Bank of England; the Bank of Canada was simply the safe-keeper. To this end, the Bank in Ottawa developed a standard response to anyone inquiring about their gold in Canada: "The arrangement which is being made by the Bank of England is entirely in their hands and the whole administration of the offer is being centralized with them."[87]

Problems and confusions however continued. The Bank of Canada began receiving letters from refugees holding gold in the account asking that their gold be delivered to them. Their stories were often heart-rending. Many reported that their flight from their homeland had now carried them to one of Europe's neutral countries or to the United States, where, having deposited all or most of their wealth in the Bank of England's sundry persons account, they were consequently no longer able to support themselves and were becoming desperate. Many of these requests went directly to the Bank of England, which had promised to consider early release of gold in exceptional cases. Others mistakenly approached the Bank of Canada with their requests for release of their wealth. A Bank of Canada official candidly admitted to a Canadian diplomat that there was "considerable confusion and misunderstanding regarding the availability of the gold."[88] These requests were invariably forwarded to London, where the British usually turned them down, reiterating the original commitment to free the gold soon after the Emergency Powers Act lapsed. Ottawa was never told of the criteria by which these decisions were reached, although the correspondence authorizing release seems to suggest why a minority of deposits were in fact freed before the end of the war. Some cases seemed to indicate that the gold was freed if it seemed destined to be applied to the Allied war effort. One applicant received a release of his gold after he made it known that he intended to apply the proceeds to the purchase of oil tankers.

Other cases indicate that extreme hardship also seemed to carry some weight with the Bank of England, especially if the refugee had acquired U.S. resident status. In July 1942, the Canadian trade commissioner in New York, Douglas Cole, reported to Ottawa that he had been approached by a Czechoslovakian refugee couple now resident in New York. The husband told Cole that he had "taken out his first [U.S. residency?] papers and as such is subject to the American draft and their funds are running low as they are exhausting the proceeds of American securities which they owned before escaping to this country." Cold told the Bank of Canada that "this couple have gone through murderous experiences and their papers appear to be in order" and asked the Bank to assist them.[89] To reinforce his request, Cole passed on a letter from the refugees. Since 1924, the Czech couple had lived in Vienna, where they owned a cotton and wool factory. It was confiscated in 1938 after the German takeover of Austria. Within a year, their remaining properties and "the fortune of my husband's father" in Czechoslovakia were also confiscated. The couple themselves fled to Paris and after the German invasion of France made their way "with great difficulty" to Lisbon. Finally, in March 1941 they arrived in New York. Just before the outbreak of war, the couple transferred two gold bars they had in an Amsterdam bank to England, from whence they found their way into the sundry persons account in Ottawa. Now they needed the gold. The letter concluded:

> We feel that the British Empire never meant to involve such a hardship on people who have suffered tremendously through the action of the axis powers. We can assure you that our financial position, prior to invasion, was one that did not give us any concern at all, but we, along with thousands of others, found ourselves suddenly removed from a position of security to one bordering on actual want. If we could receive the monetary value of these bars of gold, we would be in a position to establish a business here in the United States which would afford us an opportunity to start a new life which would settle us completely for the future.[90]

Ottawa forwarded the letter to the Bank of England, which decided to grant their request. On September 2, 1942, the couple received their gold in Ottawa.

Between late 1941 and 1945 there were 34 such early releases of gold from the sundry persons account. Others would not be so lucky.

After the initial burst of activity in 1940–42, the sundry persons arrangement slipped into a kind of mid-war quiescence. There were sporadic requests for release from clients and routine correspondence with the Bank of England, but most holders of gold in the account seemed to have settled down for the end of the war and the much-awaited expiration of Britain's Emergency Powers Act that would follow the coming of peace. The account's existence seemed to attract no publicity outside the Bank's walls, nor was there any trace of concern over the account within Ottawa's wartime bureaucracy. Within the Bank, the prevalent attitude seemed to be that once again the Bank of Canada was extending its warm relationship with its British central bank ally.

GOLD FOR FRANCS: THE ANGLO-SWISS SWAP AGREEMENT OF 1942

Britain's rush to earmark gold in Canada in the anxious years of 1938 to 1940 was primarily driven by the need to put a significant amount of the country's monetary wealth out of harm's reach. This transatlantic placement of gold had the fortunate side effect of allowing Britain a means of meeting the cost of its initial purchases from the still-neutral United States. Between September 10 and 18, 1939, for instance, the Bank of England ordered that $100 million of its Ottawa earmarked gold be shipped to the Federal Reserve Bank of New York, where it was converted into U.S. dollars to help meet the cost of "cash and carry" purchases from the Americans.[91] The pattern continued through the early phase of the war with the United States maintaining its official neutrality while acting out an unofficial friendship with the Allies. When the Lend-Lease Agreement between Britain and her allies and the United States came into effect in the spring of 1941, Britain's appetite for U.S. dollars eased somewhat, as war purchases could now be covered by the British-bases-for-American-equipment swaps that Lend-Lease made possible.

Britain, however, was making war purchases elsewhere and needed other types of hard currency to cover them. Switzerland was one of these suppliers. Even before the war, Britain had traded heavily with Switzerland, running an average annual trade deficit there in the last two years before the war of 50 million Swiss francs.[92] With war, Britain cut its luxury purchases in Switzerland and concentrated on buying war-oriented matériel, such as Swiss-made Oerlikon-Buehrle guns. As a result, the deficit in Anglo-Swiss trade burgeoned. Even when Switzerland found itself surrounded by the Axis in 1940, Britain still managed to smuggle goods out of Switzerland. At the same time, other British activities in Switzerland – legation costs, funding intelligence operations and propaganda activities – ate heavily into Britain's holdings of Swiss francs. Through all this, the Swiss franc remained one of Europe's most durable currencies. While war ravaged the worth of most European currencies (thereby, of course, placing a premium on the value of gold), the Swiss franc remained stable and convertible. The British Treasury in London did its best to conserve Britain's waning supply of Swiss francs, even to the point of applying, in direct contravention of the conditions it had agreed to under Lend-Lease, its holdings of U.S. dollars to Swiss purchases. To avoid tipping off the Federal Reserve to this use of American currency, the British drew these dollars from their account at the Chase National Bank in New York.

But in March 1942, even this expedient and devious means of supporting Britain's purchases in Switzerland came to an end. Switzerland refused to accept any more U.S. dollars. Anxious to deny Germany any means of feedings its war machine with raw materials, such as tungsten, from neutral Portugal and Spain, the United States had prohibited the use of U.S. dollars in such transactions. Since these transactions had often been arranged through Swiss financial channels, the Swiss willingness to accept U.S. dollars declined sharply. At the same time, Switzerland began to guard its monetary reserves in an effort to curb inflationary pressures in Switzerland. The Swiss central bank, the Banque Nationale Suisse, committed itself to maintaining a reserve of 40% of the money in circulation in the country in foreign currencies and/or gold to anchor the domestic performance of the franc and thereby cool inflationary pressures. Since both the Americans and British had also put in place regulations embargoing Swiss holdings of gold and foreign currency held abroad, chiefly in London and New York, the Swiss were unwilling to accumulate any more blocked gold and currency out of the country, where it could not be applied to domestic monetary operations or to pay for its own imports. Thus, while Switzerland could freely export, its ability to import was restricted, thereby creating inflationary pressures. By the spring of 1942, the pressures conspiring to create what one historian has described as Britain's "perennial shortage of Swiss francs" had reached a chronic impasse.[93]

On March 9, 1942, Graham Towers received a coded cable from Montagu Norman at the Bank of England. "For a long time," Norman confided, "we have only been able to obtain our essential Swiss franc requirements against U.S. dollars. Difficulties have lately arisen owing to United States freezing policy. Swiss are now reluctant to accept U.S. dollars without a special licence for their transfer to third party which United States authorities are reluctant to give. We must obtain Swiss francs and are therefore suggesting to Swiss that they sell us Swiss francs against gold [held by the Bank of England in Ottawa]." Norman then stated that the Swiss had asked "in general" whether any gold they acquired title to in Ottawa would be "at the free disposal of the Swiss" and in particular whether it could be sold, transferred or exported to other central banks. Norman already sensed that such gold would have to be blocked and even suggested the wording of a response to the Swiss central bank, the Banque National Suisse:

> Gold deposited in Canada is subject to an export licence system, permits being based on general allied policy. Transfers to the accounts of any neutral central bank would normally be permitted although there might be some difficulty about Portugal or Spain. Licences would probably be given for exports of gold earmarked for your account to central banks of the western hemisphere. It is most unlikely however that licences would be granted for exports to Europe.[94]

Two days later Towers cabled back: "We agree with reply suggested . . ." Reading into Norman's message, the Swiss seemed to be probing whether they could obtain Allied gold and not be bound by the blocking arrangements that they had encountered elsewhere. Norman's readiness to confound this expectation indicates that it was only a probe. On March 18, Norman cabled that the Swiss had a fall-back position: "... they are willing for the time being to renounce condition that gold deposited in in Canada must be free for exportation to central banks of neutral European countries," but "they require certainty that such gold deposited in Canada must be free for exportation to central banks of neutral European countries," but "they require certainty that such gold can be exported to other central banks of Western Hemisphere and transferred to central banks of Western Hemisphere and of neutral countries Sweden, Portugal, Spain." Norman said that the Swiss should be made to understand that "transferred" would mean not a physical transfer but a book transfer in Ottawa. Could the Bank of England tell the Swiss that Ottawa agreed to such terms?

A second cable followed on the heels of the first. "It is realized here," Norman wrote, "that undertaking required by Swiss is not wholly satisfactory to us and involves some risk of eventual transfer for enemy benefit."[95] In his reply the next day, Towers said that he could immediately see what this risk was: before any other neutral country in Europe might accept payment in gold from Switzerland it would seek assurance that any gold it took ownership of in Ottawa could be exported within the Western Hemisphere and that the gold might therefore find its way to a country of questionable neutrality, like Argentina. Norman had anticipated this loophole in his previous cable, but had to bow to the exigencies of war. "But after discussion with Whitehall it is felt that necessity to obtain Swiss Francs largely needed for direct war purposes must override these objections."[96]

The same day that Towers gave his tacit approval to Norman he telephoned and then wrote to Deputy Minister of Finance W. C. Clark to gain his department's approval of the arrangements suggested by Norman. This was an automatic obligation. An export licence would be required for any earmarked gold held by a foreign bank at the Bank of Canada and experience had shown that the client would want assurance of such a licence in advance. Towers laid out the conditions that the Swiss would accept: "certainty that such gold can be exported to other central banks of the western hemisphere, and transferred to central banks of the western hemisphere and of neutral European countries – Sweden, Portugal and Spain." Towers told Clark that the U.K. government "is not wholly satisfied with the proposals, inasmuch as they involve some risk of eventual transfer for enemy benefit, and they intend to try to make a better deal with the Swiss." But "in the circumstances," Towers concluded, "I do not think that we should refuse to facilitate such transactions."[97] Towers' letter indicated that Clark was in accord with this reading of the situation.

Clark in Finance did not reply formally to Towers until April 7, in a short letter that betrayed no undue concern and concluded that "there is nothing we can do but to facilitate the transaction . . ."[98] Two weeks later, the Bank of England inquired whether the Bank of Canada had secure, coded communications with Switzerland. Ottawa said it did not and said that it would "gladly agree to leave all necessary technical arrangements to you."[99] It was not April 28 that the first direct communication was received in Ottawa from the Banque Nationale Suisse (BNS) in Zurich. The BNS was no stranger to Ottawa. It had maintained a drawing account in Ottawa since 1935 and had made quiet enquiries in 1939 about earmarking gold in Ottawa. Now the BNS had some definite inquiries. Was it possible "under actual Canadian legislation" that a Swiss commercial bank could open a gold account in Canada? And could that deposit contain gold owned by Swiss commercial banks? Towers immediately turned to Norman in London for advice. Ottawa, he suggested, would accept deposits from a Swiss commercial bank but would not feel bound to respect the hemispheric conditions it had extended to the BNS for shipping such gold out of Canada. Or, as an alternative, Ottawa might open a special account for such gold in the name of the BNS but accept no "fiduciary" responsibility to the Swiss commercial banks actually owning the gold. Towers admitted to being mystified by "what gave rise to the inquiry."[100]

Not until May 1 did Towers hear back from Norman and what he got was a tutorial in the *realpolitik* of the war's convoluted financial affairs. London was obviously locked in tough negotiations with the Swiss, negotiations driven by its desperate need for francs. The "recent provisional arrangements" made for an account for the BNS "represented a concession by the Swiss National Bank to avoid a breakdown in the financial relations between the sterling area and Switzerland." Despite the concession, Norman had his suspicions about Swiss motives in wanting an Ottawa account. "We suspect therefore that the Swiss National Bank proposes to buy gold in Switzerland irrespective repeat irrespective of origin and ownership either against sales of equivalent gold in Canada or a guarantee to the original holders that the Swiss National Bank holds the equivalent gold in Canada to his order." (Significantly, this was the only instance in the entire post-1935 correspondence between Norman and Towers that Norman had repeated a phrase to add emphasis). Norman feared the "approach made to you tends to confirm our suspicions and we feel that the intention may be to evade the strict freezing measures in Washington, and London." In short, Norman feared that Switzerland would use the combination of a central bank account in Ottawa with a parallel Swiss commercial bank account beside it to move gold of unknown origin – and Norman must have known that gold looted from occupied countries by Germany was finding its way into Switzerland – into legitimate financial channels. The swapping, either by paper transfer or actual physical transfer, of legitimate gold in the vaults of the Bank of Canada for gold held offshore might fit such designs exactly. "I therefore suggest," Norman sternly advised, "that you avoid giving the Swiss National Bank any help or encouragement whatsoever either to transfer gold in Canada to the names of private residents or commercial banks in Switzerland or to hold gold in their own names for private Swiss interests." Canadian commercial banks should be asked to conform to this injunction. Once the possibility of private citizens or Swiss commercial banks moving gold through Canada had been blocked, Norman concluded, then the original "provisional arrangements" might be applied to the BNS alone and gold allowed to come to Ottawa.

Towers got the message. The next day, May 2, the BNS was told by Ottawa that "under existing conditions there are obstacles in the way of acceptance of gold deposits unless the gold is the property of a central bank." Neither the Bank of Canada nor Canadian commercial banks would be able to deal gold on the basis suggested by the Swiss.[101] During this negotiation, Towers had learned that two of Canada's commercial banks had received inquiries "of the same character from Swiss correspondents." Now he understood their purpose. "Present regulations in the United States," he confided to Clark at Finance, "provide that gold will only be accepted for safekeeping if it is the property of a central bank or a Government. The Swiss are evidently trying to find out whether our policy is less restrictive." Towers then despatched a circular letter to the general managers of all Canada's commercial banks. It was "the desire of the Government that no new gold safekeeping accounts should be opened for non-resident banks, corporations or individuals."[102]

Thus, by early May 1942 the Bank of Canada had worked out the terms under which it would accept gold under earmark from the Banque Nationale Suisse and potentially hold it for other neutral central banks in Europe. It had also shut the door on any of these arrangements being extended to European commercial banks. Much of policy-making on the run was done with advice from the Bank of England. Both Ottawa and London were aware that there remained loopholes in the arrangement – the possibility, for instance, that Ottawa gold might find its way to Argentina – but given London's desperate need for francs, the Bank of Canada was prepared to defer dealing with such eventualities "unless and until" they materialized.

What is remarkable is that even while these arrangements were being framed, refined and set in place between early March and early May 1942, the Bank of England and the Banque Nationale Suisse were in fact implementing their gold-for-francs swap. Such was the haste of implementing this transaction that there is no document in the Bank of Canada records that indicates the exact date on which the BNS account was opened. Nor is there any written communication between London and Ottawa detailing the sealing of the Anglo-Swiss agreement. The Bank of Canada gold ledger books (the ledgers in which all gold movements – arrivals, departures and transfers of gold – at the Bank were recorded) do indicate that on March 25, 1942, the first transfer instruction was received from the Bank of England. On that day, London asked that 66,815 fine ounces of gold – 166 bars – be moved from its earmark account to the account of the BNS. Thus began a rolling swap of English gold for Swiss francs that was to stretch out in 155 individual transactions until December 31, 1943. On each occasion, gold was transferred by ledger entry from the earmark account of the Bank of England and credited to that of the BNS. It was literally a paper transfer; actual gold bars in the vault stayed where they were and only a bookkeeping alteration was made. By the end of the series, 4,506 gold bars – 1,816,372 fine ounces or over 56 tons – had passed from English to Swiss ownership.[103] The individual swaps were remarkably evenly paced, usually taking place on a weekly or slightly less than a weekly basis. The amounts were also relatively steady, with occasional upward blips. The largest transfer came in March 1943

when 80,088 fine ounces changed accounts. The smallest 3,618 fine ounces –
came on February 17, 1943. Most transfers were in the range of 6,000–10,000
fine ounces.

The Anglo-Swiss gold-for-francs swap attracted no public attention. Nor did
it occasion any unusual bureaucratic deliberation beyond the telephone calls
and exchange of memoranda between the governor of the Bank of Canada and
the deputy minister of finance. The Anglo-Swiss agreement and its implications
for the earmarking of gold by Canada's central bank is never mentioned in the
records of the Cabinet War Committee, the political control room of Canada's
war effort. Nor is the agreement or its implications mentioned in the listing of
Cabinet conclusions. There is no direct correspondence on the matter from
Finance Minister J. L. Ilsley to Bank of Canada Governor Towers, only *pro forma*
correspondence on such things as gold export licences channelled through his
deputy minister. There is no mention of any matters relating to foreign gold in
the famous diary of Prime Minister W. L. Mackenzie King. Beyond the original
justification given by Norman to Towers that the whole deal was made necessary by Britain's acute shortage of francs, there is no written rationale for the
swap in any of the Bank of Canada's files. Only once is there a ray of illumina-
tion. On June 22, 1942, the full board of the Bank of Canada convened in
Ottawa. War had made the full board's meetings less frequent; the board's executive committee met more frequently. The June meeting was therefore the first
full meeting since the Anglo-Swiss arrangements were mapped out. When the
board turned to "business arising out of the minutes," Governor Towers was
asked to explain the new Swiss earmark arrangements. They had, he told the
directors, been established "for the purpose of acquiring Swiss francs, which
enabled the [British] authorities to assist prisoners of war."[104] The matter was
not raised again.

Even before the Bank of Canada had spelled out in its cable to Zurich of May
2 the final conditions by which the BNS could hold earmarked gold in Ottawa,
the Swiss bank began issuing instructions for the transfer of gold to another neutral country account. On April 22, the Bank of Canada received instruction
from the BNS in Berne to take "approximately 64,310 ounces" – two tons of
gold – out of its new earmark account and place them "at the disposal of Banco
de Portugal."[105] Although the Banco de Portugal had not as yet established a
formal account (for instance, lists of signatures authorized to activate transactions had not yet been exchanged), the Bank of Canada honoured the Swiss
request. Because Ottawa did not have secure, coded communications with
Lisbon, it was obliged to communicate with the Portuguese central bank via its
cable link with the Bank of England.[106] A week later, the Banco de Portugal initiated formal contact with the Bank of Canada. It acknowledged that it had
been "advised" by the BNS that the two tons of gold it had received title to from
the Swiss bank was "free to be exported, from Canada, to Central Banks of
countries in the Western Hemisphere and of neutral European countries." They
forwarded a list of authorizing signatures and concluded with a wish for "a fruitful co-operation between our two Institutions."[107] They did not provide – nor
would there have been an expectation of such – any explanation of the purpose

of their swap for Swiss gold, no sense of what item or service they had surrendered for the gold. Towers was not subsequently quizzed about this new account by the Bank's board.

On May 4, the BNS requested that another 64,837 fine ounces of gold be transferred to the Banco de Portugal account. The transfer was executed on May 5, leaving the Portuguese with approximately four tons of gold resting in the Bank of Canada vault. On May 15, Towers wrote to acknowledge the formal opening of the Banco de Portugal account and its recognition of the conditions set on the movement of their gold in Canada. Towers reciprocated Lisbon's good wishes by "expressing our pleasure in the establishment of business relations with your esteemed institution."[108] The next day W. C. Clark at the Finance Department reconfirmed that an export licence would be given to the Portuguese under the prescribed conditions "in accordance with the original arrangement approved at the request of the Government of the United Kingdom."[109]

After the intense flurry of account openings and gold swaps in the March to May period of 1942, the foreign earmark accounts at the Bank of Canada settled into a quiet mid-war routine. The steady, almost mechanical transfer of Bank of England gold into the BNS earmark account continued. Across the Atlantic in London, Anglo-Swiss negotiations continued as Britain continued to try to find ways to obtain Swiss francs. The Portuguese earmark account became inactive through the rest of 1942 and 1943, with its 321 bars of gold sitting undisturbed. There were no more requests from Switzerland that gold be transferred to the Portuguese or any other account.

In November 1942, a secret cable arrived from Montagu Norman in London shed more light on the tenor of the Anglo-Swiss negotiations that had driven the gold-for-francs swap of the spring. Norman informed Towers that the Swiss delegation that had been parked in London all summer long negotiating the issue of British access to Swiss francs was still at the bargaining table. A "financial agreement" was seemingly at hand "which will have the effect of guaranteeing the sterling area's ascribed requirements of Swiss francs over the next three years at a fixed rate of 17.35."[110] Towers cabled back that Norman could give "the Swiss the assurance they require."[111]

The Swiss negotiations, however, continued to prove arduous and Towers did not again hear from Norman directly until the following December. By then, Britain's desperate appetite for francs had obliged it to relax its vigilance. "Negotiations are at advanced stage with the Swiss for the provision of Swiss Francs to meet the requirements of the sterling area including refugee Allied Governments," Norman cabled. The British would "probably" soon allow the direct sale of gold to the Banque Nationale Suisse "at a Swiss Franc price delivery London with an unconditional export licence for shipment of such gold to any non-enemy territory." The Swiss, however, wanted yet another confirmation of the status of the gold they had accumulated in Ottawa *prior* to the upcoming agreement. More precisely, they wanted assurance that their gold in Ottawa could be moved to Berne "six months after the conclusion of hostilities between the United Kingdom and Germany . . ."[112]

The import of Norman's cable was dramatic. If Britain was now willing to sell its gold directly onto the continent to "non-enemy territory" like Switzerland, Portugal and Spain, then the protective necessity of earmarking gold in Canada evaporated. Whatever the implication of Norman's request, Towers was as usual quick to oblige it. The next day he wrote to Deputy Minister of Finance Clark asking for a reconfirmation of his department's willingness to issue an export permit for the postwar export of Switzerland's Canadian gold. On December 20, Clark reported back that he had discussed the matter with his minister, J. L. Ilsley, and that there would be "no objection," especially since the assurance would help to pave the way for Britain to receive "an adequate supply of Swiss francs..."[113] The same day, Towers gave the nod to London. By that day Britain had already reached agreement with the Swiss for the direct provision of francs for British gold. Britain had finally eased its severe liquidity problems with Switzerland; Britain's purchase of war matériel, like Portuguese tungsten, had become immensely easier, but this had been achieved at the expense of Britain bending its insistence that Allied gold not be traded directly onto the continent while hostilities lasted.

On December 30, 1943, the Bank of England made its last transfer to the Banque Nationale Suisse account in Ottawa – 10,076 fine ounces of gold. As the year thus closed, the BNS had a total earmark deposit of gold in Ottawa of 4,617 bars or 1,861,817 fine ounces of gold, all conditioned by the terms set down in the spring of 1942 and all available for unimpeded export once the war was over. The BNS account did not, however, become inactive. On January 7, 1944, the pattern of relatively regular, relatively same-sized transfers of gold into the BNS resumed. This time, however, the correspondent or originator of the transfer was Canada's minister of finance. Realizing that the British had set a precedent for selling gold directly to European neutrals, Ottawa decided to begin covering its own needs for Swiss francs by selling gold to the Swiss and placing it on earmark until the end of the war. Having alleviated their own need for gold to bolster the domestic performance of the franc, the Swiss now renewed their willingness to build up their offshore reserves of gold, ready for postwar applications. Thus, on January 7, the Swiss took title to 4,445 fine ounces or 11 bars of Canadian gold in Ottawa. This gold was sold out of the Minister of Finance Special (Exchange Fund) Account, reflecting the Finance Department's traditional exclusive right to market Canadian gold from the Canadian Mint.

This pattern of Canadian gold passing to Swiss earmark continued until April 1947. By then, 109 transfers had taken place, all in the general range of 6–8,000 fine ounces.[114] This flow had fattened the BNS earmark account in Ottawa to 4,867 bars by the end of 1944 and to 5,479 bars by the end of 1945. With each swap, the BNS in Berne cabled Ottawa that payment for the gold (calculated at 150,074 francs for each 1,000 fine ounces of gold) had been deposited to the Bank of Canada's account at the BNS. The francs were then made available to Canadian banks to meet their Swiss-franc needs to cover Canadian commercial relations with Switzerland. The Canadian banks paid U.S. dollars into the Bank of Canada's account at the Federal Reserve Bank of New York for these francs. Canadian buyers of Swiss francs were thus required to go through Canadian currency controls. In 1944, for instance, Canadians bought US$5,674,754 worth of Swiss francs in this manner.[115] Thus, the Swiss earmark account in Ottawa found a new purpose and a new, relatively unstrained rhythm for the duration of the war.

GOLD FOR KRONOR:
THE PORTUGUESE-SWEDISH SWAP AGREEMENT OF 1944-45

There was, however, one more episode of activity around the neutral country earmark accounts before the war finished. On February 12, 1944, the Swedish ambassador to Canada paid a call on the Bank of Canada. Sweden's central bank, the Sveriges Riksbank, had maintained an operating account with the Bank of Canada since soon after it had opened in 1935: early in the war there had been inconclusive discussion of another account that would act as assurance of Sweden's monetary stability in the event of an attack on the country. Dating back to 1668, the state-owned Sveriges Riksbank was Europe's oldest central bank and as such clearly commanded respect in Ottawa. The ambassador inquired whether the Bank of Canada would be interested in selling the Riksbank Canadian gold for earmark in Ottawa. Bank officials were receptive to the inquiry. They told him that Ottawa's "ability to deal in gold" depended on "whether we actually had gold in Canada surplus to our requirements which we were prepared to place under foreign earmark. We intimated also that, from time to time, there were other buyers in the market." Nonetheless, the Bank was prepared to offer a deal: gold at a discount rate of six cents per ounce off the New York price. The Swedes seemed particularly interested in having gold that could eventually be moved to New York. The ambassador also asked about the Riksbank's freedom to export the gold and was told that the minister of finance would have to be consulted, but it was likely that exports out of the hemisphere would not be permitted.[116]

Early in March, the Riksbank let the Bank of Canada know that it wanted to buy US$15 million in gold bars for Ottawa earmark. Sweden was prepared to hold gold in Ottawa subject to conditions devised in 1942 to cover other neutral country earmark accounts in Ottawa.[117] By March 15, the Riksbank had taken legal delivery in Ottawa of 1,076 bars or 429,111 fine ounces of Canadian mined gold. Thus another neutral European central bank anxious to accumulate gold had arrived in Ottawa to avail itself of the Bank of Canada's earmarking services.

Late in August, the Bank of Canada received an inquiry from the Banco de Portugal, via London, asking if its gold in Ottawa was "good delivery, New York." It was. A week later, on September 6, the Portuguese instructed Ottawa to transfer "about 1,000 kilos gold fine...good delivery New York and earmarked under the conditions laid down in your letter of May 15th 1942.[118] In a second transaction a day later, 32,174 fine ounces – about a ton or 80 bars of gold – was credited to the Riksbank account from the Portuguese account. This was the first activity in the Portuguese account since it had received its original gold from the BNS in 1942. But then twelve days later on September 19 instructions arrived by cable from the Banque Nationale Suisse for 64,386 fine ounces – about two tons – of gold to be placed in the Portuguese account.[119] Thus, having shed one ton of gold to Sweden, the Portuguese almost immediately acquired another two tons from Switzerland.

On September 30, the Portuguese queried Ottawa whether the gold they had just taken title to was "good delivery New York" and whether it was held under the May 1942 conditions. Ottawa replied yes to both questions.[120] Two days later, on October 2, the Banco de Portugal instructed Ottawa to transfer "about 500 kilos fine gold" to the Riksbank. Ottawa duly transferred 16,108 fine ounces to the Swedes.[121] Through all this staccato shifting of gold, the Bank of Canada simply followed the instructions it received. Since all parties involved openly acknowledged their compliance with the conditions laid out in the spring of 1942 for neutral earmark accounts, there was no obligation to pass the transactions past the minister of finance. Indeed, there was no written record of any internal consultation or querying of the Portuguese and Swiss requests.

Following the Riksbank's initial receipt of 120 bars – one and a half tons – of Portuguese gold in the fall of 1944, the two central banks then engaged in a series of shuffle trades of what appears to be essentially the same amount of gold back and forth between their Ottawa accounts. All of these transactions were paper transfers. They began in late November 1944 and early January 1945, when Sweden transferred back to Portugal the ton and a half of gold it had acquired in the fall of 1944. On January 26, Portugal sent half a ton back to Sweden, which was then returned by Sweden on February 28. Then in a series of six transfers from Portugal to Sweden beginning on May 7, 1945, and ending on September 13, 1945, Portugal transferred a total of 80,486 fine ounces to the Riksbank.[122] The purpose of these shuffle trades is nowhere made apparent, nor did they seem to occasion any undue attention in Ottawa. Once again, the late 1943 slackening of the early war injunction against direct trades of gold into neutral Europe had diminished Allied vigilance over gold trades between neutrals taking place outside of Europe. All of these Portuguese-Swedish swaps took place without delay or inquiry imposed by Ottawa.

Thus, a year after the Banco de Portugal and the Sveriges Riksbank first swapped gold, the Riksbank had acquired about two and a half tons of gold from Portugal. In January and June 1945, the Riksbank bought another 1,230 bars of gold from the minister of finance in Ottawa, so that by the end of 1945 the Swedes, through their direct buying and their transfers from Portugal, had accumulated 2,537 bars or 1,015,595 fine ounces of gold in their Ottawa earmark account. By the same date, the Banco de Portugal earmark in Ottawa had dwindled to 281 bars or 113,133 fine ounces of gold. Neither bank had physically moved gold out of Ottawa.

EARMARKING IN VICTORY:
EUROPEAN CENTRAL BANK ACCOUNTS IN OTTAWA, 1945–55

Throughout the war, much of the anxiety that had surrounded the earmarking of gold in Ottawa had revolved around differentiating ally, neutral and foe. All the conditions that were built into the agreements by which neutral and "occupied" countries were permitted to earmark gold in Ottawa were predicated on the eventual return of peace and a return to prewar normalcy, after which the earmarking of gold would revert to a straightforward, no-questions-asked central banking procedure. The most prominent example of the kind of wartime conditioning of the earmarking of gold was, of course, the guidelines laid down in the spring of 1942 and applied to the rights of Switzerland, Portugal and eventually Sweden to hold gold in Canada. Beyond such blanket injunctions, there had been much tailoring of the earmark procedure to the peculiar wartime situation of individuals and countries. France saw its gold frozen in Canada, largely as a result of political rather than moral or legalistic reasoning. Other occupied nations had been permitted to earmark as usual, even though their governments were in exile. And, in perhaps the greatest departure from normal central bank practice, the Bank of Canada had allowed the lodging of gold belonging to individual European refugees in its vaults. For all of these parties, the return of peace promised the return of normal banking arrangements.

Perhaps strangely, the end of the European war did not signal a scramble to Ottawa to unravel the awkward implications of wartime earmark banking. There were no sudden closings of accounts, no hurried exodus of blocked gold out of Canada and no recriminations. For some nations, the impositions of wartime banking were lifted early. The Allied liberation of France cleared the way for the restoration of legitimate government under General de Gaulle and consequently under the provisions of P.C. Order #8965 the custodian of enemy property returned control of 11,135,127 fine ounces of gold to the control of the Banque de France on December 28, 1944.[123] Similarly, the liberation of Europe allowed other central banks to return to normal operation from similarly arduous, if less stringent, wartime constriction. The Bank of Canada was therefore quick to recognize the return of normal central banking authority to Norway, the Netherlands and Belgium. In some cases, there were changes in name – the Norwegian government, for instance, established the Norges Bank in 1946 to act as its new central bank – but for purposes of recognizing control over earmarked gold stored in Ottawa, these presented no problem. Only in the case of Bank Polski were there jurisdictional problems. The exiled central bank of Poland had been recognized by the Allies and allowed to operate its accounts during the war, but the postwar provisional government was of a different ideological stripe than its prewar predecessor. At first, Canada delayed honouring the new government's request that Polish gold in Canada be shifted to its authority. But such resistance flew in the face of the new geopolitical map of Europe and finally in July 1946 the Bank of Canada released control over gold earmarked in Ottawa to the authority of a new Polish central bank.[124]

Switzerland had perhaps the most to expect in Ottawa from the return of peace. Beyond England, it had the largest gold holding in Canada and, unlike England, its gold was blocked. Not surprisingly, not long after peace came to Europe, the Swiss inquired about their gold at the Bank of Canada. On July 11, Ottawa received a cable from the BNS in Zurich. For some years, the Swiss pointed out, they had made francs available to Ottawa free of restriction in return for gold that was blocked in Ottawa. "We suppose that these restrictions have lost their importance for you since the end of European war so that we may hope that our existing and future deposits with you will from now on be entirely free for use for transfer and eventual transport to Switzerland."[125] After checking with the acting deputy minister of finance, Dr. W. A. Mackintosh, the Bank replied that export licences would be granted to any "existing or future deposits" the Swiss held in Canada, except for those destined for "enemy countries," a provision that reflected the continuing war in the Pacific.[126] Despite this clearance, the Swiss did not empty their Ottawa earmark account overnight. Instead, it in fact grew. By year's end in 1945, Switzerland had 5,479 earmarked gold bars in Ottawa. A year later, the total had climbed to 6,259 bars.

There is no documentary record that either Portugal or Sweden sought to clarify the status of their Ottawa gold in the months following the peace. In June, the Riksbank did write to query postwar exchange arrangements between Stockholm and Ottawa, but there was no mention of earmarked gold, except that Sweden might sell such gold to generate U.S. dollars.[127] Neither Sweden nor Portugal cleaned out their gold accounts in Ottawa with the peace. In fact, at year-end 1945 and year-end 1946, they had exactly the same earmark balances − 2,537 Swedish bars and 281 Portuguese bars.

The earmarking of gold in Ottawa hit its peacetime stride with remarkable ease. Only a handful of small earmarks that had only wartime rationales (e.g., the Bank of Bolivia and the Banque Melli of Iran) left completely. Otherwise, earmarking flourished at the Bank of Canada. New European clients arrived − Austria and Denmark in 1951 and West Germany[128] in 1954.

While normal earmarking reestablished itself after the war, one last legacy of wartime earmarking was quietly wound down. The sundry persons account had been holding gold since 1940–41 for as many as 155 depositors who had sought to protect their personal wealth by moving it across the Atlantic and placing it in the safekeeping of the Bank of Canada. In point of law, these deposits were included in the Bank of England's earmark account in Canada and those who had entrusted their gold to the arrangement were beholden to London, not Ottawa, in matters of control over their deposits. Throughout the war, inquiring depositors were invariably told that their gold would not be "allowed free disposal until one month after the expiry of the Emergency Powers (Defence) Act, 1939" in Britain, except in exceptional conditions. The minority − about 22% − of the depositors were successful during the course of the war in convincing the Bank of England that their need, and presumably their *bona fides* in the eyes of the Allies, outweighed any risk of releasing their assets during hostilities. The rest of the depositors quietly waited out the war.

On December 12, 1945, the British Parliament voted for the repeal of the Emergency Powers Act on February 24, 1946. The Bank of England soon began to receive requests for the release of gold under the sundry persons account in Ottawa. From the outset, the release process worked smoothly and without obstacle. Once London approved the release, depositors had various options in reclaiming their gold or its equivalent value. The Bank of Canada made it clear that it would not earmark gold for private citizens and that the gold would have to be claimed and taken away. Upon release, gold could be shipped to England or another European country through the intermediary of a Canadian chartered bank. This would necessitate the obtaining of an export permit and the payment of shipping charges. The Bank of Canada itself offered on behalf of the minister of finance to buy small amounts of gold, but warned that this might snare foreigners in Canada's non-resident foreign exchange controls and thereby make the proceeds of the sale non-convertible. It was also suggested that if the central bank of the depositor's homeland had an Ottawa earmark account, the gold might be sold to it and the depositor receive payment in the national currency. It was, for instance, suggested by the Bank of Canada that the Banque Nationale Suisse might buy the gold of Swiss nationals in return for francs.

By May 1946, instructions began arriving at the Bank of Canada for the disposition of gold held in the sundry persons account. By 1955, 107 such requests were received and processed. In all these cases of release, the Bank of Canada had received assurance from the Bank of England that London had satisfied itself that none of the claimants were of enemy origin. Sometimes these claims came directly from the depositor or his/her agent. Sometimes they came from a Canadian chartered bank that had been instructed to collect the gold and forward it or sell it in behalf of the depositor. Whatever the instruction, the Bank acted expeditiously. Demand for transfer not surprisingly peaked in 1946 and 1947, with 84 requests processed, but claims were registered throughout the rest of the decade. In 1949, for instance, a lawyer in London, England, wrote to claim gold in the account on behalf of the sole heir of a wartime depositor in the sundry persons account who had subsequently died. The Bank of England had approved the release and a New York lawyer had been designated to collect the gold. "We understand," the letter concluded, "that Mr. Katz [the client's lawyer] has already been in direct communication with you regarding the form in which the gold will be handed over, and we should be greatly obliged if you would give him any information he may require in this connection."[129] A Bank of Canada official pencilled at the bottom of the letter: "We have done so."

On June 7, 1955, the last sundry persons deposit was claimed and settled. When the Bank of Canada informed the Bank of England of this transaction, London replied that "the repayments under the Foreign Owned Gold Scheme are now complete." The account should therefore be closed. Since the Bank of England had also employed the same account to hold various small amounts of gold for other purposes, it instructed Ottawa to transfer the residue of the account – some gold coin – into its main Bank of Canada account. The chief cashier of the Bank of England ended his letter of instruction to Ottawa by noting: "I should like to take this opportunity of expressing the Bank's thanks for your co-operation over the years in the administration of the Scheme." The Bank of Canada's June 28 acknowledgement of this instruction is the last piece of correspondence in the sundry persons account file. In effect, it marks the end of the Bank of Canada's involvement in the earmarking of foreign gold in World War II.

The European Perspective:
1942–45

Any deal has two sides. There are buyers and sellers. In the case of earmarking gold in foreign central banks, there are in fact often more than two parties. That is to say, an initial deposit of earmarked gold naturally involves the depositor and the host bank. If the depositor, however, subsequently decides to transfer ownership to another central bank and requests the host bank to do so, three parties become involved in the process. While the old owner of the gold and its new holder may be fully aware of the circumstances prompting the transfer, the host bank will usually know no more than the bare terms of the transfer instruction. For the host bank, it is a simple custodial function. Elsewhere in this report, it has been argued that the advent of war in 1939 obliged the Bank of Canada to modify the conditions under which it would take instruction from its earmark clients, but the relationship still largely remained one of instruction without explication of purpose. Only the Bank of England, with its intimate contacts with the senior officers of the Bank of Canada, usually revealed the pressures behind its needs. Hence, the Bank of Canada was in many instances a blind participant in fiscal transactions that touched the gold in its vaults. As a result, the Bank of Canada's records tell only one side of a story and cast only a partial light on the motivations of its European partners.

GATHERING HISTORICAL INFORMATION IN EUROPE

Creating some sense of the European side of these gold swaps presented formidable challenges. Time was precious and the logistics were daunting. There was no assured access to the archives of European central banks. Language barriers loomed. Records procedures would undoubtedly be unfamiliar. Other countries had their own access-to-information and privacy protocols. There was, however, one very encouraging sign. Since 1995, European central and commercial banks in England, Switzerland, Portugal and Sweden had been prompted by public controversy over the issue of Nazi gold and dormant bank accounts to launch historical investigations into their own roles in wartime financial arrangements. By the summer of 1997, these investigations were well under way and receptive to outside inquiry. They were largely staffed by independent professional historians and accountants who had been given a wide mandate to present as thorough and transparent an analysis of each bank's wartime role as their records made possible. In light of this opportunity, it was decided that the most expedient means of creating some sense of a European perspective was to approach each of these institutions or commissions with a detailed request for information on the 1942–44 gold swaps.

Approaches were therefore made to five historical commissions/teams currently active in Europe. Four are working under the auspices of their central banks: the Bank of England, the Banco de Portugal, Sveriges Riksbank and the

Banque Nationale Suisse (BNS). The fifth was the Commonwealth and Foreign Office in London, a group that has been actively reporting its wartime gold research under the title Nazi Gold. The requests from Canada were tailored to the particular role played by each nation in wartime financial arrangements, with a special eye to its contacts with Canada and its central bank. These requests all contained some common elements. Were there records of the specific transactions that involved the Bank of Canada in the 1942–1944 period? Were there other references to Canada's role in wartime transatlantic financial arrangements? Did their files contain any memoranda or background papers that shed light on how Canada fit, if at all, into their country's overall wartime financial strategy? Could their research provide any sense of the real motivation that lay behind these swap transactions? In each case, the request contained detailed information, drawn from Bank of Canada records, guiding the recipient to the specific events that involved Canada (e.g., the Anglo-Swiss francs-for-gold swap and the subsequent gold transfer from Switzerland to Portugal in the spring of 1942). These requests were all despatched to Europe in the last week of August 1997.

Without exception, all the requests met with a cooperative response. All were quickly acknowledged and brought some sense of when a detailed response could be expected. Most of the respondents commented on the heavy pressure under which they themselves were operating in trying to fulfil the mandates set by their own central banks. It should be acknowledged that the archives of the Bank of England and the Banque Nationale Suisse were especially forthcoming in responding to our requests. The Bank of England, for instance, arranged for large sections of their files relating to Canada to be microfilmed and sent by courier to Canada. Not one of the respondents set any condition on their willingness to furnish us with information. (In the wake of the recent controversies surrounding the Nazi gold issue in Europe, there now appears to be broad understanding of the high price in public credibility that banks will pay for being unwilling to be open to public attention in these matters).

The subsequent arrival throughout September of dossiers of information from the five historical groups in Europe allowed a fairly coherent picture of the European perspective on the gold swaps of 1942–44 to be reliably pieced together. As these reports became available, one fairly common trait emerged: there was very little documentary trace or present-day consciousness of Canada or the Bank of Canada in the European historical work on this issue. With the exception of the Bank of England, which reported the existence of ten files relating to Canada, the other respondents all invariably commented that their search for documents and their examination of their own research yielded little on Canada. In all of their minds, Canada seemed to occupy a marginal role in the reconstruction of wartime financial relations that they were undertaking. A good example of this was provided in the prompt and cooperative response to our August inquiry by Dr. Gill Bennett, head of historians, at the Foreign and Commonwealth Office in London. Bennett's group has been busy researching Britain's part in wartime gold for over a year and has produced two studies of their findings under the title *Nazi Gold : Information from the British Archives*, published in September 1996 and May 1997. Bennett wrote in response to our inquiry:

> ... I have looked through the documentation we have collected on Nazi gold for any references of gold to Canada before or during the Second World War, but without success. There may be references to such transfers in files at the Public Record Office [Britain's national archive], but the Foreign Office Index for 1942, for example, does not indicate the presence of such information either under headings for Banks and Banking, Canada, or Switzerland. It would be necessary to check each reference to Canada and Switzerland under the broader heading of 'Gold' to be sure ... The fact that we have found no references in the large amount of material we already hold here leads me to think, however, that such an effort may well yield disappointing results.[130]

It bears reiteration that the massive American study of wartime gold commissioned by President Clinton and headed by Under Secretary of Commerce Stuart Eizenstat – *U.S. and Allied Efforts To Recover and Restore Gold and Other Assets Stolen or Hidden by Germany During World War II* (Washington, 1997) – does not contain a single reference to Canada. The Eizenstat report was based on research among some 15 million pages of documents in the National Archives in Washington. When this trove of documents was reviewed by researchers from the World Jewish Congress, only a single document implicating Canada was uncovered – the 1944 "From a very Confidential Source" memorandum alleging gold laundering through Ottawa. It was that document that quite appropriately triggered this project.

The scant impression left in Europe of Canada's wartime role in gold in no way deterred our efforts to reconstruct the motivation that lay behind the actions of the European parties to the swaps of 1942–44. In the material supplied to us, three distinct episodes were examined: the initial swap of British gold for Swiss francs between 1942 and 1943, the 1942 swap of part of this gold from Switzerland to Portugal and the 1944 swap of Portuguese gold to Sweden in company with a further transfer of Swiss gold to Portugal. The following reconstructions were therefore based on a mixture of original central bank documentation, documents emerging out of the postwar Allied effort to identify looted gold and present-day historians' opinion.

THE ANGLO-SWISS GOLD-FOR-FRANCS SWAP OF 1942–43

It was the 56 tons of gold that England provided Switzerland with through 1942–43 in exchange for Swiss francs that provided the feedstock of bullion for the subsequent contentious swaps between the Swiss and the Portuguese and, ultimately, between the Portuguese and the Swedes. This gold never physically left Ottawa. It was part of the Bank of England's earmark account at the Bank of Canada, built up by outright purchase and actual transfer from England in the late 1930s and the early war years. There is therefore absolutely no possibility that the gold in question was tainted in the sense of containing gold looted by the Germans in Europe. This was clean gold. What is more appropriately in question is the motivation that first led Britain to begin transferring ownership of the gold to neutral Switzerland in 1942, thereby putting the neutral Swiss in a position to redeploy some of this gold to the earmark accounts of other neutral powers in Ottawa.

Two factors above all else explain the Anglo-Swiss swap of 1942: Britain's desperate need for Swiss francs and Switzerland's need for gold and British trade to stabilize its commercial and financial performance. As has been explained in an excellent paper by Professor Neville Wylie of Cambridge University, "London's acute shortage of Swiss currency" in the early years of the war coloured its entire attitude to neutral Switzerland.[131] This shortage was "perennial" and was rooted in Switzerland's prewar balance of trade surplus with Britain. In 1938, for instance, Switzerland exported SFr149.7 million in goods to Britain, but imported only SFr97.2 million. By 1940, the gap had narrowed – SFr96.6 million in exports to SFr89.6 million in imports.[132] What had changed in war was Britain's ability to find the francs to cover its purchases of Swiss goods, many of which were directly related to Britain's war economy and military needs. Even after her ability to trade directly with Switzerland was restricted by the Axis encirclement of the neutral Swiss in 1940, Britain kept trading with the Swiss, even if this necessitated smuggling goods out of the country.[133] Other invisible expenses, such as the cost of maintaining a legation and possibly supporting covert operations based in Switzerland, also placed demands on Britain's supply of francs. To replenish its supply of francs, Britain sold sterling, Bank of England gold and eventually drew on its own cache of U.S. dollars to procure francs.

By early 1942, francs were becoming harder to procure. The United States had issued injunctions against the use of its dollars in European trade for fear that they would find their way into Axis coffers. For a while, Britain even skirted these regulations by drawing dollars out of commercial banks in New York so as not to alert the U.S. Federal Reserve to its activities. However, Britain's obligation to the United States under the 1941 Lend-Lease Agreement and America's subsequent entry into the war ended this expedient and deceptive means of securing hard currency for trading with Switzerland.

In a parallel subterfuge, the British ignored Swiss requests that the Bank of England transfer part of its store of earmarked gold from London to safer New York. Instead, the Bank of England added some of the Swiss gold to its own transfers of earmarked gold to Ottawa and retained the rest in London. Thus, the British retained control over Swiss gold either in London or in Ottawa, thereby providing themselves with a possible hedge in their commercial relations with the Swiss. Thus, as Professor Wylie has pointed out, by "the winter of 1941–42, the Bank of England was doubly compromised," having gone counter to American currency regulations and at the same time undermined Swiss efforts to find safe haven for their gold in the United States.

This delicate situation became worse when in early 1942 the Swiss, heeding American warnings, refused to take any more U.S. dollars from the British. This coincided with British anxiety that Switzerland was trading too heavily with the Axis. In July 1941, a Swiss-German economic agreement had provided Germany with a credit of SFr850 million that the British viewed with alarm and immediately countered with restrictions on exports of British raw materials to Switzerland. If Switzerland limited its exports to the Axis or increased its shipments of strategic goods to Britain, the British said that they would ease their restrictions on exports to Switzerland. At this awkward juncture, the British hit on the idea of raising francs by selling their gold earmarked in Ottawa or sterling blocked in foreign banks in exchange for Swiss francs. This was exactly the import of Montagu Norman's March 8, 1942, cable to Bank of Canada Governor Graham Towers: ". . . Difficulties have lately arisen mainly owing to United States freezing policy. Swiss are now reluctant to accept U.S. dollars without special license for their transfer to third party . . ."[134] Negotiations were under way to test the Swiss reaction to this offer, Norman reported.

The Swiss were not enthusiastic. As Switzerland's central bank, the Banque Nationale Suisse were tasked with keeping Swiss inflation under control, and in an economy being fanned by wartime demand this meant maintaining a reserve of gold and/or foreign currency within Switzerland's borders. The yardstick for this was a gold or foreign currency reserve equal to 40% of the money in circulation in Switzerland. This operation was already proving difficult because so much – between 33% and 50% by some estimates – of Switzerland's gold was already situated *outside* Switzerland, blocked in London and New York until the end of hostilities and therefore useless for purposes of internal monetary control. As Professor Wylie concludes: "The last thing the National Bank [BNS] wanted was to accumulate further quantities of sterling or gold in London which could not be touched until the end of the war." Adding to the pressure on the franc was the fact that Switzerland had in late 1941 agreed to take responsibility for protecting British assets blocked in Axis territories. This too required francs to flow from Britain to Switzerland and, to the dismay of the BNS, most of these francs went to non-commercial circulation, thereby exerting inflationary pressure on the Swiss economy. Rather than further jeopardize the internal stability of the Swiss economy, the BNS in March 1942 adopted an adamantly vigilant attitude toward any further release of francs for blocked gold beyond Switzerland's borders.

A protracted negotiation thus began in London. In February 1942, Berne appointed a delegation – composed of a government minister and two academics – to treat with the English. For both sides the issue was currency liquidity – the British appetite for francs and the Swiss desire to conserve francs and gold within their borders. Throughout 1942 and 1943, several tentative agreements were drafted but fell apart, usually because of disagreements over what materials were to be allowed to enter Switzerland in the wake of sterling/gold-for-francs swaps.

This impasse opened the way for the swap of British gold held in Ottawa for Swiss francs that began on March 25, 1942, with an initial transfer of 66,815 fine ounces from the Bank of England earmark account in Ottawa to the newly established account of the BNS in Ottawa. Both sides regarded the Ottawa arrangement as a *pro tem* measure, designed to feed the British with a minimum supply of francs to cover their basic needs (e.g., legation expenses) until some more durable arrangement could be negotiated in London. As a Bank of

England official noted in a letter of April 15, 1943: "... This is a purely temporary arrangement and one which the Swiss, with a declining gold stock at home, accept reluctantly."[135]

The Swiss were indeed extremely reluctant to enter this swap arrangement. As a BNS internal memo noted in mid-January: "While, on the one hand, the National Bank must hand over freely available Swiss francs and pay them out on behalf of the Bank of England in Switzerland and other countries, in return, it receives non-transferable pounds and gold stocks stored in Ottawa that, for all practical purposes, cannot be used by the Swiss economy during the war. The grave danger that this development represents for the Swiss price structure is clear. The question is whether it will be possible to eliminate the inflationary effects for the Federation or prevent the bank of issue from continually issuing new money via taxation and other measures that tie up market resources."[136] In short, blocked gold in New York or Ottawa could not be fed back into the Swiss economy or used to pay for its imports. Thus, Switzerland was unable to satisfy all of its internal demand for imports and inflation resulted from the fact that wartime demand outstripped supply. A Swiss exchange of francs for earmarked gold in Canada was a way of mopping up Swiss francs and reducing potential inflationary pressures in Switzerland.

The board of the BNS was by early February of 1942 still "not much in favour of a transfer of gold stocks to Canada."[137] The Swiss were eventually persuaded to accept this temporary gold-for-francs arrangement because, while the gold they were to receive by it was still blocked in the sense that it could not be brought directly to Switzerland, it was nonetheless freer to move than the blocked gold they had in London and New York, which was frozen hard *in situ* until the end of the war. As the minute book of the BNS board of directors noted on March 26, the gold it received on earmark in Canada "could be exported to other central banks in the Western Hemisphere and transferred to the same central banks, as well as to the central banks of the neutral European countries, Sweden, Spain and Portugal."[138] To some degree, therefore, the gold in Ottawa was portable and might through some combination of circumstances ultimately be brought home indirectly before the end of the war.

The swap of gold for francs in Ottawa thus satisfied, albeit temporarily and imperfectly, the needs of both Berne and London. The arrangement was the product of London's desperation and ingenuity and was clearly accepted *faute de mieux* by the Swiss. As Montagu Norman of the Bank of England noted, Swiss agreement "represented a concession by the Swiss National Bank to avoid a breakdown in the financial relations between the sterling area and Switzerland."[139] It provided the rationale for the 155 regular and relatively equal transfers of gold from British to Swiss ownership that followed throughout 1942 and 1943, feeding francs to the British, thereby keeping their financial lifeline to Switzerland in place. There is no documentary evidence, in either the Bank of Canada records or in the Bank of England files sent to us, that the Anglo-Swiss swap was designed to help Britain "assist prisoners of war in Germany," as Graham Towers told the Bank of Canada board of directors in June 1942. It is possible that some of the francs secured by the deal went to humanitarian payments via the Red Cross in Switzerland, but no proof of this has been found. Switzerland was also, for instance, a much-used gateway to freedom for escaped British prisoners of war, such passages to freedom required Swiss francs.

In December 1943 the British negotiators, still facing a chronic shortfall of francs in England, finally broke the deadlock by offering the Swiss what they had wanted all along: the ability to bring gold into neutral Europe. In practice, British gold would now be placed at the disposal of the Swiss, who could use it to satisfy their commercial accounts in Spain and Portugal, thereby conserving their hard currency and gold reserves at home. The agreement also freed hitherto blocked gold acquired in London by the Swiss during 1943 and placed it at Switzerland's disposal in neutral Europe. Significantly, the accord did not free Switzerland's accumulated earmarked gold in Ottawa, but instead reconfirmed the original conditions set upon it in 1942. The Ottawa gold would not be free for patriation to Switzerland until six months after the end of Britain's war with Germany. Not surprisingly, as soon as the Anglo-Swiss accord came into operation on January 1, 1944, the Swiss stopped accepting gold in Ottawa for francs. Ottawa gold was still blocked gold. Gold available in London was now more versatile.

What is striking from the perspective of this report is that both the Bank of England records submitted to us and the lengthy commentary and packet of documentation supplied by the Banque Nationale Suisse were in spontaneous agreement over the above course of events and the motivation behind it. Both saw Anglo-Swiss relations from 1939 to 1943 as essentially an ongoing liquidity crisis. The principal concern was to keep the flow of Anglo-Swiss wartime trade going and, particularly from the Swiss perspective, to allow the BNS to restrain inflationary pressures in the Swiss economy.[140] Anxiety over the possibility that looted German gold might find its way into the mainstream of European finance seemed to take a distinctly secondary role in these proceedings. The imposition of conditions that confined Swiss gold earmarked in Ottawa to movement within the Western Hemisphere and paper transfer to European neutrals seemed to provide London with the assurance that the integrity of its dealings with Switzerland was being protected.

THE SWISS-PORTUGUESE GOLD SWAP OF 1942

Thus, in the spring of 1942, gold owned by a European neutral power began to accumulate in Ottawa under earmark: 66,815 fine ounces on March 25, another 6,862 ounces on March 28, 13,328 ounces on April 7 – the payments quickly became regular. By the end of 1943, the transfers would equal 56 tons of gold. Ottawa became one of Switzerland's offshore gold havens, never rivalling New York and London in the magnitude of its holdings, but joining Stockholm and Buenos Aires as secondary locations of earmarked gold. Despite the delicate balance of its internal monetary affairs, Switzerland continued to be a net purchaser of gold from the Allies throughout the war. The United States was the principal seller of gold to the Swiss, selling some SFr178.2 million from 1939 to 1945. Britain followed with sales (that would have included the gold earmarked for Switzerland in Ottawa) of SFr580 million, while the French Vichy government sold SFr117 million in gold to the Swiss during the war (although their sales were packed into 1942 and 1945). Even Canada sold Canadian-produced gold to the Swiss, some SFr5.3 million worth, much of it sold after the British and Swiss struck their January 1944 deal to allow Allied gold freer access into Europe.[141]

Only one country sold more gold to the Swiss than the Americans – Germany. From 1939 to 1945, the Reichsbank sold SFr1,210.3 million worth of gold to the Banque Nationale Suisse. A large portion of this passed through Switzerland to other neutral countries in Europe that were trading with the Axis. Portugal took SFr451.5 million and Spain SFr185.2 million.[142] Gold transfers into Switzerland were paralleled by a flow of usable foreign currencies into Switzerland. Much of the gold looted from the vaults of European countries that had fallen under Axis occupation; some small amount of it was already probably non-monetary gold stripped from citizens of these same countries.

By late 1941, the Allies, sensing that Germany's meagre prewar reserve of gold was long spent in the initial years of the war, began suspecting that Germany was financing its war effort with looted gold. The British Ministry of Economic Warfare and the newly created Office of Strategic Services in the United States began to monitor gold flows out of Germany. In mid-1942, the British began pressuring the other Allies for some sort of diplomatic injunction against countries accepting looted goods in trade with the Axis. These early efforts were piecemeal and the knowledge of the full extent of Axis bartering of looted gold still vague. But one of the first clear realizations was that the Banco de Portugal was the primary recipient of Banque Nationale Suisse exports of gold, a fact that was quickly linked to the belief that much of this Iberian-bound gold was of Axis origin. At the heart of this early intelligence was the discovery that the Banco de Portugal maintained four accounts at the BNS: Accounts 'A', 'B', 'C' and 'D'. Allied intelligence and postwar account reconstructions have strongly tended to the view that it was accounts B, C and D that the Banco de Portugal employed to carry looted gold from Berne to Lisbon, leaving account A as a legitimate account. For example, a British intelligence report dated August 31, 1944, noted that "intercepts" of coded Portuguese communications indicated that "the gold sold by the Bank of Portugal came from their Account 'B' at the National Bank of Switzerland, i.e., gold with a German taint."[143] Another Allied intelligence document dated September 22, 1944, recapitulated the "estimated gold holdings of the Bank of Portugal at 30/6/44" and indicated that the overwhelming amount of gold "consigned to Portugal" was both received from the BNS and drawn to Lisbon from accounts B and C. Account A registered minimal activity with few transfers to Lisbon and was generally believed to contain only clean (i.e., untainted by Axis looting) gold.[144] While this pattern of moving gold from the Reichsbank through Switzerland to Portugal was only imperfectly understood by Allied intelligence in 1942, its contours were of course familiar to the BNS.

Despite the fact that the Anglo-Swiss gold-for-francs swap was in place in the late spring of 1942, Switzerland still faced the same monetary dilemma. It need-

ed gold and hard currency to secure the internal stability of its wartime economy. Negotiations in London had bogged down. Thought therefore soon turned
to ways in which the BNS's mounting store of gold in Ottawa could be directed
to Switzerland's monetary advantage. Could the unique hemispheric conditions
imposed upon is physical movement and paper transfer be somehow turned to
Switzerland's pressing monetary needs? Probably the first test of these conditions came on April 28, 1942 – just a month after the first swap payments
entered the BNS's new Ottawa account – when the BNS cabled the Bank of
Canada to inquire whether a Swiss commercial bank could open a gold account
at the Bank of Canada or if the Bank of Canada would permit the BNS to make
a "special gold deposit with your bank under our name," such deposit to contain gold owned by a Swiss commercial bank.[145] The request aroused suspicion
in Ottawa. Towers cabled Norman: "We are curious to learn what gave rise to
the inquiry and before replying should like to know if you have any comments
to offer."[146] The Bank of England answered that the purpose of the BNS proposal was all too apparent. Dual BNS-Swiss commercial bank accounts in
Ottawa would allow the BNS to transfer gold between these accounts in
Ottawa, thereby allowing it to take gold in Switzerland acquired by commercial
banks (possibly from dubious sources) in return for legitimate, but blocked, gold
in Ottawa. When Graham Towers referred the proposition to Montagu
Norman in London, the Bank of England adamantly opposed the idea. "We
suspect," Norman told Towers, "therefore that the Swiss National Bank proposes to buy gold in Switzerland irrespective repeat irrespective of origin and
ownership either against sales of equivalent gold in Canada or a guarantee to
the original holders that the Swiss National Bank holds the equivalent gold in
Canada to his order."[147] On May 2, the Bank of Canada shut the door on the
Swiss proposal: "... under existing conditions there are obstacles in the way of
acceptance of gold deposits unless the gold is the property of a central bank. We
regret to advise therefore that it would not be possible for us to enter into the
arrangements mentioned in your cable."[148] In the wake of this decision,
Governor Towers sent a circular letter to all the general managers of Canada's
chartered banks requesting that, in deference to the government's wishes, they
not open any new gold earmark accounts for non-residents and to report any
such requests to the Bank of Canada.[149]

The BNS, however, already had an alternative plan. A week before it tested
the idea of opening Swiss commercial accounts in Canada, it instructed the
Bank of Canada on April 21 to transfer 64,395 fine ounces of its newly acquired
Ottawa gold to the Banco de Portugal. There was evident haste in this request,
since the Portuguese did not as yet officially have an account in Ottawa. Once
that was accomplished on April 30, the BNS cabled that another 64,837 fine
ounces be credited to the new Portuguese account.[150] Thus, within two weeks
the Banco de Portugal acquired four tons of earmarked gold in Ottawa. Since
the transfer took place entirely within the terms of the original Anglo-Swiss
swap – the gold had been transferred to the central bank of another European
neutral power and was not physically leaving the country – the deal occasioned
no undue comment in Ottawa. Ottawa had no idea of what transaction lay

behind the BNS transfer of four tons of its gold; the host to an earmark account merely followed the instructions transmitted to it by a client.

What the Canadians did not know was that in releasing four tons of its blocked gold in Ottawa the BNS had gained possession of a similar quantity of gold in Berne out of the account of the Banco de Portugal. Four tons of gold blocked in Ottawa until the end of hostilities had thus been in effect patriated to support the domestic requirements of the BNS. Before striking this deal with the Portuguese, the BNS had offered a similar trade to the Riksbank in Stockholm, but the Swedes had declined.[151] Why would the Banco de Portugal facilitate such a deal, a deal that left it with gold blocked on the other side of the Atlantic? Principally because the Swiss were prepared to pay a hefty commission to Portugal on the transaction. The initial April 22 swap of Berne-for-Ottawa gold cost the BNS a commission of 1.5% and the subsequent swap of May 5 brought a handsome 2.5% commission. The total cost of these commissions was therefore approximately SFr428,000 on a total sale of SFr19.56 million. At its May 7, 1942, meeting, the BNS board of directors decided that such commissions were "too high to speak about" and dropped any further thought of swapping gold in Ottawa with the Portuguese.[152] With negotiations with the British still producing little result in London, the BNS was still sorely tempted to parlay its Canadian earmarked gold to its European advantage. In June of the same year, the BNS learned that the Riksbank in Stockholm had an ample supply of Swiss francs – francs that if patriated could serve the BNS's domestic needs – and suggested that it might acquire some of these by selling the Swedes gold in Ottawa. The Swedes declined. Later, in September 1942, the BNS sent a delegation to Lisbon and then Stockholm again to try to swap gold in Ottawa for francs in neutral Europe. Again, the offer was spurned; blocked gold in Ottawa had little allure.[153]

What was the origin of the four tons of Portuguese gold that the BNS now owned in Berne? Nobody in Ottawa asked. Neither did the Bank of England signal any interest in its cables across the Atlantic, even though it was acting as the Banco de Portugal's intermediary with the Canadians. Others closer to the actual swap did wonder. On June 25, 1942, David Eccles at the British Embassy in Lisbon expressed his concerns to the Ministry of Economic Warfare – the arm of government that oversaw Britain's economic campaign against the Axis – in London:

> You will have seen the reports of the gold transactions between the Bank of Portugal and the Swiss National Bank, whereby the former has taken over gold belonging to the latter in Canada and released to the Swiss Bank gold belonging to itself deposited in Switzerland. As far as I see, the result of this transaction is to free gold in Switzerland, which the Germans may now get hold of. I do not know what are the estimated quantities of gold available to the Germans, but if there is any question of their running short for purposes including selling gold to Bank of Portugal, I should have thought we should not allow the Bank of Canada to oblige the Bank of Portugal in this way.
>
> As I am not properly informed on this subject it may well be that such transactions are completely harmless . . .[154]

In July, Eccles got a reply from the ministry in London, a reply that reiterated the facts of the original deal struck between the British and the Swiss:

> . . . The Swiss refuse to give us Swiss francs against dollars which they could not use to pay to Portugal . . . since they have to meet a deficit with Portugal. It is essential for us to obtain the Swiss francs we need and we reached a provisional arrangement to obtain them against gold in Canada which would be available to be earmarked in Canada for Portugal. As you rightly say, this prevents the Swiss from having to deplete their gold reserves in order to pay Portugal, and naturally we should like Switzerland to have as little gold as possible for fear Germany may get hold of it. However, the Swiss have told us that they do not supply the Germans with gold and we have no reason to believe that up to the present they have done so.[155]

This interpretation apparently retained its currency in London's corridors of wartime economic power. In August 1944, a memorandum prepared by the Overseas and Foreign Office – a memorandum that drew on intercepted communications between Lisbon and Berne – again described the origin of the gold the Portuguese had delivered to the BNS in 1942:

> . . . The Ports obtained gold in Canada from the Swiss, by means of an exchange of Account A * gold against gold in Ottawa.

Central to the British reading of the Banco de Portugal's financial dealings with the Banque Nationale Suisse in the mid-war years was the role of its various accounts in Berne. Of the four Portuguese accounts maintained at the BNS – A, B, C, and D – British intelligence usually identified account A as a clean account. Accounts B and C, however, were usually described as containing "gold with a German taint."[157]

There was persistent commentary in the communications between British diplomats in Lisbon and London about the use of these accounts as conduits for tainted gold moving from the BNS to the Banco de Portugal deposit in Switzerland and thence being physically shipped to Lisbon. A memorandum of September 1944 entitled "Gold Imports into Portugal" and signed by Sir Stanley Wyatt, British ambassador to Lisbon, for instance, suggested that the Banco de Portugal held gold – about 11,000 kilos acquired in 1942 from the BNS – bearing Soviet markings and that "the greater part of this gold originated from occupied countries."[158] Throughout the mid-war, the Allies made periodic attempts to calculate the extent and origin of the growing Portuguese holdings of gold. One estimate in September 1944 furnished a summary that suggested that Portugal had acquired 363.5 thousand kilos of gold through Switzerland. The two largest streams of gold reaching Portugal, besides gold purchased for dollars in the United States, were described as "purchased from B.N.S. against Sfcs (? from Reichsbank) and consigned from deposit 'B' with B.N.S." and as being "purchased from Reichsbank and consigned from deposit 'C' with B.N.S." Gold in account A was described as "purchased from B.N.S. against escudos and consigned from deposit 'A' with B.N.S."[159]

---

* Thought to be without German taint.[156]

Historical data released by the Banco de Portugal in April 1997 confirm these patterns. The largest European acquisitions of gold by the Banco de Portugal were made through its accounts B and C at the BNS, the latter account in particular serving as the channel for gold acquired from the Reichsbank. Gold movement figures for 1942 show two entries representing the transfers involving Canada: one for 2,018 kilos of gold in account A and a second for 2,000 kilos of gold in account B. This obviously partially contradicts the opinion in the minds of British commentators that all the 1942 transfer was drawn out of account A. Nonetheless, *none* of the transactions appears to have been drawn from the principal Reichsbank account, C.[160] The commentary accompanying these statistics – commentary ultimately presented to the United States House of Representatives Committee on Banking and Financial Services in June 1997 – stressed the fact that gold accumulation was Portugal's preferred strategy of shoring up the external value of Portugal's currency, a policy applied to "any trade partner of the country."[161] It is perhaps worth noting that, when the war in Europe drew to a close in mid-1945, Bank of Canada Governor Graham Towers drew up a report on the financial condition of Europe. "Portugal," he reported, "has done well out of the war, accumulating $75 millions and large amounts of gold and dollars."[162]

Did Canada unwittingly facilitate the laundering of tainted German gold in the spring of 1942? The swap of Swiss gold earmarked in Ottawa for Portuguese gold deposited in Switzerland was first and foremost driven by Swiss monetary needs, *not* Portuguese needs. The imperative of bolstering the domestic requirements of the Banque Nationale Suisse in its fight against inflation was the paramount motive in the whole transaction. This need was sufficiently powerful to persuade the Swiss to pay a stiff transfer commission to prod the Banco de Portugal into accepting gold on the other side of the Atlantic that was blocked until the end of the war. The commission was daunting enough to dissuade the BNS from pursuing the strategy of further using its clean gold in Canada as a bargaining chip in its European operations.

It is, however, impossible to say with absolute surety that the four tons of gold that the Banque Nationale Suisse received in Europe from the Banco de Portugal in return for its Ottawa gold was also untainted. Contemporary intelligence reports reflected the belief that the gold was "without German taint". Similarly, the gold appeared to be drawn from accounts maintained by the Banco de Portugal that were not generally perceived as being the principal conduits for tainted Nazi gold on its journey from its looted origins to the mainstream of legitimate finance. If swapping gold in Switzerland for clean, if blocked, gold in Canada was an effective means of laundering gold, why did Portugal not employ the tactic again, especially in light of the handsome commission the Swiss were prepared to pay on the transaction? After all, Switzerland still had gold left in Ottawa after the first four tons had been transferred. But there is no record whatsoever of the Portuguese ever asking to duplicate the transaction. In fact, the Banco de Portugal spurned the BNS's offer of further sales in mid–1942. Other contemporary intelligence reports and a convincing burden of more recent research indicate that Portugal had more expedient ways of moving gold from Germany's borders through Switzerland to Portugal. There was little inclination or incentive to detour through distant Ottawa.

THE PORTUGUESE-SWEDISH-SWISS GOLD SWAPS OF 1944-45

During 1942-43, growing recognition that gold looted by the Germans was making its way to the outside world through neutral countries began to be reflected in a tightening of Allied policy around the countries believed to the middlemen in the trade. In January 1943, 17 nations signed the "Inter-Allied Declaration Against Acts of Dispossession." The signatories reserved the right to declare invalid any transfers of property taken out of countries occupied by the Axis when peace returned to Europe. The declaration did not specifically mention looted gold, but a subsequent February 1944 declaration by the United states emphatically stated that the Americans, who would plainly be the driving force of postwar economic activity, would not recognize title to any gold that had been moved by Germany onto world markets during the war. Britain and the Soviet Union quickly echoed this policy, thereby sending European powers that were alleged to be involved in the trade clear warning that they did so at their own financial peril. In the spring of 1944, the search for Nazi gold became active as the U.S. Treasury Department initiated its Safehaven program, which began to actively seek evidence of the dispersement of looted gold. Despite these early injunctions, the Banco de Portugal's gold reserves continued to rise steadily through the 1943-45 period.[163]

Paralleling its acquisition of gold, Portugal had been an active participant in European wartime trade, capitalizing on its strength in such strategic minerals as tungsten – used to harden steel – while at the same time maintaining its more normal commercial relations with European trading partners. These included trade with its oldest trading partner, Britain, which since signing a 1940 agreement between their two central banks had allowed its trade with Portugal to be conducted in sterling. The settling of Portugal's trade accounts with other countries was, however, less straightforward and more problematic. Once the war had made the reichmark an unconvertible currency, Portuguese trade with the Axis was generally financed by German payment in gold, gold usually transferred through accounts at the BNS in Switzerland. In 1941, the Banco de Portugal and the BNS signed a central bank agreement that regulated payment between the two countries. At the same time, Portugal tried to maintain its commerce with other European trading partners such as Sweden by using gold to secure hard currency to satisfy its accounts with these countries.

Throughout 1944, the turning tide of the war began to have a constricting effect on the financing of inter-European commerce. Looted gold had now acquired a second taint; few would accept it as a form of payment for fear that its true origins might be exposed with the peace, opening the way to Allied confiscation. At the same time, countries with large holdings of such gold grew anxious to rid themselves of the liability they represented. "Source states," a British secret report copied to the Bank of England warned in August 1944, "that the

Bank of Portugal is now endeavouring to liquidate the larger part of its gold holdings in Switzerland. These consist almost exclusively of German gold deposited by the Reichsbank. The Bank intends to utilize these deposits to cover imports from Switzerland or Sweden."[164] A month later there were even reports of German gold being transported by air via Spain to Portugal, where it was being smelted into Portuguese ingots and hoarded for "a postwar credit for the Germans."[165]

Amid these pressures and rumours, Canada again found a small role in the disposition of European gold. It began innocuously enough in mid-February 1944, when the Swedish ambassador to Canada paid a visit to the Bank of Canada and inquired into opening an account in Ottawa. The purpose of the account would be to allow the Sveriges Riksbank, Sweden's central bank, to buy newly minted Canadian gold and earmark it in Canada. This the Canadians were prepared to do at six cents below the going New York rate (a discount made possible by the saving of not shipping the gold to New York) as long as gold was available surplus to Canada's own needs. Early in March, the Riksbank exercised this option, buying 1,076 bars of Canadian gold for earmark and agreeing to the usual condition that it could physically export the gold only within the Western Hemisphere or transfer the gold on paper to central banks of Allied or neutral European powers.[166] The deputy minister of finance routinely approved the transaction. The Bank of Canada had another wartime earmark client. There is nothing in the correspondence covering the opening of this new account to suggest that there was an ulterior motive behind the Swedish initiative. Sweden appeared to be applying some of its U.S. dollar holdings to the acquisition of gold at a good price.

Events in Europe would soon create a new purpose for the account. By the summer of 1944, Portugal was experiencing real difficulty converting gold into the hard currencies that fuelled its trade with Switzerland and Sweden. The exchange rate in Lisbon on the Swiss franc and the Swedish krona climbed in relation to the Portuguese escudo. In early August, the Banco de Portugal instructed local banks not to sell francs or kronor except for the purpose of "conventional transactions." Under the agreement signed in 1941 between the Banco de Portugal and the BNS, the Portuguese had the right to sell gold to the Swiss in exchange for francs that would then be applied to financing Swiss-Portuguese trade. In August 1944, however, the Swiss learned that the Portuguese were in fact selling them gold for francs, but then using the francs to purchase Swedish kronor to finance their trade with Sweden. The Swiss complained and reminded the Portuguese that francs obtained for gold must be fed back into Swiss trade with Portugal. The Banco de Portugal assured the Swiss that the gold sales were to cover commercial transactions with Sweden only. The BNS did allow one such gold-for-francs-for-kronor swap to take place, but then insisted that the Portuguese respect the 1941 agreement. In desperation, the Portuguese then suggested various schemes to the Swedes, all of which revolved around the Swedes buying some form of Portuguese gold in return for kronor or swapping gold in Stockholm for gold in Berne. The Swedes proved very reluctant to accept any form of Portuguese gold in Europe and in fact were even reluctant to acquire escudos. The Swedes may have sensed what Allied intercept had already revealed: the Portuguese were selling gold out of their B account – gold with German taint.

Confronted with Swiss intransigence and Swedish hesitancy, the Portuguese then struck upon the idea of offering the Swedes gold – gold that was undeniably clean – in their Canadian earmark account in return for kronor in Stockholm. The Swedes replied cautiously, asking whether the Portuguese would promise to spend the kronor they received from the deal solely for trade with Sweden. On August 30, the Banco de Portugal, possibly responding to a Swedish request about the quality of the gold in Ottawa, asked the Bank of Canada to reconfirm that the 321 bars in its earmark were "good delivery New York." They were. With these assurances, the Swedes and the Portuguese struck a deal. On September 6, the Banco de Portugal instructed Ottawa to transfer "about 1000 kilos gold fine" – 32,174 fine ounces – into the Riksbank account in Ottawa. On October 2, another 500 kilos – 16,108 fine ounces – followed.[167] The Riksbank agreed as long as the kronor it received were derived from "normal commercial transactions." The Swedes agreed to honour this reswap arrangement for six months until April 26, 1945, at which time they would be "prepared to reconsider the matter."

On November 21, the new agreement was activated. A half ton of gold was returned to the Banco de Portugal's account. On November 24, another half ton followed. Another half ton was returned on January 5, 1945, in effect cancelling the original 1944 Portuguese-Swedish swap. But then the tide turned again, and in six separate transfers between May 7 and September 13, 1945, the Portuguese transferred gold totalling two and a half tons back to the Swedes in Ottawa.[169] Coincidentally, the Riksbank bought more gold – 1,230 bars – directly from the mint in Ottawa through the minister of finance.

This tango of Portuguese-Swedish swaps was accompanied by one last Portuguese-Swiss swap. On September 19, the Banque Nationale Suisse instructed the Bank of Canada to transfer two tons – 64,386 fine ounces – of gold to the Banco de Portugal's earmark account in Ottawa.[170] Unlike the 1942 transactions, the BNS paid a much lower commission on this transfer, only ³⁄₈%.[171] Once again, the Portuguese drew their gold from their A account at the BNS, the account generally believed to be without German taint. Statistics supplied by the Banco de Portugal show a withdrawal of 2,001 kilograms from account A in 1944.[172] There is no definitive explanation for this Portuguese-Swiss swap. Coming a week after the initial Portuguese swap with Sweden, it may have been occasioned by a Portuguese desire to replenish its Ottawa stock of clean gold in case its need of kronor necessitated further Swedish swaps, swaps that would take it beyond the two tons it by then had left in Ottawa. Hence Portugal's willingness to accept a much lower commission. Switzerland may well have been ready to facilitate this swap because it promised to ease Portugal's liquidity problems, thereby easing Switzerland's own strained exchange situation with Portugal. This is, however, only speculation. The BNS's own recent interpretation of the swap suggests that it "seems to have been motivated by a desire to avoid the cost of transporting gold from Bern to Portugal."[173]

Thus ended Ottawa's role in the wartime swapping of gold between the accounts of the central banks of neutral Europe at the Bank of Canada. The flurry of late-war swaps between Portugal, Sweden and Switzerland passed with absolutely no undue concern in the Bank of Canada. These swaps followed a pattern that was by 1944 familiar to the Bank's officials and to the deputy minister of finance. There is no written record of any sense of anxiety or alarm over the requests for transfer received from European central banks. Similarly, the record of these events supplied to us by the European banks involved – a record admittedly viewed at arm's length – gives every indication that the gold swaps that took place through the auspices of the Bank of Canada from 1942 to 1945 were driven by liquidity concerns, not by a desire to launder dirty gold into clean gold. There were too many other ways to pass off bad gold under the cover of war in Europe for the route through Ottawa to ever have had much appeal as a site for laundering gold. Documents can, however, lie. And it is in the nature of human deviousness that some acts are never captured for posterity in the first place. We can never therefore be absolutely sure that Ottawa did not unwittingly aid the designs of gold launderers, but the burden of evidence would suggest otherwise.

On July 11, 1945, the Banque Nationale Suisse cabled Ottawa to inquire whether the restrictions that had since 1942 conditioned their ability to dispose of their Canadian gold were finally in abeyance. Peace, they suggested, meant that "these restrictions have lost their importance." Ottawa concurred, but reminded the BNS that an export licence was still required and that until peace returned in the Pacific some countries were still considered "enemy." No dramatic withdrawals of gold followed. The Swedes, Portuguese and Swiss all kept their Ottawa accounts after the peace.

In 1955, a ripple of horror spread through the Bank of Canada when it was discovered that deep in its vault was a small holding of what were described as "Prussian gold bars." There was concern that the 597 bars might be "tainted" and had somehow slipped into the Bank's gold reserves as a result of wartime acquisition. A quick check revealed that they had in fact come to the Bank as part of a shipment from the Bank of England and that they were tainted only in that they were not "good delivery London" (i.e., they had been manufactured by a prewar German refiner, whose products were, in the 1950s, no longer acceptable in international gold markets). The "Prussian" bars were subsequently remelted and integrated into the supply of acceptable gold.[174] In a real way, this was probably as close as the Bank of Canada ever got to actual tainted gold crossing the portal of its vault.

Commentary: Due Diligence?

Like gold, public policy can be assayed – its purity tested and reported. This study has focused almost exclusively on the origin and disposition of six tons of gold in the vault of the Bank of Canada, gold that began the war as British property and ended the war in the accounts of the Portuguese and Swedish central banks. By the standards of Allied and Axis gold movements in World War II, this small cache of gold was relatively insignificant. The moral dimensions of this small flow of gold through Canada's central bank are, nonetheless, today possibly as momentous as the largest wartime transfers of Reichsbank gold across the Swiss border.

The issue of Nazi gold in Canada has never been one of absolute taint – the physical acceptance of looted gold and its subsequent legitimization. Nor have the recent controversies over dormant bank accounts and heirless assets touched Canada. Instead, the controversy over Canada's part in wartime gold movements has been defined in legalistic and bureaucratic terms – a questioning of the procedures by which ownership of gold was transferred on paper by one central bank to another. It involves an evaluation of the diligence that Canadian officials in Ottawa applied to overseeing the transfer of earmarked gold in Canada, in exchange for unknown commercial and financial transactions in Europe. At root, it is a matter of the morality and competence that Canada's wartime bureaucrats brought to one small aspect of their work. That competence must be weighed in terms of both the overall wartime context in which the transfers took place and the actual mechanics of the transfers.

SIX TONS OF GOLD IN A BROADER CONTEXT

Overall Gold Movements in Wartime Ottawa

Some may fault this study for its excessive myopia – the dogged pursuit of six tons of earmarked gold through the course of the war. In war, one could point out, more than in most human endeavours, decisions are made in light of the broad context – the quest for survival and ultimate victory. This study has instead begun with the premise that in war the means, however seemingly insignificant, should measure up to the moral end of war. This said, there is every reason to set the gold transfers of 1942–45 in a broader context.

In this respect, it is crucial to place the gold trades of 1942–45 in the context of the Bank of Canada's overall activity as an earmarker of foreign gold during the war. The six tons of gold – 480 bars – that were traded from Switzerland to Portugal in 1942 and 1944, and then partially on to Sweden later, represent the smallest fraction of the foreign gold that the Bank of Canada handled during the war. Even if one broadens the focus of this study to embrace the 56 tons – 4,506 bars – of English gold transferred to Switzerland in 1942–43, the ratio remains very small. The careful reconstruction of the Bank of Canada's gold ledgers over the years 1935–56 that has accompanied this research has revealed that the Bank of Canada handled approximately *565,000 bar transactions*. A "bar transaction" measures the arrival and eventual shipping out of every bar. Defined more narrowly, between 1938, when the prewar scramble to earmark foreign gold in Ottawa began, and the end of the war in 1945 the Bank of Canada received

186,332 bars of gold, plus another 8,291,032 ounces of gold coins. Another perspective on the 1942–45 transfers is offered by the fact that, over the years 1939
to the early 1950s when the last vestiges of wartime earmarking were wound up,
the Bank of Canada carried 39 earmark accounts, only four of which – England,
Switzerland, Portugal and Sweden – were involved in the trades examined here.
It is worth noting that only one further question about gold in Ottawa has
emerged from the intensive scouring of wartime records that has taken place in
Washington and Europe over the last year and a half.[175] Nor has the intensive
search of the Bank of Canada archives since August 1997 revealed any further
hint of improper transactions. Thus, the gold swaps of 1942–45 constitute only a
tiny fraction of the Bank of Canada's overall gold transactions in World War II.

Gold Swaps at the High Noon of War

The 1942 Anglo–Swiss agreement to swap gold for francs and the subsequent
transfer of Swiss gold to Portugal came at the darkest hour of the war. As the
preeminent historian of Canada's war effort, J. L. Granatstein, has noted, "A
pall of frustration hung heavily over Canada in 1941. The war was going from
bad to worse."[176] The secret, coded cables that arrived from the Bank of
England initiating the swap in March 1942 arrived just months after Pearl
Harbour, an event that shunted the Allies into a two-theatre war. On the home
front, the spring of 1942 saw Canada engaged in a national plebiscite campaign
over the thorniest of Canadian issues – whether Canadian manpower should be
conscripted to fight the Axis. There was a mood of political rancour and anxiety throughout the land. All this came after a year of desperate effort to gear up
the Canadian economy for the immense challenge of beating the Axis on the
economic front. While plans had been laid, there was still no assurance that
Canada's economy could meet the challenge of total war. In the words of historian C. P. Stacey, "The harvest then sown [in 1940] began to be reaped on a
large scale only in 1942 . . . By the end of 1943, the Canadian effort, built up
gradually through four years, was almost at its peak."[177]

   Through these days of national strain, there was still no sense that victory was
assured. Every day brought decisions of momentous import. There were decisions about war production, manpower, allocation, rationing and price controls.
The question of paying for the war was ever present. These decisions were often
made by the same senior politicans and bureaucrats whose names appeared on
the memoranda and cables that permitted gold to be earmarked in Canada –
Bank of Canada Governor Graham Towers, Finance Minister J. L. Ilsley and
Deputy Minister of Finance W. C. Clark. Every day in 1941–42, as Granatstein
has pointed out, these so-called mandarins "came to solutions to the fiscal problems that threatened to destroy the Canadian war effort."[178] The Bank of
Canada became the focal point of much of the nation's monetary war effort –
the Foreign Exchange Control Board was administered under its umbrella of
jurisdiction, the national War Bond drives were coordinated by its officials and
Canada's public debt, including Canada's famous billion-dollar gift to Britain in
early 1942, were orchestrated by the Bank of Canada. On occasion, Governor

Towers abandoned his usually dry manner of communication to reveal the pressure under which he found himself as wartime decisions crowded in upon him. "The administrative difficulties of the task which is being undertaken," he confided to Bank of England Governor Montagu Norman after wage and price controls were introduced in Canada, "are, of course, terrific. I hope that a good job will be done – or perhaps it would be better to say that a good job must be done."[179]

The Bank of England's request that the Bank of Canada facilitate a swap of its gold for Swiss francs thus arrived on the desk of a man besieged with worry. His counterpart in the Department of Finance, Deputy Minister W. C. Clark – whose assurance of the granting of an export licence was necessary before a foreign client would earmark gold in Ottawa – was similarly bowed under the burden of wartime decision-making. How diligent therefore were they in the face of yet another demand on their authority? Or did the pressures of war allow a series of gold transfers of questionable integrity to slip across the desks of Ottawa's fiscal and monetary mandarins without the exercise of due diligence? What conditioned their response to the transfer requests from England, Switzerland, Portugal and Sweden? Even before the war began, one factor clearly preconditioned Ottawa's response to England's needs in 1942.

Obliging the Motherland: Heeding Montagu Norman's Call

Since its inception in 1935, the Bank of Canada had found itself in a filial relationship with the Bank of England. Not only was the Bank of England old, experienced and at the crossroads of global finance, but it was the central bank of the senior member of the new-born Commonwealth. "Not a day passes without my thinking of some question which I should like to ask you," the deputy governor of the Bank of Canada wrote to a confrere at the Bank of England in 1935. "I must take a list of them and get your replies in a year or so when I next visit what is always referred to here as 'the Old Country'."[180] From the outset, relations between the world's newest central bank and its most seasoned practitioner were trusting, cordial and candid. Learning the ropes of central banking, one Canadian confided to London in 1936, was easier if "one has a friend from whom advice can be sought unofficially."[181] The principal link in this bond was the friendship of Montagu Norman and Graham Towers. While Towers was always his own man, intellectually active and innovative, he was at the same time constantly reliant on his friend "Monty" in London. The opening of the Bank of England's earmark account in Ottawa in 1936 and the massive prewar transfers of gold across the Atlantic in 1938 and 1939 attested to the workability of this intimacy.

The advent of war drew the two banks closer together. When England was at war, so too was Canada. When England called, the inclination of the Bank of Canada was to heed. England's gold was welcomed into the Canadian central bank's vaults. Its senior officials were accommodated in the grim days of 1940, and there were even tentative plans to establish a "shadow" Bank of England in Ottawa if Hitler's army made it across the Channel. Not everybody in Ottawa shared Towers' instinctive trust of his British counterpart. Prime Minister Mackenzie King detected a colonialism in the relationship, a closeness that he believed endangered the Canadian autonomy he had long sought to build up at England's expense. "It does seem to me," he wrote in his famous diary in late 1941, "particularly in matters that come from the Bank of England . . . that too much of our policy is being dictated purely in British interests and not sufficiently in our own."[182] King's principal foreign affairs adviser, O. D. Skelton, shared the prime minister's autonomist instincts. Together they had battled Towers in 1940 over the issue of whether France's earmarked gold in Canada should be applied to Allied needs or put under the custodian of enemy property. Towers had written in his own diary that Skelton had taken a "pretty inimical view" to obliging the Bank of England's request that French gold be pressed into the cause of war.[183]

In the end, the prime minister prevailed, illustrating that there were checks and balances on Canada's central bank relationship with England. Canada would not follow blindly if its own, in this case political, needs were put at risk. The governor of the Bank of Canada nonetheless remained attuned to London's wartime needs. Thus, when London asked Ottawa to assist it in operating the foreign-owned gold arrangement in Ottawa in September 1940, the Bank of Canada could see "no particular difficulty about the arrangement proposed." Similarly, when Montagu Norman's cable arrived in March 1942, outlining Britain's liquidity crisis with Switzerland, it was not surprising that Towers cabled back almost immediately that his Bank would facilitate the plan.

Cautious Policy from Careful Mandarins

A preconditioned inclination to respond positively to the Bank of England's wishes did not, however, mean that Ottawa proceeded without careful consideration of its course of action. From the outset, Towers and his counterparts could see risk in the British proposal. It was not the risk that the Anglo-Swiss swap agreement might open the door to the laundering of looted gold by a neutral power on the borders of the Axis. Instead, the anxiety from the outset was centred on Ottawa, not Europe. Switzerland might obtain control of clean gold – ultimately 56 tons of it – and might therefore be put in a position to move that gold across the Atlantic to where it might somehow find its way into the service of the Axis. When the Swiss inquired whether the gold they would receive in Ottawa would be at their "free disposal" to be sold, transported or exported, London and Ottawa quickly formed a defensive strategy to contain the risk": earmarked gold held in Ottawa might be exported to other central banks in the Western Hemisphere or transferred on paper to these same central banks or those of European neutral powers, namely Portugal, Sweden and Spain. It was not perfect – the gold might physically be shipped to Argentina – but in the face of Britain's wartime needs, it was a suitably pragmatic response. As Montagu Norman noted to Towers, Britain's "direct war purposes must override these objections." Ottawa concurred. Any problem with the policy would be deferred "unless and until it is raised by one of the European neutrals."

Ottawa hardly had an alternative to this pragmatism. To have denied the Bank of England's request would have severely strained, if not irreparably damaged, the Bank of Canada's relationship with the senior bank in London. Such a denial would also have run completely against the grain of Canada's commitment to the Allied cause. It would also have soured England's chances of successfully resolving its liquidity problems with Switzerland and might possibly have shunted the Swiss further in the direction of the Axis. It bears emphasis that when Ottawa and London failed to see eye-to-eye in 1940 over the disposition of the French earmarked gold in Ottawa, matters had immediately escalated to the prime ministerial level of discussion. Thus, Ottawa's central bankers and finance department mandarins devised a policy that shrewdly reflected the often divergent exigencies of war. As Deputy Minister of Finance W. C. Clark noted in approving the conditions of the Swiss earmark, ". . . there is nothing we can do but to facilitate the transactions as outlined . . ." by the British.

There are no visible signs in the letters, cables and memoranda that convey any sense of undue concern over what was at stake in the bureaucratic handling of these gold transfers. There is, for instance, no marginalia conveying disquiet over what was being requested. Neither is there any indication of disagreement over principles or tactics. Historians often look for tip-off phrases that indicate deeper concerns below the surface of any correspondence – for instance, mention of long telephone conversations, the sense of which need capturing on paper. None of this is evident here. Instead, Towers, Clark and those advising them quickly devised conditions that they knew contained possible loopholes, but in the light of wartime exigencies, were realistic and workable and allowed all parties to the transaction to consider that their ends had been met.

The men who took these decisions have come down in history as the "Ottawa" men. They were perhaps quintessential Canadians: not given to flamboyance or hasty judgement, but brilliant gradualists capable of judging a policy initiative from all its perspectives, while never losing sight of the greater end. As J. L. Granatstein has argued in his book *The Ottawa Men*,[184] these men were the architects of Canada's response to the social and economic disaster of the Depression and the challenge of the war in its wake. They fashioned the welfare state and the mixed economy that supported it. Clark in Finance had been on the job since 1932, Towers since 1935. Clark's minister, J. L. Ilsley, across whose desk the gold transfer requests passed, has been described as possessing ". . . the sharpest mind . . . in the government." He "worried incessantly about everything, but he would accept no advice from his deputy minister, Clifford Clark, that he did not understand well enough to put before the Cabinet."[185]

There was a close parallel between the historians' esteem for these wartime mandarins and opinions spontaneously volunteered in the interviews conducted during this research. Louis Rasminsky, a young economist trained at the London School of Economics who had joined the Foreign Exchange Control Board at the Bank of Canada in 1940, remembered Towers as "one of the ablest people [he] ever had contact with . . . very thoughtful and very rigorous in his thinking." The bank governor and the deputy minister of finance worked on "intimate terms as a team." Reflecting on the mid-war gold transactions, Rasminsky said that he could not "imagine Towers and Clark would have agreed to a transaction without making themselves aware of the risks."[186] Rasminsky himself had no recollection of any undue concern over these same transactions, nor could he recall any residual concern over or echo of them after the war. Rasminsky would eventually become governor of the Bank of Canada in 1961. The theme of bureaucratic rectitude surfaced elsewhere: Towers and Clark, said an economist who worked at the Bank of Canada in the 1950s, were "some of the cleverest men we have ever seen in Canada."[187]

There was, it must be admitted, a measure of moral leniency about the decisions surrounding the Ottawa gold transfers. There is, for instance, little hard evidence to support Towers' claim to the Bank of Canada board of directors in June 1942 that the Anglo-Swiss swap was necessitated by humanitarian needs, although it is plausible that some of the francs bought with British gold in Ottawa were applied to the business of freeing prisoners of war. Nonetheless, in the remaining years of the war, the policy devised in 1942 to condition the movement of gold held by neutrals in Ottawa fulfilled its intent. No gold owned by Switzerland ever left Canada and found its way across the Atlantic, let alone into the service of the Axis. No gold was ever transferred to Argentina. And only twice did the Swiss ask to transfer earmarked gold to another European neutral. When Switzerland tested the conditions governing their earmark by asking in 1942 if Swiss commercial banks could open parallel earmark accounts in Ottawa, the answer was a quick and firm no. With characteristic Canadian caution and pragmatism, the Bank of Canada, backed by the Department of Finance, had exercised due diligence without jeopardizing Britain's financial imperatives in Europe or undermining overall Allied solidarity.

Thus, one can conclude that the Bank of Canada handled its end of the gold transfers of 1942–45 with admirable due diligence. Risks were identified and policies were devised to minimize their potential. What happened in Europe was beyond Ottawa's direct influence. But as British diplomatic documents originating in Portugal during these years reveal, the British were vigilant to the ultimate purpose of subsequent gold swaps between neutral powers in Europe. The burden of proof would suggest that the gold transferred between Switzerland, Portugal and Sweden in the period 1942–45 was not looted gold, but instead clean gold. There are flickers of contrary evidence, notably the possibility that some of the gold passed from Portugal to Switzerland in 1942 was drawn from a Portuguese account – account B – that the Banque Nationale Suisse reputed to contain tainted gold. This morally positive conclusion was not the product of Allied policy, for these transfers took place beyond the practical reach of the Allies. Instead, the dynamic was supplied by imperatives within the neutral powers themselves. Switzerland's appetite for clean gold to support its monetary operations and Portugal's need of hard currency to finance its trade with Switzerland and Sweden were the *key determinants* behind the European paper transfers of gold. By 1944, Allied injunctions against the trading of looted gold carried some weight in neutral Europe and probably coloured the nature of the 1944–45 swaps.

Earmarking Foreign Gold: Canada's Unsung Wartime Victory

Amid all the intense investigation of these wartime gold swaps, the big picture perhaps slips out of focus. Between 1938 and 1945, the Bank of Canada received almost 83 million fine ounces of foreign gold for safekeeping. Almost all of this gold was from nations facing the deadliest threat to their existence in the twentieth century. Some were in fact under the heel of the Axis; others were locked in combat with the Reich. Gold in Ottawa was the ultimate insurance policy for these nations, the ultimate assurance that if all was lost in Europe, there would still be capital to continue the struggle beyond the homeland. For the Dutch, Norwegian, Polish and Belgian governments, an earmark account in Ottawa provided the wherewithal of survival and, with victory, the beginnings of reconstruction. For France, the outcome – gold frozen under the custodian of enemy property – was somewhat different, but the ultimate prospect of gold available for reconstruction was the same.

Despite its largely dormant nature, earmarked gold in Ottawa was on occasion pressed into a more active and morally commendable wartime role. It was used in 1942 to ease Britain's chronic liquidity problems with Switzerland. Even earlier, earmarking had been employed to meet the needs of the European refugees in their quest to find safe haven for their personal wealth in the face of the Nazi onslaught. For 155 sundry persons deposits, Ottawa offered a destination that instilled a sense of security and fairness in Europeans who no longer felt safe in their native Europe. Their holdings in Ottawa offered hope of postwar rehabilitation and, for the minority who secured release of their gold before the war ended, a chance to establish a new life while war raged in Europe.

For all this, the Bank of Canada charged nothing beyond minimal shipping charges. The earmarking of gold was hardly a glamorous aspect of war. It was a prosaic bureaucratic procedure, quietly and efficiently performed by one central banker on behalf of another. Yet, it was an important facet of the Allied financial strategy for the war. And Canada was the principal instrument of this policy in the Commonwealth. Particularly in the early years of the war when America remained neutral, gold in Ottawa provided the beleaguered Allies in Europe with a vital element of insurance. What is perhaps remarkable is that of the 2,586 tons of gold earmarked in Ottawa by foreign clients between 1938 and 1945, only six tons have ever been questioned in terms of their ultimate application.

Historians of Canadian foreign policy have often criticized the low morality of Canadian foreign policy in the 1930s – a policy framed by a parochial pursuit of autonomy from the British and an easy adoption of appeasement. The war, they argue, nursed a new, more constructive role for Canada in the world. Canada was a "middle power" that had useful roles to play in the world. This "functionalism" would quickly manifest itself in such roles as peacekeeping and foreign aid in the postwar years. In this light, Canada's efficiency as a safe-keeper of Allied gold in times of trouble can perhaps be seen as a foreshadowing of this new functionalism, a constructive, independent response to international needs.

Canada and the Postwar Search for Looted Gold: Bringing Closure

It was perhaps because the Ottawa men felt that they had done such a competent job of earmarking gold through the war that they felt little inclination to join in the search for looted gold after the war. In February 1944, U.S. Treasury Secretary Henry Morgenthau issued a "Declaration on Gold Purchases" that stated that the United States would not recognize the transfer of title of gold believed to have been looted by the Axis. Within days the American ambassador in Ottawa began exerting pressure on the Canadian government to take parallel action. Governor Towers at the Bank of Canada was reluctant to act. "We have never had occasion to buy gold from any country which has not broken relations with the Axis," he wrote to Undersecretary of State Norman Robertson at External Affairs, "or from countries which have acquired gold from any country which has not broken relations with the Axis."[188] Opinion in Ottawa tended to the view that Canada had signed the January 1943 first Allied declaration on looted gold and that this would suffice. Towers at the Bank of Canada had, in the words of the Bank's secretary, D. G. Marble, "never felt that there was any need for a declaration on the subject of looted gold . . ."[189] Officials at External Affairs concurred. Norman Robertson believed that "there would appear to be no urgent need for us to take the parallel action suggested by the United States. . ."[190] The same opinion prevailed at the Department of Finance. A memorandum to a senior departmental official, R. B. Bryce, noted that ". . . we have gone much further than merely protecting assets located or controlled in Canada or being disposed of here."[191] Thus, Ottawa's attitude to the issue of looted gold was that it was a European problem, to be solved by Europeans.

In the end, Canada did issue a declaration on looted gold early in 1945. This was done, as several internal memoranda made clear, as "a gesture of solidarity" with the other Allied powers, especially the Americans.[192] Canada's declaration on looted gold was, however, Canadianized to highlight its special role as an earmarker of European gold. "The Canadian Government has already taken measures," it read, "to protect the assets of the invaded countries located or controlled in Canada and to prevent the Axis from disposing in Canada of looted currencies securities and other assets, and has co-operated fully with the other Allies in all measures to prevent the disposal of looted assets on the world market."[193]

After the return of peace in 1945, Canada took an arm's-length attitude to the American, British and French campaign to identify and recover looted gold. While the Tripartite Commission on the Restitution of Monetary Gold was established in September 1946, Ottawa concentrated on tidying up the loose ends of its wartime activities in foreign gold. The Bank of Canada efficiently cleared the remaining sundry persons deposits, while the larger European earmark accounts were returned to a normal peacetime footing. When the Tripartite Commission made its first restitution of looted gold in 1947, the Department of External Affairs dutifully circulated the press release.[194] Ottawa saw itself as a spectator to these developments. In 1948, for instance, the "Big

Three" struck a deal with Switzerland that in effect saw the Netherlands repatriate only part of their monetary gold that had found its way to Switzerland in the war, allowing the Swiss to retain a large portion of what was generally believed to be looted gold. When a Montreal *Gazette* clipping describing the deal was circulated around the Department of Finance, one official scribbled the following comment:

> Could we poke our noses into this? As a creditor of the Netherlands we have a definite third party interest. I think we should lend the Netherlands every support – the Swiss have done well enough out of the war without making this kind of profit.[195]

But Canadian involvement in the complex postwar negotiations over looted gold never went beyond this level of commentary. Neither did the various American, British and French investigations into looted gold ever turn in Ottawa's direction. And when the ardour of the "Big Three" for the hunt cooled in the early 1950s, Ottawa too lost its tenuous connection with the issue.

For the next half century, the question of looted gold lived in the shadows. But, as the summer of 1997 was to reveal, Canada had not escaped implication in the issue entirely. Somewhere in the thousands of files generated by the intense postwar, Allied campaign to identify and recover Europe's looted gold lay an anonymous document – "From a very Confidential Source" – that alleged that the Bank of Canada had played a small part in the laundering of looted Axis gold. The weight of evidence belies this lone contention. This report has addressed this last vestige of Canada's handling of foreign gold in World War II and found that, given the context of the times and the burden of evidence, the Bank of Canada and other senior offices of Ottawa's wartime bureaucracy exercised due diligence in carrying out these difficult duties. In doing so, they performed a useful, if generally unnoticed, financial service to the Allies and at the same time offered, for a small group of refugees fleeing persecution in Europe, a measure of humanitarian relief.

The Documents

It is appropriate that some commentary be provided on the nature of the wartime documents from which this report has drawn its conclusions. This report has all primary material (i.e., material from the hands of the participants in the actual events) footnoted so that readers may know its exact origins and thereby return to these same documents to draw their own conclusions. Some generic consideration of the overall breadth, completeness and candidness of these documents is also in order.

THE NATURE OF CENTRAL BANK DOCUMENTS

This report draws almost exclusively on central banker's documents. Of all institutional records, banking records are perhaps the most predictably regular and complete. Their creation is driven by a series of regulatory, fiduciary and administrative obligations, all of which reflect a response to the systematized accountability that our society demands of its banking system. There is much evidence in this report of documents produced by *regulatory* obligation: the requirement, for instance, stipulated under the 1932 Gold Export Act that the Bank of Canada obtain an export licence every time an earmark client sought to remove gold from the Bank's vault and take it out of the country. The absence of correspondence to the Department of Finance requesting such a permission would constitute a breach of regulatory obligation.

Fiduciary obligation is similarly represented in the Bank's written dealings with its clients: the entitlement of any client to have a written confirmation of the disposition of the assets they have placed in the care of a bank. A good example of such an obligation in the context of this report would be the regular production of account statements that provided foreign central banks with precise month-end and year-end reckonings of their earmarked gold holdings in Ottawa. Within its own structure, the Bank of Canada responded to various *administrative* pressures by producing, as a matter of automatic procedure, internal documentation that supported its functions. For instance, this report has relied heavily upon documents generated by the chief of the Currency Division, the division of the Bank charged with overseeing the safekeeping of earmarked gold. Currency Division's reports on the arrival and departure of gold to and from these accounts therefore provided a meticulous record of foreign clients' dealings with the Bank.

Given these pressures, the nature of the Bank of Canada's historical activities is documented in a highly patterned and predictable way. Any gap in or departure from procedure quickly becomes evident. Similarly, the client-driven nature of earmark banking tended to create neatly compartmentalized series of documents that permit the historian to compare the treatment of one account against the treatment apparent in another. The record of any one account may be similarly traced, thanks to bankers' ingrained habit of copying correspondence and memoranda pertaining to one account to other relevant file series. For instance, month-end reports on earmarked gold in a client's account can be found in the files of that particular client as well in files of the Currency Division of the Bank of Canada, which oversaw the safekeeping of that gold.

Bankers' documents are also generally terse and to the point in nature. Driven as they are by regulatory, fiduciary and administrative demands, they seldom deviate from their purpose: to report and record bank activity. By this measure, any concerns on the part of the banker over any irregularity in procedure, any dilemma of interpretation or any ethical anxiety tends to emerge in the form of a departure from the usual economical style of the record – marginalia, additional paragraphs of explication, references to clarifying telephone calls, etc. Such departures from the norm are readily apparent. Similarly, one looks for out-of-the ordinary background memoranda that help bank officials shape the decisions reflected in the documents (e.g., the exchange of memoranda between Bank of Canada Governor Graham Towers and foreign affairs adviser O. D. Skelton over the fate of French gold trapped in Canada in 1940).

Research for this report extended well beyond the bounds of the Bank of

Canada's strongly patterned documentary history. The records of other government departments – Finance and External Affairs, in particular – that played a role in Canada's wartime financial policies were consulted with the full cooperation of the departments involved. Thus, the ripple effect of any earmarked gold transaction could be traced elsewhere in Ottawa's wartime bureaucracy. The Finance Department records could therefore be expected to yield evidence of consultations with the Bank of Canada over the export of earmark gold. Similarly, documents from the Department of External Affairs could be expected to yield some sense of where financial policy trespassed into the territory of diplomacy, as, for instance, was the case of the postwar disposition of Polish earmarked gold held in Ottawa. As with the Bank's own records, documentation from other departments could be scrutinized in other ways. Internal memoranda, marginalia or references to politicians might tip off the historian to anxieties bred in other government officials by Bank of Canada decisions. Similarly, the absence of such ad hoc commentary in these documents suggests that the Bank's decisions did not occasion undue concern.

THE BREADTH OF THIS DOCUMENTARY INVESTIGATION

With these observations on the *nature* of the documents consulted in mind, something should be said of the *breadth* of the investigation. Shortly after learning of the World Jewish Congress's discovery of documents connecting Canada to wartime gold movements between the Allies and European neutrals, the Bank of Canada launched a vigorous and wide-ranging review of its records to identify all material relating to its wartime gold operations. An *ad hoc* task force of Bank officers was created to compile as thorough a catalogue of documents as possible in preparation for their review by an independent historian and eventually for other researchers and the general public. At the heart of this effort was the Bank's own archival and records-management staff.

There is ample evidence that the Bank of Canada has long made a conscious effort to maintain a documentary record of its wartime activities. As early as late 1943, the Bank's assistant deputy governor and its deputy secretary drew up a set of criteria for deciding which records of wartime activities would be retained. Records of "a purely routine nature" were to be kept for two years. At the other end the spectrum were, "our most important files and those relating to transactions and business in connection with the war. For instance files on gold movements, conditions of accounts and various arrangements with Banks and the Dominion Government War Finance, Cash Reserves, taxation, Safe and Vaults, etc." were to be retained "indefinitely." Such files, it was noted, should be "examined again after the war is over" and a "permanent record is to be kept of all material destroyed . . ."[196] Following this initial commitment to records retention, there are sporadic indications of the Bank's determination to retain its records in a systematic fashion. For instance, this handwritten annotation was found on the cover of the Banque Nationale Suisse gold earmark account file: "It was suggested this file be destroyed to 1944 but Mr. St. A. wouldn't touch it. B. Le. M. March 12/49[47?]"[197] It should also be noted that every working file in the Bank had the following injunction stamped on its front cover: "Officers are requested not to remove letters from the files."

With these initial hints at the comprehensiveness of the records available, a search of the Bank of Canada documents pertinent to this report was launched. The search can only be described as painstakingly thorough. Every gold-related file was examined, catalogued and entered in a finding aid. Every document was examined by myself and/or my research assistant, Matthew Bellamy. Many of the files consulted in fact contained no material of any relation to the gold transactions in question in this report. The complete finding aid of these documents is being made available upon request to the general public by the Bank of Canada. The finding aid will reveal that a virtually complete record of the Bank's earmarked gold transactions, organized on a client-by-client basis, has survived intact to support this investigation. There is absolutely no evidence of document tampering. Given the nature of banking documents (as described earlier in this section), removed material would be glaringly evident.

There is, however, *one crucial gap or departure in record-keeping procedure* in the documents underlying this report. Clearly one of the central hinges of the Bank of Canada's wartime earmark operations was its relationship with the Bank of England. This relationship left a documentary trail in many files. Perhaps the most important of these was the "arrangements" file (file A18-17-Arrangements) for the Bank of England's earmark account in Ottawa. It stretches back to the opening of the account in 1936 and carries the relationship through the prewar tensions and into the birth of wartime earmarking. And then the file suddenly stops in February 1941 and does not restart until June 1945. Thus the crucial events of the 1942–44 period – England's negotiations with the Swiss, the francs-for-gold swap, the subsequent Portuguese and Swedish gold trades – are not wholly chronicled from the perspective of the Bank of England. There is no official record of the sanctioned destruction of this file. It should be noted that one is able to piece together much of the Bank of England's relation with Ottawa in these mid-war years from copies of the correspondence in other Bank of Canada files (e.g., the Banque Nationale Suisse arrangements file).

There are several suggestions of where the missing correspondence has gone. Given the magnitude of the events, this correspondence probably filled one, possibly two full files. It has been speculated that the file(s), because of its special ongoing sensitivity in the war, was kept in the governor's office or the Bank secretary's office, where it could be accessed easily and was never ultimately returned to its rightful place in the main file. There were occasional references in other files to a "secret authorization file" that was kept in the Bank secretary's safe. Possibly the file was kept there and never returned to its rightful parent file. It is also possible that correspondence for the Bank of England arrangements file was in fact filed in the Bank of England routine correspondence file, because most of the mid-war decisions concerning the account were of a routine nature (e.g., transfers to the Federal Reserve Bank of New York).

There is no definitive answer to the problem of the missing section of file A18–17. The saving grace, however, is that the significant transactions reached between the Bank of Canada and the Bank of England in these years were copied to other Bank of Canada files and quite frequently to the Department of Finance files and are therefore traceable. For instance, the Anglo-Swiss gold swap of early 1942 is completely chronicled in the Banque Nationale Suisse account file at the Bank of Canada. Secondary corroboration of these transactions was also found in the Bank of England files made available to us by the bank in London. It seems very unlikely that these traces of such crucial transactions would have survived in companion document series had there been a concerted effort to erase any written record of the Bank of England's mid-war dealings with the Bank of Canada. The loss of part of file A18–17 therefore seems more accidental than deliberate.

ACCESS TO INFORMATION AND PRIVACY LEGISLATION IMPLICATIONS

It bears emphasis that in its initial commitment in July 1997, to investigate its role in wartime gold transfers, the Bank of Canada undertook to make available to "other researchers, interested groups and the general public" as complete a documentary record of these activities as possible. Such release will necessarily be subject to the Canadian federal government's Access to Information and Privacy Acts, that require obtaining the consent of non-Canadian central bank clients of the Bank of Canada. The principle of client confidentiality undeniably rests at the centre of all banking operations. As the recent controversies that have embroiled Switzerland's banking record in World War II have illustrated, the principle of client confidentiality can be used in a conscious way to serve ends other than its original intent. The rights of the Bank of Canada's clients cannot, however, be taken lightly, and to this end the Bank is engaged in a consultative effort to obtain the consent of parties involved in the events chronicled in this report to ensure as full a disclosure as possible of the documents used in this report.

THE SEARCH FOR DOCUMENTS BEYOND THE BANK OF CANADA

Parallel to the search undertaken at the Bank of Canada, other searches were launched at the Department of Finance and at the National Archives of Canada, where records of federal departments have been sent once they cease to have active relevance to government operations. On July 28, Finance Minister Paul Martin informed the Canadian Jewish Congress that he had instructed his department "to begin gathering all the files on wartime gold from the archives" of his department. The subsequent search was impressively thorough, but it did not unearth documents that departed from the pattern already evident at the Bank of Canada. Finance Department files that focused on earmarked gold were double-checked as part of this report's preparation. In 1963, certain Finance Department documents were ordered destroyed, but these would appear to have been correspondence of a routine nature. A finding aid to the Finance Department documents consulted has been added to the catalogue of Bank of Canada documents described above.

Searches of other collections of federal documents yielded similar results – either a carbon copy of Bank of Canada records or no mention whatsoever of the gold transactions in question. Particular attention was paid to those collections that might have revealed consciousness of action on these issues in the highest echelons of Canada's wartime bureaucracy and its political masters. The War Cabinet Committee Minutes, the Mackenzie King diary and papers of individual ministers (e.g., Minister of Finance J. L. Ilsley) were surveyed and in all instances yielded no results. Back at the Bank of Canada, similar leads were pursued on the periphery of the main records. There were some tantalizing possibilities. Bank Governor Towers, for instance, kept a diary, but it stopped abruptly in 1940. None of these efforts yielded any significant insights.

ORAL EVIDENCE

Attempts to identify concerns about or consciousness of gold transfers in the senior echelons of government were matched by an attempt to contact Bank employees who might have witnessed these wartime events. At half a century's distance, it seemed unlikely that senior Bank officials (i.e., those who had risen to positions of authority in the 1940s) would still be available for interviewing. Nonetheless, the Bank's pension lists were consulted and a list of retired interviewed. Without exception, these interviews yielded no recollection of the gold swaps in contention, nor was there any memory of postwar gossip, folklore or inquiry into these events. The only gold memory of the war that most retained was the sudden and immense influx of earmarked gold coming to the Bank in the late 1930s and early war years from Europe. The interviews were, however, useful in providing a vivid sense of the corporate culture of the Bank during the war and in shedding light on the procedures by which gold was stored, recorded and moved in the vaults.

This attempt to collect oral evidence prompted thought about other ways in which wartime Bank officials might have obtained or transmitted information or opinion during the course of the war. The evidence used in this report is almost exclusively written. The written record is undoubtedly a candid one. All overseas communication by cable was coded and therefore secure (e.g., instructions for the transfer of gold from one earmark account to another were encoded). Here the exception proves the rule: Banco de Portugal did not have a secure, coded cable link with Ottawa, so all of its communications with Canada were transmitted through the Bank of England. Were there other methods of communication that are not reflected in the written record? Several such media suggest themselves.

Prewar records suggest that the transatlantic telephone was occasionally employed to trade opinion between London and Ottawa. Conclusions drawn from these contacts usually appeared in written form after the fact, either as a memorandum dictated to capture the sense and outcomes of the conversation or in allusions to such discussions in subsequent written communication. War seemed to cramp this style of communication, possibly because telephone communications was considered insecure. There are few indications of telephone conversations during the war; coded cables seem to carry the crucial decisions. There seems to be more likelihood that personal contact between central bank officials, especially those from the Bank of England, served to inform the decisions taken on earmarked gold policy. In the dark days of 1940, Ottawa received long visits from British officials such as Sir Frederick Phillips of the Treasury and Bank of England directors like Sir Otto Niemeyer. There are written records of these contacts (e.g., discussions between Phillips, Prime Minister King and Graham Towers over the fate of French gold and currency in Ottawa). Similarly, Canadians went to London. There are, for instance, terse reports of Graham Towers' visits to London and the Bank of England (e.g., the minutes of the Bank of Canada board of directors on February 9, 1940, record that Towers had recently been to London "at the request of the Government" during which visit "negotiations with the British authorities respecting financial arrangements with Canada had been satisfactorily concluded."). These references suggest that the written record is not entirely hermetic and that other exchanges may have lain behind the wartime decisions and that these may have escaped posterity's reach. There is, however, evidence that a strong bureaucratic instinct to commit important oral communication to paper persisted throughout the war.

RECONSTRUCTING THE BANK OF CANADA'S GOLD LEDGERS, 1935–56

All the foregoing efforts to reconstruct a narrative of the decisions surrounding the gold accounts of the Bank of Canada have been accompanied by an effort to reconstruct the actual physical movement of gold into and out of the Bank of Canada in the years 1935–56. Every gold bar stored in the Bank of Canada, whether owned by the Bank itself or earmarked for an outside client of the Bank, was meticulously recorded in the Bank's gold records. Thus, every bar arriving at the Bank was duly recorded, and every subsequent movement of that bar – either its actual physical departure from the Bank or its book transfer from the account of one client to that of another – could be tracked in the original records as well as in their companion transaction files (e.g., paper notification of gold movements to clients).

Part of the Bank of Canada's decision in July 1997 to thoroughly investigate its role in wartime gold transactions was the determination to reconstruct its gold records on an aggregated basis that would allow it to show overall gold flows in and out of the Bank, while at the same time allowing it to trace any individual bar's history with the Bank. This was a massive undertaking. To meet this challenge the Bank assembled a team of seconded current employees, mainly from its Currency Division, and recently retired officers who had deep experience in the Bank's gold procedures. Their challenge was to capture in computer data bases the entire gold storage operations of the Bank from 1935 to 1956. This entails the account activities of 39 Bank of Canada clients – two domestic clients, 19 other central banks, 6 international institutions and governments and 12 suspense accounts. It involves tracking approximately 565,000 "bar transactions" (i.e., any movement of a bar either physically in or out of the Bank). In the period from 1938 to 1945 alone, the Bank of Canada received 186,332 bars of gold. Some gaps exist in the Bank's records, but it is anticipated that a very high percentage of total gold transactions will be recreated. This project was thus in a position to make a valuable contribution to this report, especially in providing exact figures for the gold held in earmark accounts. The statistics in this report are principally from this source. A separate report prepared by the Bank covers the methodology and final results of the gold ledger reconstruction project and is appended to this report.

CONCLUSION

The foregoing review leads to the conclusion that a largely complete record of the Bank of Canada's wartime gold policies and practices has been preserved or is in the process of being accurately reconstructed. There is no evidence of document tampering, and those gaps that do exist may in large part be filled by reference to companion series of documents. To this researcher's satisfaction, the Bank of Canada has displayed an entirely open and cooperative attitude in making its history accessible. Much of this record will shortly be made available for public inquiry so that new minds may test the results of this report against their own reading of the documents.

Acknowledgements

I would like to acknowledge the assistance given me by so many of the Bank of Canada's staff in the preparation of this report. I was assured before I undertook this research that I would have full and unrestricted access to the Bank's records and personnel. Without exception, this proved to be the rule. Retired Bank of Canada employees also gave freely of their time to my inquiries. The same courtesy and candour was extended by officers of the Department of Finance. The National Archives of Canada responded with speed and efficiency to all my requests for material pertaining to gold transfers in World War II. My thanks also to the historians at the Department of Foreign Affairs and International Trade. Beyond Canada's borders, I am most grateful for the information and documents provided by the Bank of England, the Banque Nationale Suisse, the Banco de Portugal and the Sveriges Riksbank, and for the help of historians at the Records and Historical Services Group at the Foreign and Commonwealth Office. In England, special thanks to Henry Gillett and Sarah Millard of the Bank of England Archives and Gill Bennett of the Foreign and Commonwealth Office. In Sweden, special thanks to Peder Bjursten of the Sveriges Riksbank. Thanks also to Vincent Crettol and Patrick Halbeisen of the Banque Nationale Suisse in Switzerland. I certainly wish to acknowledge my debt to Professor Neville Wylie of New Hall at the University of Cambridge for his insights on Anglo-Swiss financial relations during the war, and I am grateful to Dr. Irving Abella and Dr. Edward Neufeld for their candid and constructive comments on earlier drafts of this report. All opinions contained in this report are, of course, my own.

Nearer home, I owe sincere thanks to Matthew Bellamy for his stalwart work as a research assistant and to Joan White, who so ably managed the graduate programme in history at Carleton University during my frequent absences. And at home, my wife Sandy Campbell bore history's latest incursion into our family life with her usual love and intelligence.

NOTES

[1] Stuart Eizenstat, coordinator, *U.S. and Allied Efforts To Recover and Restore Gold and Other Assets Stolen or Hidden by Germany During World War II*, Washington, May, 1997, p.iii.

[2] Adam LeBor, *Hitler's Secret Bankers: The Myth of Swiss Neutrality During the Holocaust*, New York, 1997, pp. 237–241. These proportions reflect a 1946 Allied estimate. Throughout the years covered by this report, the price of gold was fixed at US$35 an ounce.

[3] Ibid., p.iv.

[4] Eizenstat, op. cit., pp.iv–v.

[5] "The Swiss National Bank's (SNB) gold operations during the Second World War," notes prepared by the Swiss Federal Department of Foreign Affairs, August 1997, http://www.eda-tf.ethz.ch/topics/top33_e.htm.

[6] See: Eizenstat, op. cit., pp. xxxv–xxxix and Chapters 3–6, and *History Notes – Nazi Gold : Information from the British Archives*, Foreign and Commonwealth Office General Services Command, London, Part I, Septembr 1996 and Part II, May 1997.

[7] Eizenstat, op. cit., p.x.

[8] LeBor, op. cit., p.6.

[9] *Report of the Royal Commission on Banking and Currency* , Ottawa, 1933, p. 493.

[10] R. S. Sayers, The Bank of England 1891–1944, Vol.II, London, 1976, p.513-4.

[11] H. A. Siepmann to J. A. C. Osborne, April 24, 1936, Bank of Canada [hereafter BOC] file A18–17.

[12] Sayers, op. cit., p. 515.

[13] Ibid., p. 654.

[14] M. Norman to G. Towers, December 22, 1934, BOC file GFT75–9.

[15] Minute Book of the Bank of Canada Board of Directors [hereafter MBBOC], full board, November 27, 1935.

[16] Ibid., September 3, 1935.

[17] See, for instance, MBBOC full board October 23, 1936 and June 22, 1937.

[18] MBBOC, executive committee, July 5, 1935.

[19] Sayers, op. cit., ppp. 103–8.

[20] Towers to Norman, February 6, 1936 and Norman to Towers, February 19 and April 29, 1936, BOC file A18–17.

[21] Siepmann to Osborne, op. cit., April 24, 1936.

[22] J. A. C. Osborne, "Earmarked Gold," April 30, 1936, BOC file RD 1B–640.

[23] Bank of Canada Act, 24–25 George V, Chapter 43.

[24] See BOC file RD 1A–640.

[25] Ibid.

[26] An Act respecting the Export of Gold, 22–23 George V, Chapter 33 and An Act to amend The Gold Export Act, 25–26 George V, Chapter 21.

[27] J. A. C. Osborne to W. C. Clark, deputy minister of finance, March 5, 1936 and Clark to Osborne, March 11, 1936, BOC file A18–17. Whenever the Finance Department issued such assurances, it always included one proviso: "If at some future time Parliament should desire to change the present policy in regard to export licences, you will be informed in ample time to make satisfactory arrangements for the export of the gold which you may then hold earmarked

for the Bank of England."

[28] Norman to Towers, February 19 and March 30, BOC file A18–17.

[29] Memo for Mr. Gordon, May 7, 1936 from the Chief of the Currency Division, BOC file 18–17–1.

[30] Cable, Towers to Norman, April 29, 1936, BOC file A19–17.

[31] MBBOC, Executive Committee March 19, 1937.

[32] Osborne to Siepmann, June 2, 1936, ibid.

[33] Siepmann to Towers, November 20, 1936, ibid.

[34] All statistics relating to earmark accounts at the Bank of Canada are drawn from the gold record reconstructions produced by the Gold History Project, Bank of Canada, 1997.

[35] See, for instance, Norman to Towers, April 14, 1939, BOC file A18–17.

[36] Manager & Assistant General Manager, BIS, to Bank of Canada, March 9, 1935, BOC file A1–5A.

[37] Siepmann to Towers, March 31, 1938, BOC file A18–17.

[38] Towers to Siepmann, April 2, 1938 and Towers to Dunning, April 4, 1938, ibid.

[39] Towers to Siepmann, April 4, 1938, ibid.

[40] Norman to Towers, April 19, 1939, ibid.

[41] Osborne to Siepmann, May 11, 1938, ibid.

[42] Gordon to Siepmann, October 20, 1938, ibid.

[43] All dollar figures cited in this report are in Canadian dollars, unless otherwise indicated.

[44] See, for instance, MBBOC, full board May 30, 1938 and June 26, 1939, ibid.

[45] Memo by G. F. Tower, March 22, 1939, BOC file 31.

[46] Bolton to Osborne, April 13, 1939, A6–3/1.

[47] See, for instance, the opening of a 10,000 Swiss-franc Banque Nationale Suisse cash account reported in MBBOC, December 20, 1935.

[48] Towers memo 251, April 18, 1939, Towers Papers, BOC Archives.

[49] Interview with Forbes Hirsch, September 4, 1997. See: John Ibbotson, "Bullion Boy: How a Junior Accountant Herded a Wartime Armada of Gold," *The Ottawa Citizen*, December 4, 1995.

[50] "Gold Held in Safekeeping for the Bank of England, 1938–Aug. 1941," BOC file A18–17–9.

[51] Towers to Clark, April 15, 1939 and Clark to Towers, April 15, 1939, BOC file SEC/OS 91–19.

[52] Towers to Governor, Banque de France, May 1, 1939, BOC file A6–3.

[53] See: the *Toronto Star*, May 15, 1939, The *Wall Street Journal*, July 5, 1939 and the Montreal *Gazette*, August 22, 1939.

[54] Donald Gordon to Ivar Rooth, Sveriges Riksbank, January 3, 1940, BOC file A16–2.

[55] O. D. Skelton to Chairman of the Foreign Exchange Control Board, July 14, 1940, BOC file A6–4.

[56] J. L. Ilsley to Towers, August 1, 1940, BOC file SEC/OS 91–19.

[57] Churchill to W. L. M. King, August 25, 1940 and King to Churchill, September 3, 1940, BOC, Towers Papers, GFT 75–12.

[58] Memo by O. D. Skelton in response to G. F. Towers, September 14, 1940, ibid.

[59] Notes on Dr. Skelton's Memorandum of September 9, and discussion which took place on that date, September 10, 1940, ibid.

[60] Memo by O. D. Skelton in response to GFT, September 14, 1940, ibid.

[61] Ilsley to Towers, November 16, 1940, BOC file SEC/OS 91–19.

[62] W. L. M. King to Churchill, October 25, 1940, ibid.

[63] Erik Colban to Bank of Canada, BOC file 515–11–5.

[64] D. G. Marble to N. A. Robertson, July 6, 1940, ibid.

[65] Towers to Ilsley, August 15, 1940 and Ilsley to Towers, August 19, 1940, BOC file SEC/OS 91–19.

[66] D. B. Mansur to Robertson, August 24, 1940, ibid.

[67] At times, there are slight discrepancies between gold figures cited in correspondence and the actual final transaction record. Client banks would instruct Ottawa to take delivery or sell "approximate" amounts of gold and the final book entry would reflect precise fine ounces.

[68] All July 1940 Bank Polski, Bank of Canada and Bank of England in BOC file A13–2.

[69] Towers to Ilsley, August 15, 1940 and Ilsley to Towers, August 19, 1940, BOC files SEC/OS 91–19 and A13–2.

[70] "Gold Held for Bank Polski, 1940–45," dated June 27, 1946, BOC file A13–2.

[71] The request came from "Phillips," presumably Sir Frederick Phillips, who had visited the Bank of Canada that summer (MNBOC, full board, September 9, 1940). Towers to B. G. Catterns, July 16, 1940, BOC file A25–1.

[72] Secret cable Norman to Towers, July 18, 1940, ibid.

[73] BBOC, Executive Committee, July 11, 1942, August 21, 1942, April 9, 1943 and May 4, 1945.

[74] Towers to Ilsley, October 16, 1940, BOC file A23–1.

[75] BOC file A34–5A.

[76] Towers to Ilsley, August 14, 1943 and W. C. Clark to Towers, August 14, 1943, BOC file A3–1.

[77] This included 8,663 bars held on account for the Canadian minister of finance.

[78] George Watts, "A Note on the 'Shadow' Bank of England in Ottawa, 1940" and "The 'Shadow' Bank of England in Canada and Other Related Matters, 1940," Memos of George Watts, BOC Archives.

[79] See: BOC file 135–7.

[80] G. L. F. Bolton to Donald Gordon, September 18, 1940, BOC file A18–17–8.

[81] F. E. C. Notice 234/44, September 12, 1940, copy in BOC file A18–7–8.

[82] Bolton to Gordon, November 4, 1940, ibid.

[83] Gordon to Bolton, October 10, 1940, ibid.

[84] BOC file 1062–A. Another four such deposits were received into this account after the war.

[85] Bolton to Gordon, November 4, 1940, ibid.

[86] Bolton to D. G. Marble, October 30, 1940, ibid.

[87] See, for example, Donald Gordon to New York lawyer representing a gold client, November 4, 1940, ibid. Name withheld in deference to privacy legislation.

[88] S. Turk to New York Trade Commissioner D. S. Cole, July 2, 1942, ibid.

[89] D. S. Cole to S. Turk, June 30, 1942, ibid.

[90] Sundry persons account holder to D. S. Cole, June 27, 1942, ibid. Name withheld in accordance with Canada's Access to Information and Privacy Acts (ATIP).

[91] BOC file A18–19–9.

[92] My interpretation of the Anglo-Swiss trade and monetary relationship relies heavily on an excellent article, "The Swiss Franc and British policy towards Switzerland, 1939–1945," by Neville Wylie, New Hall & Centre of International Studies, University of Cambridge. A copy of this article was kindly forwarded by the Foreign and Commonwealth Office in London.

[93] Wylie, "The Swiss Franc . . .," p.2.

[94] Norman to Towers, March 9, 1942, BOC file A17–1. It should be noted that this quotation is taken from the file containing the arrangements and correspondence for the Banque Nationale Suisse earmark account that was about to be opened at Bank of Canada in 1942. The file for the Bank of Canada's arrangements with the Bank of England (BOC file A18–17) is missing for the period February 1941 to June 1945. This gap in documentation is discussed in the section of this report entitled "The Documents."

[95] Norman to Towers, March 18, 1942, ibid.

[96] Towers to Norman, March 19, 1942, ibid.

[97] Towers to Clark, March 19, 1942, ibid.

[98] Clark to Towers, April 7, 1942, ibid.

[99] Towers to Norman, April 23, 1942, ibid.

[100] Towers to Norman, April 28, 1942, ibid.

[101] Bank of Canada to BNS, May 2, 1942, ibid.

[102] Towers to Clark, May 2, 1942, ibid. and circular letter from G. F. Towers to general managers of Canadian chartered banks, May 4, 1942, BOC file 135–15.

[103] All statistics in this section taken from the gold record reconstructions undertaken by the Bank of Canada Gold History Project, 1997.

[104] MBOC, full board June 22, 1942. There had been no mention of the Swiss arrangements at the board's April 24 meeting.

[105] BNS to Bank of Canada, April 22, 1942, BOC file 515–17–5.

[106] Bank of Canada to BNS, April 21, 1942, ibid.

[107] Banco de Portugal to Bank of Ottawa, April 30, 1942, ibid.

[108] Towers to Banco de Portugal, May 15, 1942, BOC file 515–17–5.

[109] Clark to D. G. Marble, May 16, 1942, BOC file A–17–1.

[110] Norman to Towers, November 28, 1942, BOC file A17–1. Some words in this cable ("ascribed...Francs") were possibly garbled and were being checked by the cable company.

[111] Towers to Norman, December 2, 1942, ibid.

[112] Norman to Towers, December 17, 1943, ibid.

[113] Clark to D. G. Marble, December 20, 1943, ibid.

[114] A complete listing of these swaps is attached to L. P. J. Roy to BNS, June 13, 1945, ibid.

[115] Foreign Exchange Control Board memo by S. Turk and C. D. Blyth, February 7, 1945, ibid.

[116] Chief of Foreign Currency Division to Secretary, Bank of Canada, February 14, 1944, BOC file A16–3.

[117] Sveriges Riksbank to Bank of Canada, March 8, 1944 and D. G. Marble to W. C. Clark, March 8, 1944, ibid.

[118] Bank of England to Bank of Canada, September 6, 1944, BOC file A16–3. All Banco de Portugal communications to Ottawa passed through the Bank of England.

[119] BNS to Bank of Canada, September 19, 1944, BOC file A17–1.

[120] Bank of Canada to Bank of England. September 30, 1944, BOC file 515–17–5.

[121] Ibid., October 2, 1944.

[122] All these transfers are documented in BOC files 515–17–5 and A16–3.

[123] BOC file A6–4.

[124] BOC file A13–2.

[125] BNS to Bank of Ottawa, July 11, 1945, BOC file A17–1.

[126] Bank of Canada to BNS, July 12, 1945, ibid.

[127] Bank of Canada to Sveriges Riksbank, June 11, 1945, BOC file A16–3.

[128] The West German central bank, the Bank deutscher Länder, had been created in 1948 and was totally distinct from the wartime Deutsche Reichsbank. There is no connection between the 1954–56 gold transactions conducted by the Bank deutscher Länder and any gold transactions that took place during World War II and immediately after the end of that war.

[129] London lawyer representing sundry persons account holder to Bank of Canada, August 29, 1949, BOC file A18–17–8.

[130] Gill Bennett, Head of Historians, Foreign and Commonwealth Office, London, to Duncan McDowall, September 8, 1997. Copy available on request.

[131] Neville Wylie, "The Swiss Franc and British Policy towards Switzerland, 1939–1945," no date, p. 1. A copy of this paper was kindly supplied by the Foreign and Commonwealth Office in London.

[132] All statistics from the Swiss Federal Department of Foreign Affairs.

[133] In these matters, Professor Wylie's paper, op. cit., is excellent.

[134] Norman to Towers, March 8, 1942, BOC file A17–1.

[135] File OV63/4, Bank of England Archives.

[136] Translated from *Swiss Diplomatic Documents*, Vol. 14 (1941–1943), Document #292, appendix II.

[137] Minutes of the BNS Board of Directors, February 12, 1942.

[138] Minutes of the Bank Committee, March 26/27, 1942, p. 103, BNS Archive.

[139] Norman to Towers, May 1, 1942, BOC file A17–1.

[140] "Response to Professor McDowall's questionnaire on gold swaps carried out between the Swiss Nationale Bank and the Bank of Portugal," September 12, 1997 [translated from the original German]; microfilmed files OV63/3 (parts 1 & 2) and OV63/4, Bank of England Archives and Wylie, "The Swiss Franc . . .," op. cit.

[141] All statistics from the Swiss Federal Department of Foreign Affairs.

[142] Ibid.

[143] Note of August 31, 1944, Bank of England file OV62/24.

[144] "Estimated Gold Holdings of the Bank of Portugal at 30/6/64," ibid. and "Movimento do Ouro do Banco de Portugal no Estrangeiro – ouro fino (kgs.), 1937–1946" and bar graph "Banque Nationale Suisse: Movimento do ouro de 1941 a 1946" for accounts A, B, C, and D, taken from Ouro: 1937 a 1946, Banco de Portugal, Lisbon, 1997. A September 1943 cable from the Ministry of Economic Warfare in London to the British Embassy in Lisbon provided a more definitive breakdown of the purposes of the Banco de Portugal accounts in Berne. Account A was intended for "gold sold to the Bank of Portugal by Swiss for escudos, without evidence of German interest." Account B was "for gold purchased by Banco de Portugal for Swiss francs." Account C was for "gold sales by Reichsbank to Banco de Portugal." See J. R. Culpin to S. D. Wyatt, September 29, 1943, Bank of England file OV62/23.

[145] BNS to Bank of Canada, April 28, 1942, BOC file A17–1.

[146] Towers to Norman, April 28, 1942, BOC file A17–1.

[147] Norman to Towers, May 1, 1942, ibid. As has been pointed out earlier in this report, this is the only instance in which Norman repeated a phrase for emphasis in a communication with Towers.

[148] Bank of Canada to BNS, May 2, 1942, ibid.

[149] Towers to various general managers, BOC file 135–15.

[150] Bank of England to Bank of Canada, May 4, 1942, BOC file A31.

[151] Overseas and Foreign Office, "Secret: Regarding Gold in Canada," November 13, 1942, Bank of England file OV63/3.

[152] Minutes of the BNS Board of Directors, April 9, 1942, #279 and May 7, 1942, #350.

[153] Ibid., meetings of June 11, 1942, #428, June 25, 1942, #470, September 17, 1942, #658 and November 5–6, 1942, #769.

[154] David Eccles, British Embassy, Lisbon to Harry Lucas, Ministry of Economic Warfare, London, June 25, 1942, Bank of England file OV62/23 (part 2).

[155] S. D. Waley to David Eccles, July, 1942, ibid.

[156] Memorandum from Overseas and Foreign Office, August 31, 1944, Bank of England file OV62/24.

[157] See, for instance, Note of August 31, 1944, Bank of England file OV62/24.

[158] Secret – "Gold Imports into Portugal – Measures Taken to Eliminate Evidence of Origin of Gold Bars," signed by Sir Stanley Wyatt, September 9, 1944, Bank of England file OV62/24.

[159] "Estimated Gold Holdings of the Bank of Portugal at 30/6/44." Bank of England file OV62/24. There was much discussion about all such estimates and their accuracy. Each commentary reported different sources. The overall effect was, however, of large outflows of gold to Portugal from Switzerland.

[160] Banco de Portugal, "Ouro 1937 a 1946," Lisbon, 1997. Tables" "Movimento do Ouro do Banco de Portugal no Estrangeiro," "Movimento do Ouro do B. Portugal no B. Nationale Suisse" and "Ouro em Barra: Depositado no Banque National Suisse – C/'A', C/'B' and C/'C'."

[161] Testimony of Prof. Joaquim Da Costa Leite before the House of Representatives Committee on Banking and Financial Services, June 25, 1997, appended to Ouro: 1937 a 1946.

[162] Memorandum #487, Towers Papers, Bank of Canada Archives.

[163] Banco do Portugal, "Balanco do Banco de Portugal em 31 de Dezembro: Disponibilidades en Ouro e em Moeda Estrangeira," in Ouro 1937–46, Lisbon, 1997.

[164] Secret – "Gold Imports into Portugal," August 17, 1944, Bank of England file OV62/64.

[165] Ibid., September 2, 1944.

[166] Memo of February, 14, 1944 and Bank of Canada to Sveriges Riksbank, March 9, 1944, BOC file A16–3.

[167] All transaction details in BOC files A31 and A16–3 and Allied commentary on this deal in Overseas and Foreign Office Memo of August 31, 1944 and Overseas and Foreign Office Memo "Swedish Kronor Transactions of the Bank of Portugal," November 22, 1944, Bank of England file OV62/24.

[168] "Swedish Kronor Transactions . . .," op. cit.

[169] All transactions recorded in BOC file A16–3.

[170] Bank of Canada to Bank of England, September 19, 1944, BOC file 515–17–5.

[171] Minutes of the BNS Board of Directors, September 22, 1944, #985.

[172] Banco de Portugal, "Movimento do Ouro do Banco de Portugal no Estrangeiro, 1937–46."

[173] "Response to Professor McDowall . . ." September 12, 1997, op. cit.

[174] Details in BOC files A1–5A, A19–18, 1057–1 and 135C. As this report was close to printing, a 1956 memorandum of the Federal Reserve Bank of New York referring to these same "Prussian gold bars" was located in the U.S. archives. The specific transactions and bar numbers are being verified by the Bank, but it appears that the U.S. document does not contain any new evidence that "tainted" gold was handled by the Bank of Canada.

[175] See "European Perspective," p. 18, footnote 45.

[176] J. L. Granatstein, *Canada's War: The Politics of the Mackenzie King Government 1939–1945*, Toronto, 1975, p. 159.

[177] C. P. Stacey, *Men, Arms and Government: The War Policies of Canada 1939–1945*, Ottawa, 1970, p. 51.

[178] Granatstein, op. cit., p. 160.

[179] Towers to Norman, November 5, 1941, file GFT75–9, Towers Papers, Bank of Canada Archives.

[180] J. A. C. Osborne to G. F. Bolton, March 19, 1935, Bank of England file C43/284.

[181] S. Turk to G. F. Bolton, March 22, 1935, ibid.

[182] W. L. Mackenzie King diary, December 18, 1941, National Archives of Canada.

[183] Towers diary, September 1940, GFT75–39, Towers Papers, Bank of Canada Archives.

[184] J. L. Granatstein, *The Ottawa Men: The Civil Service Mandarins 1935–1957*, Toronto, 1982.

[185] Granatstein, *Canada's War*, p. 160.

[186] Interview with Louis Rasminsky, September 3, 1997.

[187] Interview with David McQueen, September 10, 1997.

[188] Towers to Robertson, February 26, 1944, BOC file 135.

[189] Marble to R.B. Bryce, July 6, 1944, BOC file 135.

[190] Robertson to W. C. Clark, June 13, 1944, ibid.

[191] A. N. McLeod to R. B. Bryce, May 30, 1944, Department of Finance Central Registry WAC file 1515–005–001.

[192] See, for instance, Memo by Louis Rasminsky to Towers, no date, BOC file 135 and Scott Macdonald, External Affairs, to W. C. Clark, February 29, 1944, Department of Finance Central Registry file WAC 1515–005–001.

[193] Department of the Secretary of State of Canada, "Declaration by Canada on Gold Looted by the Axis and Subsequently Acquired by Third Countries," January 24, 1945, copy in BOC file 135.

[194] October 23, 1947, copy in BOC file 135.

[195] Montreal *Gazette*, July 16, 1948. Comment by "D.H.F." R. B. Bryce commented on the same clipping that he thought that Canada did have a right, as a participant in the Inter-Allied Reparations Agency, to intervene.

[196] Assistant Deputy Governor L. P. Saint-Amour and Deputy Secretary L. P. J. Roy to D. G. Marble, November 24, 1943, BOC file 10-6, copy held in BOC Archives.

[197] BOC file A17–1.

APPENDIX

BANK OF CANADA

Reconstruction of Gold Safekeeping Records 1935-56

Summary of the methodology and results

On July 28, 1997, the Bank of Canada released an interim report outlining the results of an initial search of the Bank's wartime gold records. The search was in direct response to questions raised by the Canadian Jewish Congress with respect to information contained in recently declassified U.S. Government documents. These documents implied that a 1942 transfer of ownership of gold held in safekeeping at the Bank of Canada may have facilitated a separate, parallel transfer in Switzerland of looted Nazi gold between the central banks of Switzerland and Portugal.

The interim report outlined the results of the Bank's preliminary review of its gold records while recognizing that more extensive research of its records was needed to fully respond to concerns about the Bank's possible involvement in transactions related to looted Nazi gold. In mid-July, the Bank assembled a project team of current and retired officers and support staff to begin the arduous task of reconstructing the central bank's gold records for the period 1935-1956. The broad range of the reconstruction period was deemed necessary to identify and establish the proper context for gold transactions involving the Bank's 39 clients[1] in the prewar, wartime and postwar period.[2]

The principal focus of the group's research was the Bank's gold records, which include both correspondence and transaction files. The reconstruction process was possible because most of the necessary' records and documents were available for retrieval from the Bank's archives and operations files. The major documents used in the reconstruction process were:

1. Accounting ledgers
2. Transaction files
3. Other supporting records (e.g., gold bar lists)
4. Correspondence files

The accounting ledgers were examined in detail. The relevant correspondence and transaction files[3] were linked back to each physical movement of gold bars received for a client's account or released from the account. A similar process was followed for book-entry (i.e., "paper") transfers of gold between two clients. Using the transaction and correspondence files as source documents, most of the 4,400 transactions processed by the Bank in the 1935-56 period were captured in a database. However, one minor gap exists in the records for two clients[4] in 1935. The table opposite (top) summarizes the number of gold safekeeping transactions processed by the Bank.

Perhaps the most ambitious and daunting task undertaken by the project group was the attempt to track the movement of every gold bar physically shipped in or out of the Bank during the 22-year span of the reconstruction period. The Bank processed approximately 565,000 bar transactions[5] in the 1935-56 period. Tracking some half-million bar transactions was further complicated because very few of the original bar lists that accompanied incoming gold shipments were still intact. The project team faced consid-

Number of Gold Safekeeping Transactions – 1935–56

Year	Domestic Clients	Foreign Central Banks	Governments & Other Institutions	Internal Suspense Accounts	Total
1935–38	378	65	3	2	448
1939–45	751	978	189	19	1937
1946–56	1017	569	158	286	2030
Total	2146	1612	350	307	4415

erable challenges in trying to reestablish the integrity of the original bar lists. Nevertheless, by the end of the project, the Bank was successful in tracing more than 90% of all incoming and outgoing gold bars in the 1935–56 time frame.

The Bank encountered another hurdle in trying to decipher the melter/assayer numerical codes on bar lists received from the Bank of England, our largest foreign safe-keeping client. Despite extensive research, the Bank was unable to find a comprehensive list of melters/assayers and their associated Bank of England codes for this period. However, we have developed a list of melter/assayers who were accredited by the London Gold Market during this time frame. Further research into melter/assayer coding systems of this era may shed more light on this issue.

Two tables follow. Table I illustrates the significant volumes of gold received from foreign clients in the immediate prewar period and during the war. Table II shows the year end position in total fine ounces for each gold safekeeping client during the project period 1935–56. This table also shows the number of gold bars held at year-end by clients.

A more detailed report on the methodology and results is available in the Gold History Project file at the Bank.

Table I   Gold received for foreign earmarked accounts – 1938–45

Year	No. of bars	Bars (fine ozs)	Coins (fine ozs)**	Total (fine ozs)
1938	6,924	2,751,863.068		2,751,863.068
1939	40,885	16,494,059.529	520.294	16,494,579.823
1940	134,798	53,798,785.675	8,101,025.206	61,899,810.881
1941	3,198	1,192,663.370	189,339.911	1,382,003.281
1942			51.014	51.014
1943				0.000
1944	525	214,186.961	67.207	214,254.168
1945	2	811.383	29.294	840.677
Grand total	**186,332**	**74,452,369.986**	**8,291,032.926**	**82,743,402.912**

** Includes miscellaneous gold items such as gold buttons and gold clips

Table II - Client Year End Holdings in Fine Ozs 1935–56 (page 1 : 1935–38)

Client names	Date		1935	
	Opened	Closed	Bars	Y/E Holdings
Domestic Clients				
Bank of Canada	1935	1940		5,157,638.199
Minister of Finance	1935			105,973.538*
Foreign Central Banks				
Bank of England	1936			
Banque de France	1939			
Bank Polski	1940	1950		
Banque Melli Iran	1940	1948		
Banco Central de Bolivia	1940	1951		
*Exempt under Section S-13(1) ATIA***				
Banque Nationale Suisse	1942			
Banco de Portugal	1942			
De Surinaamsche Bank	1942			
Norges Bank	1942			
Banque Nationale de Belgique	1943			
Sveriges Riksbank	1944			
De Curacaosche Bank	1945			
Banco de Mexico	1945			
Narodni Banka Ceskoslevenska	1949	1950		
De Nederlandsche Bank	1946			
Danmarks Nationalbank	1951			
Oesterreichische Nationalbank	1951			
Bank Deutscher Lander	1954			
Foreign Govts & Other Institutions				
Bank for International Settlements	1935		0	0.000
Royal Norwegian Government	1940	1942		
Royal Netherlands Government	1940	1949		
Bank of London & S.America Ltd	1940	1947		
Polish Government	1940	1948		
Netherlands Indies Government	1943	1946		
Internal Suspense Accounts				
Guaranty Trust Co	1938	1938		
Sundry Persons	1941	1953		
Royal Bank of Canada	1941	1956		
Bank of Montreal	1946	1952		
Canadian Bank of Commerce	1946	1952		
Imperial Bank of Canada	1946	1947		
Bank of Toronto	1946	1947		
Barclays Bank (Canada)	1946	1948		
Bank of Nova Scotia	1947	1956		
Bankers Trust Co	1947	1947		
International Monetary Fund	1948	1948		
Federal Reserve Bank of New York	1952	1952		
GRAND TOTAL			0	5,157,636.199

The number of bars held at year end by the Bank of Canada is unavailable due to missing transaction information for the period of March 11 to September 11, 1935.

Date closed - Blank indicates that the account is still open at year end 1956.

Total Year End Holdings include gold bars, gold coins and miscellaneous gold items

1936		1937		1938	
Bars	Y/E Holdings	Bars	Y/E Holdings	Bars	Y/E Holdings
	5,159,419.759		5,159,752.223		5,282,641.907
10	109,310.597	0	773.393	72	34,657.615
3,304	1,335,588.323	4,748	1,915,435.580	10,219	4,087,731.141
42	16,908.875	42	16,908.875	42	16,908.875
				0	0.000
3,356	**6,621,299.554**	**4,790**	**7,092,870.071**	**10,333**	**9,421,939.538**

* Converted from dollar value to fine ounces at the standard rate of $20.671834
** Pending results of consultation under "Access to Information Act"

Table II - Client Year End Holdings in Fine Ozs 1935–56 (page 2 : 1939–43)

Client names	1939		1940	
	Bars	Y/E Holdings	Bars	Y/E Holdings
Domestic Clients				
Bank of Canada		5,888,072.585		0.0
Minister of Finance	909	369,477.497	8,663	3,912,471.2
Foreign Central Banks				
Bank of England	17,930	7,194,138.845	60,575	24,071,172.3
Banque de France	17,531	7,088,094.328	10,581	11,135,127.9
Bank Polski			608	241,818.6
Banque Melli Iran			0	0.0
Banco Central de Bolivia			0	0.0
*Exempt under Section S-13(1) ATIA** *			50	20,271.4
Banque Nationale Suisse				
Banco de Portugal				
De Surinaamsche Bank				
Norges Bank				
Banque Nationale de Belgique				
Sveriges Riksbank				
De Curacaosche Bank				
Banco de Mexico				
Narodni Banka Ceskoslevenska				
De Nederlandsche Bank				
Danmarks Nationalbank				
Oesterreichische Nationalbank				
Bank Deutscher Lander				
Foreign Govts & Other Institutions				
Bank for International Settlements	42	16,908.875	0	0.0
Royal Norwegian Government			1,335	1,098,263.8
Royal Netherlands Government			5,732	2,812,124.6
Bank of London & S.America Ltd			0	0.0
Polish Government			180	71,855.4
Netherlands Indies Government				
Internal Suspense Accounts				
Guaranty Trust Co				
Sundry Persons				
Royal Bank of Canada				
Bank of Montreal				
Canadian Bank of Commerce				
Imperial Bank of Canada				
Bank of Toronto				
Barclays Bank (Canada)				
Bank of Nova Scotia				
Bankers Trust Co				
International Monetary Fund				
Federal Reserve Bank of New York				
GRAND TOTAL	**36,412**	**20,554,692.130**	**87,724**	**43,363,105.6**

The number of bars held at year end by the Bank of Canada is unavailable due to missing transaction information for the period of March 11 to September 11, 1935.

Date closed - Blank indicates that the account is still open at year end 1956.

Total Year End Holdings include gold bars, gold coins and miscellaneous gold items

1941		1942		1943	
Bars	Y/E Holdings	Bars	Y/E Holdings	Bars	Y/E Holdings
8,615	3,894,381.181	10,115	4,445,235.078	15,132	6,437,092.859
50,417	20,074,083.826	45,653	17,994,473.023	42,940	16,903,030.121
10,581	11,135,127.979	10,899	11,135,127.979	10,899	11,135,127.979
489	194,007.877	444	176,887.838	422	168,190.584
0	0.000	0	0.000	0	0.000
0	0.000	0	0.000	0	0.000
197	79,597.770	197	79,597.770	197	79,597.770
		1,679	677,369.882	4,617	1,861,817.112
		321	129,233.430	321	129,233.443
		75	30,306.356	113	45,671.528
		1,335	1,098,263.842	1,335	1,098,263.842
				474	191,261.918
0	0.000	0	0.000	0	0.000
1,335	1,098,263.842	0	0.000		
3,491	1,921,836.178	2,762	1,631,744.646	714	806,975.786
0	0.000	0	0.000	0	0.000
118	47,505.687	75	30,146.023	75	30,146.023
				941	379,574.260
0	0.000	0	0.000	0	0.000
0	0.000	0	0.000	0	0.000
75,243	38,444,804.340	73,555	37,428,385.867	78,180	39,265,983.225

* Converted from dollar value to fine ounces at the standard rate of $20.671834
** Pending results of consultation under "Access to Information Act"

Table II - Client Year End Holdings in Fine Ozs 1935–56 (page 3 : 1944–48)

Client names	1944		1945	
	Bars	Y/E Holdings	Bars	Y/E Holdings
Domestic Clients				
Bank of Canada				0.0
Minister of Finance	20,113	8,432,987.947	24,349	10,125,689.0
Foreign Central Banks				
Bank of England	42,195	16,602,523.473	40,100	15,760,001.2
Banque de France	10,899	11,135,127.979	4,038	8,374,710.3
Bank Polski	904	365,332.881	947	382,536.8
Banque Melli Iran	0	0.000	0	0.0
Banco Central de Bolivia	0	0.000	246	99,472,.2
*Exempt under Section S-13(1) ATIA***	197	79,597.770	197	79,597.7
Banque Nationale Suisse	4,867	1,963,252.456	5,479	2,208,104.1
Banco de Portugal	441	177,524.282	281	113,133.6
De Surinaamsche Bank	113	45,671.528	113	45,671.5
Norges Bank	1,335	1,098,263.842	1,335	1,098,263.8
Banque Nationale de Belgique	0	0.000	470	189,666.9
Sveriges Riksbank	1,116	445,207.676	2,537	1,015,595.0
De Curacaosche Bank			0	234,188.6
Banco de Mexico			4,676	1,878,416.8
Narodni Banka Ceskoslevenska				
De Nederlandsche Bank				
Danmarks Nationalbank				
Oesterreichische Nationalbank				
Bank Deutscher Lander				
Foreign Govts & Other Institutions				
Bank for International Settlements	0	0.000	0	0.0
Royal Norwegian Government				
Royal Netherlands Government	0	284,315.309	0	50,126.6
Bank of London & S.America Ltd	0	0.000	0	0.0
Polish Government	75	30,146.023	30	12,371.4
Netherlands Indies Government	941	379,574.260	941	379,574.2
Internal Suspense Accounts				
Guaranty Trust Co				
Sundry Persons	0	0.000	0	0.0
Royal Bank of Canada	0	0.000	3	961.1
Bank of Montreal				
Canadian Bank of Commerce				
Imperial Bank of Canada				
Bank of Toronto				
Barclays Bank (Canada)				
Bank of Nova Scotia				
Bankers Trust Co				
International Monetary Fund				
Federal Reserve Bank of New York				
GRAND TOTAL	**83,196**	**41,039,525.426**	**85,742**	**42,048,083.7**

The number of bars held at year end by the Bank of Canada is unavailable due to missing transaction information for the period of March 11 to September 11, 1935.

Date closed - Blank indicates that the account is still open at year end 1956.

Total Year End Holdings include gold bars, gold coins and miscellaneous gold items

1946		1947		1948	
Bars	Y/E Holdings	Bars	Y/E Holdings	Bars	Y/E Holdings
37,906	15,379,052.311	19,999	8,223,771.123	28,227	11,514,995.596
28,444	11,315,061.647	21,000	8,373,596.862	20,841	8,314,433.813
0	0.000	14	6,169.086	18	7,750.420
947	382,536.851	947	382,536.851	977	394,908.261
0	0.000				
246	99,472.272	246	99,472.272	246	99,472.272
197	79,597.770	197	79,597.770	197	79,597.770
6,259	2,522,019.425	4,746	1,908,479.513	4,591	1,845,954.668
281	113,133.671	281	113,133.671	281	113,133.671
113	45,671.528	113	45,671.528	75	30,317.523
1,335	1,098,263.842	1,303	1,098,277.674	850	723,201.157
470	189,668.991	470	189,668.991	630	254,185.363
2,537	1,015,595.071	0	0.000	0	0.00
0	234,188.640	0	234,188.640	0	234,188.640
4,676	1,878,416.822	2,120	853,275.285	0	0.000
941	379,574.260	618	249,298.787	618	249,298.787
0	0.000	0	0.000	10	139,891.411
0	50,126.669	0	50,126.669	0	50,126.669
0	0.000	0	0.000		
30	12,371.410	30	12,371.410	0	0.00
0	0.000				
0	0.000	0	0.000	0	0.000
16	3,964.822	0	0.000	0	0.000
1	382.498	632	254,238.834	0	0.000
0	0.000	0	0.000	0	0.000
0	0.000	0	0.000		
0	0.000	0	0.000		
0	0.000				
		0	0.000	0	0.000
		0	0.000	0	
					0.000
84,399	34,799,098.500	52,716	22,173,874.966	57,561	24,051,456.021

* Converted from dollar value to fine ounces at the standard rate of \$20.671834
** Pending results of consultation under "Access to Information Act"

Table II - Client Year End Holdings in Fine Ozs 1935–56 (page 4 : 1949–53)

Client names	1949		1950	
	Bars	Y/E Holdings	Bars	Y/E Holding
Domestic Clients				
Bank of Canada				
Minister of Finance	34,321	13,955,245.446	33,887	13,779,776.
Foreign Central Banks				
Bank of England	23,686	9,458,926.236	64,156	25,694,497.
Banque de France	18	7,750.420	18	7,750.
Bank Polski	977	394,908.261	0	0.
Banque Melli Iran				
Banco Central de Bolivia	246	99,472.272	246	99,472,.
*Exempt under Section S-13(1) ATIA***	197	79,597.770	197	79,597.
Banque Nationale Suisse	4,625	1,859,528.135	4,737	1,904,492.
Banco de Portugal	281	113,133.671	281	113,133.
De Surinaamsche Bank	75	30,317.523	75	30,317.
Norges Bank	850	723,201.157	850	723,201.
Banque Nationale de Belgique	550	221,909.939	550	221,909.
Sveriges Riksbank	0	0.000	0	0.
De Curacaosche Bank	0	234,188.640	0	234,188.
Banco de Mexico	0	0.000	0	0.
Narodni Banka Ceskoslevenska	0	27,000.034	0	0.
De Nederlandsche Bank	628	303,498.105	628	303,498.
Danmarks Nationalbank				
Oesterreichische Nationalbank				
Bank Deutscher Lander				
Foreign Govts & Other Institutions				
Bank for International Settlements	345	136,413.436	768	308,597.
Royal Norwegian Government				
Royal Netherlands Government	0	0.000		
Bank of London & S.America Ltd				
Polish Government				
Netherlands Indies Government				
Internal Suspense Accounts				
Guaranty Trust Co				
Sundry Persons	0	0.000	0	0.
Royal Bank of Canada	0	0.000	0	0.
Bank of Montreal	0	0.000	0	0.
Canadian Bank of Commerce	0	0.000	0	0.
Imperial Bank of Canada				
Bank of Toronto				
Barclays Bank (Canada)				
Bank of Nova Scotia	0	0.000	0	0.
Bankers Trust Co				
International Monetary Fund				
Federal Reserve Bank of New York				
GRAND TOTAL	66,866	27,645,091.045	106,393	43,500,432.

The number of bars held at year end by the Bank of Canada is unavailable due to missing transaction information for the period of March 11 to September 11, 1935.

Date closed - Blank indicates that the account is still open at year end 1956.

Total Year End Holdings include gold bars, gold coins and miscellaneous gold items

1951		1952		1953	
Bars	Y/E Holdings	Bars	Y/E Holdings	Bars	Y/E Holdings
52,281	21,143,911.255	61,791	24,954,963.469	69,389	27,999,056.371
83,921	33,611,780.778	37,563	15,044,345.845	37,563	15,043,754.118
702	178,466.519	702	178,466.519	702	178,466.519
0	0.000				
197	79,597.770	0	0.000		
4,737	1,904,492.907	4,737	1,904,492.907	4,258	1,711,008.512
281	113,133.671	281	113,133.671	281	113,133.671
75	30,317.523	75	30,317.523	75	30,317.523
850	723,201.157	1,085	736,766.395	1,180	711,148.953
550	221,909.939	550	221,909.939	550	221,909.939
484	192,950.130	484	192,950.130	885	353,378.927
0	234,188.640	0	234,188.640	0	234,188.640
0	0.000	0	0.000	0	0.000
790	367,798.128	790	367,798.128	790	367,798.128
159	64,302.975	159	64,302.975	159	64,302.975
450	180,000.073	450	180,000.073	450	180,000.073
720	289,306.884	485	195,270.805	825	384,509.037
0	0.000	0	0.000	0	0.000
0	0.000	0	0.000	0	0.000
0	0.000	0	0.000		
0	0.000	0	0.000		
0	0.000	0	0.000	0	0.000
146,197	**59,335,358.147**	**109,152**	**44,418,907.019**	**117,107**	**47,572,971.386**

* Converted from dollar value to fine ounces at the standard rate of $20.671834
** Pending results of consultation under "Access to Information Act"

Table II - Client Year End Holdings in Fine Ozs 1935–56 (page 5 : 1954–56)

Client names	1954		1955	
	Bars	Y/E Holdings	Bars	Y/E Holding
Domestic Clients				
Bank of Canada				
Minister of Finance	75,961	30,626,061.853	78,937	31,793,435
Foreign Central Banks				
Bank of England	39,698	15,900,632.582	40,762	16,313,719
Banque de France	702	178,466.519	702	178,468
Bank Polski				
Banque Melli Iran				
Banco Central de Bolivia				
*Exempt under Section S-13(1) ATIA***				
Banque Nationale Suisse	3,458	1,388,869.114	3,458	1,388,869
Banco de Portugal	281	113,133.671	281	113,133
De Surinaamsche Bank	75	30,317.523	75	30,317
Norges Bank	851	634,125.849	989	633,862
Banque Nationale de Belgique	550	221,909.939	550	221,909
Sveriges Riksbank	2,965	1,189,963.335	3.319	1,332,893
De Curacaosche Bank	0	234,188.640	0	234,188
Banco de Mexico	0	0.000	0	0
Narodni Banka Ceskoslevenska				
De Nederlandsche Bank	790	367,798.128	790	367,798
Danmarks Nationalbank	159	64,302.975	159	64,302
Oesterreichische Nationalbank	450	180,000.073	450	180,000
Bank Deutscher Lander	375	150,310.053	1,083	436,186
Foreign Govts & Other Institutions				
Bank for International Settlements	570	228,794.874	762	306,912
Royal Norwegian Government				
Royal Netherlands Government				
Bank of London & S.America Ltd				
Polish Government				
Netherlands Indies Government				
Internal Suspense Accounts				
Guaranty Trust Co				
Sundry Persons				
Royal Bank of Canada	0	0.000	0	0
Bank of Montreal				
Canadian Bank of Commerce				
Imperial Bank of Canada				
Bank of Toronto				
Barclays Bank (Canada)				
Bank of Nova Scotia	0	0.000	0	0
Bankers Trust Co				
International Monetary Fund				
Federal Reserve Bank of New York				
GRAND TOTAL	**126,885**	**51,508,875.108**	**132,317**	**53,595,997**

The number of bars held at year end by the Bank of Canada is unavailable due to missing transaction information for the period of March 11 to September 11, 1935.

Date closed - Blank indicates that the account is still open at year end 1956.

Total Year End Holdings include gold bars, gold coins and miscellaneous gold items

1956	
Bars	Y/E Holdings
78,271	31,494,928.140
43,128	17,266,466.069
702	178,466.519
3,458	1,388,869.114
281	113,133.671
75	30,317.523
989	633,862.769
550	221,909.939
3,319	1,332,893.704
0	234,188.640
0	0.000
790	367,798.128
159	64,302.975
450	180,000.073
2,251	907,142.494
364	146,329.952
0	0.000
0	0.000
134,787	**54,560,609.710**

* Converted from dollar value to fine ounces at the standard rate of $20.671834
** Pending results of consultation under "Access to Information Act"

NOTES TO APPENDIX

[1] The Bank of Canada's clients in the 1935–56 period included: 2 domestic clients; 19 foreign central banks; 6 foreign governments and other institutions; and 12 Bank of Canada internal suspense accounts.

[2] The usefulness of this reconstruction exercise is illustrated by our ability to analyse the transactions involving "Prussian gold bars" referred to in the January 12, 1956, memorandum of the Federal Reserve Bank of New York discovered in late November 1997. Our examination of reconstructed records shows that close to 90% of these bars were originally shipped to the Bank of Canada by the Bank of England in 1940 and therefore could not have been tainted by wartime activities. The reconstruction of these transactions continues.

[3] The Gold History Project Team reviewed more than 300 files containing in excess of 50,000 documents, and examined over 500 ledger pages.

[4] Bank of Canada and Minister of Finance gold account records for the first six months of the Bank's operations March 11 – September 11, 1935) have not been located despite searches in both Bank of Canada and the National Archives of Canada.

[5] A "bar transaction" is generally defined as the physical movement of one gold bar "in" or 'out" of a client's safekeeping account. "Book-entry" transfers of ownership between two clients did not involve gold bars being shipped in or out of the Bank and thus were not included. Given the project's focus on bars shipped from Europe, we also did not track some 63,000 bars purchased by the Minister of Finance from the Royal Canadian Mint in the 1950–56 period.

Finding Aid
Gold Arrangements and Transactions Files

BANK OF CANADA, GOLD HISTORY PROJECT

CONTENTS

Introduction	184
Bank for International Settlements	185
Banque Nationale de Belgique	186
Banque de France	187
Norges Bank	190
Bank Polski	191
Sveriges Riksbank	192
Banque Nationale Suisse	193
Bank of England	194
Federal Reserve Bank of New York	203
Banco Central de Bolivia	204
Danmarks Nationalbank	205
De Nederlandsche Bank	205
Banco de México	207
Bank Van de Nederlands Antillen	207
Oesterreichische Nationalbank	208
Deutsche Bundesbank	209
Banque Centrale de la République de Turquie	210
Banco de Portugal	211
Banque Melli Iran	212
De Surinaamsche Bank	212
Narodni Banka Ceskoslovenska V Praze	212
Minister of Finance – Gold	213
Other Relevant Records	215
Material Received from Central Banks, International Financial Institutions, Governments, and Others	230
Appendix: Department of Finance Documents	233

INTRODUCTION

The present finding aid is intended to serve as a guide for researchers to the archival records of the Bank of Canada that relate to gold transactions by the Bank between March 11, 1935, the day on which the Bank first opened its doors for business, and December 31, 1956, by which time the Bank had concluded its own involvement in various wartime gold transactions and Allied efforts to identify and to restore the monetary gold that had been looted by the Axis powers had effectively come to an end. As such, the finding aid is an enlarged version of the inventory of gold arrangements and transactions files that was compiled by the Bank to assist Professor Duncan McDowall of Carleton University, who was commissioned by the Bank in July 1997 to carry out an independent investigation of the Bank's handling of foreign gold during World War II. The finding aid is being published as part of the commitment by the Bank to opening archival records that relate to wartime gold transactions to the public in order to make the source material for Professor McDowall's report available and to facilitate further research into this subject.

In order to open those archival records to the public, it was necessary for the Bank of Canada to obtain the approval of former and existing clients for services involving gold to release their files. Clients have given their approval for the period March 11, 1935 to December 31, 1956 because of the overriding public interest in gold transactions that occurred during those years. Accordingly, archival records and current working files that relate to the provision of client services involving gold after December 31, 1956 will continue to be closed to the public.

Between March 1935 and December 1956, the Bank of Canada engaged in gold transactions for its own account (until 1940) and provided client services involving gold to the federal Minister of Finance and to a number of foreign central banks and governments.

The bulk of the files that are enumerated and described in the finding aid consists of those files that relate to the provision of client services involving gold to foreign central banks and governments. Generally, there are three types of files – viz., arrangements files, which document the opening of and the terms and conditions for the operation of a gold safekeeping account with the Bank of Canada; correspondence files, which contain the orders, advices and confirmations that document the day-to-day operation of an account; and transactions files, which contain the detailed accounting records for an account. In the instances of small, low-volume clients, the arrangements and correspondence files were frequently combined in one file.

Typically, the file numbers for arrangements and correspondence files begin either with the letter "A" or with the number "515" and those for transactions files with the number "580". For convenience, all three types of file have been brought together in the finding aid on a client-by-client basis.

The file titles that appear in the finding aid are those that were specified in the Bank of Canada's classification manual of the period. They sometimes differ from the titles that were actually used on the files.

It would appear that, despite a very thorough search, some relevant files are missing. For example, no arrangements or correspondence files from the period have been found either for De Surinaamsche Bank (now the Centrale Bank van Suriname) or for Narodoni Banka Ceskoslovenska V Praze, although the transaction files have been. Where a file has not been located, that fact is noted in the rightmost column of the finding aid.

Personal information is scattered throughout the files and, indeed, one file – A18-17-8, "Gold Delivered to Individuals and Companies at Request of Bank of England" – consists largely of such information. Personal information is protected under Section 19 (1) of *the Access of Information Act* and cannot be released unless certain conditions are met. The treatment of files and records under the Act is also noted in the rightmost column of the finding aid.

File# or Name	File Titles/Scope notes	Year/ Month	Document Indexes	Access Notes*
BANK FOR INTERNATIONAL SETTLEMENTS (BIS)				
A1-5	BIS – Gold Earmarked – Banco Central de Reserva de El Salvador	Vol. 1 3601-4810	All correspondence relates to 1936, with some misfiled items from 1948 that relate to transactions involving German gold coins with the Norges Bank.	
A1-5A	BIS – Gold Arrangements File documents the opening of and arrangements for the routine operation of a gold safekeeping account for the BIS with the Bank of Canada.The file also contains a considerable amount of correspondence between the BIS and the Bank of Canada concerning the periodic updating of a BIS publicationentitled "Conditions governing Gold Operations".	Vol. 1 3501-6512	Letter dated June 22, 1956, MacDonald (BIS) to Rasminsky, concerning Prussian Mint bars in the possession of the Bank of Canada. There are two annotations to the letter. The The first, on bottom of first page, records the transfer that involved the bars. The second near the bottom of the second page by Rasminsky, indicates that the bars were not "tainted". Letter dated August 29, 1956, Rasminsky to MacDonald, gives a brief history of how the bars came to be in the Bank of Canada's possession.	
A1-5A Routine	BIS - Gold Routine - Arrangements	Vol. 1 3601-5103		1 record exempt under S. 19 (1) ATIA.
	File documents the routine operation of a gold safekeeping account for the BIS with the Bank of Canada	Vol. 2 5104-5312		
		Vol. 3 5401-5512		
		Vol. 4 5601-5712		

File# or Name	File Titles/Scope notes	Year/ Month	Document Indexes	Access Notes*
Bank for International Settlements (BIS) – continued				
A1-5A Routine	Currency Division Gold Ledger - Bank for International Settlements	3509-5509	There are 6 pages of ledgers	
	Currency Division Gold Safekeeping Location Ledger		There are 12 pages of ledgers.	
580-43-3A	Gold held for BIS	440-5212		
580-43-3B	Gold Received from the Banco Central de Reserva de El Salvador, and held for safekeeping on account of the BIS	3501-3612		
580-42-3A	Gold transfers for BIS	440-5212		
580-42-3B	Gold Shipments from Gold Held in safekeeping for BIS	3501-4012		
580-43-3C	Bank for International	5601-5912		
580-43-3D	Bank for International Settlements - Shipments and Transfers - Bullion and Coin	5301-5512		

BANQUE NATIONALE DE BELGIQUE

File# or Name	File Titles/Scope notes	Year/ Month	Document Indexes	Access Notes*
A3-1	Gold Earmarked for Banque Nationale de Belgique	Vol. 1 3501-5512	Letter dated March 23, 1939, Towers to Dunning, (Minister of Finance), asking if he "is willing to extend the arrangements in respect to Bank of England gold to cover gold held by [Bank of Canada] for account of the National Bank of Belgium".	
	File documents the opening and routine operation of a gold safekeeping account for Banque Nationale de Belgique with the Bank of Canada		Letter dated March 27, 1939, Clark (Finance) to Towers, noting that the Minister is willing to extend the arrangement.	
		Vol. 2 5601-8112	Letter dated August 14, 1943, Towers to Isley Minister of Finance), asking if the gold earmarked in the name of Banque Nationale de Belgique can be regarded as outside the control of the Custodian of Enemy Property.	

File# or Name	File Titles/Scope notes	Year/ Month	Document Indexes	Access Notes*
Banque Nationale de Belgique – continued				
A3-1			Letter dated August 18, 1943, Clark (Finance) to Towers, stating that the gold is outside the control of the Custodian.	
	Currency Division Gold Ledger - Banque Nationale de Belgique	4308-6011	There is one page of ledgers.	
	Currency Division Gold Safekeeping Location Ledger		There are 2 pages of ledgers.	
580-43-5A	Banque Nationale de Belgique, Brussels - Gold held in Safekeeping	4301-6012 6101-6212		
580-42-5A	National Bank of Belgium - Gold Shipments and Transfers	4401-6012		

BANQUE DE FRANCE

File# or Name	File Titles/Scope notes	Year/ Month	Document Indexes	Access Notes*
A6-3	Gold Earmarked for Bank France File documents the opening and routine operation of a gold and other safekeeping accounts for the Banque de France and the Government of the French Republic with the Bank of Canada	Vol. 1 3901-3912	Letter dated April 15, 1939, Clark (Finance) to Towers, noting that the Minister of Finance (Dunning) "is willing to extend to gold held by the Bank of France the arrangement outlined in previous correspondence covering Bank of England and National Bank of Belgium gold."	
		Vol. 2 4001-4412	Letter dated January 16, 1940, Marble to Rousseau (Banque de France), informing Rousseau that the Bank of Canada "shall be pleased to receive gold which may be held by banks in Canada for account of French citizens and place it in safekeeping for the Banque de France, Account T. Such deposits would be acceptable whether gold is in bars or in coin."	

File# or Name	File Titles/Scope notes	Year/ Month	Document Indexes	Access Notes*
Banque de France – continued				
A6-3			Internal memorandum dated November 27, 1940, Secretary to Chief of the Currency Division, noting that the gold, bills and notes held in safekeeping for the Banque de France are now subject to the control of the Custodian of Enemy Property. (Control was released at the end of December 1944. See A6-4 for details.)	
		Vol. 3 4501-4912		1 record exempt under S.19 (a) ATIA.
		Vol. 4 5001-6812		2 records exempt under S.13 (1) ATIA.
A6-4	Banque de France "T" at the Bank of Canada	Vol. 1 3904-7208		1 record exempt under S.19 (1) ATIA.
	There is considerable duplication between this file and A6-3. The only new information contained in this file relates to the work of account reconciliation that took place after the Liberation.			
	Date range is misleading. Substantive material ends November 1951, with two misfiled items (?) from 1972.			
	Currency Division Gold Ledger - Banque de France	4503-4912	There are 6 pages of ledgers.	
	Currency Division Gold Safekeeping Location Ledgers		There are 5 pages of ledgers.	
580-43-7B	Gold received to be held in safekeeping for Banque de France	Vol 1. 4501-3912		
580-43-7A	Gold held in safekeeping - Banque de France	Vol. 1 3904-3912		

File# or Name	File Titles/Scope notes	Year/ Month	Document Indexes	Access Notes*
Banque de France – continued				
580-43-7A	Routine internal correspondence between Secretary's Department and Currency Division relating to shipments received for safekeeping.	Vol. 2 4001-8508		5 records exempt under S. 19 (1) ATIA.
580-42-7A	Gold Shipments and Transfers - Banque de France	Vol. 1 4005-4210		
	Routine internal correspondence between Secretary's Department. Foreign Exchange Division, and Currency Division.	4510-4912		
580-42-7B	Gold held in safekeeping Banque de France	3908-4006		
580-42-7C	Banque de France Main File	3904-8909	Internal memorandum dated January 19, 1940, from Secretary to Chief, Currency Division, advising of arrangements concluded with the Banque de France that gold held by chartered banks in Canada for citizens of France may be deposited for safekeeping and that Banque de France will settle in francs with the owners. Letter dated December 30, 1944, from the Secretary of State (Canada) - Office of Custodian of Enemy Property, releasing control over gold and other assets maintained by the Bank of Canada for the Banque de France.	

File# or Name	File Titles/Scope notes	Year/ Month	Document Indexes	Access Notes*

NORGES BANK

File# or Name	File Titles/Scope notes	Year/ Month	Document Indexes	Access Notes*
515-11-5	Norges Bank - Safekeeping Account File documents shipments of gold from the Bank of England to the Bank of Canada on account of the Royal Norwegian Government during mid-1940 and the routine operation of a gold safekeeping account for that government. The gold was transferred on October 16, 1942 to a new account in the name of the Bank of Norway. Annotation on the inside front cover notes that: "Gold held in safekeeping for the Bank of Norway transferred by the Government of Norway back to the Norges Bank, Oslo - Jan. 21/46."	Vol. 1 4001-8312	Letter dated August 15, 1940, Towers to Isley (Minister of Finance), indicating that the Bank of Canada is "taking the view that (the Royal Norwegian Government) are, for the time being, domiciled in London and that the assets which they have with us are freely disposable and do not come within the control of the the Enemy Property Custodian" and asking Isley whether or not he agrees with that view. Letter dated August 19, 1940, Isley to Towers, noting that he (Isley) agrees with the view that is being taken by the Bank of Canada.	
A12-4	Gold in safekeeping for Norges Bank File documents the opening and routine operation of a gold safekeeping account for the Norges Bank with the Bank of Canada.	Vol. 1 4601-5312 ——— Vol. 2 5401-7212		
	Currency Division Gold Ledger - Norges Bank	4210-5806	There are 5 pages of ledgers.	
	Currency Division Gold Safekeeping Location Ledger		There are 10 pages of ledgers.	
	Currency Division Gold Ledger - Royal Norwegian Government	4007-4210	There are 2 pages of ledgers.	
58-85-4	Audits and Auditing - Gold - Section 9, Sub-section 10 - Norges Banks	Vol. 1 4001-8712		

File# or Name	File Titles/Scope notes	Year/ Month	Document Indexes	Access Notes*
Norges Bank – continued				
580-42-12B	Bank of Norway - Norges Bank, Oslo, - Norway - Gold - Coin/General - Correspondence	5201-8712		
580-42-12A	Gold Shipments and Transfers - Norges Bank	4810-7009		

BANK POLSKI

File# or Name	File Titles/Scope notes	Year/ Month	Document Indexes	Access Notes*
A13-2	Bank Polski Gold in safekeeping (State Gold) File documents the opening, routine operation, and closing out of a gold safekeeping account for Bank Polski with the Bank of Canada.	Vol. 1 4001-4712 ——— Vol. 2 4801-5112	Letter dated October 7, 1940, Towers to Isley (Minister of Finance), indicating that the Bank of Canada is taking the view that the assets that the Government of Poland domiciled in London have with the Bank of Canada are freely disposable and do not come under the control of the Custodian of Enemy Property and asking Isley whether or not he agrees with that view. Isley notes in a subsequent reply that he does agree. (Copies in A13-4)	1 record exempt under S. 19 (1) ATIA.
A13-4	Polish Government Gold in safekeeping File documents the opening routine operations, and closing out of a gold safekeeping account and Canadian and U.S. dollar current accounts for the Polish Government with the Bank of Canada	Vol. 1 4001-4812		
	Currency Division Gold - Polish Government	4010-4805	There is one page of ledgers.	
	Currency Division Gold Safekeeping Location Ledger		There is one page of ledgers.	
	Currency Division Gold - Bank Polski	5003-5010	There are 3 pages of ledgers.	
	Currency Division Gold Safekeeping Location Ledger		There are 2 pages of ledgers	

File# or Name	File Titles/Scope notes	Year/ Month	Document Indexes	Access Notes*

SVERIGES RIKSBANK

File# or Name	File Titles/Scope notes	Year/ Month	Document Indexes	Access Notes*
A16-2	Sveriges Riksbank Accounts - Arrangements File documents the opening and routine operation of drawing and special accounts for the Sveriges Riksbank with the Bank of Canada and the operation of an informal transfer arrangement between the Bank of Canada and the Sveriges Riksbank "to facilitate the settlement of certain outstanding Swedish credits in Canada and Canadian credits in Sweden".	Vol 1. 3501-5012	Letter dated January 3, 1940, Gordon (on behalf of Towers) to Rooth (Governor, Sveriges Riksbank), replying to a letter dated December 11, 1939 asking about the opening of a U.S. dollar account for the Sveriges Riksbank with the Bank of Canada, the opening of U.S. dollar accounts for Swedish commercial banks with the Bank of Canada, and the operational response of the Bank of Canada in the event that Sweden were to be invaded.	File is not relevant, except for one record quoted by Professor McDowall. A copy of this record is available in a separate folder.
A16-3	Sveriges Riksbank - Gold File documents the opening and operation of a gold safekeeping account for the Sveriges with the Bank of Canada.	Vol. 1 4401-4712 ——— Vol. 2 5101-6412	File includes correspondence between Marble and Clark (Finance) during early March 1944 about the opening of a gold safekeeping account for the Sveriges Riksbank.	
	Currency Division Gold Ledger - Sveriges Riksbank	4403-6312	There is one page of ledgers.	
	Currency Division Gold Safekeeping Location Ledger		There are 5 pages of ledgers.	
580-43-16B	Gold received - Sveriges Riksbank, Stockholm, Sweden	4403-5103		
580-43-16A	Gold transferred - Sveriges Riksbank, Stockholm, Sweden	4501-4704		
580-42-15A	Sveriges Riksbank	5306-6407		

File# or Name	File Titles/Scope notes	Year/ Month	Document Indexes	Access Notes*

BANQUE NATIONALE SUISSE

File# or Name	File Titles/Scope notes	Year/ Month	Document Indexes	Access Notes*
A17-1 Arr.	Gold Earmarked for Banque Nationale Suisse File documents, though not fully, the establishment of the arrangements that enabled the Bank of to transfer gold from its gold accounts with the Bank of Canada to a gold account of the Banque Nationale Suisse with the Bank of Canada and, subsequently, the Banque Nationale Suisse to transfer gold from its gold account with the Bank of Canada to a gold account of the Banco de Portugal with the Bank of Canada.	Vol. 1 4201-4612		
A17-1 Routine	Gold Earmarked for Banque Nationale Suisse File documents the routine operation of a gold safekeeping account for Banque Nationale Suisse with the Bank of Canada	Vol. 1 4401-4512	Three cables all dated September 19, 1944 between Banque Nationale Suisse and the Bank of Canada, that relate to a transfer of gold from the gold account of the Banque Nationale Suisse to that of the Banco de. Portugal. Letter dated June 13, 1945, Bank of Canada to Banque Nationale Suisse, to which is attached a list of transactions involving gold that was earmarked for the Banque Nationale Suisse between November 6, 1942 and May 14, 1945.	
		Vol. 2 4601-4612		1 record exempt under S. 19 (1) ATIA.
		Vol. 3 4701-4812		
		Vol. 4 4901-5912		
515-12-5	Banque Nationale Suisse - Gold - Safekeeping Account	Vol. 1 5001-8312		

File# or Name	File Titles/Scope notes	Year/ Month	Document Indexes	Access Notes*
Banque Nationale Suisse – continued				
515-12-5	Currency Division Gold Ledger - Banque Nationale Suisse	4203-6402	There are 8 pages of ledgers.	
	Currency Division Gold Safekeeping Location Ledger		There are 7 pages of ledgers.	
58-81-7	Audits and Auditing - Gold - Section 9, Sub-section 6 - Banque Nationale Suisse	Vol. 1 4801-9312		
58-82-6	Audits and Auditing - Gold - Section 9, Sub-section 7 - Banque Nationale Suisse	Vol. 1 4801-8312		
580-43-10A	Gold received - Swiss National Bank, Berne	Vol. 1 4203-4212		
		Vol. 2 4301-4312		
580-43-10B	Gold shipments and transfers - Swiss National Bank, Berne	4401-5008		Several records exempt under S. 19 (1) ATIA.

BANK OF ENGLAND

| A18-17 Arr | Gold Earmarked for Bank of England - File documents both preliminary and final arrangements for gold held by the Bank of Canada earmarked for the account of the Bank of England. | Vol. 1 3601-4512 | Letter dated March 5, 1936, Osborne to Clark (Finance), noting that: "We have a general undertaking from your Department that gold held for the B.I.S. will, at all times, be granted an export license [Annotation: See 135, March 11, 1935] and perhaps you will kindly let us have a similar letter in connection with the Bank of England's gold or, if you prefer, in more general terms to cover any gold earmarked here." | |

File# or Name	File Titles/Scope notes	Year/ Month	Document Indexes	Access Notes*

Bank of England – continued

A18-17 Arr
                                        Vol. 2
                                        5101-5212   Letter dated March 11, 1936,
                                                     Clark to Osborne, noting
                                                     that Finance is willing to
                                                     grant licenses for export
                                                     of newly mined gold.

                                                     Cable dated April 4, 1938,
                                                     Towers to Siepmann (Bank
                                                     of England), noting, in Para. 4,
                                                     that the Minister of Finance
                                                     is "prepared to license the
                                        ——————   re-export of gold which might
                                        Vol. 3   be brought in, as well as
                                        5405-5904   newly mined Canadian gold
                                                     purchased for earmark."

                                                     Letter dated August 26, 1940,
                                                     Isley (Minister of Finance) to
                                                     Towers, setting out general
                                                     policy of Canadian Government
                                                     "with respect to gold delivered
                                                     to the Bank of Canada by the
                                                     Bank of England in connection
                                                     with payments arrangements
                                                     completed by the United
                                                     Kingdom."

A18-17-1   Gold Earmarked for   3601-3612   Cable dated July 30, 1942,
Routine   Bank of England   ——————   Bank of Canada to Banque   ——————
            (Transfer of Bullion)   3701-3712   Nationale Suisse, advising
                                        ——————   the Banque Nationale Suisse   ——————
            File documents sales of   3801-3812   that the Bank of Canada has
            gold to or for the Bank of ——————   earmarked 13,692.33 fine
            England by the Bank of   3901-3912   ounces of gold for its account 2 records exempt
            Canada, the receipt of   by order of the Bank of   S. 19 (1) ATIA.
            gold to be held in   England.   ——————
            safekeeping by the Bank   4001-4005
            of Canada for the Bank of   ——————   ——————
            England, and shipments   4006-4007
            of gold from the Bank of   ——————
            Canada to the Federal   4008-4009   2 records exempt
            Reserve Bank of New York   S. 19 (1) ATIA.
            on behalf of the Bank of   ——————
            England. Annotations   4009-4012
            suggest that further details ——————   ——————
            on pre-war shipments of   4101-4412   3 records exempt
            gold from Europe are to be   S. 19 (1) ATIA.
            found in the papers of   ——————
            Governor Towers.   4503-4612   ——————

                                        4701-5112

File# or Name	File Titles/Scope notes	Year/ Month	Document Indexes	Access Notes*
Bank of England – continued				
A18-17-2	Gold Earmarked for Bank of England. Shipped via Vancouver	Vol. 1 3911-4006		
	File documents the receipt of gold from India and Australia to be held in safekeeping by the Bank of Canada to the Federal Reserve Bank of San Francisco and the Federal Reserve Bank of New York on behalf of the Bank of England.	Vol. 2 4007-4012 Vol. 3 4101-4103		
A18-17-3	Gold Earmarked for Bank of England "L" Account File contains merely the few routine documents required to effect a transfer of gold from one of the Bank of England's	Vol. 1 4001-4012	Cable dated September 20, 1940, Bank of England to Bank of Canada, noting that: "Gold in the [new] account to be available to meet certified claims in respect of Lloyd's Canadian dollar policies in the event of an emergency."	1 record exempt under S. 19 (1), ATIA.
A18-17-4	Gold Earmarked for Banque Melli, Iran File documents the routine operation of a gold safekeeping account for Banque Melli Iran with the Bank of Canada and shipments of gold from the Bank of Canada to Irving Trust Company, New York, on behalf of Banque Melli Iran. The account was used by the U.K. government to make periodic payments of oil royalties to the Iranian government.	Vol. 1 4001-5812	Letter dated October 16, 1940, Towers to Ilsley (Minister of Finance), referring to Isley's letter of August 26, 1940 [copy in A18-17 Arr] "with respect to gold delivered to the Bank of Canada by the Bank of England in connection with payments arrangements completed by the United Kingdom". Letter also notes the opening of gold safekeeping accounts for Banque Melli Iran and for the Banco Central de Bolivia. Letter dated December 31, 1940, Marble to Rowe (Irving Trust Company), noting that the Minister of Finance has informed the Bank of Canada that export permits for the gold of Banque Melli Iran "would be freely granted".	1 record exempt under S. 19 (1) ATIA.

File# or Name	File Titles/Scope notes	Year/ Month	Document Indexes	Access Notes*
Bank of England – continued				
A18-17-6	Gold Earmarked for Bank of London and South	Vol. 1 4001-4112		5 records exempt under S. 19 (1) ATIA.
	File documents the routine operation of a gold safekeeping account for the Bank of London and South America Limited with the Bank of Canada.	Vol. 2 4201-4412		
	The account was used by the U.K. government to make periodic payments to Bolivian tin producers, the Bank of London and South America acting as an agent for the producers.	Vol. 3 4501-4707		
A18-17-7	Gold Earmarked for the Independent Tin Companies in Bolivia.	Vol. 1 4001-4207		
A18-17-8	Gold delivered to Individuals and Companies at request Bank of England #2 Account.	Vol. 1 4001-4412	Letter dated September 18, 1940, Bolton (Bank of England) to Gordon, announcing the Bank of England's decision to refuse permission to export gold	Accessible records photocopied. Most records exempt under S. 13 (1) or 19 (1) ATIA.
	On September 12, 1940, the Bank of England made an offer whereby it was possible for foreign-owned gold, deposited in London, to be delivered to the Bank of England for the purpose of evacuation to Canada and to be made available at the Bank of Canada one month after expiration of *Emergency Powers (Defence) Act 1939*. File documents the involvement of the Bank of Canada in this scheme.	Vol. 2 4501-4612	held in England on behalf of resident in Europe. Cable dated January 30, 1946, Bank of Canada to Bank of England, and reply dated January 31, 1946, Bank of England to Bank of Canada, suggest that Bank of England did satisfy itself regarding non-enemy declarations before authorizing the release of foreign-owned . gold	Most records exempt under S. 13 (1) or 19 (1) ATIA.
		Vol. 3 4701-4712		ibid.
		Vol. 4 4801-5512		ibid.
A18-17-9	Bank of England Gold in Safekeeping at Bank of Canada	Vol. 1 3901-4412		

File# or Name	File Titles/Scope notes	Year/ Month	Document Indexes	Access Notes*
Bank of England – continued				
A18-17-9	This file contains copies of the monthly statements of account that were sent by the Bank of Canada to the Bank of England. Attached are working papers that document shipments of gold both into and out of the Bank of England's various gold accounts.	Vol. 2 4501-5112 Vol. 3 5201-5712		
A18-17-10	Gold Earmarked for Bank of England, shipments from West Indies. File documents small-value shipments of gold, mainly coin, to the Bank of Canada from the Bank of England and from the Caribbean branches of Canadian chartered banks and of a U.K. bank.	Vol. 1 3901-4512		
A18-17-14	Special shipments of Bank of England Gold from Federal Reserve Bank. File documents the policy discussions and arrangements for shipments of gold that were intended to reduce the Bank of England's unduly high gold holdings in New York by transfers to Ottawa.	Vol. 1 5007-5112		
A18-17-15	Bank of England Gold Special Account File documents the opening and routine operation of a gold safekeeping account - designated "Special Account" - for the Bank of England. The account was apparently closed in February 1952.	Vol. 1 5009-5112 Vol. 2 5201		

File# or Name	File Titles/Scope notes	Year/ Month	Document Indexes	Access Notes*
Bank of England – continued				
A18-17-15	Gold in the account was repatriated against the Bank of Canada's holdings of sterling and the balance in the account resold to the Bank of Canada.			
A18-29	Bank of England Gold with Bank of Canada Account #8	Vol. 1 5001-5212		
	File documents the opening and routine operation of a gold safekeeping account for the Bank of England between October, 1950 and January 1952.			
	Currency Division Gold Ledger - Bank of England	3602-6109	There are 42 pages of ledgers.	
	Currency Division Gold Safekeeping Location Ledger		There are 74 pages of ledgers.	11 records exempt under S. 19 (1) ATIA.
	Currency Division Gold Ledger - Bank of London and South America Limited	4012-4707	There are 5 pages of ledgers.	
	Currency Division Gold Safekeeping Location Ledger.		There are 3 pages of ledgers.	
	Currency Division Gold Ledger - Sundry Persons (on behalf of Bank of England)	4101-5304	There are 2 pages of ledgers.	Personal information that appears in these particular ledger pages is exempt under S. 19 (1) ATIA.
	Currency Division Gold Safekeeping Location Ledger		There are 3 pages of ledgers.	3 records exempt under S. 19 (1) ATIA.
58-81-5	Audits and Auditing - Gold - Section 9, Sub-section 6 - Bank of England	Vol. 1 4801-9312		
58-82-4	Audits and Auditing - Gold - Section 9, Sub-section 7 - Bank of England	Vol. 1 4801-8312		

File# or Name	File Titles/Scope notes	Year/ Month	Document Indexes	Access Notes*
Bank of England — continued				
58-84-3	Audits and Auditing - Gold - Section 9, Sub-section 9 - Bank of England	Vol. 1 4801-9312		
55-85-3	Audits and Auditing - Gold - Section 9, Sub-section 10 - Bank of England	Vol. 1 4801-9312		
Gold Safe-Keeping	Bank of England Gold held in Safekeeping	3901-4612		
Gold Shipments	Gold shipments to England	3501-4012		
580-43-14D	Bank of England Gold shipments and Release (Coin) - Account #2 - A/C #1	5302-6004		3 records exempt S. 19 (1) ATIA.
580-43-14C	Bank of England - Gold received to be held in Safekeeping - Account #1, #1A	5405-6408		
580-43-14A	Gold shipped to London, England on account of the Receiver General of Canada	3501-3807 (12 vols.)		
	Bank of England Lodgement Forms	4009-4106		All records exempt under S.13(1) and S.19(1) ATIA.
580-43-14	Gold shipments to England	3806-3806 (3 vols.)		
580-43-14B	Gold held in Safekeeping for Bank of England and BIS, 1935, 1936, 1937	3506-3506		
580-42-14A	Gold held in Safekeeping for Bank of England	Vol. 1 3601-3612		
		Vol. 2 3701-3812		
580-42-14B	Gold held in safekeeping for Bank of England received from Royal Canadian Mint, Bank of Canada, and Minister of Finance	3601-3612		

File# or Name	File Titles/Scope notes	Year/ Month	Document Indexes	Access Notes*
Bank of England – continued				
580-42-14E	Bank of England - Gold shipments and transfer	Vol. 1 5601-5912		
580-42-14C	Shipments made from Gold held in Safekeeping for Bank of England - shipments and transfers - Bank of England	Vol. 1 3711-3912 Vol. 2 4001-4008		
		Vol. 3 4001-4002	Internal memorandum dated July 8, 1940, Secretary to Chief of Currency Division, noting that "in order to save on express charges, you may divert shipments where possible". Reference to subsequent practice of Bank of England shipments to Bank of Canada being diverted at Montreal to Federal Reserve Bank of New York.	
		Vol. 4 4101-4109		2 records exempt under S.19(1) ATIA.
		Vol. 5 4201-4212		4 records exempt under S.19(1) ATIA.
		Vol. 6 4301-4312		2 records exempt under S.19(1) ATIA.
		Vol. 7 4401-4512		
		Vol. 8 4601-4612		Several records exempt under S.19(1) ATIA.
		Vol. 9 4701-4712		Several records exempt under S.19(1) ATIA.
		Vol. 10 4801-5112		Several records exempt under S.19(1) ATIA.
		Vol. 11 5201-5212		Several records exempt under S.19(1) ATIA.

File# or Name	File Titles/Scope notes	Year/ Month	Document Indexes	Access Notes*
Bank of England – continued				
580-42-14D	Bank of England - Gold received from Overseas and Chartered Banks	Vol. 1 3805-4001		5 records exempt under S.19(1) ATIA..
		Vol. 2 4001-4007 (file 8)		1 record exempt under S.19(1) ATIA.
		Vol. 3 4007-4011 (file 9)		1 record exempt under S.19(1) ATIA.
	Bank of England - Gold received to be held in	Vol. 4 4107-4112 (file 10)		4 records exempt under S.19(1) ATIA.
		Vol. 5 4301-4312 (file 11)		
		Vol. 6 4301-4612 (file 12)		2 records exempt under S.19(1) ATIA.
		Vol. 7 4701-5012 (file 13)		4 records exempt under S.19(1) ATIA.
		Vol. 8 5101-5212		
580-44-14A	Gold held in Safekeeping for Bank of England	Vol. 1 3908-4612		
		Vol. 2 4601-5212		
580-44-14B	Statements - Re: Gold transferred from Bank of England to Minister of Finance Special (Exchange Fund) Gold shipped to Federal Reserve Bank of New York	5101-5212		

File# or Name	File Titles/Scope notes	Year/ Month	Document Indexes	Access Notes*

FEDERAL RESERVE BANK OF NEW YORK

File# or Name	File Titles/Scope notes	Year/ Month	Document Indexes	Access Notes*
A19-14	Special shipments Gold Coin to Federal Reserve Bank of New York	Vol. 1 4201-4312		
	File documents initial proposals for the minting and subsequent shipment of Canadian gold coin to the Federal Reserve Bank of New York "as a secret and important measure", two subsequent shipments of French gold coin to the Federal Reserve Bank of New York for the use of U.S. forces in North Africa, and one shipment of sovereigns and half sovereigns to the Federal Reserve Bank of New York.			
A19-17	Bank of Canada Gold Account 'G' with Federal Reserve Bank of New York	Vol. 1 5001-5412		
	File documents the routine operation but not the opening of a gold safekeeping account for the Bank of Canada with the Federal Reserve Bank of New York. The account was closed in November 1955 - See A19-18, below.			
A19-18	Bank of Canada, Gold Account #1 and 2 with FRB.	Vol. 1 5501-5604		
	File documents the opening and routine of two gold safekeeping accounts for the Bank of Canada with the Federal Reserve Bank of New York.	Vol. 2 5605-5612		
Gold Ship- ments	Gold shipments to New York	3501-4012		

File# or Name	File Titles/Scope notes	Year/ Month	Document Indexes	Access Notes*
Federal Reserve Bank of New York – continued				
Gold Ship-ments	Currency Division Gold Ledger - Federal Reserve Bank of New York	5201-5210	There is one page of ledgers.	
	Currency Division Gold Safekeeping Location Ledger.		There is one page of ledgers.	
580-43-15A	Gold shipments to New York by the Bank of Canada on behalf of the Receiver General	3501-4212 (28 volumes)		Vol. 10 - Vol. 11 All records with personal informa-tion are exempt under S.19(1) ATIA.

BANCO CENTRAL DE BOLIVIA

| A23-1 | Banco Central de Bolivia - Gold

File documents the opening and routine operation of a gold safekeeping account for the Banco Central de Bolivia with the Bank of Canada. | Vol. 1 4009-5009 | Letter dated October 16, 1940, Towers to Isley (Minister of Finance), noting that: "In accordance with the general agreement contained in your letter of August 26th with respect to gold delivered to the Bank of Canada by the Bank of England in connection with payments arrangements completed by the United Kingdom. I have to advise you that the Bank has opened gold accounts for Banque Melli Iran, Tehran, and for the Central Bank of Bolivia." | |
|---|---|---|---|---|
| | Currency Division Gold Ledger - Banco Central de Bolivia | 4010-5108 | There is one page of ledgers. | |
| | Currency Division Gold Safekeeping Location Ledger | | There is one page of ledgers. | |
| 580-42-16 | Gold received to be held in safekeeping for Central Bank of Bolivia | 4001-4512 | | |
| 580-43-17 | Gold shipments and transfers - Central Bank of Bolivia | 4001-5112 | | |

File# or Name	File Titles/Scope notes	Year/ Month	Document Indexes	Access Notes*

DANMARKS NATIONALBANK

File# or Name	File Titles/Scope notes	Year/ Month	Document Indexes	Access Notes*
A24-2	Danmarks Nationalbank Gold File documents the opening and routine operation of a gold safekeeping account for the Danmarks Nationalbank with the Bank of Canada. (A second account was opened during January 1959).	Vol. 1 5101-6812	File includes correspondence between the Bank of Canada and the Bank for International Settlements relating to the sale of gold by the Bank for International Settlements to the Danmarks Nationalbank that initially led the latter to open a gold safekeeping account with the Bank of Canada.	
	Currency Division Gold Ledger - Danmarks Nationalbank	5103-5901	There is one page of ledgers.	
	Currency Division Gold Safekeeping Location Ledger		There are 2 pages of ledgers.	
580-42-8	Danmarks Nationalbank, Copenhagen - Gold held in Safekeeping	5101-9012		

DE NEDERLANDSCHE BANK

File# or Name	File Titles/Scope notes	Year/ Month	Document Indexes	Access Notes*
A25-1	Netherlands Government Gold in Safekeeping at Bank of Canada File documents the opening, routine operation, and closing out of a gold safekeeping account for the Royal Netherlands Government with the Bank of Canada. Gold in the account was transferred on July 11, 1949 to an account in the name of De Nederlandsche Bank.	Vol. 1 4001-4412	Letter dated July 18, 1940, Towers to Isley (Minister of Finance), indicating that the Bank of Canada might "shortly be asked to hold gold in safekeeping for the Netherlands Government, and to give that Government assurance that gold in question will be freely disposable by them" and asking Isley if those assurances can be given. Letter dated July 23, 1940, Isley to Towers, indicating that assurances can be given.	

File# or Name	File Titles/Scope notes	Year/ Month	Document Indexes	Access Notes*
De Nederlandsche Bank – continued				
A25C	Gold Earmarked for De Nederlandsche Bank	Vol. 1 4601-6912		
	File documents the opening and routine operation of a gold safekeeping account for De Nederlandsche Bank with the Bank of Canada.			
58-77-5	Audits and Auditing - Gold - Section 9, Sub-section 2 - De Nederlandsche Bank "ordinary"	Vol. 1 4801-8612		
58-84-6	Audits and Auditing - Gold - Section 9, Sub-section 9 - De Nederlandsche Bank "ordinary"	Vol. 1 4001-8312		
	Currency Division Gold Ledger - Royal Netherlands Government	4008-4907	There is one page of ledgers.	
	Currency Division Gold Ledger - De Nederlandsche Bank N.V.	4605-6011	There are 2 pages of ledgers.	
	Currency Division Gold Safekeeping Location Ledger		There are 6 pages of ledgers.	
	Currency Division Gold Ledger - Netherlands Indies Government Javabank	4304-4605	There is one page of ledgers.	
58-42-9	Gold received to be held in safekeeping for Netherlands Embassy	4001-4712		
580-43-9A	Royal Netherlands Government - Gold shipments and transfers to others	4101-4912		

File# or Name	File Titles/Scope notes	Year/ Month	Document Indexes	Access Notes*
De Nederlandsche Bank – continued				
580-43-9B	Gold received - Netherlands Indies Government Javabank Account changed to De Nederlandsche Bank N.V. Amsterdam changed to Nederlandsche Bank - June 23, 1951	6301-6612 6901-6912 7001-7212 9001-9012		
580-43-9C	Gold shipments or transfers - De Nederlandsche Bank N.V. Amsterdam, Netherlands changed to Nederlandsche Bank (June 23, 1951)	4701-5112		

BANCO DE MEXICO

File# or Name	File Titles/Scope notes	Year/ Month	Document Indexes	Access Notes*
A34-5A	Banco de México Gold (Routine)	Vol. 1 4301-4412		
	File documents sales of gold to the Banco de México and, subsequently, the opening and routine	Vol. 2 4501-4712		1 record exempt under S.19(1) ATIA.
	operation of a gold safekeeping account for the Banco de México with the Bank of Canada.			
	Currency Division Gold Ledger - Banco de México	4506-4807	There is one page of ledgers.	
	Currency Division Gold Safekeeping Location Ledger		There is one page of ledgers.	

BANK VAN DE NEDERLANDS ANTILLEN

File# or Name	File Titles/Scope notes	Year/ Month	Document Indexes	Access Notes*
A40	Bank Van De Nederlands Antillen - Gold in Safekeeping	Vol. 1 4504-7312		
	File documents the opening and routine operation of a gold safekeeping account for the Bank van de Nederlands Antillen with the Bank of Canada.			

File# or Name	File Titles/Scope notes	Year/ Month	Document Indexes	Access Notes*
Bank van de Nederlands Antillen – continued				
A40	Currency Division Gold Ledger - Curacaosche Bank (Changed to Bank Van De Nederlands Antillen - January 1, 1962)	4504-4504	There is one page of ledgers.	
	Currency Division Gold Safekeeping Location Ledger		There is one page of ledgers.	
58-76-4	Audits and Auditing - Gold Section 9, Sub-section 1 - Bank Van de Nederlands Antillen	Vol. 1 4001-8802		

OESTERREICHISCHE NATIONALBANK

File# or Name	File Titles/Scope notes	Year/ Month	Document Indexes	Access Notes*
A49-1	Oesterreichische Bank (Vienna) - Gold	Vol. 1 5001-7612		
	File documents the opening and routine operation of a gold safekeeping and U.S. dollar current account for the Oesterreichische Nationalbank with the Bank of Canada.			
58-81-3	Audits and Auditing - Gold - Section 9, Sub-section 6 - Oesterreichische Nationalbank	Vol. 1 4801-9512		
	Currency Division Gold Ledger - Oesterreichische Nationalbank	5101-5110	There is one page of ledgers.	
	Currency Division Gold Safekeeping Location Ledger		There are 4 pages of ledgers.	
580-42-11	Oesterrichische Bank - General Correspondence	5101-9012		

File# or Name	File Titles/Scope notes	Year/ Month	Document Indexes	Access Notes*

DEUTSCHE BUNDESBANK

File# or Name	File Titles/Scope notes	Year/ Month	Document Indexes	Access Notes*
A52C	Deutsche Bundesbank - Gold File documents the opening and routine operation of a gold safekeeping account for the Bank deutscher Länder - as the Deutsche a gold safekeeping account Bundesbank then was - with the Bank of Canada.	Vol. 1 5410-6105	File includes correspondence between the Bank of Canada and the Bank for International Settlements relating to the sale of gold by the Bank for International Settlements relating to the sale of gold by the Bank for International Settlements to the Bank deutscher Länder that that initially led the latter to open with the Bank of Canada	The Deutsche Bundesbank in giving approval for the release of its files, has asked the Bank of Canada to draw the attention of researchers to the following background information "At the time of its establishment in 1948, the Bank deutscher Länder possessed no gold holdings at all (neither was it the legal successor of the Deutsche Reichsbank). Gold holdings were shown for the first time in the balance sheet as at December 31, 1951.At that time, the accounting methods practised within the European Payments Union (EPU) were of particular importance for the accumulation of the German gold reserves: up to 1958, the EPU cleared the bilateral surpluses and deficits of the individual member states. The resulting excess accounting balances had to be offset in gold or US dollars in certain proportions which continuously increased. For this

File# or Name	File Titles/Scope notes	Year/ Month	Document Indexes	Access Notes*
Deutsche Bundesbank – continued				
A52C				purpose, the Basle-based Bank for International Settlements acted as an agent and clearing house. As the Federal Republic of Germany found itself in a surplus position in the EPU from 1951 onwards, it received consider-able quantities of gold in the course of the settlement of balances. That also accounts for the transactions undertaken with Canada from 1954 onwards."
	Currency Division Gold Ledger - Bank deutscher Länder	5410-6311	There is one page of ledgers.	
	Currency Division Gold Safekeeping Location Ledger		There are 7 pages of ledgers.	
580-43-13	Bank deutscher Länder, Frankfurt, Germany - Gold held - Gold release (name changed to: Deutsche Bundesbank, Frankfurt, August 21, 1957)	5401-6012 1963 6601-6812		

BANQUE CENTRALE DE LA REPUBLIQUE DE TURQUIE

File# or Name	File Titles/Scope notes	Year/ Month	Document Indexes	Access Notes*
A60-2	Banque Centrale de la République de Turquie - Gold	Vol. 1 4001-5212		
	File documents the opening and routine operation of a gold safekeeping account for the Banque Centrale de la République de Turquie with the Bank of Canada.			

File# or Name	File Titles/Scope notes	Year/ Month	Document Indexes	Access Notes*
Banque Centrale de la Republic de Turquie – continued				
A60-2	Currency Division Gold Ledger - Banque Centrale de la République de Turquie	4012-5209	There are 4 pages of ledgers.	
			There is one page of ledgers.	
	Currency Division Gold Safekeeping Location Ledger			

BANCO DE PORTUGAL

515-17-5	Banco de Portugal - Gold Safekeeping Account File documents the routine operation of a gold safekeeping account for the Banco de Portugal with the Bank of Canada.	Vol. 1 4201-6812	The file includes correspondence during late April and early May 1942 relating to two transfers of gold from the account of the Banque Nationale Suisse to that of the Banco de Portugal by the Bank of Canada. The file also includes correspondence from October 1944 until November 1945 between the Bank of Canada and the Banco de Portugal - sent mainly via the Bank of England - and between the Bank of Canada and the Sveriges Riksbank relating to about a dozen transfers of gold between the accounts of the Banco de Portugal and the Sveriges Riksbank with the Bank of Canada.	
	Currency Division Gold Ledger - Banco de Portugal	4204-4509	There is one page of ledgers.	
	Currency Division Gold Safekeeping Location Ledger		There are 3 pages of ledgers.	
58-81-8	Audits and Auditing - Gold - Section 9, Sub-section 6, Bank of Portugal	Vol. 1 4801-9312		
58-82-7	Audits and Auditing - Gold - Section 9, Sub-section 7 - Bank of Portugal	Vol. 1 4801-8312		

File# or Name	File Titles/Scope notes	Year/ Month	Document Indexes	Access Notes*
Banco de Portugal – continued				
580-43-4A	Gold received for Bank of Portugal, Lisbon	4204-9006		
580-43-4B	Gold transferred from Bank of Portugal, Lisbon	4409-4509		

BANQUE MELLI IRAN

	Currency Division Gold - Banque Melli Iran	4610-4612	There is one page of ledgers.	
	Currency Division Gold Safekeeping Location Ledger		There is one page of ledgers.	
580-43-1A	Gold received to be held in safekeeping for Banque Melli Iran	4001-4012		
580-43-1B	Gold shipments - Banque Melli Iran	4001-4012		

DE SURINAAMSCHE BANK

	Currency Division Gold Ledger - De Surinaamische Bank	4209-5703	There are 2 pages of ledgers.	
	Currency Division Gold Safekeeping Location Ledger		There are 3 pages of ledgers.	

NARODNI BANKA CESKOSLOVENSKA V PRAZE

580-42-1	Narodni Banka Ceskoslovenska V Praze	4901-5012		
	Currency Division Gold - Narodni Banka Ceskoslovenska V Praze	4907-5008	There is one page of ledgers.	
	Currency Division Gold Safekeeping Location Ledger		There is one page of ledgers.	

File# or Name	File Titles/Scope notes	Year/ Month	Document Indexes	Access Notes*
MINISTER OF FINANCE – GOLD				
	Currency Division Gold Ledger - Minister of Finance	3509-5706	There are 63 pages of ledgers.	
	Currency Division Gold Safekeeping Location Ledger		There are 81 pages of ledgers.	
58-82-2	Audits and Auditing - Gold - Section 9, Sub-section 7 - Minister of Finance Special (Exchange Fund) - Account	Vol. 1 4801-9312		
580-41-4 Gold held	Gold held in Safekeeping for Minister of Finance - Exchange Fund Account	3901-4012		
580-41-4 Gold received	Gold received for Minister of Finance - Exchange Fund Account - Special	4401-4512		
580-41-4 Gold shipments	Minister of Finance Gold shipments to New York	4101-4212		
580-41-4 Gold shipments	Minister of Finance Gold shipped by Chartered Banks	3912-4706		
580-41-4 Gold safe-keeping	Gold held for Minister of Finance - Exchange Fund Account	4101-4612		
580-41-4C	Minister of Finance (Exchange Fund) Gold received from the Royal Canadian Mint	Vol. 1 5501-5512		
		Vol. 2 5601-5612		
580-41-2C	Minister of Finance (Exchange Fund) Gold Received - Miscellaneous	Vol. 1 5404-5512		1 record exempt under S.19(1) ATIA 1 record exempt under S.13(1) ATIA
		Vol. 2 5601-5612		

File# or Name	File Titles/Scope notes	Year/ Month	Document Indexes	Access Notes*
Minister of Finance – Gold – continued				
580-41-2D	Lists of Gold Bars shipped from Currency Division - Minister of Finance - Royal Canadian Mint	Vol. 1 3101-3512		
		Vol. 2 3601-3712		
580-41-2B	Gold held in Safekeeping for Minister of Finance	3506-35-06		
580-41-2A	Gold received to be held in safekeeping for the Minister of Finance Special Exchange Fund Account	Vol. 1 3910		
		Vol. 2 4005-4006		Several records exempt under S.19(1) ATIA.
		Vol. 3 4007-4012		
		Vol. 4 4101-4112		Several records exempt under S.19(1) ATIA.
		Vol. 5 4201-4212		Several records exempt under S.19(1) ATIA.
		Vol. 6 4301-4312		Several records exempt under S.19(1) ATIA.
		Vol. 7 4401-4512		Several records exempt under S.19(1) ATIA.
		Vol. 8 4601-4612		Several records exempt under S.19(1) ATIA.
		Vol. 9 4701-4712		Several records exempt under S.19(1) ATIA.
		Vol. 10 4802-4912		Several records exempt under S.19(1) ATIA.
580-41-4D	Minister of Finance Special Exchange Fund Accounts "Gold Shipment"	5511-5611		
580-41-4A	Gold shipments - Minister of Finance Special Exchange Fund Account	Vol. 1 4001-4012		

File# or Name	File Titles/Scope notes	Year/ Month	Document Indexes	Access Notes*
Minister of Finance – Gold – continued				
580-41-4B	Gold shipments and transfers - Minister of Finance Special Fund Account	Vol. 1 4001-4009		
		Vol. 2 4005-4012		
		Vol. 3 4102-4112		
		Vol. 4 4204-4211		Several records exempt under S.19(1) ATIA.
		Vol. 5 4301-4312		
		Vol. 6 4401-4612		
		Vol. 7 4701-4712		
		Vol. 8 4812-5212		

OTHER RELEVANT RECORDS

	Minute Books of the Board of Directors of the Bank of Canada and the Board's Executive Committee.	1935-1949		All personnel information exempt under S.19(1) ATIA. 1949: Portion of one record exempt under Section 23 ATIA.
	Currency Division Gold Ledger - Royal Bank of Canada	4104-5611	There are 3 pages of ledgers.	1 record exempt under S.19(1) ATIA.
	Currency Division Gold Safekeeping Location Ledger		There are 7 pages of ledgers.	1 record exempt under S.19(1) ATIA.
	Currency Division Gold Ledger - Bank of Montreal	4609-5203	There is one page of ledgers.	3 records exempt under S.19(1) ATIA.
	Currency Division Gold Safekeeping Location		There are 5 pages of ledgers.	3 records exempt under S.19(1)

File# or Name	File Titles/Scope notes	Year/ Month	Document Indexes	Access Notes*
Other relevant records – continued				
	Currency Division Gold Ledger - Canadian Bank of Commerce	4609-5203	There is one page of ledgers.	3 records exempt under S.19(1) ATIA.
	Currency Division Gold Safekeeping Location Ledger		There are 3 pages of ledgers.	
	Currency Division Gold Ledger - Imperial Bank of Canada	4611-4701	There is one page of ledgers.	
	Currency Division Gold Safekeeping Location Ledger		There are 2 pages of ledgers	
	Currency Division Gold Ledger - Bank of Toronto	4612-4710	There is one page of ledgers.	
	Currency Division Gold Safekeeping Location Ledger		There are 2 pages of ledgers.	
	Currency Division Gold Ledger - Barclays Bank Canada	4609-4610	There is one page of ledgers.	
	Currency Division Gold Safekeeping Location Ledger		There are 2 pages of ledgers.	
	Currency Division Gold Ledger - Bank of Nova Scotia	4709-5612	There is one page of ledgers.	
	Currency Division Gold Safekeeping Location Ledger		There are 2 pages of ledgers.	
	Currency Division Gold Ledger - Guaranty Trust Co. of New York	3802-3803	There is one page of ledgers.	
	Currency Division Gold Ledger - Bankers Trust Co. New York	4703-4703	There is one page of ledgers.	
	Currency Division Gold Ledger - Total Gold held for Customers in Safekeeping Account "A"	4010-4704	There is one page of ledgers.	1 record exempt under S.19(1) ATIA.
	Currency Division Gold Ledger - Gold held by Royal Canadian Mint in Safekeeping for Customers	3607-3607	There is one page of ledgers.	

File# or Name	File Titles/Scope notes	Year/ Month	Document Indexes	Access Notes*
Other relevant records – continued				
	Currency Division Gold Ledger - Gold held by Royal Canadian Mint	5404-5704	There is one page of ledgers.	
	Currency Division Gold Ledger - Foreign and Mutilated Gold Coin held by the Royal Canadian Mint	4001-4001	There is one page of ledgers.	
	Currency Division Gold Ledger - Gold in transit	3705-3706	There is one page of ledgers.	
	Currency Division Gold Ledger - Suspense re: Gold Settlements outstanding	3705-3709	There is one page of ledgers.	
	Currency Division Gold Ledger - Gold under Earmark abroad Account no. 13	3808-3809	There is one page of ledgers.	
	Currency Division Gold Ledger - Gold Adjustment Account	3808-3809	There is one page of ledgers.	
	Currency Division Gold Ledger - Gold Shipping Charges Reserve	3808-3809	There is one page of ledgers.	
	Currency Division Gold Ledger - Bank of Canada	3807-4005	There are 23 pages of ledgers.	
135	Gold - General	Vol. 3 4401-4806	File contains correspondence during the period February 1944 - February 1945 between the Bank of Canada, the Department of External Affairs, and the Department of Finance documenting the background to the issuance of "Declaration by Canada on Gold Looted by the Axis and Subsequently Acquired by Third Countries". File also contains the text of a press release issued October 17, 1947 by the Tripartite Commission for the Restitution of Monetary Gold.	With the exception of the documents noted in the adjacent column, this file is not otherwise relevant to the question of client services involving gold. Copies of these records are available in a separate folder.

File# or Name	File Titles/Scope notes	Year/ Month	Document Indexes	Access Notes*
Other relevant records – continued				
135C	Internal Memoranda on Gold File documents discussions with the Bank of Canada about such matters as the pricing of gold services, the conditions of governing the storage of gold for customers, and procedures for handling gold held in safekeeping.	Vol. 1 4501-5812	File includes internal memoranda from early 1956 on Prussian Mint and Russian gold bars held by the Bank of Canada in safekeeping.	Portions of 7 records S.13(1) exempt under ATIA.
135-4	Gold shipments by Bank of Canada for all Accounts	Vol. 1 3501-4012		
135-4-1	Gold shipments by Bank of Canada for all Accounts	Vol. 1 3801-3803		
		Vol. 2 3803-3806		
		Vol. 3 3806-3809		
135-4-2	Gold shipments to New York File documents the logistics of the shipments. The run of the volumes suggests that some volumes might be missing. However, a note on the inside front cover of the second volume indicates that there were no shipments during 1954.	Vol. 1 5001-5212 Vol. 2 5501-5705		
135-4-2A	Sales of Gold (other than International Monetary Fund) The file documents the sale of gold by the Bank of Canada to other central banks between February 1953 and October 1957. As such, the file consists of offers, bids, confirmations and advices.	Vol. 1 5302-5510 Vol. 2 5511-5710		

File# or Name	File Titles/Scope notes	Year/ Month	Document Indexes	Access Notes*
Other relevant records – continued				
135-4-3	Gold expenses and packing - Arrangements - Gold shipments for all Accounts by Bank of Canada - expenses and packing arrangements The title of the file concisely describes the file's scope.	Vol. 1 3501-5912		
135-4-4	Gold statistics of U.S. and Canadian Funds paid for express charges The title of the file concisely describes the file's scope.	Vol. 1 4001-4212		
135-5	Gold Export Act and Orders-in-Council The file contains copies of *The Gold Export Act* and the various regulations issued under it.	Vol. 1 3201-5212		
135-6	Gold under Earmark Abroad File documents the establishment and operation of arrangements for the Bank of England to deposit gold intended for the Bank of Canada under earmark for the Bank of Canada's account with the Federal Reserve Bank of New York and for the Bank of Canada to earmark the same number of ounces for the Bank of England in Ottawa.	Vol. 1 3801-3812		

File# or Name	File Titles/Scope notes	Year/ Month	Document Indexes	Access Notes*
Other relevant records – continued				
135-7	Gold stored and purchased in Canada by Private Interests	Vol. 1 3801-4612	Letter dated July 11, 1938, Towers to Dunning (Minister of Finance), setting out the issues.	1 record exempt under S.19(1) ATIA.
	File documents the development and implementation of a policy for gold held in Canada for the account of foreigners or foreign interests.	Vol. 2 4601-4612	Extract sheet dated December 21, 1938 summarizing the policy: "The Government will now sell to the banks and trust companies, who are acting on behalf of foreigners, gold bullion, provided that they will declare it to be for foreigners' account, and also subject to their making reports to us in order that our export figures will not be distorted."	
		Vol. 3 4701-5012	Form letter dated November 3, 1939, Bank of Canada to chartered banks, noting that it is no longer necessary to make regular reports on gold held in Canada for foreigners.	
135-7-1	Gold Bar sales to Chartered Banks	Vol. 1 3801-3912		
	File documents sales of gold bars by the Bank of Canada, in its "capacity as Agent for the Dominion Government", to various chartered banks for the account of non-residents of Canada, with payment in . U.S funds to the Federal Reserve Bank of New York for the credit of the Bank of Canada's account with it.			

File# or Name	File Titles/Scope notes	Year/ Month	Document Indexes	Access Notes*

Other relevant records – continued

135-12 — Gold Revaluation

The *Bank of Canada Act, 1934* provided for the transfer to the new institution of the gold held by the Dominion Government and the chartered banks at a price of $20.67 per ounce. The chartered banks objected to not receiving the profit when the price of gold was raised to $35 per ounce. Eventually, it was decided that the banks would receive the higher price on that portion of their gold holdings against foreign assets. The first two volumes of the file document the long negotiations and intricate calculations with the banks. The third volume contains a small amount of material on the 1946 and 1950 revaluations.

Vol. 1 3501-3506

Vol. 2 3507-3512

Vol. 3 4601-5012

135-15 — Gold deposits to be refused from Foreign Countries

The title of the file concisely describes the file's scope

Vol. 1 4201-5112

Form letter dated May 4, 1942, Towers to general managers of the chartered banks, noting that banks have recently received messages from correspondents in a neutral European country asking whether the banks would accept deposits of gold in safekeeping and noting the "desire of the Government that no new gold safekeeping accounts should be opened for non-resident banks, corporations, or individuals." The form letter also asks that the banks alert the Bank of Canada about any future requests from non-residents to open gold safekeeping accounts.

File# or Name	File Titles/Scope notes	Year/ Month	Document Indexes	Access Notes*
Other relevant records – continued				
135-15			Undated internal memorandum providing background to the form letter of May 4, 1942. [Memorandum was probably written during October 1945]	
			Form letter dated October 26, 1945, Towers to general managers of the chartered banks, referring to the form letter of May 4, 1942 and noting that there would now be no objections to the acceptance of deposits of gold for safekeeping for non-residents, provided beneficial ownership, at present and since September 3, 1939, is established to the satisfaction of the Custodian of Enemy Property.	
135-16	London Gold Market File documents in a fairly comprehensive manner the institutional framework and operation of the London Bullion Market between January 1953 and August 1964	Vol. 1 5301-6412		
175-2	Arrangements with Express Traffic Association and Board of Railway Commissioners - Express shipments - Miscellaneous	Vol. 1 3401-4412 Vol. 2 4501-5812		
220-25C-6	International Monetary Fund (IMF) - Gold	Vol. 1 4601-4712 Vol. 2 4801-6012		File is not relevant, except for eight records. Copies of these records are available in a separate folder.
	Currency Division Gold Ledger - International Monetary Fund		4811-4811	There is one page of ledgers.
	Currency Division Safekeeping Location Ledger			There is one page of ledgers.

File# or Name	File Titles/Scope notes	Year/ Month	Document Indexes	Access Notes*

Other relevant records – continued

File# or Name	File Titles/Scope notes	Year/ Month	Document Indexes	Access Notes*
CB1-14	Chartered Banks Gold Transfer to Bank of Canada - General	Vol. 1 3501-5312		

Under the provisions of
the *Bank of Canada Act,
1934,* every chartered
bank was required to
transfer to the Bank of
Canada, on the day on
which the Bank was
authorized to commence
business (March 11, 1935),
all gold coin or bulliion
then owned and held by
it in Canada. Subsequently,
Order in Council P.C. 4189
(December 29, 1939),
a copy of which is in
CB-14-1, required every
chartered bank, on or
before January 15, 1940,
to transfer to the Bank
all gold coin held in
Canada that it owned on,.
December 20, 1939.

This file documents some
of the policy discussions
took place in the aftermath
of the first transfer,
especially settlement for
foreign and mutilated gold
coin with the banks from
which it had been received.
(As such, the file contains
some of the documents
that are also in 135-12.)
The file contains very little
material on the second
transfer, although the
issue of settlement is
raised once again.

| CB-14-1 | Chartered Banks - Gold transfer to Bank of Canada - C.O (Currency Office) | | | |

The file contains the
receipts and advices for
the transfers during 1935
and 1940.

File# or Name	File Titles/Scope notes	Year/ Month	Document Indexes	Access Notes*

Other relevant records – continued

File# or Name	File Titles/Scope notes	Year/ Month	Document Indexes	Access Notes*
AUD.1	Record of Gold Bar Control (transferred to Archives by the External Auditor when he was retired.) - Ledger - Gold Vault 9 Sub-section 9 - External Auditors Records - Ledger - Gold Vault 9 Sub-section 1 - External Auditors Records - Ledger - Gold Vault 9 Sub-section 9 - Gold Coin External Auditors Records - Ledger - Gold Vault 9 Sub-section 9 - External Auditors Records - Ledger - Gold Vault 9 Sub-section 7 - External Auditors Records			
1A-640	Gold Correspondence and Memoranda and Gold Movements File consists of worksheets and internal memoranda that provide monthly figures, between January 1939 and February 1951, for such transactions as sales of gold bars to chartered banks, sales of gold by the Mint either to the Bank of Canada for its own account or through the agency of the Bank of Canada, foreign gold received by the Bank of Canada for safekeeping, shipments to New York from gold held in safe-keeping, and gold received by the Bank of Canada and transferred to Minister of Finance Special (Exchange Fund) Account.	Vol. 1 3101-6012		

File# or Name	File Titles/Scope notes	Year/ Month	Document Indexes	Access Notes*
	Other relevant records — continued			
1A-640	Gold Movements	3901-5112		
1B-640	Gold Safekeeping	Vol. 1 3901-3912		

1B-640 Gold Safekeeping: File comprises three parts. The first part contains the monthly reports, bank by bank, that banks were asked to submit to the Bank of Canada on gold holdings for non-residents - See 135-7, for background - and some worksheets on statistics on the production and prices of non-ferrous metals in the post-war period. The second part contains internal Bank of Canada correspondence between the Secretary's and Research Departments on the amount of earmarked gold held at the Bank of Canada between the end of May 1939 and the end of October 1939. The third and final part is a collection of worksheets and statements on gold held in safekeeping for various client central banks during the war and post-war years and on gold bars sold to the chartered banks during 1939. (On the latter, see also 135-7-1.)

| 1B-642 | Gold Canadian Gold Statistics - Background - 1940s and Prior | Vol. 1 3501-4012 | | |

1B-642: File consists mainly of worksheets, one of which gives, for calendar 1940, monthly data on gold received by the Bank of Canada for safekeeping and the amount of gold in safekeeping that was shipped to New York and a second one that gives, for December 1939 to January 1941 the net amount of gold in safekeeping for various clients

File# or Name	File Titles/Scope notes	Year/ Month	Document Indexes	Access Notes*
Other relevant records – continued				
C-640	Gold	Vol. 1 3501-4712		
4-1 file and Folder	Administration - Audit of Gold and Silver Holdings	Vol. 1 3501-6512		
SEC/OS. 91-19	Office of The Secretary: Gold and Silver

File consists of two types of material - copies of the annual Order in Council suspending the operations of Subsection 1 of Section 25 (and its successors) of the *Bank of Canada Act* and the originals of many of the by letters that were written Towers in the second half of 1940 to the Minister of Finance asking the Minister if he agrees with the view that is being taken by the Bank of Canada that the assets of various Allied governments domiciled in London have with the Bank of Canada are freely disposable and do not come under the control of the Custodian of Enemy Property. | Vol. 1 3501-6712 | | |
	Gold held in Currency Division - June 21 1939	June 21/39		
	Gold held in Currency Division - Sept 9 1939	Sept 9/39		
	Letterbrook - June 1942	4206	Letter dated March 9, 1942, Towers to Clark (Finance), about selling of Swiss Francs against gold. Such gold can be exported to other Central Banks of the Western Hemisphere and transferred to Central Banks of the Western Hemisphere and of neutral European - Sweden, Portugal and Spain.	

File# or Name	File Titles/Scope notes	Year/ Month	Document Indexes	Access Notes*
Other relevant records – continued				
JOURNAL	Private Journal - Ledgers, Special Exchange Fund, Securities, Gold, Money employed, Journal.	Vol. 1 3501-4012		
236-1-1 Binder	Gold - General (Canadian Gold Statistics)	Vol. 1 2601-5312		
236-2-2	Gold Legislation - Canadian Legislation - Regulations and Guidelines (Export/Import Permits Act)	Vol. 1 4801-8212		
Gold Holdings	Revaluation of Gold Holdings	3801-4012		
Gold Holdings	Bank of Canada Gold Holdings	3601-3912		
580-41-1I Gold Lodgement	Lodgement Forms for Foreign Owned Gold -	4014-4106		All records exempt under S.13(1) and S.19(1) ATIA.
580-40-1H Gold shipment	Gold shipments and transfers to Chartered Banks	4101-5612		
580-40-1G	Correspondence - Gold	Vol. 1 3401-4812		Several records exempt under S.19(1) ATIA.
		Vol. 2 5007-5206		
		Vol. 3 5304-5512		Several records exempt under S.19(1) ATIA.
		Vol. 4 5601-7312		
580-40-1M	Gold Revaluation Letters	3501-3812		
580-40-2A	Troy Weights	3501-5212		
580-40-1C	Bank of Canada Gold Holdings Gold coins received from Canadian Chartered Banks (Order in Council P.C. 4189 - December 20, 1939)	Vol. 1 3503-35-03		
		Vol. 2 3506-3507		
		Vol. 3		

File# or Name	File Titles/Scope notes	Year/ Month	Document Indexes	Access Notes*
Other relevant records – continued				
580-40-1C		Vol. 4 4001-4012		
		Vol. 5 4002-4005		
580-40-1A	Revaluation of Gold Holdings	Vol. 1 3501-3612		
		Vol. 2 3701-3712		
		Vol. 3 3801-3812		
		Vol. 4 3901-3912		
		Vol. 5 4001-4012		
580-40-1B	Bank of Canada Gold Holdings	Vol. 1 3602-3910		
		Vol. 2 4001-4005		
580-40-1D	Gold - Sales of Gold to Canadian Chartered Banks	Vol. 1 3801-3912		
		Vol. 2 3801-3912		
		Vol. 3 3801-3912		
580-40-1E	Gold shipped or transferred from Gold held in safekeeping for Banks. Gold delivered to Chartered Banks	Vol. 1 4101-4612		Most records exempt under S.19(1) ATIA.
		Vol. 2 4701-4912		
580-40-1F	Chartered Banks - Gold shipments and transfers Gold held in safekeeping for banks Gold - Sundry Persons - Shipments and transfers Chartered Banks - Gold shipments and transfers	Vol. 1 4101-5212		Most records exempt under S.19(1) ATIA.
580-40-1T	Mr. Butler's Gold File	5001-6012		
580-40-1P	Shareholder's Auditors	3801-3812		

File# or Name	File Titles/Scope notes	Year/ Month	Document Indexes	Access Notes*
Other relevant records – continued				
580-40-1N	Original lists of American Gold Coins	Vol. 1 3701-3812		
580-40-1O	Original lists of British Gold Coins	3701-3712		
580-40-1	Currency Division Copies of memos, letters	5001-5203		
580-40-1	Chartered Banks - Gold shipments and transfers	4701-4912		
580-40-1K	Gold held in safekeeping for banks	Vol. 1 4101-4912		Most records exempt under S.19(1). 1 record exempt under S.13(1) ATIA.
580-40-1J	Gold - Sundry Persons shipment and transfers	Vol. 1 4101-4912		All records exempt under S.13(1) and S.19(1) ATIA.
580-40-1Q	Vault Location Cards	3501-4912		
580-40-1R	Gold held for safekeeping Statements of Holdings for various clients	3901-4712		
580-40-18	Gold Vouchers	Vol. 1 5301-5312		
		Vol. 2 5401-5412		
		Vol. 3 5501-5512		
		Vol. 4 5601-5612		
580-40-1L	- Gold Transfers - Gold Shipment from New York - Gold Coin received from Ottawa Agency - Receipt of Weights for use in connection with Gold Scale (Montreal Agency)	5101-5212		

File# or Name	File Titles/Scope notes	Year/ Month	Document Indexes	Access Notes*

MATERIAL RECEIVED FROM CENTRAL BANKS, INTERNATIONAL FINANCIAL INSTITUTIONS, AND GOVERNMENTS, AND OTHERS

File# or Name	File Titles/Scope notes	Year/ Month	Document Indexes	Access Notes*
	Notes on gold shipments and gold exchanges organized by the Bank for International Settlements. 1 June 1938 - 31 May 1945	Aug 27/97		
	The Regulations and Practice of Gold Clearing in Central Banking - Bank for International Settlements - Central Banking - Replies to a questionnaire addressed to various Central Banks also - Replies to a questionnaire addressed to various Central Banks	1931 1955		
C43/287 C43/288 C43/287	Bank of England Archives microfiles			
C43/285 C43/286				
C43/284 OV62/24				
OV29/29 OV62/23 Part 1				
OV62/23 Part 2 OV63/3 Part 1				
OV62/23 Part 2 OV63/4				
OV63/28				
	Fax dated July 28, 1997, Bank of England to Bank of Canada, enclosing historical information on the specifications of bars acceptable on the London Gold Market.			

File# or Name	File Titles/Scope notes	Year/ Month	Document Indexes	Access Notes*
Other materials received – continued	Faxes dated July 17, 1997, Banque Nationale Suisse to Bank of Canada, enclosing a brief account of and statistics on gold transactions between the two central banks between April 1942 and December 1945.			
	Fax dated July 24, 1997, Sveriges Riksbank to Bank of Canada, enclosing statistics on and supporting documentation for gold transactions between the two central banks between March 1944 and September 1945.			
	Fax dated July 14, 1997, Canadian Jewish Congress to Bank of Canada, enclosing a copy of a declassified U.S. government document that suggests that a transfer of ownership of gold held in safekeeping by the Bank of Canada during 1942 might have facilitated a parallel transfer in Switzerland of gold looted by the Nazis between the Banque Nationale Suisse and the Banco de Portugal.			
	Fax dated November 19, 1997, Canadian Jewish Congress to Bank of Canada, enclosing a copy of a declassified document of the Federal Reserve Bank of New York dated January 15, 1955 concerning Prussian Mint bars.			

*   All records dated later than 31/12/56 are not accessible.

•   •   •   •   •

The papers of Graham Towers, Governor of the Bank of Canada between 1934 and 1954, will also be of interest to researchers. Those papers are held in the Archives of the Bank.

For information about issues related to access to information and privacy, please contact Louise Nantel, (613) 782-8322.

For information about the Archives of the Bank of Canada, please contact Corrinne Miller, (613) 782-8673.

A summary of the report by Professor McDowall on the handling of foreign gold by the Bank of Canada during the Second World War is available at the Bank's web site: http://www.bank-banque-canada.ca

Files that are available through the Department of Finance are listed in an appendix.

APPENDIX   Department of Finance Documents

File Number	File Title	Volume Number	Document Information
WAC 1515-005 -001	Trading with the Enemy	Closed	Draft 1944 declaration by Canada on looted gold acquired from the Axis by third countries. *The Gold Export Act.*
700-13	Central files: General	2733	A 1941 article from *The New Republic* outlining the problem of the excessive influx of gold into the U.S. There is some discussion about gold policy and foreign policy in the U.S. Possible remarks in answer to inquiries about the future of gold. Gives some insight into payment in gold that is believed to be coming from enemy sources. Letter to W. C. Clark from 1939 mentioning Canada's role in safekeeping large amounts of gold, cash and securities for foreigners.
RG 19 E 2(h)	Bryce's Personal correspondence	3444	Article published in *The Canadian Financial and Mining Reporter* that was sent to R. B. Bryce in 1939. Mentions the significant amount of earmarked gold on deposit in the Bank of Canada for foreigners.
B-2-6-2	Bank of Canada Gold Holdings - Earmarked	3970	Correspondence between Finance and Bank of Canada regarding arrangements for transfer of gold from Bank of England account to Swiss National Bank's account at the Bank of Canada. Correspondence concerning the Sveriges Riksbank, Stockholm and gold transfers on paper.
RG 19	Establishment of Foreign Exchange Control in Canada	651	Letter to G. A. Newman, Acting Director, Export Division, Department of Trade and Commerce from 1948 regarding gold imported to Portugal for industrial use.
	Canada's Gold Export Policy	639 Closed	Memo to W. C. Clark from 1947 concerning Gold Export Act.

**   The file WAC 1515-005-001 is located at the Department of Finance (contact Mario Perrier at 943-0914). All other files are located at the National Archives Reference Services at 992-3884).

***   The closed files are being reviewed so that documents in the files are opened, in conformity with Access to Information and Privacy legislation.

REPUBLIC OF CROATIA

Statement by the Croatian delegation

The Republic of Croatia welcomes the idea of holding this Conference and gives credit to the British Government, which, in conjunction with the governments of USA and France as members of the 1946 Tripartite Commission for Restitution of Monetary Gold, has organised this important gathering. Croatia shares their wish to shed more light on one of the darkest pages in European and world history.

Nazi persecutions also took place in the area of Croatia, but it is important to point out that the Croatian people fought Nazi invaders on a massive scale and thus made a significant contribution to the victory of antifascist forces. Croatian President Dr. Franjo Tudjman was an active member of antifascist resistance from the very outset.

The Republic of Croatia attaches special importance to historical research related to World War II events, including the fate of the Nazi victims. This, of course, comprises the issues concerning the restitution of seized property. The degree in which the Croatian Government is aware of this problem is illustrated by the fact that a special commission has been set up to investigate historic facts about the property of Nazi victims. The commission's task is to finally establish facts related to the property seized by the Nazis from States or individuals and to review measures taken so far and those to be taken in the future with the aim of returning or compensating this property.

The commission's work will be facilitated by the fact that the 1941–45 archives have been largely preserved. For example, complete files of movable and immovable Jewish property are available. The Croatian State Archive harbours valuable and extensive materials which allow thorough investigation of the Holocaust in Croatia in general and the fate of Jewish property in particular. It should be noted that the research work carried out so far has produced more facts about the Holocaust itself than what happened to the Jewish property.

A pilot project undertaken by the Croatian State Archive over the period 1978 to 1985 on the basis of archive sources was called "Dotršćina" and tasked to comprise all fascist victims and antifascists associated with Zagreb who had been killed during World War II in concentration camps or prisons or as antifascist fighters. This project involved the study of 7,027 archive boxes, 67 boxes of files, 1,200 leaflets, posters and announcements, complete NDH press and 97 books. Based on research results, a register for each person was made containing general CV data and the place and way of death. The study is concluded with references covering each person. The result of the project is biographies of 40,000 victims including 6,537 Jews. It is planned to make a database out of it. We feel that is the right way to proceed: name every victim of World War II. We owe it to the historic truth and to the victims.

The mentioned archive materials are wholly accessible to scientific research. A part of them have been microfilmed. The Croatian State Archive has made an agreement with the Holocaust Memorial Museum in Washington and systematic copying of the Holocaust documentation in Croatia is being made for them.

At the international conference held in Paris last year on the theme "Sources for the Holocaust" detailed data were provided on the archives kept in Croatia which can be used to establish the facts related to the seized Jewish property. However, a part of these archives are still not available to us as they are stored in Belgrade as files of the former federal bodies. This particularly applies to the documents related to war reparations and compensations after World War II, including funds already received from the Tripartite Commission for compensation to Nazi victims, as well as funds related to the gold which wound up in the treasury vaults of the then National Bank of Yugoslavia.

Namely, 32 cases of gold were left over in Zagreb after 1945, stored in the Franciscan Monastery, Kaptol, Zagreb. In February 1946 this gold was handed over to the National Bank of Yugoslavia, Zagreb Branch Office, Department for People's Property of the Government, Presidency of the People's Republic of Croatia. The gold was specified in 22 lists which have remained untraceable up to now, so that the actual quantity cannot be stated. Therefore, complete gold held by NDH, with the exception of 13 cases taken abroad on 7 May 1945, was taken by Tito's Yugoslavia. It is to be hoped that additional documents plus the lists of the mentioned 32 cases hidden in the Franciscan Monastery in Zagreb will be found as part of the archives of the National Bank of Yugoslavia.

These facts repudiate all the untrue stories spread in the international and Croatian press in late July and early August 1997 about some Croatian gold stored in the Vatican. Rumours like this could have emerged only because there were no explored and published documents about the Croatian Treasure and the Croatian State Bank covering the 1941–45 period.

Anyway, the final destination of this gold as well as other seized property should still be determined, along with the destination of the funds received for compensation. According to the Steering Committee of the Jewish Communities in Croatia, so far Jews in Croatia have not received any compensations such as received by the Jews, Holocaust victims and survivors, in other countries. Besides, the property of Jews in Croatia was seized on two occasions: first during World War II and then by the Yugoslav communist authorities, never restituted as yet.

According to the documents in the archive of the Jewish Community of Zagreb as well as those kept elsewhere in Croatia, the gold and other jewellery taken from Jews by as early as 31 October 1941 amounted to 1,065,339 kg. It is reasonable to suppose that a part of this gold is kept with the fund of the

Tripartite Commission for the Restitution of Monetary Gold. The distribution of it is also on the agenda of this Conference.

According to the records of the members of the Jewish communities in Croatia, about a half of the membership are persons born before 1945, considered as Holocaust victims. In Croatia there are about 1000 to 1200 Holocaust survivors eligible for compensation. About a half of the Holocaust survivors are persons aged 70 plus.

The Croatian Government supports the idea that the remaining funds of the Tripartite Commission should be used exclusively for compensation to Nazi victims. Consequently, the Croatian Government has decided, as reported to the Tripartite Commission, to renounce its share in the distribution of the remaining funds in favour of the Jewish victims of Nazi persecution.

As for the share in the remaining funds of the Tripartite Commission due to the former Yugoslavia, our position is that one should not wait for the final outcome of the current succession procedure to determine the portion of the funds due to individual successor states of the former Yugoslavia. These are all people in an advanced age, let alone their health condition certainly affected by the aftermaths of internment, imprisonment and participation in the National Liberation Struggle, so any further delays would result in the diminishing number of those entitled to compensation such as received a long time ago by the Jews in other countries. Any arguments for a deferred distribution on the grounds that the succession procedure has not been completed with regard to the assets and archives of the former Yugoslavia are wholly unjustified. At this stage already there are criteria accepted by the international community (including IMF) for distribution of assets among successor states of the former Yugoslavia and applicable to this specific case. Moreover, in the last analysis the funds will go not to the states, but to the individuals, the actual Nazi victims.

The Croatian delegation welcomes the efforts and good will of all the participants in this Conference, who, guided by the spirit of understanding and cooperation, departing from the principles of humanity and justice, are assembled here to find the best possible way of compensating the Holocaust victims, at this stage perhaps only symbolically, for at least a part of the ordeal they underwent.

Supplement to the Report of the Croatian Delegation

SOURCES FOR THE HISTORY OF THE HOLOCAUST AND THE FATE OF JEWISH PROPERTY IN CROATIA

Archives concerning the holocaust of the Jews in World War II and the fate of their property in Croatia have been quite well preserved.

1. The archives which can shed light on the fate of the Jews in World War II can be divided into five categories:
   a. Official documents (laws, provisions, archives of different administrative bodies) generated during Paveliæ's regime in Croatia in 1941–45. This group is the largest in volume and contains lists of names of Jews. Information on camps and perishing and treatment of Jews in public life. The archives of the Ministry of State Treasury, Department for State Property, Assets and Liabilities, the Office for Nationalised Property (PONOVA) 1941–45 deserve special mention here. These archives have 751 bundles with some 720 leaves of which almost 50% relate to Jews. This documentation contains files on the confiscation of Jewish movable property and real estate with mandatory property registration forms. Information on the real estate of the Jews who left the territory of the Independent State of Croatia (NDH), documentation on the registration of the nationalised Jewish property, and filled-in forms with personal data and property of Jews.
   b. The second group includes documents generated by the antifascist Partisan movement, showing the efforts made by the antifascists in Croatia to help Jews during the war.
   c. The third group includes documentation of the Commission of the People's Republic of Croatia for the Establishment of the Atrocities committed by the Occupying Forces and their Collaborators (1944–47). This Commission investigated all war crimes and the responsibility of the perpetrators.
   d. The fourth group includes documents generated by the operation of the State Security Service in investigations conducted after 1945 against those accused of atrocities during World War II.
   e. The fifth group includes collections of printed matter, photographs, memories, archives of Jewish municipalities, and private archives.

The basic data on these archives was published in an article by J. Kolanoviæ, *Holocaust in Croatia. Documentation and Research Perspectives* in: Arhivski vjesnik (Zagreb) 39 (1998), 157–174.

2. For the research on the fate of the monetary gold and currency reserves during World War II and the fate of gold, there are the bank archives, principally: the Zagreb based Croatian State Bank (1941–45) with subsequent liquidation and claims files until 1965. The archives of this bank alone have 1688 bundles, i.e. 388 metres of documents.

3. Part of the archival material which may shed light on the holocaust of Jews

and the question of monetary gold is obviously in Belgrade, notably the documentation on war reparations and the fate of the property which was within the jurisdiction of the federal bodies and the Bank of the Federal Republic of Yugoslavia.

RESEARCH ON THE HOLOCAUST AND JEWISH PROPERTY IN CROATIA

The first research on the Holocaust was carried out at the end of World War II and immediately after the War. A very detailed research on all crimes committed during World War II was conducted by the Committees for Determining Crimes Committed by Occupying Forces and Their Collaborators. These Committees were set up at all levels (municipality, city, district) and were responsible to the Regional Commission. The most extensive documentation preserved was gathered in the archive fund of the Regional Commission of the People's Republic of Croatia, set up by the decision of the Presidency of ZAVNOH (Antifascist Council of National Liberation of Croatia). The Council was responsible for gathering data and evidence of crimes, types of crimes, time, place and method of crimes committed, as well as responsibility of perpetrators and their collaborators. The punishment was meted out by relevant courts after a conducted trial. The Commission terminated its work on 31 October 1947. The Investigative section of the Croatian public prosecutor's office continued and completed the Commission's work. The gathered documentation also contains documentation on Jews, data on Jewish property and data on camp victims in the territory of Croatia[1].

After 1945, further research on crimes committed in World War II was carried out, but not enough attention was paid to Jewish property. Research was mostly conducted in particular camps, focusing on the number of victims. In the territory of the former Yugoslavia, data on victims was often manipulated. For instance, it was often stated that more than 700,000 Serbs had been killed at the notorious ustasha camp in Jasenovac. Subsequent research showed that this number is in fact ten times less. This huge number was first used when the Federal People's Republic of Yugoslavia (FNIU) reported to the International Reparation Commission in Paris its estimate of war casualties in the whole of Yugoslavia as 1,706,000.

This number was protected until the authority of the state, Tito, died in 1980, because he had been the first to come out with the number during his speech held in Ljubljana in May of 1945. Research by Dr. Bogoljub Koéoviæ, a Serb, and Vladimir Lerjaviæ, a Croat, showed that real population losses in the whole territory of ex-Yugoslavia were half that number, whereas the estimates put the number of Serbs, Croats, Jews and Romanies killed in pits, prisons and camps (including Jasenovac) at 78,000.[2]

A pilot project named "Dotršćina" was undertaken by the Croatian State Archive from 1978 to 1985 and was based on archive sources. It was tasked to comprise all fascist victims and antifascists associated with Zagreb who had been killed between 10 April, 1941 and 15 May, 1945 in concentration camps or prisons or as antifascist fighters. The project set as its task to name all the victims. To this end all relevant records kept with the Croatian State Archive as well as other Zagreb and Belgrade institutions were carefully examined. A total of 7,027 archive boxes, 67 boxes of files, 1,200 leaflets, posters and announcements, complete NDH press and 97 books were studied. Based on research results, a register for each person was made, containing general CV data. The study is concluded with archive references and literature. The result is 105 typewritten books with biographies of 40,000 victims including 6,537 Jews of whom 86 were killed in partisan units.

Croatian historians feel that this course of action should be continued and that every victim of World War II should be named, regardless of religion, nationality or political conviction. It is in this context that the research on Jewish victims in the area of NDH should be completed.

The Croatian State Archive has made an agreement with the U.S. Holocaust Memorial Museum in Washington on the submission of microfilms of all archival records related to the Holocaust in the area of Croatia. The microfilmed CVs of the above mentioned 6,537 Jews have already been submitted to the Museum. Another 50,765 microfilms related to the Holocaust were prepared by the end of 1997.

NDH'S MONETARY GOLD AND MONEY TAKEN ABROAD

Based on documents kept with the Croatian State Archive, research was on the fate of NDH's gold and money undertaken. The most important documents have been published in a book by Jere Jareb, entitled *Gold and Money of NDH Taken Abroad*, published in Zagreb by the Croatian History Institute in 1997 (393 pp).

The documentation includes the assets and liabilities balance of the Croatian State Bank and the deposits in the State Treasury Ministry (the book gives only examples), plus a review of the Croatian State Bank as of 8 May 1945.

Special attention is paid to the problem of the NDFI gold transferred to Switzerland in May and August of 1944 and the gold taken abroad during the 1945 retreat.

1. The Croatian State Bank

The Croatian State Bank did not possess any major quantities of gold or money, founded as it was in 1941, and no significant deposits were made in the meantime.

The principal asset of the Croatian State Bank during World War II, according to preserved information, was gold in quantities ranging from 1,200 to 1,500 tons that the Croatian State Bank acquired in 1941 from the treasury of the Sarajevo Branch of the National Bank of Yugoslavia.

On 12 May 1944, Germany handed over to the Croatian State Bank in Zagreb 358.42 kg of gold against payment of transit traffic over the territory of NDH. This quantity was legally exported to Switzerland, approved by the German State Bank, and deposited in the treasury of the Swiss Bank on 31 May 1944.

The Croatian State Bank illegally imported – i.e. without prior Swiss approval – 980.45 kg gold and deposited it in the treasury of the Swiss Bank on 2 August 1944. The Croatian authorities tried to get it back to Croatia as early as September 1944, but the attempt failed because of the illegal import into Switzerland.

Finally, under an agreement of 7 June 1944 between the Swiss Bank and the Croatian State Bank, on 2 August 1944, Croatia sold to 25,000 kg silver coins estimated at 1,997,560 Swiss Francs the Swiss Bank. By the end of the war, in May 1945, the Croatian State Bank held about 2,700,000 Swiss Francs on its account with the Swiss Bank, plus about 50,000 Swiss Francs with private Swiss banks.

Therefore, by the end of the war, in May 1945, the Croatian State Bank had in 1,338,87 kg gold and about 2,750,000 Swiss Francs Switzerland.

These assets were handed over to the National Bank of Tito's Yugoslavia on 10. July 1945[3].

2. Gold and money taken abroad at the beginning of May, 1945

    a. On 6. May, Croatian prime minister, Dr. Nikola Mandiæ, took with him to exile 220,000 Swiss Francs and 150 Gold Napoleons. This was seized from him by the Yugoslav army in Škofja Loka camp, Slovenia, on 19 May 1945, after the British authorities in Austria extradited him to Yugoslavia.

    b. On Monday 7 May 1945, the following valuables were taken away from the Croatian State Bank at Jurišiæva St., Zagreb, loaded on two trucks and a motorcar:

       – 18 boxes of stamp collections owed by the Post Office Directorate
       – about 290 kg gold in bars and gold coins packed in 13 boxes
       – various currencies of lesser value, such as Italian lira and German marks, with a case of jewellery in one box
       – valuable currencies such as US dollars, Swiss francs in the car of Dr. Mirko Puk[4].

3. What is the fate of the mentioned gold, money and valuables?

Nothing has been learned about the stamp collection.

The gold and money transported in Dr. Mirko Puk's car fell into the hands of partisans. According to some data published in Revija 92, Belgrade, partisans took hold of 2 boxes of gold.

The remaining 11 boxes of gold and 1 box of currencies of lesser value reached Wolfsberg, where Major Josip Tomljenoviæ opened a box of gold coins and distributed them among the refugees. In the Wolfsberg Franciscan Monastery, 10 boxes of gold and one box of valuable currencies including a case of diamonds, were stored. Of this, Dr. Krunoslav Draganoviæ took to Rome two boxes of gold in early July. The remaining 8 boxes of gold wound up later in the hands of the Croatian refugees[5].

4. Gold that remained in Zagreb

32 cases of gold and other valuables remained in Zagreb, stored in the Franciscan Monastery, Kaptol, Zagreb. In February 1945, this gold was handed

over to the National Bank of Yugoslavia, Zagreb Branch Office, Department for People's Property of the Government Presidency of the People's Republic of Croatia. The gold was specified in 22 lists which have remained untraceable up to now and are probably kept among the archives of the National Bank of Yugoslavia.

Therefore, complete NDH gold, with the exception of 13 cases taken to exile abroad on 7 May 1945, ended up in the National Bank of Yugoslavia. It is to be hoped that additional documents, plus the lists of the mentioned 32 cases hidden in Franciscan Monastery in Zagreb, will be found among the archives of the National Bank of Yugoslavia.

These facts exclude any possibility that the NDH gold was stored in the Vatican as alleged by some international newspapers in late July and early August. Such rumours probably stem from a report by a U.S. intelligence agent who must have heard something about two boxes of gold which had reached Rome, but not the Vatican, in the hands of Dr. Krunoslav Draganoviæ, with a part thereof in his possession and the other part ending up later with General Peènikar. According to the testimony of Dr. Lovro Susiæ, Dr. Krunoslav Draganovæ held for himself no more than 10% thereof[6].

5. Did the gold, jewellery and currencies include the property of Croatian Jews?

There is no doubt that the deposits of the State Treasury Ministry stored in the treasury of the Croatian State Bank included the gold, jewellery and money handed over by the Jews as a compulsive contribution to NDH over the period from May to October, 1941.

The records of the Commission of the People's Republic of Croatia, marked GUZ 2235/45–28–30 (box No.17) – the original ZAVNOH reference was 1535 of 4 June 1945 –includes a report of 31 October 1945 on the state of requisition of Jewish property to NDH with complete enclosures, filed by a committee set up for the purpose. This report estimates all the collected valuables to an equivalent of 1,065.33 kg gold. This documents has 36 pages[7]. By the end of October 1941 all this Jewish property was in the possession of the Directorate for Public Order and Security.

During the period of the former Yugoslavia the fate of Jewish property was never thoroughly investigated. Based on available documentation, it should be determined how much of the Jewish property was handed over to the State Treasury by the said Directorate and how much the Directorate itself retained and spent. The deposits of the State Treasury stored in the treasury of the Croatian State Bank also included the valuables confiscated from arrested individuals (Jews, Serbs and Croats), the smuggled property confiscated by the Commercial Police, the illegally exported or imported property confiscated by the Croatian customs authorities. Some citizens of Zagreb were reported to have granted gold coins to the Croatian army. Therefore, the question of the Jewish compulsory contributions and the confiscated property of Croatian citizens will have to be carefully explored, and the documentation analysed and published. It should also be noted that the Croatian State Bank did not own any confiscated or forcibly granted property because such property was handed to the deposits of the State Treasury. Each deposit, protocoled and specified, was entered in the State Treasury's records under sign S and a reference number[8].

NOTES

[1] Box No.17 contans a study on the seizure of Jewish property (p.27), a study determining the total value of the Jewish property in the territory of the Federal People's Republic of Croatia (p.9), a summary review on the take-over of valuables and money from the Croatian State Bank by the Police Directorate of Zagreb and a list of savings booklets and securities handed to the police district in Zagreb on 26 January 1942 (p.5), the Minutes on the take-over of gold and valuables by the police district in Zagreb (19 January 1942), Minutes on the take-over of cessions of claims abroad by the police district in Zagreb. List of forwarded supplements related to the Jewish property (14 November 1945). Report of the Police Administration on the condition of requisition of Jewish property by 31 October 1941. Instructions for detailed registration of nationalised property. Initial collection of papers on value of nationalised property. Periodical reports on collection and keeping of data on nationalised property.

[2] Cf Vladimir Serjaviæ: *Population Losses in Yugoslavia in WWII*, Yugoslav Victims' Society, Zagreb, 1989, English and French translations by Croatian History Institute, Zagreb, 1997; Dr. Bogoljub Koèoviæ: *Victims of World War II in Yugoslavia*, Naše delo Library, London, 1985; Also see V. Serjaviæ: *Obsessions and Exaggerations with Jasenovac and Bleiburg*, Globus, Zagreb, 1992. Vladimir Serjaviæ: Demographic Figures on the Plight of Jews in NDH, *Almanac on Antisemitism, Holocaust and Antifascism, Studia Iudaco-Croatica*, Jewish Community of Zagreb, 1996, 133–138.

[3] J. Jareb, ibid., p.247–248; documents published on p.145–246.

[4] For the inventory taken abroad by Dr Mirko Puk see: J. Jaren, ibid., p.264–267.

[5] Cf J. Jareb, ibid., p.348–359 with documents published on p. 249–347.

[6] Cf. J. Jareb, ibid., p.325.

[7] It was published by Josip Paver and Petar Strèiæ the Sarajevo magazine *DALJE*, No. 29–30 (1990) under the title "A thousand kilograms of gold. plundered from Jews by ustashas in Zagrcb in 1941".

[8] J. Jareb, ibid., p.159

CZECH REPUBLIC

Czechoslovak gold reserves and their surrender to Nazi Germany

EDUARD KUBU

Institute of Economic and Social History,
Faculty of Philosophy of Charles University Prague

Until the creation of the National Czechoslovak Bank in 1926, the function of the bank of issue in the Czechoslovak Republic had been undertaken by the Bank Office of the Ministry of Finance. This office had also been responsible for monitoring and managing Czechoslovak gold reserves. At first, very modest, and according to Bank Office data amounting in 1920 to a mere 6,457.6 kg of gold,[1] these reserves arose almost continuously. The source of the relatively rapid and large-scale accumulation of gold reserves was not, however, simply state-organised purchase of the metal. It also owed much to a broad public campaign that elicited gifts from firms and institutions, and above all, in 1919 and 1924, to organised collections among the population who were asked to contribute to what was known as "The Gold Treasure of the Czechoslovak Republic".[2] The creation of gold currency reserves thus acquired a special emotional colouring linked to the building of the young Czechoslovak state, and it became a public matter.

Gold resources at the end of 1924 already amounted to 40,737.3 kg. This total included the 112,053.7 kg transferred from the former Austro-Hungarian bank.[3] During the economic boom it proved possible to increase gold reserves to 68,858.1 kg.[4] Reserves continued to rise even in the 1930s. By 29th September 1938, i.e. at the time of the Munich Conference which imposed on Czechoslovakia the cession of extensive border areas to the German Reich, the overall gold reserve was 94,772.0 kg. The National Czechoslovak Bank, however, in response to the growing German menace to the state, had been preventively increasing the amount of gold deposited abroad.[5] For this reason, at the time of Munich only 6,336.6 kg was to be found in domestic vaults, while the remaining 88,435.4 kg was distributed among several foreign depositaries generally regarded as secure.[6] Nevertheless, not only to the detriment of the CSR and its citizens, but also to the detriment of the states that were soon forced into war against Hitler, Germany ultimately managed to gain control of most of the Czechoslovak gold reserves.[7] The amounts of gold transferred, and the ways in which they were appropriated, are specified below.

I. Gold backing Czechoslovak tender circulating in the border territories occupied under the Munich Agreement of 29.9.38

While implementing the Munich *Diktat,* Germany demanded that the National Czechoslovak Bank give up gold backing the tender circulating in the territory occupied by German forces. In the annexed areas 1250.6 million Kč in bank-issued notes and 1,502.7 million Kč in state-issued notes was withdrawn. After difficult negotiations characterised by high German demands and pressure, compensation was extracted from the Czechs in the form of "purchase" of assets belonging to the rump Czechoslovakia (especially of the industrial interests of Prague banks in the border areas) and takeover of the Czechoslovak armaments which the Germans wanted.

In negotiations over the bank-issued portion of the tender withdrawn, Germany demanded gold and valuable foreign currency while refusing discussion of the proportion represented by cash orders and clearing. In January the Germans resorted to threats, which on 23rd February 1939 culminated in ultimatum demands sent to Prague. Five days later, a Czechoslovak delegation was sent to Berlin where it submitted to German pressure. On 4th March 1939 a document was signed on the basis of which 769 million Kč was to be covered by Czechoslovak real property in the occupied borderlands and by monetary loans provided there, while the remainder was covered by gold. On 7th March 1939, the National Czechoslovak Bank sent a telegram to the Bank for International Settlements in Basle, requesting that the latter should convey 47 ingots (579.8 kg) of the gold deposited in Brussels, and 125 ingots (1,468.36 kg) of the gold deposited in Berne, to the Deutsche Reichsbank: it also requested that Swiss National Bank to transfer 1,031 ingots (12,488 kgs) of the gold deposited in Berne.[8]

Since the Munich agreement has been rightly regarded by Czechoslovak law as null and void from the very beginning, these transfers were branded as unacceptable and unjustified. The claim for the return of this gold was also, of course, strengthened by the fact that the occupied territories were themselves returned to the Czechoslovak Republic in 1945.

II. Gold surrendered directly after the occupation of the Czech lands on 15th March 1939

In a warning of impending German occupation delivered on 14th March 1939 to the Czechoslovak ambassador in Berlin, Vojtěch Mastný, by the French embassy, mention was made of German interest in Czechoslovak gold.[9] The following day was to prove the French information correct. The task of securing the Czechoslovak gold for Germany was entrusted to Dr. Muller as special commissioner of the German Reichsbank attached to the command of military group 3 (Sonderbeauftragte der Reichsbank beim Heeresgruppenkommando 3). Muller, after his arrival at the National Bank, forced directors Peroutka and Malík, under threat of immediate execution, to draw up and send two orders for the transfer of the Czechoslovak gold deposited in Great Britain.[10]

The first, to the Bank of England in London, requested the transfer of 26,793 kg of gold to the Bank for International Settlements in Basle, and the second requested the Bank for International Settlements to transfer 23,087.30 kg of a deposit of 28,309,30 kg. at the Bank of England to the account of the Deutsche Reichsbank there. At the same time, however, a request was made to the British Embassy to ensure that the implementation of a forced and therefore void order should be quashed by the competent British authorities. Nevertheless, the order for the transfer of 23 tons of gold was promptly fulfilled on 20th March.[11] The property of the victim of an act of violence – an act which the British government had not recognised – was irresponsibly surrendered to the perpetrator. The second order was not, fortunately, carried out . . . because of a shift in the political view of the matter.

The issue soon attracted the attention of the British press, and on 18th May 1939 it was the subject of debate in the British House of Commons. It aroused criticism not only of the Bank of England, but also of the Treasury and the whole government. The Member of Parliament, Brendan Brecken declared it to be "a very squalid form of financial appeasement, because they are appeasing the Germans with the money of the unfortunate Czechs." Winston Churchill also expressed outrage: "If at the same time our mechanism is so butter-fingered that this 6 million pounds of gold can be transferred to the Nazi government of Germany, which only wishes to use it, and is only using it, as it does all its foreign exchange, for the purpose of increasing its armaments [...] it stultifies altogether the efforts our people are making in every class and in every party to secure National Defence and rally the whole forces of the country."[12]

III. The removal of gold coinage to Germany in 1940

The National Bank of Bohemia and Moravia – the new name for the bank of issue under the Protectorate – had only limited competence and minimal gold reserves. The trumped-up accusation and arrest of its director Sadflek by the Gestapo, which ended in his suicide, became the excuse for the transfer to Berlin of the remainder of Czech gold deposited in the vaults of the National Bank on 12th June 1940. Officials of the Deutsche Reichsbank removed 6,375.86 kg of gold, this time in the form of gold coins, part of which were numismatic collections of major historical value.[13]

IV. The decentralised part of Czechoslovak gold reserves

The final case of unlawful transfer of Czechoslovak gold to the benefit of Germany happened in the Autumn of 1940, with the transfer of 1,008.9 kg of gold administered for the National Bank within the framework of the so-called "customs autonomy of the Skoda Works and Brno Munitions Factory Inc". The gold deposited in the safes of these concerns was used to purchase foreign currency for the import of industrial raw materials.[14]

*　　*　　*　　*　　*

The total amount of Czechoslovak gold stolen by the Nazis exceeded, as is shown by the simple addition of individual items, 45 tons. This represented approximately one half of all the gold currency reserves of the National Bank as recorded at the time of the Munich Conference. Damages of this amount were also declared by the Czechoslovak government to the Tripartite Commission for the Return of Gold. This commission recognised nearly the whole of this claim as legitimate (43,999.4 kg) and also accepted it as the basis for restitution proceedings.[15] In view of the emotional charge of the problem, the Czechoslovak public followed these proceedings and the implementation of restitution with keen attention, and the issue still remains of great interest to the public.

NOTES

[1] Czech National Bank Archives (CNBA), History of The Golden Treasure of the Czechoslovak Republic – Report for the President of Czech National Bank J. Tošovský, Prague 23.10.1990. No. 2040/1990.

[2] For Collection for Gold treasure see: CNBA, Czechoslovak National Bank, carton 425, sign. NB P XVII–334, central accounting office.

[3] Report for the President of Czech National Bank J. Tošovský as quoted above.

[4] For more details see: La prèmiere période decennate de l'activité de la Banque Nationale de Tchécostovaquie, Prague 1937, p. 302–303.

[5] War preparations of the Czechoslovak National Bank started in 1936. See Jaroslav Šůla, Přehled československé měny 1918–1989 [Survey of the Czechoslovak Currency from 1919 to 19389], in: Currency Systems in Czech Lands 1892–1993, Opava – Praha 1995, p. 20.

[6] Leopold Charles. Hospodářská okupace Československa, její methody a důsledky [Economic Occupation of Czechoslovakia, Its Methods and Consequences], Praha 1946, p. 17.

[7] For further information on economic consequences of German occupation of Czech lands in general see: Václav Král, Otázky Hospodářského a sociálního vývoie v českých zemích v letech 1938–1945. [Problems of Economic and Social Development in Czech Lands from 1938 to 1945], parts I and II, Praha 1957: Alice Teichová, Německá hospodářská politika v českých zemích v letech 1939–1945 [German Economic Policy in Czech Lands from 1939 to 1945], Studie z hospodářských dějin Vysoké školy ekonomické v Praze – vol. no. 1, Praha 1998.

[8] CNBA. Memorandum of the Czechoslovak National Bank for the Ministry of Finance, Prague 15 April, 1947, NB, carton 430a, sign. NB P XVII–432, no. 69538/47–III/2; transfer orders, NB, carton 430b, sign. NB P XVII–332, folder – zlato [gold]; I. Chmela, o.c., p. 26.

[9] Ministry of Foreign Affaires of the Czech Republic - Archives (MFA CR-A), dispatches received. no. 222/1939.

[10] CNBA, Memorandum of the Czechoslovak National Bank from 15 April 1947 as quoted above: transfer orders, NB. carton 430b, sign. NB P XVII-332, folder – zlato [gold]: L. Chmela, o.c., p. 148.

[11] Eduard Táborský, Ňase věc. Československo ve světle mezinárodního práva za druhé světové války [Our Concern. Czechoslovakia in the Light of International Law], Praha 1946, p. 91; MFA CR-A, London Archive – nonconfidential part., carton 209, Memorandum of E. Táborský on Czechoslovak Gold Reserves and related documents [1941/421].

[12] Martin Gilbert and Richard Gott, The Appeasers, London 1963, p. 208–211: Harold Macmillan, Winds of Change 1914–1939, London 1966, p. 597.

[13] CNBA, Memorandum of the Czechoslovak National Bank from 15th April 1947 as quoted above: accounting documents, NB, carton 430a, sign, NB P SVII-332, folder - ńčetni doklady [accounts].

[14] Ibid: handover records, NB, carton 430a, sign NB P XVII–432, folder – Zlato Škodovky a Zbrojovky [Gold of Škoda Works and Zbrojovka].

[15] Jan Krejči, Několik poznámek k historil navráceni československého měnového zlata [Comments on the History of Czechoslovak Gold Reserves Recovery], Právník, volume CXXXV (1996), no. 7, p. 675.

Steps taken hitherto to compensate occupied countries and individual victims

MILAN BERANEK

Head of Delegation Czech Republic

It is a sad, bitter but true fact that neither former Czechoslovakia nor the Czech Republic ever received any reparation or any compensation for the victims of Nazi persecution. Czech and also Slovak individual victims have not yet been given anything – despite the explicit international obligation overtaken by Germany in the so called Settlement Convention saying among other things that "the compensation shall be assured without discrimination against any groups or classes of persecuted persons" (Part IV, par.2, lit.d/11). It is also of utmost importance that there be a general, immediate, full and definitive stop to the practical application of one of the elements of the so called Hallstein doctrine: namely that persons who currently reside in the countries of the former Eastern Bloc are not eligible for compensation. This application is, even in the year 1997, totally unacceptable.

* * * * *

I'd now rather concentrate on very short presentation or to certain extent reduced overview of facts that my country – former Czechoslovakia now the Czech Republic – has done in the sphere of compensation of individual victims of Nazi persecution mostly on her own, without waiting for the primary compensation that should have logically come from abroad.

Firstly in 1946 the Czechoslovak was charged together with the governments of the USA, Great Britain, France and Yugoslavia (and worked very actively) to prepare an agreement on plan and measures to be taken in favour of so-called non-repatriable victims of Nazi violence. The plan included also treatment of the identifiable non-monetary gold that was further distributed to the entitled individuals. The rest of this gold was transferred to the non-governmental Jewish organisations.

Secondly, Act No.255 regulated in the year 1946 compensation of Nazi victims in Czechoslovakia for the first time. It was done in the form of granting fixed amounts of money, but also in the form of repeated flow of money – especially – increased or special rents, social contributions and other social benefits including non-monetary forms.

Thirdly in the year 1994 – when seeing that the international compensation was even after almost 50 years not available for the Czech victims, the Czech authorities decided to make another gesture of goodwill and solidarity with the Nazi victims and their families. Through Act No. 217/1994 the Czech Republic offered again from its regular state budget further compensation to Nazi victims in all categories. The entitled persons had the possibility to ask for their share within a period of 6 months. The total sum that has been paid to them exceeds 2 billions of Czech crowns.

Last, but not least, these were only several selected examples of steps – perhaps the most visible – taken to compensate the individual victims. There are, of course, other ongoing activities being undertaken or supported – both directly and indirectly – by the Czech government that have not the strict character of individual compensation of victims but that express the solidarity of the society with them in other ways. On 23 July this year the Czech government decided (Decision No. 450) to offer a donation for the purpose of charity education and social activities to the Jewish organisations and communities in the Czech and the Slovak Republics. It was agreed that the amount of money coming from the Czech government will represent 20 million crowns and that coming from the Slovak government a further 10 million crowns.

*   *   *   *   *

Negotiations are underway at various levels on special projects that could contribute to clarify at least some of the still publicly unknown pages of history on the one hand and – on the other hand – to help and to contribute to the improvement of the personal situation of the generation of victims (which is diminishing very rapidly and counts today in our case about 7,500 people still surviving) and to offer them at least a moral and, where possible also material satisfaction. In this connection I should mention the ongoing negotiations on the establishment of the Common Czech-German Fund for the Future, the very important common project of Czech state and non-governmental institutions on cooperation with Memorial Museum of Holocaust in Washington on microfiching, conservation and further necessary work enabling access to documents. Other activities include cooperation with the Yat Washem in Jerusalem, the worldwide highly appreciated activities of the Jewish Museum in Prague or those of the Museum of Holocaust in Terezín (Theresienstadt).

DENMARK

Statement by the Danish Delegation

The Danish delegates at the Conference made a short statement on the themes of the Conference. They stated that part of the gold reserves of the Danish National Bank which at the time was deposited in Denmark, Norway and Sweden was transported from Bergen in Norway to the United States shortly before the German invasion of Denmark on 9 April 1940 and deposited in the Federal Reserve Bank in New York. The gold stayed in the United States during the war and the Germans thus did not seize Danish monetary gold.

Against this background Denmark never made any claims to the Tripartite Gold Commission. Instead the Danish claims or reparations for the losses suffered by the Danish people and society as a result of the war and the German occupation of Denmark were presented to the Paris Conference on Reparation in 1945. These claims amounted to a total of 11.6 billion Danish Kroner, of which 9.2 billion were losses in connection with the occupation.

The Danish delegates also made a short account of the fate of the Danish Jewish population during the war.

At the time the Danish Jewish community amounted to around 80,00 persons. In October 1943, when the Germans initiated an action against the Danish Jews in order to deport them to Germany, more than 7,000 Danish Jews succeeded in fleeing to Sweden where they stayed until the end of the war. 481 Danish Jews were, however, caught and sent to the concentration camp Theresienstadt. Of these 53 died during their stay in the camp while 423 survived and were sent back to Denmark shortly before the end of the war in 1945 (5 had been sent back earlier). When the Danish Jews returned to Denmark they found that in general their property was intact. There were therefore only few claims of a private nature for compensation of lost values and these were settled shortly after the end of the war.

It is important to state that Denmark – in contrast to the other occupied countries – remained under Danish administration during the occupation so that no legal or administrative measures against Jews or Jewish property took place.

In 1959 Denmark also signed an agreement with the Federal Republic of Germany on payments for the benefit of Danish citizens who were victims of Nazi persecution. Under this agreement the Federal Republic of Germany paid an amount of 16 million Deutsche Mark to Denmark for the said purpose.

The Ministry of Foreign Affairs has also looked into the possibility of making a contribution to the fund which was established in connection with the London

Conference and which will be used for the relief of needy victims of Nazi persecution.

While the Ministry of Foreign Affairs does not have special funds making it possible to make a direct contribution to the fund, the Danish Democracy Fund administered by the Ministry will be willing to support concrete projects that comply with the guidelines for the said fund. These would include visits to Denmark in connection with seminars etc. arranged by the Jewish Community in Denmark for victims of Nazi persecution. In this way Denmark will make its special contribution to projects falling within the purview of the international fund.

FEDERAL RESERVE BANK OF NEW YORK

The following materials reflect the main historical involvement of the Federal Reserve Bank of New York (New York Fed) with Nazi gold, namely, our role as depository for the Tripartite Gold Commission (TGC). They include a summary of the TGC's current holdings (Attachment A); a bar-by-bar inventory (Attachment B); a history of all TGC account activity since 1947 (Attachment C); and a copy of an account document concerning one of the deposits to the TGC's account in 1952 (Attachment D).

CURRENT HOLDINGS

The TGC currently has about $54.5 million worth of gold in its accounts. Of this amount, about 4 metric tons, worth about $34.7 million, are held at the Bank of England, and approximately 2 metric tons, worth about $19.8 million, are held in the TGC's account at the New York Fed. The TGC has authorized the release of the following statement about its current holdings at the New York Fed:

> "The TGC account at the New York Fed currently holds a total of 162 gold bars. The Swedish central bank deposited 158 of these bars into the TGC account between 1949 and 1955 and the U.S. High Commissioner for Germany deposited 4 bars into the account in 1952. Of the 158 bars received from Sweden, 83 were produced by the Rand Refinery, South Africa, and bear no year-stamp; 66 were produced before 1937 by the Rand Refinery, South Africa; and 8 were produced in 1933 by Rothschilds, Great Britain. Of the 4 bars from the U.S. High Commissioner for Germany, 2 were produced in 1921 by the U.S. Assay Office; and 2 were produced by the Societe de Banque Suisse Le Locle and bear no year-stamp".

In addition to this statement, Attachments A and B further detail the current holdings on a bar-by-bar basis, describing the deposits from which the current holdings came; the refiner for each bar; and year markings, if any, on each bar. These Attachments were prepared in conjunction with a physical inspection of the gold last January.

The current holdings came from three deposits, in 1949, 1952 and 1955. The 1949 deposit was accomplished by a transfer of bars from the holdings of the Swedish central bank at the New York Fed to the account of the TGC. These bars, 108 of which remain in the account, entered the Swedish central bank's account in 1947, in two shipments to the New York Fed, one from the Swedish central bank's holdings in Sweden and one from its holdings in Argentina. All of these bars appear to have been originally produced in South Africa by the Rand Refinery, though some were apparently later re-assayed by the Kungel Mint in Sweden.

The 1952 deposit was received from the U.S. High Commissioner for Germany, and consisted of 17 boxes of miscellaneous gold bars, coins and smaller gold pieces. Of this gold, 4 bars remain in the account, 2 produced by the U.S. Assay Office, and 2 produced by a Swiss refiner, the Societe de Banque Suisse Le Locle. This deposit is discussed further below.

The 1955 deposit was made by the Swedish central bank, again from holdings which had entered its account at the New York Fed in 1947, after having been shipped to New York from Sweden. Of the 50 bars from this deposit which remain in the TGC account, 42 were produced in South Africa by the Rand Refinery; and 8 appear to have been originally produced in Great Britain by Rothschilds, though some also bear an assay stamp from the Kungel Mint in Sweden.

In summary, the country of origin and year of production for the gold bars are as follows:

150	South Africa
8	United Kingdom
2	Switzerland
2	United States
162	

85	Bear no year-stamp
66	Produced before 1937
1	Produced before 1948
8	Produced in 1933
2	Produced in 1921
162	

The question may arise whether the TGC's current holdings contain any "tainted" gold, that is, gold which was produced by the Reichsbank or others from the personal gold of the Nazi victims. We simply do not know the answer to this question. The New York Fed operates a gold custody service only, which is essentially limited to receiving, safekeeping and delivering gold. The New York Fed does not assay, refine, conduct scientific tests, or otherwise process the gold it receives and holds in gold custody accounts, and has no expertise in such matters.

ACCOUNT HISTORY

The TGC account history (Attachment C) shows every deposit and withdrawal from the TGC account since its establishment in 1947. There are a number of items in the account history which are worth noting.

First, the initial Swiss deposit, which formed the bulk of the TGC's holdings at the New York Fed, consisted entirely of gold bars produced by the U.S. Assay office. Records indicate that these gold bars had been in the Swiss National Bank's account at the New York Fed from at least 1944 or 1945, before being transferred to the TGC's account in 1947.

Second, on several occasions the TGC sold small amounts of gold to the U.S. Treasury. We understand that the proceeds of these sales were used by the TGC for its operating expenses.

Third, in several instances, at the direction of the TGC, gold that was deposited into the TGC account was sent to the U.S. Assay office to be resmelted. These deposits consisted of gold bars that did not meet international "good delivery" standards in the European or U.S. markets, mutilated coins, and small pieces of gold. After being resmelted into good delivery bars and re-deposited into the TGC account, all of this gold was later distributed to claimant countries. This sort of resmelting operation was not uncommon among participants in the gold markets during the period in question and still occurs to some extent today. In general, the purpose of such resmelting is to produce bars that meet the standards of eligibility for acceptance in gold transactions.

1952 DEPOSIT

The account history indicates that a deposit received from the U.S. High Commissioner for Germany on February 26, 1952, consisted of 17 boxes of various gold bars, coins and miscellaneous items referred to in the gold trade as "finger bars," "chips," "sheets," "buttons," etc. Regrettably, our records do not provide any further information as to the nature or origin of the deposit. However, because the deposit contained smaller gold items collected by American authorities and sent from Germany, we thought it would be of particular interest, and specially requested the TGC to authorize us to release an account document describing the deposit (Attachment D).

At the instruction of the TGC in May 1952, much of this gold was sent to the U.S. Assay office, where it was converted into 43 bars of gold, or about .08 percent of all the gold ever held by the TGC at the New York Fed. All 43 bars were later disbursed to claimant nations. As noted above, 4 bars from this deposit – 2 U.S. Assay, 2 Swiss – remain in the TGC account.

COMMITMENT TO OPENNESS

The New York Fed has worked aggressively over the past year to promote complete openness with regard to records related to Nazi gold. Along with the attached materials, the New York Fed provided over 2,500 pages of documents to the National Archives in April concerning the movements of gold and other assets by central banks during World War II. We will continue to seek the release of all remaining TGC records. In addition, the New York Fed has worked closely with other U.S. Government agencies, Ambassador Eizenstat, members of

Congress, and others seeking the truth about Nazi gold. Most recently, we have cooperated with the State Department to facilitate the establishment of a fund for needy Holocaust survivors from the remaining assets of the TGC. In all our actions we have sought to contribute to the development of a complete and accurate public record and to foster a better understanding of a tragic era.

Contacts

Peter Bakstansky, Senior Vice President, Public Information Office, 212-720-6109; James Hennessy, Counsel, Legal Group, 212-720-8195.

Attachment A

SUBJECT: INSPECTION OF TGC GOLD BARS

Attached is a listing of the information obtained during the inspection of gold bars that was conducted on Monday, January 6, 1997. The bars are listed in alphabetical order by refiner (based on FRBNY's records) and then in bar number order. FRBNY's records show:

19	bars with refiner =	Kungel
2	bars with refiner =	LeLocle
131	bars with refiner =	Rand
8	bars with refiner =	Rothschild
2	bars with refiner =	U.S. Assay Office

The inspection revealed that the 19 Kungel bars also include the Rand Refinery stamp. Because we have not seen any evidence that Kungel was a recognized producer of 400 ounce bars, it appears that these bars were originally produced by Rand, and subsequently passed through the Kungel Mint, where it appears that they were re-assayed. Similarly, of the 131 Rand bars on FRBNY's records, 48 bars also bear markings made by the Kungel Mint. It appears, then that 67 bars (48 + 19) originally produced by Rand passed through the Kungel Mint, where they were re-assayed. In so doing it seems that Kungel also stamped the bars with their own bar number, as well as a date (presumably the date of the re-assay). The date stampings are all 1935 or 1936, with one exception: one bar is stamped 1947. During this re-assaying process, Kungel apparently established for 36 bars a different fineness than that stamped on the bar by the original refiner. The differences are not significant, with the difference in all but one case only +/- .0001; the other bar has a difference of .0003. It has been the practice of the Bank to "book" the bars for deposits based on the depositor's manifest. In the absence of a copy of the original manifests from the deposits in 1949, 1952 and 1955, it is reasonable to assume that the manifests showed the Kungel finenesses for the bars in question.

The LeLocle bars bear no year stamps.

The Rothschild bars also seem to have been re-assayed by Kungel, but no fineness differences appear as those bars do not have a fineness stamped on them. These bars bear two year stamps; 1933, apparently affixed by Rothschild, and 1935, apparently by Kungel.

The U.S. Assay bars are stamped with the year 1921.

It should also be noted that most bars that passed through the Kungel Mint re-assay process (Rand and Rothschild) also bear an additional set of identifying numbers. It is not clear who might have added those bar numbers.

Attachment B

BAR-BY-BAR INVENTORY

Tripartite Commission for the Restitution of Monetary Gold ("TGC")

The TGC Account at the FRBNY currently holds:

       162   bars of various refiners weighting
65,525.620   fine troy ounces, and said to contain
65,238.098   fine troy ounces

The remaining gold on deposit in the TGC Account at FRBNY originated from three deposits

1. December 12, 1949
Sweden deposited a total of 571 bars of various refiners said to contain 230,049.065 flo. 108 bars remain in the account from the original deposit, which is broken down into two sections,1a and 1b below.

2. February, 28, 1952
The U.S. High Commissioner for Germany deposited 17 boxes of miscellaneous gold bars, coins and pieces said to contain 20,999.769 flo. Four bars from this deposit remain in the account.

3. April 29, 1955
Sweden deposited a total of 479 bars of various refiners said to contain 192,904.484. Fifty bars remain in the account from the original deposit.

Deposit No. 1 – 12/12/49

December 12, 1949
Sweden deposited a total of 571 bars of various refiners said to contain 230,049.065 flo. This deposit was made by transferring bars from the of the Sveriges Riksbank at FRBNY to the TGC Account at FRBNY.

KEY:

The bars that were transferred to the TGC Account were deposited to the account of Sveriges Riksbank on two dates:

- -   a. *October 15, 1947*: The Steamship Drottningholm sailing from Stockholm delivered gold bars for deposit to the account of Sveriges Riksbank at FRBNY, by order of Sveriges Riksbank.

o   b. *December 10, 1947*: The Steamship Mormacrio sailing from Buenos
Aires delivered gold bars for deposit to the account of Sveriges Riksbank
at FRBNY, by order of Banco Central de la Republica Argentina.

1a. Sweden/Sweden
Of the deposit made by Sweden on 12/12/49 from the import from Stockholm on
10/15/47, 80 bars remain in the TGC Account at this time. These 80 bars all appear to
have been originally produced by the Rand Refinery in South Africa, but many appear
to have been re-assayed by the Kungel Mint in Stockholm, Sweden.

1b. Sweden/Argentina
Of the deposit made by Sweden on 12/12/49 from the import from Buenos Aires on
12/10/47, 28 bars remain in the account. These bars all appear to have been originally
produced by the Rand Refinery in South Africa.

Deposit No. 2 – 02/26/52

KEY:

÷   *February 26, 1952* The U.S. High Commissioner for Germany deposited
17 boxes containing miscellaneous gold bars, coins and pieces, said to
contain 20,999.769 flo. Of this deposit, most of the gold was withdrawn
at the direction of the TGC and delivered to the U.S. Assay Office in
NYC and converted into standard "400 ounce" bars. Of these
"re-smelted" bars, none currently remain in the TGC Account: all of
them had been released to one of the claimant countries that received
gold from the TGC Account at FRBNY subsequent to February, 1952:
France, Netherlands, Poland and Czechoslovakia. Four bars from the
original February 26, 1952 shipment were NOT sent out for re-smelting.
Those bars, listed below, remain in the account.
  2 bars produced by the Societe de Banque Suisse Le Locle
  2 bars produced by the U.S. Assay Office

Deposit No. 3 – 04/29/55

KEY:

x   *April 29, 1955* Sweden deposited a total of 479 bars of various refiners
said to contain 192,904.484 flo. This deposit was made by transferring
bars from the account of the Sveriges Riksbank at FRBNY to the TGC
Account the bars that were transferred were deposited to the account of
Sveriges Riksbank on September 30, 1947, having apparently been
shipped to NYC from Sweden. Of the deposit made by Sweden on
04/29/55 from the import from Sweden, 50 bars remain in the
account. These 50 bars are made up of:
42 bars that appear to have been produced by the Rand Refinery, South
Africa, and
8 bars that appear to have been produced by Rothschild, Great Britain,
but that also bear an assay stamp from the Kungel Mint.

Bar by bar description (sorted by refiner, bar number), based on FRBNY's gold ledger records

FRBNY OFFICIAL RECORDS REFLECT: INFORMATION BELOW REFLECTS ADDITIONAL MARKINGS ON BARS/COMMENTS, ETC.

Key	Refiner/Assayer	Bar No.	Gross weight	Fine-ness	Fine weight	Refiner	Year markings if any	
--	Kungel Mint	1816	404.180	0.9960	402.563	Rand	Rand Bar No. AD6938	Kungel Assay Year 1936	Additional Bar No's UY943
--	Kungel Mint	1817	405.170	0.9960	403.549	Rand	Rand Bar No. AD6939	Kungel Assay Year 1936	Additional Bar No's UY944
--	Kungel Mint	1818	404.950	0.9960	403.330	Rand	Rand Bar No. AD6940	Kungel Assay Year 1936	Additional Bar No's UY945
--	Kungel Mint	1819	403.970	0.9960	402.354	Rand	Rand Bar No. AD6941	Kungel Assay Year 1936	Additional Bar No's UY946
--	Kungel Mint	1820	403.620	0.9960	402.006	Rand	Rand Bar No. AD6942	Kungel Assay Year 1936	Additional Bar No's UY947
--	Kungel Mint	1823	403.680	0.9958	402.980	Rand	Rand Bar No. AD6421	Kungel Assay Year 1936	Additional Bar No's UY589
--	Kungel Mint	1824	404.240	0.9958	402.461	Rand	Rand Bar No. AD6422	Kungel Assay Year 1936	Additional Bar No's UY590 Fineness on bar shows .9958
--	Kungel Mint	1825	405.130	0.9956	403.347	Rand	Rand Bar No. AD6423	Kungel Assay Year 1936	Additional Bar No's UY591
--	Kungel Mint	1826	405.660	0.9956	403.875	Rand	Rand Bar No. AD6424	Kungel Assay Year 1936	Additional Bar No's UY592
--	Kungel Mint	1827	405.880	0.9956	404.094	Rand	Rand Bar No. AD6425	Kungel Assay Year 1936	Additional Bar No's UY593
--	Kungel Mint	1828	404.100	0.9964	402.645	Rand	Rand Bar No. AD6426	Kungel Assay Year 1936	Additional Bar No's UY594
--	Kungel Mint	1829	404.470	0.9964	403.014	Rand	Rand Bar No. AD6427	Kungel Assay Year 1936	Additional Bar No's UY595
--	Kungel Mint	1831	404.400	0.9964	402.944	Rand	Rand Bar No. AD6429	Kungel Assay Year 1936	Additional Bar No's UY597
--	Kungel Mint	1832	404.690	0.9964	403.233	Rand	Rand Bar No. AD6430	Kungel Assay Year 1936	Additional Bar No's UY598
--	Kungel Mint	1833	405.510	0.9964	404.050	Rand	Rand Bar No. AD6431	Kungel Assay Year 1936	Additional Bar No's UY599
--	Kungel Mint	1834	406.670	0.9964	405.206	Rand	Rand Bar No. AD6432	Kungel Assay Year 1936	Additional Bar No's UY600
--	Kungel Mint	1836	405.120	0.9962	403.581	Rand	Rand Bar No. AD6386	Kungel Assay Year 1936	Additional Bar No's UY602 Fineness on bar shows .9961
--	Kungel Mint	1839	405.290	0.9962	403.750	Rand	Rand Bar No. AD6389	Kungel Assay Year 1936	Additional Bar No's UY605 Fineness on bar shows .9961
--	Kungel Mint	1840	408.150	0.9962	406.599	Rand	Rand Bar No. AD6390	Kungel Assay Year 1936	Additional Bar No's UY606 Fineness on bar shows .9961
+	Le Locle Suisse	7743L-4357	400.420	1.0000	400.420			
+	Le Locle Suisse	7742L-40503	401.680	1.0000	401.680			
--	Rand	BA-642	401.920	0.9956	400.152			
--	Rand	BA-644	402.090	0.9954	400.240			
--	Rand	BA-648	402.810	0.9954	400.957			
--	Rand	BA-649	402.700	0.9966	401.331			
--	Rand	BA-650	404.900	0.9966	403.523			
--	Rand	BA-814	400.340	0.9962	398.819			
--	Rand	BA-922	404.890	0.9966	403.513			
--	Rand	BA-923	405.550	0.9966	404.171			
--	Rand	BA-924	404.990	0.9966	403.613			
--	Rand	BA-925	404.190	0.9966	402.816			
--	Rand	BA-926	403.670	0.9963	402.176			
--	Rand	BA-927	407.000	0.9963	405.494			

Bar by bar description - *continued*

FRBNY OFFICIAL RECORDS REFLECT:

INFORMATION BELOW REFLECTS ADDITIONAL MARKINGS ON BARS/COMMENTS, ETC.

Key	Refiner/Assayer	Bar No.	Gross weight	Fine-ness	Fine weight	Refiner	Year markings if any	
- -	Rand	BA-928	402.660	0.9962	401.130		Kungel Assay Year 1947	Fineness on bar shows .9963
- -	Rand	BA-929	405.930	0.9963	404.428			
- -	Rand	BA-930	407.940	0.9963	406.431			
- -	Rand	BA-931	403.200	0.9963	401.708			
- -	Rand	BA-932	405.650	0.9963	404.149			
- -	Rand	BA-933	406.630	0.9963	405.125			
- -	Rand	BA-934	402.550	0.9963	401.061			
- -	Rand	BA-935	405.540	0.9963	404.040			
- -	Rand	BA-936	403.680	0.9963	402.188			
- -	Rand	BA-937	402.930	0.9963	401.439			
- -	Rand	BA-938	404.310	0.9965	402.895			
- -	Rand	BA-939	406.330	0.9965	404.908			
- -	Rand	BA-940	402.520	0.9965	401.111			
- -	Rand	BA-941	405.600	0.9965	404.180			
- -	Rand	BA-942	405.760	0.9965	404.340			
- -	Rand	BA-943	403.520	0.9965	402.108			
- -	Rand	BA-944	406.170	0.9963	404.667			
- -	Rand	BA-945	403.850	0.9963	402.356			
- -	Rand	BA-946	405.010	0.9963	403.511			
- -	Rand	BA-9590	406.690	0.9962	405.145			
- -	Rand	BA-9591	407.360	0.9962	405.812			
- -	Rand	BA-9592	404.200	0.9962	402.664			
- -	Rand	BA-9593	403.200	0.9962	401.668			
- -	Rand	BA-9594	403.620	0.9956	401.844			
- -	Rand	BA-9595	404.560	0.9956	402.780			
- -	Rand	BA-9596	401.540	0.9956	399.773			
- -	Rand	BB-9597	404.740	0.9956	402.959			
- -	Rand	BB-9598	406.010	0.9956	404.224			
- -	Rand	BB-9599	407.210	0.9954	405.337			
- -	Rand	BB-9600	402.260	0.9954	400.410			
- -	Rand	BB-9601	401.410	0.9954	399.564			
- -	Rand	BB-9602	404.190	0.9954	402.331			
- -	Rand	BB-9611	405.400	0.9960	403.778			

Bar by bar description - *continued*

Key	Refiner/Assayer	Bar No.	Gross weight	Fine-ness	Fine weight	Refiner	Year markings if any
- -	Rand	BB-9612	402.710	0.9960	401.099		
- -	Rand	BB-9613	404.740	0.9960	403.121		
- -	Rand	BB-9614	407.710	0.9960	408.079		
- -	Rand	BB-9615	403.390	0.9960	401.776		
- -	Rand	BB-9616	409.020	0.9964	407.548		
- -	Rand	BB-9617	406.770	0.9964	405.306		
x	Rand	BB-9618	408.770	0.9964	407.298		
x	Rand	BB-9619	409.820	0.9964	408.345		
- -	Rand	BB-9621	402.470	0.9963	400.981		
x	Rand	BB-9622	407.840	0.9963	406.331		
- -	Rand	BB-9623	404.050	0.9963	402.555		
o	Rand	BN-6824	401.530	0.9960	399.924		
o	Rand	BN-6876	406.070	0.9960	404.446		
o	Rand	BN-6881	402.820	0.9959	401.168		
o	Rand	BN-6882	404.310	0.9959	402.652		
o	Rand	BN-6883	407.000	0.9959	405.331		
o	Rand	BN-6884	405.150	0.9966	403.772		
o	Rand	BN-6885	403.570	0.9966	402.198		
o	Rand	BN-6886	405.690	0.9966	404.311		
o	Rand	BN-6887	404.270	0.9966	402.895		
o	Rand	BN-6888	406.570	0.9966	405.188		
o	Rand	BN-6889	405.270	0.9966	403.892		
o	Rand	BN-6690	405.600	0.9966	404.221		
o	Rand	BN-6891	404.020	0.9966	402.646		
o	Rand	BN-6892	404.670	0.9966	403.294		
o	Rand	BN-6893	406.000	0.9966	404.620		
o	Rand	BN-6894	406.060	0.9966	404.679		
o	Rand	BN-6895	405.410	0.9966	404.032		
o	Rand	BN-6897	405.000	0.9958	403.299		
o	Rand	BN-6898	404.900	0.9958	403.199		
o	Rand	BN-6899	405.500	0.9958	403.797		
o	Rand	BN-6900	406.250	0.9958	404.544		
o	Rand	BN-6901	404.450	0.9958	402.751		

Bar by bar description - *continued*

	FRBNY OFFICIAL RECORDS REFLECT:					INFORMATION BELOW REFLECTS ADDITIONAL MARKINGS ON BARS/COMMENTS, ETC.			
Key	Refiner/Assayer	Bar No.	Gross weight	Fine-ness	Fine weight	Refiner	Year markings if any	Additional Bar No.	
o	Rand	BN-6902	405.950	0.9958	404.245				
o	Rand	BN-6903	404.910	0.9958	403.209				
o	Rand	BN-6904	403.120	0.9958	401.427				
o	Rand	BN-6905	407.400	0.9958	405.689				
o	Rand	BN-6906	402.810	0.9958	401.118				
o	Rand	BN-6945	401.520	0.9961	399.954				
x	Rand	1063	405.700	0.9962	404.158	Rand Bar No. AD2152	Kungel stamp year 1936	Additional Bar No. NZ673	Fineness on bar shows .9961
x	Rand	1064	406.160	0.9962	404.617	Rand Bar No. AD2153	Kungel stamp year 1936	Additional Bar No. NZ674	Fineness on bar shows .9961
x	Rand	1065	407.570	0.9960	405.940	Rand Bar No. AD2154	Kungel stamp year 1936	Additional Bar No. NZ675	Fineness on bar shows .9961
x	Rand	1066	407.570	0.9962	406.021	Rand Bar No. AD2155	Kungel stamp year 1936	Additional Bar No. NZ676	Fineness on bar shows .9961
x	Rand	1067	405.700	0.9962	404.158	Rand Bar No. AD2156	Kungel stamp year 1936	Additional Bar No. NZ677	Fineness on bar shows .9961
x	Rand	1068	405.890	0.9962	404.348	Rand Bar No. AD2157	Kungel stamp year 1936	Additional Bar No. NZ678	Fineness on bar shows .9961
x	Rand	1069	404.770	0.9962	403.232	Rand Bar No. AD2158	Kungel stamp year 1936	Additional Bar No. NZ679	Fineness on bar shows .9961
x	Rand	1070	405.570	0.9960	403.948	Rand Bar No. AD2159	Kungel stamp year 1936	Additional Bar No. NZ680	Fineness on bar shows .9961
x	Rand	1071	405.470	0.9962	403.928	Rand Bar No. AD2160	Kungel stamp year 1936	Additional Bar No. NZ681	Fineness on bar shows .9961
x	Rand	1072	407.930	0.9960	406.298	Rand Bar No. AD2161	Kungel stamp year 1936	Additional Bar No. NZ682	Fineness on bar shows .9961
x	Rand	1074	404.060	0.9962	402.525	Rand Bar No. AD2163	Kungel stamp year 1936	Additional Bar No. NZ684	Fineness on bar shows .9961
x	Rand	1075	405.410	0.9960	403.788	Rand Bar No. AD2164	Kungel stamp year 1936	Additional Bar No. NZ685	Fineness on bar shows .9963
x	Rand	1076	403.970	0.9962	402.435	Rand Bar No. AD2165	Kungel stamp year 1936	Additional Bar No. NZ686	Fineness on bar shows .9963
x	Rand	1077	407.680	0.9964	406.212	Rand Bar No. AD2166	Kungel stamp year 1936	Additional Bar No. NZ687	Fineness on bar shows .9963
x	Rand	1078	403.690	0.9964	401.639	Rand Bar No. AD2167	Kungel stamp year 1936	Additional Bar No. NZ688	Fineness on bar shows .9963
x	Rand	1079	401.560	0.9962	400.034	Rand Bar No. AD2168	Kungel stamp year 1936	Additional Bar No. NZ689	Fineness on bar shows .9963
x	Rand	1080	404.180	0.9962	402.644	Rand Bar No. AD2169	Kungel stamp year 1936	Additional Bar No. NZ690	Fineness on bar shows .9963
x	Rand	1081	404.130	0.9964	402.675	Rand Bar No. AD2170	Kungel stamp year 1936	Additional Bar No. NZ691	Fineness on bar shows .9963
x	Rand	1082	404.510	0.9964	403.054	Rand Bar No. AD2171	Kungel stamp year 1936	Additional Bar No. NZ692	Fineness on bar shows .9963
x	Rand	1083	405.790	0.9962	404.248	Rand Bar No. AD2172	Kungel stamp year 1936	Additional Bar No. NZ693	Fineness on bar shows .9963
x	Rand	1084	403.770	0.9964	402.318	Rand Bar No. AD2173	Kungel stamp year 1936	Additional Bar No. NZ694	Fineness on bar shows .9963
x	Rand	1085	403.570	0.9964	402.117	Rand Bar No. AD2174	Kungel stamp year 1936	Additional Bar No. NZ695	Fineness on bar shows .9963
x	Rand	1086	403.640	0.9964	401.190	Rand Bar No. AD2175	Kungel stamp year 1936	Additional Bar No. NZ696	Fineness on bar shows .9963
x	Rand	1087	403.710	0.9964	402.257	Rand Bar No. AD2176	Kungel stamp year 1936	Additional Bar No. NZ697	Fineness on bar shows .9963
- -	Rand	1771	403.630	0.9958	401.935	Rand Bar No. AD6741	Kungel stamp year 1936	Additional Bar No. UY898	
- -	Rand	1773	404.410	0.9958	402.711	Rand Bar No. AD6743	Kungel stamp year 1936	Additional Bar No. UV900	
- -	Rand	1774	403.910	0.9958	402.214	Rand Bar No. AD6744	Kungel stamp year 1936	Additional Bar No. UV902	Fineness on bar shows .9959

FRBNY OFFICIAL RECORDS REFLECT:

INFORMATION BELOW REFLECTS ADDITIONAL MARKINGS ON BARS/COMMENTS, ETC.

Key	Refiner/Assayer	Bar No.	Gross weight	Fine-ness	Fine weight	Refiner	Bar No.	Year markings if any	
- -	Rand	1775	402.080	0.9958	400.391		Rand Bar No. AD6745	Kungel stamp year 1936	Additional Bar No. UY902 — Fineness on bar shows .9959
- -	Rand	1778	403.930	0.9954	402.072		Rand Bar No. AD6749	Kungel stamp year 1936	Additional Bar No. UY905
- -	Rand	1782	403.750	0.9960	402.135		Rand Bar No. AD6902	Kungel stamp year 1936	Additional Bar No. UY909
- -	Rand	1788	403.400	0.9956	401.625		Rand Bar No. AD6908	Kungel stamp year 1936	Additional Bar No. UY915
- -	Rand	1790	402.540	0.9956	400.769		Rand Bar No. AD6911	Kungel stamp year 1936	Additional Bar No. UY917
x	Rand	1821	404.540	0.9956	402.760		Rand Bar No. AD6955	Kungel stamp year 1935	Additional Bar No. UZ031
x	Rand	1822	403.770	0.9956	401.993		Rand Bar No. AD6956	Kungel stamp year 1935	Additional Bar No. UZ032
x	Rand	1823	407.760	0.9956	405.966		Rand Bar No. AD6957	Kungel stamp year 1935	Additional Bar No. UZ033
x	Rand	1824	403.660	0.9956	401.884		Rand Bar No. AD6958	Kungel stamp year 1935	Additional Bar No. UZ034
x	Rand	1826	404.630	0.9960	403.011		Rand Bar No. AD6966	Kungel stamp year 1935	Additional Bar No. UZ036
x	Rand	1827	404.420	0.9960	402.802		Rand Bar No. AD6967	Kungel stamp year 1935	Additional Bar No. UZ037
x	Rand	1828	406.510	0.9960	404.884		Rand Bar No. AD6968	Kungel stamp year 1935	Additional Bar No. UZ038
x	Rand	1829	408.910	0.9960	407.274		Rand Bar No. AD6969	Kungel stamp year 1935	Additional Bar No. UZ039
x	Rand	1830	408.290	0.9960	406.657		Rand Bar No. AD6970	Kungel stamp year 1935	Additional Bar No. UZ040
x	Rand	1831	403.100	0.9964	401.649		Rand Bar No. AD6971	Kungel stamp year 1935	Additional Bar No. UZ041 — Fineness on bar shows .9965
x	Rand	1832	405.300	0.9964	403.841		Rand Bar No. AD6972	Kungel stamp year 1935	Additional Bar No. UZ042 — Fineness on bar shows .9965
x	Rand	1833	404.750	0.9964	403.293		Rand Bar No. AD6973	Kungel stamp year 1935	Additional Bar No. UZ043 — Fineness on bar shows .9965
x	Rand	1834	403.010	0.9964	401.559		Rand Bar No. AD6974	Kungel stamp year 1935	Additional Bar No. UZ044 — Fineness on bar shows .9965
x	Rand	1835	405.980	0.9964	404.518		Rand Bar No. AD6975	Kungel stamp year 1935	Additional Bar No. UZ045 — Fineness on bar shows .9965
x	Rand	1836	405.410	0.9956	403.626		Rand Bar No. AD2165	Kungel stamp year 1936	Additional Bar No. UZ046 — Fineness on bar shows .9957
x	Rothschild	1792	404.080	0.9964	402.625	Rothschild	Rothschild Bar No. R11079	Rothschild stamp year 1933	Additional Bar No.UZ002 — No fineness stamped on bars
x	Rothschild	1793	404.680	0.9964	403.223	Rothschild	Rothschild Bar No. R11080	Rothschild stamp year 1933	Additional Bar No.UZ003 — No fineness stamped on bars
x	Rothschild	1794	400.030	0.9976	399.070	Rothschild	Rothschild Bar No. R11081	Rothschild stamp year 1933	Additional Bar No.UZ004 — No fineness stamped on bars
x	Rothschild	1795	406.520	0.9994	406.276	Rothschild	Rothschild Bar No. AD11213	Rothschild stamp year 1933	Additional Bar No.UZ005 — No fineness stamped on bars
x	Rothschild	1796	407.090	0.9994	406.846	Rothschild	Rothschild Bar No. AD11214	Rothschild stamp year 1933	Additional Bar No.UZ006 — No fineness stamped on bars
x	Rothschild	1797	404.380	0.9994	404.137	Rothschild	Rothschild Bar No. AD11215	Rothschild stamp year 1933	Additional Bar No.UZ007 — No fineness stamped on bars
x	Rothschild	1798	403.290	0.9994	403.048	Rothschild	Rothschild Bar No. AD11216	Rothschild stamp year 1933	Additional Bar No.UZ008 — No fineness stamped on bars
x	Rothschild	1799	403.810	0.9994	403.568	Rothschild	Rothschild Bar No. AD11217	Rothschild stamp year 1933	Additional Bar No.UZ009 — No fineness stamped on bars
+	U.S. Assay	13395-02286	385.190	0.9975	384.227			US Assay stamp year 1921	
+	U.S. Assay	14789-03080	380.150	0.9976	379.238			US Assay stamp year 1921	

GRAND TOTAL

ALL HOLDINGS	162	65,525.620		65,283.098

Attachment C

A HISTORY OF ALL TGC ACCOUNT ACTIVITY SINCE 1947

Date	Transaction Type	Transaction Description	Fine Troy Ounces
June 6 1947	Deposit	Initial deposit of gold transferred from the gold account of Banque National Suisse @ FRBNY. This deposit appears to represent the equivalent of Swiss Francs 250 million, in accordance with the Washington Agreement of May 25, 1946 between the Allies and Switzerland, wherein the Swiss Government agreed to place Swiss Francs 250 million at the disposal of the Allies, payable on demand in gold in New York. All the bars included in this deposit were U.S. Assay bars; that is, they were all refined by a U.S. Assay Office, part of the U.S. Treasury. In order for FRBNY to record bars as U.S. Assay-type, they had to be delivered to FRBNY directly from a U.S. Assay Office or U.S. Treasury location. Available records indicate that the gold had been in a Banque Nationale Suisse account @ FRBNY from at least 1944 or 1945. **Balance:**	1,659,121.321 **1,659,121.321**
Nov 20 1947	Withdrawal	Transferred to Banque de France gold account @ FRBNY. All bars were U.S. Assay bars. **Balance:**	(539,673.638) **1,119,447.683**
Nov 20 1947	Withdrawal	Sold to U.S. Treasury **Balance:**	(3,503.693) **1,115,943.990**
Nov 24 1947	Withdrawal	Transfer to gold account of De Nederlandsche Bank @ FRBNY. All bars were U.S. Assay bars. **Balance:**	(209,201.609) **906,742.381**
Feb 2 1948	Withdrawal	Transfer to gold account of the Direktorium der Osterreichische Nationalbank @ FRBNY. All bars were U.S. Assay bars. **Balance:**	(152,630.007) **754,112.374**
Mar 2 1948	Withdrawal/ Redeposit	Gold withdrawn, delivered to U.S. Assay Office for individual weighing, then re-deposited. **Balance:**	(9,269.816) 9,269.816 **154,112.374**
Mar 3 1948	Withdrawal	Sold to U.S. Treasury **Balance:**	(5,919.923) **748,192.451**

Date	Transaction Type	Transaction Description	Fine Troy Ounces
Apr 7 1948	Withdrawal	Transfer to gold account of the Direktorium der Osterreichische Nationalbank @ FRBNY.	(244,221.408)
		Balance:	**503,971.043**
May 17 1948	Withdrawal	Transfer to gold account of the Narodni Bank Ceskoslovenska @ FRBNY. All bars were U.S. Assay.	(195,283.854)
		Balance:	**308,687.189**
Mar 7 1949	Deposit	Purchased from U.S. Treasury	434.934
		Balance:	**309,122.123**
July 22 1949	Withdrawal	Sold to U.S. Treasury	(434.934)
		Balance:	**308,687.189**
Dec 12 1949	Deposit	Transfer made to TGC Account from the gold account of Sveriges Riksbank @ FRBNY. Total deposit = 571 bars of various refiners comprised as follows: 401 bars originally imported from Sweden aboard the steamship Drottningholm and credited to Sweden's gold account @ FRBNY on 10/15/47; and 170 bars originally imported from Argentina aboard the steamship Mormacrio and credited to Sweden's gold account @ FRBNY on 12/10/47.	230,049.065
		Balance:	**538,736.254**
Jan 10 1950	Withdrawal	Transfer to gold account of De Nederlandsche Bank @ FRBNY. All bars were U.S. Assay.	(225,055.148)
		Balance:	**313,681.106**
Feb 15 1950	Withdrawal	Sold to U.S. Treasury	(408.888)
		Balance:	**313,272.218**
July 10 1950	Withdrawal	Sold to U.S. Treasury	(784.463)
		Balance:	**312,487.755**
Nov 22 1950	Withdrawal	Sold to U.S. Treasury	(397.191)
		Balance:	**312,090.564**

Date	Transaction Type	Transaction Description	Fine Troy Ounces
Mar 1 1951	Deposit	Six packages containing 150 gold bars in various sizes, consigned to FRBNY for account of the TGC by the Tripartite Advisory Committee on German Assets, Tokyo representing the disposal of German assets in Japan. Several 60 ounce bars minted by the Imperial Mint, Osaka as well as approximately 110 10 ounce bars of unknown refiner. These bars were later shipped in their entirety to the U.S. Assay Office on March 16, 1951 for conversion into U.S. Assay bars. **Balance:**	4,817.224 316,907.788
Mar 16 1951	Withdrawal	Release of gold bars deposited on March 1, 1951 from Japan; sent to U.S. Assay Office for conversion to U.S. Assay bars. **Balance:**	(4,817.224) 312,090.564
Apr 3 1951	Deposit	Re-deposit of gold sent to the U.S. Assay Office on March 16, 1951. **Balance:**	4,813.463 316,904.027
June 7 1951	Withdrawal	Sold to the U.S. Treasury **Balance:**	(797.810) 316,106.217
Nov 14 1951	Withdrawal	Sold to the U.S. Treasury **Balance:**	(406.529) 315,699.688
Feb 26 1952	Deposit	Shipment of 17 boxes containing various bags of gold coin and gold bars received from the United States High Commissioner for Germany. **Balance:**	20,999.769 336,699.457
Mar 20 1952	Withdrawal	Sold to the U.S. Treasury **Balance:**	(799.010) 335,900.447

Date	Transaction Type	Transaction Description	Fine Troy Ounces
May 1 1952	Withdrawal and Redeposit	Withdrawal of February 26, 1952 deposit & redeposit with new weights after verification.	(20,999.769)
		- four 400 oz bars (2 U.S. Assay, 2 "LeLocle"; these bars are still held in the TGC account as 10/96)	1,565.565
		- Various U.S. gold coins: these were later released to Czechoslovakia on 2/19/82	601.560
		- Various foreign gold coins: these were later released to Czechoslovakia on 2/19/82	1,679.433
		- Miscellaneous gold consisting of: ~ 14 bars of unrecognized refiner ~ 75 mutilated (fused) foreign gold coins ~ miscellaneous pieces such as small bars, chips, sheets, buttons, etc.: these pieces were all sent to the U.S. Assay Office on 5/20/52 for conversion to U.S. Assay bars	17,218.459
		Balance:	**335,965.695**
May 20 1952	Withdrawal	Release of miscellaneous gold pieces received on February 26, 1952, sent to U.S. Assay Office for conversion to U.S. Assay bars.	(17,218.459)
		Balance:	**318,747.236**
June 17 1952	Deposit	Redeposit of gold sent to the U.S. Assay Office on May 20, 1952 after conversion to U.S. Assay bars.	16,936.742
		Balance:	**335,683.978**
Sept 30 1952	Withdrawal	Sold to U.S. Treasury	(1,201.450)
		Balance:	**334,482.528**
Oct 24 1952	Deposit	Deposit of 21 various small gold bars (30 oz.) and various gold coins (5,324 pieces). These bars and coins were seized at the end of the war from the German Legation in Lisbon and held in trusteeship by the U.S. Treasury in Washington; Miscellaneous coins seized from the German Embassy in Madrid.	1,864.299
		Balance:	**336,346.827**
Oct 29 1952	Withdrawal	Adjustment on fine weight of February 26, 1952 deposit of bars.	0.210
		Balance:	**336,347.037**
Oct 29 1952	Withdrawal	Adjustment on fine weight of February 26, 1952 deposit of coins. The coins were later released in full to Czechoslovakia on 21/19/82.	(2.564)
		Balance:	**336,344.473**

Date	Transaction Type	Transaction Description	Fine Troy Ounces
Dec 4 1952	Withdrawal	Release to U.S. Assay Office of bars received in the 10/24/52 deposit, to be converted to U.S. Assay. **Balance:**	(645.510) **335,698.963**
Dec 19 1952	Deposit	Redeposit of gold sent to the U.S. Assay Office after conversion **Balance:**	644.116 **336,343.079**
Feb 7 1953	Withdrawal	Sold to the U.S. Treasury **Balance:**	(808.498) **335,534.581**
Aug 24 1953	Withdrawal	Sold to the U.S. Treasury **Balance:**	(801.337) **334,733.244**
Feb 26 1954	Withdrawal	Sold to the U.S. Treasury **Balance:**	(644.116) **334,089.128**
Aug 6 1954	Withdrawal	Sold to the U.S. Treasury **Balance:**	(770.374) **333,318.754**
Feb 2 1955	Deposit	Deposit of 63 bags of foreign gold coin from Austria via KLM. These coins were later released in full to Czechoslovakia on 2/19/82. **Balance:**	3,149.812 **336,468.566**
Apr 29 1955	Deposit	Transfer of 479 bars of various refiners from the gold account of Sveriges Riksbank @ FRBNY. **Balance:**	192,904.484 **529,373.050**
June 30 1958	Withdrawal	Transfer to Banque de France gold account @ FRBNY. Withdrawal comprised of 110 U.S. Assay bars and 129 bars of various refiners. **Balance:**	(96,451.906) **432,921.144**
Aug 21 1973	Withdrawal	Transfer to De Nederlandsche Bank gold account @ FRBNY. Withdrawal comprised of 19 U.S. Assay bars and 117 bars of various refiners. **Balance:**	(53,460.758) **379,460.386**

Date	Transaction Type	Transaction Description	Fine Troy Ounces
Aug 1976	Withdrawal	Exported to Narodni Bank Polski, Warsaw, in three separate shipments on August 3, and August 19, 1976. Withdrawal comprised of 115 U.S. Assay bars and 7 bars of various refiners. **Balance:**	(16,831.479) (17,036.493) (16,369.855) **329,222.559**
Feb 19 1982	Withdrawal	Exported to Czechoslovakia Bars: Coin: From 2/26/52 deposit (from Germany) From 10/24/52 deposit (from U.S. Treasury) From 2/2/55 deposit (from Austria)	(257,292.221) (601.560) (1,679.433) (1,216.435) (3,149.812)

CURRENT BALANCE AS OF OCTOBER, 1996: 65,283.098
162 bars of various refiners, no gold coin.

Attachment D

AN ACCOUNT DOCUMENT CONCERNING ONE OF THE DEPOSITS
TO THE TGC'S ACCOUNT IN 1952

Statement covering various gold bars, coins, and miscellaneous pieces of gold earmarked for Account Triparte Commission for the Restitution of Monetary Gold on February 26th 1952

Refiner	Description	Gross Troy Ounces	Indicated Fineness
U.S. Assay	1 bar	385.19	997.5
U.S. Assay	1 bar	380.15	997.6
Le Locle (Suisse)	2 bars	802.10	1000.
Preuss State (German)	9 bars	3,655.25	999.
Preuss State (German)	1 bar	420.64	1000.
Da Gussa (German)	376 and 1 piece	10,366.51	1000.
Da Gussa (German)	3½ finger bars		
gensine Pforsheim	8 and 1 chip		
Schaideanstalt	1 finger bar		
Unknown	2 commercial bars	328.54	1000.
Unknown	4 bars	1,214.58	Unknown
		17,552.96	

Refiner	Description	Gross Troy Ounces	Indicated Fineness
Da Gussa	7 finger bars		
Unknown	1 finger bar		
Allgemeigne Pforsheim	6 finger bars and 3 ends of bars		
Unknown	5 finger bars and 1 chip		
Unknown	7 small flat bars		
Unknown	5 peanut bars	361.41	Unknown
Unknown	1 flat bar having appearance of silver or white gold	20.10	Unknown
—	72 pieces, including small bars, very small bars, thick flat bars, bands, sheets, thin sticks, chunks, etc.	195.30	Unknown
—	10 pipes, eight inches long, one inch wide	378.11	Unknown
—	32 pieces, including plates, peanut bars, spikes, finger bars, bar ends, nuggets, buttons, chips, sheets, one commercial bar	109.35	Unknown
—	Various burnt and fused together coins and clinkers	186.75	Unknown

No. of pieces	Description	Gross Troy Ounces	Indicated Fineness
33	20 Francs – Belgium	6.81	990.0
183	20 Francs – Swiss	37.94	900.0
?	10 Francs – Swiss	9.12	900.0
6	5 Guilders – Dutch	.65	900.
147	10 Guilders – Dutch	31.75	900.0
1	5 Guilders (Mutilated) – Dutch)		
2	10 Guilders (Mutilated) – Dutch)	.54	900.0
1	Eagles (Mutilated) – U.S.A.)		
115	Eagles – U.S.A.)	62.28)	900.0
268	½ Eagles – U.S.A.)	71.84	900.0
60	¼ Eagles – U.S.A.)	8.03	900.0
490	Double Eagles – U.S.A.)	526.25	900.0
97	Piastre – Turkish		
	Various sizes – denominations Unknown	20.30	916.6
367	5 Rubles – Russian	50.69	900.0
6	7½ Rubles – Russian	1.24	900.0
217	10 Rubles – Russian	60.04	900.0
15	15 Rubles – Russian	6.21	900.0

No. of pieces	Description	Gross Troy Ounces	Indicated Fineness
1	5 Rubles – (odd) – Russian		900.0
1	10 Rubles (mutilated) – Russian		900.0
1,713	Sovereigns – England		916.6
1	Sovereign (Mutilated) – England	439.25	916.6
26	½ Sovereign – England	3.32	916.6
1,166	10 Korona – Austrian		
2	10 Krona (Mutilated) – Austrian	126.91	900.0
127	20 Krona – Austrian		
1	20 Krona (Mutilated) – Austrian	27.84	900.0
5	100 Korona – Austrian	5.44	
4	20 Francs – Hungarian	.82	900.0
3	10 Francs – Hungarian	.30	900.0
8	100 Shillings – Austrian		900.0
7	25 Shillings – Austrian	1.32	900.0
1	Leva – Bulgarian		900.0
2	25 Pesetas – Spanish	.51	900.0
1	20 Pesetas – Spanish	.20	900.0
1	100 Reales – Spanish	.26	900.0
1	100 Lira – Italian	.11	900.0
14	20 Lira – Italian	2.89	900.0
2	100 Lira – Italian		900.0
3	10 Kroner – Danish	.44	900.0
1	20 Kroner – Danish	.28	900.0
3	20 Kronor – Swedish	.87	900.0
4	10 Kronor – Swedish	.57	900.0
5	5 Kronor – Swedish	.36	900.0
1	20 Drachma – Greek		900.0
47	Ducat – Austrian (coin reads 10 francs)	5.26	900.0
		14.19	900.0
3	Ducat – Austrian (coin reads 10 francs)	23.93	900.0
998	20 Marks – German		900.0
1	20 Marks (Mutilated) – German		900.0
1	Carone – Austrian	255.31	900.0
2,056	Marks – German		900.0
7	10 Marks (Mutilated) – German	261.93	900.0
999	20 Marks – German		900.0
1	20 Marks (Mutilated) – German		900.0
1	Dukstan – German	255.12	900.0
4	20 Marks – German		900.0
15	20 Marks (Mutilated) – German		900.0
1	10 Marks – German	163.33	900.0
312	20 Francs – French	64.57	
114	10 Francs – French	11.70	900.0
3	20 Francs – Tunisia		
40	20 Francs (Mutilated) – French	8.90	900.0
		21,345.22	

Upon invitation from us to inspect these coins, Mr. Vernon Brown, head of Money Exhibit Department of Chase National Bank, 11 Broadway, advised Mr. N. P. Davis that these particular coins may have some numismatic value.

FRANCE

Plunder of Jewish Property in France and its Restitution

In 1939, France had 41.5 million inhabitants. When World War II ended in 1945, as well as the 380,000 of its citizens dead on the various battlefields, France lost 330,000 civilians, including 180,000 people deported from our national territory.

While the 1940 and 1941 censuses, which were forced on them, listed 310,000 Jews in France, we can, in fact, agree with the lawyer Serge Klarsfeld, who has compiled the history of this deportation, on the more realistic estimate of around 330,000, of whom nearly 40% had come from central and eastern Europe to seek refuge in our country in which they had put all their hopes.

Of that total, 80,000 disappeared in the turmoil:

- 76,000 were exterminated in the Nazi camps from which only 2,564 returned.
- 3,000 died from hunger or illness in our country's internment centres;
- 1,000 were mown down by bullets of the German armed forces or French militia.

Finally, there were also those who were killed in the Resistance, the Maquis, irrespective of origin or nationality.

So a quarter of the Jews living in France were victims of this deliberate insanity of the Nazis which led to the "invention" of the *"final solution"*. From the *Vélodrome d'Hiver* where many of the 13,000 people, of whom the large majority were women and children, were *rounded up* and crowded together on 16 and 17 July 1942, to *Drancy*, the internment and reprisals camp set aside for Jews from August 1941, the *"selection station"* and departure point for almost all the 80 death trains, France too has no shortage of places of remembrance connected with the tragedy of the Shoah.

I think it useful to accompany this reminder of the history of these events with a brief chronological list of the legislation passed, on its own initiative or at German request, by the Vichy regime, against the Jewish community, designed to organise the supervision and internment of its members and the confiscation of both their movable and immovable property.

- 03.10.40 – Act on the *status of Jews* and excluding them from both a whole range of public service jobs and the professions. The majority of those to whom it applied were French Jews and the Act was replaced – and strengthened – by that of 02.06.41.

- 04.10.40 – Act providing for the possibility of interning *"foreign Jews"* in *"special camps".*
- 07.10.40 – Act abrogating the Crémieux Order of 24.10.1870 concerning the situation of the Jews of Algeria. French citizens, they numbered 120,000 in 1940 (the French protectorates of Morocco and Tunisia had, respectively, 200,000 and 80,000).
- 29.03.41 – Act creating the General Board for Jewish Affairs (CGQJ) – *Commissariat général aux questions juives),* which was to be headed by a notorious anti-Semite. The CGQJ was responsible for all matters to do with the Jewish community, its members and their property.
- 02.06.41 – The Act ordering a *census of the Jews* in the unoccupied zone. A German order of 27.09.40 had required a census of the Jews living in the occupied zone.
- 22.07.41 – Act concerning the *enterprises,* shops, firms, real estate and securities belonging to the Jews. *"With a view to eliminating all Jewish influence in the national economy",* the CGQJ was permitted to appoint provisional administrators.
- 29.11.41 – Act establishing the French Jewish Union (UGIF – *Union générale des Israélites de France)* which, for the Jewish institutions, became the compulsory intermediary between them and the regime.
- 14.12.41 – Following attacks against German officers and soldiers, 95 people were shot, including 51 Jews. The Military Command in France also imposed a *fine of one billion francs* on Jews in the occupied zone.

This network of regulatory bodies and measures, established in a way which deliberately and relentlessly tightened the screw, paved the way for the second phase of the programme for eliminating the Jews mounted by the Nazis and their French henchmen: the first convoy of Jews deported from France to Germany and Central Europe left Drancy on 27 March 1942, three days later, it arrived in Auschwitz. Of the 1,146 people it transported, there were 23 known survivors in 1945.

The first preoccupation of the Government of liberated France was to manifest its concern for the welfare of the repatriates by allocating them regular financial assistance. Alongside the *déportés résistants* (deported resistance fighters), a category of *déportés politiques* (political deportees) was created, which embraced the Jews. Entitlement under the provisions of the General Pensions Code was extended to all French citizens, without exception, based on the fact that they belonged to this group of victims. Survivors' pensions were awarded to widows, and even the children of those who had disappeared. Irrespective of their nationality, the vast majority of children who had lost both their parents became war orphans cared for by the State. It is, however, conceivable that the situation of some children of foreign Jewish parents who were living in or had taken refuge in France has still not been resolved.

Concurrently, the search began for the property confiscated from members of the Jewish community during that black period of the occupation. As soon as a legally constituted government was restored in summer 1944, all the confiscations, as well as their subsequent legal effects, carried out during the occupation were declared null. Government orders permitted the restitution to the victims of their unsold possessions and apartments; in the case of the latter the decisions were sometimes the subject of painful dispute, since a number of occupants, some of whom had moved in good faith, initially refused to leave them. Subsequently, the restitution was extended to include the money obtained from the liquidation of businesses and sale of possessions.

RESTITUTION OF THE GOLD

Set up in 1918 to manage the reparations paid following the end of World War I, the Office for Personal Property and Interests (OBIP – *Office des biens et intérêts privés*) was reactivated in 1945 to ensure the restitution of *"certain categories of property seized by the enemy on French territory"*. In 1953 and 1958, on the evidence of the OBIP's files, 1,444 people received 2,231 kilograms of "personal" monetary gold, following a redistribution carried out by the Brussels Tripartite Gold Commission.

The situation of "monetary" gold in the hands of States is different. Indeed, on the outbreak of the hostilities the *Banque de France* had taken the judicious decision to place its substantial reserves in places of safety overseas. These were recovered in full. And while France is today awaiting the return of 2.2 tonnes – worth about 125 million francs – out of the 5.5 tonnes still on deposit in the United States and Great Britain, it is in fact exercising the rights previously pertaining to Belgium and Luxembourg to which it had reimbursed in full the quantities of gold these countries had entrusted to it in 1939 and which the Vichy regime had, in turn, handed over to the Germans in the winter of 1940–41. The French government intends to regain possession of the exchange value of this remaining monetary gold. We hope that this will be as soon as possible. The work of the Tripartite Gold Commission can then be wound up and its archives opened to anyone who wishes to consult them. In this respect, we listened with interest to the statement the British representative made yesterday afternoon. We totally subscribe to what he said. As regards the allocation of the sum which France is expecting to receive, this will be determined, at the appropriate moment, by the French authorities who will, of course, be guided by the absolute need for ethical and fair criteria.

REIMBURSEMENT OF THE BILLION FRANC FINE

The billion franc fine imposed on the Jews of the occupied zone had to be paid in four monthly instalments. The Jewish community had been unable to get together such a large sum in such a short time. To pay this fine, the Jews had to go through the *Administration des Domaines* (State Property Department) and the *Caisse des dépôts et consignations* (the State bank which manages National Savings Bank funds and local community funds). The payment was made by withdrawals from frozen accounts and transfers of shares belonging to Jews.

In December 1949, the *Caisse des dépôts et consignations*, through which the bulk of the sums demanded, then refunded, had passed, sold the remainder of the shares it still held. The State, on its side, had to contribute to ensure the full reimbursement of the billion franc fine.

ECONOMIC ARYANIZATION

A report of the German military administration on the situation in France, dated 21 July 1943, estimated that 28,000 industrial concerns and 11,000 buildings owned by Jews had been placed under provisional administration pursuant to the legislation passed by the Vichy authorities. A year later, in June 1944, CGQJ archives refer to 47,000 files opened for the whole of the territory with a view to the *"economic aryanization"* of *"Jewish enterprises"*.

From 1941 to 1944, over 7,000 provisional administrators were engaged in *aryanizing* the property of those whom the Vichy authorities regarded as Jews; this consisted of industrial, commercial, property and artisan concerns, as well as real estate, land rights, tenants' rights to leases, moveable assets, shares and bonds.

The archives of the CGQJ, which, under the Act of 19 May 1941, was commissioned to *"manage and liquidate Jewish property"* are stored at the French National Archives *(Archives nationales de France)*. These include some 62,500 files and the complicated task of examining them all is going to continue for a long time.

As regards Paris, in February 1996, the municipal authorities set up a *Conseil du patrimoine privé de la Ville*, to study the real estate under private ownership in the city. According to its preliminary report issued on 12 November, its investigation of the expropriations decided on between 1940 and 1944 which were classified as being in the public interest – because of their insalubrity – has not yet brought to light any evidence of confiscation or discrimination between Jewish and non-Jewish owners.

DORMANT ACCOUNTS AND SAFETY DEPOSIT BOXES

Every years, the ownership of several thousand dormant accounts and safety deposit boxes held by the French banks reverts to the French State. Searches have been instigated to try and find out which of those not reclaimed immediately after the war might have belonged to Jews. Mergers and even collapses, nationalisations or privatisations have radically changed the banking scene over the past half century. This has obviously not been facilitating the task.

OBJETS D'ART

Recently, the question of works of art seized, sold and transferred to Germany and of their restitution has been the subject of much comment. Today, we have a new opportunity to take stock of this sensitive issue.

As soon as French territory was occupied, the plundering of artworks began. The operation had been prepared well in advance and the German authorities took immediate steps to try to seize paintings and objects of whose existence and whereabouts they were extremely well informed. In the very first months of the war, however, a far-sighted national museums directorate had placed the most precious artworks in places of safety. While there were some seizures, nothing was lost track of.

Most at risk, therefore, were private collections and, in that category, those belonging to Jews, as well as items either stolen from apartments which had to be abandoned in haste by their occupants, or which simply had to be sold on the market owing to tragic necessity and at prices distorted by the circumstances. The Jeu de Paume museum on the Place de la Concorde acted as a general warehouse. Reichmarschall Goering was seen there on several occasions admiring superb paintings . . . and taking his pick. This organised pillage was recorded, sometimes at the risk of her life, by a remarkable woman, Rose Valland, who later recounted the story.

France had still not been entirely liberated when the Commission for the Recovery of Works of Art (CRA – *Commission de récupération artistique*) was set up on 24 November 1944. It operated until 31 December 1949. After that, the OBIP was commissioned to take over the unresolved cases and deal with any which might subsequently come to light. Indeed, it is the government's view that, while restitution operations have not been fully completed, the CRA did a good job. 750 boxes of records, for which the OBIP is currently responsible, are deposited at the French Foreign Ministry.

Statistically, and on the basis of statements taken just after the war, the present situation as regards such works of art – paintings, drawings, sculptures, books and illuminated manuscripts, ceramics, silverware, tapestries, etc. – is as follows for the approximately 100,000 objects which were seized, stolen or fraudulently acquired:

61,257 have been recovered, of which:

45,441 have been restored to their owners or other people with legal entitlement to them;

13,758 have been sold by the *Administration des Domaines;*

and 2,058 (almost half of them paintings) have been entrusted to the French Museums Directorate, which has classified them in specific categories, the best known of which are MNR *(Musées nationaux Récupération)* for classical paintings and OAR *(Objet d'art Récupération)*. Of this remainder, with the addition of 28 works which Germany handed back to France in 1994, a further 37 were returned to their owners between 1950 and 1997.

So starting even before the end of the war and in the five years of its operation, the CRA managed to restore to their owners or heirs three quarters of the works of art seized or stolen during the occupation. This shows the considerable and remarkable work accomplished in the immediate postwar period.

Furthermore, for four years, between 1950 to 1954, all works not yet returned were exhibited in the Château de Compiègne. Despite the long duration of the exhibition, its prestigious setting and accessibility to all, which ensured it wide publicity, only a few works were claimed. Most of the subsequent restitutions have essentially been the result of research by French government departments. In spring 1997, new exhibitions were held in the major museums of Paris and the Paris region. Finally, an exhaustive catalogue already available on the Internet – the Ministry of Culture's server – will shortly be published.

MISSION D'ETUDE SUR LA SPOLIATION DES JUIFS DE FRANCE

(Working party on the plunder of the property of French Jews)

On 25 January 1997, following the concern aroused among the French public by certain reports in the media both in France and abroad, the Prime Minister, at the time Alain Juppé, announced the establishment of a *"working party to look into the circumstances under which movable and immovable property belonging to Jews living in France was confiscated or, generally speaking, acquired by fraud, violence or deceit, either by the occupying power or the Vichy authorities, between 1940 and 1944."*

To this end, a working party was set up on 25 March 1997 by order of the Prime Minister who appointed M. Jean Mattéoli, Chairman of the Economic and Social Council, as its chairman. Working with him are a vice-chairman and six other members from a variety of professional backgrounds. Confirmed by M. Lionel Jospin, the working party's remit is:

- to assess the *scale* of the plunder;
- to indicate the specific categories of *natural and legal persons* who or which benefited from it;
- to determine the *fate* of this plundered property from the end of the war to the present day;
- to seek to identify its current *whereabouts* and legal status;
- to draw up an *inventory* of assets seized on French soil which are still in the possession of French or foreign public institutions and authorities;
- to make *proposals* to the government on the future of these assets.

Furthermore, the Prime Minister has told the working party that it will enjoy the full support of the relevant government departments in carrying out its work.

Finally, in accordance with the request he made at the outset, the Prime Minister will, at the end of the current year, i.e. very shortly, receive a *progress report* on the work completed and suggestions on how it will be continued. In the framework defined by the Prime Minister, the working party is focusing its attention on all the categories of property confiscated from France's Jewish population, in one way or another, during the war.

Chairman, as I'm sure you will understand, our delegation cannot, at this moment, tell you more. The Prime Minister is, of course, the person responsible for the Commission's work, its research, the direction its efforts take and its future guidelines. M. Lionel Jospin has, in fact, just been talking about these issues at the dinner to which the Representative Council of Jewish Institutions in France (CRIF – *Conseil représentatif des Institutions Juives de France)* – with which we maintain close contact – annually invites the head of Government.

GERMANY

Introductory statement

DR HANS-WERNER LAUTENSCHLAGER

Head of the German Delegation

The German Government accepted the invitation to attend this conference on Nazi gold because it has a profound interest in clarifying to the greatest possible extent this dark chapter of German and European history.

Germany supports the efforts to trace assets belonging to the victims and return them to their rightful owners or to use them to alleviate the material want of the survivors. This has been the objective of German restitution policy ever since the Federal Republic of Germany came into being. Restitution is part of a comprehensive national compensation legislation which the Federal Republic has developed in the post-war decades in permanent contact with the representatives of Nazi victims. That policy is consistent with Germany's other broad-ranging responsibilities in the pursuit of peaceful objectives in Europe.

As we understand it, our part in this conference is to reassemble and present the documentary material still in Germany. We make all factual material that will help throw light on the subject of Nazi gold available for international research. Our archives have been opened for decades.

The director of our Institut für Zeitgeschichte, Professor Möller, will now inform you about the German research on the subject of this conference. He will also speak about available files and archives and make suggestions with regard to future clarification.

Statement

PROF. DR HORST MÖLLER

Institut für Zeitgeschichte, München

1. INTRODUCTION

No other historical subject has occupied politicians, public opinion and scholars to such a degree since the founding of the Federal Republic of Germany in 1949 as the Nazi dictatorship. As early as 1949, the Federal Government and the governments of West Germany's Länder established in Munich the Institut für Zeitgeschichte (Institute for Modern History) which was first required to focus its research on National Socialism but already in the fifties its terms of reference were extended to include 20th century history since the First World War.

The number of studies on this subject is legion. The most recent one, Michael Ruck's *Bibliographie zum Nationalsozialismus*, which appeared in 1995, contains more than 22,000 titles. Most of the research carried out in the Federal Republic Germany has concentrated on the abortive Weimar democracy and on the Nazi seizure of power, the establishment of a totalitarian "Fuhrer" dictatorship, the system imposed by the Nazi regime, the instruments of terror such as the Gestapo and SS, concentration camps, anti-Semitism, persecution of the Jews and the extermination of Europe's Jews, post-1933 emigration, foreign policy, the economy, the Second World War, the conduct of the war and the role of the Wehrmacht, occupation policy in the conquered European states, and also everyday life under the dictatorship. But there were also many other areas of research.

The great interest in this research shown by the public and the political classes has always been apparent. Over the past 52 years there have been numerous revisions and updates which have kept this continuous historical review process at the centre of public interest. An example is the debate on Nazi crimes, which have been the object of investigation by the central registration centre established in Ludwigsburg in 1958.

Highlights of the public debate were the Auschwitz trial (1963–65) held in Frankfurt, the Majdanek trial (1975–81), and the Holocaust film of the late seventies. Others are annual events such as those marking the fiftieth anniversary of the ending of the Second World War or the Nuremberg trials.

Although the bulk of this material is discussed by specialists only, new topics keep cropping up which had previously attracted little attention. Questions arise mainly as a result of access to hitherto unknown or closed sources and changing academic and public interest. This also applies to our central topic of this conference, Nazi gold, which, despite having been dealt with on previous occasions, has not been researched by international experts with the same degree of intensity as the other subjects I have mentioned. The reasons are that:

1. the Tripartite Commission for the Restitution of Monetary Gold set up by the three Western Allies on 27 September 1946 had already begun to classify and seek the return of the looted gold;

2. 98.6 % of the gold still hidden in Germany after the war had already been

confiscated by the Americans so that no looted gold remained in Germany itself; and

3. to this day still, not all files outside Germany are accessible.

Most of the research on this subject has taken place in those countries to which large amounts of looted gold had been transferred up to 1945.

II. ORIGIN AND WHEREABOUTS OF THE NAZI GOLD LOOT

The German gold shipments to Switzerland during the Second World War were not some peripheral topic of Nazi conquest and exploitation policy or Nazi economic policy, rather, the substantial German gold transfers indeed represented the binding element for these political fields which, thus bonded, created a system which temporarily, at least, gained its own inherent momentum. The gold funded the Germany economy, which for its part facilitated Germany's conquests; and so on. Four reasons can be identified which were responsible for this development:

- The Reichsbank was almost bankrupt when war broke out; indeed, as early as on 7 January 1939 Reich Finance Minister Schacht had reported to Hitler that "gold and foreign currency reserves [...] are no longer available" here. The Nazi economic and social policy, in particular the hasty arming process, had depleted the German gold and foreign currency reserves, as well as the gold reserves of Austria (US$ 103 million) and Czechoslovakia (US$ 44 million), which Germany had confiscated in 1938–39. At the end of 1938, Germany's gold and foreign currency reserves totalled no more than RM 70.8 million. Hence the economic and financial problems which Germany faced as a consequence of the Second World War were diametrically opposed to its financial capacity.

- During the Second World War Germany's troops repeatedly managed to seize the considerable assets of its enemies; the gold reserves of some national banks took pride of place within this process.

- Even before the war began, Germany's arms industry had been highly dependent on foreign currency reserves, and the objective of an autarchic, self-sufficient German or Central European economic area was never achieved. Even the 1939 German-Soviet Non-Aggression Pact failed to fully compensate for these deficits, so that the German Reich continued to rely on supplies from, for instance, Portugal (tungsten), Turkey (chrome), Sweden (iron ore) or Romania (mineral oil). A largely similar dependency on certain industrial products evolved during the war, such as ball bearings, which were largely imported from Switzerland from 1943–44 onwards.

These three factors clearly show that Germany's leadership was faced by the following cardinal financial problem during the Second World War: How could it – irrespective of the (loot)gold embargo imposed by some neutral states – transform the looted gold into foreign currency in order to be able to acquire from neutral countries those raw materials and products which were indispensable for the German arms industry?

Switzerland, which was to take a leading role in this field of business, was predestined for a number of reasons:

- Its political neutrality had just as long a tradition as did its competence and renown as an international financial market; also – and particularly so during the Second World War – the Swiss Franc (CHF) was a means of payment recognized throughout the world.
- Switzerland could be more easily extorted by the foreign policy and military dominance of the Greater German Reich, because once France had been occupied Switzerland had become completely encompassed by the German sphere of influence. And there were strong links between German and Swiss capital and economic interests before 1939, with Swiss capital investments in Germany running to CHF 9 billion in 1939. While Switzerland remained protected from Germany's foreign trade policy measures during the first phase of the war, it was seriously affected by the Allied blockade policy. Furthermore, the United States froze all the assets of neutral European states on 14 June 1941 – all measures which pushed Switzerland, in its military and foreign policy isolation, towards the German Reich.
- Finally, Switzerland's close geographical location was a decisive factor: a long, shared border enabled both sides to complete their business transactions without risk, loss and, above all, largely unnoticed by the public at large.

When we consider these four very special starting conditions, then it becomes clear why the Reichsbank only established a depot at the Swiss National Bank (SNB) as late as on 5 May 1940, into which a first shipment of 144 gold ingots valued at CHF 8.9 million was transferred. The enemies' great assets only fell into the hands of the Germans after this. The reserves of the Polish national bank had been transported to France in 1939, Denmark and Norway had no gold reserves worthy of note, and finally, several enemy central banks managed by 1940 to transfer, and thereby save, gold reserves worth a total of CHF 13 billion abroad, above all to the United States, Canada and Africa (plus private gold shipments worth a total of CHF 8 billion). Only when the Belgium and Dutch national banks were taken did significant gold reserves fall into the hands of the Nazi regime (with the help of a simulated purchase), whereby 300 tonnes of Belgian gold had been transferred by May 1942 from Dakar via Oran and Marseilles to Berlin in an equally complicated and fantastic diplomatic operation, which also involved the help of Vichy France.

After this, these sources were initially exhausted. Nevertheless, the gold from the German extermination camps seems to have played a *relatively minor role* at least in *these* transactions. Werner Rings, for example, cites gold reserves valued at CHF 2 million which annually came from the extermination camp at Treblinka, camps Smith writes that from August 1942 onwards the SS had transferred 76 sums, largely comprised of foreign currency and gold, to a special depot at the Reichsbank with a total value of US$ 14,500,000.

III. RESEARCH

The Nazi state's international gold policy first came under the scrutiny of German researchers in 1978. Willi A. Boelcke's *Beitrag zur deutschen Wahrungs- und*

Außenwirtschaftspolitik 1933–1945, in: Manfred Funke (ed.), *Hitler, Deutschland und die Mächte. Materialien zur Außenpolitik des Dritten Reiches*, Dusseldorf 1978, pp. 292–309 was based on an evaluation of West German and a knowledge of East German archives.

The real breakthrough was achieved by the work of Werner Rings, *Raubgold aus Deutschland. Die "Golddrehscheibe" Schweiz im Zweiten Weltkrieg*, Zürich 1985. In researching his book, Rings was for the first time able to examine the relevant documents of the SNB and those of other Swiss authorities, as well as the relevant German and American records, of course. The high standard of his evaluation of the German-Swiss gold transactions would also appear unsurpassed, with the one exception of the Eizenstat Report. After having comprehensively studied the source material and clearly assessing the motives, Rings comes to the conclusion that the SNB's cooperation hardly derived from any general sympathy for National Socialism but rather from an anti-Bolshevist stance, and of course from profit-making considerations.

One must also mention, of course, the fact that the SNB was able to conduct its business for the most part independently. Even the Swiss Government was only informed in exceptional cases. In March 1944 one of the directors of the SNB stated that it would be "intolerable to combine the affairs of the Central Bank with trade and foreign policy interests". Rings clearly demonstrates the extent to which Switzerland was dependent, both politically and militarily, on Germany during the Second World War, and what huge economic and financial constraints the war placed on Switzerland as well.

In a way complementary is the work of Arthur L. Smith Jr., *Hitler's Gold. The Story of the Nazi War Loot*, Oxford 1989, since he examined in detail the Safehaven Programme and the post-1945 restitution negotiations.

Details on the fate of the gold holdings of the Banca d'Italia are provided by Lutz Klinkhammer, Zwischen Bündnis und Besatzung. Das nationalsozialistische Deutschland und die Republik von Salò 1943–45.

More recent journalistic publications, such as those by Tom Bower (1997), Peter Ferdinand Koch (1997) and Jean Ziegler (1997) do not substantially add to the body of academic research on the subject.

The following German sources have so far been researched and evaluated:

- Werner Rings based his work on the principal files of the Third Reich, which are kept at the National Archives of the United States, Washington. They include, for instance, films made by the Military Procurements and Armaments Office and the Wehrmacht Supreme Command West.

  He also studied reports by the German armistice delegation (economic matters) and on the progress of the economic negotiations with Switzerland, documents prepared by the German Industrial Commission in Switzerland, as well as files of the Supreme Command West (external department).

- Lutz Klinkhammer mainly researched the files of the political archives in the Federal Foreign Office, Bonn, concentrating on the files of the Commander of the Security Police and the SD in Italy, the Home Affairs Department and the ADAP (Files on German Foreign Policy) edition.

- Finally, there is the Source-material available to foreign researchers who used German archives. Smith for instance, was able to examine in the Bundesarchiv, Koblenz, the estate of the Reich Commissioner for Enemy Assets, Johannes Krohn, the files of the Party Headquarters, the Reich Ministry of Finance, the Reich Office for Precious Metals and the departments of the Deutsche Reichsbank.
- Gian Trepp had access to further files for his study on the Bank for International Settlements during the Second World War, i.e. the card index of members of the NSDAP in the Berlin Document Centre (now the Bundesarchiv Berlin), the files of the Deutsche Reichsbank and the Deutsche Bank in the former State Archives of the GDR, as well as the Historical Archives of the Deutsche Bundesbank. Frankfurt/Main.

IV. OPEN QUESTIONS, PERSPECTIVES FOR FURTHER RESEARCH

In assessing the hitherto available research literature, we find a general problem: the German gold transfers became a subject for extended diplomatic negotiations immediately after the war and accordingly also of detailed examination and research. This meant that academic research and treatment of the topic, and hence a process of public information based closely on the sources, only set in at a much later date. Before this, only those German records located in the western hemisphere were accessible; yet, many German records had been lost altogether or were scattered at various locations or were subjected to access restrictions in the archives of the GDR or the Soviet Union. By contrast, many foreign institutions were given the opportunity to keep their participation in these transactions secret. It is therefore necessary to open all records which provide information on the role of the Allies and, above all, on the activities of the Tripartite Commission.

To date, the German gold transfers during the Second World War have been primarily reconstructed on the basis of the records of the SNB as well as on the known German and, in some cases, American records (especially those from the OMGUS archives). In order to be able to produce a truly comprehensive picture of all the appropriate movements, the files of the Swiss *private* banks must also be included in the evaluation, as must the records on foreign state or private assets confiscated by the German authorities or on the recipients of German payments. Particular interest in this would above all be directed towards the records of neutral foreign countries, especially Sweden, Portugal, Spain and Turkey as well as the German allies, especially Romania, Hungary, Slovakia and Finland. Finally, a complementation and completion of the relevant German records by specific searches in the archives of the former Warsaw Pact would be greatly welcomed and appreciated. Particular importance must be attached to the records of the following German institutions:

- Reichsbank
- Reich Ministry of Economics
- Reich Ministry of Finance

- The Office responsible for the Implementation of the Four-Year Plan
- Foreign Office, especially
  - Trade Policy Section
  - Bern Legation
- Reich Office for Foreign Trade
- Reich Office for Precious Metals
- Military Procurements and Armaments Office at the Wehrmacht Supreme Command
- Central Distribution and Administration Office of the SS

Only after a systematic evaluation of all these named records could the gold transactions from 1939 through to 1945 be substantiated with absolutely reliable figures. This would also have to include those private accounts opened by high-ranking Nazi party functionaries, no doubt mostly in Switzerland. New information on the problem in general is likely to emerge from a post-doctoral degree project recently begun by Rolf Banken at the University of Cologne concerning the financing of external trade during the Third Reich. This study is mainly based on the archives of the DEGUSSA Group.

The fact that the figures in the available research literature differ is not only a consequence of the very patchy source situation. The problem of currency conversion becomes clear when Smith reports that Germany transferred gold worth US$ 378 million to Switzerland between 1940 and 1945, while Rings for his part gives figures of CHF 1716.1 and 1638.2 million respectively. Although both figures *roughly* correspond when an exchange rate of US$1= CHF 4.20 (as of 1946) is applied, it, would nevertheless be essential to define a specific conversion rate or respectively a specific cut-off date as a basis for all future conversions. Calculation of the gold value on the basis of present-day values is historically and legally problematical.

Research to date in all probability gives us only an *approximate* idea of the magnitude of the German transactions. More precise figures, which could then possibly serve as a basis for restitution claims, can only be produced once all sources have been considered.

Finally, the records of the still operating Tripartite Commission in Brussels to which Smith was denied access before 1989 and to which access is probably still denied, are essential to the precise clarification of the reimbursement problem surrounding the looted gold.

German Restitution for
National Socialist Crimes

From the time of its founding in 1949, the Federal Republic of Germany assumed responsibility for making reparation for crimes committed during the Nazi era to the extent that this is possible.

This sense of responsibility was expressed by the first chancellor of the Federal Republic Konrad Adenauer, in a statement made on September 27, 1951

> *"The federal goverment and the great majority of the German people are deeply aware of the immeasurable suffering endured by the Jews of Germany and by the Jews of the occupied territories during the period of National Socialism. The great majority of the German people did not participate in the crimes committed against the Jews, and wish constantly to express their abhorrence of these crimes. While the Nazis were in power there were many among the German people who attempted to aid their Jewish fellow-citizens in spite of the personal danger involved. They were motivated by religious conviction, the urgings of conscience, and shame at the base acts perpetrated in the name of the whole German people. In our name, unspeakable crimes have been committed and they demand restitution, both moral and material, for the persons and properties of the Jews who have been so seriously harmed . . ."*

In the forty-six years since Adenauer made this statement, the government of the Federal Republic of Germany has striven to make amends to those who suffered at the hands of the National Socialists on account of their race and their religion, their political beliefs. their physical disabilities, their sexual orientation, or simply because of their refusal to comply with the norms of Nazi ideology.

No matter how large the sum, no amount of money will ever suffice to compensate for National Socialist persecution. But in dealing with the legacy of the Hitler regime, the Federal Republic of Germany has, since 1951, established a precedent for legislating and implementing a comprehensive system of restitution for the injustices of the Nazi era.

Since 1990, unified Germany has continued and extended the restitution policies of the pre-unification Federal Republic. *By early 1997, Germany had provided more than DM 100 billion in restitution and compensation and it expects the figure to increase to approximately DM 124 billion by the year 2030.* Additional reparation is being made to German-speaking Eastern European Jewish victims of National Socialist persecution in the form of social security payments and war victims relief payments. These expenditures, which supplement the disability pensions already being paid are estimated to reach a total of DM 10–13 billion.

THE BEGINNINGS

After the war, the occupation powers enacted laws in their individual zones that restored property confiscated by the Nazis to the original owners. These laws were restricted to property. They did not apply to personal damage to the victims of Nazi persecution, which encompassed physical and psychological suffering, unjust deprivation of freedom, or injury to a person's professional or economic potential. Nor did these laws provide for assistance to the families of those who died as a result of Hitler's policies. The occupation forces foresaw the German state assuming responsibility for reparation for such damages.

The focus on restitution for property losses during the first years after the war soon shifted to individual restitution for personal losses, however. This initially took the form of social assistance on a local level for victims of National Socialist persecution.

THE LUXEMBOURG AGREEMENT BETWEEN GERMANY AND ISRAEL

The Luxembourg Agreement between the government of the Federal Republic of Germany and the State of Israel, and the Conference on Jewish Material Claims Against Germany, known simply as the Claims Conference, defined the shape of the legislation eventually enacted to regulate restitution. Negotiations on the agreement took place in Luxembourg on September 10, 1952. Among the agreement's provisions was the requirement that the government of the Federal Republic of Germany pay DM 3.45 billion to the state of Israel and various Jewish organizations. Payments to Israel, particularly in the form of goods, recognized the fact that the young nation bore the tremendous financial burden of providing for the many victims of Nazi persecution who had settled there. Monetary payments to the Claims Conference were designed to aid Jewish organizations throughout the world in resettling Jews who lived outside Israel.

LEGISLATION

The "Supplementary Federal Law for the Compensation of the Victims of National Socialist Persecution" of October 1, 1953, was followed by the "Federal Law for the Compensation of the Victims of National Socialist Persecution" (Bundesentschädigungsgesetz or BEG) of June 29, 1956 which substantially expanded the scope of the 1953 law. The "Final Federal Compensation Law" enacted on September 14, 1965 increased the number of persons eligible for compensation as well as the assistance offered.

On May 1, 1992, two years after German unification, the "Law on Compensation for Victims of National Socialism in the Regions Acceding to the Federal Republic" (Gesetz uber Entschädigungen für Opfer des National-sozialismus im Beitrittsgebiet) was enacted. It supersedes, in a modified version, the compensation legislation of the German Democratic Republic. Under this law persons who had been persecuted by the Nazi regime and who, for reasons inimical to the rule of law, had been denied compensation by the authorities of the former German Democratic Republic, may submit fresh applications. An additional regulation was enacted on the basis of this law in favour of victims – as defined by the BEG – who had not received any compensation due to their residency in the former German Democratic Republic.

Indemnification for persecution of individuals

The BEG laws compensate individuals persecuted for racial, religious, or ideological reasons and also apply to persons who were persecuted because of their nationality. The laws focus on reparation payments for

- physical injury and damage to health
- restrictions on personal freedom
- damage inflicted upon economic and professional growth
- damage done to personal property

The laws include provision for compensation to artists and scholars whose work disagreed with Nazi tenets. They also provide compensation to people who were persecuted merely because they were related to or friendly with victims of the Nazis. Finally, they guarantee assistance to the survivors of the deceased victims.

The BEG legislation extends far beyond the responsibilities assumed by the government of the Federal Republic of Germany in the Luxembourg Agreement. *Of the approximately 4.4 million claims submitted under this legislation, all except an insignificant number have been settled. Approximately 40 percent of those receiving compensation under the provisions of BEG laws live in Israel, 20 percent in the Federal Republic of Germany, and 40 percent in other countries.* The amount of restitution paid under BEG and other restitution laws is shown in Table 2 at the end of the text.

Restitution for lost property

Claims for property lost as a result of National Socialist persecution are handled according to the provisions of the Federal Restitution Law (Bundesrücker-stat-tungsgesetz, or BRüG) of July 19, 1957. *As of January 1, 1987, 735,076 claims had been made on the basis of BRüG: with a few exceptions, they have all been settled.*

As noted earlier, the original restitution statutes were issued by the three Western allies in their zones of occupation to expedite the return of still-existing property and to settle related legal questions. Difficulties arose, however, in handling claims for property that no longer existed, and there was no common policy for resolving such claims. The BRüG legislation represented official recognition by the Federal Republic of Germany of its obligation to pay compensation for objects confiscated by the Third Reich that no longer existed in their original state and thus could not be returned.

The BRüG legislation was further developed in four supplementary laws, the last of which was enacted on September 3, 1969. Compensation for lost property is made according to the estimated replacement value as of April 1,1956. The BRüG legislation is also applicable to property confiscated outside the territory of the Federal Republic of Germany, provided that at the time of confiscation it was brought into or held in territory covered by BRüG legislation. With the achievement of German unity a law regulating unresolved issues of property and assets within the area of the former German Democratic Republic (Gesetz zur Regelung offener offener Vermögensfragen) was passed. This law established a framework for the return of assets taken from individuals and associations between January, 30 1933 and 1990. In cases where restitution is not possible, compensation will be made for the loss of property in eastern Germany. Part of the regulations applying to people persecuted by the Nazis were negotiated with the Claims Conference and are now set out in the "Law on Compensation and Adjustment" (Entschadigungs-und Augletchsgesetz), which went into force on December 1, 1994.

An agreement with the United States was concluded on May 13, 1992, to settle approximately 1,900 claims based on U.S. Public Law 94–542 of October 18, 1976 and the "International Claims Settlement Act." Claims could be made by U.S. citizens for confiscated property in the former German Democratic Republic and East Berlin. The agreement provides for a lump-sum payment of $102 million to the U.S. for distribution to claimants who are not otherwise eligible for restitution, or in cases where the applicant elected to receive a portion of the lump sum instead of restitution. The claims are administered by the Foreign Claims Settlement Commission.

International agreements had initially limited the Federal Republic's financial obligations under BRüG to DM 1.5 billion. The amount actually paid to date exceeds DM 3.9 billion. *When all claims for loss of property have been settled, the Federal Republic of Germany will have paid DM 4 billion in restitution for lost property.*

Additional compensatory laws and agreements

To supplement this basic legal framework, several additional compensatory laws have been enacted to aid those who suffered as a result of the discrimination practised by the Nazi regime. On August 22, 1949, a law was passed restoring the rights and privileges of those who had been discriminated against in Nazi social legislation. That same day, another law was approved extending the assistance to war victims ineligible for such benefits by Nazi law. A law of May 11, 1951, provided for restitution to members of the civil service who had suffered injustice at the hands of the Nazis. The scope of each of these three laws has been considerably expanded by subsequent revisions.

Mention must be made as well of the lump sum payments made to former concentration camp internees who were the objects of medical experimentation and to prisoners of war from Palestine who, because of their Jewish background, did not receive the humane treatment guaranteed prisoners of war under international law. A special fund was set up to assist individuals persecuted by the Nazis for having Jewish ancestry although they themselves were not of Jewish faith.

The Bundestag supplemented the provisions of the BEG in December 1979 with an allocation of DM 400 million. This sum was earmarked for payments to Jewish individuals whose health was seriously impaired by the Nazi regime but who had not been able to obtain restitution previously because they missed the deadline for filing claims or did not meet residency requirements. Shortly thereafter, the Bundestag made up to DM 100 million available for payments to non-Jewish victims of the Nazi regime who likewise had not been able to receive restitution.

Existing provisions guaranteeing compensation were confirmed and partly expanded during the 1990 negotiations on German unification. The Federal Republic of Germany and the German Democratic Republic agreed in Article 2 of the "Agreement on the Enactment and Interpretation of the Unification

Treaty" of September 18, 1990 that unified Germany would continue the Federal Republic's pre-unification policy on restitution. It was also agreed to establish an additional fund for persons who had not yet received restitution or who had received little compensation. United Germany recognized the fact that the German Democratic Republic had not, on economic and ideological grounds, made consistent compensation for injustices perpetrated by the Nazi regime. The regulations were specified in an agreement with the Claims Conference in October 1992. Hardship payments to victims of Nazi persecution had begun under guidelines introduced in October 1980. The new regulations maintained the eligibility requirements and payment amounts set out in those guidelines, but they also made provisions for aid, especially by regular monthly payments, to victims of the Nazi regime in economic need who had not received help under the Federal Republic's pre-unification compensation provisions. The agreement is intended primarily to provide additional monthly payments for individuals. It does not extend indemnification for Nazi persecution to persons who live in the former communist countries of Eastern Europe, but applicants from those states who now reside in other countries may be eligible if they meet the requirements.

In early 1996, the German Bundestag approved agreements with Israel and the United States allowing formerly German-speaking Holocaust survivors in those countries to receive German old-age pensions. The individuals in question, estimated to be some 35,000 in number, are not now and have never been German citizens. In most cases, they were originally Romanian or Latvian citizens. However, because German law allows persons of German origin from Eastern Europe to come to Germany and grants them numerous benefits, the German government agreed in negotiations with Israel and the U.S. to grant similar pension benefits to German-speaking Eastern European Jews living in those two countries. The prerequisite is retroactive payment into social security funds. Total costs are expected to reach some DM 2.3 billion.

GLOBAL AGREEMENTS

Between 1959 and 1964, the Federal Republic of Germany concluded "global agreements" with eleven European nations; today, there are 15 agreements with European nations and one with the U.S. As a result of these agreements, the Federal Republic of Germany provided over DM two billion to those nations to enable them to compensate citizens not eligible under the BEG for damages incurred as victims of Nazi policies. The victims' survivors also became eligible for compensation.

The most recent of these agreements include one with Poland in 1991, in which Germany agreed to pay DM 500 million to the "Foundation for German-Polish Reconciliation" to compensate Polish citizens who had been victims of Nazi persecution. A similar arrangement was made to compensate victims in three of the successor states to the Soviet Union. Belarus, the Russian Federation, and Ukraine. Under the agreement, Germany has contributed DM

Table 1: Funds pledged by the Federal Republic of Germany as a result of global agreements with European nations and with the United States

Country	Date of agreement	Approx. amount in millions DM
Luxembourg	July 11, 1959	18
Norway	August 7, 1959	60
Denmark	August 24, 1959	16
Greece	March 18, 1960	115
Holland	April 8, 1960	125
France	July 15, 1960	400
Belgium	September 28, 1960	80
Italy	June 2, 1961	40
Switzerland	June 29, 1961	10
United Kingdom	June 9, 1964	11
Sweden	August 3, 1964	1
Poland	October 16, 1991	500
Belarus	March 3, 1993	200
Russian Federation	March 3, 1993	400
Ukraine	March 3, 1993	400
United States	September 19, 1995	3
Total:		**DM 2.379 billion**

Table 2: Public expenditures in restitution for Nazi damages, in billions DM (as of January, 1997):

1. Expenditures thus far:

Compensation of victims (BEG)	76.998
Restitution for lost property (BRüG)	3.940
Compensatory pensions (ERG)	0.803
Israel Agreement	3.450
Global agreements with 16 nations	2.500
Other (civil service etc.)	8.600
Payments by German states (not BEG)	2.434
Final restitution in special cases	1.296
Subtotal	**100.021**

11. Estimated future expenditures:

Compensation of victims (BEG)	18.002
Restitution for lost property (BRüG)	0.060
Compensatory pensions (ERG)	0.797
Estimated total	**123.744**

1 billion to a "Foundation for Understanding and Reconcilliation." With these payments, Germany has spent an additional DM 1.5 billion for victims of Nazi persecution living in former communist countries.

Austria

The Federal Republic of Germany made available to the Austrian Government DM 102 million for compensatory payments. Of this amount, DM 96 million were used for the establishment of two funds: one to pay victims of political persecution in Austria for the loss of income, and the second to aid such victims in other countries. The remaining DM 6 million were set aside to pay claims for lost property.

ADDENDUM:

This survey of restitution laws and measures does not include payments (in billions) made according to the provisions of laws such as the "Law on the Treatment of Victims of National Socialist Persecution in the Area of Social Security" (Gesetz über die Behandlung der Verfolgeten des Nationalsozialismus in der Sozialversicherung) or "Federal Law on the Reparation for National Socialist Injustice in the Area of War Victims' Relief" (Bundesgesetz zur Wiedergutmachung nationalsozialistischen Unrechts in der Kriegsopferversongung einschließlich des Sondergesetzes für Berechtigte im Ausland), or the "General Law on the Consequences of War" (Allgemeines Kriegsfolgengesetz).

In addition to expenditures totalling more than DM 100 billion as of January 1997, the government of the Federal Republic of Germany has committed itself to making the following payments:

- The German-Czech Declaration signed in Prague on January 21, 1997 stipulates the establishment of a German-Czech Future Fund. The Fund will be used to finance projects of mutual interest such as care of the elderly, the building and operation of sanatoria, the presention and restoration of monuments and cemeteries, and partnership projects. The German contribution is set at DM 140 million. The projects are to benefit victims of Nazi violence in particular.
- From 1998 until the year 2000, an additional DM 80 million will be made available for humanitarian assistance to Nazi victims in other Eastern European countries who have not received any compensation. Victims in the Baltic states of Estonia, Latvia and Lithuania receive compensatory payments through two German-funded "Foundations for Understanding and Reconciliation" in Minsk and Moscow. The federal government has also made available DM 6 million for projects such as hospitals and nursing homes that care for Nazi victims.

Total payments to victims in Eastern European countries – including contributions to foundations in Poland, Belarus, the Russian Federation and Ukraine, as well as allocations for victims of pseudo-medical experiments – amount to DM 1.848 billion.

GREECE

Speech by Ambassador Alexandros Philon
HEAD OF THE GREEK DELEGATION

It is not a coincidence that the sense of tragedy has been given its most power-ful expression by Greek poets, who have witnessed the dramatic fate of my coun-try during her long history; a country located as it is on a rocky but beautiful land, where she was destined to both thrive and suffer.

One of the most recent examples of such tragedy was the fate that befell Greece during the Second World War and the four years of Nazi occupation, when she endured pain, sacrifice and destruction.

It is not the purpose of this Conference to assess and evaluate each country's contribution to the gigantic fight against Nazism which we should leave to the historian. I will therefore limit my remarks to the questions set by the present Conference.

As far as the sharing of the remaining Nazi gold amongst beneficiaries is con-cerned, my country responded positively, right from the beginning, to the pro-posal of creating a Fund aiming at bringing some relief to the survivors of Nazi persecution. At the same time Greece announced her decision in principle to transfer her rights on the remaining gold to the Fund which is being established.

This is a decision of principle, for as the ancient Greek saying goes: ου γαρ περι χρηματων, αλλα περι αρετηςτον αγωνα ποιουμεθα (the struggle is not for money but for virtue).

The technical details of the Fund management as well as the procedure of choosing poor individuals in need of special assistance, who would be the ben-eficiaries of this initiative, will be examined by another forum to which we will present our proposals in detail. I'm sure that, when this matter will be examined by our representatives, their proposals will include the Israelite Community of Thessaloniki and its members who have survived the holocaust as well as other communities of Greece that were victimized.

I would like to seize this opportunity, especially in view of the presence here of representatives of the victims of Nazism, to state that my country, even though she considers that human pain and human life cannot be estimated, neverthe-less believes that not everything that could have been done has really been done, both as a sign of respect for those who sacrificed their lives but also as a sign of moral and indeed material support to those who have survived and can bear witness to the tragedy that befell them.

For this reason, and without going into any details, I believe that it is impera-tive to take all possible supplementary measures in favour of the victims of Nazism. This Conference gives us an opportunity to consider this matter and to suggest – and there should be a follow up to these suggestions – ways of how we could offer whatever is humanly possible in memory of those who sacrificed their lives and to their families as well as to the survivors, who have been so severely traumatized.

When we consider human pain there cannot be any distinction on the basis of race, sex, religion, and beliefs. For this reason, the people of Greece witness-ing the persecution of their fellow Jewish citizens, at the risk of their own safety, and while enduring themselves great suffering, did whatever they could to pro-tect their Jewish compatriots, often by hiding them in their own homes.

Moreover Greece is possibly the only country that did not confiscate Jewish properties even during the occupation period; after the war, the properties of those who did not return and who had no descendants were not considered to be state property. On the contrary all such property, by special legislation adopt-ed right after the war, was handed over to the Israelite Council of the Jewish Community of Greece to be managed by them for the benefit of the survivors.

Furthermore, although it is not within the immediate scope of this conference, I would like to indicate that my country maintains historically confirmed, legal-ly founded and morally justified claims for war compensation and reparations.

Greece also maintains claims concerning the restitution of stolen archeologi-cal treasures and other assets not only based on the principles of compensation and reparation but also on a "quasi-contractual" obligation imposed at the time on Greece under duress.

This conference gives the participants the opportunity to ask again many of the questions that for more than half a century have still not received a full answer. Public opinion in our countries, the victims of Nazi crimes, their fami-lies and their communities, are all eagerly expecting at least some of the answers. The message is simple: We have not forgotten, nor will we forget.

Contribution of the Historical Archive Directorate of the Hellenic Ministry of Foreign Affairs

In the great tragedy experienced by the peoples of Europe on the outbreak of World War II, the share of suffering and loss which fell to the lot of Greece was inversely proportionate to the size of its population, its wealth, and the area of the country.

Greece suffered in the War and under foreign occupation as did no other country. It had a higher percentage of human losses and a greater degree of material damage than any of the allied states – and even perhaps than any of those which were finally defeated.

A historian who wishes to study the period of the War and each step which the country took towards its recovery after the War has at his disposal an exceptional wealth of archive material. This deals with:

a. the day-to-day struggle of the Greek people to survive and its resistance against the invaders (General Archive of the State Archives of Modern Social History, Archives of the Literature and Historical Society, Private Archives);

b. the country's diplomatic manoeuvres and attempts to recover its national sovereignty and the laying of the foundations which would make possible its economic reconstruction.

Included in this second group of historical testimonies is the collection of diplomatic documents belonging to the Historical Archives Directorate of the Hellenic Ministry of Foreign Affairs.

These documents can be found in two major groups:

a. the general correspondence of the specific period

b. the German, Italian and Bulgarian reparations.

As he delves into the first group, the historian undergoes an intense personal experience (H.I. Marrou defined History as an intellectual adventure in which the whole of the personality of the historian takes part): 160 files and 749 sub-files on the period of the War (1940–45), from the dawn of 28 October 1940, when war was declared in Greece, until 9 May 1945, describe in detail, supported by documentation, often unexpected by the researcher, the suffering, the misery, the grief and the struggles of a people in the four years, six months and thirteen days that this unjust war lasted.

The basic categories of these documents which follow the rules of a careful chronological classification, are:

– The documents of the quisling government;

– The documents of the Cairo government (the lawful Greek Government in exile took refuge in Cairo);

– The documents of the London government (for certain periods a team of ministers of the Greek Government, together with the then King, resided in London, in order to have direct consultations with the British Government).

In addition to the large group of documents which deal with the concern of the Greek Government in exile over the progress and development of the country's territorial interests, a large number are concerned with persecutions, executions, arrests and the taking hostage of Greek citizens and losses of their property.

A special place is occupied, not only on the cold shelves of the state archives but above all, in the hearts of the Greek people by the sufferings, which appear to go even beyond the ultimate limit to which human irrationality can attain, of the weaker elements in society, among whom the Fascist conquerors systematically reserved the first place for citizens of Jewish descent. A considerable number of the files of the Historical Archive of the Ministry of Foreign Affairs refer exclusively to the tribulations, the sacrifices and the looting of the property of Greek Jews, whose communities once flourished in the major urban centres of Thessaloniki, Volos, Athens, Ioannina, Chania (Crete) and elsewhere. The bonds of friendship which the citizens of Greece have always felt with their Jewish fellow-citizens (in July 1917, five months before the historic declaration of the British Prime Minister Arthur Balfour, the Greek Prime Minister Eleftherios Venizelos had been the first to call attention to the need to set up an independent Jewish state[1]) not only were relaxed, but reached their closest during the War and the foreign occupation. One in every two Greek families had its own story to tell of helping in the concealment and escape of wanted Jews. In the end, the reckoning was a terrible one: of the 60,000 Greek Jews, only 2,000 survived. Together with most of them, the families of those who had concealed them also paid the ultimate price. There is, however, a further piece of evidence, unfortunately unknown to many, of the humanitarian feelings of the Greeks towards their fellow-citizens: the official Greek state was first, and perhaps alone, in restoring, immediately after it had recovered its liberty, the confiscated properties of Jews to the heirs of their owners, and not including them in the property of the Greek State. Furthermore: the government of George Papandreou, at the meeting of the Council of Ministers of 24 August 1944, determined that any item of Jewish property which had remained uninherited because of the absence of Jewish heirs who had died in the concentration camps and elsewhere would be used to support destitute Jews. In March 1945, General Plastiras declared that Greece was a poor country, but an honourable one; it would never wish to benefit by the fact that some of its citizens had been wiped out as a means of filling its State Treasury. On the contrary, on 8 May 1947, the Council of Ministers decided to grant eight million drachmas as a contribution on the part of the Greek State to meet the educational and religious needs of the Jewish communities.

The War came to an end, and Greece, small in numbers but great in its sacrifices and efforts, having, by the general admission of the Allies, played a vast role in the development and outcome of this terrible war, sat down at the table with the victors, who were seeking compensation from the Axis in order to reconstruct their economies.

Greece's demands were just and reasonable. It did not seek to be compensated either for the population which it had lost or for non-pecuniary and other forms of mental and moral prejudice. It could not accept blood-money. And a civilisation – there were hundreds of instances of damage to and looting of antiquities – cannot be exchanged for or weigh its values against any sum of money. Greece asked only to be compensated for its material losses, in order to be able to stand on its feet again. Constantly at the side of her firm allies, the forces of progress and democracy, from the Balkan Wars, after the First World War and from the Asia Minor disaster, Greece received only wounds, and it was only wounds that she was seeking to heal. When the Second Great War came, it found seven million, three hundred thousand Greeks striving to establish a proper homeland, a sound economy, a state which could take its rightful place among the other European states. When the War ended, it left behind a ruined country whose economic resources were non-existent and which was unable to feed its population, even when it was now reduced by 12%.

The 38 files and 322 sub-files of the major archival unit on German reparations of the Foreign Ministry's Historical Archive speak, with specific data, of the following losses:

In agricultural production: A reduction of up to 75%.

Forests: From woodcutting and planned fires, reduction of 25%.

Stockbreeding: Small and large animals, reduction of 50 to 80%.

Mines: Materials already mined were taken to Germany. The mines were destroyed by the resistance forces to prevent the mining of fresh materials to support the forces of the Axis.

Foreign trade: Non-existent. Goods left the country only by the route of requisitioning and theft.

Industrial production: Reduced to zero.

Railway network: Of the country's railway network, of a length of 2,679 km in 1940, only 680 km remained in 1945.

Wheeled transport: Damage to state and private equipment (in 1938 dollars): $4,200,000. Damage to roads, road surfaces, infrastructures, unfinished roads, damage to bridges, etc., total: $54,410,000.

Ports: (Damage in 1938 dollars)

Piraeus	4,700,000
Volos	1,350,000
Thessaloniki	1,200,000
Kalamata	360,000
Corfu	300,000
Alexandroupoli	200,000
Irakleio	200,000
Stylida	110,000
Karlovasi	100,000
Vathy, Samos	90,000

Corinth Canal: Damage 860,000 (1938 dollars)

Telephone – telegraph network: Damage: 100%

Civil aviation: Greece's small but well-organised civil aviation fleet ceased to exist.

*Merchant marine:*Totally disrupted. Of the 583 merchant vessels which Greece had in 1939, 434 were lost. The country lost 3,000 merchant seamen.

Buildings: The northern provinces of Greece lost, from bombing and fires, approximately 79,000 homes. Kalavryta was levelled to the ground. The country lost 23% of its total buildings. Eighteen per cent of the population (1,200,000 people) were homeless, 16,000 farming families were living in ruins, and 100,000 urban families were housed in wretched conditions.

Monuments and archaeological sites destroyed: Nineteen large Byzantine churches, monasteries, museums and libraries. Twenty-six improvised excavations were carried out by German and Italian soldier-archaeologists; hundreds of objects were stolen and sent abroad from 42 museums by Germans, from 33 museums by Italians, and from nine museums by Bulgarians[2] (all recorded in detail and with a full descriptions).

Reduction in the population: The reduction in the population was dramatic. Apart from the mass slaughter at Kalavytra (1,436 people were massacred in half an hour) and Distomo, losses on the field of battle and of the civilian population through bombing and reprisals, there were deaths from hunger, exhaustion and hardship. Thousands of people were taken hostage, were forcibly displaced, and, of course, never returned to their homes.

Schools: Damage caused by the Germans: 2,529 schools were requisitioned, 156 were looted, 492 were bombed and 492 were burned. Included in these were two teachers' training colleges where new teachers intended to staff the schools were trained.

Schools: Damage caused by the Italians: 1,948 schools were requisitioned, 68 were looted, 249 were bombed and 111 were burned. Included in these was one teachers' training college.

Greece was a poor country when war broke out. It was unable to satisfy the insatiable appetite of the invaders for the pure gold which they managed to loot from other, rich, European countries with a flourishing economy and steady rates of development. But the occupying forces themselves did not expect more of it: the property and the valuables (jewellery, money, objets d'art, gold teeth) of Greek citizens promptly appeared on the markets of nearby Europe. The country's national wealth (timber, minerals, transport, raw materials) was employed to improve the quality of life of the citizens of the Third Reich. Greek antiquities were defaced out of contempt for them (some masterpieces in marble still bear the marks) or carried off by the aesthetic tastes of German amateur antiquarians.

Apart, however, from the recording of damage and losses sustained by Greek citizens, the files of the Hellenic Ministry of Foreign Affairs also include details which concern the property in Greece of citizens of other countries, living in America, the Netherlands, etc., and that of Greeks living abroad (France, Germany, South Africa, etc.). Also included in this category are files with the case law and correspondence from third countries, which are revealing as to the manoeuvres and the considerations of expediency which finally guided each country in the implementation of a specific policy on the major issue of war reparations. There are, for example, documents which describe the desperate efforts made by George Marshall to impose the policy and the Programme for Economic Recovery in Europe and to overcome the stubborn resistance of Republican representatives and congressmen. These saw with dismay a Germany weakened by demands that it should pay compensation to the Allies and, on the other hand, an all-powerful and rapidly developing Russia, which, in their eyes, would at the very next step attempt to grip Western Europe in its stranglehold.

Greece has every moral and legal right to be sitting at the table of today's discussion on the gold looted by the Nazis. And it will be in a real position to weigh its losses if it can have an answer to two questions:
 – How many bars of gold correspond to one human life?
 – How many bars of gold are needed to set up a Parthenon?

History has as its purpose and raison d'être the quest for a truth which it knows from the very start will be relative. However, the inherent imperfection of the means which the historian possesses to reach that truth should not be a cause of discouragement, but, on the contrary, an incentive to draw closer to it.

Intellectual honesty and moral fortitude are basic characteristics of the true historian. It is with these two virtues that we have tried to approach the historical material contained in the diplomatic files of the Hellenic Ministry of Foreign Affairs.

Cicero said that the first law incumbent upon a historian is not to dare to say anything which he knows to be erroneous and the second is to dare to say that which he believes to be true.

We have dared to reveal what we believe to be true. In Greece at the moment, historical research is being intensified in this particular field. In addition, Greek scholars have for years been carrying out a systematic study of German, Italian and (former) Soviet sources. More particularly, it is expected that the archives of the countries of the former Eastern Bloc, closed to us until recently, will bring to light important facts about a great human sacrifice and the incalculable harm done to the progress of European civilisation.

NOTES

[1] Asher Moissis (1899–1975). Greek lawyer, author, translator, and leader of the Jewish community. He survived the Holocaust and was recognised as the first diplomatic representative of Israel in Athens in 1945. On Venizelos and his policy, see his article entitled 'El Mouvimento Sionista Enias Otras Sivdades de Grecia' (in the Ladino language). This article contains specific information as drawn from the weekly Sionist journal *Pro-Israel* (July 1917), which was brought out in France.

[2] On the damage to antiquities, see the publication of the Ministry of Religious Affairs and Education, Directorate for Antiquities and Historical Monuments, entitled *Damage to Antiquities caused by the War and the Armies of Occupation* (in Greek), Athens 1946, by the archaeologists C. Karouzos, M. Kalligas, I. Miliadis, G. Androutsopoulos and N. Zafeiropoulos.

See also *Works of Art in Greece, the Greek Islands and the Dodecanese. Losses and Survivals in the War*, London, HM's Stationery Office, 1946.

Results of the steps taken to compensate the country and individual victims

G. B. DERTILIS

Of the gold claimed by Greece in 1946–47, approximately 80% was actually restituted, 83 kgs, almost exclusively monetary gold. Sixteen kgs, representing looted private holdings, were not restituted on the grounds that the proofs supporting the claim were incomplete.

To this rather modest compensation, I would now like to juxtapose those claims of Greece that have not been met so far:

1. A claim for 19,000 kgs of looted monetary silver.

2. A claim for about 150 million dollars, corresponding to a loan, duly signed by the Nazi government and, in reality, imposed upon Greece by the occupation forces.

3. A claim concerning the immediate and disastrous effects of this loan. This should be further explained.

A well known method of forcefully financing public expenditure and the costs of war can be resumed in a simple sentence: when you have no gold left, use inflation. Therefore, having looted the gold, the occupation forces used hyper-inflation. Against the loan they had imposed they obliged the Greek government to pay, at various intervals, advances in cash. These were, in reality, fresh paper-money printed liberally under the orders of the occupation forces and then used immediately to literally drain the market by purchasing everything that was available – mainly, of course, raw materials, energy, and food. This practice had two direct and immediate repercussions: one of the highest hyper-inflations ever recorded in world history; and one of the most severe famines in World War II, in relative terms, a famine that caused 200,000 deaths, in a few months, in a country of 6½ million people.

4. The last category of claims that were not compensated (with some exceptions), are the claims of Greek citizens for human (and material) losses during the occupation. In addition to our 160,000 Jewish-Greek fellow-citizens, neighbours and friends, Greece "contributed" to the Holocaust, if one may say so, tens of thousands of people tortured, sent to concentration camps, or executed, for taking part in the resistance, or merely for their beliefs – the most extreme cases being those of whole villages burnt down to ashes, and of their defenceless population executed on the spot, in retaliation for the acts of the resistance movement.

Greece was among the countries that suffered the most severe losses during World War II: 7% of its population dead (a 12% demographic reduction); about 70% of its economy ruined; total losses estimated at more than thirty times her annual GNP; and about 75% of its large merchant fleet sunk in the service of the Allies, a fact comparable, perhaps, to the ships and trains of neutral countries happily supplying the Axis forces and being handsomely paid for it – in looted gold. And all this hardship fell upon a country which, alone in Europe, as early as 1940–41, resisted for 5 months the fascist Italian invasion and for nearly a month the Nazi invasion.

In consideration of these facts, one may rightly ask a question which may sound, but is not, rhetorical. Among those present in this Conference, including perhaps the historians, how many know or remember these historical facts? And is this not one more reason to open all the inaccessible archives, with no exception?

The value of the gold restituted to Greece corresponds to the amount an insurance company would have to pay, nowadays, for a sunken super-tanker. These, in Greece's case, were the results of the "Steps Taken to Compensate the Country and Individual Victims".

HUNGARY

Contribution from the Hungarian delegation

As the representatives of the Republic of Hungary, I would like to express our gratitude to the Government of Britain, for organizing this London Conference on Nazi Gold. The Conference presents an excellent opportunity to gather and evaluate the historical facts related to gold looted by the Nazis from occupied countries during the war and to consider ways in which to reimburse countries as well as individual victims.

In Hungary, following the signature of the Paris Peace Treaty, and respectively in connection with the implementation of point 2 of paragraph 27 of Law XVIII on the ratification of the Paris Peace Treaty, the question of the indemnification of the jewellery and gold articles confiscated from the Jews or from people of the Jewish faith has emerged several times. On the basis of available documents the following facts can be stated.

Hungary entered the war in June 1941. Although there had been several discriminatory legal acts against Jews since 1938, practically the first Government Decree on confiscation of Jewish property entered into force only after the German army virtually occupied the country in March 1944.

In the Spring of 1944 Decree No. 1600/1944 on the registration and sequestration of Jewish property ordered that all the Jews living in the country should register all their available assets by 30 April, 1944. The registered claims could as well be sequestrated. On the basis of the registration the banks blocked the safes hired by Jewish individuals. The Minister of Finance was authorized to take stock of the contents of the safes and, according to the decree, to deposit the securities, bank books, valuables and cash belonging to Jewish individuals. The registrations and deposits were to be performed by any of the banks being a member of the Central Corporation of Banking Companies, by any public office or by the Hungarian Royal Post Office Savings Bank.

In April 1944 according to further decrees (decree No. 6138/1944.V.BM and order No. 6163/1944.IV) members of the Jewish population were forced into ghettos and confiscation of assets still in their possession was ordered. The Hungarian Royal Highest Audit Office ordered the investigation and collection of the gold, platinum and silver jewels and other assets taken from the Jewish population. During the summer of 1944 all the assets taken from Jewish citizens were deposited in the stores of the individual financial directorates (executive organs of the Ministry of Finance). With a regard to the approaching front-line assets from the Eastern part of Hungary were transferred to the Budapest Office of the Hungarian Royal Post Office Savings Bank. Part of the assets taken from the Jewish population were later taken to the city and village offices of the Nazi party. With the development of the war all these assets and the assets in the Financial Directorate were delivered by special decree to the western part of the country. The valuables were then selected and classified. The notes indicating the owners of the confiscated assets were removed from the various parcels and deposits. The consignment was loaded and progressed by train on 30 March, 1945 through Salzburg to the destination of Hallein.

In addition two lorries set off with another part of the property assets. In May 1945 – stationed in a part of Austria occupied by the French – they were seized by the American army and later delivered to Paris. According to the documents available the two lorries were carrying the gold assets and jewels, however the museum pieces, Persian carpets, chinaware, other valuables and probably a part of the gold assets were loaded on the train. After the conclusion of the Peace Treaty, in the Spring of 1948, the French returned the assets which were loaded on the two lorries. Concerning the fate of the train there are no available documents.

The documents returned from Paris, which presumably contained information about the forced deposits and other confiscated Jewish gold articles and jewels or those registered as criminal deposits, were followed by four volumes of notes. These did not indicate names, only the assets in bulk selected into classes. The assets following their receipt were deposited with the National Bank of Hungary as deposits partly of the Ministry of Justice and the Ministry of Interior, but mostly as deposits of the Ministry of Finance.

In addition to the Paris documents the committee set up to investigate Jewish assets were able to find and bring back some Jewish assets taken abroad. In this way the so called Bezdan, Tatabánya, Nagykőrös and Bechenwald documents were returned. As well as these documents, with the indication of the names and articles, the notes were also preserved.

From the documents it can be concluded that the valuables deposited and sequestrated according to decree 1600/1944.ME were selected by classes already prior to transportation abroad and the notes containing the names were removed. So, when the material was returned in 1948, according to the attached notes, it was kept in bulk. The identification of the owners concerned was not possible by this time.

After the war the Hungarian Government among its first decrees repealed decree 1600/1944.ME and the other discriminating decrees. As regards the effective indemnification, until the enactment of the compensation acts enacted in 1991–92 (Act XXV of 1991. Kpt.I, and Act XXIV of 1992. Kpt.II) only certain legal or effective measures have been taken in order to return the jewels and assets sequestrated by decree 1600/1944.ME, or to indemnify the previous owners. On 15 November, 1946 Act XXV on the condemnation of the persecution of the Jews and the extenuation of its consequences entered into force. According to paragraph 2 of this Act the state undertook to transfer the legacy of the former owners without legal successors it acquired or will acquire to a fund to be later established. Point 2, paragraph 27 of the Peace Treaty also obliged the state to transfer the claims of the former owners without legal successors to the interest organizations of the victims, and to grant the legacy it acquired or will acquire – in the absence of other successors – due to death of persons affected by racial laws. In order to execute this obligation the National Jewish Indemnification Fund was established.

But the enactment of the laws necessary for the national fulfillment of the provisions of the Paris Peace Treaty – due to the well-known historical changes – has never occurred. Neither has the legal settlement of the National Jewish Indemnification Fund.

Only concerning the so called Bezdan, Nagykőrös, Tatabánya and Buchenwald deposits, on the direction of the Minister of Finance, have some payments occurred.

The Constitutional Court in one of its decisions gave notice to Parliament to lift this unconstitutional state, and on the basis of a consensus with the Jewish organizations, Act X of 1997 and Government decree 1635/1997. (IV.10) were enacted for this purpose. According to these the execution of point 2, paragraph 27 of Act XVIII of the 1947 Paris Peace Treaty will be performed within the framework of a fund raised by the government. For the purposes of the Fund the government is to employ indemnification vouchers of 4 Mrd forints (13 million GBP), which has been transferred to the Hungarian Jewish Inheritance Fund, the utilization of which is decided by the Board of Trustees. At the same time the government transferred the ownership of 7 immovables properties to the Fund. It gave over 10 objects of art and ensures a yearly budgetary contribution to the operational expenses of the Fund. In 1997 this was 30 Million forints (90,000 GBP). The Republic of Hungary through the enactment of the above laws fulfilled its obligation taken under paragraph 27 of the Paris Peace Treaty.

The Constitutional Court of the Republic of Hungary held several sittings on this matter. The Minister of Finance and the Chairman of the National Bank of Hungary were heard, and the Court examined the documents made available by the Ministry of Finance, the notes attached to the assets returned from Paris, research carried out by the Bank Centre, documents sent by the National Bank of Hungary and the documents of the Contemporary Collection of the Hungarian National Archives. The facts stated above were confirmed by Decision No. 16/1993 of the Constitutional Court.

Most of the documents concerned disappeared during the war. All the remaining documents, that were also available to the Constitutional Court with respect to their date of origin, have already been given to the Hungarian National Archives. Research on the documentation is still unfinished and continues. These documents, according to the Data Protection law and Act LXVI of 1995 on public documents, archives and private archives, are available for research with the permission of the Hungarian National Archive body.

INTERNATIONAL ROMANI UNION

Statement by the Hon. Ian F. Hancock

INTERNATIONAL ROMANI UNION, AND MEMBER OF
THE U.S. HOLOCAUST MEMORIAL COUNCIL

During the period of the Third Reich the Roma and Sinti, people of Romani ("Gypsy") descent, were targeted for extermination as part of the Nazi Final Solution. In the years preceding World War II, and during the Holocaust, untold numbers of Romani people were arrested for incarceration and transportation to the death camps. Part of this processing involved the confiscation of personal possessions, especially personal items of value.

The Romani people, like the Jewish people before 1948, have lived in Europe as a non-territorial population since their arrival in the West from Asia in the 14th Century. The Romani population today numbers in the millions, and supports a language and a culture having their roots in northern India. Because of their distinctive history, the Roma and Sinti have lacked political economic, national and military strength, a situation which remains unchanged today. For this reason, they have been easy prey to legislation against them, and have been powerless to defend themselves against it.

The earliest laws against the Romani people in the German-speaking lands date from the 15th Century, and have continued to be created and enforced into the present time. While the most extreme of these laws have called for the extermination of the Roma and Sinti, they typically required their expulsion from the region. Because of this, the Romani presence in western Europe has been characterised by constant movement, and the subsequent lack of access to establishment institutions such as banks.

As a result of having therefore to carry personal wealth on one's person, in the form of gold necklaces, rings, bracelets, coins serving as buttons on clothing, etc., no documentation exists in the form of bank records for property stolen by the Nazis from the Romani people. Receipts were generally not provided and the paperwork available to us today is scant. This situation is *particularly* characteristic of the Romani victims of these appropriations, and should be taken into account.

Scholarship on the Romani victims of the Holocaust is in its infancy. Only now is the recognition growing that Roma and Sinti were the only people besides the Jews singled out for extermination as a racially defined population

We are still unclear as to the total number of Romani victims of the Holocaust; almost all of those in Germany were exterminated. No Romani witness was called to testify on behalf of his own people at the Nuremberg Trials, and little has ever been paid to the Romani survivors of the Holocaust by way of war crimes reparation In Europe today, the word "genocide" is once again being used in connection with the Roma, who are increasingly the target of fascist and neo-Nazi attacks. In the years since 1945, programmes of deportation, incarceration and sterilization have all been implemented against the Roma – all techniques employed in Hitler's pre-war Germany.

The Romani people remain poorly-equipped to make their case forcefully, lacking the finances, education and governmental backing which would allow us to do so. We are not asking for anything not rightfully due to us; monies returned to the Romani people would help us break this cycle of powerlessness and redress a terrible historic wrong.

INTERNATIONAL UNION OF
FORMER JUVENILE PRISONERS
OF FASCIST CONCENTRATION CAMPS

By the International Union of Former Juvenile Prisoners of Fascist Concentration Camps (uniting more than 550 thousand citizens from nine CIS States and Baltic Republics) at the conference on "Nazi gold" and the following conference on determining its future.

World War II, the most dreadful for its all-encompassing devastating consequences, the bloodiest for its scale and effects, the most secretive for its circumstances which were not revealed until the end, is once again on our minds. This time the reason is so-called "Nazi gold". From time immemorial this has been regarded as unlawfully acquired treasures from the looted European States, the personal fortunes of peace-loving citizens, above all those who were regarded as enemies of the *Reich* and were persecuted as a mark of political, ideological and racial and nationalistic intolerance.

The broad, animated and polemically fierce discussion of the problems of "Nazi gold" is underway around the world, particularly in view of the International Conference taking place on 2–4 December in London whose remit is to resolve those problems once and for all. In that context the Members of our Union – the citizens of the Commonwealth of Newly Independent States (those States were Hitler's largest prey in the war he unleashed and had to endure the greatest loss of human life and material damage) had no choice other than to comment on the nature of those problems.

Let us recall those problems.

The people of the former USSR lost 27 (or at least 30 according to other estimates) million human lives during World War II. These losses are infinitely painful and irretrievable. During Hitler's occupation of republics, regions and districts of the former USSR, 1,710 towns and more than 70 thousand villages were ruined, destroyed, burnt down and looted. The once flourishing areas were transformed into deserted wasteland. 17 million cattle, 7 million horses, 20 million pigs, 27 million sheep and goats, 9.2 thousand tonnes of grain and flour were removed to the *Reich*. Hundreds of trains carrying coal, metal and building materials were sent to Germany. Troops specialised in farming dispatched the most fertile Ukrainian and Russian chernozem to Germany. The citizens and national economy of the USSR suffered direct material damage to the value of 679 thousand million roubles, including 285 thousand million in the Ukraine, 249 in

Russia, 75 in Belorussia, 20 in Latvia, 17 in Lithuania, 16 in Estonia and 11 thousand million roubles in Moldavia (based on the 1941 State value of money).

The description of the black night of the Occupation which suffocated our States would have been fundamentally incomplete, inaccurate and, most importantly, extremely unfair and an insult to the soldiers killed in action and those victims of fascism who miraculously survived if nothing was mentioned about the gigantic machine of organised violence conceived and operated by the Nazis and inflicted on the peaceful population. Allow us to mention just a few facts.

More than 4 thousand concentration camps, *Gestapo* prisons, ghettos and other vile creations from the unnatural imagination of the usurpers under Hitler who spread their brown plague across the continent, where day and night, in winter and summer, the peaceful citizens were taken, thrown inside and incarcerated, were counted in Europe. Furthermore, in that enormous territory, that is from the British island of Alderney in the west to the Russian town of Belaya Kalitva in the east, from the Norwegian town of Gruni in the north to the Greek River Acheloös in the south, our people were subjugated, suppressed and humiliated. The actual figures show that there were almost 6 million Soviet Union citizens among the 18 million prisoners of fascist concentration camps (every third person), two million of those did not live to see liberation. In many cases, the places where our compatriots are buried will remain forever unknown.

The lists published in the world press of persons holding so-called "dormant accounts", the familiarity with the presentation prepared on the initiative of the USA's Department of Commerce concerning the search for and restitution of the treasures of victims of fascism stolen and hidden by Germany during World War II, the political declarations made in that regard by statesmen of some countries in whose banking institutions these funds are kept, reminded prisoners of the realities of the past which cannot be eradicated from memory.

The Nazis became wealthy through the non-paid work, the life and even death of all those imprisoned behind the wire fencing of Hitler's concentration camps, irrespective of their nationality, citizenship, religion and political leanings. Even SS experts can testify to this. For example, a prisoner whose average life expectancy was approximately 270 days made Germany a net profit of 1,430 *reichsmark*. Furthermore, all people who were forced to exchange their everyday clothing for the striped uniform of a prisoner had their property, money, jewellery and other valuables confiscated. After death, even the bodies of the prisoners were "exploited" – their gold crowns were extracted and fertiliser was produced from the bones and ashes. Even soap was manufactured from the "biological raw material".

News of the "gold-extracting" activity of Nazis in the occupied territories and in the concentration camps has survived. In Lviv, as reported by the witnesses of the "death squad", which over a period of five months operated in the places where there was mass extermination of peaceful citizens, "spreading" took place (after the corpses had been burnt) and 110 kgs of the gold was sent to Germany. Those kinds of squads worked equally productively in Kiev, Minsk, Novgorod, Riga, Vilnius and Simferopol too. There are further more general details: in 1944 the concentration camps melted and handed over more than two tonnes of gold to the State coffers. In Germany there was the specialised DEGUSSA (German Gold and Silver State Institute) state structure which specialised in the processing of precious metals which had been "extracted" in the concentration camps, prisons and other such establishments.

The unequivocal conclusion which immediately suggests itself is that the looting of the occupied States, of their peaceful citizens, was total and unrelenting. That is the reason why the Nazis' gold stocks grew from 189 to 415 million dollars in the Swiss banks alone between 1939 and 1945. Moreover, stocks accrued despite the enormous expenditure on warfare.

As early as 1946, as a result of the democratic States' traditional devotion to the ideals of humanism and driven by the desire to restore justice which had been disregarded and suppressed, Great Britain, the United States of America and France discussed the problem of restituting to their rightful owners the riches stolen from them by the Nazis. A special committee was even set up which would exclusively undertake practical tasks in that regard. The harsh realities of the post-war era, the resulting hostility between the Soviet Union and the countries of the West made it impossible to undertake the measures required by the human attitude to the victims of Nazism.

And now we are observing the new round of discussions of the old, dramatic problem which is extremely painful for the victims of fascism.

Apart from the countries already mentioned (Great Britain, the USA and France), the representatives of Switzerland, Sweden, Spain, Portugal, Turkey – countries where the Nazis bought foodstuffs and goods in exchange for stolen items – and those of Argentina and Brazil – the States where Nazis hid after the end of the war – are invited to the conference in London. The conference organisers have also invited the Russian Federation, as the legal successor to the USSR, and the Ukraine to take part. Representatives of the Jewish Holocaust Victims Support Fund are also expected to be there. Today, even before the conference work has begun, there are very great expectations for the success of this conference.

The representatives of Russia and Ukraine, like representatives of most other participating States, will attend in an advisory capacity. In that respect it is also very important that the opinion of almost one million survivors of fascist brutality – the citizens of CIS States and Baltic countries – on a just resolution of the problem of "Nazi gold" will also be heard at the conference.

Our opinion is clear and easily understood. Based on a deep respect for all victims of fascism without exception, driven by the sincere desire to support the statutory rights and interests of each of them, separate from all efforts to obtain or negotiate some kind of unilateral preferences or advantages or privileges, it consists of the following points:

FIRST: In today's multicultured world, which has been freed from the harsh and dangerous resistance of military-cum-political blocs with their dividing walls and notorious "Iron Curtain", the opportunity finally arose of resolving the problem of restituting to their rightful owners the riches stolen from them at that time by the Nazis. It is essential that good use is made of this opportunity, which mankind has been given half a century after Hitler unleashed the greatest world war in world history. We are convinced that in this respect the old ideological prejudice whereby applicants were divided into "own" and "foreign" according to national dependence and other non-objective characteristics must be ruled out. At the same time it is necessary for the citizens of every country and those affected by fascist persecution to have a full and clear understanding of the past, thereby making it possible to achieve the most satisfactory results for all those involved and affected.

SECONDLY: Very large numbers of former victims of fascism live in Russia, the Ukraine, Belarus and other CIS and Baltic States. According to the situation in mid-October 1997, a total of 990,000 people were counted in those regions, that is 600,000 in the Ukraine, 220,000 in Russia, 100,000 in Belarus, 60,000 in Moldavia, Latvia, Lithuania, Estonia and other CIS States. The main categories are: 780,000 people subjected to forced labour, 60,000 concentration camp prisoners, 35,000 people who suffered in *Gestapo* prisons and other specialised medical institutions, 30,000 people condemned to be housed in ghettos, and others amounting to 85,000. As regards classification by nation, the nations are represented as follows: Ukrainians–560,000; Russians–220,000; Belarussians–90,000; Jews–45,000; Poles–15,000; Tatars–2,000; Germans–2,000; other peoples–56,000. All victims of Nazism – the citizens of the CIS States and Baltic States – are entitled to their share of "Nazi gold". The amount to which they are entitled is determined against a scale and by the severity of the crimes committed against the peaceful population: full-scale plundering, mass deportation, merciless exploitation, bloody reprisals. It must be noted that only one person out of every six prisoners or extradites to the *Reich* is still alive today. In determining a country's share, the main importance is to be given to such criteria as the standard of living and real income of victims of fascism as well as their age and state of health. In the CIS States, the average income of victims of fascism is 40 dollars per person per month. The overwhelming majority of victims are pensioners, persons unfit for work, the sick, the disabled. Thus far the question of fair compensation payments on the part of Germany and the question regarding pensions in respect of damage to health suffered and non-material suffering have not been solved.

THIRDLY: Provided that there is no doubt as to the illegal, rapacious, criminal origin of "Nazi gold", all necessary measures must be taken for it to be fairly distributed on a basis where account is taken of historical and social events and where there are no moral objections. All instances of discrimination and disregard for the suffering of each victim of Nazi persecution are excluded. In the meantime allegations which are incorrect in form and inaccurate in content can sometimes be heard. According to those allegations, everything looted by the Nazis belong exclusively to citizens of Jewish nationality. It is not possible to agree with such claims since they contradict the truth, the actual facts and fundamental analysis. Doctor Gerchard Moser, an expert from Baden-Baden who is officially involved in the investigations into the bank lists in Swiss banks, takes the view that only 30% of all accounts which have been "dormant" since 1945 belong to Holocaust victims. And what about the rest? Such proposals, which are too rash and not so well-founded, regarding the transfer of finances appropriated by criminal means by the Nazis only to the funds of Holocaust victims are hurtful to persons of other nationalities affected by Fascism, detract from the matter and can only lead to the proliferation and intensification of anti-Semitic feeling in different States, something which we, reminded of the *Führer's* zoological anti-Semitism and its tragic consequences for Germany, Europe and the entire world, can under no circumstances allow to happen. We therefore call for practical advice, sober assessments and realistic practical measures.

FOURTHLY: So that the distribution of "Nazi gold" does not turn into the immoral hunt for riches (thousands of millions of dollars are at issue), so that it does not lead to the outbreak of unwanted negative emotions and extremist feeling and does not detract from the normal work of the institutions entrusted with implementing the decisions reached in London, the following points are to be determined clearly and unambiguously, taking historical facts and the norms of international law as the starting point:

* *Account holders, i.e. the accused.* These may include the accounts opened at Swiss and at some other banks after the beginning of World War II. These accounts have not been called for thus far. The group of defendants will be determined in this way: they will include the state structures of Germany and its allies and trading partners as well as the legal and natural persons of those States;

* *Claimants for funds, i.e. applicants.* These are the States which belonged to the anti-Hitler coalition and the legal and natural persons (irrespective of nationality) of those States;

* *Claim period.* This means the period from the beginning of the war till the end of the national economy's reconstruction, period of imprisonment and period of forced labour, duration of medical treatment after the war, period of general and professional training – for juveniles;

* *Group of defendants (account holders) in respect of natural persons (claimants, applicants).* This is the state structures of Germany and its allies and trading partners as well as the legal and natural persons of those States;

* *Origins of the deposits made by the account holders (defendants).* This concerns the realisation of the appropriated assets, the profit gained from the operation of those assets, profit made from the exploitation of the work of natural persons (applicants), confiscation from natural persons (applicants) of personal items of property (foreign currency, shares, bills of exchange, jewellery, works of art), the exploitation of precious metals after the death or extermination of natural persons (applicants);

* *Principles of the distribution of bank deposits.* Bank deposits whose origins are verified in documentation are handed over to their rightful owners or to their heirs. Deposits whose origins cannot be verified are distributed in proportion to the period of imprisonment and forced labour.

We are making this statement in advance on behalf of the victims of Nazism – the citizens of Belarus, Kazakhstan, Latvia, Lithuania, Moldavia, Russia, Uzbekistan, Ukraine, Estonia, the Members of the International Union of Juvenile Prisoners of Fascist Concentration Camps – to the States taking part in the special international conference in London to determine the future of the riches looted by the "Third *Reich*".

ISRAEL

Bobby Brown's Speech

The Holocaust cries out as one of the most horrific events in human history. It culminated in a thousand years of hatred toward the people who taught the world to believe in one G–d. We are chilled by the barbarism of the perpetrators, the indifference of the bystanders and the apathy of governments great and small.

By the late 1930s life had become untenable for the thousands of Jews of Central Europe. The only question was where could they go? What country would admit the Jews of Germany – Jews whose roots could be traced back over 1,600 years?

In the summer of 1938, the hopes of our people rose as the world convened a conference to discuss the plight of refugees. The delegates met in the French spa of Evian to determine the fate of millions of Jewish men, women and children. While there was sympathy for the Jews there was no compassion. No country was ready to grant sanctuary to more than a handful. It was at Evian that the entire world learned that Hitler was not mistaken when he claimed: "No one wants the Jews."

"We on our part," declared the Fuehrer, "are ready to put all these criminals at the disposal of these countries, for all I care, even on luxury liners." But there was no need for the ships. The Jews were not welcome anywhere. The hopes of our people were dashed against the reality of indifference.

Golda Meir, who would one day become prime minister of the as yet unborn Jewish state, was present at the refugee conference and described what she witnessed:

> Sitting there in that magnificent hall and listening to the delegates of thirty-two countries rise, each in turn, to explain how much they would have liked to take in substantial numbers of refugees and how unfortunate it was that they were not able to do so, was a terrible experience. I felt sorrow, rage and frustration.

But the sorrow, rage and frustration moved no-one. No country was willing to grant the Jews sanctuary. The doors were slammed shut. The Jews of Europe were left to their fate, including members of my own family. Miraculously, my mother and grandmother succeeded in fleeing Germany at the last possible moment. In February 1940, they were among the last refugees to get out of Germany. They were allowed to escape – with their lives and with 10 Reichmarks.

Here is my mother's passport. It is branded with the letter "J" that the Swiss police persuaded their German neighbors to stamp on the passports of German

Jews. It was often the presence of this "J" in a refugee's passport that meant the difference between admission or rejection – between life and death. The "J" that yesterday stood for "Jude", today, as in the days of Dreyfus, stands for "J'accuse"!

Great Britain, committed by the League of Nations to facilitate the creation of the Jewish National Home, enacted the infamous White Paper, closing the door to significant Jewish immigration, sealing the fate of the Jews of Europe.

Recently we have learned the magnitude of the theft which accompanied the slaughter. Theft by individuals and governments – from the lowliest peasant to the loftiest banker. A suitcase, a dozen gold coins, a factory or synagogue, even the Torah – the scrolls of Law – the spiritual heritage of a thousand years of Jewish life in Europe. Looted!

Before his death, the Polish Jewish underground leader Mordechai Tenenbaum-Taroff reported, "Today every peasant woman has Jewish jewelry, a Jewish piano and furniture from Jewish salons." But who could have imagined that governments would seize the opportunity to profit from the six million Jews who were brutally murdered.

Sixty years have elapsed since Evian. The nations of the world have again gathered, this time in London. We cannot turn the clock back. We cannot erase from history the fact that the first shot fired by the British Navy in World War II was aimed not at the Nazi enemy, but across the bow of a rusty boat filled with Jews fleeing the Nazis. We cannot bring back the six million innocents – one and a half million of them children – whose lives were not considered worth saving.

Nothing can compensate for the loss of ⅓ of our people and the systematic attempt to annihilate our culture. But here we *can* demonstrate that times have changed since Evian; that we are living in a better world; that hatred and apathy have given way to humanity and compassion.

Give us back our heritage. Give us back our history. Give us the justice that was for so long denied.

Speech of MK Avraham Hirschenson

More than 35 years ago the security service of the State of Israel tracked down one of the architects of the so-called Final Solution – the sinister plan to destroy the Jewish people. Israel brought that beast – Adolf Otto Eichmann – to Jerusalem, the capital of the State of Israel and the spiritual heart of the Jewish people. The capture and trial of Eichmann reminded the world – a world that wished to forgive and forget – that the Jewish people would do neither. The Holocaust could not be swept away.

Eichmann's defense attorney claimed that the State of Israel had no right to try his client, because it came into existence after Eichmann's crimes were committed, and not on its own soil. The Supreme Court of Israel, however, explained the connection between Israel and the Holocaust. Israel, the Jewish State, which arose out of the ashes of the Holocaust, claimed the judges, is the heir to the Jewish people of Europe who had not lived to see the dawn of redemption. Moreover, had the German armies reached the land of Israel, the Jews then living in the Holy Land would have shared the fate of their brethren in Europe. The world recognized then as it does today that the connection between Israel and the Holocaust cannot be ruptured.

Over the course of the last 50 years Israel absorbed the largest number of Holocaust survivors. Hundreds of thousands of survivors of camps and ghettos, of struggles in the partisans; those who lived on false papers; those who survived thanks to non-Jewish neighbours or in spite of them – found homes in the State of Israel. That absorption process was far from painless. The survivors generally arrived with nothing but anguished memories of the torment to which they were subjected … of families gone without a trace … and above all a determination to build a secure home for their children.

Most arrived in the midst of Israel's struggle for independence and many of them gave their lives to ensure it existence. Not a few of those survivors died on the battlefield and their names were lost to posterity. All we remember is the numbers branded on their arms…

It is on their behalf – on behalf of these "brands that plucked from the fire" – on behalf of their children, and grandchildren, proud citizens of the Jewish State – that I speak to you this evening.

More than 50 years have passed since the collapse of Nazi Germany and the breakdown of the machinery that destroyed one third of the Jewish people. Yet only now – and not voluntarily – has the world begun to turn inward – to reflect not only on the enormity of the crime and the extent of their participation in it – by omission or commission – but also on the extent to which justice was done after the guns fell silent and the smoke had cleared.

How quickly life returned to "normal" – as if their could be a "normal life" after the systematic, cold-blooded murder of six million men, women and children!

But let us not forget that the Shoah went beyond the murder of six million innocents – people whose only crime was that they were Jews. The Shoah was also the most sinister, cynical and grand act of larceny the world has ever known. And here one recalls the burning words of the scriptures: "Thou has murdered and also inherited!"

All over Europe, Jewish assets, great and small, were plundered not just by the Germans and their henchmen who carried out the murders, but also by greedy opportunists who saw the slaughter of their neighbors as an unprecedented occasion to enrich themselves. Indeed, El Dorado was brought to cities and towns throughout Europe. Houses, synagogues, factories, workshops, furniture, tools, a myriad of items both sacred and secular – the wealth of an entire people accumulated over the course of centuries of toil.

Even that did not satisfy the rapacious hyenas bent on spoil. Even the bodies of the victims were not wasted. Vast quantities of hair and gold teeth were "harvested" for the benefit of the killers. Tellingly in the Majdanek Camp – the bath water of the crematorium operator was heated by bodies being burned in the furnaces!

Neutral countries which were spared the horror of war – countries in which life went on undisturbed – were prepared to dispense with any moral considerations and to fence this ill-gotten gain. While Jewish children were being gassed and burned, the vaults of the so-called neutrals were being swelled with gold and other valuables.

When the dust had cleared and the remnant returned to their hometowns, if anyone survived they were greeted in the best cases with cold indifference and in the worst cases open hostility. Could they be blamed for having survived? Those that dared to claim their property were treated not with sympathy but like creatures who had cheated fate and had crawled out of the abyss. How dare they survive! "How much more comfortable would it have been had nobody lived to bear witness and perhaps seek the return of what was theirs." What they had earned by the sweat of their brows. That was the full mead of compassion the Jews received from their neighbors. And make no mistake, this was the reaction of people not in any one country but across the breadth of Europe.

Those survivors, busy with getting about putting together the pieces of their lives, did not have the energy or self-confidence to pursue the struggle to recover their property, and how can anyone blame them? It took 50 years for the issue to appear on our agenda. But appear it has and these survivors of the survivors cannot be put off any longer. As they come to the end of their earthly journey, justice and decency demand that their claims be satisfied. No matter how uncomfortable or awkward their presence is, they cannot be fobbed off.

There are those beneficiaries of stolen property who hope that time will solve the problem. Most of the survivors are in their 80s and 90s. In the corridors of banks, insurance companies and even government offices, there is a feeling that "If we wait long enough – if we prevaricate and procrastinate – time will solve the problem."

No, time will not solve the problem. I pledge to you that we will not rest, we will not tarry, until justice is done and these people are given their due. Justice and decency – even if it is 50 years in coming – demands nothing less. Rabbi Nachman of Bratslav, a great Jewish spiritual leader, wrote: "Even the hardest rock will yield to those who drill with determination." We will drill with that determination and the rock of deception and complacency will yield. Before our very eyes it has begun to crumble...

We are not here to carry out an exercise in bookkeeping. That will be done in due time, as it should be. The economists and the historians will chronicle and debate the magnitude of the robbery – how much was stolen from whom, where and when. But this gathering is not about the sums. It is about justice and morality. And above all it is for future generations.

Every year thousands of Jewish youth from all over the world come to visit the sites of the death camps as a part of the March of the Living. When I initiated that program, over 10 years ago, my objective was not only to teach these young people about their past but to give them hope for the future. Will we be able to look these youngsters in the face and tell them that we have done everything to right this historic wrong? The answer depends on us.

Speech by Nili Arad
on behalf of the Israeli delegation

On behalf of the Israeli delegation, I would like to convey our most sincere thanks and appreciation to the British Government for hosting this historic conference.

We would like to express our deep gratitude to Secretary of State, Mr Robin Cook, whose personal involvement enabled this conference to be convened. Furthermore, we extend our heartfelt thanks to Lord Janner who has been the initiator and driving force behind this important event.

Mr Chairman, the State of Israel was founded in the aftermath of the Holocaust as a national home for the Jewish people, a haven for the victims and survivors of the Holocaust, the greatest human tragedy.

Therefore, this conference is of the utmost importance to the State of Israel and Jewish people all over the world. In many ways, this conference is the fulfillment of the vow we made to the victims of the Holocaust. Their legacy is our firm resolution that the world should know and never forget the atrocities inflicted upon them in body and soul.

Mr Chairman, allow me to thank you personally for the diligence with which you have led the presentations and discussions on such an important, complex and painful matter. We were comforted by the discovery that the Conference feels a sense of obligation to face the whole truth as a pre-condition to the next steps, painful as this may be. In that respect, the tragedy inflicted upon the Jewish people by the Nazi regime has taken its rightful place in history at this conference too. For this we thank you all.

Accordingly, from today, we propose that the goal and outcome of this conference should be to open all archives, unlock the bolted doors of the past and allow history to write the last pages of its darkest years. We suggest mutual and co-ordinated actions by all governments concerned, with no exception. Our goal should be to establish an information centre in which all the historical knowledge accumulated will become common knowledge to mankind, as it is discovered.

In addition to opening archives to public scrutiny, we suggest at this time and moment that the remainder of the looted gold should be returned to its rightful owners. In that respect, too, we should never forget the survivors who are alive today, people who were robbed of their families, their youth, their health, their property and their dignity; individuals and communities alike.

In this respect, the State of Israel supports the World Jewish Restitution Organisation in their activities, both as a result of this conference and their bilateral endeavours to gain compensation for the property stolen from the Jews.

Over the last three days of this conference, it has been established that at the signing of the Washington Accord in 1946, between the Allies and Switzerland, not all the relevant facts were revealed and known. However, now it is obvious that at the time Switzerland did not disclose vital information, taking advantage of the prevailing climate of the time in order to achieve its own economic goals, without taking into account the moral aspects of the issue. The time is right to re-open the discussions concerning the Accord that was established in Washington, in order to ensure that Holocaust victims, survivors, legitimate heirs and the Jewish people as a whole are entitled to their rightful share of the looted gold.

We are sure that each and every one of you in this room has learnt about the gold treasures that were looted from the Jewish communities, from the victims of the Holocaust and extracted from the bodies of the victims of Treblinka, Majdanek, Auschwitz and the other concentration camps.

Mr Chairman, on behalf of the Government of Israel and, if I may suggest, on behalf of all of us gathered here today, we would like to pay tribute to the Righteous Among the Nations, the few who gave shelter and life to persecuted Jews during the Holocaust. The few just and outstanding people across Europe who risked their lives and those of their families and never forgot the essence of humanity. These people were islands of hope and life for children, women and men in their struggle for survival.

Where there is love and compassion, there is hope. We will never forget and will forever remember and be grateful to those Righteous People Among the Nations.

I would like to conclude with the words of Chaim Nachman Bialik, our national poet. In his poem "On the Slaughter", written after the Kishniev Pogroms:
"Im Yesh Tzedek, Yufa Miyadi"
(If there is justice, let it show itself at once.)

ITALY

The story of the gold deposited at the Bank of Italy (1943–58)[1]

THE TRANSFER OF THE GOLD RESERVES FROM ROME TO MILAN

In September 1943, immediately following the Armistice, the German military command in Rome ordered the transfer of the Bank of Italy's gold reserves to the North in order to keep it out of the hands of the Allies, who appeared about to advance in central Italy. With no power to resist the German demands,[2] the Bank was forced to organize the transfer of all the gold held in the vault of the Cashier's Department at its Head Office[3] to the Milan regional office.

For technical reasons, the gold was shipped in two stages on 22 and 28 September and stored in the vault of the Milan office under the full control of the Bank.

The gold included:

- fine bars (more than .900 fine) each containing an average of 12 kg of fine gold;
- .900 fine bars with the same average fine content as above;
- smaller bars of widely varying dimensions made of resmelted gold from coins and gold objects, some of which also contained a percentage of silver;
- coins of various fineness and type (some of which were recorded by weight and some by piece).[4]

The gold transferred from the Cashier's Department included gold owned by the Bank (89,072.021418 kg)[5] and a number of other consignments deposited in the Bank's vaults. In particular, the Bank held gold as collateral for a loan to the National Foreign Exchange Institute (INCE – Istituto Nazionale Cambi con l'Estero, sometimes referred to in the documentation as 1st Cambi) from the Swiss National Bank (SNB); gold held in the name of the Bank for International Settlements (BIS); gold owned by the Royal Mint;[6] gold deposited by the Ministry of Trade and Foreign Exchange and gold held on behalf of INCE.[7]

The breakdown of the gold shipments is given in Table 1 (compiled using the procedures and sources outlined in the "methodological note"), which summarizes all gold movements between September 1943 and May 1945. The table shows shipments of a total of 626 boxes of bars and 543 sacks of coins. The total amount of fine gold shipped to Milan was 119,251.967623 kg.

THE TRANSFER OF THE RESERVES FROM MILAN TO FORTEZZA

At the end of 1943 the Germans demanded that the gold be moved out of Milan, citing the poor security of the Milan site in the case of bombardment. An armoured tunnel inside a military fort in the town of Fortezza in Alto Adige was selected as the most appropriate secure site.

The transfer, which involved all the gold that had been moved from Rome to Milan, began on 16 December and the gold was placed at the Fortezza tunnel on 18 and 19 December. The Bank of Italy's Historical Archive contains two documents recording the two stages of the operation, the first of which was drafted in Milan, the second in Fortezza. The documents are copies and give the number of boxes (626) and sacks (543) transferred. They only record the *gross* weight, including the *tare*, of the boxes (110,239.1 kg) and the sacks (36,598.1). The Milan document makes reference to the duplicate consignment lists (which have not survived) that accompanied the shipments, while the Fortezza document notes that the weight given was that declared by the Bank's Cashier's Department.[8]

The number of containers sent to Fortezza exactly corresponds to the number taken from the vaults in Rome in September.

Confirmation of the transfer of *all* the gold from Milan to Fortezza is provided by the 10-day reports of the Bolzano branch, which recorded the gold shipments received from Milan. Comparing the report for 10 December 1943 (prior to the beginning of the transfer) with that of 20 December (immediately following the shipment), there is an increase in the item comprising gold reserves and certain other deposits, while the same items in the Milan reports show a corresponding decrease.[9]

It is important to emphasize that the gold transferred to Fortezza remained the property of the Bank of Italy, which continued to record the metal in its own accounts[10] even though physical control of the metal was exercised jointly the German authorities and Bank officials.[11] In order to exercise more effective control over the reserves, the Bank established a full-fledged agency in Fortezza; nevertheless, the German command could have entered the armoured tunnel without the knowledge of the agency's staff.

THE FIRST SHIPMENT TO BERLIN

On 5 February 1944 an agreement between Germany and the Italian Social Republic* was signed in Fasano making "the entire amount of gold owned by the Bank of Italy available to the Ambassador and Plenipotentiary of Greater Germany in Italy".[13] The document also provided for the immediate delivery of gold totalling 141,000,000 Reichsmarks (RM) as "a contribution to the joint war effort".[14] The terms of this clause were fulfilled with an initial shipment of gold bars and coins to Berlin at the end of February.

---

* The *de facto* government,[12] headed by Mussolini and supported by the German occupying forces, was founded in Northern Italy in December 1943, three days after the armistice between the Kingdom of Italy of the Allies. At the time, the Kingdom controlled the southern part of the country.

Based on the fine gold content of the German gold mark (0.358423 g), the amount of gold to be moved was 50,537.643 kg, and this was in fact the amount recorded in the shipment list made out at Fortezza on 29 February 1944.[15] The same amount was reported by the Governor to the Bank's Board of Directors the following April[16] and the corresponding value was entered in the accounting forms. In reality, however, the amount actually shipped was significantly less: 49,634.659630 kg (see the methodological note to Table 1 for the calculation of this amount).

It is not easy to explain the difference of nearly 900 kg between the amount shown in the accounts and that effectively shipped. According to a report drafted in April 1945 by the Bank's Financial Operations and Foreign Exchange Department,[17] the Germans were deliberately given inflated figures in an attempt to save at least part of the gold.

While plausible,[18] the hypothesis does not explain the absence in official documents of any protest from Berlin regarding the discrepancy in the amount delivered and that recorded at Fortezza. The fact that the shipment list explicitly provided for verification of the consignment's fine gold content makes this lack of response all the stranger.

According to a memorandum drafted in the sixties by Paolo Carlo Dalla Torre,[19] an employee of the Bank of Italy who had a direct role in the events, the German authorities did remonstrate after the metal was weighed in Berlin: nevertheless, there is no trace of these complaints in the available documentation.

We must also bear in mind the difficulty of establishing the precise amount of gold to ship owing to the lack of information shown on the boxes and sacks. The director of the Bolzano branch, Fortunato Gigli, reporting to Azzolini on 2 March that the gold had been shipped, emphasized that "in the absence of any indication on the wrappings, the quantity of gold to ship was jointly agreed by Dr. Bernhuber[20] and myself as 435 sacks and 175 boxes, with any positive or negative adjustments to be made following verification in Berlin".[21]

THE SHIPMENT OF GOLD TO SWITZERLAND

On 20 April 1944 a second shipment of gold left Fortezza, this time headed for Switzerland. The shipment involved two consignments of gold being sent in settlement of debts owed by Italian agencies to banks operating in Switzerland.

The debt with the SNB arose out of a loan made on 2 September 1940 to INCE by a pool of Swiss banks,[22] while the gold deposited in the name of the BIS was held as collateral for the portfolio discount operations of the Consorzio Sovvenzioni su Valori Industriali with the BIS.

The SNB and the BIS had already asked the Bank of Italy to transfer the gold[23] at the end of 1943. The German authorities, who had a strong interest in maintaining access to the Swiss market for their foreign exchange and trade needs, allowed the transfer. In a number of documents drafted by Azzolini during this period,[24] the Governor emphasized that he had intervened with the German authorities, who exercised *de facto* control over the activities of the

Italian Social Republic, to make the shipment possible, arguing that honouring such debts would safeguard Italy's international creditworthiness. The gold was transferred by rail via Chiasso on 20 April 1944.

Two consignments were transferred: the first went to the SNB and totalled 10,784.052293 kg. extinguishing the debt in full; the second represented partial repayment of the loan and amounted to 12,604.72793 kg. The gold required to complete repayment (3,189.877656 kg) was drawn directly from Italian gold held at the BIS.[25] A total of 163 boxes containing 23,388.780223 kg of fine gold were shipped.[26]

On 27 April the BIS sent Azzolini a letter acknowledging receipt of the 89 boxes of gold and informing him of the verification that was then under way, expressing appreciation for the Bank's efforts to fulfil its international obligations despite the extremely difficult conditions.[27] The following day the SNB sent a similar letter acknowledging the arrival of the other 74 boxes.[28]

THE SECOND SHIPMENT TO BERLIN

The February 1944 shipment of gold to Germany was not sufficient to meet the demands of the Germans, who sought to gain control over the Bank's entire reserve, as provided for in the Fasano agreement.[29] In response to repeated requests from the Germans, a temporary compromise was reached that limited the shipment to RM 60 million, the equivalent of 21,505.380000 kg of fine gold.[30]

The consignment was shipped on 21 October. The Bank's Historical Archives possess the records for the shipment drafted at Fortezza,[31] which do not show the overall weight of the gold moved, indicating only the number of boxes (135) and sacks (53).

According to calculations based on the available documentation and the method described in the methodological note to Table 1, the amount of fine gold actually transferred to Germany with this consignment was equal to 21,463.351183 kg.

The amount entered in the records was significantly higher in this case as well, equal to 21,656.17917 kg of fine gold.[32] The latter figure was also reported by the Governor at the Annual General Meeting for 1944.[33] As with the previous shipment, the Germans reserved the right to verify the gold content and the Bank of Italy does not hold any documents mentioning a request for compensation.

The figure of 71,098.010813 kg for the two Fortezza consignments to Berlin in 1944 is also confirmed by a detailed list of the gold shipped on those occasions. The document is an original giving the identification number, content and fine weight of each box and sack.[34]

THE GOLD IN GERMANY

The Bank of Italy's archives contain two sources that describe what happended to the Italian gold once it left Italy. The first is the Dalla Torre memoir mentioned earlier, while the second is the translation of a memorandum sent to the Bank of Italy in the spring of 1957 by Herbert Herzog,[35] an Austrian citizen who some years earlier had helped recover a consignment of Italian gold hidden in Austria and later included in the gold pool (see Appendix B).

It must be emphasized that neither document is official; the Dalla Torre report was drafted when, as mentioned, its author had already retired, while the Herzog note is a non-Bank of Italy source and although the writer appears to be well-informed about the Italian gold, the information provided on Italian gold reserves in Germany cannot be verified through other Bank of Italy documentation.

As regards the *first shipment* in February 1944, both sources agree in stating that much of the gold was acquired by the Reichsbank, excepting 135 sacks of coins, equal to 7 tons of fine gold, which were taken by the German Foreign Ministry as soon as the gold arrived at the Berlin railway station. The Ministry's action apparently took the Reichsbank officials by surprise and Dalla Torre's account reports their disapproval.

The coins contained in the 135 sacks (*deposited at the Foreign Ministry*) were verified in part in the presence of Dalla Torre. He described in detail the condition of the sacks and notes that once the contents had been verified, the seals and identification tags affixed by the Bank of Italy were placed inside the sacks. The Reichsbank inspectors then marked the sacks with their own numbers before handing them over to the Foreign Ministry.

The gold held at the Reichsbank was verified in the presence of Dalla Torre, who then returned to Italy. As mentioned earlier, there is no trace of any German complaint about the amount of gold shipped.

The primary source of information on the *second shipment* of gold is the Herzog memorandum, as Dalla Torre's report does not provide any significant news, saying only that he was present when the gold content was verified before returning to Fortezza.

According to the Herzog memorandum, the gold in the second consignment was all stored at the Reichsbank, which recorded it in a number of accounts.

The document also gives information on subsequent events regarding the Italian gold. In particular:

- one lot was delivered between 3 and 26 October 1944 to the Prussian Mint for resmelting. The consignment comprised 1607 bars from the gold owned by the Bank of Italy. The document also claimed that 3.4687 kg of gold were lost in the smelting process.
- resmelted gold, together with other bars from the first shipment and 300 sacks of coins (the coins from the first shipment that remained after the Foreign Ministry had removed the sacks at the Berlin railway station) were held in a deposit labelled "German Foreign Ministry Deposit – Italian gold I";
- the INCE gold consignment was held separate from the others;
- the coins and bars of the second shipment were held in a deposit labelled as "German Foreign Ministry Deposit – Italian gold II";
- a consignment of gold with a value of RM 10 million was held on behalf of the Italian embassy in Berlin.[36]

At the beginning of 1945 all the Italian gold was moved from Berlin. The gold acquired by the German Foreign Ministry was divided into two lots; one consignment of about 5 tons was hidden in Austria, while the remainder, about 2 tons, was shipped to Schleswig-Holstein. The gold held at the Reichsbank (about 64 tons of fine gold) was sent to the Merkers salt mine together with other gold, property and valuables looted by the Germans from other countries during the course of the war.

The gold hidden in Austria was recovered and erroneously delivered to the Allies at the Austrian National Bank. At the beginning of the 1950s, following Herzog's report, Italy made a claim for the gold, which was sent to the gold pool for distribution among the claimant countries. According to the Herzog document, the gold coins hidden in Schleswig-Holstein were handed over to the British Army and presumably transferred to the gold pool. The Merkers gold was discovered by the Allied forces in April 1945 and included in the gold pool.

THE DISCOVERY OF THE REMAINING GOLD AT FORTEZZA

In the first half of May 1945, just after the end of the war, the Allies returned the gold remaining at Fortezza, which had never left the control of the Bank of Italy.[37] The gold consisted of 153 boxes of bars and 55 sacks of coins, which were transferred to the Bank in Rome under Allied escort on 17 May. On 24 May the gold was inspected and the contents verified.[38] The boxes recovered also included those of the Ministry for Trade and Foreign Exchange and the 13 containers of the gold belonging to the Royal Mint, whose weight had never been verified by the Bank of Italy. The seals were unbroken on all of the boxes save one, whose contents were nevertheless intact. The inspection report gives the numbers of the sacks and boxes and the fine weight of the two sorts of gold, which had been verified in the original shipment lists from 1943. The gold owned by the Bank of Italy amounted to 22,941.224274 kg of fine gold (19,618.724018 kg in bars and 3,322.502569 kg in coins). To this can be added the gold belonging to the Ministry of Trade and Foreign Exchange (146.950000 kg) and the Mint (1,677.000000 kg).

On 13 October two coins that had not been noticed at the time the rest of the Fortezza gold was returned to Rome were found in a crack in the tunnel floor.[39]

The gold recovered at Fortezza totalled 24,765.176587 kg, which is exactly the difference between the amount of gold that entered in December 1943 after the shipment from Milan and the amount sent to Germany and Switzerland in 1944.

Once it had arrived in Rome, the gold was held in a vault at the Bank of Italy under the control of the Allied command. On 15 October 1947[40] the Bank of Italy regained possession of the gold after the Allies had confirmed that the gold was in fact owned by the Bank of Italy and have never left the country.[41]

That same year the Dutch government made a claim against the gold that had just been returned, stating that the Italian reserves contained gold looted by the Germans during the occupation of the Netherlands. The dispute lasted a number of years and ended with the rejection of the Dutch claim (see Appendix C).

THE REQUEST FOR RESTITUTION FROM THE GOLD POOL

The Tripartite Commission for the Restitution of Monetary Gold was established in 1946 to handle the return of gold to countries whose reserves had been looted by the Germans. The Commission, commonly called the Tripartite Gold Commission (TGC), had access to a quantity of gold known as the " gold pool", part of which consisted of gold discovered in Germany and part (about $60 million) from German deposits in Switzerland whose probable origin was countries occupied by the Nazis during the war. The gold in the pool was deposited at the Bank of England, the Bank of France and the Federal Reserve Bank of New York.

Since the amount of gold available was much less than the total claims of the countries seeking restitution, the TGC decided to base its allocation on the principle of compensation rather than full restitution, with the gold to be distributed in proportion to the recipient countries' losses.

Italy was initially excluded from the list of recipient countries as it was not a signatory country of the Paris Reparations Agreement, but after negotiations it was admitted in December 1947.

Italy had already been requested at the beginning of 1947 to complete the so-called "gold questionnaire" as the basis for its claim on pool assets, which totalled 71,098.009211 kg of fine gold, of which 69,320.7 kg belonged to the Bank of Italy and 1,777.3 kg to INCE.[42]

It is important to emphasize that the amount of gold claimed did not correspond to the amount recorded for the two Berlin shipments but rather the amount actually shipped to Germany. An annex to the questionnaire describing the movement of the reserves attributes the difference to unspecified "subsequent inspections" without providing any explanation for the inaccuracy of the accounting records.[43]

The difference between the official claim and the amount sent to Berlin as calculated using the methods described in the methodological note to Table 1 (71,098.010813 kg), equal to 0.001602 kg, is probably due to rounding or the loss of a few coins in transit.[44]

The restitution was to be carried in several stages; first, each country's claim on the gold pool was examined and its legitimacy determined. Once the claim was accepted, the gold was returned in two phases, the theoretical allocation and the actual restitution.

Following the TGC's decision on a claim, the theoretical allocation was notified to the recipient country and the gold to meet the claim was set aside in account in the name of the recipient until delivery could be made. Any disputes between the recipient country and other claimants were adjudicated during this stage.

In most cases, more than one allocation was made to each country owing to subsequent acquisitions of looted gold by the gold pool, which then became available for restitution.

Actual restitution occurred with the physical transfer of the gold from the pool to the recipient country.

ALLOCATIONS BY THE POOL

Italy claim was judged legitimate; in fact, even before it was officially admitted to the gold pool the TGC had set aside 3,805.318200 kg of gold to meet future Italian claims.[45] In April 1948 the Governor of the Bank of Italy was informed of another allocation of 27,862.210300 kg of gold.[46]

Italy renounced its claim of to the actual restitution of 1,777.3 kg in relation to INCE's gold in return for a payment of $3,021,120 (see Appendix C).[47]

In 1958 Italy was allocated a further 12,749.965168 kg of gold[48] (for a summary of the gold allocations to Italy, see Table 2), the last such allocation it has received.

The total allocations made so far to Italy amount to 46,194.822994 kg, of which 44,417.484668 kg belonging to the Bank of Italy and 1,777.33829 kg belonging to INCE, equal to 64.97 per cent of Italy's initial claim (71,098.009211 kg).[49] This percentage is in line with that received by the other claimant nations. The amount of the claim that has not been met to date is equal to 24,903.186217 kg, or 35.03 per cent (see Table 2).

THE RESTITUTION OF GOLD TO ITALY

The material restitution of the gold to Italy by the gold pool took place in two tranches (see Table 2).

In 1949 the Bank of Italy received 11,370.906765 kg of fine gold, which arrived from London in six successive shipments between 17 and 24 October.[50]

The amount of gold actually delivered to Italy did not correspond to the total amount allocated up to 1949 (31,667.519500 kg, sum of the first two allocations), since Italy had been required to return French and Yugoslav gold that had entered Italy between 1941 and 1942. The French gold originated in a shipment from the Vichy government to Italy, whereas the Yugoslav gold had been taken to Italy as "war booty". Both amounts were included in the reserves in 1942[51]. As a result, 14,421.5 kg[52] of fine gold was set aside for France and 8,393 kg[53] were set aside for Yugoslavia out of the Italian allocation.

However, Yugoslavia subsequently renounced its claim for restitution to 30 per cent of the gold (2,517.9 kg) in exchange for Italy's opening a lira account of equivalent value in Yugoslavia's name. The amount of gold actually returned to Yugoslavia was therefore equal to 5,875.1 kg. The amount of the first restitution was therefore the result of the difference between the 1947–48 allocations (31,667.519500 kg) and the gold set aside on behalf of France and Yugolslavia (20,296.612735 kg).

Italy took delivery of the second allocation of gold (12,749.965168 kg) in three separate shipments in August 1958.[54]

Appendix A

Other movements of gold at Bank of Italy branches during the war

Following the Armistice, there remained small quantities of gold in some of the Bank's branches besides that kept in the vaults in Rome. It should be emphasised that none of these deposits was acquired by the German authorities. Documents held in the Historical Archives confirm the existence of a number of deposits on both Italian and colonial premises.

A report of gold shipments during the war drawn up in December 1944 shows the quantities held in some of the Bank's colonial branches (Addis Ababa, Asmara, Aseb, Benghazi, Massawa, Mogadishu, Rhodes), for an overall total of 136.863353 kg of fine gold[55]. The quantities and whereabouts of gold kept in the colonies is confirmed in a letter from Introna to De Gasperi, then Minister for Foreign Affairs, informing him of the existence of these small deposits for the purposes of notifying the Allies[56].

Documents reporting the state of the reserves as of 1 June 1944 show that small quantities of gold were also held in Bologna and Modena, and that a further amount was on its way from Milan to Turin[57].

Little is known of the gold held in Bologna, except that it consisted of bars and sovereigns weighing 51.131179 kg belonging to the Bank. Nothing is known of the date on which the gold was deposited or of its provenance.

Information concerning the gold held in Modena is more precise; a shipment from Rome of gold consisting of coins, bars, assorted pieces and objects for a value of Itl. 999,562.94 (46.747875 kg of fine gold) had been announced as imminent in April. It has so far not been possible to ascertain either the actual date this consignment arrived or its further destination. A document from July 1944 describing this lot bears a pencil note datable to mid-1946 that "Modena has shipped it to Milan", while a document of October 1944 drawn up by the branch refers to it under a list headed "monetary gold, gold bars, objects and scrap to be sent to A.C. – Servizi Monetari Bergamo…"[58]

Information relating to the gold held by the Milan branch is more substantial and confirms the efforts of some Bank employees to defend the reserves threatened by the Germans. This lot consisted of about 517,588.179 kg (it is not specified whether this was the gross or fine weight) of gold belonging to the Bank and entered in the accounts as reserves, and 156,125.800 kg of gold belonging to third parties. During the night of 7–8 September 1943, the two lots were hidden in a well on the order of the Branch Manager, Scorza, in consideration of the imminence of the Armistice and probable German reprisals. In order to show that the gold had been moved, a report was drawn up "….intentionally undated……" showing that the gold had been shipped to the Turin branch and was therefore en route to that city. The intention of the Bank's employees was that, should the German authorities order the handing over of reserves (an order that in the event never came) the report could have been duly completed with the addition of a date immediately prior to the order, thereby, explaining the gold's non-arrival at destination.[59]

Another consignment of gold was shipped from Fiume to the Cashier's Department at the Rome Head Office via the Ancona branch. Documents held by the Historical Archives show that the gold held in Fiume had mostly been deposited for safekeeping by the Prefecture of Carnaro-Civilian Administration of annexed territories. On 11 September the Fiume branch of the Bank forwarded the consignment of coins, one bar and some "wrought objects" to Ancona. From Ancona the gold was taken to Teramo and from there to Rome, where it was taken in charge by the Cashier's Department on

10 November 1943. Some gold coins purchased officially by the Fiume branch were entered in the accounts, and the remaining gold, for a value of Itl.1[60], was placed in a "T" deposit.

Appendix B

Italian gold discovered in Austria and Schleswig-Holstein

At the beginning of the fifties the Bank of Italy was informed by an Austrian citizen named Herbert Herzog of the discovery in 1945 of a consignment of about 5 tons of Italian gold in Austrian territory. The informant maintained that the origins of the gold had been unequivocally recognized by the Allied forces that had recovered it, but that it had nonetheless been consigned to the Austrian National Bank without the gold pool being involved.

According to the information supplied by Herzog, the gold was part of the consignment forwarded by rail from Fortezza in February 1944 and, specifically, the lot held at the German Ministry for Foreign Affairs (see Section 6), which totalled 135 sacks.[61]

In July 1944 the Ministry forwarded 38 of those sacks to the Reichsbank to be verified, after which the coins were sealed in 368 bags. On their return to the Ministry, these bags were packed into sacks.

In November of the same year the Ministry sent another 15 sacks to the Reichsbank for verification, but these coins were not returned to the Ministry; instead, they were kept at the Reichsbank in a deposit marked "Number 5, German Min-Foreign Affairs 2126g 44". Together with all the other Italian gold kept at the Reichsbank, they were transferred in 1945 to the Merkers salt mine.

The remaining 82 sacks were kept in their original packing and were never verified.

The coins kept at the Foreign Ministry (368 bags of German origin and 82 sacks of Italian origin) were transferred in 1945 on Ribbentrop's orders.

Specifically:

- the 368 bags were taken to Schleswig-Holstein, where they were buried in three crates. Following the arrival of the British troops the person to whom the gold had been entrusted, the wife of the Minister, Mai, reported their presence, the gold was dug up and its Italian origins acknowledged. It was then presumably consigned to the gold pool.
- the 82 sacks were transferred by the Ministry and taken in charge in Austria by a German diplomat, Gottfriedsen. At the end of April, 81 sacks, sealed in two crates, were buried at Hintersee, in Austrian territory. The eighty-second sack had broken during the transfer from Berlin to Austria, and was hidden in a cellar in Badgastein, together with some bags that had fallen out of another of the sacks transferred to Hintersee. In June 1945 the Allies recovered both these lots, containing about 5 tons of fine gold, and they were consigned to representatives of the Austrian National Bank by General Geoffrey Keyes, on instructions from the US government.

Following verification of the accuracy of this information, Italy initiated legal proceedings against Austria; these were concluded some years later and the entire lot of gold was handed over to the TGC.

Appendix C

Claims on gold by Dutch government

In December 1947 the Italian government was handed a *note verbale* by the Dutch government concerning 312 gold bars allegedly stolen by the Germans during their occupation of the Netherlands and subsequently transferred to Italy. The note requested information regarding the quantity of gold and asked if officials from the Dutch central bank could visit the Bank of Italy in order to continue their research into the matter.

Given the vagueness of the request, the initial response from the Italian Ministry for Foreign Affairs was a note denying knowledge of the gold referred to, but admitting the possibility that gold looted by the Germans to augment the resources of their Italian command could have been transferred to Italy without the knowledge of the Italian authorities. The note also affirmed a willingness to allow experts from the Nederlandsche Bank to pursue their enquiries in Italy[62].

In May 1949 the representatives from the Dutch bank arrived in Rome, bringing a list of the bars concerned, their identification numbers, weights and origins. It was thus possible to retrace the movements of the disputed gold, which for various reasons had in fact passed through Italy and a very small part of which was still there.

The 312 bars were divided into two lots:

1. 150 had been taken by the German occupying forces;
2. the remaining 162 had been resmelted by the occupying forces, mostly from confiscated Dutch guilders.

Thanks to the identification numbers, it was possible to ascertain that gold had on various occasions been sent by the Reichsbank to Italy to comply with the German bank's commitments to a number of Italian counterparties.

Specifically:

* 147 bars (all of which formed part of the resmelted gold) had been forwarded in February 1943 by the Reichsbank to INCE and held on the latter's behalf in the vaults of the Bank of Italy. The operation behind the transfer had begun in 1940, when INCE had assigned American banknotes for a total of $7,000,000 to the German embassy in Washington on behalf of the Reichsbank. During 1941 the Reichsbank had on several occasions reimbursed INCE a total of $3,978,880. In January 1942 INCE asked for restitution of the outstanding sum ($3,021,120) in gold and Swiss francs. Initially the German bank did not wish to comply with this request, stating that the residual amount had not been used and was therefore still at the disposal of the INCE at the German embassy in Washington. A smaller operation amounting to $2,000,000, or two thirds of the sum outstanding, was subsequently completed and the equivalent in fine gold – 1,777.338326 kg (at $35/oz. of fine gold) was transferred to Italy by the Reichsbank in the form of 147 bars as an advance against INCE's claim on the German bank for the larger sum of $3,021,120[63].

* 165 bars (including 15 resmelted bars) were sold between 1942 and February 1943 to the Bank of Italy by Consorzio Italiano Aeronautico, which had acquired possession of it as a result of commercial transactions. The Consorzio represented a number of Italian firms that in 1940 and 1941 had supplied the Swedish government against payment in dollars, which were then converted into payment in gold. The Consorzio had been authorized by the Ministry for Trade and Foreign Exchange to trade in gold and the metal had subsequently been sold to the Bank of Italy. The Swedes had used an account in their name with the Reichsbank to

pay the Consorzio. The actual transfer of the gold from Berlin to Rome was completed in several consignments and was handled by Banca Commerciale Italiana, which also handled its sale to the Bank of Italy once the latter had completed the assay procedures.

Nothing in the documents held by the Bank of Italy's Historical Archives suggests that the Bank was aware that the bars involved in both these operations had originally either been taken from the Dutch National Bank or resmelted from coins confiscated from a nation occupied by German troops.

During the visit of the Dutch experts it was possible not only to retrace the events just described, but also to discover the details of the operation to resmelt the Dutch guilder, which became 162 bars. It thus emerged that the Prussian Mint had mixed the coins looted in the Netherlands with a percentage of gold from the "Melmer" account, a gold deposit held by the SS to which gold objects and coins looted from private individuals was directed.

The documents on this subject held by the Bank of Italy's Historical Archives all date from after the end of the war. They include, in particular, a document from 1946, presumably of US origin, drawn up with the help of Albert Thoms, Head of the Precious Metals Department of the Reichsbank and describing the resmelting operation by the Prussian Mint that generated, among others, the bars that were sent to Italy in 1943[64].

According to this document the resmelting operation involved a total of 9,107.1124 kg of fine gold, from which 764 bars were made. Of these, 162 bars, weighing 1,946.1887 kg of fine gold, were sent for various purposes to Italy (see above). The gold transferred to Italy was thus 21.36 per cent of the entire resmelting operation. The vast majority of the gold used for resmelting consisted of Dutch guilders taken by the Germans from the Dutch National Bank. In order to ensure that the final fineness of the resmelted bars was not less than 900/1000, the Prussian Mint added a small quantity of extra fine gold, weighing 40.9126 kg. Of this, 36.9046 kg or 0.4052 per cent of the total came from the Melmer deposit.

It may therefore be presumed that the resmelted bars sent to Italy contained a total of 7.8828 kg (21.36 per cent of 36.9046 kg) of gold from the Melmer deposit.

So far as the 312 bars of Dutch origin are concerned, it was possible to ascertain that the Bank of Italy had sold part of this gold (146 unresmelted bars) in April 1943 to the SNB in Berne in exchange for Swiss francs; the remaining bars had found their way to Fortezza; the 147 bars belonging to INCE had been transferred to Berlin; of the 19 belonging to the Bank of Italy, 4 (unresmelted) went the same way and 15 (from the smelted lot) were found by the Allies in the Fortezza tunnel at the end of the war.

The legal proceedings between Italy and the Netherlands dragged on and were decided in Italy's favour in December 1963, when the Italian-Dutch Reconciliation Commission finally rejected the Dutch application for compensation[65].

METHODOLOGICAL NOTE TO TABLE I

The table summarizing gold movements from September 1943 to May 1945 (Table I) was prepared by examining and comparing a large number of archive documents. This note reviews the sources and explains how they were used.

Column I – Gold sent to Milan and Fortezza

This column regards the transfer of the gold reserves from Rome to Milan (and then Fortezza). The gold is listed by type on the left:

a) bars of varying fineness (in boxes)
b) coins recorded by weight (in bags)
c) coins recorded by piece (in bags)
d) gold from the Royal Mint (not recorded in the accounts; only entrusted to the Bank for shipment to the North).

The column was compiled with the aid of the following sources:

(A) Summary forms from the Cashier's Department (mod. 10 CC[66]), which record the operations carried out for the shipment of the gold to Milan. The documents list the gold that was transferred and provide other specific information. In particular:

- for bars and the coins recorded by weight they give the gross weight, fine weight and value;
- for the coins recorded by piece, which were never weighed, they give only the currency, quantity and value. The fine content shown in the table is easily obtained by dividing the value (Itl. 539,555,653.16) by the official price of gold (Itl. 21,381.227 per kg);
- for the gold from the Royal Mint, they give the number of the boxes and the weight declared by the Mint's representatives.

(B) Detailed lists, container by container, of the bars and coins recorded by weight shipped North; the lists were prepared at the time of shipment from the Cashier's Department and correspond perfectly with the information in the summary forms.
In particular:

- the bar gold is described in various lists, one for each type of bar (purchased bars and bars resmelted from other gold, .900 fine bars owned by the Bank of Italy, etc.). A general summary of each type of bar is given. All the bars are listed and each is accompanied by the following information: the number of the bar and the box that contained it, gross weight, fine weight, the value (in the case of resmelted bars, the weight and value of the silver in each piece is also given);
- the coins recorded by weight are described in a list that gives: the number of the sack, the details of the individual smaller bags (each sack contained 10) including currency and quantity, fineness and gross weight of each bag. This document also gives a general summary.

(C) Since there is no source document drafted in September 1943 for the coins recorded by piece, the entire list of the sacks that left the Cashier's Department (now available on computer disk) has been reconstructed by merging the list of the containers of coins subsequently sent to Germany[67] with that of the coins left at Fortezza and recovered by the allied forces at the end of the war.[68]

Thanks to these sources a detailed list could be drawn up of the identification numbers, contents and fine gold weight of each container (box or sack) that left the Cashier's Department. The list was an essential instrument for determining the precise amount of gold movements between 1944 and 1945 (first shipment to Berlin, shipment to Switzerland, second shipment to Berlin, recovery of gold at Fortezza) and verifying the amounts shown in other documents from the same period.

Finally, there is no detailed information on the contents of the boxes of gold belonging to the Mint because it was only transferred together with the reserves and not included in the Bank's accounts. The lack of detailed information on the 13 boxes did not hinder the verification of the movements of gold since the consignment was not shipped abroad and was found intact at the end of the war.

Column 2 – Gold sent to Berlin

This column shows the details of the gold moved to Berlin in 1944, distinguishing between the first and second consignments in February and October respectively. The

Table 1 – Summary of gold movements   (Amounts in kilograms)

			(1) Gold sent from Milan to Fortezza (22/28.9.1943) (16.12.1943)				(2) Gold sent to Berlin First Shipment (29.2.1944)			

BARS

Box numbers at the time of shipment		Avg fineness	Number			Fine weight	Number			Fine weight
			Boxes	Bars	Sacks		Boxes	Bars	Sacks	
1.32	Bank of Italy	999.6	32	384	0	4623.474344	0	0	0	0.000000
33.444	BI (held for BIS)	990.1	112	1344	0	15794.605586	0	0	0	0.000000
145.275	Bank of Italy	992.3	131	1572	0	18530.499834	105	1260	0	14862.83381
276.349	BI (held for SNB)	998.2	74	891	0	10784.052293	0	0	0	0.000000
350.361	INCE	905.7	12	147	0	1777.338326**	12	147	0	1777.338326
362.376	BI (smelted bars)	713.6	15	776	0	1467.462916	13	693	0	1275.775099
377	Ministry Trade and Foreign Exchange (bars, coins)		1	0	0	146.950000	0	0	0	0.000000
01.0130	Bank of Italy	899.9	130	1560	0	17140.387493	34	408	0	4290.699106
0131,0236	Bank of Italy	900.1	106	1271	0	14936.075805	11	132	0	1568.619968
Total movement of bars			**613**	**7945**	**0**	**85200.846597**	**175**	**2640**	**0**	**23775.266312**

COINS

			Number			Fine weight	Number			Fine weight
	BI: coins by piece		0	0	432	25235.018232	0	0	355	20714.588904
	BI: coins by weight		0	0	111	7139.102794	0	0	80	5144.804414
Total movement of coins			**0**	**0**	**543**	**32374.121026**	**0**	**0**	**435**	**25859.393318**
SUB TOTAL			**613**	**7945**	**543**	**117574.967623**	**175**	**2640**	**435**	**49634.659630**
	Mint		13	0	0	1677.000000*	0	0	0	0.000000
TOTAL			**626**	**7945**	**543**	**119251.967623**	**175**	**2640**	**435**	**49634.659630**

(*) Weight declared by the Mint; never verified by the Bank of Italy.

	Second Shipment (21.10.1944)				(3) Gold sent to Berne (20.4.1944)				(4) Gold found at Fortezza (17.5.1945)			
	Number			Fine weight	Number			Fine weight	Number			Fine weight
	Boxes	Bars	Sacks		Boxes	Bars	Sacks		Boxes	Bars	Sacks	
	0	0	0	0.000000	0	0	0	0.000000	32	384	0	4623.474344
	0	0	0	0.000000	89	1068	0	12604.727930	23	276	0	3189.877656
	0	0	0	0.000000	0	0	0	0.000000	26	312	0	3667.666021
	0	0	0	0.000000	74	891	0	10784.052293	0	0	0	0.000000
	0	0	0	0.000000	0	0	0	0.000000	0	0	0	0.000000
	0	0	0	0.000000	0	0	0	0.000000	2	83	0	191.687817
	0	0	0	0.000000	0	0	0	0.000000	1	0	0	146.950000
	78	936	0	10370.41863	0	0	0	0.000000	18	216	0	2479.269760
	57	684	0	7900.707417	0	0	0	0.000000	38	455	0	5466.748420
	135	1620	0	18271.126044	163	1959	0	23388.780223	140	1726	0	19765.674018
	0	0	39	2289.047401	0	0	0	0.000000	0	0	38	2231.381927
	0	0	14	903.177738	0	0	0	0.000000	0	0	17	1091.120642
	0	0	53	3192.225139	0	0	0	0.000000	0	0	55	3322.502569
	135	1620	53	21463.351183	163	1959	0	23388.780223	140	1726	55	23088.176587
	0	0	0	0.000000	0	0	0	0.000000	13	0	0	1677.000000
	135	1620	53	21463.351183	163	1959	0	23388.780223	153	1726	55	24765.176587

(**) The amount comprised 1,766.9365 kg of bars and 10.4018 kg of coins (37,580 francs).
    The latter were presumably contained inside the boxes

Cashier's Department lists[69] give full details of all the gold but *do not provide separate details for the two shipments*. The total quantity amounted to 71,098.010813 kg.

In order to arrive at a precise figure for each of the two consignments the following method was used:

a) the German report of the arrival of the first shipment of gold was available (Asbi.Segretariato Generale.pratt.n.995, fasc.2), providing the identification numbers of each container sent to Berlin. Summing the weight of fine gold in each container (175 boxes and 435 sacks), derived from the general list described in the note on column 1, it is a simple matter to determine the amount of gold transferred in February 1944 (94,634.659630 kg of fine gold).

b) the size of the second shipment was obtained by subtracting the amount transferred in the first consignment from the total sent to Germany.[70]

Column 3 – Gold sent to Berne

This column shows the transfer of gold for the SNB and the BIS.

The size of the transfer is verified by the documents with which the SNB and BIS acknowledged receipt of the gold. Two detailed lists of the boxes sent to Berne are also extant. These confirm the exact quantity of gold noted in the acknowledgements received from the Swiss banks.

The lists, one regarding the gold sent to the BIS and the other detailing that transferred to the SNB, are both typewritten and unsigned. The first page of both is marked with the stamp of the Financial Operations and Foreign Exchange Department, the unit of the Bank of Italy that handled funds transfers. The lists give the identification numbers of the boxes, the number of the individual bars, fineness, and gross and fine weight.[71]

Column 4 – Gold recovered at Fortezza

The last column documents the gold recovered at Fortezza by the Allies at the end of the war.

The information on this gold was drawn from the report of the discovery of the gold (Asbi. Segretariato Generale, pratt., n. 1378, fasc. 4), which was drafted at the time of the return of the gold from Fortezza to Rome. The document, of which both the original and the copy are available, gives the identification number of the boxes and the sacks and the total weight of the bars and coins. Here too the weight of their individual lots were verified and summed. The document also mentions the 13 boxes belonging to the Mint and the verification of their contents by the representatives of that institution.

Table 2 – Relations between Italy and the Gold Pool (amounts in kilograms)

Gold claimed by Italy (1)		Gold allocated from the Pool (2)		Gold returned from the Pool (3)		Gold still missing (4) = (1−2)
Belonging to the Bank of Italy	69,320.671	Allocation of 1947	3,805.318			
		Allocation of 1948	27,862.201			
		Total allocation through 1948	31,667.520	Allocation through 1948	31,667.520	
				Gold set aside for France	14,421.500	
				Gold set aside for Yugoslavia	8,393.000	
				Gold claim renounced by Yugoslavia in exchange for opening of lira	2,517.887	
				Gold actually returned in 1949	11,370.907	
		Allocation of 1958	12,749.965	Gold returned in 1958	12,749.985	
		Total allocations to the Bank of Italy	44,417.485	Total gold belonging to the Bank of Italy actually returned	24,120.872	
Belonging to INCE	1,777.338	Allocation of 1956	1,777.338	Cash diburstment to INCE (1) $3,021,120		
	71,098.009	Total allocations	46,194.823	Total returns	$3,021,120 24,120.872	24,903.186

(1) Italy renounced its claim to the corresponding quantity of gold following the allocation of its value in dollars.

NOTES

[1] Prepared by the Historical Archive of the Bank of Italy.

[2] In reality, an attempt to save the reserves was made on the eve of its removal. The events were described in detail by Niccolo Introna, the then Deputy Director General of the Bank of Italy, during the criminal proceedings against Vincenzo Azzolini, the Governor, in 1944. Introno testified that a few days before 20 September 1943 he proposed hiding the gold to the Governor in view of the likelihood that the Germans would remove it. The proposed stratagem involved hiding the gold in an underground vault, whose door would be walled over, and the preparation of false documents recording the shipment of the gold for safekeeping to the Bank's branch in Potenza, which was then on the verge of being liberated. Azzolini approved the project, but decided to limit its scope to half of the gold. The gold was secreted in the vault between 19 and 20 September and work began on "covering the door (…) with a wall 0.25-m thick. In order to ensure that the wall dried as completely as possible and did not appear freshly built, it was made of reinforced concrete and plaster and dried with fans and electric lamps" (Asbi.Direttorio-Introna, pratt., cart. 83). On 20 September, however, Azzolini was called to the Ministry of Finance, where he got the impression that the Germans knew the exact size of the Bank's reserves. Fearing German reprisals, Azzolini ordered the wall to be torn down and the gold returned to its normal location.

[3] Some small lots of gold remained deposited at other Bank branch offices, including those in the colonies (see Appendix A).

[4] Coins of the following currencies were present: French francs (sometimes called "Napoleons"), dollars, 1931 lire (sometimes called "newly minted" lire), marks, pounds sterling, Turkish lire, Austrian crowns and florins and Dutch guilders. The quantity of fine gold for each type of coin recorded by weight was determined by multiplying the gross weight by the coin's fineness; for coins recorded by piece (which were never weighed), the quantity of fine gold was decided to be that theoretically present in each currency.

[5] The Bank of Italy's gold reserves included gold from France (14,421.5 kg of fine gold) and Yugoslavia (8.393 kg). The gold came into the Bank's possession between 1941 and 1942 from the Vichy government and as "war booty" from Yugoslavia and had been recorded in the reserves in 1942 (see Historical Archive of the Bank of Italy (Asbi). Segretariato Generale. Pratt. 1063. fasc. 1). At the time the reserves were moved to Milan this gold was considered to be the rightful property of the Bank of Italy. At the end of the war Italy would be required to return all of this gold to its original owners (see "Restitution of Gold to Italy").

[6] The Bank of Italy never verified the actual quantity of fine gold in this consignment, simply recording the gross quantity indicated by the Royal Mint. The archive of the Milan regional office contains the records for the 13 boxes with the gross weight of each, while a record for the shipment of 22 September (Asbi. Segretariato Generale. pratt. n. 1062. fasc. 3) gives the amount as 1.670 kg of fine gold. The find content of another small lit (8.1 kg gross) is not given, but using the same ratio we can estimate its fine gold content at about 7 kg.

[7] The INCE lot, composed of 147 ingots, arrived at the Bank of Italy following an operation begun by INCE in 1940 involving the transfer of US banknotes totalling $7 million to the German embassy in Washington on behalf of the Reichsbank. The Reichsbank did not fully repay INCE in 1942 as agreed and INCE requested repayment of the amount outstanding ($3,021,120). The Reichsbank did not return the entire amount but did agree to repay at least $2 million. The amount equal to 1,777.33826 kg of fine gold (at the price of $35 per fine ounce) was subsequently transferred to Italy by the Reichsbank (Asbi. Segretariato Generale. pratt. n. 1017. fasc. 5).

[8] Asbi. Segretariato Generale. pratt. n. 995. fasc. 1.

[9] Asbi. Ragioneria. regg. mod. 14 cont. s.n. On 14 December the Bolzano branch was sent instructions for recording the different lots (in Asbi. Ragioneria. pratt. n. 46).

[10] The Bank's accounting records showing the transfer of the gold from the Milan office to Bolzano are held at the Bank's Bolzano branch.

[11] Both had a key to the specially-built armoured door of the tunnel.

[12] On the definition of the Italian Social Republic as the "*de facto* government", see C. Mortati.*Istituzioni di Diritto Pubblico*. Padua. 1960. pp. 145 ff: M.S. Giannini. "*Repubblica Sociale Italiana*" in *Enc.Dir.*, vol. XXXIX. Milan.1962. pp. 894 ff.

[13] Asbi. Segretariato Generale. pratt. n. 995 and 1043.

[14] Ibid. The Fasano agreement also made a part of the gold available to the Italian embassy in Berlin once it was transferred to Germany. For more on the events surrounding the gold in Germany, see the relevant section in the text.

[15] Asbi. Segretariato Generale. pratt. n. 995. fasc. 2.signed original.

[16] Asbi. Segretariato Generale.Consiglio Superiore. regg. n. 637. tornata n. 720 of 28 April 1944.

[17] Asbi. Rapporti con l'Estero. pratt. n. 340. fasc. 3.

[18] A number of other sources report at least one other attempt to hide the gold before it could be seized by the Germans. The episode occurred at the Milan regional office (see Appendix A).

[19] Banca d'Italia.Archivio di deposito. Segretariato. pratt. n. 237. Dalla Torre, appointed to head the Fortezza agency, had a good knowledge of German and accompanied the gold shipments to Berlin in February and October. He wrote his note in 1967 after he had retired, hoping eventually to publish the work. In recounting the event surrounding the first shipment, Dalla Torre claimed that it was not possible to determine the exact weight of each box and sack and that "after prolonged discussion with the German representatives" (ibid. p. 19) it was decided to take the 175 boxes and 435 sacks, assuming a final weight that proved to be "a couple hundred kilos" short (ibid. p. 20).

[20] Massimiliano Bernhuber was the Reichsbank's representative in Italy and the main German contact with the management of the Bank of Italy in this period.

[21] Asbi. Direttorio – Introna. cart. 83. fasc. 2.

[22] The loan, which was needed to raise foreign exchange for the war effort, was made on 2 September 1940 and totalled SF 125,000,000. On an explicit order of Mussolini, the Bank of Italy earmarked a deposit of gold from its own reserves as collateral in the name of the SNB but whose beneficiaries were the lending banks (the pool of Swiss banks consisted of Societe de Banque Suisse, Credit Suisse, UBS and the Swiss Federal Bank). The value of the deposit was equal to 26,966.940980 kg of fine gold, which corresponded to the amount of the loan increased by 5 per cent. at a price of SF 4,869.8 per kilogram of fine gold. On the due date (31 August 1941), the loan was extended for another year. The loan was subsequently extended to 31 December 1943 with a supplementary agreement on 31 July 1942. Yet another agreement on 31 January 1943 redefined the terms of the collateral, reducing the gold backing to 40 per cent of the loan amount, with the remaining 60 per cent to be guaranteed by Italian Treasury bills maturing 31 December 1943. Consequently, the Bank of Italy was able to free 16,182.888597 kg of fine gold, reducing the gold collateral to 10,784.052293 kg. On the 31 December 1943 due date INCE was unable to obtain another extension and was not able to repay the debt outstanding, equal to SF 107,000,000 that the SNB had advanced to the creditor banks (Asbi. Rapporti con l'Estero. pratt. n. 405. fasc. 7).

[23] On 6 December Governor Azzolini reported the SNB and BIS requests to Pellegrini, the Minister of Finance, underscoring the advisability of complying swiftly (Asbi. Segretariato Generale. pratt. n. 995. fasc. 1).

[24] The documents were accounts of meetings between Azzolini and representatives of the Reichsbank and others involved in the transfer of gold (Asbi. Segretariato Generale. pratt. n. 995. fasc. 1); the Governor underscores his efforts to ensure compliance with international obligations in the face of the opposition to restitution from the Germans and Minister Pellegrini. Azzolini maintained this position in a memo he presented to the President of the High Court of Justice on 3 October 1944 during criminal proceedings against him for having allowed the Germans to seize the gold (Asbi. Direttorio-Intronro. cart. 84. fasc. 1).

[25] Asbi. Segretariato Generale. pratt. n. 995. fasc. 2. unsigned typewritten copy.

[26] Asbi contains a variety of sources recording the transfer to Berne. In particular, the archive holds Azzolini's letter of 21 April 1944 to Giacomeili, the Bank's Inspector General, who had remained in Rome, in which he communicated the settlement of the debts with the Swiss banks, and a subsequent letter of 25 April to the Giampietro Pellegrini, the Minister of Finance, reporting the shipment. Asbi also contains the copies of the letters that the Governor sent to the two Swiss banks a few days before the gold was shipped, advising them of the upcoming transfer (Asbi. Rapporti con l'Estero.pratt.n.181.fasc.10). Finally, there are also two detailed lists of the bars sent to Switzerland (the record of the 1068 bars sent to the BIS in Asbi. Rapporti con l'Estero. pratt. n. 215. fasc. 10. and that of the 891 bars shipped to the SNB in Asbi. Rapporti con l'Estero. pratt. n. 405. fasc. 7).

[27] Asbi. Direttorio-Introno. cart. 83. fasc. 2.

[28] Ibid.

[29] The Germans' aim of gaining control over the entire gold reserve is also substantiated by a account of a meeting between Azzolini and Bernhuber on 1 June. During the meeting, the Governor was informed that even before the Fasano agreement "the Republican government and the Reich had agreed that all of the Bank of Italy's gold would be transferred to Germany to defray the cost of fighting the war and other expenditure on activities of common interest" (Asbi. Direttorio-Introna. pratt. cart. 84. fasc. 10).

[30] The fine gold content of the gold mark was then equal to 0.358423 g.

[31] Asbi. Segretariato Generale. pratt. n. 995. fasc. 2.

[32] Asbi. Segretariato Generale. pratt. n. 995. fasc. 2. copy with annotations.

[33] Asbi. Raccolta delle Relazioni, vol. 94. p. 22.

[34] Asbi. Cassa Centrale. pratt. n. provv .03. The source is discussed in more detail in the methodological note to Table 1.

[35] Asbi. Directtorio – Menichella. pratt. cart. n. 93. fasc. 2.

[36] According to the Herzog memorandum, the Italian embassy used the gold in this deposit on more than one occasion. This claim is not confirmed by archive documents; in fact, it appears to be ruled out by Italy's statement in relation to its claim on the gold pool that the article of the Fasano agreement providing for the creation of a deposit for the Italian embassy was never actually implemented (Asbi. Segretariato Generale. pratt. n. 1030. fasc. 1. annex to the questionnaire).

[37] During the war the gold stored at Fortezza continued to be considered reserve gold; the value of the gold was reported in the Annual Reports for 1944 and 1945 (Asbi. Relazioni Annuali.voll.nn.94 and 95.

[38] Asbi. Segretariato Generale. pratt. n. 995. fasc. 3.

[39] Asbi. Segretariato Generale.pratt. n. 1378. fasc. 4.

[40] The signed original of the document of restitution and the detailed list of the gold returned to the Bank of Italy are in Asbi. Segretariato Generale. pratt. n. 1060. fasc. 1.

[41] In June 1945 the Allied command asked the Bank of Italy to demonstrate that it owned the gold recovered at Fortezza, that the gold had never left Italy and that it was part of the gold moved from Rome to Milan and then to Fortezza in 1943. A series of documents proving that the Fortezza gold was part of the Bank's reserves were given to the Allies. The negotiations for restitution continued over the next two years and became entwined with those regarding Italy's admittance to the countries eligible for restitution from the gold pool. In September 1947 the Ministry for Foreign Affairs communicated the United States' desire to return Fortezza gold "as soon as the ratifications of the peace treaty were deposited". The protocol for restitution was signed on 10 October. Information on the entire affair can be found in Asbi. Segretariato Generale. pratt. nn. 995. 996 and 997.

[42] A copy of the gold questionnaire and part of the material prepared for Italy's official claim are to be found in Asbi. Segretariato Generale.pratt.nn.1016,1030 and 1034.

[43] Asbi. Segretariato Generale. pratt. n. 1030. fasc. 1.

[44] See section entitled 'The Discovery of the Remaining Gold at Fortezza'.

[45] Asbi. Segretariato Generale. pratt. n. 997. fasc. 2. the document is a copy of a letter to the Minister for Foreign Affairs dated 18 October 1947. The archive also contains the original accompanying letter to the Bank of Italy's delegate in Brussels.

[46] Asbi. Segretariato Generale. pratt. n. 997. fasc. 1. copy with original markings and signed copy of wire message from the Ministry for Foreign Affairs.

[47] Asbi. Segretariato Generale. pratt. n. 1023. fasc. 2.

[48] The allocation included Italy's share (586.8 kg) of the lot of Italian gold (totaling about 5 tons) found in Austria and erroneously handed over to the Allies at the Austrian National Bank. As described in Appendix B, this gold was acquired by the pool following the claim advanced by Italy after Herbert Herzog's report.

[49] The figures, which have been obtained from the available documentation, are confirmed by Governor Menichella, who at the 31 July 1958 meeting of the Bank's Board reported on the overall status of the allocations of gold to Italy, a situation that has not changed since then.

[50] The related correspondence and the original shipment documents (mod. 10 CC) are in Asbi. Segretariato Generale. pratt. n. 1060. fasc. 3.

[51] Asbi. Segretariato Generale. pratt. n. 1063. fasc. 1.

[52] Asbi. Rapporti con l'Estero. pratt. n. 338. fasc. 5. typewritten copy.

[53] Ibid.typewritten copy.

[54] The related correspondence and the original shipment documents (mod. 10 CC) are in Asbi. Segretariato Generale. pratt. n. 1060. fasc. 2.

[55] Asbi. Segretariato Generale. pratt. n. 1029. fasc. 1.

[56] Asbi. Segretariato Generale. pratt. n. 996. fasc. 2.

[57] Asbi. Segretariato Generale. pratt. n. 1029. fasc. 1.

[58] Ibid.

[59] Asbi. Segretariato Generale. pratt. n. 1062. fasc. 4.

[60] Asbi. Segretariato Generale. pratt. n. 1028. fasc. 4.

[61] Asbi. Direttorio – Menichella. pratt. cart. 93. fasc. 2.

[62] Asbi. Segretariato Generale. pratt. n. 1017. fasc. 6.

[63] The cash owned by INCE was subsequently found at the German embassy in Washington and INCE renounced its claim on the gold pool in exchange for restitution of the sum in dollars. Information on this matter is contained in Asbi. Segretariato Generale. pratt. n. 1017. fasc. 5.

[64] Asbi. Segretariato Generale. pratt. 1029. fasc. 8. The document in question is a photocopy, probably a page from the report "*Looted Netherlands Guilders Resmelted in early 1943*".

[65] Correspondence and copies of the decision (in French) in Asbi. Segretariato Generale. pratt. n. 1018.

[66] Asbi. Segretariato Generale. pratt. n. 1062. fasc. 3. The forms, which are originals, are signed by the Head Inspector and Head Cashier.

[67] The information is in the lists (Asbi. Cassa Centrale. pratt. n. provv. 03) giving the details of the gold sent to Berlin, making no distinction between the first and second consignments. The lists give the sack number, the number of the bags in each sack, the content of the bags (currency and quantity), the fineness of the coins and weight. The lists of the Berlin shipments are also available for the bars and the coins recorded by weight.

[68] The information is drawn from a document entitled "Monete a pezzo. Rimanenze" in Asbi. Rapporti con l'Estero. pratt. n. 340. fasc. 7. The document was drafted at Fortezza after the first shipment to Berlin and gives the list of the sacks remaining at the end of February 1944. Following the second consignment other items on the same list were checked off. The sacks that were not checked off therefore represent the coins that remained at Fortezza. Here too the information given includes the identification number of the sacks, the content of each sack (currency and quantity) and weight.

[69] See 'The Second Shipment to Berlin' and note 2 of this section.

[70] The report of the arrival of the October 1944 shipment, drafted in Berlin, is available (Asbi. Segretariato Generale. pratt. n. 995. fasc. 2), but it does not give the identification numbers of the boxes and sacks, reporting only the total number of containers.

[71] The list of the boxes actually sent to the BIS (89 out of the 112 held for the bank) is in Asbi. Rapporti con l'Estero, pratt. n. 215. fasc. 10. The list of gold sent in repayment of the debt with the SNB, which corresponds perfectly with the amount shipped in September 1943 from Rome, is in Asbi, Rapporti con l'Estero, pratt., n. 405, fasc. 7. This list is accompanied by a provisional receipt signed in Chiasso by the Director and the Head Cashier of the SNB.

LUXEMBOURG

Luxembourg gold despoiled by Germany during the Second World War

On 10 May 1940 German troops invaded Luxembourg, violating the country's disarmed neutrality for the second time in a quarter of a century. Luxembourg was under military administration until the end of the month of July 1940. By a decree of 20 May 1940[1] foodstuffs, raw materials and semi-finished products were sequestrated. The list annexed to the decree also included gold and other precious metals. A second implementing decree of 2 August 1940[2] required all gold (ingots, coin) to be declared and and offered for sale for the benefit of the Reichskreditkasse (Credit Bank of the Reich). The *Feldkouirnandant* (Field Commander), who was on the point of leaving Luxembourg, did not order any confiscations or requisitions, however. From 29 July 1940 the Grand Duchy of Luxembourg was put under the authority of a 'Chef der zivilverwaltung' (Head of the Civil Administration) (Cdz) in the person of Gauleiter (Head of District) Gustav Simon of the Gau (District) of Coblence-Treves. The new master of Luxembourg was answerable directly to Hitler and was thus able to avoid interference by the Berlin ministries in the administration of Luxembourg[3]. In appointing a Gauleiter as head of the civil administration, Hitler had put a man from the Nazi party in charge of preparing Luxembourg's annexation to the Reich. A formal (*de jure*) annexation was never declared.

From 27 August 1940 the CdZ published a decree on currency[4] which promulgated the German laws on the subject in Luxembourg. Paragraph 3 of that decree forced all private persons resident in Luxembourg to offer, sell and transfer currency (US dollars, Swiss francs, Swedish krona, French francs) and gold (coin, fine gold and alloy gold) owned by them to certain listed banks. The decree on currency had set 15 September 1940 as the deadline for making such declarations. Reminders of the deadline were given in the press on several occasions[5]. This general economic measure on the part of the occupier gave rise to compensation in reichsmarks. The measures taken against Jews at the beginning of September 1940[6] introduced the 'Nuremberg laws' and the discriminatory economic laws of 1938 in Luxembourg. The situation of the Jews in Luxembourg was then identical to that of Jews in the Reich.

The decree of 5 September 1940[7] on Jewish wealth required every Jew resident in Luxembourg to declare his wealth. Paragraph 7 forbade Jews of Luxembourg or German nationality to purchase, mortgage, or sell items made of gold, platinum or silver, precious stones and pearls, or any objet d'art of a value in excess of RM 1000.

On 12 December 1940 the CdZ announced that a new section had been set up in his administration. This was Section IVa, a section called 'Verwaltung des judischen Vermögens' (Administration of Jewish Property), headed by a man from the party, Gauinspekteur (District Chief of Staff) Josef Ackermann[8]. On the same day a notice in the press required all persons resident in Luxembourg to notify Section IVa of any acquisitions and donations they had received from Jews since 10 May 1940.

By a decree of 7 February 1941[9] the CdZ placed all property belonging to Jews under German administration from the date on which those Jews emigrated. He reserved the right to confiscate that same property. The decree had a retrospective effect to 10 May 1940. Thus it had its effect as Jews left Luxembourg, taking with them a maximum of 50 kilos of luggage. Two months later the Jewish property of persons still resident in Luxembourg was likewise declared to be confiscated by the CdZ[10]. In this way, little by little, Section IVa confiscated all Jewish property. No report which we have received expressly mentions the gold confiscated from Jews.

When the 'Wirtschaftstrupp' (Economic Squad) of the Feldkommandantur (Field Commander's Office) began to draw up the list of raw materials and stocks of finished or semi-finished products, it was obliged to note that the gold belonging to the Luxembourg State was no longer in Luxembourg.

In fact, the gold which had been bought by the Caisse d'Epargne de l'Etat (State Savings Bank) (CEE) since 1931, 319 bars in all, containing 3,854.7487 kgs of fine gold, like the gold bought in November and December 1938 by the Luxembourg Government, 30 bars in all, containing 368.9553 kgs of gold, and 8 bars containing 93.4988 kgs of fine gold belonging to the Pescatore Foundation, had been consigned to the Banque nationale de Belgique (National Bank of Belgium) (BNB). With regard to these 357 bars containing 4,317.2028 kgs of fine gold packed in 90 cases, the BNB had undertaken to store "this deposit of gold with the same care and attention as if it was our own gold"[11]. Consequently the BNB gave notice that it would transport "your deposit of gold abroad at your expense and risk in the event that we decide ourselves no longer to keep any quantity of gold in Belgium." On 14 May 1940 the BNB consigned the 90 cases containing the Luxembourg gold to the Banque de France (Bank of France) (BdF). The Banque de France signed an acknowledgement of receipt which it returned to the BNB. The 90 cases were then added to the cases of Belgian gold from which the BdF was not subsequently able to separate them. Together with the Belgian gold, the Luxembourg gold was then transferred to Dakar, where the local French authorities took charge of it on 28 June 1940.

In Luxembourg the CdZ attempted to extend his control to the banking system. Although he did not interfere with the private banks yet, the CEE seemed as easy prey to him. By eliminating the candidate proposed by Hengst, the 'Oberburgermeister' (Mayor) who had been in office in Luxembourg since 13 August 1940, the CdZ left the field free for the representative of the 'Rheinischer Sparkassen- und Giroverband' (Rhine Association of Savings Banks and Giro Institutions), Dr. Ernst Unbehend, who had worked in this managerial post since his arrival in Luxembourg on 2 September 1940. On 14 September 1940 the Gauleiter appointed him to the position of Commissioner to the CdZ at the CEE. The Luxembourg Director of the CEE, Kerschen, and the Deputy Director, Goergen, had been dismissed on 6 September, while a head of department at the CEE, Schroeder, had been put in charge of managing day-to-day business.

On the question of the Luxembourg gold, the Director of the Caisse d'Epargne had submitted to the BNB a request dated 31 August 1940 with a view to recovering the gold deposited in Brussels in order to be able to declare it to the Reichskreditkasse in accordance with the decree of 27 August 1940[12]. The BNB replied that it was unable to return the gold because it had been transported abroad pursuant to the agreements signed in 1939[13]. On 11 October 1940 the CEE, under the signature of Director Schroeder, declared its gold to the Reichskreditkasse of Luxembourg[14]. By ordinances of 21 October 1940 and 15 January 1941 the CEE was liquidated and replaced with three 'Kreissparkassen' (district savings banks) and one 'Stadtsparkasse' (town savings bank') to which the CEE's assets and liabilities were transferred.

In the meantime the Germans had gathered all the information about the Luxembourg gold and from February 1941 they tried to recover this gold. Dr. Unbehend asked for the CEE's 319 ingots for the new savings banks. The Government's 30 ingots were to return directly to the CdZ, and the Pescatore Foundation's 8 ingots were sought by the 'Stillhaltekommissar' (Standstill Commissioner), who had just got his hands on the property of all Luxembourg's foundations and other sporting, cultural and social associations[15].

The Stillhaltekommissar's staff had contacted the 'Oberkriegsverwaltungsrat' (Senior War Administration Councillor), Dr. Hofrichter, the German commissioner to the BNB, and had secured an undertaking that the BNB would return the Pescatore Foundation's 8 ingots. They had also been informed that all the gold would be transferred to the Berlin Reichsbank, to which the various owners were supposed to offer to sell the gold[16]. On 5 February 1941 Schroeder, the Director of the CEE, applied to the BNB for it to "make the ingots deposited under our file with you over to the Reichsbank in Berlin"[17]. The BNB then applied to the BdF on 17 April 1941 for it to follow up the CEE's demands. On 13 May the Governor of the BdF asked the BNB to supply it with "the information necessary to identify the cases containing the ingots to be withdrawn". Moreover, it asked the BNB "to authorise the Banque de France to open the said cases and verify their contents and to mandate it to send the ingots in question to the Deutsche Reichsbank"[18]. On 24 May the Governor of the BdF notified the CEE of this exchange of letters. The Governor of the BNB, however, did not deliver the information required or the authorisations requested. On 11 June 1941 Director Schroeder applied again to the Governor of the BNB, asking him "to authorise the Banque de France to make these three deposits of gold available to the Caisse d'Epargne and not to deliver them to the Reichsbank in Berlin"[19]. As the Germans had the impression that the Governor of the BNB was using delaying tactics in order to gain time and to avoid refusing to hand the gold over to the Reichsbank, which was not the owner of the gold, Director Schroeder changed his instructions in order to hasten the procedure. The BNB then asked for written instructions bearing the signature of two authorised representatives of the CEE. On 4 July the instructions in question were sent to the BNB and on 11 July 1941 those instructions were sent to the BdF which itself received instructions from officials of the CEE. Dr. Unbehend even went to Paris to hasten the delivery of the gold ingots. He had taken the lists of the numbers of the ingots with him, but had to return to Luxembourg empty-handed because the gold which the Vichy Government had handed over to Germany was at that moment in Dakar, Marseille, Algeria or Berlin. It was consequently decided to wait for all the gold to arrive in Berlin and then to look for the Luxembourg ingots[20]. As Dr. Unbehend still did not receive any news of the Luxembourg ingots he went to Paris on 23 September[21] to see how it might be possible to disregard the question of legal succession raised by the BdF, which took the view that the Luxembourg Government alone was able to ask for the gold deposit to be returned. As all the Dakar gold was being shipped to Berlin, the German representative to the BdF, the President, Dr. Schaeffer, took the view that the Reichsbank, as the holder of the gold, was now the CEE's interlocutor. Consequently Dr. Unbehend went to Berlin on 4 October to negotiate preferential treatment of the issue. On 7 November 1941 the Reichsbank informed Dr. Unbehend that 45 cases of Luxembourg gold were already in the treasuries of the Reichsbank in Berlin. At a meeting with the directors of the Reichsbank in Berlin on 28 and 29 November Dr. Unbehend tried to negotiate a higher price for the Luxembourg gold, but did not win his case because the Reichsbank considered the price of RM 2,784.00 per kg it was offering to be higher than the world market rate[22]. Dr. Unbehend therefore gave the Reichsbank the order to purchase the Luxembourg gold as it arrived in Berlin. By letters of 4 and 27 February 1942 the Reichsbank confirmed the purchase of the Luxembourg gold and the payment of the value of the gold, RM 12,018,380.01 in all, to the 'Deutsche Girozentrale –Deutsche Kommunalbank Berlin' (German Giro Centre –German Municipal Bank, Berlin) in favour of the 'Rheinische Girozentrale und Provinzialbank, zweigstelle Kbln' (Rhine Giro Centre and Provincial Bank, Cologne Branch) on behalf of the 'Staatssparkasse Luxemburg' (Luxembourg State Savings Bank), which was being liquidated. This sum was subsequently used as follows: RM 10,732,230.47 was divided between the four German savings banks established in Luxembourg; RM 1,026,122.16 was transferred to the 'Chef der Zivilverwaltung Zentralkasse, Teil B' (Head of the Civil Administration, Central Credit Institution, Section B), and RM 260,027.38 was handed over to the 'Stillhaltekommissar fur das Organisationswesen in Luxemburg' (Standstill Commissioner for Organisation in Luxembourg).

By letter dated 16 June 1942 Dr. Unbehend advised the BNB that the Reichsbank had received the Luxembourg gold. In the same letter he stated that the CEE had been liquidated and that all the lists of signatures lodged with the BNB to accredit its officials to the BNB should be regarded as null and void.

Despite the solidarity measures taken by the governors of both the BNB and the BdF to prevent or at least delay the Luxembourg gold being handed over to the Germans, the Germans finally succeeded in seizing it. On 5 February 1944 the Luxembourg Government in exile took the decision to strip the statutory bodies of the Caisse d'Epargne of the right to administer and dispose of the gold deposited at the Banque nationale de Belgique by the Caisse d'Epargne and to transfer those rights to the Luxembourg State, represented by the Government of Luxembourg[23]. Finally, it appears to us interesting to return to a second thread of the negotiations which led more directly to the Belgian gold and therefore also the Luxembourg gold being handed over to the Germans.

On 29 October 1940 the Germans imposed on the French, Armistice Delegation an agreement demanding the return of all the cases (4,944 in all, 90 of them containing Luxembourg gold) which the BNB had consigned to the Banquet de France. An additional protocol of 11 December 1940 laid down the terms of the agreement. The Stillhaltekommissar's officials had approached the economic section of the German Armistice Delegation in Paris to put pressure on the BdF. Parallel to Dr. Unbehend's repeated interventions at the BdF and the BNB, the Stillhaltekommissar continued his interventions at the German Armistice Delegation in Wiesbaden and Paris, without having the same success as Dr. Unbehend. At one point this parallel strategy even provoked irritation and a fairly serious imbroglio because of a failure to exchange information.

NOTES

[1] Official gazette for the occupied territory of the Grand Duchy of Luxembourg, published by the army group, no. 3, 28.5.1940, p. 9–11. Decree on seizure in the occupied territories of the Netherlands, Belgium, Luxembourg and France.

[2] Official gazette of the Military Commander for Belgium, Northern France and Luxembourg, 1940, no. –, p. 2. Implementing decree on the currency decree for Belgium and Luxembourg of 2 August 1940.

[3] Paul Dostert, Luxembourg Between Self-Assertion and National Self-Relinquishment. The German Policy of Occupation and the Ethnic German Movement 1940–1945, Luxembourg 1985, pp. 64–70.

[4] Official gazette for Luxembourg, published by the Head of the Civil Administration in Luxembourg, no. 2, 24.9.1940, pp. 6–7. Decree on the currency law to be used in Luxembourg. This decree had already been published in the press on 28 August 1940, the date of its entry into force.

[5] See for example Luxemburger Zeitung newspaper of 9, 11 and 13 September 1940.

[6] Official gazette 1940, no. 2, pp. 10–11. Decree on measures in the field of law on Jews.

[7] Official gazette 1940, no. 2, pp. 11–13. Decree on Jewish property in Luxembourg.

[8] Luxemburger Zeitung newspaper of 12.12.1940.

[9] Official gazette 1941, no. 12, p. 90. Decree on measures concerning the property of emigrants and Jews.

[10] Official gazette 1941, no. 31, p. 208. Decree implementing the decree on measures concerning the property of emigrants and Jews of 7 February 1941.

[11] Ministry of Finance: File: Gold: Copy of a letter of 15 November 1939 from the Banque nationale de Belgique to the Director of the CEE.

[12] Ministry of Finance: File: Gold: Copy of the letter of 31 August 1940.

[13] Ministry of Finance: Ibidem: Copy of the BNB's letter of 5 September 1940.

[14] Document reproduced in 'L'Independant' of 20 March 1947.

[15] P. Dostert, op. cit., p. 88–91.

[16] Ministry of Finance: Gold file: Copy of an internal memorandum of 28 January 1941 for the Stillhaltekommissar.

[17] Ministry of Finance: Gold file: Copy of the letter of 5 February 1941 to the Governor of the BNB.

[18] Ministry of Finance: Gold file: Copy of the letter of 13 May 1941 from the Governor of the BdF to the Governor of the BNB.

[19] Ministry of Finance: Gold file: Copy of the letter of 11 June 1941. See also the letter of 18 June 1941 from Dr. Unbehend.

[20] Ministry of Finance: Gold file: Letter of 25 July 1941 from Gaurevisor (District Auditor) Balaumerl to Reichsoberrevisor (First Revisor of the Reich) Baum of the Stillhaltekommissar in Strasbourg.

[21] Ministry of Finance: Gold file: Note of 6 October 1941 from Dr. Unbehend on the negotiations in Paris.

[22] Ministry of Finance: Gold file: Letter of 2 December 1941 from Dr. Unbehend to the Stillhaltekommissar in Luxembourg. Report on the discussions held in Berlin on 28 and 29 November 1941 on the Caisse d'Epargne's gold.

[23] Memorial, offical journal of the Grand Duchy of Luxembourg, 1944, no. 3.

The restitution of the monetary gold stolen from Luxembourg by the Nazis

On 10 September 1944 the soldiers of the 5th Armoured Division entered the town of Luxembourg, ending more than four years of Nazi occupation. On 23 September 1944 the members of the Luxembourg Government returned from exile and resumed their offices. From 7 October 1944 the Belgian Minister for Finance, Camille Gutt, informed his Luxembourg opposite number of the negotiations which had taken place between the Banque de France (Bank of France) (BdF) and the Banque Nationale de Belgique (National Bank of Belgium) (BNB) concerning the deposit of gold made by the latter and during which the deposit of Luxembourg gold had been touched on as well. The Minister from France in Brussels had made the following oral declaration at that time: "The French Government will not refuse if the Belgian Government so requests, itself to supply a quantity of gold corresponding to the Luxembourg gold. This will imply the Caisse d'Epargne (Savings Bank) having addressed a similar request to the Banque nationale de Belgique and having specified that it has found itself entirely bereft of the gold whose withdrawal was requested in 1941."[1] The Director of the Caisse d'Epargne de l'Etat (State Savings Bank) (CEE), Kerschen, was irritated by the condition indicated by the French Minister, considering "that if the Banque de France has made difficulties about restituting the gold deposit which the Banque Nationale had handed over to it, [that] does not affect the depositor and depository relationship which exists between the Caisse d'Epargne de Luxembourg [Luxembourg Savings Bank] and the Banque nationale."[2] At a meeting with the Governor of the BNB the Director of the CEE requested precise written explanations of the condition indicated in the letter of 7 November 1944. The start of the Battle of Ardennes on 16 December 1944 interrupted the negotiations concerning the deposit of Luxembourg gold at the BNB until February/March 1945. In a note to the Minister for Finance the Director of the CEE recalled that Luxembourg had undertaken not to demand its gold deposit until the end of the war. By letter of 9 March 1945 the Luxembourg Minister for Finance accordingly confined himself to asking the Governor of the BNB "to be so good as to give us an assurance that the Caisse d'Epargne's gold is indeed at the disposal of the latter or of the Luxembourg Government in your treasuries."[3] Several meetings between the Deputy Director of the CEE and the Governor of the BNB took place after Germany's capitulation, and on 21 July 1945 Luxembourg's Minister for Finance addressed to the Governor of the BNB the request "to be so good as to restore our deposit [of gold] in its weight as at the end of May 1940"[4]. The Governor of the BNB passed this letter to the Governor of the BdF. The latter informed his supervising Minister thereof. On 8 November 1945 Mr. Pleven, the Minister for Finance, gave his agreement to satisfying the CEE's demand. On 4 December 1945 the Governor of the BdF informed the Governor of the BNB of the conditions on which the BdF was prepared "to satisfy the demand formulated by the Caisse Générale (sic) d'Epargne of the Grand Duchy of Luxembourg."[5] In return the Caisse d'Epargne was to undertake "to give its full support to the Banque de France and to the Banque nationale de Belgique in any steps and in any actions which these latter would consider useful to undertake against the German Government, against the Reichsbank or against any third party holder with a view to having restituted to it the Luxembourg gold surrendered to the Reichsbank." Moreover, at the request of the BdF or the BNB, "and following the instructions of these latter", the CEE was to agree to institute "at its own expense and risk any legal actions which may appear appropriate against the Reichsbank or against any third party holder as though its rights had not been fulfilled." The CEE declared itself to be in agreement with these proposals but considered it necessary to set a ceiling for the costs of any legal action against the German Government or the Reichsbank.[6] The Governor of the BNB accordingly went to Paris on 11 and 12 January 1946 to discuss this matter with the Governor of the BdF. The Governor of the BdF was of the opinion "that it would be dangerous to call into question with Mr. Pleven the offer which has been made to us [the BNB and the CEE]."[7] On 30 January 1946 Luxembourg's Minister for Finance informed the Governor of the BNB "that both the Luxemboug Government and the Caisse d'Epargne of the Grand Duchy accept the conditions laid down by Mr. Monick, Governor of the Banque de France, in the matter of the restitution of our gold deposit to the Banque nationale de Belgique." On 21 February 1946 the Governor of the BNB sent Luxembourg's Minister for Finance the Convention between the Banque de France and the Banque nationale de Belgique, to which the Caisse d'Epargne de l'Etat was to become a party. The signatures were appended on 20 February 1946 by Maurice Frere, the Governor of the Banque nationale de Belgique, on 23 February 1946 by Ernest Goergen, the Deputy Director of the Caisse d'Epargne de l'Etat, and on 2 March 1946 by Emmanuel Monick, the Governor of the Banque de France.[8] Rather laborious negotiations finally resulted on 12 September 1946 in the sending of the letter by which "the Luxembourg Government undertook to support the French Authorities in all steps and actions which these latter might consider appropriate to undertake in order to obtain restitution of the gold belonging to the Caisse d'Epargne de l'Etat of the Grand Duchy of Luxembourg".[9]

This letter, dated 28 August 1946, which was necessary to bring the Convention into force, reached its addressee a few days before the announcement to the press of the constitution of a Tripartite Commission for the Restitution of Monetary Gold. By letter of 3 October 1946 the Deputy Governor of the BNB informed the Luxembourg Minister for Finance that the BdF had put on the BNB's file, for the CEE, "a 4,317.2028 kg weight of fine gold". Luxembourg had regained all the gold it had deposited at the BNB before the invasion.

The Tripartite Commission for the Restitution of Monetary Gold had been set up pursuant to Part III of the Agreement on Reparation from Germany, on the Establishment of an Inter-Allied Reparation Agency and on the Restitution of Monetary Gold, signed at Paris on 14 January 1946. Luxembourg had signed this Agreement, which was ratified by the Chamber of Deputies on 1 June 1949.[10]

At the Paris Conference on Reparation, Luxembourg had presented a memorandum which valued the confiscations of gold and currency at $5,050,838.00 (value in 1945) and the requisitions of gold and currency at $5,316,453.00 (value in 1945).[11]

As the requisitions were considered to be permitted by the Conventions of The Hague because the Germans had paid an indemnity, Article 55 of the Luxembourg Law on Compensation for War Damages stipulated: "Transfers of gold, currency, securities and bills of value in the possession of the occupier in accordance with the provisions enacted by him shall not give rise to compensation".[12] Article 58 of the same Law precluded from any indemnification "luxury or speculative objects such as precious metals, jewellery, natural pearls, furs, carpets, lace, statues, pictures, etc., collections of objets d'art and rare and precious objects, stamp collections and stores of wine and liqueurs".[13] Thus, Luxembourg's archives are unlikely to enable a detailed list of the confiscations perpetrated by the German occupier to be drawn up. As regards works of art, it should be pointed out that thanks to close collaboration with the Belgian Recovery Mission a number of pictures and works of art have been found in German depots and brought back to Luxembourg. Statements by persons having suffered despoilment in this field are few, fifty or so, and virtually all the objets d'art have been found and returned. Nevertheless, it seems that some objets d'art and/or books have ended up in Russia. We have not had confirmation of certain rumours, however.

A number of pictures belonging at that time to Prince Felix of Luxembourg had been despoiled from his house in Italy. The Italian Government compensated the Prince at the time. This year (1997), however, now that the house no longer belongs to the Grand-Ducal family of Luxembourg, one of the pictures was sold at auction in Vienna, Austria. It has not been possible to find out who either the vendor or the purchaser was.

On 13 March 1947 the Tripartite Gold Commission addressed a letter to all the signatory States informing them that it had been set up. Attached to this communication was a questionnaire which the Prime Minister of Luxembourg returned duly completed and with supporting documentation on 5 May 1947. After examining Luxembourg's case the Commission dismissed the demand for the 8 ingots belonging to the Pescatore Foundation because the latter was considered to be a private institution and its gold could not be considered to be monetary gold of Luxembourg. Finally, the Commission recognised that "4,223.7040 kgs of fine gold were despoiled by Germany or unlawfully transferred to German territory".[14] Finally, an initial award granted the Grand Duchy 1,929.4999 kgs of fine gold. On 28 October 1947 the documents relating thereto were signed at Brussels. At the same time Luxembourg, like Belgium, transferred its gold to France as provided for in the agreements signed in February/March 1946. The second assignment of gold in 1958 awarded Luxembourg 750 kgs of fine gold which were immediately transferred to France pursuant to the abovementioned agreements. That is still the legal position today, and any gold awarded to the Grand Duchy of Luxembourg would be transferred to France pursuant to the 1946 agreements.

NOTES

[1] Ministry of Finance: Gold file: Letter of 7 October 1944 from Camille Gutt to Pierre Dupong.

[2] Ministry of Finance: Gold file: Draft letter of 13 November 1944 to be sent to the Banque nationale de Belgique. The letter sent was dated 14 November.

[3] Ministry of Finance: Gold file.

[4] Ministry of Finance: Gold file: Letter of 21 July 1945.

[5] Ministry of Finance: Gold file: Copy of the letter of 4 December 1945 from the Banque de France to the Governor of the Banque nationale de Belgique.

[6] Ministry of Finance: Gold file: Note of 7 January 1946 from the CEE.

[7] Ministry of Finance: Gold file: Letter of 21 January 1946 from the Governor of the BNB to the Minister for Finance in Luxembourg.

[8] Ministry of Finance: Gold file: Copy of the Convention.

[9] Ministry of Finance: Gold file: Copy of the Note of 13 August 1946 from the Legation of France to the Luxembourg Ministry for Foreign Affairs.

[10] National archives of Luxembourg: MAE 8253: Draft law and opinion of the Council of State.

[11] Ministry of Finance: Gold file: Letter of 4 October 1946 from Paul Bastian, a member of the Study Committee for War Reparations to the Minister for Finance. In this letter Mr. Bastian proposed a detailed inquiry into the requisitions and confiscations. The files we have been able to consult contain no indication of any such inquiry.

[12] Memorial no. 21 of 27 March 1950, pp. 509–526. Commentary on Article 55: "It was a general, even economic, measure which made the victim lose a speculative value for which he was indemnified by the occupier: this measure is permitted by the Convention of The Hague."

[13] National Resistance Council: File 819: Reparations. The first draft had provided for compensation "in accordance with the real market value of these objects on 10.5.1940 multiplied by an index number of 2." Following the Council of State's opinion Article 55 was amended to the form in which it was voted.

[14] Ministry of Finance: Gold file: Decision taken by the Tripartite Commission for the Restitution of Monetary Gold following a request submitted by the Government of the Grand Duchy of Luxembourg with a view to the restitution of 4,317.2028 kgs of fine gold.

THE NETHERLANDS

Introduction by Count Jan d'Ansembourg

HEAD OF THE NETHERLANDS DELEGATION

My delegation is of the opinion that this conference offers a unique opportunity to collect a maximum of knowledge of the historic facts related to the gold that was stolen by the Nazis, in learning how victims have been compensated and how this can be done in the future.

The issue of stolen gold (both monetary and private gold) has lain dormant in the public perception for a considerable time and re-emerged only recently, after the end of the Cold War.

The long period of inactivity has created the necessity to establish or to re-establish structures coordinating the activities of ministries, other official agencies and non-governmental organizations. In this context today's conference can be extremely useful since it will familiarize us with solutions and initiatives other countries have undertaken to meet these challenges.

My delegation intends to contribute six papers to this conference. They are entitled:

- Dutch gold;
- Looting and restitution;
- Compensation schemes for victims of persecution;
- Concern for Dutch groups of war victims from World War II;
- Bank balances in the Netherlands' Indies;
- Information on the activities of the Contact Group World War II deposits.

With these papers we intend to provide elements of answers to the three questions which mark the three separate parts of our conference. They will be introduced by different members of my delegation.

In order to give you an overall view of the subject of this Conference in relation to The Netherlands I should like to formulate brief answers to the three questions.

1. Where did the looted gold come from and what happened to it?

During the Second World War 146 tons of Dutch gold were stolen from the Dutch Central Bank by the German Occupation Forces and was subsequently partly sold to Switzerland in order to pay directly or indirectly for the importation of goods. The Tripartite Gold Commission which was established after World War II to organise the restitution of monetary gold recognised only 110 tons of The Netherlands claim as being monetary gold. The remaining 36 tons consisted of gold that was involuntarily sold by individuals to the bank of The Netherlands during the war and was considered by the Tripartite Gold Commission to be stolen private gold. This has contributed to a large part to the fact that The Netherlands recovered less than 50% of its claim, and therefore, in relative terms, less than any other country. During the Second World War Jewish properties were robbed in a systematic and thorough fashion. With the help of fake legal constructions money, securities, jewelry and artefacts were transferred in many ways to Germany. After the war The Netherlands Council for the Restitution of Legal Rights was entrusted with the task of restoring property rights to the rightful owners or their heirs. By 1951 approximately 90% of moneys and securities had been repaid.

In the former Netherlands Indies under Japanese occupation gold and property was also stolen even though this took place in a less systematic way than from the Jewish population in The Netherlands. Since this issue has never been clearly settled The Netherlands will start a new investigation regarding these valuables.

2. What steps have been taken to compensate occupied countries and individual victims?

After the Second World War a unique system of legislation for war victims was established in The Netherlands, comprising a separate regulation for each category. According to this legislation members of the Resistance and sailors were entitled to pensions as if they had been in government service. The benefit legislation has its legal basis in a special form of commitment to solidarity between the Dutch society and the civilian war victims. Several establishments dispensing immaterial support to war victims were also instituted.

Victims of persecution form a separate category for whom the Victims of Persecution Benefit Act was passed in 1973. This act provides financial support for this category.

3. What should be the next steps?

In order to monitor all developments concerning war deposits and to advise the government on these issues The Netherlands has instituted an independent committee called Contact Group World War II deposits. This committee, headed by Mr. Van Kemenade, *inter alia*, monitors investigations conducted abroad into war deposits and reviews whether Dutch residents might put in claims in respect of such funds.

Another committee, headed by Mr. Scholten, is tasked with investigating the actual system of legal redress applied by Dutch banks and insurance companies on the basis of records in the archives.

Apart from these committees there is a committee dealing with artifacts stolen during the war and a committee which will be appointed shortly to deal with material losses inflicted on Dutch citizens in the former Dutch East Indies during the war.

One of the issues on which the committee of Mr. Van Kemenade will advise the government is destination of the Dutch part of the final distribution of gold by the Tripartite Gold Commission.

Dutch gold*

1. At the end of the Second World War, the Allies soon turned their attention to retrieving the gold stolen by the Nazis during the war and returning it to its rightful owners. The Reichsbank's gold that was still in Germany was collected, and an investigation was launched into the gold that had been sold in Switzerland or used to pay for imports from neutral countries like Switzerland, Portugal, Spain and Sweden.

The Paris Reparation Act, which regulated reparation payments and included passages on the restitution of the stolen gold, was signed in January 1946. The Netherlands was among the 18 signatories. The Act also set up a Tripartite Gold Commission (TGC) which consisted of France, the United Kingdom and the United States, to which all countries that had been the victims of Nazi theft could submit a claim for the restitution of their stolen gold. It also stipulated that the gold retrieved would be distributed in proportion to the loss that they had suffered as a result of looting by the occupying forces. The agreement would apply only to monetary gold (i.e. gold belonging to states or their central banks).

Claims submitted by the following countries were recognised: the Netherlands, Belgium, Italy, Austria, Czechoslovakia, Luxembourg, Poland, Yugoslavia, Greece and Albania. Belgium was a special case, since Belgian gold had been taken to France and had been returned by the French after the war. These countries claimed a total of 552 tonnes of gold with a current value of $622 million. However only 232 tonnes of gold (with a value of $263 million at today's prices) was eventually found, with Belgium, the Netherlands and Austria having the largest claims (see Table 1).

One problem was that Nazi Germany had sold a large proportion of the stolen gold most of which came from Belgium and the Netherlands – to Switzerland. Germany had only a fairly small gold reserve at the beginning of the war (over 100 tonnes and part of this, along with some of the stolen gold, was transferred to Switzerland to pay for imports and to purchase Swiss francs which were then used to buy goods from Sweden, Portugal, Spain etc.

The TGC therefore entered into negotiations with Switzerland on 18 March 1946 with the aim of retrieving as much of the gold as possible. However, Switzerland was of the opinion that, as a neutral country, it had obtained the gold legally. The Swiss did nevertheless acknowledge that the Allied victory had been extremely important for Switzerland and that they had a certain responsibility to help with the reconstruction of Europe. The Allied-Swiss Accord, in which Switzerland stated that it could not recognise the Allied claims to the gold, but expressed its willingness to make CHF 250 million available to the three governments of the TGC, was signed in Washington on 25 May 1946.

---

* The tables in this text are taken from: W.F.V. Vanthoor and C. van Renselaar (ESB 1997, pp.51–53), *Het is niet alles goud wat er blinkt* ("All that glitters is not gold").

Table 1. Monetary gold stolen by Germany during World War II

	In tonnes of gold
Belgium	198
Netherlands	146
Italy	46
Austria	92
Czechoslovakia	39
Others[1]	31
Total gold stolen	552
Gold retrieved	232
Net amount stolen	320
German gold reserve, end 1939	107
Total available	427
of which, to Switzerland in World War II	364

[1] Albania, Greece, Luxembourg, Poland and Yugoslavia.
Source: A.L. Smith Jr., *Hitler's Gold. The Story of the Nazi War Loot*, Oxford/New York, 1989

In return, these three governments declared that "they would refrain from making any further claims on behalf of themselves or the countries they represented (including the Netherlands)".

2. The Netherlands had submitted a claim for 145,649 kg of gold to the TGC. This was only a fifth of the total Dutch monetary gold reserve at the beginning of the war, because the rest had either been deposited abroad or taken out of the country in May 1940. However, the TGC recognised only 110,174 kg as a legitimate claim, stating that only this proportion was monetary gold. The rest was gold that Dutch residents had sold to De Nederlandsche Bank for guilders after May 1940. The TGC ruled that although these sales had been made under duress or in the face of intimidation from the occupying forces, they involved gold stolen from individuals, which could not therefore be regarded as monetary gold.

The Netherlands ultimately received compensation for 70,367 kg of gold. The third, 1958, instalment was accepted only in 1973, in the hope that the rejected part of the claim could still be recognised. In total, the Dutch received less than 50% of their gold claim from the Inter-Allied Reparation Agency fund (see Table 2).

3. The Netherlands disputed the rejection of part of its claim at the time. Finance minister Lieftinck and his successors also attempted to secure this part of the claim as well, basing their argument on the moral principle that the gold had, after all, been stolen and the fact that the Swiss authorities should have

Table 2. Size and distribution of the IARA's gold fund

	In tonnes of gold
Deposited in Switzerland	53
Deposited in Sweden	7
Found in Germany	232
Total	292
Spain 1950[1]	42.5
Total for distribution	334.5
Total paid out[2]	329
Belgium	121
Netherlands	71
Italy	44
Austria	50
Czechoslovakia	28
Others[3]	15
Remaining	5.5

[1] Spain was the only neutral country that returned gold to the IARA.

[2] The amounts in dollars are based on the quantities.

[3] Albania, Greece, Luxembourg, Poland and Yugoslavia.

Source: Verhandlungen um Rückerstattung mit den Neutralen in: *Neue Zürcher Zeitung*, 16 November 1996

realised this, as they had known how small Germany's gold reserve was at the beginning of the war. They also argued that, when it was stolen, the gold was in the possession of De Nederlandsche Bank. The Netherlands has never officially withdrawn its claim for this non-monetary gold.

Looting and restitution

A brief history of the theft of property from Dutch Jews during the Second World War and its post-war restitution*

INTRODUCTION

During the Second World War, some 135,000 Dutch Jews were robbed of their possessions. Of the approximately 107,000 people deported, only some 5,200 returned. The theft of the property of Dutch Jews was extremely systematic. It was generally based on ordinances (Verordnungen) that had the force of statute law and sometimes on 'measures', 'decrees' or 'orders' issued by the Sicherheitsdienst (SD). The SD's orders usually sanctioned the theft of bicycles, radios and household effects. The SD also sold the so-called 120,000 stamps, which I shall return to in a moment. The occupying forces went to remarkable lengths to give the theft, often euphemistically referred to as 'surrender', a semblance of legality.

The ordinances governed:

a. Individuals
b. Companies
c. Non-commercial Associations and Foundations

The Jews were forced to surrender their property to the Lippmann & Rosenthal bank, Sarphatistraat (Liro). Companies and non-commercial associations and foundations had to hand their property in to the Vermögensverwaltung und Rentenanstalt (VVRA). The theft was comprehensive – everything from household effects to art collections was looted.

The term 'Jew' was defined in Ordinance 189/1940 (article 4) as:

1. [...] a person with at least three grandparents who are full-blooded Jews by race.
2. A Jew is also a person with at least two grandparents who are full-blooded Jews and who was either a member of the Jewish religious community on 9 May 1940 or who subsequently became a member, or was married to a Jew on 9 May 1940 or subsequently married a Jew,
3. A grandparent shall be a full-blooded Jew if he or she was a member of the Jewish religious community.

The definition may seem precise, but article 4 of Ordinance 189/1940 allowed many borderline cases. Mixed marriages (Mischehen), in particular, caused the Liro organisation many administrative problems, which could only be resolved by a deluge of provisions, exemptions and individual measures. This may have delayed the theft slightly, but it certainly did not prevent it.

---

* Conference paper of the Van Kemenade Committee submitted by the Netherlands State Institute for War Documentation.

ORDINANCES

On 24 June 1940, Ordinance 26/40 on Enemy Property was issued, governing the businesses and possessions of Dutch people who had fled the country in May of that year. Many Jews had left the country, but so had citizens of other states with which Germany was at war. Enemy property had to be registered with the Deutsche Revisions- und Treuhand AG in The Hague and then surrendered to the General Kommissar für Finanz und Wirtschaft. Ordinance 26/40 related to all property, both movable and immovable.

Non-commercial associations and foundations had to be registered under Ordinance 145/40 of 20 September 1940, Jewish companies about a month later (Ordinance 189/40, 20 September 1940). Administration of the companies was taken over from the first quarter of 1941 onwards. All Jewish associations and foundations without exception were liquidated. Jewish companies were 'Aryanised' to 'purify' the Dutch economy of Jewish elements. Small companies were liquidated, usually by the Omnia Treuhand. Large companies proved difficult to sell owing to the risks attaching to them: if Hitler were to lose the war the sale would be reversed. Most of them, along with the smaller, prosperous Jewish companies, continued to operate under an administrator. Companies were sold by the administrator or through the mediation of the Niederlandische Aktiengesellschaft für Finanz und Wirtschaft (NAGU). The proceeds of the sales were deposited in full with the Vermdgensverwaltung und Rentenanstal (VVRA).

The VVRA was responsible for repaying the original Jewish owners in 100 quarterly instalments, i.e. over 25 years, or at 4% per annum without interest. In practice, the length of the repayment term was immaterial because when Seyss-Inquart, the German-appointed commissioner of the Netherlands during the occupation, established the VVRA in May 1941 – with a founding capital of just one hundred guilders – there were already plans to deport the Dutch Jews. The repayment was farcical but entirely in keeping with the Germans' desire for a veneer of legality. They also wished to avoid sowing panic or confusion among their victims.

Jewish agricultural property, land, houses and mortgage loans were also expropriated by means of ordinances (March, May and August 1941) and sold to German and Dutch people (usually black marketeers and NSB collaborators). The so-called Liro Ordinances, named after the Lippmann & Rosenthal bank, Sarphatistraat, were particularly notorious. Nearly every Jew came into contact with Liro. The First Liro Ordinance (Ordinance 148/41, 8 August 1941) forced Jews to open an account with Liro, Sarphatistraat (as opposed to Lippmann & Rosenthal, Nieuwe Spiegelstraat, a reputable Jewish bank). Under this Ordinance, which governed mainly private property, the Jews had to surrender their cash, cheques, bank balances and securities to Liro. Bank and giro services were compelled to transfer the balances in the accounts of their Jewish customers to Liro. Whether a customer was Jewish was determined by means of a questionnaire that was sent to every account holder. The Jews lost virtually all control of their bank balances at Liro. It would be beyond the scope of this brief history to consider the many special provisions.

The Second Liro Ordinance (Ordinance 58/42, 21 May 1942) demanded the surrender of all amounts receivable (including insurance benefits), rights (including patents, copyrights, trade marks, concessions and rights of inheritance), collections of all kinds, works of art, precious metals, and jewels. Amounts receivable from third parties (including international claims) also had to be registered. Horses, vehicles and vessels had to be registered with the Zentralstelle fürjudische Auswanderung.

The occupying forces were worried that the Jews might conceal such valuables as foreign currency (pounds, dollars, etc.), precious metals and precious stones – illegal property in their eyes. In the summer of 1943 the SD sold 120,000 stamps for 25,000 guilders (at today's prices approximately 250,000 guilders) that granted exemption from deportation 'until further notice'. In practice, the stamp offered no more than a brief respite. In the 1950s Stichting Sieraden-Comité (the Jewellery Committee) managed to obtain some compensation from Germany.

It cannot be said how much the Jews managed to conceal in the form of cash, jewels and securities, but it is safe to assume that practically all the immovable property was registered.

Post-war restitution has been a protracted and, for the Jews, often painful process, complicated by many legal claims and counterclaims. Furthermore, the process was initially retarded by a lack of legal precedent. Restitution, particularly of securities, took more than a quarter of a century; the Securities Registration Division was not closed until 1 October 1971.

RESTITUTION

The restoration of property rights was entrusted to the Council for the Restitution of Legal Rights, appointed under the London Restitution of Legal Rights Decree (Bulletin of Acts and Decrees E 100). The Council was an umbrella organisation that met on only one occasion, namely on the day of its inauguration, 20 August 1945. The Council consisted of a:
- Judicial Division
- Securities Registration Division
- Property Administration Division (including the Netherlands Property Administration Institute, NBI)
- Missing Persons Division
- Legal Persons Division
- Movable Property Division

The Council's executive committee was made up of the Chairman of the Council together with the chairmen of the various departments.

Everyone in the Netherlands with information that could lead to the restitution of property was obliged to report to the authorities, not only the victims themselves, but also their families, friends, acquaintances, banks, insurance companies, etc. Banks, for example, had to report the safe-deposit boxes of Jewish customers who had not returned (the contents of which had not, of course, been registered with Liro). Under the supervision of a notary, the boxes were then opened and the contents taken into custody.

A number of bodies played an important role in the restoration of the Jews' legal rights. After the War, the NB administered enemy property that had been seized by the Dutch government under the special criminal jurisdiction. In practice, this was the property of collaborators and 'enemy subjects' (from Germany, Austria, Italy, Japan, etc.).

It has already been noted that Liro and the VVRA were at the heart of the German looting machine. The NBI appointed administrators/liquidators to return the property from these two organisations to the rightful owners or their heirs. Liro was administered by a body named the Liquidatie van Vermdgensverwaltung Sarphatistraat (LVVS); the VVRA retained its name.

The LVVS was immediately faced with an enormous problem. Rather than keep separate accounts for 'full-blooded Jews', since 1 January 1943 Liro had deposited everything in a single Sammelkonto. When the LVVS commenced its work in May 1945 only 2,000 account holders were known; by the time the Sammelkonto had been unravelled, four years later, there were 70,000 accounts.

CASH, GIRO BALANCES, BANK BALANCES AND SECURITIES

Cash, giro balances and bank balances were deposited with Liro. The most important sales channel for securities was the Amsterdam Stock Exchange. Many securities were also sold in France. At the time of the liberation, those that had not been sold were lying in Liro's vaults or had been deposited with banks in Amsterdam or Germany. Some had been handed over to German institutions. The securities that had been sent to Germany were never recovered after the war. When the Soviets took Berlin, they seized securities and sold at least some of them on the international market. During the occupation, too, a relatively small number of securities had been stolen. The restitution of securities was an extremely complex and protracted process, which had several goals in addition to restoring the rights of the 'dispossessed', such as tracing enemy property, informing the tax authorities of security holdings and taking stock of the Netherlands' foreign exchange reserves.

Under the Restitution of Legal Rights Decree, all securities issued in the Netherlands, located either at home or abroad, and all foreign securities (also at home or abroad) that were owned by, held in the name of or held on behalf of Dutch citizens had to be registered with the authorities. Dutch embassies were used to register the securities. The intention, of course, was to establish ownership and to gain information on illegal acts committed during the occupation. All securities had to be handed in to a designated office for registration before 14 April 1946 (the reference date). Securities that were not registered ('missing' securities) were cancelled by having their numbers published in the Government Gazette. They were replaced with duplicates that had to be handed in to the Agent of the Ministry of Finance.

This decree did not govern foreign securities since they did not fall under Dutch jurisdiction. The Committee for the Restitution of Foreign Securities

(CRBE) was established for foreign securities. Agreements were concluded with foreign states, including Switzerland. It would be beyond the scope of this paper to consider the methods and procedures for registering securities in detail. Furthermore, it would require many pages of text. It is important to note, however, that the 'dispossessed' accepted 90% compensation from the Securities Restitution Guarantee Fund and other bodies. Part compensation for foreign securities was provided by the former FRG under the German Bundesruckstatt-ungsgesetz, Brüg (the so-called Wiedergutmachung). Where the rightful owners could not be found, the securities devolved upon the State.

Part of the capital surrendered to Liro was used to maintain and enlarge the camps at Vught and Westerbork, to cover the running expenses of the Hausraterfassungsstelle (which stripped Jews' houses after the occupants had been deported) and to pay 'bounties' to people who betrayed Jews. In addition it went to cover the costs of the extensive Liro while the Jewish Council and the Jüdische Unterstützungstelle were paid from Liro's resources.

In 1951, after much legal and administrative wrangling, an agreement was reached under which most account holders would receive 90% of the securities they had surrendered to Liro. The average account holder lost 10% and, since interest was not paid, about 10 years' interest.

HOUSEHOLD EFFECTS

In total, some 29,000 families were forced out of their homes. Chairs, tables, etc. disappeared in most cases to Germany, where they were given to the victims of the Allied bombings. In 13,000 cases, those forced out of their homes received partial compensation from the government under the War Damage Act (WMO). In the other cases, the heirs could not be traced or the beneficiaries were no longer living in the Netherlands.

The WMO did not provide for the complete reinstatement of all household effects but only for a contribution towards the most basic necessities. There was therefore no compensation for libraries, works of art, jewellery, etc. The same applied to loss of businesses; no compensation was provided, for example, for loss of company stocks. The WMO was applicable to all Dutch citizens, not only to Jews. Some compensation was also provided under the Wiedergutmachung and some compensation was available for jewellery, works of art, collections and foreign securities under the Brüg.

INSURANCE POLICIES

22,368 insurance policies were registered with Liro. The insurance companies were forced to surrender all the policies of their Jewish customers and deposit the cash value with Liro. After the war, a number of test cases were held which generally led to the restoration of the policyholders' rights. It is unclear how many of those entitled to do so actually sought legal redress.

COMPANIES

About 2,000 companies were 'Aryanised' and a further 13,000-plus were liqui-dated. It is virtually impossible to put a figure on their value. The purchase prices were usually far lower than their true value and no account was taken of goodwill. Jews suffered the greatest financial losses in this area because they received virtually no compensation for their companies and absolutely none under the WMO. If the premises were owned (i.e. not rented), the rights of the original owners were restored in that they recovered possession of the premises.

IMMOVABLE PROPERTY AND AGRICULTURAL LAND

In general, immovable property and agricultural land were restored. With regard to mortgages, claims were granted against the Niederländische Grundstückverwaltung (in liquidation). The actual outcome is not known.

EINSATZSTAB REICHSLEITER ROSENBERG

Not all works of art were seized under the Second Liro Ordinance. In many cases Einsatzstab Reichsleiter Rosenberg (ERR) or Dienststelle Mühlmann had already struck. ERR looted libraries, art collections, ceremonial objects and archives under a Führererlass issued in June 1940. Both ERR and the Dienststelle were active before the Liro Ordinances took effect. There were very few famous Jewish art collections in the Netherlands (apart from that of Fritz Mannheimer, who died shortly before the war). The Netherlands Office for Fine Arts was responsible for the recovery of art after the war. A great deal has never been recovered: about 20% of the first class works and about 80% of works of the second rank. It can be assumed that these are now scattered throughout the world. It recently became known that many of them are in Russia. The Erlass was directed at Freemasons as well as Jews.

UNCLAIMED PROPERTY

If the rightful owners were not known, natural persons (lawyers, notaries) were initially appointed to administer unclaimed property; later, foundations estab-lished by the NBI were also appointed as administrators. If it was established that the rightful owners were no longer missing, which in practice usually meant that they were dead, the administration was wound up. Notification was often a question of chance. Anyone who had information about unclaimed property, usually a relative, was obliged to notify the authorities.

Heirs were traced by the Registrar of Births, Marriages and Deaths or by means of notices published in national newspapers. When an heir was found, the case was usually handed over to a notary, who attended to its further settle-ment. A recurrent problem was that the Jews who were murdered in the con-centration camps did not have death certificates. In 1949 this problem was resolved by the Death Certificates (Missing Persons) Act (Bulletin of Acts and Decrees J.227). Administration was nonetheless continued in many cases, sometimes by the notary concerned and sometimes by the Foundation for the Administration of Missing Persons and Unclaimed Property (BAON) in Amsterdam.

If administration was wound up, many estates were managed for a given period in accordance with the Civil Code, particularly if there was uncertainty regarding the fate of the heirs, their place of residence, identity or the primacy of their right of succession. In the last case, it was important to know whether the husband or wife had died first.

In many cases, the balance of the estate was ultimately transferred to the State Consignation Fund. No exceptions were made for Jewish estates from the period 1940–45 and they, too, were subject to the provisions of the Consignation of Monies Act. At the end of a given period, the estates devolved upon the State. Such estates were published in the Government Gazette.

As far as is known, the government has not carried out any investigation other than through the offices of the Council for the Restitution of Legal Rights. It cannot be ruled out, however, that banks and/or insurance companies have carried out investigations on their own initiative.

Compensation schemes for victims of persecution in the Netherlands and the former colony of the Netherlands East Indies

The schemes for assistance to the victims of war in the Netherlands go back to World War II. A temporary scheme was introduced as long ago as 1944. Under the scheme, financial support was given to the victims of war, which included all those who as a result of war or the circumstances of war or as a result of actions or measures taken by the occupier were wholly or partially unable to provide for their own subsistence.

This scheme was replaced in 1961 by a piece of legislation called the Government Group Scheme for the Victims of War 1940–45. Under this scheme, victims of war refers specifically to those who as a result of war, the circumstances of war or as a result of actions or measures by the occupying force in the Netherlands has become wholly or partly disabled. The scheme was converted in 1965 into a scheme based on the National Assistance Act which had meanwhile come into force and which provided financial support to all Dutch citizens who were unable to provide for their own subsistence. The opportunity was also seized to declare the scheme applicable to victims of war in the former Netherlands East Indies.

Meanwhile, increasing attention had been called to a special category of war victims, namely those who had been exposed to persecution on the basis of race, religion, sexual proclivity or philosophy. This ultimately led to a separate piece of legislation being passed in 1973 for this special category: the Victims of Persecution Benefit Act 1940–45 (Wuv). The Act controls the allocation of payments to those who underwent persecution during the German or Japanese occupation on account of their race, religion, sexual proclivity or philosophy and to those who experienced persecution during the Japanese occupation on account of their European origins or disposition. The Act defines persecution as follows: deprivation of freedom by confinement in concentration camp, prisons or other establishments where termination of life or permanent control was intended. Being subject to sterilisation and going underground to avoid being deprived of one's freedom were also included in the definition. The description therefore embraces various groups of victims of persecution, such as the Jews, Jehovah's Witnesses, gypsies, homosexuals and political prisoners.

The Wuv guarantees an income which enables the victims of persecution to continue to live within reasonable limits at the level to which they were accustomed before being afflicted by the consequences of persecution. Apart from a monthly benefit, special payments can also be claimed; these include reimbursement for the cost of medical assistance, social facilities, domestic help, etc.

As to the scope of the Wuv, the scheme is unique, as payments and benefits are awarded throughout the world to victims of persecution in the Netherlands and the former Netherlands East Indies who have now made their home else-where in the world, but still have a link with the Netherlands.

Compensation to the Netherlands and former Netherlands East-Indies after the Second World War

On April 8, 1960 the governments of Holland and the Federal Republic of Germany concluded a treaty concerning a settlement for financial problems and payments in favour of Dutch victims of the Nazi persecution. It was agreed that Germany would pay Holland 280 million D-mark including an amount of 125 million D-mark on behalf of claims of Dutch citizens who were persecuted on account of their race, religion or philosophy. With this payment was agreed that the Dutch government would give up all future claims. Individual claims of Dutch citizens however remain possible.

The circumstances concerning the back-pay obligations of Japan to the Netherlands were quite different. On December 27, 1949 the Kingdom of the Netherlands carried over the sovereignty of the former Netherlands East Indies to the new Republic of Indonesia. This assignment included all claims of Dutch subjects. This applies also the claims on Japan. In 1951 a peace-treaty was closed in San Francisco which prescribed that Japan was only due to backpay those countries whose current territory was occupied by Japan during the Second World War. Japan was forced to carry over all assets to the International Red Cross who would divide the money among the military victims of war. There was no settlement on behalf of the civil victims. During the peace-treaty confer-ence the former Japanese Prime Minister Mr Yoshida and the Dutch Prime Minister Mr Stikker concluded an agreement in favour of the Dutch civil vic-tims of war. In 1965 a small amount of money was transferred to Holland.

Concern for Dutch groups of war victims from the Second World War

One third of the Dutch now alive experienced World War II. In broad terms, anyone born in 1942 has conscious memories of that period. Even slightly younger members of society often had experiences that radically affected the rest of their lives, even though they did not have those experiences consciously.

The Netherlands not only has victims of the Nazi regime, for there are also many victims of the Japanese occupation of the former colony of the Netherlands East Indies, nowadays called the Indonesian Republic, during World War II.

Dutch (civil) victims of war can be classified in five categories:
- Members of the resistance in the Netherlands
- Members of the resistance in the former Netherlands East Indies
- Maritime war victims
- Victims of persecution
- Civil victims of war

Over the years, the Dutch government has developed a unique system of legislation for those affected by war. There is a separate Act for each category. The basic principle underpinning all legislation concerning victims of war is to guarantee an income for resistance members, seamen, victims of persecution and civil victims of war, and their next of kin, who have become physically or mentally disabled through the events of war. This income will enable them to continue, within reasonable limits, to live at the level to which they were accustomed before the consequences of the disaster of war became manifest. The general principle is enshrined in different ways in the various pieces of legislation. There are three pension acts which find their legal basis in a "notional employment contract". The resistance worker or seaman is dealt with as if he were in government service during the war. On the basis of this contract of employment, the government is obliged to provide reimbursement and care, if the resistance worker or seaman has become disabled or died as a result of his active participation in the war effort.

There are two pieces of benefit legislation which have their legal basis in a special form of commitment to solidarity between Dutch society and the victims of persecution and the civil victims of war. The guiding principle in these acts is that the level of benefit is based on the income formerly enjoyed and is related to family circumstances. Further details on the Victims or Persecution Benefit Act can be found in a separate paper on the compensation schemes for the victims of persecution.

The application and implementation of acts covering the victims of war has been entrusted to a single organisation since 1990: the Pension and Benefit Council, which even today employs more than 300 full-time staff.

At present, some 50,000 people receive a benefit or pension under the legislation covering war victims. Furthermore, there are various government-financed institutions focused on non-material assistance to war victims.

In 1980, an information and coordination body for services to war victims was set up with the aim of improving assistance and services to war victims from World War II. This body provides information and advice to war victims and mediates in the provision of assistance. A further aspect of its operations is the provision of information on the specific problems of war victims, particularly for the benefit of aid workers and aid bodies.

There are four institutions which employ social workers specialised in the specific problems of the various groups of war victims.

In 1973, a centre was set up for the medico-psychological treatment of resistance workers and war victims from World War II. The treatment is mainly psychotherapeutic in nature. Apart from a clinic, the centre offers out-patient and day treatment.

Bank balances in the Netherlands East Indies

BANKING SYSTEM DURING THE WAR

In September 1942, the Japanese authorities decided to entirely liquidate non-Japanese (savings) banks. This was carried out in three separate areas: Java, Sumatra and the rest of Indonesia. In their attempts at liquidation, the Japanese focused primarily on collecting debts – Dutch safes were broken open and the contents sold, with owners of the appropriated goods being officially given claims against the Nanpo Kaihatso Ginko (Nanpobank). The Nanpobank became the bank of circulation; payment to hostile subjects was forbidden. The Yokohama Speciebank focused in particular on the needs of the army.

Allied citizens had to pay an extra war tax. When the Dutch were interned, any gold or silver objects and coins were confiscated. Shares and securities were not impounded as a rule. Internees had to pay for their own camp set-up and maintenance: they had to surrender their gold and were allowed to retain 10 guilders. They were to receive wages for voluntary work. Real estate and immovable property were seized. The governments of the US, UK and the Netherlands transferred funds for internees in 1944 via Sweden, Switzerland and the Vatican.

BANKING SYSTEM AFTER THE WAR

By Royal Decree of 3 May 1944, the Bank for the Netherlands East Indies (founded at Paramaribo) was given the right to operate as a monopoly in Indonesia. The bank worked to a limited degree only. On 2 January 1946, other banks were allowed to resume operations. Curiously enough, Japanese banks continued to work more or less as usual: in some cases in smaller units, and sometimes under a different name.

In 1945, a Dutch delegation left for the United States to see – under the auspices of the Far Eastern Commission – whether goods confiscated by Japan could be recovered. The Dutch delegation set up a military mission in Japan; talks were held with the liquidator of the banks on Java between 1942 and 1945.

A "Freezing of Assets Ordinance" came into force in Indonesia in 1945 and was sustained until 30 March 1948. Payments to (pre-war) creditors were temporarily prohibited. A pre-war balance could only be released if an exchange permit or a credit licence had been issued, or if the funds requested could be put to a productive purpose.

The "Restoration of Legal Transactions Ordinance" of 8 May 1947 boiled down to the fact that pre-war claims against banks retained their value after the war. Payments on debts made to banks during the war were recognised as 'discharging'.

After 1948, the banks were free to make payments. Within the parameters of the transfer scheme, funds could be transferred to the Netherlands from as early as February 1947.

This fact and other indicators reveal that there was no question of total seizure by the Japanese.

In 1949, a round-table conference was held between the Netherlands and Indonesia. The literature speaks of the transfer of interest, dividends, contributions and payments. If Dutch creditors requested payment of old claims, termed arrears, this would be enabled to proceed following further talks. Bank balances held by Dutch citizens who had worked in Indonesia were not included among the arrears but were deemed part of capital transactions. It is unclear whether this also applies to bank balances from before 1942.

The term 'gurni accounts' was used for outstanding bank balances held by Dutch citizens. Balances in Dutch guilders could be paid, subject to Indonesian currency measures In 1956, Indonesia served notice on the financial arrangements surrounding the round-table conference.

In 1950, a monetary reform was introduced in Indonesia which effectively meant that bank balances were halved.

After the war, it was found that the Japanese had seized more than 52 million guilders in cash (ie not bank balances) from the liquidated banks. This amount was virtually identical to the balance of the liquidation account of the Nanpobank. The Javasche Bank maintained supervision of the Nanpobank after the war. The closing balances of the Javasche Bank branches were handed over to the Government after the war. It is not clear even today to what extent the claims against the Nanpobank have been honoured.

What happened to the bank balances in the Bersiap and Revolution period is a separate story. The same is true for the nationalisations that occurred between 1951 and 1960.

CONCLUSION

One provisional conclusion could be that there was no question of systematic plundering by the Japanese of the balances of Dutch citizens or Indonesian Dutch, save in so far as safe contents are concerned. As regards claims against the Nanpobank, after conducting archive studies in the Netherlands contact could be established with Indonesia and/or Japan to review the scale on which the archives have remained intact. This would require the archive of the Nanpobank, which was liquidated by the "Netherlands-Indonesia Currency Institute", to be tracked down.

It seems that the Japanese, in conjunction with the Dutch Boards, quietly and calmly proceeded to attempt to liquidate the banks. That process was not yet concluded at the time of the capitulation in August 1945. Claims to bank balances should be dealt with by the legal successors to the banks operating in 1942.

Information on the activities of the Contact Group World War II deposits

1. The Contact Group World War II deposits was officially installed on 10 March last by the Dutch Finance Minister Zalm. The Contact Group consists of: Dr J.A. van Kemenade (chairman), Prof Dr J.C.H. Blom, Drs V. Halberstadt, Mr F. Korthals Altes, Dr J. Krant, Drs J.F.M. Peters, Prof Dr A. Schilder, Drs T. de Swaan, Drs H.H.F. Wijffels and Prof L.C. van Zutphen RA (secretary).

2. The terms of reference of the Contact Group provide for:
   - Critically monitoring the investigations conducted abroad into war deposits. If so warranted by these investigations, the Contact Group will review whether Dutch residents might put in claims in respect of the funds so revealed. In that event, the Contact Group will advise the Government on an apportionment system.
   - The system of postwar legal redress in respect of financial deposits of war victims at banks and insurance companies in the Netherlands.
   - The looted monetary gold of the Netherlands.

3. The activities of the Contact Group may be divided into the following elements:

(a) Monitoring

Maintaining contacts with sister committees and commissions in Europe and the United States, such as the Independent Committee of Eminent Persons headed by Paul Volcker and the Unabhängige Expertenkommission Schweiz-Zweiter Weltkrieg headed by Professor Jean-François Bergier. In this context, various meetings have been attended over the past few months seeking to achieve a broader exchange of information.

(b) Research

At the request of the Contact Group:
   - the Dutch National Institute for War Documentation will provide a brief general overview of the plunder of notably Jewish property during the occupation and the post-war legal redress in that respect. The overview will focus on financial assets.
   - a special committee, the Scholten-committee, is investigating the actual system of legal redress applied by Dutch banks and insurance companies on the basis of – available – records in the archives. The investigation centres on the private client business of banks and insurance companies. The research team is headed by Prof Dr P.W. Klein. The set-up of the investigation is such that the Contact Group does not deal with individual claims.
   - legal research is being conducted into the Washington Agreement (May 1946) and the legal position of the Netherlands in this respect.
   - research is being conducted into different statutes of limitation and other legal issues.

(c) Advice

The Contact Group had advised Dutch Minister of Finance, Zalm:
  - that the Dutch share in the remainder of the TGC gold pool (to an amount of about 20 million guilders) should be used for the benefit of Dutch victims of the persecution. Considering the provenance of the gold, it is fair to think in this respect of Jewish (organisations of) persecution victims. With regard to potential specific allocations, the Contact Group is considering provisions for the – meanwhile elderly – victims in the Netherlands – and those living abroad – and, in addition, organisations furthering the needs of the Jewish community in the Netherlands. The Dutch government had decided not to take up for the time being the US proposal establishing an international fund for needy persecution victims (Nazi Persecutee Relief Fund).
  - that a preliminary investigation should be conducted into the issue of the war victims from the former Netherlands East Indies. The problems involved are complex and differ in material respects from those of the persecution victims in Europe but also have in common with the latter that they essentially concern – financial – suffering inflicted on Dutch citizens during World War II.

Just last week the Dutch government decided to appoint a separate committee to deal with this issue.

(d) Handling letters

The Contact Group had received more than 70 letters from private individuals and organisations. In consultation with the Netherlands Bankers' Association and the Association of Insurance Companies, it has been agreed that letters offering sufficient clues will be passed to the relevant bank, insurance company or legal successor concerned. Letters containing information and/or documentation are passed, subject to the prior approval of the sender, to the Scholten committee. Furthermore, letters have been received which could be used to advantage at a later stage in respect of policy counselling.

4. In the autumn of 1998, when the report from the Dutch National Institute for War Documentation and the interim report from the Scholten committee are available, the Contact Group hopes to be able to issue a final report containing policy recommendations.

NORWAY

The Committee's mandate is to establish what happened to Jewish property during World War II. This includes a description of the rules laid down by the Quisling regime concerning the seizure of Jewish property, the procedure for such seizures, and the estimated value of the property seized. The Committee is also instructed to determine how and to what extent seized assets/property were restored after the war, and their value.

The Committee has divided into a *majority* and a *minority*.

Summary of the Majority Report

The *majority* (the Committee's chairman Oluf Skarpnes and members Thor Falkanger, Eli Fure, Ole Kristian Grimnes, and Guri Sunde) present the following summary of their shared views:

Of the roughly 2,100 Jews who according to the minority's calculations were in Norway at the time of the German invasion, over one-third lost their lives and about 1,300 fled to Sweden. Most Jews – whether they died, fled or in a small number of cases survived in Germany or Norway – had their property seized.

In the opinion of the majority, the Committee's main task is to attempt to calculate the total financial loss sustained by the Jews as a result of having their property seized during World War II. To do this means finding the difference in value between what was taken from them during the war and what was returned to them after the war. It is this difference which in the event will make up the uncovered losses.

The first step, establishing what was taken from the Jews during the war, is the most difficult. In this connection we have in general two types of information to build on: information dating from the occupation period, and the source material available concerning what was returned to the Jews or what compensation they received after the war. The first material presents the greatest difficulties, being to some extent rather incomplete, and accordingly requiring closer examination. Determination of values must therefore to a considerable extent be based on estimates. The material we have derives principally from the Nasjonal Samling (i.e. the Norwegian Nazi Party) agency which registered and took charge of the estates confiscated from Jews, i.e. the Liquidation Board. Several problems attach to this material. One relates to the valuation of what was seized. This applies especially to movable property and stock of goods. A second problem is that not all the estates are documented. Thirdly, uncertainty attaches to items which were not registered because in one way or another they disappeared before registration was carried out. One important means of checking and correction is available, however, in the reports of losses presented after the war, cf. below.

The second step in the assignment has been to obtain information concerning what was returned to the Norwegian Jews after the war. Information on this point is more reliable, but pressure of time has prevented us from examining all the material in the archives with a bearing on the Committee's work. This source material principally originated with the three institutions which returned and paid compensation for what had been seized from refugees and deportees: the Reparations Office, the Office for war damage, and the Settlements Division of the Ministry of Justice. This material chiefly describes what was restored to the Norwegian Jews after the war. However, it also contains a considerable amount of information on what was taken from them. very many injured parties applied to the Office for war damage for compensation for losses they had sustained, and some also applied to the Settlements Division of the Ministry of Justice. Naturally they had to state what they had lost and were seeking compensation for. Consequently we have not only the registrations and information of the Nazi authorities on which to base our conclusions, but also the information submitted by Jews themselves when they claimed compensation after the war. In many cases all the members of a Jewish household were killed during deportation. That makes information relating to them less certain, because relatives or others applying on their behalf could not have had detailed knowledge of the scale of the losses.

Nor do we know how much private individuals and public bodies had to return to their rightful owners after the war. Provisions issued by the Nazi authorities and the occupying power were invalid, and everything that had been confiscated could be claimed back by its rightful owner irrespective of the good faith of the person who had acquired it.

Subject to the reservations mentioned above, the Committee's majority has calculated what can be regarded as the uncovered losses sustained by the Norwegian Jews in consequence of having their property seized during the war. The majority's assessment of uncovered losses is to a large extent based on registrations carried out at the Committee's request. Under Committee auspices, extensive research has been carried out into archives, especially at the National Archives of Norway but also at other institutions which hold archives, aimed at arriving at the best possible answers to the questions raised in the mandate. The National Archives hold a large quantity of material which has been of major importance in the Committee's work. To ensure that the archive research was as thorough as possible, the Committee, with the help of hired project assistants, examined all the wartime and postwar estate files, i.e. the documents from the Liquidation Board and from the Reparations Office. Material has also been obtained from, among other places, the postwar administration of estates relating to Jews who were killed. Using computers, the project assistants registered the equivalent value in money of confiscated and returned assets and compensation at the individual level. Confiscated assets were registered under the following headings: cash, bank deposits, policies, shares/bonds, other (collected claims, rent revenues, yields on real property), stocks, and movable property. In the opinion of the majority, loss of earnings, if any, sustained during the war because the enterprises of Jews were seized and realised, and after the war because their enterprises had to restart, falls outside the mandate. The same applies to other forms of loss of income during the period of seizure.

The majority has calculated possible uncovered losses for the various categories of assets confiscated from Norwegian Jews. Despite the relatively extensive archive research which has been carried out, and on which the valuations are based, the valuations must for most categories of assets to some extent be discretionary. For the various categories of assets, moreover, the valuations are aggregates. They do not provide a basis for estimating uncovered losses sustained, as the case may be, by individual Jews or Jewish enterprises.

The greatest uncertainty attaching to the majority's calculations of the amount of the loss relates to the valuations in the stock of goods and movable property (furniture and other movable property) categories. This is explained in more detail in the majority's reasons. The uncertainty in these categories arises in part because it has to be assumed that in a number of cases assets were concealed or removed in other ways prior to registration, whereas the amounts involved are not known. A further consideration is that the liquidation sales that were carried out usually entail lower value in money than normal sales. The majority has therefore been obliged to devise ways of adjusting the value upwards, especially where those categories of assets are concerned, as explained in the reasons given for the majority's calculations.

In the public debate on this issue, it has been maintained that Norwegian Jews only received 68% after the war of what they had lost during the war. The majority argues that this is to take too narrow a view. In the opinion of the majority, it is not possible to express what they lost as a percentage. One reason is that many assets, such as real estate and some movable property, were restored. In addition, bank deposits were re-established with interest, and insurance policies were also restored. Compensation was also paid by the Office for war damage and by the Settlements Division of the Ministry of Justice.

The majority is moreover of the opinion that the task of restoration and compensation after the war was well and thoroughly performed. But not only was Norwegian society economically in dire straits, it also had to face enormous reconstruction costs. The rules for the Office for war damage, for instance, had for those reasons been drawn up so as to give them a social profile, which implied among other things that injured parties who were well off received reduced compensation. In this connection the majority adds that in its opinion it was generally assumed internationally that the state was under no legal obligation to cover damage sustained by the civilian population as a result of encroachments by the occupying authority or its Nazi helpers. Our lawful government in London had no means of preventing the encroachments, but objected to them strenuously.

The majority notes that the rules for compensation to Norwegian Jews and non-Jews were the same and must be viewed in the light of the historical conditions prevailing in 1945. Ten thousand Norwegians had lost their lives through acts of war 1939–45; forty to fifty thousand persons had been political prisoners; Finnmark and Nord-Troms had been laid waste; and according to calculations available today, overall real capital had been reduced by 14%. Society had a self-evident duty to help those who were unable to manage because of the war, or whose financial losses had been so great that it would be difficult for them to get started again after the occupation. Such assistance was both a part of the "reconstruction" and a contribution to it: people had to be given the necessary means of participation in the country's recovery. It was not economically possible to grant full compensation, either to Jewish or to non-Jewish Norwegians, for the losses they sustained during the war. The nation as a whole had lost. Individual citizens accordingly had to accept that their postwar lives would begin with financial loss and diminished welfare.

Despite the extensive investigations that have been carried out, it has proved impossible to quantify the Jewish losses precisely. On the contrary, it needs to be emphasised that the Committee's majority has to a large extent had to exercise judgement. The majority has, however, attached great importance to making clear where it has exercised discretion, and on what assumptions.

The Committee's majority has estimated that the total loss amounts to NOK 6,538,200 in 1946–47 krone values. It is proposed, on a discretionary overall assessment, that the amount be raised to NOK 8,000,000. Applying the present krone value (May 1997), this amounts to NOK 108,3 million. The majority proposes that this figure is rounded off to NOK 110 million.

The Committee is not instructed in its mandate to recommend the amount of a central government allocation, if any, or the form in which a payment should in the event be made. A majority within the majority (Falkanger, Fure, Grimnes and Sunde) discuss some models for dealing with the matter: settlement in full, cover for losses sustained by Jews because the application of the same rules for Jewish and non-Jewish Norwegians worked in the Jews' disfavour, or a sum in token of acknowledgement. A payment or token payment can be made either individually or collectively. The chairman of the Committee, Skarpnes, recommends that central government allocate the amount of the financial loss estimated by the majority, and that *ex gratia* compensation payments be made to injured parties or their descendants in respect of such individual losses as may be reported and shown to be probable. The remainder of the allocation can then be devoted to collective Jewish purposes. The other members of the majority do not wish to take a position on whether any amount should be paid or in the event how much or to whom.

Summary of the views of the Minority of the Committee of Inquiry, consisting of Berit Reisel and Bjarte Bruland

The economic liquidation of the Norwegian Jews during World War II was total. The Norwegian Jews were deprived of all rights of ownership and any kind of business base. This led to economic losses in the broadest sense of the term, in that an entire religious, cultural, economic and social community was destroyed. The Committee's mandate was to conduct a survey of the facts of the case and of the amount of funds which were returned to the Norwegian Jews after the war. In the view of the minority, this means that all circumstances with a bearing on the case must be brought to light. It also means that the entire situation must be examined without regard to whether or not the present-day Norwegian authorities can be regarded as legally responsible for the losses incurred, and without regard to the extent to which other Norwegian citizens also suffered losses.

The methods employed by the Committee in its investigation were a study of general source materials, examination of registrations in estate files (i.e. the files that were opened on each estate) and a study of the records relating to the administration of estates. These approaches provide different sorts of information and have different kinds of limitations. They must therefore be seen in context if they are to contribute to an overview of the entire liquidation and reparation process.

In 1941–42 the Jewish population of Norway consisted of approximately 1,000 households numbering a total of 2,173 individuals. These families lived mainly in Oslo and Trondheim, but the sources show that there were Jews living in over 60 municipalities throughout the country. The Jewish minority was primarily involved in the business sector. Norwegian Jews owned 401 enterprises. Approximately 40 individuals were members of professions (doctors, dentists and lawyers). The remainder were craftsmen and artists. Few were employed in the public sector, or as farmers or fishermen. There were two main communities in Oslo and Trondheim. In both cities the Jewish population enjoyed a lively cultural life, and the Jewish communities operated many religious institutions and cultural organisations which ran various educational and welfare programmes. There were also old-age homes and an orphanage. In Oslo and Trondheim there were three synagogues as well as centres for religious studies. Both communities had mortuaries, and there were three cemeteries.

In order to understand the economic losses incurred by the Jewish minority during World War II, the physical and economic liquidation of the Jews must be regarded as two aspects of the same crime, sharing the following systematically organised features: restriction of rights, segregation and isolation, confiscation and economic liquidation, deportation, and physical liquidation. In other words, the liquidation was compound, and its objective was the complete annihilation of the Jews as a group. The methods used to achieve the economic part of the goal ensured that the religious and cultural centres, together with the property and businesses of Jewish families, were liquidated as though they were bankrupt estates. The purpose of this was to enable the Nazi authorities to seize control of the property while also ensuring that all Jewish business operations ceased.

These economic measures were carried out as a result of the Norwegian Act of 26 October 1942 relating to the confiscation of property belonging to Jews. This Act must not be regarded as an example of ordinary legislation, but as a way of legitimising certain types of actions within an ideological system. Through this Act the economic liquidation was formalised, but source materials indicate that the liquidation process as such began before it was given formal expression in the Act. As a result, many Jewish estates were liquidated without having been formally registered. The process of formalising the economic liquidation was closely connected with the process of physical liquidation of the Norwegian Jews, and indeed, the deportations began immediately after the economic liquidation process had begun. It would obviously not have been possible to implement such a complete liquidation of the property and assets of an entire group of people if plans for internment or deportation had not been prepared in advance. A total of 767 Jews were deported from Norway. Thirty survived. The remainder of the Jews who had lived in Norway fled the country.

The formalised liquidation process was based on the principle that each estate would be settled as though it were bankrupt. For the same reason, each individual household was converted into a joint ownership with one individual in the home, usually the husband, designated as the owner. This meant that each unit (household or business) was transformed into a fixed quantity, on the condition that the unit continued to exist as a legal person, so that the current expenses could continue to be charged to the estate even after liquidation had taken place.

The collective aspect of the economic liquidation of the Norwegian Jews was of major significance. It meant that households were often merged, and income and expenditures resulting from the liquidation were allocated at the discretion of the authorities. This was often done to ensure the most efficient and time-saving procedures possible for those in charge of the liquidation. Many Jewish businesses were also merged in this way. Another aspect of this collective form of liquidation was that the property was distributed according to certain distribution formulas, in which a large proportion of the most valuable assets were not registered. This included, in particular, gold, silver and jewellery, which were given as "a voluntary contribution to the war effort" under the terms of an agreement between the Quisling regime and the German authorities in Norway. Nor were watches, furs, paintings, office equipment, wholesale stocks of goods, or many other valuable objects registered. In addition, a large amount of valuable assets were looted.

The assets which were registered were, in theory, to be sold. Many assets, however, were stolen or distributed to Nazis or Nazi organisations. The profits from the assets which were sold formed the basis for what is called the joint Jewish assets. By the end of the war the Liquidation Board had used approximately 30 per cent of these assets for its own administration.

After the war the complicated process of reparation began. Everyone from whom property had been stolen, Jews and non-Jews alike, should, in principle, have been able to demand its return. However, this proved to be impossible, one of the reasons being that the financial basis for reparation was no longer intact. In addition, the authorities established a complex system of regulations based on two main principles which they regarded as important in postwar reparation efforts: equalisation and reconstruction. The rules laid down according to these principles were designed to determine the amount of reparation each applicant should receive in proportion to what he had lost. The equalisation principle was implemented by calculating reductions according to a special scale. The result of this system was that the greater the loss, the smaller the percentage of compensation. The reconstruction principle was implemented by making special reductions in the estate for each family member who had died.

These principles of compensation had particularly far-reaching consequences for the Jews, due to the collective and total nature of the liquidation, and to the unique pattern of deaths. Thus, 230 families were totally annihilated, and the remaining families experienced serious losses. According to the reparations agencies, the survivors were not considered eligible for full compensation, because this compensation was based on assumptions about the applicants' ability to reconstruct their pre-war lives and businesses. They were either given reduced compensation or were simply not taken into consideration at all when compensation was paid out, even when they were legal heirs. Another area of concern for the reparations agencies was that if Jews were to inherit from their deceased relatives, "they would acquire funds to which they would not have had access under normal circumstances".

As a result of the unique pattern of deaths, the compensation paid out by the registered as having funds in the joint Jewish assets, and one for the heirs of those thus registered. People in the second category might be members of the same household as the registered owner of funds in the joint Jewish assets, but since they were not registered as the owner, they had no right to claim their inheritance until the registered owner was declared legally deceased. Because the Jewish people had been the victims of genocide, not of ordinary acts of war, there was no information available as to the date of death. Moreover, no death certificates had been issued. This meant that rather than being regarded as legally deceased, the murder victims were, until the autumn of 1947, classified as missing. In 1947 efforts were begun to reclassify those missing as dead, and to devise an order of deaths for each family. For instance, in cases where a mother and her children had been sent into the gas chamber together, the reparations agencies had to determine in which order they died, so as to determine the heir's place in the order of inheritance. All of these complications meant that the process of settling the estates was protracted, usually lasting from eight to ten years, or even longer; the last settlements for which we have information took place in 1987. Due to the length of this process, the expenses charged to the estates were extremely high. The estates of the deceased amounted to half of the estates which were awarded funds from the reparations agencies.

It is not unusual to define estates of deceased persons as legal persons with a financial obligation, as if they were part of the normal fellowship of society and bound by its rules. This is a normal legal procedure. However, this situation was not normal; it was motivated by the intention to annihilate the whole Jewish minority in Europe, i.e. Shoah (the Holocaust). Annihilation on this scale cannot be equated with ordinary deaths, and ordinary legal procedures for settling estates are thus not appropriate in such a context.

The economic losses which can be documented were from those parts of the property which were registered and sold. This applied to property which had belonged to approximately 75 per cent of the Jewish population. However, the material indicates that the value of estates which were not registered was at least as large. The total of the joint Jewish assets can thus be estimated, and amounted to NOK 23 million in 1940 values. According to the Statistics Norway price index, this amount multiplied by 19.07 equals today's value. And as previously mentioned, not all property was included in the joint Jewish assets. The categories not included were the value of the property distributed according to the distribution formulas, losses incurred due to the destruction of the Jewish enterprises which formed the economic basis of the Jewish community, and other losses which cannot be quantified but which clearly had economic consequences. The total scope of the economic loss, therefore, is considerably higher than the calculated estimate of the joint Jewish assets would indicate.

The reparations agencies awarded NOK 7,854,758.10 in 1947 values to 893 of the total of 1381 seized households and businesses. Today's value can be obtained by multiplying this sum by 13.59. A total of 35.3 per cent of the estates received no reparations, and 55.5 per cent received less than NOK 1,000 each. In the case of 163 estates, the settlement ended in a debit balance. In other words, the estate was in debt to the reparations agencies because the current expenses had exceeded the value of the original estate.

However, the total economic burden placed on the Norwegian Jews through the procedure of liquidating estates during the war, and through the settlement and division of estates after the war, was greater than the amount eventually awarded by the reparations agencies. Although not all expenses charged to the estates reverted to the state treasury, most did so, and in addition, the State itself inherited several estates. The special nature of this situation was due to the character and extent of the economic liquidation of property, as well as to the unique pattern of deaths caused by the systematic physical liquidation of the Norwegian Jews.

PINK TRIANGLE COALITION

AN INTERNATIONAL COALITION FOR COORDINATING AFFAIRS
RELATING TO NAZI PERSECUTION OF GAY MEN AND LESBIANS

Submitted on behalf of the Pink Triangle Coalition
by the European Jewish Congress

INTRODUCTION

The ideological basis for the persecution of homosexual men and women
stemmed directly from Nazi racial theories[1], together with their conception of
gender roles. Prior to Hitler coming to power, gay and lesbian community life
flourished more in Germany than in any other European country. Within weeks
of taking over, the Nazis had destroyed community institutions, expunged books
and organised activities designed to instil terror.

This paper outlines the unique pattern of persecution that developed; one
which relied not just on the activities of the Gestapo or SS, but on civil institutions – the police, law courts and judiciary. This was a pattern of persecution
which meant that people could be imprisoned purely for being suspected
of being gay; could suffer terrible deprivations and experimentation whilst
detained; and could even find themselves persecuted by other prisoners.

In the immediate post-war period, neither the Allies nor the German or
Austrian States recognised homosexuals as victims alongside other groups. They
were not eligible for the same compensation and restitution. Nor was property
of a communal nature properly compensated for. Indeed the Nazi version of the
§175 stayed in force in West Germany until 1969. Unsurprisingly very few victims came forward in such circumstances, and comparatively few known victims
are still alive today.

For those concerned to promote greater awareness of Nazi patterns of persecution and for those who wish to make amends, it is important to appreciate that
in addition to making gay and lesbian survivors' lives easier much needs to be
done to research, memorialise and educate in this field – out of respect for those
who died, those who survived, and those gay men and lesbians who grew up in
the Nazi period.

And precisely because of the distinctions which were drawn after the War
between different victim groups, and the unfortunate failure to admit any rep-

resentation for gay victims in the London Conference on Nazi Gold itself, we respectfully submit this paper to be included in the formal Conference Report.

THE SITUATION IN GERMANY BEFORE 1933

Homosexual acts had been punishable in Germany under Paragraph 175 of the Reich Penal Code since 1871. As with other aspects of the Penal Code, police practice and case law developed over time to define which acts – between whom and in what circumstances – would come under the purview of §175. In 1929 – as a consequence of a decades-long campaign by sexual reform organisations and the gay movement (from 1897) and growing popular support for law reform – the Reichstag Committee on Criminal Law recommended the abolition of §175.[2] This recommendation had not been approved by parliament by 1933, the time of the Nazi take-over of power in Germany.

Notwithstanding these formal legal barriers, thriving gay and lesbian communities had developed in Germany between the turn of century and the early 1930s. Berlin, Hamburg and other big cities were major centres for these communities, and were the sites of both organised and informal collectives and networks. Lesbian and gay organisations, magazines and other publications, cafes and bars, cultural events, and other expressions of a community were to be found in significant numbers. Such community structures provided lesbians and gay men with means of expressing their identity, engaging in political activities, and ensuring mutual support.

NAZI IDEOLOGY AND ANTI-HOMOSEXUAL POLICY DEVELOPMENT

The NSDAP from the outset was ideologically hostile to homosexuality and homosexuals. For instance, in 1930 the *Völkischer Beobachter*, its official newspaper, wrote that "all foul urges of the Jewish soul" come together in homosexuality, and the law should recognise [them] for what they are – utterly base aberrations of Syrians, extremely serious crimes that should be punished with hanging and deportation".[3]

Nazi ideas on race, gender and eugenics played a central role in the formulation of the regime's policy vis-à-vis homosexuality. Homosexual men and women were blamed for lower birth rates, and for polluting the 'hereditary flow'. The Nazis' declared aim was the eradication of homosexuality. To this end, over the twelve years of its rule, a wide-ranging series of measures were put into place in support of the Nazi regime's population policy.

They included:[4]

- The ordering and carrying out of police activities and of measures designed to instil terror;
- The sharpening of penal sanctions [In 1935 §175 was extended to punish every act of *Unzucht* (lewdness). This widened its scope from homosexual acts to simply being homosexual as grounds for punishment. Penalties were increased to a maximum of 10 years of detention.[5] After the beginning of the war, the death penalty was introduced for 'especially serious cases'.]

- The creation of special administrative bodies to carry out prosecutions [In 1934, a special division, the so-called *Sonderdezernat Homosexualität*, was created within the *Staatspolizeiamt* Berlin, Division II.[6] Following Himmler's reorganisation of the police force, in 1936 a *Reichszentrale zur Bekämpfung der Homosexualität und Abtreibung* (Reich Office for the Combating of Homosexuality and Abortion) was established as a department of the criminal police.];
- Deportation and isolation in concentration camps;
- Extension of the grounds for compulsory castration; and
- The organisation of para-medical experiments, up to and including 'reversal of hormonal polarity'.

THE PATTERN OF PERSECUTION

After the NSDAP had secured power in 1933, repression against homosexuals and their collectives increased dramatically. Raids by police and Gestapo throughout the country led to the arrest of significant numbers of gay men. Lists of 'homosexually active' persons were established by the police (Reich Office and Gestapo records of 'suspects' for just the three years 1937–40 include the names of over 90,000 individuals). Most bars known as meeting places for gay men and lesbians were closed throughout the country and the few remaining ones served as sources of information for the police and the Gestapo. Libraries and bookshops were purged of 'indecent' scientific and literary materials relating to homosexuality. Emancipatory organisations had to cease their activities, including the publication of their magazines; publishers' stocks were confiscated, forcing them into bankruptcy. The *Institut für Sexualwissenschaft*, a driving force behind the campaign for law reform, was destroyed on 6 May 1933. The writings of its President and Founder, Dr Magnus Hirschfeld, and other scientists were publicly burned on 10 May 1933.

Historians estimate that some 50,000 men were sentenced to severe jail sentences by Nazi judges on the basis of §175. Between 1937 and 1939 alone, 24,447 men were sentenced to jail sentences under §175; no reliable data exist for the years after 1943. Rates of acquittal declined sharply after 1933 and fines were increasingly replaced by imprisonment or penal servitude; clear indications of the heightening of repression.

Up to an estimated 15,000 homosexual men were deported to concentration camps for 're-education through labour'. In the camps they were often subjected to the harshest regime and assigned the most hazardous work duties. As a result, an unknown but large number of these Pink Triangle detainees died in the camps, often from exhaustion. Many were castrated and some subjected to so-called 'medical experiments'. Instances of collective murder actions against homosexual detainees, in which hundreds were exterminated at a time, are well-documented.[7] An as yet undetermined number were forced into military service in so-called punitive battalions, whose high-risk duties included clearing mine fields.

Even those who escaped legal persecution saw their life drastically altered, if not destroyed. Unknown numbers fled abroad, entered into marriages in order to appear to comply with prevailing norms, and/or had to cope with severe psychological disturbances as a result of the general climate of terror.

Since female homosexuality was not included in the criminal code in Germany, lesbians did not suffer from the same forms or degree of persecution as gay men. However, some historical evidence exists of police records being collected on lesbians and the presence has been documented of a small number of lesbians in concentration camps on the grounds of their sexual orientation and because of 'anti-social behaviour' (Green Triangle detainees).[8] Lesbians did suffer the same destruction of clubs and organisations, banning of publications, closure of meeting places, and destruction of informal community networks as gay men. Furthermore, as all women, lesbians did not, according to Nazi ideology, have any role to play in public life. Lesbians, who could often not rely on a male breadwinner, were at a double economic disadvantage.

PERSECUTION IN NON-GERMAN TERRITORIES

Outside Germany, the persecution of homosexuals differed according to the territory in which they lived. Territories annexed to the Reich, including West Prussia and Posen [Poznan] in Poland, the districts of Eupen, Malmédy and Moresnet in Belgium, and Alsace-Lorraine in France fell under the jurisdiction of the German Penal Code. In Austria, following a conflict on the application of the Austrian Penal Code, and in the 'Protectorate' of Bohemia and Moravia, the Reich penal code was applied, although with the inclusion of lesbians within its terms.[9] In the 'Generalgouvernement' area of Poland, only homosexual acts involving German men were punishable, although Poles found to have engaged in such acts could be deported from Poland (to a concentration camp) because they were seen as a danger to 'Germanhood'. In the Netherlands, a combination of existing Dutch legislation and German law was applied. Prosecution was generally the responsibility of the Dutch police authorities except in cases involving members of the German SS or Wehrmacht. Between 1940 and 1943 proceedings were initiated against 138 men, of whom 90 were found guilty by Dutch courts.

THE POST-WAR PERIOD AND THE ISSUE OF COMPENSATION

In the Federal Republic of Germany, the Nazi Paragraph 175 remained in force unamended until 1969. In the German Democratic Republic, the Nazi version of §175 was suspended in 1950 and replaced by the previous law. Between 1949, when the Bundesrepublik was founded, and 1969, more than 100,000 men were exposed to preliminary proceedings for violations of §175. It is not surprising, then, that very few individuals came forward to claim compensation. First, homosexuality remained illegal and prospective claimants would have to consider the very real risk of opening themselves up to renewed state persecution. Second, the majority of compensation provisions did not include persecution on the basis of homosexuality as grounds for compensation. According to the most reliable statistics available, no more than 22 gay men have been acknowledged as victims of persecution by the Nazi regime and have received compensational payments from the German authorities.

The continued presence on the statute books of the unaltered Nazi §175, meant that in the democratic Bundesrepublik entire generations of post-war gay men suffered grave problems, be they psychological, social, or direct prosecution. As Dr Grau succinctly put it: 'The long-term effects [of Nazi repression] are still today largely unknown, especially with regard to the hardening of prejudices after 1945. Nor do we know how the individual gay survivor – and the majority did survive – psychologically worked through the experience of those times, or what consequences they had for his (homo-) sexual identity. At any event they were all victims, whether they were interned in a concentration camp, imprisoned by a court or spared actual persecution. For ultimately the racist Nazi system curtailed the life-opportunities of each and every homosexual man and woman.'[10]

The Pink Triangle Coalition currently includes the following organisations:
- Homosexuelle Initiative Wien, Austria
- International Gay and Lesbian Human Rights Commission
- International Lesbian and Gay Association – Europe
- Pink Cross, Switzerland
- World Congress of Gay and Lesbian Jewish Organisations

NOTES

[1] Professors Burleigh and Wipperman eds *The Racial State*, London, 1991.

[2] Dr Günther Grau (ed.), *Hidden Holocaust? Gay and Lesbian Persecution in Germany 1933–1945*, London, 1995, p.1.

[3] Quoted in H. Stümke and R. Finkler; *Rosa Listen, Rosa Winkel. Homosexuelle und 'gesundes Volksempfinden' von Auschwitz bis heute*, Reinbek, 1981, p.96.

[4] Dr Gunther Grau op. cit., p.4.

[5] Dr Andreas Sternweiler et al., op. cit. *Goodbye to Berlin. 100 Jahre Schwulebewegung*, Berlin, 1997, p.161

[6] Dr Ilse Kokula, *Der homosexuellen NS-Opfer gedenken*, Berlin, Senatsverwaltung für Jugend und Familie, 1995, p.8.

[7] Dr Andreas Sternweiler et al., op. cit. pp.182–189. See also: *Strafkommando und Außenlager Klinkerwerk 1938–1945*, Informationsblatt 8, Gedenkstätte und Museum Sachsenhausen, Oranienburg, Stiftung Brandenburgische Gedenkstätten, 1997.

[8] Claudia Schoppmann, in Günther Grau, op. cit., pp.8–15.

[9] Soon to be published research by Claudia Schoppmann.

[10] Dr Gunther Grau op. cit., p.7.

POLAND

Statement of the Polish delegation

The Government of the Republic of Poland considers this conference as an event of fundamental importance. We are convinced that what has been started here will be continued until a just and fair solution of the problems that have been discussed for the last two days is found.

No efforts should be spared to bring justice to those who suffered, were killed and tortured during World War II.

It is vital for any suggested solution to be based on truth, honesty and a genuine desire to compensate the suffering of Nazi victims.

We believe that this Conference on Nazi Gold is also a conference about all that "Gold" symbolises that is about various kinds of valuables and stolen property and about all those who enriched themselves at the expense of war victims.

The Government of the Republic of Poland is strongly committed to seek a solution to all financial and material problems linked to the tragic events of World War II. We must keep in mind the complexity of these issues. In Poland's case, due to the extent of destruction, loss of one fifth of the population, changes of borders, mass forced migration and last but not least due to the fact that more than fifty years have passed since the end of the war.

The extent of the Holocaust tragedy, the indescribable suffering which occurred, justifies the great importance which is attached to these issues by the Polish Government and indeed by other governments. We believe that it is necessary to move in the direction of returning properties which once belonged to Jewish communities as well as to make substantial progress in the field of reprivatisation.

I have already stressed that it is my government's intention to proceed in a spirit of justice and fairness which also means that we will not be procrastinating in solving numerous legal details in this field.

I wish to reiterate that we seek justice, dialogue and a solution to these painful problems for their own sake and not for political profits.

The Government of the Republic of Poland welcomes with satisfaction the creation of the International Fund for Victims of the Nazi Persecution. We declare our readiness to contribute to this fund with the gold put to our disposal by the Tripartite Commission. A formal decision in this matter will be taken by the Polish authorities in the near future. However we would like to make the following reservations:

- we propose not to use the term "needy victims", we are convinced that it would be unjust to demand from people subjected to such suffering to provide evidence of their poverty;

- we believe it is also necessary to clarify the criteria for those who will benefit from the Fund, e.g. former prisoners of concentration camps, those who were in ghettos, those who were forced to hide in inhuman conditions, victims of pseudo-medical experiments, children born in prisons or concentration camps;
- we see a need to make benefits of this Fund available to the Righteous Among the Nations;
- we believe that there is also a genuine need for Polish NGOs representing Nazi victims, in particular those representing Jewish survivors of the Holocaust as well as Holocaust children to have a voice in the debate;
- it is extremely important to create a possibility for the Fund to contribute to the maintenance of places of martyrdom and commemoration of Holocaust victims.

The Government of the Republic of Poland declares furthermore its readiness to declassify all documents and correspondence linked to the previously mentioned matters making our archives accessible.

Finally, we would like to declare our mention to organise a seminar/conference which would focus on the moral and ethical dimensions of the problems which have been discussed at this conference.

RUSSIA

Victims of Nazism and the issue of compensation

VIKTOR ALEKSANDROVICH KNYAZEV
Chairman of the Board of the Russian Federation Fund for
Mutual Understanding and Reconciliation

Victims of Nazism. The term "victims of Nazism" applies to persons who suffered as a consequence of the criminal activities of the Nazis during World War II. Under international law these activities include: crimes against peace, war crimes, crimes against humanity, and membership in a criminal group or organisation (Charter of the International Military Tribunal, Article 11). "*Crimes against humanity*: namely, murder, extermination, enslavement, deportation, and other inhumane acts committed against any civilian population, before or during the war, or persecutions on political, racial or religious grounds in execution of or in connection with any crime within the jurisdiction of the Tribunal, whether or not in violation of the domestic law of the country where perpetrated".

Murder, enslavement, imprisonment, and persecution on political or racial grounds took place on a massive scale during the occupation of the Soviet Union. The "Ost" plan stated that: "It is not merely a question of crushing the state which is centred on Moscow, it is a question of exterminating the Russian people".

Eighteen million people passed through the horrific system of concentration camps which the Nazis established in Europe; over seven million of them were citizens of the former Soviet Union. Only 500–550 thousand survived, around 200 thousand of whom were Soviet citizens. Taking an annual mortality rate of 1.4%, fifty years on about 60 thousand people should still be alive. No-one knows how many of them are now living in Russia. However, by 1 November 1997 some 20 thousand former prisoners of the concentration camps had received compensation from the Fund for Mutual Understanding and Reconciliation.

The Nazis killed about six million Jews during World War II, two million of whom lived in the former Soviet Union. Mass extermination of the Jewish population, after they had been rounded up into ghettos, took place in Ukraine, Belarus and the Baltic States. There were some 80 thousand Jewish people living in Riga for instance before the occupation, but by the time the city was liberated by the Red Army only 140 of them remained.

The forced deportation of labour to Germany began in the early months of 1942. In March 1942 the Office of the Plenipotentiary General for the

Utilisation of Labour was set up under Fritz Sauckel. On 20 April he personally ordered that all foreign workers should receive only enough food and shelter to enable them to be exploited to the highest possible extent with the lowest degree of expenditure.

Four thousand, nine hundred and seventy eight Soviet citizens were deported from the former Soviet Union to be employed, according to instructions contained in secret circulars, to perform extremely hard labour, and of the total number of Soviet people forced to work in Germany 2165 thousand died. In all, fourteen million people from different countries were deported for forced labour by the Fascists. Nine million foreigners were employed in Germany in 1944, six million of whom were civilians, two million prisoners of war and five hundred thousand prisoners of concentration camps.

A telegram marked "secret", sent to Sauckel by the Under-Secretary of State at the Ministry for the Occupied Eastern Territories, read as follows: "'Centre' Military Headquarters for the Utilisation of Labour must under all circumstances continue to recruit young Byelorussian and Russian labourers to meet the military requirements of the Reich. Furthermore, it is the task of the Headquarters to send to the Reich young people aged between 10 and 14." This task was laid down in a special Nazi plan named "Operation Hay", which involved the seizure of some forty to fifty thousand Soviet children and youths in order to deport them to Germany with the purpose of "Germanizing" them.

Sometimes the term "recruitment on a voluntary basis" is used as a synonym for "conscription", but any delusions one might have in this regard are dispelled when one reads the following instruction from Sauckel dated 20 April 1942: "Where the appeal for volunteers does not suffice, obligatory service and drafting must be resorted to". When people stopped co-operating in such measures Sauckel resorted to quota allocation, i.e. selecting a specific number of people who were "healthy and aged between 15 and 50 years" from each inhabited locality. As Fritz Sauckel himself admitted at a conference: ". . . out of the five million foreign workers who arrived in Germany, not even two hundred thousand came voluntarily".

"*Ostarbeiter*", meaning "Eastern workers", was a term used by the Nazis to refer not to people but to "the workforce of non-German nationality conscripted in the Reichskornnissariat of Ukraine and the general administrative district of Byelorussia, or in the regions situated to the east of those regions, together with the former free states of Latvia and Estonia, which following their occupation by the Wehrmacht became part of the German Reich, including the protectorates of Bohemia and Moravia".

The rules of the German authorities on the treatment of civilian foreign workers dated 1 October 1942 contain the following passage: "'Eastern workers' includes persons from the former Soviet regions except for Latvia, Lithuania, Estonia, and the Byelostok and Lvov regions. No distinction is to be made between Ukrainians, Caucasians, Georgians, Armenians, etc".

In our terminology, the expression "Eastern workers" is used to mean people forcibly deported by the Nazis from the occupied territory of the former Soviet

Union and employed as slave labour in Germany and the protectorates of Bohemia and Moravia.

Compensation. Compensation constitutes full indemnity for physical and mental suffering, and for forced labour. The amount of compensation for forced labour must be calculated on an individual basis according to the rules which existed at that time for the German population working in the relevant industries. The amount of compensation for physical and psychological damage should be calculated on the basis established by international practice. Any other payments, including lump sums, are by way of humanitarian aid, in part compensation. Full compensation is a lump sum equal to the sum of all the individual payments, made on the basis of a calculation of the physical and mental suffering and the damage to health and loss of freedom caused by slave labour.

Up until now victims of Nazism living in the countries of Eastern Europe have only received financial assistance at a level assessed by dividing a lump sum by the number of actual or estimated victims of Nazism.

1. BACKGROUND TO THE PROBLEM

The problem of compensation for Nazi persecution was raised at international level immediately after the war, if one takes the logical conclusion of the war to be the Nuremberg trials. Sessions of the International Military Tribunal took place between 20 November 1945 and 1 October 1946 (the day the judgement was announced). The judgement of the International Tribunal has become the basis "for the establishment of new moral principles in relations between people and nations". One of the actions confirming these principles was the adoption of a decision concerning compensation for victims of the National-Socialist regime. The first claimants for compensation were French nationals who had been imprisoned in concentration camps. When these people were liberated they were treated as martyrs and national heros in France. They underwent careful medical examinations and were registered. The results of this were used in order to submit a detailed and accurate account to the Germans.

Victims of Nazism who happen to be in the West receive a single payment of DM5,000 or a monthly pension of DM500, and often both (Spiegel, No 30, 1997).

Things were different in this country, however. The authorities greeted those who returned home from concentration camps and slave labour with suspicion and accusations of treachery. Many were subjected a second time to unjustified repression and spent their entire lives branded with the stigma of inferiority in their own country. As you can imagine, there could be no question of compensation under such circumstances.

Nevertheless, these people needed not only financial assistance but psychological help too. According to the data from sociological research carried out in six oblasts (the Bryanskaya, Leningradskaya, Nizhegorodskaya, Omskaya and Rostovskaya oblasts) former *Ostarbeiter* have found it very difficult to piece together their personal lives. They are almost twice as likely as the rest of the Russian population to be single; they are more likely to live apart from their wives and children; many of them have even been deprived of the happiness of having any children; almost fifty per cent of them suffer from ill health; and the proportion of them who are relatively healthy is only a third of that of the other people interviewed.

Only with the changes which have taken place in the Soviet Union has there been any alteration in the attitude towards the victims of Nazism, and the possibility of raising the issue of compensation; this met with a positive response at the meeting between Chancellor Kohl and the Russian President, Boris Yeltsin. The outcome of the discussion of the problem was that Germany agreed to allocate a thousand million marks to the countries of the CIS. How the total amount was to be allocated was decided at a special conference of representatives of Belarus, Russia and Ukraine (DM200, DM400 and DM400 respectively).

So far, assistance to the countries of Eastern Europe has been limited to the payment of lump sums – DM500 million to Poland, DM400 million each to Russia and Ukraine, and DM200 million to Belarus. At present the Funds for Mutual Understanding and Reconciliation have registered 120 thousand victims of Nazism in Belarus, 280 thousand in Russia (in view of the country's vast area and the difficulty in informing the public it is expected that this figure will rise to 300–330 thousand), and 593 thousand in Ukraine (this is expected to rise to 658 thousand).

The average payment has been DM1,360 in Belarus, around DM900 in Russian (with the additional payments envisaged this is likely to rise to around DM1,100–1,200) and DM600 in Ukraine.

In addition, Germany has paid in the region of DM100,000 million in compensation and allowances to victims of Nazism, although over 90% of this sum has gone to German victims of Nazism (Spiegel No 30 1997).

For all of the 14 million foreigners deported to forced labour in Germany during World War II, there is less than DM10,000 million left from the above-mentioned sum, i.e. DM700 per person.

However, for the five million people forcibly deported from the former Soviet Union there was only DM1,000 million, i.e. an average of only DM100 per person. The smaller number of German victims of Fascism (the exact figure is not known) received almost ten times as much as the rest. The nine million victims of Nazism from the countries of Western Europe received less than the Germans, but seven times as much as their Eastern European brothers and sisters who shared their fate.

"The injustice experienced by the Eastern Europeans in comparison with the position of their brothers in misfortune living in the West is too great..."

2. NEW OPPORTUNITIES TO RESOLVE THE MATTER OF COMPENSATION FOR VICTIMS OF NAZISM

Apart from the funds already allocated, which have been discussed above, the victims of Nazism from Eastern European countries, and also the German public, are trying to use money from various sources to supplement the amounts that have already allocated. "The bird in the hand" is still only 194 million dollars in the Swiss Fund for the Assistance of Victims of the Holocaust and 70 million dollars available to the Tripartite Reparations Commission (USA, Britain and France).

2.1 Compensation from the German Federal Budget

It cannot be said that the German Government remains deaf to appeals from the public. A reply from the German Ministry of Finance dated 3 April 1996 to a letter from a victim of Fascism – Valentina Afaniseva, living in Klaipeda (Lithuania), states for example that assistance will not be restricted to what the Russian and Belarusian Funds pay out. Thus, under an agreement with the Government of Estonia dated 22 June 1995, the German Government has expressed its readiness to fund specific social projects for victims of Nazism. It plans to set up a Gerontology Unit with the Lithuanian Government for victims of Nazism and to organise free health-improving courses for them. The Latvian Government is planning to set up Rehabilitation Units. All these projects are to be funded by the Germans from the DM2 million already allocated to each of these Republics.

In addition, DM62500 has been allocated to the Jewish community in Tallinn and DM500 thousand to the university hospital and the Sapego Hospital in Latvia.

These facts show that the German Government has softened its position in assessing the question of the "final settlement" of the problem of compensation.

2.2 The resolution of the European Parliament and involvement of German firms which employed slave labour in making compensation payments

The Resolution of the European Parliament of 16 January 1986 (Official Journal of the European Community No C36/129 of 17 February 1986 doc. V–2–1475/85/rev) recognised that "the firms which have employed slave labour have a clear *moral and legal* obligation to pay compensation". The second paragraph of the Resolution contains a clearly-worded "request" to firms which have still not made such payments to do so "forthwith". In a separate paragraph (paragraph 4) the European Parliament "calls on all German firms who employed slave labour to set up a fund for compensation payments to the victims of forced labour".

The European Parliament has used the term "victims of Nazism" to mean persons who were persecuted "on grounds of a politically hostile attitude towards National Socialism or on racial, religious or philosophical grounds", and also victims of forced labour due to the existence and implementation of the Nazi "Extermination through Labour programme".

The Resolution of the European Parliament on the recognition of the rights of persons formerly employed as slave labour to financial and moral compensation has formed the basis for corresponding approaches to the leaders of Germany's major companies which employed slave labour.

Some German firms (IG-Farben, Krups, AEl/Telefunken, Siemens, Rheinmetall) have made payments to Jewish workers living in the United States and Israel of an average DM1,500–5,000 per person as a humanitarian gesture.

However, in other cases "emphasis on the humanitarian aspect of the problem" in talks with the leaders of German firms which employed slave labour under Nazism, is proving to have little effect.

2.3 The activity of local government bodies in Germany

Especially effective in Germany have been measures carried out by local government bodies in recent years with regard to studying the history of the use of forced labour under Nazism; an invitation to former *Ostarbeiter* who were employed as slave labour in the local towns; the erection of memorial boards; the making of films, etc. So, as part of a special programme, every year since 1990 the municipal authorities in Cologne have invited ten to fifteen people from different countries who were employed as slave labour to visit the city. As the Mayor of Cologne emphasised in his speech on 11 September 1995 at one of the most recent of such meetings, the organisers of the event want ". . . to shed light on the dark episode of employment of slave labourers, who were degraded and deprived of their rights".

As part of these events, and also in view of the desire of the Russian Federation's Fund that municipal authorities should provide assistance by establishing direct contacts with firms which employed forced labour during World War II, during the visit by a representative of the Fund to Cologne a special agreement was signed on co-operation between the Fund and the Centre for the documentation of the period of National-Socialism. Similar events were begun in October this year with the German authorities in the city of Karlsruhe.

The main drawback of this type of activity is its limited scale; assistance of this kind is given to only a handful of people in token amounts.

2.4 The contribution by German charitable funds

Certain German Funds, including such well-known ones as the Maximilian Kolbe Fund (Frankfurt), provide fairly substantial financial assistance to certain categories of victims of Nazism. The Kolbe Fund, for example, pays people who were held in concentration camps, prisons or ghettos DM300 each and also sends them gifts (clothes, shoes, bedding, medicines, etc). Unfortunately, this help is given spasmodically and only to a limited number of victims of Nazism.

2.5 Individual court cases to obtain payment of pensions

For the first time in history, the Social Court in Hamburg delivered a ruling in a claim brought by a Polish Jew from the former ghetto in Lodz that work in the ghetto constitutes "an employment relationship giving rise to social-insurance obligations which now justify the pension claims of the applicant". Eventually, in June this year the Federal Social Court upheld this ruling. "The pension claims of former *Ostarbeiter* from Ukraine recognised by the Hamburg court may soon may soon also be recognised by the Federal Social Court" (Spiegel, No 30, pp. 36–46, 1997).

2.6 Sources of accumulated gold kept in accounts with western banks

There is still no reliable information available about the number of accounts in western banks held by Nazis or under false identities during World War II. One thing is indisputable, the amounts held in such accounts will probably turn out to be very large. Even leaving aside the crimes which the Nazis committed against states, and considering only those they committed against individuals, the proceeds represent colossal wealth for the Nazis. Within Germany and the countries it occupied there were over 14 thousand concentration camps, gestapo prisons and ghettos. On the admission of the SS officers themselves, a prisoner (whose life lasted on average less than a year) brought the Nazis 1430 Reichsmarks profit. When prisoners were handed over by concentration camps to German undertakings the SS levied a tax of 6 Reichsmarks a day for a skilled worker, and 4 Reichsmarks for an unskilled worker. In addition, all their property (including foreign currency and valuables) was confiscated. Even after his death a prisoner was of value to the Fascists – gold teeth would be extracted from the corpse, the flesh was made into soap and the ashes into fertiliser. So, for example, those who survived from the "death brigade" have testified that in Lvov, after the corpses had been incinerated, 110kg of gold was collected from the mass burial places of peaceable citizens five months later and sent to Germany. Just think how many of these places there were in Minsk, Kiev, Novgorod, Simferopol and other occupied areas of the former Soviet Union! In 1944 alone the Reich concentration camps handed over to the Treasury over 2 tons of gold. There were even organisations in Germany specialising in the processing of precious metals "reclaimed" from places where peaceable citizens of Europe were forcibly detained.

2.7 Fair distribution of funds

The statement made by the International Union of Former Young Prisoners of Fascism to those attending the conference in London on the fate of the "Nazi gold" correctly points out that a discriminatory approach to the victims of Nazism is intolerable. Funds allocated by Swiss banks and money kept in Nazi accounts must be distributed among all categories of victims of Nazism, irrespective of their nationality. As was correctly pointed out in the "Statement", a discriminatory approach to resolving this question will provoke justified indignation among the various categories of victims of Nazism and the "strengthening of anti-Semitic feelings, which we, remembering the brutal anti-Semitism of the Führer and its tragic consequences . . . must not permit in any event". Jews have received compensation from the Funds for Mutual Understanding and Reconciliation of Belarus, Russia and Ukraine, according to the same rules as all the other victims of Nazism. The suspicions expressed by some people that the Funds of Poland, Russia, Belarus and Ukraine are not paying any money to

Jews who have suffered is an "outright lie". The truth is that Jews, like all the other victims, are being paid only pitiful sums, but the reason is not due to any kind of discrimination but to the slender financial resources of the Funds. However, payments of one thousand dollars each are now being made from the Swiss Fund to Jews in Latvia.

The Swiss Fund to assist needy victims of the holocaust intends initially to make foreign currency payments to people living in Eastern Europe. Moreover, all Jews living in territory occupied by the Nazis will receive one thousand dollars each irrespective of their present financial situation. In Russia a thousand such persons have been located and in total the Fund has 30 thousand Jewish victims of the holocaust. They will receive 30 million of the 194 million available in the Fund.

It remains to be seen when payments will start to be made to former concentration camp prisoners of other nationalities.

2.8 Guilt of neutral states

Whatever justifications the governments of the countries which were neutral during World War II may come up with, their guilt as regards the victims of Nazism is undeniable. It lies not only in the fact that they betrayed to the Nazis fugitives from Germany who were hiding in their territories, their main guilt lies in the fact that they prospered from the sufferings of the victims of Nazism.

Switzerland kept in its banks, and in their foreign subsidiaries (including those in the United States), Nazi gold bars melted down from stolen gold. Turkey, Sweden, Portugal and Spain received stolen goods from the Nazis, providing Germany with items which were in short supply and raw materials, including strategic Portuguese wolfram and Swedish ore. Argentina and Brazil sheltered Nazi criminals after the fall of the Third Reich. Sweden bought cut diamonds transported from Germany on submarines in the diplomatic bag, and sold high-quality steel for money obtained from the sale of stones which the Nazis took from their victims before sending them to the gas chambers.

Lastly, the whole world knows that even the Vatican helped Nazis to escape to Spain and Latin America after the fall of the Third Reich, receiving gold from them in exchange.

It would be fair if these countries and the Vatican were to set up a Fund to help the former victims of Nazism, and not only Jewish victims.

3. A FAIR ASSESSMENT OF THE AMOUNT OF COMPENSATION

3.1 Unpaid slave labour

As regards the law, Eastern workers had no legal contractual relationship with their employers. As they were not covered by German labour law they were in essence slaves. A letter from the Wehrmacht Supreme Command to the

Plenipotentiary-General for the Utilisation of Labour, F. Sauckel, dated 23 March 1942 (marked "secret") reads as follows: "Such a high tax is charged on the wages of Russian civilian workers … only 10 to 17 German marks are left from their weekly pay, from which the manager of the company takes another 1.5 German marks each day for food and lodging". Multiplying 1.5 marks by the number of days in a week gives 10.5 marks. So an *Ostarbeiter* with only 10 marks left found himself in debt to his employer. If he had 17 marks left he should have been 6.5 marks in pocket, but in practice more often than not he received nothing.

Even worse conditions were experienced by those who were imprisoned in concentration camps and being employed as forced labour. For one day's work by a skilled prisoner the SS levied a tax of 6 Reichsmarks, and by a non-skilled prisoner 4 Reichsmarks. The prisoner himself received nothing. If he died at the end of a year he left the Nazis DM1,430 in profit.

Moreover, slave labourers from the countries of Western Europe (Dutchmen, etc.) received 5 Reichsmarks a day or more. An undertaking paid the Reich for the use of the labour of a prisoner of war from Eastern Europe (a Russian or a Pole) 1.5 times less than for that of a French, Belgian or British prisoner of war. The prisoners of war themselves were paid 3.2 times less.

3.2 Impoverished old-age

The youngest victims of Nazism, born at the end of the war, are now 52 years of age. But there are only a handful of these. The overwhelming majority are now 65–70. They are pensioners and invalids. According to a survey of the living conditions of people who suffered Nazi persecution:

- former victims of Nazism are in an "extremely poor situation … in fact all of them have scarcely enough money for food and fifty per cent of them are half-starving".
- "… the people who were deported to Germany during the war as forced labour endure a significantly lower standard of living than the rest of the population. This is indicative of the radical differences between the present living conditions of those who suffered persecution under Nazism and those who did not".

From information contained in surveys by the Centre for Social Forecasting and Marketing.

In Moscow the poverty line, according to data from the Moscow Federation of Trade Unions in October 1997 was 810, 292 roubles, whilst the pensions of the vast majority of victims of Nazism are no more than 400–450 thousand roubles.

3.3 A preliminary assessment of the amount of compensation

When estimating the overall amount of compensation it is necessary to take into account unpaid slave labour, and physical and psychological damage. However, it is not possible to give a complete quantitative assessment of the last two parameters at present, so we shall simply work on the basis that, in view of the damage caused to health, we shall discount from our calculations that element of the wages which was deducted by the employer for meagre board and lodgings. This will in some way compensate for lost health.

We shall make a quantitative evaluation of unpaid labour on the basis of comparative data between the wages of Eastern workers and German workers, using an official document of the Reich – *The Imperial Law Gazette* of 30 June 1992 *(sic)* (i 3 and i 10).

According to this document:

Wages of a German worker in Reichsmarks	Wages of an Eastern worker for the same work	Amount deducted from these for board and lodging	Remaining disposable pay	Eastern tax (i 10)
Per working day				
up to 1.4	*1.6*	*1.5*	*0.1*	–
4.1–4.25	2.25	1.3 *(sic)*	1.05 *(sic)*	1.6
6–6.2	3.05	1.5	1.55	3
10–10.25	3.9	1.5	2.4	6.05
12.75–13	4.45	1.5	2.95	8.25
Per month				
up to 42	*48*	*45*	*3*	–
100.57–105	69	45	24	33
150–156	84	45	39	67.5
240–247.5	105	45	60	133.5
382–390	133.5	45	88.5	247.5

The above figures show that the amount of disposable pay which remained was between 7.1% and 25% of what a German worker received. The rest was deducted by way of the so-called "Eastern tax" (between 39% and 65%) and also for board and lodging (between 12% and 37%). If one takes into account the fact that the average pay of a German worker was 7.2 Reichsmarks per day (from RM1.4 to 13.0) and an Eastern worker actually had on average 1.5 Reichsmarks disposable pay (from RM0.10 to 2.95), he was underpaid each week by 5.7 Reichsmarks. It is possible to calculate it in another way. Deductions by way of the "Eastern tax" came to 4.9 Reichsmarks on average per day (between RM1.6 and 8.25) and 1.5 Reichsmarks were deducted each week for board and lodging. That amounts to 6.4 Reichsmarks per day. The average of the two methods comes to 6.0 Reichsmarks per day (5.7 + 6.4÷2).

With a six-day working week the amount of unpaid slave labour is DM150 per month at 1941–44 prices, and with an average duration for a Russian citizen of two years this makes DM 3,600. In view of the threefold reduction in the value of the mark over fifty years, the minimum amount of compensation, without taking any physical or psychological damage into account, in 1997 prices is DM10,800.

This corresponds more or less to the levels of payments to former slave labourers which the "Green" Party is seeking in the German Bundestag.

In 1993, when the Russian Fund for Mutual Understanding and Reconciliation was set up, it was estimated that around 500 thousand victims of Nazism were still alive in Russia. The mortality rate among elderly and infirm people is very high however. Although during the first few years after the war the mortality rate among victims of Nazism was 1.5–2%, it is now estimated to be 10%.

With the anticipated numbers of claimants in Russia at the date when the first payments are made standing at 330 thousand people, the total amount of essential payments will be:

at 1941–45 prices – DM1,200,000.
at 1997 prices – DM3,600,000.

So DM3,600,000 is the minimum amount which can be estimated as the current value of unpaid labour in respect of the number of Russians who are still alive. Each year's delay in payment will remove up to thirty thousand victims of Nazism, but in ten or so years' time very few of them will still be alive and the problem of compensation will be resolved because there will no longer be anyone left to claim it from among the people who are owed a debt of justice.

CONCLUSIONS

The Russian Federation's Fund will take steps to make active use of available opportunities in order to make contact both with the voluntary organisations for victims of Nazism and with the German firms which employed forced labour during World War II, in order to find ways of attracting German funds to improve the financial position of those who suffered Nazi persecution. A great deal of work is being done to devise equitable ways of resolving the issue of compensation. The main task is to prevent discrimination in the levels of compensation awarded to victims of Nazism living in Russia in comparison with those in Western countries.

SLOVAK REPUBLIC

SLOVAK REPUBLIC

Statement from the Ministry of Foreign Affairs

The Ministry of Foreign Affairs of the Slovak Republic welcomes the realisation of the International Conference on Nazi Gold hosted by the British Government in London 2–4 December 1997. The aim of the Conference is to pool all available knowledge on gold looted by Nazis from both occupied states and persecuted individuals, especially victims of the Holocaust, and to consider the issue of their compensation.

The Ministry of Foreign Affairs of the Slovak Republic in this connection reminds the Federal Republic of Germany that it has not yet compensated the Slovak victims of either the Holocaust or any other form of Nazi persecution.

The Federal Republic of Germany has since its establishment adopted a number of compelling measures to the benefit of victims of the Holocaust and signed the bilateral treaties with several countries concerning the victims' reimbursement. The issue of compensation was recently solved by bilateral negotiations also with the Czech Republic. It is embarrassing that the Federal Republic of Germany refuses even to negotiate any compensation with the Slovak Republic, the equal successor of the former Czecho-Slovak state.

The Ministry of Foreign Affairs of the Slovak Republic considers different treatment of the victims of Nazism in individual countries to be inhuman and inequitable. Slovak victims of Nazism have the right to obtain the same treatment as victims in other countries.

The Ministry of Foreign Affairs of the Slovak Republic expresses its belief that the London Conference – besides clarifying the issue of Nazi gold – will also contribute to the swifter compensation for those victims of Nazism who have not yet been reimbursed.

German occupational regime and the history of monetary and non-monetary gold in Slovakia 1944–45

PHDR. JÁN KORČEK

Military Historical Institute, Department of Military-
Historical Researches, Bratislava

In 1939–45 the Slovak Republic (SR) belonged to the allied states with satellite status in the aggressive pact of the fascist Axis Berlin–Rome–Tokyo. Formally proclaimed internal and international sovereignty or "independence" of this state was hidden but also visibly limited by a rewritten system of its control where the Third Reich used various forms, methods and tools of pressure, threat, exploitation and open power interventions. Both Reichs – German institutions and German national minority organisations in Slovakia – were used for this purpose. German advisers ("beraters"), members and associates in steering and other bank brands with tens of their junior colleagues controlled and directed activities also in the central institutions and bodies organising economic, financial, monetary, bank and other policies of the SR.

The Slovak National Bank (SNB), which had its head office in Bratislava and which after the break of the second Czecho-Slovak Republic on 14–15th March 1939 inherited all functions of the National Bank of Czechoslovakia, was strongly dependent on German financial capital. From 100 million Slovak crowns (Ks) of the share-holding capital, 40% were owned by the Reichsbank and 60% by the Slovak State. All important measures adopted by the leadership of the SNB had to be approved by a special member of the eight-member bank board who was formally introduced by the Slovak Government but in fact he represented the Reichsbank.

Especially in the mentioned bank-financial and economic sphere there were a large number of Slovak experts operating, whose thoughts and activities rose during the years of 1939–43–44 from an opposition platform against the "Ludak" (nationalistic and totalitarian) regime and against politico–military collaboration with Berlin to the co-operation with all parts of the resistance against fascism at home and in exile (in London and Moscow) on the platform of re-establishing the Czechoslovak Republic. In the time of deepening internal crisis of the regime in the first half of 1944 they already actively worked in the resistance within the preparations for the military uprising against the Germans and their internal collaborators. Let me name at least the top economist Dr. Ing. Peter Zaťko, the chairman of the Headquarters for Economy, Industry and Raw Materials and Prof. Dr. lmrich Karvaš, the governor of the SNB and the chairman of the Supreme Delivery Office. Thanks to these men and tens of other activists of the resistance, whose operational measures were practically realised, the economic and financial base for the prepared antifascist uprising with its centre in Banská Bystrica (Central Slovakia) was secured.

Increasing concern about the military occupation of Slovakia in the summer of 1944 inspired the governor of the SNB, I. Karvaš and his deputy Prof. Dr. Jozef Fundárek, to transport more than 3,000 kgs of monetary gold deposited in safes of the SNB in Bratislava via the branch office of the Reichsbank in Vienna. From there, after afination, resmelting and remarking with new stamps in Frankfurt uber Mohan, it was deposited to the account of the SNB in the Swiss National Bank in Zurich. At the same time, before the rise of the Slovak National Uprising, they connected various bank and financial operations with hidden focus on strengthening of the Slovak gold reserves abroad and diminishing a chance of their confiscation or forced, wrongful removal by the Germans disadvantageously only for the SR. The main results of the aforementioned operations were (1) purchase of 1,000.6542 kgs of gold by the Swiss National Bank to the account of the SNB from a so-called "Giro-account" held in Swiss Francs, (2) transfer of 1,793.7758 kgs of gold from the Reichsbank to the SNB account in the Swiss National Bank, (3) transfer of 1,398.7859 kgs of gold from the Reichsbank. According to the material prepared in 1948 for the Tripartite Commission for the Restitution of Monetary Gold, a total of 7,107.4417 kgs of gold were on the SNB account in the Swiss National Bank before the end of the war. After the liberation of ČSR this amount was equivalent to more than 700 millions of Czechoslovak crowns.

So even though the Germans tried from the beginning of the occupational regime in Slovakia from September 1944 to May 1945, they did not manage to possess the monetary gold of the SR. They looted only the remains of the bank – monetary and economy–financial reserves in Slovakia. Funds, re-deposited to the safety of banks in neutral countries abroad, were out of German reach during the final stages of the war. After five months of intensive pressure to the Allies the Swiss Government officially declared that all actives of Hungary, Slovakia and Croatia were blocked by its decree from 20th December 1944.

The value of the gold treasure of the SR increased extremely during the last year of its existence from 46 millions to 243 millions Ks (from 1.4 to 7.5 tons). This rise shows the great level of plundering of the Slovak currency by Nazi Germany before the blocking of monetary reserves in Switzerland, for instance by overvaluing of the Reichs Mark and undervaluing of the Slovak crown. On the other hand this confirms that the Slovak Government itself used the strong and "clean" value of the gold during the war for decreasing of inflation, of continuously rising state debt and growing budget deficit, for stabilising of the trade balance between export and import and so on.

What were the origins of the monetary and non-monetary gold of the SR and what financial value did it represent? The primary establishing base was created from 579.8323 kgs (47 bars), which the SNB gained as a part of a restitution of Czechoslovak monetary gold on 10 May 1939 from the Bank for International Settlements in Basle via the National Bank of Belgium in Brussels. Up today not specifically quantified amount was gained by smelting of objects from the national collection for the fund of the economic independence of the Slovak State. This is how the monetary reserves were infiltrated by jewellery made of gold and other precious metals (including wedding rings), antiques, coins with historical numismatic value and miscellaneous items from the private property of inhabitants. Solid base of the "gold treasure" was made from monetary bars smelted in the State Mint in Kremnica from gold and silver mined in Slovak mines (Banská Štiavnica, Kremnica). Then there were golden bricks and ingots gained by active balances in the international trade with Germany, neutral and dependent states as well (Switzerland, Sweden, Denmark, Spain, Romania, Turkey, Holy See). Satellite status of the SR and unequal realisation of a Slovak – German clearing allowed Berlin strongly to damage the weaker partner and by this indirectly looted from regular transactions in foreign currencies and in gold exchange rates of international trade.

One of the insufficiently examined questions of the composition of Slovak monetary and non-monetary gold remains the issue of its contamination by Jewish gold. Gold, pearls, gems, platinum, jewellery and other valuables taken from the Jewish citizens during the first period of deportations (March–October 1942), during the time of their internment in concentration (centring) and labour camps and centres or during the so-called aryanisation process at ceasing of the Jewish property were collected under supervision of the Ministry of Finance in the Central State Treasury. SNB governor I. Karvaš admitted plans for their incorporation in to the "Gold Treasury" Fund. He forbade even their storage in the SNB safes. 22 boxes and 2 safe cases with this material were finally transported and deposited in safes of the State Mint of Kremnica.

Contamination of monetary gold was indirect – from gains of taken Jewish enterprises, if their activities included export or foreign trade. Capital profits were then laundered through accounts in foreign – mainly Swiss – banks to gains in foreign currency or directly in gold. The suspicion of mixing in of looted property to the value of monetary gold cannot be today excluded for the second period of deportations of Jews to the concentration camps (September 1944 – March 1945) when only German police-security forces were responsible for the organisation (contrary to the first period). Germany had already installed full occupational regime with only fictive and some formal features of the state sovereignty. Contamination of German monetary gold was at least at minimal level of "atomic elements" caused by valuables of individuals belonging to the Slovak Jews and political prisoners who were deported to the concentration camps on the territory of Germany, Austria or the Protectorate of Bohemia and Monrovia (Terezin) shortly before the liberation of Slovakia in the spring of 1945.

Development during the Slovak National Uprising evidently influenced further faith of monetary and financial reserves of Slovakia because blocked gold and foreign currency of the SR did not represent the whole amount of its "gold treasure". In the time of the uprising its part was hidden in the Kremnica State Mint in Slovakia. The Germans decided to get it at any price. A new central monetary institution on the insurgent territory – branch office of the SNB and its director K. Markovič personally supported saving the treasury. After interruption of contacts with the SNB Centre in Bratislava the director of its branch office

K. Markovič personally controlled the operation. He was at the same time charged with the responsibility for financial affairs by the Slovak National Council (Governmental-Parliamentary state body for territory liberated by the insurgents).

The mint in Kremnica was unable to realise immediate single transfer of stock of precious metals and all already minted coins to Banská Bystrica. Their transfer by military vehicles was then divided into five runs. The last, most dramatic one was made only few hours before the occupation of Kremnica by German advancing troops.

In the second decade of October 1944 a surrounding circle around the uprising central area unstoppably narrowed. In a fear of Germans seizing the gold treasure, the Slovak National Council Chairmanship ordered the air transfer of all gold and valuables deposited in the branch office of the SNB in Banská Bystrica to the custody of the Soviet Union to the address of the Gossudarstvenyj Bank in Moscow. It was a part of the monetary gold and precious metals that were in possession of the SNB as well as precious metals from the storage of the State mint in Kremnica. The transfer was made from the airport Tri Dub (Three Oaks) on the night of 14th October 1944. After re-weighing the consignment the Moscow bank took into deposit 21 boxes in total brutto weight of 1,062.255 kg of mixed precious metals.

It is remarkable that the Jewish valuables freely and without any protection stored in the corridors of the branch office of the SNB could be transferred from Banská Bystrica only after the town was occupied by German military troops after suppressing the uprising. They were taken in sealed boxes and cases as "old state stocks and securities" back to Kremnica carried by employees of the Mint escorted by an armed troop of the fascist Hlinka's Guard. There in a yard covered by a layer of metal scrap in silence survived even the investigations of Nazi police-security commandos of SIPO and SD that were searching very intensively the destiny of the Slovak gold treasure and Jewish valuables at the end of autumn and winter of 1944–45. They wanted to take it to the Reich at any price.

Neither deep interrogation in SD, RSHA and Gestapo prisons nor hardship in Nazi concentration camps broke imprisoned I. Karvaš and K. Markovič to indicate to their investigators anything concerning their activities by which they wanted to prevent the Slovak currency from ruining before and after introduction of the occupational regime.

The director of the State Mint in Kremnica L' Gavora gave the top secret order to relocate all Jewish gold and jewellery from Kremnica to Bratislava. These valuables, looted from the Slovak Jews, had their own official evidence cards and registers made by the bank clerks. They spent all the hard time during the period of liberation in a big underground safe of the Ministry of Finance in the capital of the SR Bratislava. Only very little part of these mysterious 20 boxes and 2 safe cases were lost or stolen during their manipulations before and after the end of World War II. Nevertheless, this story belonged to the very rare cases in the history of plundering of the Jewish property in European countries. In this context we have not forgotten the fact that the various bodies of power-repressive apparatus robbed Jewish people directly during the realisation of racial-repressive measures without any bureaucratic control. In 1944–45 on the

Slovak territory there were most of all such organisations as SS. Einsatzgruppen of SIPO and SD, "Volksdeutsch" or Slovak domestic paramilitary units called Emergency Troops of Hlinka Guard and Hlinka Youth (POHG, POHM), Special Units of Slovak Labour Service (ŠJ SPS), Freiwillige Shutzstaffel (FS), Heimatschutz and others.

SLOVENIA

Some crimes committed by the German occupying force in Slovenia

By virtue of his guidelines Adolf Hitler on 3 and 12 April 1941 dismembered Yugoslavia; the largest part of Slovenia or the Province of the Drava Banovina came under the rule of the German Reich (10,261 km with approximately 798,700 inhabitants), while Italy and Hungary were granted half less. The occupying force intended to annex the occupied territory to the German Reich in a formally-legal manner, which it eventually failed to do. However, the two chiefs of the civil administration, appointed by and hence directly responsible to Hitler, administered Lower Styria and other occupied areas of Carinthia and Carniola as if they had been annexed and particularly by the forcible denationalisation severely violated the international law. Under the German occupation Slovenia experienced all kinds of gravest violence, which Europe witnessed during World War II. Among the first deadly victims there were 583 mentally sick and elderly people from the social institutions of Lower Styria, executed in June 1941 in Hartheim near Linz in the so-called false euthanasia. This group was followed by 194 groups, comprising 2,860 hostages, in the period from July 1941 to May 1945. According to the data produced by the Commission on establishing crimes committed by the occupation forces and their accomplices there were over 20,000 executed persons in total in the German occupying area. More detailed data is still being gathered.

A special feature distinguishing Slovenia under the German occupation is a large share of expelled persons, amounting to 10% of the inhabitants under the German occupation, the largest share in occupied Europe. By virtue of denationalisation purposes the German occupying force expelled with 139 transports around 63,000 persons into Serbia, the so-called Independent State of Croatia (ISC) and Germany, which confiscated their entire property. Persons expelled to Serbia and ISC (around 15,000) were stripped before the expulsion of all their gold and silver jewellery and similar articles, like the captives and prisoners in the concentration camps. Around 17,000 persons managed to escape expulsion by fleeing to the other occupation area, and were thus bereft of their entire possessions. The occupying force also confiscated all the property of the so-called hostile legal persons: the Catholic Church, the Yugoslav State, the Province of the Drava Banovina, Slovenian societies, organisations, associations, funds etc. which were also forcefully dismissed. The expelled persons in the German camps Volksdeutsche Mitteistelle were exploited by the German Reich as cheap labour force. The majority of people were expelled, in order for the occupying force to gain space for the German colonisation, which was assigned the first-class role in the denationalisation; around 25,000 persons were expelled on political and racial grounds, among them 600 children, separated from the elderly and taken to the so-called re-educational institutions or the NS homes Lebensbornö. Over 20,000 Slovenians were detained in German prisons and more than 10,000 also in German concentration camps, most of those in Dachau, Mauthausen, Auschwitz and Ravensbruck. Particularly the prisoners in Auschwitz were killed very soon, among them over 400 Jews, taken from the Prekmurje area upon the German occupation of Hungary. Several hundreds of Slovenians were killed in the gravest manner without the relevant court proceedings, in the prisons of the rice-husking plant San Sabba in Trieste.

The German occupying force burnt down several tens of Slovenian villages and market-towns. Among them there were 12, which were upon being burnt down even flattened with ground, dead bodies of the shot men were thrown into fire while the remaining population was expelled. This happened in 1942 which was marked in Slovenia by the gravest violence on the part of the occupying force.

Flagrantly violating the international law, the German occupying force mobilised Slovenians in the paramilitary formations and in the army. Already the first year of the occupation saw the inclusion in the so-called Wehrmannschaft as the preparatory stage to the Sturmabteilungen (SA) 112,752 of the adult men and out of these 35,000 were in the years 1942–45 mobilised in the German state working service (Reichsarbeitsdienst) and in the German army (born between 1908–29). Around 5,000 forcefully mobilised Slovenians fell in the German army. Those which were on political, racial and free-from-hereditary-disease grounds not intended for the Germanisation, were assigned the special working obligation (Sonderdienstpflicht) in special camps, which represented the intermediate stage between the camps for foreign workers and the concentration camps, and were foreseen for the post-war sterilisation.

Yugoslav monetary gold 1939–51

DR DUŠAN BIBER

As early as in May 1939, on the eve of World War II, the Government of the Kingdom of Yugoslavia sent by the destroyer Beograd to the British port of Portsmouth 7,344 ingots of fine gold, i.e. the large part of the monetary gold reserves of the National Bank of Yugoslavia. Although this gold, later deposited with the Federal Reserve Bank in the USA, was transferred in strictest secrecy, this shipment could not, however, have been concealed from the Third Reich intelligence services.

According to the report by the National Bank of the Democratic Federative Yugoslavia, of 5 April 1945, the remaining Yugoslav monetary gold was transported from the vaults of the National Bank branch in Užice to Montenegro in 204 boxes during the night from 13 to 14 April 1941, in a week after the aggression by the Axis powers. This shipment contained 166 boxes of coins in net weight 7,982.20298 ounces and 38 boxes of bars of fine gold in net weight of 1,612.46805 ounces. The Italian occupying forces confiscated 124 boxes of gold; 42 boxes on the road between Cetinje and Hercegnovi, and 82 boxes in the building of the district office in Nikšić. The German occupying forces later discovered and confiscated 10 boxes of gold, hidden in the Ostrog monastery. There is still no knowledge about the further movements of the 50 boxes stored in the vaults of the National Bank branch in Cetinje. Escaping to Greece, the Yugoslav Government was able to evacuate by air merely 20 boxes of gold.

The Finance Minister of the Yugoslav Government in exile, Dr Juraj Šutej, reported at the Cabinet meeting in Jerusalem on 29 April 1941 that 9,200 kg of gold remained in Yugoslavia, while 30,000 kg of gold had been evacuated earlier. Thus barely 60,000 kg of gold remained in the Federal Reserve Bank in New York; the Government decided to exchange 300 kg of gold, stored in Cairo, for pounds. Prior to signing the Protocol on Yugoslavia's adhesion to the Tripartite Pact on 25 March 1941, the Royal Yugoslav Government attempted to transfer the gold stored in the USA to other neutral countries. In the middle of March 1941 it issued an order that the gold, valued at $10 million, be transferred from the Federal Reserve Bank in the USA to the Bank of Brazil, and further $15 million to the Central Bank in Argentina. Upon the intervention of the US President Roosevelt and the warning by the Yugoslav Minister Konstantin Fotic that Yugoslav assets would be frozen in the USA, the Government in Belgrade cancelled the order for the transfer of gold to Argentina.

On 9 March 1944, Marshal Josip Broz Tito, as chairman of the National Committee of the Liberation of Yugoslavia, requested the British Government to prevent the transfer of gold in the possession of the National Bank of Yugoslavia at the value of $11,250,000, deposited with the Bank of Brazil. Yugoslav gold, deposited with the Bank of England totalling $19,000,000, should also be frozen. The same goes for Yugoslav gold, of unknown value, deposited with the Federal Reserve Bank in New York and with the National Bank in

Turkey. A similar request was conveyed by the National Committee of the Liberation of Yugoslavia to the Governments of the USA and of the USSR. Upon this, the Turkish Government on 29 March 1944 and the Brazilian Government on 16 April 1944, notified the Royal Yugoslav Government that they had frozen Yugoslav assets. In summer 1944, according to Dr Juraj Šutej, Minister of Finance in the Royal Yugoslav Government in exile, 2,194 bars of fine gold were stored at the Federal Reserve Bank, weighing 876,294,991 ounces and 3,956 sacks of coins at the weight of 463,320,360 ounces; 11.5 tons of fine gold, however, were frozen in Brazil. The US Government did not impose embargo on the deposits of the Royal Yugoslav Government in exile. However, it did so in March 1945 upon the establishment of the Provisional Government of the Democratic Federative Yugoslavia.

The issue of restitution of the Yugoslav monetary gold, deposited with the Federal Reserve Bank in the USA, was settled by way of agreements between the Yugoslav and US Governments, signed on 19 July 1948 in Washington. The Yugoslav Government agreed to pay $17 million in compensation for the American property nationalised in Yugoslavia and 45 million dinars to settle the lend-lease and pre-UNRRA accounts while the US Government defrosted Yugoslav assets in the United States including the gold amounting to a value of approximately $50 million. Yugoslav monetary gold, confiscated by the Italian occupying forces in April 1941 in Montenegro was transferred to Rome and after Italy's surrender looted by the Germans along with other Italian monetary gold. In conformity with the London Protocol of 16 December 1947, the Tripartite Gold Commission had retained 8,857 kg of gold from the quota allocated to Italy, until the decisions on the restitution of this gold to the Yugoslav Government were adopted. In compliance with the provisions of the peace treaty and the agreement between both Governments, in June 1948, 8,393 kg of fine gold had to be restituted. However, the Yugoslav Government subsequently renounced its claim for restitution to 30% of the gold (2,517.9 kg) in exchange for Italy's opening a lira account of equivalent value in Yugoslavia's name. The amount of gold actually returned to Yugoslavia was therefore equal to 5,875.1 kg.

The previously mentioned 10 boxes of gold, confiscated by the Germans in the Ostrog monastery in Montenegro, in April 1941 – according to the official data of the post-war Yugoslav Government – contained 500 kg of fine gold, out of altogether 9,600 kg of fine gold, stored at the National Bank branch in Užice. Under the German occupation, the National Bank of Serbia purchased 100 kg of gold from private persons, which the Germans took with them upon their withdrawal from Serbia. The State Bank of the so-called Independent state of Croatia also had 100 kg of fine gold at its disposal, which was allegedly taken in 1945 by the Ustashis to Germany. In the Bor Mines during the occupation, the Germans acquired, by processing copper, either in Serbia or in Germany, 2,700 kg of fine gold. The Tripartite Gold Commission temporarily validated the claim only to the extent of 2,900 kg, however it did not clarify its position on the gold of the central banks of Serbia and Croatia, nor on the 23 bars or 300 kg of gold from the Bor Mines, subsequently demanded by the Yugoslav Government.

In January 1951, the Counsellor of the Yugoslav Embassy in London, Mr

Zlatarić, stated that there were three categories of gold: (1) gold of the National bank of Yugoslavia; (2) gold from the Bor Mines, and (3) the Ustashi gold. However, the Reichsbank, via Switzerland, transferred gold to Croatia worth $400,000.

The Bank for International Settlements in Basel, for instance, transferred to the National Bank of Yugoslavia 3,138.28017 kg of fine gold between 7 June 1940 and 29 April 1941. There are no data as to whether, or how much, gold was transferred from Switzerland to Belgrade after 6 April 1941, i.e. following the German aggression and occupation, or if that gold was transferred to any account of the National Bank of Yugoslavia abroad. Sidney Zabludoff states on behalf of the World Jewish Congress that in Yugoslavia the Nazis looted monetary gold of as much value as $3,800,000, including the forced buyout of gold through central banks, paid in Reichsmarks. The same figure appears also with reference to the non-monetary gold which includes monetary gold. The proportion is neither clearly set nor evaluated. The research of the captured German documents, microfilmed at Alexandria, Virginia in the USA, Microcopy T-75, Rolls 1-89, Generalbevollmächitgte für die Wirtschaft in Serbien, could clarify much about the seizure of Jewish property in Serbia in the years from 1941 to 1944, the transactions of the National Bank of Serbia, and also about the exploitation of the Bor copper mines and the German purchase of Compagnie Française de Mines de Bor. Following the end of World War II, Mr Halpern, a solicitor of this French company, disputed the claims by the Yugoslav Government. The gold, originating from the Bor Mines (2,094,597 kg) should be registered as the gold reserve, as provided under an Order of 1934. Solicitor Mr Halpern asserted that this gold had always been the property and under control of French company agents, and never in possession or under control of the German authorities. The British Foreign Secretary Ernest Bevin did not agree with the French claim for the handing over of 23 bars of fine gold refined from ore in the Bor Mines. The handing over of these bars of gold totalling 282.979 kg was claimed by the Yugoslav Government. At first, 39 bars of fine gold were originally claimed and 16 of those were restituted. The conclusion was adopted at the Brussels Gold Conference in January 1950 that all 39 bars of gold had to be put into the gold pool, and that 16 of the bars of gold had been wrongly restituted directly to the Yugoslav Government. This gold was therefore deducted from the contingent approved for restitution to Yugoslavia. Several letters and diplomatic notes on this issue were exchanged.

According to its records, the Bank of England carried out – on behalf of the Tripartite Gold Commission established by the Governments of the USA, UK and France – the following transfers to the National Bank of the Federative People's Republic of Yugoslavia: 23 September 1948 – 69,841.059 oz coins and 6,919.692 oz bars; 4 January 1951 – 1,629.648 oz bars; 5 November 1958 – 31,613.597 oz bars and 24,650.190 oz coins, which amount to 334,654.186 oz of gold and coins.

The sources and available literature provide no data indicating that the monetary gold of the National Bank of Yugoslavia was deposited in the territory of the Republic of Slovenia. There are also no official data concerning the precise amount of non-monetary gold plundered, confiscated or perhaps even purchased by the occupying forces. According to the data submitted on 28 September 1945 to the Presidency of the National Government of Slovenia by the official Commission for war damage in Slovenia, confiscations from private persons by the German occupying forces during the occupation (1941–45) amounted to 647 million dinars in cash, 326 million dinars in securities and 114 million dinars in valuables – to the total value of one billion 87 million dinars, or $24,704.545

REFERENCES

Jacob B. Hoptner, Jugoslavija u krizi 1934–1941 (Yugoslavia in Crisis 1934–1941, Columbia University Press, New York, London 1962), Rijeka, 1972, p. 172; Akten zur deutschen auswärtigen Politik, D, VI, Nr. 680, 691.

Dušan Pienča, Medjunarodni odnosi Jugoslavije u toku drugog svetskog rata (International Relations of Yugoslavia during the Second World War), Beograd 1962, p. 10.

Bogdan Krizman (editor), Jugoslovanske vlade v izbjeglištvu, (Yugoslav Governments in Exile 1941–1945) 1941–1943, Vol. 1, Beograd, Zagreb 1981, pp. 111, 115. Prime Minister Dušan Simović, referring to the minutes of the Cabinet meeting of 21 April 1941, states in his memoirs that the Government managed to transfer one ton of gold to Jerusalem by aircraft; 66,863 kg of gold were deposited in the Federal Reserve Bank in New York, and additional 1,250 kg of gold in the Bank of Brazil (D. Pienča, op. cit., 14).

Constantin Fotich, The War We Lost, New York, The Viking Press 1948, pp. 61–64.

Public Record Office (PRO), London, PREM 3/536/11; Josip Broz –Tito, Sabrana djela (Collected Works), Vol. 19, Beograd 1984, pp. 263–265.

B. Pienča, op. cit., pp. 297–298.

PRO, FO 371/72568, R 153, 367, 1254, 2403, 2799, 2970, 3467, 7284, 7461, 8189, 8766, 9641/153/92.

PRO, FO 371/71059, CJ 3364, 3740/552/182.

Bank of Italy, notes 51–54.

PRO, FO 371/94034. Cfr. Nazi Gold: Information from the British Archives; Part II, Monetary gold, non-monetary gold and the Tripartite Gold Commission, Historians, LRD, No. 12, May 1997, p.23.

PRO, FO 371/94033, CJW 1494/5.

Unabhängige Expertenkommission, Schweiz. Zweiter Weltkrieg, Goldtransaktionen im Zweiten Weltkrieg. Kommentierte statistische Übersicht, Bern, December 1997, p. 5.

The Bank of International Settlements during the Second World War, Dr Piet, p. 15.

World Jewish Congress, Movements of Nazi Gold, By Sidney Zabludoff, Table 1 and 2.

PRO, FO 371/86117, CJ 192, 572, 3561, 4416/192/182; FO 371/94034, Aide Memoire, 10 January 1951.

Bank of England's Role as Custodian of the Tripartite Gold Commission's Holdings of Gold, Bank of England Transactions – according to the TGC Gold Book, pp. 2, 3, 4. Unfortunately, neither this report, nor the report by the Tripartite Gold Commission, presented at the Nazi Gold Conference, held in London from 2 to 4 December 1997, includes tables showing the amount of gold claimed by individual states, the validated number of accepted and of effected claims, or the residual share to be allotted among individual states.

Arhiv Slovenije, fond Vlada Slovenije (Archives of Slovenia, the Fund of the Government of Slovenia) No. 13. Data are also given on the curtailment of freedom under German occupation affecting 584,207 persons in total duration of 11,932,780 months, and the lost income, which by the average monthly income of 2,000 dinars would amount to the total of 23,865,560,000 dinars or $542,399,000 (according to the to days value amounting to almost $6 billion). According to the above data, there were 216,325 people in prison, 14,224 in P.o.W. camps, 41,214 persons were in concentration camps, 163,780 were submitted to forced labour, 56,324 were forcibly mobilised, and 92,340 persons were deported. The total number of these persons amounts to 73,14% of the population (798,700) of the parts of Slovenia under German occupation in 1941, or 47,19% (1,237,846) of the entire population of Slovenia, occupied by the Germans after the surrender of Italy on 8 September 1943. These figures are obviously unrealistic.

SPAIN

Approach and views of the Spanish Commission in the light of the London Conference

The Spanish Government decided to set up the Commission in July 1997, in line with the concern which the Spanish parliament and public opinion were voicing through the many news items which, since 1996, had been appearing in the media about the transactions involving that gold which took place during World War II.

As long ago as 1996 and 1997, indisputably sound historical reports were officially published, outstanding among which were those of the British Foreign and Commonwealth Office and the study co-ordinated by the U.S. State Department (known as the "first Eizenstat Report").

The Spanish Government shared the concern of many other countries which have set up various types of commissions to investigate the plundering of those dramatic years and to try to obtain as accurate a picture as possible of what took place at that time, in its historical and human dimensions. In so doing, and in looking at the past through present-day eyes, it is in fact necessary to take into account the climate of the time. With regard to Spain, it was a country divided and devastated by the circumstances of the Civil War; a country whose population was struggling for economic survival from day to day and which did not want to be drawn, in any way, into the suffering of an involvement in the world conflict. In a way, those in power themselves, aware of that, although burdened by the mortgages of the Civil War – including the influence of the fascist powers which contributed powerfully to the victory of the insurgents over the Government of the Republic – were obliged, at times in spite of themselves, to maintain neutrality. Spain was, in fact, a passive subject of the conflict, with all the consequences of that: for example, the belligerents brought their economic pressures to bear within the framework of their respective war strategies.

Against that background, it should also be stressed that, over and above the political circumstances and the affinities which found their way into Spanish governmental attitudes, it is a recognised fact that our country made full use of its neutrality in order to help and protect many Jews and communities who were victims of the holocaust persecution. The historical roots which link Spain with Judaism, and more specifically with the Sephardic Jews, found their human expression in that task, in which the Spanish people, and also the authorities of the time (principally the diplomatic service) joined forces and ran risks together.

Unlike other countries, Spain has never had any racial anti-Semitism and, having emerged from the historical turmoil of religious origin which led to the drama of the expulsion of 1492, which provided for the option of conversion, the first Spanish Constitution of 1812 saw the start of the process which was to lead to full reunion with our Jewish roots, the most recent proof of which was the meeting of minds explicitly declared at the 5th Centenary celebrations in 1992.

The Royal Decree 1136/97 of 11 July 1997 determined the nature, composition and objectives of the Commission:

1. It is a governmental Commission of which Mr Enrique Mugica Herzog, a Deputy of the Partido Socialista (PSOE), now in opposition in the Cortes Generales (National Assembly), and a former Minister of Justice, has been appointed Chairman by the Prime Minister.

2. Apart from the Chairman, it is made up of eight Members and a Secretary: a Deputy of the governing Partido Popular (PP), Mr Francisco de Cáceres; the Researchers, Professors Martin Acefia and Marquina; Mr Mauricio Hatchwell; Ambassador López Aguirrebengoa, and the representatives of the Administration, Mr Areilza (Prime Minister's Office), Mr Fernandez (Economic Affairs) and Mr Palacio (Justice). The post of Secretary is held by Minister Plenipotentiary Galainena.

3. The Commission is charged with submitting a report on the matter to the Government.

The Spanish Commission has received a dual mandate: openness and ethical conduct. Since its formation, it has shown its determination to examine with complete rigour and objectivity the documentation of the period held in Spanish official archives. It is doing so not only by adopting a purely factual approach, but with a critical spirit, in order to determine exactly what Spain's policy was, during those years, in its economic relations and dealings with the parties to the conflict and with third countries, and whether there was, in this sphere, any Spanish conduct which was not in accordance with international legitimacy and was injurious to the rights of third parties. Although the present Spanish democratic regime is clearly different from that which was in power in this country at that time, the continuity of the State cannot be left aside. The Spanish Government has expressed its willingness to co-operate with other Governments and Institutions in the effort to establish the historical truth and its inherent justice.

In interpreting its mandate, the Commission has focused its work on four specific areas:

1. **Monetary gold:** On this matter, it has had available to it a detailed study produced in April 1997 by one of its members, Prof. Martin Acefia, covering the formation of the Spanish official gold reserves during the years of World War II. Prof. Acefia presented a summary of his study in an appearance before the United States House of Representatives on 25 June 1997:
   • Monetary gold operations were the exclusive responsibility of the Spanish Foreign Currency Institute (IEME), which ceased to exist in the 1960s.

That institution tried to reconstitute, as far as possible, the Bank of Spain's gold reserves which had completely disappeared in 1939, at the end of the Spanish Civil War, having been disposed of by the Government of the Republic, which transferred 510 tonnes of fine gold to the former Soviet Union as well as lesser quantities to the Bank of France. In 1939, Spain recovered 52.7 tonnes of gold from the Bank of France and, between 1939 and 1945, acquired 67.419 tonnes of gold abroad (38.594 t from the National Bank of Switzerland; 14.92 t from the Bank of England; 9.126 t from the Bank of Portugal; 2.507 t from the Transatlantic German Bank; 0.838 t from the Bank for International Settlements[1] and 1.434 t from the Foreign Trade Bank of Spain).

- The Allied Tripartite Gold Commission[2] reviewed all those movements with the Spanish authorities of the time and established that 101.6 kg of gold came from the Nazi plundering of the National Bank of the Netherlands; that quantity was handed over to the said Commission in pursuance of Bretton Woods Resolution VI.

One subject under consideration is pursuit of the final destination of the State gold reserves existing in 1945, which gradually declined until they were practically exhausted at the end of the 1950s by the economic crisis which this country had experienced since the 1936–39 Civil War and by the consequences of the World War itself.

2. Non-monetary gold:

- The Commission is preparing the first systematic study ever undertaken in this country on the subject. It covers the movements of gold carried out, which are detected through analysis of the IEME's balance sheets – including individuals' deposits in the Bank of Spain, gold held by Correspondent Banks and gold belonging to the Bank of Spain; the data on the Embassy of the Third Reich in Madrid; and the data on the German undertaking SOFINDUS and its connection with the trade in wolfram as a strategic material.
- The Commission still needs to complete the work in order to be able to reach the point of completing its overall picture in this field.

3. German assets: their freezing, expropriation and liquidation.

- In this field, the Commission has been able to carry out a research project of an unprecedented nature on the liquidation of the German State's assets in Spain since the War, a process which started in 1945 and concluded in 1958, and on the liquidation of privately-owned German assets, a process which started three years later and also ended in 1958.
- This research is at a very advanced stage.

4. Spain's economic and trading relations with the outside world.

- This is a much more researched topic in the specialist economic literature, and the picture of international trade during that period is well-known. The Commission has focused on Spain's economic and trading relations with Third Reich Germany which, together with the United Kingdom and the United States, were all important traditional customers and suppliers of Spain. It has also made a thorough study of economic and trading relations with Switzerland. The study of Spain's economic relations with those four countries gives quite a full picture, highlighting two aspects: Spain's involvement in their commercial transactions and the systems used to finance transfers of goods and services through clearing systems, other types of set-off, and actual flows of foreign currency and other means of payment. Two facts have proved especially significant: the constant trade surplus with Germany during those years did not give rise to any significant movement of foreign currency, because of the recoupment of Spanish Civil War debt; however, such movement is obvious in the case of the Spanish trade surplus with the two allied countries, being directly related to the acquisition of monetary gold. The study is quite illuminating with regard to trade in services.

When completed, the Commission's Report will be submitted to the national Government in accordance with its terms of reference.

The Commission, also interpreting its terms of reference, hopes that the exchanges held during the London Conference will represent a useful contribution to its own work and to the common search for the truth, as a necessary step towards being able finally to put behind us the tragedy of those years and its consequences, so that humanity can look to the future of peace, justice and co-operation which we all desire.

Starting from this basis, the Spanish Commission is open to a fruitful dialogue leading to the exchange of knowledge and views.

NOTES

[1] Spanish wording of the Bank's name incorrect but nevertheless assumed to refer to the BIS.

[2] Literal translation of the Spanish. The nearest reference found to this body has been to the Tripartite Commission for the Restitution of Monetary Gold, which may or may not be the same thing.

The translations of the names of the other banks are unofficial.

SWEDEN

Statement by the Swedish delegation

I would like to thank the British Government and Foreign Secretary Cook for organising this conference on the Nazi gold. The Swedish Government considers this conference as a significant contribution to the efforts to shed as much light as possible on a unique chapter in mankind's history of evil, the Holocaust. Every nation has a duty to face all facts with regard to its own role in the years when Jewish communities all over Europe were destroyed and extinguished. Transparency is vital to enable us to establish all facts. My Government for its part is committed to leaving no stone unturned in this pursuit. We intend to continue a policy of total openness as regards the actions of the Swedish authorities during World War II.

Last week the Swedish prime minister, Mr Göran Persson, made a speech in our parliament about the Holocaust. He stressed that the crimes of the past may never be forgotten. We can not guarantee that something as terrible as the Holocaust will ever happen again. But by keeping our knowledge about what happened alive we can decrease the risks that our children and grandchildren will live through something similar. Human dignity and democracy cannot be defended through silence. We must actively discuss it at home, in schools, in the political life. To forget, to tolerate neo-nazi and racial tendencies would be a betrayal against those who survived and those who died.

An action programme has been launched in Sweden by the Government and the political parties in our Parliament against racism, xenophobia, for human dignity and democracy. It is called Living History – an information project about the Holocaust. This action programme is directed primarily to our schools where, the children of today will always need more information about what actually happened in a not too distant past and about what may happen if we do not learn to respect the inherent dignity of every individual.

To this conference my delegation has produced a paper with the title *Sweden and the Nazi gold* which briefly outlines what was done in the past and what is being done now regarding this issue. But before going into the details of this paper, something my delegation will do during the course of this conference, allow me, Mr Chairman, to make a comment of a general nature.

In February 1997 the Bank of Sweden, the Riksbank, appointed an independent investigator to carry out a new examination of documents in the archives of the Riksbank related to gold transactions during World War II. The findings of this investigation will be presented on 17 December this year. In March this year the Swedish Government decided to set up an official commission, The Commission on Jewish Assets in Sweden during the Second World War. The terms of reference of the Commission were formulated in close co-operation with the Jewish community in Stockholm. The Commission consists of 23 persons: special advisers, experts, historians, two full-time research secretaries. Among the special advisers are the Secretary General of the World Jewish Congress, Dr Israel Singer and representatives of the Jewish communities in Sweden. The Commission has a very broad mandate to look into all possible aspects of Jewish assets that have gone missing. One question of particular interest concerns unclaimed bank accounts. Inquiries were undertaken in the 1960s in order to ascertain what accounts in Swedish banks had remained untouched since 1945. However, this matter will be examined afresh. The Commission will also analyse and take a position on the facts that emerge from the Riksbank's investigation. The Commission will make supplementary investigations if it finds this to be beneficial to its own inquiry with particular emphasis on the question of gold that may have belonged to Jews. The Commission will report to the Government on the autumn of 1998.

*   *   *   *

I would like to state clearly that we feel that no country did as much as it might have or should have to save innocent victims of Nazis persecution. Sweden's record in this respect is far from spotless. The prevailing attitude before the war and at the beginning of the war was a lack of real concern. This is quite clear from an official report which came out in 1946 concerning the treatment of refugees. Its straightforward conclusion was that our refugee policy at the outset lacked generosity. The policy was changed in 1941 but then it was too late for many.

Once it became known, however that the Nazi regime had begun a program of mass extermination of European Jews, the Swedish Foreign Ministry organised a systematic effort to save Jews.

But were these endeavours sufficient to compensate for the moral ambiguities inherent in a position of neutrality during World War II? This issue has been debated many times in Sweden, and this conference will certainly add yet another dimension to the discussion.

*   *   *   *

I would like to sketch very briefly how monetary gold from Germany came into Swedish possession during World War II. Sweden managed to stay out of the war, which of course made its fate considerably different from that of our Nordic neighbours. However, it goes without saying that Sweden's national economy was fundamentally affected by the war. After the German occupation of Norway and Denmark in April 1940 Sweden was cut off from the West, which normally accounted for some 70% of our foreign trade.

We became utterly dependent upon Germany and countries under German control to get coal for our industry and artificial fertilisers for our agriculture. Without this trade, our economy fairly soon would have been close to a breakdown. I think it is fair to say, Mr Chairman, that foreign trade became close to a question of survival since we did not have any coal or oil resources of our own and thus had to rely on imports from Germany for our energy needs.

Our trade with Germany was based on a clearing system. In some periods when Germany was not able to export as much to Sweden as she should have done according to the clearing arrangements, the German government asked for trade credits which Sweden refused. Germany also wanted to pay in Reichsmarks, which Sweden of course also refused. Gold, however, was accepted as an international means of payment without question by the Swedish authorities until the Allies made known their suspicions that Germany was using looted gold from occupied countries.

In January 1943, upon the initiative of the British Government, 17 nations signed a declaration generally known as the Inter-Allied Declaration against Acts of Dispossession. This declaration, however, did not directly address the matter of German gold exports, but a year later in February 1944, the Swedish Government was informed of a statement issued by Henry Morgenthau, US Treasury Secretary, warning persons in neutral countries against dealing in gold that had been looted by the enemy. The warning came via the American Legation in Stockholm. A note to the same effect was presented by the British Legation.

It seems that at the time the Bank of Sweden, The Riksbank, tried to limit its transactions with Germany in gold. This is something that is presently being investigated.

In the summer of 1944 the Allies arranged a conference at Bretton Woods on monetary and financial matters. The conference adopted Resolution VI which recommended that neutral countries take certain steps with regard to property looted in occupied countries, including gold. The Resolution was presented to the Swedish Government in early October 1944. At the Potsdam conference in the summer of 1945 an American proposal was adopted to establish a "gold pot", where all looted monetary gold from Germany and neutral countries would be recovered for subsequent distribution to those countries occupied during the war and from whose central banks the gold had originally been removed.

Negotiations between Sweden and the Allies started in Washington in 1946. With regard to the gold the Swedish party made it clear from the outset of the negotiations that Sweden was prepared to return gold that had been looted from occupied countries by the Germans. The allied standpoint was that all gold that had been acquired after January 1943 should in principle be regarded as looted gold since the Germans were by that time considered to have used up all legitimately acquired gold reserves in their possession. Sweden contested the allied hypothesis that all gold purchased from Germany after a certain date should be deemed to be looted.

After much discussion, especially on the question on how to deal with looted gold that the Swedish Riksbank had purchased from the German Reichsbank but later sold to a third country, an agreement was reached which was approved by the Swedish Riksdag in December 1946. According to this agreement Sweden was committed to return looted gold but only such gold as remained in the possession of Sweden on 1 June 1945.

This Mr Chairman is a brief summary of a series of events which is described in detail in the paper we have presented to this Conference. This paper also outlines the issues of the Belgian and Dutch gold which ended up in the vaults of the Swedish Riksbank. The Belgian gold was transferred to the TGC in 1949 and the Dutch gold in 1955.

The question of whether or not gold stolen from Jews, Romani or others ever came into the possession of the Swedish Riksbank has not yet been answered.

WHAT HAS BEEN DONE TO COMPENSATE?

As pointed out by my delegation yesterday, Sweden reached an agreement with the Allies in Washington in 1946 on looted gold and on assistance to war ravaged countries.

As a result of this Agreement, the German assets in Sweden were requisitioned, examined and liquidated through the auspices of the Foreign Capital Control Office and the Restitution Board, special agencies set up in Sweden for these purposes. From the proceeds of liquidation, which were estimated to total 378 million Swedish Crowns, 150 million Crowns were paid into a special account at the Bank of Sweden for purchases of essential commodities for the economy of occupied Germany. Sweden also provided 125 million Crowns in financial aid, money which did not come from the German assets. Of these 125 million Crowns, 50 million went to the International Refugee Organisation in London and was used for reparations to and the resettlement of the non-repatriable victims of the Nazis.

The remaining 75 million were part of Sweden's continued support to reconstruction in the war ravaged countries primarily in form of depreciation on past and future credit payments. The 75 million Crowns were distributed as follows: to Denmark 15 million, France 12 million, Norway 15 million, Greece 2 million, the Netherlands 9 million, Yugoslavia 10 million and to Czechoslovakia 5 million Crowns, all mainly by writing off debts. The remaining 7 million Crowns were intended for Belgium and Luxembourg. However, these two countries declared in 1952 that they renounced the sum. The 7 million were instead donated to the UNHCR.

As regards gold, Sweden agreed to return gold considered to be looted and which remained in the possession of Sweden by 1 July 1945. Claims for such gold had to be made by the governments of the occupied countries or their central banks before 1 July 1947. The Governments of Belgium and of the Netherlands made such claims.

As has been said before, Belgium had deposited gold with the Bank of France in 1939 and 1940. Some of this gold, 7.1 tons, ended up in the possession of the Bank of Sweden during the war. In 1949 a corresponding amount of gold was transferred to the TGC in New York. The issue of the Dutch claim took a longer time to solve. At the outset, Sweden questioned whether the Dutch gold could be considered to be looted. Eventually an agreement was reached in 1954 and gold, approximately 6 tons, was returned to the TGC in 1955.

The inquiry concerning the archives of the Bank of Sweden, which my delegation mentioned yesterday, has focused its work on all gold transactions during the war with Germany directly and indirectly including amounts, dates, places of delivery, storage, transfer, reasons for the transactions.

The investigation has also studied the amounts of looted gold acquired by the Bank including total quantity, quantity of looted gold of Belgian and Dutch origin and possible evidence on looted non-monetary gold.

The investigation has also looked into what information was available to decision makers at the time, measures taken in consequence and also the role of the Swedish Government.

The investigation will publish its report on 17 December this year. Its results will be submitted to the Government Commission on Jewish Assets which, as was said before, will report in the autumn of 1998. More information is available in the document my delegation has submitted to this Conference.

Sweden and the Nazi Gold

The question has been put as to whether Sweden (as one of several countries), fully aware of what it was doing, received gold from Nazi Germany as payment for transactions before and during World War II, although officials knew, or should have known, that the gold had either been appropriated from the central banks of occupied countries or stolen from Jews in connection with Nazi persecution of the Jews, so-called looted gold.

The transactions conducted by the Swedish Central Bank – the Riksbank – during the war have attracted the greatest attention. After the war had ended an investigation was undertaken. The Riksbank returned approximately 7 tons of gold to the Banque Nationale de Belgique in 1949 and 6 tons of gold to De Nederlandsche Bank in 1955, gold which was considered to have been looted.

In February 1997, the Riksbank appointed an independent investigator to carry out a new examination of documents in the archives of the Riksbank in order to ascertain if they contain more information about the Riksbank's acquisition of looted gold during World War II. The findings will be presented on 17 December this year.

In March this year, the Swedish Government decided to set up an official government commission, the *Commission on Jewish Assets in Sweden at the Time of the Second World War*. The terms of reference for the Commission were formulated in close cooperation with the Jewish Community in Stockholm. The Commission has a very broad mandate to look into all possible aspects of Jewish assets that have gone missing. One question of particular interest concerns unclaimed bank accounts. Inquiries were undertaken in the 1960s in order to ascertain what accounts in Swedish banks had remained untouched since 1945. However, this matter will be examined afresh.

One of the Commission's tasks is to analyse and to take a position on the facts that emerge from the Riksbank's investigation. The Commission will make supplementary investigations, if it finds this to be beneficial to its own inquiry, with particular emphasis on the question of gold that may have belonged to Jews.

The Commission will report to the Government on its findings in the autumn of 1998.

The first part of this report to the London Conference describes the Swedish negotiations with the Allies after the war and the results thereof. The second part contains a description of the investigations into dormant bank accounts and other private property which took place in the 1960s. Finally, two progress reports describe the work of the Riksbank and the Commission so far and the next stages in the process.

THE GOLD ISSUE

Sweden's negotiations with the Allies after the war

Allied declarations

On 5 January 1943, upon the initiative of the British Government, 17 nations signed a declaration generally known as the *Inter-Allied Declaration against Acts of Dispossession*. This declaration stated that "the Allies intended to do their utmost to obstruct the enemy's looting" and therefore reserved the right to declare invalid all transactions, regardless of their formal framework ("transfers of or dealings with, property, rights and interests of any description whatsoever"), entailing property in enemy-occupied territory. The Declaration was submitted to the Swedish Government in a note from the British Legation in Stockholm.

In the declaration it was stated that one of the methods employed by the Axis Powers had been unlawful appropriation of large quantities of gold belonging to occupied nations. According to the declaration, the Axis Powers had sold gold of this type to various states with which they continued to have diplomatic relations, thus securing for themselves an important source of foreign currency for the import of coveted goods from these countries. The US therefore declared that it would not recognise any acquisition of looted gold held by the Axis Powers or which they had disposed of on the world market. The US Treasury Department would follow the rule not to buy any gold located outside the US from any country that had not broken relations with the Axis, or from any country that subsequent to the announcement of the declaration acquired gold from any country that had not broken relations with the Axis. The Soviet Union issued a similar declaration on 23 February, and the Swedish Ministry for Foreign Affairs received notification of this via the Embassy in Moscow on 29 February 1944. In May and June 1944 respectively, the governments-in-exile of Norway and Belgium announced that they supported the American declaration.

In the summer of 1944, the Allies arranged a monetary and financial conference in Bretton Woods in the US. The conference was divided into three commissions. On 10 July 1944, the third of these, Commission III, appointed a committee enjoined with the task of discussing such issues as "enemy assets, looted property and related matters." The various proposals put forward by the committee led to the conference adopting Resolution VI, which was presented to the Swedish Government in documents from the British and American emissaries on 2 October 1944. Resolution VI recommended certain steps in relation to the neutral countries with regard both to property that had its origins in occupied countries and enemy property in general. It urged the neutral countries to take steps on their territory to prevent the transfer of property or other transactions involving property (*inter alia* gold) that had been taken from occupied areas, to acquire and separate such property and to keep it available for the relevant authorities after liberation. Furthermore, the Resolution declared that the neutral states should prevent enemy property from being concealed and take steps to ensure that property would be surrendered to the Allies. Resolution VI was a description of the Safehaven Programme[1] which had been drafted in the USA. The Resolution came to form a common foundation for the Allies on which British and American cooperation on the Safehaven Programme could be intensified.

Sweden responds to the Bretton Woods Resolution

The Swedish Government declared that it was prepared to take internal measures to meet with the recommendations contained in the Resolution, at the same time referring to the successive tightening of Swedish currency controls designed to control enemy property, and in particular to amendments to the Foreign Exchange Ordinance made in October 1944. On 29 June 1945, the Act on the Restitution of certain Property originating from Occupied Territories (SFS 1945:520)[2] was promulgated. This instituted a special procedure for the restitution of property that, in contravention of international law, had been seized from citizens in occupied countries even in cases where the property was in the possession of someone who had acquired it in good faith. At the same time, the Act on the Control of certain foreign Property (SFS 1945:522) was passed along with ordinances generally prohibiting the sale or dispersal of German property in the country and making it compulsory to declare German property. The "Control Act" made it possible to prescribe the seizure of property that formally appeared to be Swedish, for example property belonging to a Swedish legal person, with a foreign controlling interest. An authority, the Foreign Capital Control Office (Flyktapitalbyrån), was set up to handle statements of ownership. A special committee was also established, the Restitution Board (Restitutionsnämnden), whose primary task was to examine matters pertaining to the restitution of looted property and decrees on the seizure of property.

Allied agreements 1945–46

At the Potsdam Conference, which took place between 16 July – 1 August 1945, the occupying powers decided to charge the Allied Control Council in Berlin with the task of initiating suitable measures for claiming custody of such German-owned assets abroad that were not already under Allied supervision. At the same time, the four powers agreed upon a division of these assets, whereby the Soviet Union waived its claims to German external assets with the exception of property in Bulgaria, Finland, Hungary, Romania and the eastern part of Austria. German property in former neutral countries would therefore fall to the Western Allies. In addition, the Potsdam Conference adopted an American proposal to establish a "gold pot" where all looted monetary gold from Germany and the neutral countries would be recovered for subsequent distribution to the countries which had been occupied during the war and from whose central banks the gold had originally been removed.

The question of a "gold pot" was considered in greater detail at the Paris Reparations Conference which took place in November and December 1945 with the participation of 18 nations. The concept of a Gold Pool launched at the

Potsdam Conference was confirmed, and the USA, Great Britain and France were appointed to assume responsibility for the administration of the pool, the work to be carried out by a specially appointed commission – the *Tripartite Gold Commission*[3] (TGC). The TGC was set up to implement the provisions concerning the return of monetary gold as agreed at the Paris conference. The agreement did not define what was meant by monetary gold (apart from stating that gold coins should be treated as monetary gold). In a questionnaire from 1947 the TGC gave the following definition of monetary gold:

> "All gold which at the time of its looting or wrongful removal was carried as part of a claimant country's monetary reserve, either in the accounts of the government itself, or in the accounts of the claimant country's central bank or other monetary authority at home or abroad."

The Paris Conference also decided to create a fund of at least USD 25 million for aid to the non-repatriable victims of the Nazi regime. Thus, the intention was that Jews and other victims who had survived the Nazi persecutions, but who had no government to which they could turn, would be given the opportunity to receive some portion of German reparations. The plan was to build up the fund with the proceeds of the non-monetary gold, which the Allies had found in Germany, together with proceeds from German assets in the neutral states, which were to be the subject of coming negotiations. An action plan was to be prepared by the governments of the USA, Great Britain, France, Czechoslovakia and Yugoslavia in consultation with the Intergovernmental Committee on Refugees, IGCR (later the International Refugee Organisation, IRO).

The implementation of the convention concerning German reparations that was signed in Paris in January 1946 presupposed agreements with each of the neutral states where German assets were being held. To this end, the neutral states were invited to Washington to take part in negotiations. In March 1946, negotiations were opened with Switzerland. These negotiations led to an agreement entered into on 25 May 1946.

The Allies also sought to make similar agreements with the other neutral countries, which meant that after agreement had been reached with Switzerland and Sweden – regarded as being the two countries with the largest assets – they would turn to Spain, Portugal and Ireland followed by Argentina and Turkey.

1946 Swedish-Allied Washington negotiations

Negotiations with Sweden in Washington started on 31 May 1946. As had been the case in earlier rounds of negotiations, the Allies tried to bring about some form of joint Swedish-Allied control of the German assets. On the Swedish side, officials adhered to its original position, i.e. to reject a joint control mechanism. They also asserted that responsibility for such controls should devolve solely upon the Swedish bodies: the Foreign Capital Control Office and the Restitution Board. After negotiations it was finally agreed that the German assets in Sweden would be requisitioned, examined and liquidated through the auspices of the Foreign Capital Control Office. On 18 July 1946, an agreement was made with the following main content. From the proceeds of liquidation, which were estimated to total SEK 378 million, SEK 150 million were to be paid into a special account at the Swedish Riksbank for purchases of essential commodities for the German economy. At the same time, Sweden declared that it was prepared to also provide up to SEK 125 million in financial aid – money which did not come from the German assets. Of these SEK 125 million, 50 million were to go to the International Refugee Organisation in London to be used for reparations to and the resettlement of the non-repatriable victims of the Nazis. The remaining SEK 75 million were intended to be part of Sweden's continued support for reconstruction in the war-ravaged countries, primarily in the form of depreciation on past and future credit payments.[4] The SEK 75 million were eventually distributed as follows: to Denmark 15 million, France 12 million, Norway 15 million, Greece 2 million, the Netherlands 9 million, Yugoslavia 10 million and to Czechoslovakia 5 million, mainly by writing off debts. The remaining 7 million were intended for Belgium and Luxembourg. However, these two countries declared in 1953 that they renounced the sum. The 7 million were instead donated to UNHCR.[5]

Contribution to the German economy

As stated above, according to the terms of the Washington Accord of 1946, the sum of SEK 150 million was to be deposited in a special account at the Riksbank for purchases of essential commodities for the German economy. A study of the archives of the Riksbank provides the following information:

In the course of deliberations with the Allies in 1947 it was decided that the sum should be divided up, with the Americans and British occupied zones each receiving SEK 63 million, while SEK 24 million were paid to the French zone. The funds were allocated in the following way:

American Zone: In 1947 SEK 6.8 million were spent on the purchase of cellulose from Sweden. In the 1947 agreement regulating payments between Sweden and the British-American occupation powers in Germany, it was decided that the remainder should be handled so that 1/18 of the sum should be transferred every month to the current account, allowing the funds to be used for the purchase of commodities in Sweden for use in the British-American zones. In June 1949, it was decided that the remaining sum, which amounted to around SEK 35 million, should be used for German purchases of timber and wooden manufactured goods from Sweden. Deliveries of this type worth approximately SEK 20 million were made. In 1951, it was decided that the remaining SEK 15 million should be used to pay for running imports from Sweden to the Federal Republic of Germany. The sum was transferred, and by January 1951, had been used up.

British Zone: SEK 63 million were transferred to the English Treasury in April 1947 via the Bank of England's account at the Riksbank. It was stated that the sum was earmarked for purchases of commodities for the German economy pursuant to the Washington Accord.

French Zone: Upon the request of the French occupying authority, SEK 14 million and SEK 8.5 million respectively were transferred on the 9 January and 2 August 1948, that is a total of SEK 22.5 million, to a special account at the Riksbank which had been opened for *l'Office du Commerce Extérieur de la Zone Française d'Occupation en Allemagne*. In connection with Sweden's 1949 agreement with the emerging Federal Republic of Germany, French access to the account was interrupted, at which time the account contained SEK 8.4 million. Of the total sum of SEK 24 millions, a further SEK 1.5 million remained. On 8 December 1951, the Riksbank informed the *Bank deutscher Länder* that a special account had been opened at the Riksbank in the German bank's name and that the remaining funds, amounting to SEK 9.9 million, had been transferred to that account.

With regard to the question of gold, the Swedish party made it clear at the commencement of negotiations that Sweden was prepared to return gold that was proved to have been looted from occupied countries by the Germans. The Allied standpoint at the opening of the Washington negotiations was that all gold that had been acquired after January 1943 should in principle be regarded as looted gold since the Germans were considered by that time to have used up all legitimately acquired gold reserves in their possession. The Allied line of reasoning was based on the following points. Before the seizure of the Austrian central bank's gold, Germany had not more than approximately USD 100 in gold at its disposal (the publicly acknowledged German gold reserve amounted to a mere USD 29 million). With the addition of approximately USD 23 million acquired legitimately from the Soviet Union before the outbreak of the war and the USD 53 million taken from Austria and the 33 million from Czechoslovakia, this last portion seized forcibly, Germany began the war with some USD 210 million in gold. According to information from the British and American intelligence services, it was estimated that between the outbreak of the war and June 1943 Germany had sold gold amounting to USD 220 million. From this could be deduced, according to the Allies, that by some point prior to June 1943, Germany had not only disposed of its legitimately acquired gold but also the Austrian and Czechoslovakian deposits, and therefore from some time around the beginning of 1943 had only looted gold to spend. Sweden contested the Allied hypothesis that all gold purchased from Germany after a certain day should be deemed to be looted.

After much discussion, especially on the question of how to deal with looted gold that the Swedish Riksbank had purchased from the German Reichsbank but later sold to a third country, the Washington Accord was agreed upon, and was approved by the Swedish Riksdag on 17 December 1946.[6] The Swedish commitments to return looted gold were based on the following provisions laid down in the Washington accord:

I. Statement from the chairmen of the allied delegations to the chairman of the Swedish delegation, 18 July 1946:

"§4 (a) In pursuance of its policy to restitute looted property, the Swedish Government will effect restitution to the Allies of all gold acquired by Sweden and proved to have been taken by the Germans from occupied countries, including any such gold transferred by the Swedish Riksbank to third countries. Any claims by Governments of the occupied countries or their banks of issue not presented before July 1, 1947, shall be considered to be barred.

(b) On the basis of present evidence, subject to further checking, it is assumed that the gold the Swedish Government has to restitute amounts to 7,155.32664 kilograms of fine gold, corresponding to the quantity of gold deriving from the Bank of Belgium which was acquired by the Swedish Riksbank and which is to be restituted in accordance with the foregoing.

(c) The Allied Governments undertake to hold the Swedish Government harmless from any claims deriving from transfers from the Swedish Riksbank to third countries of gold to be restituted according to the above declaration."

II. Statement on the same day by the Chairmen of the Allied delegation with regard to the implementation of the so-called Gold Declaration.

"In connection with the paragraph in the letters exchanged today dealing with looted gold, we wish to confirm to you our understanding that, in view of the evidence already produced and checked, no further claim will be presented to Sweden by the Government signatory to the Paris Reparation Agreement or their banks of issue with regard to any gold acquired by Sweden from Germany and transferred to third countries prior to June 1, 1945."

Thus, Sweden's commitment to return looted gold would only apply to such gold as remained in the possession of Sweden on 1 June 1945, and if claims for gold proved to be looted were made by the governments of the occupied countries or their central banks before 1 July 1947. Already in Washington, claims for the restitution of certain quantities of gold which the Germans had seized from Belgium had been made, and before the set period elapsed, the Government of the Netherlands had also submitted significant claims.

The Belgian gold

Background

The National Bank of Belgium, which did not have the character of a central bank, took steps already in 1938 to secure the part of the gold funds that exceeded the prescribed gold backing, if the need were to arise. Thus, before the war, certain gold consignments had already been deposited in the US and England. In the middle of November 1939, the National Bank of Belgium deposited gold worth approximately FRF 6 billion (4,449 cases) with the Bank of France, and in May 1940 a further consignment consisting of the remaining gold was also deposited with the Bank. In all, the Bank of France received 4,989 cases. At the end of May 1940, the banks agreed that 135 cases from the deposit should be used in order to free funds for the exchange of Belgian francs in the possession of Belgian refugees in France, to French francs. Thus the final deposit came to consist of 4,854 cases of gold.[7] In June 1940, the Governor of the National Bank of Belgium requested of the Governor of the French bank that the Bank of France take the same steps with regard to the Belgian gold as it had done with its own gold. Thereafter, the Belgian gold was entrusted to the French Navy, which had the gold transported to Dakar in North Africa. The gold arrived there on 28 June 1940. The cases were then placed in the custody of the colonial authorities of French West Africa.

Upon the request of the Germans, negotiations were opened between the German and French Armistice Supervisory Commission, and a Franco-German agreement was made, whereby the Bank of France was enjoined to return the gold to the Belgian national bank. Neither of the banks were a party to the agreement. When the Belgian national bank refused to request the return of the gold, the German occupation forces induced the Vichy Government to order the French Armistice Commission to sign an addition to the protocol on 11 December 1940, whereby the Deutsche Reichsbank took over the deposit from the French bank. The Belgian bank, that was not a party to the agreement, did not approve its implementation. In order to protect its rights according to the deposit agreement with France, the National Bank of Belgium in New York concurred with this standpoint and at the beginning of 1941 petitioned that the Bank of France should put aside a portion of its own gold corresponding to the Belgian claim. Via its representative in New York, the Bank of France confirmed its obligation to fulfil the terms of the deposit agreement and offered to set aside a portion of its gold reserves in the US as security for the claim. However, the process came to a halt, *inter alia* owing to the fact that the Bank of France was unable to communicate with its representative in New York.

In September 1942, the German Government decided to requisition the Belgian gold, that had been transported in stages from Dakar via Marseilles to Berlin. The Bank of Belgium was notified of the requisition on 9 October 1942, and was informed at the same time that recompense for the gold would be paid at a rate of 2,784 Reichsmark per kilo, as stipulated in the German Reichsbank Act. This payment of 500 million RM, which would be provisionally credited to the account of the Bank of Belgium, could only be used for payments inside Germany. The Belgian bank replied on 28 December 1942 to the effect that the requisitioned gold did not constitute a deposit with the Reichsbank and that the Bank of France had surrendered the shipment without the consent of the Bank of Belgium and on a number of other unacceptable conditions. For that reason, the National Bank would not consider accepting any recompense for the requisition. In a series of communications exchanged during 1944 between the Reichsbank and the Bank of France, the French bank supported the Belgian standpoint and emphasised that the gold should be returned to the Belgian bank.

A memorandum from Göring's office dated 8 July 1942 and published by the Americans in 1946 shows that the legal department of Auswärtiges Amt (the German Foreign Office) had advocated the requisition of the Belgian gold via the German military commander in Belgium, with reference to the Hague Convention concerning land war from 1907, which *inter alia* deals with requisitions from individuals or local authorities in occupied territory to meet "the needs of the occupation force". However, the Convention was never cited. Instead, on 9 September 1942, Göring issued an order for the Belgian gold to be transferred to his department. The order was made out to "Oberpresident

Führungsstab Wirtschaft" under the heading: Requisition of the gold reserve of the National Bank of Belgium pursuant to the Reichsleistungsgesetz (the German requisition decree approved on 1 September 1939).

Belgian gold negotiations

After France had compensated Belgium for its losses, negotiations between *inter alia* Sweden and France began. In 1946, representatives of the French central bank visited the Swedish Riksbank, taking with them the evidence found in the archives. Among other things, photographs of 18 pages taken from the Prussian Mint's smelting ledger for the year 1943. By comparing these records with other material, it became clear that during the period 25 January – 16 June 1943, approximately 143,600 kilos (gross weight) of Belgian gold had been resmelted, and the bars given new smelt numbers with pre-war dates (1934–39).

The claim submitted by the Bank of France amounted to a total of 7,311.33339 kilos of gold.

The claims were based on the following consignments of gold from the German Reichsbank.[8]

Acquisitions by the Riksbank	Weight (kg fine gold)	Ingots
1943		
15 April	532.81105	45
2 June	500.00422	42
14 July	503.00047	42
28 July	477.00012	38
17 August	1,001.56605	80
21 September	210.01086	17
25 November	1,004.55580	81
29 November	1,995.28728	161
22 December	88.12768	7
1944		
17 January	998.96986	81
Total Claim	**7,311.33339**	**594**

Of the gold in question, 156,00685 kilos were sold to the Schweizerische Kreditanstalt on 26 July 1943 for the purchase of silver for the Swedish Mint. Since the Washington Accord meant that only such gold had to be returned as had been in the possession of the Swedes on 1 June 1945, this item was consequently deducted. Thus, the final amount of looted Belgian gold to be returned from Sweden was determined to amount to 7.155,32654 kilos of fine gold.

According to the wording of the Washington Accord, Sweden was permitted to undertake certain extra investigations of the evidence relating to the Belgian gold. At the same time, with reference to the Allied declarations of 1943 and 1944, the American side had undertaken not to raise any objections to the gold that Sweden had taken over from the Reichsbank, but required that information be made available about the bar numbers, etc.

In a document from the American Embassy in Stockholm dated 15 March 1948 , it was stated that it would be desirable if the amount of gold agreed upon in Washington were to be delivered to the TGC. In May 1948, the Government submitted a note to the American Embassy stating that further investigations were necessary. One year later, on 31 May 1949, the Riksbank sent a telegram to the Federal Reserve Bank of New York instructing officials to transfer the agreed amount of gold from the Riksbank's depository in New York to the TGC, and on 6 May that same year, the Ministry for Foreign Affairs ordered that the sum of SEK 28,986,156.67 should be paid to the Riksbank. The state's claims with regard to the returned gold were noted as a claim in the mandatory clearing system with Germany.

The Dutch gold

Background [9]

At the last minute, the Nederlandsche Bank succeeded in moving all gold stored in Amsterdam to its depository in Rotterdam before the German invasion on 10 May 1940. That same day, 11 tons of gold were loaded on board a small boat in Rotterdam. The boat hit a mine on its way to the larger ship waiting at Nieuwe Maas to transport the gold to London. In July of the same year, the Germans managed to salvage a large share, some 9.5 tons of the sunken cargo, and on the basis of a decision of a court of arbitration in Hamburg in 1941, were granted the right to the cargo although the boat had not been salvaged in open waters. An appeal was lodged against the decision of the court, but for the duration of the war, the higher court did not examine the matter. During the occupation, approximately 146 tons of gold are believed to have been transferred from the Netherlands to Germany, of which just over three-quarters came originally from the Dutch gold reserve in Rotterdam. The situation concerning the Dutch gold differs in certain aspects from that of the Belgian gold. The Dutch central bank's gold depositions consisted almost entirely of bullion that had come from outside the Netherlands, which presumably meant that the Reichsbank did not consider it necessary to resmelt the bars, which is what they subsequently did with the Belgian bars. According to the information available, only 124 bars of more than 5,000 were resmelted, while the Prussian Mint resmelted over 85 million gold coins to make ingots. Furthermore, some compensation – ostensibly at least – was often made for the confiscated gold. Pursuant to an ordinance of 24 June 1940, it was prescribed that private persons resident in the Netherlands were to sell their gold to the central bank in exchange for florins, which in turn was credited with the corresponding value in Reichsmark. The Germans held the view that a large portion of the gold constituted payment for the inner and "external" costs of the occupation. It is thought that "external" costs referred to the expenditure incurred, for example, when German troops destined to serve with the occupation forces in the Netherlands underwent training and education outside the Netherlands. In addition, the occupation forces decided that monthly payments, retroactively from 1 July 1941, would be made as contributions to "Germany's war in the East against Bolshevism".

Dutch gold negotiations

Negotiations with the Nederlandsche Bank began in May 1947, and in December of the same year, claims were specified in more detail. Documents in the Riksbank's archives show that Dutch claims referred to the following transactions with the Reichsbank:[10]

Acquisitions by the Riksbank	Weight (kg fine gold)	Ingots
1942		
11 November	3,997.49058	337
7 December	1,008.04860	84
1943		
20 January	849.24640	72
27 January	724.48819	59
15 February	998.28830	83
19 February	1,005.36678	85
28 July	24.64842	2
Total	**8,607.57727**	**722**

Of this gold, a shipment of 1,088.04860 kilos brought to Stockholm was sold to Swedish industry during the period August 1943 – July 1944. According to the Riksbank's estimations, taking into account the appointed date of 1 June 1945, the amount of Dutch gold that Sweden was required to return therefore should amount to 638 ingots weighing a total of 7,599.52867 kilos.

In addition to the difficulties encountered by the Dutch central bank in presenting evidence to support its claims – among other things claims referred to resmelted gold coins – negotiations came to be protracted owing to other circumstances that distinguished the Dutch gold from the Belgian. At the outset, the Swedish parties questioned whether the Dutch gold could be considered to have been looted, since it was clear that Germany had paid for it. However, the main objection was based on the Swedish claim that the acquisitions made prior to the Allied declaration in 1943 had been made in good faith, at the same time as the Swedish officials referred to the fact that the Allies had assumed at the beginning of the gold negotiations that Germany had issued looted gold from the beginning of 1943 and that the Allies had proposed that all gold from a certain day that year should be regarded as looted gold. Taking these aspects into account, the Washington Accord, in the Swedish view, should be read in such a way that only gold transactions after January 1943 should be the subject of possible restitution.[11]

After further exchanges of correspondence on the matter of Dutch gold, the Western powers declared that they were prepared to reduce claims by just over one quarter if a voluntary agreement could be made. On the Swedish side, it was deemed more favourable to enter into an agreement than to be obliged to follow the arbitration procedures as prescribed in the Washington Accord. This compromise meant that approximately 6 tons of gold were to be handed over to the TGC. After Riksdag approval, the gold was returned in 1955 pursuant to the agreement.

An agreement was reached on 16 September 1954. The Allies declared that this quantity of gold was the full and final settlement of their claims against Sweden according to paragraph 4(a) of the Washington Accord.

SWEDISH INVESTIGATIONS INTO DORMANT BANK ACCOUNTS AND OTHER PRIVATE PROPERTY IN THE 1960s[12]

Bank accounts

At the outset it seems appropriate to comment on two circumstances of special relevance in this context. Firstly, foreigners were only permitted to place their assets in Swedish banks until February 1940. In February 1940, a currency regulation was introduced primarily aimed at preventing foreign flight capital from finding its way to Sweden. Thus, after February 1940, it was no longer possible for foreigners to make deposits in Swedish banks.

The second circumstance relates to the management of bank accounts generally. Formally speaking, a person who deposits money in a Swedish bank, has a claim on that bank for the amount deposited plus the agreed interest that accrues. However, such a claim lapses after ten years. Thus, a person who has not been in contact with his or her debtor for ten years forfeits the right to the claim. This applies also to bank accounts. In principle this means that the banks can appropriate the sums deposited with them that have not been demanded for ten years. However, in practice, Swedish banks do not utilize this option. Instead, dormant accounts are transferred to special accounts along with accrued interest. If after, say 15 years, an account-holder or his or her successor, gets in touch with the bank with a request to withdraw the money, the bank makes a payment together with the interest that has accrued over a ten-year period.

In May and June 1963, the organization IWÖ "Intressegemeinsschaft in der Wiedergutmachung der in Schweden lebende Österreicher", sent a number of communications to the Swedish Government and the Prime Minister requesting that steps be taken to trace and take charge of unclaimed property deriving primarily from foreign victims of Nazi persecution.

The Minister of Finance passed the document from the IWÖ to the Bank Inspection Board for a statement. In its turn, the Bank Inspection Board urged the banks and savings banks to supply information. The Swedish Bankers' Association, which is the joint organization for all banks except the savings banks, requested details from the banks on two counts. Firstly, details relating to the number of deposit accounts belonging to foreigners, where there had been no transactions after 31 December 1945 together with the balance in these accounts. Secondly, details concerning the number of foreign accounts placed with the banks' trust departments, where the bank had not had any contact with the account or title-holder after 31 December 1945.

The Swedish Bankers' Association presented the findings of its investigation in January 1964. This showed that a total of 902 such accounts had been found with a balance totalling SEK 3,091,000, as well as 30 accounts with trust departments worth a total of SEK 332,935 as well as seven safe-deposit boxes. The Bankers' Association also described how the accounts and amounts were distributed among the various banks. The Bankers' Association explained in an official letter that it had been impossible to establish to what extent Jewish or other flight capital was involved. According to the Association, certain circumstances indicated that this was the case only to a limited extent.

The savings banks reported two deposit accounts worth a total of SEK 23,179.

Thus, the total value of unclaimed foreign property reported to the Ministry of Finance amounted to just over SEK 3.4 million. There was also the additional value of the unspecified contents of the seven safe-deposit boxes.

Later in 1964, the Ministry of Justice raised the question of the establishment of a foundation. The unclaimed assets in question would be placed in this foundation provided that the banks were willing to co-operate. The Swedish Bankers' Association's comment on the proposal was that it could not be taken for granted that the entire sum in the accounts, SEK 3.1 million, was flight capital from countries occupied by the Nazi regime, but if upon closer investigation, it seemed likely that the assets had belonged to victims of Nazi persecution, then the banks would be willing to transfer the corresponding sum to a humanitarian foundation placed under public management and control. The Bank Inspection Board supported the establishment of a foundation on the conditions stipulated by the Bankers' Association.

In 1966, the Government dealt with the question of the unclaimed property once again. The matter was described in a memorandum of 16 March. The matter had been brought up by the Jewish community. Representatives of the Jewish groups had asked for a clearer description of the methods used to select the accounts, and had stated that a new examination of the lists should be undertaken by an independent person in a position of trust. In addition, they inquired after the calculation of interest and the possibility of access to the contents of safe-deposit boxes and open security accounts. Finally, the representatives asked if it would be possible to make payments directly to the recipients instead of a trust fund.

According to the memorandum, the Swedish Bankers' Association had declined an examination of the lists by an outsider and had also taken a negative position with regard to the proposal to make the contents of safe-deposit boxes and open security accounts available.

The same memorandum shows that an agreement had been made in January 1966 between the Central Council of the Jewish Community in Sweden, various Jewish charitable organizations, the World Jewish Congress, the American Joint Distribution Committee and the Jewish Agency that would allow the two last-named organizations to dispose of the assets by channelling them through their extensive humanitarian operations. In March of the same year, the organizations agreed that 25 per cent of the assets should remain in Sweden and 75 per cent should go to the World Jewish Congress.

However, in the opinion of the Bank Inspection Board, a large number of the accounts reported previously were in all probability not of Jewish origin. Therefore, in June 1966, the Bank Inspection Board requested fresh information from the banks, *inter alia*, a specification of the balance in unclaimed accounts and trust departments. The Bank Inspection Board submitted the requested information to the Ministry of Finance in December. Among other things, the Inspection Board asserted that the contents of the trust department accounts and safe-deposit boxes were not subject to the period of limitation. It also claimed that a legal representative should be appointed for the owners of the safety deposit boxes.

The findings of the 1966 investigation were at variance with facts that had emerged in the 1964 investigation. Firstly, the number of accounts had fallen from 902 to 618. The reason for this was that several account holders had been in touch with the banks. The total amount in the 618 accounts was SEK 2,164,000. Of these, 192 accounts worth a total of SEK 943,000 were deemed to have belonged to victims of the Nazi regime, Jews and others. The value of the assets in the trust departments had increased thanks to a number of additional contributions, and amounted now to SEK 590,000.

Via the Swedish Bankers' Association, the banks proposed to the Ministry of Justice that the balance of the accounts, plus a certain amount of interest – a total of SEK 1,217,827 – should be transferred to Swedish and foreign refugee organizations on the condition that the question of the recipients could be resolved once and for all. After several rounds of discussion, which finally led to the various potential recipient organizations being unable to come to any form of agreement, the Swedish Bankers' Association turned to the Ministry of Justice requesting that a humanitarian foundation be set up under public management and control to which the assets could be transferred. The point of departure for the Association was that the assets in such a fund would be used primarily to assist the victims of Nazism.

Finally in 1972, the banks transferred the sum of SEK 1,184,528 to the Swedish Red Cross, the intention being that this sum should form a special fund for financial aid to the victims of Nazism and their relatives, both in Sweden and abroad. The difference between this amount and the sum originally quoted was accountable to the fact that certain amounts had been paid directly to account-holders or their beneficiaries. The fund was placed under the supervision of the Red Cross auditors, one of whom had been appointed by the Swedish National Audit Office. The following year, the Red Cross announced that the money had been distributed in accordance with the conditions.

The way in which the matter had been handled and concluded became the target of criticism from many organizations, including the World Jewish Congress, the Jewish Agency, the Joint Distribution Committee and the Federation for Jewish Victims of the Nazis in Sweden. The criticism focused on three main issues. Firstly, the amount, which was considered to be too small. Critics also thought that the balance in trust department accounts and the safe-deposit boxes should have been included in the estimations. The second objection was related to the fact that the recipient was the Red Cross. Critics felt that the money should have gone to the acknowledged Jewish organizations. For example, the Jewish Community in Stockholm refused to be involved in the distribution of funds on account of the methods used by the Swedish Bankers' Association. Finally, the Government came in for a share of the criticism, since it was considered to have been far too passive, and it was felt that the Government should have instituted legislation to support demands vis-à-vis the banks.

Other private property

In 1965, the Swedish section of the World Jewish Congress submitted a petition to the King about the unclaimed Jewish assets. The petition was passed on to the Swedish Association of Stockbrokers, the National Federation of Swedish Insurance Companies, Folksam, the Swedish Federation of Forwarding Agents, the Swedish Association of Furniture Movers, the Stockholm Movers Association, the Swedish Association of Jewellers and Goldsmiths, the Swedish Association of Art and Antique Dealers, the Swedish Bar Association, the Institute of Authorized Public Accountants, the Association of Accountants (SSH), the Swedish Association of Professional Accountants and Auditors (YRF) and the Swedish Society of Public Accountants (SRS).

The Swedish Federation of Forwarding Agents, the Swedish Association of Furniture Removers and the Swedish Association of Professional Accountants and Auditors did not reply to the communication. The Stockholm Movers Association merely stated that none of its members had any assets in storage for the groups in question.

The Swedish Association of Jewellers and Goldsmiths stated that they had undertaken an extensive investigation among all their member companies. In their reply, they wrote that jewels and other items of value had not been deposited on behalf of persons who had tried to escape Nazi persecution and subsequently been unable to claim their property.

The Swedish Association of Art and Antique Dealers replied that they would inform their members of the letter. The outcome of that measure is unknown.

The Swedish Association of Stockbrokers carried out an investigation among those of its members who were not members of the Swedish Bankers' Association. The result was negative.

The National Federation of Swedish Insurance Companies does not appear to have undertaken any investigation. Its representatives said that it seemed highly unlikely that persons persecuted by the Nazis would have transferred assets to life insurance policies. However, if such sums did exist, the Federation was in favour of the proposal put forward by the Swedish Bankers' Association to establish a fund for support to the victims of the Nazis.

The co-operative insurance company, Folksam, replied that they had no special routines for the registration of foreigners. However, Folksam did examine cases where the beneficiary of a life insurance policy had not been found in spite of investigations. There were no foreigners in this category.

In November 1965, representatives of the Swedish Bar Association stated that it was up to individual members to determine whether or not information could be submitted. An inquiry went out to members in 1972 asking whether anyone was holding assets, that might have belonged to victims of Nazi or other persecution, and that had remained dormant since the end of the war. The Bar Association received no answers.

The Institute of Authorized Public Accountants replied that it, in contrast to the lawyers, did not normally handle administrative assignments of this type. If, in spite of that, someone had been charged with such an assignment, client confidentiality would make it impossible to pass on information about it to outsiders.

The Association of Accountants (SSH) replied that it was willing to co-operate in cases where individual accountants were also prepared to do so. However, representatives stipulated that guarantees should be made for subsequent claims. No such guarantees were made and the matter does not seem to have been pursued any further.

Nor does the matter seem to have been pursued with regard to the Swedish Society of Public Accountants (SRS). The society made a positive statement about conducting inquiries among its members, but did not consider that it was able to make any binding commitments when it came to the question of what should happen to such property.

THE PRESENT INVESTIGATIONS

The Swedish Riksbank's inquiry into the Bank's acquisitions of gold from Germany during the Second World War: "The Archives Inquiry"

Background

On 9 January 1997, the Board of Governors of the Riksbank decided that an investigation should be made into the Bank's acquisition of gold from Germany during the period 1939 to 1945. The committee of inquiry was to consist of three persons, all free of any previous connection with the Riksbank. The Board of Governors entrusted the Governor of the bank with the task of determining the composition of the committee.

The committee which started work on 17 February is headed by Jan Heuman, former Justice of the Supreme Court. In March, two new members joined the group: Harry Flam, Professor of International Economics, and Ingvar Pramhäll, authorized public accountant. The committee has two research secretaries at its disposal and since June, also, a special auditors' group.

The committee's assignment is to compile the information contained in the Riksbank archives about the bank's acquisition of gold from Germany during World War II. The report will be made public on 17 December 1997.

Since the investigation is based on the archives of the Riksbank, a comprehensive picture may be obtained only after the Commission on Jewish Assets in Sweden at the time of World War II has analysed and taken a position on the findings in the "Archives Inquiry". The Riksbank's committee of inquiry is in continuous contact with the Government Commission on Jewish Assets. Among other things, discussion focuses on how, upon completion of its assignment, the committee can put its findings at the disposal of the Commission in the most suitable manner.

The work has focused on the following issues:

1. All gold transactions with Germany, directly and indirectly, including
   a) amounts
   b) dates
   c) places of delivery, storage, transfer, etc., and
   d) reasons for the transactions
2. Amount of looted gold acquired by the Riksbank, including
   a) total quantity
   b) quantity of looted gold of Belgian and Dutch origin, and
   c) evidence on looted non-monetary gold.
3. Information in the hands of the Riksbank about looted gold and measures taken in consequence, including
   a) nature of information,
   b) information about non-monetary gold,
   c) when the information was received, and
   d) the role of the government.

Working methods

The method of investigation has largely been determined by the structure and organization of the archives of the Riksbank. Over the years, the archives have suffered a number of losses. This is primarily due to the fact that until 1991, no legal provisions regulating the administration of the bank's archives existed. Filing and sorting took place rather haphazardly in the various departments of the Riksbank. Furthermore, it is impossible to restore the original structure of the archives on account of a succession of moves and new listings. This means that the working method applied has largely consisted of systematic examination of volumes containing documents from the period in question. The archives of the Riksbank in their entirety have been placed at the disposal of the committee. The material that was examined – corresponding to ca. 75 running metres – was largely classified as confidential information until a few years ago.

The committee has primarily focused its attention on the following series in the archives of the Riksbank:

THE SPECIAL MINUTES OF THE BOARD OF GOVERNORS

Two sets of minutes were taken at the meetings of the Board of Governors, general and special minutes, the latter being classified. A systematic examination of these minutes has been undertaken for the period 1937–1950.

THE PRIVATE ARCHIVES OF CERTAIN HIGH-RANKING CIVIL SERVANTS

Ivar Rooth (Governor of the Riksbank from 1929 to 1948) was an assiduous note-taker. In his private archives, which were kept at the Riksbank, the committee has found, in addition to the usual correspondence, travel notes, memos, etc. An examination of Rooth's archives during the period 1937–1948 has been carried out. In addition, Ivar Rooth's hand-written journals for the period 1939–1945 have been examined.

The archives of the former head of the bank's Foreign Department, *Knut Wessman,* were incorporated into the central archives at the beginning of the 1990s. In the volumes that have been examined the committee has found a great deal of information about the Riksbank's gold dealings during World War II. The archives also contain a large number of memos etc. about Sweden's gold negotiations with the Allies after the war.

The auditors' group

As a part of the investigation, a group of authorized public accountants has examined the Riksbank's ledger with respect to the purchase and sale of gold during the period 1937 to 1946. The archives of the Riksbank have been weeded out, and consequently there are no books of prime entry, books of account or supporting vouchers for the period in question. Information in other sections of the Riksbank's archives, especially in the archives of Knut Wessman, is collated with the auditors' findings. Statistics for each year showing purchases and sales of gold and the balance in various depots are being compiled.

The Commission on Jewish Assets at the Time of the Second World War

Background

A decision on the Commission's terms of references was taken by the Government in February 1997. All the members of the Commission including specialist advisers and experts were appointed in March and April.

In brief, the Government's assignment to the Commission is to *clarify as far as possible what can have happened to property of Jewish origin* brought to Sweden in connection with the persecution of the Jews before and during World War II.

Thus the tasks of the Commission are:

- to conduct research into all *public archives and a number of private ones* that can conceivably have relevant information on these matters with a view to clarifying to what extent the actions of *authorities, individuals or companies* before and during World War II caused Sweden to become involved with *looted gold of Jewish origin,*

- to present an account of the findings of earlier investigations with regard to *unclaimed bank accounts and other private property* that can be assumed to have belonged to Jews, and to conduct the *supplementary investigations* necessary in order to obtain a comprehensive picture in the matter of such Jewish assets,
- to examine whether or not Jewish property came to be covered by the operations of the Foreign Capital Control Office (that is to say, the activities that were conducted over a ten-year period following the war for the purpose of liquidating German-owned property in Sweden in order to make payments to Swedish creditors and to the Western Allies for humanitarian reconstruction of West Germany),
- to deal with *other questions which can help to clarify* what has happened to property of Jewish origin brought to Sweden in connection with the Nazi persecution of the Jews,
- to list and describe property referred to in the terms of reference and that might be retrievable.

In addition, the Commission is to:
- *analyse and take a position* on the findings of the *Riksbank's inquiry* into trading in gold during World War II,
- *undertake supplementary investigations* into the matter with special focus on the question of gold that may have belonged to Jews, if this is of benefit to the inquiry.

Methods

The Commission is headed by Mr. Rolf Wirtén, a former member of the cabinet and former County Governor. In addition to special advisers, experts and two full-time research secretaries, it consists of 23 people. One of the special advisers is the Secretary-General of WJC, Dr. Israel Singer. Others are e.g. representatives of the Jewish communities in Sweden, former Swedish ambassadors, historians from various fields, archivists, bankers, auditors and lawyers. External consultants have been engaged for special tasks.

The Commission has on several occasions invited guest lecturers to attend its meetings.

The *schedule* comprises the following stages:

A. PREPARATION:
This includes analysis of the tasks, taking stock, discussion of methods and planning.

B. FACT-FINDING:
The Commission is divided into project groups with responsibility for the various sections of the terms of reference presented by the Government. As the various assignments are completed, new project groups will be set up.

In addition, two persons have been appointed to be in continuous contact with Jewish organizations in Sweden and abroad.

C. ANALYSIS:

Research findings are analysed continuously. The project groups will submit status reports to the Commission in *plenum* regularly every month.

D. COMPILATION:

This includes background briefs, accounts of method, research findings, processing and evaluation.

PUBLIC ARCHIVES

In Sweden, the principle of public access to official records is laid down in one of the country's constitutional laws which goes back to 1766. Thus, everyone has free access to official documents held by public authorities such as the Ministries. Although there are some obvious restrictions with regard to this principle, there are probably no documents from the 1933–1945 period in the official archives that still are classified.

PRIVATE ARCHIVES

A private archive is private property. There is in principle no legal obligation for individuals or private companies to keep documents in archives for the future. However, thanks to several farsighted industrialists and bankers and people who held high offices in different private companies there are today quite a number of interesting private archives in Sweden. Some are still kept in the various companies, some have been transferred to different depots.

It is up to the owner of the archives to decide whether a researcher will have access to the archives.

The first four projects

Different working parties within the Commission are responsible for the various projects. The work proceeds mainly through studies of various archives with the aim of finding as many facts as possible which are relevant to the Commission's assignment. The first four projects will be finished this autumn, and the findings of the groups will be handed over to new groups/working parties.

FOREIGN CAPITAL CONTROL OFFICE

The main purpose is to ascertain whether German-Jewish property came to be liquidated as a result of the Office's activities. The Office was active mainly from 1945 until 1956. Apart from the records of the Foreign Capital Control Office, the records of several authorities will be studied. Contact has been taken with the German Foreign Office in order to be granted access to certain German records which might be of interest when the Swedish documents are to be evaluated.

THE BANK INSPECTION BOARD

As has been stated above, in the 1960s and 1970s, the Bank Inspection Board and the Swedish Bankers' Association undertook investigations into bank accounts that had not been touched since 1945. Their findings resulted in the transfer of just over one million Swedish Kronor to the Red Cross for distribution among the victims of Nazism. There was some criticism of the inquiry at this time. The material is being studied once again, supplementary inquiries are being made, inter alia, into whether there are more unclaimed assets in the banks, what might have happened them, and how the Red Cross has allocated the funds.

THE FOUNDATION FOR ECONOMIC HISTORICAL RESEARCH IN BANKING AND BUSINESS, I.E. THE ARCHIVES OF THE STOCKHOLM'S ENSKILDA BANK AND THE WALLENBERG FAMILY

The Commission has been granted full access to the archives, including documents from members of the Wallenberg family who held high offices in the bank. The working party responsible for this project has completed its study of the archives' "Germany files". In addition, the correspondence of Jacob and Marcus Wallenberg from 1932–1949 is being examined. A special study of Marcus Wallenberg's diary (starting in August 1938) has begun. The entire material has also been systematically spot-checked in order to identify information concerning the Enskilda Bank's business dealings with German enterprises and individuals whose assets originally could have been Jewish.

THE ARCHIVES OF THE MINISTRIES

Studies have been undertaken primarily in the archives of the Ministry for Foreign Affairs, the Ministry of Trade and the Ministry of Finance. Studies have also been undertaken in the private archives left by Dag Hammarskjöld and Ernst Wigforss, the then Minister of Finance. Work has primarily focused on questions about what information might be available with regard to assets in banks, personal assets, gold in the Riksbank and matters concerning the liquidation of German property in Sweden.

The following projects

The results of the first four projects will be followed up by five new working parties which started in October 1997.

BANK ASSETS

The working party on Bank Assets is to present the findings of previous investigations with regard to unclaimed bank accounts and other bank assets that can be assume to have belonged to Jews. Supplementary investigations will be carried out when the Commission so decides. If such bank assets are found, the assets should be listed and described.

OTHER PRIVATE PROPERTY

The working party on Other Private Property is to present the findings of previous investigations concerning other private property, such as insurance policies, furniture, art and jewellery, that can be assumed to have belonged to Jews. Supplementary investigations will be carried out when the Commission so decides. If such private property is found, it should be listed and described. One important source in these investigations will be the information provided by individual members of the Jewish community in Sweden as well as information from the general public. A questionnaire will be sent to the members of the Swedish Jewish communities and an advertisement has been published in the largest morning newspaper in Sweden, *Dagens Nyheter*.

POTENTIAL BUSINESS TRANSACTIONS WITH JEWISH ASSETS

The working party on Potential Business Transactions with Jewish Assets is to investigate if, how and to what extent Swedish enterprises and companies in their normal business dealings took part in the transfer to Sweden of assets of Jewish origin. In addition to the archives of the Foundation for Economic Historical Research in Banking and Business, certain other banks and large export companies may have documents of relevance to the assignment, and the Commission has approached some of these companies concerning access to their archives.

THE RIKSBANK'S GOLD

The working party on the Riksbank's Gold will analyse the facts and findings that emerge after the examination of the documents in the archives of the Riksbank which was initiated in order to shed light on the Riksbank's acquisition of looted gold during World War II. When the Commission so decides, the working party will make supplementary investigations with particular emphasis on the question of gold that may have belonged to Jews. The archives of certain foreign central banks will be among the sources in these investigations.

THE LIQUIDATION OF GERMAN PROPERTY IN SWEDEN

The working party on the Foreign Capital Control Office will investigate if Jewish property was liquidated by the office, which was active between 1945 and 1956.

PROGRESS REPORT

The Commission plans to present its report to the Government in the autumn of 1998. A draft exists and is updated and supplemented continuously. Preliminary reports are not planned at present. However, the Commission intends to publish a list of unclaimed bank accounts in the near future.

NOTES

[1] The programme, which implied an ambition to thwart German efforts – primarily in neutral countries – to find a safe haven for German capital, war spoils and patents, came to be administered mainly under the management of the US Government.

[2] SFS, Svensk författningsamling, the Swedish Code of Statutes.

[3] Originally called: *The Tripartite Commission for the Restitution of Monetary Gold*.

[4] The amounts of SEK should today be multiplied by the relevant factor 18.2 (1996).

[5] Government Bill 1956 no. 190.

[6] Government Bill 1946 no. 367.

[7] According to information in the relevant archives the gross weight seems to have amounted to 208,027.2863 kilos, 143,634.5765 kilos in ingots, the remainder in gold coins. On 1 April 1949, in a supplement to memorandum 8/3 -48, the following note is made about the gold coins: "Perhaps it is worthwhile to mention, that the Franco-Belgian side never tried to prove in its contacts with the Riksbank that the gold taken from France and Belgium had been looted, although the Germans took from them no less than approximately 57,958.0 kilos of fine gold in the form of gold coins."

[8] All the acquisitions were made by exchanging gold in Berlin to gold in Bern.

[9] The information was taken from Rooth's notes after discussions with de Jong, Nederlandsche Bank on 30 May 1946, F. A1:74, memorandum written in the Hague on 12 September 1947, F4A:23, Werner Rings: *Raubgold aus Deutschland*, München 1985 ("Looted Gold from Germany"), and for the statistics, Thomas Maissen: *Raubgold aus den Niederlanden als Präzidenzfall?* ("Looted Gold from the Netherlands as a Test Case?) Neue Zürcher Zeitung 23/24 August 1997.

[10] All the acquisitions were made by exchanging gold in Berlin to gold in Bern. The acquisition 7 December 1942 was however made in Berlin and this gold was later transferred to Stockholm.

[11] In a memorandum dated June 1947, Dag Hammarskjöld, then Chairman of the Board of the Riksbank, stated: "To claim now that the acquisition was made in good faith before the allied declaration of 1943, if this claim was not made before, or at least during the course of negotiations in Washington, would seem unfeasible. Every attempt to avoid payment after the set time smacks of casuistry".

[12] Main sources: The archives of the Bank Inspection Board (Bankinspektionen), file 532/66 and Konseljakt 1971-12-03, nr 11, RA/1201.01, Justitiedepartementets huvudarkiv (Cabinet Document 1971-12-03, No.11, The Archives of the Ministry of Justice, stored in the National Archives).

The gold transactions of Sveriges Riksbank with Nazi Germany

Summary

REPORT TO THE RIKSBANK BY THE
INDEPENDENT ARCHIVES INQUIRY

INTRODUCTION

The Board of Governors of Sveriges Riksbank decided on 9 January 1997 that an investigation should take place into the Riksbank's acquisition of gold from Germany from 1939 to 1945. The Inquiry was to consist of from one to three persons who had no connection with Riksbank. Former Justice of the Supreme Court Jan Heuman was appointed as chairman and the Inquiry began its work on 17 February. In March, a further two members were appointed to the Inquiry, Professor of International Economics, Harry Flam, and authorised public accountant, Ingvar Pramhäll. The Inquiry has had two secretaries at its disposal and, since June, a special auditor's group.

Sweden's role during World War II has been, and is, the subject of a large number of studies. Interest has *inter alia* been focused on such topics as refugee policy, the German leave transports from July 1940 to August 1943, the Engelbrecht Division in 1941, the export of iron ore and ball bearings to Germany, and the coalition government's press policy. The task of the Inquiry has been to examine an issue which has recently attracted considerable attention, namely Sweden's and its central bank's gold transactions with Germany during World War II. This issue can naturally not be viewed in isolation but must be seen in the context of the picture produced by the whole body of research.

The remit of the Inquiry has been limited to compiling a report of the contents of the Riksbank's archives on the bank's acquisition of gold from Germany during the second world war. According to the guidelines (Dir 1997:31) to the Commission appointed on Jewish Assets in Sweden at the Time of the Second World War, the Commission is to analyse and take a position on the findings of this report. Our work should therefore be viewed as part of a larger whole.

The working methods of the Inquiry have largely been determined by the order and archival formation of the Riksbank's archives. The Riksbank's archives have suffered losses over the years. This circumstance can primarily be viewed in the light of the fact that until 1991, there were no statutory provisions regarding the keeping of the Riksbank's records, so that archiving and sorting out took place more or less at random at the various departments at the Riksbank. Furthermore, it has not been possible to rediscover the original order of the archives due to moves and reallocations (recatalogisation). These circumstances have entailed that the working method has largely consisted of a systematic review of volumes containing documents from the relevant period.

The Inquiry has had access to the whole of the Riksbank's archives. A large part of the material examined, equivalent to around 75 shelf metres, was classified until a few years ago.

Besides the minutes of the Board of Governors during the relevant period of time, the Inquiry has in its work collected facts of significance for its work focusing on documents from Ivar Rooth (Governor of the Riksbank form 1929 to 1948). Documents filed by the then head of the foreign department, Knut Wesson, have also been very important. This part of the archives contains a great deal of information on the Riksbank's trade in gold during the second world war, and a number of memoranda, etc. relating to Sweden's negotiations on the gold issue with the allies after the end of the war.

The work of going through the Riksbank's archives has mainly been focused on providing an account of:

1. Direct or indirect gold transactions with Nazi Germany, containing
   – quantities,
   – dates,
   – deposits and
   – reasons for the transactions.

2. The Riksbank's acquisition of looted gold, containing
   – quantities,
   – quantities of looted gold of Belgian and Dutch origin, and
   – looted non-monetary gold.

3. The Riksbank's knowledge of looted gold and measures taken due to this, consisting of
   – the kind of information,
   – the date the information was received,
   – information about non-monetary gold and
   – the role of the government.

The auditors' group has examined the general ledgers of the Riksbank with respect to purchase and sale of gold during the period in question. After sorting out of the Riksbank's archives, the books of first entry, books of account and all vouchers from the period in question are missing. The information that has emerged from the auditors' inquiry has been checked against information in other archival material at the Riksbank, primarily from foreign exchange reports and to some extent from Wessman's documents.

Despite the work that the Riksbank has put in from 1992 onwards in ordering and listing these records, the Inquiry has found it difficult in a limited period of time to go through all the relevant material for the period in question. Careless sorting out and the losses that the archives have suffered over the years have made the work difficult and mean that the Inquiry cannot assert with certainty that all material from a particular department has been examined. The Inquiry must also enter a reservation that there may be documents that have never been

filed or which have been placed in the archives unsystematically and have therefore not come to our attention. Neither does the Inquiry consider that it is able
to express an opinion as to whether any sorting out has taken place with the aim
of concealing sensitive information. The Inquiry has, however, not found anything to indicate that any such sorting out has taken place. The fact that, *inter
alia*, Ivar Rooth's archives have been filed outside and brought to the Riksbank's
central archives in conjunction with the reconstruction work which began some
years ago is a circumstance that is per se remarkable. A probable explanation is
probably to be found in the fact that the Riksbank did not have any archival tradition and that the officials who regarded the material as being of value have
kept it at their own initiative for future generations.

THE RIKSBANK'S GOLD TRANSACTIONS
DURING THE SECOND WORLD WAR

During the greater part of the 1930s, the Swedish krona was linked to the British
pound. After the outbreak of war in September 1939, the krona was instead tied
to the U.S. dollar at an exchange rate of approximately 4.20 kronor to the dollar. This arrangement lasted throughout the war. A number of other countries
also linked their currencies to the dollar. In this way, these currencies and the
krona had a fixed value in relation to one another. Exchange rates were in this
way fixed and substantially stable throughout World War II, although some
exchange rate adjustments did take place. The U.S. dollar had in turn a fixed
value in relation to gold of 35 dollars per ounce (approximately 28.35 grammes)
pure gold. In this way, the currencies linked to the dollar also had a fixed gold
value. In Sweden the price was approximately 4.726 kronor per kilo.

   At the beginning of World War II, the Riksbank's gold and currency reserves
(consisting of gold, foreign currencies, foreign government bonds, and net
claims on foreign banks and bankers) amounted to 2 billion kronor. At the end
of the war, the reserves amounted to over 2.8 billion.

   The gold and foreign currency reserve should be viewed in relation to commodity imports, which amounted to 2.5 billion in 1939, when considerably
hoarding took place, and 1.1 billion in 1945, as import had successively been
restricted by the prevailing wartime conditions. During the war, a strong build-
up took place of the gold and foreign exchange reserves in relation to imports.
This was in accordance with the Riksbank's task of safeguarding the import
requirements of strategic goods (arms, raw materials for industry, foodstuffs, etc.)
by having at its disposal sufficient, acceptable means of payment. In order to fulfil this task, the Riksbank also had to allow the composition of the gold and foreign currency reserve to be determined to some extent by the expected composition of import with respect to the countries and currencies of payment. Certain
import transactions were so large that they required special initiatives to be
taken by the Riksbank. Examples were the import of aircraft and ships from
Italy on a couple of occasions.

   A considerable part of the Swedish gold and currency reserves was kept

Table 1. Gold and foreign exchange reserves in SEK million.

	1938	1939	1940	1941	1942	1943	1944	1945
Foreign exchange reserves	750	301	750	760	551	652	567	758
Gold reserves at current price	1,332	1,293	672	938	1,407	1,627	1,943	2,024
Total gold and foreign exchange reserves	2,082	1,594	1,422	1,698	1,958	2,279	2,510	2,782
Gold reserves at standard price[1]	707	679	353	492	738	854	1,019	1,062
Gold reserve (difference) between standard price and current price)	625	614	319	446	669	773	924	962
Gold reserves in tonnes	285	274	142	199	298	344	411	428

[1] The gold has been stated at the standard price SEK 2,480/kg of fine gold.

abroad. There was at various stages of the war an obvious risk that parts of the gold and currency reserve would fall into alien hands and be confiscated. In order to reduce this risk, a lot of gold and currencies were relocated geographically. At the beginning of the war, for example, a considerable quantity of gold was moved from London to New York. The Riksbank, also planning for a possible invasion of Sweden, moved gold *inter alia* from Stockholm to places in southern and western Sweden. As a further emergency measure, the right of disposal to the gold reserve in the USA was transferred in May 1940 to officials at the Swedish embassy in Washington as representatives of the Swedish state. From 1941 the Riksbank also built up a gold reserve in Switzerland and South Africa. After the blocking of foreign assets in the USA in June 1941, the importance of the reichsmark increased and above all Swiss francs as a means of payment, which led to a successive build-up of gold reserves in Switzerland and to a lesser extent in Berlin. In 1939 approximately 79 per cent of the gold reserve was in Sweden. At the end of the war, the proportion in Sweden was only 18 per cent.

Foreign exchange regulations were already introduced in autumn 1939, legislation was promulgated in February 1940 and made more stringent in 1944. Currency regulation meant control of sale, purchase and possession of foreign currency and foreign securities. Exporters of goods and services were compelled to sell foreign currency earned to the commercial banks or to the Riksbank. Importers were obliged to purchase foreign currency from the commercial banks and in that connection, an assessment was made of the need for imports. In this way, access to foreign currency could be regulated and the use of currency steered towards priority imports. The Riksbank could also regulate capital flows to and from Sweden. For the same reasons, the Riksbank had a monopoly on purchase and sale of gold across national borders.

THE RIKSBANK'S GOLD TRANSACTIONS WITH NAZI GERMANY

Definitions

Trade with gold bars (synonymous term is ingots) can be briefly described by the bar having an average weight of 12.5 kg and being marked by a stamp showing the institution that has melted the gold, the smelting number, degree of purity and an identification number that does not comply with any special international system. The pure weight of the bar is obtained by the gross weight being multiplied by the percentage rate of the pure weight. On sale of the bar, it is most often accompanied by a consignment note and not by a certificate. Re-smelting of bars can take place confidentially whereupon the bar is given new stamps and number. It is therefore not possible with certainty to say anything about the origin of gold bars. Even without re-smelting a bank can give the bar its own control number. The Inquiry has noted that the Reichsbank often provided gold bars with control numbers, and that paper slips with a special German control number were attached to a large part of the gold from the Reichsbank placed in the Riksbank's deposit in Switzerland.

Gold transactions between central banks take place by purchase and sale or by exchange for the equivalent quantity and often entail physically moving the gold.

However, gold transactions can also take place without a physical move by a central bank, for example, by specially earmarking a particular quantity of gold in a special established deposit on behalf of another central bank (earmarked gold).

The Inquiry has opted to use the expression looted gold as an overall concept for both central bank gold, confiscated gold from private persons among others as well as for gold from the victims in concentration camps.

The definition of the concept monetary gold was *inter alia* for practical considerations the object of a number of discussions during the post-war period. In this report monetary gold refers mainly to such gold that formed part of a country's gold reserves or, to put it simply, central bank gold. Other gold is referred to as non-monetary gold.

Nazi Germany and looted gold

Monetary gold

Deutsche Reichsbank, which was founded in 1875, was an independent institution until Hitler's assumption of power in 1933. A new banking act gave Hitler the power to appoint the representatives of the Reichsbank Board of Governors and in 1939 the Reichsbank was made wholly subordinate to Hitler.

At the time of the annexation of Austria in 1938, the Austrian national bank and its gold reserve were placed at the disposal of the Reichsbank. In a similar way, the Reichsbank also took over the gold reserve from the Free City of Danzig in 1939. Confronted by the threat of war, a number of European countries moved large parts of their gold reserves to Great Britain or New York. The Central Bank for Bohemia and Moravia entrusted its gold before the German invasion to BIS (Bank for International Settlements) which deposited the gold *inter alia* at the Bank of England. After the German invasion, the gold was sent back to the national bank in Prague and thus fell into German hands. During World War II Germany confiscated monetary gold, both bars and coins from other countries as well such as Belgium, the Netherlands, Luxembourg and Italy. At the end of the war, the focus was first on Belgian gold.

After the war, the allies claimed that Germany during 1943 must have used up all gold acquired by legitimate means basing their argument on the following line of reasoning. Before removal of the Austrian central bank's gold, Germany did not have more than 100 million dollars worth of gold at its disposal (the officially announced German gold reserve amounted to only 29 million dollars). With the addition of around 23 million dollars legitimately acquired from the Soviet Union prior to the outbreak of war, and 53 million dollars taken from Austria and 33 million dollars taken from Czechoslovakia, Germany began the war with around 210 million dollars of gold. Through information from the British and American intelligence agencies, it was further calculated that Germany sold gold for around 220 million dollars from the beginning of the war until June 1943. From this, according to the allies, Germany had some time prior to June 1943 not only disposed of its legitimately acquired gold but also the Austrian and Czech gold.

It has later emerged that the then President of the Reichsbank, Hjalmar Schacht, and seven of the members of the Board of Governors for Reichsbank, had already in January 1939 informed Hitler in writing that there were no longer any currency or gold reserves at the Reichsbank. Schacht was later replaced by Walter Funk as President and five of the members of the Board of Governors who had signed the letter had to resign. Of the other two members of the Board of Governors Emil Puhl was later appointed as vice-president of the Reichsbank and was the real representative of the Reichsbank in the international bank world.

THE BELGIAN GOLD

Before the war the Belgian National Bank had deposited certain gold consignments in the USA and England. In mid-November 1939, the Belgian National Bank deposited 4,449 boxes of gold at the Banque de France and in May 1940 the remaining gold was deposited at the French National Bank. After a withdrawal, the final deposit consisted of 4,854 boxes equivalent to a gross weight of approximately 208,000 kg, of which approximately 143,600 kg was in bars and the rest in gold coins. In June 1940, the Belgian National Bank requested that the French National Bank should take the same measures regarding the Belgian gold as regards its own gold. The Belgian gold was thereafter transported to Dakar where it arrived at the end of June 1940.

At the request of Germany, a German-French agreement was reached which entailed that the French National Bank was instructed to restore the gold to the Belgian National Bank. Neither bank was a party to the agreement. Since the Belgian National Bank refused to request the restitution of the gold, the German occupation force persuaded the Vichy government to order the French commission to sign a supplementary protocol in December 1940, whereby the Reichsbank took over the deposit instead of the French National Bank. The Belgian National Bank which was not a party to the agreement, did not recognise its implementation.

In September 1942 the German government decided to requisition the Belgian gold, which in various ways had been transported from Dakar via Marseilles to Berlin. The Belgian National Bank was informed about the requisition at the beginning of October 1942 and was informed at the same time that compensation would be paid for the gold. The compensation amount, which was provisionally to be credited to the National Bank at 500 million reichsmark, could, however, only be used for payments within Germany. The Belgian National Bank answered in December 1942 that the requisitioned gold did not constitute any deposit at the Reichsbank and that its transfer through the Banque de France had taken place without the consent of the Belgian National Bank and under conditions that could not be accepted so that the National Bank could not consider accepting any compensation for the requisition.

From a later published memorandum from Goering's office, dated 8 July 1942, it emerges that the Auswärtiges Amt's legal department recommended requisition of the Belgian gold through the German military commander in Belgium with reference to the 1907 Hague Convention's rules on land wars which among other things dealt with requisitions in occupied countries "for the needs of the occupying power". This basis for requisition was not applied, however. Instead Goering issued on 9 September 1942 an order that the Belgian gold should be placed at the disposal of his department pursuant to the Reichsleistungsgesetz (the German requisition decree adopted on 1 September 1939).

The Belgian gold was re-smelted in Berlin during the first half of 1943 and was then given pre-war year dates.

THE DUTCH GOLD

Nederlandsche Bank transferred all the gold kept in Amsterdam to its deposit in Rotterdam shortly before the German invasion. During the occupation, altogether around 146 tons gold would have been transferred from the Netherlands to Germany, of which slightly more than three quarters originated from the Dutch gold reserve in Rotterdam.

The same day that the Germans started the invasion of the Netherlands, around 11 tons of gold was loaded on a small ship which struck a mine on its way to the larger ship waiting at Nieuwe Mass to transport the gold on to London. In July the same year, the Germans succeeded in salvaging the major part, around 9.5 tons of the sunk cargo, whereupon the gold on the basis of a decision in 1941 by the Prize Court in Hamburg, gave the Germans the right to the cargo despite the ship not having been salvaged on the high seas. The Prize Court's decision was appealed against, but the higher court did not take up the matter during the war.

The circumstances concerning the Dutch gold differ in a number of respects from the Belgian gold. The Dutch Central Bank's gold deposit consisted predominantly of bars with another country of origin than the Netherlands, which meant that the Reichsbank did not find it necessary as in the case with the Belgian gold to re-smelt the bars. According to information received, only 124 of over 5,000 ingots were re-smelted while over 85 million gold coins were re-smelted to ingots by the Prussian mint. Furthermore, compensation was most often paid, if only illusory, for the confiscated gold. According to an ordinance of 24 June 1940, it was provided that private persons domiciled in the Netherlands should sell their gold in exchange for florins to the central bank, which in turn was credited with the equivalent value in reichsmark. A large part of the gold was considered by the Germans to constitute payment for internal and "external" costs of occupation. External costs of occupation probably referred to the cost that arose for example for training and education outside the Netherlands of German troops who were destined for service in the occupying forces in the Netherlands. Furthermore, the occupying power decided that monthly payments should be made retroactively from 1 July 1941 as a contribution to "Germany's war in the east against bolshevism".

ALLIED DECLARATIONS

At British initiative, 17 nations signed a declaration on 5 January 1943 generally entitled "Inter-Allied Declaration Against Acts of Dispossession". This declaration stated that the allied nations intended to do their utmost to defeat the methods of dispossession practised by the enemy and therefore reserved the right to declare all transactions as invalid, regardless of their formal appearance ("transfer of or dealing with property, rights and interests of any description whatsoever"), relating to property in the areas occupied by the enemy. This declaration was delivered to the Swedish government by a note from the British embassy in Stockholm.

The declaration of 5 January 1943 did not contain any direct statement on the German gold exports. In November 1943, the Treasury in USA raised the issue in a statement concerning the neutral states' gold transactions with Germany and on 22 February 1944 a declaration was issued containing a warning, especially to neutral countries, in relation to dispositions made by the enemy with respect to looted gold. The Swedish government was informed via the American embassy, and declarations with the same content were also delivered through the Berlin and Soviet missions. In the declaration it was stated that one of the methods practised by the Axis powers had consisted of unlawful misappropriation of large quantities of gold belonging to occupied nations. The Axis powers had, according to the declaration, sold such gold to various states with whom they continued to have diplomatic links and in that way obtained an important source of foreign currency for import of desired goods from these countries. The USA declared that they did not intend to recognise any acquisition of looted gold which the Axis powers held or had sold on the world market, and that the US Treasury would apply the rule of not purchasing any gold which was outside the USA from any country, that had not broken its links with the Axis powers at the latest at the time of the declaration's publication.

In the summer of 1944 the allied nations held a conference for monetary and financial issues at Bretton Woods, USA. At this conference a committee was appointed with the task of dealing with issues such as "Enemy Assets, Looted Property and Related Matters". The various recommendations of the committee led to the conference adopting Resolution No.VI, which was handed over to the Swedish government by letters from the British and American ambassadors on 2 October 1944. Resolution No.VI recommended certain measures in relation to neutral countries relating to property from occupied countries and enemy property in general. The neutral countries were urged within their respective areas to take action to prevent transfers or other disposals of property (including gold) that had been looted from the occupied areas, to get hold of and separate the same and keep it available for the appropriate authorities after liberation.

Sweden declared that it was prepared by internal action to comply with the recommendations of the resolution and referred at the same time with respect to control of enemy property to the successive tightening-up of Swedish foreign exchange control, especially the changes in October 1944 in the Foreign Exchange Ordinance. In June 1945 the Act concerning Restitution of Certain Property originating from Occupied Countries and the so-called Control Act were promulgated, as well as official pronouncements on a general prohibition against dispersion of German property in Sweden and an obligation to declare German property. For dealing with the control legislation, an agency was set up, the Foreign Capital Control Office, and a special committee, the Restitution Committee, which was mainly responsible for considering matters relating to the restitution of looted property.

Non-monetary gold

Beside central bank gold, Nazi Germany also appropriated gold from private persons and companies, etc. For example, the German Jews were according to legislation from 1939 obliged to give up gold to the German Reich. Compensation was paid for the gold at a price below value and larger payments were deposited in blocked accounts. In the Netherlands it was provided that private persons should sell their gold to the central bank and in a number of the occupied countries, the so-called Devisenschutz-kommandos confiscated large quantities of gold coins, smaller gold bars and other gold items.

In spring 1945, American troops found 2,007 boxes containing some of the Reichsbank's gold reserve, currencies and other valuable items in some abandoned salt mines at Merkers in Thüringia.

In one of the mines 18 sacks were found with various silver and gold bullions and 189 larger boxes containing, among other things, jewellery, watches and other gold objects, including dental fillings. The head of the Reichsbank department responsible for precious metals, Albert Thoms, was also at Merkers. He explained that the sacks and boxes were part of the so-called Melmer system named after the SS officer, Bruno Melmer. From the information provided by Thoms, Puhl and Melmer among others during subsequent interrogation, it emerged that in 1942 an account had been opened at the Reichsbank in the name of Melmer in which stolen goods from *inter alia* the concentration camps were deposited. The first SS consignment had arrived at the Reichsbank in summer 1942. At the Reichsbank, the goods were sorted so that the larger gold and silver bars were taken care of by the Reichsbank directly, the smaller items, for example, gold rings, were sent to the to Prussian mint for re-smelting and the larger items, such as jewels, were sent to the municipal pawning office in Berlin which in turn disposed of the goods in return for foreign currency or sent them on to the precious metals company Degussa (Deutsche Gold und Silber Scheideanstalt) for re-smelting. The funds received through the Melmer system were deposited in an account belonging to the SS called "Max Heiliger". The Allies found similar finds as those at Merkers at a number of other places, including concentration camps and at some of the Reichsbank's local offices.

The Inquiry has not, either in correspondence, memoranda and similar documents, or in Rooth's notes, found any evidence that the issue of non-monetary gold was the subject of any real discussion at the Riksbank. In connection with Puhl's visit to Stockholm in June 1944, Rooth made a note that the Scandinavian gold coins which were then offered for sale by the Reichsbank were not from Jews or similar, which could indicate at any rate that the issue of confiscated gold from Jews and other private persons was called into question. Regarding gold from the concentration camps, the Inquiry notes that this matter does not seem to have been discussed at the Riksbank after the end of the war either.

The Riksbank's gold transactions with the Reichsbank

Sweden concluded a clearing agreement with Germany in 1934. According to this agreement, payments in German reichsmark from German importers to Swedish exporters were made to a special account at the Reichsbank. These payments were notified to the Swedish clearing committee, which in turn paid the exporters in Swedish kronor. In this way Sweden built up claims in reichsmark at the Reichsbank. Payments from Swedish importers to German exporters were made by the importers paying in Swedish kronor to the clearing committee and the Reichsbank then paying the equivalent amount in reichsmark to the German importers. In this way, the Reichsbank in turn built up claims on Sweden.

If the value of exports and imports balanced, claims could be exactly set off against each other. If instead the value of Swedish exports was greater than the value of imports, Sweden acquired net assets in Reichsmark at the Reichsbank.

From autumn 1941, a large German deficit arose in clearing. The problem was solved by Sweden granting commodity credit in especially the wood, paper and pulp sectors. At the year-end 1942–43, total credit amounted to almost 40 per cent of the total export value to Germany in 1943. In the negotiations with Germany at the end of 1942, Sweden adopted a restrictive position on the credit issue, which led to the credit not being renewed. From the German side, it was promised that clearing would be balanced, which could take place through an increase of German export, a reduction in Swedish export or by payment taking place outside clearing in gold. From the Swedish side, it was requested that compensation should take place in the first place by gold sales. Swedish credit to Germany was largely repaid in gold in autumn 1942 and spring 1943.

Gold transactions with the Reichsbank took place from 1940 until August 1944 and can be divided into two phases. The first phase covers the period from 1940 until December 1941 and the second phase the subsequent period, when the deficit in clearing arose, until the final purchase in August 1944.

Gold transactions with the Reichsbank 1940–41

The first gold transactions with the Reichsbank concerned Swedish part payments for purchase of war material from Germany for 25 million reichsmark. According to an agreement in principle of 29 January 1940, a certain portion of the purchase was to be paid for in gold and in February the same year the Board of Governors decided that gold to a value equivalent to 7 million reichsmark would be allowed to be exported from Sweden to a deposit labelled "Gold deposited in Berlin".

In May 1940 the Riksbank purchased approximately 2,000 kg gold from the Reichsbank. This gold had been acquired by the Reichsbank from BIS's deposit in Stockholm which in turn had been created by transfer from Eesti Pank's deposit in Stockholm in 1939 and by the Riksbank from BIS by exchanging gold in the USA for the equivalent gold to BIS in Stockholm.

In June 1940 the Reichsbank deposited approximately 3,003 kg of gold in Stockholm.

In autumn 1940 a transaction was carried out which entailed that Germany re-purchased 1930 Kreuger bonds at a nominal amount of approximately 40 million dollars. The Government viewed the transaction positively and instructed the Riksbank to try to obtain as many dollars as possible and accept gold for the remainder. The final agreement meant that the Riksbank in addition to currencies took possession of approximately 8,620 kg of gold as follows (approximate weights):

88 kg	in Berlin	Resold to the Reichsbank autumn 1940
3,003 kg	in Stockholm	The gold deposited in June 1940
1,403 kg	in Berlin	Transported in December 1940 to Bern
4,125 kg	in Berlin	Intended to be used for clearing

With respect to the last consignment of approximately 4,125 kg it was not included in the accounts under the heading gold but under "various assets" since the consignment, according to the Riksbank, was to be sold back to Germany at the same price instead of the free currencies which were to be placed at Germany's disposal, under the clearing agreement. Gold was placed in the deposit in Berlin which was concluded when the Reichsbank took back the consignment for clearing purposes in January 1941. At the year-end 1940–41, the deposit "Gold deposited in Berlin" had accordingly been terminated. No new gold purchases from the Reichsbank took place during 1941.

On 15 April 1941 an agreement was entered into between the Air Force Materiel Administration and Consorzio Italiano Esportazioni Aernautiche in Italy regarding Italian air matériel-deliveries to Sweden. After payment was initially being made in dollars, it was agreed at Italian request that payment as a rule should be made by 65 per cent in gold and the remainder through payment into the Swedish-Italian clearing. The Italians declared that they were prepared to accept gold delivered in Berlin at the Reichsbank.

In connection with the start of gold payments to Italy, a "gold account" was opened at the Reichsbank in Berlin. Gold transactions from Sweden were credited to the gold account held in the name of the Riksbank and payments to Italy were charged to this account. The gold account thus functioned as a bank account where the transactions took place in gold instead of in foreign currencies. It has not been possible to establish on the basis of the documents found in the archives to what extent the Riksbank had the right of ownership to a particular quantity of earmarked gold bars in the gold account.

In 1941 altogether 3,682 kg of gold was shipped from Sweden to Berlin, including the greater part of the 3,003 kg of gold that had been deposited by the Reichsbank in Stockholm in June 1940 and which was taken possession of by the Riksbank in connection with the Kreuger bond transaction the same year. During 1941 the gold account was used predominantly for payments to Italy on behalf of the Air Force Materiel Administration (2,540 kg).

The gold quantity of 1,403 kg which at the year-end 1940–41 had been transported from Berlin to a deposit in Berne was sold in July 1941 to the Swiss National Bank. During autumn of the same year, the Riksbank shipped 12,525 kg gold from Sweden to the deposit in Switzerland, of which 3,331 kg was sold to the Swiss National Bank.

Gold transactions with the Reichsbank 1942–44

Representatives of the Reichsbank also took part in trade negotiations between Germany and Sweden in December 1941. Gold purchases for 1942 were initially agreed upon from the Reichsbank at 25 million kronor. Puhl visited Stockholm at the turn of the month April–May 1942 and met representatives of the government *inter alia*. During the visit Puhl requested that the Riksbank should make available free Swedish kronor for disposal in return for gold and at the meeting on 30 April, the Board of Governors allowed purchase of gold from the Reichsbank up to a maximum amount of 35 million kronor. This amount was increased at the Board of Governors' meeting on 8 October at the request of the Reichsbank to a total of at most 70 million kronor. Gold transactions in 1942 can be summarised as follows:

- During the year 799 kg was transferred via Malmö to the gold account in Berlin and 3,958 kg gold was sold to Italy.
- At the Board of Governors' meeting on 25 February, Rooth stated that Germany and Turkey had concluded an agreement that Germany would make available approximately 2,138 kg gold at Turkey's disposal in Stockholm for a period of nine months. From the German side, it was requested that the Riksbank should place the aforesaid amount at Turkey's disposal in Stockholm. In return, the Reichsbank placed the equivalent amount at the Riksbank's disposal in Berlin. From the accounts compared to other documents in the archives, the transaction would seem to have meant that the quantity that was made available to the Riksbank in Berlin (2,143 kg) was used by the Riksbank, mainly in connection with payment to Italy. After the stipulated period the Riksbank therefore acquired a further 2,138 kg gold in Berlin from the Reichsbank while the gold that had been placed at Turkey's disposal in Stockholm went back to the Riksbank. In all the transaction meant that the Riksbank acquired 4,281 kg gold from the Reichsbank. There is nothing to indicate otherwise than that the gold consignment in Stockholm was only earmarked during the period and that no physical relocation of this gold has been involved.
- During the autumn, the Riksbank and the Reichsbank agreed that purchases of gold would take place with delivery either in Stockholm, Berlin or Berne.
- In August 1942 the deposit "Gold deposited at the Reichsbank" was set up. The balance increased through purchases from the Reichsbank totalling approximately 6,027 kg. Furthermore, gold was transferred from the gold account at the same time as the balance during the year was reduced by transfers to the gold account.
- In November an exchange took place of approximately 3,997 kg (337 ingots) in such a way that the Riksbank transferred to the Reichsbank 337 ingots from the deposit "Gold deposited in Berlin" and received in exchange 337 other ingots from the Reichsbank's deposit in Switzerland, which were placed in the Riksbank's deposit in Switzerland and which subsequently proved to be Dutch gold in the form of smelted gold coins.
- The Riksbank took possession of 1,007 kg of gold from BIS in Switzerland.

The same day as the allies issued their warning, 5 January 1943, the Riksbank purchased approximately 1,006 kg of gold from the Reichsbank. According to various information in the archives, the Riksbank had not received the warning before 13 or 18 January. On 13 January a further 998 kg was purchased from the Reichsbank.

The allied warning led the Riksbank management to conduct informal discussions with the Government regarding the question of whether a declaration from the Reichsbank should be obtained that they would in future only deliver gold that originated from unoccupied countries.

The Government through the Minister of Commerce and Industry, Herman Eriksson, declared on 12 February that there were insufficient grounds for obtaining a declaration but that there would be no obstacle to Rooth meeting Puhl in person "in order to mention the subject in passing". After a request from the Reichsbank on 15 February that the Riksbank should agree to raising the limit for gold purchases from 70 to 105 million kronor, the issue was again discussed by both the Board of Governors and with the Government. The Government stated, *inter alia*, that since the Swedish negotiators wanted a German promise in 1941 and 1942 on liquidation of the clearing balance by gold transfers, Sweden could not refuse accepting gold to a reasonable extent from Germany for clearing compensation.

Jacob Wallenberg, who was in Berlin in the capacity of member of the Swedish government Inquiry, presented on 18 February to Puhl the wish that no gold bars originating from occupied countries should be included in deliveries to Sweden. Puhl told Jacob Wallenberg that he was glad that the Swedish point of view had been put forward to him personally and not in an official form and Puhl declared at the same time that he was prepared to ensure personally that future deliveries to Sweden did not contain gold from occupied countries. The day after, on 19 February, Jacob Wallenberg was informed by Puhl that the "necessary arrangements" had already been made.

At the meeting of the Board of Governors the same day, the Board of Governors decided to increase the limit for purchases of gold from the Reichsbank to a total amount of 105 million kronor. The Riksbank's Board of Governors would subsequently take up the issue of further gold purchases from Germany on a number of occasions. The Riksbank declared, however, that it was not prepared to purchase more gold during 1943.

In 1943 the gold transactions took place in largely the same way as during 1942. From documents in the archives, it has emerged that the Reichsbank offered to exchange the Riksbank's gold deposited in Berlin for gold in Berne without cost to the Riksbank. Further, it has emerged that on purchase of the gold in Berlin, the gold was placed in the Berlin deposit whereupon the Reichsbank had the opportunity to replace it by new gold in Switzerland. The slight weight differences were settled via the gold account.

In 1943 no gold was transferred from Sweden to the gold account and payments to Italy only amounted to approximately 421 kg. Altogether the Riksbank purchased 11,268 kg gold in Berlin during the year. At the same time, an exchange took place of gold from the Reichsbank's deposit in Switzerland and approximately 11,531 kg (949 bars) was deposited in the Riksbank's deposit in Switzerland. The difference in weight was regulated by the gold account. From the deposit in Switzerland approximately 156 kilo gold was sold to Crédit Suisse Zürich for Hungarian silver on behalf of the Mint and from the deposit in Berlin approximately 1,008 kg of gold was brought home to Malmö and then sent to Stockholm and sold for industrial use.

In January 1944 approximately 998 kg of gold was delivered directly from the Reichsbank to the Riksbank's deposit in Switzerland. This was the last consignment of gold bars from Reichsbank. At the end of the year the Riksbank sold approximately 2,055 kg gold from the deposit in Switzerland to the Swiss National Bank.

At the meeting of the Board of Governors on 2 March 1944, the content of the gold declaration that had been issued in February by USA, England and the Soviet Union was discussed whereupon the Board of Governors decided that the Riksbank should inform the Reichsbank by telegram that the Riksbank could not accept additional gold, but that the bank was willing instead to accept Swiss Francs within the previously decided maximum limits. In March the Reichsbank requested that the Riksbank should accept gold for the approximately 9 million kronor that remained within the agreed limit of 105 million kronor. Furthermore, it was requested that the Riksbank should consider an increase of the limit by a further 35 million kronor or a total of 140 million kronor. The Board of Governors declared that it was not willing to change its previous standpoint on this issue.

During his visit to Stockholm during June 1944 Puhl requested that the Riksbank should accept gold from the Reichsbank for the remaining approximately 9 million kronor and offered, on the part of Germany, to deliver gold in the form of Scandinavian gold coins, which had been in the Reichsbank's possession since before the outbreak of war, and German gold coins, that the Reichsbank had possessed since 1923–24. At the meeting of the Board of Governors on 29 June, it was informed that the Swedish Ministry for Foreign Affairs and the head of the Ministry of Trade had informally declared that they had no objections to make to the Riksbank complying with Puhl's request. The Board of Governors decided to grant Puhl's request on condition that the amount in free Swedish kronor, which was deposited in Sweden by the Germans, was not used for such payments, which should be met by Swedish-German clearing.

During the period 23 July – 7 August the Riksbank accepted 1,501 kg in German 20-mark gold coins.

The main purpose of the foreign exchange regulations introduced in February 1940 was primarily to regulate payments from Sweden to other countries to enable Sweden's currency assets to be used primarily to meet essential import requirements. The changes in the foreign exchange ordinance that came into effect on 30 October 1944, provided greater possibilities for controlling the import of capital into Sweden and disposal of existing foreign assets in Sweden. In connection with the sharpening of the foreign exchange regulations, an import prohibition was introduced for inter alia crude gold and platinum. Due to the sharpening of the foreign exchange regulations, Puhl wrote to Rooth in November stating that in his way "finden unsere früheren Absprachen über die Goldkäufe ihre Erledigung, so dass sich ein nochmaliges Eingehen auf diese Frage erübrigt."

At the end of November 1944, the Government discussed the issue of certain transfers from Germany to the Reichsbank's general account at the Riksbank. In this connection, the issue arose, whether Germany should have the right to repurchase a part of the gold that the Riksbank had received from the Reichsbank which was deposited in Switzerland for the funds deposited in the general account. Rooth notified that the Riksbank would refuse such a request from the Reichsbank and at a meeting on 14 December 1944, the Board of Governors refused a request from the Reichsbank to making use of its assets at the Riksbank to purchase gold to a value equivalent to 10 million kronor.

A summary of transactions entered in the "Gold account", "Gold deposited at the Reichsbank" and "Gold deposited at the Swiss National Bank" is shown in Tables 2, 3 and 4.

Table 2. Gold account – specification in kg

	1941	1942	1943	Total
Deposits on account				
Transfers from the Riksbank's depots in Sweden	3,682	799	–	4,481
Transfers from the Riksbank's depots with the Reichsbank, including differences on exchange	–	2,755	297	3,052
Deposits through purchases for which sellers have not been identified	–	32	–	32
Deposits through purchases from the Royal Swedish Airforce Matériel Administration	–	–	185	185
Purchases of gold from the Reichsbank including exchange	–	4,149	–	4,149
Total deposits on account	3,682	7,735	482	11,899
Withdrawals from account				
Payments to Italy relating to the Royal Swedish Airforce Matériel Administration	2,540	3,958	421	6,919
Withdrawals for sales for which no buyers have been identified	317	230	1	548
Withdrawals transferred to the Riksbank's depot in Switzerland, including differences on exchange	–	–	283	283
Withdrawals transferred to the Riksbank's depots with the Reichsbank (reversals)	–	4,149	–	4,149
Untraced withdrawals	–	0	–	0
Total withdrawals from account	2,857	8,337	705	11,899

Table 3. Gold deposited with the Reichsbank – specification in kg

	1942	1943	Total
Opening reserves	–	1,284	
Deposits in depot			
Purchases from the Reichsbank	6,027	11,268	17,295
Transfers from Gold account	4,149	–	4,149
Total deposits in depot	10,176	11,268	21,444
Withdrawals from depot			
Transfers to Switzerland	3,998	11,247	15,245
Withdrawal in connection with Tripartite transaction	2,139	–	2,139
Transfers to Gold account	2,755	297	3,052
Transfers to Sweden	–	1,008	1,008
Total withdrawals from depot	8,892	12,552	21,444
Closing reserves	1,284	–	–

Table 4. Gold deposited in Switzerland – specification in kg

	1940	1941	1942	1943	1944	Total
Opening reserves	–	1,403	9,194	14,98	25,573	
Deposits in depot						
Exchanges and transfers from depots in Berlin	1,403	–	3,997	11,247	–	16,647
Transfer from Gold account	–	–	–	283	–	283
Transfer from Sweden	–	12,525	–	–	–	12,525
Purchase from the Reichsbank	–	–	–	1	998	999
Purchase from BIS	–	–	1,007	–	–	1,007
Total deposits in depot	1,403	12,525	5,004	11,531	998	31,461
Withdrawals from depot						
Sales to Switzerland and the Royal Swedish Mint	–	4,734	–	156	2,055	6,945
Total withdrawals from depot	–	4,734	–	156	2,055	6,945
Reserves in depot	1,403	9,194	14,198	25,573	24,516	24,516

As has been seen, a large part of the Riksbank's acquisition of gold from the Reichsbank took place by exchanges, which were mainly carried out during the period November 1942 to December 1943. These exchanges took place in such a way that the Riksbank transferred a certain number of specific gold ingots from the deposit in Berlin and received instead other gold ingots from the Reichsbank's deposit in Switzerland, which were placed in the Riksbank's deposit there. The total quantity of gold that the Riksbank transferred to the Reichsbank in Berlin in this way amounted to 15,281 kg. This gold was often held by the Riksbank only for a limited period before it was exchanged. Through these exchanges the Riksbank acquired gold from the Reichsbank deposited in Switzerland amounting to a total of 15,527 kg.

Table 5 contains a compilation of the reconstructed accounts with respect to the gold acquired by the Riksbank from the Reichsbank during the period in question. The acquisition that took place through exchanges has been recomputed to gross amounts.

Table 5. Total acquisitions of gold from the Reichsbank

	1940	1941	1942	1943	1944	Total
Recorded as purchases	6,494	–	8,038	11,268	2,500	28,300
Parts of repurchase of bonds recorded on temporary account	4,126	–	–	–	–	
Net purchases and exchanges via gold account converted into gross purchases	–	–	3,997	11,530	–	15,527
Tripartite transaction[1]	–	–	2,138	–	–	2,138
Tripartite transaction	–	–	2,138	–	–	2,138
Other acquisitions via gold account[2]	–	2,856	4,189	423	–	7,468
Total acquisitions	10,620	2,856	20,500	23,221	2,500	59,697

1. The gold amounted to 2,143 kg; of that item 5 kg has been recorded as purchase and is included in the total of 28,300 kg.

2. Payments to Italy 6,919 kg. Sales 549 kg.

Further on in this paper, a reconstruction is made of German gold in the Riksbank's deposits on 1 June 1945.

Sweden's negotiations with the allied powers after the end of the war

Background

At the Potsdam Conference in summer 1945, the occupying powers decided to instruct the Control Council in Berlin to take suitable measures for exercise of control and the right of disposal of such German assets abroad that were not already under allied supervision. In the allocation of these assets, the Soviet Union waived its claim on German assets *inter alia* in former neutral states. Furthermore, an American proposal was accepted at the Potsdam conference to establish a gold pot in which all stolen monetary gold from Germany and the neutral countries was to be collected for subsequent distribution among the former occupied countries from whose central banks the gold had been looted.

The issue of the gold pot was developed in more detail during the Paris Reparations Conference that was held in autumn 1945. The decision from the Potsdam Conference on a gold pot was confirmed and USA, Great Britain and France were appointed as being responsible for management of the pool. Implementation was to take place through a specially created Commission, the Tripartite Commission for the Restitution of Monetary Gold (TGC).

The implementation of the convention signed in Paris in January 1946 on German reparations was conditional agreements with each of the neutral states where there was German property. For this reason, the neutral countries were invited to negotiations in Washington. In March 1946, negotiations were initiated with Switzerland. These negotiations resulted on 25 May 1946 in an agreement which meant among other things that Switzerland was to transfer 250 million Swiss francs in gold to the Tripartite Gold Pool, whereupon the allied claims for restitution of looted gold would be considered as having been finally settled.

On the part of the allies, similar agreements were striven for with the other neutral countries. After an agreement had been reached with Switzerland and Sweden – which were considered to be the two countries where the most important assets were – the intention was to turn to Spain, Portugal and Ireland and to Argentina and Turkey.

Swedish-allied negotiations in Washington in 1946

Negotiations with Sweden in Washington began on 31 May 1946. At these negotiations, Sweden and the allies were in agreement that the German assets in Sweden should be taken charge of, checked and liquidated through the auspices of the Foreign Capital Control Office set up in 1945. On 18 July 1946 an agreement was concluded concerning among other things the disposal of the funds flowing in on liquidation.

With respect to the gold issue, on the part of Sweden, it was made clear at the beginning of the negotiations that Sweden was prepared to restore gold which had been looted by German actions from occupied countries. The allied view at the beginning of the negotiations that all gold purchased from Germany after a certain date should be regarded as looted, was contested from the Swedish side.

After a number of discussions, especially on the issue of how to deal with the looted gold that the Riksbank had purchased from the Reichsbank and subsequently sold to a third country, the so-called Washington agreement was reached, which was approved by the Riksdag on 17 December 1946. According to the agreement, Sweden's undertaking to return looted gold should only apply to the extent that such gold was still in Swedish possession on 1 June 1945 and that claims for provably looted gold had been put forward by the governments of the occupied countries or their central banks before 1 July 1947. Already at Washington demands were put forward for restitution of certain quantities of gold taken from the Belgians by Germany and before the end of the period of respite, the Dutch government had also made substantial demands.

Negotiations on the Belgian gold

After France had compensated Belgium for its loss, negotiations took place *inter alia* between France and Sweden. In 1946 representatives of the French National Bank visited the Riksbank and presented evidence including photographs of 18 pages from the Prussian Mint's Smelting Record for 1943. From these compared with other material, it emerged that during the period 25 January to 16 June 1943 approximately 143,600 kg (gross) of Belgian gold had been smelted whereupon the new ingots had been marked with new but incorrect dates (from 1934–39).

The claims put forward by the French National Bank for Sweden's part concerned a total of 7,311.3 kg of gold distributed over a number of gold deliveries from the Reichsbank (all acquisitions by exchange of gold in Berlin for gold in Berne). The details are shown in Table 6.

Table 6. The Riksbank's acquisition of Belgian gold

Year	weight (kg pure)	bars
1943		
15.4	532.8	45
2.6	500.0	42
14.7	503.0	42
28.7	477.0	38
17.8	1,001.6	80
21.9	210.0	17
25.11	1,004.6	81
29.11	1,995.3	161
22.12	88.1	7
1944		
17.1	998.9	81
	7,311.3	**594**

Of the gold in question, 156.0 kg was sold on 26 July 1943 to Crédit Suisse Zürich for purchase of silver on behalf of the Royal Swedish Mint. Since the Washington agreement only entailed that only such gold should be returned which was still in Swedish possession on 1 June 1945, this consignment was deducted whereupon the final quantity of looted Belgian gold to be returned by Sweden was set at 7,155.3 kg pure.

According to the Washington agreement's wording, consent was given for Sweden for some further investigation of the evidence relating to the Belgian gold. In reply to a reminder from the American Embassy in Stockholm on 15 March 1948 the Government issued a note in May 1948 in which it was stated that further investigations were necessary. A year later on 31 May, 1949, the Riksbank instructed the Federal Reserve Bank of New York by telegram that the agreed quantity of gold should be transferred from the Riksbank's deposit in New York to TGC and on 6 May of the same year, the Minister for Foreign Affairs ordered that an amount of 28,986,156 kr and 67 öre should be paid out to the Riksbank. The state's claim due to the gold transferred was taken up as a claim in the mandatory clearing with Germany.

Negotiations on the Dutch gold

Negotiations with Nederlandsche Bank began in May 1947 and in December the same year the bank's claims were specified in more detail. The Dutch claim was based on the Swedish transactions with the Reichsbank shown in Table 7 (all acquisitions by exchange of gold in Berlin for gold in Berne except the acquisition of 7 December 1942 which took place in Berlin and was later taken to Stockholm).

Table 7. The Riksbank's acquisition of Dutch gold

Year	weight (kg pure)	bars
1942		
11.11	3,997.5	337
7.12	1,008.0	84
1943		
20.1	849.2	72
27.1	724.5	59
15.2	998.3	83
19.2	1,005.4	85
28.7	24.6	2
	8,607.5	**722**

Of the gold in question, the consignment taken to Stockholm of 1,008.0 kg for Swedish industry was sold during the period August 1943 – 14 July 1944. In the Riksbank's view, taking into consideration the return date 1 June 1945, the amount of Dutch gold to be returned by Sweden should be 638 ingots with a total weight of 7,599.5 kg.

Besides the difficulties for the Dutch central bank to produce the proof called for the claim, *inter alia* with respect to that the acquisitions of 11 November 1942 and on 15 and 19 February 1943 referred to smelted gold coins, negotiations were prolonged due to the circumstances that differentiated the Dutch gold from the Belgian gold. Among other things, it was initially called into question from the Swedish side, whether the Dutch gold could be regarded as having been looted, as it emerged that compensation had been paid by Germany.

The principal objection was, however, the Swedish allegation that the acquisitions that took place before the allied declaration in January 1943 had taken place in good faith. At the same time, reference was made to the fact that the allies initially in negotiations on the gold issue had assumed that Germany since early 1943 had transferred looted gold and that from the allied side, it had been proposed that all gold after January 1943 should be considered as looted gold. Changing its previous position on the allied proposal, Sweden accordingly alleged that the Washington agreement should be interpreted as meaning that only gold transactions after January 1943 were to be subject to restitution. Sweden's position was commented on in June 1947 by the then chairman of the Riksbank's Board of Governors Dag Hammarskjöld: "It would seem to be impossible to claim 'acquisition in good faith' now if it had not been claimed before or at the latest by the Washington agreement. Every attempt to avoid payment according to the line stated will easily assume the character of casuistry."

After further exchanges of documents on the issue of the Dutch gold, the western powers declared that they were prepared to reduce their claim by just over a quarter if a voluntary agreement could be reached. From the Swedish side it was regarded as more favourable if an agreement could be reached rather than the arbitration procedure provided for in the Washington agreement. The compromise entailed that approximately 6 tons of gold should be transferred to TGC. After the Riksdag's approval, the gold was transferred in 1955 in accordance with the agreement.

Reconstruction of German gold in the Riksbank's deposits on 1 June 1945

The work of reconstructing the accounting of gold transactions has only been possible up to 22 January 1945 since the Riksbank then changed its accounting principle. The changed arrangement entailed a simplification with regard to registration of different items, but on the other hand it was no longer possible to read off any details from the general ledgers. As has previously emerged, the final gold transaction between the Riksbank and the Reichsbank took place in summer 1944 when 1.5 tons of German gold coins were delivered to Sweden.

On 22 January 1945 there were, beside gold coins, German gold in Swedish possession held at the Riksbank's deposit in Switzerland.

The auditors have compiled and compared the weight lists regarding the German gold which have been found in the archives. This material consisted of German signed carbon copies and Swedish certified copies. It has not been possible to establish with certainty whether these weight lists are original material or whether they have been drawn up retrospectively, especially with regard to the Swedish copies. Furthermore, copies of documents have been found from the Swiss National Bank which have come to the Riksbank in connection with the Riksbank's investigations as a result of claims by the Allies after the end of the war.

In their work with the weight lists, the auditors have noted the stated smelting numbers, ingot numbers and control numbers respectively for each gold ingot in a purchased consignment. Moreover, the degree of purity has been followed up and noted. In this way, it has been possible for the Inquiry to make observations on the common characteristics for different consignments of gold.

At the negotiations on the Belgian gold in 1946 and on the Dutch gold in 1947 a considerable amount of evidence was presented to the Riksbank. A review of the archives does not show otherwise than that the Riksbank, with respect to the two claims on Sweden for looted gold, would seem to have accepted that it held or had possessed the quantities claimed by Belgium and the Netherlands. With respect to the Belgian gold, the quantity of gold claimed back was also noted in the Washington agreement.

All the German gold in the Swedish deposit in Switzerland on 22 January 1945 has been verified against weight lists (see Appendix).

With reservation for the uncertainty that exists regarding the reliability of the weight lists examined – a greater reliability would be obtained from a comparison with other notes on the smelting numbers and degree of purity etc. in foreign archives – the Inquiry has in an examination of the weight lists and other material been able to make the following observations regarding the gold remaining in Switzerland:

- The Belgian ingots were re-smelted in spring 1943. The ingots included in the Belgian claim on Sweden were often characterised as having been given a special three or four-digit number as smelting number. The degree of purity is predominantly high. Three smaller consignments of approximately 500 kg each which were delivered to the deposit in Switzerland in spring and summer 1943 show a lower degree of purity, however.
- Ingots in the Dutch Central Bank's gold deposit had predominantly another country of origin than the Netherlands. Only a few of these ingots were re-smelted. The Dutch bars which were included in the claim and which were not smelted gold coins are characterised by the smelting numbers beginning with a letter and a number combination that does not follow any special series. The degree of purity is high.
- The Dutch ingots included in the claim which consisted of smelted gold coins are characterised by the smelting number consisting of a special four-digit series. They have a low degree of purity.

The Riksbank's holding of German gold on 22 January 1945 consisted of 1.5 tons of gold in Sweden and 16.4 tons of gold in the deposit of Switzerland, or a total of 17.9 tons of German gold.

In the Washington agreement, it was agreed on 1 June 1945 as the return date for gold in Swedish possession. Between 22 January 1945 and up to 1 June 1945 the same year the Riksbank did not acquire any gold from Germany. During the same period, 4.1 tons of gold were sold from deposit in Switzerland to the Swiss National Bank. According to the notes in Wessman's archives compared with a list compiled by the Swiss National Bank the consignment sold consisted of 4.1 tons probably of Swedish gold. Accordingly, it does not seem that any change took place regarding the German gold in the deposit in Switzerland between January and June 1945.

The deposit in Switzerland consisted on 1 June 1945 of 16.4 tons of German gold of which 7.2 tons was looted Belgian gold. The original demand from the Nederlandsche Bank was 8.6 tons of gold. This quantity should be reduced by the consignment of approximately 1 ton which was taken home from Berlin in 1943 and which according to the Riksbank's records should have been sold to industry. There was accordingly 7.6 tons of looted Dutch gold in the deposit.

Through the auditors' compilation of weight lists and the different characteristics that have been noted, the Inquiry can with respect to the remaining 1.6 tons of gold in the Swiss deposit state that a total of approximately 1 ton of gold, that was placed in the deposit in spring 1943, bore the same characteristics as the consignments of gold claimed by the Nederlandsche Bank which according to the information consisted entirely of smelted gold coins. The remaining 0.6 tons of gold in the Swiss deposit did not bear any special characteristics.

German gold in the Riksbank's deposit in Switzerland as per 1 June 1945 (ton)

German gold deposited in Switzerland	16.4
Belgian origin	−7.2
Dutch origin	−7.6
(Claim 8.6 – taken home to Sweden 1.0)	
	1.6
The remainder consists of:	
Gold ingots which bear the same characteristics as the looted Dutch gold consisting of smelted gold coins	1.0
Other German gold deposited in Switzerland	0.6
	1.6

The consignments of gold coins at 20 Reichsmark taken over from the Reichsbank in summer 1944 consisted of a total 4.2 million Reichsmarks with a total pure weight of 1,501 kg. According to a certificate issued by Riksbank officials dated 6 February 1946 no coins were found on random sampling with a later date than 1914. Further, it was noted that the coins were worn so that the conclusion was drawn that these had been in circulation.

The Riksbank transferred to TGC the equivalent of 7.2 tons of gold for the looted Belgian gold in 1949 and the equivalent of 6 tons of gold for the looted Dutch gold in 1955.

With regard to non-monetary gold, it emerges from the American so-called Eizenstat report of May 1997, among other things, that at the Prussian Mint's smelting in 1943 of Dutch florins to gold bars, 37 kg of gold shall have originated from the so-called Melmer system. The gold bars in question shall predominantly have been received by the Swiss National Bank; a smaller part was delivered to Italy. The report has not found any information in the Riksbank's archives to indicate that the possibility was discussed that any non-monetary gold was included in, for example, the two claims on Sweden.

OBSERVATIONS OF INTEREST WITH REGARD TO LOOTED GOLD

The task of the Inquiry has been to make a compilation of what the Riksbank's archives contain on the Riksbank's acquisition of gold from Germany during the second world war. Following this task, the ambition of the Inquiry has been to provide an account of relevant material and to give the reader scope to evaluate and interpret the content of selected documents. Below are presented some observations, especially regarding the Riksbank's and Government's knowledge of and steps taken in respect of the looted gold.

Introduction

The Riksbank discussed in autumn 1939 the consequences for the international central bank trade in gold in the event of occupation and confiscated central bank gold being offered for sale. At the end of 1940 or beginning of 1941 the Riksbank got to know that the USA would probably refuse to purchase German gold. Notes have been found in the Governor of the Riksbank's archives from May 1941 and June 1942 with the content that gold bars purchased from Germany during the war should be kept separately and that "these gold ingots should be used in the first place for sales to goldsmiths, etc.".

The Allies declared on 5 January 1943 that they intended to do their utmost to frustrate Germany's looting and reserved the right to declare invalid all transactions with property in the areas occupied or controlled by the enemy. Since the Riksbank could no longer be regarded as being in "good faith" regarding gold purchases from Germany, the Government was consulted to obtain an assurance from Germany as to the origin of the gold. The Government did not comply with this request, but declared that there was no obstacle to the Riksbank taking up the matter with the Reichsbank in passing. When the Reichsbank on 15 February 1943 requested that the Riksbank should purchase more gold, the Bank referred the matter to the Government, which informed the Riksbank that it should comply with the German request but that it wished to "avoid an official request to the German Reichsbank". On 18 February the wish was presented informally to the deputy-governor of the Reichsbank, Puhl, that no gold bars originating from occupied countries should be included in deliveries to the Riksbank. Puhl promised to personally ensure that this did not happen and declared the following day that he had made the necessary arrangements.

The Riksbank continued in accordance with previous undertakings to purchase gold from the Reichsbank. The final gold ingots were bought in January 1944. The Allies warned the neutral countries in February about trading with stolen monetary gold. In March the Reichsbank again requested that the Riksbank should purchase more gold. The Riksbank declined but declared that it was possibly willing to purchase Swiss francs. During a visit to Stockholm in June, Puhl offered instead gold coins that the Reichsbank had had in its possession since before the war. After the Government had declared that it had no objection, 1.5 tons of German gold coins were purchased in summer 1944. This was the last delivery of German gold.

The time before the allied declaration in January 1943

- According to Ivar Rooth's notes from autumn 1939 a discussion took place about the possibility that the (Dutch) central bank gold would be confiscated as a result of the war and the consequences that this would have for the central banks' trade in gold; it was feared that there would be restrictions.
- In June 1940 a number of boxes containing 248 gold ingots were deposited on behalf of the Reichsbank at the Riksbank. The boxes were opened for inspection. All ingots were from the Reichsbank in Berlin and were equipped with number labels in a series, stuck on by the Reichsbank. After checking with the notes from Berlin, the ingots were put back in the boxes, "which were closed and sealed in and for possible swift transport". It is unclear why this inspection took place. There may be a number of conceivable explanations. Information has been noted on the weight lists of this consignment of foreign smelters, which has not been done on other weight lists.
- The so-called Kreuger bond transaction took place in autumn 1940. In brief, this transaction entailed that the Reichsbank was to repurchase the existing German Kreuger bonds in Sweden for payment partially in gold. Either the sellers of the bonds or the Riksbank would take over the gold. The Riksbank, which would possibly send the gold immediately to

America for sale, then calculated the risk that the Americans would refuse to purchase the gold since it came from Germany. Rooth writes:

> "...It is conceivable that the transaction, when it becomes known in America, will be presented in such a way that Sweden helped Germany to dispose of the gold. This can easily be presented in America as a non-neutral action and consequently damage Sweden. It is also conceivable that America will draw the consequence that we are prevented from selling not only this gold but also other gold belonging to us..."

On the part of the Government, it was considered that it would be of great benefit to the country if the bond sale could go ahead. The Riksbank should try to get the Germans to pay in dollars and, if this was not possible, to take possession itself of the quantity of gold required to carry out the transaction. Certain individual interested parties also wanted the transaction to be carried out. Rooth noted:

> "...Wallenberg replied that L.M. Ericsson, which had liabilities to the banks at 18 million kr, would be able to pay off its bank debts through this transaction. L.M. Ericsson would therefore be very interested in the transaction coming about and would therefore be pleased to consider accepting the gold as payment, provided that they were able to find an outlet to sell it. A condition was, however, that the Riksbank was prepared to exchange the German gold for other gold, which they could sell in America, as they were not sure that they could sell German gold in the U.S.A."

It is to be noted that a part of the gold taken over from the Reichsbank in connection with the Kreuger bond transaction, a consignment of 18 million kronor, was not taken up in the accounts under the heading of gold but under "various assets". According to Rooth, the gold was to be used as payment for the amounts which during the first half of 1941 were to be paid to Germany in free currencies according to the Swedish-German clearing agreement.

In November 1940 a telegram arrived from the Bank for International Settlements, BIS, with an enquiry as to whether the Riksbank could sell gold bars in Berne which had been "neutral property before September year 1939". The quote has been underlined with green pen by someone at the Riksbank.

In autumn 1940, Rooth asked Marcus Wallenberg to talk to the Treasury, the Federal Reserve Bank and the private banks in USA to "sound out the American attitude to gold and its future value". Wallenberg informed Rooth that the USA would perhaps refuse to purchase such gold which they called "stolen". For this reason, Rooth considered that the Riksbank should separate gold that the Riksbank owned itself at the outbreak of war and acquired from Boliden after that from the gold that the Riksbank had acquired from countries in Europe after the outbreak of war.

In the light of the information Rooth received from Marcus Wallenberg, Rooth informed the Board of Governors in February 1941 that the American authorities would probably not be prepared to purchase gold which an occupying power had taken possession of. If it was subsequently desired to sell gold in USA, it had to be taken into account that the American authorities would make a careful investigation of the issue of ownership rights.

The following typed note dated May 1941 is included in Rooth's archives under the heading "Discussions".

"...The gold bars purchased by the Riksbank after the outbreak of war should be kept separately. When gold is sold as ingots to goldsmiths etc. the bars purchased from Germany should be used in the first place. The reason for this is that it would seem likely that America will not be prepared to purchase gold, which has been in German ownership after the outbreak of war, and at any rate will require an investigation that the gold that we will sell to America, is really not of German origin..."

Rooth informed Puhl and Wilhelm at the Reichsbank in June 1942 that the Swiss National Bank had requested that the Reichsbank's need for kronor should be paid in gold instead of in Swiss francs. The explanation for this request is probably that they wished to restrict the quantity of Swiss francs in circulation to prevent inflation. The Reichsbank complied with the Swiss request, but also wanted to purchase Swiss francs from the Riksbank for gold. To the extent that the Riksbank needed gold for payments to Italy, the Riksbank should accept gold in Berlin or in Switzerland and place Swiss francs at the disposal of the Reichsbank.

In the discussion with Puhl, he had stated that the Riksbank should immediately inform the Reichsbank if any of the Reichsbank's wishes conflicted with Swedish neutrality.

Bearing in mind any future complications regarding gold bars that had been purchased from Germany or from another country in Europe during the war Rooth noted in June 1942 that a careful account should be kept of these. In deliveries of gold to Italy and sale to jewellers, these ingots should be supplied in the first place.

Rooth asked Per Jacobsson to inform him in August 1942 if he, when visiting the USA, or on any other occasion, had heard whether the Allies would refuse to purchase confiscated gold after the war. Rooth had "now and again" heard information that the Allies "even after victory" would refuse to accept such gold in payment, which according to Rooth, could have some importance for Sweden among other countries since

"...we could hardly refuse in our transactions with the Swiss National Bank and the German Reichsbank, to accept gold as payment, which has been in German or German occupied ownership..."

The Allies' declaration of 5 January 1943 and Puhl's assurance

On 5 January 1943 a declaration was issued by a number of the Allies concerning property deriving from the occupied countries. This declaration contained an explanation that the allied countries intended to do their utmost to frustrate the enemy's looting methods and therefore reserved the right to declare invalid all transactions regarding property in the areas occupied or controlled by the enemy.

After the allied declaration, Rooth wanted to draw the Board of Governors' attention to the fact that Germany would probably in the very near future make a request for increased gold sales to Sweden and stated that the Riksbank should observe some caution on purchase of gold from *inter alia* Germany, since the Riksbank now could no longer be considered to be in "good faith". Rooth wanted – "to avoid trouble and losses for the Riksbank" – to obtain a declaration from the Reichsbank to only deliver such gold that came from non-occupied countries and referred the matter to the government. On 12 February the Minister for Industry and Commerce, Herman Eriksson, answered

> "...that the Government was unanimously of the opinion that there were insufficient grounds to take up the matter in any of the ways that I had suggested. However, there was no obstacle to me mentioning the matter in passing if I met Puhl in person..."

On 15 February the Reichsbank requested that the limit for gold purchases should be increased from 70 to 105 million kronor. The Riksbank did not want to take this responsibility and Rooth again referred the matter to the Government. On 22 February, the Government informed, through the head of the Ministry for Foreign Affair's Trade Department, Gunnar Hägglöf, that the Riksbank should comply with the German demand for further gold transactions but that it was wished to "avoid an official request to the German Reichsbank". Hägglöf writes:

> "...Instead bank director Jacob Wallenberg, who is a member of the Swedish government Inquiry, on a visit to the German deputy-governor of the Reichsbank, Puhl, on 18 February 1943 informally put forward the wish that no gold bars originating from occupied countries were to be included in deliveries to Sveriges Riksbank. Herr Puhl said that he was glad that the Swedish points of view had been put to him personally and not in an official manner, in which case the matter could have been insoluble. Puhl declared that he was willing to personally ensure that no gold from occupied countries was included in future deliveries to Sweden. On a visit to Puhl the following day, he informed that he had already made the necessary arrangements..."

Rooth has made a report on the matter to the Board of Governors already on 18 February 1943, but it was not minuted. According to Rooth's own notes, the Board of Governors considered that "the Government dismissed the risks rather lightly". On 23 February, the Board of Governors agreed that a paragraph should be included in the minutes for the 19th according to which the Board of Governors approved Rooth's proposal to increase purchases of gold from the Reichsbank.

The period after the allied declaration in January 1943

In summer 1943 Weber of the Swiss National Bank wrote to Rooth and stated that he had received information that it had been stated on the British radio that the Swedish government had prohibited import of gold from abroad. Weber wanted an explanation. Rooth informed Weber that no such import prohibition had been issued but that the Riksbank naturally had misgivings over taking possession of gold for other reasons than foreign exchange policy. Rooth stated, however, that he personally considered that the greatest caution was called for.

In a special declaration of 22 February 1944, issued by the Americans, British and Soviet ministries of finance, the neutral countries were warned about transaction with respect to looted monetary gold; the so-called gold declaration. On 25 February 1944 the declaration was handed over to the Governor of the Riksbank Rooth for information.

Due to an enquiry from the Reichsbank on taking possession of further gold the Board of Governors noted in March 1944 that the Riksbank had made use of 96 million of the 105 million kronor in gold that the Riksbank had declared itself willing to accept from the Reichsbank. Due to the allied declaration of 22 February 1944, the Board of Governors decided to inform the Reichsbank that the Riksbank could not accept any more gold but that the bank would possibly be willing to take over Swiss francs instead within the framework of the previously set limit.

However, the Reichsbank wanted the Riksbank to accept gold for the remaining amount. Puhl offered during a visit to Stockholm 20–22 June 1944 that the gold delivery could take place in the form of Scandinavian gold coins, that had been in the possession of the Reichsbank since the period before the outbreak of the war, and German gold coins that the Reichsbank had possessed since 1923–24. After the Government had informally declared that it had nothing to object to the Riksbank complying with the request, the Board of Governors decided that the Riksbank should accept gold in the form of Swedish and German gold coins up to an amount of 9.1 million kronor.

On 21 June 1944 Rooth made the following note:

> "...The Scandinavian gold coins not from Jews or the like which would not be approved by the Allies..."

In Wessman's archives there is a document with an arrival stamp in March 1944 from which it emerges that the Riksbank estimated "Maximum risk" and "Risk-free" with respect to gold that had been purchased from the Reichsbank after the outbreak of war on 1 September 1939. "Maximum risk", which was calculated at over 20,000 kg, referred to approximately 16,000 kg gold that had been exchanged for gold in Switzerland, approximately 1,000 kg gold that had been taken to Sweden, which was on sale to industry, and approximately 1,500 kg gold that had been sold to the Swiss National Bank. Subsequently, approximately 1,500 kg German gold coins to be acquired during 1944 had been added. On the document, which is typed, notations have been made, *inter alia*. "Maximum risk" and "Risk-free" have been noted in ink.

In August 1944 Jacob Wallenberg notified Rooth that a financial director of the company Otto Wolff had asked Wallenberg whether the Germans could be permitted to sell to 20 million kronor worth of gold. According to Wallenberg, Puhl had explained that the Germans would provide a guarantee that the gold had belonged to Germany since long before the present war. Wallenberg considered that it would be in the country's interests if German bonds could be replaced by gold. Rooth informed Dag Hammarskjöld that he was personally against the Riksbank purchasing gold to be used in payment for bonds.

> "…However, one could conceive of a possibility, by which individual Swedes purchased gold and were allowed to keep it until peace had been concluded so that it could be seen whether the gold could be used…"

In September 1944 Rooth stated in a letter to Per Jacobsson that many central banks did not want to buy gold in Europe or at other places in the world before peace had been declared where there was a risk of receiving "tainted gold".

At the Bretton Woods conference in summer 1944, the Allies adopted resolution no.VI, according to which issues were taken up regarding the enemy's property in neutral states. This resolution was handed over to the Swedish government in October the same year. Rooth informed the deputy governor of the Riksbank Böök of the content in a note from the Allies and said *inter alia*:

> "…The Allies say that they have proof that Germany's "pre-war gold stocks" are exhausted and that Germany consequently now only has "looted gold" (the conclusion is not completely correct. Germany can have sold the gold that was "looted" or a part of it and consequently still have some of its "pre-war stocks")…"

APPENDIX

The following tables form a summary of the German gold left in depot "Gold deposited with Schweizererische Nationalbank" as at 22 January 1945.

German gold left in depot "Gold deposited with Schweizererische Nationalbank" as at 22 January 1945

Purchase recorded in general ledger	Weight dated	ID number according to weight list		Fineness interval	Fine weight of weight list		As per requirements from		Similarities with Dutch remelted coins	Other gold
		lowest	highest		per page	total lot	the Netherlands	Belgium		
16 Nov 42	11 Nov 42	1565/2B	1565/17B	900,0	189,10413					
16 Nov 42	11 Nov 42	1565/18B	1565/27B	900,0						
16 Nov 42	11 Nov 42	1566/1B	1566/10B	900,0	235,20495					
16 Nov 42	11 Nov 42	1566/11B	1566/27B	900,2						
16 Nov 42	11 Nov 42	1567/1B	1567/3B	900,2	236,04180					
16 Nov 42	11 Nov 42	1567/4B	1567/23B	900,2	235,88522					
16 Nov 42	11 Nov 42	1567/24B	1567/27B	900,1						
16 Nov 42	11 Nov 42	1568/1B	1568/16B	900,1	238,93490					
16 Nov 42	11 Nov 42	1568/17B	1568/28B	900,1						
16 Nov 42	11 Nov 42	1569/1B	1569/25B	900,1	240,96839					
16 Nov 42	11 Nov 42	1569/9B		900,1						
16 Nov 42	11 Nov 42	1570/1B	1570/3B	900,1	243,68468					
16 Nov 42	11 Nov 42	1570/4B	1570/23B	900,1	238,91356					
16 Nov 42	11 Nov 42	1570/24B	1570/25B	900,1						
16 Nov 42	11 Nov 42	1571/1B	1571/18B	900,1	234,58721					
16 Nov 42	11 Nov 42	1571/19B	1571/30B	900,1						
16 Nov 42	11 Nov 42	1572/1B	1572/8B	900,0	236,56410					
16 Nov 42	11 Nov 42	1572/9B	1572/25B	900,0						
16 Nov 42	11 Nov 42	1573/1B	1573/3B	900,0	237,41046					
16 Nov 42	11 Nov 42	1573/4B	1573/23B	900,0	235,93707					
16 Nov 42	11 Nov 42	1573/24B	1573/25B	900,0						
16 Nov 42	11 Nov 42	1574/1B	1574/18B	900,0	235,92006					
16 Nov 42	11 Nov 42	1574/19B	1574/29B	900,0						
16 Nov 42	11 Nov 42	1575/1B	1575/9B	900,0	235,65924					
16 Nov 42	11 Nov 42	1575/10B	1575/27B	900,0						
16 Nov 42	11 Nov 42	1576/1B	1576/2B	900,0	236,53602					
16 Nov 42	11 Nov 42	1603/3B	1603/22B	899,9	235,25687					
16 Nov 42	11 Nov 42	1603/23B	1603/27B	899,9						
16 Nov 42	11 Nov 42	1604/1B	1604/16B	900,0	250,88192	3,997,49058	3,997,49058 (The lot refers to remelted Dutch coins according to Wessman)			

German gold left in depot "Gold deposited with Schweizerische Nationalbank" as at 22 January 1945

Purchase recorded in general ledger	Weight dated	ID number according to weight list		Fineness interval	Fine weight of weight list		As per requirements from		Similarities with Dutch remelted coins	Other gold
		lowest	highest		per page	total lot	the Netherlands	Belgium		
25 Jan 43	20 Jan 43	30838	30843	997,9						71,27451
25 Jan 43	20 Jan 43	AA8245	AA8.258	997,6	233,40137		162,12686			
25 Jan 43	20 Jan 43	AA8.259	AA8263	997,6						
25 Jan 43	20 Jan 43	AA8226	AA8.240	997,9	233,62061		233,62061			
25 Jan 43	20 Jan 43	AA8.241	AA8.244	997,9			47,30145			
25 Jan 43	20 Jan 43	AA9,628	AA9.643	995,5	231,78322		184,48177			
25 Jan 43	20 Jan 43	AA8.224	AA8.225	997,4			23,77951			
25 Jan 43	20 Jan 43	30826	30827	997,9						23,67118
25 Jan 43	20 Jan 43	AC2,792	AC2794	999,6			38,35945			
25 Jan 43	20 Jan 43	AC2.801	AC2.803	999,6			37,71541			
25 Jan 43	20 Jan 43	C9.644		999,7			12,74468			
25 Jan 43	20 Jan 43	C9.668		999,7			11,90543			
25 Jan 43	20 Jan 43	C9,670		999,7			12,24033			
25 Jan 43	20 Jan 43	76627	76623	999,9	245,38689		84,97090			
25 Jan 43	20 Jan 43	30,833	30,837	997,9	59,52184	1,003,71393				59,52184
30 Jan 43	27 Jan 43	12918	12925	997,4						94,83829
30 Jan 43	27 Jan 43	39,286	39,297	997,5	239,96128		145,12299			
30 Jan 43	27 Jan 43	32,298	32,303	997,5			73,89330			
30 Jan 43	27 Jan 43	39,265	39,277	996,9-997,0			154,51531			
30 Jan 43	27 Jan 43	6,089		996,9	240,18948					11,78087
30 Jan 43	27 Jan 43	6,087		996,9						11,87457
30 Jan 43	27 Jan 43	6,090		996,9						11,88145
30 Jan 43	27 Jan 43	6,317		996,9						11,86959
30 Jan 43	27 Jan 43	6,093		996,9						11,95931
30 Jan 43	27 Jan 43	6,095		996,9						11,91345
30 Jan 43	27 Jan 43	6,091		996,9						11,66323
30 Jan 43	27 Jan 43	22,272		996,3						12,60569
30 Jan 43	27 Jan 43	75,647		997,3						11,98705
30 Jan 43	27 Jan 43	8,331		995,8						11,42183

German gold left in depot "Gold deposited with Schweizerische Nationalbank" as at 22 January 1945

Purchase recorded in general ledger	Weight dated	ID number according to weight list		Fineness interval	Fine weight of weight list		As per requirements from		Similarities with Dutch remelted coins	Other gold
		lowest	highest		per page	total lot	the Netherlands	Belgium		
30 Jan 43	27 Jan 43	R227	R229	997,0			37,53794			
30 Jan 43	27 Jan 43	T8413	T8,417	996,2–996,6			62,71135			
30 Jan 43	27 Jan 43	T9,761	T9,763	997,3	244,96234		37,53688			
30 Jan 43	27 Jan 43	12,913	12,917	997,4						59,41962
30 Jan 43	27 Jan 43	S9,041		999,9			12,51645			
30 Jan 43	27 Jan 43	SS324		999,0			12,72027			
30 Jan 43	27 Jan 43	SA2,339	SA2,340	999,8			25,00809			
30 Jan 43	27 Jan 43	SA2,345		999,8			12,50030			
30 Jan 43	27 Jan 43	AD2,889		997,8			12,52389			
30 Jan 43	27 Jan 43	AC9,067		999,9			12,53025			
30 Jan 43	27 Jan 43	S8,8898		999,8			12,50950			
30 Jan 43	27 Jan 43	U2,195	U2,200	996,0			75,24213			
30 Jan 43	27 Jan 43	92,128	92,129	997,0			25,07405			
30 Jan 43	27 Jan 43	S9,005		999,8	272,59004	997,70314	12,54549			
16 Feb 43	15 Feb 43	2031/6B	2031/26B	900,0	276,46800					
16 Feb 43	15 Feb 43	2032/1B	2032/2B	900,2	242,01957					
16 Feb 43	15 Feb 43	2032/3B	2032/22B	900,2						
16 Feb 43	15 Feb 43	2032/23B		900,2						
16 Feb 43	15 Feb 43	2033/1B	2033/19B	900,2	240,46819					
16 Feb 43	15 Feb 43	2033/20B	2033/25B	900,2						
16 Feb 43	15 Feb 43	2034/1B	2034/14B	900,1	239,33254	998,28830	998,28830 (the lot refers to remelted Dutch coins according to Wessman)			
22 Feb 43	19 Feb 43	2024/25B	2024/26B	900,2	239,36865					
22 Feb 43	19 Feb 43	2025/1B	2025/18B	900,2						
22 Feb 43	19 Feb 43	2025/19B	2025/27B	900,2						
22 Feb 43	19 Feb 43	2026/1B	2026/11B	900,3	237,48107					
22 Feb 43	19 Feb 43	2026/12B	2026/22B	900,3	130,04564					
22 Feb 43	19 Feb 43	2026/23B	2026/27B	900,3						
22 Feb 43	19 Feb 43	2027/1B	2027/15B	900,2	232,44925					
22 Feb 43	19 Feb 43	2027/16B	2027/27B	900,2						

German gold left in depot "Gold deposited with Schweizerische Nationalbank" as at 22 January 1945

Purchase recorded in general ledger	Weight dated	ID number according to weight list		Fineness interval	Fine weight of weight list		As per requirements from		Similarities with Dutch remelted coins	Other gold
		lowest	highest		per page	total lot	the Netherlands	Belgium		
22 Feb 43	19 Feb 43	2028/1B		900,2						
22 Feb 43	19 Feb 43	2024/24B		900,2	166,02217	1.005,36678	1.005,36678			The lot refers to remelted Dutch coins according to Wessman
17 Apr 43	15 Apr 43	1982/10B	1982/27B	900,2						
17 Apr 43	15 Apr 43	1983/1B	1983/2B	900,2	239,82389				239,82389	
17 Apr 43	15 Apr 43	1984/16B	1984/25B	900,1						
17 Apr 43	15 Apr 43	1985/1B	1985/10B	900,3	237,53406				237,53406	
17 Apr 43	15 Apr 43	882/18B	882/26B	900,4						
17 Apr 43	15 Apr 43	883/1B	883/14B	900,3	274,29496			274,29496		
17 Apr 43	15 Apr 43	883/15B	883/26B	900,3						
17 Apr 43	15 Apr 43	884/1B	884/10B	900,3	258,51609	1,010,16900		258,51609		
21 May 43	20 May 43	1972/21B		900,1						
21 May 43	20 May 43	1973/2B		900,2						
21 May 43	20 May 43	1973/5B	1973/6B	900,2						
21 May 43	20 May 43	1973/8B	1973/9B	900,2						
21 May 43	20 May 43	1976/14B		900,1						
21 May 43	20 May 43	1976/17B	1976/18B	900,1						
21 May 43	20 May 43	1976/24B	1976/25B	900,1						
21 May 43	20 May 43	1977/1B	1977/9B	900,0	238,07223				238,07223	
21 May 43	20 May 43	1977/10B	1977/20B	900,0					130,06782	
21 May 43	20 May 43	2040/18B	2040/25B	900,0					94,51044	
21 May 43	20 May 43	2041/1B	2041/4B	900,2	271,92986	510,00209			47,35160	
5 Jun 43	2 Jun 43	903/2B	903/21B	900,3	238,55879					
5 Jun 43	2 Jun 43	904/15B	904/17B	900,4						
5 Jun 43	2 Jun 43	904/19B	904/22B	900,4						
5 Jun 43	2 Jun 43	904/24B	904/26B	900,4						
5 Jun 43	2 Jun 43	905/1B	905/8B	900,4						
5 Jun 43	2 Jun 43	909/3B		900,4						
5 Jun 43	2 Jun 43	909/11B		900,3						

Gold deposited with Schweizerische Nationalbank" as at 22 January 1945

German gold left in depot "Gold deposited with Schweizerische Nationalbank" as at 22 January 1945

Purchase recorded in general ledger	Weight dated	ID number according to weight list		Fineness interval	Fine weight of weight list		As per requirements from		Similarities with Dutch remelted coins	Other gold
		lowest	highest		per page	total lot	the Netherlands	Belgium		
5 Jun 43	2 Jun 43	909/13B		900,3						
5 Jun 43	2 Jun 43	909/17B		900,3	261,44543	500,00422		500,00422		
17 Jul 43	14 Jul 43	820/20B	820/21B	916,6				12,39793		
17 Jul 43	14 Jul 43	820/22B	820/25B	916,6				73,51718		
17 Jul 43	14 Jul 43	821/1B	821/14B	916,4	241,92196					
17 Jul 43	14 Jul 43	821/15B	821/26B	916,4						
17 Jul 43	14 Jul 43	822/1B	822/8B	916,4	237,49853			237,49853		
17 Jul 43	14 Jul 43	848/7B	848/8B	916,4	23,57998	503,00047		23,57998		
Of the lot, the following ingots have been disposed of:										
		820/20B	820/20B		(11,83101)					
		820/22B	820/25B		(47,53918)					
		821/3B	821/4B		(24,41821)					
		821/7B	821/12B		(72,21845)	(156,00685)				
31 Jul 43	28 Jul 43	992/18B	992/28B	997,7	256,20450			256,20450		
31 Jul 43	28 Jul 43	993/1B	993/9	997,4						
31 Jul 43	28 Jul 43	994/1B	994/18B	998,3						
31 Jul 43	28 Jul 43	J3,847	J3,848	995,1	245,44404	501,64854	24,64842	220,79562		
20 Aug 43	17 Aug 43	931/1B	931/20B	997,4	249,57503					
20 Aug 43	17 Aug 43	931/21B	931/26B	997,4						
20 Aug 43	17 Aug 43	932/1B	932/14B	996,8	250,43990					
20 Aug 43	17 Aug 43	932/15B	932/28B	996,8						
20 Aug 43	17 Aug 43	933/1B	933/6B	977,1	251,28709					
20 Aug 43	17 Aug 43	933/7B	933/26B	997,1	250,26403	1,001,56605		1,001,56605		
21 Sep 43	21 Sep 43	929/2		998,4						
21 Sep 43	21 Sep 43	929/4		998,4						
21 Sep 43	21 Sep 43	929/6	929/8	998,4						
21 Sep 43	21 Sep 43	929/11	929/15	998,4						

German gold left in depot "Gold deposited with Schweizererische Nationalbank" as at 22 January 1945

Purchase recorded in general ledger	Weight dated	ID number according to weight list		Fineness interval	Fine weight of weight list		As per requirements from		Similarities with Dutch remelted coins	Other gold
		lowest	highest		per page	total lot	the Netherlands	Belgium		
21 Sep 43	21 Sep 43	929/20	929/23	998,4						
21 Sep 43	21 Sep 43	929/27		998,4						
21 Sep 43	21 Sep 43	930/2		996,2						
21 Sep 43	21 Sep 43	930/5		996,2	210,01086	210,01086		210,01086		
01 Dec 43	25 Nov 43	872/28	872/29	995,8						
01 Dec 43	25 Nov 43	873/1	873/12	995,9						
01 Dec 43	25 Nov 43	873/13	873/28	995,9						
01 Dec 43	25 Nov 43	1447/1	1447/4	995,9	175,69780					
01 Dec 43	25 Nov 43	1447/5	1447/24	995,9	247,80234					
01 Dec 43	25 Nov 43	1447/25	1447/28	995,9	247,75065					
01 Dec 43	25 Nov 43	1448/1	1448/16	996,1	246,74073					
01 Dec 43	25 Nov 43	1448/17	1448/23	996,1	86,56428	1,004,55580		1,004,55580		
04 Dec 43	29 Nov 43	ND912	ND919	995,5–995,8	100,35027					100,35027
04 Dec 43	29 Nov 43	863/6	863/26	996,0	257,10286			257,10286		
04 Dec 43	29 Nov 43	864/18	864/31	995,7						
04 Dec 43	29 Nov 43	865/1	865/6	996,5	246,78843			246,78843		
04 Dec 43	29 Nov 43	865/7	865/26	996,5	250,73368			250,73368		
04 Dec 43	29 Nov 43	866/19	866/30	996,6						
04 Dec 43	29 Nov 43	867/1	867/8	996,9	247,09326			247,09326		
04 Dec 43	29 Nov 43	867/9	867/28	996,9	247,56725			247,56725		
04 Dec 43	29 Nov 43	867/29		996,9						
04 Dec 43	29 Nov 43	868/1	868/19	997,3	247,97916			247,97916		
04 Dec 43	29 Nov 43	868/20	868/29	997,3						
04 Dec 43	29 Nov 43	869/1	869/10	997,1	249,42422			249,42422		
04 Dec 43	29 Nov 43	869/11	869/30	997,1	248,57842	2,095,63755		248,57842		
22 Dec 43	22 Dec 43	977/20		999,4				11,78393		
22 Dec 43	22 Dec 43	845/14		996,6				76,34375		
22 Dec 43	22 Dec 43	R2349	R2356	997,9–998,8	188,57807	188,57807				100,45039

German gold left in depot "Gold deposited with Schweizererische Nationalbank" as at 22 January 1945

Purchase recorded in general ledger	Weight dated	ID number according to weight list		Fineness interval	Fine weight of weight list		As per requirements from		Similarities with Dutch remelted coins	Other gold
		lowest	highest		per page	total lot	the Netherlands	Belgium		
17 Jan 44	17 Jan 44	1431/7	1431/26	996,3	250,79201					
17 Jan 44	17 Jan 44	1431/27	1431/29	996,3						
17 Jan 44	17 Jan 44	1432/1	1432/17	996,9	246,72957					
17 Jan 44	17 Jan 44	1432/18	1432/29	996,9						
17 Jan 44	17 Jan 44	1433/1	1433/8	996,5	244,65437					
17 Jan 44	17 Jan 44	1433/9	1433/28	996,5						
17 Jan 44	854/10			996,1	256,79391	998,96986		998,96986		
Total						16,370,69839	7,599,52867	7,155,32654	987,36004	628,48314

Lot sold in Sweden, acquired on 8 December 1942.
The lot is accounted for in Appendix A under the heading "Gold recorded as purchases"   1,008,04860

Original Dutch demand   8,607,57727

SWITZERLAND

Switzerland – World War II

INDEPENDENT COMMISSION OF EXPERTS

Ascona Declaration

DECLARATION OF THE PARTICIPANTS AT THE ASCONA MEETING

On 28/29 October 1997, an Informal Working Meeting of historical fact-finding commissions and research groups took place in Ascona, Switzerland. The meeting, which was organised by the Independent Commission: Switzerland – World War II chaired by Prof. Jean-François Bergier, was attended by nearly thirty historians and archivists from ten countries (Argentina, Belgium, Canada, France, the Netherlands, Portugal, Sweden, Switzerland, UK and USA).

Despite the diversity of mandates and the difference in composition of the commissions and research groups, common problems and challenges were acknowledged by all participants. Considering the need for co-ordination and cooperation from both a pragmatic and practical point of view, a variety of measures that could increase the efficiency of the ongoing research were identified, *inter alia:*

- the publication of a booklet containing the mandate, members and researchers, time-frames and telephone/fax plus e-mail addresses of the different commissions/research groups;
- the publication and exchange of special finding aids on archival documents relevant for the topics of these commissions/research groups;
- the set-up of www-homepages by the commissions/research groups with indications on the links between themselves;
- bilateral and multilateral exchange of information on specific topics, including contents and access conditions to archives, exchange of non-restricted documents, sharing of definitions and standards, as well as advice on methodology;
- the holding of special meetings aimed at comparing notes and trying to reach common interpretation in specific areas.

In order to carry out the research and to achieve the aims specified in the respective mandates, some prerequisites must be fulfilled. The participants stressed the crucial importance of unrestricted access to archival sources both in public and private archives relevant to their research. They therefore appeal to both governments and private organisations, enterprises and other private groups to grant access to relevant documents. They also underline the importance of favourable working conditions in archives in general and adequate photocopying facilities in particular, in order to expedite the huge amount of research work that needs to be accomplished.

In this respect, they ask governments, members of parliament, politicians, representatives of NGOs and society at large for their understanding of the complexities and difficulties involved with this type of fact-finding concerning events that happened more than 50 years ago. Historical research requires a thorough review and analysis of thousands and millions of documents which inevitably is time-consuming and difficult. It is evident that comprehensive and serious studies cannot generate immediate results, but rather need time to be carried out. On the other hand, the historians at Ascona recognised the importance and urgency of their research to the ongoing international dialogue regarding the responsibilities of governments and people to acknowledge the events of 50 years ago and their efforts to render justice for victims where possible.

The participants view the Ascona Meeting as a first step in an international process of dialogue, co-ordination and cooperation. This process is open to all commissions and research groups willing and able to participate in and contribute to the ongoing process of historical fact-finding in this area. The participants will consult, co-ordinate and co-operate bilaterally and informally in areas of common interest. They agree to consider holding another informal working meeting at the beginning of summer 1998, for the purpose of broadening and deepening their cooperation in an informal and pragmatic manner.

Address by Ambassador Thomas G. Borer

HEAD OF THE TASK FORCE SWITZERLAND – WORLD WAR II

I would like to begin by expressing my great pleasure that this Conference is being held and that my country has been invited as an active participant. It is an honour for me to be here and I would like to thank the British Government for making this important event possible. My country sees this Conference as a unique opportunity for all those concerned to pool their knowledge on this subject and to work together to achieve a deeper understanding of the historical questions still awaiting answers. The task of establishing historical facts on these extremely delicate and complex issues is colossal and requires close international co-operation. We sincerely hope that the Conference will make a major contribution to clarifying the historical context of gold transactions and elucidating their complex nature.

Tragically, the passage of time is irreversible. However, we can still go beyond noble utterances and demonstrate our solidarity with the survivors by expressing our respect and compassion in more practical terms. Switzerland did not participate in the Holocaust. Nevertheless the memory of the victims and the sufferings of the survivors place a duty on us to keep remembering, for our conscious awareness of the mechanisms of history and of the roots of human evil is all we have to protect us against a resurgence of such monstrous insanity.

Personally, I have absolute confidence that the London Conference will offer us the opportunity to pursue a constructive dialogue on how to advance in harmony towards a greater understanding of our common past. The study of history has been the sole preserve of academia for too long. It is now high time that governments devote appropriate attention to what we can learn from history. My country has been the target of widespread criticism and questions over recent months. We are now in the process of meeting the challenge ahead with courage and determination. The demand for greater understanding has now gone beyond the bounds of the academic, economic and political spheres in Switzerland. An in-depth debate has taken root throughout our society as well as in the media, schools and universities – something my Government is proud to point out.

This Conference stands as evidence of the work being done by historians around the world to fill the gaps in our knowledge of Nazi Germany's gold transactions and to place these in an accurate context. It is not my intention to speak for the historians but before handing over to Professor Jean-Francois Bergier, Chairman of the Independent Commission of Experts, it nevertheless seems necessary to me to mention briefly three important points of historical relevance.

Firstly, Switzerland's situation during World War II differed from that of the other neutral and non-belligerent states due to its total encirclement by the Axis powers. This fact placed Switzerland in a state of absolute dependence on

Germany's good will for its supplies. Faced with the military threat of the Third Reich, Switzerland had recourse to all the instruments of dissuasion which its precarious geo-political situation imposed on it. The mobilisation of its army, strict respect for its neutrality, as well as maintaining the economic and financial channels with Germany – at all times the principal economic partner of Switzerland – were the essential elements in this.

Secondly, Switzerland is often thought to have kept the gold which it acquired from Germany. In fact the major part of the gold delivered by the Reichsbank did not stay at the SNB, but was transferred onwards to other European central banks either to pay for Swiss imports or because these banks demanded that Swiss francs received from Germany be converted into gold. By the end of the War, the SNB had thus resold almost all of the gold it had acquired from the Reichsbank, mainly to other European central banks. The gold transactions were not carried out with the aim of enriching the SNB. The latter recently assessed the profits realised through transactions with Germany during the War at around 20 million Swiss francs at 1945 values.

The third point concerns the prevailing idea that the SNB traded principally with Germany. It has been known for a long time that the SNB was the main purchaser of gold from the Reichsbank. But the fact is that the SNB did business with the central banks of 16 countries. It may come as a surprise to find that it bought much more gold from the Allies than from the Axis powers: to be specific, the SNB bought gold valued at Sfr. 1.8 billion from the Allies compared to Sfr. 1.4 billion from the Axis powers.

For Switzerland, German gold became a vital means of paying for its imports from Romania, Hungary, Portugal and Turkey. From 1941 onwards, Switzerland was unable to use the gold it purchased from the Allies due to the freeze placed on its gold reserves deposited in New York, Ottawa and London. At the beginning of 1942, a Swiss request to unblock its gold accounts was vetoed by the American State Department. This attitude, albeit comprehensible, contributed to reinforcing Switzerland's dependence on the Third Reich which, as we all know, had completely encircled our country.

The large volume of gold transactions was carried out by the SNB for one crucial reason: the Swiss franc had become the only universally accepted means of international payment. The belligerent nations thus needed Swiss francs to enable them to finance, among other things, their espionage operations, imports of Swiss products and of strategically important raw materials such as tungsten and manganese metals for which the exporting countries would only accept payment in gold or Swiss francs.

For obvious reasons this trade in gold between Switzerland and Germany angered the Allies. Were the Swiss authorities aware of this? By 1943, certainly. The SNB's gold purchases from Germany peaked in 1942, diminished somewhat in 1943 and fell off dramatically the following year. But the Swiss authorities insisted that they were unable to curtail them completely for reasons of neutrality as well as out of fear of German retaliation. In particular, Switzerland feared a total halt to German deliveries of coal on which the country was dependent for its economic survival. The Swiss therefore let the Allies know that they should bring pressure to bear on countries exporting strategic raw materials to Germany which were under far less direct Nazi military threat, to the effect that they should stop supplying Germany.

In many respects, comparing the gold transactions that Switzerland carried out with the Allies in the same light as those with the Axis powers shocks us nowadays. Our moral sense no longer tolerates the idea of coldly balancing off one set of figures representing financial support for the forces of democracy against another set representing dealings with the Nazi regime. But in Switzerland during the war years, the question was not seen in these terms, although the sentiment of the Swiss population was massively pro-Allied. Instead, Switzerland kept to the strictly legalistic attitude which had ensured its survival through the centuries. Such a stance also enjoyed the backing of international law which at the time was profoundly influenced by *realpolitik*. Switzerland thus responded to the imperatives of its geographical and military vulnerability combined with an unquestioning wish to protect its population from the horrors of world conflict.

Since last year, Switzerland has been implementing an unprecedented series of measures to come to terms with the painful and recurring questions which have remained unanswered since 1945. Our objective is to shed all possible light on the role Switzerland played in the context of World War II and to bring about the restitution of dormant assets still held in Swiss financial institutions. Switzerland has also demonstrated its profound sense of compassion towards the survivors of the worst tragedy in the history of human kind by setting up a humanitarian fund endowed with Sfr. 275 million. The first payment from the Fund to needy victims of the Holocaust in Eastern Europe was made on November 18 this year in Riga. This event, which my country was proud to witness, constituted the first stage of a wide-ranging programme whose efforts are being concentrated initially on the countries of Central and Eastern Europe. The programme is being implemented in close co-operation with the World Jewish Restitution Organisation, local Jewish communities and organisations of Holocaust survivors.

By focusing all its efforts on carrying out these measures efficiently and rapidly, Switzerland has demonstrated an unambiguous and profound commitment to dealing with this issue. To this end, my country has created direct links with the NGOs concerned whose co-operation is essential to ensure success.

The obviously international dimension of the complex question of financial transactions underlines the need for the London Conference. In this context, it must be unequivocally acknowledged that the commercial dealings with Germany carried out by all neutral and non-belligerent countries, and the financial transactions, are two sides of the same coin. It is therefore essential that all countries concerned work together with the aim of facilitating historical research, in particular through ensuring unrestricted access to all the relevant archives, and encouraging co-operation between the various institutions and commissions involved. I am pleased to announce that Switzerland will make a constructive proposal on the third day of this Conference with the aim of supporting and enhancing historical research, bearing in mind that the success of the latter is, in our view, the condition *sine qua non* for a future that will not merely be a sad repetition of past mistakes.

My Government would like to take the opportunity of expressing the very strong hope that our discussions over the next three days will be held in a spirit of openness and objectivity, and that they will mark the first step in the desired direction.

Measures taken by Switzerland relating to the problem of Nazi gold and unclaimed assets

Switzerland has taken a number of constructive steps in response to the recent discussion on its role during and immediately following World War II, as an expression of the three principles: *truth, justice and solidarity.*

Office for Unclaimed Assets headed by the Ombudsman for the Swiss banks (Swiss Bankers Association (SBA))

After the adoption of the September 8, 1995 guidelines on handling unreported Swiss bank accounts, deposits and safety-deposit boxes, the Swiss Bankers Association carried out an investigation of bank accounts opened before 8 May 1945 and dormant for more than 10 years. This led to the creation of a claims office headed by the bank's ombudsman. To date, the ombudsman has discovered about CHF.17 million in Swiss banks of which CHF.10 million belongs to Holocaust victims.

On 23 July and 29 October 1997 the SBA released the lists of unclaimed accounts opened before 1945 by both Swiss and foreign nationals. The list of accounts and other information is available on the World Wide Web (http://www/dormantaccounts.ch) or at ATAG Ernst & Young offices in New York, Tel Aviv, Basle, Budapest, and Sydney. The list published in July concerns more than 1700 accounts opened by foreign nationals with a total value of CHF 60.2 million. The October list contains the unclaimed accounts opened by Swiss nationals, amounting to CHF 12.84 million. This list also includes an update on accounts opened by non-Swiss nationals, containing about 3,500 names, with a total value of CHF 6 million.

An independent Claims Resolution Foundation has been set up to provide an international, independent and objective forum to adjudicate claims to dormant accounts. To hear claims under relaxed standards of proof that recognise the difficulty of presenting evidence in the tragic circumstances of the Holocaust and World War II, up to 15 foreign and Swiss arbitrators with experience in international adjudication will preside over a fast-track procedure, cost-free to claimants.

Independent Committee of Eminent Persons (ICEP – Volcker Committee)

The ICEP was created on 2 May 1996 by a Memorandum of Understanding between the SBA on one hand and the World Jewish Restitution Organisation (WJRO) and World Jewish Congress (WJC) on the other. It is chaired by Paul

Volcker and consists of six members, of whom three are named by the SBA and three by the WJRO/WJC. The ICEP sets as its goal *to identify all unclaimed assets in Swiss banks deposited by victims of the Nazis* which have not been reported to date. This investigation will also seek to determine if accounts have been closed, either by oversight, intentionally, in violation of legal regulations or auditing obligations.

The ICEP has engaged three auditing firms authorised by the Federal Banking Commission (Arthur Andersen, KPMG Peat Marwick, and Price Waterhouse). These three firms are bound by professional confidentiality and have unlimited access to the bank's books and archives. The auditing firms' inquiries extend to the effectiveness of the SBA guidelines, the ombudsman's methodology, and the manner in which the forms conveyed by the ombudsman to the banks are processed. The ICEP reports to federal authorities on all violations it observes, on any discovery of assets stolen by the Nazis and deposited in Switzerland, and generally on any element of importance to studies by the Independent Commission of Experts.

Independent Commission of Experts ("Bergier Commission")

The Bergier Commission was set up on December 13, 1996 to look into the *general problem of unclaimed assets of Nazi victims as well as the question of assets deposited by the Nazi regime and its intermediaries in Switzerland*. It is also investigating the issue of stolen art treasures, gold transactions with the Reichsbank and Swiss refugee policy during this period. In addition, it may broaden its area of research, either on its own initiative or by extension of its mandate. These research tasks extend to banks, insurance companies and intermediaries (auditors, lawyers, notaries etc.) as well as the Swiss National Bank (SNB). Finally this commission also examines measures taken by federal officials in this regard since 1945. The Commission has access to all data it may deem useful, including that normally protected by Swiss banking secrecy. The Federal Council will transmit directly to the individuals concerned all information uncovered by the Commission which could be used as the basis for a claim to inheritance.

The Independent Commission of Experts is under the chairmanship of Prof. J.-F. Bergier and numbers nine members in all – eight historians and one legal expert. Four members originate from foreign countries (USA, Great Britain, Israel and Poland). It has engaged around 30 researchers in Switzerland and abroad. The Commission assumed its task at the beginning of March 1997. The Commission will release two intermediate reports. The first on the Swiss National Bank's gold transactions should appear in January 1998. The second on refugee policy will be made public in the spring of 1998.

In October 1997, the Commission organised an international conference in which 30 to 40 experts from about 10 countries participated. The main goal of this conference was an exchange of views and discussion about archival data between members of various national commissions.

Swiss Fund for Needy Victims of the Holocaust/Shoah

The **Swiss Fund for Needy Victims of the Holocaust/***Shoah* was established by decree on February 26, 1997. The object of the Fund is *to support needy people who were persecuted* for racist, religious, political or other reasons *or became victims in other ways of the Holocaust/Shoah*. It applies to their needy descendants as well.

The Fund is not concerned with individual applications for support. These should be directed to institutions and relief organisations for potential recipients of support who, for their part, can submit applications for support to the Fund.

At the current time the Fund is capitalised at CHF 270 million which the three major Swiss banks, others in the private sector, and the Swiss National Bank (SNB) have made available to it.

The Fund Executive Board announced the immediate release of CHF 17 million as a first instalment destined for "double victims" – people living in Central and Eastern European countries who were victims of both Nazi oppression and the Communist regimes. The first distribution to 80 needy survivors of the Holocaust in Latvia took place on 18 November 1997.

Distribution of the money in Latvia and in the rest of Central and Eastern Europe is occurring through a comprehensive WJRO programme carried out in close cooperation with local Jewish communities and survivors' organisations as well as those representing the interests of non-Jewish Holocaust victims.

The Hug/Perrenoud Report

On October 23, 1996, the Federal Council requested that the Federal Department of Foreign Affairs issue an immediate mandate to a small group of experts. The group was directed to proceed at the shortest possible notice with in-depth research on compensation agreements between Switzerland and Eastern European countries with the objective of accelerating research currently being undertaken on the subject. Historians Peter Hug and Marc Perrenoud published their report on December 19, 1996. The lists of account holders involved in these agreements were sent to these countries – in particular Poland and Hungary.

The Federal Department of Foreign Affairs Task Force

The Task Force (http://www/switzerland.taskforce.ch) was set up on the decision of the Federal Council on October 23, 1996. It is an integral part of the Federal Department of Foreign Affairs. It comprises around 25 members and is headed by Ambassador Thomas Borer.

The Task Force's mission is to initiate promptly and in a co-ordinated manner at federal-authority level all measures relating to the complex field of assets which found their way into Switzerland as a result of National Socialist tyranny. It establishes contacts with people from all walks of life and all organisations concerned with this issue, both in Switzerland and abroad (Jewish organisations, associations of victims of Nazism, banks, insurance companies etc.).

The "Swiss Foundation for Solidarity" Project

While the measures mentioned above have been taken to correct events that happened in the past, another initiative was launched in spring 1997 oriented to the future. As its name suggests, the Foundation as now conceived would be used to relieve the suffering of the most desperate victims of poverty: cata-strophic victims in Switzerland and abroad; victims of genocide, torture, and other violations of human rights (including but exclusively needy victims of the Holocaust and their needy descendants) as well as to give financial support to institutions engaged in preventing the emergency situations noted above.

The working groups preparing to launch the Foundation submitted their report on October 31, 1997. This report defines four priorities for future actions: preventing the growth of poverty and violence; promoting future perspectives for children and youth; rebuilding destroyed social structures; understanding and reconciling tensions and conflicts. To this end, three instruments will be available to the Foundation: medium-term project support, emergency campaigns and an annual Solidarity Prize endowed with CHF 1 million.

The planned Foundation could be capitalised at CHF 7 billion which stems from a revaluation of SNB gold reserves. However, it is not this capital but the prudently managed annual yields from it which should become available for future beneficiaries (http://www.solidarity.admin.ch).

Private initiatives

The discussion, centred around Switzerland's role during and immediately after World War II, has aroused the concern of Swiss citizens whose response was manifested by actions of solidarity in the humanitarian tradition of the country.

- Association of the "Solidarity Fund for Holocaust Victims" (January 1997): initiative by a high school in Berne. Since January 27, 1997, it has collected more than CHF 140,000 and donated these to relief organisations working with Holocaust victims. One example: a donation of CHF 50,000 to AMCHA (http://www.space.ch/fonds/eng.htm).
- Foundation for "Funds for Humanity and Justice" (January 1997): CHF 1.5 million collected for needy victims of the Nazi regime and their descendants. Supports the campaigns of organisations active in this area as well as individuals on an *ad hoc* basis (http://www.menschen.ch/engl/index.html)
- Fund in Favour of Holocaust Survivors and Jewish people in distress: collects for the benefit of Holocaust survivors and their descendants (CHF 270,000).

Statement by Ambassador Thomas G. Borer

HEAD OF THE TASK FORCE SWITZERLAND – WORLD WAR II

The views exchanged today bear witness to the complexity of issues being discussed. In the case of Switzerland, a number of measures have addressed these issues since the end of the War, which I would like to briefly bring to your attention.

The question of looted gold was settled by the Washington Accord of May 1946 under which Switzerland handed over gold valued at Sfr. 250 million. In return, the United States, Great Britain, France and the 15 other countries represented at the negotiations renounced all further claim to gold acquired by Switzerland from Germany during World War II.

While the amount is today deemed inadequate by some, it must be stressed that the negotiating parties agreed on the sum with full knowledge of all relevant facts and figures. The Swiss Government of the time agreed to make this transfer on the understanding that it was to be seen as a contribution towards European reconstruction and not as a form of compensation.

At this time, I would like to add that during the period between 1944 and 1948 my country made a substantial and parallel gesture of solidarity with the victims of the conflict: the Swiss Donation to the Victims of the War, amounting to more than Sfr. 200 million or 1.5% of the annual national product. Because of this donation, rescue work in 18 countries, hospitalisation of 13,000 persons in Switzerland, including concentration camp survivors, and other humanitarian initiatives could thus be implemented. My country's contribution to European relief and rehabilitation – including public and private credits to European states, humanitarian gifts and material help – amounted to half a billion dollars of that time, a very significant sum indeed.

Regarding looted works of art, two laws – adopted in December 1945 and February 1946 respectively – initiated the process of restitution by granting victims the right to reclaim stolen property, which had been deposited in Switzerland, by the new owner, even if the latter had acquired the assets in good faith. Almost 600 people, in particular French, exercised this right. Besides, all residents in Switzerland had an obligation to report the known existence of stolen art works, under penalties in cases of failure to comply. Professional and banking secrecy laws were lifted for the purpose of searching for stolen assets, and the investigating body was authorised to demand the opening of safes and deposit boxes.

Regarding unclaimed assets, the Swiss Parliament adopted a federal decree in December 1962, providing for an obligation to declare assets on which there had been no activity since May 9, 1945, and whose owners had fallen victim to racist, religious, or political persecution during the Nazi period in Germany. A Claims Registry was set up by the Government in order to carry out account audits, open safes, and put assets found in these safes under custody. In total, assets in value of 9.9 million Swiss francs could be identified.

Obviously, these measures needed to be complemented by a more comprehensive approach. This is why the Swiss Government, the Swiss Parliament and the Swiss people are committed to establishing the truth about our country's history in the context of World War II, to rendering justice, and to acting in a spirit of humanity and solidarity towards the victims of the Holocaust.

For the sake of truth, justice and solidarity, Switzerland has taken unprecedented steps, so far unmatched by any other country. Let me avail myself of this opportunity to remind you briefly of these measures.

First, in order to shed full light on the role of Switzerland in the context of World War II the Swiss Parliament unanimously passed a law on December 13, 1996, creating an independent commission of nine international experts mandated to study all legal and historical aspects of Switzerland's role as a financial centre before, during, and after the war years, and its relations with Nazi Germany. For the purposes of this investigation, Swiss banking secrecy regulations have been lifted. The Commission is chaired by one of Switzerland's leading historians, Professor Jean-Francois Bergier, and includes internationally noted historians such as Harold James, Professor at Princeton University, and Saul Friedlaender, Professor at the University of Tel Aviv. More than two dozen additional researchers are presently at work, in Switzerland as well as in other countries. Let me remind you that the Commission is conducting historical and scientific research, based on tons of documents to be compiled. It is thus unfair to accuse the Commission of dragging its feet, as it is wrong to address criticism to my Government to try to influence its work in any way: the Bergier Commission is totally independent. It will soon publish its first interim report on gold transactions with Nazi Germany. At this Conference, the Commission has made a substantial contribution to the historical fact-finding in its field, namely on where the gold looted by the Nazis came from and what happened to it. A second report on Swiss refugee policy during the war years has been scheduled for the beginning of next year.

Secondly, no effort has been spared to intensify the search for heirless assets and to ensure full restitution to either Holocaust survivors, their heirs or to organisations representing survivors of Nazi atrocities. In May 1996, the Swiss Bankers Association, together with the World Jewish Restitution Organisation, created an Independent Committee of Eminent Persons headed by Paul Volcker, the former Chairman of the Federal Reserve. Its task is to search for dormant assets that may still remain in Swiss banks. A comprehensive forensic investigation of all Swiss banks will allow identification of all assets that could possibly have belonged to Holocaust victims. To this end, the Volcker Committee has hired three well-known auditing firms. These firms enjoy unlimited access to the banks' books and records. This ongoing process has already begun to bear fruit, and, as the banks have promised, not one penny that may have belonged to a Holocaust victim will remain in a Swiss bank. The investigation should be completed by next year.

Meanwhile, concrete steps forward have been taken. On 23 July and 29 October 1997, the Swiss Bankers' Association, in an unprecedented move, released lists of unclaimed accounts opened before 1945. The list published in

July concerns more than 1,700 accounts opened by foreign nationals with a total value of 60.2 million francs. The October list contains the unclaimed accounts opened by Swiss nationals, amounting to 12.84 million Swiss francs. This list also includes an update on accounts opened by non-Swiss nationals, containing about 3,500 names with a total value of 6 million francs. I cannot stress enough the significance of this measure which will ease and accelerate the process of identifying the rightful owners in complete openness. An Independent Claims Resolution Foundation has been set up to provide an international, independent, and objective forum to adjudicate claims to dormant accounts. To hear claims under relaxed standards of proof that recognise the difficulty of presenting evidence in the tragic circumstances of the Holocaust and World War II, up to 15 foreign and Swiss arbitrators with experience in international adjudication will preside over a fast-track procedure.

The first restitution of dormant accounts are expected soon, that is, before the end of the year. However, allow me to add that the question of heirless assets is in no way only a Swiss problem. As various reports show, this is also an issue in the process of being addressed in other countries, such as the USA, Great Britain and Israel.

Thirdly, Switzerland has also decided to take measures to support Holocaust survivors. This humanitarian move to alleviate the distress of needy survivors underscores the commitments we have made. Thus, in close co-operation and consultation with all interested groups and thanks to the significant financial contribution of the three major Swiss banks, the Swiss National Bank, and Swiss industry, we have established a humanitarian fund for the survivors of the Holocaust and their families. The Fund has an endowment of 275 million Swiss francs (approximately USD 200 million). Priority in the Fund's allocations will be guaranteed to "double victims" – people living in Central and Eastern European countries who were victims of both Nazi oppression and the Communist regimes. I am pleased to announce here that the Fund is now fully operational: 15 million francs were transferred on November 10 to the WJRO for distribution in Eastern Europe and, most important of all, the first cheques were handed over to 80 needy survivors of the Holocaust in Latvia on 18 November 1997. Our Fund shares with the Fund newly established by the Tripartite Commission, the same commitment to bring a measure of relief to needy Holocaust survivors. In view of the great material distress endured by the survivors, we cannot but welcome this complementary intensification of international endeavours in favour of a population to which we all are – in one way or another – indebted. Apart from its humanitarian function, the Swiss Fund is also a sign of the gratitude of my people for having been spared from the War.

Another project bears witness to Switzerland's commitment to strengthening our humanitarian tradition and our solidarity, with a future-oriented proposal to contribute to the prevention and resolution of human suffering and conflicts in Switzerland and abroad. I am referring to the idea of a Swiss Foundation for Solidarity, which was presented on March 5, 1997 by the President of Switzerland Arnold Koller, and which could have an annual income of several hundred million francs at its disposal. According to the concept recently submitted to the Government, the Foundation is to be defined through its activities and not through recipient groups. Since no recipient groups are to be excluded *a priori*, the Foundation will also be able to consider projects to aid victims of the Holocaust. The Swiss Government will present its concrete proposal in due course to Parliament, which remains free to decide on its form and content. Once approved by Parliament the Foundation will be subject to the Swiss people's consent. The Foundation has nothing to do with the Swiss Fund for Needy Holocaust Victims, whose sole objective is to provide immediate individual assistance to those victims.

These far-reaching measures encompass all aspects of the issues at stake. They aim to offer a full view of our past; to show solidarity with elderly survivors now while helping them and their descendants to regain possession of their assets; and to keep alive and strong our humanitarian spirit in the future. They are a clear sign that nothing is more important for my country than truth, justice and solidarity.

Declaration of the Federal Council on the Eizenstat Report

Overall acknowledgement of the report

American officials on 7 May 1997 made public the Eizenstat Report on financial transactions of the Nazi regime. On the same day the Federal Council offered a first assessment. Because the Federal Council unfortunately had insufficient opportunity for inspection and co-ordination, this was necessarily of a preliminary nature.

After detailed examination the Federal Council has concluded that the Eizenstat Report provides added elements for judging the conduct of Switzerland, the other neutrals, as well as the United States itself during and after World War II. The American administration recognises the great efforts of Switzerland in coming to terms with its history in a positive way. Knowing of the great services of the United States in liberating Europe and of the sacrifices made by this country, but also in knowledge of the unspeakable suffering of Holocaust victims, Switzerland desires to pursue this reappraisal jointly with the USA and other countries. Yet among friends there is also a self-evident need to speak openly about differences in outlook. Therefore it is a matter of concern to the Federal Council that it expresses its critical position on comments in the report's foreword.

The report as such contains numerous information items of great interest from American sources previously inaccessible in publications. It thus confirms and supplements knowledge essentially at hand already. The assessment is entrusted to the Independent Commission of Experts (Bergier Commission) and free historical research. The Federal Council is convinced that the report in this way contributes to better understanding of conduct of individual countries at the time. Hence it enriches historical work already available which may not have gained the political recognition it deserves. The Ludwig Report on refugee policy, the Bonjour Report on neutrality policy, or work on the gold trade topic could be cases in point. As repeatedly supported in word and deed, the Federal Council wants to do all it can to promote further research on our history during World War II. This research is not merely a question of historical interest but expresses readiness to come to terms with the dark side of recent Swiss history as well.

Reservations on Foreword

The Federal Council concentrated its criticism on the foreword. It also contains political and moral values which go beyond the historic report. They require clarification.

Tough Negotiating during the Postwar Period

The harshest criticism concerns the conduct of Switzerland during the postwar period. It concerns a chapter in history which especially preoccupies the Federal Council and to which it wants to dedicate its undivided attention. It involves the question whether Switzerland's conduct at the time was appropriate in a moral and material sense to the situation in destroyed Europe and the privation of a people exhausted by war. The results of various negotiations are known; the background and special interests of the various parties require a deeper historic explanation.

Here the Federal Council points out: at the conclusion of the Washington Agreement in 1946 the parties to the signing realised all essential facts. Thanks to their intelligence sources, the Allies even had precise knowledge of the Swiss negotiating position. Regarding the agreement's implementation the report confirms in writing that Switzerland had paid the settlement sum at the prevailing value of Sfr. 250 million agreed to in the gold negotiations.

We must judge more critically from today's outlook the liquidation of German assets. When reading the report, the impression arises of a country which could not or would not empathise with the needs of a war-torn Europe. Even so, the result of the 1952 settlement contract was also a mutual compromise the partners had agreed to on economic and political grounds. As the report also clearly notes, the rebuilding of West Germany was urgent, given the background of the Cold War. It will be the task of the historians to assess comprehensively if the Swiss action pursued an all too narrow legalistic approach or if it was based on comprehensible difficulties and national and international law principles. Confiscation of German assets in Switzerland belonged at that time among the particularly disputed issues. While the USA envisioned a process without compensation, Switzerland demanded appropriate compensation for the owners based on the rule of law.

During and after the war Switzerland also proved its humanitarian commitment, above all with the unmentioned "Swiss Donation to War Victims" valued at the time at more than Sfr. 200 million. This was the outcome of a common effort by officials and the people to express solidarity with war victims.

Criticism of Financial Profits

The foreword also criticises Switzerland for having profited economically from World War II. That Switzerland traded with the Axis Powers as well as the Allies was a question of national political and economic survival. Yet it is true that the Swiss business community had also pursued its own interests with the Axis and the Allies. At the same time there were also questionable deals which did not affect the survival of Switzerland. Only hypotheses are possible to question whether Switzerland in 1943–44 would have been in a situation to break off business ties with the Axis Powers without provoking the risk of an invasion. The same applies to the question of logistical alternatives. Evidence that Switzerland emerged from World War II as one of the wealthiest nations of Europe raises questions about the initial situation and possible reasons which require detailed clarification. This is missing in the report. It should also be taken into consideration that Switzerland was one of the few European countries which was not destroyed economically after World War II.

The Federal Council regards the representation of Switzerland as the banker of the Nazis as a one-sided package judgment. However, it is justified to criticise financial transactions known to be questionable. Yet a more comprehensive analysis would also have little difficulty in showing that the financial community and the Swiss National Bank not only cultivated close relationships with Germany after the Nazis had seized power. The German neighbor was previously and even today remains an economic partner of paramount importance. The same ties to the Allies were also very intensive for similar reasons.

The Issue of Prolonging the War

It is suggested in the foreword that the neutral countries may have prolonged the Third Reich's ability to wage war by trading with it. At least based on the report contents this comment must be referred to as unsupported. Such a comment would only be justified – if at all – if it were based on a comprehensive study of the German war economy, mutual dependencies, and economic relationships with the Allies. Such a study is not available. It is also not evident that the difficult situation faced by Switzerland had relaxed accordingly with the turn in the war by 1943.

Neutrality and Morality

Also not historic but clearly of a political nature are comments contained in the foreword on the importance of neutrality in World War II. It is asserted that neutrality and morality contradicted each other at the time. Behind the criticism stands the outlook that neutrality between countries committed to good and countries which embody evil is immoral. Yet for Switzerland neutrality had a towering national function for centuries. The neutrality policy pursued by the Federal Council had the central goal of keeping Switzerland out of World War II and protecting its citizenry from destruction and persecution from the Nazis. A powerful army was an essential means toward this end. Thus Switzerland also maintained itself as a haven for tens of thousands of refugees and as an oasis of democracy and freedom in a totalitarian Europe. Would Switzerland have achieved this goal better if it had taken the initiative militarily as a party favoring the Allies? All current insights suggest the contrary. Moreover, the Swiss people have never understood neutrality as mere indifference in convictions. This showed itself most clearly in the case of the reports and commentaries of the media at the time. It courageously expressed the attitude of an overwhelming portion of the people against the Nazis. Due to their independence, the voices of commentators Rodolphe von Salis and René Payot resounded throughout all Europe.

Viewed all in all, neutrality led to a difficult tightrope walk between adaptation and resistance. Today we know that this also led to mistakes. The fainthearted refugee policy concerning Jews was inexcusable. In the business and financial sector concessions were sometimes made to the Axis Powers which are very hard to comprehend today in view of the inner convictions of the population and measured by absolute necessity.

It must not be forgotten that Switzerland's neutral stance also served Allied interests. Switzerland took on numerous protective mandates on their behalf in order to serve their interests in enemy countries. Thanks to its neutrality, Switzerland could assume wide-ranging humanitarian tasks such as visiting prisoner-of-war camps in Germany and Japan and tending to civilians interned in Switzerland.

Current efforts in Switzerland

In conclusion the Federal Council maintains that impartiality on all sides presumes success in researching a difficult historical chapter and one that will be shouldered jointly by the people. The Federal Council has constantly committed itself to openness without reservation in further enlightening our past. With this purpose in mind, it assigned the task to the Independent Commission of Experts, the international group of specialists led by Professor Bergier, after Parliament speedily and unanimously provided the legal basis for it. This Commission has access to all relevant documents it deems relevant. For its investigation it also has access to documents which would normally be subject to bank secrecy. In addition, the Volcker Committee engaged by the Swiss Banker's Association and the international Jewish organisations is undertaking intensive examinations of any possible remaining financial claims against Swiss banks. Furthermore, the Federal Council has announced Switzerland's readiness to take part in an international conference of historians and other experts. The Federal Council also decided to create a Special Fund to provide prompt relief to surviving victims of the Holocaust. In addition to the major banks, other sectors of the Swiss business community are participating in this Fund. The Federal Council supports the intent of the Swiss National Bank to make a major contribution as well.

Over the years Switzerland has linked neutrality to humanitarian concerns and solidarity. Moreover, the planned Swiss Foundation for Solidarity should express Switzerland's will to strengthen its humanitarian commitment even more in the future.

The report lauds the leading role of Switzerland today in coming to terms with its history. In this sense the Federal Council is pleased to accept the offer of dialog and joint cooperation which the American president expressed recently as the newly named Swiss ambassador presented his credentials. Three basic principles will guide us further in this regard: truth, justice, and solidarity.

Reaction of Federal Councillor F. Cotti to Eizenstat Report on behalf of the Federal Council

Today the so-called Eizenstat Report on financial transactions of the German Reich has been published. The Federal Council welcomes the study as another important contribution to clarification of transactions with gold and other assets during and after World War II. It evaluates sources which for the most part have been available to the American and other governments for half a century but which have been impossible for us to know about completely. The report is very comprehensive. An all-embracing assessment cannot be provided today. We will now review the report thoroughly. This applies especially to the general conduct of Swiss authorities during the war.

The Federal Council welcomes the efforts of those responsible for the study to present the situation objectively. At first glimpse, however, it is lacking a measured recognition of the extremely difficult situation in which our country found itself militarily and in supply terms at that time.

The small Swiss nation, ladies and gentlemen, experienced an extremely difficult time during World War II. Imagine the situation: our country was encircled and threatened by the Nazis and the fascists. And indeed with no weak link in the surrounding chain. Switzerland had no choice: to survive, it had to trade with the Axis Powers too. Under these conditions neutrality was the only possibility for survival. In those dramatic days this neutrality policy meant for Switzerland a tightrope walk between adaptation and resistance, always with the goal of saving the country and its human population from war as well as to preserve freedom and democracy. And that included hundreds of thousands of refugees who found themselves here. But let us not forget: practically the entire population was emotionally against the Nazis. It is notable that the Eizenstat Report also refers to the great economic and political importance of Switzerland for the Allies.

The report confirms the facts and figures already reappraised by the Swiss National Bank and various historians on gold transactions between the German Reichsbank and the Swiss National Bank as well as with central banks of other countries.

On the other hand, the report contains evidence that the Swiss National Bank bought gold bar from the German Reichsbank during World War II which contained so-called "victim gold". Ladies and gentlemen, if this is really true, it is grave news of the most shocking nature. The degree of cynicism and cold-bloodedness it would take for the Nazi brutes to resmelt their victims' gold and resell it as regular central bank gold is almost beyond our comprehension. The report of Undersecretary Eizenstat confirms that those responsible at the Swiss National Bank were not aware that "victim gold" was also smelted into their gold bars.

The report made public today helps to cast light on one of the worst chapters of human history. It has always been stressed in Switzerland that this country wants the complete truth. Therefore we have assigned the Internal Commission of Experts under the leadership of Professor Bergier to clarify questions still open on the role of Switzerland at the time of World War II. The Commission – which has already begun its research activity – has free access to all relevant documents. The Federal Council asks the Commission to include the Eizenstat Report in its investigations.

The report by Undersecretary Eizenstat expressly recognises the steps which Switzerland has taken recently. At the same time it stresses the leading role which our country has assumed in reappraising this difficult time by introducing these various measures. I am referring in this context to the Volcker Committee set up by the Swiss Banker's Association and the international Jewish organisations. The Committee is carrying out intensive inquiries on potential financial claims still valid against Swiss banks. I also wish to recall the Special Fund, capitalised at Sfr. 165 million, to benefit Holocaust victims and their needy families. The Federal Council emphatically supports the intent of the Swiss National Bank to contribute another Sfr. 100 million to this Fund. Furthermore, the Federal Council launched the creation of a Swiss Foundation for Solidarity. It should serve to relieve severe human need in Switzerland and abroad. Moreover – and independent of government initiatives – private persons, churches, and students in Switzerland have already collected hundreds of thousands of francs to benefit Holocaust victims.

In order to show its national and international solidarity for the future, the Federal Council has also led the way toward creating a Swiss Foundation for Solidarity.

The Eizenstat Report also sheds light on the role of other countries as well as those of the Tripartite Commission (on gold). The Federal Council hopes that study commissions active in other countries will work closely with each other, co-operate in the quest for truth, and thus contribute to clarifying still unanswered questions.

The Federal Council endorses what it has always emphasised: we want truth and justice. Inquiries must be carried out with openness and without reservations in all countries involved. Switzerland is prepared for this and has introduced the necessary steps.

Gold Transactions in the Second World War: Statistical Review with Commentary

INDEPENDENT COMMISSION OF EXPERTS SWITZERLAND – SECOND WORLD WAR[*]

SUMMARY

I. General remarks

The Independent Commission of Experts: Switzerland – Second World War has been entrusted with the mandate of conducting an investigation into the fate and the volume of assets, including gold, which reached Switzerland as a result of the National-Socialist regime. This work is to represent a contribution to shedding light on a difficult phase of Switzerland's history.

The present report is a contribution to the Conference on Nazi Gold held in London from 2 to 4 December 1997. The Commission will deal with other significant aspects in a detailed interim report scheduled for publication in early 1998.

II. The most important results

The usual distinction between monetary and non-monetary gold as found in the literature, tends to reproduce an approach which is fixed on states and central banks. The Commission proposes a new approach with five categories of German gold: gold which was collected through duress of the state, confiscated and plundered gold, victim gold, gold from the currency reserves of central banks, and gold from holdings which came into the possession of the Reichsbank before 1933 or were acquired through regular transactions before the outbreak of the War.

The flow model developed by the Commission shows that the gold which was confiscated or plundered from private persons and subsequently delivered to the Reichsbank amounts to a sum of $146 million.

The most important recipients of gold shipments from the German Reichsbank were the Swiss National Bank (SNB) ($389.2 million), Swiss commercial banks ($61.2 million), the Romanian National Bank ($54.2 million), branch offices of the German Reichsbank ($51.5 million), and the German

[*] *Executive coordination:* Jean-François Bergier (Chairman); Sybil Milton, Joseph Voyame (Vice-chairmen); Wladyslaw Bartoszewski, Saul Friedländer, Harold James, Georg Kreis, Jacques Picard, Jakob Tanner

Researchers – Editorial staff: Jan Baumann, Petra Barthelmess, Geneviève Billeter, Linus von Castelmur, Michèle Fleury, James Gillespie, Benedikt Hauser, Martin Meier, Marc Perrenoud, Bertrand Perz, Hans Safrian, Thomas Sandkühler

Secretariat & Documentation: Estelle Blanc, Regina Deplazes, Armelle Godichet

banking and commercial enterprises Dresdner Bank, Deutsche Bank, Sponholz & Co., and Degussa ($14.2 million).

At a figure of $61.2 million, the German Reichsbank's shipments to Swiss commercial banks are significantly greater than what has been supposed to date. The point remains open as to how much of this was acquired on their own accounts.

The largest recipients of the German Reichsbank's shipments to major Swiss banks were the Swiss Bank Corporation ($36.6 million), the Bank Leu & Co. ($12.0 million), the Union Bank of Switzerland ($8.5 million), the Basler Handelsbank ($2.2 million), the Credit Suisse ($1.8 million) and the Eidgenössische Bank ($0.03 million).

III. Open questions

- The policy of the Tripartite Commission for the Restitution of Monetary Gold (TCG).
- The role of the central banks of countries like Portugal, Spain, and Romania.
- Gold transactions between Russia, Germany, and Switzerland in the years 1939 to 1941, and those before December 1941 between the USA, Germany, and Switzerland.
- The significance of the role played by the black market with respect to national and international gold trade.
- The question of the use of Swiss francs exchanged for gold by the states waging the War.

CONTENTS

1. Preliminary Remarks 510

2. Presentation and Terminology..510

3. Gold Transactions of the Reichsbank 513

4. Gold Transfers of the Reichsbank to the SNB 519

5. Gold Operations of the SNB 520

6. Gold shipped to Swiss Commercial Banks by the German Reichsbank ..525

7. Gold Transactions between Switzerland and the Allies 527

8. Summary..529

Annex: Archives 529

Notes 531

Abbreviations

BAR	Bundesarchiv, Berne
BIS	Bank for International Settlements
CS	Credit Suisse
CSSO	Central State Security Office
DFFD	Département fédéral des Finances et des Douanes
DFJP	Département fédéral de Justice et Police
DoSt	U.S. Department of State
DPF	Département politique fédéral (aujourd'hui Département fédéral des Affaires étrangères)
EDI	Eidgenössisches Departement des Innern
EFV	Eidgenössisches Finanzverwaltung
EFZD	Eidgenössisches Finanz- und Zolldepartement
EIBA	Eidgenössisches Bank
EJPD	Eidgenössisches Justiz- und Polizeidepartement
EMD	Eidgenössisches Militärdepartement
EPD	Eidgenössisches Politisches Departement (heute Eidgenössisches Departement für Auswärtige Angelegenheiten)
ICE	Independent Commission of Experts: Switzerland – Second World War
IfZ	Institut für Zeitgeschichte, München
OMGUS	Office of Military Government for Germany, United States
RM	Reichsmark
RSHA	Reichssicherheitshauptamt
SBC	Swiss Bank Corporation
SBVg	Schwiezerische Bankvereinigung
SDD	Swiss Diplomatic Documents
SFr	Swiss Franc
SHAEF	Supreme Headquarters Allied Expeditionary Forces
SHIV	Schweizerischer Handels- und Industrieverein (Vorort)
SNB	Swiss National Bank
SS	Schutzstaffel (der NSDAP)
SVB	Schweizerische Volksbank
SVSt	Schweizerische Verrechnungsstelle
UBS	Union Bank of Switzerland
UEK	Unabhängige Expertenkommission: Schweiz-Zweiter Weltkrieg
UNO	United Nations Organisation
Vol.	Volume
WJC	World Jewish Congress

1. PRELIMINARY REMARKS

The present working paper has been conceived as a scientific contribution by the Independent Commission of Experts: Switzerland – World War II for the London Conference on Nazi Gold. To establish a clear foundation for discussions, the Commission is proposing definitions for the various categories of gold which Germany placed on the international market. They are followed by several tables of statistics specifying the gold holding of the Reichsbank between 1939 and 1945, the use to which they were put, the transactions which were undertaken via the Swiss National Bank and the transfers which were effected via Swiss commercial banks. Gold purchases by the Swiss National Bank and the Confederation are taken into account as well.

This working paper does not contain an exhaustive analysis of Swiss transactions in gold. It is not meant to anticipate the findings to be published by the Commission in an interim report on gold at the beginning of 1998. The Commission intends to use the remaining time to complete its investigation, to amplify the present results with an evaluation of additional archival material, and to include new knowledge gained from the London Conference.

This is the reason why this working paper will not describe the sequence of gold transfers in chronological detail. It will not specify the structural reasons which made Switzerland the centre of international gold movements and the Swiss franc the only freely convertible currency in Europe. It does not analyse the role of gold in the monetary and commercial relations of Switzerland. It does not discuss the policy of the Swiss National Bank and the role of the Swiss authorities nor the arguments which legitimised them. It poses no question as to the knowledge of those responsible with regard to the gold's origin. These elements, both complex and essential, will be approached by the Commission in its forthcoming interim report.

2. PRESENTATION AND TERMINOLOGY

The definition of categories is a necessary prerequisite for a presentation of statistical material. Herewith are a number of comments on the establishment of terminology.

2.1 Establishment of terminology and categories of gold

The literature often distinguishes between "monetary" and "non-monetary" gold. The former was at the disposal of the central banks. It served as a national currency reserve and was an integral part of monetary systems based on a gold or a gold-foreign exchange standard. The term "non-monetary" relates to a less differentiated residual category in which all other gold, obtained or traded from private persons or companies, is subsumed. The distinction also formed the basis of the restitution efforts of the *Tripartite Commission for the Restitution Gold (TGC)*.

Focusing on the central banks demonstrates that the entire problem of resti-tution, raised by the Third Reich's economic system of looting and plundering, has been primarily defined by states which are affected by payment of war costs and the return of stolen national property. The victims, the dispossessed, have had to take second place behind official reparation claims and the formation of alliances during the Cold War. Even today, the difference between "monetary" and "non-monetary" tends to reproduce an approach which is fixed on states and central banks. In particular, it does not do justice to the transformation which gold underwent as a result of various forms of its use. The Commission is using "looted gold", a term characterising this discussion, in general and com-prehensively, for that gold which the National Socialist regime has seized since the onset of militant expansion abroad through the confiscation of property as authorised by its racial laws.

2.1.1 Definitions for Gold from the Area of National Socialist Hegemony

A distinction assumes a definition of gold categories which is primarily based on origin, and then goes on to examine the use of gold and the resulting transfor-mations in its form and function.

1. *Gold* which came under the control of the Reichsbank through *duress of the state*. In the Third Reich, an entire group of organisations and administrative offices were involved in the registration, appropriation and extortion of gold. Measures extended from tax laws and foreign currency regulations to compulsory mea-sures based on the wartime economy. Previous owners could be of German Jewish or non-Jewish origin as well as other disenfranchised persons, groups or institutions in Germany.

2. *Confiscated and plundered gold.* This includes, on the one hand, the assets confis-cated from the Jewish population beginning with 1938 in the context of the N.S. racial legislation in Germany and in Austria (gold, jewelry, and other precious metals). Furthermore, it encompasses the theft from residents and citizens of annexed and occupied areas resulting from the arbitrariness of the state or plun-dering by individuals. The plundered gold was either transferred to the reserves of the Reichsbank, used on the black markets, or hoarded.

3. *Victim gold.* This is a general term used to denote the gold assets which the regime confiscated from the victims of concentration and extermination camps who had either survived or been murdered. "Concentration and extermination camps" is to be understood as a comprehensive term. Victim gold includes property from various camps and ghettos in Eastern Europe.[1] The mass exter-mination of European Jews was at the same time a "large-scale hunt" for jewel-ry, gold, precious stones and foreign currencies. The SS, headed by the com-mercial administrative headquarters (WVHA), was the leading participant in the plundering of victims in the ghettos, and in concentration and extermina-tion camps. It also raises the question of embezzlement and plundering on the part of people involved in the extermination process.

4. *Gold from currency reserves of the central banks.* Already before the war, the Third Reich was able to appropriate gold reserves of other states through its territorial expansion. During the Blitzkrieg in the spring and summer of 1940, substantial gold holdings came under the control of the National Socialist state. In the years of occupation by the German Wehrmacht which followed, gold continued to flow from the monetary reserves of the European central banks to the Reichsbank.

The last three categories (2, 3, 4) are indicated here, comprehensively as "looted gold".[2] Apart from these, a category of non-looted gold must be defined:

5. *Gold* from holdings which came into the possession of the Reichsbank *before 1933* or which were *acquired* through regular transactions *before the outbreak of war.*

2.1.2 Definitions for gold transactions with the Allies

Because the gold taken over from the Allied central banks came from regular holdings and were indisputably acquired by legal means, it is clear that another category applies to them. The gold which came from commercial dealings with the Allies does not present the same problems as gold purchased from the Axis powers. It is thus not permitted to try to neutralise the difficult questions which are posed in connection with looted gold from Germany by a reciprocal setoff of incommensurate categories.

Gold shipments from the United States are quantitatively the most important. *Three categories*, which provide information not only on the origin of the gold but also on the reasons for its acceptance by the Swiss National Bank, are of importance. *First of all*, there was gold from the Swiss National Bank which originated in the *flight of capital*. It includes a large part of the gold which the National Bank accepted in the United States against dollars accruing from transactions on the capital market and which then was subjected to the American financial blockade. *Secondly, export-induced receipts of gold* resulting from the economic exchange relations with the United States. The Swiss National Bank was obliged to accept dollars against francs. These were returned to the Federal Reserve in exchange for gold. The gold shipments, in which the Swiss Confederation intervened can be interpreted in a functional was as a form of export financing. *Thirdly*, there were transactions of gold against foreign currency which guaranteed *payment* of services essential for war and for humanitarian efforts.

2.2 Tables of coherence of data

The following tables illustrate the magnitude, the institutional trails and the geographical structure of the gold transactions. They include an extensive compilation, for the Third Reich and Switzerland, of all gold transactions between September 1, 1939 and June 30, 1945. The relationship between the tables is explained in the following.

Table I provides an overview of the origin and use of the Reichsbank gold. *Table II* juxtaposes those sums which are listed under "Deliveries to Switzerland" in Table I with the "Shipments from Germany" on the Swiss side. There are certain problems of compatibility and deviations between the Swiss and the German statistics which are not serious. *Table III* provides information on the gold purchases and sales of the Swiss National Bank. Analogous to the presentation in Table I, a distinction is made between origin and utilisation. Gold transactions with the Allies and the non-belligerent states are identified on the side of origin. The remaining Reichsbank shipments to the Swiss National Bank, which were not bought by this bank but rather recorded as deposit on account of other central banks and managed in its Bern depot, are dealt with in *Table IV. Tables Va – Vc* list the shipments to Swiss commercial banks, or in other words, the major banks. *Tables VI* and *VII* provide an overview of gold transactions with the Allied states.

The following overviews and compilations are based essentially on sources of the U.S. National Archives in Washington, the archives of the Swiss Confederation and the archives of the Swiss National Bank.

All figures are calculated at the 1945 dollar price of \$35 per fine ounce of gold, or \$1,125 per kilogram of fine gold (kgf). In the period under investigation, the official purchase price for gold of the Swiss National Bank amounted to Sfr4,869.80 per kilogram, or an exchange rate of Sfr/\$4.3287.

3. GOLD TRANSACTIONS OF THE REICHSBANK

In recording the gold movements of the central banks, the Commission has used a two part compilation. It has the advantage that they must lead to two identical sum totals (origin or input = use or output), allowing a reciprocal control of both rows of figures.

Information on the origin of the gold which the Reichsbank was able to bring under its control appears in the left column of Table I. Its use can be seen in the right column. Both columns refer to the same period, extending from September 1, 1939 until June 30, 1945. The following equations are valid for this overview:

Initial holdings before the outbreak of war

Residual holdings found by Allies in spring of 1945

Initial holdings before the outbreak of war		Residual holdings found by Allies in spring of 1945
+ Gold purchases at foreign central banks		+ Gold sales to foreign central banks
+ Shipments and seizures of central bank gold		
+ Gold confiscated or plundered from private persons	=	+ Sales to the private finance sector both at home and abroad
+ Victim gold		+ Internal commercial use

Table I: Overview of the gold transactions of the Reichsbank

September 1, 1939 until June 30, 1945 (in $ millions)

I.	**Initial Holdings**			**V.**	**Holdings at the End of the War**	
I/1.	Published Reserves	31.1		V/1.	Gold Recovered in Germany	198.0
I/2.	Secret Reserves	82.7		V/2.	Gold from Italy (partly in Germany)	64.8
I/3.	Other German Note Banks	12.1		V/3.	Gold from Hungary	32.2
I/4.	Austrian Gold Reserves	99.0			*Total*	*295.0*
I/5.	Czechoslovak Gold Reserves	33.8				
	Total	*258.7*		**VI.**	**Gold Shipped Abroad**	
				VI/1.	Swiss National Bank	389.2
II.	**Gold from other Central Banks**				Swiss Commercial Banks	61.2
	(as of September 1939)			VI/2.	Other Foreign Banks	
II/1.	National Bank of Netherlands	137.2			National Bank of Belgium	9.1
II/2.	National Bank of Belgium	225.9			National Bank of the Netherlands	2.2
	National Bank of Luxembourg	4.8			Swedish Riksbank	4.6
II/3.	National Bank of Hungary	32.2			National Bank of the USSR	7.0
	National Bank of Italy	64.8			Central Bank of the Turkish Republic	5.7
II/4.	Other Central Banks				Consorzio Italiano Estero Aero	5.6
	Total	*475.0*			National Bank of Italy	3.6
					National Bank of Croatia	0.4
					National Bank of Romania	54.2
III.	**Gold from Individuals**			VI/3.	Reichsbank Branches Abroad	51.5
III/1.	Four-Year Plan Activity	71.8			*Total*	*594.3*
III/2.	"Melmer Gold"	2.5				
III/3.	Other Private Holdings	71.7		**VII.**	**Domestic Commercial Use**	
	Total	*146.0*		VII/1.	Degussa	3.3
					Sponholz & Co.	3.4
				VII/2.	Deutsche Bank	3.6
IV.	**Purchases of Gold Abroad**				Dresdner Bank	3.9
IV/1.	Soviet Union	23.0			*Total*	*14.2*
	Japan	4.2				
IV/2.	Bank for International Settlements	2.3		**VIII.**	**Government Use**	
	Total	*29.5*		VIII/1.	Auswaertiges Amt	3.1
					Amtsgruppe Ausland Abwehr	2.2
				VIII/2.	Reichssieherheitshauptamt (RSHA)	0.1
					Wehrmacht	0.3
					Total	*5.7*
	Total	*909.2*			*Total*	*909.2*

COMMENTS ON THE FIGURES:

I. Initial Holdings. The Overview takes the first day of war as the initial date for the accounting period. As a result, gold obtained by the Reichsbank prior to the official declaration of war is included in the 'Initial Holdings', including gold incorporated into the German reserves from the state banks of Austria and Czechoslovakia, and gold taken earlier from German citizens by various confiscation measures.

I/1. *Published Reserves.* Under the gold standard, all central banks made public the amount of gold with which they backed the value of their paper currency. With the imposition of exchange controls in July 1931, Germany effectively abandoned the gold standard. In any case, Germany had forfeited a large part of its reserves during the worldwide depression. The published figure for

Germany's gold reserves began to fall in December of 1933, and became constant at $31.1 million at the end of 1937.[3] The published amount did not change throughout the war.[4]

I/2. *Secret Reserves.* In 1933, Reichsbank President Hjalmar Schacht began a policy of accumulating gold secretly in several different accounts.[5] Widely believed by Reichsbank employees to be a war-preparation fund, those secret reserves were worth 582.7 million by September of 1939.[6]

I/3. *Other Note Banks.* Several banks-of-issue survived in Germany from the pre-unification financial system of the nineteenth century, such as the Bavarian State Bank. These banks together held $12.1 million worth of gold which was placed at the disposal of the German government.[7]

I/4. *Austrian Gold Reserves.* After the "Anschluss" with Germany in 1938, the gold reserves of the National Bank of Austria, worth $99 million, were amalgamated with those of the Reichsbank and were physically transferred to Berlin.[8] Subsequently, Austrians became subject to German laws requiring private citizens to turn their gold holdings over to the government. Such private gold received before September of 1939 is included in the 'Secret Reserves'; later private gold receipts are accounted for in the 'Four-Year Plan Activities' described later.[9]

I/5. *Czechoslovak Gold Reserves.* Unlike the National Bank of Austria, the Czechoslovak central bank was never absorbed by the Reichsbank. Instead, it was reorganised as the National Bank of Bohemia and Moravia and its gold, though subject virtually to confiscation by the German government, was recorded in separate accounts in the Reichsbank. Withdrawals from those accounts by Germany were always reimbursed with paper Reichsmarks. Some Czechoslovak gold reserves had been transferred to Bern, London and New York prior to the invasion, but were brought back into German control through swaps within the Bank for International Settlements (BIS). German reserves benefited from $33.8 million worth of gold.[10] The Czechoslovak reserves held in Switzerland were transferred to the account of the Reichsbank by telegraphic order on March 7, 1939, one week before the German invasion.[11]

II. Gold Seized from Central Banks. In each of the states occupied by Germany during the war, it became a key objective of the German government to gain control of national gold reserves. It is interesting to note that pains were taken to maintain a semblance of legitimacy throughout this process; the Reichsbank attempted (unsuccessfully in the case of the Belgian National Bank) to obtain signatures from each state's responsible bank officials agreeing to the transfer of gold to Germany. It is possible in addition that some of the central bank numbers include gold seized from individuals and surrendered to the national authorities rather than to the agencies of the German Four-Year Plan.

II/1. *National Bank of the Netherlands.* The Netherlands managed to send part of their gold reserves to London and New York prior to the outbreak of war, but the gold remaining in Amsterdam was shipped to Berlin for the Reichsbank and reimbursed with paper currency. The gold coins and bars from the Netherlands were worth $137.2 million.[12] Much of this gold was resmelted by the Prussian Mint, stamped with prewar dates to obscure its origin, and sold to neutral states in return for foreign exchange. Some of the postwar U.S. studies give higher figures for the gold seized from the Netherlands. A U.S. governmental memo from June of 1946, for example, states this amount to be $164 million.[13] The larger amount includes gold taken by the Four-Year Plan from individuals, gold which is shown separately in the present tabulation.[14] In the process of resmelting, some amounts of other gold, including "victim" gold from inmates of the concentration camps, was added to the Netherlands gold.[15]

II/2. *National Banks of Belgium and of Luxembourg.* Belgium and Luxembourg had both entrusted their gold reserves to the Bank of France prior to the war, and with the invasion of the Low Countries in 1940 their gold had been shipped to French colonies in Africa. The case of the Belgian gold was particularly problematical, and was already widely discussed and known during the war. At the outset of hostilities, most of Belgium's gold reserves had been transferred to Britain and United States, but part went to France from where it was transported, after the German invasion to

Dakar. Vichy France moved this gold back across the Sahara, and the Banque de France, under pressure from head of government Pierre Laval, agreed to its transfer to the Reichsbank. The Reichsbank tried to pay the Banque National de Belgique in Reichsmarks, but the Banque's directors refused to sign the receipt which would have given the transfer a nominal legality.[16] Instead, the gold was seized in France and taken to Berlin where it was melted into new bars at the Prussian State Mint and provided with smelting certificates dated from the mid-1930s. Belgium lost $225.9 million to Germany, and Luxembourg was forced to relinquish $4.8 million.[17]

II/3. *National Banks of Hungary and of Italy.* The gold reserves of Hungary and of Italy, allies of Germany in 1940, came to the Reichsbank after the fall of Mussolini's government in 1943 and the occupation of Hungary by Germany in 1944. Italy's gold reserves contained, in turn, gold obtained from the national banks of Yugoslavia and of Greece, taken by the Italians during the first years of the war. Hungary's gold was worth $32.2 million, and Italy's reserves, including gold seized by Italy from other states, amounted to $64.8 million.[18]

II/4. *Other State Banks.* Several other national banks were overrun by the Germans and had their gold reserves seized. These included Greece, Yugoslavia, Danzig, and Albania.[19] While each state alone yielded relatively little to the Reichsbank, the total amount seized was valued at $10.1 million.[20]

III. Gold Seized from Individuals. From the early 1930s, the German government made a concerted attempt to increase its gold holdings by restricting the possession, or by confiscating, privately owned gold. During the war, as the need for gold became more pressing, these measures became more draconian and were enforced both on German citizens and on individuals in the occupied states. Considerable amounts of gold were also taken from the inmates of concentration camps, dead and alive, including wedding rings, gold watches, spectacle-rims, jewelry, religious objects, and gold from dental work.

III/1. *Four-Year Plan Activities.* The German government enacted several decrees requiring all German citizens (and later all citizens of occupied states) to turn over their gold in return for paper currency, and these regulations were followed by more general levies on assets, including personal gold. The penalties for non-compliance with these regulations were severe. Documents from the Four-Year Plan Directorate state that $71.8 million was collected from individuals through these regulations.[21]

III/2. *"Melmer Gold".* Starting in 1942, an SS captain named Bruno Melmer initiated the 76 deliveries of valuables including gold to the Reichsbank for credit to an account of the SS revenue office (section AII).[22] The gold which he turned over to the Reichsbank consisted of personal effects of both dead and living inmates of Auschwitz and other concentration camps in the East. The Melmer deliveries of gold (bars and coins) eventually amounted to at least $2.5 million. Estimates until now have been strongly disparate. Whereas Hersch Fischler calculated total deliveries of $3 million,[23] Sidney Zabludoff's study refers to $4 million.[24] The figure of $2.5 million used here corresponds to a minimum and includes only those amounts from the Reichsbank holdings which are on microfilm in the National Archives in Washington and which can be clearly attributed to the Melmer Account.[25] The fact that Melmer deliveries appear in the books of the Reichsbank only as of December 1942 can possibly be explained by records referring to the first deliveries as "Sonderkonto Max Heiliger" and not as "Melmer". In documents, it is generally difficult to distinguish between deliveries of gold, silver and foreign currency. The apparatus was obviously not fully co-ordinated until the end of 1942.[26] Apart from these questions, it would be incorrect to assume that the gold listed as "Melmer" included all of the gold stolen in the eastern concentration and extermination camps. A part of the Melmer gold was resmelted by the Prussian Mint and taken abroad.[27]

III/3. *Other Private Holdings.* The sum of $71.7 million is calculated as the residual balance necessary to equalise total credits and debits of the Reichsbank during the war. It includes gold seized from individuals through executive fiat, levies, laws not falling under the jurisdiction of the Four-

Year Plan, and gold taken from concentration camp victims but not accounted for above.[28] In addition, gold was bought by Germany on the black market – in occupied Europe as well as in neutral countries, including Switzerland – by selling other property (in particular diamonds) taken from the victims of persecution and referred to unashamedly in German documents as Jewish jewelry or "Judenschmuck," and selling bank notes, chiefly French occupation currency.

IV. Purchases of Gold Abroad. The Reichsbank purchased a relatively small amount of gold from foreign banks during the war.

IV/1. The Soviet Union and Japan. Purchases of gold from banks in the Soviet Union and Japan were probably needed by Germany's allies, in return for Reichsmarks, to purchase goods from German corporations. All the purchases from the Soviet Union were prior to June of 1941. Germany purchased gold worth $23 million from the Soviet Union and $4.2 million from Japan.[29]

IV/2. The Bank for International Settlements. The BIS sold £2.3 million worth of gold to the Reichsbank in November of 1939. This gold was transported to Berlin from the BIS account in Bern at the Swiss National Bank. The gold was sold by the BIS in order to obtain German currency for payments to German organisations and corporations.[30]

V. End-of-Period Balance. The gold remaining in the possession of the Reichsbank at the time of Germany's collapse can be considered as the end-of-period balance for accounting purposes. Toward the end of the war, the Reichsbank began moving its gold to hiding places throughout Germany and Austria to protect it from the air raids which were damaging Reichsbank buildings. Most of this gold was seized by the Allies.

V/1. Gold Recovered by Germany. The largest cache of gold within Germany was found in April 1945 at the Kaiseroda Mine in the Thuringian town of Merkers. Smaller gold stocks were subsequently seized at Reichsbank branches throughout Germany and Austria and in German embassies abroad. The Allies recovered $198 million of gold in Germany, and centralised it at the Foreign Exchange Depository at Frankfurt am Main, where it was held by the Financial Division of the Office of the Military Government of Germany on behalf of the Tripartite Gold Commission.[31]

V/2. Gold Recovered in Italy. Gold seized by the Germans from the Italian government after the fall of Mussolini was transferred to an Italian castle at Fortezza in northern Italy, where it was discovered and captured by Allied forces. This gold was worth $64.8 million.[32] Gold belonging solely to the Italian government was captured by the Americans in Rome, but was never considered part of the German gold reserves.

V/3. Gold Recovered in Hungary. Allied forces captured $32.2 million worth of precious metals in Spital am Pyhrn (Austria) which had been seized from the Hungarian government by Germany.[33]

VI. Gold Shipped Abroad. Germany's desire for gold stemmed from its need for foreign exchange, both to buy goods for import, including war-related material, and to make payments abroad. These payments included routine items such as the cost of diplomatic representation, postal payments, and railroad charges, and war-related expenses for propaganda and espionage.

VI/1. Swiss Banks. The most important recipient of German gold was Switzerland which was not only able to sell the Germans vital supplies such as machinery and armaments, but also Swiss francs which were the only internationally accepted form of foreign exchange. The Swiss banks also served as conduits for transferring German gold to third parties, especially Spain, Portugal, and Sweden. The Swiss commercial banks were used by Germany as late as the spring of 1941 to make substantial dollar payments to the USSR and to the United States, as well as smaller payments to Japan and China.[34] Swiss banks received $450.4 million in gold. Gold shipments to the Swiss National Bank were relatively small at the beginning of 1940 and reached a peak in 1943. After early 1943 deliveries to Bern declined rapidly, and no gold was sent directly to the Swiss

National Bank from Berlin in 1945 (though some gold was taken from the Constance branch of the Reichsbank to Bern). The increased difficulty of selling gold on foreign markets after the end of 1943 meant that more gold was shipped to Reichsbank branches for use in South-East Europe. By the last year of the war, Germany's gold holdings were still very substantial, but the German authorities were less and less able to use them to obtain foreign resources, and the strategic usefulness of gold declines in consequence.

VI/2. *Other Foreign Banks.* Swiss banks were not the only recipients of German gold shipments. During the war, Germany sent abroad $92.4 million worth of gold to foreign banks not in Switzerland, primarily central banks. These gold shipments enabled the import of oil, machinery, arms and goods into Germany, as well as paying for diplomatic representatives, espionage, and covert military activity. The large gold shipments to Romania were intended to prolong that state's adherence to the Axis.[35]

VI/3. *Reichsbank Branches Abroad.* The Reichsbank maintained many offices throughout occupied Europe, and during the war $51.5 million worth of gold was shipped to these bank branches. A large portion of these shipments was in gold coin, and the majority of the gold was sent to the Reichsbank branch in Vienna. This gold was used to finance German military and espionage activity in southeastern Europe.[36]

VII. Domestic Commercial Use. Privately owned or semi-private corporations and banks within Germany received certain amounts of gold from the Reichsbank during the war, both for financial and industrial purposes.

VII/1. *Degussa and Sponholz & Co.* Degussa was primarily engaged in smelting gold and purifying it for industrial use. It purchased gold at slightly higher prices than the Prussian State Mint and resold it either to the Reichsbank or to licensed private purchasers. Sponholz & Co. was a German bank founded in 1835 and operated during the war by Hamel, a close friend of Reichsbank President Walther Funk. It was involved with international shipping of gold, generally in small quantities, and worked with the Reichsbank to sell jewelry abroad in return for hard currency. During the war, Degussa receive a net transfer of $3.3 million in gold, and Sponholz & Co. received a net $3.4 million.[37]

VII/2. *Deutsche Bank and Dresdner Bank.* Germany's two largest commercial banks received $3.6 million and $3.9 million worth of gold respectively from the Reichsbank.[38] These transfers were probably defrayed by the sale of German paper Reichsmarks, and the gold was used in financial transactions throughout occupied Europe and with the neutral states. Several other financial institutions, such as Dego (the German Gold Discount Bank) and the Prussian State Mint, also received large sums of gold from the Reichsbank, but they returned almost all the gold to the Reichsbank almost immediately (after smelting) and the net transfers were negligible.

VIII. Government Use. The German government itself used gold as a means of payment, mostly in regions where military operations made other forms of currency unacceptable or to directly finance governmental activity in foreign countries.

VIII/1. *The Auswaertiges Amt and the Amt Ausland Abwehr.* The Auswaertiges Amt (Foreign Office) received $3.1 million in gold from the Reichsbank, mostly in gold coins. This gold was transferred to various embassies and was used both to pay for diplomatic expenses in foreign countries and to finance espionage activity. The Amtsgruppe Ausland Abwehr (Foreign Military Intelligence branch) received $2.2 million in gold, mainly in gold coins, to pay for espionage and perhaps military activities.[39]

VIII/2. *The RSHA and the Wehrmacht.* The RSHA (Central State Security Office) and the Wehrmacht received $0.1 million and $0.3 million in gold respectively.[40] This gold was probably used to finance espionage and military activity in zones of warfare where paper Reichsmarks were not a widely accepted currency.

4. GOLD TRANSFERS OF THE REICHSBANK TO THE SNB

Table II provides details of the available information on the gold acceptances by the Swiss banks, and the agreement or difference with regard to data from the documents of the Reichsbank.

Table II: Gold imports into Switzerland 1939–45 (in Swiss franc millions)

Sources	Shipments from the Reichsbank to Switzerland (books of the Reichsbank) (1)		Swiss trade statistics (supplemented) (2)	Swiss trade statistics (according to Rings) (3)	Shipments from the Reichsbank to the depot at the SNB in Bern (SNB computations) (4)
1939	–		17.1	1.8	–
1940	222.0	(92.0)	126.3	125.9	103.2
1941	349.9	(215.1)	279.4	268.9	192.9
1942	493.2	(493.2)	474.6	458.4	497.5
1943	609.3	(609.3)	596.9	588.9	588.0
1944	275.4	(275.4)	258.2	258.2	257.3
1945	–	–	15.8	15.8	15.7
Total only					
1940–45	*1949.8*	*(1685.0)*	*1751.2*	*1716.1*	*1654.6*

(1) Shipments from Constance in the spring of 1945 have not been recorded here. The value of the Reichsbank shipments are given in parentheses, excluding shipments to the commercial banks. For 1939, no shipments are indicated in those books of the Reichsbank which have been examined until now (U.S. National Archives, Reichsbank).

(2) Column (3) supplemented by industrial gold (excluding 1944 and 1945). Source: Ilandelsstatistik.

(3) Only gold for banking transactions. 1940–45 according to Rings 1996, p.197 and Fior 1997, p. 24. Rings' source was the internal gold statistics of the Customs Administration. A copy of these statistics was provided to Rings in 1984 by the Swiss Federal Archives. 1939 according to trade statistics.

(4) Incoming transfers from Berlin according to a press documentation of the Swiss National Bank (1997), Table 5, Gold transaction of the German Reichsbank via Bern. It includes direct shipments to depts at the Swiss National Bank of other central banks and institutions.

COMMENTS ON TABLE II:

Figures used in research until now (Rings, see Column 3) are based on trade statistics but include only position 869a1 (gold for bank transactions). In 1939, the figures still appeared in the published trade statistics, but as of 1940 were for official internal use only.[41]

The Commission has supplemented the figures with position 869a2 (industrial gold) which were published in the trade statistics through 1943 (see Column 2). These figures are missing for 1944 and 1945 and are presently inaccessible. As in the previous years, the values are probably on the low side.[42]

A comparison of Column 2 (Imports of gold into Switzerland according to Swiss trade statistics) with Column 1 (Figures of the Reichsbank on deliveries to Switzerland) shows an approximate agreement for 1942–44, but substantial differences for 1940 and 1941.[43]

There is a plausible thesis to explain the difference between the figures of the Reichsbank and those of the Swiss trade statistics (according to the Customs Administration). It is peculiar that an unusual amount of gold from Russia, or respectively from the Soviet Union, entered Switzerland precisely in 1940 and 1941.[44] The federal attorney's office conducted an investigation in 1940 into the "German gold transports of ca 5,000 kg gold [...] which have been turned over to the Swiss Bank Corporation in Le Locle for smelting. It concerns Russian gold purchased in Germany; this is already the second shipment which has arrived in Le Locle."[45] These deliveries concerned Russian gold which Germany received for exports in the wake of the Ribbentrop-Molotow-Pact. They were sent in Russian cases through Germany to Switzerland.[46] It can be assumed that this gold will appear in the records of the Reichsbank as German gold (Germany was actually the owner), whereas the Swiss customs statistics (or respectively the Swiss recipient) considered it as Russian.[47]

For a comparison between Column 1 and Column 4, the figures in parentheses in Column 1, which apply only to the deliveries to the SNB, must be taken out. Deviations in 1940 amounted to 12% and in 1941 to 10%, and are thus quite high. The Commission's clarification of these deviations has not yet been completed.[48] The fact that in 1942, according to the Swiss National Bank, more gold from the Reichsbank arrive in Bern (Column 4) than Swiss trade statistics reported as total gold imports from Germany (Column 2) must be more closely examined.

5. GOLD OPERATIONS OF THE SNB

Analogous to the presentation used for the Reichsbank, the following Table III is also based on a comparison of origin and use of the gold by the Swiss National Bank. The largest part of the gold which arrived in Switzerland was taken over by the Swiss National Bank.

The presentation is structured as follows:

Holdings at the beginning of the war

+ Gold purchases at foreign central banks
+ Gold purchases from the BIS
+ Gold purchases from the private sector (banks and industry)
+ Gold purchases from the Swiss Confederation

=

Gold holdings of the SNB at the end of the war

+ Gold sales to foreign central banks
+ Gold sales to the BIS
+ Gold sales to the private sector (banks and industry)
+ Gold sales to the Swiss Confederation

5.1 Gold sales and purchases of the Swiss National Bank

The following tables show the transactions in Sfr of the Swiss National Bank for the period between September 1, 1939 and May 30, 1945.

Table III: Gold purchases and sales by the Swiss National Bank
September 1, 1939 – June 30, 1945 (in Sfr thousands and $)

I. Gold Reserves (rate of 4869.8 per refined kg)	on 1.9.1939		on 30.6.1945	
	2,860,224	660,758	4,626,300	1,068,750
	Sfr Purchases	$ Purchases	Sfr Sales	$ Sales
II. Axis				
II/1. Germany	1,231,850	284,577	19,495	4,504
II/2. Italy	150,036	34,661	0	0
II/3. Japan	0	0	4,956	1,145
Total	*1,381,886*	*319,238*	*24,451*	*5,649*

Table III: – continued

I. Gold Reserves (rate of 4869.8 per refined kg)	on 1.9.1939		on 30.6.1945	
	2,860,224	660,758	4,626,300	1,068,750
	Sfr Purchases	$ Purchases	Sfr Sales	$ Sales
III. Allies				
III/1. United States	2,242,917	518,150	706,055	163,110
III/2. Great Britain	668,454	154,424	0	0
III/3. Canada	65,283	15,081	0	0
Total	2,976,654	687,655	706,055	163,110
IV. Other countries purchasing gold				
IV/1. Portugal	85,101	19,660	536,601	123,964
IV/2. Spain	0	0	185,149	42,772
IV/3. Rumania	9,757	2,254	112,093	25,895
IV/4. Hungary	0	0	16,740	3,867
IV/5. Slovakia	0	0	11,254	2,600
IV/6. Turkey	0	0	14,847	3,430
Total	94,857	21,914	876,684	202,528
V. Other countries selling gold				
V/1. Argentina	33,585	7,759	0	0
V/2. France	193,261	44,646	0	0
V/3. Greece	486	112	0	0
V/4. Sweden	94,520	21,836	20,009	4,622
Total	321,851	74,353	20,009	4,622
VI. Various				
VI/1. BIS	61,508	14,209	18,201	4,205
VI/2. Swiss Banks, industrial and other clients	71,206	16,450	701,1981	61,988
VI/3. Swiss Confederation	269,305	62,214	1,087,873	251,316
VI/4. Swiss Mint	42,150	9,737	45,794	10,579
Total	444,168	102,610	1,853,065	428,088
VII. Corrections				
VII/1. Corrections in sale of gold on the market	39,085	9,029	0	0
VII/2. Differences in weight	3	1	87	20
VII/3. Revaluation transactions 1.9.1939–31.12.1939	0	0	8,729	2,017
VII/4. Other differences	0	0	3,350	774
Total	39,088	9,030	12,166	2,811
Total purchases and sales	5,258,504	1,214,800	3,492,431	806,808
Total	8,118,728	1,875,558	8,118,731	1,875,558

COMMENTS ON TABLE III:

A. General Notes

1. The figures for the purchase and sale of gold by the National Bank are based on the National Bank's gold transactions for its own account. Other sources such as movements of the Currency Equalisation Fund[49], the gold reserve statement[50], and the "Quarterly Reports" have been included. Minor differences still exist between these sources and the German documents which can be

consulted in the U.S. National Archives. These differences are probably due to deviations in the accounting figures.

2. The figures given here differ from those published in March 1997 by the Swiss National Bank for two reasons. On the one hand, the period considered by the Commission (1.9.1939–30.6.1945) is shorter than that of the SNB (1.1.1939–30.6.1945). On the other hand, the Commission's figures are based on the gold transactions for the SNG's own account, while those of the SNG are based on the "Quarterly Reports". The deviations, however, are minimal.

3. In the case of gold bars, the gold is posted in the following table at a price of Sfr 4,639.13 per fine kilogram until 31.12.1939 and a price of Sfr 4,869.80 per fine kilogram effective from 1 January 1940. The correction was carried out by means of the item "Revaluation of dealings". Sales of gold coins on the open market were posted at the selling price and not at the gold price. The item "Correction for gold sales on the open market" therefore permits the difference to be balanced.

4. It is necessary to draw a distinction between gold consignments from the Reichsbank to Switzerland in general and consignments to its own depository in Bern. The former actually exceed the latter as certain commercial banks bought gold directly in Germany without going through the Reichsbank's depository in Bern.

5. Moreover, it is necessary to draw a distinction between the *deliveries* by the Reichsbank to its depository in Bern, and the *sales* which it made to the Swiss National Bank. In fact, from its Bern depository, the Reichsbank sold gold to various countries (Portugal, Sweden, Romania, Slovakia, Spain, BIS, various other) for a total value of Sfr 445 million. The table takes into account only the purchases by the SNB from the Reichsbank, and not the total amounts shipped by the latter to Switzerland or to the Reichsbank depository in Bern.

6. The figures quoted in the table compromise all of the gold taken over by the SNB, including items resold to the Swiss Confederation and whose total appears under the heading "Swiss Confederation".

7. The operations undertaken using the Currency Equalisation Fund have been taken into account.

COMMENTS ON THE FIGURES IN TABLE III

I. Gold Reserves
Gold reserves on September 1, 1939 amounted to Sfr 2,860 million on September 1, 1939 (including the Currency Equalisation Fund) and represented the monetary reserves which had grown to Sfr 4,626 million by the end of the war. The increase thus amounted to Sfr 1,766 million.

II. Axis Countries
The net purchases of gold from the Axis powers amount to net Sfr 1,357 million, the great majority of which represented dealings with Germany.

II/1. Consignments from the Reichsbank to various depositories managed by the SNG totalled Sfr 1,654.6 million. Of these consignments, the SNB acquired a total of Sfr 1,231.9 million, and the balance was sold by the Reichsbank to various banks with depositories in Bern.

II/2. Of the Sfr 150 million acquired from Italy, Sfr 50 million forms part of the loan guarantee for a sum of Sfr 125 million granted in 1940. Since Italy was unable to repay all the sum, the Bank of Italy, under the influence of the German occupation authorities, sent the gold collateral to Switzerland on 20 April 1944. The balance of Sfr 98 million was acquired by the SNB in five transactions, two in September 1939, one in March 1942, one in May 1942 and the last in April 1943.

II/3. Gold to the value of Sfr 5 million was sold to Japan (Depository of the Yokohama Specie Bank) on 9 April 1945.

III. Allies

The SNB's gross purchases of gold from the Allies totals Sfr 2,977 million. They were used to cover the need of the Allies for Swiss francs (expenditures for diplomatic and secret service activities, representation of interests, humanitarian aid) and also for the balance of payments deficit result-ing from the freezing of Swiss assets as of June 14, 1941. Gold transactions by the SNB were there-fore significant from the summer of 1941 onwards and intensified at the start of 1944.

III/1. From the United States alone, the National Bank purchased gold with a gross value of Sfr 2,243 million. From the beginning of 1939 to the summer of 1940, the SNB *sold* gold to the value of several hundred million Swiss francs.

III/2. The SNB took delivery of a quantity of gold worth Sfr 668 million from the United Kingdom. In this case too, the total of all gold transfers cannot be equated with the sums of money offered to the United Kingdom. By March 1942, the SNB had bought dollars in London for Sfr 263 million.

III/3. Sfr 65 million in gold was purchased from the Canadian central bank.

IV. Other Countries as Purchasers of Gold

The SNB traded in significant quantities of gold with various European countries including Portugal, Spain and Romania. Portugal, the main purchaser, acquired gold to the net value of Sfr 451 million, mainly until the end of 1942. Spain acquired Sfr 185 million from the beginning of 1942, while Romania bought gold with a net value of Sfr 102 million. Other countries undertook similar transactions, though on a less significant scale. Hungary bought gold for Sfr 17 million, as did Slovakia (Sfr 11 million) and Turkey (Sfr 15 million).

V. Other Countries as Sellers of Gold

Net dealings with Argentina totalling Sfr 34 million took place in 1941, 1943 and 1944. Purchases by France for a total of Sfr 193 million were effected mainly between early 1941 and the end of 1942. 1942 transactions were for various gold coins (Vreneli, Napoléons, Sovereigns, Eagles), with a purchase value of Sfr 29 million. The transactions with Greece took place in early 1941 (gold coins in dollars – Sfr 0.5 million). Various transactions with Sweden were undertaken by the SNG between the end of 1941 and the beginning of 1942, and between the end of 1944 and the first half of 1945. In addition, it sold 50 gold bars to Stockholm on February 24, 1942. Total net purchases by the SNB came to Sfr 75 million.

VI. Miscellaneous

VI/1. Several sale and purchase transactions with the Bank for International Settlement (BIS) took place throughout the war. The SNB purchased gold, mainly between late 1940 and early 1941, to a net total of Sfr 43 million.

VI/2. The SNB's gold transactions also included sales on the Swiss market via the commercial banks (Sfr 550 million). These sales were intended to absorb available cash payment and to sta-bilise the Swiss franc. Due to the strong demand on the Swiss market, Swiss industry was also sup-plied directly by the SNB with gold totalling Sfr 80 million. Only 4th quarter figures for 1939 have been taken into account for gold coins.

VI/3. The term "Swiss Confederation" refers to the sums of gold which the SNB sold to federal authorities, basically as part of the "sterilisation" measures. This policy, which was applied from 1943 onwards, consisted of financing purchases of gold by issuing bonds to the public. At the end of the period under consideration, transactions by the Swiss Confederation totalled a net Sfr 819 million.

VI/4. With the exception of a purchase at the end of 1939 for Sfr 323,000, the position of "feder-al mint" refers to all movements connected with the minting of "Vreneli" gold coins from the beginning of 1945 onwards. The various mintings were in line with the SNB's policy of fighting inflation, and consisted of absorbing available cash by selling gold coins on the market.

VII. Corrections

VII/1. Corrections of sales on the market (profit from sales of gold coins).

VII/2. Corrections which the SNG undertook to offset differences in weighting.

VII/3. Corrections for transactions in 1939 (adjustment in the gold price valid from the 1940 one). See General Notes, note 3).

VII/4. This item for Sfr 3 million refers to the combined exchange rate and rounding differences.

5.2 Gold transactions of the Reichsbank via the SNB

Of the 1,654.6 million francs in gold delivered by the Reichsbank to Bern, the SNB acquired 1,224.2 million, corresponding to about three quarters of all Reichsbank deliveries during the war (all figures according to the SNB press documentation with respect to the period running from January 1, 1939 to June 30, 1945).[51] As is well known from the literature, there were also extensive movements of gold at the Bern depot of the Reichsbank without the SNB appearing as purchaser.[52] Large amounts of German gold were thus able to flow into the depots of other central banks, especially the Portuguese and Swedish national banks, as well as into the gold depot of the BIS. Table IV gives an overview of these operations in Bern.[53]

Table IV: Gold Transactions of the Reichsbank via its Depot at the SNB (net) in Bern 1940–45

Inflows (in Swiss franc millions)	1940	1941	1942	1943	1944	1945	Total
Transfers from Berlin	103.2	192.9	497.5	588.0	257.3	15.7	1,654.6
Turkish Central Bank				15.0			15.0

Outflows (in Swiss franc millions)	1940	1941	1942	1943	1944	1945	Total
SNB	67.1	142.7	428.4	374.2	182.1	29.8	1,224.2
Portuguese Central Bank			42.0	197.6	34.9		214.6
Swedish Central Bank		6.9	19.7	56.7	4.9		88.2
BIS	20.3	6.4	5.4	13.3	13.6		59.1
Rumanian Central Bank					51.1		51.1
Slovakian Central Bank		7.9			15.7		23.6
Spanish Central Bank				7.1			7.1
Various	−3.8		−0.1	5.7			1.7

Source: SNB Press Documentation (1997). Table V according to the SNB inventory accounting. A rate of 4920.63 per kilogram of fine gold has been used for this calculation. The figures cannot be directly compared with those in Tables I and III.

6. GOLD SHIPPED TO SWISS COMMERCIAL BANKS BY THE GERMAN REICHSBANK

Table Va: Shipments from the Reichsbank to Swiss banks 1940–41

Period	Swiss franc millions	dollar millions	refined gold kg
1st Semester 1940	115.2	26.6	23,654
2nd Semester 1940	14.8	3.4	3,046
Total 1940	*130.0*	*30.0*	*26,700*
1st Semester 1941	81.4	18.8	16,710
2nd Semester 1941	53.4	12.3	10,959
Total 1941	*134.8*	*31.1*	*27,669*
Total 1940–41	*264.8*	*61.2*	*54,369*

Source: Reichsbank records, U.S. National Archives

Table Vb: Shipments from the Reichsbank to Swiss banks 1940–41

	Swiss franc millions	dollar millions	refined gold kg
Swiss Bank Corporation (SBC)	158.6	36.6	32,571
Bank Leu & Co.	51.9	12.0	10,660
Union Bank of Switzerland (UBS)	37.0	8.5	7,593
Basler Handelsbank (BHB)	9.5	2.2	1,946
Credit Suisse	7.7	1.8	1,573
Eidgenössische Bank (EIBA)	0.1	0.03	26
Total	*264.8*	*61.13 (61.2*)*	*54,369*

Source: Reichsbank records, U.S National Archives: *rounding difference $0.07 million

COMMENTS ON THE TABLES Va AND Vb

It is important to draw a distinction between shipments of gold to commercial banks and actual purchases of gold by recipients. The above figures relate to the physical transfer (delivery) of gold to recipients in Switzerland. However, they do not provide any information on a possible change of ownership (purchase/sale), nor do they indicate the parties for whose account the banks received the gold delivered to them.

Immediately after the war, the U.S. occupying forces seized Reichsbank records for examination. The figures for shipments of gold to Swiss banks obtained from these records were made available during the negotiations on the 1946 Washington Agreement, and are documented in the relevant literature on the subject.[54] The study by S. Zabludoff published in October 1997 on transfers of the Swiss banks is also based on American sources and repeats the same figures: according to calculations of 1946, gold valued at about 20.3 million dollars, or 87.3 million Swiss francs (exchange rate: 1:4.3), was delivered to Swiss commercial banks between mid-1940 and May 1945.[55]

Table Vc: Gold shipments from the Reichsbank to Swiss commercial banks 1940–41 according to American sources 1946

	In dollars*
Swiss Bank Corporation	7,999,047
Bank Leu & Co.	6,183,931
Credit Suisse	1,749,740
Basler Handelsbank	1,081,958
Eidgenössische Bank	28,835
Other Banks	3,282,145
Total	*20,325,656*

Source: U.S. National Archives, RG 59,800.515.4201.

* Details of values and descriptions according to original sources.

The American occupation forces (1946), as well as the Commission, have based their information on copies of the Reichsbank records. In comparing the results of the two analyses, substantial differences can be found. According to calculations of the Commission, it appears that significantly larger amounts of gold were shipped to Swiss commercial banks in 1940 and 1941 than was previously believed. According to the U.S. figures, gold valued at about 20 million dollars was delivered, whereas the Commission estimates the gold to be worth a total of 61 million dollars (see Table Va).[56]

This discrepancy can partly be attributed to the limited time period reviewed by the Allies in 1946. If the Allies' examination period of 1946 is taken into consideration (as of mid 1940 only), these deviations can be partly explained. According to the study of the Commission, most of the gold was delivered to Swiss commercial banks during the first few months of 1940. It was exactly this period of substantial deliveries from the Reichbank which were only partly taken into consideration in the Allied survey of 1946. As various sources have suggested U.S. figures used during the hearings on the Washington Agreement relate only to the period from the beginning of May 1940. And in all likelihood, they only take into account gold shipped by the Reichsbank from June 30, 1940 on.[57]

Table Va shows transfers of German gold to Switzerland over six-month periods. As the figures indicate, of the 61.2 million dollars in gold delivered to the banks, 26.6 million dollars was shipped during the period prior to the end of June 1940. About 34.6 million dollars was then shipped during the subsequent 18 months until the end of 1942 (the period for which deliveries to banks were recorded). The latter figure is 14 million dollars greater than the figure obtained by the Allies directly after the war. From the present stand of investigation, it is not possible that a part of the shipments to the banks in Switzerland consisted of physical transfers, without the banks appearing as purchasers. It is also conceivable that the Allied investigators knew which shipments referred to transfers only. Perhaps they excluded the corresponding amounts from their calculations of Swiss gold receipts. A more thorough analysis of the documents, forming the basis of American sources cited by the authors, could clarify the question.

7. GOLD TRANSACTIONS BETWEEN SWITZERLAND AND THE ALLIES

The SNB purchased significant quantities of gold from the Allied central banks for the following reasons:

- From the end of the 1930s to June 1941, substantial capital sums crossed the Atlantic. The flows of money in both directions necessitated intervention by the SNG which successively sold, and then bought, dollars.
- Despite the embargo by the Allies, Switzerland depended for its essential supplies on imports from Great Britain, the United States and other Allied states.
- The United Kingdom and the United States established rules on commercial and financial dealing but did not conclude clearing agreements with Switzerland. Exchanges of goods were paid in currency and not by any offsetting procedures.
- Where major sums were involved, the Allied governments needed to use the Swiss franc, which was replacing the dollar and sterling as the internationally accepted currency. The American and British governments were therefore using the Swiss franc to finance their diplomatic service, humanitarian aid and intelligence activities in Europe, to support allied governments, and to finance the role of Swiss diplomacy as a force protecting the interest of various Allied countries occupied by the Axis powers.
- Industrial and commercial circles continued to pressure Switzerland to buy gold from the United States. Industries, especially the watchmaking industry, wanted to finance their exports, while financial creditors were demanding the return of the considerable U.S.A. investments back to Switzerland.[58]

All these factors contributed to the increases in gold purchases by the SNB from the United States and United Kingdom, as can be seen in Tables VI and VII.

After the freezing of Swiss assets in the United States in June 1941, a ruling on the dollar-based economy was discussed by the Swiss National Bank, the Swiss Bankers Association, the commercial banks and the Swiss Confederation. In order to obviate the inflationary effects of gold purchases, the SNB requested the Swiss Confederation to purchase gold from the Allies in order to "sterilise" the notes in circulation. These dealings involved Confederation expenditures which were financed by bonds issued on the Swiss market.[59]

Table VI: Growth of the Confederation's gold holdings *(in Sfr millions, as of December 31)*

	U.S.A.	U.K.	Canada	Total
1943	11.6			11.6
1944	266.4	195.3		461.7
1945	636.3	379.8	11.9	1,027.9

Source: Swiss National Fiscal Administration and Accounting Authority, summary of foreign assets March 5, 1949. BAR E 6100 (B) 1972/96/241/37.

Because of the economic war (blockades and restrictive measures) and military operations which made transport of valuables almost impossible, these gold deposits remained in the United States and contributed to the growing internationalisation of Switzerland's financial services industry.

Table VII: Development of the gold reserves of the SNB and the Confederation
1 January 1939 – 31 December 1945 (in Sfr)

	1.1.1939	31.12.1945
Swiss National Bank's accounts		
Home:		
Total Home	*1,654,096,481*	*1,127,592,202*
Abroad:		
Paris	11,932,959	
London	976,650,052	789,848,960
New York	246,743,545	2,561,652,429
Buenos Aires		37,906,791
Ottawa		260,039,615
Total Abroad	*1,235,326,556*	*3,649,447,795*
Total SNB	*2,889,423,037*	*4,777,039,997*
Swiss Confederation's accounts:		
London	104, 981	317,440,010
New York		638,448,809
Ottawa		74,416,906
Total Confederation's accounts	*104,981*	*1,030,305,725*

Source: SNB (Ed.) Goldtransakaonen für eigene Rechnung, 1939–45, Zürich 1997. Gold price for 1939: Sfr 4,639.13 per kg fine gold. For 1939, the Currency Equalisation Fund amounting to Sfr 430 million (according to the new gold price set in 1940) has not been taken into account. Tables VI and VII cannot be directly compared.

After the war, statistical tables were drawn up to show that gold purchases by the SNG from the Reichsbank were lower than its gold purchases from the Allies.[60] Nonetheless, these statistics mask the fundamental differences between the quantities of gold acquired under the abnormal conditions of war on the one hand, and the holdings of gold whose origin is incontestable and whose immobilisation was therefore limited to the duration of hostilities, on the other. Purchases by Switzerland of gold from the Allies and the Axis powers were fundamentally different, both in terms of the gold's provenance as well as the use of the Swiss francs obtained thereby.

8. SUMMARY

The most important results of the present report can be summarised as follows:
- The part which Switzerland contributed to the gold operations of the Reichsbank with foreign countries for the reporting period (September 1, 1939 until June 1, 1945) amounted to 76% (Table I, Point VI). Of this amount, 86% went to the SNB and 14% to the Swiss commercial banks.
- Of the gold amounting to Sfr 1,684.9 million ($389.2 million) which was delivered to it, SNB net purchases were Sfr 1,212.4 million ($280.1 million), see Tables I, II, and III. It corresponds to 62% of the total shipments by the Reichsbank to Switzerland, or respectively 72% of the shipments to the SNB.
- With $61 million, shipments of gold by the Reichsbank to commercial banks between 1939 and 1945 are a good three times higher than at first assumed. Amounts purchased for their own accounts are unknown. Complete figures are not yet available.
- The gold shipments from the Reichsbank cannot be compared with those from the Allied side. In contrast to gold purchased by Germany, these amounted to means of payment legally acquired by the Allies. They came from international movements of capital and served to finance exports. They were also used for humanitarian purposes and for services needed by the war effort.
- This working paper, which has concentrated on a presentation of statistical data, has not addressed important aspects of the subject. Remarks on Switzerland as a financial centre and the problem of the freely convertible franc, the question of the motives and degree of awareness of the participants, and the effect of gold transactions on security policy are lacking in particular.
- To be able to clarify the responsibility and co-operation of all those involved, previously inaccessible documents and sources must be included and evaluated.
- The Commission will deal with other essential aspects in a details interim report to be published at the beginning of 1998.

ANNEX: ARCHIVES

1. Archives taken into consideration

Switzerland

Bundesarchiv, Berne
Archiv der Schweizerischen Nationalbank, Zurich
Archiv der Eidgenössischen Oberzolldirektion, Berne
Archiv der Credit Suisse Group, Zurich

Archiv des Schweizerischen Bankvereins, Basle
Archiv der UBS, Zurich
Archiv der Schweizerischen Bankierverinigung, Basle
Archiv für Zeitgeschiehte, ETH Zurich

U.S.A.

United States National Archives, College Park, Maryland
Federal Reserve Bank of New York Archives, New York
Franklin D. Roosevelt Library, Hyde Park, New York
Library of Congress, Washington, DC

Germany

Bundesarchiv, Berlin
Bundesarchiv/Militärarchiv, Freiburg i. Br.
Politisches Archiv des Auswärtigen Amtes, Bonn
Archiv der Bundesbank, Frankfurt
Institut für Zeitgeschichte, Munich

Italy

Archivio della Bankca d'Italia, Rome
Archivio del Ministero degli Affari Esteri, Rome
Archivio Centrale dello Stato, Rome

2. Archives not considered in this report

Switzerland

Archiv der Bank für Internationalen Zahlungsausgleich, Basle

France

Archives du Ministère des Finances, Paris
Archives du Ministère des Affaires Etrangères, Paris

Great Britain

Public Record Office, Kew Gardens
Archives of the Bank of England

3. Archives unable to be consulted to date

Archives of the Tripartite Gold Commision, Brussels
Zentrum für die Sicherung historisch-dokumentarischer Sammlungen (ACHIDK), Moscow

NOTES

[1] See Weinmann, Martin (ed.): Das nationalsozialistische Lagersystem (Catalogue of Camps and Prisons, ND), Frankfurt s.M., 1990, p715 ff.

[2] The Commission is using the term looted gold as a description of a historical fact. It is expressing no opinion at the present time on the juridical illegitimacy of the appropriation of gold from national banks (category 4).

[3] For the Reichsmark (RM), an exchange rate of 2.479 RM/$ has been used.

[4] Documents, "Goldbestand am 1.9.1939" and "Sanderdeviseneingagn Zwischen dem 1.9.1939 und dem 1.11.1944", Four-Year Plan Memoranda, 28.11.1944, Centre for the Safekeeping of Collection of Historical Documents (ZCHUDK), Moscow, Inventory 700-1-97. In the following sited as "Four-Year Plan Memoranda".

[5] The first of these was the Konversionskasse, begun in 1933, followed by the Asservaten Sanderkento in 1934. These two accounts were closed out in 1935; a third account, the Goldankauf, was opened in 1934 and received most of the gold from the Konversionskasse and the Asservaten Soncerkonto. Treuhandgesellschaft von 1933, a fourth secret gold account, was begun in 1935, and the fifth account, Asservat "DER" (Devisen Reserve), was opened in 1937. These secret reserves were sometimes described by Reichsbank employees as the new "Juliusturm," in reference to pre-World War I hidden gold reserves intended for war preparation. U.S. National Archives. RG260, Box 444, Office of the Financial Division and the Finance Advisor, File 940.62 Work Papers, Table I. "Balances of Six Hidden Gold-Reserve Accounts of the Reichsbank." Hereafter cited as "Six Hidden Gold-Reserve Accounts."

[6] "Four-Year Plan Memoranda"

[7] "Four-Year Plan Memoranda"

[8] U.S. National Archives. RG43, 88-M, Box 201, Memorandum from O.F. Fletcher, "Revised Estimate of German Gold Movements from March 1938 to May 1945," June 12, 1946. Hereafter cited as "Fletcher Memorandum."

[9] See I/2, and III/1, infra. While Austrian gold reserves were eventually incorporated into the general gold reserves of the Reichsbank, there seems to be no danger of double-counting the Austrian and secret gold reserves in 1939. There was no large increase in hidden reserves in 1938, indicating that Austrian gold was at that point still recorded separately in the Reichsbank accounts. "Six Hidden Gold Reserve Accounts."

[10] "Four-Year Plan Memoranda."

[11] SNB Archiv

[12] "Four-Year Plan Memoranda."

[13] "Fletcher Memorandum."

[14] See III/1, infra.

[15] U.S. National Archives. RG260, Folder 940.60, "Netherlands Gold Bars Resmelted in 1942," 26 October 1946.

[16] SNB Archiv, 119.8, Brief, Gouverneur A. Goffin (Banque Nationale de Belgique) an die Reichsbank, 5. Mai 1943.

[17] "Four-Year Plan Memoranda."

[18] U.S. National Archives. RG43, International Conference, Lot File M-88, Council of Foreign Ministers. Box 257, Folder "Italian Gold." Division of Financial Affairs, Department of State, "German Gold Position" (approx. 1946).

[19] Poland enjoyed substantial gold reserves prior to the war; however, it was able to get the larger part out of the country before it could be confiscated by the Germans.

[20] "Four-Year Plan Memoranda."

[21] "Four-Year Plan Memoranda."

[22] Bruno Melmer was the leader of the SS office AII, Wirtschaftsverwaltungshauptamt.

[23] Fischler, Hersch: Erläuterungen zur Zahlenauswertung SS-Gold/Melmer-Lieferungen.

[Commentary on the evaluation of figures related to SS gold/Melmer shipments] Manuscript to the attention of the ICE Commission, Düsseldorf 1997. Fischler has mainly evaluated the Omgus records.

[24] Zabludoff, Sidney: Movements of Nazi Gold, Report June 1997, Table 1, p. 6A.

[25] With regard to gold credits for the Reichsbank, III/2 Victims of Concentration Camps (= "Melmer Gold"), $2.5 million. The information is based on an evaluation of the records of the Reichsbank "Bestandskontrolle des Goldkaufs, 1940–1945", which can be seen in the U.S. National Archives on microfilm in Inventory RG56, Entry 66A816, Box 3, Roll 5. Only those entries under the heading of "Delivered by", which unequivocally bear the handwritten notation "Melmer", have been evaluated. It is possible that there were other entries from Melmer which, in this particular source, were not identifiable due to the unsatisfactory quality of the copy.

[26] Institut für Zeitgeschichte, NID-13817; ZS 1216 (notation Melmer from 11.2.48).

[27] U.S. National Archives, RG56, Entry 66A816, Box 3, Microfilm "Records of the German Reichsbank", rolls 5, 25, 49–53, and 62, cited in the following as "Records of the German Reichsbank. These books cover the period from January 1, 1940 until 1945. The figure of $2.5 million cited here includes only gold coins and ingots which, according to the entries of the precious metal section of the Reichsbank, were delivered by Melmer. The value of victim gold, such as dental gold, watches and rings, which was brought from Auschwitz and other Eastern camps is listed under "other private objects". None of these figures take into consideration non-gold valuables such as paper money. See III/3 below.

[28] Because exact figures for the actual accumulation of this gold is lacking, the calculation of this figure is an accounting process. The debit and credit side of the balance sheet must be equal. Hence the residual, or 'Other Private Holdings' category, is equal to the difference between the total gold debits and all the known gold credits.

[29] Zabludoff, Sidney: "Movements of Nazi Gold," October 1997.

[30] Bank for International Settlements, "Note on Gold Operations Involving the Bank for International Settlements and the German Reichsbank," May 1997, section 2.4(a). Hereafter cited as "BIS" Note."

[31] "Fletcher Memorandum."

[32] "Fletcher Memorandum". According to Smith, Arthur L., Hitler's Gold. The Story of the Nazi War Loot, Oxford 1989, p. 101, this amounts to $25 million. The remainder of the Italian gold was found in Frankfurt.

[33] "Fletcher Memorandum."

[34] A memorandum by Federal Reserve Bank of New York Vice-President Knoke gives details of $558,008 paid throught the Swiss Bank Corporation in March 1941 for U.S. exports of petroleum to Germany. Federal Reserve Bank of New York Archives. File C261 Germany-Reichsbank, Memo to File from L.W. Knoke, 7 July 1941.

[35] "Records of the German Reichsbank." This sum may include oil payments as well as outright bribery.

[36] "Records of the German Reichsbank."

[37] "Records of the German Reichsbank."

[38] "Records of the German Reichsbank."

[39] "Records of the German Reichsbank." The figures cited for Reichsbank transfers to financial institutions are somewhat more precise than those for transfers to non-bank government or industrial organisations, due to differences in Reichsbank accounting techniques. Because of the small quantities involved, however, the net error will probably be insignificant.

[40] "Records of the German Reichsbank."

[41] Import and export of gold for banking trasactions and for coined silver in 1940 (Position 869a and 869e), in possession of the Customs Administration; Gold transactions of Switzerland with Germany (BAR E 7110 1973/134, Vol. 7) as well as several documents in BAR E 6100 (A)

25, Vol. 2316. See Fior, Michel: Die Schweiz und das Gold der Reichsbank. Was wusste die Schweizerische Nationalbank? Zurich 1997. See Rings, Werner: Raubgold aus Deutschland. Die "Golddrehscheibe" Schweiz im Zweiten Weltkrieg, Zurich 1996.

[42] The gold statistics of the Customs Administration for internal use includes Position 869a1 only.

[43] Shipments in 1945 were no longer entered in the books of the Reichsbank.

[44] Russia/Soviet Union in the trade statistics: as of 1926 including Ukraine; 1941 including Latvia, Lithuania, Estonia; as of 1942 excluding Latvia, Lithuania, Estonia (Länderverzeichnis Aussenhandelsstatistik der Schweiz [1925–1950], compiled by the Federal Customes Administration, Foreign Trade Statistics). Import figures are in Sfr million:

1937:	0
1938:	0
1939:	12.3
1940:	121.9
1941:	38.4
1942:	0
1943:	no information
1944:	0
1945:	0

[45] Public Prosecutor's Office to the Federal Department of Finance and Customs 23.2.1940, in: BAR E 6100 (a) 19/1484, (Letter printed in SDD, Vol. 13, p. 576. See also SDD, Vol. 13, p. 652, note 2). See also SDD Vol. 13.p.652, note 2).

[46] "Les envois d'or provenant d'Allemagne à destination de la Société de Banque Suisse, siège du Locle, sont arrivés à plus d'une reprise dan cette ville. Il S' agissait d'or russ qui était fondu et transformé en métal suisse. Il repartait ensuite pur New-York et ne venait done en Suisse qu'en transit." (Notice of the Federal Public Ministry. Department of Police. 18.5.1940, in: BAR E 4320 (b) 1968/195, Vol.41.

[47] The 5,000 kilso mentioned had a value of just under Sfr 25 million. It amounted to about one fifth of the value reported for Russia. The value of gold imports from Russia and Germany together in 1940 and 1941 amounted to somewhat more than the figures indicated in the books of the Reichsbank.

[48] Amazingly enough, the figure in Column 4 for 1942 is higher than in Column 1. This means that, according to the inventory records of the SNB, gold receipts from the Reichsbank were more highly estimated for this year than was evidenced by our investigations in the books of the Reichsbank.

[49] SNB Archives, 122.0, "Gold of the Currency Equalisation Fund"

[50] SNB Archives, 122.0, "Gold of the Currency Equalisation Fund"

[51] Source: SNB Press Documentation (1997), 4, 11, Table 5. See also SDD, Vol. 15, p. 1124 ff.

[52] See Rings, Werner: Raubgold sus Deutschland. Die "Golddrehscheibe" Schweiz im Zweiten Weltkerig, Zurich 1996, p. 56; Vogler, Robert U.: Der Goldverkehr der Schweizerischen Nationalbank mit der Deutschen Reichsbank 1939–1945, in: Gold, Währung und Konjunktur 1 (1985), p. 70–71.

[53] This data stems from SNB Press Documentation of March 1997 and is based on the Bank's original accounting figures.

[54] von Castelmur, Linus: Schweizerisch-Allierte Finanzbezichungen im übergang vom Zweiten Weltkrieg zum Kaltern Krieg. Die deutschen Guthaben in der Schweiz zwischen Zwangsliquidierung und Freigabe (1945–1952), Zurich 1997, p. 59, notes 144 and 145; Durrer, Marco: Die schweizerisch-amerikanischen Finanzbezichungen im Zweiten Weltkrieg. Von der Blockeirung der schweizerischen Guthaben in den USA über die "Safehaven"-politik zum Washingtoner Abkommen (1941–1946). Bern 1984, p. 268–270.

[55] According to Zabludoff, Sidney: Movements of Nazi Gold, October 1997. p.6a Table I.

[56] This discrepancy is at first glance all the more amazing since the calculation made by the Commission for Reichsbank shipments to the SNB – as opposed to those to commercial banks – are generally in agreement with the values known. The remaining differences in values for Reichsbank shipments to the SNB can be explained in a satisfactory manner as resulting from minor methodological problems and from the dissimilar value of gold in the books of the two Central Banks.

[57] The date of 30 April 1940 was chosen as the starting point where Allied claims for restitution of gold by Switzerland began. The calculations themselves were made for the time beginning 30 June 1940, as emerges from a report of the Department of the Treasury in 1946. "For the purpose at hand June 30, 1940 has been chosen as the base date in order to make the case as favorable as possible to the Swiss and eliminate any uncertainty as to legitimate acquisitions of gold by Germans prior to the attack on the low countries". U.S. National Archives RG59, 800.515,4201. See Durer, Mareo: Die schweizerisch-amerikanischen Finanzbeziehungen im Zweiten Weltkrieg. Von der Blockierung der schweizerischen Guthaben in den USA über die "Safehaven"-Politik zum Washingtoner Abkommen (1941–1946), Bern 1984, p. 268 ff.

[58] See Perrenoud, Marc: Banques et diplomatie suisses à la fin de la Deuxième Guerre mondiale. Politique de neutralité et relations financières internationales, in: Studien und Quellen, Hg. Schweizerisches Bundesarchiv, Nr. 13/14 (1987/88). p. 7–128.

[59] See Tanner, Jakob: Bundeshaushalt, Währung und Kriegswirtschaft. Eine finanzsoziologische Analyse der Schweiz zwischen 1938 und 1953, Zürich 1986, p. 248–257.

[60] See SDD, Vol. 15, especially p.394–399, 920–937 and 1108–1141.

The Swiss National Bank's gold operations
during the Second World War

1. The general scope of gold operations

The Swiss National Bank

The Swiss National Bank (SNB) is not a commercial bank; it is a central bank responsible, since its establishment in 1907, for implementing the country's monetary policy within the framework of the applicable exchange rate system. Until the fifties, the monetary system was based on the gold standard, under which the SNB was required to stabilise the Swiss franc rate around the gold parity. Following the devaluation of the Swiss franc in 1936, this parity was fixed at approximately 205 mg of fine gold (Sfr 4,900 per kilogram).

Switzerland's monetary policy aims during the War

When the War broke out in 1939, the general insecurity made it exceedingly difficult to preserve the country's monetary stability. The SNB concentrated its efforts on maintaining confidence in the Swiss franc in order to prevent a collapse of the country's financial system, which would have undermined its capacity for military defence. To this end, maintaining the gold convertibility of the Swiss franc was considered to be of the essence.

Beyond this primary objective, it was necessary to support the country's war economy, namely:

- to permit the import of products vital to the country by holding adequate and freely disposable gold reserves in Switzerland;
- to secure employment and social peace by encouraging exports.

Moreover, the principle of neutrality required Switzerland to maintain business relations with all sides engaged in the conflict.

Later on, when Switzerland was completely surrounded by the Axis forces, the Swiss authorities came to realise that a stable Swiss franc, freely convertible and accepted everywhere, represented an additional safeguard in view of the threat of a German invasion.

The risk of a financial collapse when hostilities broke out

When the conflict began, the fear of witnessing a breakdown of the Swiss franc was considerable given the massive outflows of capital. The SNB was obliged to intervene in support of the Swiss franc. In the first few months of 1940, gold sales and outflows of foreign exchange assumed such proportions that Switzerland seriously considered introducing general foreign exchange controls in line with most other European countries. After the signing of the armistice treaty between

France and Germany (in June 1940), however, the situation became more relaxed. Capital ceased to leave the country, and this in turn eased the pressure to introduce additional administrative measures.

Growing use of the Swiss franc in European payments

In May 1941, when the assets of continental Europe in the United States were blocked, the Swiss franc was profoundly affected. It was increasingly substituted for the dollar in international payments, particularly for business transactions in continental Europe. Thus the German Reichsbank sold gold in the Swiss market in exchange for Swiss francs which it then used to pay for German imports, notably tungsten and manganese from Portugal and Spain. The central banks of these countries subsequently requested the SNB to convert the Swiss francs they had received from Germany into gold.

These three-sided operations were a cause for concern to the SNB in several respects:

First, they led to a continued diminution of its gold stock in Switzerland (see Chart 1), and this at the very moment when its assets on the other side of the Atlantic were blocked. Consequently, In October 1941, the SNB asked the Reichsbank to acquire its Swiss francs from the SNB rather than in the market. The Reichsbank only partially complied with this request. In December 1942, when gold holdings in Berne had reached a critical level, Switzerland decided to go still further and centralise all international gold transactions at the SNB. This would finally help to solve the problem of a continued depletion of the country's gold stock.

Second, from 1942 onwards, the question of the illegal origin of German gold began to arise. In this respect, it is obvious that the centralisation of international gold transactions at the SNB had the effect of increasing the risk of the Bank's receiving gold confiscated in occupied countries. Nevertheless, the SNB did not wish to call its strategy of free convertibility of the Swiss franc in question again. It simply asked the Reichsbank to transact its foreign payments by direct gold transfers to the countries concerned without recourse to the Swiss franc. Here again, the Reichsbank only partly complied with the SNB's request. While it had in fact begun to transfer gold direct to Portugal from the summer of 1942 onwards, it still continued to use the Swiss franc for its payments to other European countries. German gold purchases thus remained on a high level until spring 1944.

The implications of the freeze on Swiss assets in the United States

The gold transactions with the Allies caused monetary problems of a different order. Beginning in mid-1941, the Allies' demand for Swiss francs assumed considerable proportions due to their growing trade deficit vis-à-vis Switzerland and their need for Swiss francs to effect certain international payments.

Accordingly, the United States, the United Kingdom and Canada sold the SNB substantial amounts of gold for Swiss francs.

Chart 1
Development of Swiss gold holdings
(in metric tons)

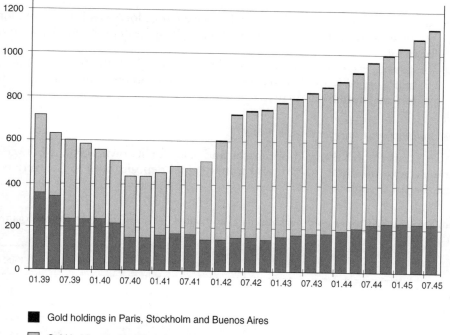

■ Gold holdings in Paris, Stockholm and Buenos Aires

▢ Gold holdings in New York, London and Ottawa

■ Gold holdings in Switzerland

During the War a metric ton of gold was worth 4.87 million Swiss francs or 1.13 million US-Dollars

Since the Swiss francs which were supplied to the Allies were used in large part for the payment of products manufactured in Switzerland they led to an expansion of domestic liquidity. The SNB, concerned about the inflationary consequences of this money creation, tried to neutralise the effects by selling gold coins on the Swiss market. From 1941 to 1945 the SNB sold Sfr 420 million worth of gold coins on the market. For its part, the Confederation agreed to siphon off liquidity by issuing loans in the capital market; subsequently, it sterilised the proceeds of these loans by repurchasing part of the SNB's gold frozen in the United States.

Increasing gold purchases from the Allies and the impossibility of disposing freely of its gold holdings outside continental Europe made the SNB all the more dependent on gold deliveries from the Reichsbank.

2. The extent of the SNB's gold transactions

Two types of transactions

As shown in Chart 2, the SNB carried out two separate types of gold transactions:

- on the one hand, it bought and sold, in exchange for Swiss francs, gold for its own account to the credit or debit of its gold deposits in Berne and abroad;
- on the other hand, it administered gold deposits which the BIS and sixteen foreign central banks had set up in the Berne head office in order to facilitate their mutual payments.

Gold purchases and sales for its own account

Table 1 lists the SNB's gold purchases and sales for its own account between January 1939 and June 1945 to and from its gold deposits both in Switzerland and abroad.

Table 1 The SNB's net gold purchases (+) and sales (−)* from 1.1.1939 to 30.6.1945
(in metric tons)

	1939	1940	1941	1942	1943	1944	1945	Total
Argentina			1.2		3.0	2.5		6.7
Canada				2.3	3.2	5.2	2.8	13.5
Germany		13.6	29.0	87.1	76.0	37.0	6.1	248.8
France	−16.5	0.1	13.8	19.7			6.2	23.2
Greece			0.1					0.1
Hungary			−2.0		−1.2	−0.2		−3.4
Italy	5.3			10.0	5.0	10.8		31.1
Japan							−1.0	−1.0
Portugal			−42.6	−56.5	0.5	5.9		−92.7
Rumania			−8.1	−0.9	−14.0	2.0		−21.0
Slovakia			−1.3			−1.0		−2.3
Spain				−15.2	−17.9	−3.3	−1.6	−38.0
Sweden			9.6	−0.5		2.1	4.1	15.3
Turkey					−3.0			−3.0
UK	−19.1	0.1	0.0	22.8	33.7	42.4	38.3	118.2
USA	−116.2	−113.3	170.7	137.4	34.6	70.0	47.9	231.1
B.I.S.	−0.3	1.8	3.5			2.6	1.0	8.6
Swiss government		−4.1	−13.8	−26.3	23.2	−74.0	−73.1	−168.1
Industry			−1.3	−3.8	−5.0	−3.8	−2.5	−16.4
Market	−5.8	−12.1	−13.9	−35.0	−13.3	−19.7	−13.3	−113.2

B.I.S. : Bank for International Settlements

* Including the purchases and sales of the Exchange Stabilisation Fund.
During the war a metric ton of gold worth was 4.87 million Swiss francs or 1.13 million US-Dollars.

Chart 2 Principal net gold flows recorded by the SNB from 1939 to 1945
(in metric tons)

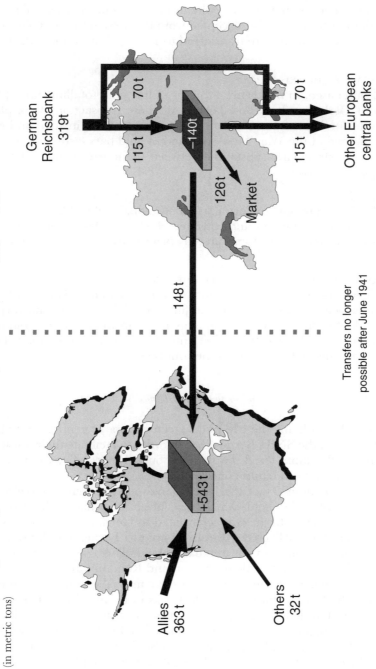

German
Reichsbank
319t

70t

115t

−140t

126t

Market

115t

70t

Other European
central banks

148t

+543t

Allies
363t

Others
32t

Transfers no longer
possible after June 1941

During the War a metric ton of gold was worth 4.87 million Swiss francs or 1.13 million US-Dollars

OPERATIONS WITH THE ALLIES

The SNB acquired, in net terms, 363 tons of fine gold to the amount of Sfr 1.8 billion from the United States, the United Kingdom and Canada. This gold was added to the deposits in London, New York and Ottawa where it remained frozen until the end of the War; excepted from this were 6 tons of gold from the deposit in Ottawa, which were transferred to Portugal's account with the Bank of Canada.

OPERATIONS WITH THE AXIS FORCES

The SNB purchased, in net terms, 279 tons of fine gold totalling almost Sfr 1.4 billion from Germany, Italy and Japan. All these transactions took place in Switzerland. Purchases from Germany (249t) commenced in 1940 and continued until the end of the War. They consisted of gold bars (210t) and gold coins (39t) and were particularly substantial between the fourth quarter of 1941 and the first quarter of 1944.

OTHER OPERATIONS

The SNB sold gold mainly to Portugal (93t) and Spain (38t). Market sales began in earnest from 1942 onwards and consisted chiefly of sales of gold pieces. Gold sales to industry totalled 16.4 tons and took place between July 1941 and the end of the War.

IMPLICATIONS FOR THE GOLD RESERVES OF THE SNB

As a result of these operations, Switzerland's gold holdings expanded by more than 400 tons between January 1939 and June 1945. This increase, however, only became evident from 1941 onwards, mainly in the form of blocked gold in New York, London and Ottawa. In Switzerland, the gold stock remained stable as purchases and sales balanced each other out (see Chart 1).

Operations carried out for account of foreign central banks

The German Reichsbank, the BIS and sixteen European central banks had set up gold deposits at the SNB's Berne office in order to facilitate their mutual payments. The SNB administered the deposits but all transactions were initiated exclusively by the central banks concerned.

Table 2 gives a summary of the Reichsbank's gold movements registered at the SNB. In 1939, the gold which Czechoslovakia had delivered to the Reichsbank's deposit in Berne was repatriated to Germany. Between 1940 and 1945, the Reichsbank delivered 336 tons of gold to Berne. The SNB acquired 249 tons of this gold, other major purchasers being Portugal (44t), Sweden (18t), the Bank for International Settlements (12t) and Rumania (10t).

As a consequence of the imbalances in their mutual payments a number of central banks had to replenish their gold stocks in Berne while others accumulated surpluses. This led to numerous gold transports from and to Switzerland. The biggest consignments of gold originated from Germany and France. Conversely, the central banks of Portugal and Spain repatriated large quantities of gold to their respective countries (Portugal 129t, Spain 38t).

Table 2 Gold flows from the German Reichsbank via Berne (in metric tons)

	1939	1940	1941	1942	1943	1944	1945	Total
Incoming								
Transfers from Berlin		21.0	39.2	101.1	119.5	52.3	3.2	336.3
Narodni Banka Cekoslovenska	12.5							12.5
B.I.S.	4.5							4.5
Central Bank of Turkey					3.0			3.0
Outgoing								
Transfers to Berlin	17.0							17.0
SNB		13.6	29.0	87.1	76.0	37.0	6.1	248.8
Central Bank of Portugal				8.5	28.0	7.1		43.6
Central Bank of Sweden			1.4	4.0	11.5	1.0		17.9
B.I.S.		4.1	1.3	1.1	2.7	2.8		12.0
Central Bank of Rumania						10.4		10.4
Central Bank of Slovakia			1.6			3.2		4.8
Central Bank of Spain					1.4			1.4
Others		0.8			−1.1			0.3

B.I.S. : Bank for International Settlements

During the war a metric ton of gold was worth 4.87 million Swiss francs or 1.13 million US-Dollars.

3. General assessment

This survey sheds light on the central role played by gold in Switzerland in the conduct of monetary policy during the Second World War. The gold standard was the pivot on which the monetary regime rested and a guarantee of the internal and external stability of the Swiss franc. Gold transactions represented the SNB's principal intervention instrument. Moreover, the gold stock at Berne filled two needs at the same time: it guaranteed adequate provision for the country and strengthened public confidence in the currency. From 1942 onwards, when the question of the origin of the German gold first arose, these elements, together with considerations of neutrality and conduct in the face of the German threat, carried considerable weight in explaining the gold purchases from the Reichsbank.

The gold transactions during this period were not prompted by motives of enrichment but by the need to maintain the stability of the country and to protect it against a possible foreign invasion. This policy was the subject of discussion, both in Switzerland and abroad, during and after the War. Negotiations in this connection were conducted with the Allies in 1946 and led to the so-called Washington Agreement. In this agreement Switzerland undertook to contribute Sfr 250 million towards European reconstruction while the Allies waived all future claims in any way connected to the gold acquired by Switzerland during the War.

The SNB finds it difficult to understand why its management of the time did not sufficiently take into account the moral and political implications of their strategy of free convertibility of the Swiss franc in a Europe dominated by Germany. They were aware of the risk that the Reichsbank was supplying Berne with gold looted in the occupied countries. *A posteriori*, the measures taken to prevent such acquisitions seem to have been altogether too half-hearted in the face of these risks. It must, however, be admitted that it is very difficult to judge their decisions outside the historical context. In particular, we do not know what their perception of the threat of a German invasion was. It is, moreover, beyond doubt that their legal argumentation was based on an interpretation of the law of neutrality that we no longer subscribe to today.

Monetary gold confiscated by Germany in occupied countries is a well-documented chapter in the history of World War II. On the other hand, the question of the origin of non-monetary gold does not appear to have been investigated with the same amount of care. Thus we can no longer rule out today that the SNB may have bought – albeit, unwittingly – gold originating from concentration camps. This, together with the material distress afflicting many survivors of the Holocaust from behind the former "iron curtain" reinforced the SNB's decision to contribute an amount of Sfr 100 million to the fund set up by the Swiss business community for the benefit of victims of the Holocaust.

Statement by Professor Jean-François Bergier

PRESIDENT OF THE INDEPENDENT COMMISSION OF EXPERTS
SWITZERLAND – WORLD WAR II

For nearly two years, Switzerland has been confronted with the image of its past and of its role during World War II. Heavy criticism has been levelled at it from abroad: first at its banks for their negligence in the treatment and restitution of escheated assets which they still hold; then at other sectors of the economy for what was considered the excessively close links which they allegedly maintained with the National Socialist economy, thereby furthering Germany's war effort; and lastly at the Federal State itself for conducting, under cover of its neutrality, a policy which was overly opportunistic. The very principle of Swiss neutrality is retrospectively called into question.

In order to be able to give a well-founded reply to the criticisms levelled at it, and also to provide the Swiss people, who are disconcerted and deeply troubled, with all of the clarification which they demand, the Federal Authority resolved to draw up a detailed record. In December 1996, it entrusted that task to an Independent Commission of Experts, historians and Swiss and foreign legal experts who were selected on the basis of their competence and reputation and who are independent of any links with Governments or non-governmental organisations. The Commission received very broad terms of reference, with a view to clarifying all of the actions of Switzerland and Swiss nationals before, during and immediately after the World War which could give rise to controversy. At the same time, it received the legal means (lifting of secrecy, access to private archives) and the financial resources necessary in order to accomplish its mission.

The Commission decided to give priority to the question of gold transactions, which was the subject of our Conference. At present, we have still not been able to close the file and publish the whole of our report: too many questions remain open, and moreover we hope to receive information which will allow them to be answered. That is also, in our view, the aim of this conference. Because we are convinced that only close international cooperation which is objective and free of any political intent can lead to the solution of the questions raised. What we have been able to bring to London, in the absence of a report, is a working document in which we have collected together and explained the statistical data which has come to our attention with regard to movements of gold through the Reichsbank and Switzerland. For the first time, I think, we have been able to take into account Swiss and German data of that period, in addition to statements made by the Allies immediately after the War; we have collated and ordered them.

There is no doubt that Switzerland played a central role in the gold question, acting as the pivot in international transactions of that time. Immediately following World War I, Switzerland became an important international financial centre and the Swiss franc a strong and relatively stable currency. The elimination of sterling by its devaluation in 1931, and of the dollar in 1941, as standards of international trade, made the Swiss franc the last freely convertible currency, remaining stable and thus an international medium of payment for which gold was the reserve. Thus, it was the structural situation and a series of short-term economic events resulting from the 1930s crisis which placed Switzerland at the heart of the gold system, rather than a deliberate desire on the part of Switzerland's Government or its monetary authority. The Axis countries, particularly Germany, the Allies and the neutral countries used gold to buy Swiss francs with which they could make their purchases of primary materials, equipment (in particular armaments) and services outside their area of sovereignty or influence.

We know that from June 1940 Switzerland found itself surrounded by the Axis forces, under siege, with its territorial integrity and independence directly threatened. It remained, in the vast majority of its people and its leaders, fundamentally hostile to fascism and even more so to Nazism, determined to defend itself against the aggressor. However, it was subjected to the blockade and counter-blockade of the Allies and the Germans. In order to safeguard its resupplies, its minimum resources of primary materials and energy, and the continuation of its exports, on which its industrial economy and its labour market depended, Switzerland had to make a number of concessions to both sides. In that balancing act, which the rush of war events constantly called into question, its immediate neighbours, Germans and Italians, by the nature of things played the leading role, since they controlled all of the access routes of Swiss trade.

A number of operators emerged on the Swiss gold market: watchmakers, goldsmiths and manufacturers, who used it in their products; the public, for the purpose of saving; and the State itself, which purchased gold from the National Bank in order to stabilise the currency, that is, to reduce the amount in circulation and to avoid the risk of inflation, which was dreaded almost as much as invasion. However, supplies were via the banks, they were therefore the main protagonists.

Our research has not yet revealed anything regarding the possible role of private bankers or the regional or cantonal banks. Gold did not really play a part in their ordinary activities (other than as a relay between the National Bank and the public); their participation was certainly very marginal. The investment banks, or large banks, are important in this regard. Unfortunately, they did not often keep evidence of their transactions. If, despite that, we have been able to piece together the gold purchases of those banks in Germany during the war, it is thanks to the Reichsbank archives. The amounts calculated by us ($61 million) are much higher than the estimates ($20 million) made by the Allies in 1946 and generally accepted by historians. That sizeable difference is explained in part by the fact that the Allies' estimates did not include transactions prior to June 1940 (about $26 million). In any case, gold purchases by the commercial banks from the Reichsbank ceased after December 1942, from then on, they were limited solely to the National Bank. It is possible that after that date the commercial banks may have continued to purchase small amounts of gold on the black market. They were above all interested, therefore, in lucrative trans-actions carried out in other neutral financial centres such as Istanbul and Buenos Aires, often with the subsidiaries of German banks. Those transactions, which were quite modest, apparently had no other purpose than profit.

The transactions of the National Bank were a different matter. Their volume was considerable; they decreased only from the end of 1943 (with regard to Germany) and ceased altogether only with the end of hostilities. Those opera-tions were motivated not by profit but by monetary, commercial and financial policy considerations. It is necessary to distinguish carefully here between the gold which the National Bank purchased on its own behalf and that which was deposited in its coffers and which it managed on behalf of the central banks of third countries, such as Romania, Portugal, Sweden – and even the Bank for International Settlements, which has its headquarters in Basel (see table on page 15 of our working document). It is likewise necessary to distinguish between the gold which physically passed through Bern and that which was purchased from the Allies but which was blocked in New York, Ottawa or London and whose utilisation was subject to restrictive conditions. The book amounts received from the Allies and those actually transferred from Germany credited to Switzerland's account may appear similar in terms of size. However, they are not comparable either as regards the origin of the gold received (a large part of the German gold was looted) or as regards the allocation of the foreign curren-cy provided in exchange.

As far as the Allies were concerned, the Swiss francs sold against gold served to clear the balance of payments surplus; to pay for the importation of resup-plies from overseas and to which the Allies agreed to grant passage; and to finance American and British humanitarian and diplomatic expenditure, intel-ligence services on the continent, and probably also resistance movements in the occupied countries. International cooperation should make it possible to clarify this aspect.

As far as Germany was concerned, the foreign currency acquired financed purchases of primary materials and oil from neutral countries which did not accept gold in payment; purchases of goods and services in Switzerland itself; and interest payments on German debts and diplomatic expenses.

The major problem posed by those transactions lies in the illegitimate origin of the German gold (confiscation of Belgian and Dutch reserves; gold extorted or confiscated from individuals, in particular from the Jews of Germany and the occupied countries); or its decidedly criminal origin (gold taken by force from victims of the Nazi genocide). On the eve of war, the Reichsbank had reserves equivalent to $258.7 million; during the war it appropriated, according to our calculations (set out on page 4 of the working document), the gold equivalent of $653.5 million; that is, a total of $909.2 million of which 76% ended up in Switzerland, 62% being credited to the account of the National Bank. The National Bank therefore received a significant share of stolen gold.

It is known that senior executives at the National Bank knew of that fact, even if they never had formal proof of it. From 1941, there were growing indications, and from 1943 warnings from the Allies. However, they were heeded only with delays and hesitations and never taken fully into account. Those responsible took refuge after the event in their legal good faith: rightly or wrongly, they regarded the seizures of gold from the occupied countries' central banks as legitimate because of the war. However, they do not at any time appear to have suspected that even a very small part of that gold might come from private victims.

Those senior executives have argued in order to justify their policy that their terms of reference obliged them to give priority to safeguarding the stability of the Swiss franc and the effective operation of the country's economy in the exceptional circumstances of war, and that they had little, if any, room for manoeuvre. There is no doubt that, strictly on a domestic level, they succeeded in their task. They also argued that the gold transactions which they carried out with Germany were useful enough to that country to constitute a deterrent: an act of aggression against Switzerland would have deprived the National Socialist economy of an unrestricted foreign currency. That argument cannot for the moment be conclusively proven.

It is difficult and questionable to pass a moral judgement on that attitude on the basis of hindsight. The criteria of today are not the same as they were then. Faced with a dilemma, the executives made a choice which in conscience they considered right. However, they were then prisoners of that choice while the danger overshadowing Switzerland remained, and even after that. They lacked political instinct and failed to anticipate the moral dimension of their action or the questions which the post-war period would raise. They did not have the imagination needed to identify more precisely and make the most of their room for manoeuvre. Moreover, they did not receive, or request, any signal from the country's political authority. In this as in other matters, the Federal Council of the war period proved weak.

The Independent Commission of Experts – Switzerland – World War II is willing to cooperate closely in a spirit of trust with all of the countries and institutions involved. It has already taken the initiative with the conference in Ascona last October. With everyone, the Commission intends to assume its full scientific, political and moral responsibility.

TRIPARTITE GOLD COMMISSION

The Tripartite Commission for the Restitution of Monetary Gold

1. The Tripartite Commission has its origins in the Agreement on Reparation which was signed in Paris on 14 January 1946. The Paris Agreement covered various aspects of reparations from Nazi Germany but it was Part III alone which gave rise to the establishment of the Tripartite Commission. This part of the Agreement was concerned exclusively with monetary gold and in effect deputed the US, French and British Governments to deal with it. Part III reads (in part):

   A. All the monetary gold found in Germany by the Allied Forces and that referred to in paragraph G below (including gold coins, except those of numismatic or historical value, which shall be restored directly if identifiable) shall be pooled for distribution as restitution among the countries partici- pating in the pool in proportion to their respective losses of gold through looting or by wrongful removal to Germany.

   . . .

   G. Any monetary gold which may be recovered from a third country to which it was transferred from Germany shall be distributed in accordance with this arrangement for the restitution of monetary gold.

2. The former Soviet Union played no part in the Paris Conference or in the activities of the Tripartite Commission, having at the Potsdam Conference in July 1945 renounced all claims to gold recovered by the Allied forces in the Western zones of Germany. For their part, the Western Allies did not apparent- ly seek to discover whether any monetary gold was recovered by the Soviet Union in its zone of occupation in Germany or elsewhere.

3. One of the surprising problems met by the three Governments, and the Tripartite Commission was that there was at that time no standard accepted definition of the term "monetary gold". There was no doubt a general under- standing that the term "monetary gold" meant gold which was the backing for a national currency. But, the Signatories to the Paris Agreement, having made provision for the restitution of monetary gold, failed to define precisely what they meant by "monetary gold". The three Governments were left to work it out for themselves. A definition was quickly formulated for the purposes of the

Tripartite Commission's enquiries and investigations of claims. It was a very specific, tightly drawn definition:

> All gold which, at the time of its looting or wrongful removal, was carried as part of the claimant country's monetary reserve, either in the accounts of the claimant Government itself or in the accounts of the claimant country's central bank or other monetary authority at home or abroad.

4. In order to assist them in carrying out their responsibilities, the three Governments established on 27 September 1946 the Tripartite Commission for the Restitution of Monetary Gold – in Brussels in co-location with but independent of the Inter-Allied Reparation Agency. The Commission was to comprise representatives, known as Commissioners, from the three Governments. Its operating mandate is to be found in the announcements made simultaneously by the US, French and British governments on 27 September 1946. The functions of the Tripartite Commission were defined as:

   a. To request the submission of and to receive from the Governments claiming the right to participate in the division of monetary gold found in Germany or which may be recovered from a third country to which it was transferred by Germany, claims for restitution of gold looted by or wrongfully removed to Germany, supported by detailed and verifiable data regarding such losses.
   b. To scrutinize claims received and to determine the share of each claimant Government in the pool of monetary gold to be distributed by way of restitution in accordance with Part III of the Paris Agreement on Reparation and any other pertinent agreements.
   c. In due course to announce the total value of the pool of monetary gold which will become available for distribution by way of restitution.
   d. When all the claims for restitution have been received and adjudicated upon, to announce the share in the pool of monetary gold available for restitution to each country entitled to participate in the pool.
   e. In such other ways as shall be decided by the three Governments establishing the Commission, to assist in the distribution of the pool of monetary gold available for restitution.
   f. To perform such administrative acts as may be necessary to carry out the functions referred to in sub-paragraphs (a) through (e) above, including, without limiting the generality of the foregoing, the opening and maintaining of bank accounts, and the making of contracts for the performance of necessary services. Expenses of the Commission incident to the carrying out of its functions shall be a first charge against the fund of monetary gold to be distributed.

5. It should be noted that, given the terms of Part III of the Paris Agreement and the Tripartite Commission's mandate of 27 September 1946, the Commission was not empowered to and did not at any stage deal with claims from private citizens, commercial banks or companies for their losses, either directly or through claimant Governments acting on their behalf – however well documented the claim. It would appear that the intention was that such claims should be covered by other parts of the Paris Agreement.

6. In accordance with its mandate, the Tripartite Commission itself was not at any stage involved with the process of the recovery of gold within Germany or from other countries such as Switzerland, Sweden, Spain, Portugal, Romania, or from the Bank for International Settlements. This onerous task remained in the hands of the three Governments. They also had the difficult responsibility of deciding what in practice constituted monetary gold for the purposes of the gold pool. The circumstances surrounding the recovery of gold for the gold pool were complex and frustrating. They are described in some detail in the research papers produced over the last year by the US and British Governments. These papers both point out how the Allied occupation forces in Germany, contending with confusion and urgency, expanded the definition of monetary gold to regard any gold in bar form as monetary gold. One does not have to have lived through that era to understand the immensity of the problems facing the Allies in post-war Germany and Europe generally, not to mention other parts of the world.

7. Given the presence here of so many distinguished historians and researchers, a point which should be made is that, as may be clear from the above, the archives of the Commission are almost entirely concerned with the detailed and highly technical examination of adjudication on the claims from the various Governments and the distribution of gold at various times to them. The archives do not comprise a great treasure trove of unique information concerning the origins of the gold in the pool. Indeed, the archives are small, occupying only a few cupboards in the Tripartite Commission's office in Brussels. In fact, the Commission was never a large organisation. At the height of its activity, in the late 1940s through to 1958 when it delivered the adjudications, it can have had no more than a dozen full-time and part-time staff. For some years, it has comprised no more than one member of staff and three part-time Commissioners.

8. The Tripartite Commission has been understandably criticised for not making its archives available to the public over the years. It is however right to point out in its defence that most of its documentation concerns confidential negotiations with the individual governments about their claims. These negotiations went into considerable detail about central bank gold holdings and losses. These were matters which the claimant countries themselves regarded as sensitive and confidential. It is also the case that the work of the Commission has not yet been completed. From the Commission's point of view therefore, its documentation is still very much in current use. Given, furthermore, that the archives are all in the single office occupied by the Commission, throwing the archives open to examination by researchers has not been a practical proposition.

9. It is a fair question to ask what the Tripartite Commission has achieved over the fifty-one years of its existence.

10. By September 1996, the amount of gold recovered by the US, French and British Governments in Germany and elsewhere, which they deemed to be

monetary within the meaning of Part III of the 1946 Paris Agreement and there-fore placed in the gold pool established by the Tripartite Commission, totalled something over 10.8 million ounces, ie over 336 tons. This gold pool was set up at the Federal Reserve Bank of New York, the Bank of England and the Banque de France. The Tripartite Commission archives have little in the way of detail about the origins of the gold in the gold pool – and then only information which originated with the three Governments. The first contribution to the gold pool was in fact the 250 million Swiss francs' worth of gold, about 1.7 million ounces, resulting from the negotiations between the Tripartite Governments and the Swiss Government in 1946. This was credited to the TGC account at the Federal Reserve Bank of New York in June 1947.

11. However, by far the greater part of the gold pool, some 7.5 million ounces entered the pool from the Frankfurt Exchange Depository, where it had been collected for safe-keeping by the US Military Authorities. In November 1947, some 3.4 million ounces were transferred direct from Frankfurt to the Netherlands, Belgium and Luxembourg as advances on their preliminary shares. In 1948, the rest of the monetary gold in Frankfurt, some 4.2 million ounces, was transferred to the Tripartite Commission account at the Bank of England. According to information supplied to the Tripartite Commission by the Governments, most of the gold in Frankfurt had been discovered by the US Army in the Merkers mine in Thuringia before the end of the war.

12. Additional significant amounts of gold were subsequently obtained from (in round figures):

Sweden	423,000 ounces
Spain	3,300 ounces
Romania	578,700 ounces
Portugal	128,600 ounces
BIS	120,200 ounces
Military zones Austria	145,500 ounces
Military zones Germany	96,200 ounces

A further 119,300 ounces recovered direct from Switzerland by Czechoslovakia were also deemed to have been part of the pool.

13. The Commission sent out to the potential claimant countries in March 1947 a questionnaire designed to elicit as much information as was possible in the cir-cumstances of the monetary gold "looted by Germany or, at any time after March 12, 1938, was wrongfully removed into German territory." The definition of monetary gold used was that referred to in paragraph 2 above. Ten countries responded: Albania, Austria, Belgium, Czechoslovakia, Greece, Italy, Luxembourg, the Netherlands, Poland and Yugoslavia. Although they had not participated in the Paris Conference on Reparation, claims were accepted from Austria, Italy and Poland. Indeed Part III of the Paris Agreement made specif-ic provision for the participation in the gold pool of countries not represented at

the Paris Conference. Paragraph D of Part III reads:

> D. The question of the eventual participation of countries not represented at the Conference (other than Germany but including Austria and Italy) in the above mentioned distribution shall be reserved, and the equivalent of the total shares which these countries would receive, if they were eventually admitted to participate, shall be set aside to be disposed of at a later date in such manner as may be decided by the Allied Governments concerned.

Austria, Italy and Poland subsequently adhered to the arrangement for the restitution of monetary gold.

14. The information provided by the claimant countries was painstakingly assessed and conclusions reached – some with considerable difficulty: one case indeed required the services of an independent arbitrator. The Commission's formal adjudications were all signed in June 1958, except for one, which for reasons to do with the Governments concerned rather than the Commission, was not signed until 1982. However, already by 1952, about 80% of the eventual total gold pool, ie about 266 tons, had been distributed to claimant countries on the basis of preliminary findings. By 1959 the total distributed had risen to 299 tons. There were further distributions in 1974 (to the Netherlands), 1976 (to Poland), 1982 (to Czechoslovakia) and 1996 (to Albania). These delays were caused by various factors attributable to Governments rather than the Commission.

15. As stated above, the total amount of gold recovered by the Tripartite Governments in pursuance of their responsibilities under Part III of the Paris agreement was about 10.8 million ounces or 336 tons. The total originally claimed by the ten claimant countries amounted to over 735 tons. The total amount of claims validated by the Tripartite Commission, however, amounted to about 16.5 million ounces or 514 tons. As a result, by the time the Commission has completed its work, each claimant country will have received from the Commission only some 64% of its validated claim.

16. The current situation is that only about 5.5 tons of the gold pool remain – ie about 1.5% of the gold pool. In the circumstances and given the constraints within which the Tripartite Commission had to operate it is reasonable to conclude that the vital restitution of monetary gold to the central banks which had been looted during the war took place as speedily as could be permitted by the need for careful consideration of the competing national claims.

TURKEY

Conference Paper *1*

The Jews of Turkey

(Historical Background)

PROF. DR. İLBER ORTAYLI

" . . . Almost from the moment Pope Urban II launched the First Crusade in 1095, zealots plundered their way toward Palestine, *slaughtering unbelievers including thousands of European Jews.* "

Life Magazine, Fall 1997

The Ottoman Empire was the state who actively supported and protected the Jews of Europe; Jews expelled from Spain in 1492 and those who had to leave the countries of Eastern Europe. The Ottoman Empire during these ages had to fulfil its historical task, namely the mission of anti-Christianism. So that the expelled Jewish masses took their asylum in the lands of the Turkish Empire. Even at the eve of its collapse, the Jews migrated from any Turkish province captured by the Christians, and took their asylum in the main land of the Turks, together with their Turkish-Muslim neighbours. The Turks were not anti-Semites, and took their countermeasures against Christian anti-Semitism, such as those taken during the weeks of Pesah (Passover) in different Ottoman towns, and did not give way to any discrimination in the courts of sharia.

During the Ottoman centuries, Turkey was the only country where the Jewish nation could seek their peace; and they shared the destiny of the Turks against the Christian world.

In the course of the 19th century, the Turkish Jewish community took its venture of modernisation. However, this modernisation didn't impose any nationalist atmosphere on the community, which otherwise could cause a struggle against the Turks. Both under the regimes of Abdulhamid II and the Young Turks, the Jewish element kept its fidelity upon the Turkish Muslim state and social order.

From several important perspectives, the position of Ottoman Jewry presented a unique case in the social and political history of the late Ottoman Empire. When the Second Constitutional Period was inaugurated in 1908, the sociopolitical situation of the Jewish community was similar in some respects to that of the Muslim Turks. Turks and Jews were both under the economic submission of the Ottoman Greeks up to the 17th century, where foreign trade was carried out by the Greeks of the Ottoman Empire. Within the Jewish community, there were some who actively supported the constitutional government, whereas others were staunch sympathisers of the fallen Harnidian (Sultan Abduihamid) regime. This duality was apparent on the highest administrative levels of the Jewish community. The most significant and widely known incident reflecting this duality was the resignation of the Acting Chief Rabbi Moshe Levi (Halevi), who later opted to relinquish his power to the party supporting the Young Turks, without provoking any kind of dramatic incident within the Community.

The general situation of Ottoman Jewry during the Second Constitutional Period may be summarised as follows: geographically, the Jews were the most widely spread group in the Empire. They lived throughout most of the Arab provinces and in Anatolia. Their presence was particularly noticeable in Izmir and in almost every other urban centre in Western Anatolia. As to the European provinces, in addition to the important cities of Istanbul, Thessalonica, Adrianopolis and Gallipoli, Jewish communities were found in the urban centres of Bosnia, southern Bulgaria and Macedonia. Ottoman Jewry was also the most culturally diverse ethnic group in the Empire. In the European and Anatolian provinces, the Judeo-Spanish speaking Sephardim predominated. However, with the increased recent immigration of East European Jews, primarily from Russia and Romania, Yiddish speaking Ashkenazi groups became increasingly noticeable. In addition, in the large port cities of Istanbul, Izmir and Thessalonica, there existed congregations of Italian Jews. Elsewhere in the Empire, there were Jews who spoke Arabic, Kurdish and even Aramaic. Indeed, there was no other ethnic element as polyglot as the Jews. These two factors, great physical dispersion and cultural and linguistic diversity, could not become easily conducive to the emergence of a national Jewish movement, as in the case of other ethnic groups.

It is possible to state that Turks and Jews were two groups within the Empire that were among the least exposed to nationalism. Ottoman Jews became exposed to European culture only in the second half of the nineteenth century, later than any other non-Muslim minority. For this reason, it was slow to accept nationalism as an abstract notion to be applied in practise. On the other hand, the Balkan nations, and especially the Christian elements, had been influenced by, and had supported each other in their national aspirations since the end of the eighteenth century. The Greek rebellion owed much to the Serbia; Bulgarian nationalism owed much to the Greek Heteairia: and the role played by Bulgarian volunteers in the Greek rebellion is well known. However, it was not possible for the Ottoman Jews, who remained outside the pale of Christian brotherhood and who generally were in economic competition with the Christian elements of the Empire, to feel an interest in and sympathy for these other nationalist movements.

In short, during the demise of the Empire, the objective conditions that would draw Ottoman Jewry to the intellectual currents of contemporary nationalism appear to have been absent. It would seem that Ottomanism – that is, a modern political theory advocating Ottoman patriotism, which was a product of the nineteenth century – held great promise for Jewish needs and aspirations. Ottoman Jewry entered the modernisation period under the guidance of Western Jewish educational and charitable organisations, whose primary concern was to prepare young Jews to become useful and productive members of the general society in which they lived. The most active organisations in the Ottoman Empire were the *Alliance Israélite Universelle* (established in 1860) and the *Hilfsverein der Deutschen Juden* (founded in 1901). The ideology of these organisations was primarily assimilationist and anti-nationalist; although by their structure and curricula they made it easier for young Jews trained in their institutions to assimilate into Western, rather than Ottoman society. There were, however, significant numbers of young Jews, especially among the lower classes, who for economic reasons attended Ottoman secondary schools, where a liberal system of financial aid was in existence. A significant number of those later went on to study in Ottoman institutions of higher learning, such as the Faculty of Law and the Medical Schools. This, in turn, led to the emergence of an Ottomanised Jewish element within the Jewish elite and also within the Ottoman bureaucratic elite. Although no Jews ever attained the offices of minister, ambassador, or governor, the number of Jews in the upper levels of the various ministries, and in particular in the financial and medical administration, and even in the army became significant toward the end of the empire.

During the Republican period, Jews of Turkey are the first, who refused the protective statute of the Lausanne treaty for minorities; and proclaimed themselves as citizens of a secular (laic) republic. During World War II, Turkey became an asylum for German-Jewish intellectuals and scholars. The surtaxation of the so called "Varlik Vergisi-property tax", however wrongly propagated as an anti-Semitic law, aimed to confiscate the properties of both Muslims and non-Muslims alike and therefore it was not an intentionally anti-Semitic law, despite the fact that it was an unjust financial operation for the whole population. During World War II, Turkish diplomatic missions protected the Jews from the Nazi Holocaust; providing them Turkish visas, or even passports as quickly and much as possible. The Turkish Consul in Rhodes, Mr. Ülkümen (decorated by Israel for his service to humanity) and Ambassador Necdet Kent were two distinguished diplomats who actively tried to save the Jews from the Nazis. Today 25,000 Turkish Jews live in welfare and many of them are among the leading scholars, intellectuals and industrialists of the country as well.

ADDENDUM 1

Presidential Message from the Honourable George Bush
The White House
of the Quincentennial Foundation Celebration
April 27, 1992 – New York City

It is my pleasure to salute the Quincentennial Foundation as you gather to commemorate and celebrate the 500th anniversary of one of the most merciful acts in history – the Ottoman Empire's offer of refuge to the persecuted Jews in Spain.

For Americans, the year 1492 is a year of discovery, of new beginnings. However, 1492 was a gloomy time in Europe. In that year came the expulsion of Spain's large Jewish Community. In a time when, in Western Europe, religious tolerance were all too rare, the Ottoman Empire extended the hand of friendship to a persecuted minority of a faith and culture different from its own.

Today, in this time of conflict and turmoil in the Middle East, the world would do well to recall this example of Muslims and Jews living side by side in harmony and respect. Your celebration tonight recalls just one example of the harmonious coexistence of people in the Ottoman Empire and the Turkish Republic that succeeded it.

The Turkish people have a long and honourable tradition of welcoming refugees, be they the Jews from Spain of 500 years ago, the Germans fleeing the Nazi regime of the 1930s or the Kurds fleeing the despotic Saddam Hussein.

Turkey is our ally and our friend, and I am honoured to salute the Turkish people in commemorating a great moment in their history.

Turkey and the United States share a history of offering refuge to the oppressed and it is a great pleasure for me to join you tonight in this celebration.

May God bless you all.

———————— • ————————

The White House, Washington

May 15, 1992

I am delighted to send warm greetings to all those who are gathered in New York City to celebrate Turkish-American Day and to commemorate the 500th anniversary of the Ottoman Empire's offer of refuge to the persecuted Jews of Spain.

For Americans, 1492 represents a year of discovery – the dawning of a new age of unprecedented opportunity and promise. However, that same year was one of hardship and despair for some 170,000 Spanish Jews, who were expelled ruthlessly from their homes. During a time when religious tolerance was all too rare, the Ottoman Empire extended a hand of friendship to this persecuted minority, to a faith and culture different from its own. Today, in this era of conflict and turmoil in the Middle East, the world community would do well to recall that example of Muslims and Jews living side-by-side in a spirit of mutual cooperation and respect.

Indeed, the Turkish people are to be commended for a tradition of welcoming refugees – be they Jews from Spain in 1492, or German Jews fleeing the Nazi regime in the 1930s.

Turkey is a strong ally of the United States, and we are grateful to the many Turkish Americans who have helped to foster the spirit of friendship that exists between our two peoples. It is but one of the many contributions that Turkish Americans have made to this country, and I am pleased to send best wishes as you commemorate a great moment in history.

George Bush

———————————— • ————————————

UNITED STATES OF AMERICA

CONGRESSIONAL RECORD

Proceedings and Debates of the 101st Congress, Second Session

Vol. 136, Washington, Monday, September 17, 1990, No. 114 (E2873)

Extensions of Remarks

An Example to Mankind

Hon. Stephen J. Solarz of New York – In the House of Representatives

MR. SOLARZ. Mr Speaker, at a time when the headlines of the day are filled with news about conflict in the Middle East, I think it is important that we pay tribute to a historical event which clearly indicates that it is possible for people of different creeds to live together peacefully under one flag.

For most Americans, the mention of the year 1492 sparks thoughts of Christopher Columbus' discovery of North America. However, few people know that at the same time Columbus sailed West, seeking riches and glory in the name of Spain, there were others who were fleeing for their lives from that country, driven by the senseless and cruel religious persecution of the Inquisition. These individuals were Sephardic Jews, who were welcomed into the overwhelming Islamic society of the Ottoman Empire by the Sultan Bayezid II and settled in its capital Istanbul.

The Sultan's actions predate by almost four centuries the American immigrant ideal, emblazoned on the Statue of Liberty, which eloquently states "give me your tired, your poor, your huddled masses yearning to breathe free." However, his actions were worthy of that high standard. Specifically, he ordered his provincial governors "not to refuse the Jews entry or cause them difficulties, but to receive them cordially," and added that "Spanish Jews are received with full sincerity and those who behave otherwise and treat the new immigrants badly are [to be] punished at once." The Sultan was later reported to have said, "The Catholic monarch Ferdinand . . . impoverished Spain by the expulsion of the Jews, and enriched Turkey."

The 500th anniversary celebration of that gracious humanitarian act, and the ensuing flowering of the Jewish community and its culture in Turkey, is now being organized by the Quincentennial Foundation and its president, Jak Kahm. This organization has planned an ambitious 3-year program of conferences, exhibitions, symposiums and studies designed to highlight the 500 years of harmonious cooperation between Turks and Jews.

To better put the Sultan's act of humanitarianism in its proper perspective, it should be remembered that the Spanish Jews, who were willing to sacrifice everything for the sake of their beliefs, were welcomed with open arms by a country where the population was overwhelmingly different in terms of language, religious, race, and culture. Clearly, as the Quincentennial Foundation notes, the embrace of the Spanish Jews by the Government and the people of the Ottoman Empire, and later, modern Turkey, is an ongoing demonstration of the highest ideals of human existence. Therefore, I think it is quite fitting that the Quincentennial Foundation has adopted as its slogan "An Example to Mankind."

In the five centuries which have passed since 1492, the community of Turkish Jews has grown and flourished, living peacefully side-by-side with their Moslem neighbors. Joined by their brethren fleeing oppression in other countries in Europe, the community expanded as word spread that Turkey was a safe haven for Jews fleeing all too frequent pogroms. This tradition has continued into modern times, as demonstrated in 1935 by the invitation of Kemal Ataturk, the founder of modern Turkey, to prominent German Jewish professors fleeing the scourge of Nazism. While most of the world turned its back on the Jews and condemned them to the horrors of the Nazi genocide, Turkey welcomed them much as they had in 1492. While much of the Jewish communities in neighboring European countries were being exterminated by the Nazis and their allies, the Jews of Turkey remained secure.

Jewish culture in Turkey also continues to flourish. During the years of the Ottoman Empire, Turkish Jews regularly served as physicians to the Sultan. Additionally, Ottoman diplomacy was often carried out by Jews, such as Salomon ben Nathan Eskenazi, the diplomat who negotiated the first diplomatic ties between the Ottoman Empire and the British Empire.

Moreover, in the free air of the Ottoman Empire, Jewish literature prospered. Joseph Caro compiled the "Shulhan Arouh", Shlomo-ha-Levi Alkabes composed the "Lekhah Dodi" a hymn which welcomes the Sabbath according to both Sephardic and Ashkenazi ritual. Jacob Cull wrote the famous "Me-am Lo'az." Rabbit Abraham ben Issac Assa became known as the father of Judeo-Espagnol literature. Throughout the centuries, a conscious effort has been made to preserve the heritage of Judeo-Espagnol, both in the spoken and written word, and today, the weekly newspaper Shalom continues to be published by and for the Jewish community in Istanbul.

Sixteen synagogues, including Ahrida in the Balat areas which dates from Byzantine times, continue to serve this vibrant community. Ably led by the Chief Rabbi, Rav David Asseo, a religious council made up of a Rosh Bet Din and three Hahamim, and 35 lay-counselors who handle the secular affairs of the community, the Jews of Turkey have many accomplishments for which they have the right to be proud.

I believe it is entirely appropriate that we in the United States do what we can to make sure the 500th anniversary of the pivotal offer of asylum to the Jews of Spain is successful I hope that my colleagues and the American people will recognize the importance of this event, and do what they can to make sure that this shining example of tolerance is placed in the pantheon of noble human acts in history.

UNITED STATES OF AMERICA

CONGRESSIONAL RECORD

Proceedings and Debates of the 102nd Congress, Second Session

Vol. 138, Washington, Tuesday, March 31, 1992, No. 47 (S4489)

Edict for the Expulsion of the Jews from Spain

MR. METZENBAUM. Mr. President, today marks a grim anniversary.

This day echoes with the pain of centuries, with the sorrow of half a millennium.

Mr. President, 500 years ago this very day, on March 31, of the year 1492, a decree was issued by the royal family of Spain. The decree was entitled "Edict for the Expulsion of the Jews From Spain."

The terms of the decree were simple: After hundreds of years in Spain, Jews were forced to pack up, get out, and never return. The alternative was equally clear: summary execution.

And any non-Jews who out of decency and kindness sheltered a Jew suffered immediate forfeiture of all property and possessions.

Mr. President, we recall this day with pain, with pride, and with concern.

Our pain derives from the centuries of tradition and of uncommon tolerance that were shattered by the expulsion decree. This was no peripheral community.

For centuries, the Jewish community of Spain had been the preeminent Jewish community in the world.

Even today, those centuries are recalled as a golden age, a time that produced Moses Malmonides, a giant of philosophy and of medicine, a man who served as a bridge between ancient Greek philosophy and the stirring of the modern age:

It was a time during which Jews served as counselors to kings, wrote poetry that is read and recited to this day, a time when Jews developed scientific methods and instruments that were breakthroughs of the day.

Indeed, the navigational instruments on which Columbus depended when he made his voyage to the New World were perfected by two Spanish Jews.

Mr. President, this terrible tragedy forced the Jews of Spain to flee, and it was not easy for them. The doors of Europe were, with few exceptions, closed.

The prime exception was Turkey. We cannot recall the tragedy of Spanish Jews, without recalling as well the wisdom of Turkey, to which Jews worldwide will ever be grateful.

Mr. President, our pride derives from the fact that the Jews did what Jews had learned from their earlier history, and were to learn again and again from their later history.

They learned how to move on, carrying with them their meager possessions and their wisdom.

Their passion for justice, their devotion to God, their learning and their lore.

They established new homes, built new communities, and contributed immensely to the nations where they came to dwell.

Mr. President, I do not raise this anniversary merely to mark the day.

It is to the concern arising from this day that I would call my colleagues' attention.

Mr. President, Spain did what it did 500 years ago because its rulers had come to the view that there was room in Spain for only one culture, one people, one religion.

And I fear terribly that this disease of intolerance did not end in 1492, that it has not ended in 1992, 500 years later.

In nations and regions around the world, intolerance is precisely the disease that threatens unprecedented de-stabilization and, ultimately, bloodshed.

Our own country is founded on very different principles. Here, we celebrate our pluralism, and rightly so.

We understand that the diversity of cultures we embrace is a source of great strength, perhaps our greatest strength as a nation.

However, even here, ugly voices are raised that promote intolerance, bigotry.

Whether the voice be that of David Duke:

Whether the voice that of the marginally more subtle demagogues:

Whether it be TV ads calculated to appeal to racism and ethnic prejudice.

We cannot hide from America's would-be inquisitors, and from their voices of bigotry and hate.

Indeed, even in our national election campaigns, intolerance is peddled as bait to catch a few votes:

In 1998, television ads were used to inject race as an issue in our Presidential decision:

In 1990, voters were offered the image of of a white worker losing his paycheck to an unqualified minority:

And in the 1992 campaign, voices of intolerance are back with renewed vigor:

Intolerance of foreigners:

Intolerance of ethnic and religious minorities; and

Intolerance of economic minorities.

There is also the continuing scandal of racism in this country.

It causes so many of our fellow citizens to suffer the insults and the injuries of bigotry and intolerance each and every day.

And then there is the newest type of racism:

It is cloaked with terms like "Buy American" and "America For Americans."

But let's not kid ourselves. The Japan-bashing of recent months is no more than Japanese-bashing. The free-trade fair-trade rhetoric is picking up an anti-Japanese racist flavor. It is there, and it is as dangerous as any other kind of discrimination.

We should be tough with our international competitors.

But our fight should be on business, not racial terms.

Mr. President, how many more centuries must we wait before we will all fully absorb the bitter lessons of 1492?

I am happy that Spain has heeded the lessons of its history, and has moved decisively away from its transgression against decency.

In 1954, the first new synagogue since 1492 was opened.

The Jewish community of Spain has sought to reclaim its past vitality.

And today, on this anniversary day, King Juan Carlos will visit the Madrid Synagogue to mark the brutal past and the new day that has come to Spain and to its Jews.

It is, I might add, no accident that Spain hosted the opening round of the Arab-Israeli peace talks last fall.

So there is hope and there is celebration. But who would deny that there is, at the same time, cause for concern?

If an anniversary is to mean anything, it must be more than an act of remembering:

It must also be an act of rededicating.

What we learn from our remembering is a lesson that we have yet fully to embrace.

A lesson to which we as a Nation must urgently give heed;

A lesson that all over the world must lead to a rededication to tolerance:

To decency: and

To the acceptance of human diversity.

This lesson is about rejecting our bias and our fear:

Who among us will resist the urge to fear someone who is different –

A different color:

A different religion:

A different accent: and

A different nationality.

How many Americans easily accept those who are made in a mirror image, but quickly reject those who are not a perfect match?

Mr. President, facing up to intolerance and fear is a fight for both our statehouses and for our homes.

It is a fight that each of us must take on.

Let both our hearts and our doors be ever open to our neighbors, whatever their faith,whatever their race: let both hearts and doors be open to the victims of hate who wander in our midst.

Mr. President, I ask unanimous consent that an English copy of the Expulsion Decree of 1492 be printed in the Record .

There being no objection, the material was ordered to be printed in the Record, as follows:

XIII. Edict for the Expulsion of the Jews from Spain – Granada, 31 March 1492

Whereas, having been informed that in these our kingdoms, there were some bad Christians who judaized and apostalized from our holy Catholic faith, the chief cause of which was the communication of Jews with Christians: at the Cortes we held in the city of Toledo in the year 1480 , we ordered the said Jews in all the cities, towns, and places in our kingdoms and dominions, to separate into Jewries and places apart, where they should live and reside, hoping by their separation alone to remedy the evil. Furthermore, we have sought and given orders, that inquisition should be made in our said kingdoms which, as is known, for upwards of twelve years has been, and is done, whereby many guilty persons have been discovered, as is notorious. And as we are informed by the inquisitors, and many other religious, ecclesiastical, and secular persons, that great injury has resulted, and does result, and it is stated, and appears to be, from the participation, society, and communication they held and do hold with Jews, who it appears always endeavour in every way they can to subvert our holy Catholic faith, and to make faithful Christians withdraw and separate themselves therefrom, and attract and pervert them to their injurious opinions and brief, instructing them in the ceremonies and observances of their religion, holding meetings where they read and teach them what they are to believe and observe according to their religion; giving them books from which they may read their prayers; and explaining to them the fasts they are to observe; assembling with them to read and to teach them the histories of their law; notifying to them the festivals previous to their occurring, and instructing them what they are to do and observe thereon: giving and carrying to them from their houses unleavened bread, and meat slaughtered with ceremonies: instructing them what they are to refrain from, as well in food as in other matters, for the due observance of their religion, and persuading them all they can to profess and keep the law of Moses, giving them to understand, that except that, there is no other law or truth, which is proved by many declarations and confessions as well of Jews themselves as of those who have been perverted and deceived by them, which has greatly redounded to the injury, detriment, and opprobrium of our holy Catholic faith.

Notwithstanding we were informed of the major part of this before, and so knew the certain remedy for all these injuries and in conveniences was to separate the said Jews from all communication with Christians, and banish them from all our kingdoms, yet we were desirous to content ourselves by ordering them to quit all the cities, towns, and places of Andalusia, where, it appears, they had done the greatest mischief, considering that would suffice, and that those of other cities, towns and places would cease to do and commit the same.

But as we are informed that neither that, nor the execution of some of the said Jews, who have been guilty of the said crimes and offences against our holy Catholic faith, has been sufficient for a complete remedy to obviate and arrest so great an opprobrium and offence to the Catholic faith and religion:

And as it is found and appears, that the said Jews, wherever they live and congregate, daily increase in continuing their wicked and injurious purposes: to afford them no further opportunity for insulting our holy Catholic faith, and those whom until now God has been pleased to preserve, as well as those who had fallen, but have amended and are brought back to our holy mother church, which, according to the weakness of our human nature and the diabolical suggestion that continually wages war with us, may easily occur, unless the principal cause of it be removed, which is to banish the said Jews from our kingdoms.

And when any serious and detestable crime is committed by some persons of a college or university, it is right that such college or university should be dissolved and annihilated and the lesser suffer for the greater, and one be punished for the other; and those that disturb the welfare and proper living of cities and towns, that by contagion may injure others, should be expelled therefrom, and even for lighter causes that might be injurious to the state, how much more then for the greatest, most dangerous, and contagious crimes like this.

Therefore we, by and with the counsel and advice of some prelates and high noblemen of our kingdoms, and other learned persons of our council, have maturely deliberated thereon, resolve to order all the said Jews and Jewesses to quit our kingdoms, and never to or come back to them, or any of them. Therefore we command this our edict to be issued, whereby we command all Jews and Jewesses, of whatever age they may be, that live, reside, and dwell in our said kingdoms and dominions, as well natives as those who are not, who in any manner or for any cause may have come to dwell therein, that by the end of the month of July next, of the present year 1492, they depart from all our said kingdoms and dominions with their sons, daughters, man-servants, maid-servants, and Jewish attendants, both great and small, of whatever age they may be: and they shall not presume to return to nor reside therein, or in any part of them, either as residents, travellers, or in any other manner whatever, under pain that if they do not perform and execute the same, and are found to reside in our said kingdoms and dominions, or should in any manner live therein, they incur the penalty of death, and confiscation of all their property to our treasury, which penalty they incur by the act itself, without further process, declaration, or sentence.

And we command and forbid any person or persons of our said kingdoms, of whatsoever rank, station, or condition they may be, that they do not presume publicly or secretly to receive, shelter, protect, or defend any Jew or Jewess, after the said term of the end of July, in their lands or houses, or in any other part of our said kingdoms and dominions, henceforward for ever and ever, under pain of losing all their property, vassals, castles, and other possessions: and furthermore forfeit to our treasury any sums they have, or receive from us.

And that the said Jews and Jewesses during the said time, until the end of the said month of July, may be the better able to dispose of themselves, their property, and estates, we hereby take and receive them under our security, protection and royal safeguard: and insure to them and their properties, that during the said period, until the said day, the end of the said month of July, they may travel in safety, and may enter, sell, barter, and alienate all their movable and immoveable property, and freely dispose thereof at their pleasure.

And that during the said time, no harm, injury, or wrong whatever shall be done to their persons or properties contrary to justice, under the pains those persons incur and are liable to, that violate our royal safeguard.

We likewise grant permission and authority to the said Jews and Jewesses, to export their wealth and property, by sea or land, from our said kingdoms and dominions, provided they do not take away gold, silver, money, or other articles prohibited by the laws of our kingdoms, but in merchandise and goods that are not prohibited.

And we command all the justices of our kingdoms, that they cause the whole of the above herein contained to be observed and fulfilled, and that they do not act contrary hereto,: and that they afford all necessary favour, under pain of being deprived of office, and the confiscation of all their property to our exchequer.

MR. METZENBAUM, Mr. President, I suggest the absence of a quorum.

THE PRESIDING OFFICER. The absence of a quorum having been suggested, the clerk will call the roll.

The legislative clerk proceeded to call the roll.

MR. MITCHELL. Mr. President, I ask unanimous consent that the order for the quorum call be rescinded.

THE PRESIDING OFFICER. Without objection, it is so ordered.

———————————— • ————————————

B'NAI B'RITH INTERNATIONAL CONVENTION
August 26–30, 1990, Dallas Texas

Proposal No. 90–6–h

In Re: Celebration of the 500th Anniversary of the Presence of Sephardic Jews in Turkey

Proposed by: Committee on Public Affairs "C"

WHEREAS, the Jewish people were expelled from Spain in 1492 during the inquisition, and Sephardic Jews were warmly welcomed to the Ottoman Empire by the Sultan Beyazit II and have lived there in peace and security during 500 years, at a time when Jews in Europe were frequently subject to persecutions and pogroms: and

WHEREAS, B'nai B'rith takes note the Jews in Turkey are preparing the celebration of this most gracious welcome inside and outside Turkey:

THEREFORE, be it resolved, that B'nai B'rith call on all friends and members to participate in the 1992 celebration in Turkey.

———————————— • ————————————

FEDERATION OF JEWISH MEN'S CLUBS BIENNIAL CONVENTION
August 11–15, 1991, Loch Sheldrake, New York

WHEREAS, the Sephardic Jews were expelled from Spain in 1492 during the Inquisition: and

WHEREAS, Sultan Beyazit II warmly welcomed the Sephardic Jews to the Ottoman Empire; and

WHEREAS, the Sephardic Jews have lived in peace and security for a period of 500 years when other Jews in Europe have been frequently subject to persecutions and pogroms.

THEREFORE BE IT RESOLVED, that the Federation of Jewish Men's Clubs urges its constituent clubs to engage in discussions, dialogues, lectures and exhibitions in commemoration of this Quincentennial.

——————————— • ———————————

AMERICAN SEPHARDIC FEDERATION CONVENTION
October 11–15, 1991 in Los Angeles California

WHEREAS resolutions were passed at the American Sephardic Federation Conventions in Miami on November 21, 1989 and in Chicago in September 2–5, 1990, recognizing:

The Ottoman Empire's warm and humanitarian welcome to the Jewish refugees of Spain in 1492.

The tolerance of the Ottoman Empire that enabled the Jewish Community to perpetuate the Sephardic culture for five centuries.

The American Sephardic Community's gratitude to the people and government of Turkey.

The activities planned by the Jewish Community of Turkey to celebrate the quincentennial of this magnificent togetherness, and supporting participation in this celebration.

BE IT RESOLVED THAT THE American Sephardic Federation reiterates to its members and friends its request to participate in 1992 celebrations and to take, if possible, active part in the events organized in Turkey.

ADDENDUM 2

FURTHER SUGGESTED READING

1. *Studies on Turkish-Jewish History: Political and Social Relations. Literature and Linguistics – The Quincentennial Papers* New York. Sepher-Hermon Press, INC for the American Society of Sephardic Studies. 1996:
   a. *Two Turkish Diplomats who Saved Jews during World War II* by Rachel A. Bortnick pp. XIX–XX
   b. *Welcoming Immigrants and Refugees: Aspects of the Balkan Jewish Experience from Byzantine to Post-Ottoman Times* by Steven Bowman pp. 1–11
   c. *Mutual Needs, Mutual Benefits* by Walter Weiker pp. 130–134
   d. Poetry pp. 193–201

2. *Constantinople – City of the World's Desire (1453–1924)* by Philip Mansel. John Murray, 50 Albemarle Street, London , 1995, Chapter 5 – City of Gold pp. 110–127

3. *The Jews of The Ottoman Empire and the Turkish Republic* by Stanford J. Shaw Ipswich Book Co. Ltd. Ipswich, Suffolk, 1991

4. *Turkey and the Holocaust* by Stanford J. Shaw, The Macmillan Press Ltd. Hong Kong, 1993

5. *Abraham Galante – A Biography* by Albert E. Kalderon, Sepherr-Hermon Press, INC. New York, 1983, pp. 52–53, 60–61

——— EXCERPT 1 ———

(From "Studies on Turkish-Jewish History – Political and Social Relations – Literature and Linguistics – The Quincentennial Papers")

Welcoming Immigrants and Refugees: Aspects of the Balkan Jewish Experience from Byzantine to Post-Ottoman Times

STEVEN BOWMAN

"As we approach the Fifth Centennial of 1492, the historian as well as the Holocaust survivor cannot avoid a metathesis which recalls 1942. If the first date represents the great exile from Spain, the second signifies the second exile of Sephardic Jews, only this time to their death. These dates, too, will define the parameters of our story of their migration eastward through the Mediterranean and the reception of the Sephardim by the Ottoman Turks and the local Romaniote Jews. In turn the Sephardim, once settled, welcomed their nearly lost Marrano brethren (more properly conversos, although the Hebrew anusim –"forced", is more correct). In subsequent centuries they all assisted the refugee victims of Eastern and Western European persecutions either to settle in their Aegean centers or to pass on to the Jewish homeland in Israel. The following story will highlight several chapters in the crowning hospitality of Ottoman Jewry.

Let us recall, although it is obvious as we approach the symbolic date 1992, why we so designate it after half a millennium. Three key events of 1492 have affected Jewish history to the present day. The conquest of Granada symbolised the eclipse of Arabic-speaking Muslims until the twentieth century. The voyage of Christopher Columbus eventually opened a New World to Jewish creativity. And the expulsion of the Jews from Spain ended a millennial symbiosis and initiated a Sephardic diaspora." *(page 1)*

———

"It was the massive influx of Sephardic Jews into the region at the end of the fifteenth century that changed the cultural identification of Aegean Jews for nearly 450 years. In the wake of his conquest of Constantinople in 1453, Mehmet II forcibly relocated the Romaniote communities of Anatolia and northern Greece to repopulate his new capital. About this time the demographic weight of the Sephardic migration transformed the political and religious structure of Ottoman Jewry from its mixture of Romaniote, Sephardic, and Must'arabi congregations (the latter Arabic-speaking Jews in Syria and Egypt) to a Jewry dominated commercially, politically, and religiously by the Sephardim (cf. Bowman 1985 and Hacker" 1978) *(page 3)*.

———

"The Jewish understanding of this Ottoman policy, at least as recorded by the new immigrants, was one of hospitality, and it praised the Ottomans accordingly. Several circular letters from the mid-fifteenth through the mid-sixteenth centuries emphasize this understanding. Isaac Zarfati (ca. mid-1450s) wrote to the communities of Ashkenaz that "Turkey is a land wherein nothing is lacking, and where, if you will, all shall yet be well with you. Is it not better for you to live under Moslems than under Christians? Here every man may dwell at peace under his own vine and fig tree . . . Arise! and leave this accursed land for ever." David dei Rossi wrote to his Italian brethren in 1535: "Hatred of the Jews is, in contrast to our homeland, unknown here, and the Turks hold the Jews in esteem." And the Provençal Jews in Salonica wrote to their brethren in 1550 that 'The Turk does not let us suffer any evil or oppression . . . Therefore . . . do not hesitate to come hither and to enjoy the best of this land." Below, we shall note some of the reasons for the positive Ottoman attitudes (full texts can be found in Kobler 1989; see also Ben-Sasson 1960.)" *(pp. 3–4)*

"The seventeenth and eighteenth centuries witnessed a concretization of both local Jewish hospitality and the Ottoman open-door policy toward Jewish immigration. The tragic events affecting Polish Jewry during the period of the "Chmielnickl massacres" (1648–1658) sent waves of refugees and captives south to the Ottoman Empire. Local communities supported special funds which were used for ransoming Jews captured by pirates at a fixed rate. Periodically, other communities were either taxed or solicited to replenish the fund in particularly adverse times such as the second half of the seventeenth century. During the eighteenth century, the Venetian Jewish community, as well as the Istanbul leadership, supported the Sephardic communities in Palestine both financially and politically before the Sublime Porte (c f. Marcus 1983: 454–58 and Barnal 1982/1991; see also Halperin 1960)"

"The massive dislocation of Jewish survivors of the Cossack and Swedish incursions into Poland during the decade of the Deluge brought to the Ottoman Empire a large influx of Ashkenazic Jews. They were received and integrated into the local communities." *(pp. 4–5)*

"The last decades of the nineteenth century initiated a tremendous upheaval for the Ashkenazi Jews of Eastern Europe. During the generation from 1881–1914, millions left to create the diaspora that characteries contemporary Jewry. While the majority of these Ashkenazim resettled in the United States, a significant number (although a small percentage) emigrated to other areas under Ottoman control, whether the Balkans or the Land of Israel. Hence the welfare of these Jews, in terms of representing them before the Porte, fell under the aegis of the Istanbul leadership. Herein lies the source for the present authority of the Sephardic Chief Rabbi of Israel, whose Ottoman predecessor had taken the title of Haham Bashat the end of the 1830s. His counterpart, the Ashkenazic Chief Rabbi of Israel, resulted from the British Mandate policy in Palestine during the 1920s." *(p. 5)*

"An interesting letter housed in the archives of the Alliance Israelite Universelle in Paris points out the continued toleration of the Ottomans toward Jewish immigration on the eve of World War I. Leon Semach of the Ecole de Garçons in Rhodes wrote to the AIU on 28 March 1907 that Nazim Pasha, Governor General of the Archipelago, responded to the pogroms in Russia by inviting the Alliance to send "une colonie serieuse" to "philanthrope" and "grand philosemite," who disseminated articles about Jews among his acquaintances and also offered to settle Russian emigres in Rhodes. On another level there had already been negotiations between Theodor Herzl and the Porte regarding the bailing out of the Ottoman economy in return for a Jewish homeland in Palestine. The special relationship between Jews and Turks interfaced on a number of levels, earnestly sought even if historically unsuccessful (Paris, AIU Archives, Greece, I.C. 32, Rhodes 1884–1939)

"Insofar as the Jewish community was concerned, any assistance was eagerly welcomed from Jewish groups, the Christian government of Greece, and the Ottoman Porte. Since the 1880s, thousands of Russian refugees had overburdened local resources in Crete and Salonica. In the former, both the French and British consuls were giving some aid to the refugees, but only the resources of the French Alliance and soon thereafter the American Joint Distribution Committee could help in their resettlement or in their continued trek toward a new life, hopefully in the Land of Israel. This is the beginning of a chapter of the Greek and Turkish Jewish efforts, which was to last until 1941, with the assistance of international Jewish organisations, to aid first the Russian and later the Central European refugees who made it to the safe havens of the Mediterranean and Aegean.

Many of the immigrants from Eastern Europe and the Balkans to Palestine in the period after World War I passed through the Bosphorus stopping either at Istanbul or Salonica before continuing their journey . . ." *(p. 6)*

———

"The following summarizes the Turkish Jewish aid to Greek refugees. In late 1943 and 1944, after the Salonica community had already been deported, the Germans turned against the Athens community, which included approximately 4,000 Spanish and Italian Jews who had escaped from Salonica. With the assistance of the Greek Resistance, and the Hagganah representing the Jewish Agency of Palestine, a ferry service was established that brought some 1,500 Jews from occupied Greece to Izmir during this period. There the local Jewish community undertook the feeding and clothing of these refugees and sent them to Palestine via Syria. At the same time, the community of Izmir was receiving certificates for immigration to Palestine as part of the British White Paper policy. Thus, the elder Jewish community of Izmir was supporting both its own emigrating children, as well as the refugees from Greece. Their coreligionists in Istanbul continued the relief efforts for those Jews who had succeeded exiting the Balkans via the Straits, just as they had done since the late 1930s." *(p. 8)*

———

"Thus, as we approach 1992, we should acknowledge that the past five hundred years, among the Jewish communities that surrounded the Aegean Sea, have witnessed a continuum of service to many scattered Jewish communities that suffered from those vicissitudes of inhospitality that constitute the traditional "lachrymose view of Jewish history." In our own days the Americas have taken over this sadly needed task, whether welcoming Jewish immigrants and refugees or assisting them to return to Israel, as had their Aegean forebears from the sixteenth through the twentieth century." *(p. 8)*

——— EXCERPT 2 ———

(From "The Jews of the Ottoman Empire and the Turkish Republic")

STANFORD J. SHAW

Turkish Jewry During World War II

Turkey managed to remain neutral during World War II. The sympathies of President Ismet Inönü and most other Turkish leaders were clearly with the western Allies, with whom alliances were signed shortly before the war began. But the Allies' clear inability to provide assistance if an open war declaration had led to a German invasion from Greece caused the Turks to maintain an uneasy neutrality until Germany's impending defeat finally led it to join late in 1944. Thus Turkey emerged from the war among the victors, as Greece had been forced to do during World War I.

While the Nazis largely exterminated the remaining Jewish populations of the former Ottoman possessions of Greece during World War II, thus culminating the persecutions begun in these countries following their achievement of full independence during the nineteenth century, neutral Turkey defended its Jews and rejected Nazi demands for them to be deported for extermination in the death camps. *(p. 255)*

———

" . . . Muslim Turks themselves never at any point showed any anti-Semitism either before, during, or after the program was in force. Turkish Jews not affected by the tax continued their lives normally, Jewish youths joined their Muslim fellow citizens in accepting conscription into the army, and Nazi-sponsored anti-Semitic publications were suppressed by the government.

Throughout the war, moreover, and despite continual Nazi pressure, the government of Turkey refused German demands that it turn over the Jewish refugees for internment in the death camps. Instead it went out of its way to assist passage into its territory of Jews fleeing from Nazi persecution in Poland, Greece and Yugoslavia as well as in western and central Europe. Turkish soldiers in Thrace turned the other way when Jewish refugees managed to slip across the borders of Nazi-occupied Greece and Bulgaria, as related by a number of veterans of Turkey's Thracian border guards, . . . " *(p. 256)*

———

"Turkey condoned the presence in Istanbul starting in the summer of 1940 of fifteen Zionist Aliyah agents led by Hayim Barlas, including the subsequent mayor of Israeli Jerusalem, Teddy Kollek and Moshe Shertok (Sharret), who from their office in the Continental Hotel collected information about Nazi treatment of Jews all over southeastern Europe. With the passive approval of the Turkish government they mounted rescue operations, providing false passports as well as transportation to Turkey of thousands of Jewish refugees who managed to flee from Nazi horrors in Poland, Yugoslavia, Bulgaria, Greece, Hungary, Romania, and Czechoslovakia, and during the Nazi invasion of the East, from Estonia, the Ukraine and Russia. They maintained them through the remainder of the war and facilitated the onward passage of those who wished to go on to Palestine. It was through these Zionist agents that Adolph Eichmann's offer came to the Zionist Organization to liberate the remaining Jews of Poland, after 3.5 million had already been killed, in return for war equipment and money, and it was through these same agents that the offer of S.S. officers in Budapest was passed on to the Allies to arrange for an early peace. Turkey allowed all this activity to go on despite strong and vehement opposition by Great Britain and the Vatican due to fears of Arab reaction against their nationals and interests, though a few local British officials as well as the Vatican's Istanbul representative, Angelo Roncalli, later Pope John XXIII, did secretly provide assistance to the Zionist agents on their own initiative. Britain urged the Balkan States, before they were taken over by Germany, to prevent Jewish emigration to Turkey and Palestine and it went on to pressure the governments of both Turkey and Greece to refuse landing privileges to ships carrying Jewish refugees." *(pp. 256–257)*

———

" . . . For the most part, however, in the face of all this pressure, the Turkish government allowed the Zionist agents to use its facilities to smuggle diamonds, gold coins, and currency into the Nazi occupied lands to help feed and house Jews who were not able to flee, with the Turkish ambassadors and consular representatives at times helping and even arranging for Jews to flee to Turkey. While Nazi and British pressure at times forced Turkey to overtly limit these Zionist rescue activities by closing the Aliyah office and limiting Jewish immigration to those who could show British permission for them to enter Palestine, the Turkish government allowed the same Zionists to maintain the unofficial Aliyah Bet organization to continue to bring in Jewish refugees and send them on to Palestine on an 'illegal' basis.

Moshe Shertok later stated that from the Jewish perspective, Istanbul was far more important as a base for gathering information and providing refuge for Jews fleeing from the Nazis than were the other neutral centres in Europe, Geneva, Stockholm or Lisbon, since only Istanbul provided direct connections between European Jewry and the Yishuv in Palestine. Zionist agents who were active in Istanbul during the war remain convinced to the present day that, in the absence of assistance from the great Jewish communities of Britain, America and South Africa, it was their activities alone, done with the full knowledge and silent support of the Turkish government, that provided European Jews with the feeling that some people still remembered them and were trying to help them." *(pp. 257–258)*

——— EXCERPT 3 ———

(From "Turkey and the Holocaust")

STANFORD J. SHAW

Turkey and the Jews, 1933–1945

"Neither the people of the Republic of Turkey nor those of Europe and America fully realise the extent to which Turkey, and the Ottoman Empire which preceded it, over the centuries served as major places of refuge for people suffering from persecution, Muslims and non-Muslims alike, from the fourteenth century to the present. In many ways the Turks historically fulfilled the role subsequently taken up by the United States of America beginning in the late nineteenth century." *(p.1)*

———

"During the nineteenth century the Ottomans received over one and a half million Muslim and Jewish refugees fleeing from massacre and persecution in the Christian provinces of south-eastern Europe as they revolted and won their independence from Ottoman rule, a situation which seems destined to be repeated, insofar as Jews are concerned, in the last decade of the twentieth century as the nations of the Soviet Union and its satellites in Eastern Europe recover their independence after seventy years of Communist rule, in the process allowing the revival of anti-Semitism which seemingly had been forgotten during the interval" *(p.2)*

———

"The Greek occupation of Ottoman western Thrace and Salonica in 1912 during the First Balkan War led to new persecutions of the Muslims and Jews living there. Many of the survivors fled into Ottoman territory, particularly after the Muslim and Jewish quarters of Salonica were burned in the great fire of 1917, after which the Greek government refused to allow anyone but Greek Christians coming from Anatolia to resettle in their homes, while the ancient Jewish cemetery of Salonica was desecrated as it was covered over by the construction of the new Greek University of Salonica."

"The brutal Russian invasion of eastern Anatolia in the early years of World War I caused those who survived to flee westward into the territories still controlled by the Ottomans. The Bolshevik Revolution and the Russian Civil War that followed led to new migrations of thousands of Jews and Muslims as well as Russians who fled across the Black Sea following attacks on them by both Reds and Whites."

"During the Turkish War for Independence, which went on at the same time, from 1918 to 1923, Istanbul and the Marmara islands were crowded with thousand of refugees in flight from southern Russia, with the Allied armies then in occupation of the old Ottoman capital doing little to alleviate the suffering while preventing the weak government of the sultan from providing help on its own initiative."

"Through all these centuries, however, Turkey faced no greater challenge nor responded more nobly, than it did in response to Nazi persecution of the Jews of Europe starting in 1933 and continuing until the end of World War II." *(p.3)*

———

Turkey shelters professionals dismissed by the Nazis in the 1930s

"The Turkish Republic took in hundreds of refugees from Nazi persecution during the 1930s, including leading professors, teachers, physicians, attorneys, artists and laboratory workers as well as thousands more less well known persons. For the most part they were brought to Turkey and given senior positions within six months of their dismissals by the Nazis. Most were appointed to major professorships in Istanbul University, then being intensively reformed and modernised, and in the newly-established faculties of Ankara University. Others were given the opportunity to found and direct important scientific research institutes, where several generations of Turkish scholars and scientists were trained." *(p.4)*

———

There is no Jewish question in Turkey

"To start with, we can say at once that there is no problem at all regarding Jews who are Turkish citizens. The Constitution of the Turkish Republic gives full political rights for Jews who have been living and working in Turkey for centuries. The Constitution of the Republic makes no distinction among its citizens in regard to religion and race. All the native sons of this country enjoy equal liberty of conscience and the right and duty to contribute together to the happiness and welfare of the fatherland of all. Though the welfare and good of the nation require that the affairs of the Republic be carried out by a single party (The Republican Peoples' Party), this principle has been applied in a very generous manner, since there are independent deputies in the Grand National Assembly who do not belong to this party, and among them are some who adhere to religion of Moses."

"All the schools of the state are open to Turkish citizens who are Jewish. They can attend them in full freedom and in large numbers. They may also hold all kinds of official positions, travel in all parts of the country, and publish newspapers. In sum, they can live in this country without being considered separately from the mass of citizens who are Muslims. These words are not a problem nor a wish, nor do they have any particular objective. They express the simple reality of today." *(pp. 26–27)*

Turkish Jewry in World War II

"While many Jews in most countries occupied by the Nazis in Western Europe were able to conceal themselves throughout the war with local assistance, and while the Italians assisted the Jews to escape deportation and death in the territories that they occupied jointly with German forces, because of the overwhelming anti-Semitism which continued to predominate in most of Greece, Yugoslavia and Romania, the Nazis and their local puppets there were largely able to exterminate the Jewish minorities, thus culminating the persecutions begun in these countries following their achievement of full independence during the nineteenth century. On the other hand, neutral Turkey defended its Jews and rejected Nazi demands for them to be deported for extermination in the death camps." *(pp. 34–35)*

"In the darkest days of World War II, moreover, after German forces had occupied Greece, Hungary, Romania, Yugoslavia and Bulgaria and pushed to the Turkish borders in Thrace, as the Turkish government was contemplating the evacuation of Istanbul in response, as each new German advance led to the arrival of hundreds more refugees flooding into Edirne and Istanbul, and as Muslim and Jewish Turks alike wondered where Hitler would move next, across the English Channel against England, or eastward against Turkey as the first step toward overrunning the Middle East, rumours were spread by Balat's Christian inhabitants and neighbours that as soon as the Nazis arrived in Istanbul they would use the ovens of the local Balat bakery, called Los Ornos de Balat by the Jews, to cremate Turkish Jews." *(pp. 35–36)*

"Nazi propaganda efforts in Turkey during World War II attracted few Turks other than the pan-Turkic exiles from Central Asia who were entranced by the possibility of restoring their homelands with German assistance rather than by the German anti-Semitic appeals. The only significant Turkish convert to Nazi anti-Semitic ideas during the war was the pan-Turkish ideologist and racist Nihal Atsiz, a high school teacher who, modelling himself after Hitler in word and dress, advocated an alliance with Germany as the first step toward '…ridding ourselves of Jews, communists and freemasons'. Turks such as Atsiz who did succumb to the Nazi appeal were suppressed by the Ankara government, and many were thrown into jail, but the Nazis did manage to attract some Armenian nationalists to join their military and propaganda activities as well as their occupation of southern France and invasion of the Soviet Caucasus in the hope of creating an Armenian state in the East, making many Turks fear a repetition of the events in the World War I, when, they believed Armenian uprisings around Lake Van starting in 1914 led to destructive and devastating Russian invasion of Eastern Anatolia in the years before the Bolshevik Revolution."

Turkey's Role in Rescuing Jews from the Nazis during the Holocaust

Jewish Turks in France at the start of the German Occupation
"Just as important as providing a haven for Jews who had lived in the Ottoman Empire for centuries was Turkey's role in helping rescue many Jewish Turks who were resident in Nazi-occupied western Europe during the Holocaust." *(p.46)*

––––––

Issuance of Turkish passports and certificates of citizenship to Jewish Turks who had lost their citizenship
"It was against this background that Turkish diplomats stationed throughout Nazi-occupied western Europe did all they could, both at an official level and even more behind the scenes, and often at risk to their own lives, to protect those Jews who were Turkish citizens, and even those Jewish Turks who had forsaken their Turkish citizenship for what had seemed at the time the greater advantages of citizenship of one of the countries of western Europe and who as a result were now in great mortal danger." *(p.60)*

––––––

Istanbul Activities In Rescuing European Jews from the Nazis

"In evaluating Turkey's role in rescuing European Jewry from the Holocaust it is instructive to compare its position as a neutral country in relation to the Jewish Agency for Palestine and other such rescue organisations with those of neutral Switzerland and Romania whose situation and policies were quite different. Istanbul and Geneva were the leading cities of the most important neutral countries in Europe during World War II, a situation which enabled them to become the major rescue centres of the time. In the face of wartime pressures, however, each had to limit the rescue operations in different ways in accordance with their understanding of the dangers which might have to be faced if their neutrality was breached by these operations. Switzerland never was under direct Nazi threat of invasion, so it was able to follow a policy of theoretical neutrality, enabling the Jewish Agency to operate with little restriction, though the Swiss did something that the Turks never did. They usually refused to accept Jewish refugees fleeing across the border from Germany if their passports had been marked "Jew" by the Nazis. Romania, on the other hand, in the light of its historic anti-Semitism, fully accepted and approved the Final Solution, and in response to British pressure to prevent Jews from leaving so they would not go to Palestine, imposed a prohibition on Jewish refugees passing through Romanian ports and cooperated with Adolph Eichmann's agents in deporting its large Jewish population to the extermination camps until the impending Allied victory convinced it to alter its policy."

"Turkey on the other hand was compelled to be a neutral state in practice since it was under immediate threat of Nazi invasion from Greece or across the Black Sea and through the Caucasus, initially by the Soviet Union and later by the invading German army. It also was being pressured by its British ally to prohibit all aid to Jewish refugees, and in fact not to admit them at all, even when Germany was allowing them to leave, because of Britain's fear that they would go on to Palestine. In response to these pressures and dangers, Turkey at times officially prohibited all activities by foreign rescue organisations such as the Jewish Agency, and closely watched the activities of all foreign groups operating in the country, but even at such times it in fact condoned and even assisted the rescue operations far more significantly than any other neutral country in Europe throughout the war."

"Turkey was of unique importance to all those who wanted to help European Jews being subjected to increasing persecution by the Nazis. It was close to Nazi-occupied south-eastern and eastern Europe. It was the locale of representatives not only of the western Allies but also of most of the European governments in exile. It was the key, moreover, to the only escape route left for Jewish refugees going from Europe to Palestine once the route previously used by the Jewish Agency's Geneva Office through France to Marseilles, and from there across the Mediterranean to Palestine, was closed as result of the German occupation of France and Italy's entry into the war during the summer of 1940. Turkey consequently came to constitute a true "Bridge to Palestine" a transit centre that enabled Jews being persecuted in their own countries to go on to the Holy Land both by land and sea making possible the salvation of thousands who would otherwise have been exterminated."

"The Geneva office of the Jewish Agency, directed by Richard Lichtheim and Chaim Pazner, remained a centre of Jewish efforts to help and rescue Jews in western Europe, but the Istanbul office became far more important and active as the war and the Holocaust progressed. Part of the reason for this was, simply, its location. It was far closer to Palestine than was Switzerland. Switzerland was surrounded by the Nazis on all sides, while Turkey had direct access by land to Europe on one side and to Iraq and Syria on the other, as well as to the Black Sea and across the Mediterranean, to Palestine. Moreover Switzerland in many ways shared Nazi hatred of the Jews and in any case was determined not to compromise its neutrality by going out of its way to help them in any way. Turkey also did not wish to stimulate a Nazi attack but much of its restrictive policies seem to have been only for show while it in fact assisted the Jewish Agency in a massive way to carry out its activities."

"Because of its strategic location and the willingness of its government to help, then, Istanbul replaced Geneva as the centre of the Jewish Agency refugee operations just as Germany shifted from a policy of deporting Jews or encouraging their emigration, to one of extermination, the Final Solution." *(pp. 255–257)*

"Those refugees who did not have official permission to enter Palestine were sent through Turkey to the Mediterranean coast, particularly to the ports of Marmaris and Bodrum, from which they were sent 'illegally' on small boats to Palestine. The Turkish government as well as private Turkish citizens, Jewish and non Jewish alike, provided fuel and food to these ships despite constant British objections, on the grounds that failure to do so would subject Turkey to even more international criticism if the ships were sunk or their passengers starved to death, since in such cases the British invariably tried to blame Turkey for the disasters. As a result, 4,400 Jewish refugees passed through

Turkey on their way to Palestine during 1941 alone and even greater numbers in subsequent years reaching a total of as many as an estimated 100,000 by the end of the war."

"Even after the Final Solution was put into effect Germany allowed thousands of Jews to leave the countries under its control for Turkey and Palestine as the result of the Exchange Plan which was negotiated through the good offices of the International Red Cross representatives in Geneva and Ankara, according to which groups of German citizens who had been stranded at the start of the war in the British colonies, in particular in South Africa and Australia, were sent to Istanbul, where they were sent on by train to Germany in exchange for Jewish refugees coming mainly from Germany, Austria and France. It was these Jewish refugees brought to Turkey on what came to be known as the Istanbul Lists who were the first eye-witnesses to tell the outside world of the mounting Nazi atrocities against the Jews of central and western Europe once the Final Solution had been put fully into effect. Their stories were reported from Istanbul to America and elsewhere with the full cooperation and assistance of the Turkish government."

"In addition to these fortunate few, hundreds of other refugees without entry or transit visas or visas for them to go on to other countries were allowed to pass across the border into Turkey, often without any papers at all, and this despite the Kararname and other regulations to the contrary, since there was nowhere else that they could go. Such refugees were allowed to remain in the country throughout the war, assisted by the local Jewish self-help organisations the Jewish Agency and other rescue groups working with it as well as by the Turkish Red Crescent and behind the scenes agencies of the Turkish government." *(pp. 266–267)*

"Even as Turkey moved to facilitate the passage of Jewish refugees on their way to Palestine, however, in one of the darkest moments in British history, His Majesty's Government moved to limit or halt the rescue movement, basing its Palestine policy on the consideration that if it angered the Arabs, they could always change sides and go over to the Nazis, for whom many Arab nationalists had already expressed considerable sympathy because of common hostility to the Jews, whereas the latter had nowhere to go. Thus N. Butler, of the North American Department of the British Foreign Office, stated:

> If we antagonise the Arabs, they are free to change sides so to speak, and throw in their lot with the Axis who will certainly be ready to welcome them. If on the other hand we antagonise the Jews, they have no such alternative, and will be forced still to adhere to our cause, since the whole of their racial future is wrapped up in our victory. Every Jew must realise this, including the Zionists in the U.S.A.

"In order to pacify the Arabs, then, descendants of those who had come out of the Arabian peninsula to conquer Palestine and other parts of the Middle East in the seventh century A.D., Great Britain refused to allow Jewish refugees to enter Great Britain 'unless in some quite rare and exceptional cases it can be shown that the admission of the refugee will be directly advantageous to our war effort, or to provide more than a small number of them with visas which would enable them to enter Palestine or any other Mediterranean area which it controlled.' In addition, it pressured Turkey and the countries of south-eastern Europe to refuse them entry and to turn back those arriving by ship, train or land, going on then to blame Turkey when, in the light of constant threats of German invasion and consequent budgetary problems, the Turkish Prime Minister declared that he would admit them only if they were allowed to go on to Palestine."

"Insofar as the British Government was concerned, there was no point in rescuing these Jews since there was no place to put them. As the British Ministry of Economic Warfare informed the United States Embassy in London on 15 December 1943, The Foreign Office are concerned with the difficulties of disposing of any considerable number of Jews should they be rescued from enemy occupied territory . . . Britain thus, albeit for its own reasons, actively cooperated with German implementation of the Final Solution by using all its influence to enforce the German prohibition against Jewish emigration from Europe so that they could be exterminated in the camps then being set up in the East. Turkey, however, saved the lives of most of these refugees by recognising visas for Palestine issued by the Jewish Agency in Istanbul which, since the British in many cases would not honour them when they went beyond the annual quotas for Jewish immigrants established by the 1939 White Paper, meant that they would be allowed to remain in Turkey through the remainder of the war or at least until means were provided for them to emigrate illegally from the ports along the coast of southern Turkey across the Mediterranean to Palestine, evading the British naval blockade, landing secretly on the shores of the Holy land, and vanishing into friendly Jewish settlements and houses throughout the country." *(pp. 278–280)*

———

On 1 April 1943 the British War Cabinet on Refugees, chaired by subsequent Prime Minister, Clement Attlee and including Home Secretary Herbert Morrison, agreed to try to persuade the United States and others in Africa and North and South America to take the refugees, but on condition that efforts would be made to make quite sure that these refugees would stay in Turkey, and would not be passed on, e.g. to Palestine. Turkey, thus, would have to keep the Jewish refugees because no-one else wanted them, and if Turkey were to refuse to accept more refugees, it would be criticised for a lack of humanity."

"Nor was the United States, because of its developing oil interests in the Arab Middle East, much more sympathetic than Great Britain to the idea of either admitting Jewish refugees to its own country or allowing them to go on to Palestine. When in November 1941 the Turkish Minister to Bucharest proposed to the American Minister that 300,000 Romanian Jews then being subjected to persecution by the Iron Guard as well as the dictatorial government of Antonescu, be shipped to safety in Palestine, the American State Department strongly opposed the plan".

"Despite persistent British as well as German efforts to get Turkey to close the Jewish Agency office in Istanbul, then, it continued to be allowed to use Turkish facilities to smuggle diamonds, gold coins, and currency into the Nazi-occupied lands to help feed and house Jews who were not able to leave, with the Turkish ambassadors and consular representatives at times helping and even arranging for Jews to flee to Turkey. All of this activity took place at a time when British assistance of money and food to the persecuted Jews of Hungary and Bulgaria was strongly opposed by Foreign Secretary Anthony Eden, who stated that "The majority of the adults who would benefit are Jews, and the political difficulties involved in this are obvious . . . ," and who went on to even oppose a public British declaration condemning the Nazi atrocities against the Jews because 'these repeated threatenings might debase the currency.' German and British pressure on Greece, Bulgaria and Yugoslavia to limit the Zionists' ability to charter ships for the dangerous trip through the Black Sea to Turkey and Palestine or to allow the ships of other nations to carry Jewish refugees through their territorial waters severely limited their ability to transport refugees, since all these nations put up very little resistance." *(pp. 285–286)*

———

"Turkey, however, resisted similar pressure, refusing to close the Straits to refugee ships on the grounds that this would violate the basic principles of freedom of navigation to which all the nations involved had subscribed before the war. When Nazi and British pressure at times forced Turkey to overtly limit these Zionist rescue activities by closing the Jewish Agency office and limiting Jewish immigration into and through Turkey, the Turkish government allowed the same Zionists to maintain the unofficial Aliyah Bet organisation established by the Mossad committee to continue to bring in Jewish refugees and send them on to Palestine on an "illegal" basis."

"Turkey moreover helped rescue non-Turkish Jews in Romania and Hungary, where almost a million and a half Jews had lived when the war began. Both were ruled by Fascist governments, in various forms of alliance with Germany, so that though they were not occupied by the Germans, they instead undertook their own means of persecuting their Jews. In both countries the Turkish diplomats worked to help protect Jews of all nationalities, even though most were not Turkish citizens. It was not that easy for the refugees to escape."

"Trains, however, were found, and Turkish and other ships carried hundreds of refugees from the coasts of Romania and Bulgaria, sometimes to Istanbul, sometimes to the Black Sea port of Samsun or the Aegean port of Izmir, and from there to Palestine."
(pp. 288–289)

"Thousands of refugees arrived in Turkey by boat and train and on foot during the remainder of 1943 and 1944 from Greece, Bulgaria, Romania, Poland and Hungary, particularly after the latter was occupied by Germany in March 1944 and as the gas chambers of Auschwitz and elsewhere geared up to carry out the Final Solution.

"It was only in early 1944 that the United States government finally realised the extent of the Holocaust and moved to provide substantial support to the task of rescuing the surviving Jews in Eastern Europe. In response to increasing political pressure for action in the United States, American Ambassador to Turkey Laurence Steinhardt, himself a Jew, was asked by the Secretary of State whether the limited number of refugees who were arriving was due to Turkey's blocking their passage, and whether it might be possible to get Turkish assistance for the transport of Jews coming from south-eastern Europe as well as camps to house them in Turkey until they were sent on to Palestine.

Steinhardt responded that the failure of large numbers of Jewish refugees to pass through Turkey previously was due not to Turkish reticence but to the refusal of the Balkan countries to allow them to leave as well as the difficulty they had encountered in finding adequate transportation even when they had received permission to move on. It was not that Turkey was unwilling to give them transit visas. It always had been willing to do so if only Britain would allow them to go on to Palestine. Turkey, moreover, was even ready to provide ships to transport them from the Bulgarian and Romanian coasts. It had already done so. But it was a poor country which would be using a substantial part of its merchant marine in the effort, and it needed guarantees that if the ships were sunk, the United States would provide replacements."

"As a direct result of Steinhardt's report, on 22 January 1944 President Franklin Delano Roosevelt established the War Refugee Board (WRB), composed of representatives of the departments of State, Interior and War, to facilitate this task. British Prime Minister Winston L. S. Churchill regarded the Middle East a primary British sphere of influence and an important element in maintaining the British Empire, so he deeply resented this American entry into the area. Due to the need to maintain Anglo American cooperation in Europe and elsewhere in the world, however, the British had no choice but to cooperate and to change their policy to one of issuing group visas for these refugee groups massed in Istanbul so that they could go on to Palestine without further difficulty. On 29 January 1944, the British Embassy at Ankara therefore informed the Turkish Ministry of Foreign Affairs:

1. Assurance is being given to the effect that Jewish immigrants arriving to Turkey under the scheme of 5,000 certificates will be granted visas to Palestine within twenty-four hours of their arrival in Istanbul.
2. Mr. Barlas, Representative for the arrangements regarding transportation of the immigrants to Palestine as well as their maintenance during their stay in Istanbul.
3. It is being understood that the transportation will be arranged in groups of seventy five children (including five adults as conveyors) every ten days, according to an itinerary to be agreed on." *(pp. 291 –292)*

Britain continued to strongly resent American intervention in what it considered to be its affairs, but in the light of the efforts of the WRB and of Ira Hirschmann in particular, it was compelled to continue to relax its immigration polices and support the effort to rescue the Jews." *(pp. 299–300)*

"The Turkish Ambassador to Romania throughout the war, Hamdullah Suphi Tannöver, played an important role in stopping Romanian plans to send its 600,000 Jews to the Nazi death camps. The Turkish Red Crescent and the Jewish Agency in Istanbul sent medical supplies and clothing to Eastern Europe on a regular basis, but at times Bulgaria refused to allow these supplies to be given to its Jewish citizens. In addition, starting in the summer of 1940, the Turkish government sent trucks, trains, and the steamship Sakarya on regular rescue missions through the Black Sea, bringing several hundred Jewish refugees from throughout eastern Europe to Istanbul on each trip. Similar rescues were made by the steamships Europe, Vitornal, Pacific and Atlantic as well as many small motor boats and sail boats sent from Turkish ports on the Black Sea. The refugee ships were allowed through Turkish waters by the authorities whether or not they had regular papers, or even when the latter were obviously forgeries or invalid documents sold to the Aliyah Bet agents, for the most part by clerks in the consulates of many of the countries of Central and South America."

"Most of the refugees landed at the Black Sea port of Samsun, from which they were sent overland to Konya, Nigde and Mersin, where they remained while passport and visa formalities were completed for their subsequent passage to Palestine. Other refugees from Yugoslavia, Bulgaria and Greece as well as many fleeing from the death camps at Bergen-Belsen and Vittel and a few from Denmark, Sweden, Switzerland and Slovakia came by sea from Salonica across the Aegean to Izmir, and from southern Greece, Rhodes and the eastern Mediterranean islands to southern Anatolia's Mediterranean ports of Antalya, Bodrum, Iskenderun and Mersin. From there they went on in groups to Palestine on steamers and small boats arranged by the Jewish agency and the Turkish government as well as overland through Syria by trains of the Turkish railroads.

On 1 February 1941, Haim Barlas estimated that about 4,594 Jewish refugees from Eastern Europe had received Turkish visas as a result of thirty lists submitted to the Ankara government."(p.302)

"Thousands more came in subsequent years, though exact figures lack for the years before 1944. The American Jewish Joint Distribution Committee reported that between

January and October 1944, they helped 4,404 Jewish refugees go to Turkey, of whom 691 were from Bulgaria, 160 from Hungry, 2,732 from Romania, 539 from Greece, and 282 from Holland. All came by the following steamers: the Milca (239 passengers), Maritza (334), Bella Cita (153), Milca (272), Martiza (318), Kazbek (752), Morina (308), Bulbul (391), Turkish Railroads (35), and five saved from the steamship Metkure, which was sunk. In the final analysis, a total of 16,474 "official" Jewish immigrants passed through Turkey during the war on their way to Palestine, in addition to approximately 75,000 unofficial refugees, while the Jewish Agency, in Istanbul and its affiliated groups distributed some 523,547 pounds sterling to Jews in Nazi-occupied Europe in 1943 and 1944. According to American figures, a total of $215,000 was distributed in Turkey for Jewish refugees by various American relief organisations from January 1944 until February 1945, much of which was raised in emotional campaigns led by Hirschmann after he returned to the United States."

"Turkey's role in the war went beyond its help to Europe's suffering Jews. It was through the Jewish agents in Istanbul that Adolph Eichmann's offer came to liberate the surviving Jews of Hungary, in return for war equipment and money. It was through these same agents that the offer of Helmuth von Moltke representing the underground German anti-Nazi opposition, for an early peace immediately after the failure of their attempt against the life of Adolph Hitler, was passed on to the Allies in October 1943, through the agency of one of the leading refugee professors, political scientist Alexander Rüstow. Similarly, it was to Istanbul in February, 1944 that agents from Hungary came to offer a separate peace if only their nation could be rescued from the deadly Nazi embrace." *(pp. 303–304)*

Conclusion

"Turkey most certainly did not remain neutral during World War II in order to save the Jews of Europe. It did so because it was allied with Britain and France, which were unable to promise assistance if its entry into the war led to a German invasion. The resulting Turkish neutrality, however, did make it possible for its diplomatic agents in Nazi occupied Europe to significantly assist in saving thousands of Jews from persecution and death and for Turkey to constitute the most important bridge for Jewish refugees fleeing from Eastern Europe on their way to Palestine." *(p.305)*

"Jewish Turks have continued to live in Turkey in peace and prosperity to the present. Turkey moreover has remained an important place of refuge to which those fleeing from persecution in the Middle East have been able to go, whether Kurds from Iraq, Jews and Bahais from Khomaini's Iran, or Turks from Greece, Armenia, Azerbaijan, Greek Cyprus and Bulgaria." *(p.305)*

Conference Paper 2

When the Turkish authorities decided to attend this important conference, which we think has high humanistic aims and a sense of justice to rectify the atrocities perpetrated against the Jews during World War II, we believe that we do not find our presence appropriate at this conference. The two reasons that led us to attend this conference at the last moment are: (a) not to put our American friends and the British authorities, who are organising this conference, in an uncomfortable situation and to encourage them in their difficult task; and (b) that we have reason to believe that we may have to react to some unfounded allegations directed against Turkey or to some unnecessary references which were voiced in the morning session.

We observe a tendency to extend one's own crimes upon others in order to externalise certain crimes (ethnical ones) especially.

If we understand correctly, this conference has three different issues, rightly or wrongly intermingling with each other, namely: (1) the investigation of the whereabouts of the Nazi gold during World War II; (2) the interconnection of this gold or money with the Jewish victims of the war; and (3) a new review of World War II with a different approach. This is the most important point, as the honourable delegate of Israel expressed his ideas "It is more important to remember the violation of Jewish dignity and honour by the Nazis than to discuss the amount of gold looted by them." Now I am saying that we, the Turks, do not deserve the reputation of being the profiteer of the material heritage of the Holocaust victims.

During World War II, Turkey had to follow an extremely passive policy as the equipment of the Turkish army has been very poor and the industrial structure of the country was extremely backward. Turkey was scared of any kind of provocation which would have caused a German or a Soviet invasion. While the belligerent countries were not able to provide Turkey with imported goods, Turkey had been asked by all of the warring parties for any kind of raw materials they needed, which caused the rise of an active trade balance in Turkey.

It is well known to economic historians that Turkey had during this period, therefore, the highest amount of gold reserves in its recent history.

Regarding the first issue of this conference, which also seems to be the main theme of the conference, Turkey played no part in any kind of clandestine gold dealings with the Nazi regime and to have a share of their plunder. The gold belonging to Turkey mentioned in the report of May 7 1997 was acquired in good faith with the rightfully earned foreign currency savings of Turkey. We have already given an extensive explanation on this matter to our American friends. My colleague from the Turkish Central Bank will convey his explanation after my speech.

The report's section on Turkey was written with certain defects of historiographical methodology. To author the structure of monetary history, clearing the system and commodity exchange, seem to have been unknown in those times. Furthermore, we were not contacted about the content of the report's section about Turkey before its circulation.

As to the gold coins deposited by the German Reich Embassy in Ankara to the Swiss Embassy in Ankara, which, at that time, was representing the German interests after the end of the war, these were entrusted to the Turkish authorities only for safekeeping. The same amount of those gold coins of concern were returned to the Federal Republic of Germany between 1960 and 1963. There were two economic protocols between Turkey and the F.R.G., one concluded in 1960 and the other in 1963, testifying this transaction. The texts of these two protocols were also submitted to our American friends.

Therefore, if there are any claims by the three allied countries of World War II or their Tripartite Gold Commission on the above mentioned two amounts, we believe that they have to resort to the German authorities, not to Turkey. Everybody should keep in mind that when Turkey adhered to the Bretton Woods Agreement and its VIth protocol, the Turkish authorities made the necessary legal reservation at that time with a view to "respect the gold acquitted in good faith".

We would like to remind you that the British judiciary system has its own law concerning the "respect of good faith" embodied in the British law, "The Sale of Goods Act" dated 1893. Another important fact we have to emphasise is that the negotiations conducted between Turkey and the three allied countries between 1947 and 1953, were purely of an economic nature and these negotiations were conducted only between Turkey and the three allies. Therefore if these countries put the matter aside themselves in 1953 because of the escalation of the "Cold War", they should apply to Turkey again diplomatically with the understanding that should still exist between two nations who have been friendly allies for almost half a century.

Our counterpart to explain the details of this matter is not an international conference in which we should not have been taking part.

Concerning the Jewish element of this conference, Turkey is proud of its well known historical heritage of being a safe haven and a refuge for the European Jews uninterruptedly after 1492 until modern times and especially during World War II.

Turkey became the asylum place for the Austro-German Jewish intelligentsia, who became our beloved and respected teachers at the Turkish universities, whereas some countries were scared to fulfil their immigration quotas by rejecting the delivery of visas to many Austro-German intellectuals, thus causing those Jews to be exterminated at the concentration camps.

(We have a paper on this issue, prepared solely on scientific grounds and we submit this paper to the conference this morning.)

On the other hand, we have learned through the Turkish Jewish community that the enduring Turkish-Jewish solidarity in our history has been registered in the recent meetings of the World Jewish Congress.

When the Jewish Congress convened recently in Oslo on this same issue, there was no mention of Turkey there. It is difficult for us to interpret which purpose and which source attempted to lure Turkey unjustly into their embroil.

It is not only the Turkish authorities who are offended, but also, and more profoundly, our Turkish Jewish community.

Regarding this second issue, anybody is able to contact the honourable representative of the Turkish Jewish community who is also taking part in our official delegation.

During our research we have studied some few thousand pages which are not comparable to the number of documents studied by the authors of this report. Studying 15 million pages from a histigraphical methodology point of view, it is not easy to evaluate Turkey's position. We are disappointed at the unsatisfactory evidence (almost nothing) provided in order to cover the claims about Turkey in the above mentioned report.

On the other hand, everybody has forgotten the infamous Ribbentrof-Molotov Pact. When the three so-called neutral countries of Europe, namely Sweden, Spain and Portugal had to encounter and protect themselves only from the Nazi regime, Turkey was facing two different evils from two different directions, namely the Nazi regime and the Stalinist Soviet Union, which had high ambitions over Turkey and tried to partition it with the Nazis. These ambitions of the Soviets were not exclusive only for the war period but continued ever forcefully after the end of the war. When we were admonishing of this danger, even during the war, perhaps our American and British friends thought we were just "crying wolf".

In short, it is not justifiable to blame Turkey for its conduct during the war. When Norway was being invaded by the Hitler armies through the safe passage of helpless Sweden, Turkey was not giving any transit to the same German army to support the Nazi sympathisers in Iraq.

European Jews were massacred because of the failures of Western countries for the 1938 Munich Agreement and because of their late entry into the war. Thank heavens, Turkey was present there, at least to save the Jews from the Middle East. Now I give the floor to my colleague, Mr Ethem Seckin, representing the Central Bank of Turkey.

THE GOLD REPORT

The gold assets of the Central Bank of the Republic of Turkey (CBRT) had increased considerably from a level of 27.4 metric tons in 1939 to 216.2 metric tons by the end of 1945.

The main reasons for CBRT's extraordinary efforts to increase its gold assets were to meet instant demands for foreign currency and to protect its foreign holdings against possible depreciation under the war conditions.

When the foreign trade figures of Turkey was examined, it was realised that the trade deficit experienced during 1938 turned to a surplus in 1939 and this surplus continued till 1946.

In 1940, the increases in cotton harvest and coal production and the discovery of petroleum fields were the main reasons for the trade surplus. The existence of cash buyers for our export goods and the limited level of our imports had positive effects on our foreign currency holdings. As a result of these positive developments our Government had decided to make all exports and imports on a cash basis. On the other hand the trade agreement with the British Government dated December 2, 1940 was another factor in increasing our trade volume. Due to similar developments in the following years CBRT could manage to increase its gold assets.

The foreign trade surplus of Turkey for the years 1939–46 was in total around 341.5 million US Dollars. When this trade surplus of Turkey during World War II was expressed in terms of gold, it was around 304 metric tons and it could be clearly understood that the trade surplus of Turkey was invested in gold because of the reasons mentioned before.

In order to increase its gold assets, CBRT had decided to make an arrangement with the Swiss National Bank in March 1942. According to this arrangement, in case CBRT's foreign currency deposits with the Swiss National Bank exceeded a certain amount, the surplus would be automatically invested in gold or vice versa. Subsequently, under the provisions of this arrangement the foreign currency holdings of CBRT exceeding the certain amount were invested in gold by the Swiss National Bank.

Replies to allegations concerning the gold acquisitions of Turkey during World War II

Turkey was unjustly accused for purchasing Nazi gold in three different parties. As I mentioned before, the trade surplus gave Turkey the opportunity to purchase gold on cash basis during World War II and the total of these allegations were only 3% of the total acquisitions of Turkey during this period.

1. The first party was a purchase of gold bars weighing 2.0 metric tons from Reichsbank in 1942 prior to the Allied Declaration on January 5, 1943.

On July 6, 1942 CBRT had bought 2,010.1717 kilograms of gold from Reichsbank and ordered Sveriges Riksbank and Swiss National Bank to credit Reichsbank's accounts with themselves for SEK 4,500,000 and SFR 5,183,673.28 respectively.

2. The second party was the acquisition of 249 gold bars weighing approximately 3 metric tons in 1943.

CBRT was planning to purchase gold for SFR 10,000,000 in the beginning of May 1943. In those days due to war conditions it was quite hard to transport gold to Turkey. Taking the high transportation costs into consideration, the Board had later decided to increase the amount to SFR 15,000,000 in order to decrease the transportation costs per kilogram. At that point Reichsbank had offered to sell gold for SFR 5,000 per kilogram which was quite expensive when compared with the SFR 4,920.63 per kilogram price of the Swiss National Bank. At the Board of Directors' meeting the Governor had suggested buying gold from Switzerland and leaving it with the Bank for International Settlements to be safeguarded or buying gold from the USA against payments in Swiss Francs, in case it would not be possible to bring it home. Finally, the Swiss National Bank had purchased 3,048.40672 kilograms of gold on our behalf for SFR 15,000,081 on May 8, 1943 according to the provisions of the arrangement mentioned before and debited our account accordingly.

In searching a way to bring the gold to Turkey, the Reichsbank offered to supply 249 bars of gold weighing 3,047.32 kilograms in total to Turkey against the gold purchased by Swiss National Bank on behalf of CBRT. This offer was accepted by CBRT and in order to settle the transaction, CBRT instructed the Swiss National Bank on May 25, 1943 to transfer the 3,048.40672 kilograms of its gold to Reichsbank against 249 gold bars weighing 3,047.32 kilograms received on June 3, 1943.

3. The third party was the acquisition of 243 kilograms of gold bars and 32,000 gold coins.

As it was known, these gold bars and coins were handed by the German Embassy to the Swiss Embassy in Ankara and then they entrusted them to CBRT.

The records show that this gold was fully returned to the German side under the provisions of the Article 3 of the Protocol signed in Bonn on November 3, 1960 between the delegations of the Federal German and Turkish Governments. This Article ruled that Turkey should return all German assets that were handed to the Turkish Government by the Swiss authorities under the provisions of the Protocol dated February 28, 1946. According to this Protocol the Ministry of Finance of Turkey had returned 100 kilograms of gold bars and 20,000 coins to Deutsche Bank and Dresdner Bank on June 22, 1960 and the rest – 123 kilograms of gold bars and 12,799 coins – to the Federal German Government on November 11, 1960.

ANNEX 1

The Return of Cultural Treasure

J. GREENFIELD

Cambridge, 1989, p. 102

The Sale of Goods Act 1893 embodied the principles of English law relating to transfer of title upon the sale of goods. This was amended in 1979 and provides in Section 23 for "sale under voidable title".

When the seller of goods has a voidable title to them, but his title has not been avoided at the time of sale, the buyer acquires a good title to the goods, provided he buys them in good faith and without notice of the seller's defect of title.

The operative words in the present context would be "voidable title", "in good faith", and "without notice of the seller's defect of title". If it can be shown that property can be stolen and there is no title in the vendor, then even a purchaser in good faith would not acquire title against a party who had a superior title.

ANNEX 2

Protocol

From 18 to 31 October 1960, talks were held at the German Ministry of Foreign Affairs in Bonn between a delegation of the Turkish Government and a delegation of the Government of the Federal Republic of Germany in the framework of the letter of November 1958 sent by the German State Secretary at the Ministry of Foreign Affairs to His Excellency the Turkish Ambassador.

The purpose of the talks was to subject the Turkish wishes to a technical examination of the extent to which they have a basis in international law or in German national legislation and whether compliance with them would be compatible with the Federal Republic's international agreements.

ARTICLE I

(1) Both delegations came to the view that the following matters fall within the scope of the above mentioned letter and can form the subject of further negotiations to begin from January 1961:

   (a) Prior clarification of economic problems which, in the event of Turkey's accession to the London Debts Agreement, would for the most part have to be settled under Annex IV thereto,

   (b) Conversion of Reichsmark balances of the Turkish Government and Turkish nationals at German credit institutions,

   (c) Questions concerning the application of the German Equalisation of Burdens legislation and the General War Consequences Act in relation to Turkish nationals,

   (d) Costs of the administration of German assets up to their return.

(2) A further topic of the negotiations referred to in paragraph 1 will be the result of the examination promised by the German side within a period of about two weeks regarding the questions of a social nature listed below, which is being carried out from the point of view of whether they come within the scope of the above mentioned letter of 10 November 1958; in particular, whether they have a basis in international law and whether compliance with them would be compatible with the Federal Republic's international agreements:

   (a) Accommodation of and provision for Turkish nationals of Jewish faith who were expelled during the war to Turkey from the territories occupied by the German armed forces.

   (b) Accommodation of and provision for refugees of Turkish ethnic origin from the territories occupied by the German armed forces.

   (c) Accommodation of and provision for former members of the Wehrmacht who were picked up from the IRO camps after World War II.

   (d) Expenditure in respect of German nationals interned in Turkey during the war.

ARTICLE 2

(1) Before the start of the abovementioned negotiations, the Turkish side will hand over to the German side an inventory relating to the questions mentioned in Article 1(1)(a) of this Protocol. In it will be listed: names and addresses of creditors and debtors, amounts and legal basis of claims and dates when they arose.

(2) The Turkish Government will communicate by *note verbale* before 31 December 1960 its wish already expressed for the conclusion of a lump-sum agreement under §102 of the General War Consequences Act.

ARTICLE 3

Both delegations further agreed that the following items will be placed on the agenda of the planned negotiations:
(a) The complex of questions arising out of the earlier German-Turkish clearing trans-actions, in particular settlement in respect of the amounts withdrawn from the cred-it balances of the German clearing office and audit of the book squaring other said clearing transactions. In order to prepare these negotiations, the German clearing office and the Turkish central bank will provide each other with information.
(b) Settlement of the questions concerning the railway equipment provided on lease to the Turkish State railways under pre-war contracts in so far as this question is not already dealt with between German Federal Railways and Turkish State Railways before the above mentioned negotiations.
(c) Completion of the remaining arrangements for the release of the German property in Turkey in so far as no clarification is achieved in the meantime by the German Embassy in Ankara; in particular
    aa) return of the valuables* handed over to the Turkish Government by the Swiss protecting power pursuant to Protocol of 28 February 1946,
    bb) use of the LT 350,000 handed over by the Swiss protecting power under Protocol of 12 September 1945,
    cc) resumption of the debt service and release of interest accrued in the meantime on Turkish loans, including
        $7^1/2$% State bond of 1933,
        Société du Chemin de fer d'Anatolie
        Société du Port Heydarpasa.
(d) Bank guarantees and letter of credit.

ARTICLE 4

(1) The German delegation put forward as a further wish for inclusion on the agenda of the planned negotiations settlement of the claims arising from the Treasury Bills (Bons de Trésor) issued by the Turkish Government in connection with the Credit Agreement of 31.12.1942 / 19.1.1943. The Turkish delegation stated in regard to this that the agreement in question, which was connected with the supply of war matériel and had not been put into force again after the war, could not form the subject of any negotiations. The German delegation stated that it could not consent to non-discussion and therefore had to reserve the right to comment further.

---

* *Translator's note: "Werte" could also be "securities" or "asse"*

(2) The Turkish delegation likewise put forward as a further wish for inclusion on the agenda of the planned negotiations settlement of the problem of the banknotes of the Ottoman Empire, which had arisen during World War I. The German delegation stated in regard to this that it was not authorised to discuss this matter. The Turkish delegation stated that it could not consent to non-discussion and therefore had to reserve the right to comment further.

The foregoing protocol was drawn up in two copies in the German and Turkish languages. Both texts are equally authentic.

Bonn, 3 November 1960

For the delegation
of the Government of the
Turkish Republic:

[signed]

For the delegation
of the Government of the
Federal Republic of Germany:

[signed]

Conference Paper 3

Historical Facts

CHAPTER I — TURKEY'S SITUATION DURING WORLD WAR II   588

Introduction   588
Turkish President Ismet Inönü's Analysis of Turkey's Situation During World War II   590
Soviet Explanation for the Causes of the War and the Justification for the Nazi-Soviet Pact   593
British Appreciation of Turkey's Attitude   595
American Neutrality and American Understanding Towards Turkey   602

CHAPTER II — TURKEY'S CONCERNS ABOUT SOVIET AMBITIONS   605

I. General Trends (Turkish Foreign Policy Regarding the Soviets)   605
  Introduction   605
  Churchill-Stalin Meeting of October 1944 and the Decision to Establish Spheres of
    Influence   608
  The Yalta Conference – The Ending of War   610
  A Historical Note – The Predicted Soviet Demands on Turkey   611

II. Soviets' Disclosure of their Intentions Over Turkey and Turkey's   613
Expression of its Concerns to the Allies
  Soviets Reveal their Intentions to the British and the Germans   613
  Turkey Expresses its Concerns about the Soviet Intentions   618

CHAPTER III — OVERLORD VERSUS THE BALKAN OPERATION   621

I. Prelude – Important Conferences and Talks   621
  The Casablanca Agreement and its Consequences for Turkey   621
  The Conference at Adana – a Meeting of Misunderstandings   624
  Washington Talks between Eden and Roosevelt   627
  Churchill-Roosevelt Meeting in Washington (May 1943) and the Quebec Conference
    (August 1943)   628
  British Failure at Rhodes   629
  The Moscow Conference: the Russians Try to Force Turkey into the War
    (October 1943)   631
  Menemencioğlu and Eden Meet at the First Cairo Conference – The British Play the
    Russian Hand   632
  The Tehran Conference: The Soviet Reversal   635
  The Second Cairo Conference: Inönü Confronts Roosevelt and Churchill   636

II. Overlord Operation Versus Churchill's Proposals   638
  American Opposition (Introduction)   638
  General Marshall's Opposition   639
  General Eisenhower's Opposition   641

Churchill's Defence of his Balkan Policy: "To Forestall the Russians in Central Europe"   641
The Deterioration of the Churchill-Roosevelt Relationship   642
Roosevelt's Opinions   643
Stalin's Attitude Concerning the Overlord and the Balkans   646
Conclusion   647

Notes   648

CHAPTER I

TURKEY'S SITUATION DURING WORLD WAR II

Introduction

İnönü and most of his associates and countrymen remembered all too well how the Ottoman Empire had been dragged into its destruction and the Turkish nation threatened with extinction by involvement in World War I. Nevertheless, circumstances have dictated Turkey's involvement in a number of international alliances. In the face of the Italian threat, relations with Britain had been improved in the mid 1930's culminating with the visit of King Edward VIII to Istanbul while cruising the Mediterranean in his yacht (September 4–5, 1936) and by İnönü's visit to London to attend the coronation of George VI (May 9–10, 1937). New credit agreement followed (May 27), providing in particular for British participation in the industrial development of Turkey's second Five-Year Plan and leading to a treaty of mutual guarantee between the two (May 12, 1939), which accompanied the Hatay settlement. The Turks entered these agreements mainly because of fear of Germany and Italy and also on the assumption that there would be no difficulty with the Soviet Union because of its strong opposition to Nazism and fascism. But with the Nazi-Soviet Alliance (August 23, 1939) and joint invasion of Poland, it seemed very possible that they might go on to overrun Turkey as well. Turkey attempted to secure a Russian guarantee for its territorial integrity so that its previous agreements with Britain and France could be transformed into open alliances. But Germany, facing encirclement from the south as the result of British-French agreements with Romania and Greece (April 1939), worked to prevent this and also to secure Turkish friendship or at least neutrality so that Britain could not get help to Romania through Turkish territory. Russia supported the German Policy and continued to threaten Turkey to keep the Allies out of the Balkans. It demanded Turkish agreement to close the Straits to foreign warships and garrison them with Russian troops through a mutual-assistance pact (October 2, 1939). The Turks could not accept this proposal if for no other reason than it would violate their obligations under the Montreux Convention and might lead to war with the Allies.

On October 19, 1939, Turkey entered a mutual-assistance agreement with Britain and France. But it was arranged to prevent Turkish participation in a war unless the Republic's interests were directly involved, such as aggression by a European power in a war in the Mediterranean, in which case the Allies would help Turkey. Turkey's obligations to help Greece and Romania by the terms of the pre-war Balkan Pact would also be thus honoured. Turkey was allowed to exclude any action against the Soviet Union regardless of other obligations. France and Britain promised to give loans to help Turkey rearm and settle its commercial debt. The Russians were highly critical of the agreement despite the fact that they were excluded, but their subsequent involvement in Poland and then with Germany prevented them from expressing their hostility by an open attack.

As World War II went on, its shifts and starts prevented Turkey from joining the Allies. It also avoided any entanglement with Germany, thus staying neutral. As Italy invaded and conquered Greece (October 1940) and Albania and Germany in turn conquered Yugoslavia, Greece, Romania and Bulgaria taking Crete and moving into North Africa in early 1941, Turkey was increasingly isolated from its nominal allies and exposed to the German threat without much hope of assistance except from Russia, whose opposition still was not very clear. Germany was now represented in Ankara by Franz von Papen, who had come to the Ottoman Empire during World War I as assistant to Falkenhaym.[1]

He attempted to get permission for German troops to pass through Turkey to attack the British and French in Iraq, Syria and Iran, promising in return territories in Thrace and a guarantee of Turkish security. Turkey, however realised that agreement to such terms would mean essentially a declaration of war on the Allies, thus it ultimately agreed only to a treaty of non-aggression with Germany (June 18, 1941), which specifically excluded commitments previously made by the parties. Germany following its invasion of Russia (June 22, 1941), increased its demands on Turkey to include the supply of raw materials, particularly manganese and chrome, but the Turks were able to avoid a commitment on the ground that they already had agreed to send these metals to Britain. In the end, Turkey was able to sell these metals to both sides at very high prices while avoiding a break with either. A trade agreement with Germany (October 9, 1941) provided some chrome in exchange for war equipment, but little more. In 1942 von Papen pressed the Turks once again for transit rights to the east, disclosing new Russian claims to the Straits made to Germany while they were Allies and also encouraging the surviving Pan-Turanians in Turkey to undermine the Soviet Union by stirring its Turkish minorities to revolt. Turkey avoided a final commitment on the pretext that such actions, if openly supported by its government, might cause the Russians to massacre their entire Turkish population, particularly since the Armenians had become very strong in the Communist Party. As a result, all Germany was able to get was new trade agreements, but Turkey was able to avoid any commitments that might cause an open break with the Western Allies. The Allies in the meantime encouraged Turkish neutrality, since they no longer were in any position to help Turkey in case it entered the war openly on their behalf.[2]

While Turkey thus managed to maintain itself in uneasy neutrality, its internal economic situation deteriorated rapidly as a result of the war. Because of the imminent threats of invasion, first by Russia and then by Germany, İnönü had to mobilise the Turkish army, putting over 1 million men under arms and doubling the military's share of budget. The mobilisation was a tremendous burden on an economy that had not been very strong to begin with. Withdrawal of thousands of men from the work force reduced agricultural and industrial production markedly, while the war actions and blockades in the Mediterranean halted the flow of most imports and exports, causing serious shortages of most goods and spare parts and depriving Turkey of many of its markets. The armed forces provided a new source of competition on the market, taking goods needed by civilians.[3]

The only positive economic result of the war came in the latter two years (1943–45) when Turkey, as it came closer to the Western Allies, began to receive lend-lease help to increase production and exports and accumulated a sufficient amount of foreign credit to finance much of its postwar economic recovery. In December 1942 the British began to pressure Turkey to enter the war on the Allied side, but Churchill agreed that Turkey would have to be armed first. Allied weapons and air advisers began to come to Turkey in 1943, but İnönü still held back because of quite justified fears that Germany still could bomb Istanbul without fear of Allied retaliation. The Allies appreciated Turkey's hesitations, but at the Moscow and Tehran Conferences (October–November 1943) they decided to pressure the Turks to enter the war as soon as possible. İnönü continued to put them off until the spring of 1944 when the rapidly developing German collapse led him to break the economic and political ties that von Papen had built and, finally, to declare war on Germany on February 23, 1945, just in time to become a charter member of the United Nations.[4]

Turkish President Ismet Inönü's analysis of Turkey's situation during World War II

President İnönü, in the statement he delivered to the Turkish Grand National Assembly on November 1, 1945 (after the war ended) analysed Turkey's attitude during the war as such.

1939: When the clouds of war were seen for the first time on the horizon during the spring of 1939, Turkey was the only nation among its equals to see the right direction of the ideal and has sided herself openly beside Great Britain and France.

1940: In 1940, when France fell and the war of Britain started, we were again the only nation who applauded the heroism of England and declared that we were beside England . . . However, the provisions of the Tripartite Alliance Treaty we had concluded with France and England (before the war started) forced us legally to a definite neutrality because of the incidents between our two Allies.

1941: At the start of 1941, we were waiting, mobilised against the German and Italian forces (that could attack) from Rhodes to Thrace. I want you to remember that in the meantime, an Axis state was established in Iraq and the Vichy government in Syria was openly against the British. When it is remembered with equity that, even when Turkey was surrounded all around by Axis powers, she was trying, in a self sacrificing way, to block the invasion paths of the arrogant powers that had occupied the whole of Europe with her meagre means, which consisted only of her own human resources and already depleted financial resources, then one can only appreciate the services our nation had rendered and the risks we had taken.

1942: In this part of his speech, İnönü emphasised that the Turkish attitude had been appreciated by England and USA, and specially indicated that the Soviet appreciation had been transmitted by the Soviet Ambassador on January 19, 1942.

After this, he replied to criticisms which started after 1943.

1943: As is known, within international relations, the secrets between states are not the property of only one state. However, as an expression of a simple truth, I would like to emphasise here in your presence, the injustice of the allegations made against us. We have been criticised for concluding a friendship agreement with the Germans before the war broke out between the Germans and the Soviets. The Germans, who had already reached the gates of Istanbul, had already been allied with the Soviets in a non-aggression pact. When our country was standing alone against the whole Axis power; when the USA was not yet in the war; when England had allocated all its forces against the German invasion of the (Aegean) Islands; when Soviets were aligned with Germany in a non-aggression pact; with which right and reason could anybody expect from us that we should have rejected on paper that the Germans would not attack us? (Unofficial Translation)

Turkey's Rejection of any Kind of Territorial Offers from Both Sides

Another of President İnönü's analyses of Turkey's position during the war, when she was resisting and refusing the territorial temptations offered to her from both the German and the Soviet sides – as he explained to Turkish historian Mr. Sevket Süreyya Aydemir (he had written the most accountable biographies of both Atatürk and İnönü) was as follows:

From the onset, that is even before the war broke out, we were following the policy of establishing relations with France, England and the Soviet Union as loyal Allies. However, when the Soviets came to an agreement with the Germans, this desire of ours for tripartite alliances was shattered, and negotiations started between Germany and the Soviet Union to partition Turkey.

But this German-Russian friendship did not last long. The German-Russian war started and England and the Soviet Union united on the same front. This time, the Germans started offering us (territory) at the expense of the Soviets. The Germans were even promising us Crimea.

As to the Soviets: they were offering us the south of Bulgaria, Western Thrace, the Dodecanese Islands and many other territories neighbouring Turkish borders. When the British Ambassador at Ankara transmitted to me these offers made by Stalin to Eden (British Foreign Minister) during the Moscow Conference, I asked the Ambassador:

"For the price of what ?"

"The ambassador replied that the offers were made for the price of Turkey staying neutral."

"Even after USA entered the war, they were offering targets that were aimed at tempting us and whipping our ambitions . . ."[5]

"We have always considered these offers as transitional efforts with no foundations that could occur during the war period. . . ."[5]

İnönü guided Turkish foreign policy during the war with a view to preserving Turkey's territorial integrity – as little interested in gaining ground as in losing some. This is doubly significant. If İnönü regarded Turkey as inviolable, he also accepted the converse. Firmly unwilling to cede one iota of Turkish territory, he was vehemently opposed to the forced cession of any other nation's lands. This applied to Russia as well. From the first days of German victory over Stalinist Russia to the end of 1942, German diplomacy failed to tempt İnönü into assuming a more favourable position toward Germany by holding out the bait of provinces ceded from the Soviet Union. İnönü's resistance to adventurist or irredentist nations severely limited the influence of the Pan-Turanion movement over Turkish foreign policy at this time.[6]

Explanations of the Territorial Offers

BRITISH REACTION TO GERMAN OFFERS FOR TURKEY

Churchill's telegram to Stafford Cripps on October 28 1941
". . . Meanwhile we shall presently be fighting ourselves as the result of the long-prepared plans, which it would be madness to upset. We have offered to relieve the five Russian divisions in Northern Persia which can be done with Indian troops fitted to maintain internal order but not equipped to face Germans. I am sorry that Molotov rejects the idea of our sending modest forces to the Caucasus. We are doing all we can to keep Turkey a friendly neutral and prevent her being tempted by German promises of territorial gains at Russia's expense . . ."[7]

STALIN'S OFFER TO EDEN IN MOSCOW

Mr. Eden's dispatch to Mr. Churchill of January 5, 1942, after he returned from Moscow negotiations with Stalin and Molotov:
"At my first conversation with M. Stalin and M. Molotov on December 16 M. Stalin set out in some detail what be considered should be the post-war territorial frontiers in Europe, and in particular his ideas for the treatment of Germany. He proposed the restoration of Austria as an independent State, the

detachment of the Rhineland from Prussia as an independent State or as a protectorate, and possibly the constitution of an independent State of Bavaria. He also proposed that East Prussia should be transferred to Poland and the Sudetenland returned to Czechoslovakia. He suggested that Yugoslavia should be restored, and even receive certain additional territories from Italy, that Albania should be reconstituted as an independent State, and that Turkey should receive the Dodecanese, with possible adjustments in favour of Greece as regards islands important to Greece. Turkey might also receive certain districts in Bulgaria and possibly also in northern Syria . . . " [8]

İnönü's Opening Statement at the Cairo Conference (December 1943)

"The Turkish President said that since the beginning his country had taken a clear decision – to stand beside those who were fighting the cause of the United Nations. She had been one of the first so to state her position clearly. The war had shown great fluctuations and difficulties but throughout Turkey had remained firmly anchored to her Alliance with Great Britain and to the ideas which she postulated for the future of humanity. In this decision Turkey had not been moved by any egotistical or personal interest."

"In connection with the object in view, it was equitable to think of the method which those who had provoked this war had used to convince their peoples-vengeance. etc. Turkey had been one of the greatest victims of the last war. From the first moment, however she had decided firmly and seriously to collaborate with those who were fighting for the fraternity of the peoples, and she had remained faithful throughout the years. These had not been without risks for Turkey. She had been alone and isolated. Great Britain had gone through a hard time and fought gallantly. In her own way, Turkey had done her best and she had sacrificed none of her principles."

"President İnönü said that he did not want to go over all the ground, but President Roosevelt and Mr. Churchill would remember that the Turkish attitude had been appreciated, and the Turks were very pleased at the repeated assurances of this appreciation."

From the agreed minutes between USA and UK on the First Tripartite Meeting of the Heads of Government (USA, UK, Turkey) December 4, 1943, 5 p.m., Roosevelt's villa in Cairo. [9]

Soviet explanation for the causes of the war and its justification for the Nazi-Soviet Pact

"The Munich conspiracy between Britain and France and Nazi Germany not only led to the dismemberment of Czechoslovakia; it also struck a blow at collective security in Europe. The Munich deal prepared the ground for the further expansion of Germany in the East, in the direction of Poland and the USSR.

"Nazi Germany and Fascist Italy took advantage of the Munich policy of the

Western powers to go ahead with further annexations. By the spring of 1939 the tension in Europe had reached a fresh peak. But even in these critical circumstances the Soviet Union continued its policy of organising a peace front to resist aggression. With this in mind the Soviet government proposed to the governments of Britain and France that they should conclude a treaty of mutual assistance.

"During the negotiations on this agreement and the subsequent talks on a military convention with Britain and France the Soviet Union did everything in its power to reach agreement with them, but the advocates of a deal with Germany and Japan at the expense of the USSR, who had come to power in these countries refused to reckon with the legitimate demand for guarantees of security. Only when it became convinced of the impossibility of concluding a mutual assistance pact with Britain and France, and also a military convention, did the USSR decide to sign a non-aggression pact with Germany. In doing so the Soviet Union avoided the trap into which the Munich policy-makers had hoped to lure it, and skilfully used the contradictions in the imperialist camp to preserve peace and strengthen its defence capacity. But it can not be said that the men of Munich did not inflict any damage on the USSR. The Soviet government would have preferred collective security based on cooperation between the USSR, Britain and France against Nazi aggression. Such cooperation, even if it had not prevented war, would have made it possible to fight in a more favourable strategic situation and would have forced Germany to fight on two fronts, in the West and the East. Anglo-French-Soviet military cooperation could have helped to prevent the fall of Poland and France, the seizure of which added to Germany's strength.

"It was the fault of the Western powers that events in 1939 did not tend towards collective security. But neither did they take the course desired by the men of Munich, the course of war by the imperialist states against the Soviet Union. The Nazis decided that it would be easier to fight Britain, France and Holland than to fight the USSR. So it was against them that the war was unleashed. War thus broke out within the capitalist world, between two antagonistic groups of imperialist powers."[10]

Soviet reasons for refusing Turkey's offer of a mutual pact with the Allies

"On September 25, 1939 the Turkish Foreign Minister Saracoğlu arrived in Moscow and offered the USSR a mutual assistance pact with regard to the straits and the Balkans. The USSR agreed to conduct negotiations but it soon transpired that the Turkish government was for a mutual pact with Britain and France. This meant that if the Soviet Union concluded the pact that Turkey had offered it, it might easily be drawn into war with Italy and Germany with no promise of assistance from Britain and France and in the face of an extremely hostile attitude to the Land of the Soviets on their part. Thus the Saracoğlu proposal amounted to an attempt to draw the USSR into an unequal military alliance with the Anglo-French bloc, to torpedo the Soviet-German treaty and to provoke an armed conflict between the USSR and Italy and Germany.[11]

British appreciation of Turkey's attitude (1939–43)

1939

When Turkey signed a Treaty of Alliance with both France and England after the outburst of the World War II on October 19, 1939, Mr. Churchill was praising this treaty at the House of Commons:

W. Churchill, in his speech to the House of Commons on October 5, (1939) "rejoiced in the treaty of Alliance between France and Britain with Turkey and in the repeal of the arms embargo in the United States… "The whole world is against Hitler and Hitlerism" he concluded in an optimistic outburst.[13]

1940

In his message of April 28, 1940, Mr. Churchill was writing to his Secretary of State:

Now that we have the Turks in such a friendly relationship the position is much more secure." [13]

GENERAL BRITISH POLICY TOWARDS TURKEY

In the Middle East, British policy was also checkmated by frightened and hesitant neutrals. The Soviet invasion of Finland had understandably sent a shock wave through the Soviet Union's smaller neutral neighbours. The Iranians adopted the rather curious attitude that Finland had somehow brought her troubles on herself and "had acted precipitately in breaking off their conversations here (in Moscow) and that with a little more patience and forbearance they might have reached an agreement more satisfactory both to the Soviets and to themselves."

The position of Turkey was more ambivalent since the Turks regarded the USSR as a very real threat, but like the Iranians, they were reluctant to take steps that might anger Moscow. The British ambassador in Ankara Sir Hughe Knatchbull-Hugessen consistently warned London of the Soviet threat to the British position in the Middle East and relayed Turkish fears to London. Responding to one of these dispatches, Deputy Under Secretary of State Sir Orme Sargent wrote to Knatchbull-Hugessen, "It is extremely satisfactory that the Turkish Government should not only be taking active measures to strengthen their defence against the Soviet Union, but should also be willing to discuss these measures with us." It would be best, Sargent reasoned, for Turkish-British cooperation to receive the widest possible publicity in the hopes of "deterring (the Soviets) strongly from embarking on any such adventures. Then, if deterrence failed, and if the Soviets should attack Afghanistan or Iran, we could with the support of Turkey, if the need arose, make a counter attack against the Caucasus, and in particular against the oil wells of Baku and the Batum-Baku pipe line. With Turkey as our active ally we should be able to send a force into the Black Sea; and we should also stand a much better chance of stirring up a rebellion in the Caucasus. With the Caucasus in a state of turmoil and the oil supplies cut off, we should have little to fear from the Russians anywhere else."

"The weakness of the Red Army, about which we never had any illusions," Sargent wrote, "has been abundantly demonstrated in Finland." In conclusion, he pointed out that "the success of any action we decide to take against the Soviet Union depends in the ultimate analysis upon Turkey."

With these considerations in mind, Turkey became one of the focal points of British foreign policy. British diplomats expended considerable effort trying to contact anti-Soviet elements in those areas of the USSR bordering Turkey in the hopes that should the occasion arise, these groups might cooperate with an British move against the Soviet Union. On February 2, Knatchbull-Hugessen informed the Foreign Office that the Afghan ambassador believed that "the whole Moslem element in Russia was ready for revolt if Russia's present difficulties lasted long."[14]

Regarding the Balkans the British Ambassador to Moscow, Cripps, was told that it was in the British interest for the nations there to form a "united front to resist aggression not only from Germany but also from the Soviet Union. Cripps was told quite clearly that "we should not welcome any Soviet expansion or increase of Soviet influence in the Balkans." Later in his first meeting with Stalin, Cripps forgot this last bit of advice, much to the chagrin of the Foreign Office.

In order to prevent an increase of Soviet influence in the Balkans, and in case the Baku project were ever to be revived, Cripps was informed that Turkey was to be wooed patiently to the Allied side. "Generally speaking our policy towards Turkey in regards to the Soviet Union is to put Turkey in a state of willingness . . . to help us against the Soviet Union in the event of our needing such help."[15]

CHURCHILL'S OWN EVALUATION OF TURKEY'S SITUATION

"I understood at this time how perilous the position of Turkey had become. It was obviously impossible to consider the treaty we had made with her before the war as binding upon her in the altered circumstances. When war had broken out in 1939 the Turks had mobilised their strong, good brave army. But this was all based upon the conditions of the First Great War. The Turkish infantry were as fine as they had ever been, and their field artillery was presentable. But they had none of the modern weapons which from May 1940 were proved to be decisive. Aviation was lamentably weak and primitive. They had no tanks or armoured cars, and neither the workshop to make and maintain them nor the trained men and staffs to handle them. They had hardly any anti-aircraft or anti-tank artillery. Their signal service was rudimentary. Radar was unknown to them. Nor did their warlike qualities include any aptitude for all these modern developments."

"On the other hand, Bulgaria had been largely armed by Germany out of the immense quantities of equipments of all kinds taken from France and Low Countries as a result of the battles of 1940. The Germans had therefore plenty of modern weapons with which to arm their allies. We, for our part, having lost so much at Dunkirk, having to build up our home army against invasion and to face all the continuous pressure of the Blitz on our cities as well as maintain the war in the Middle East, could only give very sparingly and at the cost of other claimant needs. The Turkish army in Thrace was, under these conditions, at as serious and almost disadvantage compared with the Bulgarians. If to this danger were added even moderate detachments of German air and armour the weight upon Turkey might well prove insupportable." [16]

BRITISH STAND TOWARDS GREECE'S FALL IN RELATION TO TURKEY'S IMPORTANCE (1940–1941)

Prime Minister to Mr Eden (at G.H.Q.) (2.11.40)
"Greek situation must be held to dominate others now. We are well aware of our slender resources. Aid to Greece must be attentively studied lest whole Turkish position is lost through proof that England never tries to keep her guarantees." [17]

Prime Minister Mr. Eden (at G.H.Q. Middle East) 3.11.40
"Gravity and consequence of Greek situation compels your presence in Cairo. However unjust it may be, collapse of Greece without any effort by us will have deadly effect on Turkey and on the future of war. . . ."[18]

Mr. Eden to Mr. Prime Minister (3.11.40)
"In general all Commanders-in-Chief were strongly of the opinion that the defence of Egypt is of paramount importance our whole position in the Middle East. They consider that from the strategical point of view the security of Egypt is the most urgent commitment, and must take precedence of attempts to prevent Greece being overrun. It is also essential if we are to retain the support of Turkey. . . ." [19]

Prime Minister to General Wavell (26.11.40)
"News from every quarter must have impressed on you the importance of 'Compass' in relation to the whole Middle East position, including Balkans and Turkey, to French attitude in North Africa, to Spanish attitude, now trembling on the brink, to Italy, in grievous straits, and generally to the whole war . . .

". . . It might be that 'Compass' would in itself determine the action of Yugoslavia and Turkey, and anyhow, in event of success, we should be able to give Turkey far greater assurances of early support than it has been in our power to do so far . . ." [20]

Mr Churchill's support to Turkey:
"We were developing airfields in Greece both to aid the Greek Army and to strike at Italy, or if necessarily at the Romanian oilfields. Similarly the active development of airfields in Turkey and technical assistance to Turks was in progress . . ." [21]

Prime Minister to General Wavell (January 10, 1941)
". . . Destruction of Greece will eclipse victories you have gained in Libya, and may affect decisively Turkish attitude especially if we have shown ourselves callous of fate of allies." [22]

Mr. Churchill's impression of Mr. Eden's talks with Turkish officials
"Mr. Eden's account of his discussions with the Turks at Angora was not encouraging. They realised their own dangers as acutely as we did but they, like the

Greeks, were convinced that the forces we could offer would not be sufficient to make any real difference to an actual battle."

Mr. Eden to Prime Minister (28 February 1941)
"C.I.G.S. and I this morning had discussion on extremely frank and friendly basis with President of the Council, Minister for Foreign Affairs, and Marshal Chakmak.

"Our decision to send Greece the maximum assistance at the earliest possible moment was well received. They reiterated Turkey's determination to fight if attacked by Germany, and stated their conviction that German attack on Greece meant that Turkey's turn would come next. But since Turkey's forces at present had no offensive power they considered the common cause would be better served by Turkey remaining out of the war until her deficiencies had been remedied and she could be employed with the maximum effect . . .

. . . They felt concerned lest Russians should attack (them) if Turkey became involved in war with Germany . . .

"The upshot of these discussions is that Turkey undertakes in any event to enter the war at any stage. She will of course do so immediately she is attacked. But if she is given time by Germans to re-equip herself she will take advantage of it, and will then make war at a moment favourable to the common cause, when her weight can be used with real effect." [23]

1941

On February 12, 1941, Mr. Churchill was writing to General Wavell
"There will always remain the support of Turkey." [24]

Mr. Churchill's letter to Stalin dated September 17, 1941 (before the Anglo-American-Russian Conference in Moscow)
". . . Again in the south the great prize is Turkey; if Turkey can be gained another powerful army will be available. Turkey would like to come with us, but is afraid not without reason. It may be that the promise of considerable British forces and supplies of technical material in which the Turks are deficient will exercise a decisive influence upon them. We will study with you any other form of useful aid, the sole object being to bring the maximum force against the common enemy . . ." [25]

Mr. Churchill's directive to the British Delegation attending the Anglo-American-Russian Conference in Moscow
". . . 13 . . . On the other hand, Turkey, if she could be gained, is the great prize. Not only would the German road to Syria and Egypt be barred by powerful Turkish armies, but the Black Sea naval defence could be maintained with great advantages, thus helping the defence of the Caucasus. The action of Turkey one way or other may be determined in the near future by the promises should she become involved, of help in troops and modern equipment, including especially aerodromes, tanks, anti-tank and anti-aircraft artillery etc. It should be made clear to the Russians that much of this equipment and the greater part of the troops would of course be withdrawn from the contribution available for Russia,

which are all we can give. In order however to induce Turkey to come in on our side, especially in the near future, it would be well worth Great Britain and Russia revising their arrangements."[26]

Mr. Churchill's letter to President Roosevelt (October 20, 1941)
". . . 13- We do not require Turkey to enter the war aggressively at the present moment, but only to maintain a stolid, unyielding front to German threats and blandishments. As long as Turkey is not violated or seduced, this great oblong pad of poorly developed territory is an impassable protection for the eastern flank of our Nile Army. If Turkey were forced to enter the war we should of course have to give her a great deal of support which might be better used else where, either in French North Africa or in the Caucasus. We are making promises of support to Turkey (contingent on the military situation) which amount to between four and six divisions and twenty or thirty air squadrons, and we are actively preparing them the necessary airfields in Anatolia. But what Turkey requires to keep her sound is British victory over Germany making all promises given real and living." [27]

Prime Minister to Prime Minister of Australia (September 7, 1941)
"Our position in Syria and Iraq may be threatened by a German advance
   a. On Syria through Anatolia;
   b. On Iraq through the Caucasus and Persia (Iran);
   c. A combination of (a) and (b).
   Through Anatolia – If Turkey does not grant passage to German forces the large land air forces necessary for conquering Turkey could hardly be withdrawn from Russia, refitted and reconcentrated, in less than six to eight weeks. Weather conditions in Anatolia virtually preclude operations from December 1 to the end of March. We therefore feel that the concentration by the Germans of sufficient forces on the Turkish frontier to overcome that country is now improbable until a date so late that an attack on Syria through Anatolia is not likely before the spring.
   If however, contrary to expectations, Turkey were to give passage to German forces, three or four German divisions might arrive on the Syrian frontier before the end of the year, and be reinforced at the rate of one division a month. This force might be supplemented if sea routes through Turkish territorial water were available. A great deal therefore depends on what help the Turks may expect from us. As to this, we have instructed our Attaches at Ankara to speak on the following lines . . ."[28]

1942

In this letter of May 13, 1942, to his Foreign Secretary, Prime Minister Churchill was outlining his policy on Turkey as follows:
   1. "The following seems to me to be the policy of munitions to Turkey: Nothing much can be done this summer or before the Russian campaign decides itself more clearly. Nor do we ask anything more of the Turks than to keep intruders out. But as soon as the Russian front shuts down with the winter an effort should be made, for which preparations must be begun forthwith, to

give them a substantial packet of tanks, anti-tank guns, and flak. By that time there should be an immense flow of munitions in the United States and our own output running higher. The figures mentioned in America are enormous, and there should be no difficulty in sparing 1,000 tanks and, 1,000 anti-tank and A.A. guns. No doubt older marks might form the bulk.

2. If a plan is prepared on this sort of scale, and deliveries begin in November, the promise will make the Turks stand neutral during the summer, and the arrival of these weapons, which they can train upon during the winter, may make them our allies in the spring.

3. If you think well of this, let us take it up with production here and in the United States." [29]

Prime Minister to General Ismay, for C.O.S. Committee (28 August 1942)

1. "I am much concerned about the account of the Turkish position given me by the Turkish Ambassador, who I saw this morning at the request of the Cabinet.

2. We should now prepare a scheme, on the assumption of definite success in the Western Desert by the middle of October, of sending more war material to Turkey. It ought to be possible to spare 200 tanks of the Valentine or other older type. These would be replaced in Egypt by the improved tanks now approaching in a regular stream. Similarly, 3,000 two-pounder anti-tank guns should be made available and 100 Bofors. If these were earmarked and prepared ready to move forward into Turkey the moment a favourable decision has been reached they would be in Turkish hands by the end of October. This might make all the difference to the Turkish will-power to resist in a situation where the Russians may have lost the naval command of the Black Sea and where Turkey may be subjected to very severe Axis pressure.

3. What is the objection to giving the Turks some Radar installations. The Germans surely know the secret, or have other equally satisfactory variants of their own.

4. We must proceed on the basis, which personally I adopt, that we trust Turkey. The whole Nile position would be greatly embarrassed if Turkey were forced to succumb.

5. Let me have a plan worked out on these lines for discussion." [30]

1943

On January 25, 1943, Mr. Churchill wrote to this Deputy Prime Minister and Cabinet regarding Turkey as follows:

"Neither the President (Roosevelt) nor I are convinced by arguments put forward. There never was any idea of persuading Turkey to come into war without regard to circumstances and conditions. These have to be created and prepared beforehand. In the first place, Turkey has to be well kitted up . . . ." [31]

Churchill's Statement given to President İnönü in Adana (January 1943)

"2 . . . I have been particularly distressed at the spectacle of the Turkish Army, which has the finest infantry and a good field artillery but has not been able to get, during the whole three and a half years of this war, the modern equipment which is decisive on the battlefield, and which the Germans, from their looted stores, have been able to give, for instance, to the Bulgarians. This has made me fully comprehend the attitude of Turkey at every stage we have so far travelled. The time has come when these disparities can and must be removed with the greatest speed." [32]

I know that Premier Stalin is most anxious to see Turkey well armed and ready to defend herself against aggression. I know it is President Roosevelt's wish as is certainly that of His Majesty's Government, that Turkey should be a full partner in the Peace Conference where all questions of changes in the existing status quo will have to be settled . . ." [33]

Mr. Churchill's explanation for the British defeat in the Aegean Sea to the Germans and its effects on Turkey:

a. "My parleys with Turkey were intended to prepare the way for her entry into the war in the autumn of 1943. That this did not take place after the collapse of Italy and with the further Russian advances against Germany north of the Black Sea was due to unfortunate events in the Aegean later in the year, which will be described in some detail later on." [34]

b. "Mr. Eden said he would like to get quite clear in his mind the demands that were to be made on Turkey. Was it understood that Turkey should go to war with Germany and no one else? If as a result the Germans made Bulgaria join them in a war against Turkey would the Soviet Government go to war with Bulgaria? Stalin agreed on both points. I said that, for myself, I would be satisfied with strained neutrality from Turkey. There was thus a very great measure of agreement on the limited steps for which I asked in order to win the great prize of bringing Turkey into the war, and it was settled that President İnönü should be invited to come to Cairo and talk it all over with me and the President. Although I felt how deeply Turkish minds has been affected by our failure to attack Rhodes, by the loss of Cos and Leros, and the consequent German command of the air in the Aegean, I left the subject, having got all I had thought it right to ask, and with fair hopes that it would not be insufficient." [35]

Letter of Prime Minister Churchill to Field-Marshal Smuts on Sept 5, 1943.
". . . I think it better not to demand entry into the war by Turkey at the present time with which we should have to fight are more usefully employed in the Central Mediterranean. The question may be put to Turkey later in the year . . ." [36]

Churchill's note of November 18, 1943 to the British Chiefs of Staff
". . . I wish to record my opinion that Turkey may be won if the proper measures are taken. Turkey is an Ally. She will wish to have a seat among the victors at the Peace Conference. She has a great desire to be well armed. Her army is in good order, except for the specialised modern weapons in which the Bulgarians have been given so great an advantage by the Germans. The Turkish army has been mobilised for three years, and is warlike. Hitherto Turkey has been restrained by fear from fulfilling her obligations, and we have taken an indulgent view of her policy on account of our inability to help . . ." [37]

Prime Minister Churchill's letter to General Ismay for C.O.S. Committee (6 December, 1943)
". . . Meanwhile it is also possible that, under the increasing pressure of events, Bulgaria will endeavour to make a separate peace with the three Great Allies. It is not suggested that Turkey should declare war at any stage: she should continue her protective re-equipment and await the enemy's actions."[38]

Prime Minister to General Ismay, for C.O.S. Committee (6 Dec 43)
OPERATION "SATURN"
1. After the Cairo Conference the Turkish Government will state that their policy is unchanged, and use all precautionary measures to allay enemy suspicions.
2. Nevertheless it is necessary that the preparation and protection of the Turkish airfields should proceed at full speed without a day's delay, and that all necessary personnel, in mufti, and materials should be sent in . . .[39]

American neutrality (1939–41)
and American understanding towards Turkey in 1943

PREFACE TO WAR – TIME MAGAZINE (SEPT. 11, 1939)

"The telephone in Franklin Roosevelt's bedroom at the White House rang at 2:50 a.m. on the first day of September. In more ways than one it was a ghastly hour; but the operators knew they must ring. Ambassador Bill Bullitt was calling from Paris. Mr. Bullitt told Mr. Roosevelt that World War II had begun. Adolf Hitler's bombing planes were dropping death all over Poland.

"Mr. Roosevelt telephoned to Secretary of State Hull at the Carlton Hotel, also to Under Secretary of State Welles, Secretary of War Wodring, Acting Secretary Edison of the Navy. Acting Secretary of the Treasury John Haynes was roused. Lights went on in all Washington's key executive offices. Before breakfast time, the President was ready with the only gesture he could think of in the face of world disaster: a plea to Germany, Poland, Britain, France, Italy to refrain from bombing "open" cities and non-combatants. Within a few hours the heads of all these nations replied, in a chorus that sounded sickeningly cynical, however truly meant: they would each do as Mr. Roosevelt suggested so long as their antagonists did likewise. Mussolini took the occasion to reiterate Italy's neutrality.

"That day Franklin Roosevelt's Press conference was a grave business. One question was uppermost in all minds. Correspondent Phelp Adams of the New York Sun uttered it: "Mr. President, can we stay out of it?" Franklin Roosevelt sat in silent concentration, eyes down, for many long seconds. Then, with utmost solemnity, he replied. "I not only sincerely hope so, but I believe we can, and every effort will be made by this Administration to do so."

Later, two years after the war started, the American Charge d'Affaires in Berlin (Alexander Kirk) wrote to Washington:
"The United States is the only power which can effectively oppose Hitler now and in the future and he knows it . . ."

The diplomat then urged that the United States line up unequivocally on the side of the Allies.

"The President was told substantially the same thing in (French Prime Minister) M. Paul Reynaud's two desperate appeals (during the invasion and fall of France under occupation of the German armies) for American intervention, but since only Congress possessed the power to declare war, he had to decline . . ." [40]

MR. CHURCHILL'S APPEAL TO USA TO ENTER THE WAR (APRIL 24, 1941)

In his message to Roosevelt of April 24, 1941, W. Churchill wrote "Mr. President I am sure that you will misunderstand me if I speak to you exactly what is in my mind. The one decisive counterweight I can see to balance the growing pessimism in Turkey, the near East and in Spain would be if the United States were immediately to range herself with us as a belligerent power. If this were possible I have little doubt that we could hold the situation in the Mediterranean until the weight of your munitions gained the day." [41]

AMERICA'S UNDERSTANDING OF TURKEY'S POSITION (1943)

Soviet Ambassador to Washington M. M. Litvinov to Soviet Foreign Minister Molotov writes memorandum on U.S. Policies (June 2, 1943):
"Some American gifts are granted to Turkey though the State Department has no illusions about enticing Turkey onto the side of the United Nations. However, considerations for Turkey will be quite sufficient if it maintains benevolent neutrality." [42]

President Roosevelt's letter to President İnönü (October 26, 43)
"I hope much that the day will come when you and I can meet or I have long had an admiration for you and all what you are doing."

"Our two Nations have, in so many ways, the same ideals of enlightened progress that it is right that we should be found with the same feelings toward this great crisis through which all of the peoples of the world are passing."

"I hope particularly, that when this war is ended, there will be not only an assurance of peace for many generations to come, but that agreements will be reached whereby smaller nations will no longer have to be concerned over the maintenance of their complete independence. In past years, the amount of money that has had to be spent on armaments, great and small, instead of on productive industry and agriculture and the arts, has been a disgrace to all of us in every part of the world."

"I think that we are both aware of each other's problems and again I wish that you and I could have the opportunity of talking over these and many other things . . ." [43]

Roosevelt's letter to Secretary of State Hull
President Roosevelt sent a letter to Secretary of State Mr. Cordell Hull on the same day (October 26, 1943) who was attending the Tripartite Conference in Moscow. The paragraph regarding Turkey was as follows:

". . . It would not be deemed advisable to push Turkey at this moment into declaration of war on the side of the Allies since the necessary compensation to the Turks in war material and war supplies including armed forces and ships would divert too much from the Italian front and the proposed OVERLORD operation. However, inquiries could be started on basis of lease by Turkey as a neutral of airbases and transportation facilities." [44]

Secretary of State Hull's view on Turkey during the Tripartite Conference in Moscow
". . . Mr. Hull suggests that Turkey remain neutral but help the Allies, and that consequently it is not advisable to induce Turkey into war. England's proposal contains many points. To fully consider these would require two more conferences?"

". . . Mr. Hull pointed out that Turkey has neither the necessary shipping nor supplies that would enable her to proceed efficiently with military movement. Furthermore, there is not enough U.S. shipping available to back up Turkey in a war at this time. He emphasised the already heavy commitments made by U.S. in the Mediterranean and in Italy, and in preparation for the coming cross-channel operations." [45]

American Ambassador Steinhardt's talks with Turkish Minister of Foreign Affairs Mr. Numan Menemencioğlu (November, 1943)
"Throughout our talk I was forcibly struck by the extreme frankness with which Numan discussed Turkey's probable entry into the war. I gained the distinct impression that the Turkish Government has already decided in principle to enter the war and to cooperate whole-heartedly with the Allies but that it is convinced that certain conditions precedent to its entry are vital not only in its own interests but in those of the Allies as well. These conditions grow out of a sober recognition by the Turkish Government of its military deficiencies and economic weaknesses and the realization that without adequate Allied forces immediately available disaster may result from the country's premature entry into the war. Numan however made it unmistakably clear to me that the Turkish Government is quite prepared and expects to make what he described as its contribution in blood, suffering and devastation of its country to the Allied victory but that such contribution should serve a useful purpose in furthering the Allied cause which Turkey wholeheartedly espouses and not entail needless sacrifices occasioned by precipitous action with inadequate forces which could only result in Turkey becoming a liability rather than an asset to the Allies." [46]

President Roosevelt's comments to Mr. Churchill at the Cairo Conference. Quadripartite Dinner Meeting, December 4, 1943, 8:30 p.m., Roosevelt's villa
No official record of the conversation at this meeting has been found. Leahl, p. 214, writes:
". . . President Roosevelt on December 4 gave a dinner in honor of the Turkish President. It was an interesting affair, all the conversation being in French, which the President spoke without hesitation.
"After the dinner, the Prime Minister joined the party and promptly laid siege to President İnönü to induce him to cast the fate of this country with the Allies.

Churchill did most of the talking, İnönü just listened. Later the President told his British colleague that if he Roosevelt, were a Turk he would require more assurance of aid than Britain had promised before abandoning neutrality and leading his nation into war." [47]

CHAPTER II

TURKEY'S CONCERNS ABOUT SOVIET AMBITIONS

I. GENERAL TRENDS
(TURKISH FOREIGN POLICY REGARDING THE SOVIETS)

Introduction

When İsmet İnönü acceded to the Presidency, Turkey and Soviet Union had undergone a period of nearly twenty years of unprecedented good will, İnönü's personal experience had taught him to be wary of Russian ambitions. İnönü, for example, had travelled to the Soviet Union in 1930, at a time when Turkish foreign policy was attempting to establish closer relations with the Western Powers but without offending Russia. When he returned, İnönü presented the following analysis to Ataturk before a caucus of the Parliamentary Group of the CHP: the Russians felt isolated particularly by the West and, as a result, were obsessed by what they believed to be the insecurity of their western borders. They desired and would continue to seek friendly relations with Turkey provided that the Turks refrained from actions which seemed calculated to put pressure upon Russia from the east. The Russians wanted their eastern front to be quiet in order to gain time to secure their borders in the west. As soon as they came to regard their western boundaries as safe, they will no longer care to be friends with us, İnönü advised. Once the Soviets felt no longer threatened by the Western Powers, they would become more aggressive in the east and quite possibly toward Turkey as well. For that reason, İnönü wanted the Soviets never to feel too secure in the west. During April and May 1939, when British and French diplomats were exploring the possibility of a Turkish-British-French-Soviet alliance, İnönü, in the words of Sir Alexander Cadogan, insisted on the necessity of Russian participation in hostilities on the ground that it would be disastrous if the Russian Army alone were left intact at the end of a European war. Russian insecurity in the west was Turkey's best protection. That protection would be removed if ever a war in Western Europe created a path for Russian dominance. İnönü predicted in 1930 that this could not in any case occur for at least 25 years. Russia was eventually implicated in the war, as İnönü had hoped; its incipient victory over German forces in 1943, however, made it seem as if the Soviets were about to become completely secure in the west twelve years earlier than Inonu had anticipated.

This perspective of his on Soviet policies may help to explain the severity of Turkey's reaction to Stalin's suggestion at the end of 1941 that the British and the Russians give to Turkey certain areas held by Greece. İnönü feared that perhaps Stalin was planning to annex parts of Turkey in the east. In short, if the one constant that guided İnönü's hand during World War II was the preservation of Turkey's territorial integrity, the variable which he perceived to most threaten it was the political ambition of the Soviet Union. During the period of German ascendancy, İnönü did not hesitate to make his apprehensions clear to British and American diplomats. His first official conversation with U.S. Ambassador Laurence A. Steinhardt, upon the latter's presentation of credentials, dealt largely with the question of Soviet influence in the postwar world. Despite the fact that German forces were advancing rapidly toward Stalingrad, the Turkish President warned Steinhardt that if Russia defeated Germany, Soviet imperialism would attempt to "over-run Europe and the Middle East". İnönü let it be known that he was concerned that Russia, if ever in a position to do so, would take possession of the Straits.[48]

The stubborn refusal of the Turkish Government to actively join in the Allied war effort represents a consistent set of interpretations of the content and meaning of its operational code that proscribed adventurism but clearly defined the Soviet Union as archenemy. Turkish neutrality was, in effect, a balance struck between the conflicting tugs of interventionism and noninterventionism with the latter constantly winning over the former. Turkish reluctance to assume a more activist diplomatic posture did not reflect satisfaction with British and American policies toward the Soviet Union. On the contrary, it testifies the extent to which the Turks believed the Western Allies to be misguided in their handling of the Russians.

For one thing, İnönü and his subordinates quietly hoped for the development of an international political system that would keep reign on Soviet expansionism through the mechanisms of a viable balance of power. The Turks perceived their security as well as that of other small nations in the postwar world to be inextricably tied to the creation of a process of systemic equilibrium among the Great Powers. Consequently, they considered Allied policy of unconditional surrender, initially enunciated by Roosevelt, to be an egregious error. True to their operational code, they perceived such a policy as an open invitation to Stalin to extend the Soviet domain. That Stalin would try to do so had been, in their view, highly, probable; British and American subscription to the doctrine of unconditional surrender made it, as far as they were concerned, inevitable. Thus with the "turning of the tide," Turkish concern became double-pronged: given their assumptions concerning Russian postwar ambitions, they feared either that the British and Americans would be forced to negotiate a spheres of influence agreement placing Turkey well within the Soviet orbit, or that an all-out conflict between Russia and Britain assisted by the United States would break out soon after the defeat of Germany, enveloping Turkey, possibly transforming it into a battlefield or, at the very least, finally giving Soviet Russia the pretext it needed to attempt to fortify the Straits. To Turkish officials, then, British and American policies toward Russia seemed to portend alternative futures that would leave them with no more an appealing choice than that of the frying pan or the fire.

The Turkish Government, however, never fully apprised British and American representatives of their anticipations of Soviet behaviour for a variety of reasons: İnönü's innate sense of caution, the nonadventurist principle of its operational code, the foreign policies of Britain and the United States that seemed to encourage Soviet expansionism. Under these circumstances, a Turkish policy initiative that involved a commission of anti-Soviet behaviour, even if only in the form of warnings to the West, seemed out of the question.

İnönü was occasionally tempted to reveal his deep-seated reservations to Churchill and to Roosevelt as well. But his meetings with these men convinced him that they were too deeply committed to their own policies towards Stalin to appreciate any interference from him. Perhaps this was inevitable. It may be that İnönü faced an impossible task in trying to alter the behaviour of the British and Americans in relation to Russia, particularly when the Allied coalition was based not only on ideological or cultural perceptions of "goodness" but on the highly instrumental grounds of a common enemy in a fight for survival. İnönü, after all, could only speak to the Western Allies of traditional Turkish fears of revisionist Russia.[49]

Given İnönü's belief in the inexorability of an expansionist Soviet foreign policy, British designs to expand the Allied coalition by bringing Turkey into the war made sense only in intracoalition competitive terms. Both British and Turkish interests might be served if Turkey, by coming into the war, could lend support to an Anglo-American attempt to contain Soviet Russia. Churchill's most cogent argument on behalf of Turkish belligerence, from İnönü's and Menemencioğlu's point of view, was that Turkey could thus play an active role in the establishment of a postwar settlement. Such a role had meaning to the Turks only in the context of British and American policy toward Russia and the systemic conditions that would prevail once Germany had been defeated. But British representatives never spoke in these terms. All pressures on Turkey to join the Allied coalition were seen in this light. As already suggested, had the Turks ever been convinced that they would be able to head off the Soviets by cooperating with an Anglo-American campaign in the Balkans that would place a ring around Russian expansionism without seeming to be purposefully anti-Soviet, they probably would have done so. The British and American governments never recognised these perceptions, however, and the diplomacy that resulted reflected the consequent breach in which the Turks stubbornly held on to their neutrality as their best protection, despite warnings and threats, promises and predictions.[50]

Turkish leaders were acting not only in conformity to the norms of their country's founding ideology but with a view to their position as representatives of a small state surrounded in a universe of war but not yet a party to its violence. For them it was enough merely to survive the war with their sovereignty intact. Perhaps they might have early and more actively joined in the Allied effort while attempting to make the British and Americans more aware of their perceptions of postwar Soviet policies. The consequences to Turkey and the world would surely have been significant. But to condemn Turkish policy-makers, notably İnönü, in this way is to judge them for playing small state diplomacy rather than Great Power politics. And is this not precisely the failure of such fallen giants as Sukarno and Nkrumah. İnönü may have tried to do more; but he could have achieved much less.[51]

Churchill-Stalin Meeting of October 1944
and the decision to establish spheres of influence

Turkish observers, caught between Greece, Eastern Europe, and the Balkans, judged events largely on the basis of what specific developments signified about the political intentions of the Great Powers. The fear that Britain and Russia would divide Europe into spheres of influence had been prevalent in Turkey, as we have seen, from the very first days the Allies began to defeat Axis armies. During the fall and winter of 1944, these fears became stronger. It was becoming increasingly evident that the Russians were the dominant force in the East, whereas the British seemed to be functioning alone in the West. Although there were geographical as well as historical reasons why this should be, apprehensions in Turkey were aroused in early 1944, by rumours that Stalin had accepted a British plan to partition Europe into spheres of influence, giving Russia supremacy over the Balkans, including Romania, eastern Yugoslavia, and Bulgaria. As Anne O'Hare McCormick reported on March 4, 1944, "Reasonably or unreasonably the Turks fear Russia. They are . . . a border state and the suspicion that Moscow seeks to erect her '*cordon sanitaire*' by drawing all the nations along the frontier in her own orbit makes them exceedingly wary." The Turks feared that a world divided into spheres of influence would diminish the viable independence of the smaller nations. They could not be certain, moreover, where Turkey would fall in such an international system. They doubted whether the British would fight to keep them out of the Russian orbit and deeply feared that they would be left to face a dominant Soviet Union alone. This also made the Pan-Slavic issue all the more vexing at the end of 1944. In any event, these fears help to explain why Turkish officials continued to try to win the good graces of Britain, despite their concerns over British policy, and why they were subdued in discussing Soviet intentions.

Some substance for believing that the Russians and the British had indeed divided Europe into spheres of influence was provided by Lincoln Macveagh, the United States envoy to the émigré Greek and Yugoslav governments in Cairo. On June 19, 1944, MacVeagh leaked a story to C.L. Sulzberger of *The New York Times*, alleging that "initial steps towards outlining zones of 'initiatives' in the Balkan peninsula have been agreed upon by the British and Soviet governments . . ." MacVeagh's report asserted that Greece would fall under British protection while Romania was to fall under that of the Soviet Union. Sulzberger suggests that there was a "private deal between London and Moscow" and wanted it made known to the world. Cevat Açikalin (Secretary General of Turkish Ministry for Foreign Affairs) has indicated that the Turkish Government did become aware of such reports and that İnönü suspected they were true. Indeed, they were: as early as May 1944, Churchill had broached the subject with Roosevelt and Stalin of assigning spheres of "responsibility" to the Great Powers.

Churchill had represented this as a temporary scheme. The Allied armies were advancing along different fronts and on-the-spot administrative decisions had to be taken. "We do not of course wish to carve up the Balkans into spheres of influence," Churchill had informed the President, "and in agreeing to the arrangement we should make it clear that it applied only to war conditions ..." Roosevelt and especially Hull were deeply sceptical about Churchill's plan. But the President, after reserving himself twice, notified the British and Soviet governments that the United States had accepted the "spheres" arrangement, but only for a three-month trial period. With this agreement in his pocket, Churchill went to see Stalin. The Moscow meeting between Churchill and Stalin has been immortalised by Churchill's own description of it:

"The moment was apt for business, so I said, 'Let us settle about our affairs in the Balkans. Your armies are in Romania and Bulgaria. We have interest, missions, small ways. So far as Britain and Russia are concerned, how would it do for you to have ninety per cent predominance in Romania, for us to have ninety per cent of the say in Greece, and go fifty-fifty about Yugoslavia ?' While this was being translated I wrote out on a half-sheet of paper:

Romania
> Russia   90%
> The others   10%

Greece
> Great Britain (in accord with USA) 90%
> Russia   10%
> Yugoslavia   50–50%
> Hungary   50–50%

Bulgaria
> Russia   75%
> The others   25%   [52]

President Roosevelt consulted Secretary of State Hull who became concerned that such an agreement, despite Churchill's intentions, would lead to a political division of Europe. At first Roosevelt agreed with Hull and informed Churchill of this. In mid-June 1944, however, while Hull was away from Washington, Roosevelt notified Churchill that he had decided to consent to the British initiative. The State Department, uninformed of the President's reversal, proceeded on the assumption that Roosevelt still objected to any proposal which implied a division of Europe and submitted an aide-memoire to the British Embassy to this effect. To make matters even more confusing, Roosevelt had a change of heart when his Secretary of State returned to Washington and wired Churchill that he could no longer accept Churchill's scheme. But the

British Government had already informed the Soviets that they had received the President's approval and were now ready to accept this temporary division of Europe. On July 15 the State Department finally agreed (Feis, Churchill, Roosevelt, Stalin, pp. 341–42).

The Yalta Conference: the ending of war

The Yalta Conference, convened on February 4 (1945) and lasting until February 11, created grave foreboding in Ankara. The Turkish Government was at this time primarily concerned that Western leaders, and Churchill in particular, intended to side with Stalin in seeking a revision of the Montreux Convention. Professor Esmer, for example, notes that "the possibility of Churchill's giving concessions to the Russians . . . worried the Turkish Government since Churchill was angry at Turkey and expressed at every opportunity his intention of having nothing further to do with the Straits." Although this does not correctly perceive Churchill's state of mind at Yalta, where he championed Turkish interests, it does correctly reflect the anxious state of isolation still felt by the Turks.

The Turkish question was not paramount at Yalta, but many of the other decisions did, directly or indirectly, affect Turkish interest and concerns. The veto power, slightly encumbered, was accepted by the Big Three as the basis for the wielding of real power in the proposed new peace-keeping organisation. Russia agreed to the American proposal that a permanent member should abstain from voting when it was itself a party to a dispute, but only in matters of "peaceful settlement." In relation to "enforcement resolutions", the Great Powers would still be in a position to cast an unfettered veto.[53]

The Yalta Conference also encompassed the future of the Balkan nations. In response to State Department directives warning that the Allied Control Commissions in Central Europe and the Balkans were not functioning properly because the Soviet Union seemed determined to bring them under its sole control Roosevelt submitted a document to the conference entitled "The Declaration on Liberated Europe". Eventually signed by Churchill, Roosevelt, and Stalin, this pledged that the Big Three would help the liberated nations meet their pressing political and economic problems through democratic means.

On top of this formally impressive but politically vacuous agreement came Roosevelt's surprising announcement to the conferees that American forces would not remain in Europe more than two years after the end of the war. Stalin had reason to feel pleased.

Although not a central issue in the minds of the three heads of state at the Yalta Conference, Turkey did receive attention in two of the eight plenary sessions, each time in a different connection. In the fifth plenary meeting, Stalin used Turkey as a symbol in raising the issue of which states should be admitted into the United Nations and which should be excluded. The President responded that only those nations that had declared war on Germany should be granted the Status of an Associated Nation and suggested March 1945 as the deadline for the as yet uncommitted to declare war on Germany. Referring to Turkey, Stalin declared that certain nations had "wavered and speculated on being on the winning side." Churchill, however, defended the Turks. He asserted that if a large group of hitherto uncommitted nations were to declare war at this time it would have an effect on Germany's morale. Turkey's candidacy "would not be greeted with universal approbation", Churchill said, but he also asserted that Turkey had entered into an alliance with them "at a very difficult time" and had proved both "friendly and helpful." Stalin agreed to allow Turkey to become an Associated Nation if it declared war on Germany by the end of February. Churchill greeted this with expressions of "gratification".

Despite Stalin's amiability, he served notice on February 10 1945 that he expected the regime of the Straits to be revised at the end of the war. Stalin declared that ". . . it was impossible to accept a situation in which Turkey had a hand on Russia's throat," adding that he did not intend to "harm the legitimate interests of Turkey." The President, apparently not fully up to the challenge of the discussion, responded irrelevantly by saying that the United States and Canada shared a frontier of over 3,000 miles without a fort and with no armed forces and expressed the hope that other frontiers would eventually exist "without forts or armed forces on any part of their national boundaries." The Prime Minister agreed that a revision of the Montreux Convention seemed to be in order, saying that ". . . the present position of Russia with their great interests in the Black Sea should not be dependent on the narrow exit." Churchill proposed that the matter be taken up at the next meeting of Foreign Ministers. He also suggested that the Turks be informed that this was being considered and that they be given an assurance that their independence and integrity would be respected. Stalin accepted these suggestions. With regard to the proposal that they immediately inform the Turks of what was afoot, Stalin remarked, ". . . it was impossible to keep anything secret from the Turks . . ." [54]

A historical note – the predicted Soviet demands on Turkey

On June 7 and 18 Selim Sarper, representing his government in Moscow, had conversations with Soviet Minister Molotov which confirmed the most dire expectations regarding Soviet postwar ambitions entertained in Ankara since the beginning of hostilities. The Russians demanded the cession of Kars and Ardahan, Turkey's easternmost provinces, the Soviet militarization of the approaches to the Dardanelles and the Bosphorus, and a revision of the Montreux Convention with a view to giving the Soviet Union greater legal control over the regime of the Straits. Thus began the Turko-Soviet confrontation of 1945, which helped to usher in the period now known as the Cold War.

It seemed diabolical to the Turks that the Russians chose the time of universal rejoicing and relief to begin their campaigning against them. Soviet timing, however, was well chosen. From San Francisco emanated the hopeful euphoria of universal peace. Soviet and American troops were embracing on the Elbe.

Turkey's obstinacy in relation to Russia – a nation that had done so much in cooperation with America and Great Britain to defeat the Axis – would seem a discordant, ungracious note.

The Turks were not abandoned, however. Surprisingly, almost instantly, the wartime grievances of the British towards the Turks vanished. On June 18, the day of the second Sarper-Molotov conversation, the British Government urged the United States to make "firm representations" to the Soviet Government, arguing that the Russians were renouncing "explicit assurances given by Stalin at Yalta to respect the sovereign integrity of Turkey. At least one Turkish fear, the fear that Great Britain would sacrifice them in order to divide Europe with the Russians into spheres of influence, did not materialise. The British, aware of Soviet intentions, became increasingly supportive of Turkish interests. This, Selim Sarper claims, was deeply appreciated in Ankara.

The Americans, however, temporarily hesitated to join the British. Although the U.S. Ambassador in Turkey, Edwin C. Wilson, along with others such as Averell Harriman, were informing Washington of the seriousness of the Soviet threat to Turkey and the West, the State Department preferred to see things in a more favourable light. In response to the British request that they both formally object to the Soviet treatment of Turkey, the State Department declared that the Sarner-Molotov talks had been conducted in a "friendly atmosphere". It also warned that an Anglo-American protest might create an "unfortunate background" to the Potsdam meeting.

These hesitations were spelled out in more precise terms on June 29, 1945, in a State Department briefing paper. Britain and Russia had eyed Turkey "jealously" for centuries, the paper argued, and British desires to bolster the Turks were really designed to induce the Turks to resist Russian overtures seeking to bring Turkey into the Soviet orbit. The United States should, the paper declared maintain "a detached but watchful attitude" while "the interplay of British and Soviet policies on the Turkish stage" took its course. The United States could exert pressure on any of the parties at any time in the future. For the time being, the paper concluded, it was "preferable" from the point of view of U.S. interests "for Turkey either to have special alliances in both directions or no alliance at all."

This subdued stance was quickly altered. At Potsdam the conflicts between Soviet and American interests and policies became more sharply drawn. By the time the Truman Doctrine was enunciated, Greece and Turkey had become the focal point of East-West confrontation. The United States was thus forced to take the lead in defending Western interests against Soviet expansionist aims which became no where clearer than in respect to Turkey. The "hand with the Turks", which Churchill had requested and received at Casablanca, was now for the Americans alone to play. [55]

NOTE: On April 26, 1970, Henry Raymont in the Sunday edition of *The New York Times* p. 30, reported that documents in the Franklin D. Roosevelt Library at Hyde Park, New York, recently made available to the public reveal that U.S. Ambassador William C. Bullitt warned the President on this account throughout the war. In a memorandum dated August 10, 1943. Bullitt counselled against "a new policy of appeasement" being advocated by certain circles inside the British Government, this time towards the Russians. As early as December 5, 1941, Bullitt advised Roosevelt, "Don't let Churchill get you into any more specific engagements that those in the Atlantic Charter. Try to keep him from engaging himself vis-à-vis Russia." The findings of the present study dictated that the Turkish Government was also deeply concerned about the possibility that after the war the British would seek to appease the Russians.

II. SOVIETS' DISCLOSURE OF THEIR INTENTIONS OVER TURKEY AND TURKEY'S EXPRESSION OF ITS CONCERNS TO THE ALLIES

Soviets reveal their intentions over Turkey and Turkey's expression of its concern to the Allies

Stalin reveals Soviet ambitions over the Straits to the British Ambassador Cripps, as early as 1940.

The British Ambassador, Cripps, after giving a message of Prime Minister Churchill to Molotov on July 1, had a conversation with Stalin, when the Soviet aims over Turkey are revealed openly for the first time.

Stalin responded to Churchill's warning about the destruction of the European balance of power by Germany with the chilling comment: "If the Prime Minister wishes to restore the old equilibrium we cannot agree with him." "The Soviets had signed the Nazi-Soviet Pact", Stalin told Cripps, "to get rid of the old equilibrium."

The rest of the conversation was no warmer. In one of his short telegrams Cripps assured the Foreign Office: "I did not, of course, touch upon the question of territories occupied by the Union of Soviet Socialist Republics since the war." This was strictly true, since the actual names of the occupied territories never came up. But in a broader sense Cripps managed to convey an unfortunate message to the Soviets. Speaking of the Balkans, Cripps told Stalin that what he had suggested to Molotov in a previous conversation was that without a lead in this part of the world by some major and neighbouring power who desired to bring these countries together, it would be difficult to ensure any stabilisation in the Balkans. M. Stalin here interjected that this was easier said than done. In what in retrospect seems an improbable scenario, the British ambassador was encouraging a reluctant Stalin to pursue a more aggressive Balkan policy. Stalin told Cripps: "In general it seems to me that anyone who gets into the Balkans with the idea of acting as a super-arbitrator has every chance of getting embroiled." Showing his historical ignorance, Cripps said that in this matter it would seem that Russia and Turkey, with their traditional friendship and extensive interests in the Balkans, might be able to assist in bringing about more stable conditions. Stalin replied that "the Turks are too fond of the political game" to be reliable partners (the man who said that "Sincere diplomacy is no more possible than dry water or iron wood was presumably not fond of the political game). Turkey, he said, "might launch an offensive against the Near East. It is difficult to say in what direction (Turkey) will make a spring. The Soviet Union has no wish to assume the role of super-arbitrator or to get embroiled in the Balkans." Stalin made it appear as though Turkey were a greater threat to the stability of the Balkans than Germany, which, he felt sure, would not "disperse her forces by sending troops to the Balkans." The general secretary appears to have been laying the groundwork for future claims against Turkey for which we know Molotov would press the Germans in November. Cripps reported that: "M. Stalin went on to say that it was wrong for the control of the Straits to be under the control of one power, which might abuse it; the other Black Sea Powers ought to have a say in the matter." The Soviets had evidently changed their minds since July 1936 when, at the end of the Montreux Conference on the Straits, Litvinov, then foreign commissar, had said: "It seems to me that all those who have taken part in the conference will leave it satisfied, and there will be none dissatisfied."

This ominous reversal in the Soviet attitude seemed to confirm Foreign Office fears that Soviet expansion into the Balkans was aimed at the Straits rather than at German oil supplies. Stalin according to his own account, felt no need to take active steps to curb German designs. In fact, Stalin explicitly played down the German threat.[56]

(Cripps's meeting with Stalin had undermined British interests. One recent historian claims that "British documentation does not permit definite conclusions about how far Sir Stafford Cripps exceeded his instructions by offering specific inducements. But in his May briefings Cripps was told that the Soviets were as great a threat to the Balkans as were the Germans and that the Turks should be patiently coaxed to resist pressure from both powers."

Instead of obeying his instructions Cripps had struck out on his own quite early in his conversation with Stalin. He had single-handedly reversed British policy raising the question of creating a Balkan bloc under a Soviet aegis and by suggesting that the British government might help by extracting concessions from the Turks as payment for a more cooperative Soviet attitude toward Britain. It was Stalin who downplayed the practicability of this line, odd as that may seem in retrospect. Stalin must have reasoned that the Germans were more likely to deliver on such promises than the British.

Cripps's first telegram to London after his talk with Stalin gave a fragmented account of the conversation and conveyed the incorrect impression that Stalin had broached the idea of pressuring the Turks. The Foreign Office was unimpressed.)[57]

Soviet designs on both Iran and Turkey

Intelligence reports of Soviet designs on both Iran and Turkey were being received regularly in London. One such report is enlightening about both Soviet aims and the ways by which the Foreign Office gathered information. Mr.

Rendel, British ambassador to Bulgaria, relayed a bit of gossip received from the Archbishop of Sofia, who had spoken to the Soviet ambassador's Bulgarian teacher, "to whom," the Archbishop said, "he speaks freely though he says little to anyone else." The Soviet had said that his country was not yet ready for involvement in the war and was busily repairing the Red Army's defects revealed during the Finnish War. "Moreover", Rendel's account continued, "both Germany and (the) British Empire were still too strong and it was desirable that the war should continue till they were both further enfeebled but Russia would keep her hands free. Germany had offered her access to the Persian Gulf but this was no substitute for control of the Straits." In early November this line gained further credibility when the British learned from a source in Belgrade that Vyshinski had told the Yugoslav ambassador that, in order to protect their interests in the Straits, the Soviets were prepared to join the Germans if the latter were to attack Turkey. The author of a Foreign Office memorandum thought this information might well be accurate, noting that "in the case of Turkey, as in that of Poland, (the Soviets) would no doubt feel that unless they staked out their claim immediately there would be no claim left to stake." [58]

In Berlin, Molotov demands from Hitler, Soviet sphere including Turkey (November 1940)

Sir Stafford Cripps's disillusionment with the Soviets would have been even greater had he known the details of the Berlin talks. Far from being bullied by the Germans, Molotov eagerly entered into the spirit of the occasion. The Germans were anxious to direct Soviet attention toward the vulnerable British Empire, which was, Hitler assured his guest, "a gigantic world-wide estate in bankruptcy." "The Russian Empire" Hitler told Molotov, who voiced no objection to the Soviet Union being referred to in terms normally used for the defunct tsarist regime, "could develop without in the least prejudicing German interests." Molotov said this was quite correct.

The Soviet-German talks appeared to contemporaries to be the apex of cooperation between the two dictators, but the veneer of mutual friendship masked a deepening rift. One American historian has, with understandable exaggeration, called Molotov's forty-eight hours in Berlin "the real turning point of World War II". This point of view, which probably results from too close a focus on Soviet motives, holds that Stalin, feeling that Hitler was in an embarrassed position with an unfinished war on his hands, pressed the Führer too closely for concessions in exchange for continued Soviet good will. Hitler, arrogant and enraged, this version claims, turned on his erstwhile ally and ordered the planning of "Case Barbarossa," the invasion of the Soviet Union.

Hitler was, most probably, angered by Soviet intransigence, though after Molotov's visit he remarked that he "hadn't expected anything of it any way." [59]

November 1940 gave the Soviets a last opportunity to at least postpone – if not prevent – a German invasion. They lost the chance of doing so by overplaying their hand, Molotov harangued Hitler and Ribbentrop about the presence of German troops in Finland and brushed aside the Führer's attempts to distract him with promises of territorial aggrandisement at Britain's expense by replying curtly that Germany and the USSR "should only contemplate a continuation of what had been begun." Molotov shunned generalities, declaring that "Stalin had given him exact instructions." He pursued these instructions with characteristic single-mindedness, criticising the Germans for their activities in Romania and demanding Soviet spheres of influence in Bulgaria, the Dardanelles, and Finland. Molotov revealed what lay in store for the latter country, asserting that is government desired a settlement there "on the same scale as in Bessarabia, "that is, annexation." Molotov extracted a promise from the German dictator that he "would be prepared at any time to help effect an improvement for Russia in the regime of the Straits." In his final meeting with Germans on November 13, the Soviet foreign commissar made it quite clear to Ribbentrop that a simple revision of the Montreux Convention, which governed the use of the Straits, would not satisfy his boss, since "paper agreements would not suffice for the Soviet Union rather, she would have to insist on effective guarantees of her security." That could, of course, only mean Soviet bases in Turkey.

Twelve days later, on November 25, showing how wrongly he had interpreted Hitler's intentions, Stalin offered to join the Tripartite Pact if certain conditions he specified were met. One historian has rightly pointed out that Stalin's offer of alliance with Nazi Germany has been "too often overlooked." [60]

The four Soviet conditions for joining the Axis cast serious doubt on the contention that Stalin was actuated purely by defensive motives during the period of the Nazi-Soviet Pact. Only the first condition was defensive, calling on the Germans to withdraw from Finland, but as Molotov had shown in Berlin, Moscow wanted the removal of German forces from Finland only to replace them with Soviet troops. The other three demands were, to say the least, frankly expansionist. The second condition demanded the scrapping of the Montreux Convention and "the establishment of a base for land and naval forces of the U.S.S.R. within range of the Bosporus and the Dardanelles." The third condition had been predicted as long ago as September by Leon Helfand "That the area south of Batum and Bakü in the direction of the Persian Gulf is recognised as the centre of the aspirations of the Soviet Union." The final condition demanded that Japan drop her claims to economic concessions in Northern Sakhalin. Hitler, of course, ignored Stalin's demands and continued to pilot his invasion of the USSR.[61]

According to Mr. Churchill, at the Tehran Conference Stalin asks for the revision of the Treaty of Sèvres (partition of Turkey after World War I)

"When Marshal Stalin raised this question of warm-water ports for Russia I said there were no obstacles. He also asked about the Dardanelles and the revision of the Treaty of Sèvres. I said that I wanted to get Turkey into the war, and this was an awkward moment for raising the question. Stalin replied that the time would come later. I said I expected Russia would sail the oceans with her Navy and merchant fleet, and we would welcome her ships. At this Stalin remarked that Lord Curzon had other ideas. I said that in those days we did not see eye to eye with Russia." [62]

Records of the Tehran Conference

ATTITUDE OF THE SOVIET GOVERNMENT ON EUROPEAN POLITICAL QUESTIONS AS EXPRESSED BY MARSHAL STALIN DURING THE TEHRAN CONFERENCE

THE DARDANELLES.

The Soviet Government would like to see the Montreux Convention in regard to the Straits replaced by a regime affording freer navigation to merchant and naval vessels both in war and in peace. This question was not pursued in any detail. [63]

P.M. Churchill's letter to Foreign Secretary of August 6, 1943

I do not think that the Russians have any anxieties about the rearmament of Turkey on its present scale. The Russians' preponderance of strength is so great that the trifling improvements we are making in the Turkish forces need not and I believe will not, disturb them.

No doubt they would be annoyed by Turkey complicating the situation in the Balkans without doing anything effective to help Russia defeat Germany.

Obviously however the Russians will not remain contented with the present state of the Straits, and I do not suppose they have forgotten that we offered them Constantinople in the earlier part of the late war Turkey's greatest safety lies in the active association with the United Nations. As you know, the time may come very soon when we shall ask her to admit our air squadrons and certain other forces to protect them in order to bomb Ploesti and gradually secure the control of the Straits and the Black Sea. There is not much basis of real conversation with Russia about Turkey till we know what line Turkey takes.[64]

The American Ambassador in Turkey (Steinhardt) reports to Washington about his talk with the Russian Ambassador (Vinogradov).

(November 6, 1943)

"Although recognising the vulnerability of Turk cities to aerial attack and Turk military deficiencies general, he was not clear as to what if any military assistance could or should be rendered the Turks by any of the Allies. He then remarked that if the Turks were still worried about Russian intentions in the Balkans, he failed to understand why Numan had not asked him to call to discuss the matter.

In conclusion Vinogradov said that unless Numan asked him to come to see him, it was his intention to await the progress of the talks between the British and the Turks before calling on the Foreign Minister.

I gained the impression that Vinogradov has been instructed to take no part in the Anglo-Turk talks but to hold himself in readiness, if called upon by Numan, to discuss Turk anxiety with respect to Russian intentions in the Balkans." [65]

Turkey expresses its concern about Soviet intentions

Adana Negotiations Between Churchill and İnönü (Jan. 43)

Mr. Churchill tells his talks with İnönü regarding Turkey's prudence for the Soviet aims:

> "The general discussion which followed turned largely on to two questions, the structure of the post-war world, and the arrangements for an international organisation, and the future relations of Turkey and Russia. I give only a few examples of the remarks which, according to the record, I made to the Turkish leaders. I said that I had seen Molotov and Stalin, and my impression was that both desired a peaceful and friendly association with the United Kingdom and the United States. In the economic sphere both Western Powers had much to give to Russia and they could help in the reparation of Russia's losses. I could not see twenty years ahead, but we had nevertheless made a treaty for twenty years. I thought Russia would concentrate on reconstruction for the next ten years. There would probably be changes: Communism had already been modified. I thought we should live in good relations with Russia, and if Great Britain and the United States acted together and maintained a strong Air Force they should be able to ensure a period of stability. Russia might even gain by this. She possessed vast undeveloped areas for instance, in Siberia.

The Turkish Prime Minister observed that I had expressed the view that Russia might become imperialistic. This made it necessary for Turkey to be very prudent. I replied that there would be an international organisation to secure peace and security, which would be stronger than the League of Nations. I added that I was not afraid of Communism. Mr. Saraçoğlu remarked that he was looking for something more real. All Europe was full of Slavs and Communists. All the defeated countries would become Bolshevik and Slav if Germany was beaten. I replied that things did not always turn out as bad as was expected; but if they did so it was better that Turkey should be strong and closely associated with the United Kingdom and the United States. If Russia, without any cause, were to attack Turkey the whole international organisation of which I had spoken would be applied on behalf of Turkey, and the guarantees after the present war would be much more severe, not only where Turkey was concerned, but in the case of all Europe, I would not be a friend of Russia if she imitated Germany. If she did so we should arrange the best possible combination against her and I would not hesitate to say so to Stalin. Molotov had asked for a treaty by which the Baltic States would be regarded as Russian provinces. We had refused to agree to this, (a) because territorial rearrangements were to be postponed for settlement after the war, and (b) because we felt it necessary to make a reservation for free determination for individuals." [66]

Cairo Talks between Turkish Foreign Minister Numan Menemencioğlu and British Foreign Secretary Eden (November 1943)

The first of these talks was held on November 5, and Mr. Eden reported to the Prime Minister that he had had a long tough day. Mr. Eden first requested Numan to furnish air bases for the use of Allied forces. He also brought up the question of Turkey's full entrance into the war. Numan refused to agree that there would be any difference between these two courses of action, contending that to furnish air bases to the Allies would be tantamount to entering the war. In this connection he said that Germany would not dare not to react if Turkey furnished bases. Mr. Eden argued that Germany was in such a position that it could attack only by air and apparently argued that the Allied air forces could handle any such attacks.

Mr. Eden reported that although Numan did not refuse to discuss the question of air bases or formal entry into the war, it was obvious that he was deeply suspicious of the Russians and greatly concerned about their possible penetration into the Balkans.

The discussions then turned to the broad issue of Turkey's formal entrance into the war. Numan pointed out that at Adana Mr. Churchill had given the Turks the impression that they would be free to make an independent decision as to whether and when they should enter the war. Did the British now feel that the Turks now had enough equipment with which to put up a fight ? In any case, if Turkey was to be involved in the war, it would wish to be in active collaboration with its allies and was not content to play a passive role by merely furnishing air bases. If the Turks were to go into the war and take an active part, where would the Allies want them to fight? In the Balkans? If the British really felt the Turks were ready, the Turks would want to know the precise part they were to play. Again and again Numan repeated that Turkey would never agree to play a passive part. He said that if the British Foreign Minister had brought from Moscow such decisions as the future treatment of Persia, Iraq and the Balkans, it would be much easier for him to meet the British views.

Mr. Eden replied that so far as Persia was concerned, the Russians and the British had a treaty under which they undertook to withdraw from Persia after the war. So far as Iraq was concerned, the British had a bilateral treaty which made things perfectly clear. So far as the Balkans were concerned, it would be obvious to the Turks that they would gain more by cooperating with the Allies than by standing aloof. Numan asked if it were not true that the Russians had withdrawn their demand for a second front in Europe in return for a free hand in Eastern Europe. Mr. Eden denied this and pointed out that the Americans, in particular, both in public and in private, had made it clear that they could not discuss frontiers until the end of the war.

Numan then inquired why the British had not accepted Romania's peace offer. What more could the Romanians do than offer to discuss peace? Mr. Eden retorted that the Allies would discuss peace with the Romanians only on the basis of unconditional surrender. Numan replied that the Turks would never suggest to the Romanians that they surrender unconditionally to the Russians.

Summing up, Mr. Eden said that the negative reply that he had received from the Turkish Foreign Minister was bound to have a deplorable effect among the Allies. Numan replied that to the first request for air bases he was bound to give a negative reply, for the reasons he had mentioned. As to the second request for formal Turkish entry into the war, he would have to report to his Government. Mr. Eden reported that he had given Numan a severe warning as to the possible consequences of the Turkish refusal to meet the British request. Mr. Eden also pointed out the unenviable position in which Turkey would find itself *vis-à-vis* the Russians in the event it declined to meet British wishes. He stressed, on the other hand, the far better position in which Turkey would be placed if it went along with the British request.

Numan answered that he must know more of Russian intentions before he could allow Turkey to play the part requested by the British. Furthermore, he did not believe that Germany was stretched as far as the British contended. In order to reassure the Turks on this point, Mr. Eden said that he was having General Wilson send one of his military intelligence experts to Ankara in an endeavour to convince the Turks that the Germans were over-extended. Mr. Eden also agreed that he would take up with the Russians and the Americans the precise role that Turkey might be expected to play if it entered the war and that a paper on this point would be passed through military channels.[68]

The second meeting of the British and the Turks at Cairo

On November 8 Numan had a further (and apparently final) conversation with Mr. Eden during which be showed himself considerably more receptive.

Eden said that the Soviet desires and the present discussions seemed to him to offer an opportunity to establish Turkish-Soviet relations on a sound basis for the next twenty-five years. Numan replied that he realised that this was so; that he thought the Soviet question was being well handled and that he had entirely welcomed the Moscow decisions, which were much more favourable than could have been expected. However, he said that a decision as regards the demands on Turkey could of course only be taken by the Government. He said that the Turks had been very disturbed by Stalin's references to Moldavia and Transylvania. It would be hard to explain to the National Assembly if Turkish assistance aided the establishment of Russia in Romania and Bulgaria under the claim that such establishment was in the interests of those peoples.

Numan continued that he had been upset by Eden's threatening tone, which had been used for the first time in the long relations between the two countries and that he had the impression that Eden was acting as spokesman not just for Britain but for Russia. Eden had asked Turkey to give bases and to come into the war without specifying exactly what would be expected of her, what Allied cooperation could be depended upon, and what assurances there would be as to the political results on implications. He said that today for her own safety Turkey must be as concerned about the situation in the Balkans as she was previously about the freedom of the Straits alone. Eden replied that they must face the facts that Britain was an ally of Turkey but she was also an ally of Russia. He said that if Turkey came into the war she would inevitably become stronger through the supply of Allied arms. Numan recognised that this was so.[68]

CHAPTER III

OVERLORD VERSUS THE BALKAN OPERATION

I. PRELUDE (IMPORTANT CONFERENCES AND TALKS)

The Casablanca Agreement (January 19, 1943) and its consequences for Turkey

An agreement which did emerge in the course of the discussions between Churchill and Roosevelt was the so-called Casablanca Agreement. The Prime Minister convinced the President to allow the British "to play the hand with the Turks," arguing that Turkey fell within Britain's traditional sphere of interest and that, besides, "most of the troops which would be involved in reinforcing Turkey would be British. . . ." [69]

Cordell Hull's opposition to Turkey being handed over to Britain

The President's agreement to this position actually accorded with his earlier tendency to let the British take the lead for the Allies in Turkey. As early as March 1941, the British Ambassador in Washington had surprised Cordell Hull by informing him that the President favoured sending all lend-lease materials consigned to Turkey through the offices of the United Kingdom.

Although he had let the earlier incident pass, Hull was deeply distressed by evidence that at the Casablanca Conference Roosevelt had given away even more to the British. His new fears were aroused by Eden who, during his visit to Washington in March 1943, conveyed the impression that the President had recognised Britain's primary role in relation to Turkey and had explicitly agreed to British handling of all Allied interests in Turkey as well as that of control over the flow of goods. Wallance Murray, a State Department adviser on political affairs, wrote that if this proved to be the case. "there would be . . . no need for maintaining an American Embassy at Ankara nor any necessity for the presence in Washington of a Turkish Embassy."

Hull was frustrated in his efforts to see the Casablanca Agreement. "The President," writes Admiral William D. Leahy, "had directed me not to divulge any information about the conference without his specific approval in each instance." As a result, there was "no copy available" for Hull who turned for information to the British Embassy. Mr. Michael Wright, British First Secretary, confirmed Hull's apprehensions by informing Murray "that the British Foreign Office understood that at Casablanca the President had given the Prime Minister primary responsibility for 'playing the cards' with Turkey." Hull continued his remonstrances.

On July 16, the President relented and Admiral Leahy sent a copy of the agreement to the Secretary. It, in part, reads as follows.

    a. Agreed that Turkey lies within a theatre of British responsibility and that all matters connected with Turkey should be handled by the British in the same way that all matters connected with China are handled by the United States.

This agreement, signed January 20 at the 63rd meeting of the Combined Chiefs of Staff, includes a final report which also indicated that the President and Prime Minister had ". . . agreed upon the administrative measures necessary to give effect to the decision that all matters connected with Turkey shall be handled by the British." Hull quickly attempted to reassert American independence with regard to Turkey. In messages to the British Embassy and to the Joint Chiefs of Staff, Hull declared that the American mission in Ankara reserved the right to act autonomously in its dealings with the Turkish Government.[70]

Turkey's concerns about the Casablanca Agreement

The U.S. War Department informed the Turkish Embassy on January 29 that in the future British military authorities were to present Turkish bids for military equipment before the Munitions Assignments Board. This news was a "stunning blow" and a "tremendous shock" to the Turks. The Turkish military attaché voiced the suspicion that the decision to allow the British to "retain control" of the flow of lend-lease goods to Turkey, "had resulted from a commitment by Great Britain to 'another Ally' (Russia) to keep Turkey weak." The Turkish air attaché stated that "the Turkish Government should immediately inform the British and American Governments that Turkey henceforth desired no assistance from either the United States or Great Britain." When Dean Acheson, at this time Assistant Secretary of State, heard of the Turkish reaction, he inquired why it had been necessary to "break the news to the Turks." Acheson was told by his subordinates that it had been made inevitable by the decision of the Combined Chiefs that discontinued certain previous kinds of collaboration with the Turks.

The specific dispute eventually became quiescent. A procedure was instituted soon after the inflamed meeting on January 29 which allowed Turkish officials to consult with American representatives concerning bids submitted on their behalf by the British. The British, however, continued to "play the hand" with the Turks until the end of the war. Yet far from stinting on supplies, as the Turks had feared, they proved willing to supply Turkey with more equipment than its infrastructure could handle or its policy of neutrality warranted, perhaps even more than the Turks wanted.

Nevertheless, Turkish officials continued to prefer to deal directly with the Americans. George V. Allen on March 16, 1943, in a general review of the Turkish scene, wrote:

"From time to time . . . Turkish officials have indicated their preference for dealing directly with us . . . they would know where they stood much better . . .
would know precisely to whom they were indebted, and would have more control. . . ."

Allen advised his superiors at State that the Turkish Government was beginning to despair that the United States was losing interest. This created a "damp-
ened enthusiasm" over Allied victories on their part, he observed. The reluctance of the United States to deal directly with Turkey except through the
British, left Turkish leaders uncomfortably uncertain as to what extent or in precisely what ways the United States would support, protect, or if necessary,
defend them.[71]

The implications of the Casablanca Agreement, especially the repercussions
of the January 22 directive of the Munitions Assignments Board, were felt in
Ankara to have a profound meaning. It was certainly not merely a question of
goods assigned to Turkey being accredited to one account rather than another.
At stake, in Turkish thinking, was nothing less than the role American policy-
makers intended to play in southeastern Europe. Roosevelt had accepted
Churchill's argument, that the British should "play the hand with the Turks," as
if the question were merely a matter of mutual British and American convenience. The British would function in Turkey as the Americans were doing vis-
à-vis China. To Turks, no such equation was desirable. Turkish policy-makers
wanted an American presence in southeastern Europe. This was due to their
fear that Russia would attempt to "Bolshevize" Europe after the war. Any
arrangement that seemed designed to cut Ankara off from Washington or that
seemed to remove Washington from direct responsibility toward Turkey troubled Turkish statesmen.

Their reaction to the Casablanca Agreement was also the result of long historical experience. In Menemencioğlu's mind, for example, it awakened memories of the days when the Ottoman Empire was "the sick man of Europe." Any
suggestion that Turkey was to be included in the sphere of influence of a single
European power deeply offended him. This was true of all leading Turkish officials. Their experience with the British occupation during World War I had
hardly prepared them for a filial relationship now.[72]

The Casablanca Agreement seemed to Turkish leaders therefore to suggest
two things: first, a gradual American withdrawal from the Turkish sphere and
second, the reassertion of Britain's right to act as a colonial power.[73]

Turkish leaders thus perceived themselves as facing a dangerous new situation
after Casablanca. The Allies had decided that Germany's power was to be
destroyed by "unconditional surrender." Russia was clearly in the ascendant
and, with Germany vanquished, would face no countervailing continental force
to restrict its appetite for Eastern Europe. The British seemed either unwilling
or unable to sense this danger, but, rather, were working in close collaboration
with the Russians to speed this outcome and, if possible, to force the Turks, by
entry into the war against Germany, to help dig their own grave. As for
America, it seemed less interested and more remote to the Turkish leaders than

ever. In the midst of these thoughts, the Turks learned that Prime Minister Churchill was planning to come to Turkey. [74]

Churchill is happy about Casablanca results and decides to come to Turkey (Adana)

Churchill's telegram of January 20, 1943 to Deputy Prime Minister and the Foreign Secretary:

> "I raised the Turkish question, having explored the ground beforehand, with President Roosevelt. It was agreed that we played the hand in Turkey whether in munitions or in diplomacy, the Americans taking the lead in China, and of course in French North Africa. You will be pleased at this . . . As soon as the President has gone I shall, if the weather is good, fly from Marrakesh to Cairo, where I propose to stay for two or three days and settle several important matter. Is this not the opportunity and the moment for me to get into direct touch with the Turks ? If you both think well of this the Foreign Secretary should make the proposal to the Turks without delay." [75]

The Conference at Adana: (January 30–31, 1943): a meeting of misunderstandings

The Adana Talks

Churchill had been emboldened by American acceptance of British plans to invade Sicily. He thus decided to pursue his plans to bring Turkey into the war, the "key" to his strategy in the Mediterranean, by visiting with Turkish statesmen. [76]

President İnönü has testified that he went to Adana to meet Prime Minister Churchill with two purposes in mind: to warn Churchill about Russian postwar intentions and to obtain an increase in British deliveries of war materials and armament. Although İnönü still feared a German attack, his real concern at Adana was the threat posed by Russia and what the British intended to do about it. This was true of the entire Turkish delegation. Saraçoğlu's experience during his fateful visit to Moscow in 1939 prompted him to seize the opportunity to act as a "strong speaker." Had not Prime Minister Churchill himself "expressed the view that Russia might become imperialistic," Saraçoğlu asked. This possibility "made it necessary for Turkey to be very prudent." What would guarantee Turkey's integrity after an Allied victory? Saraçoğlu declared that he was "looking for something more real" than an international security organisation. "All Europe was full of Slavs and Communists. All the defeated countries would become Bolshevik and Slav if Germany was beaten." [77]

Churchill, *The Hinge of Fate*, pp. 709–11; Erkin, Turkish-Russian Relations, p. 224, also writes that during the talks at Adana Prime Minister Saraçoğlu repeatedly warned Churchill of Soviet imperial intentions toward the Straits, the Balkans, and Eastern Europe and that this "was causing great anxiety in Ankara." Erkin cites Saraçoğlu as having said, "The defeat of Germany would leave a tragic vacuum which would make all the vanquished countries easy prey to communism."

Such arguments were hardly what the buoyant Prime Minister had come to Adana to hear and discuss. He immediately attempted to reassure his hosts. "Things did not always turn out as bad as was expected," he said. "I would not be a friend of Russia if she imitated Germany. If she did so we would arrange the best possible combination against her and I would not hesitate to say so to Stalin." Churchill had made it clear in his opening remarks that he was acting as spokesman for the Allied coalition. His trip to Adana had the backing of both the United States and the Soviet Union. The Russian victory at Stalingrad had marked the turning point in Allied fortunes. What Stalin wanted the Turks to do could not be shrugged off by Ankara. "I know," Churchill concluded, "that Premier Stalin is most anxious to see Turkey well armed and ready to defend itself against aggression." Aydemir has correctly suggested that Churchill should have known that "Turkish statesmen would not take these reassurances seriously." [78]

The Ambiguous Aftermath of Adana

On February Churchill wired Stalin that "there is no doubt" the Turks "have come a long way towards us" although, he added, he had "not asked for any precise political engagement or promise about entering the war on our side." He stated that Turkey would participate in the Allied cause possibly before the end of the year by a "strained interpretation of the neutrality" similar to that once invoked by the Americans. "They may allow us to use their airfields for refuelling for British and American bombing attacks" he wrote, and, "I am telegraphing you to range them more plainly than before in the anti-Hitler system." President İnönü, however, seems to some degree to have succeeded in his attempts to impress upon Churchill the extent to which he was concerned about Stalin's postwar intentions. Churchill informed the Russian Premier that the Turks were apprehensive over their political position in view of the great strength of the Soviet Republic. "They would, I am sure" he added, " be responsive to any gesture of friendship on the part of the U.S.S.R." Stalin, however, seems not to been impressed either with Churchill's close personal relationship with İnönü, which the Prime Minister claimed to have established, nor by the need to reassure the Turks. [79]

At Adana and throughout subsequent months, Turkish policymakers repeatedly warned Allied officials that "the line where Soviet forces . . . would meet Allied armies . . . in invaded Germany would determine the boundary between free Europe and that part of Europe that would be compiled to be Sovietised." Turkish leaders hastened to advise the Allies that "it was vital to the free world that this demarcation be situated as far to the East as possible." As far as Turkish statesman could tell, however, the Western Allies were refusing to heed their advice. [80]

Gradually, Turks began to reason that Britain's inability to heed good advice was the result of its unwillingness to do so. Turkish leaders, who at this time resented Britain for seeming to act paternalistically, feared the British were planning to renounce responsibility toward Turkey in favour of the Russians. Turkish leaders suspected that the British had entered into a secret arrangement giving the Russians a free hand in Turkey on condition that Stalin would fight to the end. In this event Turkey would be left alone to face the Soviet Union. The announcement of the doctrine of unconditional surrender seemed to forecast this development.[81]

In retrospect, therefore, it appears that the Adana meeting was not a success, neither from the Turkish nor the British point of view. Churchill did not succeed in committing the Turks to a policy of more direct involvement. The Turks did not convince the British that the Russians really were bent on aggressive expansion. Both sides probably thought however that they had done a little better at convincing the other than later proved to be the case and this led to much subsequent British-Turkish misunderstanding and animosity.

The feeling in Ankara after Adana, therefore, remained constant in two crucial respects. Turkish policy-makers continued to regard Soviet ambitions as the principal danger facing them and continued to believe that Britain would conceivably do nothing to restrain those ambitions. Churchill's inadroit assertions that the Soviets harboured only good intentions heightened the fear that Britain might seek to strengthen its position in Europe by a "separate agreement with Russia" and that such an agreement could come "at the expense of Turkey." [82]

What the Turks had feared at Adana, however, gradually materialised during the months following it: as the Soviet Union's fortunes of war changed, as it came to feel more powerful, it became increasingly anti-Turkish and openly threatening. Molotov rejected Turkish overtures on the grounds that they were inadequate to the task of ameliorating Turkish-Soviet relations which would improve only when Turkey entered the war. Thus the Turkish diplomatic attempt to achieve a *modus vivendi* with the Russians, prompted by Churchill, met with a rebuff. After the battle of Stalingrad and especially after Adana, the Soviet Union began to criticise Turkey's nonbelligerence vehemently.[83]

Thus the Adana Conference, which Churchill portrayed to Stalin as having brought the Turks closer to the Allies, did little to remove the distrust which had plagued Turko-Soviet and Anglo-Turkish relations. In the face of increasing Soviet resentment Turkish officials were made to remember the promise of Stalin that if Turkey were ever invaded "Russia would help." The Russian Premier had uttered this in a friendly tone at a time when the Soviet Union was losing the war against Germany. But now that the Soviet Union was becoming increasingly victorious and Stalin's tone increasingly venomous, his promise to help could mean invasion. Turkish leaders decided that no pretext must be given to the Soviets to invade, and then became more determined than ever to prevent the fighting from being waged on Turkish territory. This made them ever more reluctant to cooperate with the British.[84]

An Editorial in "The Times" newspaper concerning post-war British-Soviet cooperation
The Turks did not wait long after Churchill departed to be confirmed in their apprehensions about British policy toward Russia. An editorial in *The Times* and a speech by Churchill created consternation in Ankara. On March 10, 1943, *The Times* of London published an editorial.

After the war, the editorial reasoned, the Soviet Union would be in a position to get what it wanted anyway. What mattered was whether Great Britain would be with her or against her:

"Britain has the same interest as Russia herself in active and effective Russian participation in continental affairs; for there can be no security in Western Europe unless there is also security in Eastern Europe, and security in Eastern Europe is unattainable unless it is buttressed by the military power of Russia."

The editorial concluded unequivocally: "Russia will, at the moment of victory so largely due to her outstanding effort, enjoy the same right as her allies to judge for herself the conditions which she deems necessary for the security of her frontiers." Again, the reaction in Turkey was one of dismay. The Turkish press was clamorous in its denunciations.[85]

An editorial in "The New York Times" newspaper (on March 21, 1943) replies to The Times. On March 21, 1943, The New York Times strongly dissented from The Times editorial of March 10.

"American opinion will not look favourably on any proposal to put the small nations of Europe on the execution block in order to purchase Russian confidence and cooperation" it declared. *The New York Times* later reported that it had been gratified to learn that *The Times* had spoken only on its own behalf. The extent to which this was true remains uncertain.

Washington talks between Eden and Roosevelt (March 1943)

Had the Turks at this time possessed exact information about the substance of the discussions taking place in Washington between Foreign Secretary Eden and President Roosevelt (March 12 March 30), they would have felt even more confirmed in their bleak view of the future. During their talks concerning the shape of postwar Europe, Roosevelt declared that only the Big Three, Great Britain, the Soviet Union, and the United States, should be allowed to possess armaments, with the smaller nations, including the neutrals, allowed to possess "nothing more dangerous than rifles." Eden, for his part, assured the President that the Russians "would demand very little territory of Poland, just possibly up to the 'Curzon Line' and stated his belief that Stalin wanted a strong Poland "providing the right kind of people were running it." Eden also informed Roosevelt that the Soviet Union would probably insist upon absorbing the Baltic States, a thought which troubled the President more than Eden who accepted it more or less as a tolerable *fait accompli*. In general, Eden's views of Soviet postwar intentions appear to have been based on a presumption of Stalin's determination to be reasonable and moderate in his claims to postwar "security" for Russia. This was just as the Turks feared. As for the security of the small powers Roosevelt gave Eden the impression, somewhat alarming even to the British, that in Eden's words Roosevelt "seemed to see himself disposing of the fate of many lands, allied no less than enemy." At the end of their discussions, Roosevelt noted that many territorial questions remained, but that he "did not intend to go to the Peace Conference and bargain with Poland or the other small states. . . ." This too reflected the Turks' worst suspicions of Allied attitudes and intentions.

One event which did lend credence to Turkish apprehensions took place a few weeks after Eden returned from Washington – the Soviet rejection of the Polish Government-in-exile. On April 26 1943 the Soviets broke off diplomatic relations with the Sikorski regime in London and organised their own pro-Russian, communist-dominated government, the Union of Polish Patriots. The Turks, who immediately perceived this as the first step in Russia's attempt to annex eastern Poland, were deeply distressed yet the British, as far as the Turks could tell, remained oblivious to the dangers. Thus they watched Churchill's activities in North America during the Summer of 1943 with deep foreboding.[86]

Churchill-Roosevelt meeting in Washington (May 1943) and the Quebec Conference (August 1943)

At the Churchill-Roosevelt meeting in Washington in May 1943, and at the Quebec Conference three months later, the British Prime Minister indeed pushed for Turkish belligerence. He did this first by focusing on Italy. On May 12 1943 Churchill listed the advantages of a campaign to defeat Italy: it would require the Axis to overextend their logistics, thereby "taking the weight off" Russia; it would force Italian divisions to leave the Balkans, thus reducing Axis strength in the area, and encourage Turkey, "who had always measured herself with Italy in the Mediterranean," to enter the war. Churchill declared, "The moment would come when . . . a request might be made to Turkey for permission to use bases in her territory . . . " which, Churchill argued, "could hardly fail to be successful if Italy were out of the war." Controversy exists and perhaps always will as to what Churchill had in mind at this time. The one conclusion which emerges clearly is that Churchill wanted to occupy Italy with a view to bringing pressure upon Turkey.

The Americans were prepared, although as ever with reluctance, to agree with Churchill on an invasion of Italy, but for reasons not wholly congruent with those of the Prime Minister. American strategists considered Italy in terms of the western rather than the southeastern front as a potential airbase against enemy-occupied Europe which could be useful in connection with the opening of the Second Front. In July 1943, American planners hoped "that the measures finally adopted to eliminate Italy would yield a base area for broadcasting air operations against German controlled Europe." Thus the Americans, even after the decisions to attack the Italian mainland had been agreed upon, continued to confound the British Prime Minister. Rather than assist in the reinforcement of the Turkish defences, as Churchill had hoped, the Americans now decided to withhold support. They opposed sending US heavy bombers to Turkey on the grounds that these could be put to better use in missions based in Italy. Insofar as Churchill hoped that the decision to invade would be a stepping stone to further commitments by the Americans in the Eastern Mediterranean, his plans were not to be realised. With the Eastern Mediterranean consigned to low priority by the Americans, the British were still left to play their hand with the

Turks, but were forced to do so without tangible American strategic support.[87]

Perhaps Turkey would not have dragged its feet against Churchill's Balkan operation fantasy as it did had it been certain that a link-up between Turkish and British forces would have led to a large-scale Anglo-American thrust into the Balkans. But the British would make no such commitment and did not trust the Turks sufficiently to reveal Allied grand strategy. We know now, that, failing to secure American approval for a Balkan campaign, the British had no grand strategy to reveal.[88]

British failure at Rhodes

With the fall of Mussolini on July 25 1943 despite these other frustrations Churchill renewed his efforts, both with the Turks about the war and with the Americans about the Eastern Mediterranean. Churchill, with these considerations in mind, left ten days later, on August 5, 1943 for the Quebec Conference with the U.S. President Roosevelt and the Joint Chiefs resolved that this time they would meet Churchill with their policy firmly set. At the first plenary session of the conference, August 19 1943 elicited from the British Prime Minister an agreement to assign top priority to the cross-Channel attack. Churchill accepted this, agreeing to the target date of May 1 1944. As Henry L. Stimson the U.S. Under-Secretary of State, wrote, "from this time onward Overlord held the inside track."

The results of the meeting reflected little of Churchill's thinking about the Eastern Mediterranean. However, in their final conference report to the President and the Prime Minister, for example, the Combined Chiefs of Staff stated that "the time was not considered right for Turkey to enter the war." They agreed, however, that the United States and Great Britain should continue to supply Turkey with such equipment "as they could spare and the Turks could absorb." Although they were parties to such agreements, the British never stopped believing it would be to Allied advantage to have Turkey enter the war. There was still reason to hope that the Turks could be brought into battle. Churchill decided to play his trump card. On September 9, 1943, while he was in Washington and apparently without informing the President, Churchill cabled General Wilson, "This is the time to play high. Improvise and dare." He thus signalled his forces in the Eastern Mediterranean to launch an attack on Rhodes.

To Churchill, the combined sea and air base of Rhodes, the air base on Cos, and the sea base at Leros together offered a vantage point from which to attack German concentrations in the Balkans and northern Italy, to bomb the Romanian oil fields and refineries at Ploesti, and to defend Egypt and North Africa. Thus Churchill decided on a new initiative, if not in conjunction with the United States, then alone. He would take Rhodes. But there was still another reason for this daring to attack Rhodes. He wanted to bolster British diplomatic approaches to Turkey. British capture of Rhodes and gradual control of the Aegean might possibly persuade the Turks to enter the war. At least,

Churchill reasoned, British officials would be able to speak with greater authority in Ankara. British plans failed however, and by the end of 1943, British influence with Turkish officials hit a new low. Although the British made several later attempts in 1943 to occupy some of the islands in the Aegean, the failure to take Rhodes marks the beginning of the end of Churchill's campaign to bring Turkey into the war. Not only did the British fail to take over Italian-garrisoned Rhodes, but the Germans, meeting little resistance, took it and then went on to take Cos, Liros, and Samos from the British, who had held them almost from the beginning of the Mediterranean war.[89]

Turkey gives substantial aid to the Allied side

Although the British 1943 campaign was stillborn, and despite the fact that the British were actually having to retreat before the Germans in this sector, the Turks gave substantial aid to the Allied side, while retaining their public posture of neutrality. They supplied beleaguered British forces in the Aegean with food and equipment and helped escaping units from the Royal West Kent, Irish Fusilier and other regiments reach the Turkish mainland safely.

Supplies destined for British-held islands in the Aegean were transported by railroad through Syria across Turkey to Kusadasi, a small but excellent port south of Izmir. From October 9 to November 17 when Leros fell, 1,400 tons of emergency material were shipped to British forces through Turkish hands. From September 28 to November 16, 3,000 tons of goods actually reached Samos and 480 tons reached Leros. Turkish caiques manned by Turkish crews transported these goods. When the British evacuated their forces in the Aegean, furthermore, Kusadasi and Bodrum, further along the coast, were the first stops in their escape route. When General Wilson, for example, on November 18–19 ordered the evacuation of Samos, Turkish caiques brought such personalities as Brigadier Baird, Colonel Tzigantes, commander of the Greek Sacred Squadron, General Soldarelli, the Italian commander, the Greek Archbishop, and hundreds of British and Italian citizens to the mainland. On the evenings of November 20 and 21, Turkish caiques were able to bring more British out of Samos, plus 1,000 Greek civilians and 400 Italian troops: all this while the Germans were occupying the island.

The fact that Foreign Minister Menemencioğlu was personally in charge of these operations further strengthens the evidence that he was neither particularly a foe of Britain nor a friend to the Germans.[90]

The American ambassador's account of the Turkish support to the British operation of the Aegean Islands
The Ambassador in Turkey (Steinhardt) to the President, the Secretary of State, and the Under Secretary of State (Stetinius):

"ANKARA, November 16, 1943–6 p.m. Most secret for the President, the Secretary and the Under Secretary.

An American newspaper correspondent informed me this afternoon that the Turk censor had told the foreign correspondents this morning that no further press despatches referring to the battle on the Island of Leros would be passed by the censors.

I interpret the foregoing as indicating a desire by the Turks to conceal the increased assistance which they are rendering to the British on the Islands who are being hard-pressed, and who are said to have been out-numbered for several days as the result of the landing of German reinforcements. This interpretation is supported by the fact that the lighthouses on the Turk coast in the vicinity of Leros were extinguished last night to permit the landings on Leros by the British or Greek guerrillas".[91]

The Moscow Conference:
The Russians try to force Turkey into the war (October 1943)

The Moscow Conference of American, British, and Soviet Foreign Ministers was marked by the extraordinary vigour with which the Soviets pressed for an Anglo-American commitment to force Turkey into the war, a commitment which the United states in particular was reluctant to give but one which Molotov finally succeeded in obtaining if not as a part of the main conclusions to the conference then at least as an important codicil.[92]

Having received satisfactory response from Eden, Molotov's attention turned to Hull. The Secretary of State had listened silently to Eden's exposition of British policy toward Turkey. Now he responded with what became his standard rejoinder during the conference whenever this question arose: he preferred "not to speak on military matters." Hull, like Eden, had also cabled home for instructions after the first session. Hull's chief, unlike Eden's, was not keenly interested in the question of Turkish belligerence. Instead of replying directly to the Secretary of State's message, Roosevelt turned it over to the Joint Chiefs of Staff. The Joint Chiefs, in turn, gave it to the Joint Strategic Survey Command (JSSC) for its consideration. Response to Hull's request for instructions was further delayed by the disagreement between army planners and the JSSC which ensued over this issue.

Army planners argued against bringing Turkey into the war, restating many of the old arguments and concluding correctly, that "Turkey did not want Soviet help and would probably demand British and American guarantees to protect it against the USSR . . ." which would divert the Anglo-American forces from the cross-Channel attack. The JSSC, on the other hand, argued that it would be desirable to have the Turks join in the fighting in order to divert the Germans from the Channel defences. In the end the Joint Chiefs of Staff took the equivocal position that pending further study Turkey should be neither encouraged nor dissuaded. The Joint Chiefs wanted to ascertain what the Soviet Union would do to protect Turkey should it enter the war. It also wanted to make certain that Turkish belligerence would not jeopardise the cross-Channel attack. Since no such assurance could be given at the time of Hull's message to the President, the Joint Chiefs recommended caution.[93]

Churchill, for his part, encouraged at the outset of the conference, had already decided to launch a new campaign to facilitate Turkish entry into the war. Whereas American planners had refused to recommend that the Turks be made to fight, feeling themselves unwilling or unable to divert sufficient logistic support to a Turkish front, Churchill seems to have decided, along with the Russians, that it would be well to have the Turks fight in any case. He appears to have been much less pessimistic than the Americans about the chances of Turkish survival were they to be pushed into war with the supplies already available. This marks the beginning of the nadir in Anglo-Turkish relations during the war. Turkish policy-makers, particularly Foreign Minister Menemencioğlu soon gathered the impression that the British and Russians wished to force their country into the war, whether or not Turkish cities could be adequately protected, whether or not Turkish troops could be properly supplied and reinforced. Eden now told Molotov that he was prepared to meet the Turkish Foreign Minister in Cairo in order to request, on behalf of the Big Three, the immediate use of Turkey's airfields and to demand authority to send submarines through the Straits.[94]

Menemencioğlu and Eden meet at the First Cairo Conference
The British play the Russian hand (November 5–8, 1943)

In his memoirs, *The Reckoning*, Foreign Secretary Eden's account of the Cairo Conference was as such:

"The strength of the Turkish position lay in their doubts about Soviet intentions after the war. They feared the growth of Soviet power and that we and the United States would then be far away and unwilling to help them." Despite the secret Anglo-Soviet-American protocol that he himself had signed, Eden goes on to say "the weakness of their (the Turks) position was an unfounded suspicion that there had been some deal between us and the Russians. . . "

Eden states that the basic weakness of the the Turkish position was that they suspected that the British had made "some deal" with the Russians. He was quite correct, as subsequent research has shown. The Turks did, in fact, perceive Eden to be repeating "exactly" the Russian demands at the Moscow Conference. In their discussions Menemencioğlu very quickly concluded that Eden was doing the bidding of the Soviet Union. "I was not slow," he writes, "in becoming convinced that it was at the instigation of the Russians that M. Eden . . . insisted in Cairo on the precipitous entry of Turkey into the war." On one occasion Menemencioğlu openly accused Eden of acting as a spokesman not only for Britain but for Russia as well. Eden replied that Menemencioğlu would do well to "face facts . . . Britain was an ally of Turkey but she was also an ally of Russia." This was scarcely a winning argument and made the Turks all the more unwilling to accept British requests.

Menemencioğlu was quite candid in regard to his apprehensions about Russian ambitions, particularly in regard to the Balkan nations and Eastern Europe. He let these concerns become known to the British Foreign Secretary by continually asking him questions concerning Russian intentions. Menemencioğlu admits, without apology, that these questions "were in truth very indiscreet". Menemencioğlu's eagerness to learn about decisions at Moscow particularly centred on the fate of Poland to which he reverted repeatedly. At one point the Turkish Foreign Minister asked Eden point-blank: "What do you intend to do with Poland?" Eden "became furious," and retorted, "What business is it of yours?" Menemencioğlu replied heatedly, "For us, Poland is the *pierre de touche* (proof of the pudding)." His failure to win over Menemencioğlu would not have been particularly surprising to Eden had he better understood the basis of Turkish policy which was to safeguard now and in the postwar era, first, the independence of Turkey and, second, the independence of the Balkans, if at all possible. The Turks were not interested in fighting the Germans. They had no desire to weaken themselves unnecessarily, believing it essential to build up and conserve their strength for a possible future confrontation with a victorious Soviet Union. As already suggested, they suspected the Russians of wanting the Turks to waste their resources in a battle with Germany so as to make them, later, more vulnerable to Soviet pressures and designs. They had no territorial ambitions in the Balkans and no national animosity toward Germany, which had at least respected the essentials of their neutrality and territorial integrity during the period of Axis ascendance. If they were to fight, it would be to protect their present and future position against their only perceived enemy: the Russians. They were prepared to go war to help the British and Americans take the Balkans ahead of the Russians. But, as Menemencioğlu put it bluntly to Eden at Cairo, they were not interested in helping to aid "the establishment of Russia in Romania and Bulgaria" nor in becoming a route by which Soviet troops could enter the Eastern Mediterranean. Given these fixed policy commitments, it did not help the Allied cause to threaten Turkey with the possibility of Soviet expansionism: it was already the basic assumption in all Turkish calculations. Nor was it productive to hold out the possibility that, if they were to cooperate with Moscow now, Russia would be more restrained in their future demands toward the Turks. This was to stretch Turkish credulity beyond the breaking point. Eden thus had neither carrot nor stick with which to confront Menemencioğlu.[95]

The new Turkish strategy: a tactical shift

At Cairo, the record reveals, much of the Turkish effort to avoid being forced into the war was centred on an effort to persuade Eden that premature Turkish entry would serve only the interests of the Russians and that these interests would prove to be inimical not only to Turkey, but to the Western Allies as well. This effort, at least insofar as convincing Eden was concerned, failed dismally. Thereafter, Turkish strategy appears to have undergone a change. No longer did the Turks attempt to warn the Western Allies of future Russian designs on Eastern Europe. They now concentrated on purely logistical and military-tactical arguments to resist Allied demands while leaving their perceptions of the Soviet threat quietly in the background. They seem to have agreed that the

British and Americans were not prepared to accept their counsel or their reasoning in this respect.[96]

On the evening of November 13, three days after his return to Ankara, Menemencioğlu launched into the new strategy in a conversation with Ambassador Steinhardt. Reporting to him on his Cairo talks, he listed his disagreements with Eden in eight points which the Foreign Minister argued, militated in favour of continued Turkish neutrality. All eight are military in nature. Together, they form a kind of plea against the British effort to push Turkey into war. Not a word is said about the Soviet menace or about postwar settlements in the Balkans.

This shift in Turkish strategy – from an emphasis on the political dangers of premature entry to one on purely military concerns – was apparently accepted at face value by Ambassador Steinhardt.

This is significant because Steinhardt had, by this time, already received a full account of the Cairo discussions from Hugessen which clearly revealed the predominance of political over military concerns in Turkish thinking. Yet Steinhardt appears to have been ready not only to accept the new Turkish line put to him, but anxious to convey it to the Soviet Ambassador. The probable reason for this is not difficult to deduce. The position of the United States throughout the war – as most recently evidenced at Moscow – had been one of reluctant agreement to put pressure on Turkey to force it into the war. Cevat Acikalin states that Steinhardt placed no pressure on the Turks during this period to enter the war. At the same time, the United States was anxious that Turkish recalcitrance be interpreted to Russia as inoffensively as possible. The new Turkish line, in its emphasis on fear of German military power and the weakness of the Allies in the Eastern Mediterranean, was far more accommodating of the American position than had been the hard anti-Soviet political line pursued at Cairo. Cevat Agikalin confirms that Turkey, at this point, deliberately selected the purely military argument as the one more likely to bolster its neutrality. Once Turkish policy-makers had decided that the Americans had joined the British in placing close relations with Russia above scepticism over Russian intentions, they thereafter spoke only of military preparedness and the inadequacy of Turkish defences, no longer of the dangers of Soviet expansionism.

The Americans accepted this as at least a convenient, if not entirely convincing argument. It served to give weight to American reluctance to become embroiled in a British campaign in the Eastern Mediterranean, and it was the one argument for leaving Turkey alone which least offended the Russians. On November 20, as the President was en route to the Tehran Conference, Secretary Hull informed him that the Turks had decided in principle to enter the war but that military considerations, primarily those concerning defence against a German attack, were preventing them from taking actual steps. He also told Roosevelt that Anglo-Turkish military talks had revealed a wide divergence on estimated Axis strength. Hull suggested that this divergence reflected the self-interest of both parties and indicated that Steinhardt believed a compromise could be reached on the amount of further military assistance required to enable Turkey to withstand the Axis. [97]

The Tehran Conference: the Soviet reversal

President Roosevelt went to Tehran hoping to gain Stalin's confidence and believed that they could accomplish this by convincing the Russian Premier that he desired the opening of the Second Front as much as Stalin himself. Roosevelt almost certainly feared that this would be made more difficult by the importunities of Churchill who undoubtedly would insist upon a hearing for his Balkan and Turkish plans. The outcome of all this was that Roosevelt and Stalin did have several private meetings and, in pursuing the logic of their own ends, came to the decision that it would not be to their advantage to have the Turks fight.

At Tehran, Roosevelt became even more determined to keep the Turks from making a thrust at the Dodecanese lest they thereby involve American might in a Greek campaign and thus threaten preparations for the cross-Channel attack. The President's intention to oppose Churchill's Turkish plans became evident the first day of the Tehran Conference, November 28, in a meeting with the Joint Chiefs on the morning of the day the first plenary meeting was scheduled. Roosevelt pelted his Chiefs of Staff with questions dealing with British policy toward Turkey. "Suppose we can get the Turks in, what then," he asked. General Marshall responded by warning that much equipment and possibly much manpower would have to be diverted to the Aegean. Marshall also discounted the British claim that the Turks could alone hold the Straits against the Germans. Admiral King declared that the United States would almost inevitably get involved in the Dodecanese if Turkey entered the war. The President, apparently convinced, eventually renounced all intentions of forcing the Turks to fight.

The President carried through on this during the first plenary meeting and seems to have personally condoned operation footdrag. After promising to urge the President of Turkey to bring his country into the war, Roosevelt declared that "if he were in the Turkish President's place he would demand such a price in planes, tanks and equipment that to grant the request would indefinitely postpone OVERLORD" When Churchill suggested that it might be possible to divert some forces and supplies from the Pacific theatre to the Eastern Mediterranean, Roosevelt declared that "it was absolutely impossible to withdraw any landing craft from that area. So important did Hopkins consider this that he wrote out a statement for the record in longhand. No landing craft were available for an attack on Rhodes, he wrote, and even if any were to become available, no decision had been taken as to where they might best be used. Moreover, no promise of an amphibious landing, "implied or otherwise" was to be made to the Turks.

These tensions between the British and the Americans were not new. Ever since Casablanca the Americans had disagreed with the British on the question of the feasibility of Turkey's entrance into the war. What was striking at Tehran was that Stalin now reversed the position his Foreign Minister had so strongly taken at the Moscow Conference and, instead of supporting the British on the question of Turkey, now sided with the Americans. In the intervening months the Soviets had made more progress in the field and perhaps had by now concluded that Turkish help was likely to be more trouble than it was worth.

This conclusion is borne out by Stalin's concern as to where the Turks would fight and who would fight alongside them and in particular whether Anglo-American forces would go into Bulgaria with the Turks. Indeed, Stalin asked this directly of Churchill and the President. Churchill responded in the affirmative. Using Roosevelt's line of argument; with Churchill, Marshal Stalin admonished Churchill that it was not wise to scatter British and the American forces. He suggested that it would be better to concentrate all efforts upon OVERLORD and to consider the other campaigns as diversionary. Stalin added that he had lost hope of Turkey entering the war and was now certain that it would not "in spite of all the pressure that might be exerted".[98]

Despite this new Soviet-American combination Churchill continued to pursue his Mediterranean and Balkan policies, but to no avail. Turkey's entry into the war would divert nine Bulgarian divisions and leave the Germans alone to fight in Yugoslavia and Greece. Britain, he assured Stalin, "had no ambitious interests in the Balkans but merely wanted to pin down the German Divisions there." In his difficult position, Churchill even hit upon the surprising tactic of playing on Soviet ambitions. If the Allies could agree on an ultimatum to Turkey he would personally point out to the Turks that their refusal to accept "would have very serious political and territorial consequences for Turkey particularly in regard to the future status of the Straits." It was actually Churchill, not Stalin, who threatened at Tehran to alter the status of the Straits after the war as reprisal against the Turks. Later he noted that such a large land mass as Russia "deserved" access to a warmwater port and suggested that this could be settled agreeably "as between friends."[99]

(Turkish historian Prof. Esmer in *Turkish Foreign Policy*, p. 162, suggests that at this time, "Russia could not dwell on the subject of Turkey's neutrality. What it could do was to lessen the aid being sent to Turkey, to prevent Turkey and the Westerners (Britain and the United States) from embarking upon the Balkans with large forces.")

The Second Cairo Conference (December 4–6, 1943)
Inönü confronts Roosevelt and Churchill

Churchill left Tehran in a state of utter exhaustion. In Cairo he met with President İsmet İnönü of Turkey; in vain he pressed again for Turkey's entry into the war – the only condition that could at that time justify Balkan operations.[100]

Cairo Conference results according to David Eisenhower

"During the autumn of 1943 Churchill had high hopes of bringing Turkey into the war and thereby attacking the Germans in force from the southwest. The Turks, however, were unwilling to move until the British and Americans guaranteed to furnish them with a massive amount of supplies and equipment. At Tehran Churchill talked Roosevelt and Stalin into inviting Turkish president

İsmet İnönü to confer with the Allies at Cairo. For three days, December 4 to 6, Churchill tried every argument to persuade İnönü to bring his country into the war but the price was too high. The Allies did not have the military resources that the Turks demanded, and without Turkish support Churchill realised an attempt against Rhodes and other Aegean islands had little chance of success. (Ehrman, *Grand Strategy*, V, pp. 194–95) [101]

Roosevelt's understanding of the Turkish position

At the final meeting of the three heads of government in Cairo, Secretary of State Hopkins urged Roosevelt, to meet Turkish President İnönü for a few minutes privately in a last attempt to urge him to be ready to go to war by February 15, 1944. Roosevelt waited until the appropriate moment and adjourned the meeting. He requested İnönü to remain in order to say good-bye. Roosevelt "expressed the hope that Turkey would join the United Nations actively to defeat the Axis by February 15th." İnönü responded, "I was willing to soften my requirements to enter the war but not to relinquish them." Roosevelt "agreed that everything had to be done to protect Turkey." Roosevelt also told İnönü that "he (Roosevelt) completely understood my (İnönü's) reluctance to bring Turkey into the war." Erkin reports that President İnönü took the occasion of this private meeting to thank Roosevelt "warmly for having occupied with so much grace and skill the role of intermediary and moderator between the opposing theses that separated the British and the Turks." Well he might have been thankful for Roosevelt had, by his lukewarm support of Eden and Churchill and his receptivity to the Turkish argument, given the Turks yet another reprieve. Menemencioğlu wrote that in the American President's company "the state of my soul had been touched by grace." To Churchill and Eden it was a grace that passed all understanding. [102]

Text of the communiqué of the Cairo Conference (December 6, 1943)

"Mr. Roosevelt, President of the United States of America, M. İsmet İnönü, President of the Turkish Republic, and Mr. Winston Churchill, Prime Minister of Great Britain, met in Cairo on December 4th, 5th and 6th, 1943. Mr. Anthony Eden, His Britannic Majesty's Principal Secretary of State for Foreign Affairs, M. Numan Menemencioğlu, Minister of Foreign Affairs of Turkey, and Mr. Harry L. Hopkins took part in their deliberations.

The participation in this conference of the Head of the Turkish State, in response to the cordial invitation addressed to him by the United States, British and Soviet Governments, bears striking testimony to the strength of the alliance which unites Great Britain and Turkey, and to the firm friendship existing between the Turkish Republic, the United States of America and the Soviet Union.

Presidents Roosevelt and İnönü and Prime Minister Churchill reviewed the general political situation and examined at length the policy to be followed, taking into account the joint and several interests of the three countries.

The study of all problems in a spirit of understanding and loyalty showed that the closest unity existed between the United States of America, Turkey and Great Britain in their attitude towards the world situation.

The conversations in Cairo have consequently been most useful and most fruitful for the future of the relations between the four countries there represented.

The identity of interest and of views of the American and British democracies, with those of the Soviet Union, and the traditional relations of friendship existing between these powers and Turkey, have been reaffirmed throughout the proceedings of the Cairo conference." [103]

The importance of the Cairo Conference from Turkey's viewpoint

For all its inconclusiveness the Second Cairo Conference is important in another respect. It marks the beginning of the end of the first phase, and the beginning of the second phase of Turkish wartime diplomacy. The first phase was designed, essentially, to meet a military threat from the Soviets as well as the Nazis; the second was an attempt to curb the political influence of Russia in Eastern Europe. The Second Cairo Conference marks the turning point in Turkish foreign policy from a wartime strategy designed to ward off military dangers to a policy directed toward the potential political conflicts during the final stages of the war and in the postwar world.

In Cairo İnönü had refused to assume any obligation and promised only to consult his colleagues in Ankara. After some weeks his answer had been received. It had been merely a repetition of an agreement in principle to enter the war – on condition that the Allies first make good Turkish deficiencies in all kinds of combat equipment and provide air support and transport. Their needs in all these respects the Turks reckoned to be very large. The continuation of the talks into February had not overcome Turkish fears and plans for an Allied military campaign based on Turkey lapsed.

Churchill and his colleagues had grieved over what they regarded as a brilliant lost chance to rout the Germans from the southeast. The American government had been sorry but the Joint Chiefs were also partly relieved at the passing of a possible extra diversionary demand upon combat resources. [105]

II. OVERLORD OPERATION VERSUS CHURCHILL'S PROPOSALS

American opposition (Introduction)

To Churchill the Balkans and east Mediterranean as an area of strategic interest – and the ancillary concept of Turkish entry into the war – was something of an obsession. It reappears again and again in his strategic appreciations, like a recurring decimal. To the US Chiefs of Staff, however, and particularly to Marshall, it was like a red rag to a bull; and whenever Churchill raised it, they charged. Churchill himself realised after a while – though it took him some time to do so – that this was a dangerous subject to bring up, and not conducive to achieving his general objective of sustaining Mediterranean operations but he seemed unable to desist. In one form or another – an attack on the Dodecanese, British use of Turkish air-bases, a landing in Greece, on the Dalmatian coast, in Trieste – it continued to occupy his thoughts, and consequently to raise dire suspicions in the minds of Marshall, Stimson and, more and more as time went by, of Roosevelt himself. The reassurances that Churchill felt bound to give, that he did not wish to see a major campaign in the Balkans, were simply not believed. Churchill's pertinacity, a virtue when confronted with Hitler or indeed Stalin, became a weakness in the long-drawn argument with the Americans over Grand Strategy, and ultimately eroded what influence it possessed with Marshall, and increasingly with Roosevelt.[106]

The Americans wanted Overlord to go ahead, as agreed, on or about May 1. They had not the slightest intention of becoming bogged down in Italy or the Balkans, let alone the Dodecanese or Turkey, merely to satisfy an imperial whim of the British as they saw it. Roosevelt was counting on Stalin's help in thwarting Churchill's ambitions. Roosevelt intended to offer himself to Stalin as an "honest broker" between East and West.[107]

General Marshall's opposition

For six days as the battleship Iowa had ploughed eastward the American Joint Chiefs of Staff had conferred in the admiral's cabin. They were an oddly assorted bunch. Admiral Ernest J. King, chief of the U.S. Navy, would be sixty-five a few days later; his gaze was riveted on the Pacific theatre of war. General Hap Arnold was a happy-go-lucky aviator, who spent much of the time pencilling in a daily diary. General Marshall, the top U.S. soldier, was stern, authoritarian and incorruptible. Whatever their internal disputes all were agreed on one thing: the need to defeat the British obstinacy about Overlord. The British, it seemed, wanted to back out both from Overlord and from the simultaneous landing by two divisions in southern France, a plan called Anvil. The British obviously had plans of their own – plans for operations in the Balkans, in the Greek islands, even in Norway. The Joint Chiefs had just received a discouraging message from the British refusing to place their heavy bomber squadrons under the American who would be appointed Supreme Commander for Overlord. That seemed to confirm that the British had got cold feet. Roosevelt's chief of staff, Admiral William D. Leahy, another of the Iowa's distinguished passengers, suggested that in that case the Americans should abandon Overlord completely.

But Marshall's fear as the nine-hundred-foot-long battleship headed steadily eastward was that it was the British who might abandon Overlord. His planners had forecast that the British would try to claim that an invasion in the Balkans would knock out Germany even before May 1. Marshall urged Roosevelt to soothe Churchill's ambitions "We have now over a million tons of supplies in England for Overlord. It would be going into reverse to undertake the Balkans, and prolong the war materially. . . . May I point out that commitments and preparations for Overlord at this time in order to undertake operations in a country with practically no communications." Just as Brooke had predicted, Marshall threatened "We could say that, if they propose to do that, we will pull out and go into the Pacific with all our forces." [108]

The Americans, were "divided and frustrated" when they arrived at Casablanca, plagued by too many alternatives, none of which appeared wholly acceptable. On the one hand, they favoured a continued troop build-up of American forces in the British Isles. On the other, they felt that it would be disadvantageous to keep great numbers of troops idle in the many months before the cross-Channel attack. Admiral King and General Arnold consequently were attracted to Churchill's plans regarding the Mediterrannean. General Marshall, however, vehemently resisted, afraid that the Prime Minister's recommended course of action would involve them all in "interminable operations" in the Mediterranean and, as a result, indefinitely delay the opening of the Second Front. Marshall reacted in a similar fashion to Churchill's stated desire to create the circumstances favourable for Turkish entry into the war. [109]

In Casablanca, Churchill spared no effort to convince the Americans that it was advisable to use Turkey as a base of operations and to build up Turkish defences in the Mediterranean. Here again he met with Marshall's strong opposition. [110]

Churchill's championship of operations in the eastern Mediterranean and (possibly) the Balkans, particularly the ill-fated Dodecanese campaign which poisoned Anglo-American relations in 1943, can certainly be seen as part and parcel of his general belief in the Mediterranean strategy, but that is not a sufficient explanation. More moderate champions of that strategy – for example General Brooke – saw that the North African campaign, followed by a sustained effort in Italy, met all the most valid arguments for the Mediterranean option and most of its requisites. It could be argued convincingly that sustained pressure in the western and central Mediterranean would draw German troops away from the Eastern Front and the potential front in north-western Europe. In so doing, the Italian campaign would contribute to the gradual erosion of Axis resources, and so facilitate a successful cross-Channel attack. Marshall was too fair-minded not to accept the validity of these arguments, at least in part. The capture of the Dodecanese islands, on the other hand, made far less obvious a contribution to Overlord, was much further removed from the main scene of action, and was necessarily linked to the entry of Turkey into the war, a project of dubious utility to the Allies. [111]

Another familiar problem – that of the authority of the Supreme Commander – had taken on an added complexity. The leading candidate for the job, Marshall, had become larger than life among the military commanders. Roosevelt had wanted him to control the whole European theatre including the Mediterranean. Churchill had rejected that because of the British political implications. He insisted that the commander be appointed only for Overlord. Roosevelt knew he would have to give in on this. He also saw that this restriction would make the post somewhat smaller – no longer big enough for Marshall. It would be beneath Marshall, he believed, to accept only part of a theatre. Thus it became likely that another general would have to get Overlord.

General Eisenhower's opposition

The Americans, Eisenhower included, were not carried away either by the forecasts of momentous gains which might flow from the eastward ventures which Churchill proposed, or by his estimates of how little extra combat forces and shipping would be needed for them. Churchill, then and later, thought this the loss of a chance to earn great war prizes at small cost and the American unwillingness – especially in regard to the Aegean Islands – harsh, and unappreciative of the great value of the Italian operations which he, Churchill, had sponsored. About this Churchill later allowed himself one of his very few bitter remarks, "The American staff had enforced their view; the price had now to be paid by the British." [113]

Eisenhower had particularly disagreed with the British Mediterranean strategy.[114]

Churchill's defence of his Balkan policy:
"To forestall the Russians in Central Europe"

Equally important was the fact that the military and strategic decisions forced on Churchill by Roosevelt and Stalin in 1943 meant that there would be no Anglo-American military presence in Eastern Europe. Therefore there would be no obstacle to complete Soviet dominance in that region in 1944–45, or in the post-war world. Furthermore, the Americans resolutely refused to join with the British in their attempts to limit Soviet influence by diplomatic means and by written agreements. Roosevelt and Hull did not wish to offend Stalin by showing distrust and attempting to fetter Soviet policy, nor did they wish to put US power at the service of real or fancied British interests, as Roosevelt put it, especially if it involved "Wasting men and material in the Balkan mountains". Marshall was expressing the same thought when he said, *apropos* of Aegean operations, that if he had his way not one US soldier "should die for Rhodes". Roosevelt in fact was not worried about Russia becoming stronger in Europe. Churchill increasingly was, and it strengthened his belief in the need for such operations as the Dodecanese, or later on, the strengthening of the Italian campaign so as to make it possible for the Allies to invade central-eastern Europe through the so-called "Ljublajana Gap" or via amphibious landings in the Adriatic. Though Churchill talked of "joining hands with the Russians" in the Balkans, or the Dardanelles and Black Sea, it was less the joining of hands than "hands off Greece or Yugoslavia" that was in his mind. By September 1944, at the Second Quebec Conference, he was openly saying not only to his own chiefs of staff, but also to the Americans, "we must forestall the Russians in Central

Europe . . . it is important we retain a stake in Central and Eastern Europe, and do not allow everything to pass into Soviet hands . . . a landing in Istria or Trieste would have political as well as military advantages, in view of the Russian advance in the Balkans . . . I prefer to get into Vienna before the Russians do" and much more in this vein. At times he thought he was converting Roosevelt and the Americans to this view. He was quite wrong. [115]

The deterioration of the Churchill-Roosevelt relationship

For Churchill, lying ill in Morocco after Tehran, a more dismal reflection was the extent to which his relationship with Roosevelt had deteriorated. It would be an exaggeration to say that Roosevelt had cold-shouldered him entirely at Cairo and Tehran, but he had certainly snubbed the British leader on a number of occasions. He had so arranged matters that there could be no confidential talks with Churchill and the British Chiefs of Staff before the meetings with Chiang Kai-shek and Stalin. He had refused to meet Churchill privately until he had two meetings with the Soviet leader. At Tehran he had chosen to stay at the Soviet Embassy rather than at the British Embassy: and he had publicly needled and teased Churchill in front of Stalin. Churchill had not relished any of this. It seemed a bad omen for the future. He may or may not have realised that Roosevelt had good reasons – or reasons that seemed good to him – for these actions, reasons which had nothing to do with his personal feeling towards Churchill. Roosevelt had, after all, never met Chiang Kai-shek or Stalin before, and he wanted to get to know them, if possible to win their trust and friendship. He expected to work with both leaders after the war, and their cooperation he thought would be necessary to build the new world order he envisaged. Churchill he knew already – only too well. Roosevelt's advisers had been warning him for some time that after the war Russia would be the strongest power in Europe, while Britain would be exhausted and British power would be declining. A world statesman has to be cold-blooded about these things. Whatever sacrifices Britain had made for the common cause, one had to deal with facts as they were. Moreover, the British were heavily dependent on US aid and supplies. The US contribution to the global war effort already exceeded the British contribution in most ways, and once Overlord was launched, US ground forces in Europe would increasingly outnumber British forces. Quite simply at this point in the war it was more expedient to slight Churchill than to thwart Stalin. But it was also true that Roosevelt's attitude to Churchill had changed. He had been angered and wearied by the revival of the Overlord/Mediterranean controversy and the arguments over the Dodecanese. Possibly, also, he felt a twinge or two of regret that it had been thought necessary to leave the British forces to their fate in that area. One never likes to be made to feel guilty, and Roosevelt was not immune to the common human reaction, which is to feel resentment towards the person who makes you feel guilty. Churchill's tactless reminder that US ground forces contribution to European (i.e. Mediterranean) operations had so far been pretty small in relation on US resources had also stung. Roosevelt made a point of having the disparity in the global contribution of the two countries spelt out publicly when they met again at Cairo and Tehran.

It is noticeable how from this time forward Roosevelt gave increasingly free rein to suspicions of British policy – suspicions which would always have been latent the mind of an American liberal democrat in regard to British Imperial policy and the British pursuit of power politics as Roosevelt saw it. Moreover, he was surrounded by men who in different ways fed these suspicions – Leahy, his Chief of Staff and Chairman of the US Joint Chiefs, Admiral King, Hull, Stimson, and in his more dispassionate way, Marshall. Harry Hopkins, who, perhaps surprisingly, provided something of a counterweight to these men, was soon to be incapacitated by illness and lose his influence with the President. Whatever the reasons, it is impossible to read the US accounts of Roosevelt's discussions with his chiefs of staff on his way to the Cairo Conference, or his son's account of their conversations during the conference, without being struck by the extent to which Roosevelt harboured dire suspicions of British policy and the wildness of some, though not all, of these suspicions. Marshall and Stimson and the others had done their work only too well.[116]

Roosevelt's opinions

In Tehran Roosevelt met with his staff. The fate of Overlord was in the balance. If the British continued to insist on self-serving military digressions in the Mediterranean, the main chance in Europe might be lost. Churchill would be pained by later American descriptions of his role. Perhaps he had forgotten, or been too ill to recall. He would write in his memoirs, "It has become a legend in America that I strove to prevent . . . Overlord, and that I tried vainly to lure the Allies into some mass invasion of the Balkans, or a large-scale camping in the Eastern Mediterranean, which would effectively kill it." Of course, the key words in this *apologia* were "mass" and "large-scale". But even the small operations that he had asked for would have used up the tank landing craft needed to make Overlord a success. Admiral Leaky saw this clearly. "We can do either of two things", he said. "Either undertake Overlord, or go after Italy and Rhodes." Roosevelt was still deeply suspicious of British motives at the eastern end of the Mediterranean. He observed, "We've got to realise that the British look upon the Mediterranean as an area under British domination." And in private, he told his son Elliott: "Trouble is, the Prime Minister is thinking too much of the post-war, and where England will be. He's scared of letting the Russians get too strong. May be the Russians will get strong in Europe. Whether that's bad depends on a whole lot of factors".[117]

Roosevelt's further statements to his son concerning British intentions after the war

"Churchill admitted, in that moment, that he knew the peace could only be won according to precepts which the United States of America would lay down. And in saying what he did, he was acknowledging that British colonial policy would be a dead duck, and British attempts to dominate world trade would be a dead duck and British ambitions to play off the U.S.S.R. against the U.S.A. would be a dead duck.

Or would have been, if Father had lived." [118]

"You see, what the British have done, down through the centuries, historically, is the same thing. They've chosen their allies wisely and well. They've always been able to come out on top, with the same reactionary grip on the peoples of the world and the markets of the world, through every war they've ever been in."

"Yes."

"This time, we're Britain's ally. And it's right we should be. But . . . first at Argentina, later in Washington, now here at Casablanca . . . I've tried to make it clear to Winston and the others that while we're their allies, and in it to victory by their side, they must never get the idea that we're in it just to help them hang on to the archaic, medieval Empire ideas."

"I know what you mean," I said slowly. "I think they got the idea".

"I hope they did. I hope they realise they're not senior partners; that we're not going to sit by, after we've won, and watch their system stultify the growth to every country in Asia and half the countries in Europe to boot . . .

Great Britain signed the Atlantic Charter. I hope they realise the United States government means to make them live up to it." [119]

"Trouble is, the P.M. is thinking too much of the post-war, and where England will be. He's scared of letting the Russians get too strong."

"Maybe the Russians will get strong in Europe. Whether that's bad depends on a whole lot of factors."

"The one thing I'm sure of is this: if the way to save American lives, the way to win as short a war as possible, is from the west and from the west alone, without wasting landing-craft and men and materiel in the Balkan mountains, and our chiefs are convinced it is, then that's that!"

He smiled, but grimly. "I see no reason for putting the lives of American soldiers in jeopardy in order to protect real or fancied British interest on the European continent. We're at war, and our job is to win it as fast as possible, and without adventures. I think – I hope – that he's learned we mean that, once, finally! and for all." He closed his eyes again, and there was silence except for the ticking of a clock which reminded me of the time.[120]

I promptly headed for the White House, and Father's room, hoping to catch him before he started his day's work. He waved me to a chair; he was scowling over some official dispatches; the morning newspapers had been irritably crumpled on he floor. For some minutes he read, exclaiming every now and then, muttering his dissatisfaction. When he looked up my eyebrows were raised in curiosity.

"Greece," he said. "British troops. Fighting against the guerrillas who fought the Nazis for the last four years." He made no attempt to conceal his anger. I had seen only a vague and obviously incomplete story in one of the Washington papers: the complete story would not be printed for some weeks to come. "How the British can dare such a thing!" Father cried. "The lengths to which they will go to hang on to the past!" Beside him, his coffee was brewing: he glanced at it, noted that it was ready, and poured himself a cup, looking over to me with an invitation to join him. I've got an extra cup here," he said.

"Fine!"

"I wouldn't be surprised," he went on, "if Winston had simply made it clear he was backing the Greek Royalists. That would be only in character, but killing Greek guerrillas! Using British colliers for such a job!"

"Probably using American Lend-Lease equipment to do it, too," I reminded him.

"I'll find out about that" Father said. And then, "Though I don't suppose there's too much I can do about it."

"A public statement?"

"Condemning the British?" He shook his head. "Not now. Time enough to raise it when I see Winston in February. And anyway . . ." and his scowl disappeared.[121]

Roosevelt's ideas about Turkey as told to his son Elliott in Cairo

At that time Steinhardt was our Ambassador to Turkey, and there had been considerable speculation about Turkey's entry into the war on the side of the Allies. I asked Father if any decision had been taken yet.

"No final decision has been agreed on," he said. "But my mind is made up."

Harry Hopkins chuckled. You could tell that this subject was one on which they had talked before, and that there was disagreement on the final decision from some other, third, party. Nor was it difficult to guess that the third party was the P.M.

"Is your decision on Turkey top-secret around here, Pop?"

He laughed. "I've told about everybody, I guess," he said. "Turkey'll come in the war on our side only in the event she's given a lot of Lend-Lease equipment. What does she want it for? Just so she can be strong in the postwar world? Winston thinks she should be given the equipment and come in to the fight. Why? When Lend-Lease equipment to Turkey means less equipment for the invasion of Europe, why does he think so?"

"Maybe Turkey on our side would strengthen his argument to fight Hitler from the Mediterranean," I guessed.

"It could be," said Father sarcastically.[122]

And in the morning, when I saw him again, he told me that the question of Turkey's entry into the war had been finally decided upon. Against.

"In a sense, I guess, it was Winston's last effort to force an allied attack from the south, from the Mediterranean," he said.

I asked him whether Russia had taken any position, and he smiled.

"They agreed with me. No Lend-Lease to Turkey said Stalin, in effect, if it means any delay on the western front. Winston and I are going to draw up some sort of statement to save Turkey's face this afternoon. After all, it's been in the newspaper for nearly a month now that she was going to declare war against Germany on our side."

I wagged my head, thinking about how well Stalin and Father had got along, thinking about the identity of interests that we apparently had. And when I said something to that effect:

"The biggest thing" Father commented, "was in making clear to Stalin that the United States and Great Britain were not allied in one common bloc against the Soviet Union. I think we've got rid of that idea, once and for all. I hope so. The one thing that could upset the applecart, after the war, is if the world is divided again, Russia against England and us. That's our big job now, and it'll be our big job tomorrow, too; making sure that we continue to act as referee, as intermediary between Russia and England." [123]

At lunch, with Churchill and Harry Hopkins as Father's only guests, the talk was of the forthcoming communiqué covering İnönü's visit. The language of the communiqué had to be delicately arrived at, in view of the continued hostility between Turkey and the Soviet Union, especially inasmuch as Churchill had been hoping Turkey would become a fighting ally in the war. İnönü himself came in after we had left the lunch table, and shortly thereafter the others were joined by Vinogradov, the Soviet Ambassador to Turkey, representing Stalin. The communiqué to be drafted had to make clear that the Turkish government was in agreement with those of the Soviet Union, Great Britain, and the United States, despite the fact that Turkey would not be entering the war as had been forecast by the most perspicacious journalists. This was what led to words like: "the firm friendship existing between the Turkish Republic, the United States of America, and the Soviet Union," and "the strength of the alliance which united Great Britain and Turkey." [124]

Stalin's attitude concerning Overlord and the Balkans

In Tehran, for the start of Overlord, Stalin was not prepared to tolerate any delay beyond May 1944. He feared further backsliding by the British and he probably wanted to discourage them from encroaching into the Balkans. As they parted, Stalin shot a look across the conference table at Churchill and hurled a challenge: "I wish to pose a very direct question. Do the Prime Minister and the British staff really believe in Overlord?" Churchill equivocated but finally said he did.

Roosevelt was unimpressed by Churchill on this occasion. The British Prime minister seemed peevish, unwell, and prejudiced. "Marshall," Roosevelt commented to his son, "has got to the point where he just looks at the Prime

Minister as though he can't believe his ears. If there's one American general Winston can't abide, it's General Marshall. And needless to say it's because Marshall's right." Like a distracted eagle Churchill seemed to be swooping about the eastern end of the Mediterranean, looking for something to catch, first settling on the Dodecanase Islands, then Rhodes and finally concentrating his attention on Turkey – he wanted to get Turkey into the war on the Allied side, to serve as the air base for a British thrust against the Germans. Roosevelt would later relate to Secretary of War Henry Stimson how he had headed off Churchill time after time. "I fought hard for Overlord." he said. "With Stalin's help I finally won out."

For his part Churchill was wounded by Roosevelt's unabashed conniving with Stalin. When he heard that the two men had conferred, privately, he was apprehensive lest Roosevelt might be agitating against him. So he bearded the Soviet dictator in private and tried to reassure him. Stalin warned Churchill that the survival of the Soviet Union depended on Overlord. "If there are no operations in May 1944, then the Red Army will think that there will be no operations at all that year." His soldiers were already war weary. They would not hold on if Overlord were delayed. Perhaps he was deliberately exaggerating, but the prospect of Stalin coming to terms with Hitler was not a cheering one for the Western Powers.[125]

Conclusion

Later the Turkish leaders came to understand why the Russians had been so cool toward Turkey entering the war armed and supported by the Anglo-Americans. The Soviet Union preferred to join in an agreement of "mutual assistance", which the Turks feared would mean Soviet forces on Turkish soil from which they might never leave. The Turks also could never get the Allies to commit themselves to any kind of a Balkan compaign because all their resources were soon to be committed to OVERLORD. Consequently, Turkey did not immediately . . . declare war against Germany and only severed diplomatic relations on August 2, 1944, but later declared war in March, 1945.

The Turks were wise to avoid joining the Allied side without guarantees of adequate aid from either the British or the Americans. In the talks with the Turks, Roosevelt had appeared aloof, not wholly committed to the Turkish cause. Never would he and the Joint Chiefs of Staff disperse American military power through a landing on the shores of Turkey; their goal was OVERLORD. Had an Anglo-American force entered Turkey, Stalin would have been given an excuse to dispatch Soviet troops into Turkey in pursuit of German soldiers. He really did not care for an Allied military force landing in that part of Europe. For his part, Churchill had few resources to spare for the Turks. He was trying to trick them into war, so eager was he to get any operation under way in the eastern Mediterranean. He had been dreaming about Turkey entering the war and now the dream had ended.[126]

NOTES

[1] Stanford J. Shaw and Ezel Kural Shaw, *History of the Ottoman Empire and Modern Turkey* London, 1976, pp. 396–397

[2] Shaw and Shaw, ibid., p. 397–398

[3] ibid., p. 398

[4] ibid., p. 399

[5] Sevket Süreyya Ademir, *The Second Man* (Ikinci Adam), Remzi Kitabevi, Ankara, 1979, Vol. II, pp. 194–195

[6] Edward Weisband, *Turkish Foreign Policy 1943–1945, Small State Diplomacy and Great Power Politics*, Princeton, 1964, p. 43

[7] Winston D. Churchill, *The Second World War* (Vols. II, III, IV and V), Cassel and Co., 1952, Vol. II, p. 420

[8] op. cit., p. 558

[9] Department of State Publication, *Foreign Relations of the United States, Diplomatic Papers – The Conferences at Cairo and Tehran 1943*, Washington, 1961, pp. 692–693

[10] *Soviet Foreign Policy 1917–1980.* Vol I. 1917–1945, Progress Publishers, Moscow, 1981, pp. 378–379

[11] op. cit., pp. 397–398

[12] Joseph P. Lash, *Roosevelt and Churchill (1939–1941) The Partnership that Saved the World*, New York, 1970, p.79

[13] Churchill, ibid., Vol II. p.154

[14] Steven Merritt Miner, *Between Churchill and Stalin*, The University of North Carolina Press, 1998, pp. 16–17

[15] op cit., pp. 37–38

[16] Churchill, ibid., Vol. III, pp. 32–33

[17] op. cit.,Vol. II, p. 474

[18] op. cit.,Vol. II, p. 476

[19] op. cit., Vol. II, p. 478

[20] op. cit., Vol. II, p. 483

[21] op. cit., Vol. II, p. 553

[22] op. cit., Vol. III, pp. 16–17

[23] op. cit., Vol. III, pp. 85–86

[24] op. cit., Vol. III, p. 49

[25] op. cit., Vol. III, pp. 412–413

[26] op. cit., Vol. III, p. 767

[27] op. cit., Vol. III, pp. 482–484

[28] op. cit., Vol. III, pp. 760–761

[29] op. cit., Vol. IV, p. 768

[30] op. cit., Vol. IV, p. 788

[31] op. cit., Vol. IV, p. 628

[32] op. cit., Vol. IV, p. 632–633

[33] op. cit., Vol. IV, p. 634

[34] op. cit., Vol. IV, p. 641

[35] op. cit., Vol. V, p. 437

[36] op. cit., Vol. V, p. 114

[37] op. cit., Vol. IV, p. 623

[38] op. cit., Vol. V, p. 369

[39] op. cit., Vol. V, p. 367

[40] Lash, ibid., p. 310

[41] H. L. Trefousse, *Germany and American Neutrality – 1939–1941*, Octagon Books, New York, 1969, pp. 55–56

[42] Amos Perlmutten, *FDR and Stalin – A Not So Great Alliance 1943–1945*, University of Missouri Press, 1993, p. 242

[43] The Conferences at Cairo and Tehran, p. 43

[44] op. cit., p. 121

[45] op. cit., pp. 123–124

[46] op. cit., p. 192

[47] op. cit., p. 698

[48] Weisband, ibid, p. 44–46

[49] op. cit., pp. 319–321

[50] op. cit., pp. 325–328

[51] op. cit., pp. 288–291

[52] op. cit., pp. 288–291

[53] op. cit., p. 298

[54] op. cit., pp. 299–301

[55] op. cit., pp. 315–318

[56] Miner, ibid., pp. 63–69

[57] op. cit., p. 71

[58] op. cit., p. 95

[59] op. cit., p. 98

[60] op. cit., p. 99

[61] op. cit., p. 100

[62] Churchill, ibid., Vol. V, p. 336

[63] *The Conferences at Cairo and Tehran*, pp. 846–848

[64] Churchill, ibid., Vol. V, p. 582

[65] *The Conferences at Cairo and Tehran*, pp. 199–200

[66] Churchill, ibid., Vol. IV, pp. 635–636

[67] *The Conferences at Cairo and Tehran*, pp. 164–167

[68] op. cit., pp.180–181

[69] Weisband. ibid., pp. 123–124

[70] op. cit., pp. 124–125

[71] op. cit., pp. 126–128

[72] op. cit., pp. 128–129

[73] op. cit., p. 129

[74] op. cit., p. 132

[75] Churchill, ibid., Vol. IV, p. 627

[76] Weisband, ibid., p. 133

[77] op. cit., pp. 133–134

[78] op. cit., p. 135

[79] op. cit., p. 139

[80] op. cit., p. 131

[81] op. cit., pp. 131–132

[82] op cit., pp. 141–142

[83] op. cit., pp. 143–144

[84] op. cit., p. 145

[85] op. cit., p. 148

[86] op. cit., pp. 149–151

[87] op. cit., pp. 151–153

[88] op. cit., pp. 161–162

[89] op. cit., pp. 162–165

[90] op. cit., pp. 165–166

[91] *The Conferences at Cairo and Tehran*, p. 199

[92] Weisband, ibid., p. 167

[93] op. cit., pp. 170–171

[94] op. cit., p. 173

[95] op. cit., pp. 182–184

[96] op. cit., pp. 185–186

[97] op. cit., pp. 186–190

[98] op. cit., pp. 194–197

[99] op. cit., pp. 198–199

[100] W. Averell Harriman and Elie Abel, *Special Envoy to Churchill and Stalin (1941–46)*, Random House, New York, 1975, p. 89

[101] *The Papers of David Eisenhower – The War Years* (Vol. VIII), The John Hopkins Press, 1970, p. 1615

[102] Weisband., ibid., pp. 213–214

[103] *The Conferences at Cairo and Tehran*, pp. 831–832

[104] Weisband, ibid., pp. 214–215

[105] Herbert Feis, *Churchill, Roosevelt, Stalin – The War They Waged and the Peace They Sought*, Princeton, 1957, p. 304

[106] Keith Sainsbury, *Churchill and Roosevelt at War (The War They Fought and the Peace They Hoped to Make)*, New York, p. 36

[107] David Irving, *The War Between The Generals*, Penguin Books, 1981, p. 17

[108] op. cit., pp. 17–18

[109] Weisband, p. 122

[110] op. cit., p. 123

[111] Sainsbury, ibid., p. 38

[112] Irving, ibid., p. 21

[113] Feis, ibid., p. 153

[114] Irving, ibid., p. 22

[115] Sainsbury, ibid., pp. 42–43

[116] op. cit., pp. 50–51

[117] Irving, pp. 22–23

[118] Elliott Roosevelt, *As He Saw It*, Duel, Sloan and Pearce, New York, 1946, p. 42

[119] op. cit., pp. 121–122

[120] op. cit., pp. 185–86

[121] op. cit., pp. 222–223

[122] op. cit., pp. 148–149

[123] op. cit., pp. 206–207

[124] op. cit., p. 208

[125] Irving, ibid., pp. 23–24

[126] Keith Eubank, *Summit At Tehran*, Morrow and Co. Inc., New York, 1985, pp. 397–398

BIBLIOGRAPHY (*) AND FURTHER READING

Unpublished Archive Documents

GREAT BRITAIN:

Public Records Office, Foreign Office Correspondence: F.O. 371: Turkey.
British Cabinet Documents:
  War Cabinet Conclusions and Confidential Annexes; CAB/65. 'W.M.' series. 1939–
  1945. Vols. 1–10, 18, 19, 21–23, 26, 29, 31, 40, 42, 45, 47.
  War Cabinet Memoranda: CAB/66. 'W.P.' series. 1943–1945. Vols. 34, 41, 48, 49, 51.
Prime Ministry Documents:
  Operational Papers, PREM. 3: Vol. 447. 5A; Cairo conversations and negotiations for
  Turkish entry into war.

Published Archive Documents

GREAT BRITAIN:

Documents on British Foreign Policy 1919–1939. E.L. Woodward and Rohan Butler (eds.)

GERMANY:

Documents on German Foreign Policy (D.G.F.P.) Series D.
  Vol. VI The Last Months of Peace. March–August 1939.
  Vol. VII The Last Days of Peace. August 9–September 3, 1959.
  Vol. IX The War Years. March 18, June 22, 1940.
  Vol. X The War Years. June 23–August 31, 1940.
  Vol. XII The War Years. February 1–June 22, 1941.
  Vol. XIII The War Years. June 23–December 11, 1941.

USA:

Department of State. Foreign Relations of the United States. (U.S.F.R.)
  The Conferences at Washington 1941–1942 and Casablanca, 1943.
  (*) *Foreign Relations of the United States: Conferences at Cairo and Tehran 1941*
  Foreign Relations of the United States: Diplomatic Papers, 1944, Vol. V.
  Foreign Relations of the United States: Conferences at Malta and Yalta, 1945.
  *Foreign Relations of the United States: Diplomatic Papers, 1945, The Conference of Berlin (The
    Potsdam Conference)* Vol. I and II.
  Foreign Relations of the United States: Diplomatic Papers, 1945, Vol. VIII.
  Foreign Relations of the United States: Diplomatic Papers, 1946, Vol. VII.
Department of State, *Nazi-Soviet Relations 1939–1940: Documents from the Archives of the
  German Foreign Office,* Raymond S. Sontag and James Stuart Beddie (eds.)
(*) *The Papers of David Eisenhower – The War Years (Vol. VIII).* The John Hopkins Press, 1970.

(*) *Special Envoy to Churchill and Stalin (1941–46)* by W. Averell Harriman and Elie Abel. Random House, New York, 1975.

THE SOVIET UNION:

Documents Secrets des Affaires Etragéres d' Allemagne. La Politique Allemande (1941–1943). Traduits de Russe par Madelaine et Michel Eristov.

(*) *Soviet Foreign Policy 1917–1980. Vol. 1: 1917–1945.* (Under the editorship of A.A. Gromyko and B.N. Ponomarev). Progress Publishers – Moscow, English Translation 1981.

Official Publications

GREAT BRITAIN:

Foreign Office. *British and Foreign State Papers.* Treaty of Mutual Assistance between His Majesty in respect of the United Kingdom, the President of the French Republic, and the President of the Turkish Republic, Ankara, October 19, 1939, Cmd. 6165, Treaty Series No. 4, House of Commons Sessional Papers, Vol. XII London. Her Majesty's Stationery Office 1940.

Royal Institute of International Affairs. Foreign Research and Press Service: *Review of the Foreign Press.* Ser. B. European Neutrals and the Near East. (Allied Governments, European Neutrals – Smaller European Enemies – and the Near East). 4 October, 1939-27 June, 1943. After 1943 Ser. N. compiled by Foreign Office Research Department: The Near and Middle East. 30 June, 1943–27 June, 1945.

House of Commons. *The Parliamentary Debates* (official reports) Fifth Series 1942–1945.

History of the Second World War. *Grand Strategy.* J.R.M. Butler. Vol.11, September 1939–June 1941. HMSO. London 1957.

History of the Second World War. *Economic Blockade.* W.N. Medlicott. Vols. I and II. HMSO. London 1952–1959.

History of the Second World War. *The War at Sea.* S.W. Roskill, Vol. III, Part I. HMSO. London 1960.

History of the Second World War. *British Foreign Policy in the Second World War.* Sir L. Woodward, Vol. IV. HMSO. London 1975. Vol. V. HMSO. London 1976.

Books and Articles

Al-Quzzaz, Ayad. "The Iraqi-British War of 1941. A Review Article" in *International Journal of Middle East Studies.* Vol. 7, 1976, p.591.

(*) Aydemir, Sevket Süreyya. *Ikinci Adam [The Second Man]* Vol. I and II. Istanbul, Remizi Kitabevi, 1976.

Barker, Elizabeth. *British Policy in South-East Europe in the Second World War.* Macmillan Press, London 1976.

Bryant, Arthur. *The Turn of the Tide 1939–1943. A Study Based on the Diaries and Autobiographical Notes of Field Marshall the Viscount Alanbrooke.* Collins, London 1957.

(*) Churchill, Winston S. *The Second World War.* Vol. III: *The Grand Alliance.* Cassel and Co. 1951. Vol. V. *Closing the Ring.* Cassel and Co. 1952. Vol VI. *Triumph and Tragedy.* Cassel and Co. 1954.

Van Creveld, Martin L. *Hitler's Strategy 1940–1941. The Balkan Clue.* Cambridge University Press, London 1973.

Eden, Anthony. *The Eden Memoirs: The Reckoning.* Cassel, London 1965.

(*) Eubank, Keith. *Summit at Tehran.* William Morrow and Co. Inc, New York 1985.

(*) Feis, Herbert. *Churchill, Roosevelt, Stalin The War They Waged and the Peace They Sought.* Princeton University Press, Princeton 1957.

Gafenncu, Grigore. *The Last Days of Europe. A Diplomatic Journey in 1939.* Frederick Muller Ltd., London 1947.

Higgins, Trumbull. *Winston Churchill and the Second Front 1940–1942.* Oxford University Press, New York 1957.

Hodge Vere, Edward. *Turkish Foreign Policy 1918–1948.* Ambilly Annemasse 1950.

Hugessen, Knatchbull. *Diplomat in Peace and War.* Murray, London 1949.

Hull, Cordell. *The Memoirs of Cordell Hull,* Vol. II. The Macmilian Co., New York 1948.

Irving, David (ed.) and Watt, Donald Cameron. *Breach of Security.* William Kinber, London 1968.

Irving, David. *Hitler's War.*

(*) Irving, David. *The War Between the Generals.* Penguin Books, 1981

Kirk, George. "The U.S.S.R and the Middle East in 1939–1945; Turkey" in *Survey of International Relations. The Middle East in the War, 1939–1946,* p. 443. London, Oxford University Press, 1952.

Koliopoulos, John S. *Greece and the British Connection, 1935–1941.* Oxford University Press, Oxford 1977.

Kuniholm, Bruce T.R. *The Origins of the Cold War in the Near East. Great Power Conflict and Diplomacy in Iran, Turkey and Greece.* Princeton University Press, Princeton, New Jersey 1980.

Langer, William and Geleason, Evertt S. *The Undeclared War.* Peter Smith, Gloucester, Mass. 1968.

(*) Lash, Joseph. P. *Roosevelt and Churchill (1939–1941)–The Partnership that Saved the West.* W.W. Nonon and Company Inc., New York 1970.

Loewenheim, Francis L. Langley, Horold, D. and Jonas, Manfred (eds.) *Roosevelt and Churchill, Their Secret Wartime Correspondence.* Saturday Review Press, E. P. Dutton and Co. Inc, New York 1975.

Massigli, René. *La Turquie devant la guerre: mission a Ankara 1939–40.* Librairie Plon, Paris 1964.

(*) Miner, Steven Merritt. *Between Churchill and Stalin.* The University of North Carolina Press, 1988.

Moyzisch, L.C. *Operation Cicero.* Constantine Fitzgibbon and Hejnrich Fraenkel (trans.). Wintage, London 1950.

(*) Nadeau, Rerny. *Stalin, Churchill and Roosevelt Divide Europe.* Praeger Press, 1990.

Von Papen, Franz. *Memoirs.* Andrew Dueutsch Limited, London 1952.

Petrov, Vladimir. *June 22, 1941, Soviet Historians and the German Invasion.* University of South Carolina Press, Columbia, S.C. 1968.

(*) Perimutten, Amos. *FDR and Stalin – A Not So Great Alliance – 1943–45.* University of Missouri Press, 1993.

Phillips, Ernest. *Hitler's Last Hope: A Factual Survey of the Middle-Eastern War Zone and Turkey's Vital Strategic Position with A Special Chapter on Turkey's Military Strength* by Noel Barber. W.H.Allen and Co., London 1942.

(*) Roosevelt, Elliot. *As He Saw It.* Duell, Sloan and Pearce, New York 1946.

Sadak, Necmettin. "Turkey Faces the Soviets" in *Foreign Affairs,* Vol. 27, 1948–1949, p. 449.

(*) Sainsbury, Keith. *Churchill and Roosevelt At War (The War They Fought and The Peace They Hoped to Make).* New York University Press.

(*) Shaw, Stanford J. and Shaw, Ezel Kural. *History of the Ottoman Empire and Modern Turkey* Vol. I, Vol. II. Cambridge University Press, 1976.

Taylor, A.J.P. *The Origins of the Second World War.* Hamish Hamilton, London 1961.

Truman, Harry S. *Memoirs of Harry S. Truman.* Vol. I, *Years of Decisions,* Vol. II, *Years of Trial and Hope,* Doubleday and Co., New York 1956.

(*) Weisband, Edward. *Turkish Foreign Policy 1943–1945 Small State Diplomacy and Great Power Politics.* Princeton University Press, Princeton 1964.

Wiskemann, Elizabeth. *Undeclared War.* Constable and Co., London 1949.

Xydis, Stephen G. "New Light on the Big Three Crisis over Turkey" in *Middle East Journal,* Vol. XIV, 1960, p. 420.

Zhivkova, Ludmila. *Anglo-Turkish Relations 1933–1939.* Secker and Warburg, London 1976.

Conference Paper 4

Complementary Statement by Turkey

Why it should not have been included in the Report of May 1997

I. MISPLACEMENT OF THE EDITORS OF THE REPORT

The inclusion of Turkey as a 'neutral' European country during World War II along with Sweden, Switzerland, Spain and Portugal in the same category, in Mr. Eizenstat's report of May 1997, is a misplacement for many reasons explained below:

1. This misplacement is partially admitted even by Mr William Z. Slany himself in his report of May 7, 1997 from the onset in the Preface of the said report whereby the justification of this generalisation is stated in a footnote:

> "Technically, only Switzerland and Sweden were 'neutral' countries during the War according to generally-accepted definitions of neutrality. Spain, Portugal, Turkey and Argentina were 'non-belligerent' but not neutral. However, throughout the report (as well as in the Foreword and Summary), the neutral and non-belligerent countries are, for the sake of simplicity, referred to as 'neutrals' when mention of them is made collectively." (Report of May 1997, Preface, p. xiii, footnote, shown with an asterisk at the bottom of the page.)

Turkey cannot accept such a superfluous categorisation for many reasons.

2. Turkey was in a very different position during the course of World War II compared with the other above-mentioned four European countries as regards its relations with Nazi Germany and also with the allied Powers. Turkey had signed an Alliance Pact with England and France on October 19, 1939, right after the start of World War II, when the U.S.A was trying to keep itself out of the war until December 7, 1941.

The other differences may be explained from several historical facts such as:
   a. Turkey stopped the transportation of its chrome export to Germany on April 21, 1944; consecutively cut its diplomatic and economic relations completely with Nazi Germany on August 2, 1944 by a resolution of the Turkish Parliament and the German Ambassador Franz von Papen left Turkey on August 6, 1944; when the 3000 German citizens were asked to leave Turkey within ten days as a result of this Parliamentarian resolution, only the Germans with Jewish origin and also those who were not Nazis were allowed to stay indefinitely in Turkey.
   b. Turkey declared war on Nazi Germany and Japan on February 22, 1945 by a resolution of the Turkish Parliament and also decided to adhere to the

"United Nations Declaration" of January 1, 1942, by the same parliamentarian resolution.

The other four European countries did not have an Alliance Pact with
England and France; never declared war on Nazi Germany; and
Switzerland was even continuing its economic relations with Nazi
Germany at the end of World War II, as stated in the said report:

". . . The Swiss government explained to the press and its missions
abroad that the German-Swiss agreement of April 1945 provided for purchases other than war purchases . . ." (Report of May 1997, p. 35)

c. Whereas Turkey, as a result of its declaration of war on Germany, was invited to the San Francisco Conference which opened on April 25, 1945 and
later became a founding member of the United Nations on October 24,
1945,
– Switzerland is still not a member of the U.N.,
– Sweden was admitted to the U.N. on November 19, 1946,
– Spain, Portugal and Ireland could eventually be admitted to the U.N.
only on December 14, 1955. (It is also noteworthy that Ireland, which
may be considered a neutral or a non-belligerent European country
during World War II, is never cited in the report of May 7, 1997.)

3. Among the three "non-belligerent" European countries, Turkey held its first
democratic general elections on July 21, 1946, right after World War II.
– Portugal, which was ruled under a fascist constitution adopted in 1933 and
in practice until the coup of April 25, 1974, had its elections on April 25,
1975 for the Constitutional Assembly, and its first democratic general elections in April of 1976.
– In Spain, only after the death of General Franco in November 1975, could
the first elections be held in June 1977 for the Constitutional Assembly, and
the first democratic general elections in March of 1979. (With all due
respect to the present governments of Spain and Portugal who are also
Turkey's allies in NATO, there are historical facts that clarify Turkey's
unique position during and right after World War II.)

II. OMISSION OF THE EDITORS OF THE REPORT

Omissions of references to the verbatim records of the important international
conferences during World War II in the report of May 1977, in relation to
Turkey's exceptional and incomparable situation during World War II and
other relevant important documents are cited below:

a. International conferences and negotiations

The Allied Powers had a different approach to Turkey, starting from the end of
1942, in comparison with other neutral or non-belligerent European countries.
The Allied countries desired to have Turkey alongside the Allies and several

negotiations were made on this subject both among themselves and also with Turkey. On the other hand, there was not any similar strategic intent displayed for the other neutral or non-belligerent European countries by the Allies.

These intentions of the Allies to bring Turkey into war on their side could not be realised earlier, mainly due to the disapproval of Roosevelt and Stalin against Churchill's preference of opening a Balkan front in Europe against the Germans, instead of the "Overlord Operation" starting from France (Normany): the insufficiency of military aid and support to Turkey offered by the Allies, and lack of any substantial British guarantee to satisfy Turkey's prophetic concerns about the Soviet Union's predictable aggression and ambitions towards Turkey after the war.

These long strategic discussions about Turkey's situation were ever present in international conferences and negotiations such as:

1. *Among the Allied countries*
    a. The Casablanca Conference (14–26 January, 1943) between Churchill and Roosevelt,
    b. The Washington Conference (12–25 May, 1943) between Churchill and Roosevelt,
    c. The Quebec Conference (17–24 August, 1943) between Churchill and Roosevelt,
    d. The Moscow Conference (19–30 October, 1943) among Molotov, Eden and Hull,
    e. The Tehran Conference (28 November–1 December 1943) among Stalin, Churchill and Roosevelt,
    f. The Moscow Negotiations (9–18 October, 1944) between Churchill and Stalin.

2. *Between Turkey and the Allies*
    a. The Adana Negotiations (30–31 January, 1943) between Churchill and Ismet Inönü, President of Turkey.
    b. The First Cairo Conference (5–16 November, 1943) between Eden and Numan Menemencioğlu, Turkish Minister of Foreign Affairs,
    c. The Second Cairo Conference (7–14 December, 1943) among Churchill, Roosevelt and Inönü.

b. Important diplomatic documents

For any scientific evaluation of Turkey's position during World War II, not only are the verbatim records of the above-mentioned international conferences and negotiations indispensable to study for an accurate historical assessment, but a review of the documents of the below-mentioned diplomatic correspondences and talks are also necessary:
    1. Correspondences of K. Hugessen, the British Ambassador at Ankara during World War II to the Foreign Office in London.
    2. Correspondences of Steinhardt, the American Ambassador at Ankara during World War II to the State Department at Washington.

3. Documents of the negotiations of the Turkish Ambassador and the Turkish Military Attache at Washington with the State Department and American military officials during World War II.
4. Correspondence between Churchill and Stalin during World War II.
5. Correspondence between Roosevelt and Stalin during World War II.

III. NEGLIGENCE OF EVEN SOME IMPORTANT AMERICAN DOCUMENTS

Some important American official documents describing the reality of Turkey's position during World War II have unfortunately been neglected, and because of this neglect, some facts concerning Turkey from the viewpoints of American officials are not duly reflected.

Two of these American documents are highly illuminating:

1. In the document dated June 1, 1945 and prepared by the Office of Strategic Services (Research and Analysis Branch – Central European Section), with the title "German Economic Penetration Abroad", Turkey's relations with Germany during the war are correctly analysed below (page 12):

> "Turkey was the only country in Southeastern Europe which was successful in extricating itself from German penetration. This achievement was due, first, to the nationalistic economic policy of Turkey which prevented expansion of German business interest beyond a certain influence in banking and trade, and second, to the economic warfare conducted in Turkey by the Allies which eventually deprived Germany of the leading position it held before the outbreak of the war in Turkish foreign trade" (see Annex I).

2. In another document which is a telegram of the State Department sent to the American Embassy at Ankara on April 8, 1948, an Aide-Memoir of the State Department presented to the British and French Embassies at Washington on March 25, 1948, concerning Turkey's special position which is different from the other European countries is quoted as below:

> "Turkey requires special consideration. On December 30, 1947 the Turkish Ministry of Foreign Affairs presented notes to the three Allied Missions at Ankara agreeing to place at the disposition of the three Allied governments any balance of sums realised from German assets any balance of sums realised from German assets subject to Turkish jurisdiction. The Department suggests that the three Allied governments accept the proposal. The Department realized that by this action the three Allies probably will receive less than they originally hoped to obtain from the German assets in Turkey. However, inasmuch as no contribution from German assets in the other American Republics can be obtained, and consistent with the Department's recommendations to abandon any effort to obtain any contribution from Iraq, Iran, Lebanon, Syria, Saudi Arabia, Ethiopia, Iceland, Liberia, China and Siam, it feels constrained to treat Turkey in the same manner as nations in like or identical positions" (see Annex II).

3. Edward B. Lawson, Counsellor of the American Embassy at Ankara for Economic Affairs, in his letter of June 25, 1947, addressed to the Secretary of State, about "conversations concerning German Assets and Related Subjects

Between Representatives of the Turkish Government and Representatives of the United States, United Kingdom and France", had informed Washington of the Turkish official stance as such:

> "Accordingly the meetings were resumed, and the minutes of meetings from June 16 through June 20 record the conversations concerning the Paris Reparation Agreement, the accords concluded with Sweden and Switzerland, and arrangements under consideration with other nations. The Department's attention is invited to the fact that the Turkish representative disclaimed any concern with or interest in the provisions of the Paris Reparation Agreement concerning German assets in neutral countries, emphasizing that these provisions are not applicable to Turkey . . . "

4. The Turkish Ministry of Foreign Affairs, in its reply Note to Allied Embassies in Ankara, dated December 30, 1947, which was transmitted by Mr. Edward B. Lawson to The Secretary of State by his cover letter of letter of January 2, 1948, clarifies the Turkish Government's position as following:

> " . . . The Turkish Government is disposed:
>
> 1) to announce publicly its adherence to the Declaration of London, to that of Washington, and to Bretton Woods Resolution No. VI. and to put into effect their principles:
>
> 2) to restore their legal owners of all the property stolen or looted by the enemy located in Turkey; however, acquisitions made in good faith and in accordance with laws and regulations, national as well as international, can not be subjugated to the terms of this paragraph." . . .

5a) In a report on the subject of "Sanctions on the Forthcoming Safehaven Negotiations with the European Neutrals", prepared by the Office of European Affairs of the State Department and presented to the Secretary of State on February 15, 1946, Turkey is not referred to at all:

> "THE PRESENT CASE
>
> The present case is the application of sanctions against Western European powers who remained neutral in the last war: Sweden, Switzerland, Spain, Portugal and possibly Ireland . . ." (see Annex III)

5b) In the report of May 1997, the section (G) entitled "The Office of Strategic Services and Project Safehaven" (pp. 37–47), prepared by the History Staff in the Center for the Study of Intelligence of the Central Intelligence Agency, a large amount of information is dedicated to four neutral countries: Switzerland, Spain, Portugal and Sweden; and here again there is no reference to Turkey.

5c) In Section (F) "Safehaven After the End of War", on page 36, information is given on the 1945 War Mobilisation Subcommittee, where also Turkey was not included:

> "During the June 1945 War Mobilisation Subcommittee hearings chaired by Senator Kilgore, Henry Fowler, Chief of the Enemies Branch of the FEA, gave evidence of German wartime penetration into banking, industry, and commerce of the neutral nations, particularly Sweden, Spain, Switzerland and Portugal.

ANNEX I

OFFICE OF STRATEGIC SERVICES

Research and Analysis Branch
Central European Section

1 June 1945

German Economic Penetration Abroad

I. Introduction
The present paper seeks to outline briefly the objectives, methods, and scope of German economic penetration into foreign countries. The objective of this penetration, under the Nazis, was very distinctly preparation for war, to be achieved mainly by (a) expanding the sources of supply of foodstuffs and raw materials, secure from Allied blockade; (b) and by weakening the economic resources of the Western nations by hampering their industrial progress and expansion and their trade with other countries.

The methods applied by the Germans before the war were substantially the following:
1. Control of foreign trade and exchange
2. Granting of export credits to buyers of German goods
3. Investment of German capital in foreign enterprises
4. International cartel agreements
5. International patent and licensing agreements
6. German business organizations abroad
7. Voluntary and paid German agents

. . .

Turkey was the only country in Southeastern Europe which was successful in extricating itself from German penetration. This achievement was due, first, to the nationalistic economic policy of Turkey which prevented expansion of German business interests beyond a certain influence in banking and trade, and, second, to the economic warfare conducted in Turkey by the Allies which eventually deprived Germany of the leading position it had held before the outbreak of the war in Turkish foreign trade.

ANNEX II

OUTGOING AIRGRAM

No A–45

Department of State, Washington
April 8, 1948

American Embassy   SECRET
Ankara

Reference is made to the Department's telegrams no. 66 of February 12, 1948 and no. 99 of March 5, 1948.

On March 25, 1948 the Department presented an Aide Memoire to the British and French Embassies at Washington which contained a study that had been concluded in the Department concerning steps taken by certain governments with regard to German assets in their jurisdiction. The Department is now prepared to take concluding steps with regard to German assets in certain countries and seeks concurrence of the British and French governments in its proposals. The Aide Memoire (regarding Turkey) stated:

"Turkey requires special consideration. On December 30, 1947 the Turkish Ministry of Foreign Affairs presented notes to the three Allied Missions at Ankara agreeing to place at the disposition of the three Allied governments any balance of sums realized from German assets after all types of claims of the Turkish government and Turkish nationals against Germany have been satisfied from the German assets subject to Turkish jurisdiction. The Department suggests that the three Allied governments accept the Turkish proposal. The Department realizes that by this action the three Allies probably will receive less than they originally hoped to obtain from the German assets in Turkey. However, inasmuch as no contribution from German assets in the other American Republics can be obtained, and consistent with the Department's recommendations to abandon any efforts to obtain a contribution from Iraq, Iran, Lebanon, Syria, Saudi Arabia, Ethiopia, Iceland, Liberia, China and Siam, it feels constrained to treat Turkey in the same manner as nations in like or identical positions.

The Department would recommend, however, that the three Allies not inform the Turkish government of their acceptance of the aforementioned offer at this time. Rather, it would leave the time of acceptance to the discretion of the three Allied Missions at Ankara as of possible utility in arriving at a satisfactory settlement on the question of looted gold."

Lovett
(Acting)

ANNEX III

Department of State
Office of European Affairs
February 15, 1946

S: Mr. Secretary   SECRET

Subject: Sanctions and the Forthcoming Safehaven Negotiations with the European Neutrals

One of the major political aspects of the forthcoming Safehaven negotiations with the neutrals is that of the proposed use of economic sanctions. As you were absent during the preliminary discussions here, I feel that you will wish to know the views thereon of the Office of European Affairs, and I have therefore requested the preparation, in as concise a form as possible, of a memorandum on this complex subject. The views set out below on the use of sanctions do not in any way detract from the importance which EUR attaches to the achievement of the general Safehaven objectives. These objectives can, we believe, be attained in harmony with our general policy toward Western Europe.

General Considerations

Economic sanctions are a drastic and unfriendly means of pressure against a state. The books on International Law generally list economic sanctions among "Non amicable means of redress short of war". Perhaps because of their drastic nature, they have been used sparingly, and never wholly successfully.

a. Psychological Effect
Like all near-hostile acts, the effect on the nations against whom sanctions are applied is one of general popular resentment. As in an old fashioned siege, the entire population is affected. Internal differences tend to be forgotten, nationalism is intensified and the people are united against the economic "aggressors". Whether or not they are ulti- mately successful, sanctions destroy friendly relations between the states that apply them and the states against whom they are applied. It follows that there is reluctance to apply sanctions against states whose friendship for economic, ideological or merely geograph- ical reasons will be useful in the immediate future, and that the use of sanctions is only justified where really vital issues are at stake.

b. Effectiveness
The serious deterioration of relations between states which results from applications of economic sanctions is not worth incurring unless the sanctions will bring about the desired results. To be effective they must be participated in by all the states controlling

the supplies, facilities, credits or assets which are to be denied the state or states against whom the sanctions are directed. Sanctions have failed in the past largely because this condition was not met.

c. Economic

The Governments of the sanctions-applying states must create or maintain a rigid and effective system of supply, financial and other controls within their own borders as well as international machinery to correlate these controls.

Depending on the extent of the program, economic sanctions will disrupt normal and traditional channels of trade and finance, not only for the states against whom they are applied, but also throughout the immediately surrounding economic area and, to a lesser degree, the entire world.

The Present Case

The present case is the application of sanctions against Western European powers who remained neutral in the last war: Sweden, Switzerland, Spain, Portugal and possibly Ireland. Ideologically, we have no quarrel with any of these powers except Spain. These lying furthest to the East, Sweden and Switzerland, resemble the United States in their political and economic institutions as closely as any nations on the continent. They are firmly wedded to the Democratic way of life, and political parties with totalitarian conceptions are in the minority. They look toward the West and have deep general admiration for the United States. Because their industrial and financial structures are relatively intact, they can contribute and are contributing to European post-war rehabilitation including that of our former Allies. It is against these countries that the weight of the sanctions program will fall, and it is their resentment which we shall incur. Spain is expected to be substantially compliant with our Safehaven demands, and it is most unlikely that the Joint Chiefs of Staff will approve a sanctions program against Portugal in view of our desire to obtain Portugese-controlled bases. We should find ourselves in the curious ideological position while resisting, because of Spanish compliance, the popular demand for similar action against Franco Spain.

The total amount of German assets involved for the states – Sweden and Switzerland – against whom sanctions may thus ultimately be applied is small: Less than $75,000,000 for the former and amounts variously estimated between $250,000,000 and $500,000,000 for the latter.

Although the question of the actual machinery necessary for the application of sanctions is an economic rather than a political problem, we may have had very grave doubts as to the willingness of this Government to retain or reimpose many of the wartime controls necessary to implement the sanctions program. With the exception of financial sanctions, largely in the hands of Treasury, we do not believe that sufficient thought has been given to the mechanics involved and to possible public reaction to the continuance or reimposition of certain restrictions.

EUR was brought face to face with the question of sanctions not as a proposal to be objectively considered and adopted or rejected on its merits, but rather as a full blown program vigorously endorsed by Treasury, and to which certain of our own economic divisions were partially committed.

Since objective consideration was no longer possible, and in view of our doubts as to the necessity of sanctions to achieve the substantial accomplishment of the Safehaven program or the desirability of their use even if it were, we limited our efforts:

    a. to assuring that the program be a joint one with the British and the French.

    b. to placing the sanctions program before the British and French as a basis for objective discussion rather than urging its adoption in toto.

We were successful in having it understood within the Department and *vis-à-vis* Treasury that no sanctions would be undertaken without full agreement with and full participation of our French and British partners. We were convinced that no sanctions program could be successful without a united front and we were unwilling to have the United States bear alone the onus of coercing the Governments and peoples of democratic Western European states.

We were not successful in having our thesis adopted that British and French consideration of our sanctions proposals should be free of pressure on our part. We felt that as the nations nearest geographically to the neutrals and those having the most at stake in both the reparations and security features of the Safehaven program, they should be made at least equal judges of the disciplinary measures to be taken against their neighbors. Despite EUR's convictions in this matter, our missions in Paris and London were instructed strongly to urge unqualified adoption of our sanctions program.

As you know, Great Britain has completely rejected our proposals. France, while accepting the weakest of the proposed sanctions, has expressed general reservations as to entering an economic war with the neutrals and specific reservations as to measures affecting her trade with them. The Department has now sent a sharp note to the British urging reconsideration of their rejection. As we understand it, this Government is now committed to coercing the British – and to lesser degree the French – into a program of coercing their neighbours into accepting Safehaven in its entirety. We feel impelled to point out the dangers – both for the success of the forthcoming negotiations and our relations with Britain and France – to which this course of action is committing us. The differences in Allied ranks is already known to the neutrals. The substance of British rejection of our sanctions proposals has appeared in sarcastic dress in the London *Daily Worker*. The British and French, if pressed too hard to accept sanctions against their better judgement, cannot be expected to refrain from exculpating themselves privately to the Swedes and Swiss. This will result not only in stiffening the neutral attitude in the negotiations but in having the United States bear the full onus for the sponsorship of such sanctions as we may find ourselves committed to apply.

EUR proposes that the question of how far we are to go in attempting to force the British and French into unwilling compliance with the sanctions proposal be reconsidered. EUR recommends that, in the preliminary talks before negotiations with the neutrals start, the U.S. negotiators be instructed to refrain from pressing the French and British too far. If they show a disposition to go along willingly, well and good. If they do not, we should accept that fact and undertake with them a further consideration of the means available for obtaining neutral compliance with Safehaven objectives, with a view to agreeing to a line of procedure vis-à-vis the neutrals, to which we and the British and the French could all give our full support. There are increasing indications that the neutrals are aware of the necessity of settling the question of German assets to the substantial satisfaction of the victorious powers, and that the success of the program will be endangered more by our intransigence *vis-à-vis* our negotiating partners than by a failure to reach agreement in the use of sanctions.

H. Freeman Matthews

WE: W Wallner: rc
O Horsey

Conference Paper 5

Gold Purchased from Switzerland

I. INTRODUCTION

(a) It is apparent that in the report of May 1997, the section (D) concerning Turkey (pp. 144–147) of Chapter VII, "Allied Negotiations with Other Neutral Countries", is based on several American documents, seven of which have been forwarded also to the Turkish authorities after the publication of the said report (see Annex I).

(b) Missing American (Allied) documents concerning Turkey

Almost all of the documents concerning the correspondence between the Turkish M. F. A. and the three Allied Embassies in Ankara are present in the Turkish archives obviously with the exception of internal correspondence between the State Department and the U.S. Embassy at Ankara.

However, there are two important documents of later dates found in the Turkish archives, which may have been absent in the American archives or may not have been taken into account:

1) Allied Note of March 23, 1953 presented to Turkey on the looted gold issue (Annex II: French version of the Note)
2) Allied Note of August 11, 1953 with reference to the above Note (see Annex III).

With this in mind, a final judgement on Turkey without taking into account these two documents and other possible important documents which may be missing or not have been discovered in the American archives may be misleading. On the other hand, while the same issue has also been dealt with by the United Kingdom and France, their archives concerning Turkey have obviously not been consulted and reviewed.

(c) The contents of the two missing documents

In the report of May 1997, the section on Turkey ends with the following paragraph: (p. 147)

> "On May 21, 1952, the Allied governments presented a Note to the Turkish F.M. that agreed to settle the gold issue for one million Dollars. In return, the Allies would relinquish their claim to German assets in Turkey, remove Turkey from AHC Law 63, and consider justified to recompense to itself for the proceeds from liquidation of German assets. Turkey never turned over any monetary gold to the Tripartite Gold Commission."

As is seen, the last sentence is very judgmental and arbitrary.

This last paragraph is based on the Allied Note to Turkey, dated May 21, 1952, which is the last and the most recently dated of the above-mentioned seven American documents on Turkey.

In the Allied Note of March 3, 1953, after referring to the Allied Note of May 21, 1952, it is stated in its third paragraph that: "If this offer is not accepted by Turkey until May 15, 1953, it is decided that the three Allied countries will notify the I.A.R.A., as well as the countries whose monetary gold was looted, of the refusal of Turkey for an agreement, so that they can take appropriate measures. In this regard, the three Allied governments, without prejudice to their rights acquired by Law No: 5 of the Allied Control Commission and Law No: 65 of the Allied High Commission, agreed to give technical assistance to all those countries whose monetary gold was looted, if they can identify that their gold is in the possession of the Central Bank of Turkey, so that these governments or their central banks can claim their rights against the Turkish Central Bank or the Turkish government to recover their gold" (Unofficial translation from the original French text).

In the light of the two above Notes, the Allies have decided to give liberty to the countries whose monetary gold is looted to apply to Turkey, if they can identify that their gold is in the possession of the Central Bank of Turkey, and to give them technical assistance if they do so.

(Some observations on the question of the identification of this gold shall be dealt with later in this paper).

2. TURKEY'S POSITION ON THESE OFFERS

(a) Turkey did not reply to either the Allied note of May 21, 1952, or the Allied note of March 3, 1953, for the following reasons:
- For Turkey, the two issues of gold and the German assets were two completely different matters, because Turkey did not acquire or purchase directly any looted gold from Germany like the other countries concerned. To have accepted to settle the gold issue for one million dollars, in exchange for relinquishing the claims on German assets, would have meant conceding to the culpability of Turkey on the gold issue, to which Turkey strongly objected at that time and strongly protests to any similar revived and unfounded insinuations.
- A comprehensive explanation was given by the Turkish delegation at the London Conference of last December. (See the statement of the Turkish delegation under "Gold Report", Conference Paper 2.)

In addition to this statement, it would be helpful here to paraphrase the opinion of the Turkish Ministry of Finance on the matter given in March 1953, after the Allied Note of March 3, 1953 was received, on the two different matters alleged in the Note of January 10, 1948.

However, it would be wise to remind the source of the enquiry of these two matters, stated in the Allied Note of January 10, 1948 to the Turkish Ministry of Foreign Affairs as stated below:

> "On behalf of Belgium the primary victim of German spoliation in the matter of monetary gold, the Government of the United States in association with the Governments of the United Kingdom and France has evidence that there has come into the possession of the said Central Bank 249 bars of gold. They would wish also to see enquiries made into the nature, and subsequent history, of some 32,000 coins and 243 kilos of gold ingots (mainly monetary gold of the Latin Union or gold bars which were demonstrably minted from such coins) delivered to the Turkish authorities by Swiss officials who then had charge of German affairs."

(b) Legal opinions on the gold issue and the assets delivered by the Swiss Embassy

1) GOLD TURKEY BOUGHT FROM SWITZERLAND AND LATER TRANSFERRED TO TURKEY

As has been stated in the Turkish delegation's gold report at the London Conference, the Central Bank of Turkey had the equivalent of the same amount of gold mentioned above with the Swiss National Bank, which was exchanged from Swiss francs into gold for the surplus foreign currency account of the CBT, according to an agreement which had been concluded with the two banks, in order to avoid a possible devaluation of the foreign currency deposited at CBT's Swiss account.

When Turkey wanted to bring its own rightfully earned and acquired gold into Turkey, because of the transportation difficulties during the war, 3,048.4 kg at the Swiss Bank was transferred to Germany, and in return, 3,047.32 kg was received in Turkey from the Reichsbank, and the difference was given to the Reichsbank as commission.

As is seen very clearly, this transaction is only an exchange for the transportation of the gold and a certain commission was given for the transportation costs. It cannot be considered as a direct purchase or acquisition of gold from Germany, like the other countries concerned had done so. Therefore, this transaction is not within the scope of either the Gold Declaration of January 5, 1943, or Resolution VI of the Bretton Woods Agreement.

2) THE SWISS EMBASSY'S DELIVERY TO TURKEY

At the end of the war, the German Embassy at Ankara transferred the above-mentioned gold coins and gold ingots to the Swiss Embassy, which was taking charge of German affairs, and the Swiss Embassy delivered them to the Turkish authorities with the Protocol dated February 28, 1946 concluded between the two sides.

At those times, the opinion of the Turkish Ministry of Finance was that those amounts were not to be considered looted gold, but enemy assets, and in accordance with the reservation registered by the Turkish government during its adherence to the Bretton Woods Agreement's Resolution VI on the enemy assets, "enemy assets found within the boundaries of the Turkish territory will first be consecrated to the compensation of the losses and damage of the Turkish State and the Turkish citizens", this gold was kept within Turkey's safekeeping until a future agreement with Germany.

In the light of this legal view, this gold was fully returned to the German side, under the provisions of Article 3/c of the Protocol, signed in Bonn on November 3, 1960 between the delegations of the F.R.G. and Turkey. (See Annex II of Conference Paper 2 for the German text of this Protocol.)

3) THE SOURCE OF GOLD TURKEY BOUGHT FROM SWITZERLAND AND THE TARGET OF ITS RESPONSIBILITY

a) *Solid proof of its purchase from Switzerland*

1) A document issued by the National Bank of Switzerland, concerning the purchase of 256 bars of gold by the Central Bank of Turkey in 1943, is the most important hard evidence of this transaction (see Annexe IV).

The remaining seven bars (256 −7 = 249) may have been given as commission to the Reichsbank.

2) In the Fletcher Report of Swiss gold movements from 1/1/39 to 30/6/45, with the attached report by Mann (dated 2/5/46), the Swiss official statement was as follows:

Sold to Germany	–	4.9 tons
Sold to Portugal	–	116.6 tons
Sold to Spain	–	42.6 tons
Sold to Turkey	–	3.5 tons

Since Turkey bought no other amount of gold from Switzerland during World War II other than the 256 bars of gold in question, this verifies again Turkey's position that this gold was purchased from Switzerland, but only transferred by Germany to Turkey because of the wartime transportation difficulties. (Since fine gold weighs less, this 3.5 tons corresponds approximately to the 256 bars of gold.)

In the concluding section of this report, in paragraph (3), it is also alleged that "part of the gold that the Swiss sold during the war to Portugal, Spain and Germany, could have been looted gold."

b) *Allegations by the Allies on the source of this gold and its identification*

1) In the Allied Note of January 10, 1948 to Turkey, it is alleged that:

> "The Embassy (Allied Countries) wishes to suggest, on behalf of the nations despoiled of monetary gold, that action should be taken to restore the 249 bars of gold (or the gold equivalent thereof) known from the examination of German records to have been looted from the Belgian National Bank . . ."

2) On the other hand, in the Swiss Memorandum of April 13, 1946 on "Swiss reservations with regard to the gold problem", it is argued as follows in paragraph (5) on "Gold of the Belgian National Bank":

> "With the exception of a few general and sketchy indications given to the Swiss National Bank by Mr. Boisanger during his vacation in Switzerland, the Swiss National Bank learned only through Mr. Frere at the beginning of 1946 about the

fate of this so-called Belgian looted gold. According to this information, the Swiss National Bank would have received 378 million Swiss francs of the gold, whereas the Reichsbank would have sold directly out of its gold deposits in Switzerland an amount of 153 million Swiss francs to other purchasers. This Belgian gold was not transferred separately by the Reichsbank, but arrived in Switzerland together with other gold. In the meantime, a considerable portion of the Belgian gold has been resold by the Swiss National Bank and is no longer in Switzerland.

Switzerland reserves any commitments with regard to the identity of this gold, and numerous inconsistencies were brought to the attention of Mr. Frere on March 15, 1946. No reply has as yet been received. Even if the identity of a major portion of the 378 million Swiss francs could be established, this gold could not possibly be considered looted since its restitution would still have been possible; after having been transferred for greater safety to Dakar, the gold was nevertheless brought back by the French Government and transferred to Berlin.

For these reasons the Swiss National Bank is forced to decline the total or partial restitution of this gold. Considering the tactics of deception practised by the Germans, about which it was only in the most recent past, no one can doubt the Swiss National Bank's good faith."

3) Since the German records on the source of the gold transferred to Turkey by Germany on behalf of Switzerland have never been presented to Turkey, it is difficult to determine precisely the real source of this gold, and validate the Allied allegations.

On the assumption that even if this gold had been identified precisely as the "Belgian Gold", it is a valid question to ask (within the context of the Allied Note of March 3, 1953 to Turkey) why the concerned despoiled countries such as Belgium and France have not resorted to Turkey within the years 1953 to 1997 for the recovery of this gold.

c) *The responsibility of the gold transferred to Turkey which it purchased from Switzerland*

In the agreement signed between the three Allied countries and Portugal on October 27, 1958, on "German assets in Portugal and on certain claims regarding monetary gold", it is envisaged in Article 1/4, that:

"The payments to the three Governments referred to in paragraph (3) of this article shall not take place until it has been established that the payments to the Portuguese Government foreseen in the Portuguese/Federal German Agreement have been made."

As in this agreement and in similar agreements with other countries, it had been a general principle that restitution of even directly purchased gold from Germany is made conditional that the German government first reimburses the amount at hand to the concerned country.

As has been informed above, with the Protocol of October 31, 1960, signed between Turkey and the F.R.G., economic matters related to World War II have already been settled. However, since Turkey regards that there is no responsibility of Turkey concerning looted gold (as explained above in section (2) and sections (3) (a) and (b), and even within the context of Resolution VI of the Bretton Woods Agreement, any claimant for the Belgian gold looted by Nazi Germany should directly resort to the present German government.

ANNEX I

List of American Documents submitted to Turkey on "Allied Negotiations with Turkey"

1. U.S. Embassy's (Ankara) despatch of 29/3/46, covering the Allied Embassy's Note of 27/33/46 presented to Turkey, concerning Safehaven.

2. Ankara Embassy's despatch of 25/6/47, concerning "Allied conversations with Turkey concerning German assets and related subjects."

3. Ankara Embassy's despatch of 12/8/47, concerning Allied presentation of Note concerning German assets program in Turkey.

4. Ankara Embassy's despatch of 1/1/48, transmitting Turkey's Note (30/12/47), on compliance with the Bretton Woods Resolution.

5. Ankara Embassy's despatch of 13/1/48, covering American Note to the Turkish M.F.A. on looted gold.

6. State Department's airgram of 8/4/48 to U.S. Embassy in Ankara, concerning U.S. proposal that the Allies accept the Turkish settlement offer.

7. Ankara Embassy's despatch of 21/5/52, concerning Tripartite offer to the Turkish Government on looted gold and German assets.

ANNEX II

French Embassy in Turkey

No. 36

The French Embassy presents its compliments to the Ministry of Foreign Affairs and, with reference to its previous letters regarding the issue of plundered gold and German assets in Turkey, has the honour, by order of the French Government, to notify the Turkish Government of the following points:

1. The Governments of the French Republic, the United Kingdom of Great Britain and the United States of America wish to discharge as quickly as possible their obligations under the international agreements concerning plundered gold and German assets abroad.

2. This figure proposed in the letter of 22 May 1952 to His Excellency The Minister for Foreign Affairs by each of the ambassadors of the three governments in respect of settlement of the issue of plundered gold represents a minimum proposal on which the three powers cannot contemplate any compromise. In that letter the three powers stated that they were ready to accept from the Turkish Government the total sum of one million gold dollars by way of overall settlement for the $4 million worth of plundered

gold held by Turkey. They also mentioned that they were prepared to waive their claims to the German assets in Turkey once the gold issue is settled in the manner indicated above. The three powers have not received a reply to that letter from the Turkish Government.

3. In those circumstances, the three powers inform the Turkish Government that the offer contained in their letter of 22 May will remain open until 1 April 1953. Should the Turkish Government fail to accept that offer within the set period, the three powers will notify both the Inter-Allied Reparation Agency and the countries robbed of their monetary gold of Turkey's refusal to negotiate an agreement so that they can take the appropriate measures. In this respect, without prejudice to the rights conferred on them by Law No. 5 of the Allied Control Council and Law No. 65 of the Allied High Commission, the three powers have agreed to lend technical assistance to any country whose gold has been found to be in the possession of the Central Bank of Turkey in cases where the Government of that country or its Central Bank wishes to assert its claims against the Turkish Government or the Turkish Central Bank for the purpose of recovering that gold.

The French Embassy avails itself of the opportunity presented by this note to renew to the Ministry of Foreign Affairs the assurance of its highest consideration.

Ankara, 2 March 1953

Ministère des Affaires Etrangères, Ankara

ANNEX III

American Embassy, Ankara
August 11, 1953
No. 143

The Embassy of the United States of America presents its compliments to the Ministry of Foreign Affairs and has the honor to refer to its Note No. 2250 of May 21, 1952 which contained an offer made by the Governments of the United States, France, and the United Kingdom for the settlement of the German-looted gold issue, and to its Note No. 1106 of March 3, 1953, relative to this subject.

It will be recalled that, as stated in the Embassy's note of March 3, 1953, the offer of settlement was initially held open for acceptance by the Turkish Government until April 1, 1953 and that, following an oral request of the competent officials of the Ministry, this date was extended to May 15, 1953.

In the absence of a response from the Ministry on the subject, the Governments of the United States, France, and the United Kingdom propose to proceed with the action outlined in paragraph (3) of the Embassy's note of March 3, 1953 under reference.

Ministry of Foreign Affairs, Ankara.

ANNEX IV

GOLD TRANSACTIONS FOR THE THIRD ACCOUNT IN 1943

Deposit: Banque Centrale de la Turquie, Ankara

Presented by the Swiss National Bank to the Cental Bank of Turkey

IN

Date		Bars	Kg fine	CHF
01 Jan	Balance	0	0.00000	0
08 Mai	our assignment	256	3,048.40672	15,000,082
	Total	256	3,048.40672	15,000,082
	Balance per 31.12	0	0.00000	0

OUT

Date		Bars	Kg fine	CHF
25 Mai	Account Reichsbank Berlin	256	3,048.40	15,000,082
	Total	256	3,048.40672	15,000,082

UKRAINE

Report of the Ukraine delegation

The Second World War again reminded about itself. It was the most terrible by its comprehensive destructive consequences, the most bloody by its ruinous, mortal force, the most mysterious by its so far not disclosed behind-the-scenes manoeuvres of the representatives of the political, financial establishment. This time, by so-called Nazi gold. From time immemorial we consider it as unjust treasure that came into the world as a result of unprecedented and unheard of the total robbery of the occupied countries of Europe, plunder, gangster appropriation of valuables, personal property of citizens, first of all those, who were considered as enemies of the Reich, who were persecuted by the reasons of political, ideological, racial, national, religious intolerance and who were included in the numerous groups of people subjected to unconditional extermination.

I

Let us recall that 27, and by some estimates, not less than 30 million of human lives were lost in the past war by the peoples of the USSR, 8, and by estimates, 10 million human lives were lost in the past war by the Ukrainian people. Those losses are extremely bitter and irreplaceable. They irrefutably testify that extermination of people by Nazis bore organised, mass, purposeful and premeditated character. This was recognised by the tribunal which was established under the London Agreement of 8 August 1945 between Great Britain, USA, France and the USSR, before which the group of the main Nazi war criminals appears. Its verdict is known and it was welcome by the peoples.

As it was stated in the verdict of the tribunal sounded under the vaults of the Palace of Justice in Nuremberg more than half a century ago, committed crimes had the purpose "of getting rid of the local population by means of exile and extermination in order to colonise free territory by the Germans". In other words starting principal conclusion inevitably arises. Reprisals over the peaceful population; executions, atrocities, humiliation, forced isolation and confinement in the places of forced custody, exhaustion by hunger, cold, diseases, hard labour a long way from the native land, have been accomplished not only for the purposes of suppression of opposition and resistance to the German troops.

The main thing was in the solution on a global scale of strategic demographic, economic and financial tasks. And since the subject of the desired dreams of the Nazis was the richest gigantic territories from the Carpathian Mountains to the Urals, mainly populated by the Slavs, then they, the Slavs – Russians, Ukrainians, Belorussians, were subjected to extermination, eviction or, in the best case, to forced Germanization and enslavement.

The General plan "Ost" born in the depths of the Main Imperial Directorate of Security (RSHA) just contained those practical methods of "settlement" of quantitative and qualitative (and consequently, racial and ethnic) composition of the population on the European continent which would satisfy the aggressive expedites of Hitler and would be in full conformity with colonial strivings of Hitlerites. The above-mentioned plan envisaged, in particular, the exile to Siberia of 65 per cent of Ukrainians, 75 per cent of Belorussians, "radical liberation" from Russians, general extermination of Jews and Gypsies. The programmed fundamental numerical targets were outlined. For instance, only 14 million "natives" should survive in the occupied territories. And there were 88 million people living here before the war.

The results of the bloody "management" of the Nazis on the occupied Soviet territories testify to the realisation of the general plan "Ost" supported subsequently by a great number of the "intermediate" directives and instructions of the Nazi leadership. After the liberation of the territories where 88 million of people lived only 55 million remained. Thus, the difference is equal to 33 million. It "consisted" of the tortured persons, punished, died in the period of the occupation, those who have fallen in the struggle against the enemy, prisoners in concentration camps and prisons, condemned to penal servitude in Germany and also the evacuees.

The peculiarity of the Nazi occupation regime on the annexed territories was the combination of measures directed both at "depopulation" of these territories and their merciless economic exploitation and premeditated robbery. The looting was complete, open, cynical.

It should be said that long before the memorable Sunday of 22 June 1941, the "Barbarossa" plan has begun to find visible features, the Nazis have elaborated "The Directives on management of economy in the newly occupied eastern regions".

These "Directives" are know in history as "Green file" of H. Goering.

The German invaders annexed the territories where 45 per cent of the population lived before the war, with 47 per cent of the area under crops, 45 per cent of livestock, 55 per cent of railroads, where 33 per cent of total industrial production was produced. The Nazis, with the insatiability characteristic of them, started to swallow all that they were in need of. And they were in need of many raw materials. For example, the endowment of Germany by some kinds of raw materials of its own production on the eve of the war against the USSR made up (in per cent to the needs):

Oil – 10
Manganese – 55
Nickel – 7
Chromium – 0
Bauxites – 2
Flax – 64

Cotton –
Hemp – 11
Oil-yielding crops – 6
Wool – 16
Iron-ore – 28

The food supply problem was extremely urgent for the Reich. Hitler and his associates in the looting of the occupied European nations, first of all the Ukraine repeatedly said about it, taking into account its human and economic potential. This problem acquired more actuality and importance in the conditions of the war.

The German statistic data testify; during two years. Up to the crushing defeat of the Wehrmacht strategic grouping on the Kursk Bulge, the Nazis steadily increased the use of the natural resources of the occupied Soviet territory. In particular, it was related to oil from the regions in the West of Ukraine, timber from Belarus, iron-ore and nickel from the basins of Krivily Rih and Nikopol. (It is no mere chance, that the loss of the latter caused particular concern of the minister of armaments Speer, which he expressed in a special memorandum to Hitler of 11 November 1943). A number of mines and pits were restored, a number of enterprises was put into operation, including the metallurgical giant of the Ukrainian south – the "Azovstal" plant.

The powerful German military and economic machine which was set up in the occupied territory, aimed its efforts at providing for the efficient looting of this territory. Everywhere the measures were taken on requisition of raw materials, half-finished products, scrap, fuel, lubricants, equipment. Thus, 325,751 tons of iron ore and 438,031 tons of manganese ore were delivered to Germany. The coal industry of Donbas was technically completely rendered lifeless. The occupants took out 2,400 pit electric locomotives and petrol engines, 2,700 coal-cutting machines, 5,000 pumps, 2,800 compressors and ventilators. Machine-building plants which remained intact were robbed. 47,000 sets of lifting equipment, 34,000 hammers (with mechanical drive), presses, etc. were removed. Particular activity in the removal of the property of Ukraine, was manifested by the firms "Fridrich Krupp and K", "Herman Goering", "Siemens Shukkert", mining and metallurgical society "East", stock company group "South", "Henrich Lantz", "I.G. Farbenindustry" and many others.

As to the food supply, then in the first year of war the Wehrmacht formations, not taking into consideration the formations of satellites, were supplied mainly from the local resources; bread 80 per cent, meat – 83 per cent, fats – 77 per cent, potatoes 70 per cent. Besides this, a considerable quantity of food was requisitioned illegally. People's property in the form of soldiers' and officers' parcels flowed to Germany as a broad river.

Monster organisations appeared which specialised in the looting of the agricultural product and their deliveries. Thus, only one central trade stock company "East" "procured" in the occupied regions and sent to the Reich:

Grain – 9,200,000 tons;
Meat and meat goods – 622,000 tons;
Seeds of oil-yielding crops – 950,000 tons;
Oil – 208,000 tons;

Sugar – 400,000 tons;
Eggs – 1,075 million pcs.;
Potatoes – 320,000 tons;
Fodders – 2.500000 tons;
Seeds – 141,000 tons;
Other agricultural products – 1,200,000 tons

More than 1,400 thousand of railroad wagons and a great quantity of trade river and sea vessels of total tonnage 472,000 tons were required for transportation of food "procurements" by the central trade stock company "East".

Data on separate republics is available. Thus, as Erich Koch, the leader of Reichscolllmisariat Ukraine testifies, the territory of which due to the arbitrary but not at all inoffensive transfer by the Nazis of the borders of Ukraine essentially conceded to the territory of the pre-war Ukraine, from entrusted to him administrative formation from the beginnings of the occupation up to the end of June, 1943, exported: grain – 3,600,000 tons, leguminous plants – 100,000 tons; oil – 50,000 tons,, potatoes – 500,000 tons, honey and jam – 25,000 tons, sugar – 155,000 tons, cotton – 5,000 tons, wool – 7,000 tons, medicinal herbs – 1,500 tons, hemp and flax – 5,500 tons. The German historian W. Haupt wrote that Nazis often took away even the last things.

At the same time and simultaneously with requisition and removal to Germany raw materials, industrial equipment, livestock, agricultural products, the cultural, scientific, artistic, archives value were looted. The property of monasteries and churches, mosques, synagogues was forcibly taken. By Hitler's decree of 1 March 1942 the operative headquarters was set up in Ukraine under the authority of Reichminister A. Rozenberg who was entrusted to direct and co-ordinate the work in the sphere which interested the Nazis very much. This headquarters succeeded in all lines of its activity.

The world-wide known Kiev-Pechersk monastery, founded in 1051, was damaged. Museums and libraries of Crimea, Transdnieper, the Black Sea region and Chernihiv were subjected to plunder. The rich collections of the museum in the Bakhchisaray palace disappeared, including the Big Koran of Khan's mosque – a manuscript with unique ornaments. The pictures of the leading masters of the past, sculptures, suites of antique furniture, decorative highly glazed pottery and chinaware, jewellery, manuscripts, music materials, and theatre property were transported to Germany.

Here is a characteristic document – a secret report of G. Utikal about the plunder of cultural and scientific values, stored in the museums of Kiev and Kharkiv (G. Utikal was one of A. Rozenberg's assistants in the operative headquarters).

The document reads:

On 24 September 1943 there were loaded and dispatched: 98 Ukrainian pictures, 185 West European pictures, 12 carvings on wood and on copper, 25 carpets and tapestries;

On 27 September 1943 there were loaded and dispatched: 42 cases with 10,185 books, 7 cases of general catalogue of the Eastern library; 21 cases of selected magazines, 12 cases with pictures; 11 parcels of magazines' samples, 9 bundles and 7 rolls of paintings, 22 bundles with films, many cases with negatives and positives from photo archives;

On 1 October 1943, there were loaded and dispatched: the materials of the Ukrainian museum in Kiev, textiles of all sorts, collections of valuable embroideries, collections of brocade, numerous household articles of wood, the great part of the Museum of primitive history....

The crimes against the culture of the eastern Slavs had the purpose not only physically but also spiritually to disparage them, to bring down to the position of the slaves. On the other hand, it should be remembered that the artistic, scientific, historic values stolen by the Nazis were easily converted into gold, money. In conditions of the war Germany was in great need of both of them.

2

The civil population was ruthlessly robbed in the occupied areas of Ukraine. The property, valuables, money, clothes, household articles were requisitioned. Even the fertile black soils called "chernozem" were taken from the villages' personal plots of land. Fines, high taxes and contributions were imposed on the local residents.

The secret instruction of the German command of 17 July 1941 (it was revealed among the documents of the defeated 68th division of the Wehrmacht) stated the necessity "to bring out in every officer and soldier...a sense of personal material interest in the war".

The Nazis aroused the most brute, bestial instincts in those who by force of arms spread the "new order" in the Ukrainian land.

There are enormous quantities of materials and documents which point to Nazi invaders being barbarians and marauders who looted the property not only of the state, co-operative, public organisations but also of the civil population.

Dnipropetrovsk oblast. 137,000 heads of cattle, 3,000 horses, 67,000 pigs, 16,000 heads of sheep and goats, more than one million of poultry, 36,000 tons of grain and flour, 35,000 tons of potatoes and vegetables. 57,000 houses were burnt and destroyed. Only a few managed to save the part of the property, things and clothes for personal wear.

Sumy oblast. Having requisitioned from the population 106 thousand cattle, 5 thousand horses, 29 thousand heads of sheep and goats, 52 thousand pigs, 67 thousand tons of grain and flour, 47 thousand tons of potatoes, the occupants destroyed and burnt 130 thousand houses. The occupants sowed death and ash around. The same events took place in Zhitomir, Vinnitsa, Poltava and in other areas of Ukraine.

The search of the food by the occupants, removal of valuables, personal property of citizen, wherever produced – in the village or in town, was accompanied by tortures, mass reprisals and executions.

Extracts from act on the atrocities and robberies by the occupants in the village of Zakotno Krasholimansk district, Stalino (now Donetsk) oblast (it was made up on 27 March 1942):

"....The Nazis destroyed the village, committed unprecedented robbery and reprisal over the villagers. 173 houses were burnt, 243 heads of cattle, 160 pigs, 1,550 chickens, geese and ducks have been taken away, all warm clothing, footwear, utensils, food products have been taken away. The Germans killed the citizens: E. Sarzhevskiy, 63 years of age, I. Kupyanskiy, 18 years of age, S. Bondar, 65 years of age, P. Zakharenko – 37 years of age and many others".

From the report on the criminal proceeding over the Nazi occupants committed grave crimes in the territory of Chernihiv oblast:

"On 11 March 1943 for derangement of deliveries of bread, cattle, food products in the village of Kozary, Nosovka district on demand by the German agricultural commandant Henrich Droste a punitive operation was performed, 3 thousand people were shot and burnt. The village of 980 houses was levelled to the ground."

One more example. The city of Kiev was divided into "battle zones" and started their regular combing for the purpose that the population of Kiev "voluntarily" would carry out an order of Obershturmbanfuhrer Shpatsel (October, 1942) to hand over all gold, silver and all valuable possessions. The overall looting of the Kievites' flats began. According to the Ukrainian historian K.K. Dubyna, the city was seized with madness of robbery on the one hand, and with the despair of inability on the other.

The crimes of the Nazis in the occupied territories were a direct challenge to the code of morality, humanity and the norms of international law. It is known that special Regulations of the Hague Convention of 1907 on the laws and customs of the land warfare strictly regulated combat operations of the parties. For example, it was envisaged that:

- Life, honour and family rights of individuals should be respected (art.46);
- property of citizens are not subject to confiscation (art.46);
- robbery is unconditionally prohibited (p.47);
- no total penalty should be imposed on civil population (art.50);
- any extermination or damage of historical monuments, capture of artistic and scientific works are prohibited and should be subjected to persecution (art.56).

Nazi arbitrariness, violation, stupidity, gangsterism, raised to the rank of state policy, were condemned by the nations of the world. At present, taking into account the concrete circumstances, the specific possibilities we should speak about the recovery of losses for the victims. This loss is enormous and makes up the amount of 679 billion roubles at the state prices of 1941.

The structure of the loss is as follows:

- damage to state enterprises and organisations – 287 bn roubles
- damage to rural and town inhabitants – 192 bn roubles
- damage to collective farms – 181 bn roubles
- damage to co-operative, trade – 19 bn roubles
- damage to union and other public organisations – 19 bn roubles

The economic damage to the Ukraine equals to 285 bn roubles which is more than that of the losses suffered by the Russians – 249 billion roubles.

As it was noted in the Report of the Extraordinary State Commission, the submitted data do not exhaust all the damage caused by the Nazis. They cover only losses from direct destruction of property, whose owners were state enterprises and institutions, rural and town inhabitants, collective farms, co-operative and public organisations. Many other indices were not included in the total estimates of losses. For instance, the cost of food confiscated by the German occupation troops or the volumes of those profits which for a long time were obtained by the Nazis from the use of slave labour, from exploitation of prisoners – citizens of foreign states detained by the occupation authorities. To this latter issue, bearing in mind the subject of our conference, special attention should be given.

There were more than 14 thousand concentration camps, Gestapo prisons, ghettos established by the Nazis in Europe. Those installations covered the continental map with a thick brown rash, and to which daily and nightly, in summer and in winter, the people were thrown.

And over all this enormous area; from the English island Alderney in the west to the Russian town Belaya Kalitva in the east, from the Norwegian settlement of Greeny in the north to the lower reaches of the Greek river Aheloos on the south – our compatriots had been dying. From 18 million prisoners of fascism, almost 3 million (every sixth person) were citizens of Ukraine. 1 million of them did not live to see liberation. In many cases the places of burial of our fellow-countrymen are not even known nor do we know the places of their last confinement.

The lists of the owners of the dormant accounts published in the world press, with the report prepared on the initiative of the US Department of Trade, with regard to the search and return of the stolen assets of the fascist slaves, statements of the politicians of the states in whose bank institutions those assets are stored, revives the memories of the past. Those memories cannot be erased.

All those who suffered behind the barbed wire of the Nazi camps, regardless of nationality, citizenship, religious convictions, political preferences, by their deaths unimaginably enriched the Nazis. SS "experts" confirmed this fact. For example, it was calculated that one prisoner, whose average duration of life in the conditions of captivity was 270 days, gave to Germany 1430 Reichmarks of net profit. Besides, in everyone who was forced to change the civilian clothes for striped clothing of "heftling", they confiscated property, currency, personal things, decorations. After the prisoner's death his or her body was "utilised"; golden crowns were removed, fertilisers were produced from bones and ash. They even contrived to produce soap from "biological raw material". The relevant experiments in this field were performed at the Anatomical Institute of Danzig.

Rather remarkable information concerning the "gold-mining" activity of the Nazis is available. In Lviv, as it was witnessed by a member of "the brigade of death", the unit which served the places of mass executions of civil citizens, only within five months 110 kg of gold were "retrieved" after burning of the corpses and sent to Germany. Nazi marauders worked with the same high "productivity" in Kiev, Kharkiv, Vinnitsa, Simferopol and in other places of Ukraine. Only in 1944 the concentration camps transferred more than 2 tons of gold to the treasury. Specialised organisation DEGUSSA existed in Germany (Deutsche

Gold und Silber Staat Anstalt), which was engaged in reprocessing of precious metals, "mining" in the places of forced custody of civil citizens of Europe.

A very definite conclusion arises from this. The looting of the occupied countries, robbery of civilian population, including suffering prisoners in the camps, was total and unstoppable. That is why, only in the banks of Switzerland, as it was reported in press, the German gold reserves during the period from 1939 to 1945 increased from 189 to 415 million USD. And all that was under steadily increasing huge expenses needed to wage the war both to the east and to the west.

Back in 1946 Great Britain, the United States of America and France faithful to the principles of democratic states, induced by striving to restore the profaned and trampled justice, considered the problem of return of the riches robbed by Nazis to their legal owners. A special commission was even set up, which had exclusively practical tasks. However, severe realities of the post-war peace, the confrontation which emerged between the Soviet Union and western countries did not permit them to perform that required respectful, humane attitude to the victims of Nazism.

Here is a new round of discussion and consideration of the long standing, dramatic, extremely painful problem for the different categories of citizens who suffered from Nazism that should be borne in mind:

a. prisoners of all kinds of isolation and forced custody: concentration camps, camps of death, places of mass extermination; of Gestapo prisons, ghettos, clinics of pseudo medical experiments and hospitals of forcible donorship, establishments of ethnic cleansing and Germanization, factories of slave labour in towns, villages, in transport, in construction industry, etc.;

b. citizens, subjected to persecutions and robbed during the Nazi occupation both by the Wehrmacht units and by the bodies created by the Nazi administrative, economic, financial management; those deprived of property, and who bore excessive taxes, forced to serve labour;

c. civilians who under the threat of enemy occupation were forced to leave their places of permanent residence and evacuated to the rear, due to this they lost all their property and experienced a bitter fate of refugees.

The peculiarity of the situation is in the fact that the representatives of the most scanty but the most unfortunate group "A" (prisoners) are, as a rule, the representatives of a broader and diverse in its structure group "B" – inhabitants of the occupied territory. In other words, these persons, before they found themselves behind the camp wire or behind the bars, at first experienced all "the delights" of being under the heel of enemy soldier at home, on the place of permanent residence.

Thus, one may speak about double blow of destiny. At the same time, the persons from group "A" (prisoners) had never become the persons from group "B" (evacuees). And if they found themselves in the rear them only in the enemy one, for slave labour, to have a drink from the cup of sufferings to the end.

The exclusiveness of the fates of the prisoners of fascism – the citizens of the Ukraine, in whose vital tragedy the horrors of the two regimes were interpreted (having been liberated from Nazi captivity in Germany, they were taken in captivity of the wildest prejudices and the severest limitations in their home country due to these reasons they did not get – in many cases – education, normally paid work, had no family, did not solve, like the fellow-sufferers from the countries of Western and Central Europe, the questions of full compensation payments, additions to the scanty pensions for old age, etc. This exclusiveness puts them in a position of the people whose interests in connection with the consideration of the problems of the "Nazi gold" should be unconditionally taken into account, and their legitimate rights must be satisfied. Here, as it seems to us, any ambiguity must be excluded.

On the eve of the London conference the public associations of the prisoners made their statements concerning well-grounded solution of the problem of wealth looted by the Nazis. Their position is clear and well defined. Based on deep respect to all, without exclusion, victims of Nazism, dictated by sincere striving to contribute to the satisfaction of legal rights and interests of each of them, devoid of any craftiness, striving to get or to manage to get any benefits, privileges of advantages, is in the following.

First – In the present multi-cultural world, which is freed from strictly irreconcilable and dangerous confrontation of military political blocs, dividing walls, the infamous "iron curtain", at last, the possibility emerged to solve the problem of the return to their legal owners of the assets robbed by the Nazis. This possibility should be used in the best way, let even in half a century after the united efforts of the peoples managed to liquidate the fire of a universal armed conflict unleashed by Hitler. It is our conviction that the former ideological prejudice, division of the claimants into "friendly" and the "strangers", by the national sign, etc. At the same time a clear understanding of the hardships that the victims of Nazism endured. That understanding would make it possible to exercise maximum consideration to each of the claims.

Second – Many victims of fascism live in Ukraine presently. As of the middle of November this year, there are about 650 thousand of them. Ukrainian victims fall into the following main categories; people subjected to forced labour – 474.1 thousand; prisoners of concentration camps – 11.3 thousand; the inmates of Gestapo torture-chambers and special medical establishments – 7.7 thousand; doomed residents of ghetto – 3.5 thousand. 533.4 thousand of them are Ukrainians (88.4%); 50.06 thousand are Russians (8.3%); 4.82 thousand – Belorussians (0.8%); 4.81 thousand – Jews (0.8%); 3.9 thousand – Poles (0.7%); 0.7 thousand – Tartars (0.1%); Germans – 0.6 thousand (0.1%) and others.

All the prisoners, victims of Nazi cruelty have the equal right to their share of the "Nazi gold". Its size is determined by the scares and weight of the crimes committed against a peaceful population; total robberies, mass deportations, merciless exploitation, bloody reprisals. One should bear in mind that from every five seized and sent into captivity citizens at present alive remained only one. The principal significance in determination of the share (part) of one or other country should have such indices as the level of material provision of the prisoners, their age, health condition. In Ukraine average per head income of the victims of Nazism is equal to about $35 USD per month. The overwhelming majority of them are pensioners, disabled, ill persons, invalids.

Third – Since the robbery, illegal origin of the "Nazi gold" is beyond doubt, it is necessary to take measures to provide for its just distribution on historically true, socially clear, morally irreproachable basis. Inadmissible are the manifestations of discrimination and disrespect to the sufferings of any of the victims of Nazi persecutions. We do realise that the Jewish people were the first nation to suffer from the inhumane Nazi hatred. The Jews suffered unimaginable losses. Ukraine always respected and will respect the memory of our compatriots who fell victims of Holocaust. However, it is hard to agree with the view that the wealth looted by the Nazis belongs to one nation only. We should not ignore the facts of history.

It was not by accident that Jewish public organisations of Ukraine, hundreds of Jewish citizens – members of the largest public associations of the prisoners from the CIS countries and Baltic States – support the addresses to the organisers of the present conference to avoid selective national approach to the victims of Nazi persecutions. They emphasise that hasty imprudent and insufficiently grounded proposals with respect to the transfer of misappropriated funds of Nazis only in the funds of the victims of Holocaust offend the feelings of the Nazi victims who belong to other nationalities. To support their appeal we call for consideration, soberness of estimates and adjustment of practical steps. A just solution of the matter is possible only on the basis of harmonisation of the interests of the prisoners of the different countries, various nationalities.

Fourth – In order that the distribution of the "Nazi gold" would not turn out in indecent hunting for riches and would not cause undesired splash of emotions, would not prevent from the normal work of the institutions, to which, as we hope, will be entrusted the fulfilment of the decisions made in London, we should be proceeded from the historic realities, norms of international law and clearly to determine the following:
- owners of the accounts;
- candidates for the funds – plaintiffs;
- claim period of time;
- range of defendants (owners of accounts) for the physical persons (candidates, plaintiffs);
- sources of the formation of deposits by their owners (defendants);
- principles of allocation of the deposits.

CONCLUSION

Despite of the seeming simplicity of the Nazi gold problem or its seemingly accidental appearance, which extremely sharpened almost general interest, this issue does exist. It is part of our contemporary world, whatever feelings it may arouse – understanding, disappointment or irritation. And, naturally, it should be solved. This issue should be solved along with other problems without prejudice and in the spirit of humanity, benevolence and concern for everyone who suffered innocently. Mankind should not take this problem unsolved to the next millennium.

Nazi victims in Ukraine

INTERNATIONAL UNION OF FORMER MINOR VICTIMS OF FASCISM
UKRAINIAN UNION OF FORMER MINOR VICTIMS OF FASCISM

After the end of the war and the return of Nazi victims to their Motherland: concentration camps prisoners, Gestapo prisons inhabitants, peaceful citizens who were in the death row, patients of horrible medical clinics and donor stations, doomed inhabitants of Jewry ghettos, convicts of labour brigades who performed backbreaking journey-work on the territory of the Reich – at home they faced ultimate misunderstanding of what they had gone through, deaf irritation and even contempt towards themselves, sincere chase. As a consequence of the totalitarian-system-born prepossession of the official authorities, discrimination, deformation of the public conscience they were bearing a label of "traitors" and were subjected to abuse during long decades. Their rights were violated, interests ignored, civil and human dignity injured.

Only after the prisoners got to be spoken about not by prisoners themselves but other people too, only after on the basis of collected and systematised data and specially conducted research representatives of the intelligentsia (writers, journalists, scientists, diplomats) decisively called for historical, social and moral rehabilitation of Hitler bonds martyrs as early as in the Soviet times, – only after this the ring of the shameful blockade around Nazi victims – a ring of silence, unconcern and baleful aggressiveness – was eventually broken. Crucial changes took place.

In June 1988 in Kyiv was held the All-union Meeting of Former Minor Victims of Fascism. At the same time our public association was established. In 1989 and 1990 were issued decrees providing for privileges for victims of fascism. However, only for minors for the time being. But there were no doubts: it was a beginning. And really. After Ukraine gained independence and a law on war veterans was adopted, victims of all age categories received privileges. "Minors" as the basic "clout" in an organised advance to the bastions of the defenders of the evil memory of the old order did their great deed.

As of the end of 1997 in Ukraine there were 650 thousand registered victims of Nazism. 350 thousand of them went through the hell and tortures of the Hitler bonds being in their child and minor age.

We ought to particularly point out that:
- about 30 thousand of former victims were born behind barbed wire, in bonds;
- 585 thousand of Nazi victims, i.e. 90 percent, are pensioners;
- the age of 520 thousand of victims, i.e. 80 percent, is 70 or more;
- 130 thousand of Nazi victims (20 percent) are disabled and 390 thousand (60 percent) suffer from various dangerous chronic diseases;
- out of five citizens of Ukraine who were thrown by Nazis behind barbed wire only one survived;

- out of ten Nazi victims five remained lonely as they could have no children;
- each third woman – a former victim – did not feel the joy of being a mother;
- physical sufferings, psychological and nervous shocks experienced by Nazi victims told on their children. The genetic apparatus was broken. The majority bore disabled and sick children. They are handicapped already.

Having lost their strength and health in youth Nazi victims do not have a feeling of quiet and well-provided age now, either. Many live from hand to mouth. The death-rate among Nazi victims is twice as high as among other equivalent age groups of the population. During a year only we lost more than 30 thousand of our friends.

The largest and, in the opinion of independent experts, foreign observers, most influential organisation of Nazi victims in Ukraine is the Ukrainian Union of Former Minor Victims of Fascism. It is officially registered with the Ministry of Justice of Ukraine. Certificate No. 115 issued on 2.08.1991. It has a branch network of regional divisions in all the regions of Ukraine and in the Autonomous Republic of Crimea (more than 80). It renders practical assistance to Nazi victims – irrespective of their age, type of former bonds, nationality – in solving various living problems, first of all in the fields of social security, provision for retired, medical care, sanatorium-resort therapy, search for archive and other confirming documents.

The Ukrainian Union of Former Minor Victims of Fascism carries out its work meeting the principles of legal, organisation and financial independence. It is governed by the applicable law and the Articles of Association of the Ukrainian Union. It consistently preaches the principles of mutual assistance and support, constructive approaches towards problems solution, openness of human relations.

Being a member of the International Union of Former Minor Victims of Fascism, the Ukrainian Union actively cooperates with Nazi victims in the CIS and Baltic states, maintains its relations with kindred organisations in Austria, Bulgaria, Germany, Israel, Poland and the USA. At the present stage the basic tasks of the Ukrainian Union of Former Minor Victims of Fascism are as follows:

- promotion of quick adoption in Ukraine of the Law of Ukraine "On Nazi Victims"
- promotion of quick obtaining by Nazi victims in Ukraine and the CIS and Baltic states of fair compensation redemption on the part of Germany;
- further all-round improvement of the system of legal, social and moral protection of Nazi victims;
- consistent vindication of the rights and interests of all the Nazi victims residing in Ukraine;
- collection, systematisation, generalisation and publication of materials about all the survived Nazi victims, immortalising of the names of all the victims of fascist bonds who perished on the territory of Ukraine, which is a concrete manifestation of our care about preservation of historical memory by forthcoming generations;

- organisation strengthening of our movement through rendering of all-round and concrete assistance to the subordinate structures of the Ukrainian Union of Former Minor Victims of Fascism;
- strengthening of moral bases of the movement, its cleaning from hucksters, bribers, false victims – all those who because of their disgraceful behaviour damage the authority of the organization, defame the sainthood of our fraternity;
- broadening and strengthening of our relations with foreign organizations of victims, strengthening of our members' unity;
- steady establishment of the principles of goodness, justice, humanism, their following in all our deeds and inceptions.

The Ukranian Union of Former Minor Victims of Fascism is an organization of victims and for victims. Let us be faithful to our Union, to our camp fraternity!

UNITED KINGDOM

Allied discussions and decisions on gold, 1945–46

GILL BENNETT

Head of Historians, Foreign and Commonwealth Office

As the war in Europe drew to a close in early 1945, the Western Allies, led by the Big Three, the United States of America, the Soviet Union and the United Kingdom, were engaged both severally and jointly in detailed planning for a postwar settlement. Though their perceptions of the form this settlement might take were different, they agreed that the principles of reparation and restitution must lie at the heart of it. At the Crimea Conference held at Yalta from 4–11 February 1945, the Protocol on German Reparation established an Allied Reparation Commission (ARC), initially composed of British, American and Soviet representatives, which began work in Moscow in June 1945, joined by a French delegation in August. The ARC met on and off throughout the summer and autumn until its work was taken over the Paris Conference on Reparation which met in November 1945. Its members discussed reparations in the light of the agreement reached in July–August at the Potsdam Conference. They discussed the relationship between reparations and restitution, a matter of considerable disagreement. They discussed definitions of war booty. But although there was general agreement that gold must be dealt with as part of the post-war financial settlement, they barely discussed it. In the end they deferred discussion of gold to the Paris Conference of November–December 1945, when the Final Act, signed on 21 December 1945, made provision for the restitution of monetary and disposal of non-monetary gold without defining either of them.

Earlier in the war, the Allies had been concerned with trying to stop the enemy's traffic in gold, and to prevent enemy access to gold in non-enemy countries.[1] The question of what might happen at the end of hostilities had not been addressed in detail, apart from an implicit assumption that the priority would be to give gold back to those from whom it had been taken. In 1944, for example, when the British Government had expressed some doubts about the wisdom of issuing a gold declaration warning neutral countries against continued gold dealings with the Nazi regime, on the grounds that "any action which commits the United States or the United Kingdom to a continuing policy of discriminating against unidentifiable gold after the war may involve many embarrassments",[2] the US Government responded that

> The United Nations are already in a position which requires them in the post-war period to face the problems involved in clarifying the position of looted property including gold acquired by the neutral countries from the Axis during the war; this follows not only from the declaration of January 5 1943, but from our desire to aid our allies in obtaining the return of such property wherever possible.[3]

Whatever their concerns about future difficulties with neutral countries, the British Government were at one with the US Government in believing that gold should be given back to its former owners where possible. This implied that gold should be subject to restitution, rather than reparation. The phrase 'where possible', however, reflected a growing awareness that 'giving gold back' was not as simple as it seemed. As the Allies moved into Germany and began to discover and collect in gold, they received confirmation of what they already knew, that not all gold was clearly marked with stamps of origin, and that some had clearly been resmelted by the Prussian Mint. If identifiable gold were to be given back as restitution, would that be unfair to those countries whose lost gold had been rendered unidentifiable?

At the first meeting of the War Cabinet's Ministerial Committee on Reparations on 3 May 1945, under the chairmanship of Sir John Anderson Chancellor of the Exchequer, it was decided that all gold, identifiable or not, should be treated as available reparation and should be allocated in accordance with the criteria laid down in the Yalta Protocol.[4] Mr. Playfair, in the Treasury, had moral objections to this decision, which he thought would be unacceptable to Britain's Western European allies, and contrary to the principle that reparation should not be made out of goods taken from the recipients in the first place: 'If we extend the doctrine to cover gold plainly seen, before all the world, to be theirs, it will seem nothing less than banditry to them.'[5] The Foreign Office also objected to the inclusion of gold in an overall reparations settlement:

> From the political point of view the Department considers it of primary importance that the European Allies should be entitled to restitution of identifiable and recoverable monetary gold, valuable and securities which were their property before occupation and which were looted by the enemy. We very much hope it will prove possible to secure this. The inclusion of identifiable monetary gold in any Restitution policy agreed at Terminal [codename for Potsdam Conference] would materially lessen the bitterness with which other European Allies, especially the French, would look upon a policy settled by the Three Great Powers without consultation with them.[6]

By this time, however, the discovery by American forces of the major gold hoard in the Merkers salt mine at Kaiserode had brought the problem to a head and convinced the US Government that the idea of a 'gold pot', to be distributed to those countries who had lost gold in proportion to their losses, was the only possible way forward. To claim the Merkers hoard as war booty would 'seriously prejudice' US relations with the formerly occupied countries and although in principle gold should be restored to its former owners, the difficulties of implementing that principle equitably meant that another method of distribution had to be found.

The future destination of the Merkers gold was discussed at the Potsdam Conference in a different context for the Kaiserode mine where the gold was found fell within the Soviet, not the American Zone of occupation in Germany. The Soviet Union listed the gold amongst other property removed by the Allies from its Zone,[7] and Marshal Stalin claimed it as part of the Soviet reparation share. When Mr. Byrnes stated that 'according to his information, most of that now in the hands of the United States was identifiable as having been looted by the Germans; and the United States Government proposed that all such gold should be restored to its rightful owners', Marshal Stalin said that he would be prepared to restrict his claim to 30% of all German gold in Allied hands.[8] It seems clear from the records that the claim for gold was a bargaining counter in the Soviet campaign to secure higher percentages for reparations from the Western Zones of Germany: once the UK and US Governments agreed to these higher percentages, the Soviet Union undertook to make no claim to German external assets, nor to German gold.[9] This renunciation was formally enshrined in the Protocol of the Conference which laid down the agreement on reparations from Germany.

Among the three Western occupying powers, discussions on what to do with gold found in Germany proceeded throughout the autumn of 1945, the British Government initially maintaining the line that looted gold should be restored only to the extent that individual gold bars and gold coin could be identified. The US view, however, was that captured German gold should be distributed among all countries from which Germany looted gold, and the French thesis was that looted gold and securities should be replaced by other gold and securities. Effectively, the British were outnumbered, and in order to avoid deadlock the British delegate on the ARC, Sir David Waley, asked for authority to accept the American-French thesis.[10] The basic difficulty was what to do about gold of uncertain origin, and in the end the arguments put forward by US delegate Angell on 31 October 1945 proved unanswerable: he pointed out that the practicability of restitution was limited by the percentage of identifiable gold, and made three statements:

1. Gold is generally unidentifiable.
2. The question whether the gold of one or another origin has been used by Germany is one of chance.
3. Consequently it would be best to divide the gold found in Germany between the countries which have right to restitution in proportions according to their losses.[11]

Waley had to agree that restitution was a 'matter of chance. The only question that one could ask is to what extent chance takes a hand in each particular case.'[12]

Having decided on the pooling of gold found in Germany, whether identifiable or not, discussions in the preparatory phase of the Paris Conference on Reparation proceeded fruitfully and with little major disagreement between the three Western Powers. The proposals which were to be embodied in the Final Act of the Conference were drafted before the Conference opened and were amended only in detail before adoption.

The provisions of the Final Act of the Paris Conference in regard both to monetary and non-monetary gold found in Germany are discussed in detail in the second History Note on Nazi Gold published by the Foreign & Commonwealth Office in May 1997, and the text of the provisions is annexed to the note. They provided the authority for the three governments of France, the United Kingdom and United States to take the lead in all matters concerning the discovery, collection and disposition of German gold, in negotiating with the neutral countries who held German gold, and in establishing the Tripartite Commission for the Restitution of Monetary Gold in September 1946, and in making decisions as to which gold should go into the pool. In June 1946, they were party to the five-power agreement which provided that all non-monetary gold found in Germany, together with $25m and any heirless assets found in neutral countries, should be used to benefit non-repatriable refugees.

The three governments were faced with a series of challenging decisions regarding gold, but despite occasional differences of emphasis or approach they were on the whole able to take those decisions without serious disagreement. Whatever their views had been earlier in the war, a combination of experience, pragmatism and a strong sense of the need for a post-war settlement which was not just equitable but transparently so, influenced the evolution of Allied thinking so that when the time came for a firm decision on what to do about gold – in many ways the symbol of what so many had lost – the need to make a decision and act upon it was acknowledged as imperative.

NOTES

[1] See FCO History Note No.11, *Nazi Gold : Information from the British Archives*, 2nd edition January 1997 (hereafter *Nazi Gold*).

[2] *Ibid*, p.6.

[3] Casaday (US Embassy, London) to Rowe-Dutton (HM Treasury), 18 January 1944, Bank of England archives. For the 1943 Declaration see *Nazi Gold I*, p.4.

[4] RM (45) 1st meeting, 3 May 1945, copy taken from Bank of England files.

[5] Playfair to Waley (both Treasury), 14 May 1945, T 236/931.

[6] FO telegram. No. 133 to Berlin, 21 July 1945, printed in *Documents on British Policy Overseas*, Series I, Volume I (HMSO, 1984), No. 352.

[7] *DEPO*, Series, Vol. I, No. 455.

[8] *Ibid*, No. 495.

[9] *Ibid*, No. 498.

[10] Note by Waley on Restitution of Monetary Gold, 27 September 1945, reproduced in *DBPO*, Series I. Vol. V, No. 32.i.

[11] Minutes of 3rd meeting of prepatory conference on reparations, 31 October 1945, T 236/932; see also *Foreign Relations of the United States*, 1945, vol. iii, pp.1366-6

[12] *Ibid*.

Changes in the conceptual landscape

DONALD CAMERON WATT, FBA DLITT (OXON)

Emeritus Professor of International History

The theme of this Conference is gold, but underlying it is the analysis of what opinion in very many countries has come to see as a major injustice, committed during and after the end of the World War II. The nature of that injustice arose from the deposit with the banking systems of countries not involved in the war of sums of money by people who were robbed of their citizenships, their ability to prove their own identities, and in a great many cases of their lives before the war's end. Those who survived equally found themselves robbed of their heritage. That it has taken fifty years or more to reach the point where this injustice has achieved public recognition has itself added to the degree of indignation with which the subject is discussed in the organs of opinion in Europe and in the United States.

It is the duty of historians to ignore the temperature of indignation, even where they feel it themselves. It colours the imagination, distorts the judgement and leads to condemnation rather than comprehension. The expression of emotion should follow the establishment of understanding rather than govern and possibly misdirect it.

What has to be understood is how the question of restoration of losses experienced by those who, in the course of the war and through the policies followed by the government of Hitler's Europe, were deprived of citizenship, parentage, ability to prove their own legal identity and heritage seems so little to have engaged the attention of the governments of the victorious powers in their preparations for meeting the disorder and chaos they expected to follow their victory. After all, they had organisations concerned with the identification of those whom they regarded as war criminals. They had organisations devoted to tracing and rescuing where possible the works of art damaged or looted in war. They were informed and prepared for the issue of the restoration to the countries from which it had been plundered of their reserves of gold and specie. They had formed and prepared, however inadequately, the United Nations Relief and Rehabilitation Administration (UNRRA). They had reached agreement for the return to their own countries of persons taken by the defeated regime for the purposes of forced labour, agreements which for a time they were prepared to enforce even where it was clear that some of those concerned did not want, indeed feared for their lives in the case of, such repatriation. In fact, a good deal of attention had been paid by those planning for the post-war conditions the victors might expect to face, to the problem of restitution. Their preparations and planning however were not carried through with the same effectiveness.

This paper is going to suggest that the greatest difficulty was one of the conceptual framework that governed the thinking of government advisers, especially in the European countries when faced with what was a situation which their mental framework simply did not and could not recognise.

Government advice was conditioned and expressed within the concepts of international law and national sovereignty. For them the world was made up of a number of sovereign states, each with its own body of laws, its citizens, its government. Relations between these states were seen entirely in terms of relations between the governments which were the expression of the sovereignty of each such state. To govern such relations there were both treaties and conventions, general treaties and specific ones. To give one obvious example, extradition of an individual from one state to face charges of breach of the laws of another could and can only take place if there is a bilateral treaty between the two states setting out the procedures and the terms of accusation on which such yielding of the sovereign rights of each state can be accepted by both of them. Without such an agreement no extradition is possible.

The nineteenth and early twentieth centuries were the great period for the investment of private capital across the boundaries which divided one sovereign state from another. Much of that investment took the form of the lending of capital by organisations of private individuals in one state to the government of another. Inevitably there were cases where the recipients of the loans were unable or unwilling to observe the terms on which the loan was to be serviced. If the recipient of the loan was a private citizen then legal action in the courts of the country of which the recipient was a citizen was the first course of action to which those who advanced the loan could have resort. But if that was unsatisfactory, or if the recipient was the government of the country concerned, foreigners advancing such loans would turn to their own government or governments and pressure would be exerted by their government or governments on the government which was in default. In Britain and in the other major European countries the private interests who felt themselves damaged would band together in Councils of Foreign Bondholders or the like. The role of such organisations in British and international practice was already established when the twentieth century opened; as was the projection of such groups under the guise of national representatives onto such organisations as the International Commission for the Control of the Greek banks set up in 1896, the Chinese Maritime Customs Administration and so on.

What I cannot discover, with one exception only, was whether before 1939 any such organisations were recognised by international practice where they were not in fact the projection of groups defined by their national sovereignty. There were of course international pressure groups especially in the field of disarmament, women's rights, anti-slavery and so on, whose rise was part of the same movement that at the end of the nineteenth century produced the great international professional movements and the Olympic movement. There were also, a much older phenomenon, groups claiming to represent nations without political existence, including the Zionist movement. The Paris Peace Conference was beset by many such groups and found ways of giving them for however briefly a platform for their claims. But they too were obsessed by the issue of the sovereignty they claimed but did not yet possess.

The years after World War I did produce a large body of persons who as a result of that war and the revolutions that accompanied it had lost their citizenship. For them the Nansen passport was instituted and created. The question of recompense for their losses of money and property was very largely subsumed by that of claims against the new state of the Soviet Union. And such claims were inevitably made on a government to government basis.

The only exception I can find to this construction of an international political framework based on the institution of national sovereignty is in the case of the mandate for Palestine granted to Britain by the League of Nations Commission for Mandates, where a Jewish agency for Palestine, the members of which were not chosen from the Jewish population in Palestine, was created to act as the agency to represent their interests in London and Geneva. Its basis was the international Zionist movement, which drew its support from the Zionist-minded members of the Jewish communities of Europe and the United States. Official opinion in London resented its role as a limitation on British sovereignty; but its role and existence was part of the international agreement by which Britain exercised sovereign power in the former Palestine and was therefore unavoidable.

The creation and the subsequent destruction of the Nazi "New Order" in Europe and the determination of the British and American governments not to be led into any commitments as to the future of any part of Europe prior to the surrender of their enemies, embodied in the demand for "Unconditional Surrender", confronted both the American and British governments, and through them the exiled governments of Europe, with a Europe which, apart from the neutrals, was at war's end largely a *tabula rasa*. The group of historians, diplomats and economists responsible for developing and projecting Britain's vision of the post-war world concentrated on strengthening its international institutions, especially in the economic and financial field. In that of international security, they succeeded in neutralising the initial American desire for a radical restructuring in terms of the conferment of police powers on the "Big Four" of China, the Soviet Union, the British Empire and the United States, and substituting a system in which the second division of powers were given an enhanced role to play. They also insisted on France's inclusion among the permanent members of the Security Council and the powers occupying Germany and Austria. In a world where some Americans, including President Roosevelt, were looking to a radical restructuring of the international political system in which the sovereign rights of the individual powers were not regarded as a matter for particularly serious consideration, the British were intent on a world in which national sovereignty was the basis on which international order should be established.

Much the same phenomenon can be observed in the Anglo-American discussions on an International War Crimes Tribunal. British thinking on war crimes was conventionally bound up with the questions of the international laws of war. The initial reaction of the British cabinet to American approaches on the subject of a tribunal to try the leaders of Nazism was that the leading Nazis should be shot out of hand since there did not seem to be legal grounds on which a prosecution could rest. They were prepared to make an exception where British citizens had been the victims of traditional war crimes, shot after surrender, maltreated when in imprisonment and so on. Indeed it was notice-able that whereas after the trial of the major war criminals at Nuremberg, the United States embarked on eleven similar trials of other categories of those who could be regarded as part of the Establishment of the Nazi state, including lead-ing industrialists, soldiers, diplomatists, civil servants, and so on. Britain con-fined its action to those who had allegedly committed traditional crimes of war against British citizens. The lists of persons wanted on war crimes charges included a great many such wanted for crimes against Soviet, Jugoslav, Greek and so on, who, if found were due to be extradited to the country where the crimes had allegedly been committed. The British manifestly did not take mea-sures to collect evidence against or to try such persons before British tribunals until the early 1980s after a controversy which divided the generations. The pur-suit of war criminals was abandoned by the Labour government with the explic-it support of Winston Churchill and the leaders of the conservative opposition.

The same concentration on sovereign governments can be found in the nego-tiations on the recovery of the gold reserves of the Third Reich. Small in 1938, these had been augmented by that part of the reserves of the countries they had occupied thereafter which had fallen into their hands and which they had used as security to buy whatever they needed from and through neutral countries. This aspect of German war-time policy and the trade in gold with the neutral countries and the post-war negotiations to recover that gold has been exhaus-tively covered by recently published research, and is the subject of other papers before this conference. The question that emerges from this examination is, given that part of these reserves was know to have represented gold taken in all kinds of ways from the victims of the Holocaust, was the question of identifying the legal owners of such gold ever raised, and if not, why not?

It would appear that the question of restitution or recovery of assets belong-ing to Jewish refugees was raised by some of the organisations involved in bring-ing refugees to Britain during the war years and was indeed the subject of a con-siderable degree of forward planning by British officials. But it was not pressed and there were after all much more urgent questions exercising the principal Jewish organisations and personalities in Britain in 1943-44, recognising the appalling nature of what was happening to their fellows in Europe and attempt-ing to obtain some kind of reaction from the Allied governments. The writer, Arthur Koestler, has recorded how when he incorporated into his novel *Arrival and Departure*, published in 1944, descriptions of the death-vans which were used for executing Jews before the gas-chambers were in full action, he was attacked for manufacturing atrocity propaganda. There were efforts of comprehension which had to be made before there could be any realisation of the scale of the problem that would be faced once hostilities ended.

But the straightforward answer to these questions must be that it was assumed such claims should be collected and dealt with according to the nationality of the claimant by the sovereign states whose nationality they claimed. That there would be a stateless population whose numbers would run into the thousands was not anticipated; that in such conditions there would be no organisation to collect the claims and play a para-state role in presenting them for international negotiation is obvious to us now. But in the conditions of 1944–45 it does not seem to have arisen. The assumption was that claims might arise against a post-war German government. And indeed, in the long run they did and the West German government acknowledged these claims as part of its reparations pro-gramme. By the 1950s the return to an international system based on national sovereignty appeared to have re-established itself; though reparations in blocked East German marks seemed to acknowledge the letter rather than the spirit of such a system. In the interim the British government did indeed put aside funds to cover the question of restitution and indeed did disburse these funds. The sums concerned however amounted to not much more than a million pounds, so small a drop in the ocean that their disbursement was hardly even noticed at the time and has been largely forgotten since.

The problem was seen however in the context of state to state relations; as such it inevitably became part of the larger issue of reparations, a subject on which the British had learnt from the experience of the 1919 Peace Settlement was one to be handled with the utmost care, and became an issue which divid-ed Britain from the Soviet Union with its claims for massive reparations for the destruction wrought in European Russia by the invasions of Germany and her East European allies, Hungary and Romania. Indeed so far as the problem of the refugees was concerned, the problem of reparations for the loss of employ-ment, the forced sale or outright confiscation of private property or other such assets could only be accommodated within the framework of the successor gov-ernments to those that had carried through such measures, that is to say, not only the German government but also those of her allies who had co-operated with the measures of the Nazi Holocaust. The issue of the recovery of assets deposited in neutral countries by comparison simply was subsumed within these larger issues.

By the 1950s however it was already too late too look for the kind of interna-tional regime that the victorious Allies might have insisted on in 1945. Whether they could have extended it to cover the issue of resources deposited in neutral countries by persons who had themselves disappeared, lost their citizenship, been deprived of any chance of proving their pre-war identities, lost the whole of their families as well as the ability to prove that loss to be genuine, and the devising of a scheme by which such claims could be legitimised to the satisfac-tion of the banking institutions to whose care the funds claimed had originally been entrusted can only be a matter for conjecture.

Today, however, the gap between the conservative interpretation of interna-tional law and the contemporary reality has grown so wide that these questions are reasserting themselves. International public opinion, in so far as such an entity exists, does not wholeheartedly accept the conservative view of an international system based firmly on national sovereignty. If that national sover-eignty results in a situation that can be depicted as inherently contrary to nat-ural justice the pressure of opinion on the exercise of that national sovereignty becomes such that the opportunity costs of insisting on it can prove greater that the government concerned can accept. Under these circumstances we are returned to the field of multilateral negotiation. It will not be helped if prejudice and the accusation of prejudice, even if not indefensible, enters into the processes of negotiation. But it cannot be prevented from expressing itself once those processes are over. Even the historian is entitled to pronounce moral judgement on the outcome of historical research. Indeed, it sometimes appears as if only the historians have any right to be heard on such issues.

Documentation of the records of the Tripartite Gold Commission

STATEMENT BY THE HEAD OF THE UK DELEGATION

Several delegations have urged the early release of the Tripartite Gold Commission's records into the public domain. I cannot speak for the three TGC countries on this subject, but I should like briefly to explain the British view.

We have two separate objectives in relation to the TGC, which potentially conflict with one another. In the first place, we want to wind up the TGC's work and see its gold distributed as quickly as possible to the claimant countries. As you know, we hope that as many as possible of these claimant countries will want to contribute a high proportion of their receipts to the new Fund of which the establishment was announced yesterday. Our delegation and the US delegation have already spoken of the need to enable this Fund to start giving help to the surviving victims of war-time repression as quickly as possible, while they are still alive to receive it.

Second, we share the general wish to release the TGC's documents as quickly as possible. Those documents which relate to the origins of the gold which went into the monetary gold pool are also in national archives, and are already publicly available. But the rest relate to the process of submission, examination and adjudication of claims by the formerly occupied countries which own the gold in the pool. Negotiations on this have been conducted between the Commission and each claimant country on the basis that they would remain confidential. There is a real danger that if we were to release the information now, before the final distribution of gold, the effect would be to launch a debate among the claimant countries which could delay the distribution of the gold, and thus frustrate our first objective. The work of the Commission in its early years was substantially delayed by disputes between claimant countries: it is in nobody's interest that these should be repeated now.

We hope that the work of the TGC can be completed, and its papers released to the public, within a very few months. Thereafter, the Sectretary-General of the TGC will submit a report to the three TGC countries on the way in which the TGC has discharged its duties. I cannot speak for the other two TGC countries, but it will certainly be the hope of the British Government that that report can be made publicly available, as the Luxembourg delegate requested.

UNITED STATES
OF AMERICA

What U.S. officials knew about the movement of German monetary gold,

looted or otherwise, during World War II
and the restitution of looted gold after the War

Outline of a Study

COORDINATED BY STUART E. EIZENSTAT
Under Secretary of State for Economic, Business, and Agricultural Affairs

Prepared by a U.S. Interagency Team
DIRECTED BY WILLIAM SLANY
The Historian, Department of State

OUTLINE

Introduction

A key aspect of the U.S. Government interagency effort to research American policy on the recovery and restitution of gold and other assets looted by Germany during World War II has been our recognition of the importance of sharing the progress and results of our work with historians and experts in other countries. For the benefit of the participants at the London Conference on Nazi Gold, we are presenting below a summary account, together with detailed charts, of the factual information with respect to gold in particular. These facts and figures are drawn both from our preliminary study on *US and Allied Efforts to Recover and Restore Gold and Other Assets Stolen or Hidden by Germany During World War II*, released in the May 1997, as well as our forthcoming supplemental study which we plan to publish in January 1998.

That supplemental study will present a factual account addressing the Safehaven investigations in Portugal, Spain, Sweden, Turkey, and Argentina as well as the Allied negotiations after the war with the first four of these wartime neutral nations. These negotiations focused on the effort to restitute monetary gold looted by Germany from occupied Europe and to liquidate German external assets and apply the proceeds to European reparations and to stateless refugees. The new report will also seek to present a comprehensive picture of the broad policy context of U.S. attitudes and actions with respect to these neutral nations both during and after the war, as well as U.S. efforts during the war to curtail the economic relationships between these neutrals and Germany.

The information summarized below is confined to the wartime transfers of German monetary gold to the neutral nations and banks and attempts by the Allies to recover this gold and accomplish its restitution to the nations from which it had been looted. The narrative text is followed by tables summarizing information known to U.S. officials at the time regarding the wartime gold exchanges and the postwar restitution efforts.

Background

The United States and its Allies sought to prevent Germany from using looted gold and other assets abroad to help finance the war effort and, in the face of certain defeat, to conceal such gold and assets to help facilitate a revival of Nazism. Allied declarations in January 1943 and February 1944, together with Resolution VI of the Bretton Woods Agreement on postwar world financial arrangements, warned the neutral countries that the Allies would not recognize the acceptance of monetary gold and other assets looted by Germany from occupied Europe and outlined the need for postwar restitution. The United States and Britain, and late in the war, France, joined to negotiate Safehaven undertakings with the neutrals aimed at implementing these Allied policies and preventing the flight and concealment of stolen assets, including gold.

The postwar Allied policies for the recovery and restitution of stolen gold and other assets were developed in various postwar inter-Allied conferences. At the Potsdam Heads of Government meeting in July–August 1945, Truman, Stalin, and Churchill (and Attlee) agreed that the Western Allies would assume responsibility for the disposition of looted gold and external German assets outside the Soviet sphere. At the Inter-Allied Reparations Conference in Paris in November 1945-January 1946, agreement was reached that looted monetary gold would be recovered by the United States, Britain, and France, assembled into a gold pot under the auspices of a Tripartite Gold Commission, and distributed on a pro-rata basis to claimant countries. External German assets would be liquidated and applied to Allied reparations needs, and a fund of up to $25 million, composed of non-monetary gold and some liquidated external assets, would be used for the "non-repatriable victims of Nazism." The procedures for supporting the nonrepatriables were worked out in detail at a Five-Power Conference in Paris in June 1946.

In pursuance of the various wartime and postwar declarations and decisions, representatives of the United States, Britain, and France met in Washington with Swiss representatives from March to May 1946 to negotiate the terms of an agreement covering the restitution of looted gold acquired by Switzerland and the liquidation of German external assets and their application to European reparations and to non-repatriable victims. Following the talks with Switzerland, Swedish representatives came to Washington from June to July 1946 to negotiate a similar accord. In September 1946 other negotiations were begun by the three Allies in Madrid and Lisbon to achieve the same goals. Both the Swiss and Swedish negotiators contested the legal basis of Allied claims for gold and assets.

The Swiss denied their nation had received looted gold or that Switzerland was obliged to return such gold. Switzerland volunteered a contribution of $58 million in gold and, after five years of negotiations, had contributed a total of $28 million of liquidated assets to reparations and to non-repatriables. Both the gold returned and the funds from liquidated assets were small fractions of the amounts in Swiss possession.

The results of the negotiations with Portugal, Spain, and Sweden; the attempted negotiations with Turkey; and the consideration given to the possible wartime transfer of gold to Argentina are discussed briefly below and in the tables following. These nations likewise returned far less than the amount of looted gold and German assets they possessed. This situation resulted from a combination of recalcitrance even after the war by several of the neutrals, and distraction by the United States and its Allies, who were focused on rebuilding postwar Europe and then on meeting the Cold War threat from the former Soviet Union.

Portugal

From 1939 to 1944 Portuguese domestic gold holdings increased by $67.5 million. The Allies were certain that after early 1943 Germany was resorting to the sale of looted gold from the occupied countries to finance its trade. Both Portugal and Germany used Switzerland as an intermediary to facilitate gold transactions. When Germany needed escudos to purchase Portuguese goods, the Swiss National Bank would make transfers from its Reichsbank account to the account of the Bank of Portugal. Sometimes the gold was transferred directly; some times the Swiss National Bank used the German gold as credit and deposited equivalent amounts of Swiss francs, which the Portuguese used to buy Swiss goods. Wartime estimates of Swiss National Bank deliveries of gold to Portugal between 1939 and 1943 totaled 123.7 tons, worth about $139.2 million. There was also a significant gold trade outside the Bank of Portugal. In the second half of 1943, the partially Swiss-owned Bank Espirito Santo advanced $226.8 million escudos to the Germans to purchase Portuguese commodities in return for gold or Swiss francs from the Reichsbank. Smuggling also brought significant amounts of gold into the country. After Allied warnings in 1944 about trafficking in looted gold, the Bank of Portugal began to sell its German gold. Between June and September 1944 it reportedly sold 3,387 kilograms of its German gold holdings at the Swiss National Bank, and in August began selling 50–100 kilograms of gold a day to private concerns. In September the Bank allegedly transferred to the Portuguese Government nearly 16 tons of gold it had purchased from the Reichsbank and held in Portugal.

In preparation for the November 1946 negotiations with the Portuguese, the Allies estimated that Portugal, in its trade with Germany, received 123.8 tons of gold ($139.3 million) from the Swiss National Bank for the entire war period. According to Swiss sources, about 20.1 tons ($22.6 million) was looted from Belgium; this gold had been acquired by the Bank of Portugal directly from a Reichsbank account at the Swiss National Bank. Of the remaining gold, a minimum 72 percent or 74.67 tons ($84 million) worth was presumed to have been looted by Germany. Early in the negotiations a joint Subcommittee on Gold was established and its report, issued in March 1947, concluded that the Bank of Portugal acquired 46.76 tons of gold ($52.6 million) from Germany between 1939 and 1945. Of this amount, 38.4543.95 tons ($43.3–$49.4 million) was believed to be looted. Only 4 tons of Dutch gold was in its original form; the rest included 20.4 tons ($23 million) of re-smelted Belgian gold as well as some re-smelted Dutch coins worth almost $16 million. In November 1947 the Allies demanded that Portugal return 38.331 tons of gold ($43.1 million). The Portuguese contested all but 3.9 tons ($4.5 million), claiming they had purchased all the gold in a "good faith" belief that the Germans had not looted it. They refused to relinquish any without compensation.

A final settlement with Portugal on the restitution of looted gold was not reached until the late 1950s. Finally, in October 1958, the United States, Britain, France, Portugal, and West Germany reached agreements on Portuguese restitution of looted gold, the distribution of the proceeds of liquidated German external assets, and West German compensation to Portugal for wartime claims. In December 1959 Portugal delivered 3.998 tons of gold ($4.5 million) to the Tripartite Gold Commission.

Spain

Early estimates of Spain's wartime gold acquisitions were based on intelligence, captured Reichsbank records, statements by Swiss banking officials, and records from private corporations. The United States estimated that Spain acquired about 122.8 tons of gold ($138.2 million) between 1942 and 1945: 11 tons directly from Axis nations, 74 tons from German accounts at the Swiss National Bank, and 37.852 tons directly from the Swiss National Bank. Of that total U.S. experts estimated 72 percent or about 88 tons ($99 million) was looted, which Spain was liable to return. Most of this gold went to the German Embassy, German State offices, German-controlled institutions, and the Bank of Spain. Published figures showed that Spanish domestic gold holdings increased from $42 million to $110 million between 1941 and 1945. The OSS also reported evidence of gold entering Spain by truck from Switzerland to the Spanish Foreign Exchange Institute, the only body in Spain officially allowed to conduct gold transactions.

Allied negotiations with Spain on restitution of gold extended from November 1946 until an agreement was reached in May 1948. Some gold bars and coins worth about $1.13 million seized by Spain at war's end were turned over to OMGUS before the negotiations began. In 1947 Spain allowed a U.S. review of the gold transactions records of the Foreign Exchange Institute. The investigators determined that the Institute had acquired about 26.8 tons of looted gold (about $30.2 million) during the war from the Swiss National Bank, Bank of Portugal, and the Banco Aleman Transatlantico. Included in that total were 8 bars identifiable as Dutch gold weighing 101.6 kilograms ($114,329), which had been purchased directly from the Banco Aleman Transatlantico. In an Allied-Spanish exchange of notes on April 30 and May 3, 1948, Spain agreed to resti-tute the 101.6 kilograms of gold ($114,329) identified as looted from the Netherlands in exchange for an Allied public acknowledgement that Spain had not been aware when it acquired the gold that it was looted. In late 1948 the gold was deposited with the Tripartite Gold Commission.

In 1950 Spain proposed to use gold it held at the Federal Reserve Bank of New York as collateral for $50 million in loans from two New York banks. Some of that gold was determined to be looted from the Netherlands and Belgium by Germany, re-smelted in the Prussian Mint, and then sold to Switzerland, which in turn sold it to Spain. Because Spain had not purchased the gold directly from Germany or a German institution, it was declared eligible for purchase by the United States.

Sweden

The OSS and other agencies provided the United States and its Allies with information on the flow of gold from Germany to Sweden, but orderly and com-prehensive quantification of such transfers was not available to Allied policy-makers until late 1945. Although there were some estimates that Sweden had acquired as much as nearly $23 million in looted Belgian monetary gold, U.S. experts finally concluded that Germany had sold Sweden gold worth $18.5 mil-lion and Switzerland had purchased gold from Sweden worth $17 million.

At the Allied-Swedish negotiations in Washington in June and July 1946, agreement was quickly reached that Sweden would restitute to the Allies all gold looted by Germany from occupied Europe including such gold transferred to the Swedish Riksbank to third countries. Initial agreement was reached in Washington for Sweden to restitute over $8 million in gold, corresponding to the amount of Belgian monetary gold acquired by the Riksbank during the war. The Swedish postponed implementing the agreed restitution pending its own further investigations into the movement of the Belgian gold, and the $8.1 mil-lion was not deposited in the Tripartite Gold Commission account until December 1949. A parallel claim by the Dutch Government for the return from Sweden of about $7 million in looted monetary gold, made first in 1947 and sub-sequently pursued with the support of the U.S. Government, was not finally resolved until April 1955 when Sweden transferred $7 million in gold to the Tripartite Gold Commission account at the Federal Reserve in New York.

Turkey

U.S. officials reached various estimates of gold sold by Germany to Turkey dur-ing World War II at from $10 to $15 million. Some American officials thought all this gold was looted. Postwar investigations in captured German records revealed that 249 bars of identifiable Belgian monetary gold worth $3.4 million was resmelted and sent to the Turkish Central Bank in 1943. Allied wartime diplomatic and intelligence reports described a lively traffic in looted gold in Turkey's free gold market from 1941 through 1943. The principal German banks in Turkey acquired gold from Switzerland and later directly from the Reichsbank. One report put such free market sales at worth $5 million in the first part of 1943 alone. Some of what the German banks in Turkey were selling was suspected by the Allies to be loot. Some German looted gold reached Turkey, even after the war had ended when in September 1945 the Swiss Legation delivered to Turkish authorities various coins and ingots belonging to official German institutions and later confirmed as part of the so-called "Ribbentrop Fund" used by the German Foreign Ministry.

U.S., British, and French representatives, acting on behalf of the Allied signatories of the Paris Reparations Agreement of January 1946, formally presented to Turkey in March 1946 a program for the restitution of looted gold. During negotiations in June and July 1946, Turkish negotiators insisted that because Turkey had joined the war on the Allied side (in February 1945), it was not bound by the Paris Agreement and could dispose of German gold; it denied, in any case, that it had any looted gold. In July 1947 Turkey agreed to return $3.4 million in gold to the Allies, but the restitution offer was not carried out because Turkey would not provide additional information required by the Allies and because the Turkish Government had approached the Bank of England with a request for re-melting 8 tons of gold ingots and various gold coins worth a total of some $12.4 million. The Turkish offer to return $3.4 million was not revived. The Allies subsequently expressed a willingness to settle for $1 million, and, after April 1953, abandoned further efforts at gold restitution.

Argentina

The U.S. Treasury Department made a final Safehaven report in May 1946 regarding Argentine wartime gold acquisitions and concluded that Argentina had not become a haven for looted monetary gold from Europe. Suspicions continued, however, among State and Treasury Department officials that Argentina had acquired looted gold from Germany or the neutral European countries. In 1947 Argentina shipped $320 million in gold for deposit at the Federal Reserve Bank of New York, reviving U.S. Government concerns about the source of such gold. The United States purchased $232 million of gold, which was in the form of U.S. assay bars. The remaining $88 million fell into three categories: (1) $39 million of gold that could not be identified as having been under "earmark" in the United States in the prewar period, (2) $20 million held under "earmark" in the United States during the war but exported to Argentina prior to the February 1944 Allied Gold Declaration, and (3) $29 million under "earmark" in the United States and exported to Argentina after the February 1944 Declaration. In October 1947 the Argentine Government assured the U.S. Government that it had not obtained any gold from the Axis countries or from

Spain, Portugal, or Turkey and that it had purchased from Switzerland gold worth less than $65,000 between 1940 and 1947. The Argentine Government provided written assurance in October 1947 that the gold purchased from Switzerland never had German ownership although it declined to provide bar numbers, mint marks, or other identifying symbols.

TABLES

Statement on gold values

The dollar figures for gold assets cited in the report and in the following charts are based on the 1946 value of gold at $35 per ounce. To assist readers, dollar values have been added to the weight of gold cited in the report and the following charts, as well as to assets denominated in a foreign currency. The calculations were based on the following considerations.

With respect to gold, the original documents usually cited the weight in kilograms or tons without indicating the dollar values or whether it was in U.S., British, or metric tons. The authors of this report have assumed that all figures in the documents were in metric tons unless otherwise noted. The authors estimated the dollar value of the gold according to the formula of $35 a troy ounce, or 32,150.7 fine troy ounces of gold per ton. Thus a ton of gold was valued at $1.125 million. When the documents referred to an amount of gold in kilograms only, the authors converted these weights into tons, so that a reader could follow more easily the history of the negotiations between the Allies and the neutral countries. During 1997 the value of gold has been 8.5 to 10 times higher than in 1946.

Portugal

	Gold	Dollars
Allied estimates, July 1946	123.827 tons	$139.3 million
– of which looted from Belgium and acquired directly from Germany	20.117 tons	$22.6 million
– estimate of remainder looted	74.67 tons	$106.6 million
Gold Subcommittee estimates, March 1947	46.76 tons	$52.6 million
– estimate of amount looted	38.45–43.95 tons	$43.3–49.4 million
Allied demands in November 1947 negotiations	38.331 tons	$43.1 million
Gold Subcommittee Report estimates, March 1947, of Portugal's acquisitions, 1939–45 Germany	46.76 tons	$52.6 million
– amount "of concern" to Allies	43.95 tons	$49.4 million
– amount U.S. believed was looted	38.45 tons	$43.3 million
Turned over to Allies/TGC, 1959	3,998 kgs	$4.5 million

Spain

	Gold	Dollars
Allied estimates, August 1946, of Spain's acquisitions, 1942–45	122.852 tons	$138.2 million
– from the Axis	11 tons	
– from the Swiss National Bank (SNB)	37.852 tons	
– from German accounts at the SNB	74 tons	
Allied estimates, December 1947, of Foreign Exchange Institute acquisitions of looted gold from SNB, Bank of Portugal, Banco Aleman Transatlantico*	26.8 tons	$30.2 million
– Dutch gold liable for restitution	101.6 kgs	$114,329
Turned over to Allies/TGC, 1948	101.6 kgs	$114,329

*Does not include 2.6 tons of gold ($2.94 million) Spain purchased directly from Germany, which was later determined to have been minted into coins and thus too difficult to identify and recover.

Sweden

	Gold	Dollars
Allied estimates		$18.5–22.7 million
Amount of Belgian gold restituted, 1949	7,155.32644 kgs	$8.1 million
Amount of Dutch gold restituted, 1955	638 bars 6,000 kgs	$6.8 million
Turned over to Allies/TGC		$14.9 million

Turkey

	Gold	Dollars
FEA estimates, March 1947		$10–15 million
– held by Turkish Government		$3.5 million
– held by private individuals		$6.5–11 5 million
Estimates used in Allied-Turkish negotiations, June–July 1947*		
– Belgian origin gold	3,000 kgs	$3.4 million
– coins acquired from German Embassy, Ankara	32,799 coins 243.6 kgs	$400,000
Turned over to Allies/IARA	None	None

*Does not include 11 tons of gold (54 million TL; $12.4 million) that Turkey attempted to sell to the Bank of England July 22, 1947.

Argentina

The Allies found no conclusive evidence that looted gold reached Argentina.

Switzerland

	Dollars	Swiss Francs
Estimates of German gold reserves and movements, 1939–45 February 1946)	$781–785 million	
– amount of looted gold (74%)[1]	$579 million	
Estimates of gold traded by Germany to Switzerland[2]	$398–414 million	
– amount of looted gold to Switzerland[3]	$185–289 million	
Allied estimate presented to Switzerland of looted Nazi gold sent to Switzerland March 1946)	$200 million	860 million SF
Allied statement of Swiss liability based on amount of looted Belgian gold (April 1946)	$130 million	559 million SF
Amount of Belgian gold Swiss admit to receiving (April 1946)	$88 million	378 million SF
Amount of gold Swiss agree to transfer to the Allies (May 1946)[4]	$58 million	250 million SF
Transferred to the TGC (1947)	$58 million	250 million

[1] The 74% figure is derived from the Treasury report based on the 579/785 ratio.
[2] These figures are consistent with a recently-released Swiss National Bank report.
[3] The State Department estimated that during the war Switzerland purchased from Germany $276 million in gold, and that "the larger part was looted gold." In addition, part of the gold that Switzerland sold during the war to Portugal, Spain, and Turkey ($138–148 million) could have been looted German gold. The Treasury Department estimated the amount of looted gold that Switzerland received from Germany at a minimum of $185 million but more likely $289 million.
[4] Pursuant to the 1946 Washington Accord.

Summary

Monetary Gold

	Allied estimates	Terms of accord with the Allies	Turned over to Allies/TGC
Argentina	None	N/A	N/A
Portugal	$52.6 million ($49.5 million looted) 46.76 tons (43.95 tons looted)	3,998 kgs $4.5 million	3,998 kgs $4.5 million, 1959
Spain	up to $138.2 million ($30.3–98.7 million looted) up to 122.9 tons (26.8–87.7 tons looted)	101.6 kgs $114,329	101.6 kgs $114,329, 1948
Sweden	$17–22.7 million looted	$14.9 million	$14.9 million, 1949, 1955
Turkey	$10–15 million	N/A	N/A
Switzerland	$398–414 million ($185–289 looted)	$58 million	$58 million, 1947

Research into U.S. and Allied efforts to recover and restore gold and other assets stolen or hidden by Germany during World War II

An outline of ongoing official U.S. Government research

WILLIAM SLANY

Bureau of Public Affairs, Department of State

The fall of the Berlin Wall, the unification of Germany, and the collapse of Communism marked the end of the Cold War and the resolution of the East-West conflict in Europe. The conclusion of this long, difficult period revealed many long-neglected aspects of the final accounting of World War II and its aftermath. One very important consequence of the war in particular the unsettled fate of so many victims of Nazis – remains unresolved. Jewish groups and individuals took the lead in reminding governments and legislatures in Europe and in the United States that a terrible injustice had yet to be remedied. A new spotlight of attention was cast on these issues, and some troubling facts were thrown into sharp relief.

The remaining thousands of aging survivors of the Nazi camps, as well as the heirs of the millions who died in the camps, had never been able fully to regain their property and personal possessions looted by Nazi Germany. After the war the Allied occupation forces in Germany recovered only a small proportion of the things stolen directly from individuals. It was unclear, or at least not generally known, what share of the property, assets, and other valuables moved to wartime neutral countries by the victims or their tormentors was ever properly redeemed. Governments and banks had grown forgetful or even callous in their stewardship of such property.

In the United States, the Congress and the Executive Branch heard the call for redress for the Nazi victims and during 1996 acted to heed it. At President Clinton's direction, Under Secretary of State Eizenstat set in motion an interagency examination of the U.S. Government's documentary record bearing upon the fate of bank accounts and other assets, properties, and valuables in Europe and elsewhere of the victims of Nazi Germany. A U.S. interagency historical research team, which the Under Secretary coordinated, sought to meet the expectations of the victims and their heirs through a three-pronged effort.

- First, to ensure that all government records bearing upon these issues were moved to the National Archives and Records Administration and made available as quickly as possible for all researchers, including rapid declassification of records that still remained secret;
- Second, to identify all the documentary collections, files, and bodies of records that constituted these materials and provide usable finding aids so that individual researchers could explore the records;

- And third, to prepare a narrative report based on these U.S. records that would provide general readers with a usable understanding of the files and collections, as well as offer policy-makers information sufficient to begin to take action in responding to the unanswered questions regarding the claims of surviving victims and the children of victims.

Under Secretary Eizenstat made clear to all engaged in the project that, while the desperate plight of many of the survivors and the wholly inadequate response from governments, banks, and others made the interagency project terribly urgent, it also had to be carried out as rigorously and comprehensively as possible.

The U.S. interagency project responded to Under Secretary Eizenstat's direction and expectations. All of the known government records that seemed to bear on the issues were transferred to the National Archives and opened to public review by the end of 1996, adding up to a total of more than 15 million pages. Many of these records had already been publicly available at the National Archives for 10 or more years. But nearly a million pages of very important records from several agencies were declassified during the last month of 1996, one of the largest single declassification actions ever accomplished. A narrative account of the government perceptions and policies during and after World War II was assembled from the contributions of the State, Treasury, Justice, and Defense Departments; the Central Intelligence Agency; the Holocaust Memorial Museum; and others. The National Archives assembled a detailed finding aid of the relevant records while rushing to assist the growing body of private researchers carrying forward their own research into the historical record.

The preliminary study on *U.S. and Allied Efforts To Recover and Restore Gold and Other Assets Stolen or Hidden by Germany During World War II* was released to the public in May 1997. The study was not so much a conventional history as it was a road map through more than 15 million pages of official documents from the 1941–55 period. The study sought to identify what U.S. officials knew about the movements of looted monetary gold and other assets into neutral nations during World War II and what these officials did with their knowledge. Especially important was the U.S. role in the postwar negotiations undertaken in cooperation with its Allies to restore looted monetary gold to the liberated nations and to apply the proceeds from liquidated German assets to the reconstruction of Europe.

The preliminary study of May 1997 concluded that wartime and postwar public policy-making regarding the issues of German looted monetary gold and external assets fell into four major episodes: (1) the economic war against Germany during World War II where the neutral nations were the principal battlefields; (2) the immediate postwar policy making of the top Allied leadership on issues of restitution and reparations; (3) the efforts of the Allies to apply the high-level postwar policies in negotiations with neutral nations and achieve the desired restitution of gold and application of external assets to European reparation; and (4) the creation and use of the Tripartite Gold Commission as the vehicle to achieve the restitution of the recovered looted gold.

As a key aspect of Allied economic warfare against the Axis, including the blockade of Axis-occupied Europe, the Allies sought to cut off those exports from the neutral countries that sustained the German war effort. One aspect of economic warfare against Germany was the effort of the United States and its Allies to prevent Germany from using looted gold and other assets in the neutral nations to help finance the war effort and, in the face of certain defeat beginning in 1944, to conceal such gold and assets for some future revival of Nazism. Allied policy declarations in January 1943 and February 1944 along with Resolution VI of the July 1944 Bretton Woods Agreement on postwar world financial arrangements, made clear that the Allies would not recognize the use of German looted monetary gold in international commerce and established the need for postwar restitution. The United States and Britain, joined late in the war by France, undertook a Safehaven program in 1944 that sought to identify in the neutral nations German looted gold and external assets, to prevent their concealment, and to lay the basis for their restitution.

In the 13 months after the end of the war in Europe, the Allies adopted policies and programs aimed at ensuring that a defeated Germany bore the full burden of the restitution of looted and stolen property and served as the immediate source of reparations for the recovery of Europe. These policies and programs intended to work through governments and not deal with individual victims. At the Potsdam Heads of Government meeting in July-August 1945, President Truman, Prime Ministers Churchill and Attlee, and Marshal Stalin agreed that the Western Allies would assume responsibility for the disposition of looted monetary gold and German external assets outside the Soviet sphere. The Inter-Allied Reparations Conference of representatives of 18 Allied nations, which met in Paris from November 1945 to January 1946, resulted in agreement that looted gold would be recovered by the United States, Britain, and France, assembled into a gold pot under the auspices of a Tripartite Gold Commission, and be distributed on a pro-rata basis to claimant countries. The Reparations Conference also concluded that German external assets would be liquidated and applied to Allied reparations, and that a fund of at least $25 million, composed of all non-monetary gold and some portion of liquidated external assets, would be used for the "non-repatriable victims of Nazism" – largely the stateless Jewish survivors of the Holocaust. The procedures for supporting the non-repatriables through the Inter-Governmental Refugee Committee were worked out in greater detail at a Five-Power conference in Paris in June 1946.

The negotiations undertaken by the United States, Britain, and France in 1946 and 1947 with various neutral nations to apply the policies and programs agreed upon by the Allied leaders yielded surprisingly and disappointingly little of either looted gold or proceeds from liquidated external German assets. Allied negotiations were held in Washington with Swiss representatives from March to May 1946 and with Swedish representatives from June to July 1946 and reached firm agreements. Allied negotiations were begun with Spanish and Portuguese officials in September 1946, reached initial undertakings in 1947 and 1948, but stretched into the 1950s before final agreements could be reached. Intermittent efforts at negotiations with the Turkish Government from 1946 through 1948 had no outcome. The Swiss and Swedish negotiators in Washington in 1946 contested the legal basis of Allied claims for monetary gold and external assets. The Swiss denied that their nation had received looted gold or that Switzerland was obliged to return such gold. Switzerland did, however, volunteer a contribution of $58 million in gold and, after five years of negotiations had contributed a total of $28 million from liquidated assets to reparations and to the support of non-repatriables. Sweden eventually in 1949 and 1955 restituted almost $15 million in looted monetary gold and turned over to the Allies more than $66 million from liquidated assets between 1947 and 1955. Spain restituted a small amount of gold acquired from German institutions and over $26 million derived from liquidated German assets over a period from 1948 to 1955. Portugal's restitution of $4.5 million in looted gold was achieved in 1958, while liquidated assets in Portugal netted only about $500,000 for European reparations.

Despite the comparatively small amounts of monetary gold recovered by Allied negotiators from the neutral nations, the Tripartite Gold Commission succeeded in overseeing the restitution of a gold pot of over $350 million in gold to ten claimant nations. Over $263 million of the gold pot came from Allied-occupied Germany, and much of this amount was the Reichsbank gold reserve recovered by American forces at the Merkers mine in April 1945, where it was hidden in the closing months of the war. The Commission, whose task it was to adjudicate among the claims of 10 nations whose monetary gold had been looted, made an initial distribution of gold to Belgium, Netherlands, Luxembourg, and France in 1947. Other distributions followed, and by 1997 only $60 million remained in the gold pot.

In its haste to carry forward the program for gold restitution, the Allies swept into the Tripartite gold pool some undetermined (and indeterminable) amount of non-monetary gold, much of which was the possessions, even dental gold, of the victims of Nazi looting and murder. Postwar investigations demonstrated that the Nazi SS systematically melted victim gold into gold bars with disguised markings that were added to the Reichsbank gold holdings. Research for the May 1997 preliminary report determined that on at least one occasion victim gold could be traced in gold bars shipped to Switzerland and Italy. Postwar procedures adopted by the Allied occupation forces in Germany may also have resulted in the inclusion of non-monetary gold in gold shipped to the Tripartite Gold Commission.

The Preliminary Report of May 1997 makes clear the concern of U.S. policymakers to work at the governmental level to achieve the restitution of gold and other assets stolen by German authorities during the war. The issue of heirless assets of the individual victims of Nazism never became a significant issue in the postwar negotiations of the Allies, including the United States, nor did it become a major object of federal or state investigation or legislation in the United States.

Most of the historians and other experts involved in the preparation of the Preliminary Report of May 1997 recognized that time constraints and gaps in the documentation reviewed for the study had resulted in a published account that was incomplete. By using exclusively contemporary U.S. official sources, the Preliminary Study did not make fully clear the information and presumptions that drove U.S. policy-making and U.S. negotiations with its Allies and with all the neutral nations. Therefore a small team of historians and other researchers, far smaller than the interagency team that drafted the May report, set out to prepare a supplementary report that would provide a broader context for understanding wartime and postwar U.S. and Allied policies toward Argentina, Portugal, Spain, Sweden, Turkey, as well as the Vatican, as well as examining more closely the lengthy and complicated postwar negotiations with these states.

Like the Preliminary Report of May 1997, the supplementary study undertaken in the State Department with assistance from the Justice Department, the Treasury Department, the Federal Reserve Bank, the Center for Military History, and the CIA, and of course the National Archives and Records Administration, presents what U.S. officials, particularly those at the highest political level, knew and what attitude or action they took. It is likewise coordinated by Under Secretary of State Eizenstat. To a much greater extent than the May report, the supplementary report will expand the scope of research and fact-finding to include the broader political and economic context of major wartime economic warfare actions and postwar negotiations.

The supplementary study will not conclusively answer the question of whether the neutral nations, individually or collectively, could have halted the war by denying Germany important supplies for its war effort. It will seek to demonstrate what great importance the Allies and the neutral countries themselves assigned to the economic support reaching Germany, particularly Swedish iron ore and ball bearings, Turkish chromite, and Portuguese and Spanish wolfram, as keys to sustaining a continued German war effort. The report seeks to address how U.S. officials recognized and acknowledged the considerable differences among the various neutral nations in their relationship with Germany, their past historical policies and relationships with the Allies, and the various forms their "neutrality" took. The report further seeks to document the policy presumptions that underlay Allied efforts to bring to an end the perceived economic assistance being rendered by the neutrals to Germany.

The study will also seek to provide a clearer and more detailed description than that offered in the May 1997 report of the postwar negotiations of the United States, Britain, and France with Portugal, Spain, Sweden, and Turkey and the consideration given to negotiations with Argentina and others. There was no intention to gloss over the delays and loss of focus of these various negotiations which extended from March 1946 until well into the 1950s for all of the former wartime neutrals. The supplemental report will examine these negotiations in more detail. Special attention will be given to the context of U.S. policy-making in the postwar period, especially U.S. foreign policy considerations and perceived national interests in the establishment of military security measures against possible Soviet aggression as well as the urgent need to extend Marshall Plan assistance and get Europe back on its feet economically.

The study will examine the foreign policy context of relations with Portugal, where negotiations for permanent bases in the Azores and elsewhere for the U.S.

military paralleled protracted gold and assets discussions; in Spain where anxiety over the apparent danger of another civil war from which the Communists would benefit colored gold and assets discussions; in Turkey which was drawn early on into anti-Communist economic and military assistance program by President Truman; and in Sweden which sought a postwar interpretation of neutrality in the face of Soviet imperialism.

The study will explore how these foreign affairs undertakings intersected with the long-drawn-out negotiations and resulted in restitution of less than $20 million (in contemporary value) in looted monetary gold and the conversion of less than $100 million in German external assets (and none at all from Argentina and Turkey) into reparations, including the $25 million assigned to the support of non-repatriable victims of Nazism – compared to the estimated total of $97 to $170 million in looted monetary gold and $473 to $493 million in German external assets they possessed.

The gathering here in London of so many of my fellow historians and of others concerned about these matters gives me encouragement and confidence. A full acknowledgment of the scope and significance of role of governments and institutions in the dispossession and plundering of Europe's Jews and other rejected peoples during World War II is finally within reach.

To accomplish this, it will be essential that all countries immediately declassify their documents so the fullest understanding of their wartime can be reviewed. Those countries with historical commissions are to be complimented, and it is to be hoped they will speedily complete their work. For others, it is hoped that they will proceed quickly with establishing such a truth-seeking commission. These are very difficult and complex problems, but it may be at last possible, fifty years after the events, for men and women of all nations to bring together their efforts and knowledge and render the historical accounting that victims and survivors alike must have as their due – whatever else may be possible for all of us who must bear witness, now and in the future.

Insurance as a forcibly surrendered or plundered asset in the Holocaust

GERALD D. FELDMAN

University of California, Berkeley

Let me preface these remarks by making it clear that I am not yet an "expert" on this subject. I have been asked by the Allianz Insurance Company to undertake an independent study of its history during the "Third Reich" as well as during the de-nazification and restitution period which followed, and I began to work on the project four months ago. It would be pretentious to claim expertise in so short a time. Also, I should make it clear that I am not competent to evaluate the legal claims for restitution and compensation being made against Allianz and other insurance companies in the courts. Nor do I have the technical skills to assess the mass of insurance policies now being audited by the accounting firm of Arthur Andersen employed by Allianz for this purpose. My own task is to produce an historical study dealing with the internal and external development of the company during the period and the relationships between its executives and employees and the National Socialist regime. Needless to say, this also means studying the role of the company in aryanization within its own ranks, its involvement in the expropriation of the assets of its Jewish customers, and its acquisition of Jewish assets or involvement in the acquisition of such assets by others. It is important to recognize that such a study cannot be confined to Allianz alone and inevitably requires a consideration of the entire industry, which was highly organized and which also had substantial international subsidiaries or affiliates and engaged in a great deal of international business. Since relations with the regime were often conducted through the insurance industry's peak organization, the Reichsgruppe Versicherung and its branches, no single company, however large and important, could act in isolation. Also, Allianz was closely associated with major reinsurance companies, above all the Münchener Rückversicherungsgesellschaft, and relations with reinsurance companies and their behavior were of central importance to the industry's history in the National Socialist period. Finally, much of Allianz's business, for example, the insurance of the physical plants and German supervisory and technical personnel at SS factories set up at the major concentration camps or at the widespread network of sub-camps, involved membership in consortia of insurance companies. The same may have been true for the plants producing for the Germany army in the ghettos and their production, which were also insured.

   Leaving all legal issues and claims aside, it is essential to recognize that insurance forms a substantial and significant category of Jewish asset that further legitimizes and reinforces the arguments made at this conference for a special fund and other forms of restitution on moral grounds. A full accounting of insurance losses and of the various categories of such losses is extraordinarily difficult but it is revealing to contemplate the variety and types of such losses. The infamous *Reichskristallnacht* ("Night of Broken Glass") of November 9–10, 1938, when Nazi thugs burned, wrecked, and plundered Jewish synagogues, stores, and homes, is a monumental example of how German Jews were deprived of their just insurance compensation. Not only did the regime bar the insurance companies from fulfilling their obligations, but it also imposed a massive fine on the Jewish community to pay the costs of the damages. It is highly likely that some Jews found it necessary to cash in their life insurance in order to pay this fine and to pay for the other economic burdens imposed on them during this period. Indeed, from a moral and also from an economic point of view, one must treat as insurance losses the cashing-in of insurance policies or the non-payment of insurance premiums made necessary by the loss of livelihood and economic discrimination against Jews under the National Socialist regime. There were other ways in which Jews and other persecuted persons were deprived of their insurance investments. An important one was the use of the government's currency control regulations to make it impossible for Jewish emigrants to collect on policies denominated in foreign currencies and, ultimately, in Reichsmark which could not be used outside Germany. There is evidence that Swiss insurance companies, which worked hand-in-hand with their German counterparts, also transferred the proceeds of Jewish-owned policies to the Reich before and during the war.

As was the case with other Jewish assets, the expansion of the "Third Reich" meant that the insurance policies of non-German Jews became subject to the same measures of direct and indirect expropriation already practiced in Germany. With the implementation of the "final solution," of course, one increasingly plundered the dead rather than the living and despoiled survivors. It is highly likely, however, that insurance remained an important aspect of expropriation to the very end, not only because the SS and government agencies collected on the insurance of some of those who were murdered in the concentration camps but also because of the expropriation of such assets from Jews living in the various countries occupied or controlled by National Socialist Germany. German insurance companies pursued a very active policy of expansion in the conquered areas and were very intent on dominating the European insurance business. This was true not only in the West but also in the East, and it is very important to recognize that Austrian and Italian subsidiaries and partners were very active in this expansion as well. The Austrians and Italians, for example, were strongly engaged in Poland. Much of the aggressiveness on the part of German companies was motivated by a desire to counter the efforts of the more Socialist-minded Nazis to nationalize the insurance business by getting a foot in the door in the newly conquered territories and demonstrating the importance of the private insurance industry to the New Order. This final stage in the disintegration of business ethics and criminalization of business activity certainly must have had negative consequences for the insurance assets of Jews living in these areas and raises the important question of how Jewish insurance policies held by native insurance companies were handled either by those companies themselves if they continued to exist or by the Axis insurance companies that took them over. In any case, one may hope that this preliminary foray into the insurance problem demonstrates the need for further research and, once again, suggests the importance of insurances as a category of asset that must be taken into account when considering the despoliation of European Jewry by the National Socialists and their allies.

WORLD JEWISH CONGRESS

Indemnification and reparations: Jewish losses

World Jewish Congress
World Jewish Restitution Organization

Jewish Losses

DISPOSSESSION OF JEWS – PROCESS AND METHODS[1]

In general the dispossession or spoliation of the Jews in Nazi dominated countries followed the pattern evolved in the practice of depriving German Jews of their property and positions. But in Germany the process was comparatively slow (lasting for five or six years), in the other cases it proceeded far more rapidly. In most cases the dispossession was total, e.g. in Austria and Hungary, in Czechoslovakia, Poland and the Baltic countries, in Norway, Belgium and Holland. In some instances certain Jewish groups or individuals were robbed only partially – e.g. certain groups in Romania and Italy; the German and some other Jews succeeded in transferring an inconsiderable part of their wealth abroad.

Since the dispossession has been almost total, we may assume that the amount of wealth previously owned by Jews is equivalent to the losses they have suffered.

Many diverse measures were applied. The first employed in Germany was the boycott of 1933, which was followed by the ousting of Jews from certain positions. The general anti-Jewish policy of the Nazis weakened the economic position of the Jews and thus diminished the value of their fortunes. Threats and forcible actions against individuals, resulting in utter insecurity of person and property, worked in the same direction in Germany and the countries imitating this system. Currency restrictions and "escape" levies upon emigrants helped to deprive the emigrating German Jews of the greatest part of their wealth. Registration of property, forced administration and liquidation of commercial and industrial enterprises were direct acts of spoliation; other such measures were surrender of valuables, blocking of accounts, deprivation of the right to succession. Special levies on Jewish communities and national organisations were imposed, the best known of which is the fine of 1 billion marks levied on the Jews of Germany following the murder of vom Rath in the fall of 1938. Similar levies were imposed in almost every country under German domination (occupied countries) or influence, e.g. in Bulgaria in 1941 (amounting to 20% of the entire capital), and in Romania (where a war contribution of 1 billion lei was imposed in 1943). Direct destruction and robbery of Jewish property en masse (including extortions) was first introduced during the occupation of Austria and was followed by the pogrom in November 1938 throughout Germany; Jewish losses during the latter were estimated at hundreds of millions, possible a billion marks.[2] This wilful destruction later became quite customary; but outright confiscation of property became the favourite method of dispossession when regard for world opinion no longer appeared necessary. In this way the greatest part of Jewish owned wealth in all German occupied countries and the satellite nations was lost. Everywhere the legislative and administrative apparatus of the state was mis-used for this purpose; in essence it makes little difference whether the property was registered, put under administration, frozen, seized, or simply robbed. In case of emigrated Jews the spoliation of the fortune left behind was effected by de-nationalization combined with confiscation of property (Germany, Czechoslovakia). A very usual and cruel way of dispossession was deprivation of all property through deportation and ghettoization. The deported Jews were permitted to take with them only very small packages and were compelled to leave behind all else, which was forfeited to the Germans or local authorities and populations. Indeed, even the little the Jews were permitted to bear with them when they left their place of residence was robbed later. The wealth of those who remained was further reduced by forcible delivery of clothing and other warm goods for the army and by other means. A part of the Jewish fortune was lost by "voluntary" acts. Fearing forthcoming confiscation or other harsh spoliation measures or under direct or indirect threats, Jews disposed of their fortune or part of it to Gentiles either fictitiously or at prices often far below the actual value. In certain cases this was done in anticipation of things to come. Furthermore, in view of the deprivation of other sources of income the Jews often had to sell their valuables and belongings to cover the expenses of bare living; in other instances they needed the money to flee the country or to buy freedom. Finally the dreaded invasion sent into exile many thousands of Jews, who fled leaving their entire fortune behind.

In common with their fellow citizens in the various nations of which they were a part, Jews suffered from the war and its consequences. Thus they sustained considerable losses as a result of aerial and land warfare. Jews, as urban dwellers, have lost much of the property (either before or after spoliation) through the aerial destruction of urban settlements, which were the particular targets of bombardment for the Germans, or because of the military value of industries or communication networks located in cities.

ESTIMATES OF THE WEALTH OF THE JEWISH POPULATION
IN COUNTRIES UNDER NAZI DOMINATION

A. General Considerations

Estimates of Jewish Losses

We propose in this section to arrive at a more or less accurate approximation of the private wealth of the Jewish population in the countries where they have been despoiled of their fortunes. The estimate is based on the different data available for the several countries, which vary greatly as to their precision, provenance, and character. None of these calculations is absolutely exact, but it may be hoped that out of the conflicting figures some approximate evaluation may be reached. In most cases it may be a minimum, in others a mean, rarely if ever a maximum evaluation.

The material available consists of estimates of Jewish wealth made by the Nazis or their satellites or by private sources in Allied or neutral countries, as well as data on the total wealth of the respective national or national income figures (which we must convert into national wealth). From this total the portion belonging to Jews will have to be calculated on the basis of the ratio of the Jews to the total population and the Jewish minority, and other relevant data.

In general, the estimates of Jewish losses made by the sources cited above are hardly more than rough evaluations. It is very hard to say how far they are minimized or maximized for special political purposes; or to determine the actual basis for their computation and the degree of their correspondence to the real value of the looted Jewish wealth.

National Wealth

The data on national wealth are, unfortunately, not very much more reliable.[3] They are seldom based on a census undertaken for the specific purpose of computing the amount of wealth;[4] generally the only data available are such as have been assembled for other purposes. Even in countries where many of the necessary data are available the estimates are very uncertain. For instance the amount of national wealth of the United States in 1929–30 was described by Mr. Walter Renton Ingalls, Director of the American Bureau of Metal Statistics,[5] in the following words:

> "I suppose a reasonable estimate of our national wealth at the present time is somewhere between 310 and 558 (billion dollars). That is a wide range, and we may narrow it in a *guess* of 400 to 450, but that is only a guess."

It will not surprise us that the actual estimates vary with the source. Thus the wealth of the United States in 1930 was evaluated at 329.7 billion dollars[6] by the National Industrial Conference Board, and at 400 billion by the U.S. Chamber of Commerce,[7] a difference of about 20%. Indeed, even the same source occasionally has changed it figures. Thus in 1939 the National Industrial Conference Board revised all its previous estimates, lowering the figures for some years and raising them for others.[8] The variations just noted are even greater in the case of other nations, e.g. the national wealth of Belgium in 1926 was variously estimated at 45 and 30 billion RM, that of Hungary in the same year at 24 and 16.5 billion RM, that of Yugoslavia at 38.30 and 23 billion RM, of Germany in 1928 at 350 and 212–280 billion RM, and of Italy in that year at 119 and 88.5 billion RM.[9] Other estimates on Italy's postwar wealth vary between 450 and 650 billion lires, but there were also estimates of 335 and 400 billions;[10] and the figures for France varied between 250 and 360 billion francs.[11] In these cases differences of about 50% or more from the lower amount are registered. Sir Josiah Stamp[12] estimates that the data for national wealth in different countries vary in their accuracy from about 10% up to about 40%. This seems to be a rather conservative view.

Indeed, the fact that the different estimates vary so greatly need not surprise anyone familiar with the various methods employed in the computation and the inherent difficulties of this very complicated[13] problem of statistical research.[14] There are even certain well known economists who deny altogether the possibility of arriving at anything resembling accurate figures for national wealth.[15] The differences in computation make very difficult a comparison among the various years, and much more so among various nations. Thus the figures sometimes refer to total wealth, sometimes only to private fortune, and occasionally to both,[16] and, in certain cases there is no indication as to which one is involved. We must consider that in estimating the Jewish fraction of the national wealth of a country only figures for private wealth can normally be used, since the Jews claim only their private and communal fortune, but not their share of the public wealth. The proportion between these two classes of wealth naturally varies from state to state. Thus, according to the figures given by Gini,[17] the ratio of public to private wealth was 1:11 in Belgium, about 1:6–1:7 in Denmark, about 1:4 in Bulgaria, and almost 1:3 in Yugoslavia.

National Income

The difficulties described above are encountered to a lesser degree in calculating national income[18] Here, too, we must distinguish between total national and private income (exclusive of the income of the state and other public bodies).[19] There is also a difference between income produced and income paid out.[20] However, the real differences start with the methods of computation. As in the case of the figures for wealth, there are no statistics on primary national income and recourse must be had to available date which were originally computed for other purposed and from different standpoints than those involved in estimating the national income.[21] Because the scope of these figures is only rarely the same as that necessary for computing national income, the results cannot be accurate. For instance, with regard to Bulgaria, the statistical situation of which is roughly the same as in most Eastern European countries. Professor Tchakaloff[22] has expressed the difficulties involved as follows:

> "In the evaluation of incomes from separate branches of economic activity a
> number of errors are inevitable, made either on account of the lack of informa-

tion or because of the incompleteness of available statistical material. Furthermore, it is well-nigh impossible to estimate with any great accuracy the income of such classes as small workers on their own account. The estimates of incomes from a number of branches of the National Economy, however, are frequently only approximations. This applies particularly to the estimates of incomes from agriculture, and the arts and crafts."

The figures actually used for computing national income are those of production, income, or consumption; in many cases certain services (e.g. domestic service),[23] pensions, and domestic industries of the agricultural population[24] are not included. There is no general rule for computing the consumption by producers of their own products; this is especially true of agricultural products. Thus it is evident that it is hardly possible to arrive at completely comparable figures in view of the fact that so many diverse methods are used, and various extra-scientific consideration involved in different cases.[25]

This is well illustrated by the data published on the national income of Hungary. Nobody would be surprised to find variations in figures cited by different authors.[26] But it is quite unusual to find that figures cited by the same authors should vary greatly in different publications of the same study, as is the case with the data contained in the Hungarian and English editions respectively of the study by Matolsey and Varga. Several figures (shown in Table I) may illustrate the difference.[27]

Table I National Income in Million Pengoes

Year	According to The Hungarian Edition	According to The English Edition
1928–29	5,728.3	6,262.5
1929–30	5,655.5	6,219.8
1931–32	5,783.3	5,615.8
1933–34	5,628.9	6,067.3
1934–35	5,559.2	6,143.7

It is the consensus of opinion that the figures published on national income can be used with great reservation only. *The World Economic Survey* 1938–39 published by the League of Nations,[28] cautioned the reader on this score in the following words:

"Great care must be taken in interpreting these figures, for there are a number of differences in definition and in the method of measuring the national income, and the basic material from which the estimates are made is in many cases of a rough and approximate nature."[29]

The value of this caution is revealed by a comparison of the computations of national income in the different Balkan states, made by Professor Tchakaloff. The figures available for Yugoslavia concern the income produced and do not include all types of income; while the Romanian figures do not show total agricultural income nor pensions. The figures in Table II demonstrate how greatly these differences affect the data on income:[30]

Table II

Year	Bulgaria's national income in million levas	Bulgaria's income calculated on the same basis as that of Yugoslavia	Bulgaria's income calculated on the same basis as that of Romania
1926	49,149	41,351	–
1928	56,529	–	51,300
1930	48,541	–	43,800
1931	44,561	34,878	40,000
1933	35,633	–	31,600
1935	36,569	28,335	–

Thus in some cases differences of almost 30% are registered. If the basis of the computation were known exactly it might be possible to correct the results accordingly, but this information is rarely available.[31] Therefore, it always remains questionable whether we may assume that the available figures were computed on the same or on a different basis. There can be no question that this circumstance affects greatly the exactitude of all deductions based on these figures.

Per Capita Wealth in Various Countries

In order to ascertain what proportion of total national wealth was owned by Jews we must have adequate data regarding this wealth for all the countries in question.

Figures for one country cannot be used for another because the data of per capita wealth are too different. The figures in Table III for the years 1926–28 were given by the Dresdner Bank, indicating the range of differences.[32]

Table III National Wealth

Country	Per Capita in 1,000 RM		
	1925	1926	1928
Belgium	5.9	5.8	–
Denmark	6.7	7.2	–
Germany	–	4.9	5.5
Greece	–	1.9	–
Yugoslavia	–	2.9	–
Latvia	–	2.4	–
Norway	5.1	5.2	–
Hungary	–	2.9	2.7
Austria	–	–	3.5
France	–	–	7.2
Italy	–	–	2.9

According to these figures, the ratios of per capita wealth in Denmark, Greece, Latvia, Yugoslavia, and Hungary would be 7.2: 1.9: 2.4: 2.9, i.e., Denmark's inhabitants were on average almost four times wealthier than those of Greece, three times than those of Latvia, and 2.5 times than those of Hungary and Yugoslavia. P.E. Gourjou and Hargreaves Parkinson[33] bring the following figures (in Lstg.) regarding per capita wealth, which illustrate the variation:

Germany	Hungary	Belgium	Austria	Greece	Bulgaria	Italy
250	97	288	108	87	89	127

France	Romania	Czechoslovakia	Yugoslavia	Holland
273	129	151	114	233

Changing Valuation of Wealth

It is known that the money value of wealth changes frequently in accordance with the fluctuation of prices[34] and the economic conjuncture. These changes, which may be of great amplitude, are especially evident when one compares years of economic prosperity with those of depression. The national wealth of the United States, for instance, was estimated by the National Industrial Conference Board at 488.6 billion dollars in 1920 (the year of high prices); at 317.2 billion dollars in 1921; 362.3 billion dollars in 1925; 360.0 billion dollars in 1928 (the prosperity year) and only 247.0 billion dollars in 1932 (a depression year).[35] Moreover, there may be considerable differences even between "normal years." Thus in Germany the estimates for 1928 were 350 billions RM as again 320 billions RM for 1926 (both years of about equal conjuncture and employment); in Italy 119 billions RM in 1928 as against 101 billions RM in 1924; and in Hungary 23.5 billions RM and 15 respectively (a rise of almost 50%).[36] These facts must be taken into consideration in using figures for previous years as the basis for a later period. Since we are interested in the estimated wealth of the Jews on the eve of World War II (in the case of Germany, Austria, and Czechoslovakia, at the time of dispossession and the occupation of these regions by Germany) we can use only figures close to that time or of periods similar to it. Since 1938 and 1939 were years of good business and higher prices, it would be unwise to rely on data of a few years earlier – when low prices and bad business conditions prevailed, but the figures for the years before the great crisis may be more suitable. However, we must consider first the question of the growth of the wealth, which no doubt varies with the economic conjuncture in the country. In time of economic slumps consumption may be higher than production, consuming a part of the wealth (the stocks of industrial, agricultural and other products), and causing the deterioration of machinery, equipment, and buildings. Conversely, in years of prosperity, investments may grow rapidly since the volume of production rises considerably.[37]

It is usual and advisable (in consequence of the vast amount of work involved) to calculate national income for a certain year and to estimate the income in the following years by extrapolation, i.e., use of price and production indices, crop yield, foreign trade and unemployment figures, movement of wages, and other economic data. In the case of national wealth, this complicated method may not be absolutely necessary. Figures on the growth of wealth (investments) and price indices may suffice for a rough evaluation, although other factors (especially the rate of interest and changes in the part of income received by capital) ought to be considered. In periods of equal interest rates and income from capital, the aforementioned two constituents may give a fair picture of variations in the value of wealth.

According to Monograph No. 4 of the *Information Service on Slavonic Countries of Birmingham University*,[38] the excess of income over consumption in Poland during 1929 was 2.1 billion zlotys. In the year 1933 the same accumulation of capital represented 0.5 billion zlotys.[39] This would represent about 1.5% and 0.4% of the national wealth (as of 1927), respectively. According to the figures on the national wealth of the United States computed by the National Industrial Conference Board for the years 1919–1930, on the basis of the 1913 price level,[40] the average annual increase in wealth in these years of growing prosperity and population was about 2%. In France, which is famous for the thrift of its population, the average rate of savings was only 11.2% of national income in 1927–30, representing less than 2% of the national wealth. In Holland the average rate in 1925–30 was 1,052 million fl.;[41] the average income being 5,590 million fl.,[42] the savings represented 17.5% of income or roughly, 3% of wealth. In Germany before World War I the rate of increase in wealth was around 2%.[43] If we accept the figure of about 1% as the average annual increase in wealth over a considerable period, we shall have some means of bridging the years between the 1920s and 1930s so far as the volume of wealth is concerned, although the actual growth of wealth will differ in various countries.

It is more difficult to find a measure for price changes. Experience with devaluation of currencies has shown that it does not always affect the prices, especially of capital goods. Yet certain European currencies have suffered sharp decreases in value; in other cases the stability of the external value of a currency was achieved by restrictions on currency transfers and foreign trade, etc., which did not prevent price rises within the country. The relation between the price indices in stable national currencies and the indices multiplied by the average yearly exchange rates of the nation's currency in a stable foreign currency, may provide certain clues. However, it must be borne in mind that there is no index expressing wealth in monetary units of equal purchasing power. For certain countries there may be specific indices approaching this ideal more or less closely.[44] But in general we must rely on wholesale and retail indices. However, the latter are very often based on prices in a few cities only; and though the whole sale index is usually country-wide, it too must be used with caution.

The figures on national wealth in the United States[45] published by the National Industrial Conference Board, the wholesale price indices (Dun's Index Number),[46] and those published by the League of Nations,[47] are provided in Table IV.

We see that the dramatic drop in the original figures from 488.7 billion dollars in 1920 to 317.2 billion dollars in 1921, i.e., a decline of 35%, was accompa-

Table IV

Year	National Wealth	(New Estimates)[48]	Dun's Index	L.o.N. Index
1919	431.0	–	233	–
1920	488.7	–	260	–
1921	317.2	–	159	–
1922	320.8	306.8	173	–
1923	339.9	309.1	188	–
1924	337.9	306.2	185	–
1925	362.4 (100)	307.2	195	148 (100)
1926	356.5	310.1	186	–
1927	346.4	326.7	185	–
1928	360.1 (99)	340.6	195	139 (94)
1929	361.8	353.6	188	–
1930	329.7 (91)	344.2	171	124 (84)
1931	280.3 (77)	322.0	146	105 (71)
1932	247.3 (68)	299.0	125	93 (63)
1933	249.8	288.9	149	95
1934	286.8	286.6	167	–

nied by a decrease in the wholesale price index from 260 to 159, i.e., 39%. The decrease in wealth from 488.7 billions in 1920 to 377.9 in 1924, i.e., of 31%, was accompanied by a drop in the index from 260 to 185, i.e., of 29%; and the decrease from 360.1 billions in 1928 to 247.3 billions in 1932, i.e., of 31.3% was paralleled by a drop in the index from 195 to 125, i.e., 35.8%. These figures and a comparison between the relative figures of wealth and the League of Nations index presented in the table show that the index is easily the most important element in those evaluations. There is a considerable difference both absolutely and relatively in the figures published by the Board at a later date,[48] which are, therefore, less in accord with the indices. Yet in determining the figures on wealth the Board considers only changes in volume and prices. Since the increases in volume are minimal, the figures for the different years must be dependent on a "price index applicable to the wealth items." Clearly, the index later accepted by the Board differs from the one given above; otherwise the figures could not have changed. It is evident that prices of capital goods which, together with the stocks of goods, represent the national wealth, do not change rapidly. This comparative inertia is reflected in the new estimates, which reveal that not every increase (or decrease) in the wholesale index is accompanied by an increase (or decrease) in the valuation of wealth. Yet in the long run, changes in the general price indices must affect the value of property. The figures for the periods given above may not be conclusive, since the decrease in income from wealth must have been paralleled by a decrease in the interest rate (characteristic of depressions), which tends to raise the prices of capital goods. Consequently, if comparing prosperity with depression years the index can be used only with caution.

There is a close resemblance between the trends discernible in the available figures on Germany's wealth for 1926 and 1928[49] and those emerging from the wholesale index of the League of Nations, viz.:

Year	Wealth	Index
1926	320 (100)	134 (100)
1928	350 (109.4)	140 (104.5)

In the states with fluctuating exchange rates the wholesale indices must, as already mentioned, be multiplied by the exchange rate (combined index) in order to obtain a fair picture of the actual change in value. On the basis of such data on wealth as are available we obtain the following figures:

Country	Year	Wealth in billions of RM	Rate of Exchange	Wholesale Index	Combined Index
Italy	1924	101 (100)	.0436	554	100
	1928	119 (118)	.0526	491	107

In smaller countries, retail indices are sometimes a better reflection of changes in wealth, as appears from Table V.

Table V

Country	Year	Wealth in billions of RM	Rate of Exchange	Wholesale Index	Combined Index
Belgium	1924	50 (100)	.0464	573	100
	1925	46 (92)	.0476	559	100
	1926	45 (90)	.0326	744	91.2
	1928	45 (90)	.0279	843	89
				Retail Index	
Norway	1925	14 (100)	.1788	243	100
	1926	14.5 (103.6)	.2233	206	100
	1927	15.5 (110.7)	.2605	186	111.5
Denmark[50]	1925	23 (100)	.2113	211	100
	1926	25 (108)	.2623	184	108
Austria	1923	22.5			
	1924	20.0 (100)	Stable	88 (100)	
	1925	23.5 (117.5)		108 (123)	

Consequently, if the previously cited figures of the Dresdner Bank on wealth and other data are accepted as correct, we may obtain figures for any later period by using the wholesale or retail index in countries of stable currency, and the combined index in all other nations, with the understanding that the indices of wealth usually vary somewhat differently from those of prices.

Relation Between Income and Wealth

As stated above, we do not possess all necessary data on the national wealth of the countries in question. On the other hand, figures for national income are more abundant and in many cases come up to the year 1938. Of greatest regularity are those published by the League of Nations in the *World Economic Survey* 1938–39. These annual data are particularly useful since the income figures in the several countries do not vary, under the influence of business cycles and price levels, in the same manner. For example, the *World Economic Survey* 1935–36, pp. 104–5, has made the following estimate (in percentages) of the fall of national income (in national currency) from 1929 to 1932 in the countries concerned:

Hungary	Romania	Germany	Latvia	Greece	Austria	France	Norway
48	47	39	35	30	17	16	12

In part[51] at least, the national income is the result of national wealth. It would, therefore, seem possible to ascertain the wealth from the available figures on income. In fact several attempts to determine the relation between wealth and income have been made, the conclusions arrived at varying with the author. Vandellos,[52] using the figures on wealth and income given by Stamp, concludes that the percentage of national income in relation to wealth (apart from certain exceptions) rises as the amount of per capita wealth decreases, i.e., the poorer a country the greater the percentage. C. Gini's[53] view is about the same: "Study of the figures representing national income and wealth estimated by various authors shows that the income ratio varies from 12.5% (pre-war) to 15% (post-war) for the wealth in countries having accumulated wealth and in which national securities are already well exploited (as France), to about 20% in countries like British India with very low average of wealth and a superabundant population." However, a totally different conclusion is arrived at by the aforementioned study of the Dresdner Bank:

> "A comparison between the values of income and the value of wealth shows that national income on the whole fluctuates between 10 and 20 per cent of national wealth and that it rises the more in its proportion to national wealth the larger the latter is per head of population. Thus, in the countries with the highest quota of wealth per head of population the corresponding proportion of the national income amounts as a rule to 17–20 per cent, in countries with medium wealth per head of the population to 13–17 per cent, and finally, in those with a low quota per head to 10–13 per cent."[54]

Certainly the finding of such ratios would be of great value for our study, since it would make possible the direct transformation of the available data on national income of the different nations into figures on national wealth, which would otherwise be non-available. But it may be disputed whether either of the two conflicting views is entirely correct in this general form, especially in view of the problematic character of the figures given. However, it would appear that the view of the Dresdner Bank may be presumed to be nearer the truth, inasmuch as it is based on more extensive data and more recent figures. This conclusion would seem to be borne out in part by the well known fact that the branches of national economy less supplied with capital (agriculture, handicraft), i.e., with less wealth per gainfully employed person, very often yield smaller amounts of income per wealth unit than the others, in spite of greater application of labor. But even this fact must be considered with due caution in view of the "price scissors," which operates in disfavor of agricultural products, not because of any inherent factors, but possibly because of a slump in the price of these articles as a result of post war conditions. It is likely that this is what accounts, at least in part, for the differences between the conclusions derived from the study of the pre-war period and that immediately following World War I (Vandellos and Gini), and those of the later period (Dresdner Bank). Other reasons for the divergence in conclusions are to be sought in the difference of prevailing social conditions and the scientific methods applied.

In comparing the figures of Vandellos and Gini with those of the Dresdner Bank we must remember that they refer to different periods, viz., the first two are almost exclusively pre-war estimates, the last a calculation for the post-war period. Prof. Gini[55] admits that there are circumstances which make a comparison between the pre-war and post-war figures uncertain, viz., changes in economic and social conditions and their effects upon the evaluation of wealth or income, or both. The most important factor is the greater share of labour in the income, which reduces the monetary value of private wealth, while it leaves untouched the aggregate total income.[56] Thus for France it was estimated[57] that from 1913 to 1936 the nominal value of wealth rose (because of devaluation and other reasons) by 4.5 and that of income by 5.5, the greatest rise of income being that of salaried persons. The figures computed by W. von Hoellendorff and others[58] show the following changes in labour's share in the total national income in 1913 and in the years 1925–29:

Year	U.S.A.	Great Britain	France	Italy	Germany
1913	55%	50%	40.5%	45%	48%
1925–9	62.5%	60%	50 %	52%	63%

The Ratios of Income to Wealth

Mr. Vandellos gives the following ratios of income to wealth (in percentages):

France	Belgium	Holland	Ger-many	Denmark	Italy	Bulgaria	Yugo-slavia	Austria-Hungary
12.5	12.7–13.6	12.2–13.3	13	15.3–15.5	17.1–18	17.8–18	18.1–18.2	17.7

From the figures given by Gini in "Quelques Chiffres," the following ratios evolve:[59]

	Belgium	Holland	Denmark	Norway	Czecho-slovakia	Bulgaria	Yugo-slavia
Ratio	12.7–13.6	12.2–13.3	15.4	app. 19	app. 15	17.9	18
Wealth per capita in francs	7.200	7.100	5.400	3.500	3.500	2.150	1.850

On the basis of the figures on national wealth and income published in the study of the Dresdner Bank, which refer to the same year, we arrive at the ratios, in percentage of wealth, shown in Table VI.

Table VI

Country	1924	1925	1926	1927	1928	Wealth per Capita in RM
France	–	–	–	–	13.8	7,200
Latvia	–	–	18.7	–	–	2,400
Austria	–	–	–	–	18.7	3,500
Belgium	12.0	15.2	–	–	–	6,500 and 5,900 resp.
Germany	–	–	17.6	–	19.6	4,900 and 5,500 resp.
Hungary	18.0	–	–	–	15.8	1,800 and 2,700 resp.
Italy	–	–	–	–	20.0[60]	2,900
Norway	23.0	–	25.5	24.0	–	5,100, 5,200 and 5,500
Yugoslavia	–	–	11.6	–	–	2,900
Finland	–	–	13.3	–	–	3,300
Switzerland	–	9.7	–	–	–	12,800
Spain	11.5	–	–	–	–	5,500

In certain cases the data available for wealth and income are of different years. Since each figure varies in different years the ratio arrived at in this way must be corrected, according to other available figures. For Czechoslovakia the figures given by the Dresdner Bank are: wealth in 1924, 60 billion RM; income in 1926, 7.5 billion RM. This would provide us with a ratio of about 12.5%. Since we must assume that the income in 1924 was somewhat smaller (because nearer to the end of the war) than in 1926, the actual ratio might have been 11–12%. For Greece the Dresdner Bank has estimated the per capita national wealth in 1926 at 1900 RM; the per capita income in 1927 is set by Prof. G. Findlay Shirrass[61] at Lstg. 20. According to the yearly averages of RM and Lstg. in dollars, the figures would be 452 and 97.2 dollars, respectively, giving a ratio of 21.5%.

Frederic de Fellner[62] puts the national wealth of Hungary in 1925–27 at about 32 billion pengoes and the annual income in 1926–28 at about 4.4 billion pengoes; the ratio would thus be 13.7%. Prof. Dr. C. A. Verriju Stuart[63] has calculated Netherlands' private wealth as of May 1, 1927 at about 21.7 billion fl., and the private income in 1927–28 at about 5.1 billion fl.; the ratio for the Netherlands would therefore be 23.7%. The Polish National wealth for 1927 was calculated at 143 billion zlotys,[64] and the income at 9.4 billion RM.[65] According to the yearly averages of the RM and zloty in 1927[66] the figures amount to 16.16 billion and 2.23 billion dollars respectively. The ratio would thus be about 13.8%.

Those who have tried to find the ratios for the various nations have come to the conclusion that the ratio of income to wealth represents about 15% in Spain and Portugal,[67] about 16% in Greece,[68] and 17%–18% in Italy and Austria–Hungary.[69] If these deductions are correct, they would confirm the view of the Dresdner Bank, since Greece is more commercialized than Spain and Portugal; and Italy and Austria-Hungary are wealthier than Greece. However, if the figures of the Dresdner Dank given above are accepted, it appears that the ratio of France with a per capita wealth of 7,200 RM was smaller than that of Belgium of 1925 with an average wealth of only 5,900 RM; that the ratio for Latvia in 1928, with a per capita wealth of 2,400 was higher than Hungary's, with a per capita wealth of 2,700 RM; and that the ratio of the admittedly poorer countries of Latvia, Hungary and Austria were higher than those of the wealthier France and Belgium. The figures of Gini too cannot be regarded as exact (see the figures for Denmark and Czechoslovakia cited above). The figures we have arrived at for the Netherlands (23.7%[70] and 13%), Norway (24% and 19%), Yugoslavia (18.5% and 11.6%), and Greece (16% and 21.5%) vary so greatly that they cannot be used for a comparison with other countries; even their application to these countries makes imperative the correction and elimination of the less dependable figures.

It is, of course, probable that the ratios of various countries for the same year were influenced by differences in the state of affairs and prices in the particular countries. Naturally the differences would be more marked in ratios computed for different years. But one fact remains: since income depends not only on the use of the wealth, but also on the actual labor of the population, the capital invested (e.g., rents or loans yield less than active industrial or commercial capital),[71] the interest rate, the share of the working population in the total income – all of which may differ widely in countries of equal per capita wealth – there can hardly be such a general rule for establishing the ratio as suggested in the studies quoted above. We have already seen that the ratios vary within every country. This is the consequence of several well-known facts, among which may be mentioned the following: in periods of high employment greater income is produced with approximately the same actual amount of wealth; prices of capital goods do not necessarily parallel those of consumers' goods and wages; cheaper credit affects the valuation of wealth to a greater extent than income. For instance, using the figures on the national wealth of the United States as calculated by the National Industrial Conference Board[72] and the figures for national income produced for the years 1929, 1930, and 1932,[73] we arrive at the following ratios:

$$1929 \quad \frac{82.7}{361.8} = 22.9\%$$

$$1930 \quad \frac{69.1}{329.7} = 21.0\%$$

$$1932 \quad \frac{43.5}{247} = 17.6\%$$

Even greater fluctuations are reported by Mr. Mori for Japan in his calculation of the ratios for that country:[74]

1913	1917	1918	1924
7.29%	6.29%	6.37%	12.59%

We must therefore arrive at the conclusion that we do not possess definite ratios for various categories of countries. These ratios fluctuate somewhat inconclusively between 12 and 20%. But we can say that the national wealth is approximately 5–8 times greater than the income. Yet since the available data are only approximate and since, furthermore, we possess no other ratios, we must regard the average of the ratios we have gained for the different nations with which we are concerned as characteristic, although usually the ratios are only for one or two years and many are of conflicting nature. We must note that those relating to the years 1926–28 concern a period of comparative prosperity, not very unlike that prevalent during the years 1937–38. When no ratio was found for a particular country, we have necessarily to use the average reached for others in similar economic conditions, when estimating wealth according to income. As mentioned, the ratios are only approximate and will have to be corrected if pertinent data make it advisable. This is obvious since the data on wealth and income themselves are far from being exact and, moreover, the differences in exactitude may move in opposite directions (e.g., one figure may be 40% higher than the exact amount, the other 30% lower) or be of different scope.[75] This may account in part for the excessive difference between the ratios of Holland (23.7%) and France (13.8%), in spite of the fact that these countries are similar in many respects.

Sources for Estimates of National Wealth

In estimating the wealth of a country during the period shortly before the out-break of this war we possess, as stated above, two sets of figures: (a) direct data on national wealth for different periods[76] and (b) data on national income of recent years for almost every country in question, which have to be trans-formed into fortune. As mentioned, the greatest number of such figures are presented in the *World Economic Survey*, 1938–39. In addition, there are studies on the national income of particular countries.[77] Other relevant data are included in different studies to be mentioned below. Average figures on nation-al income for almost all countries with which we are here concerned, except Yugoslavia, are published in the study of Colin Clark, "The International Comparison of National Incomes."[78] The figures presented are supposed to be averages for 1925–34, i.e., for a decade embracing both prosperity and depres-sion years. They are given in gold dollars, thus eliminating the necessity of con-verting the different national currencies (as in the case of many studies) into a single monetary unit. Yet these figures are hardly suitable for our purpose, since we are not interested in average estimates of the income of the nations concerned for the years 1925–34, but in the total wealth shortly before it was robbed. There is no certainty that this average is even approximately equal to the actual income on the eve of the war or invasion. Furthermore, it must be stressed that these figures can be considered as averages for the years 1925–34 only in a relative sense, since there are simply no income figures for every year and every country. In fact, in many cases figures were available for only 2 or 3 years and the average figures were calculated on the basis of their being repre-sentative for the whole decade (Greece), or by converting these amounts into averages by using average prices only[79] (Bulgaria), or simply estimating the average as the mean of two years (Italy), or using only some of the data neces-sary for fair extrapolation. In certain cases the figures will be used for compar-ison and in others as corrections when this appears to be indicated or when no other reliable data are available.

Social and Occupational Distribution of the Jewish Population

Were the Jewish population a simple cross-section of the total population, we could arrive at an estimate of its wealth quite simply. Yet actually, the social and occupational stratification of the Jewish minority is quite different from that of the majority.[80] First of all, with few exceptions, the Jews are practically unrepre-sented in agriculture. Conversely, their proportion in professions and commerce is higher than their part in the total population. We possess reliable figures on the Jewish occupational and social distribution for certain countries only, since in most cases the official statistics do not classify the social groups by religion (and almost nowhere by race). Several figures may illustrate the situation:[81]

In *Bulgaria*, out of 48,398 professing Jews (in 1934), 46,972, about 97%, lived in towns and cities and only 1,426, about 3%, in rural places.[82]

In *Yugoslavia*, where the Jews represented 0.5%[83] of the total population, the occupational distribution of the Jewish population was as follows (1930):

Agriculture	Handicraft	Commerce	Liberal Professions	White Collar Workers
3%	13%	37%	8%	25%

In *Czechoslovakia*, where the Jews represented 2.4% of the total population, the percentages of Jews and non-Jews engaged in gainful occupations (without agriculture) were as follows:

	Transport and Communication	Industry and Handicraft	Commerce and Credit	Public Service and Liberal Professions	Rentiers and Others
Non-Jews	6.0	51.7	10.1	6.7	16.4
Jews	2.2	22.2	46.7	8.3	17.8

Among the Jews, 56.1% were proprietors of business enterprises, independent professionals or persons of independent means, as compared with 32.5% among the non-Jewish population. Among gainfully employed Jews, 20.8% were salaried employees; among non-Jews, 7.8%. Wage earners constituted 23.1% of persons gainfully employed as against 60.1% of non-Jews.

In *Hungary*, the Jews formed about 5.1% of the total population (1930), but constituted different ratios in the various economic branches:

Trade and Credit[84]			Industry			Liberal
Independent Workers	Employees	Physical Workers	Independent Workers	Office Employees	Physical Workers	Professions
45.6%	47.6%	29.1%	11%	33.4%	5.6%	26%

The occupational distribution of the Jewish and non-Jewish population in 1930 was as follows:

	Trade and Credit	Public Service and Professions	Industry and Handicraft	Agriculture
Jews	44.9%	8.2%	32.0%	2.7%
Non-Jews	4.5%	4.7%	21.5%	53.5%

In *Poland*, where the Jewish population came to 9.8%[85], the occupational structure of the Jews and non-Jews engaged in gainful occupations in 1931 was as follows:

	Crafts and Industry	Commerce and Credit	Transport and Communication	Public Service and Liberal Professions	Agriculture
Jews	42.2%	36.6%	4.5%	6.2%	4.4%
Non-Jews	16.9%	3.5%	3.5%	9.3% (including "other professions")	67.5%

In *Romania*, where the Jews represented 4.2% of the total population, the professional structure of the Jews and non-Jews engaged in gainful occupations (without agriculture) was as follows:

	Industry and Handicraft	Credit and Commerce	Public Service and Liberal Professions	Communication and Transport
Jews	34.8%	51.5%	2.9%	2.6%
Non-Jews	47.5%	18.1%	13.4%	10.1%

The occupational distribution of the Jewish population in *Germany* differed considerably from that of the total German population. This is evident from the following figures on the occupational distribution of the Jewish population and the total number of gainfully employed persons as of June 16, 1933.[86]

	Agriculture and Forestry	Industry and Handicraft	Commerce and Transportation	Public and Private
Percentage of gainfully employed	1.7	23.1	61.3[87]	12.5
Percentage of total gainfully employed	28.9	40.4	18.4	8.4

The social position of the Jews in the various economic branches was also different from that of the total population. Only 16.4% of the total of German gainfully employed persons were independent, but 46% among the Jews. The figures for employees (white collar workers) were 12.5% and 33.5% respectively, and for manual workers 46.3% and 8.7% respectively. The Jews were better represented in the liberal professions than the average population, e.g., while the Jews constituted 0.74% of all gainfully employed persons, their proportion in the total number of physicians, lawyers and notaries public, and dentists was 10.88%, 16.25% and 8.59% respectively.[88]

In *Austria* out of 191,481 professing Jews (1934), 176,034 lived in Vienna.[89] Their occupational distribution was as follows:

	Industry and Handicraft	Commerce and Traffic	Public Service and Liberal Professions
Jews	23.4%	54.5%	20.1%
Non-Jews	48.5%	25.1%	11.1%

Agricultural and Non-Agricultural Wealth

In estimating the Jewish wealth, the negligible proportion of Jews engaged in agriculture compels us to disregard the agricultural wealth and population of the countries concerned. Consequently, we must know what proportion of the people are agriculturists, and what proportion of the total wealth is agricultural wealth. Unfortunately, we do not possess data even for a part of the countries in question. There is more information available on the distribution of income according to the different branches of economy, but the ratios of agricultural wealth and income cannot be presumed to be the same. The majority of writers who analyze the national wealth in detail do not differentiate it according to the occupational division of the population, but only according to the kind of property, viz. they bring figures on value of land, buildings (agricultural and urban together), and movables (without distinction of proprietor), and so on. Thus, for Hungary, Frederic de Fellner[90] gives the value of soil, of buildings, movable goods, mines, and transport. For Italy, Gini[91] gives the value of land and rural buildings and livestock as separate items, but fails to differentiate between the movables and securities belonging to the agricultural and the other population; for France[92] no differentiation is indicated even in respect to the buildings. Nor do the estimates for the United States by the National Industrial Conference Board[93] give all data on this score.

More detailed figures are given by Dederko[94] for Poland in 1926–27. However, since the method employed is strictly "objective," i.e., regardless of ownership, we do not find there the real wealth of the separate economic groups, but only the values of the objects owned. Since the lands are usually burdened with debts[95] and the holders are rarely agriculturists, equipment is often bought on credit from industry and commerce, and agriculturists owe other debts to urban residents, the objective method can never reveal an even approximately exact proportion of the agricultural wealth. Dederko calculates that it represents 46.9% of the total national wealth,[96] but he includes in the total amount the value of the apparatus of traffic and transportation belonging to the state, the funds of the central bank of issue belonging to the nation and agricultural property owned by the state; these must be subtracted in estimating the proportion of private agricultural wealth to the total. If we consider these amounts, and conversely consider the problem of debts and stocks, which may have the effect of changing the amount of wealth of the agriculturists, we may set the ratio of agricultural wealth somewhat lower than Dederko, i.e., not more than 45% of the total wealth Since the agricultural working population in 1927 was 64% of the total,[97] the agricultural wealth in terms of working persons would be about 70% (45:64).

According to the figures on the distribution of Romania's wealth given by C. Sesceoreatiu, President of the Union of Romania's Chambers of Agriculture for the period around 1936,[98] the value of agricultural assets (lands, forests, livestock, and buildings) was 1,131,857 million leis.[99] The total national wealth, including railways, etc., was set at 2,315,278 million leis; thus the ratio of agricultural wealth in the total national wealth would be a little less than 50%. But, since the item of movable property (220 billion leis) includes a certain amount belonging to peasants, the actual ratio must be somewhat higher. If we take into consideration the problem of debts on the one hand, and the fact that certain state and other public property is included in the agricultural and non-agricultural wealth on the other, we will not go wrong in estimating the value of agricultural wealth at 50–55% of the total. Since, according to this source, 84.2% of all gainfully employed made their living from agriculture, 100 the ratio in terms of working persons would be about 60–65%, or almost the same as in the case of Poland. These countries have in common low standards and considerable natural wealth.

It is obvious that the ratio of agricultural wealth to the total depends not only on the position of the agriculturists, but also on that of the rest of the population. Thus in countries with great capital accumulation, which have rich natural wealth, industry, large cities, and large amounts of securities, but a not very progressive agriculture, the relative value of arable land and other agricultural wealth is much smaller than in countries which are comparatively poor in sources of non-agricultural wealth. Thus, according to Gini,[101] landed real estate[102] in 1925 represented 38% of the value of the total private property in Italy, whereas in France, it was supposed to be only 13%, although the agricultural working population was only over 1.3 greater (47.3% in Italy, as against 35.7% in France).[103] Conversely, the ratio depends on the use made of the land. For instance, although the population gainfully employed in agriculture in Great Britain (a country with great natural resources) represented only about 6% of the total in 1931, the agricultural capital was about 14% of the total in 1928,[104] apparently due to the fact that the large wealthy estates employed very few persons. The available figures for other countries show that in Canada (1921) about 30% of the total wealth was invested in farms;[105] the percentage of persons engaged in agriculture being about 30% of the total (in 1930),[106] the ratio was almost equal to 100%. In Switzerland[107] the value of agricultural property represented in 1923 about 12% of the total; since the proportion of persons employed in agricultural pursuits was (in 1930) about 21%, the ratio would be about 60%. But it must be assumed that the actual agricultural wealth was higher, since the agricultural population must also have participated in the large investments this country possesses, in goods and cash, etc.; thus, we may put the ratio at 70–80% (even if we take account of possible indebtedness). In Luxembourg, famous for its great natural wealth, the value of cultivated land alone was estimated as representing over 21% of the total of the national wealth,[108] with 36% of the population gainfully employed in agriculture.[109] Since the wealth of the agricultural population consists of other items also, the ratio must have been higher than would follow from these figures.

On the basis of these figures and taking into consideration agricultural debts, we may arrive at the conclusion that in countries with low agricultural standards the ratio of agricultural wealth to the total wealth amounted to 60–65% of the numerical proportion of persons employed in agriculture to the total of gainfully employed; but that, in countries with higher standards, the ratio must be put at 70–80%, and in cases of very high agricultural standards (Holland, Denmark), even higher.

Agricultural Income and Agricultural Wealth

Since the value of agricultural property (as any other) is not only dependent on the revenues, but in many cases is calculated on the very basis of the income (aggregate or net),[110] we may accept the view that the ratio between agricultural income to total national income in the different countries reflects approximately the ratio between the values of the corresponding branches of national economy. Account has been taken of the high valuation of agricultural property in many countries, the smaller income from extensive agriculture in comparison with the more highly organized types of economic activity, viz., industry, commerce, and transportation,[111] and of the differences in capitalization rate. Thus the figures of income can be transformed into figures for wealth by using the available figures on wealth and income and the different capitalization percentage for both categories of property.

The relation of agricultural income to the number of persons gainfully employed in agriculture[112] for various countries is shown in Table VII.[113]

It must be remarked that the ratio cannot be regarded as absolutely correct since, in addition to the aforementioned faults, it refers to different years, the years of the great crisis being characterized by a greater price decrease in agricultural products than industrial, but with greater decrease in industrial production than agricultural. Moreover, the income is partly private (France, Belgium), partly total (Poland), partly unspecified. However, we gain the general impression that with the exception of Belgium, which is characterized by a very high level of agricultural production, and Czechoslovakia (possibly in consequence of radical agrarian reforms), the ratio of the percent part of agricultural income to the proportion of agricultural working population fluctuates between 65% and 75% of the number of gainfully employed persons. Since the previously cited figures on agricultural wealth, apart from the abnormal situation in Great Britain, tend to verify the aforementioned observation of smaller income per wealth unit in agriculture than in other branches, we must estimate the wealth ratio at about 10% higher than the income ratio, when using the ratio of agricultural income to compute that of agricultural wealth.

Table VII

Country	% of Gainfully Employed Population in Agriculture	% of Income from Agriculture	Ratio of Income to Gainfully Employed Persons (Approximate)
Yugoslavia	71.2	48.3	68%
Hungary	50.8	33.9 (33.2 average 1934–7, Matolsey and Varga, p.43)	65%
Bulgaria	80.0	53.5 (51 average 1933–5, Tchakaloff, p.98)	64%
Greece	61.0	45.0 (44 in 1927– Rediadis, pp.1256)	74%
Poland (1931)	61.6	42.3[114]	70%
Germany (average 1934–1938)	26.0	18.5[115]	71%
Italy	47.3 (1931)[116] 55.8 (1921)	31.3[117] (1928) 32.0 (1925)[118]	67%
Czechoslovakia	38.3 (1930)	33.3 (1929)[119]	87%
France	35.7 (1931)	22.0 (average of 1937–9) [120]	63%
Belgium	17.1 (1930)	14.0 (1932)[121]	82%

Errors in Estimating Wealth

As indicated above, in computing the amount of Jewish wealth, we generally disregard the agricultural wealth of the country. This leads to another source of possible error: the movement of prices in agricultural fortune must not necessarily be the same as in non-agricultural wealth. However, since it is most difficult to ascertain this difference and all figures are only approximate; we will disregard it.

One more source of possible error must be noted here. We possess figures on the occupational distribution of the total population of the countries concerned, but we rarely have this information for the Jewish people. For the Jews, the figure usually available is their numerical strength, and their proportion in the total of population. The ratio of gainfully occupied persons[122] in the total population varies rather considerably from country to country,[123] depending on the age and sex structure of the population, and the economic structure of the nation, its wealth and customs. For lack of other evidence we must accept the view that the percentage of gainfully employed Jews is approximately the same as that of urban non-Jews in the same country. But in this connection it must be remembered that the number of working persons per family is greater among the peasantry than the urban population. The figures for Germany, for instance, show that in 1925 persons gainfully employed in agriculture represented 30.5% of the total, but the number of Germans dependent for their living on agriculture, i.e., working people and their families, constituted only 23% of the total population.[124] On the basis of these figures the total number of persons living from agriculture would represent only about 80% of the number of persons gainfully employed. This figure may be employed, with certain variations depending on the particular state concerned, to calculate the proportion of the Jewish population to the number of non-agricultural persons. That is, if in a certain country persons employed in agriculture represent 60% of the total, this would mean, in terms of the total population, only 48% (60 × 0.80); the rest of the population would thus be 52% of the total. If the Jews represented 5% of the total inhabitants, their relative strength in the non-agricultural population would be 5:52, about 9.6%.

B. Estimates in the Various Nations

Introduction

On the basis of the principles established above and the various figures and ratios derived therefrom, an attempt will now be made to arrive at an estimate of the total Jewish wealth in the countries under Nazi domination.

Several general remarks are in order. Whenever the number of Jews in a certain country is given, this refers to the known figures, which usually include only professing Jews. But the estimates and data on Jewish confiscated wealth include also other persons classified by the Nazis as Jews; the figures, therefore, necessarily will be much larger than those reached here on the basis of our calculations. Furthermore, most of the reported figures on wealth were published at a time when the currencies were already greatly inflated. The Germans have fixed the exchange rates of the occupied and dominated countries but this can hardly stay the deterioration of the currency. Even the strictest price regulations can scarcely check price rises in many commodities. Yet, the figures in national currency are almost invariably converted into dollars at the exchange rate prevailing before the outbreak of the war.

In most cases the data on income[125] and wealth include income of public bodies and public wealth. This part of the income and wealth must be excluded, as explained above. In most cases a reduction of 10% would be appropriate. Therefore, in comparing the figures on the different nations, this difference should be subtracted when total national wealth is given. But since the actual composition of the figures is only rarely known and all figures are approximate evaluations only, we have not done this.

The wealth of the Jewish population in every country consists of the fortunes of Jewish individuals (private wealth) and the property of their communities and organizations (public wealth). As seen above, the public property of the countries concerned represents 10–15% of the total national wealth. Jewish communities and organizations owned none of the larger assets representing public wealth, viz., means of communication, lands and forests, public utilities, mines and enterprises. Therefore, Jewish public wealth cannot be more than a small percentage of Jewish private wealth. In addition, there are few figures on Jewish public wealth. Therefore, this part of Jewish assets will not be considered when estimating Jewish owned wealth in the various countries.

Average figures are of value only in dealing with large masses. In countries with a small percentage of Jews,[126] the majority of the Jews usually belong to the middle and upper classes. Therefore the average figures on wealth we arrive at cannot be even approximately correct if in the country concerned the Jews form a small minority; in this case a certain multiplier must be applied. In general, this may vary from 2 to 5, but in certain cases, even this amount may prove to be too small. The figures we arrive at are nominal, i.e., they do not take into account the buying power of the currency which varies in different countries. Thus, according to Clark's computations, an income of 494 dollars in Greece was worth 922 dollars in the United States (the average of prices in the United States was thus 186% those in Greece). On the same basis, 100 dollars in Austria was worth 155 dollars in the United States; 100 dollars in Romania and Bulgaria, 151 dollars; 100 dollars in Poland, 125 dollars; 100 dollars in Denmark, 95 dollars; 100 dollars in Norway, 83 dollars in the United States, and so on. The prices in Norway were thus more than double those in Greece. This difference may explain certain divergencies in the amount of national wealth and income among the several nations. Yet, for our purpose, it is useless to compute the figures on wealth or income on the same price basis,[127] since the value of Jewish property in a certain country does not depend on the buying power of the unit of currency abroad, but only on the price it may command within the country.

1. Poland

No official or semi-official figures on the value of Jewish property in Poland have been published. Estimates by private Polish-Jewish persons put the value of Jewish property confiscated by Germans in Poland at 1 billion dollars.[128] Polish circles in London estimate the value of Jewish movables robbed from Jews in Warsaw at 100–150 million dollars.[129]

It would seem that the figure of 1 billion dollars is much too low. The total value of the Polish national wealth in 1926–27 was put by Dr. Dederko[130] at 137,436 million zlotys.[131] But according to *L'Economiste Européen* the national wealth of Poland was estimated at 160–180 billion zlotys at some time near this date.[132] Hence we may accept the figure of 150 billion zlotys as approximately correct. If we deduct approximately 10% for the value of state and other public property[133] the private wealth of Poland at that time might have been approximately 135 billion zlotys. Assuming that it grew in volume by approximately 1% annually, the private wealth of Poland in 1938–39 would have been approximately 150 billion zlotys at the prices of 1926–27. Unfortunately, there are no available figures on the wholesale price index for 1926–27. The nearest is for 1928, but since the retail price index was the same in 1927 as in 1928 we may use the wholesale index for the period in which the computation by Dederko was made. The wholesale indices for 1928 and 1938[134] were 100, and 56 respectively. Accepting a somewhat higher index for wealth, viz., approximately 65, the value of the private wealth in 1938 could, on the basis of the above figures, be put at around 95 billion zlotys (16.8 billion dollars).[135] There are no detailed figures on the Polish national income for the years immediately preceding the war. According to the data compiled by the National Industrial Conference Board,[136] the maximum level of national income of Poland since 1929 was 3,168 million dollars. Converting this income figure into wealth by using the multiplier 6–7,[137] we obtain a figure of 19–22 billion dollars. But since it must be assumed that these figures contain also public wealth, the private wealth must, therefore, be set at 17–20 billion dollars. On the basis of both computations we may estimate Polish private wealth for the period not far from the start of the war at 17–19 billion dollars. Of this amount, according to the figures given above,[138] about 45% may be presumed to be agricultural wealth; eliminating this part of national wealth[139] we obtain the figure of 9.5–10.5 billion dollars for non-agricultural private wealth.

The Jews represented 9.8% of the total Polish population, but approximately 21% of the non-agricultural population.[140] Therefore, the value of Jewish wealth, if the share of the Jews is on the same level as any other non-agricultural inhabitant of Poland, would amount to 1,995–2,205 million dollars. But, since the Jews were more strongly represented in the upper and middle classes than the non-jewish population, and conversely in the working classes, and since, contrary to some other countries, the basis of computation was private wealth, we may assume that a figure of 2,100 million dollars may be near the truth.

2. Romania

The most complete account of expropriated Jewish fortunes was given in *Excelsior* of October 31, 1943.[141] According to this source, the value of expropriated Jewish rural estates, forests, sawmills, timber, industrial enterprises, vessels, mortgages and urban property came to 70,866 million leis. However, this amount does not seem to include the total wealth possessed by Jews and is incomplete in various respects, e.g., the "liberated areas" are apparently not included.

According to an article in the Swiss newspaper, *St. Galler Tagblatt*,[142] the wealth of the 600,000 Romanian Jews amounted to 350 billion leis, which is supposed to represent 65.5% of the total national wealth at a conservative estimate. This ratio would seem to be in accordance with the reported ratio of the Jewish income to the total national income of Romania, supposedly amounting to 55%,[143] but both ratios are doubtless pure propaganda figures. The much lower figure of 50 billion leis of confiscated Jewish property was announced by Dr. Maniu.[144]

As mentioned above, the national wealth of Romania was estimated at 2,315,278 million leis in 1936, equal to approximately 17 billion dollars at the yearly average of the lei in dollars for that year. This figure corresponds roughly to other available estimates of Romanian wealth, e.g., that for 1928 given by the Dresdner Bank, namely 53 billions RM., equal to 12.6 billion gold dollars. However, both figures may seem to be somewhat exaggerated if we consider the known data on income.[145] Thus, according to Clark, the average yearly income of Romania in 1925–34 was 868 (or 974, if indirect levies are included) million gold dollars. This figure is much higher than the maximum income since 1929 calculated by the Conference Board Economic Record,[146] viz., 1,168 million dollars of actual value. If we convert the mean figure of about 800 million gold dollars by using the multiplier 9 (since the income from forests constituting over one third of the total wealth is very low, an unusually high multiplier is applied), the national wealth of Romania would have amounted to around 7.2 billion gold dollars, which is equal to 12.0 million "paper" dollars. On the basis of these figures we may safely estimate the actual wealth at approximately 25–30% below the official data. According to the figures cited above on Jewish wealth, the total national wealth would amount to only about 530 billion leis. Even if we assume that the figure of 2,315 billion leis may have been exaggerated and refers to pre-war Romania while the estimates of the *St. Galler Tagblatt* relates to a later period, it seems impossible that the value of the Romanian wealth should have decreased by almost three quarters in nominal figures.

The reported 350 billion leis of Jewish wealth would equal about 2,565 million dollars according to the average exchange rate in 1938,[147] but is doubtless much less if the real value of the inflated lei is taken into consideration. However, the figures cited by Maniu would be equal to 366 million dollars only.

If we accept the aforementioned figure of 2,315,278 million leis as the basis of our computation of Romania's total wealth and its subdivisions, the non-agricultural wealth of Romania would have amounted to about 1,180 billion leis.[148] Taking into consideration the growth of the wholesale index from 68.5 in 1936 to 87.6 in 1939, allowing for the recognized tendency of capital goods to follow these indices only in part, and considering the possible growth of wealth by 3–4%, the amount of non-agricultural wealth of Romania in 1939 would have amounted to some 1,400 billion leis. It is true that the Jews also owned some agricultural wealth, but their share in this was comparatively rather small[149] and may therefore be neglected. The Jewish population in pre-war Romania amounted to 4.2% of the total population;[150] since about 76% of the total working population were engaged in agriculture,[151] the non-agricultural population may represent around 35% of the total population and the Jews about 12.14% of this segment of the population. If the wealth of an average Jew is regarded as equal to that of an average non-agricultural inhabitant the total wealth of the Jews would thus amount to approximately 200 billion leis, or 1.4 billion dollars. Adjusting this figure downwards by 25%, for the reason given above, the wealth of the Jews would amount to over 1 billion dollars. Since Jews had only a small share in Romania's greatest source of wealth, i.e. forests and minerals, this figure must be regarded as rather considerable.

3. Hungary

The Budapest correspondent of the *Berliner Boersen Zeitung*[152] reported that Jewish property in Hungary (of changed boundaries) was valued at about 30 billion pengoes (approximately 6 billion dollars). However, Hungarian newspapers later estimated this property at 20 billion pengoes, or approximately 4 billion dollars.[153] Unquestionably these figures are far too high to be even approximately correct.

According to the previously quoted estimate of Fellner; the total value of the Hungarian national wealth between 1925 and 1927 amounted to about 32 billion pengoes, or 5,600 million gold dollars. The Dresdner Bank estimated the value of the wealth in 1928 at the same figure, viz., 23.5 billion marks. Converting the figure of 32 billion pengoes in accordance with the corrected wholesale index[154] and the anticipated growth of wealth (amounting in this case to some 12%), we may accept the figure of 32 billion pengoes as approximately correct for 1939. This would come to about 6.3 billion dollars.[155]

The latest figures on Hungary's national income are 4,417 million pengoes in 1937 and 4,705 millions in 1938.[156] If we accept the figure of 4,800 million pengoes as approximately correct for 1939, we may estimate the national wealth at approximately 33 billion pengoes,[157] which yields the same figure as indicated above.

According to the figure previously cited, the agricultural income was about 33% of the total; we may therefore estimate the agricultural wealth at about 40% of the total wealth. Thus the non-agricultural wealth[158] would amount to around 19 billion pengoes. Since the Jewish population was 5.1% of the total and the population engaged in agriculture 50.8%, the Jews constituted about 9% of the non-agricultural population. On the basis of the average per capita non-agricultural wealth, the wealth of the Jews amounted to 1.7 billion pengoes, or about 335 million dollars.

4. Germany

"A high Nazi source conversant with the facts as are few others in Germany" estimated the value of Jewish possessions in Germany in 1938 at about 7 billion marks,[159] which would be equivalent to 2,800 million dollars. Later in 1938, in connection with the vom Rath levy, the evaluation was about 6 billion marks;[160] other sources,[161] possibly more reliable, estimated the value for that time at approximately one half of the aforementioned figure of 7 billion marks, with the "original estimates" (i.e., for the period before 1938) running from 12 to 20 billion marks. The Royal Institute of International Affairs[162] reported the total of Jewish seizures (including the vom Rath fine of 1 billion RM) to have amounted to between 2.5 and 5 billion RM.

The Dresdner Bank estimated the value of Germany's national wealth in 1928 at 350 billion marks. This would appear to be a conservative estimate by comparison with Ballod's figure of 331 billions and Steinmann-Bucher's[163] of 376–397 billions for the period immediately before or during the war, even if due consideration is given to loss of territory and foreign investments, since prices in 1928 were much higher than in 1913.[164]

If we bridge the period from 1928 through 1939 by adding the accepted rate of increase in wealth and adjust it according to the corrected wholesale price indices[165] we arrive at a figure of somewhat over 300 billion marks. The latest figures on the national income were about 70.9 billions in 1937 and 76 billions in 1938;[166] these figures would produce, if we use the average multiplier,[167] about 400 billion marks. However, the figures for the period of rearmament can hardly be considered as reflecting the true state of affairs. We shall, therefore, retain the figure of 300 billion marks.

The 500,000 German Jews represented 0.77% of the total population. Of the total[168] German population 22% were agriculturists and their families; and Jews constituted 1% of the non-agricultural population. With average income from agriculture representing 18.5% of the total income, the share of agricultural wealth might be around 20–21%. This would give us the figure of about 240 billion marks for the total non-agricultural wealth and about 2,400 million marks for the portion owned by Jews, which is equivalent to 964 million dollars. This figure is much lower than those given above.

5. France

According to an announcement by Daquier de Pellepoix, French Commissioner for Jewish Affairs, Jewish property in the value of more than 100 billion francs has been "aryanized" in France.[169] But it would appear from the text that this amount does not represent all Jewish owned wealth in France.

At the beginning of 1939 French private wealth was evaluated at between 1,400 and 1,450 billion francs.[170] In 1938 the national income was estimated at around 260 billion francs.[171] If the multiplier of 7 is accepted,[172] the total national wealth would, on this basis, amount to 1,800 billions.[173] We may, therefore, accept the figure of 1,600 billion francs for the private wealth.

The Jewish population of France was 0.57% of the total. Inasmuch as the proportion of persons gainfully employed in agriculture was 35.7%, the non-agricultural population must be estimated as 70% of the total, with the Jews constituting 0.8% thereof. Since the section of the population engaged in agriculture produced 22% of the total income, its wealth may be calculated at about 25%, with the rest holding 75% of the total private wealth, which would be equivalent to 1200 billion francs. On the basis of figures for average wealth, Jewish wealth would, therefore, amount to some 9.6 billion francs, or 278 million dollars. The figure of 100 billion francs cited above seems to be very high compared with this amount (assuming there had been no large-scale price increase.)

6. Czechoslovakia

The Bulletin of International News published by the Royal Institute[174] estimated the value of confiscated Jewish property in Czechoslovakia at £125 million (about 500 million dollars).[175] Far higher figures would evolve from the data on Jewish wealth in the Protectorate, Sudetenland, and Slovakia. According to the Times of June 22, 1939, Jewish property in the Protectorate was estimated at 17 billion kr.[176] Narodni Noviny of August 19, 1939 put the figure at 20 billion kr., which comes to 700 million dollars. According to reports in the Nazi press, Jewish wealth in Sudetenland transferred to Aryans was valued at 8,673 million kr.,[177] which amounts to approximately 290 million dollars on the basis of the 1938 average exchange rate.

The figures on Jewish owned wealth in Slovakia are rather confusing. The Central Committee of Slovakian Jewry is reported to have evaluated it at approximately 160 million dollars.[178] Official sources in Slovakia estimated the value of Jewish property variously at 4.5 billion crowns, at 3 billions, 4.2 billions net, 5 billions, and 3,950 millions.[179] Other sources[180] put the actual value at 17 billion crowns; since they evaluate a crown at 1/30 of a dollar, the Jewish wealth in Slovakia would have amounted to 100–160 million dollars or, if one assumes the maximum value, over 500 million dollars.[181]

It would appear that the figure of the Central Committee is approximately correct.

The total figures for these three parts of Czechoslovakia would be 1,150 million dollars.

The *World Almanac*[182] estimated the national wealth of Czechoslovakia for 1928 at 9,942 million dollars, far less than the 60 billion RM (equivalent to 14.3 billion dollars) which was the evaluation by the Dresdner Bank for 1924. In 1937, the last year for which data on income are available, the income reported was 66.7 billion kr.,[183] far less than the 1929 figure (90 billions). On the basis of the general growth of incomes, the income in 1938 may be estimated at approximately 70 billion kr., which would correspond to about 500 billion kr. in national wealth, equivalent to 17.3 billion dollars.[184] The figure of 10 billion dollars in 1928 would be equivalent to about 340 billion kr.; bridging the period in accordance with the figures on capital growth and retail index,[185] we arrive at a figure of approximately 370 billion kr., or about 12.8 billion dollars. Since the figure of 10 billion dollars appears to have been low, we may well accept as fair the estimate computed on the basis of income.

The Jews represented 2.4% of the total population of the Czechoslovak Republic. Since 38.3% of all gainfully employed were in agriculture and their income amounted to 33.3%, i.e. these figures were almost equal, we must estimate the *per capita* agricultural and non-agricultural wealth as equal. Thus, on the assumption that the average Jews were as wealthy as the average non-Jewish inhabitants of Czechoslovakia, Jewish wealth would have amounted to 415 million dollars, almost equal to the figure given by the Royal Institute, and somewhat more than one third of the combined figures of the reported wealth in the Protectorate, Sudetenland and Slovakia (no attention is paid here to Carpathian Ruthenia and the part of Slovakia annexed by Hungary).

7. Austria

The estimates of Jewish wealth in Austria vary between 1 billion dollars[186] and less than 1 billion RM.[187]

The Dresdner Bank estimated the value of Austria's national wealth in 1928 at 23.5 billion marks, which is equivalent to 5.6 billion dollars, or about 40 billion schillings. If we bridge the period up to 1939 in accordance with the accepted rate of growth of national wealth and the retail index,[188] we arrive at a figure of about 44 billion schillings for 1938. The latest income figure is 5,748 million schillings for 1935; in accordance with the increase of income in neighboring countries the Austrian income for 1938 might be estimated at about 6.8 billion schillings. This would bring the national wealth to approximately 37.4[189] billion schillings. In view of the low multiplier, a figure of around 40 billion schillings, equal to 7,750 million dollars, may be regarded as representing the wealth of Austria in 1937–38.

The Jews constituted 2.8% of the total population. The persons gainfully employed in agriculture represented 31.7% of the total; approximately 76% of the total population were non-agricultural, of whom the Jews constituted 3.7%. If we assume that the share of agriculture (by percentage of employed persons) in the total wealth, was somewhat higher than in Germany (in view of the smaller industrial potential), the agricultural population may be presumed to have possessed approximately 25% of the total wealth. The wealth of the total non-agricultural population would then amount to 5,800 million dollars, and that of the Jews to 215 million dollars.

8. Lithuania

There are no reliable data on national wealth for particular years[190] and almost none on national income, except the figure of 126 million dollars for 1924 given by Fisk,[191] and of 700 million marks for 1926 by the Dresdner Bank. Clark regards 146 million dollars, equivalent to 1,460 million litas, as the average figure for the years 1925 to 1934. But obviously this figure cannot be correct for the period shortly before the war since the average index of 1925 to 1934 was 86.3 while that from 1937 to 1939, only 53. This reduction in the index, and various data for other countries do not permit us to estimate the income for the period before the war at more than 70% of this figure, i.e. 1 billion litas, or 160 million dollars of current value. In the absence of other figures we must accept the same multiplier as in the case of Poland, viz. 7. The national wealth of Lithuania would thus amount to 1.1 billion dollars.

The Jews constituted 7% of the total population. There is hardly any reason to place the *per capita* agricultural wealth lower than that of any other branch of national economy, since there were practically no large cities and industries. Thus the wealth of the Lithuanian Jews, on the average basis, would have amounted to some 80 million dollars.

9. Holland

According to an announcement in the Nazi-controlled press[192] the German authorities have taken over Dutch Jewish interests in the amount of 500 million guildens (approximately 270 million dollars). Of this sum, business enterprises totalled 150 million guildens, real estate 200 million, and securities 150 million.

The previously mentioned estimate by Stuart of Dutch private wealth in 1927 was 21,713 million fl.[193] Bridging the period until 1939 by the accepted rules,[194] we arrive at a figure of approximately 20 billion fl. The latest income figures (for 1937 and 1938) were 4.5 and 4.7 billion guildens respectively; converting the average of these amounts into wealth, we arrive, on the basis of the corrected ratio of Stuart (20%), at the figure of approximately 28 billion guildens, which may be accepted as close to the possible value.

The Jews represented about 1.8% of the total population.[195] In view of the income figures we arrived at for Czechoslovakia, there seems to be no reason for estimating the agricultural wealth on a lower level than any other type. Consequently the Jewish owned portion of the Dutch national wealth would amount to 414 million guildens (230 million dollars). Since the wealth of the average Jew must have exceeded at least slightly that of the average Dutchman, the figure of 500 million guildens mentioned above, cannot be regarded as excessive.

10. Belgium

According to a report in the *Bruesseler Zeitung*,[196] Jewish property in Belgium already "aryanized" by 1943 came to 18,327 million francs, equal to 618 million dollars. It is difficult to say whether any appreciable wealth still remained in Jewish hands at that time.

In 1928 the national wealth of Belgium was estimated at 10,769 million dollars[197] equivalent to 380 billion francs. Bridging the period up to 1939 in the customary manner,[198] we arrive at a figure of approximately 415 billion francs. The latest figures on national income are 60,200 and 65,920 million francs for 1936 and 1937 respectively; the income for 1938 may be estimated at 70 billion francs in view of the fact that in all countries the year 1938 shows an increase over 1937.[199] If this figure is converted into wealth with the help of the multiplier,[200] we arrive at the figure of 490 billion francs. The mean between this figure and the one suggested above would come to about 450 billion francs.

The Jews constituted 0.9% of the total of Belgian population.[201] Of the total gainfully employed, 17.1% were in agriculture; the non-agricultural population must thus be set at 84% of the total, of whom the Jews would constitute 1.08%. With the non-agricultural wealth valued at 380 billion francs, the Jewish share would amount to about 4,100 million francs, or 138 million dollars.

11. Latvia

The Dresdner Bank evaluated the national wealth of Latvia in 1926 at 4.5 billion RM, equivalent to 1,074 million dollars or 5,565 million lats.[202] Bridging the period up to 1939, in accordance with the accepted rules,[203] we arrive at a figure of 5.6 billion lats, which is equivalent to 1.09 billion dollars. Clark estimates the average income 1925–1934 at 178 million gold dollars or 922 million lats. *Moody's Manual* (1940, p. 1900) sets the total income for 1936 at 1,025 million lats, and for 1937 at 1,250 millions. This would bring the income shortly before the war to 250 million dollars and the national wealth, through the application of the multipliers evolved,[204] to 1,375 million dollars. In view of these figures, a mean value of about 1,200 million dollars may be regarded as fair.

Persons employed in agriculture represented 67% of all gainfully employed, and the non-agricultural population, 40% of the total. If we assume that the same proportion of the national wealth went to agriculture as in the case of Poland, i.e. that the ratio of agricultural wealth to the total wealth was 75% of the proportion of persons gainfully employed in agriculture to the total working population, the share of agriculture would be 50% of the total.[205] The non-agricultural wealth would then amount to 600 million dollars. As the Jews constituted 5% of the total population or 12.5% of the non-agricultural, their segment of national wealth would, therefore, amount to 75 million dollars.

12. Yugoslavia

There are no published figures on Jewish wealth in Yugoslavia. Indeed there is even a dearth of data on the national wealth. The Dresdner Bank estimate for 1926 was 38 billion marks, equal to around 9 billion gold dollars (or 510 billion dinars). In 1926 and 1939 the League of Nations wholesale indices[206] were about 100 and 79 respectively. Taking into account the average rate of growth of national wealth and the corrected index, we may estimate the national wealth of Yugoslavia in 1939 at approximately 500 billion dinars, which amounts to 11.5 billion dollars, at the average rate of exchange of 1938.

The national income of Yugoslavia in 1937 was 44.2 billion dinars.[207] Allowing for a growth of about 10% during the years 1938–39,[208] the national income in 1939 would be about 48 billion dinars. According to the *Conference Board Economic Record*, the maximum national income was 1,231 million dollars, which is equivalent to 5,300 million dinars. In 1926 the ratio was, according to the Dresdner Bank, 11.6%, the multiplier approximately 9. On the basis of an average of these figures, the national wealth would amount to around 450 billion dinars or approximately 10.5 billion dollars.

The Jews represented less than 0.5% of the total population. Since 71.2% of the total population were gainfully employed in agriculture, the Jews would represent around 1.4% of the non-agricultural population. In view of the fact that the income from agriculture was 48.3% of the total,[209] the non-agricultural wealth may be evaluated at about 45% of the total, i.e., approximately 5 billion dollars, and the Jewish share at 70 million dollars.

13. Greece

According to Rediadis,[210] the Greek national wealth in 1929 amounted to 212–233 billion drachmas. We shall accept the mean figure of 225 billions. Bridging the period up to 1939 in accordance with the accepted figures of the growth of national wealth and the corrected index,[211] we arrive at a figure of approximately 380 billion drachmas, equal to 3.42 million dollars. This figure may appear to be somewhat low for a country with a population of over 7 million persons, even taking into consideration the comparatively low prices there.[212] But according to the *Conference Board Economic Record*,[213] the highest income since 1929 was 530 million dollars, which would bring the national wealth to about 3.3 billion dollars on the basis of aforementioned ratio of

Rediadis. The figure of Clark is much higher, viz., 436 million gold dollars on the average, which amounts to 720 million dollars of actual value; the national wealth would then total 4.5 billion dollars. We may accept the mean figure of 4 billion dollars as probably close to the truth.

In view of the fact that agricultural income forms 45%[214] of the total, non-agricultural wealth may be estimated at around 2.0 billion dollars. Persons gainfully employed in agriculture represented 61% of the total, and the non-agricultural population of Greece constituted approximately 45% of the total. The Jews represented 1.2% of the total population, and 2.7% of the non-agricultural. On this basis the wealth of the Jews would come to some 54 million dollars.

14. Bulgaria

The Commission for Jewish Affairs valued Jewish property in Bulgaria at approximately 8 billion levas. This amount which is supposed to be equivalent to 8–13% of the entire national wealth[215] would represent approximately 100 million dollars at pre-war rates.[216]

There are no figures on Bulgaria's national wealth for recent years,[217] nor any estimates of income in the years immediately preceding the war.[218] The average annual income for the period 1925–34 is estimated by Clark at 295 million gold dollars (or 317 if indirect levies are included). The *Conference Board Economic Record*[219] estimates the maximum income since 1929 at 474 million dollars, somewhat lower than the figure of Clark. Tchakaloff's figure for 1935 is 36,596 million levas. Since the wholesale price index in 1939 was 120% of that in 1935, the production must also have been larger, and in addition the year 1938 brought to some of the neighboring countries an increase of about 30% over 1935 (Hungary), we may set the Bulgarian national income for 1938 at approximately 47 billion levas, about 580 million dollars. On the basis of these figures and of the application of the multiplier 6.5,[220] the average value of Bulgaria's national wealth would come to about 3.7 billion dollars.

The Jews represented 0.8% of the total population,[221] and about 3.0% of the non-agricultural population (80% being occupied in agriculture which contributed 51–53% of the national income).[222] On the view that agricultural wealth amounted to about 60% of the total, non-agricultural wealth might be set at about 1.5 billion dollars, and the total Jewish wealth at 45 million dollars (assuming that the average share of all Bulgarian non-agricultural inhabitants was also characteristic of the Jewish group as well).

15. Italy

There are no figures available on the losses Jews suffered under the Fascist regime. The figures published on confiscated Jewish property are concerned only with the part of Italy under German domination. Consequently, these figures cover only a part of the total Jewish wealth. According to the *Regima Fascista*[223] the value of confiscated Jewish property in the German controlled area was approximately 12 billion lires,[224] which would be equal to over 630 million dollars on the 1938 average exchange rate.

According to Gini[225] the private net wealth of Italy amounted to 475 billion lires in 1928.[226] Adjusting this amount in accordance with the data relative to the growth of wealth and the wholesale index (491 in 1938 and 482 in 1938), private wealth would reach about 525 billion lires in 1939, which comes to 27.6 billion dollars. Dr. Espinosa evaluated the wealth of Italy in 1937 at 619 billion lires[227] or 32.5 billion dollars.

The Conference Board Economic Record[228] sets the maximum income since 1929 at 4,605 million dollars, a figure which if transformed in wealth by the application of the multiplier 6 would correspond almost exactly to the sum arrived at above.[229] The figures of Clark are much higher, viz., 4.2 billion gold dollars, equal to 7.0 billion dollars, but they are based on the data for 1928 and 1931 only and must, therefore, be reduced considerably for the later period. A fair estimate would be 30 to 35 billion dollars.

The Jews represented 0.1% of the total population. The agricultural population was 47.3% of the total, and the agricultural income 31% of the total. The non-agricultural part of the population would thus amount to approximately 60% of the total, and the Jews to 0.17% of that part. We may estimate the non-agricultural wealth at approximately 20 billion dollars; assuming equal per capita wealth of Jews and non-Jews the share of the Jewish population would then be 34 million dollars, which is obviously too low for the wealthy Jewry of Italy.

16. Estonia

No reliable data on Estonia's national wealth are available.[230] The last figure on national income, referring to the year 1936, is 318 million kroons. If we consider the usual growth of income in other countries since 1936, and the 14% increase in the indices from 1936 to 1939, we may safely estimate the 1939 income at about 370 million kroons. Applying the multiplier 6, as in case of Latvia, we arrive at the figure for national wealth of 2,220 million kroons or 600 million dollars.

The Jews constituted 0.4% of the total population. Persons gainfully employed in agriculture represented 68.2% of the total. Thus the non-agricultural population represented 40% of the total, with the Jews constituting 1% of it. If we assume that the ratio of agricultural wealth to the total wealth is 75% of the ratio of persons gainfully employed in this branch of national economy to the total of gainfully employed, we arrive at a figure for non-agricultural wealth of 49% of the total wealth or about 300 million dollars. The wealth of the Estonian Jews would amount, on the basis of the average figures for *per capita* wealth, to 3 million dollars.

17. Denmark

According to Stockholm reports, German occupation authorities in Denmark have confiscated Jewish owned property in the amount of approximately 1,780 million kroners, approximately 356 million dollars.[231] This sum would seem to be exaggerated.

The national wealth of Denmark was officially estimated for 1928 at 5,360 million dollars, approximately 20 billion kroner.[232] If we bridge the period up to 1939 according to the method usually applied,[233] we arrive at a figure of around 23.5 billion kroner which is equivalent to 5,140 million dollars. The latest available figure on national income for 1936 is 4,200 million kroner. In the light of the figures regarding the growth of income in neighboring countries and of the indices,[234] the income for 1939 must have been at least 10–12% higher, i.e. about 4,700 million kroner. If we convert this figure with the help of the multiplier 6.5,[235] we arrive at a figure of over 30 billion kroner. The mean figure of 26–27 billion kroner may be regarded as approximately correct.

The Jews represented 0.2% of the total population. Thus their share would amount, on the average basis, to some 52–54 million kroner or approximately 12 million dollars.

18. Norway

In Norway the Jews were only 0.05% of the total population. Because of their minute representation in this country they could not even be regarded as constituting a cross-section of the urban population. For this reason it is futile to establish the average wealth of a Norwegian non-agricultural person, in order to arrive at some approximate amount of this fortune. The figures below are given only for the sake of comparison with other countries.

In 1927 the Dresdner Bank estimated the Norwegian national wealth at 15.5 billion marks, equivalent to 3,682 million dollars, or 14.1 billion kroner. The amount of wealth in 1939 would be about 14.7 billion kroner, or 3,612 million dollars.[236] The latest figure on income (that for 1938) is 2,879 million kroner;[237] for 1939 the income may be put at ca. 2,900 million kroner. Transforming this amount into wealth,[238] we again arrive at the aforementioned figure of 14.7 billion kroner. The proportion of the population gainfully employed in agriculture was 35.8%. According to Clark,[239] the average *per capita* income in agriculture for 1934 was about 35% of the average income for the economy as a whole. This figure is much lower than that for any country previously discussed. Even if we put it at 50%, the proportion of agricultural to the total wealth would be about 15%; accordingly the agricultural wealth would amount to 542 million dollars, and the remainder would be valued at over 3 billion dollars. The Jews represent 0.075% of the non-agricultural population and their fortune 2.25 million dollars.

SUMMARY

As indicated above, the figures regarding average wealth may be regarded as minimum or, in some instances, as only probable measurements of the wealth owned by Jews within countries where they formed a fairly large section of the population; in other cases it must be assumed that the *per capita* wealth of the Jews was larger. Consequently, if we regard certain published figures in Jewish wealth (e.g., those on Holland, Germany, Czechoslovakia) as more or less correct, we may assume that in cases when Jews constituted less than 5% of the total population a correction of the average figures appears necessary, the coefficient generally increasing as the proportion of the Jews to the total population decreases.

On this basis the wealth of Jews in the different countries may be estimated in million dollars of current value as shown in Table VIII, the first column reproducing the figures arrived at above, and the second giving the figures as corrected in the light of other data and the economic position of the Jewish population in the country concerned.

Table VIII

Country	Amount of Wealth (averages subject to the reservations indicated above)	Probable Jewish Wealth (round numbers) *
Poland	2,100	2,100
Romania	1,000	1,000
Hungary	335	400
Germany	964	2,000
France	278	600–800
Czechoslovakia	415	700–800
Austria	215	350–400
Lithuania	80	100
Holland	230	300
Belgium	138	200
Latvia	75	100
Yugoslavia	70	100
Greece	54	60–80
Bulgaria	45	50–60
Estonia	3	10
Italy	34	100
Denmark	12	50–60
Norway	2	10
TOTAL	6,050	8,230–8,620

*Discounting great individual fortunes.
The estimate of Jewish losses contained in *Hitler's Ten Year War on Jews* is based on a different method of computation and is higher than the one given here.

NOTES

[1] This section is very brief since its purpose is simply to suggest the general lines of the despoliation of the Jews practised by Germany and her satellites.
A detailed account of the process and methods of dispossession, though from a different angle, will be given in the forthcoming volume of the Institute, "War Crimes."
[2] *New York Times*, November 13, 1938.

[3] G. H. Knobbs (Commonwealth Bureau of Census and Statistics, Melbourne. *The Private Wealth of Australia and Its Growth, Melbourne, 1918)* describes the degree of accuracy of national wealth estimates in the following words: "It cannot be too strongly emphasized that by whatever means an estimate of the wealth of a community is computed, the resultant figures can never be regarded as more than rough approximation" (p. 176).

[4] It must be noted that the National Industrial Conference Board's new estimates of national wealth (*The Conference Board Economic Record,* October 5, 1939, p. 118) have lowered the official figures of the 1922 census from 320.8 to 306.8 billion dollars.

[5] "The Wealth of Nations with special reference to that of the American People." *Journal of the Franklin Institute,* July 1931, p. 55.

[6] In the cited new estimates (*The Conferences Board Economic Record,* Oct. 5, 1939) the figure was raised to 353.6 billion dollars.

[7] See Robert R Doane, *The Measurement of American Wealth,* New York and London, 1933, p.9. It is true that for other years the difference is less pronounced.

[8] *The Conference Board Economic Record, l.c.*

[9] Dresdner Bank. *The Economic Forces of the World,* Berlin, 1930, Table, "The Development of National Wealth." This publication introduces its presentation of figures on wealth with the following words: "It is a well known fact that, owing to the lack of accurate statistical data, it is impossible to establish the exact amount of national wealth, which can, therefore, only be estimated more or less accurately. Consequently, the results obtained in this field by various investigations not infrequently show rather considerable divergencies, and can only be compared in a limited sense. The following table represents a summary of those results which offer the best guarantee for their reliability. Though with reference to these figures the fact should not be overlooked that all the values given are merely approximate" (p. 169).

[10] C. Gini, *A Comparison of the Wealth and National Income of Several Important Nations (Italy, France, Belgium, United Kingdom, and United States) before and after the War,* Rome, 1925, p. 7.

[11] Kulp in *Revue de Deux Monds,* October 15, 1924.

[12] "The Wealth and Income of the Chief Powers, 4. Various Methods of Computing Wealth and Income," *Journal of the Royal Statistical Society,* Vol. LXXXII, Part IV, p. 491.

[13] "The evaluation of the national income is, together with that of national wealth, one of the most difficult problems of economic statistics." F. de Fellner, *"Le revenu national de la Hongrie actuelle," Bulletin de ÓInstitute International de Statistique* (subsequently quoted as *Bulletin*), XXV, livr. 3, p. 448. However, this view is not generally shared in regard to income (See Stamp, l.c.).

[14] For the complex of problems involved in computing national wealth (and national income) see, *inter alia, Studies on Income and Wealth,* Vol I, 1937; Vol. II, 1938, National Bureau of Economic Research, New York; Sir Josiah Stamp, *Wealth and Taxable Capacity,* London, 1922, Chapter I; J. Stamp, "The Wealth and Income of the Chief Powers, 4. Various Methods of Computing Wealth and Income," *Journal of the Royal Statistical Society,* Vol. LXXXII, part IV; "Fortune et Revenu National," *Revue d'Economie Politique,* Jan–Feb., 1939; G. H. Knobbs, *l.c.;* C. Gini, *A Comparison of the Wealth and National Income of Several Important Nations (Italy, France, Belgium, United Kingdom, and United States) before and after the War,* Rome, 1925 (hereafter cited as "Comparison"); *The Conference Board Economic Record, l.c.,* appendix.

[15] Colin Clark, *The Conditions of Economic Progress,* London, 1940. "The tedious and intractable problems of measuring real national income is a child's play in comparison with the difficulties of measuring real national wealth" (p.374).

[16] Thus in Corrado Gini's "Quelques chiffres sur la richesse et les revenus nationaux de quinze états," *Metron,* July, 1923 (hereafter cited as "Quelques Chiffres"), the private wealth alone is given for Holland and the national wealth alone for Norway, Czechoslovakia, Poland, and Romania; whereas for Belgium, Denmark, Bulgaria, and Yugoslavia, both are presented.

[17] *Op. cit.* See below the figures for Poland and Germany.

[18] See in addition to the works mentioned in footnote 14, *i.e.,,* Sir Josiah Stamp, "Methods Used in Different Countries for Estimating the National Income," *Journal of the Royal Statistical Society,* Vol,, 1934; *The National Capital and other Statistical Studies,* London, 1937, Chapter III, and *Wealth and Taxable Capacity,* London, 1922, Chapter II; W.L. Mitchell and S. Kuznets, "Current Problems in Measurement of National Income," *Bulletin,* Vol. XXVIII, 1934, pp. 280 ff.; A.L.

Bowley, *Studies in National Income,* Cambridge University Press, 1942; *The Conference Board Economic Record,* August 3, 1939, "The National Income of Principal Foreign Powers."

[19] National income must not necessarily be larger than the private. A comparison of these two figures for Germany shows that for the year 1931 (great depression) the private income was 59, 242 million RM, and the national income only 57,074 million RM (*Einzelschriften zur Statistik des Deutschen Reichs,* No. 24, 1932, "Das deutsche Volkseinkommen vor und nach dem Kriege," p.83).

[20] Depending on whether investments are made or a part of the wealth is consumed, the first or the second may be larger. See *e.g.* the figures for the United States in the *Statistical Abstract of the United States,* 1939, p. 311.

[21] *Einzelschriften zur Statistik des Deutschen Reichs, l.c.,* p. 12.

[22] *The National Income of Bulgaria 1924–35,* Publication of the Statistical Institute at the University of Sofia, 1937, No. 2, p.123.
It is very questionable whether Mr. Tchakaloff's estimates in regard to the degree of possible errors are correct. He puts (p. 84) the weighted total average error at 10.42%, that for commerce at 15%, for agriculture and animal breeding at 10.96% and 11.36% respectively, for real estate at 10%, and so on. We are much more inclined to accept the figures of Sir Josiah Stamp on this score ("Various Methods of Computing Wealth and Income," *l.c.*), who estimates (for the year 1914) the possible error at about 40% in countries like Italy, Spin, and Canada.

[23] *South-Eastern Europe, A Brief Survey.* The Royal Institute of International Affairs, Information Department Papers, No. 26, London, 1940.

[24] See below the study of Tchakaloff.

[25] "Political as well as economic considerations are believed to have influenced the official statistics upon which the estimates of certain countries are based." *Economic Record, l.c.,* p. 33.

[26] According to Jules Neubauer, "Le montant de revenu national Hongrois" in *Journal de la Société Hongroise de Statistique,* Vol. XVII (1939), p. 297, the annual national income for the years 1926–28 was estimated by Mr. Fellner (See for instance, *Le revenu national de la Hongrie démembré,* 1930; *La réparation de la charge fiscale, 1936*) at 4,383,402,000 pengoes, and by Mathias Matolsey and Stephen Varga (*The National Income of Hungary*) at 4,157,015,000; for 1932 at 3,253,951,000 and 2,573,247,000 pengoes respectively. The figure of Fellner for 1932 is thus about 24% higher than that of Matolsey and Varga.
For Italy the national income in 1928 was variously estimated at 24.3 and 18.8 billion RM; for France in 1924 at 44.2 and 40.2 billion RM; for Czechoslovakia in 1927 at 9.1 and 8.7–9.5 (Dresdner Bank, *l.c.,* Table, "Development of National Income").

[27] Jules Neubauer, *l.c.,* p. 308. Mr. Neubauer contends that the method applied in the English edition yields rather improbable results.

[28] *World Economic Survey* 1938/9, League of Nationns, p.45, note 1.

[29] Cf. also Dresdner Bank, *l.c.,* p. 171; *Einzelschriften, l.c.,* p. 12 ("the results are mere estimates and may be used with corresponding reservations only"); "Estimations des revenues privés" by L. Dugé de Bernonville in *Revue d'Economie Politique,* May-June, 1933, p. 659 ("it is necessary once more to insist on the extremely uncertain character of these evaluations").

[30] Tchakaloff, *l.c.,* p.p. 98–100.

[31] For example, Tchakaloff was unable to determine the basis of the income figures for Hungary and Greece.

[32] It must be stresses that other sources give different data in regard to the ratios for *per capita* wealth among the nations in question. Thus K. Mori, "The Estimate of the National Wealth and Income of Japan Proper," *Bulletin,* Vol. 25, lvr. 2, p.200 (following Gini and Moody) gives these figures for per capital wealth in 1925: France, 2,549; Belgium, 2,953; Denmark, 1,760; Norway, 900; Italy, 1,117 yens. Corrado Gini, "Quelques Chiffres," pp. 110–112, brings these data for the period before or shortly after World War I (in thousand francs): Belgium, 7.8; Denmark, 6.0–6.5; Norway, 3.7–4.1; Czechoslovakia, 4.0–4.2; Poland, 3.0–3.2; Romania, 2.9; Bulgaria, 2.5–2.9; Yugoslavia, 2.3–2.7: Netherlands (private wealth), 7.1.

[33] *Home, Colonial and Foreign Borrowing,* London, 1927, p.26. The figures are based on estimates made by Moody's Investors Service of New York and London. However, it is hardly probable that Romania is wealthier than Austria, and the latter poorer than Yugoslavia.

[34] See the figures given in this subsection.

[35] Doane, *l.c.*, p. 9.

[36] Dresdner Bank, *l.c.* The reason for the large discrepancy between the two figures for Hungary may be the greater stability in the later period.

[37] We do not consider the case of countries like the USSR. In Germany industrial production was (in percentages of 1928) :1926, 78.7; 1927, 101.2; 1928, 100; 1929, 100.9; 1930, 88.9; 1931, 72.8; 1932, 58.7; 1933, 65.5 (*Statistisches Jahrbuch fuer das Deutsche Reich* 1935, p. 50* and 1938, p. 55*), These production and the income statistics show how useless it may be to calculate average increases in national income, ranging allegedly (in dollars) for the period 191425, from 1% in Italy and France, and 2% in Belgium and Great Britain, to 10% in the United States (Gini: *A Comparison*).

[38] July, 1937, "The National Income of Poland," p. 3.

[39] *Concise Statistical Yearbook of Poland*, 1937, p. 54.

[40] *World Almanac*, 1934, p. 302. For annual savings in percent of income see *Conference Board Economic Record*, 1940, p. 181.

[41] Marschak and Lederer, *Kapitalbildung*, London, 1936.

[42] According to annual figures by Lindahl, quoted in Colin Clark, *The Conditions of Economic Progress*, London, 1940, p. 175.

[43] E. Fuhrmann, *Das Volksvermoegen und Volkseinkommen des Koenigreichs Sachsen*, Leipzig, 1914; A. Steinmann-Bucher, Das Reich Deutschland, Berlin, 1914, p. 61.

[44] *E.g.*, the index of Mr. Carl Snyder for the United States.

[45] *Conference Board Bulletin*, May 20, 1933 and *World Almanac* as cited below.

[46] *World Almanac*, 1934, p. 302: 1936, p.534; 1938, p. 359.

[47] Statistical Yearbook of the L.o.N., 1933/4, pp. 248–251

[48] *The Conference Board Economic Record*, Oct. 5, 1939, p. 118.

[49] Dresdner Bank, *op. cit.*

[50] The figures on Denmark's wealth in the *World Almanac*, 1932, p. 335, correspond almost exactly to the combined index obtained by using the wholesale Index:

Year	Wealth	Rate of Exchange	Wholesale Index	Combined Index
1925	5,766.5 (100)	.2113	210	100
1928	5,360.0 (93)	.2674	153	92

[51] One of the main sources of income is not included in the wealth, *viz.*, human labor.

[52] "La richesse et le revenu de la pénisule ibérique" in *Metron*, Vol. 5, No. 4, pp. 185/6.

[53] *A Comparison*, p. 3.

[54] P. 171. Mori *(l.c.,* p. 204) gives much higher figures viz., 21.16% for France, 23.14% for Italy, and 34.83% for Germany (1922). The reason for the unusually high figure for Germany may be that during the inflation year 1922 the prices of capital goods were very low.

[55] La XIX Session de l'Institut International de Statistique," *Metron* 193112, p. 119.

[56] Gini, *A Comparison*.

[57] *Revue d'Economie Politique*, Jan–Feb., 1939, p. 387.

[58] *Der volkswirtschaftliche Elementarvergleich zwischen den Vereinigten Staaten von Amerika, Deutschland, Grossbritannien, Frankreich und Italien*, Berlin, 1930, part IV, Table 1.

[59] For Italy in 1928, Gini arrives at the figure of approximately 19.9 in "La determinazione della richezza e del reddito delle nazioni nel dopo guerra e il loro confronto col periodo prebellico," *Bulletin*, Vol. XXV, lvr. 3, p. 364.

The figures on wealth for Norway and Czechoslovakia given above were obtained by reducing the figures on total wealth to private wealth, since the income figures presented are those of private income only. Judging by the figures presented for other countries the national wealth is 10–35% higher than the private. In the case of Norway and of Czechoslovakia, reductions of about 1O% and 15% respectively were made.

[60] According to Gini, *ibid.*, the ratio was about 19.9.

[61] *Revue de l'Institut Intern. d Statistique*, 1936, Vol. IV, livr. 4, p. 481.

[62] "La fortune nationale de la Hongrie actuelle," *Bulletin*, Vol. XXIV, livr. 2 (1930), p. 432. According to Matolsey and Varga the income of Hungary was almost constant during the years 1925 to 1928. Hence the difference in the year would not affect the ratio which would, however, increase to 17% if the income figures of Matolsey and Varga are used.

[63] "Volksvermoegen and Volkseinkommen in den Niederlanden," *Bulletin*, Vol. XXV, livr. 3, pp. 461 and 464. According to the figures given there, the ratio was 21% in 1925–26.

[64] Dr. Bohdan Dederko, *Majatek narodowy Polski*, Warszawa 1930. p. 47.

[65] Dresdner Bank, *op. cit.*

[66] *Foreign Commerce Yearbook*, 1938.

[67] Vandellos, *l.c.*

[68] P. D. Rediadis, "The Greek National Income and Wealth in 1929," *Metron*, June 15, 1930, pp. 121 ff.

[69] Gini, *A Comparison*.

[70] Gini *(La XIX Session, l.c.)* regards this ratio as totally improbable.

[71] This accounts for the smaller ratio in France.

[72] Doane, *l.c.*, p. 9.

[73] *Statistical Abstract of the United States*, 1939, p. 311, and Doane, p. 81.

[74] *op. cit.*, p. 203.

[75] Stamp *(Various Methods l.c.)*.

[76] In addition to the general sources for national wealth cited above (Stamp, Kulp, Dresdner Bank, Gini, Mori Gourjou and Parkinson, *World Almanac)*, figures for many countries are contained in *World Economic Chart*, 1928 (published by tine New York Stock Exchange firm of Redmond and Co.), and in *Moody's Manual of Investments American and Foreign. Government Securities*, 1927. However, the two last sources do not always give the exact year of the estimate and can, therefore, be used only in exceptional cases. On the other hand, the figures contained in later editions of *Moody's Manual* are given for particular years. The publication of the U. S. Treasury Dept. (Section of Financial and Economic Research), "Compilation of Post-War Estimates of National Wealth with Sources" (prepared in April, 1928 and revised April, 1929) contains only a few figures Paul II. Nystrom, *Economic Principles* of *Consumption*, New York, brings rata for 1922. Doane, l.c., p. 35, contains data on national wealth relating to the year 1929. These figures are not very reliable, at least in part. Thus, the wealth of Sweden is estimated to be smaller than that of Estonia; on the other hand, the figures for the Baltic states appear excessive and so on. It must be noted that the cited sources usually relate to periods before 1930. *Moody's Manual*, 1937, p.2711, has this to say about the lack of figures after 1930: "There have been no recent estimates for Germany's wealth and any attempt at establishing figures would have to be based to a large extent on highly problematic data, on account of the extremely unsettled conditions prevailing through the world since 1930. All previous estimates cannot, under the circumstances be considered to represent event fairly accurate information for present day comparison."

[77] See the studies by Tchakaloff and Matolsey and Varga already cited. Figures for Czechoslovakia can be found in *Bulletin* No. *147, 1939/1* and *156,1939/10* of the *National Bank of Czechoslovakia* and *the Nationalbank fuer Bochmen und Machren*, Prague, 1939; for France in *Revue d'Economie Politique*, 1935, 1937 and 1939 (by L. Dugé de Bernonville), etc. The aforementioned *World Economic Chart, Moody's Manual*, the study of the Dresdner Bank, the *World Almanac*, Stamp, as well as Fink, "Some New Estimates of National Income," *American Economic Review*, March 1930, pp. 20 ff., and others also bring figures on income.

[78] *Weltwirtschaftliches Archiv*, 1938, pp. 51 ff., later incorporated into The *Conditions of Economic Progress*, London, 1940.

[79] This neglects even the crucial production figures.

[80] It is not difficult to imagine what difference it makes whether the Jews are déclassés, workers and small traders on the one hand, or industrialists, bankers, on the other. For example, according to Sir Josiah Stamp *(Wealth and Taxable Capacity*, London 1922, p. 102), two thirds of the total wealth in Great Britain was held by just under 400,000 people, *i.e.*, about 1% of the population, and the top one third by 36,000 people, *i.e.*, less than 0.1% of the population.

[81] Data on the occupational and social distribution of the Jews in the different countries are contained in: *(a) Hitler's Ten-Year War on the Jews* (Institute of Jewish Affairs, New York, 1943;

(b) *Jews in Nazi Europe* (Institute of Jewish Affairs), New York 1941; *(c) The Jewish Communities in Nazi-Occupied Europe* (American Jewish Committee, Research Institute on Peace and Postwar Problems), New York, 1944; (d) *Universal Jewish Encyclopaedia*, Vol.8 ("Occupations," by Jacob Lestchinsky); (e) B.D., "Jews in Hungary," *Di Yiddishe Economic*, 1937, Volumes 4–5 and 6–8; (f) Dr. Leo Goldhammer "On the professional structure of the Jews in Vienna," *Di Yiddishe Economic*, 1937, Vol. 68; Arthur Rupin, *Jewish Fate and Future* (Chapter VIII), London, 1942.

[82] *Bulgaria, Recensement de la population* au 31 décembre 1934, Vol. 1 (Sofia, 1938), p.23.

[83] *American Jewish Yearbook*, Vol. 43. For figures on the Jewish population see also *The Jewish Yearbook*, London, and the previously mentioned *Hitler's Ten-Year War on the Jews*.

[84] *The London and Cambridge Economic Service*, Special Memorandum No. 48 ("South Eastern Europe"), London, 1939, p. 110, estimates that the Jews represented 45% and 53% respectively of independent workers and employees in trade and credit.

[85] *Maly Rocznik Statystyczny*, 1939, pp. 24–25.

[86] *Statistik des Deutschen Reichs*, Uand *451*, Heft 5. "Die Glaubensjuden im Deutschen Reich," p. 23.

[87] 47.7% of all gainfully employed Jews were engaged in commerce with goods as against 8.4% of the total. (*Wirtschaft und Statistik*, 1935, No. 22. "Die Glaubensjuden im Deutschen Reich nach Staatsangehoerigkeit, Gebuertigkeit, Alter und Beruf," p. 824.)

[88] *Statistik des Deutschen Reichs, l.c.*, p. 26.

[89] *Statistik des Bundesstaates Oesterreich*, Heft l. *Die Ergebnisse der oesterreichischen Volkszachlung vom 22. Maerz 1934*, Vienna 1935, p. 45.

[90] "La Fortune nationale de la Hongrie actuelle," *Bulletin*, Vol. 24, livr. 2 (1930), pp. 380 ff.

[91] A *Comparison*, p. 7. Cf. the data compiled by Dr. Espinosa on the national wealth of Italy for 1930 *(Moody's Manual*, 1937, p. 2830) and for 1937 *(Moody's Manual*, 1940, p.1885) containing only the items of land, urban buildings, industry and commerce, securities, and other movables. The estimate for Latvia on December 1, 1927 *(Moody's Manual*, 1937, p. 2862) is more detailed and contains figures on landed property, forests, personal property. communication, municipal real estate, rural structures, state resources, merchandise, livestock. agricultural implements, and industries.

[92] *Ibid.*, p. lı. Cf. also A. Sauvy and R. Rivet, "Fortune et Revenu National," *Revue d'Economic Politique*, January–February, 1939.

[93] *The Conference Board Economic Record*, October 5, 1939.

[94] Dr. Bohdan Dederko, *op. cit.*

[95] The amount of these debts may be judged by the fact that the agricultural indebtedness of Germany was about 11.6 billion marks in 1930 *(Foreign Commerce Yearbook*, 1938, p.48).

[96] *L.c.*, p. 48. It is worth indicating however, that the food stocks seem to be totally disregarded as an item of national wealth.

[97] *Monograph* No. 4, *l.c.* The figures concern the year 1927. J. W. Nixon, "On the Statistics Available Concerning the Occupied Population of the World and Its Distribution." Revue de l'Institut International de Statistique, 1938, pp. 384385. 388 and 392, gives the figure of 67%. *The Statistical Yearbook of the League of Nations* 1933–34, p. 40 ff. brings the figure of 75.9%; this must refer to the year 1921, as does the figure of the *Statistisches Tuschenjuhrbuch der Weltwirtschaft*, Berlin, 1939 (76.2%).

[98] *The Financial Times, Little Entente Supplement*, June 15, 1936.

[99] Over 70% of this amount (807 billion) is represented by forests.

[100] *Ibid.* Nixon,, *l.c.*, gives a somewhat lower figure for 1930, viz. about 78%; *The Statistical Yearbook of the League of Nations* 1933–34, p. 40 ff. gives 79.5%. For details, see *infra*, Section B of this chapter.

[101] A *Comparison*, p.45.

[102] This term is not clarified.

[103] In Poland, according to the figures by Dederko, landed property (soil and rural buildings) represented about 34% (excluding the forests), or about 40% (including them) of the total of wealth. The rest of agricultural property represented only 18.20% of that of landed property. The ratio must be higher in countries of greater use of machinery and better farm housing.

[104] Josiah Stamp, *The National Capital and Other Statistical Studies*, London, 1937, p.234.

[105] *Economic World,* June 21, 1924. In 1915 the value of farms, livestock and implements represented almost 40% of the total national wealth. (Data in *Journal of the Canadian Bankers Association,* 1915, cited in *Studies in Current Problems in Finance and Government,* by Sir Josiah Stamp, London, 1924, p. 328).

[106] It must be assumed that, as in all other countries, the percentage was somewhat higher in 1921.

[107] *The Economist,* January 3, 1925.

[108] Absolute figures in *Banque Nationale de Belgique, Bulletin d'Information et de Documentation,* July 25,1934, "La fortune nationale dans le Grand-Duché de Luxembourg," p. 34.

[109] *Moody's Manual, l.c.,* 1927, p.605.

[110] See, for instance, the calculation of the value of the rural and urban real estate by Fellner, *l.c., (Der Deutsche Volkswirt* June 7,1929, p.1210); also the computation of the value of the Polish industries by Dederko *(l.c.,* p.28).

[111] Fellner, *l.c.,* capitalized the value of agricultural land at 4.5% (on the basis of rentals) and urban lots at 5.5%–7%.

[112] The data are all approximate since the classifications for different countries are not always closely comparable *(Foreign Commerce Yearbook* 1938) and the percentage of the persons employed in agriculture changes with the time *(e.g.,* in Belgium it was 19.3% in 1920, and 17.1% in 1930; in France, 38.4% in 1926 and 35.7% in 1931; in Italy, 55.8% in 1921 and 46.7% in 1931, etc. *St. Taschenjahrbuch, l.c.)*

[113] The first four figures are from *South-Eastern Survey, l.c.,* p.86, and refer to periods close to World War II.

[114] *Monograph* No.4, *l.c.,* p.3. The income is estimated at 26 billion Zl. If we accept the figures on total income *of Maly Rocznik Statystyczny,* 1937, p.80, the ratio would be 38.8% and the ratio of income to gainfully employed persons, 63%. In 1933 the ratio was only about 57% (Figures in the *Concise Statistical Yearbook,* 1937, p. 54).

[115] *Vierteljahreshefte zur Wirtschaftsforschung,* 1938–9, Heft IV, p. 426.

[116] *Statistisches Jahrbuch fuer das Deutsche Reich,* 1936, pp. 37*.38*. The figure for Czechoslovakia according to the *Financial Times, Little Entente Supplement,* p. 40, was only 34.6% in the same year.

[117] According to figures by Gini in *La determinazione.*

[118] According to figures by Gini in *A Comparison,* p.46.

[119] *Nationalbank fuer Boehmen und Maehren, Monatsbericht,* 156, 1939/10, p.344.

[120] The ratio is computed from the figures on income from agriculture and agricultural salaries given by Dugé de Bernonville in *Revue d'Economie Politique* May–August, 1939, p.950, and others.

[121] The figures of professional income alone were used for the computations since the non-professional income was not differentiated. Source: Fernand Baudhuin, "Devant les statistiques fiscales," *Banque Nationale de Belgique, Bulletin d'Information et de Documentation,* December 25, 1936.

[122] The figures are based on Nixon, l.c.: *Statistisches Taschenjahrbuch der Weltwirtschaft, llc.; Statistical Yearbook of the League of Nations, l.c.;* and *Statistisches Handbuch der Weitwirtychait,* Berlin, 1936. Figures are to be found in Clark, *Conditions of Economic Progress, l.c.,* and the *International Labor Review.*

[123] Thus it was 40.1% in Holland (1930), 46.9% in Austria (1935), 52.4% in Poland (1921), 56.4% in Estonia (1922), 59.9% in Latvia (1925), and 67.6% in Lithuania (1923). (Figures from *Statistisches Handbuch der Weltwirtschaft,* pp. 53ff.)

[124] *Statistisches Jahrbuch fuer das Deutsche Reich,* 1936, p. 17, and *Wirtschaft und Statistik,* 1927, p.571.

[125] All figures on national income, unless otherwise indicated, are from World *Economic Survey,* 1938–39.

[126] As a rule the figures for the Jewish population are from the *American Jewish Yearbook,* Vol.43.

[127] A computation of income for Germany, France, and Great Britain on the basis of equal purchasing power, was made by the Royal Institute of International Affairs, in the *Bulletin of International News* of March 9, 1940, and April 6, 1940. This computation was undertaken in order to make possible a comparison of the war effort in the various countries.

[128] Memorandum by a group of Polish Jewish industrialists to the Polish Consul General in Jerusalem *(JTA,* November 21, 1943). The same figure is reported to have been estimated by the United Nations Information Office (Mowrer in *New York Post,* October 5, 1944).

[129] *Nowy Swiat,* June 16,1942.

[130] *op. cit.*

[131] The *Financial Times* estimated the Polish national wealth for 1922 at about 17 billion dollars (*L'Economiste Européen,* April 17, 1925, p.254). Since we possess no figures on the state of prices at that time, it is not possible to arrive at any conclusion as to the relation of this figure to the detailed data we possess on national wealth.

[132] The figure of 160–180 billions zlotys is about 15% higher than that of Dederko, which is not a great difference.

[133] *L'Economiste Européen,* June 20, 1930, "La fortune de l'Etat polonais," p. 396, reported that the aggregate value of the wealth of the Polish State was estimated at that time by the Committee of the Society of Polish Economists at 16,374,577,000 zlotys, with a net value of 12.5 billions. *L'Economiste Européen* estimated the national wealth at 160–180 billion zlotys. The aggregate value of state and other public wealth must be estimated as at least 10% of the national wealth. This would seem to be a moderate fraction, since for Germany in 1913 with a liberal economy the percentage was estimated at 10% (if the net value is accepted) or 20% (if the aggregate value is used). Cf *Deutschlands Volkswohlstand,* 1888–1913, by Dr. Karl Helfferich, Berlin, 1915, p.107.

[134] *Statistical Yearbook of the League of Nations,* 1933–34, pp. 248–51 and 1939–40, pp. 206–10. This source is used throughout for price indices.

[135] The yearly average of zloty in dollars on cable transfers in New York was 0.1886 in 1938 (*Statistical Abstract of the United States,* 1940, p.291).

[136] *Conference Board Economic Record,* No.21, 1939, p.198.

[137] See above, Section A.

[138] Since the ratios of agricultural income were 70% and 57%, averaging 66%, we may set the wealth ratio at about 75%.

[139] Although there are data on the Jewish agricultural population, their use will cause little change in our conclusions, since this group represented only about 4% of the total Jewish population, and the number of Jewish agricultural holdings constitutes only 0.6% of the total.

[140] The agricultural working population represented about 62% of the total. According to the above given German ratio of agricultural population to the total population of the country, the figure would be 62 × 0.8 or about 49%. We adopt the figure of approximately 55%.

[141] *News Digest.* Jan.19, 1944, C. 34.

[142] *Folkets Dagblatt* of Jan.26, 1943.

[143] *Voelkischer Beobachter* of June 16, 1943. According to an estimate by Dr. Radelescu it was exactly the same ratio, viz. 65% (*Judenviertel Europa,* ed. Hans Hinkel, Berlin, 1939, p.147).

[144] *Jewish Journal,* August 20, 1944.

[145] Owing to a lack of price indices for the whole period, we must have recourse to this system of computation.

[146] December 21, 1939, p.222.

[147] *Statistical Abstract of the United States, l.c.* This source and – for earlier years – *Foreign Commerce Yearbook,* 1935, p.288, are used throughout.

[148] To make up for the agricultural indebtedness, the total of movable property is considered as belonging to the urban population.

[149] Out of the total available area of 13,866,120 ha (*Financial Times, lc.*). the Jews seemed to have owned only about 500,000 (*Timpul in JTA,* Aug. 10, 1943), *i.e.* less than 4%, and of forests out of the assumed value of over 800 billion leis (*Financial Times, l.c.* only about 2.6 billion leis worth (*News Digest,l.c.*).

[150] *American Jewish Yearbook,* Vol.43. However, it was given as 5% in Vol.44 of the same *Yearbook,* the same figure appears in Zander, *Die Verbreitung der Juden in der Welt,* Berlin, 1937, p.159.

[151] *Financial Times, l.c.* gives the figures of 84.2. This ratio is, however, hardly correct, since Nixon estimates 78% for 1930 and the League of Nations 79.5% for all earlier period. For the period before the war 76% may be fair.

[152] *JTA,* July 19, 1944.

[153] *JTA,* August 7, 1944.

[154] In 1928, it was about 135 and in 1939 about 105.

[155] If this amount appears low it is because of the high purchasing power of money in Hungary. Taking the ratios calculated by Clark for the years 1925–1934, £19 nominal in Hungary equals

£27 in purchasing power, whereas £12–15 in Romania equals only £16 and £14–16 in Bulgaria, £15 *(South Eastern Europe, l.c.,* p.85).

[156] *Moody's Manual,* 1940, p. 1875, brings the figure of 3,631 million kr. as the total income for 1937 and 1,402 millions as the agricultural income. The share of agriculture was thus a little higher than indicated above.

[157] The ratio according to Fellner and the Dresdner Bank (1928), was 13.7% or 15.8% respectively. The mean figure gives us a multiplier of 7.

[158] Jews owned 4.9% of the landed property in Hungary *(The Jewish Communities in Nazi-Occupied Europe, op. cit.).*

[159] *New York Post,* April 28, 1938; Cf. *New York Times* November 13, 1938 and *New York Daily News,* November 14, 1938.

[160] *New York Evening Post, November* 12, 1938. The reference is evidently to the "Greater Reich."

[161] *New York Times, November* 13, 1938 and December 16, 1938.

[162] "German Exploitation of Occupied Europe. I" *(Bulletin of International News,* December 14, 1904, p.1611).

[163] *Deutschlands Volksermoegen im Krieg,* Stuttgart, 1916, p.10.

[164] The wholesale index in 1928 was 140 as against 100 in 1914; the retail prices 152 and 100 respectively *(L.o.N. Statistical Yearbook* 1933/34, pp.247 and 250). The following figures provide some indication of the differences in the evaluation of national wealth in nominal currency before and after the First World War:

Country	Wealth in 1912	Wealth in 1922
Italy	21.8 billion dollars	35.0 billion dollars *Source: Economic World, Apr.12,* 1924
Belgium	5.8 billion dollars	11.0 billion dollars (same source)
Holland	11.2 billion Fl. (1915/16)	21.7 billion Fl. (1927) *Source: C. A. Verriju Stuart, op. cit.*

The property tax returns for 1928 were 220,903 million marks (aggregate) and 140,881 million marks ("unit values-Einheitswerte"), for 1931, 231,325 and 140,601 millions and for 1935, 227,845 and 146,619 million marks respectively *(Statistik des Deutschen Reichs* Vol. 392, p.46 and Vol. 526, pp. 28–29).

[165] It was about 102 in 1928 and 77.7 in 1939.

[166] Of this, private income represented 69.7 annd 75.3 billions respectively (Laufenburger, "La vie économique en Allemagne," in *Revue d'Economie Politique* September-December, 1939, Nos. 5–6, p.1394).

[167] The ratios were 17.6% in 1926 and 19.6% in 1928 (on the basis of the figures of the Dresdner Bank).

[168] Those gainfully employed in agriculture in 1933 constituted 28.9% of the total gainfully employed *(Statistisches Jahrbuch für das Deutsche Reich,* 1936, p.17).

[169] *JTA,* March 16, 1943. The President of the Jewish Unity Committee in Paris stated that Jews in Paris have been robbed of property worth at least 10 billion francs, in addition to household articles and furniture removed from them during the occupation *(JTA,* September 26, 1944). It is not known what part of the total Jewish wealth this figure represents.

[170] P. Sauvy et T. Rivet, "Fortune et Revenue National" in *Revue d'Economie Politique,* January-February, 1939, p.385, footnote 1. The source is M. Pupin in *Capital* of January 10, 1939. This amount would seem to be in accordance with the figure of 1300 billion francs for 1936 given by Sauvy and Rivet, *l.c.,* p. 385.

For lack of available data, North Africa is not considered.

[171] *Ibid.,* p. 372. The *World Economic Survey* quotes the figure of 250 billion francs with reservation. Clark's figure for the annual national income 1925–34 is much higher, viz., 7.8 billion gold dollars. This would bring the national wealth to approximately 55 billion gold dollars.

[172] The ratio was 15% in 1924/5 *(World Almanac* and Gini), 13.8% in 1928 (Dresdner Bank).

[173] Although this figure (60 billion dollars) is smaller than that given for 1925 by the *World Almanac* (51,600 million gold dollars), for 1928 by the Dresdner Bank (70.6 billion gold dollars), and for 1929 by Doane (75 billion dollars), there seems to be no reason to set it higher. Sauvy and Rivet have put the average wealth of the French at 25,000 francs; the total would amount to only 1,050 billions.

[174] December 14, 1940. *German Exploitation al Occupied Countries I*, p. 1611.

[175] Z. H. Wachsman, *Jews After Victory* (Yiddish), New York, 1944, p. 23, reports that official German circles estimated this fortune at 3 billion marks.

[176] This report assumes that there were 200,000 Jews involved, which is 80% higher than the generally accepted figure of 117,500.

[177] *Jewish Journal*, September 8, 1943.

[178] *JTA*, January 6, 1944.

[179] *Czechoslovak Economic Council, Bulletin No. 17*, June 1, 1944; *JTA*, September 18, 1943; *National Zeitung*, Essen, August 16, 1942; *Neues Wiener Tagblatt*, August 1, 1942, and *Slovak*, September 28, 1942; *JTA*, January 19, 1942.

[180] *News Digest*, February 6, 1943, C. 61–62; *Robotnik Polski*, May 9, 1943

[181] President Tisso calculated that the Jews owned 18% of the total national wealth *(Le Temps,* August 19,1942), but received 38% of the income *(Gardista*, August 18, 1942).

[182] 1932, p. 335.

[183] *National Bank ol Czechoslovakia, Bulletin* No.147, 1939/1, p.28.

[184] The ratio was 15% (in 1924) according to Gini, and 12% (in 1926) according to the figures of the Dresdner Bank.

[185] It was 99.5 in 1928 and 98.6 in 1938.

[186] *NewYork Evening Post*, November 12,1938.

[187] *NewYork Times*, November 13, 1938 reported that the value of Jewish property in Austria and Sudetenland was estimated unofficially at 1 billion marks.

[188] It was 97.3 in 1928 and 94.3 in 1937 (the latest period available).

[189] The ratio according to the figures of the Dresdner Bank was 18.7, the multiplier 5.5.

[190] The *World Economic Chart* cites the figures of 870 million dollars; Doane, *l.c.* gives the figure of 3.8 million dollars (for 1929).

[191] "Some New Estimates of National Income," *American Economic Review*, March 1930, pp. 20 ff.

[192] *Netherlands News*, June 1, 1942, p. 189; *Neue Zuercher Zeitung*, May 31, 1942 (based on a report in *De Waag* of May 20th).

[193] This figure has been contested (see Section A). It must be regarded as too low, since the property tax returns for the year 1927–1928 showed a total of 14 billions (*Banque Nationale de Belgique, Bulletin d'Inforrnation et de Documentation*, April 10, 1932). Even if these figures are about 20% lower than the usual prices, the taxable wealth would represent 80% of the Stuart estimate.

[194] The wholesale indices were 104 and 73.9 respectively; the retail indices 100 and 83.3 respectively.

[195] The generally accepted figure is 156,009, which is given in the *American Jewish Yearbook*. According to the *Netherlands News*, June 11–25, 1943, there were 100,000 persons classified by the Nazis as non-Aryans.

[196] *Jewish Journal*, March 15, 1943.

[197] *World Almanac 1932*, *l.c.* This amount is roughly equal to the figure of the Dresdner Bank for 1926, viz, 45 billion marks, or 10,710 million dollars.

[198] The retail index was 94.5 in 1920 and 92.9 in 1939.

[199] The figures in the *Conference Board Economic Record* of August 3, 1939 are somewhat lower, viz, 59,770 and 65,270 million francs respectively. R. Ardenne, *German Exploitation of Belgium*, Brookings Institution, Pamphlet Series No. 35, states that before the war Belgium's national income was evaluated at about 65 million francs (p.32).

[200] The ratio was 12% in 1924 (Dresdner Bank) and 15.2% in 1925 (Dresdner Bank and Gini).

[201] The figure of 60,000 cited by the *American Jewish Yearbook* is evidently too low. Zander, *Die Verbreitung der Juden in der Welt*, Berlin, 1937, p.94, gives the figure of 75,000 Jews, which is more accurate.

[202] *Moody's Manual*, 1927, p.601, evaluates the national wealth in 1922 at 5,124 million lats, and

the *World Economic Chart* gives the figure of 1,047 million dollars. *Moody's Manual*, 1937, p.2862, puts the wealth at 5,423 million lats as of December 1,1927, while Doane, *l.c.*, gives the figure of 2,5 billion dollars for 1929.

[203] The earliest index figure, for 1928, was 129; the index for 1939 was 117. The income figures for 1926 and 1920 cited by the Dresdner Bank are almost the same. We must, therefore, accept the 1926 figure on wealth as approximately valid for 1928.

[204] The ratio in 1926 was 18.7%, and the multiplier can be assumed to be 5.5–6.

[205] *Moody's Manual*, 1927, p.601, reported this part of the national wealth to be 56% of the total. According to *Moody's Manual*, 1940, p.1900, the agricultural income in 1937 represented somewhat over 40% of the total.

[206] *Statistical Yearbook, l.c.*

[207] *World Economic Survey*, 1938–39, p. 84, based on Franges, *Weltwirtschaftliches Archiv*, September, 1938.

[208] The figures in 1937 and 1938 in *World Economic Survey* show an increase of 5–7%.

[209] See above, Section A. According to *Moody's Manual*, 1940, p. 1995, the income from agriculture (including live stock breeding and forestry) in 1937 was 21,383 million dinars, out of a total of 44,221 million dinars.

[210] *op. cit.*

[211] The League of Nations wholesale index was 100 in 1929 and 121.9 in 1939, but since the drachma fell during this time from 0.013 gold dollars to 0.00896 dollars, i.e., by almost 160%, the higher retail index of 160 is used.

[212] See above, Introduction to this Section.

[213] December 21, 1939.

[214] See above, Section A.

[215] *News Digest*, No. 987, November 25, 1942 *(Transocean*, November 22, 1942). The same figure of 8 billions was given by the former Bulgarian Minister of Interior in an interview with the correspondent of the *Jewish Journal (ibid.*, September 15, 1944).

[216] The average rate in 1938 was 0.0124 *(Satistical Abstract, l.c.).*

[217] Gini, *Quelques Chiffres*, estimates the private wealth of Bulgaria at 9–10 billion francs or about 2 billion gold dollars.

[218] Tchakaloff, *l.c.*, brings figures for 1935 inclusive.

[219] December 21,1939, p.222.

[220] Vandellos, *l.c.*, sets the ratio at 17.8.18%, but in the later period it may have decreased somewhat.

[221] According to the official Bulgarian census of 1934.

[222] See above, Section A of this chapter.

[223] *Jewish Journal*, December 15, 1943. Yet the figure suggested for interned Jews, i.e. 60,000 (higher than the geuerally accepted total), would indicate that almost all Italian Jews were affected by those measures, even non-professing Jews.

[224] The dispatch of *JTA*, December 30, 1943, stating that the German press had corrected this figure to 12 million lires, must be based on a confusion between milliards and billions. According to *Regima Fascista*, 24 Jews owned 100 billion lires, 82 had 100 million lires per capita, and 296 more than 1 million lires per person; the total would surpass 12 billion. Evidently all these figures are gross exaggerations and cannot be used at all, since the sum of 12 trillion lires would exceed the total Italian wealth by 25 times.

[225] *La determinazione*, p. 364. For lack of available data, the colonies are not considered.

[226] Gini *(A Comparison)* puts the total national wealth in 1925 at 550 billion lires

[227] *Moody's Manual*, 1940, p.1885.

[228] November 21, 1939.

[229] Gini *(A Comparison)* calculated the ratio at 18%. However, it must he remembered that the income may include public revenues.

[230] Doane, *l.c.*, estimates the national wealth of Estonia at 1.9 billion dollars, as of 1929.

[231] *JTA*, November 28, 1942.

[232] *Moody's Manual*, 1937, p. 2626. Thc figures of the Dresdner Bank for 1925 and 1926 were 23 and 25 billion marks, equivalent to 5,474 and 5,950 million gold dollars, respectively.

[233] The wholesale indices were 102 in 1928 and 109.3 in 1939.

[234] The wholesale index rose from 97.2 to 104.1, *i.e.*, by 7%.

[235] The ratio was, according to Gini and Vandellos, 15.3–15.5%.

[236] The indices were 112 in 1927 and 104.8 in 1939. According to estimates by Mr. Schoedt, a Norwegian barrister, the pre-war national wealth of Norway was 13 to 15 billion kroner *(News of Norway*, August 13, 1943).

[237] *Moody's Manual*, 1940, p.1926. Clark, *The Conditions of Economic Progress*, p. 143, gives the figure of 3,100 million kroner for 1937. Schoedt, *l.c.*, has set the pre-war national income at 4 billion kroner (Cf. also other Norwegian estimates in *New York Herald Tribune*, April 4,1943).

[238] The ratio was, according to Gini, 19%, and according to the figures of the Dresdner Bank, 23%–25.5%.

[239] *The Conditions of Economic Progress*, p. 356.

Movements of Nazi gold

SIDNEY ZABLUDOFF

World Jewish Congress
World Jewish Restitution Organization

Key Highlights

• The Nazis looted at least $850 million in gold from 1933 to 1945. In today's prices (shown in parentheses below) that amounts to $8.5 billion.

• Of that sum:
  - $590 million ($5.9 billion) was monetary gold held in the vaults of the central banks of occupied countries on the day the Nazis invaded.
  - $260 million ($2.6 billion) was non-monetary gold taken from individuals and private businesses. This includes:
    - $100 million ($1 billion) seized from German citizens from 1933–39 under regulations in which the maximum penalty for non-compliance was death.
    - $80 million ($800 million) coerced from individuals by the Nazi controlled central banks in occupied countries. The same stiff penalties were imposed as in Germany.
    - $80 million ($800 million) taken from individuals by the Wehrmacht, SS, etc. in occupied territories.

• Switzerland was the first stop for 85 percent of the $520 million ($5.2 billion) in gold which the Nazis expended mainly on buying strategic goods and services from foreign countries during the war years.

• Switzerland still owes at least $200 million ($2 billion) and more likely $300 million ($3 billion) if it is to conform with the January 1943 Allied declaration that all looted gold handled by neutrals must be returned after the war.

• At war's end, the Allies found more than $300 million ($3 billion) in gold in Germany and Austria or more than a third of the looted gold.

Discussion

A wealth of reliable and detailed information has been collected on the gold the Nazis looted during World War II. It started with the British early in the war. Once the United States entered the picture, several military units and civilian agencies began churning out estimates. In both cases the objective was to prevent the Nazis from using their ill-gotten gold to buy strategic materials. In January 1943, the Allies warned the neutral countries that they would be taken to task for acceptance of the looted gold once the war ended.

In 1945, Allied occupation forces set upon the task of finding the gold remaining in Germany, determining its source and returning it to its proper owners. The bulk of the unspent gold was found along with the records of the Reichsbank, the central bank charged with handling gold. Three key Reichsbank officials helped interpret these records and provided the insider information needed to track the bank's gold flows. They were the very knowledgeable Albert Thoms who for many years headed up the bank's gold department; Emil Puhl, vice president and member of the bank's directorate; and Karl Graupner, head of the Gold-Affairs Branch of the Foreign Exchange Department.

Starting soon thereafter, the issue was intensively examined for more than a decade by the Tripartite Gold Commission (TGC), an organization formed to determine the validity of the claims of the European governments from which the gold was stolen. The accumulated material was so minute that, for example, an individual stolen gold bar could be traced by its bar number as it moved from country to country. Finally, a number of books have been published since 1980 describing the Nazi plundering of gold.

Based on this rich data base, this study provides a full accounting of Nazi gold movements. Although a number of preliminary estimates of the flow were prepared during the war and partial ones thereafter, there has never been a full accounting. Moreover, no attempt has been made to estimate the vast amount of gold the Nazi regime stole from individuals throughout Europe.

THE FRAMEWORK

A simple accounting flow model is used to ensure that all elements of the gold movements are considered and to provide a framework for judging the reliability of the weakest components. It shows where the gold came from and where it went. More precisely, the model has two segments that must equal each other. The amount of gold held by the Nazis on March 12, 1938 (Austrian "Anschluss"), plus the gold looted or purchased from outside of Germany must equal the gold shipped from Germany to other countries, plus net domestic usage and the stock of gold remaining in Germany on June 30, 1945.

The study distinguishes between two sources of the looted gold. The vast majority came from central banks (so called monetary gold) throughout Europe. Most of this gold was sitting in their vaults when the Nazis invaded. An exception was gold from Belgium and Luxembourg which had been entrusted to the pre-war French monetary authorities and moved to Dakar in French West Africa. Under pressure from the Nazis, the Vichy Government allowed the gold to be shipped to Berlin.

In addition, the allies considered as monetary gold those bars and coins forcibly purchased from individuals by central banks in occupied countries. Immediately after the Nazis occupied a nation, they instituted regulations requiring all citizens to turn their gold into the central bank in exchange for currency that only could be spent domestically. A separate estimate is made for such gold obtained from individuals even though it was classified as "monetary" gold by the TGC.

The remainder of the looted gold (called non monetary) resulted from seizures instituted by the Army, SS and other police units in Germany and the nations captured by the Nazis. It includes bars and coins as well as gold contained in jewelry, art objects and dental work that was taken as war booty and from concentration camp victims. Although this non monetary category lacks sufficient information to make a reasoned estimate, its size can be gauged by allowing it to be the residual or balancing amount after considering all other elements. The estimated numbers in all other categories are considered highly reliable, reasonably accurate or too small to have a significant impact on this study's conclusions.

Unofficial looting of gold and gold laden articles unquestionably took place by individual soldiers and policeman as well as high government officials. Both Germans and their collaborators throughout the occupied territories were involved. The collaborators likely accounted for the largest share of this pilfering, as they possessed the best knowledge of where individuals in their locality stored gold and often lacked supervision. Gold looted by German soldiers seemed to have been minimized by the strict discipline imposed on them and the considerable emphasis placed by the regime on ensuring the central collection of all gold.

Most of the gold was kept by the looters and rarely entered government coffers. Since the total of these many small scale thefts is extremely difficult to gauge no estimate is made of gold seized from individuals and kept by private looters. As the war was ending, however, Nazi leaders escaping from Germany did take some gold with them and this amount is estimated.

A separate estimate is made for non monetary gold the Nazis took from German citizens between 1933 and 1939. Under Nazi regulations, gold as well as other liquid assets that could be sold abroad – such as foreign currencies, stocks and bonds – had to be turned into the Reichsbank for reichsmark, a currency that could not be spent or invested abroad. The maximum penalty for non-compliance was death. Although these regulations originally were introduced to help overcome Germany's foreign financial crisis, they soon became a means of confiscating assets. This was especially true for Jews and others who wanted to leave Germany or protect their liquid assets by depositing them abroad.

Gold is valued at $35 an ounce (fine) throughout this study. It was the official price used through much of the 1930s and all of the 1940s. Gold is now set at a daily market value. A rough approximation of today's value can be derived by multiplying the study's numbers by 10. For example, $100 million at the historic value amounts to about one billion dollars in today's prices.

The dollar amounts in this discussion are rounded to the nearest ten million dollars for major categories and million dollars for sub categories even though the table rounds to the nearest hundred thousand dollars. Although most of the gold estimates shown here are considered highly reliable, as with similar estimates there are a number of minor problems: for example, using various exchange rates (Swiss franc or reichsmark) to obtain a dollar value. Rounding the estimates in such a manner has no impact on the relative magnitude of the numbers or on the conclusions.

GOLD AND THE NAZIS

During the inter-war years, gold traditionally was used by governments to back their domestic currencies and as a means for buying and selling goods, services and financial assets in international markets. Most often, this precious metal was the major component of a country's foreign exchange holdings which also included currencies – such as the US dollar and the Swiss franc – that were considered sound and were freely convertible into gold or other currencies. Gold enjoyed a reverent aura and the stock held by a nation was a key measure of its economic prowess.

In 1930, Germany held a respectable $1 billion in gold reserves. But by mid-1934 they plummeted to $55 million as result of a financial and economic crises. To rectify the situation, the Nazi government required all Germans to turn in their gold and foreign liquid assets to the Reichsbank in exchange for reichsmark. As a result of the gold collected and the liquid assets exchanged for gold in foreign markets, the Reichsbank's gold holdings began to rise slowly during the 1930s. The rise reflected newly confiscated gold increasing somewhat faster than the amounts spent on imports to support economic recovery and an arms build-up.

Immediately before the Nazis took over Austria on March 12, 1938, gold reserves amounted to only about $150 million. By any measure these holdings were paltry. For example, France held $2,564 million in gold, the UK $2,689 million and the much smaller countries of Holland and Switzerland had $1,089 million and $648 million respectively. The inadequacy of the German gold holdings can best be gauged by how many months of imports they can buy. French gold was equivalent to 18 months imports, the UK 7 months the Dutch 13 months and the Swiss 19 months. The comparable German figure was less than one month.

Partly as a result of its foreign exchange constraints, the Nazi government in the 1930s denounced the existing gold standard. Gold no longer was used to back the reichsmark. In the international sphere, trade was conducted mainly through bilateral trade clearing arrangements. Payments via gold or convertible foreign exchange were made only as a last resort. Indeed, in the late 1930s Germany asked Switzerland and other countries to pay off any trade imbalances in commodities rather than financial assets.

Before the outbreak of World War II, major gold markets were operating in New York, London, Amsterdam and Zurich. The Germans used Zurich mainly to buy and London to sell the relatively small amounts of gold they transacted in international markets. In 1937, for example, about half its gold imports were from Switzerland and less than five percent of its foreign sales were to that country. From the Swiss perspective, less than ten percent of the gold that moved in and out of the country was from Germany.

German foreign gold movements were small and reflected special transactions during these pre-war years. Facing foreign exchange constraints in late 1936, the Nazi government declared an amnesty allowing German citizens who failed to turn in all their gold and foreign exchange under previous regulations an opportunity to do so without penalty. About one-third of the considerable foreign exchange collected was sold in Switzerland for gold in the first half of 1937 which in turn was shipped to Germany. In the last half of the year, most of the acquired gold was sold in the London market to pay for emergency imports of grain needed to overcome a drought. For the year as a whole, foreign gold sales just about equalled purchases.

Germany continued to acquire gold mainly via Switzerland. Major boosts came in 1938 and 1939 from gold held by the Austrian and Czechoslovakian central banks in Switzerland which was turned over to Germany and shipped to the Reichsbank in Berlin. Czechoslovakian gold also reached Germany via Bank of International Settlements (BIS) accounts in London and Amsterdam as described later in the looted gold section. Other German gold inflows during these two years about matched outflows.

Starting in 1940, Germany used Switzerland almost exclusively for handling its gold and other foreign financial transactions with neutral countries. The Nazis of course would not use London or New York and occupied Amsterdam fell into the reichsmark area. About $10 million in gold received from the Soviet Union in the first quarter, for example, was deposited by the Reichsbank in its account at the Swiss National Bank (SNB), the country's central bank.

ESTIMATING THE COMPONENTS

Initial Holdings

The monetary gold held by the Nazis prior to the Austrian "Anschluss" amounted to nearly $150 million. Table 1 provides a summary of all components of the gold movements. The number comes from a study prepared by the Office of Military Government for Germany (OMGUS) dated November 14, 1945. It is based upon the records of the Precious Metals Department of Reichsbank and interviews of Thoms, Graupner and Puhl.

The actual monetary gold reserve number is from January 1, 1938, since available data are semi-annual. Changes in these stocks during the next two and half months likely did not amount to more than $5 million, according to German and Swiss trade data. Thus, the possible error rate for the $150 million figure is not more than three percent.

A further breakdown of the $150 million reveals that it consists of $29 million in published reserves and $121 million in hidden reserves. These hidden reserves were further subdivided into three accounts.

Table 1 Movements of Nazi Gold, March 12, 1938 – June 30, 1945
(millions of dollars) *

Initial holdings		149.1	**End of period balance**		307.8
Looted		753.5	Reichsbank monetary	256.0	
Monetary	670.8		*of which*		
of which			In Merkers mine	238.5	
Belgium	222.9 (a)		Found elsewhere	14.0	
Netherlands	163.8 (a)		Missing	3.5	
Austria	102.6 (a)		Other monetary	32.2	
Italy	78.0 (b)		Hungary	32.2	
Czechoslovakia	42.6 (a)		Non-monetary	19.6	
Hungary	32.2		*of which*		
Greece	8.4 (a)		SS "Melmer"	2.0	
Poland	7.3 (a)		Other looted	7.0	
Luxembourg	4.8 (a)		Foreign Office	10.6	
Danzig	4.3				
Yugoslavia	3.8 (a)		**Foreign shipments**		517.6
Albania	0.1		Switzerland	438.0	
Non monetary	82.7		*of which*		
of which			SNB 4/40-6/44	378.0	
SS "Melmer"	4.0		SNB 1/40-3140	10.0	
Other looted	78.7		Banks 4/40-12/41	20.0	
			From Italy 1944	30.0	
			Other of which	79.6	
Foreign purchases		27.2	Rumania	53.8	
USSR (prior to 6/41)	23.0		Greece	8.0	
Japan	4.2		Turkey	5.5	
			Japan	3.6	
			Slovakia	2.0	
			Sweden	1.7	
			Other countries	5.0	
			Other uses		104.4
			Organizations	34.4	
			Industrial / artistic	60.0	
			Individual	10.0	
Total		929.8			929.8

*Calculated at $1,125.275 per kilo of fine gold.
(a) Includes monetary and forced purchases of private holdings in exchange for reichsmark: Greece, Poland and Yugoslavia mainly private holdings.
(b) Includes $9.4 from Yugoslavia and $7.4 from France which Italy looted.

- Trehand ($75 million). According to Albert Thoms, this hidden account was known to officials of the bank as the "new Juliussturm", a phrase which, they explained, refers to the gold reserve built up by the Reichsbank for World War II and stored in the Julius tower in Spandau. From its inception in November 1935 until war's end, the amount in this account changed little.
- Asservat "Der" ($19 million) This account was established on March 25, 1937 and was the most active. Much of the looted gold and foreign shipments were handled via this account. Although it was never entirely clear, the movements in and out of this account seemed to have been directed by Herman Goering for use in the country's Four Year Plan.
- Gold Ankauf ($27 million) This was a suspense account which took in gold from the German citizens under the exchange control laws adopted in 1933 and later from gold looted from captured countries. Although much of gold remained in this suspense account for longer than usual, it eventually was credited to other gold accounts.

Only a small share of the Reichsbank's $150 million in gold reserves was held outside of Germany. During 1938 and prior to the outbreak of war in September 1939, nearly all these limited amounts were withdrawn from New York and London. As of September 1,1939, a small (but unknown) quantity was deposited with Swiss banks including $2.1 million in the Reichsbank's account of the BIS at the SNB. Because these external holdings are already included under reserves and are relatively insignificant, they have no impact on the findings of this study.

Gold experts, including those in Switzerland, in the late 1930s clearly knew about the small size of the German reserves. Knowledgeable estimates at the time of gold held by the Germans in early March 1938 tended to be less than the $150 million actual amount. For example, the Federal Reserve Board figure was $113 million while Paul Einzig indicated in his book *Economic Warfare* that the reserve number for 1939 is 50 million pound sterling or $250 million. This, however, includes $145 million in gold taken from Austria and Czechoslovakia. The comparable number for March 1938 is $105 million.

Looted

Monetary

At a minimum, the Nazis looted $750 million in gold from the territories they occupied in Europe. Of that amount, the bulk – $670 million – came via the monetary authorities of these countries. The situation could have been much worse. Before the war most European states moved nearly all their monetary gold to safehavens, mainly the United States.

The looting started with Austria in March 1938, and by 1940 the Nazis had snatched nearly ninety per cent of the total monetary gold taken during the war. Three countries – Belgium, Netherlands and Austria – accounted for three-quarters of the looted monetary gold. The only large seizure in the latter years of the war was $78 million in Italian gold which the Nazis moved to northern Italy after the Mussolini government collapsed. In 1944, it was shipped to Germany. The Italian gold included nearly $17 million of the metal that the Mussolini regime had previously looted from Yugoslavia and France.

The stolen gold provided a more than adequate supply to meet war time needs. Indeed, Germany's gold reserve at war's end was double that of early 1938. The ability to utilize the gold to buy imports from countries outside of Europe was severely limited during the war as a result of the Allied naval blockade. Nearly all the captured gold was spent in neutral European countries for goods they produced themselves or obtained by clandestine means from other countries. Within the Nazi domain gold was rarely used to pay for imports. The major exception was Rumania which received $54 million in gold, mainly for oil.

The monetary gold numbers are highly accurate reflecting detailed records of the Reichsbank and of the European central banks that were looted. The TGC spent years combing through these figures and validating their reliability. Those controversies that did arise were not about the numbers, but mainly from determining whether gold taken from citizens via central banks after the Nazi invasion was monetary gold under the charter given the Commission. For most countries the answer was yes, but for relatively small quantities of gold seized from Greece, Poland and Yugoslavia the claims were turned down. For estimating the overall flow of Nazi gold, the distinction makes no difference. All of the loot was shipped back to the Reichsbank in Germany. In total, the amount of gold seized from citizens via central banks exceeded $80 million (see Table 2).

Special note needs to be made about the $12 million in Czechoslovakian gold originally held by the Bank of England in 1939. Under an order from officials of the new Nazi-dominated National Bank for Bohemia-Moravia, the Bank of England was asked to move the gold from the account of the old National Bank of Czechoslovakia at the Bank of England to that of the BIS. The BIS then on its own books debited the amount it held in the Bank of England and credited its account at the National Bank of Amsterdam and then had gold shipped from Amsterdam to Berlin. Thus without physically moving gold out of England, the Nazis were able to acquire the gold owned by Czechoslovakia.

In March 1939, an additional $15 million in gold was physically moved from the BIS account at the SNB to the Reichsbank in Germany. These funds had been held by the BIS for the National Bank of Czechoslovakia. After occupying the Sudetenland, the Nazis insisted that Prague transfer the gold to them. The BIS accepted the view of its German representative who indicated the BIS should not take political considerations into account in deciding how to deal with its interests in areas absorbed by Germany.

Non monetary

The amount of looted non monetary gold can not be estimated directly because only fragmentary information exists. A reasonable approximation of its size, however, can be derived by allowing this category to be a residual. All other categories are either well documented or can be estimated with a high degree of reliability. Thus, if the accounting process is to be balanced, the non monetary looted account would have to be at least $80 million. The number probably is higher because the estimate of industrial gold usage (which is the least reliable category) is very conservative (see pages "Other distribution and Usage"). A larger industrial use number would raise the non monetary gold number (the residual) by a similar amount. It is surely within the realm of possibility that both industrial use and thus the non monetary gold figure are some $50 million higher.

Table 2 Nazi Confiscation of Gold From Individuals via Central Banks in Occupied Countries*, March 12, 1938 – June 30, 1945   *(millions of dollars)***

Netherlands	39.9***
Austria	14.6***
Greece	8.4
Poland	7.3
Belgium	7.2***
Yugoslavia	3.8
Czechoslovakia	1.1***
Luxembourg	0.1
Total	84.2

*   Based on documented claims submitted by governments to the Tripartite Gold Commission; excludes seizures of gold by the Nazi military, SS and other police units.

**   Calculated at $1,125.275 per kilo of fine gold.

*** These amounts included as monetary gold as defined by the Tripartite Gold Commission.

What is known:

• Wehrmacht booty was turned into the Reich Treasury which sorted and disposed of it and received all receipts from its sale. Most goods with an artistic value, such as diamonds and jewelry, were sent by the Treasury to Municipal Pawn Shops, mainly for sale abroad. Smaller items with a high precious metal content, such as rings, were shipped to the Prussian State Mint and larger articles to Degussa, the major German precious metal smelting firm. Gold was extracted and the resulting bars sent to the Reichsbank. Seized gold bars and coins, other precious metals, currencies and stock certificates were delivered directly from the Treasury to the Reichsbank.

• SS booty from concentration camps and elsewhere was delivered to the Reichsbank for inventorying and was dispersed in the same way as the Wehrmacht booty. Gold teeth and bridges were melted down by the Prussian State Mint, refined into gold bars and returned to the Reichsbank. Some 76 shipments from the SS were received by the Reichsbank from 1942 to 1944 with an estimated value of $20 million. Its gold content was valued at some $45 million. All receipts were deposited to a secret SS account at the Treasury, under the name Max Heiliger, and referred to as the "Melmer" account after the SS officer who delivered the stolen items to the Reichsbank.

• Non-monetary gold obtained by the Reichsbank, in most instances became a part of its monetary holdings. For example, the value of the gold looted by the SS and brought to the Reichsbank would be credited to the "Melmer" account in a reichsmark equivalent. If the SS wanted gold for an overseas operation, its account would be reduced by an equivalent amount of reichsmark. The gold it received would not necessarily be the same bars or coins it originally deposited.

• SS and other loot also was found scattered throughout the former Nazi occupied areas of Europe by the Allies after the war. This was spoils that had not reached the Treasury or Reichsbank for sorting and valuing. Many bags, for example, were found at or near concentration camps.

• Safety deposit boxes in France. These boxes were sealed and checked for gold, currency and other foreign assets soon after the Nazis occupied non Vichy France. The assets in the boxes were exchanged for local currency and the gold removed to Germany. The Nazi Custom Service was in charge of this operation and was backed by the SS and other police units.

Foreign purchases

Germany received $23 million in gold from the USSR. These shipments to the Reichsbank took place between the September 1939 implementation of the Hitler-Stalin pact which divided Poland and the Baltic states between their two countries and the June 1941 Nazi invasion of the USSR. The gold received by Germany was for payment of military equipment the Nazis delivered to the Russians.

In 1941, Japan delivered $4 million in gold to Germany to repay foreign exchange advances by Germany. This transaction is confirmed in reports indicating the Reichsbank had to smelt Japanese gold bars because they did not meet international standards set by the Bank of England.

End of war balance

When the Allies took over Germany, they found more than $300 million in gold, an amount equivalent to 40 percent of the gold looted by the Nazis from occupied countries. Some 95 percent of the gold remaining was held by the Reichsbank. The non-monetary portion consisted of SS gold possessed by the Reichsbank but not yet sorted or valued, looted gold found by allies throughout Europe and that held by the German Foreign Office.

Monetary

The records of the monetary inventory are well documented. Captured Reichsbank records show that it held nearly $260 million in monetary gold. Under the direction of Colonel Bernard Bernstein, Director of the Finance

Division of the OMGUS Control Council, bars and coins were checked against the Reichsbank inventory. This process indicated that 98 percent of the monetary gold had been recovered. Most was found in the Kaiserode Salt Mine, near the town of Merkers by US troops on April 7, 1945. This large cache had been evacuated from Berlin in February. In addition, Reichsbank records showed some gold remained at its branches throughout Germany. As a result US teams were sent out to the branches and most was recovered by June 1945. Most of the nearly $4 million never found likely was stolen from the branches. A third of that missing was in Berlin and probably taken by Soviet troops.

In addition, $32 million in monetary gold from the National Bank of Hungary was discovered by US forces in Spital am Pyhrn, Austria. It had been removed from Budapest by the Nazis in mid-November 1944 and was on its way back to Germany.

There was also about $5 million remaining in Reichsbank accounts in Switzerland. This amount is not shown in the gold movements table because it already is accounted for in foreign shipments.

Non-monetary

Some $9 million in looted gold, that was not part of the Reichsbank's official monetary holdings, was found throughout Germany and Austria at war's end. In this amount was $2 million in SS "Melmer" gold or gold-laden articles that had been discovered among the Reichsbank's holdings that were stashed in the Merkers mine. This gold was being stored on behalf of the SS until it could be melted down into bars. Much of the remaining $7 million was gold found near concentration camps or en route to the Reichsbank and other gold processors.

The Nazi Foreign Office under Ribbentrop had an account at the Reichsbank (stipulated in reichsmark) from which it withdrew an equivalent amount of foreign currency or gold to meet the outlays of its embassies and consulates abroad. It also kept gold in its own vaults in Germany for similar uses. Some came from the bags of coins looted from Italy in 1944. Reports indicate that Foreign Minister Ribbentrop had a special fund but this reserve likely was equivalent to the Ministry's holdings in its own vaults. Some $11 million originating from the Foreign Office was found after the war. Of that amount, about $7 million was discovered by US and UK forces in Germany and Austria and $4 million at foreign locations. This included $1.8 million in Switzerland, $1 million in Sweden, $0.5 million in Portugal, and $0.4 million in Turkey.

Another $0.8 million in gold was brought over to Berne in Switzerland from the Lake Constance area in Germany during the closing days of the war. This shipment was undertaken in the presence of the son of the former German Minister for Foreign Affairs, Von Neurath who, according to newspaper accounts, arrived soon thereafter in Argentina. This amount is not counted in the gold flow table because it is not known whether it is part of the gold found at the German Consulate in Berne or a separate batch that might have been moved to Argentina. It is likely that another one or two million dollars of Foreign Office funds ended up in the hands of Nazi officials fleeing Germany.

No figure is included for any of this leaked gold because estimating the exact amount is difficult and the amounts are too small (although large for an individual) to have a significant impact on the conclusions of this study.

Foreign Shipments

Switzerland

Swiss banking institutions played the pivotal role in handling the looted gold sold by the Nazis. They were the initial recipient of $438 million or 85 percent of all gold Germany shipped to foreign locations from March 1938 to June 1945. In most cases, this precious metal first was shipped from the Reichsbank to its depot account at Swiss National Bank (SNB), with the heaviest flow occurring from the fourth quarter 1941 to the first quarter of 1944.

Data on these movements are highly reliable. Reichsbank records captured by the Allies in 1945 indicate a flow of $378 million between April 1940 and the end of the war. Although the Swiss Government never opened up its books, it did confirm that the overall Reichsbank figure was correct. In addition, the Reichsbank records show that $20 million in gold was shipped to Swiss commercial banks between April 1940 and December 1941. This included Swiss Banking Corporation, Leu Bank and the Basler Handelsbank. Beginning in 1942, Berne said all gold entering and leaving Switzerland must go through the SNB.

There are no Reichsbank records on gold movements to Switzerland before April 1940. Other reporting, however, does indicate a first quarter of 1940 shipment amounting to $10 million. As discussed earlier for the 1938 and 1939 period there was a net flow of gold from Switzerland to Germany as the Nazis bought gold in the Zurich market in exchange for foreign assets they forcibly acquired from their citizens. This gold was then moved to Germany to build the reserves of the Reichsbank Most of the gold sold abroad by the Reichsbank was through non Swiss markets. Since the net German foreign gold movements for 1938 and 1939 were minor, no number is included in Table 1 for that period.

In addition, the Swiss received $30 million in looted gold indirectly via the Nazi controlled regime in northern Italy. When the German troops retreated from Rome in December 1943, they took with them all the Italian monetary gold. It was held in Milan until 1944 when the decision was made to move the gold to Berlin to keep it out the hands of the advancing Allied forces. The Swiss knowledgeable about the situation asked the Nazi regime to send $30 million in this looted gold to them. Twelve million dollars worth of gold was used to repay Swiss banks for loans made to Italy and $18 million went to meet German obligations to the BIS in Basle.

A more complex issue is the gold supposedly shipped to Switzerland in April 1945. Immediately after the Allied-sponsored Currie Mission left Switzerland in early March 1945 with an agreement that restricted gold purchases from Germany to the amount needed to pay for diplomatic services and to meet its obligations to the BIS, Emil Puhl came to Berne to secure Swiss agreement for shipment of $6.8 million in gold from the Reichsbank to the SNB. On April 6, he succeeded in an arrangement allowing gold valued at $3.5 million be moved to the SNB and exchanged for Swiss francs which were deposited in a special giro account for the Reichsbank

Puhl bragged about his achievements in an infamous letter to Walther Funk, President of the Reichsbank, that was later found in captured Reichsbank files. He said, "The practical result (of the negotiations) was to free the Reichsbank accounts for payments desired by us." The Swiss, however, did not allow the gold to be shipped from Germany but insisted it be taken out of the remaining metal in the Reichsbank's depot account. This transfer means is substantiated by a April 13, 1945 message between the SNB in Bern and the Reichsbank in Berlin that was intercepted by the British Ministry of Economic Warfare. In the case of German payments to the BIS, they were met by a transfer of gold from Berlin to the BIS account at a Reichsbank branch in Constance (a German town near the Swiss border). Neither the Swiss nor the BIS transaction added to the gold flow from Germany to Switzerland.

The Reichsbank used its depot account at SNB as the central distribution point in moving gold outside of Germany. About 60 percent of this gold was sold to the SNB in exchange for Swiss franc deposits and the remainder was transferred to the BIS and central banks of neutral countries, mainly Portugal, Spain and Sweden.

Depot accounts are common in international financial centers, such as Switzerland, and play a useful role in expediting gold movements among countries. Because gold is expensive to ship, transfers between countries are made by simply moving the gold from the depot account of one country to another at the same central bank. Physically, this normally means moving the gold (referred to as "earmarked") a few yards from the locker of the country that originally owned the gold to that of the recipient country. Thus, for example, when Germany bought goods from Portugal, the Reichsbank often paid for them by instructing the SNB to transfer gold from its depot account to that of the National Bank of Portugal.

In those instances when a neutral country wanted actual possession, the Reichsbank asked the SNB to transport gold from its depot account to the recipient country. Spain and Portugal were the main destination of these shipments. According to a State Department report, from January 1942 to February 1944, 282 truckloads of German gold bars were sent from Switzerland to the two Iberian countries. For the war as a whole, the two received some $80 million in direct shipments from the Reichsbank depot at the SNB.

The Reichsbank also sold gold in its depot account to the SNB for an equivalent amount of Swiss francs deposited into a "giro" account. From this account, the Reichsbank was able to pay for goods and services bought in Switzerland as well as other countries. With the Swiss franc being freely convertible into any currency, the money could easily be transferred elsewhere. When, for example, Germany wanted to transfer funds to Spain, the Reichsbank instructed the SNB by telegram to reduce its giro account by so many Swiss francs and add the same amount to the giro account of the Banco de Espana at the SNB. The Spanish bank could then spend these Swiss francs anywhere or it could ask the SNB to convert the Swiss francs into pesos and deposit them in the Banco de Espana in Madrid. Spain and Portugal acquired nearly $100 million from the Reichsbank via giro accounts at the SNB. Whatever its final destination, the Swiss were the first recipient of the gold looted by the Nazis.

Of the total Swiss intake of gold, at least $260 million must be considered looted. This assumes the Swiss received all the so called "legitimate" gold held by the Reichsbank before March 1938. A more reasonable assumption is that other recipient countries received a proportional share (15 percent) of the "legitimate" gold. This would increase the amount of looted gold handled by the Swiss to $275 million. If gold forcibly purchased from German citizens during the 1930s is classified as looted, then the Swiss would have taken in some $375 million in looted gold. All these figures are much greater than the $58 million in gold the Swiss turned over to the Allies after the war. To understand these numbers in today's prices, they must be multiplied by about 10. Thus, after subtracting out its modest post war payment, Switzerland would now have to pay some $2 to $3 billion to compensate for taking in looted gold.

Other Countries

Besides the large gold shipments to Rumania mainly to pay for oil (already discussed), there were small movements by the Reichsbank to other countries as follows:

• Greece: In attempt to stem inflation, the Nazi rulers in Greece sold some $8 million in gold coin to the public between 1942 and 1944. The amount approximates the value of the gold already looted from this country.

• Turkey: The Germans sold more than $5 million in gold for foreign currencies on the Turkish free gold market. As this market paid a higher price in foreign currencies, the Reichsbank occasional sold gold there. Much greater use of the Turkish market was inhibited by its smallness and its long distance from Germany.

• Japan: One sale in 1941 amounting to $3.6 million.

• Slovakia: The Reichsbank turned over $2 million worth of gold in November 1943 to reduce the German trade clearing deficit it had with Slovakia.

• Sweden: Direct shipments of gold to that country amounted to less than $2 million. The other category includes the relatively small amounts of gold shipped directly from Germany to Spain, Portugal, the Middle East and North Africa.

All gold transactions between the BIS and Reichsbank from September 1939 to May 1945 were handled via earmarked (or depot) accounts held by both organizations at the SNB. Since these flows are already counted in the Reichsbank shipments to its earmarked account at SNB they cannot and are not included in Table 1. During the above war period $13.5 million in gold was moved from the

Reichsbank to the BIS account at the SNB. This money was used to pay interest payments on BIS loans secured in the early 1930s and for international postal payments. The nearly $2 million in gold deposited in the BIS account at the Constance branch (in Germany) of the Reichsbank is not included in the accounting of Nazi gold flows to Switzerland.

Other Distribution and Usage

Deliveries to government agencies and select private banks and firms under special licenses issued by the Reich's Ministry of Economics

Special licenses amounting to some $45 million during the war were granted to the Supreme Commands of military units, the Foreign Office, the Gestapo, private banks such as Deutsche Bank and Dresdner Bank, and a few private foreign exchange dealers working for government agencies. These organizations in turn used the gold to pay for their operations, mainly in neutral countries. For example, the Foreign Office maintained a $8 million revolving gold fund and the Deutsche Bank received $1.8 million in gold from the Reichsbank About $5 million was given to foreign exchange dealers Helmuth Maurer and Otto Wolff. The biggest such transactions – $2.4 million – was with Wolff in mid-1944. The gold was sold in Spain and the proceeds were delivered to the Reichsbank in the form of Swiss francs and Spanish pesetas. For this arrangement, Wolff was paid a three per cent commission.

To avoid double counting, this category has to be reduced by the $10.6 million in Foreign Office gold found in and outside of Germany at war's end. Thus, the estimate is that $34.4 million in gold remained with the various official and private organizations and was not found by the Allies, or more likely was sold by these organizations to others in Germany and elsewhere. Although a large share probably transited or was deposited in Switzerland, the only known information relates to the $2.3 million Wolff shipment to Spain.

Domestic Industrial and Artistic Applications

The most difficult category to estimate is the net amount of gold Germany used in industry and artistic endeavors. This includes gold needed in manufacturing precision devices, photography, chemical processing, in dentistry and in making jewelry. According to Albert Thoms, until August 1944, the Reichsbank provided 200 kilograms of gold per month to Degussa, which was the nation's largest precious metal smelter and supplier to industrial users. For the period March 1938 to August 1944, such an allocation would be worth $17 million. For the rest of the war Degussa probably drew down the large gold stocks it was allowed to maintain – 2,000 kilos – according to Thoms.

This industrial usage amount seems low according to experts in the field. For example, US net gold consumption was more than 15 times that of Germany during the same period, while its economy was only three times larger. Switzerland used some $19 million even though its economy is only a tenth of

Germany. Moreover, German usage included an unknown amount of gold used for industrial purposes in the occupied countries.

A number of explanations are possible. There were other precious metal smelters like Degussa, although it was the biggest. Whether they received allocations from the Reichsbank or had to depend on smelting scrap gold is unknown. Degussa also could have been highly dependent on scrap. Scrap gold is derived from the many discarded products that contain gold and on the bits and pieces left over in manufacturing new items. Since gold is valuable and can not be destroyed, scrap always plays an important role in the industrial market.

Given the Nazi penchant to build their stock of gold, there likely was considerable emphasis on utilizing scrap. Public calls by the Nazis to donate gold laden jewelry to the war effort were constantly being made and large amounts of similar items were confiscated from concentration camp and other victims. Degussa is known to have paid higher prices for gold laden items than the Prussian Mint in order to attract sufficient metal to meet market demands. Some of these items could have been smelted and sold for industrial use.

If the gold used for industrial purposes came from normal domestic scrap, there would be no change in net domestic use since the inputs and usage would offset each other. But net use would rise, if smelters were obtaining scrap from items looted outside of Germany and/or the Reichsbank was allocating gold for industrial use to more than Degussa. A very conservative estimate for net gold use is $60 million or less than $10 million a year during the war. This would be less than a fifth of the comparable US figure.

Shipments by Individuals

At a bare minimum, individual Germans on their own account likely sold $10 million in gold in foreign markets. This would involve gold they seized from others, received from other looters or removed from government holdings. Much was probably sold through Switzerland or deposited there. Considerable reporting indicates a large number of high ranking Nazi officials and industrialists took gold with them as they tried to flee to South America and other locations in the last year of the war or during the turmoil of the immediate postwar period.

THE NON MONETARY GOLD ISSUE

Determining the total amount of non monetary gold looted by the Nazis has remained a difficult and elusive issue and more recently an important and controversial one. There has never been any estimate of the amount. The definition of non monetary gold has varied with the needs of the entity dealing with the problem. In general, the TGC and other post-war organizations defined monetary gold as all gold in the possession of a central bank and non monetary as all other. This was done to make the task of the organization easier. For example, gold obtained by the Nazis from concentration camp victims was classified as monetary if it was melted down into bars and held in the inventory of the

Reichsbank. If a sack of gold teeth had been found near a concentration camp – before it was smelted into bars and sent to the Reichsbank – it would be considered non monetary.

A more appropriate non monetary definition would be all gold taken from individuals in Germany and the captured territories from 1933 to war's end. Such a category amounts to more than $260 million and includes gold:

– Taken from German citizens from 1933–39 ($100 million).

This estimate is based on the build-up of German gold reserves (including hidden) from mid-1934 to the end of 1937 of some $95 million. Nearly all these increased gold holdings came from domestic confiscations since the net gold inflow into Germany was small. Moreover, as discussed earlier the inflow largely resulted from liquid foreign assets being seized at home and sold in foreign markets for gold that was shipped to the Reichsbank In addition, most certainly an additional $5 million was taken from Jews and others during 1938 and 1939. This is a period when nearly all assets remaining in Jewish hands were seized.

– Coerced from individuals by central banks in occupied territories ($80 million).
– Seized by the Wehrmacht, SS, etc. ($80 million).

Looted monetary gold is better defined as the amount in the coffers of the central banks the day the Nazis took over a country. This involves excluding from the study's monetary gold category of $670 million (see Table 1) the $80 million the Nazis forced the central banks to collect once they occupied a country. The remainder is $590 million which can be considered the amount of gold earned by central banks through their normal balance of payments operations. The total of all looted gold is $850 million.

SOURCES

Gold and the Nazis

1. Germany's gold and devisen position, Staff Memo, Federal Reserve Bank of New York, September 30, 1937.

2. German gold movements for 1937, Staff Memo, Federal Reserve Bank of New York, February 23, 1938.

3. German gold movements for 1938, Staff Memo, Federal Reserve Bank of New York, March 27, 1939.

4. German gold movements for 1939, Staff Memo, Federal Reserve Bank of New York, July 20, 1939.

5. Swiss gold movements for 1938, Staff Memo, Federal Reserve Bank of New York, March 1, 1939.

6. Swiss gold movements for 1939, Staff Memo, Federal Reserve Bank of New York, February 7, 1940.

7. Swiss gold shipments to Germany, Staff Memo, Federal Reserve Bank of New York, April 18, 1939.

8. Recent European gold developments, Staff Memo, Federal Reserve Bank of New York, August 27, 1940.

9. Switzerland and the Axis, US Treasury Department, Division of Monetary Research, February 1, 1943.

Estimated Components

Initial Holdings

10. The Hidden Gold-Reserve Program Initiated by the German Reichsbank During Schachts Second Term of Office, Office of Military Government for Germany- US (OMGUS), Division of Investigation of Cartels and External Assets, November 14, 1945; NA RG 260, Records of Foreign Exchange Depository Group, Central Files 1945–1950, Box 440, File 940.63 (location 390/46/8-10/5-1).

11. Estimated Unreported Official Gold Holdings. Staff Memo, Federal Reserve Board, December 30, 1940.

12. Einzig, Paul, *Economic Warfare*, MacMillan and Co., London, 1940.

Looted Gold: Monetary

13. Tripartite Commission for the Restitution on Monetary Gold—Tabulation of Provisional Decisions, From US Commissioner, Trilateral Gold Commission, American Embassy-Brussels to Department of State (271), July 5, 1951; NA RG 56 Treasury Department, OAISA, Box 62, File IARA Looted Gold Restitution and Claims (location 450/80/32/01).

14. NA RG 43, Records related to the Paris Conference on Reparations, Files of Jacques J. Reinstein, 1945–1951, Box 257 (location 250/10/20/05).

15. NA RG 59, Department of State, Office of Financial Operations, Records relating to the Tripartite Commission for the Restitution of Monetary Gold, 1942–1962, Boxes 1-29 (location 631/A/04/06).

16. NA RG 84, Records of US Embassy in Brussels, Files of US Delegation to the IARA, Tripartite Gold Commission, 1946–1956; Country files, Boxes 17 (location 631/19/63/06).

17. Italy: Istcambi gold excluded from Italian looted gold because it was originally lent to Italy by Germany during the war as part of a trade credit package. NA RG 84, Records of US Embassy in Brussels, Files of US Delegation to the IARA, Tripartite Gold Commission, 1946–1956; Country files, Box 7 (location 631/19/63/06).

18. Czechoslovakia: see, Investigation concerning case: Reichsbankrat Karl Graupner August 15/16/1946, p 11; NA RG 260, Records of Foreign Exchange Depository Group, Central Files 1945–1950, Box 439, File 940.5602 (location 390/46/8-10/5-1).

Looted Gold: Non-Monetary

19. SS Loot and the Reichsbank, Supreme Headquarters, Allied Expeditionary Force, G-5 Division, 8 May 1945; NA RG 260, Records of Foreign Exchange Depository Group, Central Files 1945–1950, Box 422, File 940.1551 (location 390/46/8-10/5-1).

20. Draft Tab—Evaluation of the Loot, no date; NA RG 260, Records of Foreign Exchange Depository Group, Central Files 1945–1950, Box 423, File 940.304 (location 390/46/8-10/5-1).

21. Further Evidence on Disposition of SS Loot by Reichsbank, Monthly May 1945; NA RG 260, Records of Foreign Exchange Depository Group, Files 1945–1950, Box 423, File 940.304 (location 390/46/8-10/5-1).

22. Data Re SS Loot, no date; NA RG 260, Records of Foreign Exchange Depository Group, Central Files 1945–1950, Box 423, File 940.304 (location 390/46/8-10/5-1).

23. International Military Tribunal, Blue Series, Volume 13, pages 559–61 9; Red Series, Supplement A, 3944-PS, 3947-PS, 3949-PS, 3951-PS, pages 670–682.

Foreign Purchases

24. Russia: Table 2, no date; NA RG 56, Department of the Treasury, Special subject files, Box 1, File: Looted gold: location and recovery: (location 450/80/19/01).

25. Russia: Allied Claim against Swiss for Return of Looted Gold, page 2, no date; NA RG 43, Records of the US Delegation to the Conference on German External Assets and Looted Gold, Washington, January 6–21, 1953, Box 201, File: Swedish negotiations (location 250/10/19/04).

26. Japan: Investigation concerning case: Reichsbankrat Karl Graupner, August 15/16/1946, p 15; NA RG 260, Records of Foreign Exchange Depository Group, Central Files 1945–1950, Box 439, File 940.5602 (location 390/46/8-10/5-1).

27. Japan: Report prepared by Karl Jahnke, November 17, 1946, page 4; NA RG 260, Records of Foreign Exchange Depository Group, Central Files 1945–1950, Box 439, File 940.5602 (location 390/46/8-10/5-1).

End of Period Balance Monetary

28. Report on Recovery of Reichsbank Precious Metals, Headquarters US Group, Control Council (Germany) (Main) Finance Division, September 6, 1945; NA RG 59 Department of State, Office of Financial Operations, Records relating to the Tripartite Commission for the Restitution of Monetary Gold, 1942–1962, Box 25, File: German gold holdings (location 631/A/04/06).

29. Incoming Classified Message, from: Supreme Headquarters Allied Expeditionary Forces Main Versailles France, to War Department, May 6, 1945; NA RG 218 Records of the Joint Chiefs of Staff, Geographic file, 1942–1945, Box 72, File: CCS 386-Germany (3-2145), Control of German property and assets, 1945–1949 (location 190/1/13/02).

End of Period Balance Non-Monetary

30. Extract from *"Decision in Germany"* by General Lucius D. Clay, p308, Department of State, Embassy London, message 2496, November 20, 1950; NA RG 59, Department of State, 1950–1954 Decimal system, Box 867, File: 200.6241, gold/11-2450 (location 631/14/23/01).

31. Office of Chief Counsel for War Crimes, December 28,1948; NA RG 260, Records of Foreign Exchange Depository Group, Central Files 1945–1950. Box 440, File 940.65 (location 390/46/8-10/5-1).

32. From: US High Commissioner for Germany to Department of State (A-1082), July 13, 1950; NA RG 59, Department of State, 1950–1954 Decimal System, Box 867, File: 200.6241, gold/11-2450 (location 631/14/23/01).

Foreign Shipments

Switzerland

33. Swiss Gold Traffic with Germany 1939–1945, no date; NA RG 43, Records of the US Delegation to the Conference on German External Assets and Looted Gold, Washington, January 621, 1953, Box 201, File: Swedish negotiations (location 250/10/19/04).

34. Quarterly Value of Gold Shipments from German Reichsbank to Swiss National Bank 1940–1945, no date; NA RG 43, Records of the US Delegation to the Conference on German External Assets and Looted Gold, Washington, January 621, 1953, Box 201, File: Swedish negotiations (location 250/10/19/04).

35. First Quarter 1940 Gold Shipments from Germany to Switzerland, Department of the US Treasury; NA RG 56, Records of the Office of the Technical Assistant to the Secretary of the Treasury, Stabilization Records, Subject Files, Box 74, File: Gold Jan–June 1940 (location 450/80/22/02).

36. Summary of Shipments of Gold: Berlin to Bern, no date; NA RG 59 Department of State, Office of Financial Operations, Records relating to the Tripartite Commission for the Restitution of Monetary Gold, 1942–1962, Box 25, File: German gold holdings (location 631/A/04/06).

37. Meeting with Treasury Re Looted Gold—New Documentary Evidence, February 14, 1946; NA RG 43, Records of the US Delegation to the Conference on German External Assets and Looted Gold, Washington, January 6–21, 1953, Box 201, File: Swiss negotiations-volume I (location 250/10/19/04).

38. Statement by Emil Puhl, November 17, 1945: NA RG 153, Records of the Office of the Judge Advocate General, Safehaven Reports 1944–1945, Box 13 (location 270/1/5/04).

39. Ministry of Economic Warfare, Telegram Unit, April 13, 1945; NA RG 43, Records of the US Delegation to the Conference on German External Assets and Looted Gold, Washington, January 6–21, 1953, Box 203, File: Switzerland safehaven gold transactions (location 250/10/19/04).

40. Enclosure 1, Explanation of the Statement "Total Gold Stocks of the Reichsbank", Investigation concerning case: Reichsbankrat Karl Graupner August 15/16/1946; NA RG 260, Records of Foreign Exchange Depository Group, Central Files 1945–1950, Box 439, File 940.5602 (location 390/46/8-10/5-1).

41. Comments on cable re: Swiss gold movements, Staff Memo, Federal Reserve Bank of New York, June 3, 1940.

42. For Italian gold: NA RG 43, Records related to the Paris Conference on Reparations, Files of Jacques J. Reinstein, 1945–1951, Box 257 (location 250/10/20/05).

43. Shipments to Spain: State Department message from American Legation, Bern to Washington, August 12, 1946; NA RG 56, Treasury Department, Country and Area Records 1934–1952, Box 27, File: Switzerland gold-silver (location 450/80/35/04).

44. Shipments to Portugal: Report Relating to Negotiations for the Restitution of Looted Gold, Lisbon, September 1946; NA RG 56 , Miscellaneous Committee Records, Box 62, File: IARA-Looted Gold-Restitution and Claims Volume 1 (location 450/80/30/02).

Other Countries

45. Gold Held in Germany by Hans J. Dornburg, Division of Research and Statistics, Board of Governors of the Federal Reserve System, April 1945; NA RG 43, Records of the US Delegation to the Conference on German External Assets and Looted Gold, Washington, January 6–21, 1953, Box 198, File: external assets (location 250/10/19/04).

46. Rumania: Gold Received by the National Bank of Rumania, Bucharest, from the Reichsbank, Berlin During the War, From William G. Brey, Chief Foreign Exchange Depository to Director Finance Division, OMGUS, July 23, 1946; NA RG 43, Records of the US Delegation to the Conference on German External Assets and Looted Gold, January 6–21 1953, Box 199, File: Rumania negotiations. (Note: The Reichsbank is supposed to have deposited $11.7 million in the National Bank of Rumania's account at the Swiss bank, Union des Banques Suisses. There is no confirmation.)

47. BIS: Minute, June 14, 1946; NA RG 43, Records of the US Delegation to the Conference on German External Assets and Looted Gold, January 6–21 1953, Box 199, File: French report-BIS material.

48. Exhibit 1, Note on gold operations involving the Bank of International Settlements and the German Reichsbank, 1939–1945, October 10, 1996.

49. Sweden: Memorandum on Swedish-German Gold Transactions from January 1939 to December 1945, May 27, 1946; RG NA 59, Department of State, Division of Economic Security Controls, 1945–1947, Safehaven subject file, Box 3 (location 250/45/35/07).

50. Turkey: V. An External Security Program, German Dealings in Looted Gold, no date, page V.23.

51. Japan: Annex 2, Remarks Concerning Gold Deliveries of the Reichsbank, Investigation concerning case: Reichsbankrat Karl Graupner, August 15/16/1946, p 2; NA RG, Records of Foreign Exchange Depository Group, Central Files 1945–1950, Box 439, File 940.5602 (location 390/46/8-10/5-1).

52. Slovakia: NA RG 59, Department of State, 1950–1954 Decimal system, Box 870, File: 200.6241 (location 631/14/23/01).

Other Distribution and Usage

53. SS Loot and the Reichsbank, Supreme Headquarters, Allied Expeditionary Force, G-5 Division, 8 May 1945; NA RG 260, Records of Foreign Exchange Depository Group, Central Files 1945–1950, Box 422, File 940.1551 (location 390/46/8-10/5-1).

54. Annex 2, Remarks Concerning Gold Deliveries of the Reichsbank, Investigation concerning case: Reichsbankrat Karl Graupner, August 15–16/1946, p 2; NA RG, Records of Foreign Exchange Depository Group, Central Files 1945–1950, Box 439, File 940.5602 (location 390/46/8-10/5-1).

55. Durrer, Marco, *Die Schweizeisch-Amerikan is Ohen Finarzbeziehugen im Zweiten Weltkreig*, no date.

CLOSING STATEMENTS

Closing Statement by the Foreign Secretary, the Rt. Hon. Robin Cook MP

FOREIGN AND COMMONWEALTH OFFICE

I am delighted that this conference has achieved the objectives which the British Government set for it. First, we have gathered together at Lancaster House over the past three days an unprecedented group of Government representatives, historians, other experts and international NGOs. There has been a high quality of discussion and debate.

Second, the conference has marked a step change in the international community's effort to document the facts, gather evidence and locate the truth about this dark period of European history. A lot of new information has emerged. There is now more light and more understanding.

Third, I am pleased that the establishment of the Fund to help the victims of Nazi persecution has been so widely welcomed at this conference by the other countries and NGOs represented here. A number of Governments have committed themselves to provide a contribution, or to provide support in other ways. The British contribution of £1 million has already helped to prime the pump. The British Government will now work with its partners in the Tripartite Gold Commission to wind up the Commission's activities over the next couple of months and then release its archives and publish a final report.

Fourth, I am confident that the spirit of greater openness and fuller exchange of information will be maintained, and I warmly welcome the decision reached today to hold a further conference in the United States next year to discuss other aspects of this problem.

Closing Plenary Statement by Stuart Eizenstat

U.S. UNDER SECRETARY OF STATE

INTRODUCTION

We have just concluded three days of dialogue and learning which will be instrumental in our task of completing some of the most important unfinished business of this century as its gates close and we approach a new millennium. I believe that for years to come, the London Conference will be seen as a landmark event along the road of coming to terms with this painful period of history and doing justice for its victims.

The past three days have been truly remarkable. Remarkable in the number of countries participating; in the quality of the materials presented and the information shares; in the high level of discussions; and in the clear commitment to carry on this important work with both vigor and urgency. This Conference will have a legacy not only of cooperation in research but of commitment to action.

As I suggested in my opening plenary remarks on Monday, our greatest hope for this Conference was that it would give fresh impetus and momentum to the emerging international consensus for truth and for justice to be done. While we always had confidence that this consensus would be crystallised, I believe that over the last three days it has been truly galvanized, exceeding even our most optimistic expectations.

CONFERENCE ACCOMPLISHMENTS

There have been many significant contributions made at this conference. First and foremost has been the striking degree of acknowledgement of and agreement on the key historical facts. We have taken a hard look at the level and degree of looting, movement and disposition of Nazi gold. Each of the presentations has also given a direct sense from each country of the devastation inflicted by Nazi Germany during the World War II era, and the degree to which Nazis went to loot gold they needed to sustain their war effort. Each nation has made an important and enduring contribution.

I would especially like to commend the contribution made by our Swiss colleagues in particular. In written and oral presentations, Switzerland had demonstrated both courage in the extent of its openness and candor in the depth of its detail.

Professor Bergier's report confirmed the estimates contained in our preliminary report of last May in which we estimated gold transfers to Switzerland at more than $400 million. Our report estimated the amount of looted gold at between $185 million and $289 million. If, as Professor Bergier suggests, the gold received by Switzerland from Germany after 1941 was looted, the amount of looted gold traded to Switzerland was around $335 million. The Swiss report, as well as reports presented by several other delegations, also confirmed the nature of the post-war Allied negotiations on looted gold and assets with the wartime neutrals and the relatively small amount of monetary gold that was finally obtained after many years for the Tripartite Gold Commission.

The Swiss Report likewise confirmed the finding in our report that Swiss authorities as early as 1941 knew of the presence of looted gold transferred by Germany due to the well-known small amount of gold reserves the Reischbank possessed at the outset of the War. It also estimated gold taken from individuals at over $140 million.

The U.S. will look into the new Swiss estimates of gold transfers and this will be reflected in our forthcoming supplementary report on the other World War II neutrals. We look forward to reviewing the more complete document, due out at the beginning of the year, which is sure to add to the wealth of information now being synthesized.

The report of the German delegation confirmed our report's contention of the presence of concentration camp victim gold mixed into German monetary gold reserve of which $2.5 million was from the Melmer account "which consisted of personal effects of both dead and living inmates of Auschwitz and other concentration camps in the East."

The presentation made by the U.S. was drawn from the findings of our May 1997 preliminary report and additional historical documentation that will be presented in our supplemental report due in late January 1998 indicating the amount of Nazi gold which Argentina, Portugal, Spain, Sweden and Turkey received. The U.S. hopes the participants will study the working papers we provided. We welcome your constructive comments and we will make every effort to weigh them carefully as complete our supplemental report. The presentations made by the neutrals and non-belligerents will be fully taken into account in our second report.

In the spirit of cooperation and the hope assisting further research efforts, we encourage Conference participants to use the supplemental finding aids and materials of the national archives which are available on disk.

The spirit of this Conference established a constructive tone and tenor for our common enterprise over the coming days and months. Over the past three days, Conference participants generated an atmosphere of openness and urgency. It is in this spirit that we requested that, by the time the report of this conference is issued in February, we should have as much of the historical record in place as possible.

In this same spirit, participants supported greater access to private archives, such as the Degussa Company in Germany which resmelted stolen gold and central banks in neutral and non-belligerent countries. We are encouraged by the fact that during the conference, the Degussa Company issued a press release reporting that all its records are now publicly available.

There was also a shared sense of the conference that records from the Reischbank to other various banks and financial institutions are critical to gaining a comprehensive understanding of the Nazi Gold transfers. We emphasized the need to fulfil the long-standing request to locate and open the surviving records of the Reischbank and the Prussian State Mint. Both the Federal Republic of Germany and Austria agree that the location of these records are essential, and both are willing to cooperate in determining their current whereabouts and making them available to historical researchers. The biggest gap in our knowledge is the amount of victim gold confiscated and smelted into disguised gold bars through the "Melmer account." This newly discovered microfilm may help fill that gap, but we cannot be certain until there is further opportunity to examine them.

We urge nations represented at this Conference to immediately declassify and open the records of their respect intelligence agencies bearing on Nazi gold issues.

We fully recognize that research into all these records can be time consuming and costly, but there is a general sense among conference participants of the urgency to establish a complete historical record.

Let me note once again that Foreign Secretary Robin Cook established the positive tenor of this Conference by announcing the establishment of a fund – in consultation with our TGC partners and the TGC recipient countries – to provide relief to needy survivors of Nazi persecution. In addition to the contributions announced Tuesday by the United States and Britain, positive indications have also come in the form of announcements this week from Argentina, Brazil, Greece, Luxembourg, Croatia and Austria.

But it is beyond the discovery of the past and understanding of history that will be the true legacy of London. For this Conference not only served as the culmination of a year of discovery, but also as a launchpad for a year of action.

NEXT STEPS

In the spirit of the London Conference, we must continue to cooperate and coordinate our efforts to gain the most complete possible accounting of this issue in the coming months. I am even more confident than ever, after hours and hours of exchanges with so many distinguished participants across these three days, that we can and we will move forward.

Let me briefly outline several steps that will enable us to do so. First, we are encouraging these countries – some dozen – which have established historical commissions – to fully complete their work and to show their final results by the end of this millennium.

Second, we believe that all nations must proceed with transparency and full disclosure. To do so, we would like to participate in the establishment of a website to open a process of communication between all interested parties. This web site could include, in real time, reports and studies, informational updates, and most importantly, documents. We understand that technology exists that would restore, scan, translate, and produce documents so that all who are interested may have free use and access to this information. For a cause this important, it is essential we use all the means at our disposal to facilitate learning and foster cooperation.

Third, the U.S. Government intends to research Holocaust-era assets located in the U.S. during and after World War II. As we have called on other nations to honestly and fully examine their pasts, I want to assure you that the United States will continue to do the same. We will continue to fully review the policies and activities of U.S. government entities which played a part in the tracking, collection and disposition of Nazi gold after the War. The U.S. Treasury and Federal Reserve will continue to look into reports which have appeared in the U.S. press about the resmelting of Nazi gold by the now-defunct U.S. Assay Office. We could also seek ways to examine dormant accounts in U.S. banks which under the laws of our states, generally revert to the states when unclaimed, to try to determine how many may have included accounts of the World War II era.

Fourth, while the London Conference has appropriately focused on gold, we began to focus today on other assets – including real property, securities, bonds, insurance and artworks. The continued research and discovery of these issues is important in providing a more complete picture of this complex set of issues.

To build on this start, and to give attention to these other asset issues in particular, it is important to commit to a follow-up conference.

The U.S. Holocaust Museum had indicated a willingness to host such a conference to follow up our work here and to give these other issues and remaining questions the attention and depth of study they so richly deserve. We hope to convene such a conference in Washington in late Spring or early Summer under the sponsorship of the U.S. Holocaust Museum, and we will be in contact with all delegations and countries represented here concerning the arrangements for such a conference.

Fifth, the work of the TGC must be completed so that its documents can be declassified. We hope that the Nazi Persecutee Account opened at the Conference will prove a desirable option for all the countries represented here.

Sixth, the double victims, in Central and Eastern Europe and the former Soviet Union of both fascism and communism should receive some direct compensation before it is too late. They have a special call on our attention and on our conscience.

CONCLUSION

In an atmosphere of cooperation comes a sense of urgency to secure a measure of justice for the surviving victims. For these victims, the approach of a new millennium takes on a uniquely poignant significance. We must not enter a new millennium – when the issues of today will begin to be ancient history – without completing the work before us by December 31, 1999. We must complete the work of confronting this tragedy with compassion and urgency. We must not enter a new century without completing the unfinished business of this century. We have a collective responsibility to leave this century having spared no effort to establish the truth, and to do justice.

Today, I call on all concerned – on those here in London, and those who care about these issues – to accelerate our pace and complete this great task as we enter the new millennium. The work of the historical commission underway in so many countries should be completed. The funds which have been established, should disburse a generous portion of their contributions to the Holocaust survivors. I call on all concerned to commit themselves publicly, in the months ahead, to achieving these difficult but attainable goals, on the eve of the new millennium, by the year 2000.

In making this commitment, we harbor no illusions about the complexity and enormity of the task before us. But the magnitude of the injustice to be addressed and the manifest urgency of the victims' needs demand our immediate attention and action. Let us go forward from London determined to meet our responsibilities to history, to the past and to the future, and above all to justice.

Summing up by the Conference Chairman, Lord Mackay of Clashfern

1. I will now sum up our proceedings. As was made clear from the outset, we have not been trying to take decisions or adopt resolutions; my summing up is therefore a brief record of what has been said here. I shall produce more detailed conclusions of the Conference in due course – within the next two weeks.

2. This has been a memorable and most stimulating Conference. Attended by 40 countries (plus Holy See as observers, 4 other institutions and 6 NGOs). Would wish to note that majority of delegates were not official representatives of governments, but independent historians, representatives of independent commissions, and central banks.

3. This made for extremely useful discussion. Countries, organisations have taken the trouble to make available the people who really know most about the subjects on our agenda. Discussion throughout was free, frank and productive. I should say at this point that the atmosphere in our meetings was not one of recrimination for past events, but one of constructive examination of present actions and future plans. The spirit of solidarity which, as the FCO historian, Gill Bennett, recalled, had imbued the countries meeting in Paris in 1945–46, was repeated here.

4. We had the horrors of the persecution inflicted on a large part of Europe by the Nazi regime vividly recalled for us by a number of those who survived. The plight of some of the survivors, many still scarred by the trauma of their earlier experiences, was also most movingly described by them. Some told us that this Conference had at last given them a hope that their sufferings might be recognised and some assistance find its way to them, so that they could live out their remaining days in greater comfort and dignity.

5. It was brought home to me how the descent of the Iron Curtain across Europe had for almost 50 years prevented these questions from being properly addressed, both by delaying access to important records and by preventing large numbers of victims from receiving compensation of any kind. These "double victims" are the ones who most urgently need help now.

6. Our Conference considered first the question of where the gold looted by the Nazis came from, and what happened to it. The German delegation told us of the Third Reich's thirst for gold to pay for armaments, oil and raw materials, even before the outbreak of World War II. A number of delegations produced detailed descriptions of the process by which gold was taken from their countries by the Nazis. I will give just two examples. The delegation from the Czech

Republic described the 94 tons of gold held by pre-war Czechoslovakia, most of which had been transferred abroad by the end of 1938. The Nazis managed, however, after their invasion in 1939, to secure almost half of this gold, including the 26 tons of gold held in the Bank of England, which was transferred to the Reichsbank on the receipt of instructions which Czechoslovak Central Bank officials had been forced to sign. The Czech delegation delicately referred to the role of the British authorities involved in this episode as "complicated", though he also quoted a British Member of Parliament who called it at the time "a squalid form of financial appeasement". The Italian delegation told us of the seizure of 111 tons from the Banca d'Italia in Rome in September 1943 by a squad of 55 soldiers.

7. Question marks remain, however. We still do not know precisely how much gold the Nazis stole. The Tripartite Gold Commission was set up by the British, French and United States Governments following the Paris Agreement on Reparations of 1946 to distribute monetary gold found in Germany or recovered from neutrals to the ten countries occupied by Nazi Germany, whose central reserves were looted. The Commission established fairly accurately that the monetary gold held in these reserves beforehand totalled about 514 tons. About 336 tons of gold found in monetary form in occupied Germany and elsewhere post-war, or recovered from neutral countries, was placed in the Commission's monetary gold pool, and the great majority of this has of course already been distributed to the countries concerned.

8. The Allies in 1946 deemed monetary gold as that which had formed part of the central reserves of the countries concerned and was looted or wrongfully removed by Nazi Germany. This was the definition adopted by the Commission in assessing whether gold taken from the occupied countries qualified for restitution under the Agreement. Non-monetary gold, whose definition changed from time to time as the Allies encountered in occupied Germany forms of gold they had not previously foreseen, included gold stolen from individual victims of the Nazis, some taken by pseudo-legal confiscations, some seized from those murdered in the death camps and elsewhere. We do not know for sure how much gold of this kind the Nazis took from their victims. The World Jewish Congress stated that the total of gold seized by the Nazis was worth 7 billion dollars, of which 2.2 billion dollars was non-monetary, but the records on this are incomplete. It was noted that the missing records of the Reichsbank might produce vital further information on this. The German delegation told us that the search for these papers or microfilms (which at one time were in the custody of the United States authorities) was still going on, and a report reached us that some microfilms found recently in Austria might be relevant.

9. As the Foreign Secretary, Robin Cook, said in opening this Conference, the jigsaw may never be complete, but our work has certainly added a number of pieces to the picture and given an important stimulus to the search for those still missing.

10. We then went on to the question of measures taken hitherto to compensate occupied countries and assist individual victims. It was clear that a great deal

has indeed been done. The Western Allies after World War II decided to allocate monetary gold found in Germany or recovered from neutrals to the occupied countries who had lost it, while non-monetary gold and certain other recovered assets were applied to the resettlement of post-war refugees. Research shows that this task was tackled with energy and in good faith. There is in the documents extensive correspondence between British, French and US authorities on these subjects.

11. Since its establishment in 1951, the Federal Republic of Germany has made a unique and unprecedented national effort to apply resources to compensation and restitution of victims of the Nazis. More than 100 billion Deutschmarks have already been spent on this, and commitments to pensions will continue for many years. There have also been payments in kind. The German delegation told us of Germany's efforts since the lifting of the Iron Curtain, to extend to the countries of the former Soviet Bloc the assistance previously available only to victims living in the West. Foundations have been established in Warsaw, Moscow, Minsk and Kiev with substantial endowments from Germany. Similar efforts are being made now in the Baltic States and other Central European countries.

12. A number of other countries have done a great deal to help victims in their own territories. And more recently, Switzerland has set up a Special Fund for Victims, financed by Swiss industry, commerce, banks and the Swiss National Bank. This has already begun disbursements to needy survivors. The Swiss delegation, which included Professor Bergier of the Independent Historical Commission, and Mr Rolf Bloch, President of the Swiss Fund, gave us a historical survey which brought out clearly the extreme difficulty of Switzerland's position in World War II (confirmed by the German delegation). The Swiss delegation also confronted squarely some of the more painful memories of Swiss action in that period, and described the measures being taken by Switzerland now to assist those affected. It is particularly noticeable that the Special Fund is assisting needy victims wherever they might be – principally in the former Eastern Europe. These measures were widely welcomed by delegations.

13. In the third part of our Conference we considered the case for further compensation. Under this heading, the fund whose establishment was announced by the Foreign Secretary, Robin Cook, at the beginning of the Conference, was described. It was noted that the machinery established – an account in the Federal Reserve Bank of New York with the British Government as account holder – involves the minimum of bureaucratic machinery. It is extremely flexible. Contributions can be made by any country. They can be allocated to non-governmental organisations who accept the Fund's Terms of Reference – broadly, to assist needy victims of Nazi persecution, and to support educational projects related to this. It was noted that, if contributing countries wished, they could allocate their contributions to organisations in their own countries.

14. In the course of the Conference, a number of countries promised contributions to this Fund – subject, in some cases, to legal or other procedures. These

were Argentina, Austria, Croatia, Greece, Luxembourg, the United Kingdom and the United States. France, the Netherlands and Poland indicated that contributions by their governments might be considered. A number of countries explained that they wished to await the results of studies on the fate of the property of victims in their own territories before taking a decision on this.

15. The Conference also looked in this morning's session at the question of assets other than gold, including bank accounts, insurance policies, securities, works of art and precious stones. It was noted that these had formed an important part of the assets of victims, of which they had been systematically deprived. The question of insurance policies was particularly complicated: there were many ways in which victims had been prevented from benefiting under their policies. It was clear that more work is needed on this, and that documentation is, for the moment at least, scarce.

16. As part of the excellent and systematic presentation made by the delegation of the Netherlands, reference was made to the sufferings during World War II of the population of the former Dutch East Indies. This was not, of course, brought about by Nazi Germany, but by Japan. Nonetheless, this question clearly forms part of the unfinished business of the aftermath of World War II.

17. There was discussion about the question of whether the Tripartite Gold Commission's work should be completed quickly, or whether more time should be given for further gold to be sought for the monetary gold pool. The great majority of delegates who expressed a view on this thought the Commission should distribute its remaining gold as quickly as possible so as to make resources available for contributions to the Fund, and to enable the Commission's records to be released. Decisions on this are, of course, for the authorities of the countries concerned.

18. It was a recurring theme of the Conference that the international research effort needed to be co-ordinated and needed to be pursued further. The US delegation brought with them and made available to those attending the Conference "finding aids" on computer diskettes to assist researchers in gaining access to the 15 million or more papers which formed the database in the US archives from which US research on these issues is being done. It was proposed that work should go forward to produce, in effect, an international "finding aid" to assist access to documentation worldwide. The seminar on sources and methodology which is being held in the Conference Room this afternoon should get this work off to a flying start. A number of delegations undertook to co-operate in the production and maintenance of a Website to facilitate future research.

19. The US delegation announced that a further conference could be held in the first half of next year, sponsored by the United States Holocaust Memorial Museum in Washington, to look further at these issues, in particular assets other than gold.

20. As I said at the beginning of this summing up, the Conference which has just ended was not intended to take decisions or adopt resolutions. Decisions on the important matters we discussed are for governments and others with relevant responsibilities. All present recognised, however, the urgency of action to help the remaining and dwindling group of survivors of Nazi persecution. This Conference has undoubtedly done what it set out to do: it has made a conspicuous contribution to the process of establishing a body of fact on the basis of which the necessary decisions for the future can be taken.

21. A member of the delegation of Belarus, herself a survivor, and one who lost family members in this, the darkest episode of our Continent's history, said during her poignant intervention: "May God lead you to a just conclusion". We are not there yet, but the strong feeling of our Conference was that we must all do our utmost to get there by the end of the present century.

22. It was a great honour for me to be asked to chair this Conference. I am grateful to the Foreign Secretary for inviting me to play this role. I am grateful also to all the delegations who attended and who made such serious and useful contributions to the Conference's work. And to the Conference staff here at Lancaster House who have done all that could possibly have been done to facilitate our proceedings.

23. I am now ready to answer questions.

Conclusions by the Conference Chairman
Lord Mackay of Clashfern

INTRODUCTION

1. I was greatly honoured when the Secretary of State for Foreign and Commonwealth Affairs, Robin Cook, invited me to undertake the responsibility of chairing this unique Conference. I found it a most memorable, worthwhile and stimulating experience. The Conference was attended by delegations from 40 countries (the Holy See were present only as observers), and 6 international non-governmental organisations, which all had special knowledge of the subjects on our agenda, and between them represented surviving victims of Nazi persecution worldwide. Also present were 4 other institutions, the Tripartite Gold Commission, the Bank of International Settlements, the Bank of England and the Federal Reserve Bank of New York (the last two of which actually handled the gold assembled by the Allies post-war for the Tripartite Commission's monetary gold pool). A full list of delegates accompanies these Conclusions.

2. As was suggested in the invitations conveyed by the Foreign and Commonwealth Office to participating governments, the majority of those forming the national delegations were not official representatives of governments, but independent historians, members of independent commissions, representatives of national non-governmental organisations, and central banks. This helped greatly in setting the scene for an extremely useful discussion. The countries and organisations attending had taken the trouble to make available the people who really knew most about the subjects on our agenda. The exchanges which took place were throughout free, frank and productive. There was little sign of recrimination for past events; on the contrary, the keynote was of constructive examination of present actions and future plans. In her introductory presentation, the FCO historian, Ms Gill Bennett, recalled the practical, common-sense approach to sensitive and intractable problems and the atmosphere of solidarity that had characterised the Paris Conference on Reparations in 1945–46. That approach was repeated at Lancaster House.

3. As was made clear by Robin Cook from the outset, this was not a Conference intended to adopt resolutions or take decisions, but a concerted international effort to shed light on a tragic episode in our past. Our aim was to pool the knowledge available in all the countries involved in that episode, and thus help to establish a sound body of fact on the basis of which governments and other decision-takers would be able to take better-informed decisions in this area in the future. The papers tabled at Lancaster House represent a very substantial body of information, and constitute the main product of the Conference. In

order to allow a number of unfinished papers to be completed, and to allow participants to respond to information appearing in papers which were presented, I decided to allow delegations to continue to table papers until the end of February 1998. A full report of the Conference will then be published, including the texts of all papers tabled.

4. I shall not attempt in these Conclusions to repeat the information in the Conference papers: they speak adequately for themselves. I shall, however, attempt to give a general account of our proceedings, drawing on both the oral presentations made by those tabling papers, and what was said during the periods of free discussion. First, I shall highlight two general themes which recurred throughout our proceedings.

THE 50-YEAR DIVISION OF EUROPE

5. One theme which was powerfully brought home to me by elements in several presentations was the extent to which the descent of the Iron Curtain across Europe had for almost 50 years prevented the matters on our agenda from being comprehensively addressed, both by delaying access to important records and by preventing large numbers of individual victims of the Nazis from receiving compensation of any kind. The presence at the Conference of delegations from the countries that formerly formed the Soviet bloc was especially welcome, and their contribution to our debate most valuable.

NEED FOR OPENNESS

6. Another theme was that of the importance of the opening of archives dealing with our subject-matter, and the facilitation of research into them. The president of the World Jewish Congress, Mr Edgar Bronfman, said aptly that the accurate writing of history constituted "moral restitution". I was struck by this metaphor. In a very real sense, those whose losses and sufferings have in the past been neglected or brushed aside as too painful or too difficult to deal with, must have felt that the absence of recognition of their experiences was a grievous additional affliction. I am glad to have had the opportunity to take part in an effort to put this right.

7. A very large number of speakers at the Conference supported the principle of openness in this area, both as a desirable end in itself, and as a necessary basis for decisions on further compensation. Many delegations gave accounts of the work of special Commissions that have been set up in their countries to examine various aspects of the losses incurred by those persecuted by the Nazis. A number of delegations, including that of Sweden, urged that research, and international co-ordination of it, should continue after the Conference. The US delegation distributed to delegates "finding aids" on computer diskettes to assist researchers in gaining access to the 15 million or more papers which formed the database in the US archives from which official US research on these issues is being done. It was proposed that work should go forward to produce, in effect,

an international "finding aid" to assist access to documentation worldwide. The seminar on sources and methodology which was held at Lancaster House on 4 December set this in hand. A number of delegations undertook to co-operate in the production and maintenance of a Website to facilitate the conduct and co-ordination of future research.

8. It was noted that the need for the greatest possible openness applied both to official and to certain private archives. The US delegation welcomed the co-operation established between the World Jewish Congress and the Degussa smelting company (which smelted stolen gold for the Nazi authorities) on research into the company's archives.

9. There were a number of calls for the Holy See to open its wartime and post-war archives, which it was suggested, might contain relevant information. The Holy See delegation, which had made it clear from the outset that they were attending only as observers, did not respond.

10. The Russian delegation, noting that Russia had made its official archives available to the Bergier Commission in the preparation of the paper tabled by the latter, stated that the Russian government stood ready to assist further research. The delegation urged that governments should restrict themselves to suitably objective language when treating these sensitive issues. They commented that some of the language in the Introduction to the US State Department's "Preliminary Study" on Nazi Gold, tabled at the Conference, fell short of this standard: a sentence therein referred to gold "found" in occupied Germany by the Western Allies, but said the Red Army had "plundered" much of the remaining wealth of the countries they occupied.

11. The Israeli delegation asked whether British wartime and postwar intelligence files would be opened to researchers. Ms Bennett said she had had access to intelligence files when preparing the two Foreign and Commonwealth Office History Notes tabled at the Conference, though these had not added materially to the information in other British official archives already available publicly in the Public Record Office. The UK delegation later added that the UK was committed to a review of intelligence archives with a view to releasing these unless retention was necessary for national security reasons, for example to protect sources.

12. The US, Swedish, Israeli and Luxembourg delegations called for the immediate release of the confidential records of the Tripartite Gold Commission, which might contain information on the origins of the gold which went into its monetary gold pool. The Commission itself noted that it had never been responsible for collecting gold: its function was to take delivery of gold allocated to the pool by its member governments (France, the UK and the US), receive and adjudicate claims to the gold from the countries occupied by Nazi Germany during the War, whose gold reserves had been seized, and deliver gold to them in proportion to their proven losses. The UK delegation added that the British Government's view was that the remaining gold held by the Commission should

be distributed to the countries due to receive it, and the Commission itself should be wound up, as soon as possible, with its records being made public immediately thereafter. They said there was no information about the origins of the gold in the Commission's records which was not also in the national archives of the member countries: these were all open to the public. The remaining Commission records related to the process of adjudication of claims. This had been conducted bilaterally between the Commission and each claimant on a confidential basis. Releasing these records now would carry the risk that the adjudication process might be re-opened. This would delay the final distribution, and therefore the availability of resources to assist surviving individual victims.

13. The French delegation spoke in support of the UK on this point. The matter was not raised again except by the Head of the US delegation, Mr. Stuart Eizenstat, who suggested, among other steps to be taken in the future, that the work of the Tripartite Commission should be completed "so that its documents can be declassified".

PART I:

WHERE DID THE GOLD SEIZED BY THE NAZIS COME FROM, AND WHAT HAPPENED TO IT?

14. Our Conference considered first the question of where the gold looted by the Nazis came from, and what happened to it. The German delegation described the Third Reich's thirst for gold to pay for armaments, oil and raw materials, even before the outbreak of World War II. The World Jewish Congress said that the Nazis had looted gold worth US $ 7 billion, $ 2.2 billion of this "non-monetary", and that Switzerland had received 85% of this. On the other hand, the Bergier Commission estimated that Germany had had at its disposal during the War gold worth US $ 909 million (having started with reserves worth $ 258.7 million), and that 76% of the total had been transferred to or through Switzerland.

15. A number of delegations produced detailed descriptions of the process by which gold was taken from their countries by the Nazis. I will give just two examples. The delegation from the Czech Republic described the 94 tons of gold held by pre-war Czechoslovakia, most of which had been transferred abroad by the end of 1938. The Nazis managed, however, after their invasion in May 1939, to secure almost half of this gold, including the 26 tons of gold held in the Bank of England, which was transferred to the Reichsbank on the receipt of instructions which Czechoslovak Central Bank officials had been forced to sign. The Czech delegation delicately referred to the role of the British authorities involved in this episode as "complicated", though they also quoted a British Member of Parliament who called it at the time "a squalid form of financial

appeasement". The Italian delegation told us of the seizure of 111 tons from the Banca d'Italia in Rome in September 1943 by a squad of SS soldiers.

16. Question marks remain, however. We still do not know precisely how much gold the Nazis stole. Some of the differences between the estimates provided by different delegations may have arisen from the use of different units, different rates of exchange, and valuations made at different times. The Tripartite Gold Commission was set up by the British, French and United States Governments following the Paris Agreement on Reparations of 1946 to distribute monetary gold found in Germany or recovered from neutrals to the ten countries occupied by Nazi Germany, whose central reserves were looted. The Commission established fairly accurately that the monetary gold held in these reserves beforehand totalled about 514 tons. About 336 tons of gold found in monetary form in occupied Germany and elsewhere post-war, or recovered from neutral countries, was placed in the Commission's monetary gold pool, and the great majority of this has already been distributed to the countries concerned.

17. The Allies in 1946 defined monetary gold as that which had formed part of the central reserves of the countries concerned and was looted or wrongfully removed by Nazi Germany. This was the definition adopted by the Commission in assessing whether gold taken from the occupied countries qualified for restitution under the Agreement. Non-monetary gold, whose definition changed from time to time as the Allies encountered in occupied Germany forms of gold they had not previously foreseen, included gold stolen from individual victims of the Nazis, some taken by pseudo-legal confiscations, some seized from those murdered in the death camps and elsewhere. We do not know for sure how much gold of this kind the Nazis took from their victims; once re-smelted, its origins were concealed. It was noted that the missing records of the Reichsbank might produce vital further information on this. The German delegation told us that the search for these papers or microfilms (which at one time were in the custody of the United States authorities) was still going on; the Institute of Contemporary History was acting as the main collection centre for material on this, and on other property of victims of the Nazis. A report reached us during the Conference that some microfilms found recently in Austria might be relevant, but it has not yet been possible to confirm this.

18. The delegations of a number of wartime neutral countries, including Argentina, Portugal, Switzerland and Turkey, gave accounts of research being undertaken into their wartime dealings with Nazi Germany, and the US delegation noted that a paper being prepared by them, but not yet ready for circulation, would shed further light on this aspect.

19. As the Foreign Secretary, Robin Cook, said in opening this Conference, the jigsaw may never be complete, but our work has certainly added a number of pieces to the picture and given an important stimulus to the search for those still missing.

PART II:

MEASURES TAKEN HITHERTO TO COMPENSATE COUNTRIES
AND ASSIST INDIVIDUAL VICTIMS

20. We then went on to the question of measures taken hitherto to compensate occupied countries and assist individual victims. It was clear that a great deal has indeed been done. The French delegation recalled how France had returned to Belgium and Luxembourg after World War II gold equivalent in value to the central bank gold lodged in Paris by them beforehand for safe keeping. It was noted that the Western Allies had decided in 1945–46 to allocate monetary gold found in Germany or recovered from neutrals to the occupied countries who had lost it, while non-monetary gold and certain other recovered assets were applied to the resettlement of post-war refugees. Research shows that this task was tackled with energy and in good faith. There is in the documents extensive correspondence between British, French and US authorities on these subjects.

21. Since its establishment in 1951, the Federal Republic of Germany has made a unique and unprecedented national effort to apply resources to compensation and restitution of victims of the Nazis. More than 100 billion Deutschmarks have already been spent on this, largely as a result of discussions between the German government and the Conference on Jewish Material Claims. Commitments to pensions will continue for many years. There have also been payments in kind. The German delegation told us of Germany's efforts since the lifting of the Iron Curtain, to extend to the countries of the former Soviet Bloc the assistance previously available only to victims living in the West. Foundations have been established in Warsaw, Moscow, Minsk and Kiev with substantial endowments from Germany. Similar efforts are being made now in the Baltic States and other Central European countries, though the Slovak delegation said that they were still awaiting action in their territory.

22. A number of other countries have done a great deal to help victims in their own territories. Delegations reported on measures taken in several countries to amend laws on heirless property so that the property of deceased victims of Nazi persecution could benefit their communities instead of passing to the State in accordance with the normal rule. Investigations have been conducted in some places into the contents and origins of dormant bank accounts, and sums have been paid to the successors of the owners, or to charities benefitting victim communities. More recently, Switzerland has set up a Special Fund for Victims, financed by Swiss industry, commerce, banks and the Swiss National Bank. This has already begun disbursements to needy survivors. The Swiss delegation, which included Professor Bergier of the Independent Historical Commission, and Mr Rolf Bloch, President of the Swiss Special Fund, gave us a historical survey which brought out clearly the extreme difficulty of Switzerland's position in World War II (confirmed by the German delegation). The Swiss delegation also confronted squarely some of the more painful memories of Swiss action in that period, and described the measures being taken by

Switzerland now to assist those affected. It is particularly noticeable that the Special Fund is assisting needy victims wherever they might be – principally in the former Eastern Europe. These measures were widely welcomed by delegations.

PART III:

THE CASE FOR FURTHER COMPENSATION

23. In the third part of our Conference we considered the case for further compensation. In this session, I found it particularly moving to hear the horrors of the persecution inflicted on a large part of Europe by the Nazi regime vividly recalled for us by a number of those who survived. The plight of some of the survivors, many still scarred by the trauma of their earlier experiences, was also most tellingly described by them. Some who, for various reasons, have until now received little or no benefit from the considerable efforts that have been made since the War to help victims, told us that this Conference had at last given them a hope that their sufferings might be recognised and some assistance find its way to them, so that they could live out their remaining days in greater comfort and dignity. I think all present were agreed that the international community must look urgently and imaginatively for ways to bring relief to such people.

24. The World Jewish Congress stated its view that all the gold transferred from Germany to Switzerland during World War II was stolen property, and should be returned to its owners or their successors. The Swiss delegation noted that the Swiss government relied legally on the Washington Agreement of 1946, which provided that no further claims would be made against Switzerland in respect of German gold following the Sw. Fr. 250 million contributed to the Tripartite Commission's gold pool by Switzerland. Lord Janner, an independent member of the UK delegation, observed that any agreement could be varied with the consent of the parties; but he expressed the view that it was unnecessary at present to consider amending the Washington Agreement in the light of steps being taken to assist victims in other ways. The Swiss delegation, accepting that there was a moral dimension to these questions, noted the establishment of the Special Fund as an effort to address this dimension by means other than the re-opening of the Washington Agreement.

25. The British Secretary of State for Foreign and Commonwealth Affairs, Robin Cook, announced at the beginning of the Conference that a new Fund had been established, following discussions between the member countries of the Tripartite Gold Commission and the countries due to receive shares of its remaining gold. It was noted that the machinery established to operate this Fund – an account in the Federal Reserve Bank of New York with the British Government as account holder – involved the minimum of bureaucratic machinery, and was extremely flexible. Contributions could be made by any

country. They could be allocated to non-governmental organisations who accepted the Fund's Terms of Reference – broadly, to assist needy victims of Nazi persecution, and to support educational projects related to this. It was noted that, if contributing countries wished, they could allocate their contributions to organisations in their own countries.

26. In the course of the Conference, a number of delegations stated that their governments intended to contribute to this Fund – subject, in some cases, to legal or other procedures. These were Argentina, Austria, Croatia, Greece, Luxembourg, the United Kingdom and the United States. France, the Netherlands and Poland indicated that contributions by their governments might be considered. A number of countries explained that they wished to await the results of studies on the fate of the property of victims in their own territories before taking decisions on this.

27. The Conference also looked in this session at the question of assets other than gold, including real property, bank accounts, insurance policies, securities, works of art and precious stones. It was noted that these had formed an important part of the assets of victims, of which they had been systematically deprived. The question of insurance policies was particularly complicated: there were many ways in which victims had been prevented from benefiting under their policies. It was clear that more work is needed in relation to assets other than gold, and that documentation is, for the moment at least, scarce. It was noted that efforts had been made in some countries, for example France, to make looted works of art available to be reclaimed by the successors of their former owners. The US delegation, however, pointed out the difficulty that these successors might not know of their entitlement to this property.

28. There was discussion about the question of whether the Tripartite Gold Commission's work should be completed quickly, or whether more time should be given for further gold to be sought for the monetary gold pool. The great majority of delegates who expressed a view on this thought the Commission should distribute its remaining gold as quickly as possible so as to make resources available for contributions to the Fund, and to enable the Commission's records to be released. Decisions on this are, of course, for the authorities of the countries concerned.

29. As part of the excellent and systematic presentation made by the delegation of the Netherlands, reference was made to the sufferings during World War II of the population of the former Dutch East Indies. This was not, of course, brought about by Nazi Germany, but by Japan. This question clearly forms part of the unfinished business of the aftermath of the Second World War, but was not part of the subject matter of this Conference.

30. A number of delegations drew attention to the fact that several categories of people were systematically persecuted by the Nazis – Jews (in most countries, the great majority of victims), people of Slav or Romany origin, political opponents of Nazism, and other groups.

FOLLOW-UP

31. The US delegation announced that a further conference would be held in the first half of next year, sponsored by the United States Holocaust Memorial Museum in Washington, to look further at these issues, in particular assets other than gold.

32. As I said at the beginning of these Conclusions, the Conference over which I had the honour to preside was not intended to take decisions or adopt resolutions. Decisions on the important matters we discussed are for governments and others with relevant responsibilities. All present recognised, however, the urgency of action to help the remaining and dwindling group of survivors of Nazi persecution. This Conference undoubtedly did what it set out to do: it made a conspicuous contribution to the process of establishing a body of fact on the basis of which the necessary decisions for the future can be taken.

33. A member of the delegation of Belarus, herself a survivor, and one who lost family members in this, the darkest episode of our Continent's history, said during her poignant intervention: "May God lead you to a just conclusion". We are not there yet, but the strong feeling of our Conference was that we must all do our utmost to get there by the end of the present century.

34. I wish to record my gratitude to all the delegations who attended and who made such serious and useful contributions to the Conference's work. I am grateful also to the Conference staff in the Foreign and Commonwealth Office and at Lancaster House who did all that could possibly have been done to facilitate our proceedings.

OBSERVERS' PAPERS

Nazi gold – a call for justice

IAN K. T. SAYER

Co-author of *Nazi Gold*

INTRODUCTION

> If we are not to reflect the mistakes of the past we cannot shrink from any aspect
> of the truth of the past . . . The more nations and people are willing to face the
> truth openly and without fear, the sooner we will all be able to move forward
> . . . We strive then not for perfect justice which is beyond our power but the best
> possible justice which is within our power to achieve.

These words were spoken by U.S. Secretary of State Madeleine Albright in
Berne just over two weeks ago during a speech to the Swiss political establishment on the continuing controversy of Switzerland's World War II dealings in
looted Nazi Gold.

This paper, which deals broadly in scope with the three main aims of today's
conference, seeks to concentrate mainly on the issue of Nazi Gold recovered by
the allies within the frontiers of Germany itself.

BACKGROUND

Whilst researching for the book *Nazi Gold* which I co-authored in the early 1980s
I became aware of the existence of the Tripartite Commission for the
Restitution of Monetary Gold (TGC) and its work. With the assistance of Jeff
Rooker M.P. (now Minister of State for Agriculture Fisheries and Food) a number of Parliamentary questions were tabled on the subject beginning in May
1984 and culminating in an Adjournment Debate on the 13th July 1987. As a
result of Parliamentary procedures Mr Rooker was unable to put forward my
suggestion that the 5.5 tonnes of former Nazi Gold which would be left for the
account of the TGC after processing Albania's 40-year-old claim should be distributed to a needy cause. With the final resolution of the Albanian gold dispute
earlier this year I applaud the new initiative to consider distributing the balance
of the TGC's account to victims and survivors of Nazi persecution.

THE HOWARD REPORT

The most definitive report on Germany's holdings at the end of the war is known as The Howard Report. This document reconciles the exact closing balance of Reichsbank gold in the Berlin Precious Metals Department. According to USGCC Finance Director Colonel Bernstein U.S. Forces recovered a total of 98.6% of the closing balance. The missing 1.4% comprised 92 gold bars and 147 bags of gold coin collectively valued in 1945 at $4,434,620. In 1996 two of the missing 92 gold bars mysteriously appeared in the Bank of England's vaults.

THE ABSENCE OF OFFICIAL GERMAN RECORDS

Detailed information relating to gold held outside Germany for the account of the Reichsbank or other German agencies is unavailable. Detailed records of unofficial and official looting by German military or civil authorities in occupied countries likewise do not exist. Large quantities of gold and foreign exchange was held by the German Foreign Office and the R.S.H.A outside both the custody and control of the Reichsbank. Some S.S. loot was stored in the Reichsbank, as in the case of the Melmer account, for safekeeping.

The absence of adequate records and the resmelting of bullion, coins and miscellaneous gold was the principal reason why the US operated gold and foreign exchange depository in Frankfurt (FED) was unable to adequately respond to the many queries they received on behalf of countries who had sustained gold and currency losses during the Nazi occupation.

THE CONFISCATION OF JEWISH GOLD IN GERMANY

Apart from valuables taken from Concentration and Extermination Camps there is also the question of what happened to the gold bullion and coin which had been systematically confiscated from Jewish residents of Germany since the 21st February 1939. On that day a state decree was passed requiring all Jewish citizens to lodge all personally held gold bullion and coin with the appropriate State authorities. All valuables in this category were shipped to the Reichsbank but, as far as it can be determined no evaluation or investigation into the receipts and eventual disposition of this property was conducted following Germany's collapse in 1945.

DISCREPANCIES AND LOSSES

As a result of extensive research between 1975 and 1984 it has been possible to establish by eye witness testimony and contemporary documentation that a substantial quantity of gold bullion and foreign currency located in the U.S. and Russian Zones of Germany was misappropriated or 'lost'. Examples of these discrepancies are as follows:

1945 value

- 90 bars of gold and 4,580,878 gold coins taken from the Berlin Reichsbank by the Red Army in May 1945 — $3,434,620

- Jewels, diamonds, securities and foreign currency removed at gunpoint from the Berlin Reichsbank on the 22nd April 1945 by S.S. Brigadier General Josef Spacil (Value after deduction of known recoveries) — $8,580,143

- U.S. currency recovered in Oberau, Bavaria by U.S. Forces in June 1945 a proportion of which was last seen in the office of the Garmisch-Partenkirchen Town Major — $8,000,000

- 11 boxes of gold last seen in the area of Einsiedl, Bavaria on the 25th April 1945 — $1,856,703

- 100 gold bars recovered by U.S. Forces in the area of Mittenwald, Bavaria in June 1945. — $1,406,595

- 6.5 tonnes of Nazi Foreign Office gold last seen in the vicinity of Salzburg, Austria in May 1945. — $7,431,693

- 17 bags of foreign currency including over $1m in U.S. bills removed from mountainside caches in Bavaria during May/June 1945 by former S.S. officers dispatched to retrieve valuables from the area by the U.S. military authorities. — $1,878.711

Total $32,588,467

It is difficult to provide a present day estimate of the value of these discrepancies but it is probably fair to say that it is in the region of $350,000 when coupling the current price of gold with the relative increase in the purchasing power of the dollar.

This list is by no means exhaustive. Apart from additional similar discrepancies described in the book *Nazi Gold* many further examples can be found in contemporary documentation located at the United States National Archives. American and German investigation agencies also possess files concerning the disappearance of gold, foreign currency and other valuables formerly in the possession of the Nazi State.

FOREIGN CURRENCY FOUND IN GERMANY

In 1947 the U.S. government issued a directive on the disposition of foreign currency found in Germany. Essentially all such currency was to be returned to the country of issue. However contemporary records indicate that at least a proportion of this currency was recovered from such dubious sources as the Gestapo and might, more properly, have been handed over to the International Refugee Organisation (IRO).

INVESTIGATION OF ALLEGED MISAPPROPRIATION

Between 1945 and 1947 various allegations of misappropriation of former Nazi valuables (including gold and foreign currency) came to light. The U.S. authorities had an obligation (Sections A and G of the Single Article Part III Paris Reparations Agreement) to ensure that all monetary gold recovered in the U.S. Zone was subsequently distributed (via the TGC) to the appropriate claimant countries. In the event that any such monetary gold was either misappropriated, lost or misplaced the U.S. government would appear to be in violation of the Paris Agreement.

As early as mid 1945 U.S. military agencies began to investigate an increasing number of discrepancies and thefts of gold and currency discovered in the American occupation zone. In 1945 the FED itself began to investigate similar cases. Unfortunately, in many instances a lack of cohesion between the various agencies and the policy of redeployment did much to prevent most of these cases being brought to a satisfactory conclusion.

THE STATE DEPARTMENT INVESTIGATES A 'TEST CASE'

In 1974 the U.S. Army stated that they had no knowledge of the disappearance (or investigation) of large quantities of former Nazi gold and foreign exchange from U.S. occupied Germany. Subsequently, similar responses were received from various other U.S. government agencies including the Department of State.

In order to highlight the issue and encourage the possibility of an extensive U.S. government investigation a test case was selected which involved the disappearance of two gold bars (of Belgian origin) described in the Howard Report as having been "lost somewhere in the chain of evacuation from Erfurt to Wallgau". These two bars were a part of the 1.4% of the closing balance of the Reichsbank's Precious Metals Department which the Howard Report claims was not recovered by US Forces. Previous submissions on the same subject to the Bundesbank had been rejected "in view of secrecy regulations". On the 16th December 1983 the Department of State agreed to launch a serious investigation. Further information was requested and supplied to the Department of State during 1984. The last communication from the Department stating that they had "not been able to ascertain the disposition of the gold bars from records available to us" was received in March 1985, which is where the matter rested until August 1996. At that time a telephone call to the Department elicited the comment that the investigation was "ongoing". In May 1997 the Bank of England issued a press release stating that the Bank had received 2 bars of gold (with Nazi markings) in September 1996 from the Bundesbank. The Bank also stated that the 2 bars "may be the two referred to as having disappeared just after the war in a book called *Nazi Gold*." The Department of State, apart from not having expressed their appreciation in respect of the assistance which enabled the U.S. government to turn over their 'lost' gold to the TGC continue to avoid providing an explanation of how gold in their custody was shipped to the Bank of England by the equally reticent Bundesbank.

THE DEPARTMENT OF JUSTICE REFUSES TO INVESTIGATE 'TEST CASE'

A response from the Department of State is particularly relevant as a substantial quantity of US dollars and British pounds amounting to nearly $500,000 in 1945 and with a current purchasing power of millions of dollars was stored in the same vault as the 2 bars. This currency was the subject of a similar request for investigation to the U.S. Department of Justice in 1983. The Department of Justice rejected the request despite the provision of evidence suggesting that these former Nazi funds may also have been misplaced whilst in US custody. The origins of this cash have not been established, but the possibility exists that at least a proportion of it may have represented former S.S. assets.

U.S. GOVERNMENT POSITION REGARDING ACCOUNTABILITY

The apparent disinterest of the U.S. Department of Justice and other U.S. government agencies over the question of Nazi loot together with the indifference of the Department of State following their successful 14 year investigation into the 2 bar test case lead to the conclusion that the U.S. government are not seriously interested in pursuing the many outstanding issues with any degree of resolve. This appears to be in complete contrast to their efforts in evaluating Switzerland's dealings in Nazi Gold which culminated in the 200 page Eizenstat Report apparently compiled by 11 U.S. government agencies over 7 months following the processing of some 14 million pages of U.S. records.

A CALL FOR JUSTICE

I believe it would support the aims of this conference if the U.S., British and French government cooperate in providing an official report encompassing the following elements.

1. A full and detailed reconciliation including the origins and ultimate disposition of all monetary and non monetary gold, captured foreign exchange and Law 53 assets assembled in the Allied Occupation Zones.

2. A full schedule and evaluation of all recorded instances of the recovery of any assets referred to in Section I by combat or occupation troops.

3. A full schedule (incorporating brief reports) of all investigations undertaken by military or civilian agencies within the Occupation Zones involving cases or allegations of misappropriation or loss of any assets referred to in Section I.

4. A review of those assets specified in Section I to ensure that the ultimate disposition of all such assets was made in accordance with contemporary Allied legislation.

5. A review of specified incidents such as the Hungarian Gold Train and the Joel Brand/Kurt Beeches shipments in order to confirm that they were correctly inventoried and properly accounted for by the U.S. military authorities.

6. Confirmation that all identifiable SS funds and assets (including gold and foreign exchange stolen from Concentration Camp inmates) were released to the International Refugee Organisation for the benefit of victims of Nazi persecution.

In conclusion I can only call on Secretary of State Albright to adhere to the principle which she expressed in the Swiss Parliament just two weeks ago.

"If we are not to repeat the mistakes of the past we cannot shrink from any aspect of the truth of the past."

•　　•　　•　　•　　•

Copy: 5 August 1946

Subject: Interrogation of SS General Kurt Becher
To : American Embassy, Paris
Attn: Mr Mason

1. SS Standartenführer Kurt Becher presently interred at Civilian Internment Enclosure 3c. 409, vicinity of Nüremberg, was interrogated by a member of our Division regarding the payments in gold and valuables made to the SS in Budapest during 1944 for the release of a number of Hungarian Jews earmarked for deportation to extermination camps.

2. The affidavit attached is self explanatory. It definitely establishes the origin of the gold and valuables presently registered with the Property Control Officer United States Forces, Austria under the name: "Kurt Becher shipments".

3. Becher constantly claims to have received the ransom payments from representatives of the American Joint Distribution Committee. His judgement, however, may be faulty and it is up to Dr. Kastner and Mr. Brand with whom Becher dealt continuously to establish the origin of the valuables turned over by them to the SS in Budapest.

4. The possibility of certain portions of the gold and valuables being hidden in the process of transfer from Hungary to Austria should not be overlooked. It is now definitely established that Karl Grabau, SS Hauptsturaführer, accompanied the gold and valuables during the evacuation. Grabau is presently interred at Dachau and will be questioned in detail to reconstruct each phase of the story of the evacuation from Budapest to Bad Ischel, Austria.

Jack Bennett, Director

•　　•　　•　　•　　•

DEPARTMENT OF THE ARMY   DA10–F1 10 January 1975

Concerning the alleged Reichsbank Reserve robbery in 1945: if you choose to regard a newspaper report and a speculative (but interesting) book as verification of that allegation, that is of course, your own decision to make.

Nevertheless, based upon repeated research of the official records of that period occasioned by previous enquiries over a 10 year span, United States Army archivists regard the Guiness entry as an unverified allegation. Furthermore, there is no substantiation that either a "Captain MacKenzie" or a "Captain Borg" ever served in the Army.

By the way, how are things with the Loch Ness monster these days?

Hugh G Waite, Lieutenant Colonel

•   •   •   •   •

OFFICE MEMORANDUM UNITED STATES GOVERNMENT

To Director FBI
From SAC, San Francisco

Subject: Theft of Government Property
Date: September 19, 1947

At 10.50am, September 19, 1947 HOWARD C STATT, CID agent, Ft. Mason, San Francisco, appeared at the San Francisco office and requested a name sheet of the captioned subject, at which time he furnished the following information:

A special project of CID has been established at Garmisch-Partenkirchen, Bavaria, to determine, among other matters, the ultimate disposition of some $404,840.00 and 405 English pounds, allegedly receipted for on August 24, 1945 by one Capt. XXXXXX. F.A., CID, Third US Army.

In this connection investigation has been undertaken by CID to determine if XXX may have misappropriated funds turned over to the Army by captured prisoners of war. Agent Hyatt of CID was in possession of a photostatic copy of the purported receipt obtained from Capt. XXX. As of August 27th, 1945, however, Finance records of headquarters, European command failed to disclose such an amount of money as had been received by the US Army from Capt. XXX.

XXX was relieved from active duty on January 15, 1946 and gave his home address as XXXXX, California, with other addresses appearing in his file as XXX and XXXXX, all XXXX California. According to instructions received from CID Agent Hyatt he was to undertake a thorough investigation of former Capt. XXX financial activities prior to his entrance into the Army on active duty and up to the present time. Upon completion of this investigation XXX is to be interviewed by CID to determine the validity of the receipt and, if valid, what disposition was made of the funds involved, following which a report is to be forwarded to the office of the Provost Marshall General, War Department, Washington, DC. File number PAGPR 353.8 (20-E). Agent Hyatt explained that XXX is presently a reserve officer of the US Army XXX. XXX was born in Germany and is a naturalised citizen and at the present time is the western representative of Coin-Operated Cigarette Vending Machines in San Francisco.

The indices of the San Francisco office contain no record of XXX. Agent Hyatt advised that his investigation is proceeding and at the appropriate time the FBI would be notified in the event it became necessary for this Bureau to undertake investigation. It appears that should **XXX** exhibit a receipt regarding the disposition he made of this large sum of money, he will be temporarily in the clear and further efforts made by CID to trace these funds.

In view of the huge sum of money involved and because the Bureau may be called upon to undertake investigation, the above is being . . . at this time for its information.

●   ●   ●   ●   ●

UNITED STATES DEPARTMENT OF JUSTICE
FEDERAL BUREAU OF INVESTIGATION

Date: January 17, 1978

This is in response to your Freedom of Information-Privacy Acts Request concerning the disappearance of gold bullion and United States currency between May, 1944 and December, 1947.

Please be advised that our records show that this matter was investigated by the Army department and the FBI did not conduct an investigation.

In view of this, you may want to direct your enquiry to: Freedom of Information Center, United States Army Intelligence Agency, Army Security Agency and Security Command, Fort George G. Meade, Maryland 20755.

I hope that this will answer your questions satisfactorily.

Clarence M Kelley, Director

●   ●   ●   ●   ●

OFFICE OF THE SECRETARY TO THE TREASURY
WASHINGTON D.C.

FAC No. 85133

Your letter of April 21, 1978 refers to our letter of January 6, 1978. That letter advised that a search of our records had not disclosed any records relating to the disappearance of certain gold and currency after World War II.

Matters relating to the provision of the Tri-partite Agreement relating to gold looted by the Germans during World War II are the concern of the Department of State. Accordingly, it is suggested that that department may be able to give you some assistance.

Stanley L Somerfield, Acting Director, Office of Foreign Assets Control

●   ●   ●   ●   ●

DEPARTMENT OF STATE

July 10, 1978

Dear Mr Sayer:

I refer to your letter of June 27, 1978, enquiring about the files with respect to an episode in Germany involving narcotics and the disappearance of certain gold bullion and foreign currency.

I have been involved for many years in the operations of the Tripartite Gold Commission under the Paris Reparation Agreement of January, 1946, and I am not aware of the episode you describe or of the press item you refer to.

In view of the fact that this particular episode appears to have occurred during the military government of Germany and in view of the involvement of military personnel, I would suggest that you address any inquiry on this matter to the Department of Defense and the Department of the Army.

Ely Maurer, Assistant Legal Adviser

•   •   •   •   •

CENTRAL INTELLIGENCE AGENCY

17 October 1979

This is in response to your letter of 26 September, 1979, received in my office 9 October, in which you inquired as to the classification status of the three documents identified in my letter of 28 March, 1979. The documents have been referred to the Director of Central Intelligence and he has certified that the classification of them must be continued to protect the intelligence methods contained in them.

This Agency did not receive an original request directly from you. The information provided to you was a result of a referral from the Department of the Army of CIA documents located in Army files in the course of processing your request to them for information concerning narcotics smuggling and the disappearance of gold bullion. Your letters to the Army were dated 9, 25 and 31 January, 1978.

George W Owens, Information and Privacy Coordinator

•   •   •   •   •

June 9, 1983

Dear Sirs,

In reply to your letter of April 25, 1983 (which we received May 16th, 1983) we would advise you that in view of the secrecy regulations to which we are subject – and which you mention yourselves – we are as a matter of principle unable to give you information about the details of transactions.

Deutsche Bundesbank

• • • • •

U.S. DEPARTMENT OF JUSTICE

DMSchlitz:je
F–28–20169
F–28–31520
June 13, 1983

We are in receipt of your letter dated April 14, 1983 to the U.S. Department of Justice concerning U.S. currency recovered in Germany at the end of the Second World War. As to your enquiry whether we are able to confirm the loss of the amount stated in your letter, we are unable to do so based on the information contained in the files retained by this office.

We thank you for your interest in this matter and your offer to assist the United States.

David M Schlitz, Attorney, Office of Foreign Litigation, Civil Division

• • • • •

UNITED STATES DEPARTMENT OF STATE

December 16, 1983

I refer to your letter of October 14, 1983, with its enclosed letter of July 19, 1983, concerning two bars of gold which you believe may not have come into the gold pool administered by the Tripartite Gold Commission. Your letter with its enclosed letter, has just recently arrived in my office. Evidently, your earlier letter, if received in the department, was misplaced in the process of handling.

I have been concerned with the handling of Tripartite Gold Commission matters for many years but have no recollection of an episode involving two missing gold bars. We are prepared to make a serious effort to check U.S. Government files to ascertain the complete story on the two gold bars and whether they finally were deposited in the gold pool. In order to do this, we need copies of the documentation which furnished the basis of the facts put forth in your letter. With such documentation we would best be able to pick up the paper trail involving the gold bars. We would appreciate it if you could send us copies of such documentation so that we can initiate the requisite investigation.

Ely Maurer, Assistant Legal Adviser

•   •   •   •   •

UNITED STATES DEPARTMENT OF STATE

July 25, 1984

I refer to your letter of June 20, 1984, and to your earlier letter of March 20 relating to the two missing gold bars.

We appreciate the additional material with which you provided us in your letter of March 20. We have been carrying on in search of files in the department and elsewhere to try to ascertain what happened with the two missing gold bars. Although we have not concluded our search, thus far we have not been able to ascertain that the two gold bars found their way into the gold pool or to ascertain that the two gold bars were taken into possession of the U.S. Armed Forces. We continue our search on these possibilities.

We note that one possibility is that the two gold bars were left in the Bank at Munich and taken over by the Bank in 1955 when the Allied High Commission representative (letter of 21 February from Mr Weir M. Brown, Chairman of the Economic and Finance Committee) released remaining foreign exchange assets from the provisions of Military Government Law no. 53. In that connection we note the correspondence involving your predecessor researcher, I. K. T. Sawyer, and in particular the letter of April 13, 1983, which you sent to the Deutsche Bundesbank, pressing them for further information on this matter. We would indeed appreciate knowing if you received a reply and what the reply was.

We shall be turning also to Military records in the possession of our Archives Service either in the Archives building proper or in the Suitland, Md. You indicate you have had access to these records and, if so, we would appreciate the nature and extent of the search you engaged in and the staff persons you dealt with. It may be that in view of your search, a further search in the same records would not be worthwhile.

Finally, I note in your recent correspondence an indication that you have some documentation showing the existence of the two bars in the Bank at Munich up to 1950 rather than up to 1947. I would appreciate it if you could supply me with any such documentation.

Ely Maurer, Assistant Legal Adviser

•   •   •   •   •

UNITED STATES DEPARTMENT OF STATE

March 21, 1985

I regret the delay in answering your letters enquiring about the status of our investigation into the missing gold bars.

We have not been able to ascertain the disposition of the gold bars from records available to us. We are now approaching the German authorities to ascertain what information they may have on the subject.

Ely Maurer, Assistant Legal Adviser

•   •   •   •   •

UNITED STATES DEPARTMENT OF STATE

July 21, 1997

Dear Mr Sayer:

I am writing in response to your letters dated May 12, 1997 and July 8, 1997, addressed to Ely Maurer. I am sorry to bring you news of Mr Maurer's death in late June. His death apparently took place before he was able to reply to your letter concerning two gold bars.

Unfortunately, the loss of Mr Maurer's deep historical knowledge of this issue makes it impossible, as a practical matter, for us to respond to your request for additional information concerning the status of the two gold bars between 1948 and 1996. We suggest that you contact either the Bank of England or Mr Emrys Davies, Secretary General of the Tripartite Gold Commission, for assistance with your enquiry. As you may know, Mr Davies can be reached through the TGC Offices at the UK Embassy in Brussels.

I regret that I do not have the information you request, but I hope you will understand our response under the circumstances.

Ronald J Bettauer, Assistant Legal Adviser for International Claims and Investment Disputes

•   •   •   •   •

Mr R J Bettauer
Assistant Legal Adviser
for International Claims
and Investment Disputes
United States Department of State
Washington D.C. 20520
USA

23 September 1997

Dear Mr Bettauer

Thank you for your letter dated 21 July which reached me in mid August when I was on vacation.

I am sorry to learn of Ely Maurer's death since we had corresponded and occasionally spoken to each other over a period spanning nearly twenty years.

As you may be aware the British Foreign Secretary, Robin Cook, has announced that an international conference on Nazi Gold will take place in London between 2nd and 4th December this year. I understand that representatives of the U.S., French and British governments will be present and that one of the aims of the conference will be to pool available knowledge on the historical facts relating to gold looted by the Nazis from both countries and individuals. According to a Press Office release issued on 6 August the Department of State has carried out research into a number of 'gold related issues'.

In the light of the conference aims I feel that I should formally place on record my utter amazement that you are unable to deal with the query I raised in my letter of 12th May purely on the basis that the only information on the subject was that which was personally held by Mr Maurer. I find it inconceivable that the State Department have not retained copies of Mr Maurer's correspondence, but if that is indeed the case, this may very well prove to be a matter of grave concern not only to the governments of Great Britain and France but to all the other interested parties (including claimant countries) who may have an interest in the credibility of the U.S. Government's administrative housekeeping in connection with all the relevant gold related issues which have occurred during the past fifty odd years.

The incident that I have written to you about is directly related to my ongoing concern that vast quantities of Nazi Gold were both lost and stolen whilst directly under U.S. supervision and jurisdiction, in violation of Clauses A and F of the Single Article contained in Part III of the Paris Reparations Agreement dated 14 January 1946.

As yet there is no public awareness that the two bars of gold numbered 41919/41920 and received from the Bundesbank by the Bank of England in 1996 were originally under U.S. control before they were 'lost' for 50 years. On the basis that it was a British investigative historian who first reported the discrepancy and subsequently, at the request of the Department of State, provide information on the origins and probable final disposition of the gold I can, to some extent, understand your reluctance to acknowledge the part played by a private citizen in rectifying, at the very least, a grave and serious administrative error which culminated in a 20 year long U.S. Government investigation before the matter was finally concluded.

There are still a great many other looting issues, including the disappearance of some $500,000 worth of US dollars and British pounds that were stored in the same vault as the missing gold bars, to be resolved. Although I understand that the missing cash does not come under your jurisdiction I still possess a fatuously worded letter dated 1983 from the Department of Justice (copy enclosed) expressing complete disinterest in my enquiry. I have reason to believe that a substantial portion of this cash was formerly the property of the SS and included money removed from Holocaust victims in concentration camps. Although I appreciate that this is a separate issue it may be that it is one which should be debated as germane to the wider aims of the forthcoming conference.

In conclusion I would mention that I have spoken to Emrys Davies of the TGC who quite properly advised me, that, as an organisation set up purely to perform the physical act of restitution on behalf of the three governments, the TGC hold no documentation referring to the transportation or custodial aspects of the two bars. The Department of State would appear to retain the only information relating to these matters. I would be most grateful to receive your response at the earliest opportunity.

•   •   •   •   •

Mr R Bettauer
Assistant Legal Adviser
for International Claims
and Investment Disputes
United States Department of State
Washington D.C. 20520
USA

16 October, 1997

Dear Mr Bettauer

I wrote to you on 23rd September on several issues relating to looting Nazi Gold but as yet I have not received a reply. In case my letter has gone astray I am now enclosing a copy which I am delivering by international courier.

I would be most grateful if you would be kind enough to let me have your response to the points I have raised as soon as possible since I believe they may be germane to the stated aims of the forthcoming London Conference on Nazi Gold which is scheduled to take place at the beginning of December.

Ian K T Sayer

Present position of surviving former political prisoners of German concentration camps

Z. OGRODZINSKI AND C. A. ROMMER

Representing the Association of Former Political Prisoners of German Concentration Camps

There still remain a number of survivors of concentration camps who were incarcerated by reasons of their anti-Nazi activities and nationality, political and religious beliefs (e.g. Jehovah's Witnesses) or as members of the "intelligentsia" from occupied territories etc.

In broad terms this group has been disregarded as not fitting into acceptable categories. In the case of compensation by German authorities, a number of applications were refused on the grounds that the victims were in the camps because of their "nationality or social status", even though they had been transferred from prisons and had often survived "severe interrogations". In such cases, however, pensions were allowed for loss of health but only where supported by medical proof and confirmed by German Embassy doctors. The lack of compensation particularly applies to former nationals of Eastern European countries who are scattered all over the world, as they were regarded by the then Communist governments as potential or actual opponents of the regime and as such were not included in any national compensation schemes.

It is our view that:

1. All survivors of German Concentration Camps should be included in any assistance or compensation programme.

2. That where applications for compensation have been rejected by the German compensation office, for reasons of nationality or social standing etc., these could be reviewed sympathetically by the German Government and some compensation should be considered, perhaps based on the period of incarceration or alternatively such survivors could be considered for compensation or ex-gratia payment from any common funds established.

3. In view of the fact that property, valuables, gold rings, gold teeth etc., were confiscated or extracted from all prisoners, their position should be recognised within any funds provided by Swiss Banks.

4. Whereas claims are being made by various countries for enforced labour, no compensation or ex-gratia payments have been considered for the work carried out by individual concentration camp inmates in the construction of underground factories, work in stone quarries, synthetic rubber and other chemical factories e.g. Bunawerke (I G Farben), or indeed in aircraft and military factories in such camps as Mauthausen, Gusen, St Georgen, Steyer, and others (DEST, Messerschmit).

5. A category which has not been considered are the widows of former camp inmates who often had to endure difficult times due to the health and men-

tal problems of their husbands and are today in difficult financial circumstances.

There is a lack of accurate data as to the number and residence of survivors of prisons and concentration camps and we feel that before the question of any compensation or assistance can be sensibly dealt with, such data is essential.

We would therefore propose that:

1. A central register of survivors to be established as soon as possible in cooperation with local national associations and Jewish organisations. German Government Pension Data could provide a total number of survivors resident in different countries and receiving pensions. This would act as a crosscheck for collected data. Some form of publicity campaign will be required.
2. To avoid spurious claims, local national associations and Jewish organisations should undertake the vetting to establish if the people on the register are bona fide survivors.
3. A register of widows of survivors should also be established so that, where necessary, some assistance could be given in cases of need.

We feel that some positive action in this direction should be taken with the support of the Conference, and in conjunction with other similar organisations and Holocaust survivor organisations world-wide. Our association is now trying to establish the number and identity of survivors who are resident in the UK, as well as to liaise with other similar organisations in Europe and elsewhere.

Campaign for Jewish Slave Labour Compensation

ROMAN HALTER

I, Roman Halter, survivor of Auschwitz-Birkenau and currently representing Holocaust survivors who are seeking compensation for slave-labour have attended this conference as an observer.

Firstly I would like to express my huge gratitude to the Secretary of State, Robin Cook and to the American Under Secretary of State Stuart Eizenstat and to Lord Greville Janner for initiating this conference and to you Lord Mackay of Clashfern for your even-handed Chairing. Furthermore I would also like to thank the Foreign Office for their impeccable organisation.

We Holocaust survivors are also grateful for the fund which has been established by the United Kingdom and the United States of America which we understand will not go to nations but directly to Holocaust survivors and their families.

This conference has given survivors hope not only in material terms but also because their cause has been taken up at the highest level.

It is imperative that this matter be tackled quickly. The survivors are all aged seventy or over and if they are to see any benefits from the fund then the results should take months not years and the contact with them should be as direct as possible rather than through committees and organisations.

The build-up to the conference and the conference itself have thrown up certain truths which up till now lay hidden. Future generations will understand our times so much better and will therefore be better able to judge whether those present have been fully candid. If this is the case then perhaps they will be able to derive positive values from what has gone on here which may serve their generations.

APPENDIX

List of delegates

Chairman
Lord Mackay of Clashfern
Mrs Kathryn Colvin, FCO Assistant to Chairman
Ms Julia Painting, FCO Assistant to Chairman
Dr Liz Kane, FCO Assistant to Chairman
Press Officer
Mr Carne Ross

Albania
Mr Quirko, Head of Legal and Consular Affairs, MFA
Mr Vangel Dheri, Head of West European Division, MFA
Prof. Arben Puto (Retd), Specialist in International and Public Law
Mr Ilir Melo, First Secretary Embassy, Charge d'Affaires

Argentina
Ambassador Rogelio Pfirter
Dr Manuel Mora y Araujo, Chairman of the Academic Committee of the Commission
Mr Ignacio Klich, Co-Ordinator of the Academic Committee of the Commission for the
    clarification of Nazi activities in the Argentine Republic
Counsellor Claudio Pérez Paladino, Member of the Committee for Institutional Co-Ordination
    of the Commission for the Clarification of Nazi activities
Support Staff
Mrs Bibiana Jones, London Embassy

Austria
Mr Hans Winkler, Americas dept, MFA
Mag. Reitböck, Federal Ministry of Finance
Mag. Hanna Lessing, Senior Governor of the Austrian National Fund for Holocaust Victims
Prof. Dieter Stiefel, Dept of Social and Economic History, Univ. of Vienna
Mr Michael Rendi, First Secretary, London Embassy

Belarus
Valentin Gerasimov, Chairman of the fund "Mutual Understanding and Reconciliation
Olga Nekhai, Professor, Minsk State Linguistic Unversity
Felix Lipski, Surgeon, State Company "MTZ Medservice"

Belgium
Mr J Makart, General Affairs Unit Counsellor, Belgian National Bank
Mrs C Taquet, First Secretary Embassy, Head of Unit "International Financial Institutions"
Mr J Ph Schreiber, Historian, Member of the Investigation Commission
Mr E Laureys, Historian, Seeker at the Investigation Centre on War and Contemporary Society

Bosnia Herzegovina
Mr Mugdim Pasic, Charge d'Affairs, London Embassy
Mr Kerim Karabdic, Counsellor, London Embassy

Brazil
Dr Jose Gregori, National Secretary for Human Rights, Ministry of Justice
Mr Sarquis Jose Buainain Sarquis, Second Secretary, London Embassy
Rabbi Henri Sobel, (Observer)

Bulgaria
Dr Andrey N. Jichev, Counsellor London Embassy
Mr Luczkanov, London Embassy

Canada
Mr Paul Cliffen, Gold History Project, Bank of Canada
Mr Dan Calof, Counsellor, Canadian High Commission, London

Croatia
Mrs Snjezana Bagic, Deputy Minister of Justice
Mrs Ljerka Alajbeg, Minister Plenipotentiary, Head of International Law Department,
    MFASDr Josip Kolokovic, Director, Croatian State Archive
Mr Kusen, Ms M Juric, Counsellors, London Embassy

Czech Republic
Mr M Beranek, Head of Department of International Law, MFA
Mrs Z Vselichova, Department of International Law, MFA
Mr E Kubu, Historian, University of Prague
Mr V Rombold, Ministry of Finance
Ambassador Pavel Seifter

Denmark
Mette Kanstrup, National Bank of Denmark
Mrs Helen Dueholm, London Embassy

Estonia
Ambassador Raul Malk, London Embassy

France
M Alain Pierret, Ambassadeur, Member of the Matteoli Commission
M Michel Filhol, MFA
Mme Wieviorka, Historian
Mme Obert, Conservateur des Archives de France
M Charles Fries, London Embassy
M Bernard Chappedelaine, London Embassy
Mme Pairone, London Embassy

Germany
Dr Hans-Werner Lautenschlager, Former State Secretary (PUS) at the Auswärtiges Amt.
Professor Dr Horst Möller, Director of the "Institut für Zeitgeschichte der Universität
    München"

Herr Michael Geier, Head of Legal Department, Auswartiges Amt
Dr Siegfried Büttner, Vice-President of "Bundesarchiv"
Baron Paul von Maitzahn, Minister Counsellor, London Embassy
Mr Peter Gottwald, First Counsellor, London Embassy

Greece
Alexander Philon, Secretary General, MFA (PUS equivalent)
Prof George Dertilis, Historian, University of Athens
Prof Constantin Kostas, Historian, Unversity of Athens
Mr Nikolaos Garilidis, Counsellor, London Embassy
Ioannis Pappanicolaou, Adviser to the Minister of Foreign Affairs
Vassilios Manessiotis, Expert in Economic Affairs, Bank of Greece
Ph. Tomai-Constantopoulou, Expert Counsellor A', Scientific Director of the Historic Archive Department, MFA
Miss Konstantina Sini, Administrative Officer

Hungary
Dr Peter Kallós, Consul General, London Embassy
Dr Erzsebet Pek, Second Secretary, International Law Dept

Israel
Mr Abrahim Hirschson MK, Chair of the Knesset Committee on the Restitution of Jewish Property
Mr Bobby Brown, Adviser to PM on Diaspora Affairs
Mr Gideon Meir, Adviser to Foreign Minister on World Jewish Affairs, MFA
Ms Nili Arad, Director General, Ministry of Justice
Mr Zvi Barak, Chairman, World Jewish Restitution Organisation
Prof. Yehuda Bauer, representative of "Yad Vashem" (Holocaust Foundation)
Mr Shalom Tourgeman, Second Secretary, London Embassy
Mr Mattityahu Drobles, Chairman, World Jewish Congress, Israel
Mr Amiram Magid, Minister Plenipotentiary, London Embassy
Mr Itamar Levin, Special Adviser to Mr Hirchson (Deputy Editor "Globes")
Mr Ron Prosor, Counsellor (Press), London Embassy

Italy
Ambassador Federico Di Roberto, Director Economic Affairs, MFA
Minister Michaelangelo Pisani, MFA
Dr Roselli, Banca d'Italia

Latvia
Represented by Ambassador Normans Penke
Professor Stranga of Riga University

Lithuania
H E Mr Justas V Palechis, Ambassador, London Embassy
Mr Audrius Bruzga, Counsellor, Lithuanian Embassy
Mr Vygaudas Usackas, Director of Political Department, MFA

Luxembourg
Ambassador Joseph Weyland
Prof Paul Dostert

Former Yugoslav Republic of Macedonia
Mrs R Sekulovska, Embassy of FYROM
Mr D Nikolov, Embassy of FYROM

Netherlands
Mr J M V A Count de Marchant et d'Ansembourg, Deputy Director-General Political Affairs, MFA
Drs H D Knook, Head of Western Europe Division, MFA
MW T Blankert-van Veen, Director of the Department for Resistance Members, Victims of Persecution and Civilian Victims of War, Ministry of Health Welfar, Sport
Drs Chr Ruppert, Project Group WWII accounts, Ministry of Finance
Prof. L C van Zutphen, Commission on WWII accounts
M W Mr ACM Proost, Department for Resistance Members
MW Drs C van Renselaar, Secretary to the Commission on WWII accounts

Norway
Hans Olav Oestgaard, Assistant Secretary General, Royal Ministry of Justice and the Police
Wegger Strommen, Head of Division, MFA
Observer, Mrs Berit Reisel, The Jewish Congregation in Norway

Poland
Ambassador Krzysztof Sliwinksi
Mr Wojciech Kowalski
Mr Thomas Kozlowski
Mrs Eleonora Bergman
Mr Andrej Chmiel

Portugal
Prof Dr Joaquim Costa Leite, Historian Researcher, Member of the Commission responsible for following the research on Gold Transaction during 1936–46
Prof Dr Antónió José Telo, Historian from the University of Lisbon and researcher on the Foreign Ministry Archives
Mr Pedro Pessoa e Costa, First Secretary, London Embassy

Romania
Mr Emil Ghizari, First Vice-Governor of the Romanian National Bank
Ambassador Radu Onofrei, London Embassy
Mr D Chiriac, Counsellor, London Embassy
Mr Dragos-Viorel Tigau, Third Secretary, London Embassy

Russia
Mr Valentin Kopteltsev, Senior Counsellor, Fourth European Dept, MFA, Ambassador at Large
Mrs Tatiata Zanina, Federal Archive Service
Mr Vyacheslav Polyakov, Central Bank of Russia
Mr Victor Petrakov, Deputy Director, Dept of Cultural Assets, Minister of Culture
Mr Victor Knyazev, President, Russian Fund of Understanding and Reconciliation
Mr Anatoly Oreshin, Counsellor, Economic Relations Department, MFA

Slovakia
Dr Grexa, Head of International Law Section, MFA
Mr Jan Korcek, Historian, Slovak Academy of Sciences
Ms Katarina Zakova, London Embassy

Slovenia
Mr Aleksander Brackovic, Charge Slovenian Embassy
Mr Janez Kosak, Vice Governor, Bank of Slovenia
Prof. Dr Dusan Biber, Historian
Mrs Alenka Sz Suhadolnik, Counsellor, Slovenian Embassy

Spain
Don Enrique Múgica, President of the Spanish Commission investigating Nazi Gold
Professor Pablo Martinez Aceña, Historical Adviser to the Commission
Professor Antonio Marquina, Historical Adviser to the Commission (TBC)
Ambassador Lopez Aguirrebengoa
Don Mauricio Cachuel, President of the Jewish Association of Spain
Don Fernando Galainena, Secretary of the Spanish Gold Commission
Don Vincente J Fernández
Mr Carlos Sanchez, Press Counsellor, London Embassy

Sweden
Mr Ulf Hjertonsson, Director-General for Political Affairs
Mr Lars Maagnuson, Director-General for Legal Affairs
Mr Krister Wahlback, Professor, Ambassador, MFA
Ms Gabriella Lindholm, Director, MFA
Mr Bertil Ahnborg, Deputy Director, MFA
Mr Harry Flam, Professor, The Riksbank Investigation
Mr Salomo Berlinger, Former Chairman of the Jewish Community in Stockholm, The
    Government Commission
Ms Gertrud Forkman, Secretary of the Government Commission
Mr Björn Lyrvall, London Embassy
Mr Gösta Grassman, London Embassy

Switzerland
Ambassador Thomas G Borer, Head of the Swiss Foreign Ministry Task Force: Switzerland –
    Second World War
Jean-Pierre Roth, Vice-Chairman of the Governing Board of the Swiss National Bank
Rolf Bloch, President of the Swiss Fund for Needy Victims of the Holocaust/Shoa
Robert Reich, Deputy Head of Mission at the Swiss Embassy in London
Paul Seger, Director of International Legal Affairs
Andreas Kellerhals, Deputy Director of the Swiss Federal Archives
Prof Jean-Francois Bergier, Chairman, Independent Commission of Experts
Prof Harold James, Independent Commission of Experts

Turkey
Prof Ilber Ortayli, University of Ankara Faculty of Polictical Sciences
Mr Etem Seckin, Director of Emission and Treasury, Central Bank of Turkey
Mr Aron Habib, Deputy Chairman of Turkish-Jewish Community
Dr Mr Cefi Kamhi, Member of Parliament
Assist. Prof Dr Bahri Yilmaz, Chief Advisor to the Ministry of State, University of Bilkent
Mr Nuri Yildirim, Advisor to State Secretary Gurel
Mr Kenan Ipek, Counsellor, London Embassy

UK
Mr Francis Richards, Director Europe, FCO
Lord Janner, Chairman, Holocaust Educational Trust (independent member of delegation)

Mr Anthony Layden, Head of Western European Department, FCO
Ms Gill Bennett, Chief Historian, FCO
Prof. Donald Cameron Watt, Emeritus Professor, LSE

Ukraine
Mr Sergei Borshchevsky, Cultural Relations Department, MFA
Mr Ihor Lushnikov, Head of Department, Ukranian National Fund "Mutual Understanding and Reconciliation" attached to the Cabinet of Ministers of Ukraine
Mr Markiyan Demidov, Chairman, Ukranian Union of Former Juvenile Prisoners of Fascist Concentration Camps
Mr Vladimir Litvinov, Deputy Chairman, State Copyright Agency of Ukraine

Uruguay
Ambassador Fischer

USA
State Department:
Stuart E. Eizenstat, Under Secretary of State
Mrs Fran Eizenstat
Dr William Slany, State Department Historian
Randolph M. Bell, Director, United Kingdom, Benelux and Ireland Affairs, State Department
Bennet Freeman, Senior Adviser
Victor Comras, EUR/NAR
Marilyn Ereshfsky, State Department

Holocaust Museum:
Stan Turetsky, Legislative Affairs
Dr Peter Black, Senior Historian

Commerce Department:
Judith Barnett, Deputy Assistant Secretary

Justice Department:
Eli Rosenbaum, OSI
Barry White, OSI

National Archives:
Michael Kurts, Asst. Archivist
Author: Nazi Contraband: American Policy on the Return of European Cultural Treasures

Congress:
Greg Ricman, Sen. D'Amato staff
Greg Wierzinski, Rep. Leach staff
Ms Bodlander, Rep. Gilman staff

Authors/Academics:
Elie Wiesel
Hector Feliciano, author, Journalist based in Paris; The Lost Museum
Gerald Feldman, UC Berkeley, research project for Allianz

Yugoslavia
Mr Petar Bokun
Ambassador Milos Radulovic
Mr R Bobojevic, Minister Counsellor, London Embassy

ORGANISATIONS

TGC
Emrys Davies, Secretary General
Anne Derse, US Commissioner
Mervyn Jones, UK Commissioner

New York Fed Bank
James R Hennessy
Timothy Fogarty

Bank of England
Graham Kentfield, Deputy Director and Chief Cashier
Peter Rodgers , Secretary of the Bank
Henry Gillett, Bank Archivist
Nick Durey, Bullion Manager

BIS
Mr Guy Noppen, Manager
Mr Piet Clement, Historian

Public Records Office:
Howard Davies

NGOs

World Jewish Congress
Mr Edgar Bronfman
Mr Israel Singer
Mr Mendel Kaplan
Mr Mortimer Zuckerman
Observers:
Mr Benjamin Meed
Mr Isi J Leibler
Mr Elan Steiberg
Dr Avi Beker
Mr Sidney Zabludoff

World Jewish Restitution Org.
Mr A Burg
Mr Z Barak
Mr M Zanbar
Observers:
Ambassador Naphtali Lavi
Mr N Flug
Mr E Spanic
Mr H Ben-Yehuda
Mr Z Ramot
Adv A Abramovitch

European Jewish Congress
Eldred Tabachnik, President
Henri Hajdenberg, Vice-President
Serge Cwajgenbaum, Secretary General
Joseph Zissels, Member of the Executive
Ben Helfgott, Representative of Holocaust survivors

European Council of Jewish Communities
Mr David J Lewis, ECJC President, London
Mr Gregory Krupnikov, Member, ECJC Executive Committee, Riga
Mr Michael May, ECJC Executive Director, London

American Jewish Joint Distribution Committee
Gideon Taylor, Assistant Executive Vice-President
Eli Shashua, International Legal Counsel

International Romani Union
Mr Donald Kenrick

OBSERVERS

Holy See
Monsignor Giovanni D'Aniello, Senior Counsellor, MFA
Rev Father Marcel Chappin SJ, Vatican Historian

N M Rothschild
Sir Derek Thomas, Non-Executive Director

HET
Ms Janice Lopatkin
Charles Rommer, Association of Former Political Prisoners of German Concentration Camps
Mr Z Ogrodzinski, Association of Former Political Prisoners of German Concentration Camps
Mr Roman Halter, Claims for Jewish Slave Labourers
Mr Rudy Kennedy, Claims for Jewish Slave Labourers
Ian Sayer, Author
Ms Helen B Junz, Independent Committee of Eminent Persons

KPMG
Mr Jeremy Outen
Mr Brian Dilley

Academics:

John P Fox, Department of Hebrew and Jewish Studies, University College London
Michael Butler, School of Modern Languages, University of Birmingham
Professor David Cesarani, Department of History, University of Southampton